THE OXFORD New Portuguese Dictionary

Portuguese—English
Compiled by John Whitlam

English—Portuguese
Compiled by Lia Correia Raitt

BERKLEY BOOKS, NEW YORK

THE BERKLEY PUBLISHING GROUP
Published by the Penguin Group
Penguin Group (USA) Inc.
375 Hudson Street, New York, New York 10014, USA
Penguin Group (Canada), 90 Eglinton Avenue East, Suite 700, Toronto, Ontario M4P 2Y3, Canada
(a division of Pearson Penguin Canada Inc.)
Penguin Books Ltd., 80 Strand, London WC2R 0RL, England
Penguin Group Ireland, 25 St. Stephen's Green, Dublin 2, Ireland (a division of Penguin Books Ltd.)
Penguin Group (Australia), 250 Camberwell Road, Camberwell, Victoria 3124, Australia
(a division of Pearson Australia Group Pty. Ltd.)
Penguin Books India Pvt. Ltd., 11 Community Centre, Panchsheel Park, New Delhi—110 017, India
Penguin Group (NZ), 67 Apollo Drive, Rosedale, North Shore 0632, New Zealand
(a division of Pearson New Zealand Ltd.)
Penguin Books (South Africa) (Pty.) Ltd., 24 Sturdee Avenue, Rosebank, Johannesburg 2196, South Africa

Penguin Books Ltd., Registered Offices: 80 Strand, London WC2R 0RL, England

THE OXFORD® NEW PORTUGUESE DICTIONARY

A Berkley Book / published by arrangement with Oxford University Press, Inc.

PRINTING HISTORY
Berkley mass-market edition / July 2008

ISBN: 978-0-425-22244-7

BERKLEY®
Berkley Books are published by The Berkley Publishing Group,
a division of Penguin Group (USA) Inc.,
375 Hudson Street, New York, New York 10014.
BERKLEY is a registered trademark of Penguin Group (USA) Inc.
The "B" design is a trademark belonging to Penguin Group (USA) Inc.

PRINTED IN THE UNITED STATES OF AMERICA

10 9 8 7 6 5 4 3 2

Contents/Índice

Preface

The *Oxford Paperback Portuguese Dictionary* has been written for speakers of both Portuguese and English and contains the most useful words and expressions in use today.

The dictionary provides a handy and comprehensive reference work for tourists, students, and business people who require quick and reliable answers to their translation needs.

Thanks are due to: Dr John Sykes, Prof. A. W. Raitt, Commander Virgílio Correia, Marcelo Affonso, Eng. Pedro Carvalho, Eng. Vasco Carvalho, Dr Iva Correia, Dr Ida Reis de Carvalho, Eng. J. Reis de Carvalho, Prof. A. Falcão, Bishop Manuel Falcão, Dr M. Luísa Falcão, Prof. J. Ferraz, Prof. M. de Lourdes Ferraz, Drs Ana and Jorge Fonseca, Mr Robert Howes, Irene Lakhani, Eng. Hugo Pires, Prof. M. Kaura Pires, Dr M. Alexandre Pires, Ambassador L. Pazos Alonso, Dr Teresa Pinto Pereira, Dr Isabel Tully, Carlos Wallenstein, Ligia Xavier, and Dr H. Martins and the members of his Mesa Lusófona at St Anthony's College, Oxford.

Prefácio

O *Oxford Paperback Portuguese Dictionary* foi escrito por pessoas de língua portuguesa e inglesa, e contém as palavras e expressões mais úteis em uso atualmente.

O dicionário constitui uma obra de referência prática e abrangente para turistas, estudantes e pessoas de negócios que necessitam de respostas rápidas e confiáveis para as suas traduções.

Agradecimentos a: Dr John Sykes, Prof. A. W. Raitt, Comandante Virgílio Correia, Marcelo Affonso, Eng. Pedro Carvalho, Eng. Vasco Carvalho, Dr Iva Correia, Dr Ida Reis de Carvalho, Eng. J. Reis de Carvalho, Prof. A. Falcão, Bispo Manuel Falcão, Dr M. Luísa Falcão, Prof. J. Ferraz, Prof. M. de Lourdes Ferraz, Drs Ana e Jorge Fonseca, Mr Robert Howes, Eng. Hugo Pires, Prof. M. Laura Pires, Dr M. Alexandre Pires, Embaixador L. Pazos Alonso, Dr Teresa Pinto Pereira, Dr Isabel Tully, Carlos Wallenstein, e Dr H. Martins e os membros de sua Mesa Lusófona do St Anthony's College, em Oxford.

Introduction

The swung dash (~) is used to replace a headword, or that part of a headword preceding the vertical bar (|).

In both English and Portuguese, only irregular plural forms are given. Plural forms of Portuguese nouns and adjectives ending in a single vowel are formed by adding an s (e.g. *livro*, *livros*). Those ending in *n*, *r*, *s* where the stress falls on the final syllable, and *z*, add *es* (e.g. *mulher*, *mulheres*, *falaz*, *falazes*). Nouns and adjectives ending in *m* change the final *m* to *ns* (e.g. *homem*, *homens*, *bom*, *bons*). Most of those ending in *ão* change their ending to *ões* (e.g. *estação*, *estações*).

Portuguese nouns and adjectives ending in an unstressed *o* form the feminine by changing the *o* to *a* (e.g. *belo*, *bela*). Those ending in *or* become *ora* (e.g. *trabalhador*, *trabalhadora*). All other masculine-feminine changes are shown at the main headword.

English and Portuguese pronunciation is given by means of the International Phonetic Alphabet. It is shown for all headwords, and for those derived words whose pronunciation is not easily deduced from that of a headword.

Portuguese verb tables will be found in the appendix.

Introdução

O sinal (~) é usado para substituir o verbete, ou parte deste precedendo a barra vertical (|).

Tanto em inglês como em português, somente as formas irregulares do plural são dadas. As formas regulares do plural dos substantivos ingleses recebem um *s* (ex. *teacher*, *teachers*), ou *es* quando terminarem em *ch*, *sh*, *s*, *ss*, *us*, *x* ou *z* (ex. *sash*, *sashes*). Os substantivos terminados em *y* e precedidos por uma consoante, mudam no plural para *ies* (ex. *baby*, *babies*).

O passado e o particípio passado dos verbos regulares ingleses são formados pelo acréscimo de *ed* à forma infinitiva (ex. *last*, *lasted*). Os verbos terminados em *e* recebem *d* (ex. *move*, *moved*). Aqueles terminados em *y* têm o *y* substituído por *ied* (*carry*, *carried*). As formas irregulares dos verbos aparecem no dicionário em ordem alfabética, remetidas à forma infinitiva, e também, na lista de verbos no apêndice.

As pronúncias inglesa e portuguesa são dadas em acordo com o Alfabeto Fonético Internacional. A pronúncia é dada para todos os verbetes, assim como para aquelas palavras derivadas cuja pronúncia não seja facilmente deduzida a partir do verbete.

Proprietary terms

This dictionary includes some words which are, or are asserted to be, proprietary names or trade marks. Their inclusion does not imply that they have acquired for legal purposes a non-proprietary or general significance, nor is any other judgement implied concerning their legal status. In cases where the editor has some evidence that a word is used as a proprietary name or trade mark this is indicated by the label *propr*, but no judgement concerning the legal status of such words is made or implied thereby.

Nomes comerciais

Este dicionário inclui algumas palavras que são, ou acredita-se ser, nomes comerciais ou marcas registradas. A sua inclusão no dicionário não implica que elas tenham adquirido para fins legais um significado geral ou não-comercial, assim como não afeta em nenhum dos conceitos implícitos o seu status legal.

Nos casos em que o editor tenha prova suficiente de que uma palavra seja usada como um nome comercial ou marca registrada, este emprego é indicado pela etiqueta *propr*, mas nenhuma apreciação relativa ao status legal de tais palavras é feita ou sugerida por esta indicação.

Portuguese Pronunciation

Vowels and Diphthongs

a, à, á, â	/ã/	cham*a*m, *a*mbos, *a*ntes	1) before *m* at the end of a word, or before *m* or *n* and another consonant, is nasalized
	/a/	*a*b*a*, *à*, *a*col*á*, des*â*nimo	2) in other positions is like *a* in English r*a*ther
ã	/ã/	irm*ã*	is nasalized
e	/ẽ/	sem, venda	1) before *m* at the end of a word, or before *m* or *n* and another consonant, is nasalized
	/i/	art*e*	2) at the end of a word is like *y* in English happ*y*
	/e/	menas	3) in other positions is like *e* in English th*e*y
é	/ɛ/	art*é*ria	is like *e* in English g*e*t
ê	/e/	f*ê*mur	is like *e* in English th*e*y
i	/ĩ/	s*i*m, v*i*ndo	1) before *m* at the end of a word, or before *m* or *n* and another consonant, is nasalized
	/i/	f*i*la	2) in other positions is like *ee* in English s*ee*
o	/õ/	com, sombra, onda	1) before *m* at the end of a word, or before *m* or *n* and another consonant, is nasalized
	/u/	muito	2) at the end of a word, unstressed, is like *u* in English r*u*le
	/o/	comover	3) in other positions, unstressed, is like *o* in English pole
	/o/	bobo	4) stressed, is like *o* in
	/ɔ/	loja	English pole or *o* in shop

ó	/o/	ópera	is like o in English shop
ô	/o/	tônica	is like o in English pole
u, ú		*gu*erra, *gu*isado, *qu*e, *qu*ilo	1) is silent in *gue*, *gui*, *que*, and *qui*
	/u/	m*u*la, p*ú*rp*u*ra	2) in other positions is like *u* in English rule
ü, gü	/gw/	un*gü*ento	in the combinations *güe* and *güi* is like *g* in English *g*ot, followed by English *w*
	/kw/	tran*qü*ilo	in the combinations *qüe* and *qüi* is like *qu* in English *qu*een
ãe	/ãj/	m*ãe*, p*ãe*s, alem*ãe*s	is like *y* in English b*y*, but nasalized
ai	/aj/	v*ai*, p*ai*, s*ai*, c*ai*ta	is like *y* in English b*y*
ao, au	/aw/	*ao*s, *au*todefesa	is like *ow* in English h*ow*
ão	/ãw/	não	is like *ow* in English h*ow*, but nasalized
ei	/ej/	l*ei*	is like *ey* in English th*ey*
eu	/ew/	d*eu*s, fl*eu*gma	both vowels pronounced separately
oẽ	/õj/	eleiç*õe*s	is like *oi* in English c*oi*n, but nasalized
oi	/oj/	n*oi*te	is like *oi* in English c*oi*n
ou	/o/	p*ou*co	is like *o* in English p*o*le

Consonants

b	/b/	*b*anho	is like *b* in English *b*all
c	/s/	cinza, cem	1) before *e* or *i* is like *s* in English *s*it
	/k/	casa	2) in other positions is like *c* in English cat

ç	/s/	estação	is like *s* in English *s*it
ch	/ʃ/	*ch*á	is like *sh* in English *sh*out
d	/dʒ/	*d*izer, don*d*e	1) before *i* or final unstressed *e* is like *j* in English *j*oin
	/d/	*d*ar	2) in other positions is like *d* in English *d*og
f	/f/	*f*alar	is like *f* in English *f*all
g	/g/	agente, *g*iro	1) before *e* or *i* is like *s* in English vision
	/g/	*g*ato	2) in other positions is like *g* in English *g*et
h		haver	is silent in Portuguese, but see *ch*, *lh*, *nh*
j	/ʒ/	*j*unta	is like *s* in English vision
k	/k/	*k*it	is like English *k* in *k*ey
l	/w/	fa*l*ta	1) between a vowel and a consonant, or following a vowel at the end of a word, is like *w* in English *w*ater
	/l/	*l*ata	2) in other positions is like *l* in English *l*ike
l	/ʎ/	calhar	is like *lli* in English mi*lli*on
m		ambas/ãbuʃ/ com/kɪ/	1) between a vowel and a consonant, or after a vowel at the end of a word, *m* nasalizes the preceding vowel
	/m/	*m*ato, *m*ão	2) in other positions is like *m* in English *m*other
n		ci*n*ʒa/'sĩza/	1) between a vowel and a consonant, *n* nasalizes the preceding vowel
	/n/	beni*g*no	2) in other positions is like *n* in English *n*ear

nh	/ɲ/	ba*nh*o	is like *ni* in English opi*ni*on
p	/p/	*p*az	is like *p* in English *p*oor
q	/k/	*q*ue, in*q*uieto	1) *qu* before *e* or *i* is like English *k*
	/kw/	*q*uase, *q*uórum	2) *qu* before *a* or *o*, or *qü* before *e* or *i*, is like *qu* in English *qu*een
r	/r/	apa*r*ato, go*r*do	1) between two vowels, or between a vowel and a consonant, is trilled
	/x/	*r*ato, ga*rr*a, mel*r*o, gen*r*o, Is*r*ael	2) at the beginning of a word, or in *rr*, or after *l*, *n*, or *s*, is like *ch* in Scottish lo*ch*
s	/ʃ/	depoi*s*	at the end of a word is like *sh* in English *sh*oot
	/z/	a*s*a, de*s*de, abi*s*mo, I*s*rael	2) between two vowels, or before *b*, *d*, *g*, *l*, *m*, *n*, *r*, *v*, is like *z* in English *z*ebra
	/s/	*s*uave	3) in other positions is like *s* in English *s*it
t	/tʃ/	*t*io, an*t*es	1) before *i* or final unstressed *e* is like *ch* in English *ch*eese
	/tʃi/	ki*t*	2) at the end of a word is like *chy* in English it*chy*
	/t/	a*t*ar	3) in other positions is like *t* in English *t*ap
v	/v/	lu*v*a	is like *v* in English *v*ain
w	/u/	*w*att	is shorter than English *w*
x	/z/	e*x*ato, e*x*emplo	1) in the prefix *ex* before a vowel, is pronounced like *z* in *z*ero

	/ʃ/	*xícara, baixo, peixe, frouxo*	2) at the beginning of a word or after *ai*, *ei* or *ou*, is pronounced like *sh* in *show*
	/s/	explodir, auxiliar	3) is like *s* in English sit
	/ks/	axila, fixo	4) is like *x* in English exit
			5) in the combination *xce*, *xci*, *x* is not pronounced in Portuguese e.g. excelente, excitar
z	/s/	falaz	1) at the end of a word, is like *s* in English *sit*
	/z/	dizer	2) In other positions, is like English *z*

Pronúncia Inglesa

Vogais e Ditongos

/iː/	*see*, *tea*	como *i* em *giro*
/ɪ/	s*i*t, happ*y*	é um som mais breve do que *i* em l*i*
/e/	set	como *e* em t*é*pido
/æ/	h*a*t	é um som mais breve do que *a* em *a*mor
/ɑː/	*ar*m, c*al*m	como *a* em c*a*rtaz
/ɒ/	got	como *o* em ex*ó*tico
/ɔː/	s*aw*, m*o*re	como *o* em c*o*rte
/ʊ/	p*u*t, l*oo*k	como *u* em m*u*rro
/uː/	t*oo*, d*ue*	como *u* em d*u*ro
/ʌ/	c*u*p, s*o*me	como *a* em p*a*no
/ɜː/	f*ir*m, f*ur*	como *e* em enx*e*rto
/ə/	*a*go, weath*er*	como *e* no português europeu part*e*
/eɪ/	p*a*ge, p*ai*n, p*ay*	como *ei* em l*ei*te
/əʊ/	h*o*me, r*oa*m	é um som mais longo do que *o* em c*o*ma
/aɪ/	f*i*ne, b*y*, g*uy*	como *ai* em s*ai*
/aɪə/	f*ire*, t*yre*	como *ai* em *sai* seguido por /ə/
/aʊ/	n*ow*, sh*ou*t	como *au* em *au*la
/aʊə/	h*our*, fl*ower*	como *au* em *au*la seguido por /ə/
/ɔɪ/	j*oi*n, b*oy*	como *oi* em d*ói*
/ɪə/	d*ear*, h*ere*, b*eer*	como *ia* em d*ia*
/eə/	h*air*, c*are*, b*ear*, th*ere*	como *e* em et*é*reo
/ʊə/	p*oor*, d*ur*ing	como *ua* em s*ua*

Consoantes

/p/	sna*p*	como *p* em *p*ato
/b/	*b*ath	como *b* em *b*ala
/t/	*t*ap	como *t* em *t*ela
/d/	*d*ip	como *d* em *d*ar
/k/	*c*at, *k*ite, stoma*ch*, pi*que*	como *c* em *c*asa
/ks/	e*x*ercise	como *x* em a*x*ila
/g/	*g*ot	como *g* em *g*ato

/tʃ/	*ch*in	como *t* em *t*io
/dʒ/	*J*une, *g*eneral, *j*u*dg*e	como *d* em *d*izer
/f/	*f*all	como *f* em *f*aca
/v/	*v*ine, o*f*	como *v* em *v*aca
/θ/	*th*in, mo*th*	não tem equivalente, soa como um *s* entre os dentes
/ð/	*th*is	não tem equivalente, soa com um *z* entre os dentes
/s/	*s*o, voi*c*e	como *s* em *s*uave
/z/	*z*oo, ro*s*e	como *z* em fa*z*er
/ʃ/	*sh*e, lun*ch*	como *ch* em *ch*egar
/ʒ/	mea*s*ure, vi*s*ion	como *j* em *j*amais
/h/	*h*ow	*h* aspirado
/m/	*m*an	como *m* em *m*ala
/n/	*n*o*n*e	como *n* em *n*ada
/ŋ/	si*ng*	como *n* em ci*n*to
/l/	*l*eg	como *l* em *l*uva
/r/	*r*ed, w*r*ite	como *r* em ca*r*a
/j/	*y*es, *y*oke	como *i* em *i*oga
/w/	*w*eather, s*w*itch	como *u* em ég*u*a

ˈ indica a sílaba tônica

European Portuguese

Brazilian Portuguese, which is used in this dictionary, differs in a number of respects from that used in Portugal and the rest of the Portuguese-speaking world. These differences affect both spelling and pronunciation. Spelling variations appear on the Portuguese-English side. In so far as they affect pronunciation, the main variants are:

Brazilian Portuguese often omits the letters *b*, *c*, *m*, and *p*, which are retained by European Portuguese:

	Brazilian	**European**
b	sutil	su*b*til
c	ação	a*c*ção
	ato	a*c*to
	elétrico	elé*c*trico
m	indenizar	inde*m*nizar
p	batismo	ba*p*tismo
	exceção	exce*p*ção

Letters *c* and *p* in such variant forms are usually silent, hence acto /'atu/, baptismo/ba'tiʒmu/. However, *c* is pronounced in the combination *ect*, hence eléctrico/i'lektriku/.

The combinations *gü* and *qü* become *gu* and *qu*:

Brazilian	**European**
un*gü*ento	un*gu*ento
tran*qü*ilo	tran*qu*ilo

However, they are still pronounced /gw/ and /kw/ respectively.

The other main differences in pronunciation are:

d	/d/	*d*ar, *d*izer, bal*d*e, don*d*e	1) at the beginning of a word, or after *l*, or *n*, is like *d* in English *d*og
	/ð/	ci*d*a*d*e, me*d*roso	2) in other positions is a sound between *d* in English *d*og and *th* in English *th*is
e	/ə/	art*e*	at the end of a word, is like *e* in English quarr*e*l
r	/rr/	*r*ato, ga*rr*a, mel*r*o, gen*r*o, Is*r*ael, guel*r*a, ten*r*o, is*r*aelense	at the beginning of a word, or in *rr*, or after *l*, *n*, or *s*, is strongly trilled
s	/ʃ/	depoi*s*, a*s*co, ra*s*par, co*s*tura	1) at the end of a word, or before *c*, *f*, *p*, *qu*, or *t*, is like English *sh*
	/ʒ/	de*s*de, I*s*lã, abi*s*mo, I*s*rael	2) before *b*, *d*, *g*, *l*, *m*, *n*, *r*, or *u* is like *s* in English vi*s*ion
t	/t/	a*t*ar, an*t*es, *t*io	is like *t* in English *t*ap
z	/ʃ/	fala*z*	at the end of a word, is like *sh* in English *sh*ake

Abbreviations/Abreviaturas

adjective	*a*	adjetivo
abbreviation	*abbr/abr*	abreviatura
something	*aco*	alguma coisa
adverb	*adv*	advérbio
somebody, someone	*alg*	algúem
article	*art*	artigo
American (English)	*Amer*	(inglês) americano
anatomy	*anat*	anatomia
architecture	*arquit*	arquitetura
astrology	*astr/astrol*	astrologia
motoring	*auto*	automobilismo
aviation	*aviat*	aviação
Brazilian Portuguese	*B*	português do Brasil
biology	*biol*	biologia
botany	*bot*	botânica
Brazilian Portuguese	*Bras*	português do Brasil
cinema	*cine*	cinema
colloquial	*colloq*	coloquial
commerce	*comm/com*	comércio
computing	*comput*	computação
conjunction	*conj*	conjunção
cookery	*culin*	cozinha
electricity	*electr/eletr*	eletricidade
feminine	*f*	feminina
familiar	*fam*	familiar
figurative	*fig*	figurativo
geography	*geog*	geografia
grammar	*gramm/gram*	gramática
infinitive	*inf*	infinitivo
interjection	*int*	interjeição
interrogative	*interr*	interrogativo
invariable	*invar*	invariável
legal, law	*jur/jurid*	jurídico
language	*lang*	linguagem
literal	*lit*	literal
masculine	*m*	masculino

thematics	*mat*	matemática
mechanics	*mech*	mecânica
medicine	*med*	medicina
military	*mil*	militar
music	*mus*	música
noun	*n*	substantivo
nautical	*naut*	náutico
negative	*neg*	negativo
oneself	*o.s.*	se, si mesmo
European Portuguese	*P*	português de Portugal
pejorative	*pej*	pejorativo
philosophy	*phil*	filosofia
plural	*pl*	plural
politics	*pol*	política
European Portuguese	*Port*	português de Portugal
past participle	*pp*	particípio passado
prefix	*pref*	prefixo
preposition	*prep*	preposição
present	*pres*	presente
present participle	*pres p*	particípio presente
pronoun	*pron*	pronome
psychology	*psych/psic*	psicologia
past tense	*pt*	pretérito
relative	*rel*	relativo
religion	*relig*	religião
somebody	*sb*	alguém
singular	*sing*	singular
slang	*sl*	gíria
someone	*s.o.*	alguém
something	*sth*	alguma coisa
subjunctive	*subj*	subjuntivo
technology	*techn/tecn*	tecnologia
theatre	*theat/teat*	teatro
television	*TV*	televisão
university	*univ*	universidade
auxiliary verb	*v aux*	verbo auxiliar
intransitive verb	*vi*	verbo intransitivo
pronominal verb	*vpr*	verbo pronominal
transitive verb	*vt*	verbo transitivo
transitive & intransitive verb	*vt/i*	verbo transitivo e intransitivo

Aa

a¹ /a/ *artigo* the □ *pron* (*mulher*) her; (*coisa*) it; (*você*) you

a² /a/ *prep* (*para*) to; (*em*) at; **às 3 horas** at 3 o'clock; **à noite** at night; **a lápis** in pencil; **a mão** by hand

à /a/ = **a² + a¹**

aba /'aba/ *f* (*de chapéu*) brim; (*de camisa*) tail; (*de mesa*) flap

abacate /aba'katʃi/ *m* avocado (pear)

abacaxi /abaka'ʃi/ *m* pineapple; (*fam: problema*) pain, headache

aba|de /a'badʒi/ *m* abbot; **~dia** *f* abbey

aba|fado /aba'fadu/ *a* (*tempo*) humid, close; (*quarto*) stuffy; **~far** *vt* (*asfixiar*) stifle; muffle <*som*>; smother <*fogo*>; suppress <*informação*>; cover up <*escândalo, assunto*>

abagunçar /abagũ'sar/ *vt* mess up

abaixar /aba'ʃar/ *vt* lower; turn down <*som, rádio*> □ *vi* **~-se** *vpr* bend down

abaixo /a'baʃu/ *adv* down; **~ de** below; **mais ~** further down; **~-assinado** *m* petition

abajur /aba'ʒur/ *m* (*quebra-luz*) lampshade; (*lâmpada*) (table) lamp

aba|lar /aba'lar/ *vt* shake; (*fig*) shock; **~lar-se** *vpr* be shocked, be shaken; **~lo** *m* shock

abanar /aba'nar/ *vt* shake, wave; wag <*rabo*>; (*com leque*) fan

abando|nar /abãdo'nar/ *vt* abandon; (*deixar*) leave; **~no** /o/ *m* abandonment; (*estado*) neglect

abarcar /abar'kar/ *vt* comprise, cover

abarro|tado /abaxo'tadu/ *a* crammed full; (*lotado*) crowded, packed; **~tar** *vt* cram full, stuff

abastado /abas'tadu/ *a* wealthy

abaste|cer /abaste'ser/ *vt* supply; fuel <*motor*>; fill up (with petrol) <*carro*>; refuel <*avião*>; **~cimento** *m* supply; (*de carro, avião*) refuelling

aba|ter /aba'ter/ *vt* knock down; cut down, fell <*árvore*>; shoot down <*avião, ave*>; slaughter <*gado*>; knock down, cut <*preço*>; **~ter alg** <*trabalho*> get s.o. down, wear s.o. out; <*má notícia*> sadden s.o.; <*doença*> lay s.o. low, knock the stuffing out of s.o.; **~tido** *a* dispirited, dejected; <*cara*> haggard, worn; **~timento** *m* dejection; (*de preço*) reduction

abaulado /abaw'ladu/ *a* convex; <*estrada*> cambered

abcesso /ab'sɛsu/ *m* (*Port*) *veja* **abscesso**

abdi|cação /abidʒika'sãw/ *f* abdication; **~car** *vt/i* abdicate

abdômen /abi'domẽ/ *m* abdomen

abecedário /abese'dariu/ *m* alphabet, ABC

abeirar-se /abe'rarsi/ *vr* draw near

abe|lha /a'beʎa/ *f* bee; **~lhudo** *a* inquisitive, nosy

abençoar /abẽso'ar/ *vt* bless

aber|to /a'bɛrtu/ *pp de* **abrir** □ *a* open; <*céu*> clear; <*gás, torneira*> on; <*sinal*> green; **~tura** *f* opening; (*foto*) aperture; (*pol*) liberalization

abeto /a'betu/ *m* fir (tree)

abis|mado /abiz'madu/ *a* astonished; **~mo** *m* abyss

abjeto /abi'ʒɛtu/ *a* abject

abóbada /a'bɔbada/ *f* vault

abobalhado /aboba'ʎadu/ *a* silly

abóbora /a'bɔbora/ *f* pumpkin

abobrinha /abo'briɲa/ *f* courgette, (*Amer*) zucchini

abo|lição /aboli'sãw/ *f* abolition; **~lir** *vt* abolish

abomi|nação /abomina'sãw/ *f* abomination; **~nável** (*pl* **~náveis**) *a* abominable

abo|nar /abo'nar/ *vt* guarantee <*dívida*>; give a bonus to <*empregado*>; **~no** /o/ *m* guarantee; (*no salário*) bonus; (*subsídio*) allowance, benefit; (*reforço*) endorsement

abordar /abor'dar/ *vt* approach <*pessoa*>; broach, tackle <*assunto*>; (*naut*) board

aborre|cer /aboxe'ser/ *vt* (*irritar*) annoy; (*entediar*) bore; **~cer-se** *vpr* get annoyed; get bored; **~cido** *a* annoyed; bored; **~cimento** *m* annoyance; boredom

abor|tar /abor'tar/ *vi* miscarry, have a miscarriage □ *vt* abort; **~to** /o/ *m* abortion; (*natural*) miscarriage

aboto|adura /abotoa'dura/ *f* cufflink; **~ar** *vt* button (up) □ *vi* bud

abra|çar /abra'sar/ *vt* hug, embrace; embrace <*causa*>; **~ço** *m* hug, embrace

abrandar /abrã'dar/ *vt* ease <*dor*>; temper <*calor, frio*>; mollify, appease, placate <*povo*>; tone down, smooth over <*escândalo*> □ *vi* <*dor*> ease; <*calor, frio*> become less extreme; <*tempestade*> die down

abranger /abrã'ʒer/ *vt* cover; (*entender*) take in, grasp; **~ a** extend to

abrasileirar /abrazile'rar/ *vt* Brazilianize

abre-|garrafas /abriga'xafas/ *m invar* (*Port*) bottle-opener; **~latas** *m invar* (*Port*) can-opener

abreugrafia /abrewgra'fia/ *f* X-ray

abrevi|ar /abrevi'ar/ *vt* abbreviate <*palavra*>; abridge <*livro*>; **~atura** *f* abbreviation

abridor /abri'dor/ *m* **~ (de lata)** can-opener; **~ de garrafa** bottle-opener

abri|gar /abri'gar/ *vt* shelter; house <*sem-teto*>; **~gar-se** *vpr* (take) shelter; **~go** *m* shelter

abril /a'briw/ *m* April

abrir /a'brir/ *vt* open; (*a chave*) unlock; turn on <*gás, torneira*>; make <*buraco, exceção*> □ *vi* open; <*céu, tempo*> clear (up); <*sinal*> turn green; **~-se** *vpr* open; (*desabafar*) open up

abrupto /a'bruptu/ *a* abrupt

abrutalhado /abruta'ʎadu/ *a* <*sapato*> heavy; <*pessoa*> coarse

abscesso /abi'sɛsu/ *m* abscess

absolu|tamente /abisoluta'mẽtʃi/ *adv* absolutely; (*não*) not at all; **~to** *a* absolute; **em ~to** not at all, absolutely not

absol|ver /abisow'ver/ *vt* absolve; (*jurid*) acquit; **~vição** *f* absolution; (*jurid*) acquittal

absor|ção /abisor'sãw/ *f* absorption; **~to** *a* absorbed; **~vente** *a* <*tecido*> absorbent; <*livro*> absorbing; **~ver** *vt* absorb; **~ver-se** *vpr* get absorbed

abs|têmio /abis'temiu/ *a* abstemious; (*de álcool*) teetotal □ *m* teetotaller; **~tenção** *f* abstention; **~tencionista** *a* abstaining □ *m/f* abstainer; **~ter-se** *vpr* abstain; **~ter-se de** refrain from; **~tinência** *f* abstinence

abstra|ção /abistra'sãw/ *f* abstraction; (*mental*) distraction; **~ir** *vt* separate; **~to** *a* abstract

absurdo /abi'surdu/ *a* absurd □ *m* nonsense

abun|dância /abũ'dãsia/ *f* abundance; **~dante** *a* abundant; **~dar** *vi* abound

abu|sar /abu'zar/ *vi* go too far; **~sar de** abuse; (*aproveitar-se*) take advantage of; **~so** *m* abuse

abutre /a'butri/ *m* vulture

aca|bado /aka'badu/ *a* finished; (*exausto*) exhausted; (*velho*) decrepit; **~bamento** *m* finish; **~bar** *vt* finish □ *vi* finish, end; (*esgotar-se*) run out; **~bar-se** *vpr* end, be over; (*esgotar-se*) run out; **~bar com** put an end to, end; (*abolir, matar*) do away with; split up with <*namorado*>; wipe out <*adversário*>; **~bou de chegar** he has just arrived; **~bar fazendo** *or* **por fazer** end up doing

acabrunhado /akabru'ɲadu/ *a* dejected

aca|demia /akade'mia/ *f* academy; (*de ginástica etc*) gym; **~dêmico** *a & m* academic

açafrão /asa'frãw/ *m* saffron

acalentar /akalẽ'tar/ *vt* lull to sleep <*bebê*>; cherish <*esperanças*>; have in mind <*planos*>

acalmar /akaw'mar/ *vt* calm (down) □ *vi* <*vento*> drop; <*mar*> grow calm; **~-se** *vpr* calm down

acam|pamento /akãpa'mẽtu/ *m* camp; (*ato*) camping; **~par** *vi* camp

aca|nhado /aka'ɲadu/ *a* shy; **~nhamento** *m* shyness; **~nhar-se** *vpr* be shy

ação /a'sãw/ *f* action; (*jurid*) lawsuit; (*com*) share

acariciar /akarisi'ar/ *vt* (*com a mão*) caress, stroke; (*adular*) make a fuss of; cherish <*esperanças*>

acarretar /akaxe'tar/ *vt* bring, cause

acasalar /akaza'lar/ *vt* mate; **~-se** *vpr* mate

acaso /a'kazu/ *m* chance; **ao ~** at random; **por ~** by chance

aca|tamento /akata'mẽtu/ *m* respect, deference; **~tar** *vt* respect, defer to <*pessoa, opinião*>; obey, abide by <*leis, ordens*>; take in <*criança*>

acc-, acç- (*Port*) *veja* **ac-, aç-**

acautelar-se /akawte'larsi/ *vpr* be cautious

acei|tação /asejta'sãw/ *f* acceptance; **~tar** *vt* accept; **~tável** (*pl* **~táveis**) *a* acceptable

acele|ração /aselera'sãw/ *f* acceleration; **~rador** *m* accelerator; **~rar** *vi* accelerate □ *vt* speed up

acenar /ase'nar/ *vi* signal; (*saudando*) wave; **~ com** promise, offer

acender /asẽ'der/ *vt* light <*cigarro, fogo, vela*>; switch on <*luz*>; heat up <*debate*>

aceno /a'senu/ *m* signal; (*de saudação*) wave

acen|to /a'sẽtu/ *m* accent; **~tuar** *vt* accentuate; accent <*letra*>

acepção /asep'sãw/ *f* sense

acepipes /ase'pipʃ/ *m pl* (*Port*) cocktail snacks

acerca /a'serka/ **~ de** *prep* about, concerning

acercar-se /aser'karsi/ *vpr* **~ de** approach

acertar /aser'tar/ *vt* find <(*com o*) *caminho*, (*a*) *casa*>; put right, set <*relógio*>; get right <*pergunta*>; guess (correctly) <*solução*>; hit <*alvo*>; make <*acordo, negócio*>; fix, arrange

<*encontro*> □ *vi* (*ter razão*) be right; (*atingir o alvo*) hit the mark; ~ **com** find, happen upon; ~ **em** hit

acervo /a'servu/ *m* collection; (*jurid*) estate

aceso /a'sezu/ *pp de* **acender** □ *a* <*luz*> on; <*fogo*> alight

aces|sar /ase'sar/ *vt* access; **~sível** (*pl* **~síveis**) *a* accessible; affordable <*preço*>; **~so** /ɛ/ *m* access; (*de raiva, tosse*) fit; (*de febre*) attack; **~sório** *a & m* accessory

acetona /ase'tona/ *f* (*para unhas*) nail varnish remover

achado /a'ʃadu/ *m* find

achaque /a'ʃaki/ *m* ailment

achar /a'ʃar/ *vt* find; (*pensar*) think; **~-se** *vpr* (*estar*) be; (*considerar-se*) think that one is; **acho que sim/não** I think so/I don't think so

achatar /aʃa'tar/ *vt* flatten; cut <*salário*>

aciden|tado /asidẽ'tadu/ *a* rough <*terreno*>; bumpy <*estrada*>; eventful <*viagem, vida*>; injured <*pessoa*>; **~tal** (*pl* **~tais**) *a* accidental; **~te** *m* accident

acidez /asi'des/ *f* acidity

ácido /'asidu/ *a & m* acid

acima /a'sima/ *adv* above; ~ **de** above; **mais** ~ higher up

acio|nar /asio'nar/ *vt* operate; (*jurid*) sue; **~nista** *m/f* shareholder

acirrado /asi'xadu/ *a* stiff, tough

acla|mação /aklama'sãw/ *f* acclaim; (*de rei*) acclamation; **~mar** *vt* acclaim

aclarar /akla'rar/ *vt* clarify, clear up □ *vi* clear up; **~-se** *vpr* become clear

aclimatar /aklima'tar/ *vt* acclimatize, (*Amer*) acclimate; **~-se** *vpr* get acclimatized, (*Amer*) get acclimated

aço /'asu/ *m* steel; ~ **inoxidável** stainless steel

acocorar-se /akoko'rarsi/ *vpr* squat (down)

acolá /ako'la/ *adv* over there

acolcho|ado /akowʃo'adu/ *m* quilt; **~ar** *vt* quilt; upholster <*móveis*>

aco|lhedor /akoʎe'dor/ *a* welcoming; **~lher** *vt* welcome <*hóspede*>; take in <*criança, refugiado*>; accept <*decisão, convite*>; respond to <*pedido*>; **~lhida** *f*, **~lhimento** *m* welcome; (*abrigo*) refuge

acomodar /akomo'dar/ *vt* accommodate; (*ordenar*) arrange; (*tornar cômodo*) make comfortable; **~-se** *vpr* make o.s. comfortable

acompa|nhamento /akõpaɲa-'mẽtu/ *m* (*mus*) accompaniment; (*prato*) side dish; (*comitiva*) escort; **~nhante** *m/f* companion; (*mus*) accompanist; **~nhar** *vt* accompany, go with; watch <*jogo, progresso*>; keep up with <*eventos, caso*>; keep up with, follow <*aula, conversa*>; share <*política, opinião*>; (*mus*) accompany; **a estrada ~nha o rio** the road runs alongside the river

aconche|gante /akõʃe'gãtʃi/ *a* cosy, (*Amer*) cozy; **~gar** *vt* (*chegar a si*) cuddle; (*agasalhar*) wrap up; (*na cama*) tuck up; (*tornar cômodo*) make comfortable; **~gar-se** *vpr* ensconce o.s.; **~gar-se com** snuggle up to; **~go** /e/ *m* cosiness, (*Amer*) coziness; (*abraço*) cuddle

acondicionar /akõdʒisio'nar/ *vt* condition; pack, package <*mercadoria*>

aconse|lhar /akõse'ʎar/ *vt* advise; **~lhar-se** *vpr* consult; **~lhar alg a** advise s.o. to; **~lhar aco a alg** recommend sth to s.o.; **~lhável** (*pl* **~lháveis**) *a* advisable

aconte|cer /akõte'ser/ *vi* happen; **~cimento** *m* event

acordar /akor'dar/ *vt/i* wake up

acorde /a'kɔrdʒi/ *m* chord

acordeão /akordʒi'ãw/ *m* accordion

acordo /a'kordu/ *m* agreement; **de ~ com** in agreement with <*pessoa*>; in accordance with <*lei etc*>; **estar de ~** agree

Açores /a'soris/ *m pl* Azores

açoriano /asori'ano/ *a & m* Azorean

acorrentar /akoxẽ'tar/ *vt* chain (up)

acossar /ako'sar/ *vt* hound, badger

acos|tamento /akosta'mẽtu/ *m* hard shoulder, (*Amer*) berm; **~tar-se** *vpr* lean back

acostu|mado /akostu'madu/ *a* usual, customary; **estar ~mado a** be used to; **~mar** *vt* accustom; **~mar-se a** get used to

acotovelar /akotove'lar/ *vt* (*empurrar*) jostle; (*para avisar*) nudge

açou|gue /a'sogi/ *m* butcher's (shop); **~gueiro** *m* butcher

acovardar /akovar'dar/ *vt* cow, intimidate

acre /'akri/ *a* <*gosto*> bitter; <*aroma*> acrid, pungent; <*tom*> harsh

acredi|tar /akredʒi'tar/ *vt* believe; accredit <*representante*>; **~tar em** believe <*pessoa, história*>; believe in <*Deus, fantasmas*>; (*ter confiança*) have faith in; **~tável** (*pl* **~táveis**) *a* believable

acre-doce /akri'dosi/ *a* sweet and sour

acrescentar /akresẽ'tar/ *vt* add

acres|cer /akre'ser/ *vt* (*juntar*) add; (*aumentar*) increase □ *vi* increase;

~cido de with the addition of; **~ce que** add to that the fact that

acréscimo /a'krɛsimu/ *m* addition; (*aumento*) increase

acriançado /akriã'sadu/ *a* childish

acrílico /a'kriliku/ *a* acrylic

acroba|cia /akroba'sia/ *f* acrobatics; **~ta** *m/f* acrobat

act- (*Port*) *veja* **at-**

acuar /aku'ar/ *vt* corner

açúcar /a'sukar/ *m* sugar

açuca|rar /asuka'rar/ *vt* sweeten; sugar <*café, chá*>; **~reiro** *m* sugar bowl

açude /a'sudʒi/ *m* dam

acudir /aku'dʒir/ *vt/i* **~ (a)** come to the rescue (of)

acumular /akumu'lar/ *vt* accumulate; combine <*cargos*>

acupuntura /akupũ'tura/ *f* acupuncture

acu|sação /akuza'sãw/ *f* accusation; **~sar** *vt* accuse; (*jurid*) charge; (*revelar*) reveal, show up; acknowledge <*recebimento*>

acústi|ca /a'kustʃika/ *f* acoustics; **~co** *a* acoustic

adap|tação /adapta'sãw/ *f* adaptation; **~tado** *a* <*criança*> well-adjusted; **~tar** *vt* adapt; (*para encaixar*) tailor; **~tar-se** *vpr* adapt; **~tável** (*pl* **~táveis**) *a* adaptable

adega /a'dɛga/ *f* wine cellar

adentro /a'dẽtru/ *adv* inside; **selva ~** into the jungle

adepto /a'dɛptu/ *m* follower; (*Port: de equipa*) supporter

ade|quado /ade'kwadu/ *a* appropriate, suitable; **~quar** *vt* adapt, tailor

adereços /ade'resus/ *m pl* props

ade|rente /ade'rẽtʃi/ *m/f* follower; **~rir** *vi* (*colar*) stick; join <*a partido, causa*>; follow <*a moda*>; **~são** *f* adhesion; (*apoio*) support; **~sivo** *a* sticky, adhesive □ *m* sticker

ades|trado /ades'tradu/ *a* skilled; **~trador** *m* trainer; **~trar** *vt* train; break in <*cavalo*>

adeus /a'dews/ *int* goodbye □ *m* goodbye, farewell

adian|tado /adʒiã'tadu/ *a* advanced; <*relógio*> fast; **chegar ~tado** be early; **~tamento** *m* progress; (*pagamento*) advance; **~tar** *vt* advance <*dinheiro*>; put forward <*relógio*>; bring forward <*data, reunião*>; get ahead with <*trabalho*> □ *vi* <*relógio*> gain; (*ter efeito*) be of use; **~tar-se** *vpr* progress, get ahead; **não ~ta (fazer)** it's no use (doing); **~te** *adv* ahead

adia|r /adʒi'ar/ *vt* postpone; adjourn <*sessão*>; **~mento** *m* postponement, adjournment

adi|ção /adʒi'sãw/ *f* addition; **~cionar** *vt* add; **~do** *m* attaché

adivi|nhação /adʒiviɲa'sãw/ *f* guesswork; (*por adivinho*) fortune-telling; **~nhar** *vt* guess; tell <*futuro, sorte*>; read <*pensamento*>; **~nho** *m* fortune-teller

adjetivo /adʒe'tʃivu/ *m* adjective

adminis|tração /adʒiministra-'sãw/ *f* administration; (*de empresas*) management; **~trador** *m* administrator; manager; **~trar** *vt* administer; manage <*empresa*>

admi|ração /adʒimira'sãw/ *f* admiration; (*assombro*) wonder(ment); **~rado** *a* admired; (*surpreso*) amazed, surprised; **~rador** *m* admirer □ *a* admiring; **~rar** *vt* admire; (*assombrar*) amaze; **~rar-se** *vpr* be amazed; **~rável** (*pl* **~ráveis**) *a* admirable; (*assombroso*) amazing

admis|são /adʒimi'sãw/ *f* admission; (*de escola*) intake; **~sível** (*pl* **~síveis**) *a* admissible

admitir /adʒimi'tʃir/ *vt* admit; (*permitir*) permit, allow; (*contratar*) take on

adoção /ado'sãw/ *f* adoption

ado|çar /ado'sar/ *vt* sweeten; **~cicado** *a* slightly sweet

adoecer /adoe'ser/ *vi* fall ill □ *vt* make ill

adoles|cência /adole'sẽsia/ *f* adolescence; **~cente** *a & m* adolescent

adopt- (*Port*) *veja* **adot-**

adorar /ado'rar/ *vt* (*amar*) adore; worship <*deus*>; (*fam: gostar de*) love

adorme|cer /adorme'ser/ *vi* fall asleep; <*perna*> go to sleep, go numb; **~cido** *a* sleeping; <*perna*> numb

ador|nar /ador'nar/ *vt* adorn; **~no** /o/ *m* adornment

ado|tar /ado'tar/ *vt* adopt; **~tivo** *a* adopted

adquirir /adʒiki'rir/ *vt* acquire

adu|bar /adu'bar/ *vt* fertilize; **~bo** *m* fertilizer

adu|lação /adula'sãw/ *f* flattery; (*do público*) adulation; **~lar** *vt* make a fuss of; (*com palavras*) flatter

adulterar /aduwte'rar/ *vt* adulterate; cook, doctor <*contas*> □ *vi* commit adultery

adúltero /a'duwteru/ *m* adulterer (*f* -ess) □ *a* adulterous

adul|tério /aduw'tɛriu/ *m* adultery; **~to** *a & m* adult

advento /adʒi'vẽtu/ *m* advent

advérbio /adʒi'vɛrbiu/ *m* adverb

adver|sário /adʒiver'sariu/ *m* opponent; (*inimigo*) adversary; **~sidade** *f* adversity; **~so** *a* adverse; (*adversário*) opposed

adver|tência /adʒiver'tẽsia/ *f* warning; **~tir** *vt* warn

advo|cacia /adʒivoka'sia/ *f* legal practice; **~gado** *m* lawyer; **~gar** *vt* advocate; (*jurid*) plead ◻ *vi* practise law

aéreo /a'ɛriu/ *a* air

aero|dinâmica /aerodʒi'namika/ *f* aerodynamics; **~dinâmico** *a* aerodynamic; **~dromo** *m* airfield; **~moça** /o/ *f* air hostess; **~nauta** *m* airman (*f*-woman); **~náutica** *f* (*força*) air force; (*ciência*) aeronautics; **~nave** *f* aircraft; **~porto** /o/ *m* airport

aeros|sol /aero'sɔw/ (*pl* **~sóis**) *m* aerosol

afabilidade /afabili'dadʒi/ *f* friendliness, kindness

afagar /afa'gar/ *vt* stroke

afamado /afa'madu/ *a* renowned, famed

afas|tado /afas'tadu/ *a* remote; <*parente*> distant; **~tado de** (far) away from; **~tamento** *m* removal; (*distância*) distance; (*de candidato*) rejection; **~tar** *vt* move away; (*tirar*) remove; ward off <*perigo, ameaça*>; put out of one's mind <*idéia*>; **~tar-se** *vpr* move away; (*distanciar-se*) distance o.s.; (*de cargo*) step down

afá|vel /a'favew/ (*pl* **~veis**) *a* friendly, genial

afazeres /afa'zeris/ *m pl* business; **~ domésticos** (household) chores

afect- (*Port*) *veja* **afet-**

Afeganistão /afeganis'tãw/ *m* Afghanistan

afe|gão /afe'gãw/ *a & m* (*f* **~gã**) Afghan

afeição /afej'sãw/ *f* affection, fondness

afeiçoado /afejsu'adu/ *a* (*devoto*) devoted; (*amoroso*) fond

afeminado /afemi'nadu/ *a* effeminate

aferir /afe'rir/ *vt* check, inspect <*pesos, medidas*>; (*avaliar*) assess; (*cotejar*) compare

aferrar /afe'xar/ *vt* grasp; **~-se a** cling to

afe|tação /afeta'sãw/ *f* affectation; **~tado** *a* affected; **~tar** *vt* affect; **~tivo** *a* (*carinhoso*) affectionate; (*sentimental*) emotional; **~to** /ɛ/ *m* affection; **~tuoso** /o/ *a* affectionate

afi|ado /afi'adu/ *a* sharp; skilled <*pessoa*>; **~ar** *vt* sharpen

aficionado /afisio'nadu/ *m* enthusiast

afilhado /afi'ʎadu/ *m* godson (*f*-daughter)

afili|ação /afilia'sãw/ *f* affiliation; **~ada** *f* affiliate; **~ar** *vt* affiliate

afim /a'fĩ/ *a* related, similar

afinado /afi'nadu/ *a* in tune

afinal /afi'naw/ *adv* **~ (de contas)** (*por fim*) in the end; (*pensando bem*) after all

afinar /afi'nar/ *vt* tune ◻ *vi* taper

afinco /a'fĩku/ *m* perseverance, determination

afinidade /afini'dadʒi/ *f* affinity

afir|mação /afirma'sãw/ *f* assertion; **~mar** *vt* claim, assert; **~mativo** *a* affirmative

afivelar /afive'lar/ *vt* buckle

afixar /afik'sar/ *vt* stick, post

afli|ção /afli'sãw/ *f* (*física*) affliction; (*cuidado*) anxiety; **~gir** *vt* <*doença*> afflict; (*inquietar*) trouble; **~gir-se** *vpr* worry; **~to** *a* troubled, worried

afluente /aflu'ẽtʃi/ *m* tributary

afo|bação /afoba'sãw/ *f* fluster, flap; **~bado** *a* in a flap, flustered; **~bar** *vt* fluster; **~bar-se** *vpr* get flustered, get in a flap

afo|gado /afo'gadu/ *a* drowned; **morrer ~gado** drown; **~gador** *m* choke; **~gar** *vt/i* drown; (*auto*) flood; **~gar-se** *vpr* (*matar-se*) drown o.s.

afoito /a'fojtu/ *a* bold, daring

afora /a'fɔra/ *adv* **pelo mundo ~** throughout the world

afortunado /afortu'nadu/ *a* fortunate

afresco /a'fresku/ *m* fresco

África /'afrika/ *f* Africa; **~ do Sul** South Africa

africano /afri'kanu/ *a & m* African

afrodisíaco /afrodʒi'ziaku/ *a & m* aphrodisiac

afron|ta /a'frõta/ *f* affront, insult; **~tar** *vt* affront, insult

afrouxar /afro'ʃar/ *vt/i* loosen; (*de rapidez*) slow down; (*de disciplina*) relax

afta /'afta/ *f* (mouth) ulcer

afugentar /afuʒẽ'tar/ *vt* drive away; rout <*inimigo*>

afundar /afũ'dar/ *vt* sink; **~-se** *vpr* sink

agachar /aga'ʃar/ *vi* **~-se** *vpr* bend down

agarrar /aga'xar/ *vt* grab, snatch; **~-se** *vpr* **~se a** cling to, hold on to

agasa|lhar /agaza'ʎar/ *vt* **~lhar-se** *vpr* wrap up (warmly); **~lho** *m* (*casaco*) coat; (*suéter*) sweater

agência /a'ʒẽsia/ *f* agency; **~ de correio** post office; **~ de viagens** travel agency

agenda /a'ʒẽda/ *f* diary

agente /a'ʒẽtʃi/ *m/f* agent

ágil /'aʒiw/ (*pl* **ágeis**) *a* <*pessoa*> agile; <*serviço*> quick, efficient

agili|dade /aʒili'dadʒi/ *f* agility; (*rapidez*) speed; **~zar** *vt* speed up, streamline

ágio /'aʒiu/ *m* premium

agiota /aʒi'ɔta/ *m/f* loan shark

agir /a'ʒir/ *vi* act

agi|tado /aʒi'tadu/ *a* agitated; <*mar*> rough; **~tar** *vt* wave <*braços*>; wag <*rabo*>; shake <*garrafa*>; (*perturbar*) agitate; **~tar-se** *vpr* get agitated; <*mar*> get rough

aglome|ração /aglomera'sãw/ *f* collection; (*de pessoas*) crowd; **~rar** collect; **~rar-se** *vpr* gather

agonia /ago'nia/ *f* anguish; (*da morte*) death throes

agora /a'gɔra/ *adv* now; (*há pouco*) just now; **~ mesmo** right now; **de ~ em diante** from now on; **até ~** so far, up till now

agosto /a'gostu/ *m* August

agouro /a'goru/ *m* omen

agraciar /agrasi'ar/ *vt* decorate

agra|dar /agra'dar/ *vt* please; (*fazer agrados*) be nice to, fuss over □ *vi* be pleasing, please; (*cair no gosto*) go down well; **~dável** (*pl* **~dáveis**) *a* pleasant

agrade|cer /agrade'ser/ *vt* **~cer aco a alg, ~cer a alg por aco** thank s.o. for sth □ *vi* say thank you; **~cido** *a* grateful; **~cimento** *m* gratitude; *pl* thanks

agrado /a'gradu/ *m* **fazer ~s a** be nice to, make a fuss of

agrafa|r /agra'far/ *vt* (*Port*) staple; **~dor** *m* stapler

agrário /a'grariu/ *a* land, agrarian

agra|vante /agra'vãtʃi/ *a* aggravating □ *f* aggravating circumstance; **~var** *vt* aggravate, make worse; **~var-se** *vpr* get worse

agredir /agre'dʒir/ *vt* attack

agregado /agre'gadu/ *m* (*em casa*) lodger

agres|são /agre'sãw/ *f* aggression; (*ataque*) assault; **~sivo** *a* aggressive; **~sor** *m* aggressor

agreste /a'grɛstʃi/ *a* rural

agrião /agri'ãw/ *m* watercress

agrícola /a'grikola/ *a* agricultural

agricul|tor /agrikuw'tor/ *m* farmer; **~tura** *f* agriculture, farming

agridoce /agri'dosi/ *a* bittersweet

agropecuá|ria /agropeku'aria/ *f* farming; **~rio** *a* agricultural

agru|pamento /agrupa'mẽtu/ *m* grouping; **~par** *vt* group; **~par-se** *vpr* group (together)

água /'agwa/ *f* water; **dar ~ na boca** be mouthwatering; **ir por ~ abaixo** go down the drain; **~ benta** holy water; **~ doce** fresh water; **~ mineral** mineral water; **~ salgada** salt water; **~ sanitária** household bleach

aguaceiro /agwa'seru/ *m* downpour

água-de|-coco /agwadʒi'koku/ *f* coconut water; **~-colônia** *f* eau de cologne

aguado /a'gwadu/ *a* watery

aguardar /agwar'dar/ *vt* wait for, await □ *vi* wait

aguardente /agwar'dẽtʃi/ *f* spirit

aguarrás /agwa'xas/ *m* turpentine

água-viva /agwa'viva/ *f* jellyfish

agu|çado /agu'sadu/ *a* pointed; <*sentidos*> acute; **~çar** *vt* sharpen; **~deza** *f* sharpness; (*mental*) perceptiveness; **~do** *a* sharp; <*som*> shrill; (*fig*) acute

agüentar /agwẽ'tar/ *vt* stand, put up with; hold <*peso*> □ *vi* <*pessoa*> hold out; <*suporte*> hold

águia /'agia/ *f* eagle

agulha /a'guʎa/ *f* needle

ai /aj/ *m* sigh; (*de dor*) groan □ *int* ah!; (*de dor*) ouch!

aí /a'i/ *adv* there; (*então*) then

aidético /aj'dɛtʃiku/ *a* suffering from Aids □ *m* Aids sufferer

AIDS /'ajdʒis/ *f* Aids

ainda /a'ĩda/ *adv* still; **melhor ~** even better; **não ... ~** not ... yet; **~ assim** even so; **~ bem** just as well; **~ por cima** moreover, in addition; **~ que** even if

aipim /aj'pĩ/ *m* cassava

aipo /'ajpu/ *m* celery

ajeitar /aʒej'tar/ *vt* (*arrumar*) sort out; (*arranjar*) arrange; (*ajustar*) adjust; **~-se** *vpr* adapt; (*dar certo*) turn out right, sort o.s. out

ajoe|lhado /aʒoe'ʎadu/ *a* kneeling (down); **~lhar** *vi*, **~lhar-se** *vpr* kneel (down)

aju|da /a'ʒuda/ *f* help; **~dante** *m/f* helper; **~dar** *vt* help

ajuizado /aʒui'zadu/ *a* sensible

ajus|tar /aʒus'tar/ *vt* adjust; settle <*disputa*>; take in <*roupa*>; **~tar-se** *vpr* conform; **~tável** (*pl* **~táveis**) *a* adjustable; **~te** *m* adjustment; (*acordo*) settlement

ala /'ala/ *f* wing

ala|gação /alaga'sãw/ *f* flooding; **~gadiço** *a* marshy □ *m* marsh; **~gar** *vt* flood

alameda /ala'meda/ *f* avenue

álamo /'alamu/ *m* poplar (tree)

alarde /a'lardʒi/ *m* **fazer ~ de** flaunt; make a big thing of <*notícia*>; **~ar** *vt/i* flaunt

alargar /alar'gar/ *vt* widen; (*fig*) broaden; let out <*roupa*>

alarido /ala'ridu/ *m* outcry

alar|ma /a'larma/ *m* alarm; **~mante** *a* alarming; **~mar** *vt* alarm; **~me** *m* alarm; **~mista** *a & m* alarmist

alastrar /alas'trar/ *vt* scatter; (*disseminar*) spread ◻ *vi* spread

alavanca /ala'vãka/ *f* lever; **~ de mudanças** gear lever

alban|ês /awba'nes/ *a & m* (*f* **~esa**) Albanian

Albânia /aw'bania/ *f* Albania

albergue /aw'bɛrgi/ *m* hostel

álbum /'awbũ/ *m* album

alça /'awsa/ *f* handle; (*de roupa*) strap; (*de fusil*) sight

alcachofra /awka'ʃofra/ *f* artichoke

alçada /aw'sada/ *f* competence, power

álcali /'awkali/ *m* alkali

alcan|çar /awkã'sar/ *vt* reach; (*conseguir*) attain; (*compreender*) understand ◻ *vi* reach; **~çável** (*pl* **~çáveis**) *a* reachable; attainable; **~ce** *m* reach; (*de tiro*) range; (*importância*) consequence; (*compreensão*) understanding

alcaparra /awka'paxa/ *f* caper

alcatra aw'katra/ *f* rump steak

alcatrão /awka'trãw/ *m* tar

álcool /'awkɔw/ *m* alcohol

alcoó|latra /awko'ɔlatra/ *m/f* alcoholic; **~lico** *a & m* alcoholic

alcunha /aw'kuɲa/ *f* nickname

aldeia /aw'deja/ *f* village

aleatório /alia'tɔriu/ *a* random, arbitrary

alecrim /ale'krĩ/ *m* rosemary

ale|gação /alega'sãw/ *f* allegation; **~gar** *vt* allege

ale|goria /alego'ria/ *f* allegory; **~górico** *a* allegorical

ale|grar /ale'grar/ *vt* cheer up; brighten up <*casa*>; **~grar-se** *vpr* cheer up; **~gre** /ɛ/ *a* cheerful; <*cores*> bright; **~gria** *f* joy

alei|jado /ale'ʒadu/ *a* crippled ◻ *m* cripple; **~jar** *vt* cripple

alei|tamento /alejta'mẽtu/ *m* breast-feeding; **~tar** *vt* breast-feed

além /a'lẽj/ *adv* beyond; **~ de** (*ao lado de lá de*) beyond; (*mais de*) over; (*ademais de*) apart from

Alemanha /ale'maɲa/ *f* Germany

alemão /ale'mãw/ (*pl* **~mães**) *a & m* (*f* **~mã**) German

alen|tador /alẽta'dor/ *a* encouraging; **~tar** *vt* encourage; **~tar-se** *vpr* cheer up; **~to** *m* courage; (*fôlego*) breath

alergia /aler'ʒia/ *f* allergy

alérgico /a'lɛrʒiku/ *a* allergic (**a** to)

aler|ta /a'lɛrta/ *a & m* alert ◻ *adv* on the alert; **~tar** *vt* alert

alfa|bético /awfa'bɛtʃiku/ *a* alphabetical; **~betização** *f* literacy; **~betizar** *vt* teach to read and write; **~beto** *m* alphabet

alface /aw'fasi/ *f* lettuce

alfaiate /awfaj'atʃi/ *m* tailor

al|fândega /aw'fãdʒiga/ *f* customs; **~fandegário** *a* customs ◻ *m* customs officer

alfine|tada /awfine'tada/ *f* prick; (*dor*) stabbing pain; (*fig*) dig; **~te** /e/ *m* pin; **~te de segurança** safety pin

alforreca /alfo'xeka/ *f* (*Port*) jellyfish

alga /'awga/ *f* seaweed

algarismo /awga'rizmu/ *m* numeral

algazarra /awga'zaxa/ *f* uproar, racket

alge|mar /awʒe'mar/ *vt* handcuff; **~mas** /e/ *f pl* handcuffs

algibeira /alʒi'bejra/ *f* (*Port*) pocket

algo /'awgu/ *pron* something; (*numa pergunta*) anything ◻ *adv* somewhat

algodão /awgo'dãw/ *m* cotton; **~(-doce)** candy floss, (*Amer*) cotton candy; **~ (hidrófilo)** cotton wool, (*Amer*) absorbent cotton

alguém /aw'gẽj/ *pron* somebody, someone; (*numa pergunta*) anybody, anyone

al|gum /aw'gũ/ (*f* **~guma**) *a* some; (*numa pergunta*) any; (*nenhum*) no, not one ◻ *pron pl* some; **~guma coisa** something

algures /aw'guris/ *adv* somewhere

alheio /a'ʎeju/ *a* (*de outra pessoa*) someone else's; (*de outras pessoas*) other people's; **~ a** foreign to; (*impróprio*) irrelevant to; (*desatento*) unaware of; **~ de** removed from

alho /'aʎu/ *m* garlic; **~-poró** *m* leek

ali /a'li/ *adv* (over) there

ali|ado /ali'adu/ *a* allied ◻ *m* ally; **~ança** *f* alliance; (*anel*) wedding ring; **~ar** *vt*, **~ar-se** *vpr* ally

aliás /a'ljaʃ/ *adv* (*além disso*) what's more, furthermore; (*no entanto*) however; (*diga-se de passagem*) by the way, incidentally; (*senão*) otherwise

álibi /'alibi/ *m* alibi

alicate /ali'katʃi/ *m* pliers; **~ de unhas** nail clippers

alicerce /ali'sɛrsi/ *m* foundation; (*fig*) basis

alie|nado /alie'nadu/ *a* alienated; (*demente*) insane; **~nar** *vt* alienate; transfer <*bens*>; **~nígena** *a & m/f* alien

alimen|tação /alimẽta'sãw/ *f* (*ato*) feeding; (*comida*) food; (*tecn*) supply; **~tar** *a* food; <*hábitos*> eating ◻ *vt* feed; (*fig*) nurture; **~tar-se de** live on;

~tício *a* gêneros **~tícios** foodstuffs; **~to** *m* food

ali|nhado /ali'ɲadu/ *a* aligned; <*pessoa*> smart, (*Amer*) sharp; **~nhar** *vt* align

alíquota /a'likwota/ *f* (*de imposto*) bracket

alisar /ali'zar/ *vt* smooth (out); straighten <*cabelo*>

alistar /alis'tar/ *vt* recruit; **~-se** *vpr* enlist

aliviar /alivi'ar/ *vt* relieve

alívio /a'liviu/ *m* relief

alma /'awma/ *f* soul

almanaque /awma'naki/ *m* yearbook

almejar /awme'ʒar/ *vt* long for

almirante /awmi'rãtʃi/ *m* admiral

almo|çar /awmo'sar/ *vi* have lunch ◻ *vt* have for lunch; **~ço** /o/ *m* lunch

almofada /awmo'fada/ *f* cushion; (*Port: de cama*) pillow

almôndega /aw'mõdʒiga/ *f* meatball

almoxarifado /awmoʃari'fadu/ *m* storeroom

alô /a'lo/ *int* hallo

alocar /alo'kar/ *vt* allocate

alo|jamento /aloʒa'mẽtu/ *m* accommodation, (*Amer*) accommodations; (*habitação*) housing; **~jar** *vt* accommodate; house < *sem-teto*>; **~jar-se** *vpr* stay

alongar /alõ'gar/ *vt* lengthen; extend, stretch out <*braço*>

alpendre /aw'pẽdri/ *m* shed; (*pórtico*) porch

Alpes /'awpis/ *m pl* Alps

alpinis|mo /awpi'nizmu/ *m* mountaineering; **~ta** *m/f* mountaineer

alqueire /aw'keri/ *m = 4.84 hectares,* (*in São Paulo = 2.42 hectares*)

alquimi|a /awki'mia/ *f* alchemy; **~sta** *mf* alchemist

alta /'awta/ *f* rise; **dar ~ a** discharge; **ter ~** be discharged

altar /aw'tar/ *m* altar

alterar /awte'rar/ *vt* alter; (*falsificar*) falsify; **~-se** *vpr* change; (*zangar-se*) get angry

alter|nado /awter'nadu/ *a* alternate; **~nar** *vt/i*, **~nar-se** *vpr* alternate; **~nativa** *f* alternative; **~nativo** *a* alternative; <*corrente*> alternating

al|teza /aw'teza/ *f* highness; **~titude** *f* altitude

alti|vez /awtʃi'ves/ *f* arrogance; **~vo** *a* arrogant; (*elevado*) majestic

alto /'awtu/ *a* high; <*pessoa*> tall; < *barulho*> loud ◻ *adv* high; <*falar*> loud(ly); <*ler*> aloud ◻ *m* top; **os ~s e baixos** the ups and downs ◻ *int* halt!; **~-falante** *m* loudspeaker

altura /aw'tura/ *f* height; (*momento*) moment; **ser à ~ de** be up to

aluci|nação /alusina'sãw/ *f* hallucination; **~nante** *a* mind-boggling, crazy

aludir /alu'dʒir/ *vi* allude (**a** to)

alu|gar /alu'gar/ *vt* rent <*casa*>; hire, rent <*carro*>; <*locador*> let, rent out, hire out; **~guel** (*Port*), **~guer** /ɛ/ *m* rent; (*ato*) renting

alumiar /alumi'ar/ *vt* light (up)

alumínio /alu'miniu/ *m* aluminium, (*Amer*) aluminum

aluno /a'lunu/ *m* pupil

alusão /alu'zãw/ *f* allusion (**a** to)

alvará /awva'ra/ *m* permit, licence

alve|jante /awve'ʒãtʃi/ *m* bleach; **~jar** *vt* bleach; (*visar*) aim at

alvenaria /awvena'ria/ *f* masonry

alvo /'awvu/ *m* target

alvorada /awvo'rada/ *f* dawn

alvoro|çar /awvoro'sar/ *vt* stir up, agitate; (*entusiasmar*) excite; **~ço** /o/ *m* (*tumulto*) uproar; (*entusiasmo*) excitement

amabilidade /amabili'dadʒi/ *f* kindness

amaci|ante /amasi'ãtʃi/ *m* (*de roupa*) (fabric) conditioner; **~ar** *vt* soften; run in <*carro*>

amador /ama'dor/ *a & m* amateur; **~ismo** *m* amateurism; **~ístico** *a* amateurish

amadurecer /amadure'ser/ *vt/i* <*fruta*> ripen; (*fig*) mature

âmago /'amagu/ *m* heart, core; (*da questão*) crux

amaldiçoar /amawdʒiso'ar/ *vt* curse

amamentar /amamẽ'tar/ *vt* breast-feed

amanhã /ama'ɲã/ *m & adv* tomorrow; **depois de ~** the day after tomorrow

amanhecer /amaɲe'ser/ *vi & m* dawn

amansar /amã'sar/ *vt* tame; (*fig*) placate < *pessoa*>

a|mante /a'mãtʃi/ *m/f* lover; **~mar** *vt/i* love

amarelo /ama'rɛlu/ *a & m* yellow

amar|go /a'margu/ *a* bitter; **~gura** *f* bitterness; **~gurar** *vt* embitter; (*sofrer*) endure

amarrar /ama'xar/ *vt* tie (up); (*naut*) moor; **~ a cara** frown, scowl

amarrotar /amaxo'tar/ *vt* crease

amassar /ama'sar/ *vt* crush, squash; screw up <*papel*>; crease <*roupa*>; dent <*carro*>; knead <*pão*>; mash <*batatas*>

amá|vel /a'mavew/ (*pl* **~veis**) *a* kind

Ama|zonas /ama'zonas/ *m* Amazon; **~zônia** *f* Amazonia

âmbar /'ãbar/ *m* amber

ambi|ção /ãbi'sãw/ *f* ambition; **~cionar** *vt* aspire to; **~cioso** /o/ *a* ambitious

ambien|tal /ãbiẽ'taw/ (*pl* **~tais**) *a* environmental; **~tar** *vt* set <*filme, livro*>; set up <*casa*>; **~tar-se** *vpr* settle in; **~te** *m* environment; (*atmosfera*) atmosphere

am|bigüidade /ãbigwi'dadʒi/ *f* ambiguity; **~bíguo** *a* ambiguous

âmbito /'ãbitu/ *m* scope, range

ambos /'ãbus/ *a & pron* both

ambu|lância /ãbu'lãsia/ *f* ambulance; **~lante** *a* (*que anda*) walking; <*músico*> wandering; <*venda*> mobile; **~latório** *m* out-patient clinic

amea|ça /ami'asa/ *f* threat; **~çador** *a* threatening; **~çar** *vt* threaten

ameba /a'mɛba/ *f* amoeba

amedrontar /amedrõ'tar/ *vt* scare; **~-se** *vpr* get scared

ameixa /a'meʃa/ *f* plum; (*passa*) prune

amém /a'mẽj/ *int* amen □ *m* agreement; **dizer ~ a** go along with

amêndoa /a'mẽdoa/ *f* almond

amendoim /amẽdo'ĩ/ *m* peanut

ame|nidade /ameni'dadʒi/ *f* pleasantness; *pl* pleasantries, small talk; **~nizar** *vt* ease; calm <*ânimos*>; settle <*disputa*>; tone down <*repreensão*>; **~no** /e/ *a* pleasant; mild <*clima*>

América /a'mɛrika/ *f* America; **~ do Norte/Sul** North/South America

america|nizar /amerikani'zar/ *vt* Americanize; **~no** *a & m* American

amestrar /ames'trar/ *vt* train

ametista /ame'tʃista/ *f* amethyst

amianto /ami'ãtu/ *m* asbestos

ami|gar-se /ami'garsi/ *vpr* make friends; **~gável** (*pl* **~gáveis**) *a* amicable

amígdala /a'migdala/ *f* tonsil

amigdalite /amigda'litʃi/ *f* tonsillitis

amigo /a'migu/ *a* friendly □ *m* friend; **~ da onça** false friend

amistoso /amis'tozu/ *a & m* friendly

amiúde /ami'udʒi/ *adv* often

amizade /ami'zadʒi/ *f* friendship

amnésia /ami'nɛzia/ *f* amnesia

amnistia /amnis'tia/ *f* (*Port*) *veja* **anistia**

amo|lação /amola'sãw/ *f* annoyance; **~lante** *a* annoying; **~lar** *vt* annoy, bother; sharpen <*faca*>; **~lar-se** *vpr* get annoyed

amolecer /amole'ser/ *vt/i* soften

amol|gadura /amowga'dura/ *f* dent; **~gar** *vt* dent

amoníaco /amo'niaku/ *m* ammonia

amontoar /amõto'ar/ *vt* pile up; amass <*riquezas*>; **~-se** *vpr* pile up

amor /a'mor/ *m* love; **~ próprio** self-esteem

amora /a'mɔra/ *f* **~ preta**, (*Port*) **~ silvestre** blackberry

amordaçar /amorda'sar/ *vt* gag

amoroso /amo'rozu/ *adj* loving

amor-perfeito /amorper'fejtu/ *m* pansy

amorte|cedor /amortese'dor/ *m* shock absorber; **~cer** *vt* deaden; absorb <*impacto*>; break <*queda*> □ *vi* fade

amostra /a'mɔstra/ *f* sample

ampa|rar /ãpa'rar/ *vt* support; (*fig*) protect; **~rar-se** *vpr* lean; **~ro** *m* (*apoio*) support; (*proteção*) protection; (*ajuda*) aid

ampère /ã'pɛri/ *m* amp(ere)

ampli|ação /ãplia'sãw/ *f* (*de foto*) enlargement; (*de casa*) extension; **~ar** *vt* enlarge <*foto*>; extend <*casa*>; broaden <*conhecimentos*>

amplifi|cador /ãplifika'dor/ *m* amplifier; **~car** *vt* amplify

amplo /'ãplu/ *a* <*sala*> spacious; <*roupa*> full; <*sentido, conhecimento*> broad

ampola /ã'pola/ *f* ampoule

amputar /ãpu'tar/ *vt* amputate

Amsterdã /amister'dã/, (*Port*) **Amsterdão** /amiʃter'dãw/ *f* Amsterdam

amu|ado /amu'adu/ *a* in a sulk, sulky; **~ar** *vi* sulk

amuleto /amu'leto/ *m* charm

amuo /a'muu/ *m* sulk

ana|crônico /ana'kroniku/ *a* anachronistic; **~cronismo** *m* anachronism

anais /a'najs/ *m pl* annals

analfabeto /anawfa'bɛtu/ *a & m* illiterate

analisar /anali'zar/ *vt* analyse

análise /a'nalizi/ *f* analysis

ana|lista /ana'lista/ *m/f* analyst; **~lítico** *a* analytical

analogia /analo'ʒia/ *f* analogy

análogo /a'nalogu/ *a* analogous

ananás /ana'naʃ/ *m invar* (*Port*) pineapple

anão /a'nãw/ *a & m* (*f* **anã**) dwarf

anarquia /anar'kia/ *f* anarchy; (*fig*) chaos

anárquico /a'narkiku/ *a* anarchic

anarquista /anar'kista/ *m/f* anarchist

ana|tomia /anato'mia/ *f* anatomy; **~tômico** *a* anatomical

anca /'ãka/ *f* (*de pessoa*) hip; (*de animal*) rump

anchova /ã'ʃova/ *f* anchovy

ancinho /ã'siɲu/ *m* rake

âncora /'ãkora/ *f* anchor

anco|radouro /ãkora'doru/ *m* anchorage; **~rar** *vt/i* anchor

andaime /ã'dajmi/ *m* scaffolding

an|damento /ãda'mẽtu/ *m* (*progresso*) progress; (*rumo*) course; **dar ~damento a** set in motion; **~dar** *m* (*jeito de andar*) gait, walk; (*de prédio*) floor; (*Port: apartamento*) flat, (*Amer*) apartment □ *vi* (*ir a pé*) walk; (*de trem, ônibus*) travel; (*a cavalo, de bicicleta*) ride; (*funcionar, progredir*) go; **ele anda deprimido** he's been depressed lately

Andes /'ãdʒis/ *m pl* Andes

andorinha /ãdo'riɲa/ *f* swallow

anedota /ane'dæta/ *f* anecdote

anel /a'nɛw/ (*pl* **anéis**) *m* ring; (*no cabelo*) curl; **~ viário** ringroad

anelado /ane'ladu/ *a* curly

anemia /ane'mia/ *f* anaemia

anêmico /a'nemiku/ *a* anaemic

anes|tesia /aneste'zia/ *f* anaesthesia; (*droga*) anaesthetic; **~tesiar** *vt* anaesthetize; **~tésico** *a & m* anaesthetic; **~tesista** *m/f* anaesthetist

ane|xar /anek'sar/ *vt* annex <*terras*>; (*em carta*) enclose; (*juntar*) attach; **~xo** /ɛ/ *a* attached; (*em carta*) enclosed □ *m* annexe; (*em carta*) enclosure

anfíbio /ã'fibiu/ *a* amphibious □ *m* amphibian

anfiteatro /ãfitʃi'atru/ *m* amphitheatre; (*no teatro*) dress circle

anfi|trião /ãfitri'ãw/ *m* (*f* **~triã**) host (*f*-ess)

angariar /ãgari'ar/ *vt* raise <*fundos*>; canvass for <*votos*>; win <*adeptos, simpatia*>

angli|cano /ãgli'kanu/ *a & m* Anglican; **~cismo** *m* Anglicism

anglo-saxônico /ãglusak'soniku/ *a* Anglo-Saxon

Angola /ã'gɔla/ *f* Angola

angolano /ãgo'lanu/ *a & m* Angolan

angra /'ãgra/ *f* inlet, cove

angular /ãgu'lar/ *a* angular

ângulo /'ãgulu/ *m* angle

angústia /ã'gustʃia/ *f* anguish, anxiety

angustiante /ãgustʃi'ãtʃi/ *a* distressing; <*momento*> anxious

ani|mado /ani'madu/ *a* (*vivo*) lively; (*alegre*) cheerful; (*entusiasmado*) enthusiastic; **~mador** *a* encouraging □ *m* presenter; **~mal** (*pl* **~mais**) *a & m* animal; **~mar** *vt* encourage; liven up <*festa*>; **~mar-se** *vpr* cheer up; <*festa*> liven up

ânimo /'animu/ *m* courage, spirit; *pl* tempers

animosidade /animozi'dadʒi/ *f* animosity

aniquilar /aniki'lar/ *vt* destroy; (*prostrar*) shatter

anis /a'nis/ *m* aniseed

anistia /anis'tʃia/ *f* amnesty

aniver|sariante /aniversari'ãtʃi/ *m/f* birthday boy (*f* girl); **~sário** *m* birthday; (*de casamento etc*) anniversary

anjo /'ãʒu/ *m* angel

ano /'anu/ *m* year; **fazer ~s** have a birthday; **~ bissexto** leap year; **~ letivo** academic year; **~-bom** *m* New Year

anoite|cer /anojte'ser/ *m* nightfall □ *vi* **~ceu** night fell

anomalia /anoma'lia/ *f* anomaly

anonimato /anoni'matu/ *m* anonymity

anônimo /a'nonimu/ *a* anonymous

anor|mal /anor'maw/ (*pl* **~mais**) *a* abnormal

ano|tação /anota'sãw/ *f* note; **~tar** *vt* note down, write down

ânsia /'ãsia/ *f* anxiety; (*desejo*) longing; **~s de vômito** nausea

ansi|ar /ãsi'ar/ *vi* **~ por** long for; **~edade** *f* anxiety; (*desejo*) eagerness; **~oso** /o/ *a* anxious

antártico /ã'tartʃiku/ *a & m* Antarctic

antebraço /ãtʃi'brasu/ *m* forearm

antece|dência /ãtese'dẽsia/ *f* **com ~dência** in advance; **~dente** *a* preceding; **~dentes** *m pl* record, past

antecessor /ãtese'sor/ *m* (*f* **~a**) predecessor

anteci|pação /ãtʃisipa'sãw/ *f* anticipation; **com ~pação** in advance; **~padamente** *adv* in advance; **~pado** *a* advance; **~par** *vt* anticipate, forestall; (*adiantar*) bring forward; **~par-se** *vpr* be previous

antena /ã'tena/ *f* aerial, (*Amer*) antenna; (*de inseto*) feeler

anteontem /ãtʃi'õtẽ/ *adv* the day before yesterday

antepassado /ãtʃipa'sadu/ *m* ancestor

anterior /ãteri'or/ *a* previous; (*dianteiro*) front

antes /'ãtʃis/ *adv* before; (*ao contrário*) rather; **~ de/que** before

ante-sala /ãtʃi'sala/ *f* ante-room

anti|biótico /ãtʃibi'ɔtʃiku/ *a & m* antibiotic; **~caspa** *a* anti-dandruff; **~concepcional** (*pl* **~concepcionais**) *a & m* contraceptive; **~congelante** *m* antifreeze; **~corpo** *m* antibody

antídoto /ã'tʃidotu/ *m* antidote

antiético /ãtʃi'ɛtʃiku/ *a* unethical

antigamente /ãtʃiga'mẽtʃi/ *adv* formerly

anti|go /ã'tʃigu/ *a* old; (*da antiguidade*) ancient; <*móveis etc*> antique; (*anterior*) former; **~guidade** *f* antiquity; (*numa firma*) seniority; *pl* (*monumentos*) antiquities; (*móveis etc*) antiques

anti-|higiênico /ãtʃiʒi'eniku/ *a* unhygienic; **~histamínico** *a & m* antihistamine; **~horário** *a* anticlockwise

antilhano /ãtʃi'ʎanu/ *a & m* West Indian

Antilhas /ã'tʃiʎas/ *f pl* West Indies

anti|patia /ãtʃipa'tʃia/ *f* dislike; **~pático** *a* unpleasant, unfriendly

antiquado /ãtʃi'kwadu/ *a* antiquated, out-dated

anti-|semitismo /ãtʃisemi-'tʃizmu/ *m* anti-Semitism; **~séptico** *a & m* antiseptic; **~social** (*pl* **~sociais**) *a* antisocial

antítese /ã'tʃitezi/ *f* antithesis

antologia /ãtolo'ʒia/ *f* anthology

antônimo /ã'tonimu/ *m* antonym

antro /'ãtru/ *m* cavern; (*de animal*) lair; (*de ladrões*) den

antro|pófago /ãtro'pɔfagu/ *a* man-eating; **~pologia** *f* anthropology; **~pólogo** *m* anthropologist

anu|al /anu'aw/ (*pl* **~ais**) *a* annual, yearly

anu|lação /anula'sãw/ *f* cancellation; **~lar** *vt* cancel; annul <*casamento*>; (*compensar*) cancel out ▫ *m* ring finger

anunciar /anũsi'ar/ *vt* announce; advertise <*produto*>

anúncio /a'nũsiu/ *m* announcement; (*propaganda, classificado*) advert(isement); (*cartaz*) notice

ânus /'anus/ *m invar* anus

an|zol /ã'zɔw/ (*pl* **~zóis**) *m* fish-hook

aonde /a'õdʒi/ *adv* where

apadrinhar /apadri'ɲar/ *vt* be godfather to <*afilhado*>; be best man for <*noivo*>; (*proteger*) protect; (*patrocinar*) support

apa|gado /apa'gadu/ *a* <*fogo*> out; <*luz, TV*> off; (*indistinto*) faint; <*pessoa*> dull; **~gar** *vt* put out <*cigarro, fogo*>; blow out <*vela*>; switch off <*luz, TV*>; rub out <*erro*>; clean <*quadro-negro*>; **~gar-se** *vpr* <*fogo, luz*> go out; <*lembrança*> fade; (*desmaiar*) pass out; (*fam: dormir*) nod off

apaixo|nado /apaʃo'nadu/ *a* in love (**por** with); **~nante** *a* captivating; **~nar-se** *vpr* fall in love (**por** with)

apalpar /apaw'par/ *vt* touch, feel; <*médico*> examine

apanhar /apa'ɲar/ *vt* catch; (*do chão*) pick up; pick <*flores, frutas*>; (*ir buscar*) pick up; (*alcançar*) catch up ▫ *vi* be beaten

aparafusar /aparafu'zar/ *vt* screw

apa|ra-lápis /apara'lapiʃ/ *m invar* (*Port*) pencil sharpener; **~rar** *vt* catch <*bola*>; parry <*golpe*>; trim <*cabelo*>; sharpen <*lápis*>

aparato /apa'ratu/ *m* pomp, ceremony

apare|cer /apare'ser/ *vi* appear; **~ça!** do drop in!; **~cimento** *m* appearance

apare|lhagem /apare'ʎaʒẽ/ *f* equipment; **~lhar** *vt* equip; **~lho** /e/ *m* apparatus; (*máquina*) machine; (*de chá*) set, service; (*fone*) phone

aparência /apa'rẽsia/ *f* appearance; **na ~** apparently

aparen|tado /aparẽ'tadu/ *a* related; **~tar** *vt* show; (*fingir*) feign; **~te** *a* apparent

apar|tamento /aparta'mẽtu/ *m* flat, (*Amer*) apartment; **~tar** *vt*, **~tar-se** *vpr* separate; **~te** *m* aside

apatia /apa'tʃia/ *f* apathy

apático /a'patʃiku/ *a* apathetic

apavo|rante /apavo'rãtʃi/ *a* terrifying; **~rar** *vt* terrify; **~rar-se** *vpr* be terrified

apaziguar /apazi'gwar/ *vt* appease

apear-se /api'arsi/ *vpr* (*de cavalo*) dismount; (*de ônibus*) alight

ape|gar-se /ape'garsi/ *vpr* become attached (**a** to); **~go** /e/ *m* attachment

ape|lação /apela'sãw/ *f* appeal; (*fig*) exhibitionism; **~lar** *vi* appeal (**de** against); **~lar para** appeal to; (*fig*) resort to

apeli|dar /apeli'dar/ *vt* nickname; **~do** *m* nickname

apelo /a'pelu/ *m* appeal

apenas /a'penas/ *adv* only

apêndice /a'pẽdʒisi/ *m* appendix

apendicite /apẽdʒi'sitʃi/ *f* appendicitis

aperceber-se /aperse'bersi/ *vpr* **~ (de)** notice, realize

aperfeiçoar /aperfejso'ar/ *vt* perfect

aperitivo /aperi'tʃivu/ *m* aperitif

aper|tado /aper'tadu/ *a* tight; (*sem dinheiro*) hard-up; **~tar** *vt* (*segurar*) hold tight; tighten <*cinto*>; press <*botão*>; squeeze <*esponja*>; take in <*vestido*>; fasten <*cinto de segurança*>; step up <*vigilância*>; cut down on <*despesas*>; break <*coração*>; (*fig*) pressurize <*pessoa*> ▫ *vi* <*sapato*> pinch; <*chuva, frio*> get worse; <*estrada*> narrow; **~tar-se** *vpr* (*gastar menos*) tighten one's belt; (*não ter dinheiro*) feel the pinch; **~tar a mão de alg** shake hands with s.o.; **~to** /e/ *m* pressure; (*de botão*) press; (*dificuldade*) tight spot, jam; **~to de mãos** handshake

apesar /ape'zar/ **~ de** *prep* in spite of

apeti|te /ape'tʃitʃi/ *m* appetite; **~toso** /o/ *a* appetizing

apetrechos /ape'treʃus/ *m pl* gear; (*de pesca*) tackle

apimentado /apimẽ'tadu/ *a* spicy, hot

apinhar /api'ɲar/ *vt* crowd, pack; **~-se** *vpr* crowd

api|tar /api'tar/ *vi* whistle □ *vt* referee <*jogo*>; **~to** *m* whistle

aplanar /apla'nar/ *vt* level <*terreno*>; (*fig*) smooth <*caminho*>; smooth over <*problema*>

aplau|dir /aplaw'dʒir/ *vt* applaud; **~so(s)** *m* (*pl*) applause

apli|cação /aplika'sãw/ *f* application; (*de dinheiro*) investment; (*de lei*) enforcement; **~car** *vt* apply; invest <*dinheiro*>; enforce <*lei*>; **~car-se** *vpr* apply (**a** to); (*ao estudo etc*) apply o.s. (**a** to); **~que** *m* hairpiece

apoderar-se /apode'rarsi/ *vpr* **~ de** take possession of; <*raiva*> take hold of

apodrecer /apodre'ser/ *vt/i* rot

apoi|ar /apoj'ar/ *vt* lean; (*fig*) support; (*basear*) base; **~ar-se** *vpr* **~ar-se em** lean on; (*fig*) be based on, rest on; **~o** *m* support

apólice /a'pɔlisi/ *f* policy; (*ação*) bond

apon|tador /apõta'dor/ *m* pencil sharpener; **~tar** *vt* (*com o dedo*) point at, point to; point out <*erro, caso interessante*>; aim <*arma*>; name <*nomes*>; put forward <*razão*> □ *vi* <*sol, planta*> come up; (*com o dedo*) point (**para** to)

apoquentar /apokẽ'tar/ *vt* annoy

aporrinhar /apoxi'ɲar/ *vt* annoy

após /a'pɔs/ *adv* after; **loção ~-barba** after-shave (lotion)

aposen|tado /apozẽ'tadu/ *a* retired □ *m* pensioner; **~tadoria** *f* retirement; (*pensão*) pension; **~tar** *vt*, **~tar-se** *vpr* retire; **~to** *m* room

após-guerra /apɔz'gɛxa/ *m* post-war period

apos|ta /a'pɔsta/ *f* bet; **~tar** *vt* bet (**em** on); (*fig*) have faith (**em** in)

apostila /apos'tʃila/ *f* revision aid, book of key facts

apóstolo /a'pɔstolu/ *m* apostle

apóstrofo /a'pɔstrofu/ *m* apostrophe

apre|ciação /apresia'sãw/ *f* appreciation; **~ciar** *vt* appreciate; think highly of <*pessoa*>; **~ciativo** *a* appreciative; **~ciável** (*pl* **~ciáveis**) *a* appreciable; **~ço** /e/ *m* regard

apreen|der /apriẽ'der/ *vt* seize <*contrabando*>; apprehend <*criminoso*>; grasp <*sentido*>; **~são** *f* apprehension; (*de contrabando*) seizure; **~sivo** *a* apprehensive

apregoar /aprego'ar/ *vt* proclaim; cry <*mercadoria*>

apren|der /aprẽ'der/ *vt/i* learn; **~diz** *m/f* (*de ofício*) apprentice; (*de direção*) learner; **~dizado** *m*, **~dizagem** *f* (*de ofício*) apprenticeship; (*de profissão*) training; (*escolar*) learning

apresen|tação /aprezẽta'sãw/ *f* presentation; (*teatral etc*) performance; (*de pessoas*) introduction; **~tador** *m* presenter; **~tar** *vt* present; introduce <*pessoa*>; **~tar-se** *vpr* (*identificar-se*) introduce o.s.; <*ocasião, problema*> present o.s., arise; **~tar-se a** report to <*polícia etc*>; go in for <*exame*>; stand for <*eleição*>; **~tável** (*pl* **~táveis**) *a* presentable

apres|sado /apre'sadu/ *a* hurried; **~sar** *vt* hurry; **~sar-se** *vpr* hurry (up)

aprimorar /aprimo'rar/ *vt* perfect, refine

aprofundar /aprofũ'dar/ *vt* deepen; study carefully <*questão*>; **~-se** *vpr* get deeper; **~-se em** go deeper into

aprontar /aprõ'tar/ *vt* get ready; pick <*briga*> □ *vi* act up; **~-se** *vpr* get ready

apropriado /apropri'adu/ *a* appropriate, suitable

apro|vação /aprova'sãw/ *f* approval; (*num exame*) pass; **~var** *vt* approve of; approve <*lei*> □ *vi* make the grade; **ser ~vado** (*num exame*) pass

aprovei|tador /aprovejta'dor/ *m* opportunist; **~tamento** *m* utilization; **~tar** *vt* take advantage of; take <*ocasião*>; (*utilizar*) use □ *vi* make the most of it; (*Port: adiantar*) be of use; **~tar-se** *vpr* take advantage (**de** of); **~te!** (*divirta-se*) have a good time!

aproxi|mação /aprosima'sãw/ *f* (*chegada*) approach; (*estimativa*) approximation; **~mado** *a* <*valor*> approximate; **~mar** *vt* move nearer; (*aliar*) bring together; **~mar-se** *vpr* approach, get nearer (**de** to)

ap|tidão /aptʃi'dãw/ *f* aptitude, suitability; **~to** *a* suitable

apunhalar /apuɲa'lar/ *vt* stab

apu|rado /apu'radu/ *a* refined; **~rar** *vt* (*aprimorar*) refine; (*descobrir*) ascertain; investigate <*caso*>; collect <*dinheiro*>; count <*votos*>; **~rar-se** *vpr* (*com a roupa*) dress smartly; **~ro** *m* refinement; (*no vestir*) elegance; (*dificuldade*) difficulty; *pl* trouble

aquarela /akwa'rɛla/ *f* watercolour

aquariano /akwari'anu/ *a & m* Aquarian

aquário /a'kwariu/ *m* aquarium; **Aquário** Aquarius

aquartelar /akwarte'lar/ *vt* billet

aquático /a'kwatʃiku/ *a* aquatic, water

aque|cedor /akese'dor/ *m* heater; **~cer** *vt* heat ▫ *vi*, **~cer-se** *vpr* heat up; **~cimento** *m* heating

aqueduto /ake'dutu/ *m* aqueduct

aquele /a'keli/ *a* that; *pl* those ▫ *pron* that one; *pl* those; **~ que** the one that

àquele = **a**[2] + **aquele**

aqui /a'ki/ *adv* here

aquilo /a'kilu/ *pron* that

àquilo = **a**[2] + **aquilo**

aquisi|ção /akizi'sãw/ *f* acquisition; **~tivo** *a* **poder ~tivo** purchasing power

ar /ar/ *m* air; (*aspecto*) look, air; (*Port: no carro*) choke; **ao ~ livre** in the open air; **no ~** (*fig*) up in the air; (*TV*) on air; **~ condicionado** air conditioning

árabe /'arabi/ *a & m* Arab; (*ling*) Arabic

Arábia /a'rabia/ *f* Arabia; **~ Saudita** Saudi Arabia

arado /a'radu/ *m* plough, (*Amer*) plow

aragem /a'raʒẽ/ *f* breeze

arame /a'rami/ *m* wire; **~ farpado** barbed wire

aranha /a'raɲa/ *f* spider

arar /a'rar/ *vt* plough, (*Amer*) plow

arara /a'rara/ *f* parrot

arbi|trar /arbi'trar/ *vt/i* referee <*jogo*>; arbitrate <*disputa*>; **~trário** *a* arbitrary

arbítrio /ar'bitriu/ *m* judgement; **livre ~** free will

árbitro /'arbitru/ *m* arbiter <*da moda etc*>; (*jurid*) arbitrator; (*de futebol*) referee; (*de tênis*) umpire

arborizado /arbori'zadu/ *a* wooded, green; <*rua*> tree-lined

arbusto /ar'bustu/ *m* shrub

ar|ca /'arka/ *f* **~ca de Noé** Noah's Ark; **~cada** *f* (*galeria*) arcade; (*arco*) arch

arcaico /ar'kajku/ *a* archaic

arcar /ar'kar/ *vt* **~ com** deal with

arcebispo /arse'bispu/ *m* archbishop

arco /'arku/ *m* (*arquit*) arch; (*arma, mus*) bow; (*eletr, mat*) arc; **~-da-velha** *m* **coisa do ~-da-velha** amazing thing; **~-íris** *m invar* rainbow

ar|dente /ar'dẽtʃi/ *a* burning; (*fig*) ardent; **~der** *vi* burn; <*olhos, ferida*> sting

ar|dil /ar'dʒiw/ (*pl* **~dis**) *m* trick, ruse

ardor /ar'dor/ *m* heat; (*fig*) ardour; **com ~** ardently

árduo /'arduu/ *a* strenuous, arduous

área /'aria/ *f* area; **(grande) ~** penalty area; **~ (de serviço)** yard

arear /ari'ar/ *vt* scour <*panela*>

areia /a'reja/ *f* sand

arejar /are'ʒar/ *vt* air ▫ *vi*, **~-se** *vpr* get some air; (*descansar*) have a breather

are|na /a'rena/ *f* arena; **~noso** /o/ *a* sandy

arenque /a'rẽki/ *m* herring

argamassa /arga'masa/ *f* mortar

Argélia /ar'ʒɛlia/ *f* Algeria

argelino /arʒe'linu/ *a & m* Algerian

Argentina /arʒẽ'tʃina/ *f* Argentina

argentino /arʒẽ'tʃinu/ *a & m* Argentinian

argila /ar'ʒila/ *f* clay

argola /ar'gɔla/ *f* ring

argumen|tar /argumẽ'tar/ *vt/i* argue; **~to** *m* argument; (*de filme etc*) subject-matter

ariano /ari'anu/ *a & m* (*do signo Aries*) Arian

árido /'aridu/ *a* arid; barren <*deserto*>; (*fig*) dull, dry

Aries /'aris/ *f* Aries

arisco /a'risku/ *a* timid

aristo|cracia /aristokra'sia/ *f* aristocracy; **~crata** *m/f* aristocrat; **~crático** *a* aristocratic

aritmética /aritʃ'mɛtʃika/ *f* arithmetic

arma /'arma/ *f* weapon; *pl* arms; **~ de fogo** firearm

ar|mação /arma'sãw/ *f* frame; (*de óculos*) frames; (*naut*) rigging; **~madilha** *f* trap; **~madura** *f* suit of armour; (*armação*) framework; **~mar** *vt* (*dar armas a*) arm; (*montar*) put up, assemble; set up <*máquina*>; set, lay <*armadilha*>; fit out <*navio*>; hatch <*plano, complô*>; cause <*briga*>; **~mar-se** *vpr* arm o.s.

armarinho /arma'riɲu/ *m* haberdashery, (*Amer*) notions

armário /ar'mariu/ *m* cupboard; (*de roupa*) wardrobe

arma|zém /arma'zẽj/ *m* warehouse; (*loja*) general store; (*depósito*) storeroom; **~zenagem** *f*, **~zenamento** *m* storage; **~zenar** *vt* store

Armênia /ar'menia/ *f* Armenia

armênio /ar'meniu/ *a & m* Armenian

aro /'aru/ *m* (*de roda, óculos*) rim; (*de porta*) frame

aro|ma /a'roma/ *f* aroma; (*perfume*) fragrance; **~mático** *a* aromatic; fragrant

ar|pão /ar'pãw/ *m* harpoon; **~poar** *vt* harpoon

arquear /arki'ar/ *vt* arch; **~-se** *vpr* bend, bow

arque|ologia /arkiolo'ʒia/ *f* 5archaeology; **~ológico** *a* archaeological; **~ólogo** *m* archaeologist

arquétipo /ar'kɛtʃipu/ *m* archetype

arquibancada /arkibã'kada/ *f* terraces, (*Amer*) bleachers

arquipélago /arki'pɛlagu/ *m* archipelago

arquite|tar /arkite'tar/ *vt* think up; **~to** /ɛ/ *m* architect; **~tônico** *a* architectural; **~tura** *f* architecture

arqui|var /arki'var/ *vt* file <*papéis*>; shelve <*plano, processo*>; **~vista** *m/f* archivist; **~vo** *m* file; (*conjunto*) files; (*móvel*) filing cabinet; *pl* (*do Estado etc*) archives

arran|cada /axã'kada/ *f* lurch; (*de atleta, fig*) spurt; **~car** *vt* pull out <*cabelo etc*>; pull off <*botão etc*>; pull up <*erva daninha etc*>; take out <*dente*>; (*das mãos de alg*) wrench, snatch; extract <*confissão, dinheiro*> □ *vi* <*carro*> roar off; <*pessoa*> take off; (*dar solavanco*) lurch forward; **~car-se** *vpr* take off; **~co** *m* pull, tug; *veja* **~cada**

arranha-céu /axaɲa'sɛw/ *m* skyscraper

arra|nhadura /axaɲa'dura/ *f* scratch; **~nhão** *m* scratch; **~nhar** *vt* scratch; have a smattering of <*língua*>

arran|jar /axã'ʒar/ *vt* arrange; (*achar*) get, find; (*resolver*) settle, sort out; **~jar-se** *vpr* manage; **~jo** *m* arrangement

arrasar /axa'zar/ *vt* devastate; raze, flatten <*casa, cidade*>; **~-se** *vpr* be devastated

arrastar /axas'tar/ *vt* drag; <*corrente, avalancha*> sweep away; (*atrair*) draw □ *vi* trail; **~-se** *vpr* crawl; <*tempo*> drag; <*processo*> drag out

arreba|tador /axebata'dor/ *a* entrancing; shocking <*notícia*>; **~tar** *vt* (*enlevar*) entrance, send; (*chocar*) shock

arreben|tação /axebẽta'sãw/ *f* surf; **~tar** *vi* <*bomba*> explode; <*corda*> snap, break; <*balão, pessoa*> burst; <*onda*> break; <*guerra, incêndio*> break out □ *vt* snap, break <*corda*>; burst <*balão*>; break down <*porta*>

arrebitar /axebi'tar/ *vt* turn up <*nariz*>; prick up <*orelhas*>

arreca|dação /axekada'sãw/ *f* (*dinheiro*) tax revenue; **~dar** *vt* collect

arredar /axe'dar/ *vt* **não ~ pé** stand one's ground

arredio /axe'dʒiu/ *a* withdrawn

arredondar /axedõ'dar/ *vt* round up <*quantia*>; round off <*ângulo*>

arredores /axe'dɔris/ *m pl* surroundings; (*de cidade*) outskirts

arrefecer /axefe'ser/ *vt/i* cool

arregaçar /axega'sar/ *vt* roll up

arrega|lado /axega'ladu/ *a* <*olhos*> wide; **~lar** *vt* **~lar os olhos** be wide-eyed with amazement

arreganhar /axega'ɲar/ *vt* bare <*dentes*>; **~-se** *vpr* grin

arrema|tar /axema'tar/ *vt* finish off; (*no tricô*) cast off; **~te** *m* conclusion; (*na costura*) finishing off; (*no futebol*) finishing

arremes|sar /axeme'sar/ *vt* hurl; **~so** /e/ *m* throw

arrepen|der-se /axepẽ'dersi/ *vpr* be sorry; <*pecador*> repent; **~der-se de** regret; **~dido** *a* sorry; <*pecador*> repentant; **~dimento** *m* regret; (*de pecado, crime*) repentance

arrepi|ado /axepi'adu/ *a* <*cabelo*> standing on end; <*pele, pessoa*> covered in goose pimples; **~ar** *vt* (*dar calafrios*) make shudder; make stand on end <*cabelo*>; **me ~a (a pele)** it gives me goose pimples; **~ar-se** *vpr* (*estremecer*) shudder; <*cabelo*> stand on end; (*na pele*) get goose pimples; **~o** *m* shudder; **me dá ~os** it makes me shudder

arris|cado /axis'kadu/ *a* risky; **~car** *vt* risk; **~car-se** *vpr* take a risk, risk it

arroba /a'xoba/ *m* (*comput*) @, at sign

arro|char /axo'ʃar/ *vt* tighten up □ *vi* be tough; **~cho** /o/ *m* squeeze

arro|gância /axo'gãsia/ *f* arrogance; **~gante** *a* arrogant

arro|jado /axo'ʒadu/ *a* bold; **~jar** *vt* throw

arrombar /axõ'bar/ *vt* break down <*porta*>; break into <*casa*>; crack <*cofre*>

arro|tar /axo'tar/ *vi* burp, belch; **~to** /o/ *m* burp

arroz /a'xoz/ *m* rice; **~ doce** rice pudding; **~al** (*pl* **~ais**) *m* rice field

arrua|ça /axu'asa/ *f* riot; **~ceiro** *m* rioter

arruela /axu'ɛla/ *f* washer

arruinar /axui'nar/ *vt* ruin; **~-se** *vpr* be ruined

arru|madeira /axuma'dera/ *f* (*de hotel*) chambermaid; **~mar** *vt* tidy (up) <*casa*>; sort out <*papéis, vida*>; pack <*mala*>; (*achar*) find, get; make up <*desculpa*>; (*vestir*) dress up; **~mar-se** *vpr* (*aprontar-se*) get ready; (*na vida*) sort o.s. out

arse|nal /arse'naw/ (*pl* **~nais**) *m* arsenal

arsênio /ar'seniu/ *m* arsenic

arte /'artʃi/ *f* art; **fazer ~** <*criança*> get up to mischief; **~fato** *m* product, article

arteiro /ar'teru/ *a* mischievous

artéria /ar'tɛria/ *f* artery

artesa|nal /arteza'naw/ (*pl* **~nais**) *a* craft; **~nato** *m* craftwork

arte|são /arte'zãw/ (*pl* **~s**) *m* (*f* **~sã**) artisan, craftsman (*f*-woman)

ártico /'artʃiku/ *a & m* arctic

articu|lação /artʃikula'sãw/ *f* articulation; (*anat, tecn*) joint; **~lar** *vt* articulate

arti|ficial /artʃifisi'aw/ (*pl* **~ficiais**) *a* artificial; **~fício** *m* trick

artigo /ar'tʃigu/ *m* article; (*com*) item

arti|lharia /artʃiʎa'ria/ *f* artillery; **~lheiro** *m* (*mil*) gunner; (*no futebol*) striker

artimanha /artʃi'maɲa/ *f* trick; (*método*) clever way

ar|tista /ar'tʃista/ *m/f* artist; **~tístico** *a* artistic

artrite /ar'tritʃi/ *f* arthritis

árvore /'arvori/ *f* tree

arvoredo /arvo'redu/ *m* grove

as /as/ *artigo & pron veja* **a**[1]

ás /as/ *m* ace

às = **a**[2] + **as**

asa /'aza/ *f* wing; (*de xícara*) handle; **~-delta** *f* hang-glider

ascen|dência /asẽ'dẽsia/ *f* ancestry; (*superioridade*) ascendancy; **~dente** *a* rising; **~der** *vi* rise; ascend <*ao trono*>; **~são** *f* rise; (*relig*) Ascension; **em ~são** rising; (*fig*) up and coming; **~sor** *m* lift, (*Amer*) elevator; **~sorista** *m/f* lift operator

asco /'asku/ *m* revulsion, disgust; **dar ~** be revolting

asfalto /as'fawtu/ *m* asphalt

asfixiar /asfiksi'ar/ *vt/i* asphyxiate

Asia /'azia/ *f* Asia

asiático /azi'atʃiku/ *a & m* Asian

asilo /a'zilu/ *m* (*refúgio*) asylum; (*de velhos, crianças*) home

as|ma /'azma/ *f* asthma; **~mático** *a & m* asthmatic

asneira /az'nera/ *f* stupidity; (*uma*) stupid thing

aspas /'aspas/ *f pl* inverted commas

aspargo /as'pargu/ *m* asparagus

aspecto /as'pɛktu/ *m* appearance, look; (*de um problema*) aspect

aspereza /aspe'reza/ *f* roughness; (*do clima, de um som*) harshness; (*fig*) rudeness

áspero /'asperu/ *a* rough; <*clima, som*> harsh; (*fig*) rude

aspi|ração /aspira'sãw/ *f* aspiration; (*med*) inhalation; **~rador** *m* vacuum cleaner; **~rar** *vt* inhale, breathe in <*ar, fumaça*>; suck up <*líquido*>; **~rar a** aspire to

aspirina /aspi'rina/ *f* aspirin

asqueroso /aske'rozu/ *a* revolting, disgusting

assa|do /a'sadu/ *a & m* roast; **~dura** *f* (*na pele*) sore patch

assalariado /asalari'adu/ *a* salaried □ *m* salaried worker

assal|tante /asaw'tãtʃi/ *m* robber; (*na rua*) mugger; (*de casa*) burglar; **~tar** *vt* rob; burgle, (*Amer*) burglarize <*casa*>; **~to** *m* (*roubo*) robbery; (*a uma casa*) burglary; (*ataque*) assault; (*no boxe*) round

assanhado /asa'ɲadu/ *a* worked up; <*criança*> excitable; (*erótico*) amorous

assar /a'sar/ *vt* roast

assassi|nar /asasi'nar/ *vt* murder; (*pol*) assassinate; **~nato** *m* murder; (*pol*) assassination; **~no** *m* murderer; (*pol*) assassin

asseado /asi'adu/ *a* well-groomed

as|sediar /asedʒi'ar/ *vt* besiege <*cidade*>; (*fig*) pester; **~sédio** *m* siege; (*fig*) pestering

assegurar /asegu'rar/ *vt* (*tornar seguro*) secure; (*afirmar*) guarantee; **~ a alg aco/que** assure s.o. of sth/that; **~-se de/que** make sure of/that

assembléia /asẽ'blɛja/ *f* (*pol*) assembly; (*com*) meeting

assemelhar /aseme'ʎar/ *vt* liken; **~-se** *vpr* be alike; **~-se a** resemble, be like

assen|tar /asẽ'tar/ *vt* (*estabelecer*) establish, define; settle <*povo*>; lay <*tijolo*> □ *vi* <*pó*> settle; **~tar-se** *vpr* settle down; **~tar com** go with; **~tar a** <*roupa*> suit; **~to** *m* seat; (*fig*) basis; **tomar ~to** take a seat; <*pó*> settle

assen|tir /asẽ'tʃir/ *vi* agree; **~timento** *m* agreement

assessor /ase'sor/ *m* adviser; **~ar** *vt* advise

assexuado /aseksu'adu/ *a* asexual

assiduidade /asidui'dadʒi/ *f* (*à escola*) regular attendance; (*diligência*) diligence

assíduo /a'siduu/ *a* (*que freqüenta*) regular; (*diligente*) assiduous

assim /a'sĩ/ *adv* like this, like that; (*portanto*) therefore; **e ~ por diante** and so on; **~ como** as well as; **~ que** as soon as

assimétrico /asi'mɛtriku/ *a* asymmetrical

assimilar /asimi'lar/ *vt* assimilate; **~-se** *vpr* be assimilated

assinalar /asina'lar/ *vt* (*marcar*) mark; (*distinguir*) distinguish; (*apontar*) point out

assi|nante /asi'nãtʃi/ *m/f* subscriber; **~nar** *vt/i* sign; **~natura** *f* (*nome*) signature; (*de revista*) subscription

assis|tência /asis'tẽsia/ *f* assistance; (*presença*) attendance; (*público*) audience; **~tente** *a* assistant □ *m/f* assistant; **~tente social** social worker; **~tir (a)** *vt/i* (*ver*) watch; (*presenciar*) attend; assist <*doente*>

assoalho /aso'aʎu/ *m* floor

assoar /aso'ar/ *vt* **~ o nariz**, (*Port*) **~-se** blow one's nose

assobi|ar /asobi'ar/ *vt/i* whistle; **~o** *m* whistle

associ|ação /asosia'sãw/ *f* association; **~ado** *a & m* associate; **~ar** *vt* associate (**a** with); **~ar-se** *vpr* associate; (*com*) go into partnership (**a** with)

assolar /aso'lar/ *vt* devastate

assom|bração /asõbra'sãw/ *f* ghost; **~brar** *vt* astonish, amaze; **~brar-se** *vpr* be amazed; **~bro** *m* amazement, astonishment; (*coisa*) marvel; **~broso** /o/ *a* astonishing, amazing

assoprar /aso'prar/ *vi* blow □ *vt* blow; blow out <*vela*>

assovi- *veja* **assobi-**

assu|mido /asu'midu/ *a* (*confesso*) confirmed, self-confessed; **~mir** *vt* assume, take on; accept, admit <*defeito*> □ *vi* take office

assunto /a'sũtu/ *m* subject; (*negócio*) matter

assus|tador /asusta'dor/ *a* frightening; **~tar** *vt* frighten, scare; **~tar-se** *vpr* get frightened, get scared

asterisco /aste'risku/ *m* asterisk

as|tral /as'traw/ (*pl* **~trais**) *m* (*fam*) state of mind; **~tro** *m* star; **~trologia** *f* astrology; **~trólogo** *m* astrologer; **~tronauta** *m/f* astronaut; **~tronave** *f* spaceship; **~tronomia** *f* astronomy; **~tronômico** *a* astronomical; **~trônomo** *m* astronomer

as|túcia /as'tusia/ *f* cunning; **~tuto** *a* cunning; <*comerciante*> astute

ata /'ata/ *f* minutes

ataca|dista /ataka'dʒista/ *m/f* wholesaler; **~do** *m* **por ~do** wholesale

ata|cante /ata'kãtʃi/ *a* attacking □ *m/f* attacker; **~car** *vt* attack; tackle <*problema*>

atadura /ata'dura/ *f* bandage

ata|lhar /ata'ʎar/ *vi* take a shortcut; **~lho** *m* shortcut

ataque /a'taki/ *m* attack; (*de raiva, riso*) fit

atar /a'tar/ *vt* tie

atarantado /atarã'tadu/ *a* flustered, in a flap

atarefado /atare'fadu/ *a* busy

atarracado /ataxa'kadu/ *a* stocky

atarraxar /ataxa'ʃar/ *vt* screw

até /a'tɛ/ *prep* (up) to, as far as; (*tempo*) until □ *adv* even; **~ logo** goodbye; **~ que** until

atéia /a'tɛja/ *a & f* *veja* **ateu**

ateliê /ateli'e/ *m* studio

atemorizar /atemori'zar/ *vt* frighten

Atenas /a'tenas/ *f* Athens

aten|ção /atẽ'sãw/ *f* attention; *pl* (*bondade*) thoughtfulness; **com ~ção** attentively; **~cioso** *a* thoughtful, considerate

aten|der /atẽ'der/ **~der (a)** *vt/i* answer <*telefone, porta*>; answer to <*nome*>; serve <*freguês*>; see <*paciente, visitante*>; grant, meet <*pedido*>; heed <*conselho*>; **~dimento** *m* service; (*de médico etc*) consultation

aten|tado /atẽ'tadu/ *m* murder attempt; (*pol*) assassination attempt; (*ataque*) attack (**contra** on); **~tar** *vi* **~tar contra** make an attempt on

atento /a'tẽtu/ *a* attentive; **~ a** mindful of

aterrador /atexa'dor/ *a* terrifying

ater|ragem /ate'xaʒẽ/ *f* (*Port*) landing; **~rar** *vi* (*Port*) land

aterris|sagem /atexi'saʒẽ/ *f* landing; **~sar** *vi* land

ater-se /a'tersi/ *vpr* **~ a** keep to, go by

ates|tado /ates'tadu/ *m* certificate; **~tar** *vt* attest (to)

ateu /a'tew/ *a & m* (*f* **atéia**) atheist

atiçar /atʃi'sar/ *vt* poke <*fogo*>; stir up <*ódio, discórdia*>; arouse <*pessoa*>

atinar /atʃi'nar/ *vt* work out, guess; **~ com** find; **~ em** notice

atingir /atʃĩ'ʒir/ *vt* reach; hit <*alvo*>; (*conseguir*) attain; (*afetar*) affect

atirar /atʃi'rar/ *vt* throw □ *vi* shoot; **~ em** fire at

atitude /atʃi'tudʒi/ *f* attitude; **tomar uma ~** take action

ati|va /a'tʃiva/ *f* active service; **~var** *vt* activate; **~vidade** *f* activity; **~vo** *a* active □ *m* (*com*) assets

Atlântico /at'lãtʃiku/ *m* Atlantic

atlas /'atlas/ *m* atlas

at|leta /at'lɛta/ *m/f* athlete; **~lético** *a* athletic; **~letismo** *m* athletics

atmosfera /atʃimos'fɛra/ *f* atmosphere

ato /'atu/ *m* act; (*ação*) action; **no ~** on the spot

ato|lar /ato'lar/ *vt* bog down; **~lar-se** *vpr* get bogged down; **~leiro** *m* bog; (*fig*) fix, spot of trouble

atômico /a'tomiku/ *a* atomic

atomizador /atomiza'dor/ *m* atomizer spray

átomo /'atomu/ *m* atom

atônito /a'tonitu/ *a* astonished, stunned

ator /a'tor/ *m* actor

atordoar /atordo'ar/ *vt* <*golpe, notícia*> stun; <*som*> deafen; (*alucinar*) bewilder

atormentar /atormẽ'tar/ *vt* plague, torment

atração /atra'sãw/ *f* attraction

atracar /atra'kar/ *vt/i* (*naut*) moor; **~-se** *vpr* grapple; (*fam*) neck

atractivo (*Port*) *veja* **atrativo**

atraente /atra'ẽtʃi/ *a* attractive

atraiçoar /atrajso'ar/ *vt* betray

atrair /atra'ir/ *vt* attract

atrapalhar /atrapa'ʎar/ *vt/i* (*confundir*) confuse; (*estorvar*) hinder; (*perturbar*) disturb; **~-se** *vpr* get mixed up

atrás /a'traʃ/ *adv* behind; (*no fundo*) at the back; **~ de** behind; (*depois de, no encalço de*) after; **um mês ~** a month ago; **ficar ~** be left behind

atra|sado /atra'zadu/ *a* late; <*país, criança*> backward; <*relógio*> slow; <*pagamento*> overdue; <*idéias*> old-fashioned; **~sar** *vt* delay; put back <*relógio*> □ *vi* be late; <*relógio*> lose; **~sar-se** *vpr* be late; (*num trabalho*) get behind; (*no pagar*) get into arrears; **~so** *m* delay; (*de país etc*) backwardness; *pl* (*com*) arrears; **com ~so** late

atrativo /atra'tʃivu/ *m* attraction

através /atra'vɛs/ **~ de** *prep* through; (*de um lado ao outro*) across

atravessado /atrave'sadu/ *a* <*espinha*> stuck, **estar com alg ~ na garganta** be fed up with s.o.

atravessar /atrave'sar/ *vt* go through; cross <*rua, rio*>

atre|ver-se /atre'versi/ *vpr* dare; **~ver-se a** dare to; **~vido** *a* daring; (*insolente*) impudent; **~vimento** *m* daring, boldness; (*insolência*) impudence

atribu|ir /atribu'ir/ *vt* attribute (**a** to); confer <*prêmio, poderes*> (**a** on); attach <*importância*> (**a** to); **~to** *m* attribute

atrito /a'tritu/ *m* friction; (*desavença*) disagreement

atriz /a'tris/ *f* actress

atrocidade /atrosi'dadʒi/ *f* atrocity

atrope|lar /atrope'lar/ *vt* run over, knock down <*pedestre*>; (*empurrar*) jostle; mix up <*palavras*>; **~lamento** *m* (*de pedestre*) running over; **~lo** /e/ *m* scramble

atroz /a'tros/ *a* awful, terrible; heinous <*crime*>; cruel <*pessoa*>

atuação /atua'sãw/ *f* (*ação*) action; (*desempenho*) performance

atu|al /atu'aw/ (*pl* **~ais**) *a* current, present; <*assunto, interesse*> topical; <*pessoa, carro*> up-to-date; **~alidade** *f* (*presente*) present (time); (*de um livro*) topicality; *pl* current affairs; **~alizado** *a* up-to-date; **~alizar** *vt* update; **~alizar-se** *vpr* bring o.s. up to date; **~almente** *adv* at present, currently

atum /a'tũ/ *m* tuna

aturdir /atur'dʒir/ *vt* *veja* **atordoar**

audácia /aw'dasia/ *f* boldness; (*insolência*) audacity

audi|ção /awdʒi'sãw/ *f* hearing; (*concerto*) recital; **~ência** *f* audience; (*jurid*) hearing

audiovisu|al /awdʒiovizu'aw/ (*pl* **~ais**) *a* audiovisual

auditório /awdʒi'tɔriu/ *m* auditorium; **programa de ~** variety show

auge /'awʒi/ *m* peak, height

aula /'awla/ *f* class, lesson; **dar ~** teach

aumen|tar /awmẽ'tar/ *vt* increase; raise <*preço, salário*>; extend <*casa*>; (*com lente*) magnify; (*acrescentar*) add □ *vi* increase; <*preço, salário*> go up; **~to** *m* increase; (*de salário*) rise, (*Amer*) raise

au|sência /aw'zẽsia/ *f* absence; **~sente** *a* absent □ *m/f* absentee

aus|pícios /aws'pisius/ *m pl* auspices; **~picioso** /o/ *a* auspicious

auste|ridade /awsteri'dadʒi/ *f* austerity; **~ro** /ɛ/ *a* austere

Austrália /aw'stralia/ *f* Australia

australiano /awstrali'anu/ *a* & *m* Australian

Áustria /'awstria/ *f* Austria

austríaco /aws'triaku/ *a* & *m* Austrian

autarquia /awtar'kia/ *f* public authority

autêntico /aw'tẽtʃiku/ *a* authentic; genuine <*pessoa*>; true <*fato*>

autobio|grafia /awtobiogra'fia/ *f* autobiography; **~gráfico** *a* autobiographical

autocarro /awto'kaxu/ *m* (*Port*) bus

autocrata /awto'krata/ *a* autocratic

autodefesa /awtode'feza/ *f* self-defence

autodidata /awtodʒi'data/ *a* & *m/f* self-taught (person)

autódromo /aw'tɔdromu/ *m* race track

auto-escola /awtois'kɔla/ *f* driving school

auto-estrada /awtois'trada/ *f* motorway, (*Amer*) expressway

autógrafo /aw'tɔgrafu/ *m* autograph

auto|mação /awtoma'sãw/ *f* automation; **~mático** *a* automatic; **~matizar** *vt* automate

auto|mobilismo /awtomobi'lizmu/ *m* motoring; (*esporte*) motor racing; **~móvel** (*pl* **~móveis**) *m* motor car, (*Amer*) automobile

au|tonomia /awtono'mia/ *f* autonomy; **~tônomo** *a* autonomous; <*trabalhador*> selfemployed

autopeça /awto'pɛsa/ *f* car spare

autópsia /aw'tɔpsia/ *f* autopsy

autor /aw'tor/ *m* (*f* **~a**) author; (*de crime*) perpetrator; (*jurid*) plaintiff

auto-retrato /awtoxe'tratu/ *m* self-portrait

autoria /awto'ria/ *f* authorship; (*de crime*) responsibility (**de** for)

autori|dade /awtori'dadʒi/ *f* authority; **~zação** *f* authorization; **~zar** *vt* authorize

autuar /awtu'ar/ *vt* sue

au|xiliar /awsili'ar/ *a* auxiliary ▫ *m/f* assistant ▫ *vt* assist; **~xílio** *m* assistance, aid

aval /a'vaw/ (*pl* **avais**) *m* endorsement; (*com*) guarantee

avali|ação /avalia'sãw/ *f* (*de preço*) valuation; (*fig*) evaluation; **~ar** *vt* value <*quadro etc*> (**em** at); assess <*danos, riscos*>; (*fig*) evaluate

avan|çar /avã'sar/ *vt* move forward ▫ *vi* move forward; (*mil, fig*) advance; **~çar a** (*montar*) amount to; **~ço** *m* advance

avar|eza /ava'reza/ *f* meanness; **~ento** *a* mean

ava|ria /ava'ria/ *f* damage; (*de máquina*) breakdown; **~riado** *a* damaged; <*máquina*> out of order; <*carro*> broken down; **~riar** *vt* damage ▫ *vi* be damaged; <*máquina*> break down

ave /'avi/ *f* bird; **~ de rapina** bird of prey

aveia /a'veja/ *f* oats

avelã /ave'lã/ *f* hazelnut

avenida /ave'nida/ *f* avenue

aven|tal /avẽ'taw/ (*pl* **~tais**) *m* apron

aventu|ra /avẽ'tura/ *f* adventure; (*amorosa*) fling; **~rar** *vt* venture; **~rar-se** *vpr* venture (**a** to); **~reiro** *a* adventurous ▫ *m* adventurer

averiguar /averi'gwar/ *vt* check (out)

avermelhado /averme'ʎadu/ *a* reddish

aver|são /aver'sãw/ *f* aversion; **~so** *a* averse (**a** to)

aves|sas /a'vɛsas/ **às ~sas** the wrong way round; (*de cabeça para baixo*) upside down; **~so** /e/ *m* **ao ~so** inside out

avestruz /aves'trus/ *m* ostrich

avi|ação /avia'sãw/ *f* aviation; **~ão** *m* (aero)plane, (*Amer*) (air)plane; **~ão a jato** jet

avi|dez /avi'des/ *f* (*cobiça*) greediness; **~do** *a* greedy

avi|sar /avi'zar/ *vt* (*informar*) tell, let know; (*advertir*) warn; **~so** *m* notice; (*advertência*) warning

avistar /avis'tar/ *vt* catch sight of

avo /'avu/ *m* **um doze ~s** one twelfth

avó /a'vɔ/ *f* grandmother; **~s** *m pl* grandparents

avô /a'vo/ *m* grandfather

avoado /avo'adu/ *a* dizzy, scatterbrained

avulso /a'vuwsu/ *a* loose, odd

avultado /avuw'tadu/ *a* bulky

axila /ak'sila/ *f* armpit

azaléia /aza'lɛja/ *f* azalea

azar /a'zar/ *m* bad luck; **ter ~** be unlucky; **~ado, ~ento** *a* unlucky

aze|dar /aze'dar/ *vt* sour ▫ *vi* go sour; **~do** /e/ *a* sour

azei|te /a'zejtʃi/ *m* oil; **~tona** /o/ *f* olive

azevinho /aze'viɲu/ *m* holly

azia /a'zia/ *f* heartburn

azucrinar /azukri'nar/ *vt* annoy

azul /a'zuw/ (*pl* **azuis**) *a* blue

azulejo /azu'leʒu/ *m* (ceramic) tile

azul-marinho /azuwma'riɲu/ *a invar* navy blue

Bb

babá /ba'ba/ *f* nanny; **~ eletrônica** baby alarm

ba|bado /ba'badu/ *m* frill; **~bador** *m* bib; **~bar** *vt/i*, **~bar-se** *vpr* drool (**por** over); <*bebê*> dribble; **~beiro** (*Port*) *m* bib

baby-sitter /bejbi'siter/ (*pl* **~s**) *m/f* babysitter

bacalhau /baka'ʎaw/ *m* cod

bacana /ba'kana/ (*fam*) *a* great

bacha|rel /baʃa'rɛw/ (*pl* **~réis**) bachelor; **~relado** *m* bachelor's degree; **~relar-se** *vpr* graduate

bacia /ba'sia/ *f* basin; (*da privada*) bowl; (*anat*) pelvis

baço /'basu/ *m* spleen

bacon /'bejkõ/ *m* bacon

bactéria /bak'tɛria/ *f* bacterium; *pl* bacteria

bada|lado /bada'ladu/ *a* (*fam*) talked about; **~lar** *vt* ring <*sino*> □ *vi* ring; (*fam*) go out and about; **~lativo** (*fam*) *a* fun-loving, gadabout

badejo /ba'dɛʒu/ *m* sea bass

baderna /ba'dɛrna/ *f* (*tumulto*) commotion; (*desordem*) mess

badulaque /badu'laki/ *m* trinket

bafafá /bafa'fa/ (*fam*) *m* to-do, kerfuffle

ba|fo /'bafu/ *m* bad breath; **~fômetro** *m* Breathalyser; **~forada** *f* puff

bagaço /ba'gasu/ *m* pulp; (*Port: aguardente*) brandy

baga|geiro /baga'ʒeru/ *m* (*de carro*) roofrack; (*Port: homem*) porter; **~gem** *f* luggage; (*cultural etc*) baggage

bagatela /baga'tɛla/ *f* trifle

Bagdá /bagi'da/ *f* Baghdad

bago /'bagu/ *m* berry; (*de chumbo*) pellet

bagulho /ba'guʎu/ *m* piece of junk; *pl* junk; **ele é um ~** he's as ugly as sin

bagun|ça /ba'gũsa/ *f* mess; **~çar** *vt* mess up; **~ceiro** *a* messy

baía /ba'ia/ *f* bay

baiano /ba'janu/ *a & m* Bahian

baila /'bajla/ *f* **trazer/vir à ~** bring/come up

bai|lar /baj'lar/ *vt/i* dance; **~larino** *m* ballet dancer; **~le** *m* dance; (*de gala*) ball

bainha /ba'iɲa/ *f* (*de vestido*) hem; (*de arma*) sheath

baioneta /bajo'neta/ *f* bayonet

bairro /'bajxu/ *m* neighbourhood, area

baixa /'baʃa/ *f* drop, fall; (*de guerra*) casualty; (*dispensa*) discharge; **~-mar** *f* low tide

baixar /ba'ʃar/ *vt* lower; issue <*ordem*>; pass <*lei*>; (*comput*) download □ *vi* drop, fall; (*fam: pintar*) turn up

baixaria /baʃa'ria/ *f* sordidness; (*uma*) sordid thing

baixela /ba'ʃɛla/ *f* set of cutlery

baixeza /ba'ʃeza/ *f* baseness

baixo /'baʃu/ *a* low; <*pessoa*> short; <*som, voz*> quiet, soft; <*cabeça, olhos*> lowered; (*vil*) sordid □ *adv* low; <*falar*> softly, quietly □ *m* bass; **em ~** underneath; (*em casa*) downstairs; **em ~ de** under; **para ~** down; (*em casa*) downstairs; **por ~ de** under(neath)

baju|lador /baʒula'dor/ *a* obsequious □ *m* sycophant; **~lar** *vt* fawn on

bala /'bala/ *f* (*de revólver*) bullet; (*doce*) sweet

balada /ba'lada/ *f* ballad

balaio /ba'laju/ *m* linen basket

balan|ça /ba'lãsa/ *f* scales; **Balança** (*signo*) Libra; **~ça de pagamentos** balance of payments; **~çar** *vt/i* (*no ar*) swing; (*numa cadeira etc*) rock; <*carro, avião*> shake; <*navio*> roll; **~çar-se** *vpr* swing; **~cete** /e/ *m* trial balance; **~ço** *m* (*com*) balance sheet; (*brinquedo*) swing; (*movimento no ar*) swinging; (*de carro, avião*) shaking; (*de navio*) rolling; (*de cadeira*) rocking; **fazer um ~ço de** (*fig*) take stock of

balangandã /balãgã'dã/ *m* bauble

balão /ba'lãw/ *m* balloon; **soltar um ~-de-ensaio** (*fig*) put out feelers

balar /ba'lar/ *vi* bleat

balbu|ciar /bawbusi'ar/ *vt/i* babble; **~cio** *m* babble, babbling

balbúrdia /baw'burdʒia/ *f* hubbub

bal|cão /baw'kãw/ *m* (*em loja*) counter; (*de informações, bilhetes*) desk; (*de cozinha*) worktop, (*Amer*) counter; (*no teatro*) circle; **~conista** *m/f* shop assistant

balde /'bawdʒi/ *m* bucket

baldeação /bawdʒia'sãw/ *f* **fazer ~** change (trains)

baldio /baw'dʒiu/ *a* fallow; **terreno ~** (piece of) waste ground

balé /ba'lɛ/ *m* ballet

balear /bali'ar/ *vt* shoot

baleia /ba'leja/ *f* whale

balido /ba'lidu/ *m* bleat, bleating

balísti|ca /ba'listʃika/ *f* ballistics; **~co** *a* ballistic

bali|za /ba'liza/ *f* marker; (*luminosa*) beacon; **~zar** *vt* mark out

balneário /bawni'ariu/ *m* seaside resort

balofo /ba'lofu/ *a* fat, tubby

baloiço, balouço /ba'lojsu, ba'losu/ (*Port*) *m* (*de criança*) swing

balsa /'bawsa/ *f* (*de madeira etc*) raft; (*que vai e vem*) ferry

bálsamo /'bawsamu/ *m* balm

báltico /'bawtʃiku/ *a & m* Baltic

baluarte /balu'artʃi/ *m* bulwark

bambo /'bãbu/ *a* loose, slack; <*pernas*> limp; <*mesa*> wobbly

bambo|lê /bãbo'le/ *m* hula hoop; **~lear** *vi* <*pessoa*> sway, totter; <*coisa*> wobble

bambu /bã'bu/ *m* bamboo

ba|nal /ba'naw/ (*pl* **~nais**) *a* banal; **~nalidade** *f* banality

bana|na /ba'nana/ *f* banana □ (*fam*) *m/f* wimp; **~nada** *f* banana fudge; **~neira** *f* banana tree; **plantar ~neira** do a handstand

banca /'bãka/ *f* (*de trabalho*) bench; (*de jornais*) newsstand; **~ examinadora** examining board; **~da** *f* (*pol*) bench

bancar /bã'kar/ *vt* (*custear*) finance; (*fazer papel de*) play; (*fingir*) pretend

bancário /bã'kariu/ *a* bank □ *m* bank employee

bancarrota /bãka'xota/ *f* bankruptcy; **ir à ~** go bankrupt

banco /'bãku/ *m* (*com*) bank; (*no parque*) bench; (*na cozinha, num bar*) stool; (*de bicicleta*) saddle; (*de carro*) seat; **~ de areia** sandbank; **~ de dados** database

banda /'bãda/ *f* band; (*lado*) side; **de ~** sideways on; **nestas ~s** in these parts; **~ desenhada** (*Port*) cartoon; **~ larga** broad band

bandei|ra /bã'dera/ *f* flag; (*divisa*) banner; **dar ~ra** (*fam*) give o.s. away; **~rante** *m/f* pioneer □ *f* girl guide; **~rinha** *m* linesman

bandeja /bã'deʒa/ *f* tray

bandido /bã'dʒidu/ *m* bandit

bando /'bãdu/ *m* (*de pessoas*) band; (*de pássaros*) flock

bandolim /bãdo'lĩ/ *m* mandolin

bangalô /bãga'lo/ *m* bungalow

Bangcoc /bã'koki/ *f* Bangkok

bangue-bangue /bãgi'bãgi/ (*fam*) *m* western

banguela /bã'gɛla/ *a* toothless

banha /'baɲa/ *f* lard

banhar /ba'ɲar/ *vt* (*molhar*) bathe; (*lavar*) bath; **~-se** *vpr* bathe

banhei|ra /ba'ɲera/ *f* bath, (*Amer*) bathtub; **~ro** *m* bathroom; (*Port*) lifeguard

banhista /ba'ɲista/ *m/f* bather

banho /'baɲu/ *m* bath; (*no mar*) bathe, dip; **tomar ~** have a bath; (*no chuveiro*) have a shower; **tomar um ~ de loja/cultura** go on a shopping/cultural spree; **~ de espuma** bubble bath; **~ de sol** sunbathing; **~-maria** (*pl* **~s-maria**) *m* bain marie

ba|nimento /bani'mẽtu/ *m* banishment; **~nir** *vt* banish

banjo /'bãʒu/ *m* banjo

banqueiro /bã'keru/ *m* banker

banqueta /bã'keta/ *f* foot-stool

banque|te /bã'ketʃi/ *m* banquet; **~teiro** *m* caterer

banzé /bã'zɛ/ (*fam*) *m* commotion, uproar

bapt- (*Port*) *veja* **bat-**

baque /'baki/ *m* thud, crash; (*revés*) blow; **~ar** *vi* topple over □ *vt* hit hard, knock for six

bar /bar/ *m* bar

barafunda /bara'fũda/ *f* jumble; (*barulho*) racket

bara|lhada /bara'ʎada/ *f* jumble; **~lho** *m* pack of cards, (*Amer*) deck of cards

barão /ba'rãw/ *m* baron

barata /ba'rata/ *f* cockroach

bara|tear /baratʃi'ar/ *vt* cheapen; **~teiro** *a* cheap

baratinar /baratʃi'nar/ *vt* fluster; (*transtornar*) rattle, shake up

barato /ba'ratu/ *a* cheap □ *adv* cheaply □ (*fam*) *m* **um ~** great; **que ~!** that's brilliant!

barba /'barba/ *f* beard; *pl* (*de gato etc*) whiskers; **fazer a ~** shave; **~da** *f* walkover; (*cavalo*) favourite; **~do** *a* bearded

barbante /bar'bãtʃi/ *m* string

bar|baridade /barbari'dadʒi/ *f* barbarity; (*fam: muito dinheiro*) fortune; **~bárie** *f*, **~barismo** *m* barbarism

bárbaro /'barbaru/ *m* barbarian □ *a* barbaric; (*fam: forte, bom*) terrific

barbatana /barba'tana/ *f* fin

bar|beador /barbia'dor/ *m* shaver; **~bear** *vt* shave; **~bear- se** *vpr* shave; **~bearia** *f* barber's shop; **~beiragem** (*fam*) *f* bit of bad driving; **~beiro** *m* barber; (*fam: motorista*) bad driver

bar|ca /'barka/ *f* barge; (*balsa*) ferry; **~caça** *f* barge; **~co** *m* boat; **~co a motor** motorboat; **~co a remo/vela** rowing/sailing boat, (*Amer*) rowboat/ sailboat

barga|nha /bar'gaɲa/ *f* bargain; **~nhar** *vt/i* bargain

barítono /ba'ritonu/ *m* baritone

barômetro /ba'rometru/ *m* barometer

baronesa /baro'neza/ *f* baroness

barra /'baxa/ *f* bar; (*sinal gráfico*) slash, stroke; (*fam: situação*) situation; **segurar a ~** hold out; **forçar a ~** force the issue

barra|ca /ba'xaka/ *f* (*de acampar*) tent; (*na feira*) stall; (*casinha*) hut; (*guarda-sol*) sunshade; **~cão** *m* shed; **~co** *m* shack, shanty

barragem /ba'xaʒẽ/ *f* (*represa*) dam

barra-pesada /baxape'zada/ (*fam*) *a invar* <*bairro*> rough; <*pessoa*> shady; (*difícil*) tough

bar|rar /ba'xar/ *vt* bar; **~reira** *f* barrier; (*em corrida*) hurdle; (*em futebol*) wall

barrento /ba'xẽtu/ *a* muddy

barricada /baxi'kada/ *f* barricade

barri|ga /ba'xiga/ *f* stomach, (*Amer*) belly; **~ga da perna** calf; **~gudo** *a* pot-bellied

bar|ril /ba'xiw/ (*pl* **~ris**) *m* barrel

barro /'baxu/ *m* (*argila*) clay; (*lama*) mud

barroco /ba'xoku/ *a* & *m* baroque

barrote /ba'xɔtʃi/ *m* beam, joist

baru|lheira /baru'ʎera/ *f* racket, din; **~lhento** *a* noisy; **~lho** *m* noise

base /'bazi/ *f* base; (*fig: fundamento*) basis; **com ~ em** on the basis of; **na ~ de** based on; **~ado** *a* based; (*firme*) well-founded □ (*fam*) *m* joint; **~ar** *vt* base; **~ar-se em** be based on

básico /'baziku/ *a* basic

basquete /bas'kɛtʃi/ *m*, **basquetebol** /basketʃi'bɔw/ *m* basketball

bas|ta /'basta/ *m* **dar um ~ta em** call a halt to; **~tante** *a* (*muito*) quite a lot of; (*suficiente*) enough □ *adv* (*com adjetivo, advérbio*) quite; (*com verbo*) quite a lot; (*suficientemente*) enough

bastão /bas'tãw/ *m* stick; (*num revezamento, de comando*) baton

bastar /bas'tar/ *vi* be enough

bastidores /bastʃi'doris/ *m pl* (*no teatro*) wings; **nos ~** (*fig*) behind the scenes

bata /'bata/ *f* (*de mulher*) smock; (*de médico etc*) overall

bata|lha /ba'taʎa/ *f* battle; **~lhador** *a* plucky, feisty □ *m* fighter; **~lhão** *m* battalion; **~lhar** *vi* battle; (*esforçar-se*) fight hard □ *vt* fight hard to get

batata /ba'tata/ *f* potato; **~ doce** sweet potato; **~ frita** chips, (*Amer*) French fries; (*salgadinhos*) crisps, (*Amer*) potato chips

bate-boca /batʃi'boka/ *m* row, argument

bate|deira /bate'dera/ *f* whisk; (*de manteiga*) churn; **~dor** *m* (*policial etc*) outrider; (*no criquete*) batsman; (*no beisebol*) batter; (*de caça*) beater; **~dor de carteiras** pickpocket

batelada /bate'lada/ *f* batch; **~s de** heaps of

batente /ba'tẽtʃi/ *m* (*de porta*) doorway; **para o/no ~** (*fam: ao trabalho*) to/at work

bate-papo /batʃi'papu/ *m* chat.

bater /ba'ter/ *vt* beat; stamp <*pé*>; slam <*porta*>; strike <*horas*>; take <*foto*>; flap <*asas*>; (*datilografar*) type; (*lavar*) wash; (*usar muito*) wear a lot <*roupa*>; (*fam*) pinch <*carteira*> □ *vi* <*coração*> beat; <*porta*> slam; <*janela*> bang; <*horas*> strike; <*sino*> ring; (*à porta*) knock; (*com o carro*) crash; **~-se** *vpr* (*lutar*) fight; **~ à máquina** type; **~ à** *ou* **na porta** knock at the door; **~ em** hit; harp on <*assunto*>; <*luz, sol*> shine on; **~ com o carro** crash one's car, have a crash; **~ com a cabeça** bang one's head; **ele batia os dentes de frio** his teeth were chattering with cold; **ele não bate bem** (*fam*) he's not all there

bate|ria /bate'ria/ *f* (*eletr*) battery; (*mus*) drums; **~ria de cozinha** kitchen utensils; **~rista** *m/f* drummer

bati|da /ba'tʃida/ *f* beat; (*à porta*) knock; (*no carro*) crash; (*policial*) raid; (*bebida*) cocktail of rum, sugar and fruit juice; **~do** *a* beaten; <*roupa*> well worn; <*assunto*> hackneyed □ *m* **~do de leite** (*Port*) milkshake

batina /ba'tʃina/ *f* cassock

ba|tismo /ba'tʃizmu/ *m* baptism; **~tizado** *m* christening; **~tizar** *vt* baptize; (*pôr nome*) christen

batom /ba'tõ/ *m* lipstick

batu|cada /batu'kada/ *f* samba percussion group; **~car** *vt/i* drum in a samba rhythm; **~que** *m* samba rhythm

batuta /ba'tuta/ *f* baton; **sob a ~ de** under the direction of

baú /ba'u/ *m* trunk

baunilha /baw'niʎa/ *f* vanilla

bazar /ba'zar/ *m* bazaar; (*loja*) stationery and haberdashery shop

bê-a-bá /bea'ba/ *m* ABC

bea|titude /beatʃi'tudʒi/ *f* (*felicidade*) bliss; (*devoção*) piety, devoutness; **~to** *a* (*devoto*) pious, devout; (*feliz*) blissful

bêbado /'bebadu/ *a* & *m* drunk

bebê /be'be/ *m* baby; **~ de proveta** test-tube baby

bebe|deira /bebe'dera/ *f* (*estado*) drunkenness; (*ato*) drinking bout; **~dor** *m* drinker; **~douro** *m* drinking fountain

beber /be'ber/ *vt/i* drink

bebericar /beberi'kar/ *vt/i* sip

bebida /be'bida/ *f* drink

beca /'bɛka/ *f* gown

beça /'bɛsa/ *f* **à ~** (*fam*) (*com substantivo*) loads of; (*com adjetivo*) really; (*com verbo*) a lot

beco /'beku/ *m* alley; **~ sem saída** dead end

bedelho /be'deʎu/ *m* **meter o ~ (em)** stick one's oar in(to)

bege /'bɛʒi/ *a invar* beige

bei|cinho /bej'siɲu/ *m* **fazer ~cinho** pout; **~ço** *m* lip; **~çudo** *a* thick-lipped

beija-flor /bejʒa'flor/ *m* hummingbird

bei|jar /be'ʒar/ *vt* kiss; **~jo** *m* kiss; **~joca** /ɔ/ *f* peck

bei|ra /'bera/ *f* edge; (*fig: do desastre etc*) verge, brink; **à ~ra de** at the edge of; (*fig*) on the verge of; **~rada** *f* edge; **~ra-mar** *f* seaside; **~rar** *vt* (*ficar*) border (on); (*andar*) skirt; (*fig*) border on, verge on; **ele está ~rando os 30 anos** he's nearing thirty

beisebol /beijsi'bɔw/ *m* baseball

belas-artes /bɛlaʃ'artʃiʃ/ *f pl* fine arts

beldade /bew'dadʒi/ *f*, **beleza** /be'leza/ *f* beauty

belga /'bɛwga/ *a* & *m* Belgian

Bélgica /'bɛwʒika/ *f* Belgium

beliche /be'liʃi/ *m* bunk

bélico /'bɛliku/ *a* war

belicoso /beli'kozu/ *a* warlike

belis|cão /belis'kãw/ *m* pinch; **~car** *vt* pinch; nibble <*comida*>

Belize /be'lizi/ *m* Belize

belo /'bɛlu/ *a* beautiful

beltrano /bew'tranu/ *m* such-and-such

bem /bẽj/ *adv* well; (*bastante*) quite; (*muito*) very ▫ *m* good; *pl* goods, property; **está ~** (it's) fine, OK; **fazer ~ a** be good for; **tudo ~?** (*fam*) how's things?; **se ~ que** even though; **~ feito (por você)** (*fam*) it serves you right; **muito ~!** well done!; **de ~ com alg** on good terms with s.o.; **~ como** as well as

bem|-apessoado /bẽjapeso'adu/ *a* nice-looking; **~-comportado** *a* well-behaved; **~-disposto** *a* keen, willing; **~-estar** *m* well-being; **~-humorado** *a* good-humoured; **~-intencionado** *a* well-intentioned; **~-passado** *a* <*carne*> well-done; **~-sucedido** *a* successful; **~-vindo** *a* welcome; **~-visto** *a* well thought of

bênção /'bẽsãw/ (*pl* **~s**) *f* blessing

bendito /bẽ'dʒitu/ *a* blessed

benefi|cência /benefi'sẽsia/ *f* (*bondade*) goodness, kindness; (*caridade*) charity; **~cente** *a* <*associação*> charitable; <*concerto, feira*> charity; **~ciado** *m* beneficiary; **~ciar** *vt* benefit; **~ciar-se** *vpr* benefit (**de** from)

benefício /bene'fisiu/ *m* benefit; **em ~ de** in aid of

benéfico /be'nɛfiku/ *a* beneficial (**a** to)

benevolência /benevo'lẽsia/ *f* benevolence

benévolo /be'nɛvolu/ *a* benevolent

benfeitor /bẽfej'tor/ *m* benefactor

bengala /bẽ'gala/ *f* walking stick; (*pão*) French stick

benigno /be'niginu/ *a* benign

ben|to /'bẽtu/ *a* blessed; <*água*> holy; **~zer** *vt* bless; **~zer-se** *vpr* cross o.s.

berço /'bersu/ *m* (*de embalar*) cradle; (*caminha*) cot; (*fig*) birthplace; **ter ~** be from a good family

berimbau /berĩ'baw/ *m Brazilian percussion instrument shaped like a bow*

berinjela /berĩ'ʒɛla/ *f* aubergine, (*Amer*) eggplant

Berlim /ber'lĩ/ *f* Berlin

berma /'bɛrma/ (*Port*) *f* hard shoulder, (*Amer*) berm

bermuda /ber'muda/ *f* Bermuda shorts

Berna /'bɛrna/ *f* Berne

ber|rante /be'xãtʃi/ *a* loud, flashy; **~rar** *vi* <*pessoa*> shout; <*criança*> bawl; <*boi*> bellow; **~reiro** *m* (*gritaria*) yelling, shouting; (*choro*) crying, bawling; **~ro** /ɛ/ *m* yell, shout; (*de boi*) bellow; **aos ~ros** shouting

besouro /be'zoru/ *m* beetle

bes|ta /'besta/ *a* (*idiota*) stupid; (*cheio de si*) full of o.s.; (*pedante*) pretentious ▫ *f* (*pessoa*) dimwit, numbskull; **ficar ~ta** (*fam*) be taken aback; **~teira** *f* stupidity; (*uma*) stupid thing; **falar ~teira** talk rubbish; **~tial** (*pl* **~tiais**) *a* bestial; **~tificar** *vt* astound, dumbfound

besuntar /bezũ'tar/ *vt* coat; (*sujar*) smear

betão /be'tãw/ (*Port*) *m* concrete

beterraba /bete'xaba/ *f* beetroot

betoneira /beto'nera/ *f* cement mixer

bexiga /be'ʃiga/ *f* bladder

bezerro /be'zeru/ *m* calf

bibelô /bibe'lo/ *m* ornament

Bíblia /'biblia/ *f* Bible

bíblico /'bibliku/ *a* biblical

biblio|grafia /bibliogra'fia/ *f* bibliography; **~teca** /ɛ/ *f* library; **~tecário** *m* librarian ▫ *a* library

bica /'bika/ *f* tap; (*Port: cafezinho*) espresso; **suar em ~s** drip with sweat

bicama /bi'kama/ *f* truckle bed

bicar /bi'kar/ *vt* peck

bíceps /'bisɛps/ *m invar* biceps

bicha /'biʃa/ *f* (*Port: fila*) queue; (*Bras: fam*) queer, fairy

bicheiro /bi'ʃeru/ *m* organizer of illegal numbers game, racketeer

bicho /'biʃu/ *m* animal; (*inseto*) insect, (*Amer*) bug; **que ~ te mordeu?** what's got into you?; **~-da-seda** (*pl* **~s-da-seda**) *m* silkworm; **~-de-sete-cabeças** (*fam*) *m* big deal, big thing; **~-do-mato** (*pl* **~s-do-mato**) *m* very shy person

bicicleta /bisi'klɛta/ *f* bicycle, bike

bico /'biku/ *m* (*de ave*) beak; (*de faca*) point; (*de sapato*) toe; (*de bule*) spout; (*de caneta*) nib; (*do seio*) nipple; (*de gás*) jet; (*fam*) (*emprego*) odd job, sideline; (*boca*) mouth

bidê /bi'de/ *m* bidet

bidimensio|nal /bidʒimẽsio'naw/ (*pl* **~nais**) *a* two-dimensional

biela /bi'ɛla/ *f* connecting rod

Bielo-Rússia /bielo'xusia/ *f* Byelorussia

bielo-russo /bielo'xusu/ *a & m* Byelorussian

bie|nal /bie'naw/ (*pl* **~nais**) *a* biennial ▫ *f* biennial art exhibition

bife /'bifi/ *m* steak

bifo|cal /bifo'kaw/ (*pl* **~cais**) *a* bifocal

bifur|cação /bifurka'sãw/ *f* fork; **~car-se** *vpr* fork

bigamia /biga'mia/ *f* bigamy

bígamo /'bigamu/ *a* bigamous □ *m* bigamist
bigo|de /bi'gɔdʒi/ *m* moustache; **~dudo** *a* with a big moustache
bigorna /bi'gɔrna/ *f* anvil
bijuteria /biʒute'ria/ *f* costume jewellery
bilate|ral /bilate'raw/ (*pl* **~rais**) *a* bilateral
bilhão /bi'ʎãw/ *m* thousand million, (*Amer*) billion
bilhar /bi'ʎar/ *m* pool, billiards
bilhe|te /bi'ʎetʃi/ *m* ticket; (*recado*) note; **~te de ida e volta** return ticket, (*Amer*) round-trip ticket; **~te de identidade** (*Port*) identity card; **o ~te azul** (*fam*) the sack; **~teria** *f*, (*Port*) **~teira** *f* (*no cinema, teatro*) box office; (*na estação*) ticket office
bilíngüe /bi'lĩgwi/ *a* bilingual
bilionário /bilio'nariu/ *a & m* billionaire
bílis /'bilis/ *f* bile
binário /bi'nariu/ *a* binary
bingo /'bĩgu/ *m* bingo
binóculo /bi'nɔkulu/ *m* binoculars
biodegradá|vel /biodegra'davew/ (*pl* **~veis**) *a* biodegradable
bio|grafia /biogra'fia/ *f* biography; **~gráfico** *a* biographical
biógrafo /bi'ɔgrafu/ *m* biographer
bio|logia /biolo'ʒia/ *f* biology; **~lógico** *a* biological
biólogo /bi'ɔlogu/ *m* biologist
biombo /bi'õbu/ *m* screen
biônico /bi'oniku/ *a* bionic; (*pol*) unelected
biópsia /bi'ɔpsia/ *f* biopsy
bioquími|ca /bio'kimika/ *f* biochemistry; **~co** *a* biochemical □ *m* biochemist
biquíni /bi'kini/ *m* bikini
birma|nês /birma'nes/ *a & m* (*f* **~nesa**) Burmese
Birmânia /bir'mania/ *f* Burma
birô /bi'ro/ *m* bureau
bir|ra /'bixa/ *f* wilfulness; **fazer ~ra** have a tantrum; **~rento** *a* wilful
biruta /bi'ruta/ (*fam*) *a* crazy □ *f* windsock
bis /bis/ *int* encore!, more! □ *m invar* encore
bisa|vó /biza'vɔ/ *f* great-grandmother; **~vós** *m pl* great-grandparents; **~vô** *m* great-grandfather
bisbilho|tar /bizbiʎo'tar/ *vt* pry into □ *vi* pry; **~teiro** *a* prying □ *m* busybody;
bisca|te /bis'katʃi/ *m* odd job; **~teiro** *m* odd-job man
biscoito /bis'kojtu/ *m* biscuit, (*Amer*) cookie
bisnaga /biz'naga/ *f* (*pão*) bridge roll; (*tubo*) tube
bisne|ta /biz'nɛta/ *f* great-granddaughter; **~to** /ɛ/ *m* great-grandson; *pl* great-grandchildren
bis|pado /bis'padu/ *m* bishopric; **~po** *m* bishop
bissexto /bi'sestu/ *a* occasional; **ano ~** leap year
bissexu|al /biseksu'aw/ (*pl* **~ais**) *a & m/f* bisexual
bisturi /bistu'ri/ *m* scalpel
bito|la /bi'tɔla/ *f* gauge; **~lado** *a* narrow-minded
bizarro /bi'zaxu/ *a* bizarre
blablablá /blabla'bla/ (*fam*) *m* chitchat
black /'blɛki/ *m* black market; **~-tie** *m* evening dress
blas|femar /blasfe'mar/ *vi* blaspheme; **~fêmia** *f* blasphemy; **~femo** /e/ *a* blasphemous □ *m* blasphemer
blecaute /ble'kawtʃi/ *m* power cut
ble|far /ble'far/ *vi* bluff; **~fe** /ɛ/ *m* bluff
blin|dado /blĩ'dadu/ *a* armoured; **~dagem** *f* armour-plating
blitz /blits/ *f invar* police spot-check (on vehicles)
blo|co /'blɔku/ *m* block; (*pol*) bloc; (*de papel*) pad; (*no carnaval*) section; **~quear** *vt* block; (*mil*) blockade; **~queio** *m* blockage; (*psic*) mental block; (*mil*) blockade
blusa /'bluza/ *f* shirt; (*de mulher*) blouse; (*de lã*) sweater
boa /'boa/ *f de* **bom**; **numa ~** (*fam*) well; (*sem problemas*) easily; **estar numa ~** (*fam*) be doing fine; **~-gente** (*fam*) *a invar* nice; **~-pinta** (*pl* **~s-pintas**) (*fam*) *a* nice-looking; **~-praça** (*pl* **~s-praças**) (*fam*) *a* friendly, sociable
boate /bo'atʃi/ *f* nightclub
boato /bo'atu/ *m* rumour
boa|-nova /boa'nɔva/ (*pl* **~s-novas**) *f* good news; **~-vida** (*pl* **~s-vidas**) *m/f* good-for-nothing, waster; **~zinha** *a* sweet, kind
bo|bagem /bo'baʒẽ/ *f* silliness; (*uma*) silly thing; **~beada** *f* slip-up; **~bear** *vi* slip up; **~beira** *f veja* **bobagem**
bobe /'bɔbi/ *m* curler, roller
bobina /bo'bina/ *f* reel; (*eletr*) coil
bobo /'bobu/ *a* silly □ *m* fool; (*da corte*) jester; **~ca** /ɔ/ (*fam*) *a* stupid □ *m/f* twit
bo|ca /'boka/ *f* mouth; (*no fogão*) ring; **~ca da noite** nightfall; **~cado** *m* (*na boca*) mouthful; (*pedaço*) piece, bit; **~cal** (*pl* **~cais**) *m* mouthpiece
boce|jar /bose'ʒar/ *vi* yawn; **~jo** /e/ *m* yawn

boche|cha /bo'ʃeʃa/ *f* cheek; **~char** *vi* rinse one's mouth; **~cho** /e/ *m* mouthwash; **~chudo** *a* with puffy cheeks

bodas /'bodas/ *f pl* wedding anniversary; **~ de prata/ouro** silver/golden wedding

bode /'bɔdʒi/ *m* (billy) goat; **~ expiatório** scapegoat

bodega /bo'dɛga/ *f* (*de bebidas*) off-licence, (*Amer*) liquor store; (*de secos e molhados*) grocer's shop, corner shop

boêmio /bo'emiu/ *a & m* Bohemian

bofe|tada /bofe'tada/ *f*, **bofe|tão** /bofe'tãw/ *m* slap; **~tear** *vt* slap

boi /boj/ *m* bullock, (*Amer*) steer

bói /bɔj/ *m* office boy

bóia /'bɔja/ *f* (*de balizamento*) buoy; (*de cortiça, isopor etc*) float; (*câmara de borracha*) rubber ring; (*de braço*) armband, water wing; (*na caixa-d'água*) ballcock; (*fam: comida*) grub; **~ salva-vidas** lifebelt; **~-fria** (*pl* **~s-frias**) *m/f* itinerant farm labourer

boiar /bo'jar/ *vt/i* float; (*fam*) be lost

boico|tar /bojko'tar/ *vt* boycott; **~te** /ɔ/ *m* boycott

boiler /'bojler/ (*pl* **~s**) *m* boiler

boina /'bojna/ *f* beret

bo|jo /'boʒu/ *m* bulge; **~judo** *a* (*cheio*) bulging; (*arredondado*) bulbous

bola /'bɔla/ *f* ball; **dar ~ para** (*fam*) give attention to <*pessoa*>; care about <*coisa*>; **~ de gude** marble; **~ de neve** snowball

bolacha /bo'laʃa/ *f* (*biscoito*) biscuit, (*Amer*) cookie; (*descanso*) beermat; (*fam: tapa*) slap

bo|lada /bo'lada/ *f* large sum of money; **~lar** *vt* think up, devise

boléia /bo'lɛja/ *f* cab; (*Port: carona*) lift

boletim /bole'tʃĩ/ *m* bulletin; (*escolar*) report

bolha /'boʎa/ *f* bubble; (*na pele*) blister □ (*fam*) *m/f* pain

boliche /bo'liʃi/ *m* skittles

Bolívia /bo'livia/ *f* Bolivia

boliviano /bolivi'anu/ *a & m* Bolivian

bolo /'bolu/ *m* cake

bo|lor /bo'lor/ *m* mould, mildew; **~lorento** *a* mouldy

bolota /bo'lɔta/ *f* (*glande*) acorn; (*bolinha*) little ball

bol|sa /'bowsa/ *f* bag; **~sa (de estudo)** scholarship; **~sa (de valores)** stock exchange; **~sista** *m/f*, (*Port*) **~seiro** *m* scholarship student; **~so** /o/ *m* pocket

bom /bõ/ *a* (*f* **boa**) good; (*de saúde*) well; <*comida*> nice; **está ~** that's fine

bomba[1] /'bõba/ *f* (*explosiva*) bomb; (*doce*) eclair; (*fig*) bombshell; **levar ~** (*fam*) fail

bomba[2] /'bõba/ *f* (*de bombear*) pump

Bombaim /bõba'ĩ/ *f* Bombay

bombar|dear /bõbardʒi'ar/ *vt* bombard; (*do ar*) bomb; **~deio** *m* bombardment; (*do ar*) bombing

bomba|-relógio /bõbaxe'lɔʒiu/ (*pl* **~s-relógio**) *f* time bomb

bom|bear /bõbi'ar/ *vt* pump; **~beiro** *m* fireman; (*encanador*) plumber

bombom /bõ'bõ/ *m* chocolate

bombordo /bõ'bɔrdu/ *m* port

bondade /bõ'dadʒi/ *f* goodness

bonde /'bõdʒi/ *m* tram; (*teleférico*) cable car

bondoso /bõ'dozu/ *a* good(-hearted)

boné /bo'nɛ/ *m* cap

bone|ca /bo'nɛka/ *f* doll; **~co** /ɛ/ *m* dummy

bonificação /bonifika'sãw/ *f* bonus

bonito /bo'nitu/ *a* <*mulher*> pretty; <*homem*> handsome; <*tempo, casa etc*> lovely

bônus /'bonus/ *m invar* bonus

boqui|aberto /bokia'bɛrtu/ *a* open-mouthed, flabbergasted; **~nha** *f* snack

borboleta /borbo'leta/ *f* butterfly; (*roleta*) turnstile

borbotão /borbo'tãw/ *m* spurt

borbu|lha /bor'buʎa/ *f* bubble; **~lhar** *vi* bubble

borda /'bɔrda/ *f* edge; **~do** *a* edged; (*à linha*) embroidered □ *m* embroidery

bordão /bor'dãw/ *m* (*frase*) catchphrase

bordar /bor'dar/ *vt* (*à linha*) embroider

bor|del /bor'dɛw/ (*pl* **~déis**) *m* brothel

bordo /'bɔrdu/ *m* **a ~** aboard

borra /'boxa/ *f* dregs; (*de café*) grounds

borra|cha /bo'xaʃa/ *f* rubber; **~cheiro** *m* tyre fitter

bor|rão /bo'xãw/ *m* (*de tinta*) blot; (*rascunho*) rough draft; **~rar** *vt* (*sujar*) blot; (*riscar*) cross out; (*pintar*) daub

borrasca /bo'xaska/ *f* squall

borri|far /boxi'far/ *vt* sprinkle; **~fo** *m* sprinkling

bosque /'bɔski/ *m* wood

bosta /'bɔsta/ *f* (*de animal*) dung; (*chulo*) crap

bota /'bɔta/ *f* boot

botâni|ca /bo'tanika/ *f* botany; **~co** *a* botanical □ *m* botanist

bo|tão /bo'tãw/ *m* button; (*de flor*) bud; **falar com os seus ~tões** say to o.s.

botar /bo'tar/ *vt* put; put on <*roupa*>; set <*mesa, despertador*>; lay <*ovo*>; find <*defeito*>

bote[1] /'bɔtʃi/ *m* (*barco*) dinghy; **~ salva-vidas** lifeboat; (*de borracha*) liferaft

bote[2] /'bɔtʃi/ *m* (*de animal etc*) lunge

botequim /butʃi'kĩ/ *m* bar

botoeira /boto'era/ *f* buttonhole

boxe /'bɔksi/ *m* boxing; **~ador** *m* boxer

brabo /'brabu/ *a* <*animal*> ferocious; <*calor, sol*> fierce; <*doença*> bad; <*prova, experiência*> tough; (*zangado*) angry

bra|çada /bra'sada/ *f* armful; (*em natação*) stroke; **~çadeira** (*faixa*) armband; (*ferragem*) bracket; (*de atleta*) sweatband; **~çal** (*pl* **~çais**) *a* manual; **~celete** /e/ *m* bracelet; **~ço** *m* arm; **~ço direito** (*fig: pessoa*) right-hand man

bra|dar /bra'dar/ *vt/i* shout; **~do** *m* shout

braguilha /bra'giʎa/ *f* fly, flies

braile /'brajli/ *m* Braille

bra|mido /bra'midu/ *m* roar; **~mir** *vi* roar

branco /'brãku/ *a* white □ *m* (*homem*) white man; (*espaço*) blank; **em ~** <*cheque etc*> blank; **noite em ~** sleepless night

bran|do /'brãdu/ *a* gentle; <*doença*> mild; (*indulgente*) lenient, soft; **~dura** *f* gentleness; (*indulgência*) softness, leniency

brasa /'braza/ *f* **em ~** red-hot; **mandar ~** (*fam*) go to town

brasão /bra'zãw/ *m* coat of arms

braseiro /bra'zeru/ *m* brasier

Brasil /bra'ziw/ *m* Brazil

brasi|leiro /brazi'leru/ *a & m* Brazilian; **~liense** *a & m/f* (person) from Brasilia

bra|vata /bra'vata/ *f* bravado; **~vio** *a* wild; <*mar*> rough; **~vo** *a* (*corajoso*) brave; (*zangado*) angry; <*mar*> rough; **~vura** *f* bravery

breca /'brɛka/ *f* **levado da ~** very naughty

brecar /bre'kar/ *vt* stop <*carro*>; (*fig*) curb □ *vi* brake

brecha /'brɛʃa/ *f* gap; (*na lei*) loophole

bre|ga /'brɛga/ (*fam*) *a* tacky, naff; **~guice** (*fam*) *f* tack, tackiness

brejo /'brɛʒu/ *m* marsh; **ir para o ~** (*fig*) go down the drain

brenha /'brɛɲa/ *f* thicket

breque /'brɛki/ *m* brake

breu /brew/ *m* tar, pitch

bre|ve /'brɛvi/ *a* short, brief; **em ~ve** soon, shortly; **~vidade** *f* shortness, brevity

briga /'briga/ *f* fight; (*bate-boca*) argument

briga|da /bri'gada/ *f* brigade; **~deiro** *m* brigadier; (*doce*) chocolate truffle

bri|gão /bri'gãw/ *a* (*f* **~gona**) belligerent; (*na fala*) argumentative □ *m* (*f* **~gona**) troublemaker; **~gar** *vi* fight; (*com palavras*) argue; <*cores*> clash

bri|lhante /bri'ʎãtʃi/ *a* (*reluzente*) shiny; (*fig*) brilliant; **~lhar** *vi* shine; **~lho** *m* (*de sapatos etc*) shine; (*dos olhos, de metais*) gleam; (*das estrelas*) brightness; (*de uma cor*) brilliance; (*fig: esplendor*) splendour

brin|cadeira /brĩka'dera/ *f* (*piada*) joke; (*brinquedo, jogo*) game; **de ~cadeira** for fun; **~calhão** (*f* **~calhona**) *a* playful □ *m* joker; **~car** *vi* (*divertir-se*) play; (*gracejar*) joke

brinco /'brĩku/ *m* earring

brin|dar /brĩ'dar/ *vt* (*saudar*) toast, drink to; (*presentear*) give a gift to; **~dar alg com aco** afford s.o. sth; (*de presente*) give s.o. sth as a gift; **~de** *m* (*saudação*) toast; (*presente*) free gift

brinquedo /brĩ'kedu/ *m* toy

brio /'briu/ *m* self-esteem, character; **~so** /o/ *a* self-confident

brisa /'briza/ *f* breeze

britadeira /brita'dera/ *f* pneumatic drill

britânico /bri'taniku/ *a* British □ *m* Briton; **os ~s** the British

broca /'brɔka/ *f* drill

broche /'brɔʃi/ *m* brooch

brochura /bro'ʃura/ *f* **livro de ~** paperback

brócolis /'brɔkulis/ *m pl*, (*Port*) **brócolos** /'brɔkuluʃ/ *m pl* broccoli

bron|ca /'brõka/ (*fam*) *f* telling-off; **dar uma ~ca em alg** tell s.o. off; **~co** *a* coarse, rough

bronquite /brõ'kitʃi/ *f* bronchitis

bronze /'brõzi/ *m* bronze; **~ado** *a* tanned, brown □ *m* (sun)tan; **~ador** *a* tanning □ *m* suntan lotion; **~amento** *m* tanning; **~ar** *vt* tan; **~ar-se** *vpr* go brown, tan

bro|tar /bro'tar/ *vt* sprout <*folhas, flores*>; spout <*lágrimas, palavras*> □ *vi* <*planta*> sprout; <*água*> spout; <*idéias*> pop up; **~tinho** (*fam*) *m* youngster; **~to** /o/ *m* shoot; (*fam*) youngster

broxa /'brɔʃa/ *f* (large) paint brush □ (*fam*) *a* impotent

bruços /'brusus/ **de ~** face down

bru|ma /'bruma/ *f* mist; **~moso** /o/ *a* misty

brusco /'brusku/ *a* brusque, abrupt

bru|tal /bru'taw/ (*pl* **~tais**) *a* brutal; **~talidade** *f* brutality; **~to** *a* <*feições*> coarse; <*homem*> brutish; <*tom, comentário*> aggressive; <*petróleo*> crude; <*peso, lucro, salário*> gross ◻ *m* brute

bruxa /'bruʃa/ *f* witch; (*feia*) hag; **~ria** *f* witchcraft

Bruxelas /bru'ʃɛlas/ *f* Brussels

bruxo /'bruʃu/ *m* wizard

bruxulear /bruʃuli'ar/ *vi* flicker

bucha /'buʃa/ *f* (*tampão*) bung; (*para paredes*) rawlplug (R); **acertar na ~** (*fam*) hit the nail on the head

bucho /'buʃu/ *m* gut; **~ de boi** tripe

budis|mo /bu'dʒizmu/ *m* Buddhism; **~ta** *a & m/f* Buddhist

bueiro /bu'eru/ *m* storm drain

búfalo /'bufalu/ *m* buffalo

bu|fante /bu'fãtʃi/ *a* full, puffed; **~far** *vi* snort; (*reclamar*) grumble, moan

bufê /bu'fe/ *m* (*refeição*) buffet; (*serviço*) catering service; (*móvel*) sideboard

bugiganga /buʒi'gãga/ *f* knickknack

bujão /bu'ʒãw/ *m* **~ de gás** gas cylinder

bula /'bula/ *f* (*de remédio*) directions; (*do Papa*) bull

bulbo /'buwbu/ *m* bulb

bule /'buli/ *m* (*de chá*) teapot; (*de café etc*) pot

Bulgária /buw'garia/ *f* Bulgaria

búlgaro /'buwgaru/ *a & m* Bulgarian

bulhufas /bu'ʎufas/ (*fam*) *pron* nothing

bulício /bu'lisiu/ *m* bustle

bumbum /bũ'bũ/ (*fam*) *m* bottom, bum

bunda /'bũda/ *f* bottom

buquê /bu'ke/ *m* bouquet

buraco /bu'raku/ *m* hole; (*de agulha*) eye; (*jogo de cartas*) rummy; **~ da fechadura** keyhole

burburinho /burbu'riɲu/ *m* (*de vozes*) hubbub

bur|guês /bur'ges/ *a & m* (*f* **~guesa**) bourgeois; **~guesia** *f* bourgeoisie

burlar /bur'lar/ *vt* get round <*lei*>; get past <*defesas, vigilância*>

buro|cracia /burokra'sia/ *f* bureaucracy; **~crata** *m/f* bureaucrat; **~crático** *a* bureaucratic; **~cratizar** *vt* make bureaucratic

bur|rice /bu'xisi/ *f* stupidity; (*uma*) stupid thing; **~ro** *a* stupid; (*ignorante*) dim ◻ *m* (*animal*) donkey; (*pessoa*) halfwit, dunce; **~ro de carga** (*fig*) workhorse

bus|ca /'buska/ *f* search; **dar ~ca em** search; **~ca-pé** *m* banger; **~car** *vt* fetch; (*de carro*) pick up; **mandar ~car** send for

bússola /'busola/ *f* compass; (*fig*) guide

busto /'bustu/ *m* bust

butique /bu'tʃiki/ *f* boutique

buzi|na /bu'zina/ *f* horn; **~nada** *f* toot (of the horn); **~nar** *vi* sound the horn, toot the horn

Cc

cá /ka/ *adv* here; **o lado de ~** this side; **para ~** here; **de ~ para lá** back and forth; **de lá para ~** since then; **~ entre nós** between you and me

ca|bal /ka'baw/ (*pl* **~bais**) *a* complete, full; <*prova*> conclusive

cabana /ka'bana/ *f* hut; (*casinha no campo*) cottage

cabeça /ka'besa/ *f* head; (*de lista*) top; (*pessoa inteligente*) mind ◻ *m/f* (*chefe*) ringleader; (*integrante mais inteligente*) brains; **de ~** <*saber*> off the top of one's head; <*calcular*> in one's head; **de ~ para baixo** upside down; **deu-lhe na ~ de** he took it into his head to; **esquentar a ~** (*fam*) get worked up; **fazer a ~ de alg** convince s.o.; **quebrar a ~** rack one's brains; **subir à ~** go to s.o.'s head; **ter a ~ no lugar** have one's head screwed on; **~da** *f* (*no futebol*) header; (*pancada*) head butt; **dar uma ~da no teto** bang one's head on the ceiling; **~-de-porco** (*pl* **~s-de-porco**) *f* tenement; **~-de-vento** (*pl* **~s-de-vento**) *m/f* scatterbrain, airhead; **~lho** *m* heading

cabe|cear /kabesi'ar/ *vt* head <*bola*>; **~ceira** *f* head; **~çudo** *a* pigheaded

cabe|dal /kabe'daw/ (*pl* **~dais**) *m* wealth

cabelei|ra /kabe'lera/ *f* head of hair; (*peruca*) wig; **~reiro** *m* hairdresser

cabe|lo /ka'belu/ *m* hair; **cortar o ~lo** have one's hair cut; **~ludo** *a* hairy; (*difícil*) complicated; <*palavra, piada*> dirty

caber /ka'ber/ *vi* fit; (*ter cabimento*) be fitting; **~ a** <*mérito, parte*> be due to; <*tarefa*> fall to; **cabe a você ir** it is up to you to go; **~ em alg** <*roupa*> fit s.o.

cabide /ka'bidʒi/ *m* (*peça de madeira, arame etc*) hanger; (*móvel*) hat stand; (*na parede*) coat rack

cabimento /kabi'mẽtu/ *m* **ter ~** be fitting, be appropriate; **não ter ~** be out of the question

cabine /ka'bini/ *f* cabin; (*de avião*) cockpit; (*de loja*) changing room; **~ telefônica** phone box, (*Amer*) phone booth

cabisbaixo /kabiz'baʃu/ *a* crestfallen

cabí|vel /ka'bivew/ (*pl* **~veis**) *a* appropriate, fitting

cabo[1] /'kabu/ *m* (*militar*) corporal; **ao ~ de** after; **levar a ~** carry out; **~ eleitoral** campaign worker

cabo[2] /'kabu/ *m* (*fio*) cable; (*de panela etc*) handle; **TV por ~** cable TV; **~ de extensão** extension lead; **~ de força** tug of war

caboclo /ka'boklu/ *a & m* mestizo

ca|bra /'kabra/ *f* goat; **~brito** *m* kid

ca|ça /'kasa/ *f* (*atividade*) hunting; (*caçada*) hunt; (*animais*) game □ *m* (*avião*) fighter; **à ~ça de** in pursuit of; **~ça das bruxas** (*fig*) witch hunt; **~çador** *m* hunter; **~ça-minas** *m invar* minesweeper; **~ça-níqueis** *m invar* slot machine; **~çar** *vt* hunt <*animais, criminoso etc*>; (*procurar*) hunt for □ *vi* hunt

cacareco /kaka'rɛku/ *m* piece of junk; *pl* junk

cacare|jar /kakare'ʒar/ *vi* cluck; **~jo** /e/ *m* clucking

caçarola /kasa'rɔla/ *f* saucepan

cacau /ka'kaw/ *m* cocoa

cace|tada /kase'tada/ *f* blow with a club; (*fig*) annoyance; **~te** /e/ *m* club □ (*fam*) *int* damn

cachaça /ka'ʃasa/ *f* white rum

cachê /ka'ʃe/ *m* fee

cache|col /kaʃe'kɔw/ (*pl* **~cóis**) *m* scarf

cachimbo /ka'ʃĩbu/ *m* pipe

cacho /'kaʃu/ *m* (*de banana, uva*) bunch; (*de cabelo*) lock; (*fam: caso*) affair

cachoeira /kaʃo'era/ *f* waterfall

cachor|rinho /kaʃo'xiɲu/ *m* (*nado*) doggy paddle; **~ro** /o/ *m* dog; (*Port*) puppy; (*pessoa*) scoundrel; **~ro-quente** (*pl* **~ros-quentes**) *m* hot dog

cacife /ka'sifi/ *m* (*fig*) pull

caci|que /ka'siki/ *m* (*índio*) chief; (*político*) boss; **~quia** *f* leadership

caco /'kaku/ *m* shard; (*pessoa*) old crock

cacto /'kaktu/ *m* cactus

caçula /ka'sula/ *m/f* youngest child □ *a* youngest

cada /'kada/ *a* each; **~ duas horas** every two hours; **custam £5 ~ (um)** they cost £5 each; **~ vez mais** more and more; **~ vez mais fácil** easier and easier; **ele fala ~ coisa** (*fam*) he says the most amazing things

cadafalso /kada'fawsu/ *m* gallows

cadarço /ka'darsu/ *m* shoelace

cadas|trar /kadas'trar/ *vt* register; **~tro** *m* register; (*ato*) registration; (*policial, bancário*) records, files; (*imobiliário*) land register

ca|dáver /ka'daver/ *m* (dead) body, corpse; **~davérico** *a* cadaverous, corpse-like; <*exame*> post-mortem

cadê /ka'de/ (*fam*) *adv* where is/are...?

cadeado /kadʒi'adu/ *m* padlock

cadeia /ka'deja/ *f* (*de eventos, lojas etc*) chain; (*prisão*) prison; (*rádio, TV*) network

cadeira /ka'dera/ *f* (*móvel*) chair; (*no teatro*) stall; (*de político*) seat; (*função de professor*) chair; (*matéria*) subject; *pl* (*anat*) hips; **~ de balanço** rocking chair; **~ de rodas** wheelchair; **~ elétrica** electric chair

ca|dência /ka'dẽsia/ *f* (*mus, da voz*) cadence; (*compasso*) rhythm; **~denciado** *a* rhythmic; <*passos*> measured

cader|neta /kader'neta/ *f* notebook; (*de professor*) register; (*de banco*) passbook; **~neta de poupança** savings account; **~no** /ɛ/ *m* exercise book; (*pequeno*) notebook; (*no jornal*) section

cadete /ka'detʃi/ *m* cadet

cadu|car /kadu'kar/ *vi* <*pessoa*> become senile; <*contrato*> lapse; **~co** *a* <*pessoa*> senile; <*contrato*> lapsed; **~quice** *f* senility

cafajeste /kafa'ʒɛstʃi/ *m* swine

ca|fé /ka'fɛ/ *m* coffee; (*botequim*) café; **~fé da manhã** breakfast; **tomar ~fé** have breakfast; **~fé-com-leite** *a invar* coffee-coloured, light brown □ *m* white coffee; **~feeiro** *a* coffee □ *m* coffee plant; **~feicultura** *f* coffee-growing; **~feína** *f* caffein(e)

cafetã /kafe'tã/ *m* caftan

cafetão /kafe'tãw/ *m* pimp

cafe|teira /kafe'tera/ *f* coffee pot; **~zal** (*pl* **~zais**) *m* coffee plantation; **~zinho** *m* small black coffee

cafo|na /ka'fɔna/ (*fam*) *a* naff, tacky; **~nice** *f* tackiness; (*coisa*) tacky thing

cágado /'kagadu/ *m* turtle

caiar /kaj'ar/ *vt* whitewash

cãibra /'kãjbra/ *f* cramp

caí|da /ka'ida/ *f* fall; *veja* **queda**; **~do** *a* <*árvore etc*> fallen; <*beiços etc*> drooping; (*deprimido*) dejected; (*apaixonado*) smitten

caimento /kaj'mẽtu/ *m* fall

caipi|ra /kaj'pira/ *a* <*pessoa*> countrified; <*festa, música*> country; <*sotaque*> rural □ *m/f* country person;

(*depreciativo*) country bumpkin; **~rinha** *f* cachaça with limes, sugar and ice

cair /ka'ir/ *vi* fall; <*dente, cabelo*> fall out; <*botão etc*> fall off; <*comércio, trânsito etc*> fall off; <*tecido, cortina*> hang; **~ bem/mal** <*roupa*> go well/ badly; <*ato, dito*> go down well, badly; **estou caindo de sono** I'm really sleepy

cais /kajs/ *m* quay; (*Port: na estação*) platform

caixa /'kaʃa/ *f* box; (*de loja etc*) cashdesk ▫ *m*/*f* cashier; **~ de correio** letter box; **~ de mudanças**, (*Port*) **~ de velocidades** gear box; **~ postal** post office box, PO Box; **~-d'água** (*pl* **~s-d'água**) *f* water tank; **~-forte** (*pl* **~s-fortes**) *f* vault

cai|xão /ka'ʃãw/ *m* coffin; **~xeiro** *m* (*em loja*) assistant; salesman; **~xilho** *m* frame; **~xote** /ɔ/ *m* crate

caju /ka'ʒu/ *m* cashew fruit; **~eiro** *m* cashew tree

cal /kaw/ *f* lime

calado /ka'ladu/ *a* quiet

calafrio /kala'friu/ *m* shudder, shiver

calami|dade /kalami'dadʒi/ *f* calamity; **~toso** /o/ *a* calamitous

calar /ka'lar/ *vi* be quiet ▫ *vt* keep quiet about <*segredo, sentimento*>; silence <*pessoa*>; **~-se** *vpr* go quiet

calça /'kawsa/ *f* trousers, (*Amer*) pants

calça|da /kaw'sada/ *f* pavement, (*Amer*) sidewalk; (*Port: rua*) roadway; **~dão** *m* pedestrian precinct; **~deira** *f* shoe-horn; **~do** *a* paved ▫ *m* shoe; *pl* footwear

calcanhar /kawka'ɲar/ *m* heel

calção /kaw'sãw/ *m* shorts; **~ de banho** swimming trunks

calcar /kaw'kar/ *vt* (*pisar*) trample; (*comprimir*) press; **~ aco em** (*fig*) base sth on, model sth on

calçar /kaw'sar/ *vt* put on <*sapatos, luvas*>; take <*número*>; pave <*rua*>; (*com calço*) wedge ▫ *vi* <*sapato*> fit; **~-se** *vpr* put one's shoes on

calcário /kaw'kariu/ *m* limestone ▫ *a* <*água*> hard

calças /'kawsas/ *f pl veja* **calça**

calcinha /kaw'siɲa/ *f* knickers, (*Amer*) panties

cálcio /'kawsiu/ *m* calcium

calço /'kawsu/ *m* wedge

calcu|ladora /kawkula'dora/ *f* calculator; **~lar** *vt*/*i* calculate; **~lista** *a* calculating ▫ *m*/*f* opportunist

cálculo /'kawkulu/ *m* calculation; (*diferencial*) calculus; (*med*) stone

cal|da /'kawda/ *f* syrup; *pl* hot springs; **~deira** *f* boiler; **~deirão** *m* cauldron; **~do** *m* (*sopa*) broth; (*suco*) juice; **~do de carne/galinha** beef/chicken stock

calefação /kalefa'sãw/ *f* heating

caleidoscópio /kalejdos'kɔpiu/ *m* kaleidoscope

calejado /kale'ʒadu/ *a* <*mãos*> calloused; <*pessoa*> experienced

calendário /kalẽ'dariu/ *m* calendar

calha /'kaʎa/ *f* (*no telhado*) gutter; (*sulco*) gulley

calhamaço /kaʎa'masu/ *m* tome

calhambeque /kaʎã'bɛki/ (*fam*) *m* banger

calhar /ka'ʎar/ *vi* **calhou que** it so happened that; **calhou pegar em o mesmo trem** they happened to get the same train; **~ de** happen to; **vir a ~** come at the right time

cali|brado /kali'bradu/ *a* (*bêbado*) tipsy; **~brar** *vt* calibrate; check (the pressure of) <*pneu*>; **~bre** *m* calibre; **coisas desse ~bre** things of this order

cálice /'kalisi/ *m* (*copo*) liqueur glass; (*na missa*) chalice

caligrafia /kaligra'fia/ *f* (*letra*) handwriting; (*arte*) calligraphy

calista /ka'lista/ *m*/*f* chiropodist, (*Amer*) podiatrist

cal|ma /'kawma/ *f* calm; **com ~ma** calmly ▫ *int* calm down; **~mante** *m* tranquilizer; **~mo** *a* calm

calo /'kalu/ *m* (*na mão*) callus; (*no pé*) corn

calombo /ka'lõbu/ *m* bump

calor /ka'lor/ *m* heat; (*agradável, fig*) warmth; **estar com ~** be hot

calo|rento /kalo'rẽtu/ *a* <*pessoa*> sensitive to heat; <*lugar*> hot; **~ria** *f* calorie; **~roso** /o/ *a* warm; <*protesto*> lively

calota /ka'lɔta/ *f* hubcap

calo|te /ka'lɔtʃi/ *m* bad debt; **~teiro** *m* bad risk

calouro /ka'loru/ *m* (*na faculdade*) freshman; (*em outros ramos*) novice

ca|lúnia /ka'lunia/ *f* slander; **~luniar** *vt* slander; **~lunioso** /o/ *a* slanderous

cal|vície /kaw'visi/ *f* baldness; **~vo** *a* bald

cama /'kama/ *f* bed; **~ de casal/ solteiro** double/single bed; **~-beliche** (*pl* **~s-beliches**) *f* bunk bed

camada /ka'mada/ *f* layer; (*de tinta*) coat

câmara /'kamara/ *f* chamber; (*fotográfica*) camera; **~ digital** digital camera; **em ~ lenta** in slow motion; **~ municipal** town council; (*Port*) town hall

camarada /kama'rada/ *a* friendly ▫ *m*/*f* comrade; **~gem** *f* comradeship; (*convivência agradável*) camaraderie

câmara-de-ar /kamaradʒi'ar/ (*pl* **câmaras-de-ar**) *f* inner tube
camarão /kama'rãw/ *m* shrimp; (*maior*) prawn
cama|reira /kama'rera/ *f* chambermaid; **~rim** *m* dressing room; **~rote** /ɔ/ *m* (*no teatro*) box; (*num navio*) cabin
cambada /kã'bada/ *f* gang, horde
cambalacho /kãba'laʃu/ *m* scam
camba|lear /kãbali'ar/ *vi* stagger; **~lhota** *f* somersault
cambi|al /kãbi'aw/ (*pl* **~ais**) *a* exchange; **~ante** *m* shade; **~ar** *vt* change
câmbio /'kãbiu/ *m* exchange; (*taxa*) rate of exchange; **~ oficial/paralelo** official/black market exchange rate
cambista /kã'bista/ *m/f* (*de entradas*) ticket-tout, (*Amer*) scalper; (*de dinheiro*) money changer
Camboja /kã'bɔʒa/ *m* Cambodia
cambojano /kãbo'ʒanu/ *a & m* Cambodian
camburão /kãbu'rãw/ *m* police van
camelo /ka'melu/ *m* camel
camelô /kame'lo/ *m* street vendor
camião /kami'ãw/ (*Port*) *m veja* **caminhão**
caminhada /kami'ɲada/ *f* walk
caminhão /kami'ɲãw/ *m* lorry, (*Amer*) truck
cami|nhar /kami'ɲar/ *vi* walk; (*fig*) advance, progress; **~nho** *m* way; (*estrada*) road; (*trilho*) path; **a ~nho** on the way; **a meio ~nho** halfway; **~nho de ferro** (*Port*) railway, (*Amer*) railroad
caminho|neiro /kamiɲo'neru/ *m* lorry driver, (*Amer*) truck driver; **~nete** /ɛ/ *m* van
camio|neta /kamio'neta/ *f* van; **~nista** (*Port*) *m/f veja* **caminhoneiro**
cami|sa /ka'miza/ *f* shirt; **~sa-de-força** (*pl* **~sas-de-força**) *f* straitjacket; **~sa-de-vênus** (*pl* **~sas-de-vênus**) *f* condom; **~seta** /e/ *f* T-shirt; (*de baixo*) vest; **~sinha** (*fam*) *f* condom; **~sola** /ɔ/ *f* nightdress; (*Port*) sweater
camomila /kamo'mila/ *f* camomile
campainha /kãpa'iɲa/ *f* bell; (*da porta*) doorbell
campanário /kãpa'nariu/ *m* belfry
campanha /kã'paɲa/ *f* campaign
campe|ão /kãpi'ãw/ *m* (*f* **~ã**) champion; **~onato** *m* championship
cam|pestre /kã'pɛstri/ *a* rural; **~pina** *f* grassland
cam|ping /'kãpĩ/ *m* camping; (*lugar*) campsite; **~pismo** (*Port*) *m* camping
campo /'kãpu/ *m* field; (*interior*) country; (*de futebol*) pitch; (*de golfe*) course; **~ de concentração** concentration camp; **~nês** *m* (*f* **~nesa**) peasant
camu|flagem /kamu'flaʒẽ/ *f* camouflage; **~flar** *vt* camouflage
camundongo /kamũ'dõgu/ *m* mouse
cana /'kana/ *f* cane; **~ de açúcar** sugar cane
Canadá /kana'da/ *m* Canada
canadense /kana'dẽsi/ *a & m* Canadian
ca|nal /ka'naw/ (*pl* **~nais**) *m* channel; (*hidrovia*) canal
canalha /ka'naʎa/ *m/f* scoundrel
canali|zação /kanaliza'sãw/ *f* piping; **~zador** (*Port*) *m* plumber; **~zar** *vt* channel <*líquido, esforço, recursos*>; canalize <*rio*>; pipe for water and drainage <*cidade*>
canário /ka'nariu/ *m* canary
canastrão /kanas'trãw/ *m* (*f* **~trona**) ham actor (*f* actress)
canavi|al /kanavi'aw/ (*pl* **~ais**) *m* cane field; **~eiro** *a* sugar cane
canção /kã'sãw/ *f* song
cance|lamento /kãsela'mẽtu/ *m* cancellation; **~lar** *vt* cancel; (*riscar*) cross out
câncer /'kãser/ *m* cancer; **Câncer** (*signo*) Cancer
cance|riano /kãseri'anu/ *a & m* Cancerian; **~rígeno** *a* carcinogenic; **~roso** /o/ *a* cancerous □ *m* person with cancer
cancro /'kãkru/ *m* (*Port: câncer*) cancer; (*fig*) canker
candango /kã'dãgu/ *m* person from Brasilia
cande|eiro /kãdʒi'eru/ *m* (oil-) lamp; **~labro** *m* candelabra
candida|tar-se /kãdʒida'tarsi/ *vpr* (*a vaga*) apply (**a** for); (*à presidência etc*) stand, (*Amer*) run (**a** for); **~to** *m* candidate (**a** for); (*a vaga*) applicant (**a** for); **~tura** *f* candidature; (*a vaga*) application (**a** for)
cândido /'kãdʒidu/ *a* innocent
candomblê /kãdõ'blɛ/ *m* Afro-Brazilian cult; (*reunião*) candomble meeting
candura /kã'dura/ *f* innocence
cane|ca /ka'nɛka/ *f* mug; **~co** /ɛ/ *m* tankard
canela[1] /ka'nɛla/ *f* (*condimento*) cinnamon
canela[2] /ka'nɛla/ *f* (*da perna*) shin; **~da** *f* **dar uma ~da em alg** kick s.o. in the shins; **dar uma ~da em aco** hit one's shins on sth
cane|ta /ka'neta/ *f* pen; **~ esferográfica** ballpoint pen; **~ta-tinteiro** (*pl* **~tas-tinteiro**) *f* fountain pen
cangote /kã'gɔtʃi/ *m* nape of the neck
canguru /kãgu'ru/ *m* kangaroo

canhão /ka'ɲãw/ *m* (*arma*) cannon; (*vale*) canyon

canhoto /ka'ɲotu/ *a* left-handed □ *m* (*talão*) stub

cani|bal /kani'baw/ (*pl* **~bais**) *m*/*f* cannibal; **~balismo** *m* cannibalism

caniço /ka'nisu/ *m* reed; (*pessoa*) skinny person

canícula /ka'nikula/ *f* heat wave

ca|nil /ka'niw/ (*pl* **~nis**) *m* kennel

canivete /kani'vɛtʃi/ *m* penknife

canja /'kãʒa/ *f* chicken soup; (*fam*) piece of cake

canjica /kã'ʒika/ *f* corn porridge

cano /'kanu/ *m* pipe; (*de bota*) top; (*de arma de fogo*) barrel

cano|a /ka'noa/ *f* canoe; **~agem** *f* canoeing; **~ista** *m*/*f* canoeist

canonizar /kanoni'zar/ *vt* canonize

can|saço /kã'sasu/ *m* tiredness; **~sado** *a* tired; **~sar** *vt* tire; (*aborrecer*) bore □ *vi*, **~sar-se** *vpr* get tired; **~sativo** *a* tiring; (*aborrecido*) boring; **~seira** *f* tiredness; (*lida*) toil

can|tada /kã'tada/ *f* (*fam*) chat-up; **~tar** *vt*/*i* sing; (*fam*) chat up

cântaro /'kãtaru/ *m* **chover a ~s** pour down, bucket down

cantarolar /kãtaro'lar/ *vt*/*i* hum

cantei|ra /kã'tera/ *f* quarry; **~ro** *m* (*de flores*) flowerbed; (*artífice*) stonemason; **~ro de obras** site office

cantiga /kã'tʃiga/ *f* ballad

can|til /kã'tʃiw/ (*pl* **~tis**) *m* canteen; **~tina** *f* canteen

canto[1] /'kãtu/ *m* (*ângulo*) corner

can|to[2] /'kãtu/ *m* (*cantar*) singing; **~tor** *m* singer; **~toria** *f* singing

canudo /ka'nudu/ *m* (*de beber*) straw; (*tubo*) tube; (*fam: diploma*) diploma

cão /kãw/ (*pl* **cães**) *m* dog

caolho /ka'oʎu/ *a* one-eyed

ca|os /kaws/ *m* chaos; **~ótico** *a* chaotic

capa /'kapa/ *f* (*de livro, revista*) cover; (*roupa sem mangas*) cape; **~ de chuva** raincoat

capacete /kapa'setʃi/ *m* helmet

capacho /ka'paʃu/ *m* doormat

capaci|dade /kapasi'dadʒi/ *f* capacity; (*aptidão*) ability; **~tar** *vt* enable; (*convencer*) convince

capataz /kapa'tas/ *m* foreman

capaz /ka'pas/ *a* capable **(de** of**)**; **ser ~ de** (*poder*) be able to; (*ser provável*) be likely to

cape|la /ka'pɛla/ *f* chapel; **~lão** (*pl* **~lães**) *m* chaplain

capen|ga /ka'pẽga/ *a* doddery; **~gar** *vi* dodder

capeta /ka'peta/ *m* (*diabo*) devil; (*criança*) little devil

capilar /kapi'lar/ *a* hair

ca|pim /ka'pĩ/ *m* grass; **~pinar** *vt*/*i* weed

capi|tal /kapi'taw/ (*pl* **~tais**) *a* & *m*/*f* capital; **~talismo** *m* capitalism; **~talista** *a* & *m*/*f* capitalist; **~talizar** *vt* (*com*) capitalize; (*aproveitar*) capitalize on

capi|tanear /kapitani'ar/ *vt* captain <*navio*>; (*fig*) lead; **~tania** *f* captaincy; **~tania do porto** port authority; **~tão** (*pl* **~tães**) *m* captain

capitulação /kapitula'sãw/ *f* capitulation, surrender

capítulo /ka'pitulu/ *m* chapter; (*de telenovela*) episode

capô /ka'po/ *m* bonnet, (*Amer*) hood

capoeira /kapo'era/ *f* Brazilian martial art

capo|ta /ka'pɔta/ *f* roof; **~tar** *vi* overturn

capote /ka'pɔtʃi/ *m* overcoat

capri|char /kapri'ʃar/ *vi* excel o.s.; **~cho** *m* (*esmero*) care; (*desejo*) whim; (*teimosia*) contrariness; **~choso** /o/ *a* (*cheio de caprichos*) capricious; (*com esmero*) painstaking, meticulous

Capricórnio /kapri'kɔrniu/ *m* Capricorn

capricorniano /kaprikorni'anu/ *a* & *m* Capricorn

cápsula /'kapsula/ *f* capsule

cap|tar /kap'tar/ *vt* pick up <*emissão, sinais*>; tap <*água*>; catch, grasp <*sentido*>; win <*simpatia, admiração*>; **~tura** *f* capture; **~turar** *vt* capture

capuz /ka'pus/ *m* hood

caquético /ka'kɛtʃiku/ *a* broken-down, on one's last legs

caqui /ka'ki/ *m* persimmon

cáqui /'kaki/ *a invar* & *m* khaki

cara /'kara/ *f* face; (*aparência*) look; (*ousadia*) cheek □ (*fam*) *m* guy; **~ a ~** face to face; **de ~** straightaway; **dar de ~ com** run into; **está na ~** it's obvious; **fechar a ~** frown; **~ de pau** cheek; **~ de tacho** (*fam*) sheepish look

cara|col /kara'kɔw/ (*pl* **~cóis**) *m* snail

caracte|re /karak'tɛri/ *m* character; **~rística** *f* characteristic, feature; **~rístico** *a* characteristic; **~rizar** *vt* characterize; **~rizar-se** *vpr* be characterized

cara-de-pau /karadʒi'paw/ (*pl* **caras-de-pau**) *a* cheeky, brazen

caramba /ka'rãba/ *int* (*de espanto*) wow; (*de desagrado*) damn

caramelo /kara'mɛlu/ *m* caramel; (*bala*) toffee

caramujo /kara'muʒu/ *m* water snail

caranguejo /karã'geʒu/ *m* crab

caratê /kara'te/ *m* karate

caráter /ka'rater/ *m* character

caravana /kara'vana/ *f* caravan

car|boidrato /karboi'dratu/ *m* carbohydrate; **~bono** /o/ *m* carbon

carbu|rador /karbura'dor/ *m* carburettor, (*Amer*) carburator; **~rante** *m* fuel

carcaça /kar'kasa/ *f* carcass; (*de navio etc*) frame

cárcere /'karseri/ *m* jail

carcereiro /karse'reru/ *m* jailer, warder

carcomido /karko'midu/ *a* worm-eaten; <*rosto*> pock-marked

cardápio /kar'dapiu/ *m* menu

carde|al /kardʒi'aw/ (*pl* **~ais**) *a* cardinal

cardíaco /kar'dʒiaku/ *a* cardiac; **ataque ~** heart attack

cardio|lógico /kardʒio'lɔʒiku/ *a* heart; **~logista** *m/f* heart specialist, cardiologist

cardume /kar'dumi/ *m* shoal

careca /ka'rɛka/ *a* bald ▫ *f* bald patch

ca|recer /kare'ser/ **~recer de** *vt* lack; **~rência** *f* lack; (*social*) deprivation; (*afetiva*) lack of affection; **~rente** *a* lacking; (*socialmente*) deprived; (*afetivamente*) in need of affection

carestia /kares'tʃia/ *f* high cost; (*geral*) high cost of living; (*escassez*) shortage

careta /ka'reta/ *f* grimace ▫ *a* (*fam*) straight, square

car|ga /'karga/ *f* load; (*mercadorias*) cargo; (*elétrica*) charge; (*de cavalaria*) charge; (*de caneta*) refill; (*fig*) burden; **~ga horária** workload; **~go** *m* (*função*) post, job; **a ~go de** in the charge of; **~gueiro** *m* (*navio*) cargo ship, freighter

cariar /kari'ar/ *vi* decay

Caribe /ka'ribi/ *m* Caribbean

caricatu|ra /karika'tura/ *f* caricature; **~rar** *vt* caricature; **~rista** *m/f* caricaturist

carícia /ka'risia/ *f* (*com a mão*) stroke, caress; (*carinho*) affection

cari|dade /kari'dadʒi/ *f* charity; **obra de ~dade** charity; **~doso** /o/ *a* charitable

cárie /'kari/ *f* tooth decay

carim|bar /karĩ'bar/ *vt* stamp; postmark <*carta*>; **~bo** *m* stamp; (*do correio*) postmark

cari|nho /ka'riɲu/ *m* affection; (*um*) caress; **~nhoso** /o/ *a* affectionate

carioca /kari'ɔka/ *a* from Rio de Janeiro ▫ *m/f* person from Rio de Janeiro ▫ (*Port*) *m* weak coffee

caris|ma /ka'rizma/ *m* charisma; **~mático** *a* charismatic

carna|val /karna'vaw/ (*pl* **~vais**) *m* carnival; **~valesco** /e/ *a* carnival; <*roupa*> over the top, overdone ▫ *m* carnival organizer

car|ne /'karni/ *f* (*humana etc*) flesh; (*comida*) meat; **~neiro** *m* sheep; (*macho*) ram; (*como comida*) mutton; **~niça** *f* carrion; **~nificina** *f* slaughter; **~nívoro** *a* carnivorous ▫ *m* carnivore; **~nudo** *a* fleshy

caro /'karu/ *a* expensive; (*querido*) dear ▫ *adv* <*custar, cobrar*> a lot; <*comprar, vender*> at a high price; **pagar ~** pay a high price (for)

caroço /ka'rosu/ *m* (*de pêssego etc*) stone; (*de maçã*) core; (*em sopa, molho etc*) lump

carona /ka'rona/ *f* lift

carpete /kar'pɛtʃi/ *m* fitted carpet

carpin|taria /karpĩta'ria/ *f* carpentry; **~teiro** *m* carpenter

carran|ca /ka'xãka/ *f* scowl; **~cudo** *a* <*cara*> scowling; <*pessoa*> sullen

carrapato /kaxa'patu/ *m* (*animal*) tick; (*fig*) hanger-on

carrasco /ka'xasku/ *m* executioner; (*fig*) butcher

carre|gado /kaxe'gadu/ *a* <*céu*> dark, black; <*cor*> dark; <*ambiente*> tense; **~gador** *m* porter; **~gamento** *m* loading; (*carga*) load; **~gar** *vt* load <*navio, arma, máquina fotográfica*>; (*levar*) carry; charge <*bateria, pilha*>; **~gar em** overdo; pronounce strongly <*letra*>; (*Port*) press

carreira /ka'xera/ *f* career

carre|tel /kaxe'tɛw/ (*pl* **~téis**) *m* reel

car|ril /ka'xiw/ (*pl* **~ris**) (*Port*) *m* rail

carrinho /ka'xiɲu/ *m* (*para bagagem, compras*) trolley; (*de criança*) pram; **~ de mão** wheel-barrow

carro /'kaxu/ *m* car; (*de bois*) cart; **~ alegórico** float; **~ esporte** sports car; **~ fúnebre** hearse; **~ça** /ɔ/ *f* cart; **~ceria** *f* bodywork; **~-chefe** (*pl* **~s-chefes**) *m* (*no carnaval*) main float; (*fig*) centrepiece; **~-forte** (*pl* **~s-fortes**) *m* security van

carros|sel /kaxo'sɛw/ (*pl* **~séis**) *m* merry-go-round

carruagem /kaxu'aʒẽ/ *f* coach

carta /'karta/ *f* letter; (*mapa*) chart; (*do baralho*) card; **~ branca** (*fig*) carte blanche; **~ de condução** (*Port*) driving licence, (*Amer*) driver's license; **~-bomba** (*pl* **~s-bomba**) *f* letter bomb; **~da** *f* (*fig*) move

cartão /kar'tãw/ *m* card; (*Port: papelão*) cardboard; **~ de crédito** credit card; **~ de visita** visiting card; **~ magné tico**

swipe card; **~-postal** (*pl* **cartões-postais**) *m* postcard

car|taz /kar'tas/ *m* poster, (*Amer*) bill; **em ~** showing, (*Amer*) playing; **~teira** *f* (*para dinheiro*) wallet; (*cartão*) card; (*mesa*) desk; **~teira de identidade** identity card; **~teira de motorista** driving licence, (*Amer*) driver's license; **~teiro** *m* postman

car|tel /kar'tɛw/ (*pl* **~téis**) *m* cartel

cárter /'karter/ *m* sump

carto|la /kar'tɔla/ *f* top hat ▫ *m* director; **~lina** *f* card; **~mante** *m/f* tarot reader, fortune-teller

cartório /kar'tɔriu/ *m* registry office

cartucho /kar'tuʃu/ *m* cartridge; (*de dinamite*) stick; (*de amendoim etc*) bag

car|tum /kar'tũ/ *m* cartoon; **~tunista** *m/f* cartoonist

caruncho /ka'rũʃu/ *m* woodcorm

carvalho /kar'vaʎu/ *m* oak

car|vão /kar'vãw/ *m* coal; (*de desenho*) charcoal; **~voeiro** *a* coal

casa /'kaza/ *f* house; (*comercial*) firm; (*de tabuleiro*) square; (*de botão*) hole; **em ~** at home; **para ~** home; **na ~ dos 30 anos** in one's thirties; **~ da moeda** mint; **~ de banho** (*Port*) bathroom; **~ de campo** country house; **~ de saúde** private hospital; **~ decimal** decimal place; **~ popular** council house

casaco /ka'zaku/ *m* (*sobretudo*) coat; (*paletó*) jacket; (*de lã*) pullover

ca|sal /ka'zaw/ (*pl* **~sais**) *m* couple; **~samento** *m* marriage; (*cerimônia*) wedding; **~sar** *vt* marry; (*fig*) combine ▫ *vi* get married; (*fig*) go together; **~sar-se** *vpr* get married; (*fig*) combine; **~sar-se com** marry

casarão /kaza'rãw/ *m* mansion

casca /'kaska/ *f* (*de árvore*) bark; (*de laranja, limão*) peel; (*de banana*) skin; (*de noz, ovo*) shell; (*de milho*) husk; (*de pão*) crust; (*de ferida*) scab

cascalho /kas'kaʎu/ *m* gravel

cascata /kas'kata/ *f* waterfall; (*fam*) fib

casca|vel /kaska'vɛw/ (*pl* **~véis**) *m* (*cobra*) rattlesnake ▫ *f* (*mulher*) shrew

casco /'kasku/ *m* (*de cavalo etc*) hoof; (*de navio*) hull; (*garrafa vazia*) empty

ca|sebre /ka'zɛbri/ *m* hovel, shack; **~seiro** *a* <*comida*> home-made; <*pessoa*> home-loving; <*vida*> home ▫ *m* housekeeper

caserna /ka'zɛrna/ *f* barracks

casmurro /kaz'muxu/ *a* sullen

caso /'kazu/ *m* case; (*amoroso*) affair; (*conto*) story ▫ *conj* in case; **em todo** *ou* **qualquer ~** in any case; **fazer ~ de** take notice of; **vir ao ~** be relevant; **~ contrário** otherwise

casório /ka'zɔriu/ (*fam*) *m* wedding

caspa /'kaspa/ *f* dandruff

casquinha /kas'kiɲa/ *f* (*de sorvete*) cone, cornet

cassar /ka'sar/ *vt* revoke, withdraw <*direitos, autorização*>; ban <*político*>

cassete /ka'sɛtʃi/ *m* cassette

cassetete /kase'tɛtʃi/ *m* truncheon, (*Amer*) nightstick

cassino /ka'sinu/ *m* casino; **~ de oficiais** officers' mess

casta|nha /kas'taɲa/ *f* chestnut; **~nha de caju** cashew nut; **~nha-do-pará** (*pl* **~nhas-do-pará**) *f* Brazil nut; **~nheiro** *m* chestnut tree; **~nho** *a* chestnut (-coloured); **~nholas** /ɔ/ *f pl* castanets

castelhano /kaste'ʎanu/ *a* & *m* Castilian

castelo /kas'tɛlu/ *m* castle

casti|çal /kastʃi'saw/ (*pl* **~çais**) *m* candlestick

cas|tidade /kastʃi'dadʒi/ *f* chastity; **~tigar** *vt* punish; **~tigo** *m* punishment; **~to** *a* chaste

castor /kas'tor/ *m* beaver

castrar /kas'trar/ *vt* castrate

casu|al /kazu'aw/ (*pl* **~ais**) *a* chance; (*fortuito*) fortuitous; **~alidade** *f* chance

casulo /ka'zulu/ *m* (*de larva*) cocoon

cata /'kata/ *f* **à ~ de** in search of

cata|lão /kata'lãw/ (*pl* **~lães**) *a* & *m* (*f* **~lã**) Catalan

catalisador /kataliza'dor/ *m* catalyst; (*de carro*) catalytic convertor

catalogar /katalo'gar/ *vt* catalogue

catálogo /ka'talogu/ *m* catalogue; (*de telefones*) phone book

Catalunha /kata'luɲa/ *f* Catalonia

catapora /kata'pɔra/ *f* chicken pox

catar /ka'tar/ *vt* (*procurar*) search for; (*recolher*) gather; (*do chão*) pick up; sort <*arroz, café*>

catarata /kata'rata/ *f* waterfall; (*no olho*) cataract

catarro /ka'taxu/ *m* catarrh

catástrofe /ka'tastrofi/ *f* catastrophe

catastrófico /katas'trɔfiku/ *a* catastrophic

catecismo /kate'sizmu/ *m* catechism

cátedra /'katedra/ *f* chair

cate|dral /kate'draw/ (*pl* **~drais**) *f* cathedral; **~drático** *m* professor

cate|goria /katego'ria/ *f* category; (*social*) class; (*qualidade*) quality; **~górico** *a* categorical; **~gorizar** *vt* categorize

catinga /ka'tʃĩga/ *f* body odour, stink

cati|vante /katʃi'vãtʃi/ *a* captivating; **~var** *vt* captivate; **~veiro** *m* captivity; **~vo** *a & m* captive

catolicismo /katoli'sizmu/ *m* Catholicism

católico /ka'tɔliku/ *a & m* Catholic

catorze /ka'torzi/ *a & m* fourteen

cau|da /'kawda/ *f* tail; **~dal** (*pl* **~dais**) *m* torrent

caule /'kawli/ *m* stem

cau|sa /'kawza/ *f* cause; (*jurid*) case; **por ~sa de** because of; **~sar** *vt* cause

caute|la /kaw'tɛla/ *f* caution; (*documento*) ticket; **~loso** /o/ *a* cautious, careful

cava /'kava/ *f* armhole

cava|do /ka'vadu/ *a* <*vestido*> low-cut; <*olhos*> deep-set; **~dor** *a* hard-working □ *m* hard worker

cava|laria /kavala'ria/ *f* cavalry; **~lariça** *f* stable; **~leiro** *m* horseman; (*na Idade Média*) knight

cavalete /kava'letʃi/ *m* easel

caval|gadura /kavawga'dura/ *f* mount; **~gar** *vt/i* ride; sit astride <*muro, banco*>; (*saltar*) jump

cavalhei|resco /kavaʎe'resku/ *a* gallant, gentlemanly; **~ro** *m* gentleman □ *a* gallant, gentlemanly

cavalo /ka'valu/ *m* horse; **a ~** on horseback; **~-vapor** (*pl* **~s-vapor**) horsepower

cavanhaque /kava'ɲaki/ *m* goatee

cavaquinho /kava'kiɲu/ *m* ukulele

cavar /ka'var/ *vt* dig; (*fig*) go all out for □ *vi* dig; (*fig*) go all out; **~ em** (*vasculhar*) delve into; **~ a vida** make a living

caveira /ka'vera/ *f* skull

caverna /ka'vɛrna/ *f* cavern

caviar /kavi'ar/ *m* caviar

cavidade /kavi'dadʒi/ *f* cavity

cavilha /ka'viʎa/ *f* peg

cavo /'kavu/ *a* hollow

cavoucar /kavo'kar/ *vt* excavate

caxemira /kaʃe'mira/ *f* cashmere

caxumba /ka'ʃũba/ *f* mumps

cear /si'ar/ *vt* have for supper □ *vi* have supper

cebo|la /se'bola/ *f* onion; **~linha** *f* spring onion

ceder /se'der/ *vt* give up; (*dar*) give; (*emprestar*) lend □ *vi* (*não resistir*) give way; **~ a** yield to

cedilha /se'dʒiʎa/ *f* cedilla

cedo /'sedu/ *adv* early; **mais ~ ou mais tarde** sooner or later

cedro /'sɛdru/ *m* cedar

cédula /'sɛdula/ *f* (*de banco*) note, (*Amer*) bill; (*eleitoral*) ballot paper

ce|gar /se'gar/ *vt* blind; blunt <*faca*>; **~go** /ɛ/ *a* blind; <*faca*> blunt □ *m* blind man; **às ~gas** blindly

cegonha /se'goɲa/ *f* stork

cegueira /se'gera/ *f* blindness

ceia /'seja/ *f* supper

cei|fa /'sejfa/ *f* harvest; (*massacre*) slaughter; **~far** *vt* reap; claim <*vidas*>; (*matar*) mow down

cela /'sɛla/ *f* cell

cele|bração /selebra'sãw/ *f* celebration; **~brar** *vt* celebrate

célebre /'sɛlebri/ *a* celebrated

celebridade /selebri'dadʒi/ *f* celebrity

celeiro /se'leru/ *m* granary

célere /'sɛleri/ *a* swift, fast

celeste /se'lɛstʃi/ *a* celestial

celeuma /se'lewma/ *f* uproar

celibato /seli'batu/ *m* celibacy

celofane /selo'fani/ *m* cellophane

celta /'sɛwta/ *a* Celtic □ *m/f* Celt □ *m* (*língua*) Celtic

célula /'sɛlula/ *f* cell

celu|lar /selu'lar/ *a* cellular □ *m* mobile, (*Amer.*) cell phone **~lite** *f* cellulite; **~lose** /ɔ/ *f* cellulose

cem /sẽj/ *a & m* hundred

cemitério /semi'tɛriu/ *m* cemetery; (*fig*) graveyard

cena /'sena/ *f* scene; (*palco*) stage; **em ~** on stage

cenário /se'nariu/ *m* scenery; (*de crime etc*) scene

cênico /'seniku/ *a* stage

cenoura /se'nora/ *f* carrot

cen|so /'sẽsu/ *m* census; **~sor** *m* censor; **~sura** *f* (*de jornais etc*) censorship; (*órgão*) censor(s); (*condenação*) censure; **~surar** *vt* censor <*jornal, filme etc*>; (*condenar*) censure

centavo /sẽ'tavu/ *m* cent

centeio /sẽ'teju/ *m* rye

centelha /sẽ'teʎa/ *f* spark; (*fig: de gênio etc*) flash

cente|na /sẽ'tena/ *f* hundred; **uma ~na de** about a hundred; **às ~nas** in their hundreds; **~nário** *m* centenary

centésimo /sẽ'tɛzimu/ *a* hundredth

centí|grado /sẽ'tʃigradu/ *m* centigrade; **~litro** *m* centilitre; **~metro** *m* centimetre

cento /'sẽtu/ *a & m* hundred; **por ~** per cent

cen|tral /sẽ'traw/ (*pl* **~trais**) *a* central □ *f* switchboard; **~eólica** wind farm; **~tralizar** *vt* centralize; **~trar** *vt* centre; **~tro** *m* centre

cepti- (*Port*) *veja* **ceti-**

cera /'sera/ *f* wax; **fazer ~** waste time, faff about

cerâmi|ca /se'ramika/ *f* ceramics, pottery; **~co** *a* ceramic

cer|ca /'serka/ *f* fence; **~ca viva** hedge □ *adv* **~ca de** around, about; **~cado** *m* enclosure; (*para criança*) playpen; **~car** *vt* surround; (*com muro, cerca*) enclose; (*assediar*) besiege

cercear /sersi'ar/ *vt* restrict

cerco /'serku/ *m* (*mil*) siege; (*policial*) dragnet

cere|al /seri'aw/ (*pl* **~ais**) *m* cereal

cere|bral /sere'braw/ *a* cerebral

cérebro /'sɛrebru/ *m* brain; (*inteligência*) intellect

cere|ja /se'reʒa/ *f* cherry; **~jeira** *f* cherry tree

cerimônia /seri'monia/ *f* ceremony; **sem ~** unceremoniously; **fazer ~** stand on ceremony

cerimoni|al /serimoni'aw/ (*pl* **~ais**) *a* & *m* ceremonial; **~oso** /o/ *a* ceremonious

cer|rado /se'xadu/ *a* <*barba, mata*> thick; <*punho, dentes*> clenched □ *m* scrubland; **~rar** *vt* close; **~rar-se** *vpr* close; <*noites, trevas*> close in

certeiro /ser'teru/ *a* well-aimed, accurate

certeza /ser'teza/ *f* certainty; **com ~** certainly; **ter ~** be sure (**de** of; **de que** that)

certidão /sertʃi'dãw/ *f* certificate; **~ de nascimento** birth certificate

certifi|cado /sertʃifi'kadu/ *m* certificate; **~car** *vt* certify; **~car-se de** make sure of

certo /'sɛrtu/ *a* (*correto*) right; (*seguro*) certain; (*algum*) a certain □ *adv* right; **dar ~** work

cerveja /ser'veʒa/ *f* beer; **~ria** *f* brewery; (*bar*) pub

cervo /'sɛrvu/ *m* deer

cer|zidura /serzi'dura/ *f* darning; **~zir** *vt* darn

cesariana /sezari'ana/ *f* Caesarian

césio /'sɛziu/ *m* caesium

cessar /se'sar/ *vt*/*i* cease

ces|ta /'sesta/ *f* basket; (*de comida*) hamper; **~to** /e/ *m* basket; **~to de lixo** wastepaper basket

ceticismo /setʃi'sizmu/ *m* scepticism

cético /'sɛtʃiku/ *a* sceptical □ *m* sceptic

cetim /se'tʃĩ/ *m* satin

céu /sɛw/ *m* sky; (*na religião*) heaven; **~ da boca** roof of the mouth

cevada /se'vada/ *f* barley

chá /ʃa/ *m* tea

chacal /ʃa'kaw/ (*pl* **~cais**) *m* jackal

chácara /'ʃakara/ *f* smallholding; (*casa*) country cottage

chaci|na /ʃa'sina/ *f* slaughter; **~nar** *vt* slaughter

chá|-de-bar /ʃadʒi'bar/ (*pl* **~s-de-bar**) *m* bachelor party; **~-de-panela** (*pl* **~s-de-panela**) *m* hen night, (*Amer*) wedding shower

chafariz /ʃafa'ris/ *m* fountain

chaga /'ʃaga/ *f* sore

chaleira /ʃa'lera/ *f* kettle

chama /'ʃama/ *f* flame

cha|mada /ʃa'mada/ *f* call; (*dos presentes*) roll call; (*dos alunos*) register; **~mado** *m* call □ *a* (*depois do substantivo*) called; (*antes do substantivo*) so-called; **~mar** *vt* call; (*para sair etc*) ask, invite; attract <*atenção*> □ *vi* call; <*telefone*> ring; **~mar-se** *vpr* be called; **~mariz** *m* decoy; **~mativo** *a* showy, flashy

chamejar /ʃame'ʒar/ *vi* flare

chaminé /ʃami'nɛ/ *f* (*de casa, fábrica*) chimney; (*de navio, trem*) funnel

champanhe /ʃã'paɲi/ *m* champagne

champu /ʃã'pu/ (*Port*) *m* shampoo

chamuscar /ʃamus'kar/ *vt* singe, scorch

chance /'ʃãsi/ *f* chance

chanceler /ʃãse'ler/ *m* chancellor

chanchada /ʃã'ʃada/ *f* (*peça*) second-rate play; (*filme*) B movie

chanta|gear /ʃãtaʒi'ar/ *vt* blackmail; **~gem** *f* blackmail; **~gista** *m*/*f* blackmailer

chão /ʃãw/ (*pl* **~s**) *m* ground; (*dentro de casa etc*) floor

chapa /'ʃapa/ *f* sheet; (*foto*) plate; **~ eleitoral** electoral list; **~ de matrícula** (*Port*) number plate, (*Amer*) license plate □ (*fam*) *m* mate

chapéu /ʃa'pɛw/ *m* hat

charada /ʃa'rada/ *f* riddle

char|ge /'ʃarʒi/ *f* (political) cartoon; **~gista** *m*/*f* cartoonist

charla|tanismo /ʃarlata'nizmu/ *m* charlatanism; **~tão** (*pl* **~tães**) *m* (*f* **~tona**) charlatan

char|me /'ʃarmi/ *m* charm; **fazer ~me** turn on the charm; **~moso** /o/ *a* charming

charneca /ʃar'nɛka/ *f* moor

charuto /ʃa'rutu/ *m* cigar

chassi /ʃa'si/ *m* chassis

chata /'ʃata/ *f* (*barca*) barge

chate|ação /ʃatʃia'sãw/ *f* annoyance; **~ar** *vt* annoy; **~ar-se** *vpr* get annoyed

cha|tice /ʃa'tʃisi/ *f* nuisance; **~to** *a* (*tedioso*) boring; (*irritante*) annoying; (*mal-educado*) rude; (*plano*) flat

chauvinis|mo /ʃovi'nizmu/ *m* chauvinism; **~ta** *m*/*f* chauvinist □ *a* chauvinistic

cha|vão /ʃa'vãw/ *m* cliché; **~ve** *f* key; (*ferramenta*) spanner; **~ve de fenda** screwdriver; **~ve inglesa** wrench;

~veiro *m* (*aro*) keyring; (*pessoa*) locksmith

chávena /'ʃavena/ *f* soup bowl; (*Port: xícara*) cup

checar /ʃe'kar/ *vt* check

che|fe /'ʃɛfi/ *m/f* (*patrão*) boss; (*gerente*) manager; (*dirigente*) leader; **~fia** *f* leadership; (*de empresa*) management; (*sede*) headquarters; **~fiar** *vt* lead; be in charge of <*trabalho*>

che|gada /ʃe'gada/ *f* arrival; **~gado** *a* <*amigo, relação*> close; **~gar** *vi* arrive; (*deslocar-se*) move up; (*ser suficiente*) be enough □ *vt* bring up <*prato, cadeira*>; **~gar a fazer** go as far as doing; **aonde você quer ~gar?** what are you driving at?; **~gar lá** (*fig*) make it

cheia /'ʃeja/ *f* flood

cheio /'ʃeju/ *a* full; (*fam: farto*) fed up

chei|rar /ʃe'rar/ *vt/i* smell (**a** of); **~roso** /o/ *a* scented

cheque /'ʃɛki/ *m* cheque, (*Amer*) check; **~ de viagem** traveller's cheque; **~ em branco** blank cheque

chi|ado /ʃi'adu/ *m* (*de pneus, freios*) screech; (*de porta*) squeak; (*de vapor, numa fita*) hiss; **~ar** *vi* <*porta*> squeak; <*pneus, freios*> screech; <*vapor, fita*> hiss; <*fritura*> sizzle; (*fam: reclamar*) grumble, moan

chiclete /ʃi'klɛtʃi/ *m* chewing gum; **~ de bola** bubble gum

chico|tada /ʃiko'tada/ *f* lash; **~te** /ɔ/ *m* whip; **~tear** *vt* whip

chi|frar /ʃi'frar/ (*fam*) *vt* cheat on <*marido, esposa*>; two-time <*namorado, namorada*>; **~fre** *m* horn; **~frudo** *a* horned; (*fam*) cuckolded □ *m* cuckold

Chile /'ʃili/ *m* Chile

chileno /ʃi'lenu/ *a* & *m* Chilean

chilique /ʃi'liki/ (*fam*) *m* funny turn

chil|rear /ʃiwxi'ar/ *vi* chirp, twitter; **~reio** *m* chirping, twittering

chimarrão /ʃima'xãw/ *m* unsweetened maté tea

chimpanzé /ʃĩpã'zɛ/ *m* chimpanzee

China /'ʃina/ *f* China

chinelo /ʃi'nɛlu/ *m* slipper

chi|nês /ʃi'nes/ *a* & *m* (*f* **~nesa**) Chinese

chinfrim /ʃĩ'frĩ/ *a* tatty, shoddy

chio /'ʃiu/ *m* squeak; (*de pneus*) screech; (*de vapor*) hiss

chique /'ʃiki/ *a* <*pessoa, aparência, roupa*> smart, (*Amer*) sharp; <*hotel, bairro, loja etc*> smart, up-market, posh

chiqueiro /ʃi'keru/ *m* pigsty

chis|pa /'ʃispa/ *f* flash; **~pada** *f* dash; **~par** *vi* (*soltar chispas*) flash; (*correr*) dash

choca|lhar /ʃoka'ʎar/ *vt/i* rattle; **~lho** *m* rattle

cho|cante /ʃo'kãtʃi/ *a* shocking; (*fam*) incredible; **~car** *vt/i* hatch <*ovos*>; (*ultrajar*) shock; **~car-se** *vpr* <*carros etc*> crash; <*teorias etc*> clash

chocho /'ʃoʃu/ *a* dull, insipid

chocolate /ʃoko'latʃi/ *m* chocolate

chofer /ʃo'fɛr/ *m* chauffeur

chope /'ʃopi/ *m* draught lager

choque /'ʃɔki/ *m* shock; (*colisão*) collision; (*conflito*) clash

cho|radeira /ʃora'dera/ *f* fit of crying; **~ramingar** *vi* whine; **~ramingas** *m/f invar* whiner; **~rão** *m* (*salgueiro*) weeping willow □ *a* (**~rona**) tearful; **~rar** *vi* cry; **~ro** /o/ *m* crying; **~roso** /o/ *a* tearful

chouriço /ʃo'risu/ *m* black pudding; (*Port*) sausage

chover /ʃo'ver/ *vi* rain

chuchu /ʃu'ʃu/ *m* chayote

chucrute /ʃu'krutʃi/ *m* sauerkraut

chumaço /ʃu'masu/ *m* wad

chum|bado /ʃũ'badu/ (*fam*) *a* knocked out; **~bar** (*Port*) *vt* fill <*dente*>; fail <*aluno*> □ *vi* <*aluno*> fail; **~bo** *m* lead; (*Port: obturação*) filling

chu|par /ʃu'par/ *vt* suck; <*esponja*> suck up; **~peta** /e/ *f* dummy, (*Amer*) pacifier

churras|caria /ʃuxaska'ria/ *f* barbecue restaurant; **~co** *m* barbecue; **~queira** *f* barbecue; **~quinho** *m* kebab

chu|tar /ʃu'tar/ *vt/i* kick; (*fam: adivinhar*) guess; **~te** *m* kick; **~teira** *f* football boot

chu|va /'ʃuva/ *f* rain; **~va de pedra** hail; **~varada** *f* torrential rainstorm; **~veiro** *m* shower; **~viscar** *vi* drizzle; **~visco** *m* drizzle; **~voso** /o/ *a* rainy

cica|triz /sika'tris/ *f* scar; **~trizar** *vt* scar □ *vi* <*ferida*> heal

cic|lismo /si'klizmu/ *m* cycling; **~lista** *m/f* cyclist; **~lo** *m* cycle; **~lone** /o/ *m* cyclone; **~lovia** *f* cycle lane

cida|dania /sidada'nia/ *f* citizenship; **~dão** (*pl* **~dãos**) *m* (*f* **~dã**) citizen; **~de** *f* town; (*grande*) city; **~dela** /ɛ/ *f* citadel

ciência /si'ẽsia/ *f* science

cien|te /si'ẽtʃi/ *a* aware; **~tífico** *a* scientific; **~tista** *m/f* scientist

ci|fra /'sifra/ *f* figure; (*código*) cipher; **~frão** *m* dollar sign; **~frar** *vt* encode

cigano /si'ganu/ *a* & *m* gypsy

cigarra /si'gaxa/ *f* cicada; (*dispositivo*) buzzer

cigar|reira /siga'xera/ *f* cigarette case; **~ro** *m* cigarette

cilada /si'lada/ *f* trap; (*estratagema*) trick

cilindrada /silĩ'drada/ *f* (engine) capacity

cilíndrico /si'lĩdriku/ *a* cylindrical

cilindro /si'lĩdru/ *m* cylinder; (*rolo*) roller

cílio /'siliu/ *m* eyelash

cima /'sima/ *f* **em ~** on top; (*na casa*) upstairs; **em ~ de** on, on top of; **para ~** up; (*na casa*) upstairs; **por ~** over the top; **por ~ de** over; **de ~** from above; **ainda por ~** moreover

címbalo /'sĩbalu/ *m* cymbal

cimeira /si'mera/ *f* crest; (*Port: cúpula*) summit

cimen|tar /simẽ'tar/ *vt* cement; **~to** *m* cement

cinco /'sĩku/ *a & m* five

cine|asta /sini'asta/ *m/f* film-maker; **~ma** /e/ *m* cinema

Cingapura /sĩga'pura/ *f* Singapore

cínico /'siniku/ *a* cynical ▫ *m* cynic

cinismo /si'nizmu/ *m* cynicism

cinqüen|ta /sĩ'kwẽta/ *a & m* fifty; **~tão** *a & m* (*f* **~tona**) fifty-year-old

cinti|lante /sĩtʃi'lãtʃi/ *a* glittering; **~lar** *vi* glitter

cin|to /'sĩtu/ *m* belt; **~to de segurança** seatbelt; **~tura** *f* waist; **~turão** *m* belt

cin|za /'sĩza/ *f* ash ▫ *a invar* grey; **~zeiro** *m* ashtray

cin|zel /sĩ'zɛw/ (*pl* **~zéis**) *m* chisel; **~zelar** *vt* carve

cinzento /sĩ'zẽtu/ *a* grey

cipó /si'pɔ/ *m* vine, liana; **~poal** (*pl* **~poais**) *m* jungle

cipreste /si'prɛstʃi/ *m* cypress

cipriota /sipri'ɔta/ *a & m* Cypriot

ciranda /si'rãda/ *f* (*fig*) merry-go-round

cir|cense /sir'sẽsi/ *a* circus; **~co** *m* circus

circu|ito /sir'kuitu/ *m* circuit; **~lação** *f* circulation; **~lar** *a & f* circular ▫ *vt* circulate ▫ *vi* <*dinheiro, sangue*> circulate; <*carro*> drive; <*ônibus*> run; <*trânsito*> move; <*pessoa*> go round

círculo /'sirkulu/ *m* circle

circunci|dar /sirkũsi'dar/ *vt* circumcise; **~ção** *f* circumcision

circun|dar /sirkũ'dar/ *vt* surround; **~ferência** *f* circumference; **~flexo** /ɛks/ *a & m* circumflex; **~scrição** *f* district; **~scrição eleitoral** constituency; **~specto** /ɛ/ *a* circumspect; **~stância** *f* circumstance; **~stanciado** *a* detailed; **~stancial** (*pl* **~stanciais**) *a* circumstantial; **~stante** *m/f* bystander

cirrose /si'xɔzi/ *f* cirrhosis

cirur|gia /sirur'ʒia/ *f* surgery; **~gião** *m* (*f* **~giã**) surgeon

cirúrgico /si'rurʒiku/ *a* surgical

cisão /si'zãw/ *f* split, division

cisco /'sisku/ *m* speck

cisma[1] /'sizma/ *m* schism

cis|ma[2] /'sizma/ *f* (*mania*) fixation; (*devaneio*) imagining, daydream; (*prevenção*) irrational dislike; (*de criança*) whim; **~mar** *vt/i* be lost in thought; <*criança*> be insistent; **~mar em** brood over; **~mar de** *ou* **em fazer** insist on doing; **~mar que** insist on thinking that; **~mar com alg** take a dislike to s.o.

cisne /'sizni/ *m* swan

cistite /sis'tʃitʃi/ *f* cystitis

ci|tação /sita'sãw/ *f* quotation; (*jurid*) summons; **~tar** *vt* quote; (*jurid*) summon

ciúme /si'umi/ *m* jealousy; **ter ~s de** be jealous of

ciu|meira /siu'mera/ *f* fit of jealousy; **~mento** *a* jealous

cívico /'siviku/ *a* civic

ci|vil /si'viw/ (*pl* **~vis**) *a* civil ▫ *m* civilian; **~vilidade** *f* civility

civili|zação /siviliza'sãw/ *f* civilization; **~zado** *a* civilized; **~zar** *vt* civilize

civismo /si'vizmu/ *m* public spirit

cla|mar /kla'mar/ *vt/i* cry out, clamour (**por** for); **~mor** *m* outcry; **~moroso** /o/ *a* <*protesto*> loud, noisy; <*erro, injustiça*> blatant

clandestino /klãdes'tʃinu/ *a* clandestine

cla|ra /'klara/ *f* egg white; **~rabóia** *f* skylight; **~rão** *m* flash; **~rear** *vt* brighten; clarify <*questão*> ▫ *vi* brighten up; (*fazer-se dia*) become light; **~reira** *f* clearing; **~reza** /e/ *f* clarity; **~ridade** *f* brightness; (*do dia*) daylight

cla|rim /kla'rĩ/ *m* bugle; **~rinete** /e/ *m* clarinet

clarividente /klarivi'dẽtʃi/ *m/f* clairvoyant

claro /'klaru/ *a* clear; <*luz*> bright; <*cor*> light ▫ *adv* clearly ▫ *int* of course; **~ que sim/não** of course/of course not; **às claras** openly; **noite em ~** sleepless night; **já é dia ~** it's already daylight

classe /'klasi/ *f* class; **~ média** middle class

clássico /'klasiku/ *a* classical; (*famoso, exemplar*) classic ▫ *m* classic

classifi|cação /klasifika'sãw/ *f* classification; (*numa competição* *esportiva*) placing, place; **~cado** *a* classified; <*candidato*> successful; <*esportista, time*> qualified; **~car** *vt* classify; (*considerar*) describe (**de** as); **~car-se** *vpr* <*candidato, esportista*> qualify; (*chamar-se*) describe o.s. (**de** as); **~catório** *a* qualifying

classudo /kla'sudu/ (*fam*) *a* classy

claustro|fobia /klawstrofo'bia/ *f* claustrophobia; **~fóbico** *a* claustrophobic

cláusula /'klawzula/ *f* clause

cla|ve /'klavi/ *f* clef; **~vícula** *f* collar bone

cle|mência /kle'mẽsia/ *f* clemency; **~mente** *a* <*pessoa*> lenient; <*tempo*> clement

cleptomaníaco /kleptoma'niaku/ *m* kleptomaniac

clérigo /'klɛrigu/ *m* cleric, clergyman

clero /'klɛru/ *m* clergy

clicar /kli'kar/ *vi* (*comput*) click

clien|te /kli'ẽtʃi/ *m*/*f* (*de loja*) customer; (*de advogado, empresa*) client; **~tela** /ɛ/ *f* (*de loja*) customers; (*de restaurante, empresa*) clientele

cli|ma /'klima/ *m* climate; **~mático** *a* climatic

clímax /'klimaks/ *m invar* climax

clíni|ca /'klinika/ *f* clinic; **~ca geral** general practice; **~co** *a* clinical □ *m* **~co geral** general practitioner, GP

clipe /'klipi/ *m* clip; (*para papéis*) paper clip

clone /'kloni/ *m* clone

cloro /'klɔru/ *m* chlorine

close /'klozi/ *m* close-up

clube /'klubi/ *m* club

coação /koa'sãw/ *f* coercion

coadjuvante /koadʒu'vãtʃi/ *a* <*ator*> supporting □ *m*/*f* (*em peça, filme*) co-star; (*em crime*) accomplice

coador /koa'dor/ *m* strainer; (*de legumes*) colander; (*de café*) filter bag

coadunar /koadu'nar/ *vt* combine

coagir /koa'ʒir/ *vt* compel

coagular /koagu'lar/ *vt*/*i* clot; **~-se** *vpr* clot

coágulo /ko'agulu/ *m* clot

coalhar /koa'ʎar/ *vt*/*i* curdle; **~-se** *vpr* curdle

coalizão /koali'zãw/ *f* coalition

coar /ko'ar/ *vt* strain

coaxar /koa'ʃar/ *vi* croak □ *m* croaking

cobaia /ko'baja/ *f* guinea pig

cober|ta /ko'bɛrta/ *f* (*de cama*) bedcover; (*de navio*) deck; **~to** /ɛ/ *a* covered □ *pp de* **cobrir**; **~tor** *m* blanket; **~tura** *f* (*revestimento*) covering; (*reportagem*) coverage; (*seguro*) cover; (*apartamento*) penthouse

cobi|ça /ko'bisa/ *f* greed, covetousness; **~çar** *vt* covet; **~çoso** /o/ *a* covetous

cobra /'kɔbra/ *f* snake

co|brador /kobra'dor/ *m* (*no ônibus*) conductor; **~brança** *f* (*de dívida*) collection; (*de preço*) charging; **~brança de pênalti/falta** penalty (kick)/free kick; **~brar** *vt* collect <*dívida*>; ask for <*coisa prometida*>; take <*pênalti*>; **~brar aco a alg** (*em dinheiro*) charge s.o. for sth; (*fig*) make s.o. pay for sth; **~brar uma falta** (*no futebol*) take a free kick

cobre /'kɔbri/ *m* copper

cobrir /ko'brir/ *vt* cover; **~-se** *vpr* <*pessoa*> cover o.s. up; <*coisa*> be covered

cocaína /koka'ina/ *f* cocaine

coçar /ko'sar/ *vt* scratch □ *vi* (*esfregar-se*) scratch; (*comichar*) itch; **~-se** *vpr* scratch o.s.

cócegas /'kɔsegas/ *f pl* **fazer ~ em** tickle; **sentir ~** be ticklish

coceira /ko'sera/ *f* itch

cochi|char /koʃi'ʃar/ *vt*/*i* whisper; **~cho** *m* whisper

cochi|lada /koʃi'lada/ *f* doze; **~lar** *vi* doze; **~lo** *m* snooze

coco /'koku/ *m* coconut

cócoras /'kɔkoras/ *f pl* **de ~** squatting; **ficar de ~** squat

côdea /'kodʒia/ *f* crust

codificar /kodʒifi'kar/ *vt* encode <*mensagem*>; codify <*leis*>

código /'kɔdʒigu/ *m* code; **~ de barras** bar code

codinome /kodʒi'nomi/ *m* codename

coeficiente /koefisi'ẽtʃi/ *m* coefficient; (*fig: fator*) factor

coelho /ko'eʎu/ *m* rabbit

coentro /ko'ẽtru/ *m* coriander

coerção /koer'sãw/ *f* coercion

coe|rência /koe'rẽsia/ *f* (*lógica*) coherence; (*conseqüência*) consistency; **~rente** *a* (*lógico*) coherent; (*conseqüente*) consistent

coexis|tência /koezis'tẽsia/ *f* coexistence; **~tir** *vi* coexist

cofre /'kɔfri/ *m* safe; (*de dinheiro público*) coffer

cogi|tação /koʒita'sãw/ *f* contemplation; **fora de ~tação** out of the question; **~tar** *vt*/*i* contemplate

cogumelo /kogu'mɛlu/ *m* mushroom

coibir /koi'bir/ *vt* restrict; **~-se de** keep o.s. from

coice /'kojsi/ *m* kick

coinci|dência /koĩsi'dẽsia/ *f* coincidence; **~dir** *vi* coincide

coisa /'kojza/ *f* thing

coitado /koj'tadu/ *m* poor thing; **~ do pai** poor father
cola /'kɔla/ *f* glue; (*cópia*) crib
colabo|ração /kolabora'sãw/ *f* collaboration; (*de escritor etc*) contribution; **~rador** *m* collaborator; (*em jornal, livro*) contributor; **~rar** *vi* collaborate; (*em jornal, livro*) contribute (**em** to)
colagem /ko'laʒẽ/ *f* collage
colágeno /ko'laʒenu/ *m* collagen
colapso /ko'lapsu/ *m* collapse
colar[1] /ko'lar/ *m* necklace
colar[2] /ko'lar/ *vt* (*grudar*) stick; (*copiar*) crib □ *vi* stick; (*copiar*) crib; <*desculpa etc*> stand up, stick
colarinho /kola'riɲu/ *m* collar; (*de cerveja*) head
colate|ral /kolate'raw/ (*pl* **~rais**) *a* **efeito ~ral** side effect
col|cha /'kowʃa/ *f* bedspread; **~chão** *m* mattress
colchete /kow'ʃetʃi/ *m* fastener; (*sinal de pontuação*) square bracket; **~ de pressão** press stud, popper
colchonete /kowʃo'nɛtʃi/ *m* (fold-away) mattress
coldre /'kɔwdri/ *m* holster
cole|ção /kole'sãw/ *f* collection; **~cionador** *m* collector; **~cionar** *vt* collect
colega /ko'lɛga/ *m/f* (*amigo*) friend; (*de trabalho*) colleague
colegi|al /koleʒi'aw/ (*pl* **~ais**) *a* school □ *m/f* schoolboy (*f*-girl)
colégio /ko'lɛʒiu/ *m* secondary school, (*Amer*) high school
coleira /ko'lera/ *f* collar
cólera /'kɔlera/ *f* (*doença*) cholera; (*raiva*) fury
colérico /ko'lɛriku/ *a* (*furioso*) furious □ *m* (*doente*) cholera victim
colesterol /koleste'rɔw/ *m* cholesterol
cole|ta /ko'lɛta/ *f* collection; **~tânea** *f* collection; **~tar** *vt* collect
colete /ko'letʃi/ *m* waistcoat, (*Amer*) vest; **~ salva-vidas** life-jacket, (*Amer*) life-preserver
coletivo /kole'tʃivu/ *a* collective; <*transporte*> public □ *m* bus
colheita /ko'ʎejta/ *f* harvest; (*produtos colhidos*) crop
colher[1] /ko'ʎɛr/ *f* spoon
colher[2] /ko'ʎer/ *vt* pick <*flores, frutos*>; gather <*informações*>
colherada /koʎe'rada/ *f* spoonful
colibri /koli'bri/ *m* hummingbird
cólica /'kɔlika/ *f* colic
colidir /koli'dʒir/ *vi* collide
coli|gação /koliga'sãw/ *f* (*pol*) coalition; **~gado** *m* (*pol*) coalition partner; **~gar** *vt* bring together; **~gar-se** *vpr* join forces; (*pol*) form a coalition
colina /ko'lina/ *f* hill
colírio /ko'liriu/ *m* eyewash
colisão /koli'zãw/ *f* collision
collant /ko'lã/ (*pl* **~s**) *m* body; (*de ginástica*) leotard
colmeia /kow'meja/ *f* beehive
colo /'kɔlu/ *f* (*regaço*) lap; (*pescoço*) neck
colo|cação /koloka'sãw/ *f* placing; (*emprego*) position; (*exposição de fatos*) statement; (*de aparelho, pneus, carpete etc*) fitting; **~cado** *a* placed; **o primeiro ~cado** (*em ranking*) person in first place; **~cador** *m* fitter; **~car** put; fit <*aparelho, pneus, carpete etc*>; put forward, state <*opinião, idéias*>; (*empregar*) get a job for
Colômbia /ko'lõbia/ *f* Colombia
colombiano /kolõbi'anu/ *a & m* Colombian
cólon /'kɔlõ/ *m* colon
colônia[1] /ko'lonia/ *f* (*colonos*) colony
colônia[2] /ko'lonia/ *f* (*perfume*) cologne
coloni|al /koloni'aw/ (*pl* **~ais**) *a* colonial; **~alismo** *m* colonialism; **~alista** *a & m/f* colonialist; **~zar** *vt* colonize
colono /ko'lonu/ *m* settler, colonist; (*lavrador*) tenant farmer
coloqui|al /koloki'aw/ (*pl* **~ais**) *a* colloquial
colóquio /ko'lɔkiu/ *m* (*conversa*) conversation; (*congresso*) conference
colo|rido /kolo'ridu/ *a* colourful □ *m* colouring; **~rir** *vt* colour
colu|na /ko'luna/ *f* column; (*vertebral*) spine; **~nável** (*pl* **~náveis**) *a* famous □ *m/f* celebrity; **~nista** *m/f* columnist
com /kõ/ *prep* with; **o comentário foi comigo** the comment was meant for me; **você está ~ a chave?** have you got the key?; **~ seis anos de idade** at six years of age
coma /'koma/ *f* coma
comadre /ko'madri/ *f* (*madrinha*) godmother of one's child; (*mãe do afilhado*) mother of one's godchild; (*urinol*) bedpan
coman|dante /komã'dãtʃi/ *m* commander; **~dar** *vt* lead; (*ordenar*) command; (*elevar-se acima de*) dominate; **~do** *m* command; (*grupo*) commando group
comba|te /kõ'batʃi/ *m* combat; (*a drogas, doença etc*) fight (**a** against); **~ter** *vt/i* fight; **~ter-se** *vpr* fight
combi|nação /kõbina'sãw/ *f* combination; (*acordo*) arrangement;

(*plano*) scheme; (*roupa*) petticoat; **~nar** *vt* (*juntar*) combine; (*ajustar*) arrange □ *vi* go together, match; **~nar com** go with, match; **~nar de sair** arrange to go out; **~nar-se** *vpr* (*juntar-se*) combine; (*harmonizar-se*) go together, match

comboio /kõ'boju/ *m* convoy; (*Port: trem*) train

combustí|vel /kõbus'tʃivew/ (*pl* **~veis**) *m* fuel

come|çar /kome'sar/ *vt/i* start, begin; **~ço** /e/ *m* beginning, start

comédia /ko'mɛdʒia/ *f* comedy

comediante /komedʒi'ãtʃi/ *m/f* comedian (*f* comedienne)

comemo|ração /komemora'sãw/ *f* (*celebração*) celebration; (*lembrança*) commemoration; **~rar** *vt* (*festejar*) celebrate; (*lembrar*) commemorate

comen|tar /komẽ'tar/ *vt* comment on; (*falar mal de*) make comments about; **~tário** *m* comment; (*de texto, na TV etc*) commentary; **sem ~tários** no comment; **~tarista** *m/f* commentator

comer /ko'mer/ *vt* eat; <*ferrugem etc*> eat away; take <*peça de xadrez*> □ *vi* eat; **~-se** *vpr* (*de raiva etc*) be consumed (**de** with); **dar de ~ a** feed

comerci|al /komersi'aw/ (*pl* **~ais**) *a & m* commercial; **~alizar** *vt* market; **~ante** *m/f* trader; **~ar** *vi* do business, trade; **~ário** *m* shopworker

comércio /ko'mɛrsiu/ *m* (*atividade*) trade; (*loja etc*) business; (*lojas*) shops; **~ eletrônico** e-commerce

comes /'komis/ *m pl* **~ e bebes** (*fam*) food and drink; **~tíveis** *m pl* foods, food; **~tível** (*pl* **~tíveis**) *a* edible

cometa /ko'meta/ *m* comet

cometer /kome'ter/ *vt* commit <*crime*>; make <*erro*>

comichão /komi'ʃãw/ *f* itch

comício /ko'misiu/ *m* rally

cômico /'komiku/ *a* (*de comédia*) comic; (*engraçado*) comical

comida /ko'mida/ *f* food; (*uma*) meal

comigo = **com** + **mim**

comi|lão /komi'lãw/ *a* (*f* **~lona**) greedy □ *m* (*f* **~lona**) glutton

cominho /ko'miɲu/ *m* cummin

comiserar-se /komize'rarsi/ *vpr* commiserate (**de** with)

comis|são /komi'sãw/ *f* commission; **~sário** *m* commissioner; **~sário de bordo** (*aéreo*) steward; (*de navio*) purser; **~sionar** *vt* commission

comi|tê /komi'te/ *m* committee; **~tiva** *f* group; (*de uma pessoa*) retinue

como /'komu/ *adv* (*na condição de*) as; (*da mesma forma que*) like; (*de que maneira*) how □ *conj* as; **~?** (*pedindo repetição*) pardon?; **~ se** as if; **assim ~** as well as

cômoda /'komoda/ *f* chest of drawers, (*Amer*) bureau

como|didade /komodʒi'dadʒi/ *f* comfort; (*conveniência*) convenience; **~dismo** *m* complacency; **~dista** *a* complacent

cômodo /'komodu/ *a* comfortable; (*conveniente*) convenient □ *m* (*aposento*) room

como|vente /komo'vẽtʃi/ *a* moving; **~ver** *vt* move □ *vi* be moving; **~ver-se** *vpr* be moved

compacto /kõ'paktu/ *a* compact □ *m* single

compadecer-se /kõpade'sersi/ *vpr* feel pity (**de** for)

compadre /kõ'padri/ *m* (*padrinho*) godfather of one's child; (*pai do afilhado*) father of one's godchild

compaixão /kõpa'ʃãw/ *f* compassion

companhei|rismo /kõpaɲe'rizmu/ *m* companionship; **~ro** *m* (*de viagem etc*) companion; (*amigo*) friend, mate

companhia /kõpa'ɲia/ *f* company; **fazer ~ a alg** keep s.o. company

compa|ração /kõpara'sãw/ *f* comparison; **~rar** *vt* compare; **~rativo** *a* comparative; **~rável** (*pl* **~ráveis**) *a* comparable

compare|cer /kõpare'ser/ *vi* appear; **~cer a** attend; **~cimento** *m* attendance

comparsa /kõ'parsa/ *m/f* (*ator*) bit player; (*cúmplice*) sidekick

comparti|lhar /kõpartʃi'ʎar/ *vt/i* share (**de** in); **~mento** *m* compartment

compassado /kõpa'sadu/ *a* (*medido*) measured; (*ritmado*) regular

compassivo /kõpa'sivu/ *a* compassionate

compasso /kõ'pasu/ *m* (*mus*) beat, time; (*instrumento*) compass, pair of compasses

compatí|vel /kõpa'tʃivew/ (*pl* **~veis**) *a* compatible

compatriota /kõpatri'ɔta/ *m/f* compatriot, fellow countryman (*f*-woman)

compelir /kõpe'lir/ *vt* compel

compene|tração /kõpenetra'sãw/ *f* conviction; **~trar** *vt* convince; **~trar-se** *vpr* convince o.s.

compen|sação /kõpẽsa'sãw/ *f* compensation; (*de cheques*) clearing; **~sar** *vt* make up for

<*defeitos, danos*>; offset <*peso, gastos*>; clear <*cheques*> □ *vi* <*crime*> pay

compe|tência /kõpe'tẽsia/ *f* competence; **~tente** *a* competent

compe|tição /kõpetʃi'sãw/ *f* competition; **~tidor** *m* competitor; **~tir** *vi* compete; **~tir a** be up to; **~tividade** *f* competitiveness; **~titivo** *a* competitive

compla|cência /kõpla'sẽsia/ *f* complaisance; **~cente** *a* obliging

complemen|tar /kõplemẽ'tar/ *vt* complement □ *a* complementary; **~to** *m* complement

comple|tar /kõple'tar/ *vt* complete; top up <*copo, tanque etc*>; **~tar 20 anos** turn 20; **~to** /ɛ/ *a* complete; (*cheio*) full up; **por ~to** completely; **escrever por ~to** write out in full

comple|xado /kõplek'sadu/ *a* with a complex; **~xidade** *f* complexity; **~xo** /ɛ/ *a* & *m* complex

compli|cação /kõplika'sãw/ *f* complication; **~cado** *a* complicated; **~car** *vt* complicate; **~car-se** *vpr* get complicated

complô /kõ'plo/ *m* conspiracy, plot

com|ponente /kõpo'nẽtʃi/ *a* & *m* component; **~por** *vt/i* compose; **~por-se** *vpr* (*controlar-se*) compose o.s.; **~por-se de** be composed of

compor|tamento /kõporta'mẽtu/ *m* behaviour; **~tar** *vt* hold; bear <*dor, prejuízo*>; **~tar-se** *vpr* behave

composi|ção /kõpozi'sãw/ *f* composition; (*acordo*) conciliation; **~tor** *m* (*de música*) composer; (*gráfico*) compositor

compos|to /kõ'postu/ *pp de* **compor** □ *a* compound; <*pessoa*> level-headed □ *m* compound; **~to de** made up of; **~tura** *f* composure

compota /kõ'pɔta/ *f* fruit in syrup

com|pra /'kõpra/ *f* purchase; *pl* shopping; **fazer ~pras** go shopping; **~prador** *m* buyer; **~prar** *vt* buy; bribe <*oficial, juiz*>; pick <*briga*>

compreen|der /kõpriẽ'der/ *vt* (*conter em si*) contain; (*estender-se a*) cover, take in; (*entender*) understand; **~são** *f* understanding; **~sível** (*pl* **~síveis**) *a* understandable; **~sivo** *a* understanding

compres|sa /kõ'prɛsa/ *f* compress; **~são** *f* compression; **~sor** *m* compressor; **rolo ~sor** steamroller

compri|do /kõ'pridu/ *a* long; **~mento** *m* length

compri|mido /kõpri'midu/ *m* pill, tablet □ *a* <*ar*> compressed; **~mir** *vt* (*apertar*) press; (*reduzir o volume de*) compress

comprome|tedor /kõpromete'dor/ *a* compromising; **~ter** *vt* (*envolver*) involve; (*prejudicar*) compromise; **~ter alg a fazer** commit s.o. to doing; **~ter-se** *vpr* (*obrigar-se*) commit o.s.; (*prejudicar-se*) compromise o.s.; **~tido** *a* (*ocupado*) busy; (*noivo*) spoken for

compromisso /kõpro'misu/ *m* commitment; (*encontro marcado*) appointment; **sem ~** without obligation

compro|vação /kõprova'sãw/ *f* proof; **~vante** *m* receipt; **~var** *vt* prove

compul|são /kõpuw'sãw/ *f* compulsion; **~sivo** *a* compulsive; **~sório** *a* compulsory

compu|tação /kõputa'sãw/ *f* computation; (*matéria, ramo*) computing; **~tador** *m* computer; **~tadorizar** *vt* computerize; **~tar** *vt* compute

comum /ko'mũ/ *a* common; (*não especial*) ordinary; **fora do ~** out of the ordinary; **em ~** <*trabalho*> joint; <*atuar*> jointly; **ter muito em ~** have a lot in common

comungar /komũ'gar/ *vi* take communion

comunhão /komu'ɲãw/ *f* communion; (*relig*) (Holy) Communion

comuni|cação /komunika'sãw/ *f* communication; **~cação social /visual** media studies/ graphic design; **~cado** *m* notice; (*pol*) communiqué; **~car** *vt* communicate; (*unir*) connect □ *vi*, **~car-se** *vpr* communicate; **~cativo** *a* communicative

comu|nidade /komuni'dadʒi/ *f* community; **~nismo** *m* communism; **~nista** *a* & *m/f* communist; **~nitário** *a* (*da comunidade*) community; (*para todos juntos*) communal

côncavo /'kõkavu/ *a* concave

conce|ber /kõse'ber/ *vt* conceive; (*imaginar*) conceive of □ *vi* conceive; **~bível** (*pl* **~bíveis**) *a* conceivable

conceder /kõse'der/ *vt* grant; **~ em** accede to

concei|to /kõ'sejtu/ *m* concept; (*opinião*) opinion; (*fama*) reputation; **~tuado** *a* highly thought of; **~tuar** *vt* (*imaginar*) conceptualize; (*avaliar*) assess

concen|tração /kõsẽtra'sãw/ *f* concentration; (*de jogadores*) training camp; **~trar** *vt* concentrate; **~trar-se** *vpr* concentrate

concepção /kõsep'sãw/ *f* conception; (*opinião*) view

concernir /kõser'nir/ *vt* **~ a** concern

concerto /kõ'sertu/ *m* concert

conces|são /kõse'sãw/ *f* concession; **~sionária** *f* dealership; **~sionário** *m* dealer

concha /'kõʃa/ *f* (*de molusco*) shell; (*colher*) ladle

concili|ação /kõsilia'sãw/ *f* conciliation; **~ador** *a* conciliatory; **~ar** *vt* reconcile

concílio /kõ'siliu/ *m* council

conci|são /kõsi'zãw/ *f* conciseness; **~so** *a* concise

conclamar /kõkla'mar/ *vt* call <*eleição, greve*>; call upon <*pessoa*>

conclu|dente /kõklu'dẽtʃi/ *a* conclusive; **~ir** *vt/i* conclude; **~são** *f* conclusion; **~sivo** *a* concluding

concor|dância /kõkor'dãsia/ *f* agreement; **~dante** *a* consistent; **~dar** *vi* agree (**em** to) ◻ *vt* bring into line; **~data** *f* **abrir ~data** go into liquidation

concórdia /kõ'kɔrdʒia/ *f* concord

concor|rência /kõko'xẽsia/ *f* competition (**a** for); **~rente** *a* competing; **~rer** *vi* compete (**a** for); **~rer para** contribute to; **~rido** *a* popular

concre|tizar /kõkretʃi'zar/ *vt* realize; **~tizar-se** *vpr* be realized; **~to** /ɛ/ *a & m* concrete

concurso /kõ'kursu/ *m* contest; (*prova*) competition

con|dado /kõ'dadu/ *m* county; **~de** *m* count

condeco|ração /kõdekora'sãw/ *f* decoration; **~rar** *vt* decorate

conde|nação /kõdena'sãw/ *f* condemnation; (*jurid*) conviction; **~nar** *vt* condemn; convict

conden|sação /kõdẽsa'sãw/ *f* condensation; **~sar** *vt* condense; **~sar-se** *vpr* condense

condescen|dência /kõdesẽ'dẽsia/ *f* acquiescence; **~dente** *a* acquiescent; **~der** *vi* acquiesce; **~der a** comply with <*pedido, desejo*>; **~der a ir** condescend to go

condessa /kõ'desa/ *f* countess

condi|ção /kõdʒi'sãw/ *f* condition; (*qualidade*) capacity; **ter ~ção** *ou* **~ções para** be able to; **em boas ~ções** in good condition; **~cionado** *a* conditioned; **~cional** (*pl* **~cionais**) *a* conditional; **~cionamento** *m* conditioning

condimen|tar /kõdʒimẽ'tar/ *vt* season; **~to** *m* seasoning

condoer-se /kõdo'ersi/ *vpr* **~ de** feel sorry for

condolência /kõdo'lẽsia/ *f* sympathy; *pl* condolences

condomínio /kõdo'miniu/ *m* (*taxa*) service charge

condu|ção /kõdu'sãw/ *f* (*de carro etc*) driving; (*transporte*) transport; **~cente** *a* conducive (**a** to); **~ta** *f* conduct; **~to** *m* conduit; **~tor** *m* driver; (*eletr*) conductor; **~zir** *vt* lead; drive <*carro*>; (*eletr*) conduct ◻ *vi* (*de carro*) drive; (*levar*) lead (**a** to)

cone /'koni/ *m* cone

conecta|r /konek'tar/ *vt* connect; **~do** *a* connected; (*comput*) on-line

cone|xão /konek'sãw/ *f* connection; **~xo** /ɛ/ *a* connected

confec|ção /kõfek'sãw/ *f* (*roupa*) off-the-peg outfit; (*loja*) clothes shop, boutique; (*fábrica*) clothes manufacturer; **~cionar** *vt* make

confederação /kõfedera'sãw/ *f* confederation

confei|tar /kõfej'tar/ *vt* ice; **~taria** *f* cake shop; **~teiro** *m* confectioner

confe|rência /kõfe'rẽsia/ *f* conference; (*palestra*) lecture; **~rencista** *m/f* speaker

conferir /kõfe'rir/ *vt* check (**com** against); (*conceder*) confer (**a** on) ◻ *vi* (*controlar*) check; (*estar exato*) tally

confes|sar /kõfe'sar/ *vt/i* confess; **~sar-se** *vpr* confess; **~sionário** *m* confessional; **~sor** *m* confessor

confete /kõ'fɛtʃi/ *m* confetti

confi|ança /kõfi'ãsa/ *f* (*convicção*) confidence; (*fé*) trust; **~ante** *a* confident (**em** of); **~ar** (*dar*) entrust; **~ar em** trust; **~ável** (*pl* **~áveis**) *a* reliable; **~dência** *f* confidence; **~dencial** (*pl* **~denciais**) *a* confidential; **~denciar** *vt* tell in confidence; **~dente** *m/f* confidant (*f* confidante)

configu|ração /kõfigura'sãw/ *f* configuration; **~rar** *vt* (*representar*) represent; (*formar*) shape; (*comput*) configure

con|finar /kõfi'nar/ *vi* **~finar com** border on; **~fins** *m pl* borders

confir|mação /kõfirma'sãw/ *f* confirmation; **~mar** *vt* confirm; **~mar-se** *vpr* be confirmed

confis|car /kõfis'kar/ *vt* confiscate; **~co** *m* confiscation

confissão /kõfi'sãw/ *f* confession

confla|gração /kõflagra'sãw/ *f* conflagration; **~grar** *vt* set alight; (*fig*) throw into turmoil

confli|tante /kõfli'tãtʃi/ *a* conflicting; **~to** *m* conflict

confor|mação /kõforma'sãw/ *f* resignation; **~mado** *a* resigned (**com** to); **~mar** *vt* adapt (**a** to); **~mar-se com** conform to <*regra, política*>; resign o.s. to, come to terms with <*destino, evento*>; **~me** /ɔ/ *prep* according to □ *conj* depending on; **~me** it depends; **~midade** *f* conformity; **~mismo** *m* conformism; **~mista** *a & m/f* conformist

confor|tar /kõfor'tar/ *vt* comfort; **~tável** (*pl* **~táveis**) *a* comfortable; **~to** /o/ *m* comfort

confraternizar /kõfraterni'zar/ *vi* fraternize

confron|tação /kõfrõta'sãw/ *f* confrontation; **~tar** *vt* confront; (*comparar*) compare; **~to** *m* confrontation; (*comparação*) comparison

con|fundir /kõfũ'dʒir/ *vt* confuse; **~fundir-se** *vpr* get confused; **~fusão** *f* confusion; (*desordem*) mess; (*tumulto*) commotion; **~fuso** *a* (*confundido*) confused; (*que confunde*) confusing

conge|lador /kõʒela'dor/ *m* freezer; **~lamento** *m* (*de preços etc*) freeze; **~lar** *vt* freeze; **~lar-se** *vpr* freeze

congênito /kõ'ʒenitu/ *a* congenital

congestão /kõʒes'tãw/ *f* congestion

congestio|nado /kõʒestʃio'nadu/ *a* <*rua, cidade*> congested; <*pessoa, rosto*> flushed; <*olhos*> bloodshot; **~namento** *m* (*de trânsito*) traffic jam; **~nar** *vt* congest; **~nar-se** *vpr* <*rua*> get congested; <*rosto*> flush

conglomerado /kõglome'radu/ *m* conglomerate

congratular /kõgratu'lar/ *vt* congratulate (**por** on)

congre|gação /kõgrega'sãw/ *f* (*na igreja*) congregation; (*reunião*) gathering; **~gar** *vt* bring together; **~gar-se** *vpr* congregate

congresso /kõ'grɛsu/ *m* congress

conhaque /ko'ɲaki/ *m* brandy

conhe|cedor /koɲese'dor/ *a* knowing □ *m* connoisseur; **~cer** *vt* know; (*ser apresentado a*) get to know; (*visitar*) go to, visit; **~cido** *a* known; (*famoso*) well-known □ *m* acquaintance; **~cimento** *m* knowledge; **tomar ~cimento de** learn of; **travar ~cimento com alg** make s.o.'s acquaintance, become acquainted with s.o.

cônico /'koniku/ *a* conical

coni|vência /koni'vẽsia/ *f* connivance; **~vente** *a* conniving (**em** at)

conjetu|ra /kõʒe'tura/ *f* conjecture; **~rar** *vt/i* conjecture

conju|gação /kõʒuga'sãw/ *f* (*ling*) conjugation; **~gar** *vt* conjugate <*verbo*>

cônjuge /'kõʒuʒi/ *m/f* spouse

conjun|ção /kõʒũ'sãw/ *f* conjunction; **~tivo** *a & m* subjunctive; **~to** *a* joint □ *m* set; (*roupa*) outfit; (*musical*) group; **o ~to de** the body of; **em ~to** jointly; **~tura** *f* state of affairs; (*econômica*) state of the economy

conosco = com + nós

cono|tação /konota'sãw/ *f* connotation; **~tar** *vt* connote

conquanto /kõ'kwãtu/ *conj* although, even though

conquis|ta /kõ'kista/ *f* conquest; (*proeza*) achievement; **~tador** *m* conqueror □ *a* conquering; **~tar** *vt* conquer <*terra, país*>; win <*riqueza, independência*>; win over <*pessoa*>

consa|gração /kõsagra'sãw/ *f* (*de uma igreja*) consecration; (*dedicação*) dedication; **~grado** *a* <*artista, expressão*> established; **~grar** *vt* consecrate <*igreja*>; establish <*artista, estilo*>; (*dedicar*) dedicate (**a** to); **~grar-se a** dedicate o.s. to

consci|ência /kõsi'ẽsia/ *f* (*moralidade*) conscience; (*sentidos*) consciousness; (*no trabalho*) con-scientiousness; (*de um fato etc*) awareness; **~encioso** /o/ *a* conscientious; **~ente** *a* conscious; **~entizar** *vt* make aware (**de** of); **~entizar-se** *vpr* become aware (**de** of)

consecutivo /kõseku'tʃivu/ *a* consecutive

conse|guinte /kose'gĩtʃi/ *a* **por ~guinte** consequently; **~guir** *vt* get; **~guir fazer** manage to do □ *vi* succeed

conse|lheiro /kõse'ʎeru/ *m* counsellor, adviser; **~lho** /e/ *m* piece of advice; *pl* advice; (*órgão*) council

consen|so /kõ'sẽsu/ *m* consensus; **~timento** *m* consent; **~tir** *vt* allow □ *vi* consent (**em** to)

conse|qüência /kõse'kwẽsia/ *f* consequence; **por ~qüência** consequently; **~qüente** *a* consequent; (*coerente*) consistent

conser|tar /kõser'tar/ *vt* repair; **~to** /e/ *m* repair

conser|va /kõ'sɛrva/ *f* (*em vidro*) preserve; (*em lata*) tinned food; **~vação** *f* preservation; **~vador** *a & m* conservative; **~vadorismo** *m* conservatism; **~vante** *a & m* preservative; **~var** *vt* preserve; (*manter, guardar*) keep; **~var-se** *vpr* keep; **~vatório** *m* conservatory

conside|ração /kõsidera'sãw/ *f* consideration; (*estima*) esteem; **levar em ~ração** take into consideration; **~rar** *vt* consider; (*estimar*) think highly of □ *vi* consider; **~rar-se** *vpr* consider o.s.; **~rável** (*pl* **~ráveis**) *a* considerable

consig|nação /kõsigna'sãw/ *f* consignment; **~nar** *vt* consign

consigo = com + si

consis|tência /kõsis'tẽsia/ *f* consistency; **~tente** *a* firm; **~tir** *vi* consist (**em** in)

consoante /kõso'ãtʃi/ *f* consonant

conso|lação /kõsola'sãw/ *f* consolation; **~lador** *a* consoling; **~lar** *vt* console; **~lar-se** *vpr* console o.s.

consolidar /kõsoli'dar/ *vt* consolidate; mend <*fratura*>

consolo /kõ'solu/ *m* consolation

consórcio /kõ'sɔrsiu/ *m* consortium

consorte /kõ'sɔrtʃi/ *m/f* consort

conspícuo /kõs'pikuu/ *a* conspicuous

conspi|ração /kõspira'sãw/ *f* conspiracy; **~rador** *m* conspirator; **~rar** *vi* conspire

cons|tância /kõs'tãsia/ *f* constancy; **~tante** *a & f* constant; **~tar** *vi* (*em lista etc*) appear; **não me ~ta** I am not aware; **~ta que** it is said that; **~tar de** consist of

consta|tação /kõstata'sãw/ *f* observation; **~tar** *vt* note, notice; certify <*óbito*>

conste|lação /kõstela'sãw/ *f* constellation; **~lado** *a* star-studded

conster|nação /kõsterna'sãw/ *f* consternation; **~nar** *vt* dismay

consti|pação /kõstʃipa'sãw/ *f* (*Port: resfriado*) cold; **~pado** *a* (*resfriado*) with a cold; (*no intestino*) constipated; **~par-se** *vpr* (*Port: resfriar-se*) get a cold

constitu|cional /kõstʃitusio'naw/ (*pl* **~cionais**) *a* constitutional; **~ição** *f* constitution; **~inte** *a* constituent □ *f* **Constituinte** Constituent Assembly; **~ir** *vt* form <*governo, sociedade*>; (*representar*) constitute; (*nomear*) appoint

constran|gedor /kõstrãʒe'dor/ *a* embarrassing; **~ger** *vt* embarrass; (*coagir*) constrain; **~ger-se** *vpr* get embarrassed; **~gimento** *m* (*embaraço*) embarrassment; (*coação*) constraint

constru|ção /kõstru'sãw/ *f* construction; (*terreno*) building site; **~ir** *vt* build <*casa, prédio*>; (*fig*) construct; **~tivo** *a* constructive; **~tor** *m* builder; **~tora** *f* building firm

cônsul /'kõsuw/ (*pl* **~es**) *m* consul

consulado /kõsu'ladu/ *m* consulate

consul|ta /kõ'suwta/ *f* consultation; **~tar** *vt* consult; **~tor** *m* consultant; **~toria** *f* consultancy; **~tório** *m* (*médico*) surgery, (*Amer*) office

consu|mação /kõsuma'sãw/ *f* (*taxa*) minimum charge; **~mado** *a* **fato ~mado** fait accompli; **~mar** *vt* accomplish <*projeto*>; carry out <*crime, sacrifício*>; consummate <*casamento*>

consu|midor /kõsumi'dor/ *a & m* consumer; **~mir** *vt* consume; take up <*tempo*>; **~mismo** *m* consumerism; **~mista** *a & m/f* consumerist; **~mo** *m* consumption

conta /'kõta/ *f* (*a pagar*) bill; (*bancária*) account; (*contagem*) count; (*de vidro etc*) bead; *pl* (*com*) accounts; **em ~** economical; **por ~ de** on account of; **por ~ própria** on one's own account; **ajustar ~s** settle up; **dar ~ de** (*fig*) be up to; **dar ~ do recado** (*fam*) deliver the goods; **dar-se ~ de** realize; **fazer de ~** pretend; **ficar por ~ de** be left to; **levar** *ou* **ter em ~** take into account; **prestar ~s de** account for; **tomar ~ de** take care of; **~ bancária** bank account; **~ corrente** current account

contabi|lidade /kõtabili'dadʒi/ *f* accountancy; (*contas*) accounts; (*seção*) accounts department; **~lista** (*Port*) *m/f* accountant; **~lizar** *vt* write up <*quantia*>; (*fig*) notch up

contact- (*Port*) *veja* **contat-**

conta|dor /kõta'dor/ *m* (*pessoa*) accountant; (*de luz etc*) meter; **~gem** *f* counting; (*de pontos num jogo*) scoring; **~gem regressiva** countdown

contagi|ante /kõtaʒi'ãtʃi/ *a* infectious; **~ar** *vt* infect; **~ar-se** *vpr* become infected

contágio /kõ'taʒiu/ *m* infection

contagioso /kõtaʒi'ozu/ *a* contagious

contami|nação /kõtamina'sãw/ *f* contamination; **~nar** *vt* contaminate

contanto /kõ'tãtu/ *adv* **~ que** provided that

contar /kõ'tar/ *vt/i* count; (*narrar*) tell; **~ com** count on

conta|tar /kõta'tar/ *vt* contact; **~to** *m* contact; **entrar em ~to com** get in touch with; **tomar ~to com** come into contact with

contem|plação /kõtẽpla'sãw/ *f* contemplation; **~plar** *vt* (*considerar*) contemplate; (*dizer respeito a*) concern; **~plar alg com** treat s.o. to □ *vi* ponder; **~plativo** *a* contemplative

contemporâneo /kõtẽpo'raniu/ *a & m* contemporary

contenção /kõtẽ'sãw/ *f* containment

conten|cioso /kõtẽsi'ozu/ *a* contentious; **~da** *f* dispute

conten|tamento /kõtẽta'mẽtu/ *m* contentment; **~tar** *vt* satisfy; **~tar-se** *vpr* be content; **~te** *a* (*feliz*) happy; (*satisfeito*) content; **~to** *m* **a ~to** satisfactorily

conter /kõ'ter/ *vt* contain; **~-se** *vpr* contain o.s.

conterrâneo /kõte'xaniu/ *m* fellow countryman (*f*-woman)

contestar /kõtes'tar/ *vt* question; (*jurid*) contest

conteúdo /kõte'udu/ *m* (*de recipiente*) contents; (*fig: de carta etc*) content

contexto /kõ'testu/ *m* context

contigo = **com** + **ti**

continência /kõtʃi'nẽsia/ *f* (*mil*) salute

continen|tal /kõtʃinẽ'taw/ (*pl* **~tais**) *a* continental; **~te** *m* continent

contin|gência /kõtʃĩ'ʒẽsia/ *f* contingency; **~gente** *a* (*eventual*) possible; (*incerto*) contingent □ *m* contingent

continu|ação /kõtʃinua'sãw/ *f* continuation; **~ar** *vt/i* continue; **eles ~am ricos** they are still rich; **~idade** *f* continuity

contínuo /kõ'tʃinuu/ *a* continuous □ *m* office junior

con|tista /kõ'tʃista/ *m/f* (short) story writer; **~to** *m* (short) story; **~to de fadas** fairy tale; **~to-do-vigário** (*pl* **~tos-do-vigário**) *m* confidence trick, swindle

contorcer /kõtor'ser/ *vt* twist; **~-se** *vpr* (*de dor*) writhe

contor|nar /kõtor'nar/ *vt* go round; (*fig*) get round <*obstáculo, problema*>; (*cercar*) surround; (*delinear*) outline; **~no** /o/ *m* outline; (*da paisagem*) contour

contra /'kõtra/ *prep* against

contra-|atacar /kõtrata'kar/ *vt* counterattack; **~-ataque** *m* counterattack

contrabaixo /kõtra'baʃu/ *m* double bass

contrabalançar /kõtrabalã'sar/ *vt* counterbalance

contraban|dear /kõtrabãdʒi'ar/ *vt* smuggle; **~dista** *m/f* smuggler; **~do** *m* (*ato*) smuggling; (*artigos*) contraband

contração /kõtra'sãw/ *f* contraction

contracenar /kõtrase'nar/ *vi* **~ com** play up to

contraceptivo /kõtrasep'tʃivu/ *a & m* contraceptive

contracheque /kõtra'ʃɛki/ *m* pay slip

contradi|ção /kõtradʒi'sãw/ *f* contradiction; **~tório** *a* contradictory; **~zer** *vt* contradict; **~zer-se** *vpr* <*pessoa*> contradict o.s.; <*idéias etc*> be contradictory

contragosto /kõtra'gostu/ *m* **a ~** reluctantly

contrair /kõtra'ir/ *vt* contract; pick up <*hábito, vício*>; **~-se** *vpr* contract

contramão /kõtra'mãw/ *f* opposite direction □ *a invar* one way

contramestre /kõtra'mɛstri/ *m* supervisor; (*em navio*) bosun

contra-ofensiva /kõtraofẽ'siva/ *f* counter-offensive

contrapartida /kõtrapar'tʃida/ *f* (*fig*) compensation; **em ~** on the other hand

contraproducente /kõtraprodu'sẽtʃi/ *a* counterproductive

contrari|ar /kõtrari'ar/ *vt* go against, run counter to; (*aborrecer*) annoy; **~edade** *f* adversity; (*aborrecimento*) annoyance

contrário /kõ'trariu/ *a* opposite; (*desfavorável*) adverse; **~ a** contrary to; <*pessoa*> opposed to □ *m* opposite; **pelo** *ou* **ao ~** on the contrary; **ao ~ de** contrary to; **em ~** to the contrary

contras|tante /kõtras'tãtʃi/ *a* contrasting; **~tar** *vt/i* contrast; **~te** *m* contrast

contra|tante /kõtra'tãtʃi/ *m/f* contractor; **~tar** *vt* employ, take on <*operários*>

contra|tempo /kõtra'tẽpu/ *m* hitch

contra|to /kõ'tratu/ *m* contract; **~tual** (*pl* **~tuais**) *a* contractual

contraven|ção /kõtravẽ'sãw/ *f* contravention; **~tor** *m* offender

contribu|ição /kõtribui'sãw/ *f* contribution; **~inte** *m/f* contributor; (*pagador de impostos*) taxpayer; **~ir** *vt* contribute □ *vi* contribute; (*pagar impostos*) pay tax

contrição /kõtri'sãw/ *f* contrition

contro|lar /kõtro'lar/ *vt* control; (*fiscalizar*) check; **~le** /o/, (*Port*) **~lo** /o/ *m* control; (*fiscalização*) check

contro|vérsia /kõtro'vɛrsia/ *f* controversy; **~verso** /ɛ/ *a* controversial

contudo /kõ'tudu/ *conj* nevertheless

contundir /kõtũ'dʒir/ *vt* (*dar hematoma em*) bruise; injure <*jogador*>; **~-se** *vpr* bruise o.s.; <*jogador*> get injured

conturbado /kõtur'badu/ *a* troubled

contu|são /kõtu'zãw/ *f* bruise; (*de jogador*) injury; **~so** *a* bruised; <*jogador*> injured

convales|cença /kõvale'sẽsa/ *f* convalescence; **~cer** *vi* convalesce

convenção /kõvẽ'sãw/ *f* convention

conven|cer /kõvẽ'ser/ *vt* convince; **~cido** *a* (*convicto*) convinced; (*metido*) conceited; **~cimento** *m* (*convicção*) conviction; (*imodéstia*) conceitedness

convencio|nal /kõvẽsio'naw/ (*pl* **~nais**) *a* conventional

conveni|ência /kõveni'ẽsia/ *f* convenience; **~ente** *a* convenient; (*cabível*) appropriate

convênio /kõ'veniu/ *m* agreement

convento /kõ'vẽtu/ *m* convent

convergir /kõver'ʒir/ *vi* converge

conver|sa /kõ'vɛrsa/ *f* conversation; **a ~sa dele** the things he says; **~sa fiada** idle talk; **~sação** *f* conversation; **~sado** *a* <*pessoa*> talkative; <*assunto*> talked about; **~sador** *a* talkative

conversão /kõver'sãw/ *f* conversion

conversar /kõver'sar/ *vi* talk

conver|sível /kõver'sivew/ (*pl* **~síveis**) *a* & *m* convertible; **~ter** *vt* convert; **~ter-se** *vpr* be converted; **~tido** *m* convert

con|vés /kõ'vɛs/ (*pl* **~veses**) *m* deck

convexo /kõ'vɛksu/ *a* convex

convic|ção /kõvik'sãw/ *f* conviction; **~to** *a* convinced; (*ferrenho*) confirmed; <*criminoso*> convicted

convi|dado /kõvi'dadu/ *m* guest; **~dar** *vt* invite; **~dativo** *a* inviting

convincente /kõvĩ'sẽtʃi/ *a* convincing

convir /kõ'vir/ *vi* (*ficar bem*) be appropriate; (*concordar*) agree (**em** on); **~ a** suit, be convenient for; **convém notar que** one should note that

convite /kõ'vitʃi/ *m* invitation

convi|vência /kõvi'vẽsia/ *f* coexistence; (*relação*) close contact; **~ver** *vi* coexist; (*ter relações*) associate (**com** with)

convívio /kõ'viviu/ *m* association (**com** with)

convocar /kõvo'kar/ *vt* call <*eleições, greve*>; call upon <*pessoa*> (**a** to); (*ao serviço militar*) call up

convosco = **com** + **vós**

convul|são /kõvuw'sãw/ *f* (*do corpo*) convulsion; (*da sociedade etc*) upheaval; **~sionar** *vt* convulse <*corpo*>; (*fig*) churn up; **~sivo** *a* convulsive

cooper /'kuper/ *m* jogging; **fazer ~** go jogging

coope|ração /koopera'sãw/ *f* cooperation; **~rar** *vi* cooperate; **~rativa** *f* cooperative; **~rativo** *a* cooperative

coorde|nação /koordena'sãw/ *f* co-ordination; **~nada** *f* coordinate; **~nar** *vt* coordinate

copa /'kɔpa/ *f* (*de árvore*) top; (*aposento*) breakfast room; (*torneio*) cup; *pl* (*naipe*) hearts; **a Copa (do Mundo)** the World Cup; **~-cozinha** (*pl* **~s-cozinhas**) *f* kitchen-diner

cópia /'kɔpia/ *f* copy

copiar /kopi'ar/ *vt* copy

co-piloto /kopi'lotu/ *m* co-pilot

copioso /kopi'ozu/ *a* ample; <*refeição*> substantial

copo /'kɔpu/ *m* glass

coque /'kɔki/ *m* (*penteado*) bun

coqueiro /ko'keru/ *m* coconut palm

coqueluche /koke'luʃi/ *f* (*doença*) whooping cough; (*mania*) fad

coque|tel /koke'tɛw/ (*pl* **~téis**) *m* cocktail; (*reunião*) cocktail party

cor[1] /kɔr/ *m* **de ~** by heart

cor[2] /kor/ *f* colour; **TV a ~es** colour TV; **pessoa de ~** coloured person

coração /kora'sãw/ *m* heart

cora|gem /ko'raʒẽ/ *f* courage; **~joso** /o/ *a* courageous

co|ral[1] /ko'raw/ (*pl* **~rais**) *m* (*animal*) coral

co|ral[2] /ko'raw/ (*pl* **~rais**) *m* (*de cantores*) choir □ *a* choral

co|rante /ko'rãtʃi/ *a* & *m* colouring; **~rar** *vt* colour □ *vi* blush

cor|da /'kɔrda/ *f* rope; (*mus*) string; (*para roupa lavada*) clothes line; **dar ~da em** wind <*relógio*>; **~da bamba** tightrope; **~das vocais** vocal chords; **~dão** *m* cord; (*de sapatos*) lace; (*policial*) cordon

cordeiro /kor'deru/ *m* lamb

cor|del /kor'dɛw/ (*pl* **~déis**) (*Port*) *m* string; **literatura de ~del** trash

cor-de-rosa /kordʒi'rɔza/ *a invar* pink

cordi|al /kordʒi'aw/ (*pl* **~ais**) *a* & *m* cordial; **~alidade** *f* cordiality

cordilheira /kordʒi'ʎera/ *f* chain of mountains

coreano /kori'anu/ *a* & *m* Korean

Coréia /ko'rɛja/ *f* Korea

core|ografia /koriogra'fia/ *f* choreography; **~ógrafo** *m* choreographer

coreto /ko'retu/ *m* bandstand

coriza /ko'riza/ *f* runny nose

corja /'kɔrʒa/ *f* pack; (*de pessoas*) rabble

córner /'kɔrner/ *m* (*futebol*) corner

coro /'koru/ *m* chorus

coro|a /ko'roa/ *f* crown; (*de flores etc*) wreath ▫ (*fam*) *m/f* old man (*f* woman); **~ação** *f* coronation; **~ar** *vt* crown

coro|nel /koro'nɛw/ (*pl* **~néis**) *m* colonel

coronha /ko'roɲa/ *f* butt

corpete /kor'petʃi/ *m* bodice

corpo /'korpu/ *m* body; (*físico de mulher*) figure; (*físico de homem*) physique; **~ de bombeiros** fire brigade; **~ diplomático** diplomatic corps; **~ docente** teaching staff, (*Amer*) faculty; **~-a-~** *m invar* pitched battle; **~ral** (*pl* **~rais**) *a* physical; <*pena*> corporal

corpu|lência /korpu'lẽsia/ *f* stoutness; **~lento** *a* stout

correção /koxe'sãw/ *f* correction

corre-corre /kɔxi'kɔxi/ *m* (*debandada*) stampede; (*correria*) rush

correct- (*Port*) *veja* **corret-**

corre|diço /koxe'dʒisu/ *a* <*porta*> sliding; **~dor** *m* (*atleta*) runner; (*passagem*) corridor

correia /ko'xeja/ *f* strap; (*peça de máquina*) belt; (*para cachorro*) lead, (*Amer*) leash

correio /ko'xeju/ *m* post, mail; (*repartição*) post office; **pôr no ~** post, (*Amer*) mail; **~ aéreo** air mail; **~ eletrônico** email

correlação /koxela'sãw/ *f* correlation

correligionário /koxeliʒio'nariu/ *m* party colleague

corrente /ko'xẽtʃi/ *a* <*água*> running; <*mês, conta*> current; <*estilo*> fluid; (*usual*) common ▫ *f* (*de água, eletricidade*) current; (*cadeia*) chain; **~ de ar** draught; **~za** /e/ *f* current; (*de ar*) draught

cor|rer /ko'xer/ *vi* (*à pé*) run; (*de carro*) drive fast, speed; (*fazer rápido*) rush; <*água, sangue*> flow; <*tempo*> elapse; <*boato*> go round ▫ *vt* draw <*cortina*>; run <*risco*>; **~reria** *f* rush

correspon|dência /koxespõ'dẽsia/ *f* correspondence; **~dente** *a* corresponding ▫ *m/f* correspondent; (*equivalente*) equivalent; **~der** *vi* **~der a** correspond to; (*retribuir*) return; **~der-se** *vpr* correspond (**com** with)

corre|tivo /koxe'tʃivu/ *a* corrective ▫ *m* punishment; **~to** /ɛ/ *a* correct

corretor /koxe'tor/ *m* broker; **~ de imóveis** estate agent, (*Amer*) realtor

corrida /ko'xida/ *f* (*prova*) race; (*ação de correr*) run; (*de taxi*) ride

corrigir /koxi'ʒir/ *vt* correct

corrimão /koxi'mãw/ (*pl* **~s**) *m* handrail; (*de escada*) banister

corriqueiro /koxi'keru/ *a* ordinary, run-of-the-mill

corroborar /koxobo'rar/ *vt* corroborate

corroer /koxo'er/ *vt* corrode <*metal*>; (*fig*) erode; **~-se** *vpr* corrode; (*fig*) erode

corromper /koxõ'per/ *vt* corrupt; **~-se** *vpr* be corrupted

corro|são /koxo'zãw/ *f* (*de metal*) corrosion; (*fig*) erosion; **~sivo** *a* corrosive

corrup|ção /koxup'sãw/ *f* corruption; **~to** *a* corrupt

cor|tada /kor'tada/ *f* (*em tênis*) smash; (*em pessoa*) put-down; **~tante** *a* cutting; **~tar** *vt* cut; cut off <*luz, telefone, perna etc*>; cut down <*árvore*>; cut out <*efeito, vício*>; take away <*prazer*>; (*com o carro*) cut up; (*desprezar*) cut dead ▫ *vi* cut; **~tar o cabelo** (*no cabeleireiro*) get one's hair cut; **~te**[1] /ɔ/ *m* cut; (*gume*) blade; (*desenho*) cross-section; **sem ~te** <*faca*> blunt; **~te de cabelo** haircut

cor|te[2] /'kortʃi/ *f* court; **~tejar** *vt* court; **~tejo** /e/ *m* (*séquito*) retinue; (*fúnebre*) cortège; **~tês** *a* (*f* **~tesa**) courteous, polite; **~tesão** (*pl* **~tesãos**) *m* courtier; **~tesia** *f* courtesy

corti|ça /kor'tʃisa/ *f* cork; **~ço** *m* (*casa popular*) slum tenement

cortina /kor'tʃina/ *f* curtain

cortisona /kortʃi'zona/ *f* cortisone

coruja /ko'ruʒa/ *f* owl ▫ *a* <*pai, mãe*> proud, doting

coruscar /korus'kar/ *vi* flash

corvo /'korvu/ *m* crow

cós /kɔs/ *m invar* waistband

coser /ko'zer/ *vt/i* sew

cosmético /koz'mɛtʃiku/ *a & m* cosmetic

cósmico /'kɔzmiku/ *a* cosmic

cosmo /'kɔzmu/ *m* cosmos; **~nauta** *m/f* cosmonaut; **~polita** *a* cosmopolitan ▫ *m/f* globetrotter

costa /'kɔsta/ *f* coast; *pl* (*dorso*) back; **Costa do Marfim** Ivory Coast; **Costa Rica** Costa Rica

costarriquenho /kostaxi'keɲu/ *a & m* Costa Rican

cos|teiro /kos'teru/ *a* coastal; **~tela** /ɛ/ *f* rib; **~teleta** /e/ *f* chop; *pl* (*suíças*) sideburns; **~telinha** *f* (*de porco*) spare rib

costu|mar /kostu'mar/ *vt* **~ma fazer** he usually does; **~mava fazer** he used to do; **~me** *m* (*uso*) custom; (*traje*) costume; **de ~me** usually; **como de ~me** as usual; **ter o ~me de** have a habit of; **~meiro** *a* customary

costu|ra /kos'tura/ *f* sewing; **~rar** *vt/i* sew; **~reira** *f* (*mulher*) dressmaker; (*caixa*) needlework box

co|ta /'kɔta/ *f* quota; **~tação** *f* (*preço*) rate; (*apreço*) rating; **~tado** *a* <*ação*> quoted; (*conceituado*) highly rated; **~tar** *vt* rate; quote <*ações*>

cote|jar /kote'ʒar/ *vt* compare; **~jo** /e/ *m* comparison

cotidiano /kotʃidʒi'anu/ *a* everyday □ *m* everyday life

cotonete /koto'nɛtʃi/ *m* cotton bud

cotove|lada /kotove'lada/ *f* (*para abrir caminho*) shove; (*para chamar atenção*) nudge; **~lo** /e/ *m* elbow

coura|ça /ko'rasa/ *f* (*armadura*) breastplate; (*de navio, animal*) armour; **~çado** (*Port*) *m* battleship

couro /'koru/ *m* leather; **~ cabeludo** scalp

couve /'kovi/ *f* spring greens; **~-de-bruxelas** (*pl* **~s-de-bruxelas**) *f* Brussels sprout; **~-flor** (*pl* **~s-flores**) *f* cauliflower

couvert /ku'vɛr/ (*pl* **~s**) *m* cover charge

cova /'kɔva/ *f* (*buraco*) pit; (*sepultura*) grave

covar|de /ko'vardʒi/ *m/f* coward □ *a* cowardly; **~dia** *f* cowardice

coveiro /ko'veru/ *m* gravedigger

covil /ko'viw/ (*pl* **~vis**) *m* den, lair

covinha /ko'viɲa/ *f* dimple

co|xa /'koʃa/ *f* thigh; **~xear** *vi* hobble

coxia /ko'ʃia/ *f* aisle

coxo /'koʃu/ *a* hobbling; **ser ~** hobble

co|zer /ko'zer/ *vt/i* cook; **~zido** *m* stew, casserole

cozi|nha /ko'ziɲa/ *f* (*aposento*) kitchen; (*comida, ação*) cooking; (*arte*) cookery; **~nhar** *vt/i* cook; **~nheiro** *m* cook

crachá /kra'ʃa/ *m* badge, (*Amer*) button

crânio /'kraniu/ *m* skull; (*pessoa*) genius

crápula /'krapula/ *m/f* scoundrel

craque /'kraki/ *m* (*de futebol*) soccer star; (*fam*) expert

crase /'krazi/ *f* contraction; **a com ~** a grave (à)

crasso /'krasu/ *a* crass

cratera /kra'tɛra/ *f* crater

cravar /kra'var/ *vt* drive in <*prego*>; dig <*unha*>; stick <*estaca*>; **~ com os olhos** stare at; **~-se** *vpr* stick

cravejar /krave'ʒar/ *vt* nail; (*com balas*) spray, riddle

cravo[1] /'kravu/ *m* (*flor*) carnation; (*condimento*) clove

cravo[2] /'kravu/ *m* (*na pele*) blackhead; (*prego*) nail

cravo[3] /'kravu/ *m* (*instrumento*) harpsichord

creche /'krɛʃi/ *f* crèche

credenci|ais /kredẽsi'ajs/ *f pl* credentials; **~ar** *vt* qualify

credi|ário /kredʒi'ariu/ *m* hire purchase agreement, credit plan; **~bilidade** *f* credibility; **~tar** *vt* credit

crédito /'krɛdʒitu/ *m* credit; **a ~** on credit

cre|do /'krɛdu/ *m* creed □ *int* heavens; **~dor** *m* creditor □ *a* <*saldo*> credit

crédulo /'krɛdulu/ *a* gullible

cre|mação /krema'sãw/ *f* cremation; **~mar** *vt* cremate; **~matório** *m* crematorium

cre|me /'kremi/ *a invar & m* cream; **~me Chantilly** whipped cream; **~me de leite** (sterilized) cream; **~moso** /o/ *a* creamy

cren|ça /'krẽsa/ *f* belief; **~dice** *f* superstition; **~te** *m* believer; (*protestante*) Protestant □ *a* religious; (*protestante*) Protestant; **estar ~te que** believe that

crepe /'krɛpi/ *m* crepe

crepitar /krepi'tar/ *vi* crackle

crepom /kre'põ/ *m* crepe; **papel ~** tissue paper

crepúsculo /kre'puskulu/ *m* twilight

crer /krer/ *vt/i* believe (**em** in); **creio que** I think (that); **~-se** *vpr* believe o.s. to be

cres|cendo /kre'sẽdu/ *m* crescendo; **~cente** *a* growing □ *m* crescent; **~cer** *vi* grow; <*bolo*> rise; **~cido** *a* grown; **~cimento** *m* growth

crespo /'krespu/ *a* <*cabelo*> frizzy; <*mar*> choppy

cretino /kre'tʃinu/ *m* cretin

cria /'kria/ *f* baby; *pl* young

criação /kria'sãw/ *f* creation; (*educação*) upbringing; (*de animais*) raising; (*gado*) livestock

criado /kri'adu/ *m* servant; **~-mudo** (*pl* **~s-mudos**) *m* bedside table

criador /kria'dor/ *m* creator; (*de animais*) farmer, breeder

crian|ça /kri'ãsa/ *f* child □ *a* childish; **~çada** *f* kids; **~cice** *f* childishness; (*uma*) childish thing

criar /kri'ar/ *vt* (*fazer*) create; bring up <*filhos*>; rear <*animais*>; grow <*planta*>; pluck up <*coragem*>; **~-se** *vpr* be brought up, grow up

criati|vidade /kriatʃivi'dadʒi/ *f* creativity; **~vo** *a* creative

criatura /kria'tura/ *f* creature

crime /'krimi/ *m* crime

crimi|nal /krimi'naw/ (*pl* **~nais**) *a* criminal; **~nalidade** *f* crime; **~noso** *m* criminal

crina /'krina/ *f* mane

crioulo /kri'olu/ *a & m* creole; (*negro*) black

cripta /'kripta/ *f* crypt

crisálida /kri'zalida/ *f* chrysalis

crisântemo /kri'zãtemu/ *m* chrysanthemum

crise /'krizi/ *f* crisis

cris|ma /'krizma/ *f* confirmation; **~mar** *vt* confirm; **~mar-se** *vpr* get confirmed

crista /'krista/ *f* crest

cris|tal /kris'taw/ (*pl* **~tais**) *m* crystal; (*vidro*) glass; **~talino** *a* crystal-clear; **~talizar** *vt/i* crystallize

cris|tandade /kristã'dadʒi/ *f* Christendom; **~tão** (*pl* **~tãos**) *a & m* (*f* **~tã**) Christian; **~tianismo** *m* Christianity

Cristo /'kristu/ *m* Christ

cri|tério /kri'tɛriu/ *m* discretion; (*norma*) criterion; **~terioso** *a* perceptive, discerning

crítica /'kritʃika/ *f* criticism; (*análise*) critique; (*de filme, livro*) review; (*críticos*) critics

criticar /kritʃi'kar/ *vt* criticize; review <*filme, livro*>

crítico /'kritʃiku/ *a* critical □ *m* critic

crivar /kri'var/ *vt* (*furar*) riddle

crí|vel /'krivew/ (*pl* **~veis**) *a* credible

crivo /'krivu/ *m* sieve; (*fig*) scrutiny

crocante /kro'kãtʃi/ *a* crunchy

crochê /kro'ʃe/ *m* crochet

crocodilo /kroko'dʒilu/ *m* crocodile

cromo /'kromu/ *m* chrome

cromossomo /kromo'somu/ *m* chromosome

crôni|ca /'kronika/ *f* (*histórica*) chronicle; (*no jornal*) feature; (*conto*) short story; **~co** *a* chronic

cronista /kro'nista/ *m/f* (*de jornal*) feature writer; (*contista*) short story writer; (*historiador*) chronicler

crono|grama /krono'grama/ *m* schedule; **~logia** *f* chronology; **~lógico** *a* chronological; **~metrar** *vt* time

cronômetro /kro'nometru/ *m* stopwatch

croquete /kro'kɛtʃi/ *m* savoury meatball in breadcrumbs

croqui /kro'ki/ *m* sketch

crosta /'krosta/ *f* crust; (*em ferida*) scab

cru /kru/ *a* (*f* **~a**) raw; <*luz, tom, palavra*> harsh; <*linguagem*> crude; <*verdade*> unvarnished, plain

cruci|al /krusi'aw/ (*pl* **~ais**) *a* crucial

crucifi|cação /krusifika'sãw/ *f* crucifixion; **~car** *vt* crucify; **~xo** /ks/ *m* crucifix

cru|el /kru'ɛw/ (*pl* **~éis**) *a* cruel; **~eldade** *f* cruelty; **~ento** *a* bloody

crupe /'krupi/ *m* croup

crustáceos /krus'tasius/ *m pl* shellfish

cruz /krus/ *f* cross

cruza|da /kru'zada/ *f* crusade; **~do**[1] *m* (*soldado*) crusader

cru|zado[2] /kru'zadu/ *m* (*moeda*) cruzado; **~zador** *m* cruiser; **~zamento** *m* (*de ruas*) crossroads, junction, (*Amer*) intersection; (*de raças*) cross; **~zar** *vt* cross □ *vi* <*navio*> cruise; **~zar com** pass; **~zar-se** *vpr* cross; <*pessoas*> pass each other; **~zeiro** *m* (*moeda*) cruzeiro; (*viagem*) cruise; (*cruz*) cross

cu /ku/ *m* (*chulo*) arse, (*Amer*) ass

Cuba /'kuba/ *f* Cuba

cubano /ku'banu/ *a & m* Cuban

cúbico /'kubiku/ *a* cubic

cubículo /ku'bikulu/ *m* cubicle

cubis|mo /ku'bizmu/ *m* cubism; **~ta** *a & m/f* cubist

cubo /'kubu/ *m* cube; (*de roda*) hub

cuca /'kuka/ (*fam*) *f* head

cuco /'kuku/ *m* cuckoo; (*relógio*) cuckoo clock

cu|-de-ferro /kudʒi'fɛxu/ (*pl* **~s-de-ferro**) (*fam*) *m* swot

cueca /ku'ɛka/ *f* underpants; *pl* (*Port: de mulher*) knickers

cueiro /ku'eru/ *m* baby wrap

cuia /'kuia/ *f* gourd

cuidado /kui'dadu/ *m* care; **com ~** carefully; **ter** *ou* **tomar ~** be careful; **~so** /o/ *a* careful

cuidar /kui'dar/ *vi* **~ de** take care of; **~-se** *vpr* look after o.s.

cujo /'kuʒu/ *pron* whose

culatra /ku'latra/ *f* breech; **sair pela ~** (*fig*) backfire

culiná|ria /kuli'naria/ *f* cookery; **~rio** *a* culinary

culmi|nância /kuwmi'nãsia/ *f* culmination; **~nante** *a* culminating; **~nar** *vi* culminate (**em** in)

cul|pa /'kuwpa/ *f* guilt; **foi ~pa minha** it was my fault; **ter ~pa de** be to blame for; **~pabilidade** *f* guilt; **~pado** *a* guilty □ *m* culprit; **~par** *vt* blame (**de** for); (*na justiça*) find guilty (**de** of); **~par-se** *vpr* take the blame (**de** for); **~pável** (*pl* **~páveis**) *a* culpable, guilty

culti|var /kuwtʃi'var/ *vt* cultivate; grow <*plantas*>; **~vo** *m* cultivation; (*de plantas*) growing

cul|to /'kuwtu/ *a* cultured □ *m* cult; **~tura** *f* culture; (*de terra*) cultivation; **~tural** (*pl* **~turais**) *a* cultural

cumbuca /kũ'buka/ *f* bowl
cume /'kumi/ *m* peak
cúmplice /'kũplisi/ *m/f* accomplice
cumplicidade /kũplisi'dadʒi/ *f* complicity
cumprimen|tar /kũprimẽ'tar/ *vt/i* (*saudar*) greet; (*parabenizar*) compliment; **~to** *m* (*saudação*) greeting; (*elogio*) compliment; (*de lei, ordem*) compliance (**de** with); (*de promessa, palavra*) fulfilment
cumprir /kũ'prir/ *vt* keep <*promessa, palavra*>; comply with <*lei, ordem*>; do <*dever*>; carry out <*obrigações*>; serve <*pena*>; **~ com** keep to ◻ *vi* **cumpre-nos ir** we should go; **~-se** *vpr* be fulfilled
cúmulo /'kumulu/ *m* height; **é o ~!** that's the limit!
cunha /'kuɲa/ *f* wedge
cunha|da /ku'ɲada/ *f* sister-in-law; **~do** *m* brother-in-law
cunhar /'kuɲar/ *vt* coin <*palavra, expressão*>; mint <*moedas*>
cunho /'kuɲu/ *m* hallmark
cupim /ku'pĩ/ *m* termite
cupom /ku'põ/ *m* coupon
cúpula /'kupula/ *f* (*abóbada*) dome; (*de abajur*) shade; (*chefia*) leadership; **(reunião de) ~** summit (meeting)
cura /'kura/ *f* cure ◻ *m* curate, priest
curandeiro /kurã'deru/ *m* (*religioso*) faith-healer; (*índio*) medicine man; (*charlatão*) quack
curar /ku'rar/ *vt* cure; dress <*ferida*>; **~-se** *vpr* be cured
curativo /kura'tʃivu/ *m* dressing
curá|vel /ku'ravew/ (*pl* **~veis**) *a* curable
curin|ga /ku'rĩga/ *m* wild card; **~gão** *m* joker
curio|sidade /kuriozi'dadʒi/ *f* curiosity; **~so** /o/ *a* curious ◻ *m* (*espectador*) onlooker
cur|ral /ku'xaw/ (*pl* **~rais**) *m* pen
currículo /ku'xikulu/ *m* curriculum; (*resumo*) curriculum vitae, CV
cur|sar /kur'sar/ *vt* attend <*escola, aula*>; study <*matéria*>; **~so** *m* course; **~sor** *m* cursor
curta|-metragem /kurtame'traʒẽ/ (*pl* **~s-metragens**) *m* short (film)
cur|tição /kurtʃi'sãw/ (*fam*) *f* enjoyment; **~tir** *vt* (*fam*) enjoy; tan <*couro*>
curto /'kurtu/ *a* short; <*conhecimento, inteligência*> limited; **~-circuito** (*pl* **~s-circuitos**) *m* short circuit
cur|va /'kurva/ *f* curve; (*de estrada, rio*) bend; **~va fechada** hairpin bend; **~var** *vt* bend; **~var-se** *vpr* bend; (*fig*) bow (**a** to); **~vo** *a* curved; <*estrada*> winding
cus|parada /kuspa'rada/ *f* spit; **~pe** *m* spit, spittle; **~pir** *vt/i* spit
cus|ta /'kusta/ *f* **à ~ta de** at the expense of; **~tar** *vt* cost ◻ *vi* (*ser difícil*) be hard; **~tar a fazer** (*ter dificuldade*) find it hard to do; (*demorar*) take a long time to do; **~tear** *vt* finance, fund; **~teio** *m* funding; (*relação de despesas*) costing; **~to** *m* cost; **a ~to** with difficulty
custódia /kus'tɔdʒia/ *f* custody
cutelo /ku'tɛlu/ *m* cleaver
cutícula /ku'tʃikula/ *f* cuticle
cútis /'kutʃis/ *f invar* complexion
cutucar /kutu'kar/ *vt* (*com o cotovelo, joelho*) nudge; (*com o dedo*) poke; (*com instrumento*) prod
czar /zar/ *m* tsar

Dd

da = de + a
dádiva /'dadʒiva/ *f* gift; (*donativo*) donation
dado /'dadu/ *m* (*de jogar*) die, dice; (*informação*) fact, piece of information; *pl* data
daí /da'i/ *adv* (*no espaço*) from there; (*no tempo*) then; **~ por diante** from then on; **e ~?** (*fam*) so what?
dali /da'li/ *adv* from over there
dália /'dalia/ *f* dahlia
dal|tônico /daw'toniku/ *a* colour-blind; **~tonismo** *m* colour-blindness
dama /'dama/ *f* lady; (*em jogos*) queen; *pl* (*jogo*) draughts, (*Amer*) checkers; **~ de honra** bridesmaid
da|nado /da'nadu/ *a* damned; (*zangado*) angry; (*travesso*) naughty; **~nar-se** *vpr* get angry; **~ne-se!** (*fam*) who cares?
dan|ça /'dãsa/ *f* dance; **~çar** *vt* dance ◻ *vi* dance; (*fam*) <*pessoa*> miss out; <*coisa*> go by the board; <*crimonoso*> get caught; **~çarino** *m* dancer; **~ceteria** *f* discotheque
da|nificar /danifi'kar/ *vt* damage; **~ninho** *a* undesirable; **~no** *m* (*pl*) damage; **~noso** /o/ *a* damaging
dantes /'dãtʃiʃ/ *adv* formerly
daquela(s), daquele(s) = de + aquela(s), aquele(s)

daqui /da'ki/ *adv* from here; **~ a 2 dias** in 2 days(' time); **~ a pouco** in a minute; **~ em diante** from now on

daquilo = de + aquilo

dar /dar/ *vt* give; have <*dormida, lida etc*>; do <*pulo, cambalhota etc*>; cause <*problemas*>; produce <*frutas, leite*>; deal <*cartas*>; (*lecionar*) teach ◻ *vi* (*ser possível*) be possible; (*ser suficiente*) be enough; **~ com** come across; **~ em** lead to; **ele dá para ator** he'd make a good actor; **~ por** (*considerar como*) consider to be; (*reparar em*) notice; **~-se** *vpr* <*coisa*> happen; <*pessoa*> get on

dardo /'dardu/ *m* dart; (*no atletismo*) javelin

das = de + as

da|ta /'data/ *f* date; **de longa ~** long since; **~tar** *vt/i* date

dati|lografar /datʃilogra'far/ *vt/i* type; **~lografia** *f* typing; **~lógrafo** *m* typist

de /dʒi/ *prep* of; (*procedência*) from; **~ carro** by car; **trabalho ~ repórter** I work as a reporter

debaixo /dʒi'baʃu/ *adv* below; **~ de** under

debalde /dʒi'bawdʒi/ *adv* in vain

debandada /debã'dada/ *f* stampede

deba|te /de'batʃi/ *m* debate; **~ter** *vt* debate; **~ter-se** *vpr* grapple

debelar /debe'lar/ *vt* overcome

dé|bil /'dɛbiw/ (*pl* **~beis**) *a* feeble; **~bil mental** retarded (person)

debili|dade /debili'dadʒi/ *f* debility; **~tar** *vt* debilitate; **~tar-se** *vpr* become debilitated

debitar /debi'tar/ *vt* debit

débito /'dɛbitu/ *m* debit

debo|chado /debo'ʃadu/ *a* sardonic; **~char** *vt* mock; **~che** /ɔ/ *m* jibe

debruar /debru'ar/ *vt/i* edge

debruçar-se /debru'sarsi/ *vpr* bend over; **~ sobre** study

debrum /de'brũ/ *m* edging

debulhar /debu'ʎar/ *vt* thresh

debu|tante /debu'tãtʃi/ *f* debutante; **~tar** *vi* debut, make one's debut

década /'dɛkada/ *f* decade; **a ~ dos 60** the sixties

deca|dência /deka'dẽsia/ *f* decadence; **~dente** *a* decadent

decair /deka'ir/ *vi* decline; (*degringolar*) go downhill; <*planta*> wilt

decal|car /dekaw'kar/ *vt* trace; **~que** *m* tracing

decapitar /dekapi'tar/ *vt* decapitate

decatlo /de'katlu/ *m* decathlon

de|cência /de'sẽsia/ *f* decency; **~cente** *a* decent

decepar /dese'par/ *vt* cut off

decep|ção /desep'sãw/ *f* disappointment; **~cionar** *vt* disappoint; **~cionar-se** *vpr* be disappointed

decerto /dʒi'sɛrtu/ *adv* certainly

deci|dido /desi'dʒidu/ *a* <*pessoa*> determined; **~dir** *vt/i* decide; **~dir-se** *vpr* make up one's mind; **~dir-se por** decide on

decíduo /de'siduu/ *a* deciduous

decifrar /desi'frar/ *vt* decipher

deci|mal /desi'maw/ (*pl* **~mais**) *a & m* decimal

décimo /'dɛsimu/ *a & m* tenth; **~ primeiro** eleventh; **~ segundo** twelfth; **~ terceiro** thirteenth; **~ quarto** fourteenth; **~ quinto** fifteenth; **~ sexto** sixteenth; **~ sétimo** seventeenth; **~ oitavo** eighteenth; **~ nono** nineteenth

deci|são /desi'zãw/ *f* decision; **~sivo** *a* decisive

decla|ração /deklara'sãw/ *f* declaration; **~rado** *a* <*inimigo*> sworn; <*crente*> avowed; <*ladrão*> self-confessed; **~rar** *vt* declare

decli|nação /deklina'sãw/ *f* declension; **~nar** *vt* **~nar (de)** decline ◻ *vi* decline; <*sol*> go down; <*chão*> slope down

declínio /de'kliniu/ *m* decline

declive /de'klivi/ *m* (downward) slope, incline

decodificar /dekodʒifi'kar/ *vt* decode

deco|lagem /deko'laʒẽ/ *f* take-off; **~lar** *vi* take off; (*fig*) get off the ground

decom|por /dekõ'por/ *vt* break down; contort <*feições*>; **~por-se** *vpr* break down; <*cadáver*> decompose; **~posição** *f* (*de cadáver*) decomposition

deco|ração /dekora'sãw/ *f* decoration; (*aprendizagem*) learning by heart; **~rar** *vt* (*adornar*) decorate; (*aprender*) learn by heart, memorize; **~rativo** *a* decorative; **~reba** /ɛ/ (*fam*) *f* rote-learning; **~ro** /o/ *m* decorum; **~roso** /o/ *a* decorous

decor|rência /deko'xẽsia/ *f* consequence; **~rente** *a* resulting (**de** from); **~rer** *vi* <*tempo*> elapse; <*acontecimento*> pass off; (*resultar*) result (**de** from) ◻ *m* **no ~rer de** in the course of; **com o ~rer do tempo** in time, with the passing of time

deco|tado /deko'tadu/ *a* low-cut; **~te** /ɔ/ *m* neckline

decrépito /de'krɛpitu/ *a* decrepit

decres|cente /dekre'sẽtʃi/ *a* decreasing; **~cer** *vi* decrease

decre|tar /dekre'tar/ *vt* decree; declare <*estado de sítio*>; **~to** /ɛ/ *m* decree; **~to-lei** (*pl* **~tos-leis**) *m* act

decurso /de'kursu/ *m* course

de|dal /de'daw/ (*pl* **~dais**) *m* thimble; **~dão** *m* (*da mão*) thumb; (*do pé*) big toe

dedetizar /dedetʃi'zar/ *vt* spray with insecticide

dedi|cação /dedʒika'sãw/ *f* dedication; **~car** *vt* dedicate; devote <*tempo*>; **~car-se** *vpr* dedicate o.s. (**a** to); **~catória** *f* dedication

dedilhar /dedʒi'ʎar/ *vt* pluck

dedo /'dedu/ *m* finger; (*do pé*) toe; **cheio de ~s** all fingers and thumbs; (*sem graça*) awkward; **~-duro** (*pl* **~s-duros**) *m* sneak; (*político, criminoso*) informer

dedução /dedu'sãw/ *f* deduction

dedurar /dedu'rar/ *vt* sneak on; (*à polícia*) inform on

dedu|tivo /dedu'tʃivu/ *a* deductive; **~zir** *vt* (*descontar*) deduct; (*concluir*) deduce

defa|sado /defa'zadu/ *a* out of step; **~sagem** *f* gap, lag

defecar /defe'kar/ *vi* defecate

defei|to /de'fejtu/ *m* defect; **botar ~to em** find fault with; **~tuoso** /o/ *a* defective

defen|der /defẽ'der/ *vt* defend; **~der-se** *vpr* (*virar-se*) fend for o.s.; (*contra-atacar*) defend o.s. (**de** against); **~siva** *f* **na ~siva** on the defensive; **~sor** *m* defender; (*advogado*) defence counsel

defe|rência /defe'rẽsia/ *f* deference; **~rente** *a* deferential

defesa /de'feza/ *f* defence □ *m* defender

defici|ência /defisi'ẽsia/ *f* deficiency; **~ente** *a* deficient; (*física ou mentalmente*) handicapped □ *m/f* handicapped person

déficit /'dɛfisitʃi/ (*pl* **~s**) *m* deficit

deficitário /defisitʃi'ariu/ *a* in deficit; <*empresa*> loss-making

definhar /defi'ɲar/ *vi* waste away; <*planta*> wither

defi|nição /defini'sãw/ *f* definition; **~nir** *vt* define; **~nir-se** *vpr* (*descrever-se*) define o.s.; (*decidir-se*) come to a decision; (*explicar-se*) make one's position clear; **~nitivo** *a* definitive; **~nível** (*pl* **~níveis**) *a* definable

defla|ção /defla'sãw/ *f* deflation; **~cionário** *a* deflationary

deflagrar /defla'grar/ *vt* set off □ *vi* break out

defor|mar /defor'mar/ *vt* misshape; deform <*corpo*>; distort <*imagem*>; **~midade** *f* deformity

defraudar /defraw'dar/ *vt* defraud (**de** of)

defron|tar /defrõ'tar/ *vt* **~tar com** face; **~te** *adv* opposite; **~te de** opposite

defumar /defu'mar/ *vt* smoke

defunto /de'fũtu/ *a & m* deceased

dege|lar /deʒe'lar/ *vt/i* thaw; **~lo** /e/ *m* thaw

degeneração /deʒenera'sãw/ *f* degeneration

degenerar /deʒene'rar/ *vi* degenerate (**em** into)

degolar /dego'lar/ *vt* cut the throat of

degra|dação /degrada'sãw/ *f* degradation; **~dante** *a* degrading; **~dar** *vt* degrade

degrau /de'graw/ *m* step

degringolar /degrĩgo'lar/ *vi* deteriorate, go downhill

degustar /degus'tar/ *vt* taste

dei|tada /dej'tada/ *f* lie-down; **~tado** *a* lying down; (*dormindo*) in bed; (*fam: preguiçoso*) idle; **~tar** *vt* lay down; (*na cama*) put to bed; (*pôr*) put; (*Port: jogar*) throw □ *vi*, **~tar-se** *vpr* lie down; (*ir para cama*) go to bed

dei|xa /'deʃa/ *f* cue; **~xar** *vt* leave; (*permitir*) let; **~xar de** (*parar*) stop; (*omitir*) fail; **não pôde ~xar de rir** he couldn't help laughing; **~xar alg nervoso** make s.o. annoyed; **~xar cair** drop; **~xar a desejar** leave a lot to be desired; **~xa (para lá)** (*fam*) never mind, forget it

dela(s) = de + ela(s)

delatar /dela'tar/ *vt* report

délavé /dela've/ *a invar* faded

dele(s) = de + ele(s)

dele|gação /delega'sãw/ *f* delegation; **~gacia** *f* police station; **~gado** *m* delegate; **~gado de polícia** police chief; **~gar** *vt* delegate

delei|tar /delej'tar/ *vt* delight; **~tar-se** *vpr* delight (**com** in); **~te** *m* delight; **~toso** /o/ *a* delightful

delgado /dew'gadu/ *a* slender

delibe|ração /delibera'sãw/ *f* deliberation; **~rar** *vt/i* deliberate

delica|deza /delika'deza/ *f* delicacy; (*cortesia*) politeness; **~do** *a* delicate; (*cortês*) polite

delícia /de'lisia/ *f* delight; **ser uma ~** <*comida*> be delicious; <*sol etc*> be lovely

delici|ar /delisi'ar/ *vt* delight; **~ar-se** delight (**com** in); **~oso** /o/ *a* delightful, lovely; <*comida*> delicious

deline|ador /delinia'dor/ *m* eye-liner; **~ar** *vt* outline

delin|qüência /delĩ'kwẽsia/ *f* delinquency; **~qüente** *a & m* delinquent

deli|rante /deli'rãtʃi/ *a* rapturous; (*med*) delirious; **~rar** *vi* go into raptures; <*doente*> be delirious
delírio /de'liriu/ *m* (*febre*) delirium; (*excitação*) raptures
delito /de'litu/ *m* crime
delonga /de'lõga/ *f* delay
delta /'dɛwta/ *f* delta
dema|gogia /demago'ʒia/ *f* demagogy; **~gógico** *a* demagogic; **~gogo** /o/ *m* demagogue
demais /dʒi'majs/ *a & adv* (*muito*) very much; (*em demasia*) too much; **os ~** the rest, the others; **é ~!** (*fam*) it's great!
deman|da /de'mãda/ *f* demand; (*jurid*) action; **~dar** *vt* sue
demão /de'mãw/ *f* coat
demar|car /demar'kar/ *vt* demarcate; **~catório** *a* demarcation
demasia /dema'zia/ *f* excess; **em ~** too (much, many)
de|mência /de'mẽsia/ *f* insanity; (*med*) dementia; **~mente** *a* insane; (*med*) demented
demissão /demi'sãw/ *f* sacking, dismissal; **pedir ~** resign
demitir /demi'tʃir/ *vt* sack, dismiss; **~-se** *vpr* resign
demo|cracia /demokra'sia/ *f* democracy; **~crata** *m/f* democrat; **~crático** *a* democratic; **~cratizar** *vt* democratize; **~-grafia** *f* demography; **~gráfico** *a* demographic
demo|lição /demoli'sãw/ *f* demolition; **~lir** *vt* demolish
demônio /de'moniu/ *m* demon
demons|tração /demõstra'sãw/ *f* demonstration; **~trar** *vt* demonstrate; **~trativo** *a* demonstrative
demo|ra /de'mɔra/ *f* delay; **~rado** *a* lengthy; **~rar** *vi* (*levar*) take; (*tardar a voltar, terminar etc*) be long; (*levar muito tempo*) take a long time □ *vt* delay
dendê /dẽ'de/ *m* (*óleo*) palm oil
denegrir /dene'grir/ *vt* denigrate
dengoso /dẽ'gozu/ *a* coy
dengue /'dẽgi/ *m* dengue
denomi|nação /denomina'sãw/ *f* denomination; **~nar** *vt* name
denotar /deno'tar/ *vt* denote
den|sidade /dẽsi'dadʒi/ *f* density; **~so** *a* dense
den|tado /dẽ'tadu/ *a* serrated; **~tadura** *f* (set of) teeth; (*postiça*) dentures, false teeth; **~tal** (*pl* **~tais**) *a* dental; **~tário** *a* dental; **~te** *m* tooth; (*de alho*) clove; **~te do siso** wisdom tooth; **~tição** *f* teething; (*dentadura*) teeth; **~tífrico** *m* toothpaste; **~tista** *m/f* dentist
dentre = de + entre
dentro /'dẽtru/ *adv* inside; **lá ~** in there; **por ~** on the inside; **~ de** inside; (*tempo*) within
dentu|ça /dẽ'tusa/ *f* buck teeth; **~ço** *a* with buck teeth
denúncia /de'nũsia/ *f* (*à polícia etc*) report; (*na imprensa etc*) disclosure
denunciar /denũsi'ar/ *vt* (*à polícia etc*) report; (*na imprensa etc*) denounce
deparar /depa'rar/ *vi* **~ com** come across
departamento /departa'mẽtu/ *m* department
depauperar /depawpe'rar/ *vt* impoverish
depenar /depe'nar/ *vt* pluck <*aves*>; (*roubar*) fleece
depen|dência /depẽ'dẽsia/ *f* dependence; *pl* premises; **~dente** *a* dependent (**de** on) □ *m/f* dependant; **~der** *vi* depend (**de** on)
depi|lação /depila'sãw/ *f* depilation; **~lar** *vt* depilate; **~latório** *m* depilatory cream
deplo|rar /deplo'rar/ *vt* deplore; **~rável** (*pl* **~ráveis**) *a* deplorable
de|poente /depo'ẽtʃi/ *m/f* witness; **~poimento** *m* (*à polícia*) statement; (*na justiça, fig*) testimony
depois /de'pojs/ *adv* after(wards); **~ de** after; **~ que** after
depor /de'por/ *vi* (*na polícia*) make a statement; (*na justiça*) give evidence, testify □ *vt* lay down <*armas*>; depose <*rei, presidente*>
depor|tação /deporta'sãw/ *f* deportation; **~tar** *vt* deport
deposi|tante /depozi'tãtʃi/ *m/f* depositor; **~tar** *vt* deposit; cast <*voto*>; place <*confiança*>
depósito /de'pɔzitu/ *m* deposit; (*armazém*) warehouse
depra|vação /deprava'sãw/ *f* depravity; **~vado** *a* depraved; **~var** *vt* deprave
depre|ciação /depresia'sãw/ *f* (*perda de valor*) depreciation; (*menosprezo*) deprecation; **~-ciar** *vt* (*desvalorizar*) devalue; (*menosprezar*) deprecate; **~ciar-se** *vpr* <*bens*> depreciate; <*pessoa*> deprecate o.s.; **~ciativo** *a* deprecatory
depre|dação /depreda'sãw/ *f* depredation; **~dar** *vt* wreck
depressa /dʒi'prɛsa/ *adv* fast, quickly
depres|são /depre'sãw/ *f* depression; **~sivo** *a* depressive
depri|mente /depri'mẽtʃi/ *a* depressing; **~mido** *a* depressed; **~mir** *vt* depress; **~mir-se** *vpr* get depressed
depurar /depu'rar/ *vt* purify
depu|tação/deputa'sãw/ *f* deputation; **~tado** *m* deputy, MP, (*Amer*)

congressman (*f* -woman); **~tar** *vt* delegate

deque /'dɛki/ *m* (sun)deck

deri|va /de'riva/ *f* **à ~va** adrift; **andar à ~va** drift; **~vação** *f* derivation; **~var** *vt* derive; (*desviar*) divert ▫ *vi*, **~var-se** *vpr* derive, be derived (**de** from); <*navio*> drift

dermatolo|gia /dermatolo'ʒia/ *f* dermatology; **~gista** *m/f* dermatologist

derradeiro /dexa'deru/ *a* last, final

derra|mamento /dexama'mẽtu/ *m* spill, spillage; **~mamento de sangue** bloodshed; **~mar** *vt* spill; shed <*lágrimas*>; **~mar-se** *vpr* spill; **~me** *m* spill, spillage; **~me cerebral** stroke

derra|pagem /dexa'paʒẽ/ *f* skidding; (*uma*) skid; **~par** *vi* skid

derreter /dexe'ter/ *vt* melt; **~-se** *vpr* melt

derro|ta /de'xɔta/ *f* defeat; **~tar** *vt* defeat; **~tismo** *m* defeatism; **~tista** *a* & *m/f* defeatist

derrubar /dexu'bar/ *vt* knock down; bring down <*governo*>

desaba|far /dʒizaba'far/ *vi* speak one's mind; **~fo** *m* outburst

desa|bamento /dʒizaba'mẽtu/ *m* collapse; **~bar** *vi* collapse; <*chuva*> pour down

desabotoar /dʒiaboto'ar/ *vt* unbutton

desabri|gado /dʒizabri'gadu/ *a* homeless; **~gar** *vt* make homeless

desabrochar /dʒizabro'ʃar/ *vi* blossom, bloom

desaca|tar /dʒizaka'tar/ *vt* defy; **~to** *m* (*de pessoa*) disrespect; (*da lei etc*) disregard

desacerto /dʒiza'sertu/ *m* mistake

desacompanhado /dʒizakõpa'ɲadu/ *a* unaccompanied

desaconse|lhar /dʒizakõse'ʎar/ *vt* advise against; **~lhável** (*pl* **~lháveis**) *a* inadvisable

desacor|dado /dʒizakor'dadu/ *a* unconscious; **~do** /o/ *m* disagreement

desacostu|mado /dʒizakostu'madu/ *a* unaccustomed; **~mar** *vt* **~mar alg de** break s.o. of the habit of; **~mar-se de** get out of the habit of

desacreditar /dʒizakredʒi'tar/ *vt* discredit

desafeto /dʒiza'fɛtu/ *m* disaffection

desafi|ador /dʒizafia'dor/ *a* <*tarefa*> challenging; <*pessoa*> defiant; **~ar** *vt* challenge; (*fazer face a*) defy <*perigo, morte*>

desafi|nado /dʒizafi'nadu/ *a* out of tune; **~nar** *vi* (*cantando*) sing out of tune; (*tocando*) play out of tune ▫ *vt* put out of tune

desafio /dʒiza'fiu/ *m* challenge

desafivelar /dʒizafive'lar/ *vt* unbuckle

desafo|gar /dʒizafo'gar/ *vt* vent; (*desapertar*) relieve; **~gar-se** *vpr* give vent to one's feelings; **~go** /o/ *m* (*alívio*) relief

desafo|rado /dʒizafo'radu/ *a* cheeky; **~ro** /o/ *m* cheek; (*um*) liberty

desafortunado /dʒizafortu'nadu/ *a* unfortunate

desagra|dar /dʒizagra'dar/ *vt* displease; **~dável** (*pl* **~dáveis**) *a* unpleasant; **~do** *m* displeasure

desagravo *m* redress, amends

desagregar /dʒizagre'gar/ *vt* split up; **~-se** *vpr* split up

desaguar /dʒiza'gwar/ *vt* drain ▫ *vi* <*rio*> flow (**em** into)

desajeitado /dʒizaʒej'tadu/ *a* clumsy

desajuizado /dʒizaʒui'zadu/ *a* foolish

desajus|tado /dʒizaʒus'tadu/ *a* (*psic*) maladjusted; **~te** *m* (*psic*) maladjustment

desalen|tar /dʒizalẽ'tar/ *vt* dishearten; **~tar-se** *vpr* get disheartened; **~to** *m* discouragement

desali|nhado /dʒizali'ɲadu/ *a* untidy; **~nho** *m* untidiness

desalojar /dʒizalo'ʒar/ *vt* turn out <*inquilino*>; flush out <*inimigo, ladrões*>

desamarrar /dʒizama'xar/ *vt* untie ▫ *vi* cast off

desamarrotar /dʒizamaxo'tar/ *vt* smooth out

desamassar /dʒizama'sar/ *vt* smooth out

desambientado /dʒizãbiẽ'tadu/ *a* unsettled

desampa|rar /dʒizãpa'rar/ *vt* abandon; **~ro** *m* abandonment

desandar /dʒizã'dar/ *vi* <*molho*> separate; **~ a** start to

de|sanimar /dʒizani'mar/ *vt* discourage ▫ *vi* <*pessoa*> lose heart; <*fato*> be discouraging; **~sânimo** *m* discouragement

desapaixonado /dʒizapaʃo'nadu/ *a* dispassionate

desaparafusar /dʒizaparafu'zar/ *vt* unscrew

desapare|cer /dʒizapare'ser/ *vi* disappear; **~cimento** *m* disappearance

desapego /dʒiza'pegu/ *m* detachment; (*indiferença*) indifference

desapercebido /dʒizaperse'bidu/ *a* unnoticed

desapertar /dʒizaper'tar/ *vt* loosen

desapon|tamento /dʒizapõta'mẽtu/ *m* disapointment; **~tar** *vt* disappoint

desapropriar /dʒizapropri'ar/ *vt* expropriate

desapro|vação /dʒizaprova'sãw/ *f* disapproval; **~var** *vt* disapprove of

desaproveitado /dʒizaprovej'tadu/ *a* wasted

desar|mamento /dʒizarma'mẽtu/ *m* disarmament; **~mar** *vt* disarm; take down <*barraca*>

desarran|jar /dʒizaxã'ʒar/ *vt* mess up; upset <*estômago*>; **~jo** *m* mess; (*do estômago*) upset

desarregaçar /dʒizaxega'sar/ *vt* roll down

desarru|mado /dʒizaxu'madu/ *a* untidy; **~mar** *vt* untidy; unpack <*mala*>

desarticular /dʒizartʃiku'lar/ *vt* dislocate

desarvorado /dʒizarvo'radu/ *a* disoriented, at a loss

desassociar /dʒizasosi'ar/ *vt* disassociate; **~-se** *vpr* disassociate o.s.

desas|trado /dʒizas'tradu/ *a* accident-prone; **~tre** *m* disaster; **~troso** /o/ *a* disastrous

desatar /dʒiza'tar/ *vt* untie; **~ a chorar** dissolve in tears

desatarraxar /dʒizataxa'ʃar/ *vt* unscrew

desaten|cioso /dʒizatẽsi'ozu/ *a* inattentive; **~to** *a* oblivious (**a** to)

desati|nar /dʒizatʃi'nar/ *vt* bewilder □ *vi* not think straight; **~no** *m* bewilderment; (*um*) folly

desativar /dʒizatʃi'var/ *vt* deactivate; shut down <*fábrica*>

desatrelar /dʒizatre'lar/ *vt* unhitch

desatualizado /dʒizatuali'zadu/ *a* out-of-date

desavença /dʒiza'vẽsa/ *f* dispute

desavergonhado /dʒizavergo'ɲadu/ *a* shameless

desbancar /dʒizbã'kar/ *vt* outdo

desbaratar /dʒizbara'tar/ *vt* (*desperdiçar*) waste

desbocado /dʒizbo'kadu/ *a* outspoken

desbotar /dʒizbo'tar/ *vt*/*i* fade

desbra|vador /dʒizbrava'dor/ *m* explorer; **~var** *vt* explore

desbun|dante /dʒizbũ'dãtʃi/ (*fam*) *a* mind-blowing; **~dar** (*fam*) *vt* blow the mind of □ *vi* flip, freak out; **~de** (*fam*) *m* knockout

descabido /dʒiska'bidu/ *a* inappropriate

descafeinado /dʒizkafej'nadu/ *a* decaffeinated

descalabro /dʒiska'labru/ *m* débâcle

descalço /dʒis'kawsu/ *a* barefoot

descambar /dʒiskã'bar/ *vi* deteriorate, degenerate

descan|sar /dʒiskã'sar/ *vt*/*i* rest; **~so** *m* rest; (*de prato, copo*) mat

desca|rado /dʒiska'radu/ *a* blatant; **~ramento** *m* cheek

descarga /dʒis'karga/ *f* (*eletr*) discharge; (*da privada*) flush

descarregar /dʒiskaxe'gar/ *vt* unload <*mercadorias*>; discharge <*poluentes*>; vent <*raiva*> □ *vi* <*bateria*> go flat; **~ em cima de alg** take it out on s.o.

descarrilhar /dʒiskaxi'ʎar/ *vt*/*i* derail

descar|tar /dʒiskar'tar/ *vt* discard; **~tável** (*pl* **~táveis**) *a* disposable

descascar /dʒiskas'kar/ *vt* peel <*frutas, batatas*>; shell <*nozes*> □ *vi* <*pessoa, pele*> peel

descaso /dʒis'kazu/ *m* indifference

descen|dência /desẽ'dẽsia/ *f* descent; **~dente** *a* descended □ *m*/*f* descendant; **~der** *vi* descend (**de** from)

descentralizar /dʒisẽtrali'zar/ *vt* decentralize

des|cer /de'ser/ *vi* go down; <*avião*> descend; (*do ônibus, trem*) get off; (*do carro*) get out □ *vt* go down <*escada, ladeira*>; scroll down <*página*>; **~cida** *f* descent

desclassificar /dʒisklasifi'kar/ *vt* disqualify

desco|berta /dʒisko'bɛrta/ *f* discovery; **~berto** /ɛ/ *a* uncovered; <*conta*> overdrawn; **a ~berto** overdrawn; **~bridor** *m* discoverer; **~brimento** *m* discovery; **~brir** *vt* discover; (*expor*) uncover

descolar /dʒisko'lar/ *vt* unstick; (*fam*) (*dar*) give; (*arranjar*) get hold of, rustle up; (*Port*) <*avião*> take off

descom|por /dʒiskõ'por/ *vt* (*censurar*) scold; **~-se** *vpr* <*pessoa*> lose one's composure; **~postura** *f* (*estado*) loss of composure; (*censura*) talking-to

descomprometido /dʒiskõprome'tʃidu/ *a* free

descomu|nal /dʒiskomu'naw/ (*pl* **~nais**) *a* extraordinary; (*grande*) huge

desconcentrar /dʒiskõsẽ'trar/ *vt* distract

desconcer|tante /dʒiskõser'tãtʃi/ *a* disconcerting; **~tar** *vt* disconcert

desconexo /dʒisko'nɛksu/ *a* incoherent

desconfi|ado /dʒiskõfi'adu/ *a* suspicious; **~ança** *f* mistrust; **~ar** *vi* suspect

desconfor|tável /dʒiskõfor'tavew/ (*pl* **~táveis**) *a* uncomfortable; **~to** /o/ *m* discomfort

descongelar /dʒiskõʒe'lar/ *vt* defrost <*geladeira*>; thaw <*comida*>

descongestio|nante /dʒiskõʒestʃio'nãtʃi/ *a* & *m* decongestant; **~nar** *vt* decongest

desconhe|cer /dʒiskoɲe'ser/ *vt* not know; **~cido** *a* unknown □ *m* stranger

desconsiderar /dʒiskõside'rar/ *vt* ignore

desconsolado /dʒiskõso'ladu/ *a* disconsolate

descontar /dʒiskõ'tar/ *vt* deduct; (*não levar em conta*) discount

desconten|tamento /dʒiskõteta'mẽtu/ *m* discontent; **~te** *a* discontent

desconto /dʒis'kõtu/ *m* discount; **dar um ~** (*fig*) make allowances

descontra|ção /dʒiskõtra'sãw/ *f* informality; **~ído** *a* informal, casual; **~ir** *vt* relax; **~ir-se** *vpr* relax

descontro|lar-se /dʒiskõtro'larsi/ *vpr* <*pessoa*> lose control; <*coisa*> go out of control; **~le** /o/ *m* lack of control

desconversar /dʒiskõver'sar/ *vi* change the subject

descortesia /dʒiskorte'zia/ *f* rudeness

descostu|rar /dʒiskostu'rar/ *vt* unrip; **~rar-se** *vpr* come undone

descrédito /dʒis'krɛdʒitu/ *m* discredit

descren|ça /dʒis'krẽsa/ *f* disbelief; **~te** *a* sceptical, disbelieving

des|crever /dʒiskre'ver/ *vt* describe; **~crição** *f* description; **~critivo** *a* descriptive

descui|dado /dʒiskui'dadu/ *a* careless; **~dar** *vt* neglect; **~do** *m* carelessness; (*um*) oversight

descul|pa /dʒis'kuwpa/ *f* excuse; **pedir ~pas** apologize; **~par** *vt* excuse; **~pe!** sorry!; **~par-se** *vpr* apologize; **~pável** (*pl* **~páveis**) *a* excusable

desde /'dezdʒi/ *prep* since; **~ que** since

des|dém /dez'dẽj/ *m* disdain; **~denhar** *vt* disdain; **~nhoso** /o/ *a* disdainful

desdentado /dʒizdẽ'tadu/ *a* toothless

desdita /dʒiz'dʒita/ *f* unhappiness

desdizer /dʒizdʒi'zer/ *vt* take back, withdraw □ *vi* take back what one said

desdo|bramento /dʒizdobra'mẽtu/ *m* implication; **~brar** *vt* (*abrir*) unfold; break down <*dados, contas*>; **~brar-se** *vpr* unfold; (*empenhar-se*) go to a lot of trouble, bend over backwards

dese|jar /deze'ʒar/ *vt* want; (*apaixonadamente*) desire; **~jar aco a alg** wish s.o. sth; **~jável** (*pl* **~jáveis**) *a* desirable; **~jo** /e/ *m* wish; (*forte*) desire; **~joso** /o/ *a* desirous

deselegante /dʒizele'gãtʃi/ *a* inelegant

desemaranhar /dʒizemara'ɲar/ *vt* untangle

desembara|çado /dʒizĩbara'sadu/ *a* <*pessoa*> confident, nonchalant; **~çar-se** *vpr* rid o.s. (**de** of); **~ço** *m* confidence, ease

desembar|car /dʒizĩbar'kar/ *vt/i* disembark; **~que** *m* disembarkation; (*seção do aeroporto*) arrivals

desembocar /dʒizĩbo'kar/ *vi* flow

desembol|sar /dʒizĩbow'sar/ *vt* spend, pay out; **~so** /o/ *m* expenditure

desembrulhar /dʒizĩbru'ʎar/ *vt* unwrap

desembuchar /dʒizĩbu'ʃar/ (*fam*) *vi* (*desabafar*) get things off one's chest; (*falar logo*) spit it out

desempacotar /dʒizĩpako'tar/ *vt* unpack

desempatar /dʒizĩpa'tar/ *vt* decide <*jogo*>

desempe|nhar /dʒizĩpe'ɲar/ *vt* perform; play <*papel*>; **~nho** *m* performance

desempre|gado /dʒizĩpre'gadu/ *a* unemployed; **~go** /e/ *m* unemployment

desencadear /dʒizĩkadʒi'ar/ *vt* set off, trigger

desencaminhar /dʒizĩkami'ɲar/ *vt* lead astray; embezzle <*dinheiro*>

desencantar /dʒizĩkã'tar/ *vt* disenchant

desencon|trar-se /dʒizĩkõ'trarsi/ *vpr* miss each other, fail to meet; **~tro** *m* failure to meet

desencorajar /dʒizĩkora'ʒar/ *vt* discourage

desenferrujar /dʒizĩfexu'ʒar/ *vt* derust <*metal*>; stretch <*pernas*>; brush up <*língua*>

desenfreado /dʒizĩfri'adu/ *a* unbridled

desenganar /dʒizĩga'nar/ *vt* disabuse; declare incurable <*doente*>

desengonçado /dʒizĩgõ'sadu/ *a* <*pessoa*> ungainly

desengre|nado /dʒizĩgre'nadu/ *a* <*carro*> in neutral; **~nar** *vt* put in neutral <*carro*>; (*tec*) disengage

dese|nhar /deze'ɲar/ *vt* draw; **~nhista** *m/f* drawer; (*industrial*) designer; **~nho** /e/ *m* drawing

desenlace /dʒizĩ'lasi/ *m* dénouement, outcome

desenredar /dʒizĩxe'dar/ *vt* unravel

desenrolar /dʒizĩxo'lar/ *vt* unroll <*rolo*>

desenten|der /dʒizĩtẽ'der/ *vt* misunderstand; **~der-se** *vpr* (*não se dar bem*) not get on; **~dimento** *m* misunderstanding

desenterrar /dʒizĩte'xar/ *vt* dig up <*cadáver*>; unearth <*informação*>

desentortar /dʒizĩtor'tar/ *vt* straighten out

desentupir /dʒizĩtu'pir/ *vt* unblock

desenvol|to /dʒizĩ'vowtu/ *a* casual, nonchalant; **~tura** *f* casualness, nonchalance; **com ~tura** nonchalantly; **~ver** *vt* develop; **~ver-se** *vpr* develop; **~vimento** *m* development

desequi|librado *a* unbalanced; **~librar** *vt* unbalance; **~librar-se** *vpr* become unbalanced; **~líbrio** *m* imbalance

deser|ção /dezer'sãw/ *f* desertion; **~tar** *vt/i* desert; **~to** /ɛ/ *a* deserted; **ilha ~ta** desert island □ *m* desert; **~tor** *m* deserter

desespe|rado /dʒizispe'radu/ *a* desperate; **~rador** *a* hopeless; **~rar** *vt* (*desesperançar*) make despair □ *vi*, **~rar-se** *vpr* despair; **~ro** /e/ *m* despair

desestabilizar /dʒizistabili'zar/ *vt* destabilize

desestimular /dʒizistʃimu'lar/ *vt* discourage

desfal|car /dʒisfaw'kar/ *vt* embezzle; **~que** *m* embezzlement

desfal|ecer /dʒisfale'ser/ *vt* (*desmaiar*) faint; **~ecimento** *m* faint

desfavor /dʒisfa'vor/ *m* disfavour

desfavo|rável /dʒisfavo'ravew/ (*pl* **~ráveis**) *a* unfavourable; **~recer** *vt* be unfavourable to; treat less favourably *<minorias etc>*

desfazer /dʒisfa'zer/ *vt* undo; unpack *<mala>*; strip *<cama>*; break *<contrato>*; clear up *<mistério>*; **~-se** *vpr* come undone; *<casamento>* break up; *<sonhos>* crumble; **~-se em lágrimas** dissolve into tears

desfe|char /dʒisfe'ʃar/ *vt* throw *<murro, olhar>*; **~cho** /e/ *m* outcome, dénouement

desfeita /dʒis'fejta/ *f* slight, insult

desferir /dʒisfe'rir/ *vt* give *<pontapé>*; launch *<ataque>*; fire *<flecha>*

desfiar /dʒisfi'ar/ *vt* pick the meat off *<frango>*; **~-se** *vpr* *<tecido>* fray

desfigurar /dʒisfigu'rar/ *vt* disfigure; (*fig*) distort

desfi|ladeiro /dʒisfila'deru/ *m* pass; **~lar** *vi* parade; **~le** *m* parade; **~le de modas** fashion show

desflorestamento /dʒisfloresta'mẽtu/ *m* deforestation

desforra /dʒis'fɔxa/ *f* revenge

desfraldar /dʒisfraw'dar/ *vt* unfurl

desfrutar /dʒisfru'tar/ *vt* enjoy

desgas|tante /dʒizgas'tãtʃi/ *a* wearing, stressful; **~tar** *vt* wear out; **~te** *m* (*de máquina etc*) wear and tear; (*de pessoa*) stress and strain

desgosto /dʒiz'gostu/ *m* sorrow

desgovernar-se /dʒizgover'narsi/ *vpr* go out of control

desgraça /dʒiz'grasa/ *f* misfortune; **~do** *a* wretched □ *m* wretch

desgravar /dʒizgra'var/ *vt* erase

desgrenhado /dʒizgre'ɲadu/ *a* unkempt

desgrudar /dʒizgru'dar/ *vt* unstick; **~-se** *vpr* *<pessoa>* tear o.s. away

desidra|tação /dʒizidrata'sãw/ *f* dehydration; **~tar** *vt* dehydrate

desig|nação /dezigna'sãw/ *f* designation; **~nar** *vt* designate

desi|gual /dʒizi'gwaw/ (*pl* **~guais**) *a* unequal; *<terreno>* uneven; **~gualdade** *f* inequality; (*de terreno*) unevenness

desilu|dir /dʒizilu'dʒir/ *vt* disillusion; **~são** *f* disillusionment

desinfe|tante /dʒizĩfe'tãtʃi/ *a & m* disinfectant; **~tar** *vt* disinfect

desinibido /dʒizini'bidu/ *a* uninhibited

desintegrar-se /dʒizĩte'grarsi/ *vpr* disintegrate

desinteres|sado /dʒizĩtere'sadu/ *a* uninterested; **~sante** *a* uninteresting; **~sar-se** *vpr* lose interest (**de** in); **~se** /e/ *m* disinterest

desis|tência /dezis'tẽsia/ *f* giving up; **~tir** *vt/i* **~tir (de)** give up

desle|al /dʒizle'aw/ (*pl* **~ais**) *a* disloyal; **~aldade** *f* disloyalty

deslei|xado /dʒizle'ʃadu/ *a* sloppy; (*no vestir*) scruffy; **~xo** *m* carelessness; (*no vestir*) scruffiness

desli|gado /dʒizli'gadu/ *a* *<luz, TV>* off; *<pessoa>* absent-minded; **~gar** *vt* turn off *<luz, TV, motor>*; hang up, put down *<telefone>* □ *vi* (*ao telefonar*) hang up, put the phone down

deslindar /dʒizlĩ'dar/ *vt* clear up, solve

desli|zante /dʒizli'zãtʃi/ *a* slippery; *<inflação>* creeping; **~zar** *vi* slip; **~zar-se** *vpr* creep; **~ze** *m* slip; (*fig: erro*) slip-up

deslo|cado *a* *<membro>* dislocated; (*fig*) out of place; **~car** *vt* move; (*med*) dislocate; **~car-se** *vpr* move

deslum|brado /dʒizlũ'bradu/ *a* (*fig*) starry-eyed; **~bramento** *m* (*fig*) wonderment; **~brante** *a* dazzling; **~brar** *vt* dazzle; **~brar-se** *vpr* (*fig*) be dazzled

desmai|ado /dʒizmaj'adu/ *a* unconscious; **~ar** *vi* faint; **~o** *m* faint

desman|cha-prazeres / dʒizmãʃapra'zeris/ *m/f invar* spoil-sport; **~char** *vt* break up; break off *<noivado>*; shatter *<sonhos>*; **~char-se** *vpr* break up; (*no ar, na água, em lágrimas*) dissolve

desmantelar /dʒizmãte'lar/ *vt* dismantle

desmarcar /dʒizmar'kar/ *vt* cancel *<encontro>*

desmascarar /dʒizmaske'rar/ *vt* unmask

desma|tamento /dʒizmata'mẽtu/ *m* deforestation; **~tar** *vt* clear (of forest)

desmedido /dʒizme'didu/ *a* excessive

desmemoriado /dʒizmemori'adu/ *a* forgetful

desmen|tido /dʒizmẽ'tʃidu/ *m* denial; **~tir** *vt* deny

desmiolado /dʒizmio'ladu/ *a* brainless

desmontar /dʒizmõ'tar/ *vt* dismantle

desmorali|zante /dʒizmorali'zãtʃi/ *a* demoralizing; **~zar** *vt* demoralize

desmoro|namento /dʒizmorona'mẽtu/ *m* collapse; **~nar** *vt* destroy; **~nar-se** *vpr* collapse

desnatar /dʒizna'tar/ *vi* skim <*leite*>

desnecessário /dʒiznese'sariu/ *a* unnecessary

desní|vel /dʒiz'nivew/ (*pl* **~veis**) *m* difference in height

desnortear /dʒiznortʃi'ar/ *vt* disorientate, (*Amer*) disorient

desnutrição /dʒiznutri'sãw/ *f* malnutrition

desobe|decer /dʒizobede'ser/ *vt/i* **~decer (a)** disobey; **~diência** *f* disobedience; **~diente** *a* disobedient

desobrigar /dʒizobri'gar/ *vt* release (**de** from)

desobstruir /dʒizobistru'ir/ *vt* unblock; empty <*casa*>

desocupado /dʒizoku'padu/ *a* unoccupied

desodorante /dʒizodo'rãtʃi/ *m*, (*Port*) **desodorizante** /dʒizoduri'zãtʃi/ *m* deodorant

deso|lação /dezola'saw/ *f* desolation; **~lado** *a* <*lugar*> desolate; <*pessoa*> desolated; **~lar** *vt* desolate

desones|tidade /dʒizonestʃi'dadʒi/ *f* dishonesty; **~to** /ɛ/ *a* dishonest

deson|ra /dʒi'zõxa/ *f* dishonour; **~rar** *vt* dishonour; **~roso** /o/ *a* dishonourable

desor|deiro /dʒizor'deru/ *a* trouble-making □ *m* troublemaker; **~dem** *f* disorder; **~denado** *a* disorganized; <*vida*> disordered; **~denar** *vt* disorganize

desorgani|zação /dʒizorganiza'sãw/ *f* disorganization; **~zar** *vt* disorganize; **~zar-se** *vpr* get disorganized

desorientar /dʒizoriẽ'tar/ *vt* disorientate, (*Amer*) disorient

desossar /dʒizo'sar/ *vt* bone

deso|va /dʒi'zɔva/ *f* roe; **~var** *vi* spawn

despa|chado /dʒispa'ʃadu/ *a* efficient; **~chante** *m/f* (*de mercadorias*) shipping agent; (*de documentos*) documentation agent; **~char** *vt* deal with; dispatch, forward <*mercadorias*>; **~cho** *m* dispatch

desparafusar /dʒisparafu'zar/ *vt* unscrew

despedaçar /dʒispeda'sar/ *vt* (*rasgar*) tear to pieces; (*quebrar*) smash; **~-se** *vpr* <*vidro, vaso*> smash; <*papel, tecido*> tear

despe|dida /dʒispe'dʒida/ *f* farewell; **~dida de solteiro** stag night, (*Amer*) bachelor party; **~dir** *vt* dismiss; sack <*empregado*>; **~dir-se** *vpr* say goodbye (**de** to)

despei|tado /dʒispej'tadu/ *a* spiteful; **~to** *m* spite; **a ~to de** despite, in spite of

despe|jar /dʒispe'ʒar/ *vt* pour out <*líquido*>; empty <*recipiente*>; evict <*inquilino*>; **~jo** /e/ *m* (*de inquilino*) eviction

despencar /dʒispẽ'kar/ *vi* plummet

despender /dʒispẽ'der/ *vt* spend <*dinheiro*>

despensa /dʒis'pẽsa/ *f* pantry, larder

despentear /dʒispẽtʃi'ar/ *vt* mess up <*cabelo*>; mess up the hair of <*pessoa*>

despercebido /dʒisperse'bidu/ *a* unnoticed

desper|diçar /dʒisperdʒi'sar/ *vt* waste; **~dício** *m* waste

desper|tador /dʒisperta'dor/ *m* alarm clock; **~tar** *vt* rouse <*pessoa*>; (*fig*) arouse <*interesse, suspeitas etc*> □ *vi* awake

despesa /dʒis'peza/ *f* expense

des|pido /des'pidu/ *a* bare, stripped (**de** of); **~pir** *vt* strip (**de** of); strip off <*roupa*>; **~pir-se** *vpr* strip (off), get undressed

despo|jar /dʒispo'ʒar/ *vt* strip (**de** of); **~jar-se** *vpr* divest o.s. (**de** of); **~jo** /o/ *m* spoils, booty; **~jos mortais** mortal remains

despontar /dʒispõ'tar/ *vi* emerge

despor|tista /diʃpur'tiʃta/ (*Port*) *m/f* sportsman (*f*-woman); **~tivo** (*Port*) *a* sporting; **~to** /o/ (*Port*) *m* sport; **carro de ~to** sports car

déspota /'dɛspota/ *m/f* despot

despótico /des'pɔtʃiku/ *a* despotic

despovoar /dʒispovo'ar/ *vt* depopulate

desprender /dʒisprẽ'der/ *vt* detach; (*da parede*) take down; **~-se** *vpr* come off; (*fig*) detach o.s.

despreocupado /dʒisprioku'padu/ *a* unconcerned

despreparado /dʒisprepa'radu/ *a* unprepared

despretensioso /dʒispretẽsi'ozu/ *a* unpretentious

desprestigiar /dʒisprestʃiʒi'ar/ *vt* discredit

desprevenido /dʒispreve'nidu/ *a* off one's guard, unprepared; **apanhar ~** catch unawares

despre|zar /dʒispre'zar/ *vt* despise; (*ignorar*) ignore; **~zível** (*pl* **~zíveis**) *a* despicable; **~zo** /e/ *m* contempt

desproporção /dʒispropor'sãw/ *f* disproportion

desproporcio|nado / dʒisproporsio'nadu/ *a* disproportionate; **~nal** (*pl* **~nais**) *a* disproportional

despropositado /dʒispropozi'tadu/ *a* (*absurdo*) preposterous

desprovido /dʒispro'vidu/ *a* **~ de** without

desqualificar /dʒiskwalifi'kar/ *vt* disqualify

desqui|tar-se /dʒiski'tarsi/ *vpr* (legally) separate; **~te** *m* (legal) separation

desrespei|tar /dʒizxespej'tar/ *vt* not respect; (*ignorar*) disregard; **~to** *m* disrespect; **~toso** /o/ *a* disrespectful

dessa(s), desse(s) = de + essa(s), esse(s)

desta = de + esta

desta|camento /dʒistaka'mẽtu/ *m* detachment; **~car** *vt* detach; (*ressaltar*) bring out, make stand out; **~car-se** *vpr* (*desprender-se*) come off; <*corredor*> break away; (*sobressair*) stand out (**sobre** against); **~cável** (*pl* **~cáveis**) *a* detachable; <*caderno*> pull-out

destam|pado /dʒistã'padu/ *a* (*panela*) uncovered; **~par** *vt* remove the lid of

destapar /dʒista'par/ *vt* uncover

destaque /dʒis'taki/ *m* prominence; (*coisa, pessoa*) highlight; (*do notíciario*) headline

destas, deste = de + estas, este

destemido /dʒiste'midu/ *a* intrepid, courageous

desterrar /dʒiste'xar/ *vt* (*exilar*) exile

destes = de + estes

destilar /desti'lar/ *vt* distil; **~ia** *f* distillery

desti|nado /destʃi'nadu/ *a* (*fadado*) destined; **~nar** *vt* intend, mean (**para** for); **~natário** *m* addressee; **~no** *m* (*de viagem*) destination; (*sorte*) fate

destituir /destʃitu'ir/ *vt* remove

desto|ante /dʒisto'ãtʃi/ *a* <*sons*> discordant; <*cores*> clashing; **~ar** *vi* **~ar de** clash with

destrancar /dʒistrã'kar/ *vt* unlock

destreza /des'treza/ *f* skill

destrinchar /dʒistrĩ'ʃar/ *vt* (*expor*) dissect; (*resolver*) sort out

destro /'destru/ *a* skilful

destro|çar /dʒistro'sar/ *vt* wreck; **~ços** *m pl* wreckage

destronar /dʒistro'nar/ *vt* depose

destroncar /dʒistrõ'kar/ *vt* rick

destru|ição /dʒistrui'sãw/ *f* destruction; **~idor** *a* destructive □ *m* destroyer; **~ir** *vt* destroy

desumano /dʒizu'manu/ *a* inhuman; (*cruel*) inhumane

desunião /dʒizuni'ãw/ *f* disunity

desu|sado /dʒizu'zadu/ *a* disused; **~so** *m* disuse

desvairado /dʒizvaj'radu/ *a* delirious, raving

desvalori|zação /dʒizvaloriza-'sãw/ *f* devaluation; **~zar** *vt* devalue

desvanta|gem /dʒizvã'taʒẽ/ *f* disadvantage; **~joso** /o/ *a* disadvantageous

desve|lar /dʒizve'lar/ *vt* unveil; uncover <*segredo*>; **~lar-se** *vpr* go to a lot of trouble; **~lo** /e/ *m* great care

desvencilhar /dʒizvẽsi'ʎar/ *vt* extricate, free

desvendar /dʒizvẽ'dar/ *vt* reveal <*segredo*>; solve <*mistério*>

desventura /dʒizvẽ'tura/ *f* misfortune; (*infelicidade*) unhappiness

desviar /dʒizvi'ar/ *vt* divert <*trânsito, rio, atenção, dinheiro*>; avert <*golpe, suspeitas, olhos*>; **~-se** *vpr* deviate; <*do tema*> digress

desvincular /dʒizvĩku'lar/ *vt* free

desvio /dʒiz'viu/ *m* diversion; (*do trânsito*) diversion, (*Amer*) detour; (*linha ferroviária*) siding

desvirtuar /dʒizvirtu'ar/ *vt* misrepresent <*verdade*>

deta|lhado /deta'ʎadu/ *a* detailed; **~lhar** *vt* detail; **~lhe** *m* detail

detec|tar /detek'tar/ *vt* detect; **~tive** (*Port*) *m veja* **detetive**; **~tor** *m* detector

de|tenção /detẽ'sãw/ *f* (*prisão*) detention; **~tentor** *m* holder; **~ter** *vt* (*ter*) hold; (*prender*) detain

detergente /deter'ʒẽtʃi/ *m* detergent

deterio|ração /deteriora'sãw/ *f* deterioration; **~rar** *vt* damage; **~rar-se** *vpr* deteriorate

determi|nação /determina'sãw/ *f* determination; **~nado** *a* (*certo*) certain; (*resoluto*) determined; **~nar** *vt* determine

detestar /detes'tar/ *vt* hate

detetive /dete'tʃivi/ *m* detective

detido /de'tʃidu/ *pp de* **deter** □ *a* thorough □ *m* detainee

detonar /deto'nar/ *vt* detonate; (*fam: criticar*) pull to pieces □ *vi* detonate

detrás /de'traʃ/ *adv* behind □ *prep* **~ de** behind

detrito /de'tritu/ *m* detritus

deturpar /detur'par/ *vt* misrepresent, distort

deus /dews/ *m* (*f* **deusa**) god (*f* goddess); **~-dará** *m* **ao ~-dará** at the mercy of chance
devagar /dʒiva'gar/ *adv* slowly
deva|near /devani'ar/ *vi* daydream; **~neio** *m* daydream
devas|sar /deva'sar/ *vt* expose; **~sidão** *f* debauchery; **~so** *a* debauched
devastar /devas'tar/ *vt* devastate
de|vedor /deve'dor/ *a* debit □ *m* debtor; **~ver** *vt* owe □ *vaux* **~ve fazer** (*obrigação*) he has to do; **~ve chegar** (*probabilidade*) he should arrive; **~ve ser** (*suposição*) he must be; **~ve ter ido** he must have gone; **~v(er)ia fazer** he ought to do; **~v(er)ia ter feito** he ought to have done; **~vidamente** *adv* duly; **~vido** *a* due (**a** to)
devoção /devo'sãw/ *f* devotion
de|volução /devolu'sãw/ *f* return; **~volver** *vt* return
devorar /devo'rar/ *vt* devour
devo|tar /devo'tar/ *vt* devote; **~tar-se** *vpr* devote o.s. (**a** to); **~to** /ɔ/ *a* devout
dez /dɛs/ *a & m* ten
dezanove /dza'nɔv/ (*Port*) *a & m* nineteen
dezas|seis /dza'sejʃ/ (*Port*) *a & m* sixteen; **~sete** /ɛ/ (*Port*) *a & m* seventeen
dezembro /de'zẽbru/ *m* December
deze|na /de'zena/ *f* ten; **uma ~ (de)** about ten; **~nove** /ɔ/ *a & m* nineteen
dezes|seis /dʒize'sejs/ *a & m* sixteen; **~sete** /ɛ/ *a & m* seventeen
dezoito /dʒi'zojtu/ *a & m* eighteen
dia /'dʒia/ *m* day; **de ~** by day; **(no) ~ 20 de julho** (on) July 20th; **~ de folga** day off; **~ util** working day; **~-a-~** *m* everyday life
dia|bete /dʒia'bɛtʃi/ *f* diabetes; **~bético** *a & m* diabetic
dia|bo /dʒi'abu/ *m* devil; **~bólico** *a* diabolical, devilish; **~brete** /e/ *m* little devil; **~brura** *f* (*de criança*) bit of mischief; *pl* mischief
diadema /dʒia'dema/ *m* tiara
diafragma /dʒia'fragima/ *m* diaphragm
dia|gnosticar /dʒiagnostʃi'kar/ *vt* diagnose; **~gnóstico** *m* diagnosis □ *a* diagnostic
diago|nal /dʒiago'naw/ (*pl* **~nais**) *a & f* diagonal
diagra|ma /dʒia'grama/ *m* diagram; **~mação** *f* design; **~mador** *m* designer; **~mar** *vt* design <*livro, revista*>
dialect- (*Port*) *veja* **dialet-**
dia|lética /dʒia'lɛtʃika/ *f* dialectics; **~leto** /ɛ/ *m* dialect
dialogar /dʒialo'gar/ *vi* talk; (*pol*) hold talks
diálogo /dʒi'alogu/ *m* dialogue
diamante /dʒia'mãtʃi/ *m* diamond
diâmetro /dʒi'ametru/ *m* diameter
dian|te /dʒi'ãtʃi/ *adv* **de ... em ~te** from ... on(wards); **~te de** (*enfrentando*) faced with; (*perante*) before; **~teira** *f* lead; **~teiro** *a* front
diapasão /dʒiapa'zãw/ *m* tuning-fork
diapositivo /dʒiapozi'tʃivu/ *m* transparency
diá|ria /dʒi'aria/ *f* daily rate; **~rio** *a* daily
diarista /dʒia'rista/ *m/f* day labourer; (*faxineira*) daily (help)
diarréia /dʒia'xɛja/ *f* diarrhoea
dica /'dʒika/ *f* tip, hint
dicção /dʒik'sãw/ *f* diction
dicionário /dʒisio'nariu/ *m* dictionary
didáti|ca /dʒi'datʃika/ *f* teaching methodology; **~co** *a* teaching; <*livro*> educational; <*estilo*> didactic
die|ta /dʒi'ɛta/ *f* diet; **de ~ta** on a diet; **~tista** *m/f* dietician
difa|mação /dʒifama'sãw/ *f* defamation; **~mar** *vt* defame; **~matório** *a* defamatory
diferen|ça /dʒife'rẽsa/ *f* difference; **~cial** (*pl* **~ciais**) *a & f* differential; **~ciar** *vt* differentiate; **~ciar-se** *vpr* differ; **~te** *a* different
dife|rimento /dʒiferi'mẽtu/ *m* deferment; **~rir** *vt* defer □ *vi* differ
difí|cil /dʒi'fisiw/ (*pl* **~ceis**) *a* difficult; (*improvável*) unlikely
dificilmente /dʒifisiw'mẽtʃi/ *adv* **~ poderá fazê-lo** he's unlikely to be able to do it
dificul|dade /dʒifikuw'dadʒi/ *f* difficulty; **~tar** *vt* make difficult
difteria /dʒifte'ria/ *f* diphtheria
difun|dir /dʒifũ'dʒir/ *vt* spread; (*pela rádio*) broadcast; diffuse <*luz, calor*>; **~dir-se** *vpr* spread
difu|são /dʒifu'zãw/ *f* diffusion; **~so** *a* diffuse
dige|rir /dʒiʒe'rir/ *vt* digest; **~rível** (*pl* **~ríveis**) *a* digestible
diges|tão /dʒiʒes'tãw/ *f* digestion; **~tivo** *a* digestive
digi|tal /dʒiʒi'taw/ (*pl* **~tais**) *a* digital; **impressão ~tal** fingerprint; **~tar** *vt* key
dígito /'dʒiʒitu/ *m* digit
digladiar /dʒigladʒi'ar/ *vi* do battle
dig|nar-se /dʒig'narsi/ *vpr* deign (**de** to); **~nidade** *f* dignity; **~nificar** *vt* dignify; **~no** *a* worthy (**de** of); (*decoroso*) dignified
dilace|rante /dʒilase'rãtʃi/ *a* <*dor*> excruciating; **~rar** *vt* tear to pieces
dilapidar /dʒilapi'dar/ *vt* squander

dilatar /dʒila'tar/ *vt* expand; (*med*) dilate; **~-se** *vpr* expand; (*med*) dilate

dilema /dʒi'lema/ *m* dilemma

diletante /dʒile'tãtʃi/ *a & m/f* dilettante

dili|gência /dʒili'ʒẽsia/ *f* diligence; (*carruagem*) stagecoach; **~gente** *a* diligent, hard-working

diluir /dʒilu'ir/ *vt* dilute

dilúvio /dʒi'luviu/ *m* deluge

dimen|são /dʒimẽ'sãw/ *f* dimension; **~sionar** *vt* size up

diminu|ição /dʒiminui'sãw/ *f* reduction; **~ir** *vt* reduce □ *vi* lessen; <*carro, motorista*> slow down; **~tivo** *a & m* diminutive; **~to** *a* minute

Dinamarca /dʒina'marka/ *f* Denmark

dinamar|quês /dʒinamar'kes/ (*f* **~quesa**) *a* Danish □ *m* Dane

dinâmi|ca /dʒi'namika/ *f* dynamics; **~co** *a* dynamic

dina|mismo /dʒina'mizmu/ *m* dynamism; **~mite** *f* dynamite

dínamo /'dʒinamu/ *m* dynamo

dinastia /dʒinas'tʃia/ *f* dynasty

dinda /'dʒĩda/ (*fam*) *f* godmother

dinheiro /dʒi'ɲeru/ *m* money

dinossauro /dʒino'sawru/ *m* dinosaur

diocese /dʒio'sɛzi/ *f* diocese

dióxido /dʒi'ɔksidu/ *m* dioxide; **~ de carbono** carbon dioxide

diplo|ma /dʒi'ploma/ *m* diploma; **~macia** *f* diplomacy; **~mar-se** *vpr* take one's diploma; **~mata** *m/f* diplomat □ *a* diplomatic; **~mático** *a* diplomatic

direção /dʒire'sãw/ *f* (*sentido*) direction; (*de empresa*) management; (*condução de carro*) driving; (*manuseio do volante*) steering

direct- (*Port*) *veja* **diret-**

direi|ta /dʒi'rejta/ *f* right; **~tinho** *adv* exactly right; **~tista** *a* rightwing □ *m/f* rightwinger, rightist; **~to** *a* right; (*ereto*) straight □ *adv* properly □ *m* right

dire|tas /dʒi'rɛtas/ *f pl* direct (presidential) elections; **~to** *a* direct □ *adv* directly; **~tor** *m* director; (*de escola*) headteacher; (*de jornal*) editor; **~tor-gerente** managing director; **~toria** *f* (*diretores*) board of directors; (*sala*) boardroom; **~tório** *m* directory; **~triz** *f* directive

diri|gente /dʒiri'ʒẽtʃi/ *a* leading □ *m/f* leader; **~gir** *vt* direct; manage <*empresa*>; drive <*carro*>; **~gir-se** *vpr* (*ir*) make one's way; **~gir-se a** (*falar com*) address

dis|cagem /dʒis'kaʒẽ/ *f* dialling; **~car** *vt/i* dial

discente /dʒi'sẽtʃi/ *a* **corpo ~** student body

discer|nimento /dʒiserni'mẽtu/ *m* discernment; **~nir** *vt* discern

discipli|na /dʒisi'plina/ *f* discipline; **~nador** *a* disciplinary; **~nar** *vt* discipline

discípulo /dʒi'sipulu/ *m* disciple

disc-jóquei /dʒisk'ʒɔkej/ *m* disc-jockey

disco /'dʒisku/ *m* disc; (*de música*) record; (*no atletismo*) discus □ (*fam*) *f* disco; **~ flexível/rígido** floppy/hard disk; **~ laser** CD, compact disc; **~ voador** flying saucer

discor|dante /dʒiskor'dãtʃi/ *a* conflicting; **~dar** *vi* disagree (**de** with)

discote|ca /dʒisko'tɛka/ *f* discotheque; **~cário** *m* DJ

discre|pância /dʒiskre'pãsia/ *f* discrepancy; **~pante** *a* inconsistent; **~par** *vi* diverge (**de** from)

dis|creto /dʒis'krɛtu/ *a* discreet; **~crição** *f* discretion

discrimi|nação /dʒiskrimina'sãw/ *f* discrimination; (*descrição*) description; **~nar** *vt* discriminate; **~natório** *a* discriminatory

discur|sar /dʒiskur'sar/ *vi* speak; **~so** *m* speech

discussão /dʒisku'sãw/ *f* discussion; (*briga*) argument

discu|tir /dʒisku'tʃir/ *vt/i* discuss; (*brigar*) argue; **~tível** (*pl* **~tíveis**) *a* debatable

disenteria /dʒizẽte'ria/ *f* dysentery

disfar|çar /dʒisfar'sar/ *vt* disguise; **~çar-se** *vpr* disguise o.s.; **~ce** *m* disguise

dis|lético /dʒiz'lɛtʃiku/ *a & m* dyslexic; **~lexia** *f* dyslexia; **~léxico** *a & m* dyslexic

dispa|rada /dʒispa'rada/ *f* bolt; **~rado** *adv* **o melhor ~rado** the best by a long way; **~rar** *vt* fire <*arma*> □ *vi* (*com arma*) fire; <*preços, inflação*> shoot up; <*corredor*> surge ahead

disparate /dʒispa'ratʃi/ *m* piece of nonsense; *pl* nonsense

dis|pêndio /dʒis'pẽdʒiu/ *m* expenditure; **~pendioso** /o/ *a* costly

dispen|sa /dʒis'pẽsa/ *f* exemption; **~sar** *vt* (*distribuir*) dispense; (*isentar*) exempt (**de** from); (*prescindir de*) dispense with; **~sável** (*pl* **~sáveis**) *a* dispensable

dispersar /dʒisper'sar/ *vt* disperse; waste <*energias*> □ *vi*, **~-se** *vpr* disperse

disperso /dʒis'pɛrsu/ *adj* scattered

dispo|nibilidade /dʒisponibili'dadʒi/ *f* availability; **~nível** (*pl* **~níveis**) *a* available

dis|por /dʒis'por/ *vt* arrange □ *vi* **~por de** have at one's disposal; **~por-se** *vpr* form up □ *m* **ao seu ~por** at your disposal; **~posição** *f* (*vontade*) willingness; (*arranjo*) arrangement; (*de espírito*) frame of mind; (*de testamento etc*) provision; **à ~posição de alg** at s.o.'s disposal; **~positivo** *m* device; **~posto** *a* prepared, willing (**a** to)

dispu|ta /dʒis'puta/ *f* dispute; **~tar** *vt* dispute; (*tentar ganhar*) compete for

disquete /dʒis'ketʃi/ *m* diskette, floppy (disk)

dissabores /dʒisa'boris/ *m pl* troubles

disseminar /dʒisemi'nar/ *vt* disseminate

dissertação /dʒiserta'sãw/ *f* dissertation, lecture

dissi|dência /dʒisi'dẽsia/ *f* dissidence; **~dente** *a & m* dissident

dissídio /dʒi'sidʒiu/ *m* dispute

dissimular /dʒisimu'lar/ *vt* hide □ *vi* dissimulate

disso = de + isso

dissipar /dʒisi'par/ *vt* clear <*nevoeiro*>; dispel <*dúvidas, suspeitas, ilusões*>; dissipate <*for-tuna*>; **~-se** *vpr* <*nevoeiro*> clear; <*dúvidas etc*> be dispelled

dissolu|ção /dʒisolu'sãw/ *f* dissolution; **~to** *a* dissolute

dissolver /dʒisow'ver/ *vt* dissolve; **~-se** *vpr* dissolve

dissuadir /dʒisua'dʒir/ *vt* dissuade (**de** from)

distância /dʒis'tãsia/ *f* distance

distan|ciar /dʒistãsi'ar/ *vt* distance; **~ciar-se** *vpr* distance o.s.; **~te** *a* distant

disten|der /dʒistẽ'der/ *vt* stretch <*pernas*>; relax <*músculo*>; **~der-se** *vpr* relax; **~são** *f* (*med*) pull; **~são muscular** pulled muscle

distin|ção /dʒistʃĩ'sãw/ *f* distinction; **~guir** *vt* distinguish (**de** from); **~guir-se** *vpr* distinguish o.s.; **~tivo** *a* distinctive □ *m* badge; **~to** *a* distinct; <*senhor*> distinguished

disto = de + isto

distor|ção /dʒistor'sãw/ *f* distortion; **~cer** *vt* distort

distra|ção /dʒistra'sãw/ *f* distraction; **~ído** *a* absent-minded; **~ir** *vt* distract; (*divertir*) amuse; **~ir-se** *vpr* be distracted; (*divertir-se*) amuse o.s.

distribu|ição /dʒistribui'sãw/ *f* distribution; **~idor** *m* distributor; **~idora** *f* distributor, distribution company; **~ir** *vt* distribute

distrito /dʒis'tritu/ *m* district

distúrbio /dʒis'turbiu/ *m* trouble

di|tado /dʒi'tadu/ *m* dictation; (*provérbio*) saying; **~tador** *m* dictator; **~tadura** *f* dictatorship; **~tame** *m* dictate; **~tar** *vt* dictate; **~tatorial** (*pl* **~tatoriais**) *a* dictatorial

dito /'dʒitu/ *a* **~ e feito** no sooner said than done □ *m* remark

ditongo /dʒi'tõgu/ *m* diphthong

DIU /'dʒiu/ *m* IUD, coil

diurno /dʒi'urnu/ *a* day

divã /dʒi'vã/ *m* couch

divagar /dʒiva'gar/ *vi* digress

diver|gência /dʒiver'ʒẽsia/ *a* divergence; **~gente** *a* divergent; **~gir** *vi* diverge (**de** from); **~são** *f* diversion; (*divertimento*) amusement; **~sidade** *f* diversity; **~sificar** *vt/i* diversify; **~so** /ɛ/ *a* (*diferente*) diverse; *pl* (*vários*) several; **~tido** *a* (*engraçado*) funny; (*que se curte*) enjoyable; **~timento** *m* enjoyment, fun; (*um*) amusement; **~tir** *vt* amuse; **~tir-se** *vpr* enjoy o.s., have fun

dívida /'dʒivida/ *f* debt; **~ externa** foreign debt

divi|dendo /dʒivi'dẽdu/ *m* dividend; **~dido** *a* <*pessoa*> torn; **~dir** *vt* divide; (*compartilhar*) share; **~dir-se** *vpr* be divided

divindade /dʒivĩ'dadʒi/ *f* divinity

divino /dʒi'vinu/ *a* divine

divi|sa /dʒi'viza/ *f* (*lema*) motto; (*galão*) stripes; (*fronteira*) border; *pl* foreign currency; **~são** *f* division; **~sória** *f* partition

divorci|ado /dʒivorsi'adu/ *a* divorced □ *m* divorcé (*f* divorcée); **~ar** *vt* divorce; **~ar-se** *vpr* get divorced; **~ar-se de** divorce

divórcio /dʒi'vɔrsiu/ *m* divorce

divul|gado /dʒivuw'gadu/ *a* widespread; **~gar** *vt* spread; publish <*notícia*>; divulge <*segredo*>; **~gar-se** *vpr* be spread

dizer /dʒi'zer/ *vt* say; **~ a alg que** tell sb that; **~ para alg fazer** tell s.o. to do □ *vi* **~ com** go with; **~-se** *vpr* claim to be □ *m* saying

dizimar /dʒizi'mar/ *vt* decimate

do = de + o

dó /dɔ/ *m* pity; **dar ~** be pitiful; **ter ~ de** feel sorry for

do|ação /doa'sãw/ *f* donation; **~ador** *m* donor; **~ar** *vt* donate

do|bra /'dɔbra/ *f* fold; (*de calça*) turn-up, (*Amer*) cuff; **~bradiça** *f* hinge; **~bradiço** *a* pliable; **~brado** *a* (*duplo*) double; **~brar** *vt* (*duplicar*) double; (*fazer dobra em*) fold; (*curvar*) bend; go round <*esquina*>; ring <*sinos*>; (*Port*) dub <*filme*> □ *vi* double; <*sinos*> ring; **~brar-se** *vpr* bend; **~bro** *m* double

doca /'dɔka/ *f* dock

doce /'dosi/ *a* sweet; <*água*> fresh □ *m* sweet; **~ de leite** fudge

docente /do'sẽtʃi/ *a* teaching; **corpo ~** teaching staff, (*Amer*) faculty

dó|cil /'dɔsiw/ (*pl* **~ceis**) *a* docile

documen|tação /dokumẽta'sãw/ *f* documentation; **~tar** *vt* document; **~tário** *a & m* documentary; **~to** *m* document

doçura /do'sura/ *f* sweetness

dodói /do'dɔj/ (*fam*) *m* **ter ~** have a pain □ *a* poorly, ill

doen|ça /do'ẽsa/ *f* illness; (*infecciosa, fig*) disease; **~ da vaca louca** mad cow disease; **~te** *a* ill; **~tio** *a* <*criança, aspecto*> sickly; <*interesse, curiosidade*> morbid

doer /do'er/ *vi* hurt; <*cabeça, músculo*> ache

dog|ma /'dɔgima/ *m* dogma; **~mático** *a* dogmatic

doido /'dojdu/ *a* crazy

dois /dojs/ *a & m* (*f* **duas**) two

dólar /'dɔlar/ *m* dollar

dolo|rido /dolo'ridu/ *a* sore; **~roso** /o/ *a* painful

dom /dõ/ *m* gift

do|mador /doma'dor/ *m* tamer; **~mar** *vt* tame

doméstica /do'mɛstʃika/ *f* housemaid

domesticar /domestʃi'kar/ *vt* domesticate

doméstico /do'mɛstʃiku/ *a* domestic

domi|ciliar /domisili'ar/ *a* home; **~cílio** *m* home

domi|nação /domina'sãw/ *f* domination; **~nador** *a* domineering; **~nante** *a* dominant; **~nar** *vt* dominate; have a command of <*língua*>; **~nar-se** *vpr* control o.s.

domin|go /do'mĩgu/ *m* Sunday; **~gueiro** *a* Sunday

domini|cal /domini'kaw/ (*pl* **~cais**) *a* Sunday; **~cano** *a & m* Dominican

domínio /do'miniu/ *m* command

dona /'dona/ *f* owner; **Dona** (*com nome*) Miss; **~ de casa** *f* housewife

donativo /dona'tʃivu/ *m* donation

donde /'dõdʒi/ *adv* from where; (*motivo*) from whence

dono /'donu/ *m* owner

donzela /dõ'zɛla/ *f* maiden

dopar /do'par/ *vt* drug

dor /dor/ *f* pain; (*menos aguda*) ache; **~ de cabeça** headache

dor|mente /dor'mẽtʃi/ *a* numb □ *m* sleeper; **~mida** *f* sleep; **~minhoco** /o/ *m* sleepyhead; **~mir** *vi* sleep; **~mitar** *vi* doze; **~mitório** *m* bedroom; (*comunitário*) dormitory

dorso /'dorsu/ *m* back; (*de livro*) spine

dos = de + os

do|sagem /do'zaʒẽ/ *f* dosage; **~sar** *vt* moderate; **~se** /ɔ/ *f* dose; (*de uísque etc*) shot, measure

dossiê /dosi'e/ *m* file

do|tação /dota'sãw/ *f* endowment; **~tado** *a* gifted; **~tado de** endowed with; **~tar** *vt* endow (**de** with); **~te** /ɔ/ *m* (*de noiva*) dowry; (*dom*) endowment

dou|rado /do'radu/ *a* (*de cor*) golden; (*revestido de ouro*) gilded, gilt □ *m* gilt; **~rar** *vt* gild

dou|to /'dotu/ *a* learned; **~tor** *m* doctor; **~torado** *m* doctorate, PhD; **~trina** *f* doctrine; **~trinar** *vt* indoctrinate

doze /'dozi/ *a & m* twelve

dragão /dra'gãw/ *m* dragon

dragar /dra'gar/ *vt* dredge

drágea /'draʒia/ *f* lozenge

dra|ma /'drama/ *m* drama; **~malhão** *m* melodrama; **~mático** *a* dramatic; **~matizar** *vt* dramatize; **~maturgo** *m* dramatist, playwright

drapeado /drapi'adu/ *a* draped

drástico /'drastʃiku/ *a* drastic

dre|nagem /dre'naʒẽ/ *f* drainage; **~nar** *vt* drain; **~no** /ɛ/ *m* drain

driblar /dri'blar/ *vt* (*em futebol*) dribble round, beat; (*fig*) get round

drinque /'drĩki/ *m* drink

drive /'drajvi/ *m* disk drive

dro|ga /'drɔga/ *f* drug; (*fam*) (*coisa sem valor*) dead loss; (*coisa chata*) drag □ *int* damn; **~gado** *a* on drugs □ *m* drug addict; **~gar** *vt* drug; **~gar-se** *vpr* take drugs; **~garia** *f* dispensing chemist's, pharmacy

duas /'duas/ *veja* **dois**

dúbio /'dubiu/ *a* dubious

dub|lagem /du'blaʒẽ/ *f* dubbing; **~lar** *vt* dub <*filme*>; mime <*música*>; **~lê** *m* double

ducentésimo /dusẽ'tɛzimu/ *a* two-hundredth

ducha /'duʃa/ *f* shower

ducto /'duktu/ *m* duct

duelo /du'ɛlu/ *m* duel

duende /du'ẽdʒi/ *m* elf

dueto /du'etu/ *m* duet

duna /'duna/ *f* dune

duodécimo /duo'dɛsimu/ *a* twelfth

duodeno /duo'dɛnu/ *m* duodenum

dupla /'dupla/ *f* pair, duo; <*no tênis*> doubles

dúplex /du'plɛks/ *a invar* two-floor ▫ *m invar* two-floor apartment, (*Amer*) duplex

dupli|car /dupli'kar/ *vt/i* double; **~cidade** *f* duplicity; **~cata** *f* duplicate

duplo /'duplu/ *a* double

duque /'duki/ *m* duke; **~sa** /e/ *f* duchess

du|ração /dura'sãw/ *f* duration; **~radouro** *a* lasting; **~rante** *prep* during; **~rar** *vi* last; **~rável** (*pl* **~ráveis**) *a* durable

durex /du'rɛks/ *m invar* sellotape

du|reza /du'reza/ *f* hardness; **~ro** *a* hard; (*fam: sem dinheiro*) hard up, broke

dúvida /'duvida/ *f* doubt; (*pergunta*) query

duvi|dar /duvi'dar/ *vt/i* doubt; **~doso** /o/ *a* doubtful

duzentos /du'zẽtus/ *a & m* two hundred

dúzia /'duzia/ *f* dozen

e /i/ *conj* and

ébano /'ɛbanu/ *m* ebony

ébrio /'ɛbriu/ *a* drunk ▫ *m* drunkard

ebulição /ebuli'sãw/ *f* boiling

eclesiástico /eklezi'astʃiku/ *a* ecclesiastical

eclético /e'klɛtʃiku/ *a* eclectic

eclip|sar /eklip'sar/ *vt* eclipse; **~se** *m* eclipse

eclodir /eklo'dʒir/ *vi* emerge; (*estourar*) break out; <*flor*> open

eco /'ɛku/ *m* echo; **ter ~** have repercussions; **~ar** *vt/i* echo

eco|logia /ekolo'ʒia/ *f* ecology; **~lógico** *a* ecological; **~logista** *m/f* ecologist

eco|nomia /ekono'mia/ *f* economy; (*ciência*) economics; *pl* (*dinheiro poupado*) savings; **~nômico** *a* economic; (*rentável, barato*) economical; **~nomista** *m/f* economist; **~nomizar** *vt* save ▫ *vi* economize

écran /ɛ'krã/ (*Port*) *m* screen

eczema /ek'zɛma/ *m* eczema

edição /edʒi'sãw/ *f* edition; (*de filmes*) editing

edificante /edʒifi'kãtʃi/ *a* edifying

edifício /edʒi'fisiu/ *m* building

Edimburgo /edʒĩ'burgu/ *f* Edinburgh

edi|tal /edʒi'taw/ (*pl* **~tais**) *m* announcement; **~tar** *vt* publish; (*comput*) edit; **~to** *m* edict; **~tor** *m* publisher; **~tora** *f* publishing company; **~torial** (*pl* **~toriais**) *a* publishing ▫ *m* editorial

edredom /edre'dõ/ *m*, (*Port*) **edredão** /edre'dãw/ *m* quilt

educa|ção /eduka'sãw/ *f* (*ensino*) education; (*polidez*) good manners; **é falta de ~ção** it's rude; **~cional** (*pl* **~cionais**) *a* education

edu|cado /edu'kadu/ *a* polite; **~car** *vt* educate; **~cativo** *a* educational

EEB /ee'be/ *f* BSE

efeito /e'fejtu/ *m* effect; **fazer ~** have an effect; **para todos os ~s** to all intents and purposes; **~ colateral** side effect; **~ estufa** greenhouse effect

efêmero /e'fẽmeru/ *a* ephemeral

efeminado /efemi'nadu/ *a* effeminate

efervescente /eferve'sẽtʃi/ *a* effervescent

efe|tivar /efetʃi'var/ *vt* bring into effect; (*contratar*) make a permanent member of staff; **~tivo** *a* real, effective; <*cargo, empregado*> permanent; **~tuar** *vt* carry out, effect

efi|cácia /efi'kasia/ *f* effectiveness; **~caz** *a* effective

efici|ência /efisi'ẽsia/ *f* efficiency; **~ente** *a* efficient

efígie /e'fiʒi/ *f* effigy

Egeu /e'ʒew/ *a & m* Aegean

égide /'ɛʒidʒi/ *f* aegis

egípcio /e'ʒipsiu/ *a & m* Egyptian

Egito /e'ʒitu/ *m* Egypt

ego /'ɛgu/ *m* ego; **~cêntrico** *a* self-centred, egocentric; **~ísmo** *m* selfishness; **~ísta** *a* selfish ▫ *m/f* egoist ▫ *m* (*de rádio etc*) earplug

égua /'ɛgwa/ *f* mare

eis /ejs/ *adv* (*aqui está*) here is/are; (*isso é*) that is

eixo /'ejʃu/ *m* axle; (*mat, entre cidades*) axis; **pôr nos ~s** set straight

ela /'ɛla/ *pron* she; (*coisa*) it; (*com preposição*) her; (*coisa*) it

elaborar /elabo'rar/ *vt* (*fazer*) make, produce; (*desenvolver*) work out

elasticidade /elastʃisi'dadʒi/ *f* (*de coisa*) elasticity; (*de pessoa*) suppleness

elástico /e'lastʃiku/ *a* elastic ▫ *m* (*de borracha*) elastic band; (*de calcinha etc*) elastic

ele /'eli/ *pron* he; (*coisa*) it; (*com preposição*) him; (*coisa*) it

electr- (*Port*) *veja* **eletr-**

eléctrico /i'lɛktriku/ (*Port*) *m* tram, (*Amer*) streetcar ▫ *a veja* **elétrico**

elefante /ele'fãtʃi/ *m* elephant

ele|gância /ele'gãsia/ *f* elegance; **~gante** *a* elegant

eleger /ele'ʒer/ *vt* elect; **~-se** *vpr* get elected

elegia /ele'ʒia/ *f* elegy

elei|ção /elej'sãw/ *f* election; **~to** *a* elected, elect; <*povo*> chosen; **~tor** *m* voter; **~torado** *m* electorate; **~toral** (*pl* **~torais**) *a* electoral

elemen|tar /elemẽ'tar/ *a* elementary; **~to** *m* element

elenco /e'lẽku/ *m* (*de filme, peça*) cast

eletri|cidade /eletrisi'dadʒi/ *f* electricity; **~cista** *m*/*f* electrician

elétrico /e'lɛtriku/ *a* electric

eletri|ficar /eletrifi'kar/ *vt* electrify; **~zar** *vt* electrify

eletro /e'lɛtru/ *m* ECG; **~cutar** *vt* electrocute; **~do** /o/ *m* electrode; **~domésticos** *m pl* electrical appliances

eletrôni|ca /ele'tronika/ *f* electronics; **~co** *a* electronic

ele|vação /eleva'sãw/ *f* elevation; (*aumento*) rise; **~vado** *a* high; <*sentimento, estilo*> elevated; **~vador** *m* lift, (*Amer*) elevator; **~var** *vt* raise; (*promover*) elevate; **~var-se** *vpr* rise

elimi|nar /elimi'nar/ *vt* eliminate; **~natória** *f* heat; **~natório** *a* eliminatory

elipse /e'lipsi/ *f* ellipse

elíptico /e'liptʃiku/ *a* elliptical

eli|te /e'litʃi/ *f* elite; **~tismo** *m* elitism; **~tista** *a & m*/*f* elitist

elmo /'ɛwmu/ *m* helmet

elo /'ɛlu/ *m* link

elo|giar /eloʒi'ar/ *vt* praise; **~giar alg por** compliment s.o. on; **~gio** *m* (*louvor*) praise; (*um*) compliment; **~gioso** /o/ *a* complimentary

elo|qüência /elo'kwẽsia/ *f* eloquence; **~qüente** *a* eloquent

eluci|dar /elusi'dar/ *vt* elucidate; **~dativo** *a* elucidatory

em /ẽj/ *prep* in; (*sobre*) on; **ela está no Eduardo** she's at Eduardo's (house); **de casa ~ casa** from house to house; **aumentar ~ 10%** increase by 10%

emagre|cer /emagre'ser/ *vi* lose weight, get thinner □ *vt* make thinner; **~cimento** *m* slimming

emanar /ema'nar/ *vi* emanate (**de** from)

emanci|pação /emãsipa'sãw/ *f* emancipation; **~par** *vt* emancipate; **~par-se** *vpr* become emancipated

emara|nhado /emara'ɲadu/ *a* tangled □ *m* tangle; **~nhar** *vt* tangle; (*envolver*) entangle; **~nhar-se** *vpr* get tangled up; (*envolver-se*) become entangled (**em** in)

embaçar /ĩba'sar/, (*Port*) **embaciar** /ĩbasi'ar/ *vt* steam up <*vidro*> □ *vi* <*vidro*> steam up; <*olhos*> grow misty

embainhar /ĩbaj'ɲar/ *vt* hem <*vestido, calça*>

embaixa|da /ĩba'ʃada/ *f* embassy; **~dor** *m* ambassador; **~triz** *f* ambassador; (*esposa*) ambassador's wife

embaixo /ĩ'baʃu/ *adv* underneath; (*em casa*) downstairs; **~ de** under

emba|lagem /ĩba'laʒẽ/ *f* packaging; **~lar**[1] *vt* pack

emba|lar[2] /ĩba'lar/ *vt* rock <*criança*>; **~lo** *m* (*fig*) excitement, thrill

embalsamar /ĩbawsa'mar/ *vt* embalm

embara|çar /ĩbara'sar/ *vt* embarrass; **~çar-se** *vpr* get embarrassed (**com** by); **~ço** *m* embarrassment; **~çoso** /o/ *a* embarrassing

embaralhar /ĩbara'ʎar/ *vt* muddle up; shuffle <*cartas*>; **~-se** *vpr* get muddled up

embar|cação /ĩbarka'sãw/ *f* vessel; **~cadouro** *m* wharf; **~car** *vt*/*i* board, embark

embar|gado /ĩbar'gadu/ *a* <*voz*> faltering; **~go** *m* embargo

embarque /ĩ'barki/ *m* boarding; (*seção do aeroporto*) departures

embasba|cado /ĩbazba'kadu/ *a* open-mouthed; **~car-se** *vpr* be left open-mouthed

embate /ĩ'batʃi/ *m* (*de carros etc*) crash; (*fig*) clash

embebedar /ĩbebe'dar/ *vt* make drunk; **~-se** *vpr* get drunk

embeber /ĩbe'ber/ *vt* soak; **~-se de** soak up; **~-se em** get absorbed in

embele|zador /ĩbeleza'dor/ *a* <*cirurgia*> cosmetic; **~zar** *vt* embellish; spruce up <*casa*>; **~zar-se** *vpr* make o.s. beautiful

embevecer /ĩbeve'ser/ *vt* captivate, engross; **~-se** *vpr* get engrossed, be captivated

emblema /ẽ'blema/ *m* emblem

embocadura /ĩboka'dura/ *f* (*de instrumento*) mouthpiece; (*de freio*) bit; (*de rio*) mouth; (*de rua*) entrance

êmbolo /'ẽbulu/ *m* piston

embolsar /ĩbow'sar/ *vt* pocket; (*reembolsar*) reimburse

embora /ĩ'bɔra/ *adv* away □ *conj* although

emborcar /ĩbor'kar/ *vi* overturn; <*barco*> capsize

emboscada /ĩbos'kada/ *f* ambush

embrai|agem /ẽbraj'aʒẽ/ (*Port*) *f veja* **embreagem**; **~ar** (*Port*) *vi veja* **embrear**

embre|agem /ẽbri'aʒẽ/ *f* clutch; **~ar** *vi* let in the clutch

embria|gar /ẽbria'gar/ *vt* intoxicate; **~gar-se** *vpr* get drunk, become intoxicated; **~guez** /e/ *f* drunkenness; **~guez no volante** drunken driving

embri|ão /ẽbri'ãw/ *m* embryo; **~onário** *a* embryonic

embro|mação /ĩbroma'sãw/ *f* flannel; **~mar** *vt* flannel, string along; (*enganar*) con □ *vi* stall, drag one's feet

embru|lhada /ĩbru'ʎada/ *f* muddle; **~lhar** *vt* wrap up <*pacote*>; upset <*estômago*>; (*confundir*) muddle up; **~lhar-se** *vpr* <*pessoa*> get muddled up; **~lho** *m* parcel; (*fig*) mix-up

embur|rado /ĩbu'xadu/ *a* sulky; **~rar** *vi* sulk

embuste /ĩ'bustʃi/ *m* hoax, put-up job

embu|tido /ĩbu'tʃidu/ *a* built-in, fitted; **~tir** *vt* build in, fit

emen|da /e'mẽda/ *f* correction, improvement; (*de lei*) amendment, **~dar** *vt* correct; amend <*lei*>; **~dar-se** *vpr* mend one's ways

ementa /i'mẽta/ (*Port*) *f* menu

emer|gência /emer'ʒẽsia/ *f* emergency; **~gente** *a* emergent; **~gir** *vi* surface

emi|gração /emigra'sãw/ *f* emigration; (*de aves etc*) migration; **~grado** *a & m* émigré; **~grante** *a & m/f* emigrant; **~grar** *vi* emigrate; <*aves, animais*> migrate

emi|nência /emi'nẽsia/ *f* eminence; **~nente** *a* eminent

emis|são /emi'sãw/ *f* (*de ações etc*) issue; (*na rádio, TV*) transmission, broadcast; (*de som, gases*) emission; **~sário** *m* emissary; **~sor** *m* transmitter; **~sora** *f* (*de rádio*) radio station; (*de TV*) TV station

emitir /emi'tʃir/ *vt* issue <*ações, selos etc*>; emit <*sons*>; (*pela rádio, TV*) transmit, broadcast

emoção /emo'sãw/ *f* emotion; (*excitação*) excitement

emocio|nal /emosio'naw/ (*pl* **~nais**) *a* emotional; **~nante** *a* (*excitante*) exciting; (*comovente*) touching, emotional; **~nar** *vt* (*excitar*) excite; (*comover*) move, touch; **~nar-se** *vpr* get emotional

emoldurar /emowdu'rar/ *vt* frame

emotivo /emo'tʃivu/ *a* emotional

empacar /ĩpa'kar/ *vi* <*cavalo*> baulk; <*negociações etc*> grind to a halt; <*orador*> dry up

empacotar /ĩpako'tar/ *vt* pack up; (*pôr em pacotes*) packet

empa|da /ẽ'pada/ *f* pie; **~dão** *m* (large) pie

empalhar /ĩpa'ʎar/ *vt* stuff

empalidecer /ĩpalide'ser/ *vi* turn pale

empanar[1] /ẽpa'nar/ *vt* tarnish, dull

empanar[2] /ẽpa'nar/ *vt* cook in batter <*carne etc*>

empanturrar /ĩpãtu'xar/ *vt* stuff; **~-se** *vpr* stuff o.s. (**de** with)

empapar /ĩpa'par/ *vt* soak

empa|tar /ẽpa'tar/ *vt* draw <*jogo*> □ *vi* <*times*> draw; <*corredores*> tie; **~te** *m* (*em jogo*) draw; (*em corrida, votação*) tie; (*em xadrez, fig*) stalemate

empatia /ẽpa'tʃia/ *f* empathy

empecilho /ẽpe'siʎu/ *m* hindrance

empenar /ẽpe'nar/ *vt/i* warp

empe|nhar /ĩpe'ɲar/ *vt* (*penhorar*) pawn; (*prometer*) pledge; **~nhar-se** *vpr* do one's utmost (**em** to); **~nho** /e/ *m* (*compromisso*) pledge; (*diligência*) effort, commitment

emperrar /ĩpe'xar/ *vt* make stick □ *vi* stick

emperti|gado /ĩpertʃi'gadu/ *a* upright; **~gar-se** *vpr* stand up straight

empilhar /ĩpi'ʎar/ *vt* pile up

empi|nado /ĩpi'nadu/ *a* erect; (*íngreme*) sheer, steep; <*nariz*> turned-up; (*fig*) stuck-up; **~nar** *vt* stand upright; fly <*pipa*>; tip up <*copo*>

empírico /ẽ'piriku/ *a* empirical

emplacar /ĩpla'kar/ *vt* notch up <*pontos, sucessos, anos*>; license <*carro*>

emplastro /ĩ'plastru/ *m* surgical plaster; **~ de nicotina** nicotine patch

empobre|cer /ĩpobre'ser/ *vt* impoverish; **~cimento** *m* impoverishment

empoleirar /ĩpole'rar/ *vt* perch; **~-se** *vpr* perch

empol|gação /ĩpowga'sãw/ *f* fascination; **~gante** *a* fascinating; **~gar** *vt* fascinate

empossar /ĩpo'sar/ *vt* swear in

empreen|dedor /ẽpriẽde'dor/ *a* enterprising □ *m* entrepreneur; **~der** *vt* undertake; **~dimento** *m* undertaking

empre|gada /ĩpre'gada/ *f* (*doméstica*) maid; **~gado** *m* employee; **~gador** *m* employer; **~gar** *vt* employ; **~gar-se** *vpr* get a job; **~gatício** *a* **vínculo ~gatício** contract of employment; **~go** /e/ *m* (*trabalho*) job; (*uso*) use

emprei|tada /ĩprej'tada/ *f* commission, contract; (*empreendimento*) venture; **~teira** *f* contractor, firm of contractors; **~teiro** *m* contractor

empre|sa /ĩ'preza/ *f* company; **~ dot.com** dot-com; **~sariado** *m* business community; **~sarial** (*pl* **~sariais**) *a* business; **~sário** *m* businessman; (*de cantor etc*) manager

empres|tado /ĩpres'tadu/ *a* on loan; **pedir ~tado** (ask to) borrow; **tomar ~tado** borrow; **~tar** *vt* lend

empréstimo /ĩ'prɛstʃimu/ *m* loan

empur|rão /ĩpu'xãw/ *m* push; **~rar** *vt* push

emular /emu'lar/ *vt* emulate

enamorado /enamo'radu/ *a* (*apaixonado*) in love

encabeçar /ĩkabe'sar/ *vt* head

encabu|lado /ĩkabu'ladu/ *a* shy; **~lar** *vt* embarrass; **~lar-se** *vpr* be shy

encadear /ĩkade'ar/ *vt* chain *ou* link together

encader|nação /ĩkaderna'sãw/ *f* binding; **~nado** *a* bound; (*com capa dura*) hardback; **~nar** *vt* bind

encai|xar /ĩka'ʃar/ *vt/i* fit; **~xe** *m* (*cavidade*) socket; (*juntura*) joint

encalço /ĩ'kawsu/ *m* pursuit; **no ~ de** in pursuit of

encalhar /ĩka'ʎar/ *vi* <*barco*> run aground; (*fig*) get bogged down; <*mercadoria*> not sell; (*fam: ficar solteiro*) be left on the shelf

encaminhar /ĩkami'ɲar/ *vt* (*dirigir*) steer, direct; (*remeter*) pass on; set in motion <*processo*>; **~-se** *vpr* set out

encana|dor /ĩkana'dor/ *m* plumber; **~mento** *m* plumbing

encan|tador /ĩkãta'dor/ *a* enchanting; **~tamento** *m* enchantment; **~tar** *vt* enchant; **~to** *m* charm

encaraco|lado /ĩkarako'ladu/ *a* curly; **~lar** *vt* curl; **~lar-se** *vpr* curl up

encarar /ĩka'rar/ *vt* confront, face

encarcerar /ĩkarse'rar/ *vt* imprison

encardido /ĩkar'dʒidu/ *a* grimy

encarecidamente /ĩkaresida-'mẽtʃi/ *adv* insistently

encargo /ĩ'kargu/ *m* task, responsibility

encar|nação /ĩkarna'sãw/ *f* (*do espírito*) incarnation; (*de um personagem*) embodiment; **~nar** *vt* embody; play <*papel*>

encarre|gado /ĩkaxe'gadu/ *a* in charge (**de** of) □ *m* person in charge; (*de operários*) foreman; **~gado de negócios** chargé d'affaires; **~gar** *vt* **~gar alg de** put s.o. in charge of; **~gar-se de** undertake to

encarte /ĩ'kartʃi/ *m* insert

ence|nação /ĩsena'sãw/ *f* (*de peça*) production; (*fingimento*) playacting; **~nar** *vt* put on □ *vi* put it on

ence|radeira /ĩsera'dera/ *f* floor polisher; **~rar** *vt* wax

encer|rado /ĩse'xadu/ *a* <*assunto*> closed; **~ramento** *m* close; **~rar** *vt* close; **~rar-se** *vpr* close

encharcar /ĩʃar'kar/ *vt* soak

en|chente /ẽ'ʃẽtʃi/ *f* flood; **~cher** *vt* fill; (*fam*) annoy □ (*fam*) *vi* be annoying; **~cher-se** *vpr* fill up; (*fam: fartar-se*) get fed up (**de** with)

enciclopédia /ẽsiklo'pɛdʒia/ *f* encyclopaedia

enco|berto /ĩko'bɛrtu/ *a* <*céu, tempo*> overcast; **~brir** *vt* cover up □ *vi* <*tempo*> become overcast

encolher /ĩko'ʎer/ *vt* shrug <*ombros*>; pull up <*pernas*>; shrink <*roupa*> □ *vi* <*roupa*> shrink; **~-se** *vpr* (*de medo*) shrink; (*de frio*) huddle; (*espremer-se*) squeeze up

encomen|da /ĩko'mẽda/ *f* order; **de** *ou* **sob ~da** to order; **~dar** *vt* order (**a** from)

encon|trão /ĩkõ'trãw/ *m* bump; (*empurrão*) shove; **~trar** *vt* (*achar*) find; (*ver*) meet; **~trar com** meet; **~trar-se** *vpr* (*ver-se*) meet; (*estar*) be; **~tro** *m* meeting; (*mil*) encounter; **ir ao ~tro de** go to meet; (*fig*) meet; **ir de ~tro a** run into; (*fig*) go against

encorajar /ĩkora'ʒar/ *vt* encourage

encor|pado /ĩkor'padu/ *a* stocky; <*vinho*> full-bodied; **~par** *vt/i* fill out

encos|ta /ĩ'kɔsta/ *f* slope; **~tar** *vt* (*apoiar*) lean; park <*carro*>; leave on the latch <*porta*>; (*pôr de lado*) put aside □ *vi* <*carro*> pull in; **~tar-se** *vpr* lean; **~to** /o/ *m* back

encra|vado /ĩkra'vadu/ *a* <*unha, pêlo*> ingrowing; **~var** *vt* stick

encren|ca /ĩ'krẽka/ *f* fix, jam; *pl* trouble; **~car** *vt* get into trouble <*pessoa*>; complicate <*situação*> □ *vi* <*situação*> get complicated; <*carro*> break down; **~car-se** *vpr* <*pessoa*> get into trouble; **~queiro** *m* troublemaker

encres|pado /ĩkres'padu/ *a* <*mar*> choppy; **~par** *vt* frizz <*cabelo*>; **~par-se** *vpr* <*cabelo*> go frizzy; <*mar*> get choppy

encruzilhada /ĩkruzi'ʎada/ *f* crossroads

encurralar /ĩkuxa'lar/ *vt* hem in

encurtar /ĩkur'tar/ *vt* shorten

endere|çar /ĩdere'sar/ *vt* address; **~ço** /e/ *m* address; (*comput*) **~ço de e-mail** email address

endinheirado /ĩdʒiɲe'radu/ *a* well-off

endireitar /ĩdʒirej'tar/ *vt* straighten; **~-se** *vpr* straighten up

endivi|dado /ĩdʒivi'dadu/ *a* in debt; **~dar** *vt* put into debt; **~dar-se** *vpr* get into debt

endoidecer /ĩdojde'ser/ *vi* get mad

endos|sar /ĩdo'sar/ *vt* endorse; **~so** /o/ *m* endorsement

endurecer /ĩdure'ser/ *vt/i* harden

ener|gético /ener'ʒɛtʃiku/ *a* energy; **~gia** *f* energy

enérgico /e'nɛrʒiku/ *a* vigorous; <*remédio, discurso*> powerful

enevoado /enevu'adu/ *a* (*com névoa*) misty; (*com nuvens*) cloudy

enfarte /ĩ'fartʃi/ *m* heart attack

ênfase /'ẽfazi/ *f* emphasis; **dar ~ a** emphasize

enfático /ẽ'fatʃiku/ *a* emphatic

enfatizar /ẽfatʃi'zar/ *vt* emphasize

enfei|tar /ĩfej'tar/ *vt* decorate; **~tar-se** *vpr* dress up; **~te** *m* decoration

enfeitiçar /ĩfejtʃi'sar/ *vt* bewitch

enfer|magem /ĩfer'maʒẽ/ *f* nursing; **~maria** *f* ward; **~meira** *f* nurse; **~meiro** *m* male nurse; **~midade** *f* illness; **~mo** *a* sick □ *m* patient

enferru|jado /ĩfexu'ʒadu/ *a* rusty; **~jar** *vt/i* rust

enfezado /ĩfe'zadu/ *a* bad-tempered

enfiar /ẽfi'ar/ *vt* put; slip on <*roupa*>; thread <*agulha*>; string <*pérolas*>

enfileirar /ĩfilej'rar/ *vt* line up; **~-se** *vpr* line up

enfim /ẽ'fĩ/ *adv* (*finalmente*) finally; (*resumindo*) anyway

enfo|car /ĩfo'kar/ *vt* tackle; **~que** *m* approach

enfor|camento /ĩforka'mẽtu/ *m* hanging; **~car** *vt* hang; **~car-se** *vpr* hang o.s.

enfraquecer /ĩfrake'ser/ *vt/i* weaken

enfrentar /ĩfrẽ'tar/ *vt* face

enfumaçado /ĩfuma'sadu/ *a* smoky

enfurecer /ĩfure'ser/ *vt* infuriate; **~-se** *vpr* get furious

enga|jamento /ĩgaʒa'mẽtu/ *m* commitment; **~jado** *a* committed; **~jar-se** *vpr* get involved (**em** in)

engalfinhar-se /ĩgawfi'ɲarsi/ *vpr* grapple

enga|nado /ĩga'nadu/ *a* (*errado*) mistaken; **~nar** *vt* deceive; cheat on <*marido, esposa*>; stave off <*fome*>; **~nar-se** *vpr* be mistaken; **~no** *m* (*erro*) mistake; (*desonestidade*) deception

engarra|famento /ĩgaxafa'mẽtu/ *m* traffic jam; **~far** *vt* bottle <*vinho etc*>; block <*trânsito*>

engas|gar /ĩgaz'gar/ *vt* choke □ *vi* choke; <*motor*> backfire; **~go** *m* choking

engastar /ĩgaʃ'tar/ *vt* set <*jóias*>

engatar /ĩga'tar/ *vt* hitch <*reboque etc*> (**a** to); engage <*marcha*>

engatinhar /ĩgatʃi'ɲar/ *vi* crawl; (*fig*) start out

engave|tamento /ĩgaveta'mẽtu/ *m* pile-up; **~tar** *vt* shelve

engelhar /ĩʒe'ʎar/ *vi* (*pele*) wrinkle

enge|nharia /ĩʒeɲa'ria/ *f* engineering; **~nheiro** *m* engineer; **~nho** /e/ *m* (*de pessoa*) ingenuity; (*de açúcar*) sugar mill; (*máquina*) device; **~nhoca** /ɔ/ *f* gadget; **~nhoso** *a* ingenious

engessar /ĩʒe'sar/ *vt* put in plaster

engodo /ĩ'godu/ *m* lure

engolir /ĩgo'lir/ *vt/i* swallow; **~ em seco** gulp

engomar /ĩgo'mar/ *vt* press; (*com goma*) starch

engordar /ĩgor'dar/ *vt* make fat; fatten <*animais*> □ *vi* <*pessoa*> put on weight; <*comida*> be fattening

engraçado /ĩgra'sadu/ *a* funny

engradado /ĩgra'dadu/ *m* crate

engravidar /ĩgravi'dar/ *vt* make pregnant □ *vi* get pregnant

engraxar /ĩgra'ʃar/ *vt* polish

engre|nado /ĩgre'nadu/ *a* <*carro*> in gear; **~nagem** *f* gear; (*fig*) mechanism; **~nar** *vt* put into gear <*carro*>; strike up <*conversa*>; **~nar-se** *vpr* mesh; (*fig*) <*pessoas*> get on

engrossar /ĩgro'sar/ *vt* thicken; raise <*voz*> □ *vi* thicken; <*pessoa*> turn nasty

enguia /ẽ'gia/ *f* eel

engui|çar /ẽgi'sar/ *vi* break down; **~ço** *m* breakdown

enig|ma /e'nigima/ *m* enigma; **~mático** *a* enigmatic

enjaular /ĩʒaw'lar/ *vt* cage

enjo|ar /ĩʒo'ar/ *vt* sicken □ *vi*, **~ar-se** *vpr* get sick (**de** of); **~ativo** *a* <*comida*> sickly; <*livro etc*> boring

enjôo /ĩ'ʒou/ *m* sickness

enlameado /ĩlami'adu/ *a* muddy

enlatado /ĩla'tadu/ *a* tinned, canned; **~s** *m pl* tinned foods

enle|var /ẽle'var/ *vt* enthral; **~vo** /e/ *m* rapture

enlouquecer /ĩloke'ser/ *vt* drive mad □ *vi* go mad

enluarado /ĩlua'radu/ *a* moonlit

enor|me /e'nɔrmi/ *a* enormous; **~midade** *f* enormity

enquadrar /ĩkwa'drar/ *vt* fit □ *vi*, **~-se** *vpr* fit in

enquanto /ĩ'kwãtu/ *conj* while; **~ isso** meanwhile; **por ~** for the time being

enquete /ã'kɛtʃi/ *f* survey

enraivecer /ĩxajve'ser/ *vt* enrage

enredo /ẽ'redu/ *m* plot

enrijecer /ĩxiʒe'ser/ *vt* stiffen; **~-se** *vpr* stiffen

enrique|cer /ĩxike'ser/ *vt* (*dar dinheiro a*) make rich; (*fig*) enrich □ *vi* get rich; **~cimento** *m* enrichment

enro|lado /ĩxo'ladu/ *a* complicated; **~lar** *vt* (*envolver*) roll up; (*complicar*) complicate; (*enganar*) cheat; **~lar-se** *vpr* (*envolver-se*) roll up; (*confundir-se*) get mixed up

enroscar /ĩxos'kar/ *vt* twist

enrouquecer /ĩxoke'ser/ *vi* go hoarse

enrugar /ĩxu'gar/ *vt* wrinkle <*pele, tecido*>; furrow <*testa*>

enrustido /ĩxus'tʃidu/ *a* repressed

ensaboar /ĩsabo'ar/ *vt* soap

ensai|ar /ĩsaj'ar/ *vt* (*provar*) try out; (*repetir*) rehearse; **~o** *m* (*prova*) test; (*repetição*) rehearsal; (*escrito*) essay

ensangüentado /ĩsãgwẽ'tadu/ *a* bloody, bloodstained

enseada /ĩsi'ada/ *f* inlet

ensebado /ĩse'badu/ *a* greasy

ensimesmado /ĩsimez'madu/ *a* lost in thought

ensi|nar /ẽsi'nar/ *vt/i* teach (**aco a alg** s.o. sth); **~nar alg a nadar** teach s.o. to swim; **~no** *m* teaching; (*em geral*) education

ensolarado /ĩsola'radu/ *a* sunny

enso|pado /ĩso'padu/ *a* soaked □ *m* stew; **~par** *vt* soak

ensurde|cedor /ĩsurdese'dor/ *a* deafening; **~cer** *vt* deafen □ *vi* go deaf

entabular /ĩtabu'lar/ *vt* open, start

entalar /ĩta'lar/ *vt* wedge, jam; (*em apertos*) get; **~-se** *vpr* get wedged, get jammed; (*em apertos*) get caught up

entalhar /ĩta'ʎar/ *vt* carve

entanto /ĩ'tãtu/ *m* **no ~** however

então /ĩ'tãw/ *adv* then; (*nesse caso*) so

entardecer /ĩtarde'ser/ *m* sunset

ente /'ẽtʃi/ *m* being

entea|da /ẽtʃi'ada/ *f* stepdaughter; **~do** *m* stepson

entedi|ante /ĩtedʒi'ãtʃi/ *a* boring; **~ar** *vt* bore; **~ar-se** *vpr* get bored

enten|der /ĩtẽ'der/ *vt* understand; **~der-se** *vpr* (*dar-se bem*) get on (**com** with); **dar a ~der** give to understand; **~der de futebol** know about football; **~dimento** *m* understanding

enternecedor /ĩternese'dor/ *a* touching

enter|rar /ĩte'xar/ *vt* bury; **~ro** /e/ *m* burial; (*cerimônia*) funeral

entidade /ẽtʃi'dadʒi/ *f* entity; (*órgão*) body

entornar /ĩtor'nar/ *vt* tip over, spill

entorpe|cente /ĩtorpe'sẽtʃi/ *m* drug, narcotic; **~cer** *vt* numb

entortar /ĩtor'tar/ *vt* make crooked

entrada /ẽ'trada/ *f* entry; (*onde se entra*) entrance; (*bilhete*) ticket; (*prato*) starter; (*pagamento*) deposit; *pl* (*no cabelo*) receding hairline; **dar ~ a** enter; **~ proibida** no entry

entranhas /ĩ'traɲas/ *f pl* entrails

entrar /ẽ'trar/ *vi* go/come in; **~ com** enter <*dados*>; put in <*dinheiro*>; **~ em detalhes** go into details; **~ em vigor** come into force

entravar /ẽtra'var/ *vt* hamper

entre /'ẽtri/ *prep* between; (*em meio a*) among

entreaberto /ẽtria'bɛrtu/ *a* half-open

entrecortar /ẽtrikor'tar/ *vt* intersperse; (*cruzar*) intersect

entre|ga /ĩ'trɛga/ *f* delivery; (*rendição*) surrender; **~ga a domicílio** home delivery; **~gar** *vt* hand over; deliver <*mercadorias, cartas*>; hand in <*caderno, trabalho escolar*>; **~gar-se** *vpr* give o.s. up (**a** to); **~gue** *pp de* **entregar**

entrelaçar /ẽtrela'sar/ *vt* intertwine; clasp <*mãos*>

entrelinhas /ẽtri'liɲas/ *f pl* **ler nas ~** read between the lines

entremear /ẽtrimi'ar/ *vt* intersperse

entreolhar-se /ẽtrio'ʎarsi/ *vpr* look at one another

entretanto /ẽtre'tãtu/ *conj* however

entre|tenimento /ẽtreteni'mẽtu/ *m* entertainment; **~ter** *vt* entertain

entrever /ẽtre'ver/ *vt* glimpse

entrevis|ta /ẽtre'vista/ *f* interview; **~tador** *m* interviewer; **~tar** *vt* interview

entristecer /ĩtriste'ser/ *vt* sadden □ *vi* be saddened (**com** by)

entroncamento /ĩtrõka'mẽtu/ *m* junction

entrosar /ĩtro'zar/ *vt/i* integrate

entu|lhar /ĩtu'ʎar/ *vt* cram (**de** with); **~lho** *m* rubble

entupir /ĩtu'pir/ *vt* block; **~pir-se** *vpr* get blocked; (*de comida*) stuff o.s. (**de** with)

enturmar-se /ĩtur'marsi/ *vpr* mix in, fit in

entusias|mar /ĩtuziaz'mar/ *vt* fill with enthusiasm; **~mar-se** *vpr* get enthusiastic (**com** about); **~mo** *m* enthusiasm; **~ta** *m/f* enthusiast □ *a* enthusiastic

entusiástico /ĩtuzi'astʃiku/ *a* enthusiastic

enumerar /enume'rar/ *vt* enumerate

envelope /ẽve'lɔpi/ *m* envelope

envelhecer /ĩveʎe'ser/ *vt/i* age

envenenar /ĩvene'nar/ *vt* poison; (*fam*) soup up <*carro*>

envergadura /ĩverga'dura/ *f* wingspan; (*fig*) scale

envergo|nhado /ĩvergo'ɲadu/ *a* ashamed; (*constrangido*) embarrassed; **~nhar** *vt* disgrace; (*constranger*) embarrass; **~nhar-se** *vpr* be ashamed; (*acanhar-se*) get embarrassed

envernizar /ĩverni'zar/ *vt* varnish

en|viado /ẽvi'adu/ *m* envoy; **~viar** *vt* send; **~vio** *m* (*ato*) sending; (*remessa*) consignment
envidraçar /ĩvidra'sar/ *vt* glaze
enviesado /ĩvie'zadu/ *a* (*não vertical*) slanting; (*torto*) crooked
envol|vente /ĩvow'vẽtʃi/ *a* compelling, gripping; **~ver** *vt* (*embrulhar*) wrap; (*enredar*) involve; **~ver-se** *vpr* (*enrolar-se*) wrap o.s.; (*enredar-se*) get involved; **~vimento** *m* involvement
enxada /ẽ'ʃada/ *f* hoe
enxaguar /ẽʃa'gwar/ *vt* rinse
enxame /ẽ'ʃami/ *m* swarm
enxaqueca /ẽʃa'keka/ *f* migraine
enxergar /ĩʃer'gar/ *vt/i* see
enxer|tar /ĩʃer'tar/ *vt* graft; **~to** /e/ *m* graft
enxotar /ĩʃo'tar/ *vt* drive away
enxofre /ẽ'ʃofri/ *m* sulphur
enxo|val /ẽʃo'vaw/ (*pl* **~vais**) *m* (*de noiva*) trousseau; (*de bebê*) layette
enxugar /ĩʃu'gar/ *vt* dry; **~-se** *vpr* dry o.s.
enxurrada /ĩʃu'xada/ *f* torrent; (*fig*) flood
enxuto /ĩ'ʃutu/ *a* dry; <*corpo*> shapely
enzima /ẽ'zima/ *f* enzyme
epicentro /epi'sẽtru/ *m* epicentre
épico /'ɛpiku/ *a* epic
epidemia /epide'mia/ *f* epidemic
epi|lepsia /epilep'sia/ *f* epilepsy; **~léptico** *a & m* epileptic
epílogo /e'pilogu/ *m* epilogue
episódio /epi'zɔdʒiu/ *m* episode
epitáfio /epi'tafiu/ *m* epitaph
época /'ɛpoca/ *f* time; (*da história*) age, period; **fazer ~** make history; **móveis da ~** period furniture
epopéia /epo'pɛja/ *f* epic
equação /ekwa'sãw/ *f* equation
equador /ekwa'dor/ *m* equator; **o Equador** Ecuador
equatori|al /ekwatori'aw/ (*pl* **~ais**) *a* equatorial; **~ano** *a & m* Ecuadorian
equilibrar /ekili'brar/ *vt* balance; **~-se** *vpr* balance
equilíbrio /eki'libriu/ *m* balance
equipa /e'kipa/ (*Port*) *f* team
equi|pamento /ekipa'mẽtu/ *m* equipment; **~par** *vt* equip
equiparar /ekipa'rar/ *vt* equate (**com** with); **~-se** *vpr* compare (**a** with)
equipe /e'kipi/ *f* team
equitação /ekita'sãw/ *f* riding
equiva|lência /ekiva'lẽsia/ *f* equivalence; **~lente** *a* equivalent; **~ler** *vi* be equivalent (**a** to)
equivo|cado /ekivo'kadu/ *a* mistaken; **~car-se** *vpr* make a mistake
equívoco /e'kivoku/ *a* equivocal □ *m* mistake
era /'ɛra/ *f* era
erário /e'rariu/ *m* exchequer
ereção /ere'sãw/ *f* erection
eremita /ere'mita/ *m/f* hermit
ereto /e'rɛtu/ *a* erect
erguer /er'ger/ *vt* raise; erect <*monumento etc*>; **~-se** *vpr* rise
eri|çado /eri'sadu/ *a* bristling; **~çar-se** *vpr* bristle
ermo /'ermu/ *a* deserted □ *m* wilderness
erosão /ero'zãw/ *f* erosion
erótico /e'rɔtʃiku/ *a* erotic
erotismo /ero'tʃizmu/ *m* eroticism
er|rado /e'xadu/ *a* wrong; **~rante** *a* wandering; **~rar** *vt* (*não fazer certo*) get wrong; miss <*alvo*> □ *vi* (*enganar-se*) be wrong; (*vaguear*) wander; **~ro** /e/ *m* mistake; **fazer um ~ro** make a mistake; **~rôneo** *a* erroneous
erudi|ção /erudʒi'sãw/ *f* learning; **~to** *a* learned; <*música*> classical □ *m* scholar
erupção /erup'sãw/ *f* (*vulcânica*) eruption; (*cutânea*) rash
erva /'ɛrva/ *f* herb; **~ daninha** weed; **~-doce** *f* aniseed
ervilha /er'viʎa/ *f* pea
esban|jador /izbãʒa'dor/ *a* extravagant □ *m* spendthrift; **~jar** *vt* squander; burst with <*saúde, imaginação, energia etc*>
esbar|rão /izba'xãw/ *m* bump; **~rar** *vi* **~rar com** *ou* **em** bump into <*pessoa*>; come up against <*problema*>
esbelto /iz'bɛwtu/ *a* svelte
esbo|çar /izbo'sar/ *vt* sketch <*desenho etc*>; outline <*plano etc*>; **~çar um sorriso** give a hint of a smile; **~ço** /o/ *m* (*desenho*) sketch; (*plano*) outline; (*de um sorriso*) hint
esbofetear /izbofetʃi'ar/ *vt* slap
esborrachar /izboxa'ʃar/ *vt* squash; **~-se** *vpr* crash
esbravejar /izbrave'ʒar/ *vi* rant, rail
esbura|cado /izbura'kadu/ *a* full of holes; **~car** *vt* make holes in
esbuga|lhado /izbuga'ʎadu/ *a* <*olhos*> bulging; **~lhar-se** *vpr* <*olhos*> pop out
escabroso /iska'brozu/ *a* (*fig*) difficult, tough
escada /is'kada/ *f* (*dentro de casa*) stairs; (*na rua*) steps; (*de mão*) ladder; **~ de incêndio** fire escape; **~ rolante** escalator; **~ria** *f* staircase
escafan|drista /iskafã'drista/ *m/f* diver; **~dro** *m* diving suit
escala /is'kala/ *f* scale; (*de navio*) port of call; (*de avião*) stopover; **fazer ~** stop over; **sem ~** <*vôo*> non-stop

esca|lada /iska'lada/ *f* (*fig*) escalation; **~lão** *m* echelon, level; **~lar** *vt* (*subir a*) scale; (*designar*) select

escaldar /iskaw'dar/ *vt* scald; blanch <*vegetais*>

escalfar /iskaw'far/ *vt* poach

escalonar /iskalo'nar/ *vt* schedule <*pagamento*>

escama /is'kama/ *f* scale

escanca|rado /iskãka'radu/ *a* wide open; **~rar** *vt* open wide

escandalizar /iskãdali'zar/ *vt* scandalize; **~-se** *vpr* be scandalized

escândalo /is'kãdalu/ *m* (*vexame*) scandal; (*tumulto*) fuss, uproar; **fazer um ~** make a scene

escandaloso /iskãda'lozu/ *a* (*chocante*) scandalous; (*espalhafatoso*) outrageous, loud

Escandinávia /iskãdʒi'navia/ *f* Scandinavia

escandinavo /iskãdʒi'navu/ *a* & *m* Scandinavian

escanga|lhado /iskãga'ʎadu/ *a* broken; **~lhar** *vt* break up; **~lhar-se** *vpr* fall to pieces; **~lhar-se de rir** split one's sides laughing

escaninho /iska'niɲu/ *m* pigeonhole

escanteio /iskã'teju/ *m* corner

esca|pada /iska'pada/ *f* (*fuga*) escape; (*aventura*) escapade; **~pamento** *m* exhaust; **~par** *vi* **~par a** *ou* **de** (*livrar-se*) escape from; (*evitar*) escape; **~pou-lhe a palavra** the word slipped out; **o copo ~pou-me das mãos** the glass slipped out of my hands; **o nome me ~pa** the name escapes me; **~par de boa** have a narrow escape; **~patória** *f* way out; (*desculpa*) pretext; **~pe** *m* escape; (*de carro etc*) exhaust; **~pulir** *vi* escape (**de** from)

escaramuça /iskara'musa/ *f* skirmish

escaravelho /iskara'vɛʎu/ *m* beetle

escarcéu /iskar'sɛw/ *m* uproar, fuss

escarlate /iskar'latʃi/ *a* scarlet

escarnecer /iskarne'ser/ *vt* mock

escárnio /is'karniu/ *m* derision

escarpado /iskar'padu/ *a* steep

escarrado /iska'xadu/ *m* **ele é o pai ~** he's the spitting image of his father

escarro /is'kaxu/ *m* phlegm

escas|sear /iskasi'ar/ *vi* run short; **~sez** *f* shortage; **~so** *a* (*raro*) scarce; (*ralo*) scant

esca|vadeira /iskava'dera/ *f* digger; **~var** *vt* excavate

esclare|cer /isklare'ser/ *vt* explain <*fatos*>; enlighten <*pessoa*>; **~cer-se** *vpr* <*fato*> be explained; <*pessoa*> find out; **~cimento** *m* (*de pessoas*) enlightenment; (*de fatos*) explanation

esclerosado /isklero'zadu/ *a* senile

escoar /isko'ar/ *vt*/*i* drain

esco|cês /isko'ses/ *a* (*f* **~cesa**) Scottish □ *m* (*f* **~cesa**) Scot

Escócia /is'kɔsia/ *f* Scotland

esco|la /is'kɔla/ *f* school; **~la de samba** samba school; **~lar** *a* school □ *m*/*f* schoolchild; **~laridade** *f* schooling

esco|lha /is'koʎa/ *f* choice; **~lher** *vt* choose

escol|ta /is'kɔwta/ *f* escort; **~tar** *vt* escort

escombros /is'kõbrus/ *m pl* debris

escon|de-esconde /iskõdʒis-'kõdʒi/ *m* hide-and-seek; **~der** *vt* hide; **~der-se** *vpr* hide; **~derijo** *m* hiding place; (*de bandidos*) hideout; **~didas** *f pl* **às ~didas** secretly

esco|ra /is'kɔra/ *f* prop; **~rar** *vt* prop up; **~rar-se** *vpr* <*argumento etc*> be based (**em** on)

escore /is'kɔri/ *m* score

escória /is'kɔria/ *f* scum, dross

escori|ação /iskoria'sãw/ *f* graze, abrasion; **~ar** *vt* graze

escorpião /iskorpi'ãw/ *m* scorpion; **Escorpião** Scorpio

escorredor /iskoxe'dor/ *m* drainer

escorrega /isko'xega/ *m* slide

escorre|gador /iskoxega'dor/ *m* slide; **~gão** *m* slip; **~gar** *vi* slip

escor|rer /isko'xer/ *vt* drain □ *vi* trickle; **~rido** *a* <*cabelo*> straight

escoteiro /isko'teru/ *m* boy scout

escotilha /isko'tʃiʎa/ *f* hatch

esco|va /is'kova/ *f* brush; **fazer ~va no cabelo** blow-dry one's hair; **~va de dentes** toothbrush; **~var** *vt* brush; **~vinha** *f* **cabelo à ~vinha** crew-cut

escra|chado /iskra'ʃadu/ (*fam*) *a* outspoken; **~char** (*fam*) *vt* tell off

escra|vatura /iskrava'tura/ *f* slavery; **~vidão** *f* slavery; **~vizar** *vt* enslave; **~vo** *m* slave

escre|vente /iskre'vẽtʃi/ *m*/*f* clerk; **~ver** *vt*/*i* write

escri|ta /is'krita/ *f* writing; **~to** *pp de* **escrever** □ *a* written; **por ~to** in writing; **~tor** *m* writer; **~tório** *m* office; (*numa casa*) study

escritu|ra /iskri'tura/ *f* (*a Bíblia*) scripture; (*contrato*) deed; **~ração** *f* bookkeeping; **~rar** *vt* keep, write up <*contas*>; draw up <*documento*>

escri|vaninha /iskriva'niɲa/ *f* bureau, writing desk; **~vão** *m* (*f* **~vã**) registrar

escrúpulo /is'krupulu/ *m* scruple

escrupuloso /iskrupu'lozu/ *a* scrupulous

escrutínio /iskru'tʃiniu/ *m* ballot

escu|dar /isku'dar/ *vt* shield; **~deria** *f* team; **~do** *m* shield; (*moeda*) escudo

escula|chado /iskula'ʃadu/ (*fam*) *a* sloppy; **~char** (*fam*) *vt* mess up <*coisa*>; tell off <*pessoa*>; **~cho** (*fam*) *m* (*bagunça*) mess; (*bronca*) telling-off

escul|pir /iskuw'pir/ *vt* sculpt; **~tor** *m* sculptor; **~tura** *f* sculpture; **~tural** (*pl* **~turais**) *a* statuesque

escuma /is'kuma/ *f* scum; **~deira** *f* skimmer

escuna /is'kuna/ *f* schooner

escu|ras /is'kuras/ *fpl* **às ~ras** in the dark; **~recer** *vt* darken □ *vi* get dark; **~ridão** *f* darkness; **~ro** *a* & *m* dark

escuso /is'kuzu/ *a* shady

escu|ta /is'kuta/ *f* listening; **estar à ~ta** be listening; **~ta telefônica** phone tapping; **~tar** *vt* (*perceber*) hear; (*prestar atenção a*) listen to □ *vi* (*poder ouvir*) hear; (*prestar atenção*) listen

esdrúxulo /iz'druʃulu/ *a* weird

esfacelar /isfase'lar/ *vt* wreck

esfalfar /isfaw'far/ *vt* wear out; **~-se** *vpr* get worn out

esfaquear /isfaki'ar/ *vt* stab

esfarelar /isfare'lar/ *vt* crumble; **~-se** *vpr* crumble

esfarrapado /isfaxa'padu/ *a* ragged; <*desculpa*> lame

es|fera /is'fɛra/ *f* sphere; **~férico** *a* spherical

esferográfi|co /isfero'grafiku/ *a* **caneta ~ca** ball-point pen

esfiapar /isfia'par/ *vt* fray; **~-se** *vpr* fray

esfinge /is'fiʒi/ *f* sphinx

esfolar /isfo'lar/ *vt* skin; (*fig*) overcharge

esfomeado /isfomi'adu/ *a* starving, famished

esfor|çar-se /isfor'sarsi/ *vpr* make an effort; **~ço** /o/ *m* effort; **fazer ~ço** make an effort

esfre|gaço /isfre'gasu/ *m* smear; **~gar** *vt* rub; (*para limpar*) scrub

esfriar /isfri'ar/ *vt* cool □ *vi* cool (down); (*sentir frio*) get cold

esfumaçado /isfuma'sadu/ *a* smoky

esfuziante /isfuzi'ãtʃi/ *a* irrepressible, exuberant

esganar /izga'nar/ *vt* throttle

esganiçado /izgani'sadu/ *a* shrill

esgarçar /izgar'sar/ *vt/i* fray

esgo|tado /izgo'tadu/ *a* exhausted; <*estoque, lotação*> sold out; **~tamento** *m* exhaustion; **~tamento nervoso** nervous breakdown; **~tar** *vt* exhaust; (*gastar*) use up; **~tar-se** *vpr* <*pessoa*> become exhausted; <*estoque, lotação*> sell out; <*recursos, provisões*> run out; **~to** /o/ *m* drain; (*de detritos*) sewer

esgri|ma /iz'grima/ *f* fencing; **~mir** *vt* brandish □ *vi* fence; **~mista** *m/f* fencer

esgrouvinhado /izgrovi'ɲadu/ *a* tousled, dishevelled

esgueirar-se /izge'rarsi/ *vpr* slip, sneak

esguelha /iz'geʎa/ *f* **de ~** askew; <*olhar*> askance

esgui|char /izgi'ʃar/ *vt/i* spurt, squirt; **~cho** *m* jet, spurt

esguio /iz'gio/ *a* slender

eslavo /iz'lavu/ *a* Slavic □ *m* Slav

esmaecer /izmaj'ser/ *vi* fade

esma|gador /izmaga'dor/ *a* <*vitória, maioria*> overwhelming; <*provas*> incontrovertible; **~gar** *vt* crush

esmalte /iz'mawtʃi/ *m* enamel; **~ de unhas** nail varnish

esmeralda /izme'rawda/ *f* emerald

esme|rar-se /izme'rarsi/ *vpr* take great care (**em** over); **~ro** /e/ *m* great care

esmigalhar /izmiga'ʎar/ *vt* crumble <*pão etc*>; shatter <*vidro, copo*>; **~-se** *vpr* <*pão etc*> crumble; <*vidro, copo*> shatter

esmiuçar /izmiu'sar/ *vt* examine in detail

esmo /'ezmu/ *m* **a ~** <*escolher*> at random; <*andar*> aimlessly; <*falar*> nonsense

esmola /iz'mɔla/ *f* donation; *pl* charity

esmorecer /izmore'ser/ *vi* flag

esmurrar /izmu'xar/ *vt* punch

esno|bar /izno'bar/ *vt* snub □ *vi* be snobbish; **~be** /iz'nɔbi/ *a* snobbish □ *m/f* snob; **~bismo** *m* snobbishness

esotérico /ezo'tɛriku/ *a* esoteric

espa|çar /ispa'sar/ *vt* space out; make less frequent <*visitas, consultas etc*>; **~cial** (*pl* **~ciais**) *a* space; **~ço** *m* space; (*cultural etc*) venue; **~çoso** /o/ *a* spacious

espada /is'pada/ *f* sword; *pl* (*naipe*) spades; **~chim** *m* swordsman

espádua /is'padua/ *f* shoulder blade

espaguete /ispa'gɛtʃi/ *m* spaghetti

espaire|cer /ispajre'ser/ *vt* amuse □ *vi* relax; (*dar uma volta*) go for a walk; **~cimento** *m* recreation

espaldar /ispaw'dar/ *m* back

espalhafato /ispaʎa'fatu/ *m* (*barulho*) fuss, uproar; (*de roupa etc*) extravagance; **~so** /o/ *a* (*barulhento*) noisy, rowdy; (*ostentoso*) extravagant

espalhar /ispa'ʎar/ *vt* scatter; spread <*notícia, terror etc*>; shed <*luz*>; **~-se** *vpr* spread; <*pessoas*> spread out

espa|nador /ispana'dor/ *m* feather duster; **~nar** *vt* dust

espan|camento /ispãka'mẽtu/ *m* beating; **~car** *vt* beat up

Espanha /is'paɲa/ *f* Spain

espa|nhol /ispa'ɲɔw/ (*pl* **~nhóis**) *a* (*f* **~nhola**) Spanish □ *m* (*f* **~nhola**) Spaniard; (*língua*) Spanish; **os ~nhóis** the Spanish

espan|talho /ispã'taʎu/ *m* scarecrow; **~tar** *vt* (*admirar*) amaze; (*assustar*) scare; (*afugentar*) drive away; **~tar-se** *vpr* (*admirar-se*) be amazed; (*assustar-se*) get scared; **~to** *m* (*susto*) fright; (*admiração*) amazement; **~toso** /o/ *a* amazing

esparadrapo /ispara'drapu/ *m* sticking plaster

espargo /is'pargu/ (*Port*) *m* asparagus

esparramar /ispaxa'mar/ *vt* scatter; **~-se** *vpr* be scattered, spread

espartano /ispar'tanu/ *a* spartan

espartilho /ispar'tʃiʎu/ *m* corset

espas|mo /is'pazmu/ *m* spasm; **~módico** *a* spasmodic

espatifar /ispatʃi'far/ *vt* smash; **~-se** *vpr* smash; <*carro, avião*> crash

especi|al /ispesi'aw/ (*pl* **~ais**) *a* special; **~alidade** *f* speciality; **~alista** *m/f* specialist

especiali|zado /ispesiali'zadu/ *a* specialized; <*mão-de-obra*> skilled; **~zar-se** *vpr* specialize (**em** in)

especiaria /ispesia'ria/ *f* spice

espécie /is'pɛsi/ *f* sort, kind; (*de animais*) species

especifi|cação /ispesifika'sãw/ *f* specification; **~car** *vt* specify

específico /ispe'sifiku/ *a* specific

espécime /is'pesimi/ *m* specimen

espectador /ispekta'dor/ *m* (*de TV*) viewer; (*de jogo, espetáculo*) spectator; (*de acidente etc*) onlooker

espectro /is'pɛktru/ *m* (*fantasma*) spectre; (*de cores*) spectrum

especu|lação /ispekula'sãw/ *f* speculation; **~lador** *m* speculator; **~lar** *vi* speculate (**sobre** on); **~lativo** *a* speculative

espe|lhar /ispe'ʎar/ *vt* mirror; **~lhar-se** *vpr* be mirrored; **~lho** /e/ *m* mirror; **~lho retrovisor** rear-view mirror

espelunca /ispe'lũka/ (*fam*) *f* dive

espera /is'pɛra/ *f* wait; **à ~ de** waiting for

esperan|ça /ispe'rãsa/ *f* hope; **~çoso** /o/ *a* hopeful

esperar /ispe'rar/ *vt* (*aguardar*) wait for; (*desejar*) hope for; (*contar com*) expect □ *vi* wait (**por** for); **fazer alg ~** keep s.o. waiting; **espero que ele venha** I hope (that) he comes; **espero que sim /não** I hope so/not

esperma /is'pɛrma/ *m* sperm

espernear /isperni'ar/ *vi* kick; (*fig: reclamar*) kick up

esper|talhão /isperta'ʎãw/ *m* (*f* **~talhona**) wise guy; **~teza** /e/ *f* cleverness; (*uma*) clever move; **~to** /e/ *a* clever

espes|so /is'pesu/ *a* thick; **~sura** *f* thickness

espe|tacular /ispetaku'lar/ *a* spectacular; **~táculo** *m* (*no teatro etc*) show; (*cena impressionante*) spectacle; **~taculoso** /o/ *a* spectacular

espe|tar /ispe'tar/ *vt* (*cravar*) stick; (*furar*) skewer; **~tar-se** *vpr* (*cravar-se*) stick; (*ferir-se*) prick o.s.; **~tinho** *m* skewer; (*de carne etc*) kebab; **~to** /e/ *m* spit

espevitado /ispevi'tadu/ *a* cheeky

espezinhar /ispezi'ɲar/ *vt* walk all over

espi|a /is'pia/ *m/f* spy; **~ão** *m* (*f* **~ã**) spy; **~ada** *f* peep; **~ar** *vt* (*observar*) spy on; (*aguardar*) watch for □ *vi* peer, peep

espicaçar /ispika'sar/ *vt* goad <*pessoa*>; excite <*imaginação, curiosidade*>

espichar /ispi'ʃar/ *vt* stretch □ *vi* shoot up; **~-se** *vpr* stretch out

espiga /is'piga/ *f* (*de trigo etc*) ear; (*de milho*) cob

espina|fração /ispinafra'sãw/ (*fam*) *f* telling-off; **~frar** (*fam*) *vt* tell off; **~fre** *m* spinach

espingarda /ispĩ'garda/ *f* rifle, shotgun

espinha /is'piɲa/ *f* (*de peixe*) bone; (*na pele*) spot; **~ dorsal** spine

espinho /is'piɲu/ *m* thorn; **~so** /o/ *a* thorny; (*fig*) difficult, tough

espio|nagem /ispio'naʒẽ/ *f* espionage, spying; **~nar** *vt* spy on □ *vi* spy

espi|ral /ispi'raw/ (*pl* **~rais**) *a* & *f* spiral

espírita /is'pirita/ *a* & *m/f* spiritualist

espiritismo /ispiri'tʃizmu/ *m* spiritualism

espírito /is'piritu/ *m* spirit; (*graça*) wit

espiritu|al /ispiritu'aw/ (*pl* **~ais**) *a* spiritual; **~oso** /o/ *a* witty

espir|rar /ispi'xar/ *vt* spurt □ *vi* <*pessoa*> sneeze; <*lama, tinta etc*> spatter; <*fogo, lenha, fritura etc*> spit; **~ro** *m* sneeze

esplêndido /is'plẽdʒidu/ *a* splendid

esplendor /isplẽ'dor/ *m* splendour

espoleta /ispo'leta/ *f* fuse

espoliar /ispoli'ar/ *vt* plunder, pillage

espólio /is'pɔliu/ *m* (*herdado*) estate; (*roubado*) spoils

espon|ja /is'põʒa/ *f* sponge; **~joso** /o/ *a* spongy

espon|taneidade /ispõtanej-'dadʒi/ *f* spontaneity; **~tâneo** *a* spontaneous

espora /is'pɔra/ *f* spur

esporádico /ispo'radʒiku/ *a* sporadic

esporear /ispori'ar/ *vt* spur on

espor|te /is'pɔrtʃi/ *m* sport □ *a invar* <*roupa*> casual; **carro ~te** sports car; **~tista** *m/f* sportsman (*f*-woman); **~tiva** *f* sense of humour; **~tivo** *a* sporting

espo|sa /is'poza/ *f* wife; **~so** *m* husband

espregui|çadeira /ispregisa'dera/ *f* (*tipo cadeira*) deckchair; (*tipo cama*) sun lounger; **~çar-se** *vpr* stretch

esprei|ta /is'prejta/ *f* **ficar à ~ta** lie in wait; **~tar** *vt* stalk <*caça, vítima*>; spy on <*vizinhos, inimigos etc*>; look out for <*ocasião*> □ *vi* peep, spy

espre|medor /ispreme'dor/ *m* squeezer; **~mer** *vt* squeeze; wring out <*roupa*>; squash <*pessoa*>; **~mer-se** *vpr* squeeze up

espu|ma /is'puma/ *f* foam; **~ma de borracha** foam rubber; **~mante** *a* <*vinho*> sparkling; **~mar** *vi* foam, froth

espúrio /is'puriu/ *a* spurious

esqua|dra /is'kwadra/ *f* squad; **~dra de polícia** (*Port*) police station; **~drão** *m* squadron; **~dria** *f* doors and windows; **~drinhar** *vt* explore; **~dro** *m* set square

esqualidez /iskwali'des/ *f* squalor

esquálido /is'kwalidu/ *a* squalid

esquartejar /iskwarte'ʒar/ *vt* chop up

esque|cer /iske'ser/ *vt/i* forget; **~cer-se de** forget; **~cido** *a* forgotten; (*com memória fraca*) forgetful; **~cimento** *m* oblivion; (*memória fraca*) forgetfulness

esque|lético /iske'lɛtʃiku/ *a* skinny, skeleton-like; **~leto** /e/ *m* skeleton

esque|ma /is'kema/ *m* outline, draft; (*operação*) scheme; **~ma de segurança** security operation; **~mático** *a* schematic

esquentar /iskẽ'tar/ *vt* warm up □ *vi* warm up; <*roupa*> be warm; **~-se** *vpr* get annoyed; **~ a cabeça** (*fam*) get worked up

esquer|da /is'kerda/ *f* left; **à ~da** (*posição*) on the left; (*direção*) to the left; **~dista** *a* left-wing □ *m/f* left-winger; **~do** /e/ *a* left

esqui /is'ki/ *m* ski; (*esporte*) skiing; **~ aquático** water skiing; **~ador** *m* skier; **~ar** *vi* ski

esquilo /is'kilu/ *m* squirrel

esquina /is'kina/ *f* corner

esquisi|tice /iskizi'tʃisi/ *f* strangeness; (*uma*) strange thing; **~to** *a* strange

esqui|var-se /iski'varsi/ *vpr* dodge out of the way; **~var-se de** dodge; **~vo** *a* elusive; <*pessoa*> aloof, antisocial

esquizo|frenia /iskizofre'nia/ *f* schizophrenia; **~frênico** *a* & *m* schizophrenic

es|sa /'ɛsa/ *pron* that (one); **~sa é boa** that's a good one; **~sa não** come off it; **por ~sas e outras** for these and other reasons; **~se** /e/ *a* that; *pl* those; (*fam: este*) this; *pl* these □ *pron* that one; *pl* those; (*fam: este*) this one; *pl* these

essência /e'sẽsia/ *f* essence

essenci|al /esẽsi'aw/ (*pl* **~ais**) *a* essential; **o ~al** what is essential

estabele|cer /istabele'ser/ *vt* establish; **~cer-se** *vpr* establish o.s.; **~cimento** *m* establishment

estabili|dade /istabili'dadʒi/ *f* stability; **~zar** *vt* stabilize; **~zar-se** *vpr* stabilize

estábulo /is'tabulu/ *m* cowshed

estaca /is'taka/ *f* stake; (*de barraca*) peg; **voltar à ~ zero** go back to square one

estação /ista'sãw/ *f* (*do ano*) season; (*ferroviária etc*) station; **~ balneária** seaside resort

estacar /ista'kar/ *vi* stop short

estacio|namento /istasiona'mẽtu/ *m* (*ação*) parking; (*lugar*) car park, (*Amer*) parking lot; **~nar** *vt/i* park

estada /is'tada/ *f*, **estadia** /ista-'dʒia/ *f* stay

estádio /is'tadʒiu/ *m* stadium

esta|dista /ista'dʒista/ *m/f* statesman (*f*-woman); **~do** *m* state; **~do civil** marital status; **~do de espírito** state of mind; **Estados Unidos da América** United States of America; **Estado-Maior** *m* Staff; **~dual** (*pl* **~duais**) *a* state

esta|fa /is'tafa/ *f* exhaustion; **~fante** *a* exhausting; **~far** *vt* tire out; **~far-se** *vpr* get tired out

estagi|ar /istaʒi'ar/ *vi* do a traineeship; **~ário** *m* trainee

estágio /is'taʒiu/ *m* traineeship

estag|nado /istagi'nadu/ *a* stagnant; **~nar** *vi* stagnate

estalagem /ista'laʒẽ/ *f* inn

estalar /ista'lar/ *vt* (*quebrar*) crack; (*fazer barulho com*) click □ *vi* crack

estaleiro /ista'leru/ *m* shipyard

estalo /is'talu/ *m* crack; (*de dedos, língua*) click; **me deu um ~** it clicked (in my mind)

estam|pa /is'tãpa/ *f* print; **~pado** *a* <*tecido*> patterned □ *m* (*desenho*) pattern; (*tecido*) print; **~par** *vt* print

estampido /istã'pidu/ *m* bang

estancar /istã'kar/ *vt* staunch; **~-se** *vpr* dry up

estância /is'tãsia/ *f* **~ hidromineral** spa
estandarte /istã'dartʃi/ *m* ban-ner
estanho /is'taɲu/ *m* tin
estanque /is'tãki/ *a* watertight
estante /is'tãtʃi/ *f* bookcase
estapafúrdio /istapa'furdʒiu/ *a* weird, odd
estar /is'tar/ *vi* be; **(~ em casa)** be in; **está chovendo**, (*Port*) **está a chover** it's raining; **~ com** have; **~ com calor /sono** be hot/sleepy; **~ para terminar** be about to finish; **ele não está para ninguém** he's not available to see anyone; **o trabalho está por terminar** the work is yet to be finished
estardalhaço /istarda'ʎasu/ *m* (*barulho*) fuss; (*ostentação*) extravagance
estarre|cedor /istaxese'dor/ *a* horrifying; **~cer** *vt* horrify; **~cer-se** *vpr* be horrified
esta|tal /ista'taw/ (*pl* **~tais**) *a* state-owned □ *f* state company
estate|lado /istate'ladu/ *a* sprawling; **~lar** *vt* knock down; **~lar-se** *vpr* go sprawling
estático /is'tatʃiku/ *a* static
estatísti|ca /ista'tʃistʃika/ *f* statistics; **~co** *a* statistical
estati|zação /istatʃiza'sãw/ *f* nationalization; **~zar** *vt* nationalize
estátua /is'tatua/ *f* statue
estatueta /istatu'eta/ *f* statuette
estatura /ista'tura/ *f* stature
estatuto /ista'tutu/ *m* statute
está|vel /is'tavew/ (*pl* **~veis**) *a* stable
este[1] /'ɛstʃi/ *m a invar* & *m* east
este[2] /'estʃi/ *a* this; *pl* these □ *pron* this one; *pl* these; (*mencionado por último*) the latter
esteio /is'teju/ *m* prop; (*fig*) mainstay
esteira /is'tera/ *f* (*tapete*) mat; (*rastro*) wake
estelionato /istelio'natu/ *m* fraud
estender /istẽ'der/ *vt* (*desdobrar*) spread out; (*alongar*) stretch; (*ampliar*) extend; hold out <*mão*>; hang out <*roupa*>; roll out <*massa*>; draw out <*conversa*>; **~-se** *vpr* (*deitar-se*) stretch out; (*ir longe*) stretch, extend; **~-se sobre** dwell on
esteno|datilógrafo /istenodatʃi-'lɔgrafu/ *m* shorthand typist; **~grafia** *f* shorthand
estepe /is'tɛpi/ *m* spare wheel
esterco /is'terku/ *m* dung
estéreo /is'tɛriu/ *a invar* stereo
estere|otipado /isteriotʃi'padu/ *a* stereotypical; **~ótipo** *m* stereotype
esté|ril /is'tɛriw/ (*pl* **~reis**) *a* sterile
esterili|dade /isterili'dadʒi/ *f* sterility; **~zar** *vt* sterilize
esterli|no /ister'lino/ *a* **libra ~na** pound sterling
esteróide /iste'rɔjdʒi/ *m* steroid
estética /is'tɛtʃika/ *f* aesthetics
esteticista /istetʃi'sista/ *m/f* beautician
estético /is'tɛtʃiku/ *a* aesthetic
estetoscópio /istetos'kɔpiu/ *m* stethoscope
estiagem /istʃi'aʒẽ/ *f* dry spell
estibordo /istʃi'bɔrdu/ *m* starboard
esti|cada /istʃi'kada/ *f* **dar uma ~cada** go on; **~car** *vt* stretch □ (*fam*) *vi* go on; **~car-se** *vpr* stretch out
estigma /is'tʃigima/ *m* stigma; **~tizar** *vt* brand (**de** as)
estilha|çar /istʃiʎa'sar/ *vt* shatter; **~çar-se** *vpr* shatter; **~ço** *m* shard, fragment
estilingue /istʃi'lĩgi/ *m* catapult
estilis|mo /istʃi'lizmu/ *m* fashion design; **~ta** *m/f* fashion designer
esti|lístico /istʃi'listʃiku/ *a* stylistic; **~lizar** *vt* stylize; **~lo** *m* style; **~lo de vida** lifestyle
esti|ma /es'tʃima/ *f* esteem; **~mação** *f* estimation; **cachorro de ~mação** pet dog; **~mado** *a* esteemed; **Estimado Senhor** Dear Sir; **~mar** *vt* value <*bens, jóias etc*> (**em** at); estimate <*valor, preço etc*> (**em** at); think highly of <*pessoa*>; **~mativa** *f* estimate
estimu|lante /istʃimu'lãtʃi/ *a* stimulating □ *m* stimulant; **~lar** *vt* stimulate; (*incentivar*) encourage
estímulo /is'tʃimulu/ *m* stimulus; (*incentivo*) incentive
estio /is'tʃiu/ *m* summer
estipu|lação /istʃipula'sãw/ *f* stipulation; **~lar** *vt* stipulate
estirar /istʃi'rar/ *vt* stretch; **~-se** *vpr* stretch
estirpe /is'tʃirpi/ *f* stock, line
estivador /istʃiva'dor/ *m* docker
estocada /isto'kada/ *f* thrust
estocar /isto'kar/ *vt* stock □ *vi* stock up
Estocolmo /isto'kɔwmu/ *f* Stockholm
esto|far /isto'far/ *vt* upholster <*móveis*>; **~fo** /o/ *m* upholstery
estóico /is'tɔjku/ *a* & *m* stoic
estojo /is'toʒu/ *m* case
estômago /is'tomagu/ *m* stomach
Estônia /is'tonia/ *f* Estonia
estonte|ante /istõtʃi'ãtʃi/ *a* stunning, mind-boggling; **~ar** *vt* stun
estopim /isto'pĩ/ *m* fuse; (*fig*) flashpoint
estoque /is'tɔki/ *m* stock
estore /is'tɔri/ *m* blind
estória /is'tɔria/ *f* story

estor|var /istor'var/ *vt* hinder; obstruct <*entrada, trânsito*>; **~vo** /o/ *m* hindrance

estou|rado /isto'radu/ *a* <*pessoa*> explosive; **~rar** *vi* <*bomba, escândalo, pessoa*> blow up; <*pneu*> burst; <*guerra*> break out; <*moda, cantor etc*> make it big; **~ro** *m* (*de bomba, moda etc*) explosion; (*de pessoa*) outburst; (*de pneu*) blowout; (*de guerra*) outbreak

estrábico /is'trabiku/ *a* <*olhos*> squinty; <*pessoa*> squint-eyed

estrabismo /istra'bizmu/ *m* squint

estraçalhar /istrasa'ʎar/ *vt* tear to pieces

estrada /is'trada/ *f* road; **~ de ferro** railway, (*Amer*) railroad; **~ de rodagem** highway; **~ de terra** dirt road

estrado /is'tradu/ *m* podium; (*de cama*) base

estraga-prazeres /istragapra'zeris/ *m/f invar* spoilsport

estragão /istra'gãw/ *m* tarragon

estra|gar /istra'gar/ *vt* (*tornar desagradável*) spoil; (*acabar com*) ruin □ *vi* (*quebrar*) break; (*apodrecer*) go off; **~go** *m* damage; *pl* damage; (*da guerra, do tempo*) ravages

estrangeiro /istrã'ʒeru/ *a* foreign □ *m* foreigner; **do ~** from abroad; **para o /no ~** abroad

estrangular /istrãgu'lar/ *vt* strangle

estra|nhar /istra'ɲar/ *vt* (*achar estranho*) find strange; (*não se adaptar a*) find it hard to get used to; (*não se sentir à vontade com*) be shy with; **~nhar que** find it strange that; **estou te ~nhando** that's not like you; **não é de se ~nhar** it's not surprising; **~nheza** /e/ *f* (*esquisitice*) strangeness; (*surpresa*) surprise; **~nho** *a* strange □ *m* stranger

estratagema /istrata'ʒema/ *m* stratagem

estraté|gia /istra'tɛʒia/ *f* strategy; **~gico** *a* strategic

estrato /is'tratu/ *m* (*camada*) stratum; (*nuvem*) stratus; **~sfera** *f* stratosphere

estre|ante /istri'ãtʃi/ *a* new □ *m/f* newcomer; **~ar** *vt* première <*peça, filme*>; embark on <*carreira*>; wear for the first time <*roupa*> □ *vi* <*pessoa*> make one's début; <*filme, peça*> open

estrebaria /istreba'ria/ *f* stable

estréia /is'trɛja/ *f* (*de pessoa*) début; (*de filme, peça*) première

estrei|tar /istrej'tar/ *vt* narrow; take in <*vestido*>; make closer <*relações, laços*> □ *vi* narrow; **~tar-se** *vpr* <*relações*> become closer; **~to** *a* narrow; <*relações, laços*> close; <*saia*> straight □ *m* strait

estre|la /is'trela/ *f* star; **~lado** *a* <*céu*> starry; <*ovo*> fried; **~lado por** <*filme etc*> starring; **~la-do-mar** (*pl* **~las-do-mar**) *f* starfish; **~lar** *vt* fry <*ovo*>; star in <*filme, peça*>; **~lato** *m* stardom; **~lismo** *m* star quality

estreme|cer /istreme'ser/ *vt* shake; strain <*relações, amizade*> □ *vi* shudder; <*relações, amizade*> become strained; **~cimento** *m* shudder; (*de relações, amizade*) strain

estrepar-se /istre'parsi/ (*fam*) *vpr* come a cropper

estrépito /ɪs'trɛpitu/ *m* noise; **com ~** noisily

estrepitoso /istrepi'tozu/ *a* noisy; <*sucesso etc*> resounding

estres|sante /istre'sãtʃi/ *a* stressful; **~sar** *vt* stress; **~se** /ɛ/ *m* stress

estria /is'tria/ *f* streak; (*no corpo*) stretch mark

estribeira /istri'bera/ *f* stirrup; **perder as ~s** lose control

estribilho /istri'biʎu/ *m* chorus

estribo /is'tribu/ *m* stirrup

estridente /istri'dẽtʃi/ *a* strident

estripulia /istripu'lia/ *f* antic

estrito /is'tritu/ *a* strict

estrofe /is'trɔfi/ *f* stanza, verse

estrogonofe /istrogo'nɔfi/ *m* stroganoff

estrógeno /is'trɔʒenu/ *m* oestrogen

estron|do /is'trõdu/ *m* crash; **~-doso** /o/ *a* loud; <*aplausos*> thunderous; <*sucesso, fracasso*> resounding

estropiar /istropi'ar/ *vt* cripple <*pessoa*>; mangle <*palavras*>

estrume /is'trumi/ *m* manure

estrutu|ra /istru'tura/ *f* structure; **~ral** (*pl* **~rais**) *a* structural; **~rar** *vt* structure

estuário /istu'ariu/ *m* estuary

estudan|te /istu'dãtʃi/ *m/f* student; **~til** (*pl* **~tis**) *a* student

estudar /istu'dar/ *vt/i* study

estúdio /is'tudʒiu/ *m* studio

estu|dioso /istudʒi'ozu/ *a* studious □ *m* scholar; **~do** *m* study

estufa /is'tufa/ *f* (*para plantas*) greenhouse; (*de aquecimento*) stove; **~do** *m* stew

estupefato /istupe'fatu/ *a* dumbfounded

estupendo /iste'pẽdu/ *a* stupendous

estupidez /istupi'des/ *f* (*grosseria*) rudeness; (*uma*) rude thing; (*burrice*) stupidity; (*uma*) stupid thing

estúpido /is'tupidu/ *a* (*grosso*) rude, coarse; (*burro*) stupid □ *m* lout

estupor /istu'por/ *m* stupor

estu|prador /istupra'dor/ *m* rapist; **~prar** *vt* rape; **~pro** *m* rape
esturricar /istuxi'kar/ *vt* parch
esvair-se /izva'irsi/ *vpr* fade; **~ em sangue** bleed to death
esvaziar /izvazi'ar/ *vt* empty; **~-se** *vpr* empty
esverdeado /izverdʒi'adu/ *a* greenish
esvoa|çante /izvoa'sãtʃi/ *a* <*cabelo*> fly-away; **~çar** *vi* flutter
eta /'eta/ *int* what a
etapa /e'tapa/ *f* stage; (*de corrida, turnê etc*) leg
etário /e'tariu/ *a* age
éter /'ɛter/ *m* ether
etéreo /e'tɛriu/ *a* ethereal
eter|nidade /eterni'dadʒi/ *f* eternity; **~no** /ɛ/ *a* eternal
éti|ca /'ɛtʃika/ *f* ethics; **~co** *a* ethical
etimo|logia /etʃimolo'ʒia/ *f* etymology; **~lógico** *a* etymological
etíope /e'tʃiopi/ *a & m/f* Ethiopian
Etiópia /etʃi'ɔpia/ *f* Ethiopia
etique|ta /etʃi'keta/ *f* (*rótulo*) label; (*bons modos*) etiquette; **~tar** *vt* label
étnico /'ɛtʃiniku/ *a* ethnic
eu /ew/ *pron* I ▫ *m* self; **mais alto do que ~** taller than me; **sou ~** it's me
EUA *m pl* USA
eucalipto /ewka'liptu/ *m* eucalyptus
eufemismo /ewfe'mizmu/ *m* euphemism
euforia /ewfo'ria/ *f* euphoria
euro /'ewru/ *m* euro
Europa /ew'rɔpa/ *f* Europe
euro|peu /ewro'pew/ *a & m* (*f* **~péia**) European
eutanásia /ewta'nazia/ *f* euthanasia
evacu|ação /evakua'sãw/ *f* evacuation; **~ar** *vt* evacuate
evadir /eva'dʒir/ *vt* evade; **~-se** *vpr* escape (**de** from)
evan|gelho /evã'ʒɛʎu/ *m* gospel
evaporar /evapo'rar/ *vt* evaporate; **~-se** *vpr* evaporate
eva|são /eva'zãw/ *f* escape; (*fiscal etc*) evasion; **~são escolar** truancy; **~siva** *f* excuse; **~sivo** *a* evasive
even|to /e'vẽtu/ *m* event; **~tual** (*pl* **~tuais**) *a* possible; **~tualidade** *f* eventuality
evidência /evi'dẽsia/ *f* evidence
eviden|ciar /evidẽsi'ar/ *vt* show up; **~ciar-se** *vpr* show up; **~te** *a* obvious, evident
evi|tar /evi'tar/ *vt* avoid; **~tar de beber** avoid drinking; **~tável** (*pl* **~táveis**) *a* avoidable
evocar /evo'kar/ *vt* call to mind, evoke <*passado etc*>; call up <*espíritos etc*>
evolu|ção /evolu'sãw/ *f* evolution; **~ir** *vi* evolve
exacerbar /ezaser'bar/ *vt* exacerbate
exage|rado /ezaʒe'radu/ *a* over the top; **~rar** *vt* (*atribuir proporções irreais a*) exaggerate; (*fazer em excesso*) overdo ▫ *vi* (*ao falar*) exaggerate; (*exceder-se*) overdo it; **~ro** /e/ *m* exaggeration
exa|lação /ezala'sãw/ *f* fume; (*agradável*) scent; **~lar** *vt* give off <*perfume etc*>
exal|tação /ezawta'sãw/ *f* (*excitação*) agitation; (*engrandecimento*) exaltation; **~tar** *vt* (*excitar*) agitate; (*enfurecer*) infuriate; (*louvar*) exalt; **~tar-se** *vpr* (*excitar-se*) get agitated; (*enfurecer-se*) get furious
exa|me /e'zami/ *m* examination; (*na escola*) exam(ination); **~me de sangue** blood test; **~minar** *vt* examine
exaspe|ração /ezaspera'sãw/ *f* exasperation; **~rar** *vt* exasperate;**~rar-se** *vpr* get exasperated
exa|tidão /ezatʃi'dãw/ *f* exactness; **~to** *a* exact
exaurir /ezaw'rir/ *vt* exhaust; **~-se** *vpr* become exhausted
exaus|tivo /ezaws'tʃivu/ *a* <*estudo*> exhaustive; <*trabalho*> exhausting; **~to** *a* exhausted
exceção /ese'sãw/ *f* exception; **abrir ~** make an exception; **com ~ de** with the exception of
exce|dente /ese'dẽtʃi/ *a & m* excess, surplus; **~der** *vt* exceed; **~der-se** *vpr* overdo it
exce|lência /ese'lẽsia/ *f* excellence; (*tratamento*) excellency; **~lente** *a* excellent
excentricidade /esẽtrisi'dadʒi/ *f* eccentricity
excêntrico /e'sẽtriku/ *a & m* eccentric
excep|ção /iʃsɛ'sãw/ (*Port*) *f veja* **exceção**; **~cional** (*pl* **~cionais**) *a* exceptional; (*deficiente*) handicapped
exces|sivo /ese'sivu/ *a* excessive; **~so** /ɛ/ *m* excess; **~so de bagagem** excess baggage; **~so de velocidade** speeding
exce|to /e'sɛtu/ *prep* except; **~tuar** *vt* except
exci|tação /esita'sãw/ *f* excitement; **~tante** *a* exciting; **~tar** *vt* excite; **~tar-se** *vpr* get excited
excla|mação /isklama'sãw/ *f* exclamation; **~mar** *vt/i* exclaim
exclu|ir /isklu'ir/ *vt* exclude; **~são** *f* exclusion; **com ~são de** with the exclusion of; **~sividade** *f*

exclusive rights; **com ~sividade** exclusively; **~sivo** *a* exclusive; **~so** *a* excluded

excomungar /iskomũ'gar/ *vt* excommunicate

excremento /iskre'mẽtu/ *m* excrement

excur|são /iskur'sãw/ *f* excursion; (*a pé*) hike, walk; **~sionista** *m/f* day-tripper; (*a pé*) hiker, walker

execu|ção /ezeku'sãw/ *f* execution; **~tante** *m/f* performer; **~tar** *vt* carry out <*ordem, plano etc*>; perform <*papel, música*>; execute <*preso, criminoso etc*>; **~tivo** *a & m* executive

exem|plar /ezẽ'plar/ *a* exemplary □ *m* (*de espécie*) example; (*de livro, jornal etc*) copy; **~plificar** *vt* exemplify

exemplo /e'zẽplu/ *m* example; **a ~ de** following the example of; **por ~** for example; **dar o ~** set an example

exeqüí|vel /eze'kwivew/ (*pl* **~veis**) *a* feasible

exer|cer /ezer'ser/ *vt* exercise; exert <*pressão, influência*>; carry on <*profissão*>; **~cício** *m* exercise; (*mil*) drill; (*de profissão*) practice; (*financeiro*) financial year; **~citar** *vt* exercise; practise <*ofício*>; **~citar-se** *vpr* train

exército /e'zεrsitu/ *m* army

exibição /ezibi'sãw/ *f* (*de filme, passaporte etc*) showing; (*de talento, força, ostentação*) show

exibicionis|mo /ezibisio'nizmu/ *m* exhibitionism; **~ta** *a & m/f* exhibitionist

exi|bido /ezi'bidu/ *a* <*pessoa*> pretentious □ *m* show-off; **~bir** *vt* show; (*ostentar*) show off; **~bir-se** *vpr* (*ostentar-se*) show off

exi|gência /ezi'ʒẽsia/ *f* demand; **~gente** *a* demanding; **~gir** *vt* demand

exíguo /e'zigwu/ *a* (*muito pequeno*) tiny; (*escasso*) minimal

exi|lado /ezi'lado/ *a* exiled □ *m* exile; **~lar** *vt* exile; **~lar-se** *vpr* go into exile

exílio /e'ziliu/ *m* exile

exímio /e'zimiu/ *a* distinguished

eximir /ezi'mir/ *vt* exempt (**de** from); **~-se de** get out of

exis|tência /ezis'tẽsia/ *f* existence; **~tencial** (*pl* **~tenciais**) *a* existential; **~tente** *a* existing; **~tir** *vi* exist

êxito /'ezitu/ *m* success; (*música, filme etc*) hit; **ter ~** succeed

êxodo /'ezodu/ *m* exodus

exonerar /ezone'rar/ *vt* (*de cargo*) dismiss, sack; **~-se** *vpr* resign

exorbitante /ezorbi'tãtʃi/ *a* exorbitant

exor|cismo /ezor'sizmu/ *m* exorcism; **~cista** *m/f* exorcist; **~cizar** *vt* exorcize

exótico /e'zɔtʃiku/ *a* exotic

expan|dir /ispã'dʒir/ *vt* spread; **~dir-se** *vpr* spread; <*pessoa*> open up; **~dir-se sobre** expand upon; **~são** *f* expansion; **~sivo** *a* expansive, open

expatri|ado /ispatri'ado/ *a & m* expatriate; **~ar-se** *vpr* leave one's country

expectativa /ispekta'tʃiva/ *f* expectation; **na ~ de** expecting; **estar na ~** wait to see what happens; **~ de vida** life expectancy

expedição /espedʒi'sãw/ *f* (*de encomendas, cartas*) dispatch; (*de passaporte, diploma etc*) issue; (*viagem*) expedition

expediente /ispedʒi'ẽtʃi/ *a* <*pessoa*> resourceful □ *m* (*horário*) working hours; (*meios*) expedient; **meio ~** part-time

expe|dir /ispe'dʒir/ *vt* dispatch <*encomendas, cartas*>; issue <*passaporte, diploma*>; **~dito** *a* prompt, quick

expelir /ispe'lir/ *vt* expel

experi|ência /isperi'ẽsia/ *f* experience; (*teste, tentativa*) experiment; **~ente** *a* experienced

experimen|tação /isperimẽta'sãw/ *f* experimentation; **~tado** *a* experienced; **~tar** *vt* (*provar*) try out; try on <*roupa*>; try <*comida*>; (*sentir, viver*) experience; **~to** *m* experiment

expi|ar /espi'ar/ *vt* atone for; **~atório** *a* **bode ~atório** scapegoat

expi|ração /espira'sãw/ *f* (*vencimento*) expiry; (*de ar*) exhalation; **~rar** *vt* exhale □ *vi* (*morrer, vencer*) expire; (*expelir ar*) breath out, exhale

expli|cação /isplika'sãw/ *f* explanation; **~car** *vt* explain; **~car-se** *vpr* explain o.s.; **~cável** (*pl* **~cáveis**) *a* explainable

explicitar /isplisi'tar/ *vt* set out

explícito /is'plisitu/ *a* explicit

explodir /isplo'dʒir/ *vt* explode □ *vi* explode; <*ator etc*> make it big

explo|ração /isplora'sãw/ *f* (*uso, abuso*) exploitation; (*pesquisa*) exploration; **~rar** *vt* (*tirar proveito de*) exploit; (*esquadrinhar*) explore

explo|são /isplo'zãw/ *f* explosion; **~sivo** *a & m* explosive

expor /es'por/ *vt* (*sujeitar, arriscar*) expose (**a** to); display <*mercadorias*>; exhibit <*obras de arte*>; (*explicar*) expound; **~ a vida** risk one's life; **~-se** *vpr* expose o.s. (**a** to)

expor|tação /isporta'sãw/ *f* export; **~tador** *a* exporting □ *m* exporter; **~tadora** *f* export company; **~tar** *vt* export

exposi|ção /ispozi'sãw/ *f* (*de arte etc*) exhibition; (*de mercadorias*) display; (*de filme fotográfico*) exposure; (*explicação*) exposition; **~tor** *m* exhibitor

exposto /is'postu/ *a* exposed (a to); <*mercadoria, obra de arte*> on display

expres|são /ispre'sãw/ *f* expression; **~sar** *vt* express; **~sar-se** *vpr* express o.s.; **~sivo** *a* expressive; <*número, quantia*> significant; **~so** /ɛ/ *a & m* express

exprimir /ispri'mir/ *vt* express; **~-se** *vpr* express o.s.

expropriar /ispropri'ar/ *vt* expropriate

expul|são /ispuw'sãw/ *f* expulsion; (*de jogador*) sending off; **~sar** *vt* (*de escola, partido, país etc*) expel; (*de clube, bar, festa etc*) throw out; (*de jogo*) send off; **~so** *pp de* **expulsar**

expur|gar /ispur'gar/ *vt* purge; expurgate <*livro*>; **~go** *m* purge

êxtase /'estazi/ *f* ecstasy

extasiado /istazi'adu/ *a* ecstatic

exten|são /istẽ'sãw/ *f* extension; (*tamanho, alcance, duração*) extent; (*de terreno*) expanse; **~sivo** *a* extensive; **~so** *a* extensive; **por ~so** in full

extenu|ante /istenu'ãtʃi/ *a* wearing, tiring; **~ar** *vt* tire out; **~ar-se** *vpr* tire o.s. out

exterior /isteri'or/ *a* outside, exterior; <*aparência*> outward; <*relações, comércio etc*> foreign □ *m* outside, exterior; (*de pessoa*) exterior; **o ~** (*outros países*) abroad; **para o/no ~** abroad

exter|minar /istermi'nar/ *vt* exterminate; **~mínio** *m* extermination

exter|nar /ister'nar/ *vt* show; **~na** /ɛ/ *f* location shot; **~no** /ɛ/ *a* external; <*dívida etc*> foreign □ *m* day-pupil

extin|ção /istʃĩ'sãw/ *f* extinction; **~guir** *vt* extinguish <*fogo*>; wipe out <*dívida, animal, povo*>; **~guir-se** *vpr* <*fogo, luz*> go out; <*animal, planta*> become extinct; **~to** *a* extinct; <*organização, pessoa*> defunct; **~tor** *m* fire extinguisher

extirpar /istʃir'par/ *vt* remove <*tumor etc*>; uproot <*ervas daninhas*>; eradicate <*abusos*>

extor|quir /istor'kir/ *vt* extort; **~são** *f* extortion

extra /'ɛstra/ *a & m/f* extra; **horas ~s** overtime

extração /istra'sãw/ *f* extraction; (*da loteria*) draw

extraconju|gal /estrakõʒu'gaw/ (*pl* **~gais**) *a* extramarital

extracurricular /estrakuxiku'lar/ *a* extracurricular

extradi|ção /istradʒi'sãw/ *f* extradition; **~tar** *vt* extradite

extrair /istra'ir/ *vt* extract; draw <*números da loteria*>

extrajudici|al /estraʒudʒisi'aw/ (*pl* **~ais**) *a* out-of-court; **~almente** *adv* out of court

extraordinário /istraordʒi'nariu/ *a* extraordinary

extrapolar /istrapo'lar/ *vt* (*exceder*) overstep; (*calcular*) extrapolate □ *vi* overstep the mark, go too far

extra-sensori|al /estrasẽsori'aw/ (*pl* **~ais**) *a* extra-sensory

extraterrestre /estrate'xestri/ *a & m* extraterrestrial

extrato /is'trato/ *m* extract; (*de conta*) statement

extrava|gância /istrava'gãsia/ *f* extravagance; **~gante** *a* extravagant

extravasar /istrava'zar/ *vt* release, let out <*emoções, sentimentos*> □ *vi* overflow

extra|viado /istravi'adu/ *a* lost; **~viar** *vt* lose, mislay <*papéis, carta*>; lead astray <*pessoa*>; embezzle <*dinheiro*>; **~viar-se** *vpr* go astray; <*carta*> get lost; **~vio** *m* (*perda*) misplacement; (*de dinheiro*) embezzlement

extre|midade /estremi'dadʒi/ *f* end; (*do corpo*) extremity; **~-mismo** *m* extremism; **~mista** *a & m/f* extremist; **~mo** /e/ *a & m* extreme; **o Extremo Oriente** the Far East; **~moso** /o/ *a* doting

extrovertido /istrover'tʃido/ *a & m* extrovert

exube|rância /ezube'rãsia/ *f* exuberance; **~rante** *a* exuberant

exultar /ezuw'tar/ *vi* exult

exumar /ezu'mar/ *vt* exhume <*cadáver*>; dig up <*documentos etc*>

Ff

fã /fã/ *m/f* fan

fábrica /'fabrika/ *f* factory

fabri|cação /fabrika'sãw/ *f* manufacture; **~cante** *m/f* manufacturer; **~car** *vt* manufacture; (*inventar*) fabricate

fábula /'fabula/ *f* fable; (*fam: dinheirão*) fortune

fabuloso /fabu'lozu/ *a* fabulous

faca /'faka/ *f* knife; **~da** *f* knife blow; **dar uma ~da em** (*fig*) get some money off

façanha /fa'saɲa/ *f* feat

facção /fak'sãw/ *f* faction

face /'fasi/ *f* face; (*do rosto*) cheek; **~ta** /e/ *f* facet

fachada /fa'ʃada/ *f* façade

facho /'faʃu/ *m* beam

faci|al /fasi'aw/ (*pl* **~ais**) *a* facial

fá|cil /'fasiw/ (*pl* **~ceis**) *a* easy; <*pessoa*> easy-going

facili|dade /fasili'dadʒi/ *f* ease; (*talento*) facility; **~tar** *vt* facilitate

fã-clube /fã'klubi/ *m* fan club

fac-símile /fak'simili/ *m* facsimile; (*fax*) fax

fact- (*Port*) *veja* **fat-**

facul|dade /fakuw'dadʒi/ *f* (*mental etc*) faculty; (*escola*) university, (*Amer*) college; **fazer ~dade** go to university; **~tativo** *a* optional

fada /'fada/ *f* fairy; **~do** *a* destined, doomed; **~-madrinha** (*pl* **~s-madrinhas**) *f* fairy godmother

fadiga /fa'dʒiga/ *f* fatigue

fa|dista /fa'dʒista/ *m/f* fado singer; **~do** *m* fado

fagote /fa'gɔtʃi/ *m* bassoon

fagulha /fa'guʎa/ *f* spark

faia /'faja/ *f* beech

faisão /faj'zãw/ *m* pheasant

faísca /fa'iska/ *f* spark

fais|cante /fajs'kãtʃi/ *a* sparkling; **~car** *vi* spark; (*cintilar*) sparkle

faixa /'faʃa/ *f* strip; (*cinto*) sash; (*em karatê, judô*) belt; (*da estrada*) lane; (*de ônibus*) bus lane; (*para pedestres*) zebra crossing, (*Amer*) crosswalk; (*atadura*) bandage; (*de disco*) track; **~ etária** age group

fajuto /fa'ʒutu/ (*fam*) *a* fake

fala /'fala/ *f* speech

falácia /fa'lasia/ *f* fallacy

fa|lado /fa'ladu/ *a* <*língua*> spoken; <*caso, pessoa*> talked about; **~lante** *a* talkative; **~lar** *vt/i* speak; (*dizer*) say; **~lar com** talk to; **~lar de** *ou* **em** talk about; **por ~lar em** speaking of; **sem ~lar em** not to mention; **~lou!** (*fam*) OK!; **~latório** *m* (*boatos*) talk; (*som de vozes*) talking

falaz /fa'las/ *a* fallacious

falcão /faw'kãw/ *m* falcon

falcatrua /fawka'trua/ *f* swindle

fale|cer /fale'ser/ *vi* die, pass away; **~cido** *a & m* deceased; **~cimento** *m* death

falência /fa'lẽsia/ *f* bankruptcy; **ir à ~** go bankrupt

falésia /fa'lɛzia/ *f* cliff

fa|lha /'faʎa/ *f* fault; (*omissão*) failure; **~lhar** *vi* fail; **~lho** *a* faulty

fálico /'faliku/ *a* phallic

fa|lido /fa'lidu/ *a & m* bankrupt; **~lir** *vi* go bankrupt; **~lível** (*pl* **~líveis**) *a* fallible

falo /'falu/ *m* phallus

fal|sario /faw'sariu/ *m* forger; **~sear** *vt* falsify; **~sete** *m* falsetto; **~sidade** *f* falseness; (*mentira*) falsehood

falsifi|cação /fawsifika'sãw/ *f* forgery; **~cador** *m* forger; **~car** *vt* falsify; forge <*documentos, notas*>

falso /'fawsu/ *a* false

fal|ta /'fawta/ *f* lack; (*em futebol*) foul; **em ~ta** at fault; **por ~ta de** for lack of; **sem ~ta** without fail; **fazer ~ta** be needed; **sentir a ~ta de** miss; **~tar** *vi* be missing; <*aluno*> be absent; **~tam dois dias para** it's two days until; **me ~ta ...** I don't have ...; **~tar a** miss <*aula etc*>; break <*palavra, promessa*>; **~to** *a* short (**de** of)

fa|ma /'fama/ *f* reputation; (*celebridade*) fame; **~migerado** *a* notorious

família /fa'milia/ *f* family

famili|ar /famili'ar/ *a* familiar; (*de família*) family; **~aridade** *f* familiarity; **~arizar** *vt* familiarize; **~arizar-se** *vpr* familiarize o.s.

faminto /fa'mĩtu/ *a* starving

famoso /fa'mozu/ *a* famous

fanático /fa'natʃiku/ *a* fanatical □ *m* fanatic

fanatismo /fana'tʃizmu/ *m* fanaticism

fanfarrão /fãfa'xãw/ *m* braggart

fanhoso /fa'ɲozu/ *a* nasal; **ser ~** talk through one's nose

fanta|sia /fãta'zia/ *f* (*faculdade*) imagination; (*devaneio*) fantasy; (*roupa*) fancy dress; **~siar** *vt* dream up

□ *vi* fantasize; **~siar-se** *vpr* dress up (**de** as); **~sioso** /o/ *a* fanciful; <*pessoa*> imaginative; **~sista** *a* imaginative

fantasma /fã'tazma/ *m* ghost; **~górico** *a* ghostly

fantástico /fã'tastʃiku/ *a* fantastic

fantoche /fã'tɔʃi/ *m* puppet

faqueiro /fa'keru/ *m* canteen of cutlery

fara|ó /fara'ɔ/ *m* pharaoh; **~ônico** *a* (*fig*) of epic proportions

farda /'farda/ *f* uniform; **~do** *a* uniformed

fardo /'fardu/ *m* (*fig*) burden

fare|jador /fareʒa'dor/ *a* **cão ~jador** sniffer dog; **~jar** *vt* sniff out □ *vi* sniff

farelo /fa'rɛlu/ *m* bran; (*de pão*) crumb; (*de madeira*) sawdust

farfalhar /farfa'ʎar/ *vi* rustle

farináceo /fari'nasiu/ *a* starchy; **~s** *m pl* starchy foods

farin|ge /fa'rĩʒi/ *f* pharynx; **~gite** *f* pharyngitis

farinha /fa'riɲa/ *f* flour; **~ de rosca** breadcrumbs

far|macêutico /farma'sewtʃiku/ *a* pharmaceutical □ *m* (*pessoa*) pharmacist; **~mácia** *f* (*loja*) chemist's, (*Amer*) pharmacy; (*ciência*) pharmacy

faro /'faru/ *f* sense of smell; (*fig*) nose

faroeste /faro'ɛstʃi/ *m* (*filme*) western; (*região*) wild west

faro|fa /fa'rɔfa/ *f* fried manioc flour; **~feiro** (*fam*) *m* day-tripper

fa|rol /fa'rɔw/ (*pl* **~róis**) *m* (*de carro*) headlight; (*de trânsito*) traffic light; (*à beira-mar*) lighthouse; **~rol alto** full beam; **~rol baixo** dipped beam; **~roleiro** *a* boastful □ *m* bighead; **~rolete** /e/ *m*, (*Port*) **~rolim** *m* side-light; (*traseiro*) tail-light

farpa /'farpa/ *f* splinter; (*de metal, fig*) barb; **~do** *a* **arame ~do** barbed wire

farra /'faxa/ (*fam*) *f* partying; **cair na ~** go out and party

farrapo /fa'xapu/ *m* rag

far|rear /faxi'ar/ (*fam*) *vi* party; **~rista** (*fam*) *m/f* raver

far|sa /'farsa/ *f* (*peça*) farce; (*fingimento*) pretence; **~sante** *m/f* (*brincalhão*) joker; (*pessoa sem seriedade*) unreliable character

far|tar /far'tar/ *vt* satiate; **~tar-se** *vpr* (*saciar-se*) gorge o.s. (**de** with); (*cansar*) tire (**de** of); **~to** *a* (*abundante*) plentiful; (*cansado*) fed up (**de** with); **~tura** *f* abundance

fascículo /fa'sikulu/ *m* instalment

fasci|nação /fasina'sãw/ *f* fascination; **~nante** *a* fascinating; **~nar** *vt* fascinate

fascínio /fa'siniu/ *m* fascination

fas|cismo /fa'sizmu/ *m* fascism; **~cista** *a* & *m/f* fascist

fase /'fazi/ *f* phase

fa|tal /fa'taw/ (*pl* **~tais**) *a* fatal; **~talismo** *m* fatalism; **~talista** *a* fatalistic □ *m/f* fatalist; **~talmente** *adv* inevitably

fatia /fa'tʃia/ *f* slice

fatídico /fa'tʃidʒiku/ *a* fateful

fati|gante /fatʃi'gãtʃi/ *a* tiring; **~gar** *vt* tire, fatigue

fato[1] /'fatu/ *m* fact; **de ~** as a matter of fact, in fact; **~ consumado** fait accompli

fato[2] /'fatu/ (*Port*) *m* suit

fator /fa'tor/ *m* factor

fátuo /'fatuu/ *a* fatuous

fatu|ra /fa'tura/ *f* invoice; **~ramento** *m* turnover; **~rar** *vt* invoice for <*encomenda*>; make <*dinheiro*>; (*fig: emplacar*) notch up □ *vi* (*fam*) rake it in

fauna /'fawna/ *f* fauna

fava /'fava/ *f* broad bean; **mandar alg às ~s** tell s.o. where to get off

favela /fa'vɛla/ *f* shanty town; **~do** *m* shanty-dweller

favo /'favu/ *m* honeycomb

favor /fa'vor/ *m* favour; **a ~ de** in favour of; **por ~** please; **faça ~** please

favo|rável /favo'ravew/ (*pl* **~ráveis**) *a* favourable; **~recer** *vt* favour; **~ritismo** *m* favouritism; **~rito** *a* & *m* favourite

faxi|na /fa'ʃina/ *f* clean-up; **~neiro** *m* cleaner

fazen|da /fa'zẽda/ *f* (*de café, gado etc*) farm; (*tecido*) fabric, material; (*pública*) treasury; **~deiro** *m* farmer

fazer /fa'zer/ *vt* do; (*produzir*) make; ask <*pergunta*>; **~-se** *vpr* (*tornar-se*) become; **~-se de** make o.s. out to be; **~ anos** have a birthday; **~ 20 anos** be twenty; **faz dois dias que ele está aqui** he's been here for two days; **faz dez anos que ele morreu** it's ten years since he died; **tanto faz** it doesn't matter

faz-tudo /fas'tudu/ *m/f invar* jack of all trades

fé /fɛ/ *f* faith

fe|bre /'fɛbri/ *f* fever; **~bre amarela** yellow fever; **~bre do feno** hay fever; **~bril** (*pl* **~bris**) *a* feverish

fe|chado /fe'ʃadu/ *a* closed; <*curva*> sharp; <*sinal*> red; <*torneira*> off; <*tempo*> overcast; <*cara*> stern; <*pessoa*> reserved; **~chadura** *f* lock; **~chamento** *m* closure; **~char** *vt* close, shut; turn off <*torneira*>; do up <*calça, casaco*>; close <*negócio*> □ *vi* close, shut; <*sinal*> go red; <*tempo*> cloud over; **~char à chave** lock; **~char a cara** frown; **~cho** /e/ *m* fastener; **~cho ecler** zip

fécula /'fɛkula/ *f* starch

fecun|dar /fekũ'dar/ *vt* fertilize; **~do** *a* fertile

feder /fe'der/ *vi* stink

fede|ração /federa'sãw/ *f* federation; **~ral** (*pl* **~rais**) *a* federal; (*fam*) huge; **~rativo** *a* federal

fedor /fe'dor/ *m* stink, stench; **~ento** *a* stinking

feérico /feɛriku/ *a* magical

feições /fej'sõjs/ *f pl* features

fei|jão /fe'ʒãw/ *m* bean; (*coletivo*) beans; **~joada** *f* bean stew; **~joeiro** *m* bean plant

feio /'feju/ *a* ugly; <*palavra, situação, tempo*> nasty; <*olhar*> dirty; **~so** /o/ *a* plain

fei|ra /'fera/ *f* market; (*industrial*) trade fair; **~rante** *m/f* market trader

feiti|çaria /fejtʃi'sera/ *f* magic; **~ceira** *f* witch; **~ceiro** *m* wizard □ *a* bewitching; **~ço** *m* spell

fei|tio /fej'tʃiu/ *m* (*de pessoa*) make-up; **~to** *pp de* **fazer** □ *m* (*ato*) deed; (*proeza*) feat □ *conj* like; **bem ~to por ele** (it) serves him right; **~tura** *f* making

feiúra /fej'ura/ *f* ugliness

feixe /'feʃi/ *m* bundle

fel /fɛw/ *f* gall; (*fig*) bitterness

felicidade /felisi'dadʒi/ *f* happiness

felici|tações /felisita'sõjs/ *f pl* congratulations; **~tar** *vt* congratulate (**por** on)

felino /fe'linu/ *a* feline

feliz /fe'lis/ *a* happy; **~ardo** *a* lucky; **~mente** *adv* fortunately

fel|pa /'fewpa/ *f* (*de pano*) nap; (*penugem*) down, fluff; **~pudo** *a* fluffy

feltro /'fewtru/ *m* felt

fêmea /'femia/ *a & f* female

femi|nil /femi'niw/ (*pl* **~nis**) *a* feminine; **~nilidade** *f* femininity; **~nino** *a* female; <*palavra*> feminine; **~nismo** *m* feminism; **~nista** *a & m/f* feminist

fêmur /'femur/ *m* femur

fen|da /'fẽda/ *f* crack; **~der** *vt/i* split, crack

feno /'fenu/ *m* hay

fenome|nal /fenome'naw/ (*pl* **~nais**) *a* phenomenal

fenômeno /fe'nomenu/ *m* phenomenon

fera /'fɛra/ *f* wild beast; **ficar uma ~** get really angry; **ser ~ em** (*fam*) be brilliant at

féretro /'fɛretru/ *m* coffin

feriado /feri'adu/ *m* public holiday

férias /'fɛrias/ *f pl* holiday(s), (*Amer*) vacation; **de ~** on holiday; **tirar ~** take a holiday

feri|da /fe'rida/ *f* injury; (*com arma*) wound; **~do** *a* injured; (*mil*) wounded □ *m* injured person; **os ~dos** the injured; (*mil*) the wounded; **~r** *vt* injure; (*com arma*) wound; (*magoar*) hurt

fermen|tar /fermẽ'tar/ *vt/i* ferment; **~to** *m* yeast; (*fig*) ferment; **~to em pó** baking powder

fe|rocidade /ferosi'dadʒi/ *f* ferocity; **~roz** *a* ferocious

fer|rado /fe'xadu/ *a* **estou ~rado** (*fam*) I've had it; **~rado no sono** fast asleep; **~radura** *f* horseshoe; **~ragem** *f* ironwork; *pl* hardware; **~ramenta** *f* tool; (*coletivo*) tools; **~rão** *m* (*de abelha*) sting; **~rar** *vt* brand <*gado*>; shoe <*cavalo*>; **~rar-se** (*fam*) *vpr* come a cropper; **~reiro** *m* blacksmith; **~renho** *a* <*partidário etc*> staunch; <*vontade*> iron

férreo /'fɛxiu/ *a* iron

ferro /'fɛxu/ *m* iron; **~lho** /o/ *m* bolt; **~-velho** (*pl* **~s-velhos**) *m* (*pessoa*) scrap-metal dealer; (*lugar*) scrap-metal yard; **~via** *f* railway, (*Amer*) railroad; **~viário** *a* railway □ *m* railway worker

ferrugem /fe'xuʒẽ/ *f* rust

fér|til /'fɛrtʃiw/ (*pl* **~teis**) *a* fertile

fertili|dade /fertʃili'dadʒi/ *f* fertility; **~zante** *m* fertilizer; **~zar** *vt* fertilize

fer|vente /fer'vẽtʃi/ *a* boiling; **~ver** *vi* boil; (*de raiva*) seethe; **~vilhar** *vi* bubble; **~vilhar de** swarm with; **~vor** *m* fervour; **~vura** *f* boiling

fes|ta /'fɛsta/ *f* party; (*religiosa*) festival; **~tejar** *vt/i* celebrate; (*acolher*) fete; **~tejo** /e/ *m* celebration; **~tim** *m* feast; **~tival** (*pl* **~tivais**) *m* festival; **~tividade** *f* festivity; **~tivo** *a* festive

feti|che /fe'tʃiʃi/ *m* fetish; **~-chismo** *m* fetishism; **~chista** *m/f* fetishist □ *a* fetishistic

fétido /'fɛtʃidu/ *a* fetid

feto[1] /'fɛtu/ *m* (*no útero*) foetus

feto[2] /'fɛtu/ (*Port*) *m* (*planta*) fern

feu|dal /few'daw/ (*pl* **~dais**) *a* feudal; **~dalismo** *m* feudalism

fevereiro /feve'reru/ *m* February

fezes /'fɛzis/ *f pl* faeces

fiação /fia'sãw/ *f* (*eletr*) wiring; (*fábrica*) mill

fia|do /fi'adu/ *a* <*conversa*> idle □ *adv* <*comprar*> on credit; **~dor** *m* guarantor

fiambre /fi'ãbri/ *m* cooked ham

fiança /fi'ãsa/ *f* surety; (*jurid*) bail

fiapo /fi'apu/ *m* thread
fiar /fi'ar/ *vt* spin <*lã etc*>
fiasco /fi'asku/ *m* fiasco
fibra /'fibra/ *f* fibre
ficar /fi'kar/ *vi* (*tornar-se*) become; (*estar, ser*) be; (*manter-se*) stay; **~ fazendo** keep (on) doing; **~ com** keep; get <*impressão, vontade*>; **~ com medo** get scared; **~ de fazer** arrange to do; **~ para** be left for; **~ bom** turn out well; (*recuperar-se*) get better; **~ bem** look good
fic|ção /fik'sãw/ *f* fiction; **~ção científica** science fiction; **~-cionista** *m/f* fiction writer
fi|cha /'fiʃa/ *f* (*de telefone*) token; (*de jogo*) chip; (*da caixa*) ticket; (*de fichário*) file card; (*na polícia*) record; (*Port: tomada*) plug; **~chário** *m*, (*Port*) **~cheiro** *m* file; (*móvel*) filing cabinet
fictício /fik'tʃisiu/ *a* fictitious
fidalgo /fi'dalgu/ *m* nobleman
fide|digno /fide'dʒignu/ *a* trustworthy; **~lidade** *f* fidelity
fiduciário /fidusi'ariu/ *a* fiduciary □ *m* trustee
fi|el /fi'ɛw/ (*pl* **~éis**) *a* faithful □ *m* **os ~éis** (*na igreja*) the congregation
figa /'figa/ *f* talisman
fígado /'figadu/ *f* liver
fi|go /'figu/ *m* fig; **~gueira** *f* fig tree
figu|ra /fi'gura/ *f* figure; (*carta de jogo*) face card; (*fam: pessoa*) character; **fazer (má) ~ra** make a (bad) impression; **~-rado** *a* figurative; **~rante** *m/f* extra; **~rão** *m* big shot; **~rar** *vi* appear, figure; **~rativo** *a* figurative; **~rinha** *f* sticker; **~rino** *m* fashion plate; (*de filme, peça*) costume design; (*fig*) model; **como manda o ~rino** as it should be
fila /'fila/ *f* line; (*de espera*) queue, (*Amer*) line; (*fileira*) row; **fazer ~** queue up, (*Amer*) stand in line; **~ indiana** single file
filamento /fila'mẽtu/ *m* filament
filante /fi'lãtʃi/ (*fam*) *m/f* sponger
filan|tropia /filãtro'pia/ *f* philanthropy; **~trópico** *a* philanthropic; **~tropo** /o/ *m* phil-anthropist
filão /fi'lãw/ *m* (*de ouro*) seam; (*fig*) money-spinner
filar /fi'lar/ (*fam*) *vt* sponge, cadge
filar|mônica /filar'monika/ *f* philharmonic (orchestra); **~mônico** *a* philharmonic
filate|lia /filate'lia/ *f* philately; **~lista** *m/f* philatelist
filé /fi'lɛ/ *m* fillet
fileira /fi'lera/ *f* row
filete /fi'lɛtʃi/ *m* fillet
fi|lha /'fiʎa/ *f* daughter; **~lho** *m* son; *pl* (*crianças*) children; **~lho da puta** (*chulo*) bastard, (*Amer*) son of a bitch; **~lho de criação** foster child; **~lho único** only child; **~lhote** *m* (*de cão*) pup; (*de lobo etc*) cub; *pl* young
fili|ação /filia'sãw/ *f* affiliation; **~al** (*pl* **~ais**) *a* filial □ *f* branch
Filipinas /fili'pinas/ *f pl* Philippines
filipino /fili'pinu/ *a & m* Filipino
fil|madora /fiwma'dora/ *f* camcorder; **~magem** *f* filming; **~mar** *vt/i* film; **~me** *m* film
fi|lologia /filolo'ʒia/ *f* philology; **~lólogo** *m* philologist
filo|sofar /filozo'far/ *vi* philosophize; **~sofia** *f* philosophy; **~sófico** *a* philosophical
filósofo /fi'lɔzofu/ *m* philosopher
fil|trar /fiw'trar/ *vt* filter; **~tro** *m* filter
fim /fĩ/ *m* end; **a ~ de** (*para*) in order to; **estar a ~ de** fancy; **por ~** finally; **sem ~** endless; **ter ~** come to an end; **~ de semana** weekend
fi|nado /fi'nadu/ *a & m* deceased, departed; **~nal** (*pl* **~nais**) *a* final □ *m* end □ *f* final; **~nalista** *m/f* finalist; **~nalizar** *vt/i* finish
finan|ças /fi'nãsas/ *f pl* finances; **~ceiro** *a* financial □ *m* financier; **~ciamento** *m* financing; (*um*) loan; **~ciar** *vt* finance; **~cista** *m/f* financier
fincar /fĩ'kar/ *vt* plant; **~ o pé** (*fig*) dig one's heels in
findar /fĩ'dar/ *vt/i* end
fineza /fi'neza/ *f* finesse; (*favor*) kindness
fin|gido /fĩ'ʒidu/ *a* feigned; <*pessoa*> insincere; **~gimento** *m* pretence; **~gir** *vt* pretend; feign <*doença etc*> □ *vi* pretend; **~gir-se de** pretend to be
finito /fi'nitu/ *a* finite
finlan|dês /fĩlã'des/ *a* (*f* **~desa**) Finnish □ *m* (*f* **~desa**) Finn; (*língua*) Finnish
Finlândia /fĩ'lãdʒia/ *f* Finland
fi|ninho /fi'niɲu/ *adv* **sair de ~ninho** slip away; **~no** *a* (*não grosso*) thin; <*areia, pó etc*> fine; (*refinado*) refined; **~nório** *a* crafty;~nura *f* thinness; fineness
fio /'fiu/ *m* thread; (*elétrico*) wire; (*de sangue, água*) trickle; (*de luz, esperança*) glimmer; (*de navalha etc*) edge; **horas a ~** hours on end
fir|ma /'firma/ *f* firm; (*assinatura*) signature; **~mamento** *m* firmament; **~mar** *vt* fix; (*basear*) base □ *vi* settle; **~mar-se** *vpr* be based **(em** on); **~me** *a* firm; <*tempo*> settled □ *adv* firmly; **~meza** *f* firmness

fis|cal /fis'kaw/ (*pl* **~cais**) *m* inspector; **~calização** *f* inspection; **~calizar** *vt* inspect; **~co** *m* inland revenue, (*Amer*) internal revenue service

fis|gada /fiz'gada/ *f* stabbing pain; **~gar** *vt* hook

físi|ca /'fizika/ *f* physics; **~co** *a* physical □ *m* (*pessoa*) physicist; (*corpo*) physique

fisio|nomia /fiziono'mia/ *f* face; **~nomista** *m/f* **ser ~nomista** have a good memory for faces; **~terapeuta** *m/f* physiotherapist; **~terapia** *f* physiotherapy

fissura /fi'sura/ *f* fissure; (*fam*) craving; **~do** *a* **~do em** (*fam*) mad about

fita /'fita/ *f* tape; (*fam: encenação*) playacting; **fazer ~** (*fam*) put on an act; **~ adesiva** (*Port*) adhesive tape; **~ métrica** tape measure

fitar /fi'tar/ *vt* stare at

fivela /fi'vɛla/ *f* buckle

fi|xador /fiksa'dor/ *m* (*de cabelo*) setting lotion; (*de fotos*) fixative; **~xar** *vt* fix; stick up <*cartaz*>; **~xo** *a* fixed

flácido /'flasidu/ *a* flabby

flagelo /fla'ʒɛlu/ *m* scourge

fla|grante /fla'grãtʃi/ *a* flagrant; **apanhar em ~grante (delito)** catch in the act; **~grar** *vt* catch

flame|jante /flame'ʒãtʃi/ *a* blazing; **~jar** *vi* blaze

flamengo /fla'mẽgu/ *a* Flemish □ *m* Fleming; (*língua*) Flemish

flamingo /fla'mĩgu/ *m* flamingo

flâmula /'flamula/ *f* pennant

flanco /'flãku/ *m* flank

flanela /fla'nɛla/ *f* flannel

flanquear /flãki'ar/ *vt* flank

flash /flɛʃ/ *m invar* flash

flau|ta /'flawta/ *f* flute; **~tista** *m/f* flautist

flecha /'flɛʃa/ *f* arrow

fler|tar /fler'tar/ *vi* flirt; **~te** *m* flirtation

fleuma /'flewma/ *f* phlegm

fle|xão /flek'sãw/ *f* press-up, (*Amer*) push-up; (*ling*) inflection; **~xibilidade** *f* flexibility; **~xionar** *vt/i* flex <*perna, braço*>; (*ling*) inflect; **~xível** (*pl* **~xíveis**) *a* flexible

fliperama /flipe'rama/ *m* pinball machine

floco /'flɔku/ *m* flake

flor /flor/ *f* flower; **a fina ~** the cream; **à ~ da pele** (*fig*) on edge

flo|ra /'flɔra/ *f* flora; **~reado** *a* full of flowers; (*fig*) florid; **~reio** *m* clever turn of phrase; **~rescer** *vi* flower; **~resta** /ɛ/ *f* forest; **~restal** (*pl* **~restais**) *a* forest; **~rido** *a* in flower; (*fig*) florid; **~rir** *vi* flower

flotilha /flo'tʃiʎa/ *f* flotilla

flu|ência /flu'ẽsia/ *f* fluency; **~ente** *a* fluent

flui|dez /flui'des/ *f* fluidity; **~do** *a* & *m* fluid

fluir /flu'ir/ *vi* flow

fluminense /flumi'nẽsi/ *a* & *m* (person) from Rio de Janeiro state

fluorescente /fluore'sẽtʃi/ *a* fluorescent

flutu|ação /flutua'sãw/ *f* fluctuation; **~ante** *a* floating; **~ar** *vi* float; <*bandeira*> flutter; (*hesitar*) waver

fluvi|al /fluvi'aw/ (*pl* **~ais**) *a* river

fluxo /'fluksu/ *m* flow; **~grama** *m* flowchart

fobia /fo'bia/ *f* phobia

foca /'fɔka/ *f* seal

focalizar /fokali'zar/ *vt* focus on

focinho /fo'siɲu/ *m* snout

foco /'fɔku/ *m* focus; (*fig*) centre

fofo /'fofu/ *a* soft; <*pessoa*> cuddly

fofo|ca /fo'fɔka/ *f* piece of gossip; *pl* gossip; **~car** *vi* gossip; **~queiro** *m* gossip □ *a* gossipy

fo|gão /fo'gãw/ *m* stove; (*de cozinhar*) cooker; **~go** /o/ *m* fire; **tem ~go?** have you got a light?; **ser ~go** (*fam*) (*ser chato*) be a pain in the neck; (*ser incrível*) be amazing; **~gos de artifício** fireworks; **~goso** /o/ *a* fiery; **~gueira** *f* bonfire; **~guete** /e/ *m* rocket

foice /'fojsi/ *f* scythe

fol|clore /fow'klɔri/ *m* folklore; **~clórico** *a* folk

fole /'fɔli/ *m* bellows

fôlego /'folegu/ *m* breath; (*fig*) stamina

fol|ga /'fɔwga/ *f* rest, break; (*fam: cara-de-pau*) cheek; **~gado** *a* <*roupa*> full, loose; <*vida*> leisurely; (*fam: atrevido*) cheeky; **~gar** *vt* loosen □ *vi* have time off

fo|lha /'foʎa/ *f* leaf; (*de papel*) sheet; **novo em ~lha** brand new; **~lha de pagamento** payroll; **~lhagem** *f* foliage; **~lhear** *vt* leaf through; **~-lheto** /e/ *m* pamphlet; **~lhinha** *f* tear-off calendar; **~lhudo** *a* leafy

foli|a /fo'lia/ *f* revelry; **~ão** *m* (*f* **~ona**) reveller

folículo /fo'likulu/ *m* follicle

fome /'fomi/ *f* hunger; **estar com ~** be hungry

fomentar /fomẽ'tar/ *vt* foment

fone /'foni/ *m* (*do telefone*) receiver; (*de rádio etc*) headphones

fonema /fo'nema/ *m* phoneme

fonéti|ca /fo'nɛtʃika/ *f* phonetics; **~co** *a* phonetic

fonologia /fonolo'ʒia/ *f* phonology

fonte /'fõtʃi/ *f* (*de água*) spring; (*fig*) source

fora /'fɔra/ *adv* outside; (*não em casa*) out; (*viajando*) away ▫ *prep* except; **dar um ~** drop a clanger; **dar um ~ em alg** cut s.o. dead; chuck <*namorado*>; **por ~** on the outside; **~-de-lei** *m*/*f invar* outlaw

foragido /fora'ʒidu/ *a* at large, on the run ▫ *m* fugitive

forasteiro /foras'teru/ *m* outsider

forca /'forka/ *f* gallows

for|ça /'forsa/ *f* (*vigor*) strength; (*violência*) force; (*elétrica*) power; **dar uma ~ça a alg** help s.o. out; **fazer ~ça** make an effort; **~ças armadas** armed forces; **~çar** *vt* force; **~ça-tarefa** (*pl* **~ças-tarefa**) *f* task force

fórceps /'fɔrseps/ *m invar* forceps

forçoso /for'sozu/ *a* forced

for|ja /'fɔrʒa/ *f* forge; **~jar** *vt* forge

forma /'fɔrma/ *f* form; (*contorno*) shape; (*maneira*) way; **de qualquer ~** anyway; **manter a ~** keep fit

fôrma /'forma/ *f* mould; (*de cozinha*) baking tin

for|mação /forma'sãw/ *f* formation; (*educação*) education; (*profissionalizante*) training; **~-mado** *m* graduate; **~mal** (*pl* **~mais**) *a* formal; **~malidade** *f* formality; **~malizar** *vt* formalize; **~mar** *vt* form; (*educar*) educate; **~mar-se** *vpr* be formed; <*estudante*> graduate; **~mato** *m* format; **~matura** *f* graduation

formidá|vel /formi'davew/ (*pl* **~veis**) *a* formidable; (*muito bom*) tremendous

formi|ga /for'miga/ *f* ant; **~-gamento** *m* pins and needles; **~gar** *vi* swarm (**de** with); <*perna, mão etc*> tingle; **~gueiro** *m* ants' nest

formosura /formo'zura/ *f* beauty

fórmula /'fɔrmula/ *f* formula

formu|lação /formula'sãw/ *f* formulation; **~lar** *vt* formulate; **~lário** *m* form

fornalha /for'naʎa/ *f* furnace

forne|cedor /fornese'dor/ *m* supplier; **~cer** *vt* supply; **~cer aco a alg** supply s.o. with sth; **~cimento** *m* supply

forno /'fornu/ *m* oven; (*para louça etc*) kiln

foro /'foru/ *m* forum

forra /'fɔxa/ *f* **ir à ~** get one's own back

for|ragem /fo'xaʒẽ/ *f* fodder; **~rar** *vt* line <*roupa, caixa etc*>; cover <*sofá etc*>; carpet <*assoalho, sala etc*>; **~ro** /o/ *m* (*de roupa, caixa etc*) lining; (*de sofá etc*) cover; (*carpete*) (fitted) carpet

forró /fo'xɔ/ *m* type of Brazilian dance

fortale|cer /fortale'ser/ *vt* strengthen; **~cimento** *m* strengthening; **~za** /e/ *f* fort-ress

for|te /'fɔrtʃi/ *a* strong; <*golpe*> hard; <*chuva*> heavy; <*físico*> muscular ▫ *adv* strongly; <*bater, chover*> hard ▫ *m* (*militar*) fort; (*habilidade*) strong point, forte; **~tificação** *f* fortification; **~tificar** *vt* fortify

fortu|ito /for'tuitu/ *a* chance; **~na** *f* fortune

fosco /'fosku/ *a* dull; <*vidro*> frosted

fosfato /fos'fatu/ *m* phosphate

fósforo /'fɔsforu/ *m* match; (*elemento químico*) phosphor

fossa /'fɔsa/ *f* pit; **na ~** (*fig*) miserable, depressed

fós|sil /'fɔsiw/ (*pl* **~seis**) *m* fossil

fosso /'fosu/ *m* ditch; (*de castelo*) moat

foto /'fɔtu/ *f* photo; **~cópia** *f* photocopy; **~copiadora** *f* photocopier; **~copiar** *vt* photocopy; **~gênico** *a* photogenic; **~grafar** *vt* photograph; **~grafia** *f* photography; **~gráfico** *a* photographic

fotógrafo /fo'tɔgrafu/ *m* photographer

foz /fɔs/ *f* mouth

fração /fra'sãw/ *f* fraction

fracas|sado /fraka'sadu/ *a* failed ▫ *m* failure; **~sar** *vi* fail; **~so** *m* failure

fracionar /frasio'nar/ *vt* break up

fraco /'fraku/ *a* weak; <*luz, som*> faint; <*medíocre*> poor ▫ *m* weakness, weak spot

fract- (*Port*) *veja* **frat**

frade /'fradʒi/ *m* friar

fragata /fra'gata/ *f* frigate

frá|gil /'fraʒiw/ (*pl* **~geis**) *a* fragile; <*pessoa*> frail

fragilidade /fraʒili'dadʒi/ *f* fragility; (*de pessoa*) frailty

fragmen|tar /fragmẽ'tar/ *vt* fragment; **~tar-se** *vpr* fragment; **~to** *m* fragment

fra|grância /fra'grãsia/ *f* fragrance; **~grante** *a* fragrant

fralda /'frawda/ *f* nappy, (*Amer*) diaper

framboesa /frãbo'eza/ *f* raspberry

França /'frãsa/ *f* France

fran|cês /frã'ses/ *a* (*f* **~cesa**) French ▫ *m* (*f* **~cesa**) Frenchman (*f*-woman); (*língua*) French; **os ~ceses** the French

franco /'frãku/ *a* (*honesto*) frank; (*óbvio*) clear; (*gratuito*) free ▫ *m* franc; **~-atirador** (*pl* **~-atiradores**) *m* sniper; (*fig*) maverick

frangalho /frã'gaʎu/ *m* tatter

frango /'frãgu/ *m* chicken

franja /'frãʒa/ *f* fringe; (*do cabelo*) fringe, (*Amer*) bangs

fran|quear /frãki'ar/ *vt* frank <*carta*>; **~queza** /e/ *f* frankness; **~quia** *f* (*de cartas*) franking; (*jur*) franchise

fran|zino /frã'zinu/ *a* skinny; **~zir** *vt* gather <*tecido*>; wrinkle <*testa*>

fraque /'fraki/ *m* morning suit

fraqueza /fra'keza/ *f* weakness; (*de luz, som*) faintness

frasco /'frasku/ *m* bottle

frase /'frazi/ *f* (*oração*) sentence; (*locução*) phrase; **~ado** *m* phrasing

frasqueira /fras'kera/ *f* vanity case

frater|nal /frater'naw/ (*pl* **~nais**) *a* fraternal; **~nidade** *f* fraternity; **~nizar** *vi* fraternize; **~no** *a* fraternal

fratu|ra /fra'tura/ *f* fracture; **~rar** *vt* fracture; **~rar-se** *vpr* fracture

frau|dar /fraw'dar/ *vt* defraud; **~de** *f* fraud; **~dulento** *a* fraudulent

frear /fri'ar/ *vt/i* brake

freezer /'frizer/ *m* freezer

fre|guês /fre'ges/ *m* (*f* **~guesa**) customer; **~guesia** *f* (*de loja etc*) clientele; (*paróquia*) parish

frei /frej/ *m* brother

freio /'freju/ *m* brake; (*de cavalo*) bit

freira /'frera/ *f* nun

freixo /'freʃu/ *m* ash

fremir /fre'mir/ *vi* shake

frêmito /'fremitu/ *m* wave

frenesi /frene'zi/ *m* frenzy

frenético /fre'nɛtʃiku/ *a* frantic

frente /'frẽtʃi/ *f* front; **em ~ a** *ou* **de** in front of; **para a ~** forward; **pela ~** ahead; **fazer ~ a** face

freqüência /fre'kwẽsia/ *f* frequency; (*assiduidade*) attendance; **com muita ~** often

freqüen|tador /frekwẽta'dor/ *m* regular visitor (**de** to); **~tar** *vt* frequent; (*cursar*) attend; **~te** *a* frequent

fres|cão /fres'kãw/ *m* air-conditioned coach; **~co** /e/ *a* <*comida etc*> fresh; <*vento, água, quarto*> cool; (*fam*) (*afetado*) affected; (*exigente*) fussy; **~cobol** *m* kind of racquetball; **~cor** *m* freshness; **~cura** *f* (*fam*) (*afetação*) affectation; (*ser exigente*) fussiness; (*coisa sem importância*) trifle

fresta /'frɛsta/ *f* slit

fre|tar /fre'tar/ *vt* charter <*avião*>; hire <*caminhão*>; **~te** /ɛ/ *m* freight; (*aluguel de avião*) charter; (*de caminhão*) hire

frevo /'frevu/ *m* type of Brazilian dance

fria /'fria/ (*fam*) *f* difficult situation, spot; **~gem** *f* chill

fric|ção /frik'sãw/ *f* friction; **~cionar** *vt* rub

fri|eira /fri'era/ *f* chilblain; **~eza** /e/ *f* coldness

frigideira /friʒi'dera/ *f* frying pan

frígido /'friʒidu/ *a* frigid

frigorífico /frigo'rifiku/ *m* cold store, refrigerator, fridge

frincha /'frĩʃa/ *f* chink

frio /'friu/ *a & m* cold; **estar com ~** be cold; **~rento** *a* sensitive to the cold

frisar /fri'zar/ *vt* (*enfatizar*) stress; crimp <*cabelo*>

friso /'frizu/ *m* frieze

fri|tada /fri'tada/ *f* fry-up; **~tar** *vt* fry; **~tas** *f pl* chips, (*Amer*) French fries; **~to** *a* fried; **está ~to** (*fam*) he's had it; **~tura** *f* fried food

frivolidade /frivoli'dadʒi/ *f* frivolity; **frívolo** *a* frivolous

fronha /'froɲa/ *f* pillowcase

fronte /'frõtʃi/ *f* forehead, brow

frontei|ra /frõ'tera/ *f* border; **~riço** *a* border

frota /'frɔta/ *f* fleet

frou|xidão /froʃi'dãw/ *f* looseness; (*moral*) laxity; **~xo** *a* loose; <*regulamento*> lax; <*pessoa*> lackadaisical

fru|gal /fru'gaw/ (*pl* **~gais**) *a* frugal; **~galidade** *f* frugality

frus|tração /frustra'sãw/ *f* frustration; **~trante** *a* frustrating; **~trar** *vt* frustrate

fru|ta /'fruta/ *f* fruit; **~ta-do-conde** (*pl* **~tas-do-conde**) *f* sweetsop; **~ta-pão** (*pl* **~tas-pão**) *f* breadfruit; **~teira** *f* fruitbowl; **~tífero** *a* (*fig*) fruitful; **~to** *m* fruit

fubá /fu'ba/ *m* maize flour

fu|çar /fu'sar/ *vi* nose around; **~ças** (*fam*) *f pl* face, chops

fu|ga /'fuga/ *f* escape; **~gaz** *a* fleeting; **~gida** *f* escape; **~gir** *vi* run away; (*soltar-se*) escape; **~-gir a** avoid; **~gitivo** *a & m* fugitive

fulano /fu'lanu/ *m* whatever his name is

fuleiro /fu'leru/ *a* down-market, cheap and cheerful

fulgor /fuw'gor/ *m* brightness; (*fig*) splendour

fuligem /fu'liʒẽ/ *f* soot

fulmi|nante /fuwmi'nãtʃi/ *a* devastating; **~nar** *vt* strike down; (*fig*) devastate; **~nado por um raio** struck by lightning □ *vi* (*criticar*) rail

fu|maça /fu'masa/ *f* smoke; **~maceira** *f* cloud of smoke; **~mante**, (*Port*) **~mador** *m* smoker; **~mar** *vt/i* smoke; **~-mê** *a invar* smoked; **~megar** *vi* smoke; **~mo** *m* (*tabaco*) tobacco; (*Port: fumaça*) smoke; (*fumar*) smoking

função /fũ'sãw/ *f* function; **em ~ de** as a result of; **fazer as funções de** function as

funcho /'fũʃu/ *m* fennel

funcio|nal /fũsio'naw/ (*pl* **~nais**) *a* functional; **~nalismo** *m* civil service; **~namento** *m* working; **~nar** *vi* work; **~nário** *m* employee; **~nário público** civil servant

fun|dação /fũda'sãw/ *f* foundation; **~dador** *m* founder □ *a* founding

fundamen|tal /fũdamẽ'taw/ (*pl* **~tais**) *a* fundamental; **~tar** *vt* (*basear*) base; (*justificar*) substantiate; **~to** *m* foundation

fun|dar /fũ'dar/ *vt* (*criar*) found; (*basear*) base; **~dar-se** *vpr* be based (**em** on); **~dear** *vi* drop anchor, anchor; **~dilho** *m* seat

fundir /fũ'dʒir/ *vt* melt <*ouro, ferro*>; cast <*sino, estátua*>; (*juntar*) merge; **~-se** *vpr* <*ouro, ferro*> melt; (*juntar-se*) merge

fundo /'fũdu/ *a* deep □ *m* (*parte de baixo*) bottom; (*parte de trás*) back; (*de quadro, foto*) background; (*de dinheiro*) fund; **no ~** basically; **~s** *m pl* (*da casa etc*) back; (*recursos*) funds

fúnebre /'funebri/ *a* funereal

funerário /fune'rariu/ *a* funeral

funesto /fu'nɛstu/ *a* fatal

fungar /fũ'gar/ *vt/i* sniff

fungo /'fũgu/ *m* fungus

fu|nil /fu'niw/ (*pl* **~nis**) *m* funnel; **~nilaria** *f* panel-beating; (*oficina*) bodyshop

furacão /fura'kãw/ *m* hurricane

furado /fu'radu/ *a* **papo ~** (*fam*) hot air

furão /fu'rãw/ *m* (*animal*) ferret

furar /fu'rar/ *vt* pierce <*orelha etc*>; puncture <*pneu*>; make a hole in <*roupa etc*>; jump <*fila*>; break <*greve*> □ *vi* <*roupa etc*> go into a hole; <*pneu*> puncture; (*fam*) <*programa*> fall through

fur|gão /fur'gãw/ *m* van; **~goneta** /e/ (*Port*) *f* van

fúria /'furia/ *f* fury

furioso /furi'ozu/ *a* furious

furo /'furu/ *m* hole; (*de pneu*) puncture; (*jornalístico*) scoop; (*fam: gafe*) blunder, faux pas; **dar um ~** put one's foot in it

furor /fu'ror/ *m* furore

fur|ta-cor /furta'kor/ *a invar* iridescent; **~tar** *vt* steal; **~-tivo** *a* furtive; **~to** *m* theft

furúnculo /fu'rũkulu/ *m* boil

fusão /fu'zãw/ *f* fusion; (*de empresas*) merger

fusca /'fuska/ *f* VW beetle

fuselagem /fuze'laʒẽ/ *f* fuselage

fusí|vel /fu'zivew/ (*pl* **~veis**) *m* fuse

fuso /'fuzu/ *m* spindle; **~ horário** time zone

fustigar /fustʃi'gar/ *vt* lash; (*fig: com palavras*) lash out at

futebol /futʃi'bɔw/ *m* football; **~ístico** *a* football

fú|til /'futʃiw/ (*pl* **~teis**) *a* frivolous, inane

futilidade /futʃili'dadʒi/ *f* frivolity, inanity; (*uma*) frivolous thing

futu|rismo /futu'rizmu/ *m* futurism; **~rista** *a & m* futurist; **~rístico** *a* futuristic; **~ro** *a & m* future

fu|zil /fu'ziw/ (*pl* **~zis**) *m* rifle; **~zilamento** *m* shooting; **~zilar** *vt* shoot □ *vi* flash; **~zileiro** *m* rifleman; **~zileiro naval** marine

fuzuê /fuzu'e/ *m* commotion

Gg

gabar-se /ga'barsi/ *vpr* boast (**de** of)

gabarito /gaba'ritu/ *m* calibre

gabinete /gabi'netʃi/ *m* (*em casa*) study; (*escritório*) office; (*ministros*) cabinet

gado /'gadu/ *m* livestock; (*bovino*) cattle

gaélico /ga'ɛliku/ *a & m* Gaelic

gafanhoto /gafa'ɲotu/ *m* (*pequeno*) grasshopper; (*grande*) locust

gafe /'gafi/ *f* faux pas, gaffe

gafieira /gafi'era/ *f* dance; (*salão*) dance hall

gagá /ga'ga/ *a* (*fam*) senile

ga|go /'gagu/ *a* stuttering □ *m* stutterer; **~gueira** *f* stutter; **~guejar** *vi* stutter

gaiato /gaj'atu/ *a* funny

gaiola /gaj'ɔla/ *f* cage

gaita /'gajta/ *f* **~ de foles** bagpipes

gaivota /gaj'vɔta/ *f* seagull

gajo /'gaʒu/ *m* (*Port*) guy, bloke

gala /'gala/ *f* **festa de ~** gala; **roupa de ~** formal dress

galã /ga'lã/ *m* leading man

galan|tear /galãtʃi'ar/ *vt* woo; **~teio** *m* wooing; (*um*) courtesy

galão /ga'lãw/ *m* (*enfeite*) braid; (*mil*) stripe; (*medida*) gallon; (*Port: café*) white coffee

galáxia /ga'laksia/ *f* galaxy

galé /ga'lɛ/ *f* galley

galego /ga'legu/ *a & m* Galician
galera /ga'lɛra/ *f* (*fam*) crowd
galeria /gale'ria/ *f* gallery
Gales /'galis/ *m* **País de ~** Wales
ga|lês /ga'les/ *a* (*f* **~lesa**) Welsh □ *m* (*f* **~lesa**) Welshman (*f*-woman); (*língua*) Welsh
galeto /ga'letu/ *m* spring chicken
galgar /gaw'gar/ *vt* (*transpor*) jump over; climb <*escada*>
galgo /'gawgu/ *m* greyhound
galheteiro /gaʎe'teru/ *m* cruet stand
galho /'gaʎu/ *m* branch; **quebrar um ~** (*fam*) help out
galináceos /gali'nasius/ *m pl* poultry
gali|nha /ga'liɲa/ *f* chicken; **~-nheiro** *m* chicken coop
galo /'galu/ *m* cock; (*inchação*) bump
galocha /ga'lɔʃa/ *f* Wellington boot
galo|pante /galo'pãtʃi/ *a* galloping; **~par** *vi* gallop; **~pe** /ɔ/ *m* gallop
galpão /gaw'pãw/ *m* shed
galvanizar /gawvani'zar/ *vt* galvanize
gama /'gama/ *f* (*musical*) scale; (*fig*) range
gamado /ga'madu/ *a* besotted (**por** with)
gamão /ga'mãw/ *m* backgammon
gamar /ga'mar/ *vi* fall in love (**por** with)
gana /'gana/ *f* desire
ganância /ga'nãsia/ *f* greed
ganancioso /ganãsi'ozu/ *a* greedy
gancho /'gãʃu/ *m* hook
gangorra /gã'goxa/ *f* seesaw
gangrena /gã'grena/ *f* gangrene
gangue /'gãgi/ *m* gang
ga|nhador /gaɲa'dor/ *m* winner □ *a* winning; **~nhar** *vt* win <*corrida, prêmio*>; earn <*salário*>; get <*presente*>; gain <*vantagem, tempo, amigo*> □ *vi* win; **~nhar a vida** earn a living; **~nha-pão** *m* livelihood; **~nho** *m* gain; *pl* (*no jogo*) winnings □ *pp de* **ganhar**
ga|nido *m* squeal; (*de cachorro*) yelp; **~nir** *vi* squeal; <*cachorro*> yelp
ganso /'gãsu/ *m* goose
gara|gem /ga'raʒẽ/ *f* garage; **~gista** *m/f* garage attendant
garanhão /gara'ɲãw/ *m* stallion
garan|tia /garã'tʃia/ *f* guarantee; **~tir** *vt* guarantee
garatujar /garatu'ʒar/ *vt* scribble
gar|bo /'garbu/ *m* grace; **~boso** *a* graceful
garça /'garsa/ *f* heron
gar|çom /gar'sõ/ *m* waiter; **~çonete** /ɛ/ *f* waitress
gar|fada /gar'fada/ *f* forkful; **~fo** *m* fork
gargalhada /garga'ʎada/ *f* gale of laughter; **rir às ~s** roar with laughter
gargalo /gar'galu/ *m* bottleneck; **tomar no ~** drink out of the bottle
garganta /gar'gãta/ *f* throat
gargare|jar /gargare'ʒar/ *vi* gargle; **~jo** /e/ *m* gargle
gari /ga'ri/ *m/f* (*lixeiro*) dustman, (*Amer*) garbage collector; (*varredor de rua*) roadsweeper, (*Amer*) streetsweeper
garim|par /garĩ'par/ *vi* prospect; **~peiro** *m* prospector; **~po** *m* mine
garo|a /ga'roa/ *f* drizzle; **~ar** *vi* drizzle
garo|ta /ga'rota/ *f* girl; **~to** /o/ *m* boy; (*Port: café*) coffee with milk
garoupa /ga'ropa/ *f* grouper
garra /'gaxa/ *f* claw; (*fig*) drive, determination; *pl* (*poder*) clutches
garra|fa /ga'xafa/ *f* bottle; **~fada** *f* blow with a bottle; **~fão** *m* flagon
garrancho /ga'xãʃu/ *m* scrawl
garrido /ga'xidu/ *a* (*alegre*) lively
garupa /ga'rupa/ *f* (*de animal*) rump; (*de moto*) pillion seat
gás /gas/ *m* gas; *pl* (*intestinais*) wind, (*Amer*) gas; **~ lacrimogêneo** tear gas
gasóleo /ga'zɔliu/ *m* diesel oil
gasolina /gazo'lina/ *f* petrol
gaso|sa /ga'zɔza/ *f* fizzy lemonade, (*Amer*) soda; **~so** *a* gaseous; <*bebida*> fizzy
gáspea /'gaspia/ *f* upper
gas|tador /gasta'dor/ *a & m* spendthrift; **~tar** *vt* spend <*dinheiro, tempo*>; use up <*energia*>; wear out <*roupa, sapatos*>; **~to** *m* expense; *pl* spending, expenditure; **dar para o ~to** do
gastrenterite /gastrẽte'ritʃi/ *f* gastroenteritis
gástrico /'gastriku/ *a* gastric
gastrite /gas'tritʃi/ *f* gastritis
gastronomia /gastrono'mia/ *f* gastronomy
ga|ta /'gata/ *f* cat; (*fam*) sexy woman; **~tão** *m* (*fam*) hunk
gatilho /ga'tʃiʎu/ *m* trigger
ga|tinha /ga'tʃiɲa/ *f* (*fam*) sexy woman; **~to** *m* cat; (*fam*) hunk; **fazer alg de ~to-sapato** treat s.o. like a doormat
gatuno /ga'tunu/ *m* crook □ *a* crooked
gaúcho /ga'uʃu/ *a & m* (person) from Rio Grande do Sul
gaveta /ga'veta/ *f* drawer
gavião /gavi'ãw/ *m* hawk
gaze /'gazi/ *f* gauze
gazela /ga'zɛla/ *f* gazelle
gazeta /ga'zeta/ *f* gazette
geada /ʒi'ada/ *f* frost

ge|ladeira /ʒela'dera/ *f* fridge; **~lado** *a* frozen; (*muito frio*) freezing □ *m* (*Port*) ice cream; **~lar** *vt/i* freeze
gelati|na /ʒela'tʃina/ *f* (*sobremesa*) jelly; (*pó*) gelatine; **~noso** /o/ *a* gooey
geléia /ʒe'lɛja/ *f* jam
ge|leira /ʒe'lera/ *f* glacier; **~lo** /e/ *m* ice
gema /'ʒema/ *f* (*de ovo*) yolk; (*pedra*) gem; **carioca da ~** carioca born and bred; **~da** *f* egg yolk whisked with sugar
gêmeo /'ʒemiu/ *a & m* twin; **Gêmeos** (*signo*) Gemini
ge|mer /ʒe'mer/ *vi* moan, groan; **~mido** *m* moan, groan
gene /'ʒɛni/ *m* gene; **~alogia** *f* genealogy; **~alógico** *a* genealogical; **árvore ~alógica** family tree
Genebra /ʒe'nɛbra/ *f* Geneva
gene|ral /ʒene'raw/ (*pl* **~rais**) *m* general; **~ralidade** *f* generality; **~ralização** *f* generalization; **~ralizar** *vt/i* generalize; **~ralizar-se** *vpr* become generalized
genérico /ʒe'nɛriku/ *a* generic
gênero /'ʒeneru/ *m* type, kind; (*gramatical*) gender; (*literário*) genre; *pl* goods; **~s alimentícios** foodstuffs; **ela não faz o meu ~** she's not my type
gene|rosidade /ʒenerozi'dadʒi/ *f* generosity; **~roso** /o/ *a* generous
genéti|ca /ʒe'nɛtʃika/ *f* genetics; **~co** *a* genetic
gengibre /ʒẽ'ʒibri/ *m* ginger
gengiva /ʒẽ'ʒiva/ *f* gum
geni|al /ʒeni'aw/ (*pl* **~ais**) *a* brilliant
gênio /'ʒeniu/ *m* genius; (*temperamento*) temperament
genioso /ʒeni'ozu/ *a* temperamental
geni|tal /ʒeni'taw/ (*pl* **~tais**) *a* genital
genitivo /ʒeni'tʃivu/ *a & m* genitive
genocídio /ʒeno'sidʒiu/ *m* genocide
genro /'ʒẽxu/ *m* son-in-law
gente /'ʒẽtʃi/ *f* people; (*fam*) folks; **a ~** (*sujeito*) we; (*objeto*) us □ *interj* (*fam*) gosh
gen|til /ʒẽ'tʃiw/ (*pl* **~tis**) *a* kind; **~tileza** /e/ *f* kindness
genuíno /ʒenu'inu/ *a* genuine
geo|grafia /ʒeogra'fia/ *f* geography; **~gráfico** *a* geographical
geógrafo /ʒe'ɔgrafu/ *m* geographer
geo|logia /ʒeolo'ʒia/ *f* geology; **~lógico** *a* geological
geólogo /ʒe'ɔlogu/ *m* geologist
geo|metria /ʒeome'tria/ *f* geometry; **~métrico** *a* geometrical; **~político** *a* geopolitical
Geórgia /ʒi'ɔrʒia/ *f* Georgia
georgiano /ʒiorʒi'anu/ *a & m* Georgian
gera|ção /ʒera'sãw/ *f* generation; **~dor** *m* generator
ge|ral /ʒe'raw/ (*pl* **~rais**) *a* general □ *f* (*limpeza*) spring-clean; **em ~ral** in general
gerânio /ʒe'raniu/ *m* geranium
gerar /ʒe'rar/ *vt* create; generate <*eletricidade*>
gerência /ʒe'rẽsia/ *f* management
gerenci|ador /ʒerẽsia'dor/ *m* manager; **~al** (*pl* **~ais**) *a* management; **~ar** *vt* manage
gerente /ʒe'rẽtʃi/ *m* manager □ *a* managing
gergelim /ʒerʒe'lĩ/ *m* sesame
geri|atria /ʒeria'tria/ *f* geriatrics; **~átrico** *a* geriatric
geringonça /ʒerĩ'gõsa/ *f* contraption
gerir /ʒe'rir/ *vt* manage
germânico /ʒer'maniku/ *a* Germanic
ger|me /'ʒɛrmi/ *m* germ; **~me de trigo** wheatgerm; **~minar** *vi* germinate
gerúndio /ʒe'rũdʒiu/ *m* gerund
gesso /'ʒesu/ *m* plaster
ges|tação /ʒesta'sãw/ *f* gestation; **~tante** *f* pregnant woman
gestão /ʒes'tãw/ *f* management
ges|ticular *vi* gesticulate; **~to** /'ʒɛstu/ *m* gesture
gibi /ʒi'bi/ *m* (*fam*) comic
Gibraltar /ʒibraw'tar/ *f* Gibraltar
gigan|te /ʒi'gãtʃi/ *a & m* giant; **~tesco** /e/ *a* gigantic
gilete /ʒi'lɛtʃi/ *f* razor blade □ *a & m/f* (*fam*) bisexual
gim /ʒĩ/ *m* gin
ginásio /ʒi'naziu/ *m* (*escola*) secondary school; (*de ginástica*) gymnasium
ginasta /ʒi'nasta/ *m/f* gymnast
ginásti|ca /ʒi'nastʃika/ *f* gymnastics; (*aeróbica*) aerobics; **~co** *a* gymnastic
ginecolo|gia /ʒinekolo'ʒia/ *f* gynaecology; **~gista** *m/f* gynaecologist
gingar /ʒĩ'gar/ *vi* sway
gira-discos /ʒira'diʃkuʃ/ *m invar* (*Port*) record player
girafa /ʒi'rafa/ *f* giraffe
gi|rar /ʒi'rar/ *vt/i* spin, revolve; **~rassol** (*pl* **~rassóis**) *m* sunflower; **~ratório** *a* revolving
gíria /'ʒiria/ *f* slang; (*uma ~*) slang expression
giro /'ʒiru/ *m* spin, turn □ *a* (*Port fam*) great
giz /ʒis/ *m* chalk
gla|cê /gla'se/ *m* icing; **~cial** (*pl* **~ciais**) *a* icy
glamour /gla'mur/ *m* glamour; **~oso** /o/ *a* glamorous

glândula /'glãdula/ *f* gland
glandular /glãdu'lar/ *a* glandular
glicerina /glise'rina/ *f* glycerine
glicose /gli'kɔzi/ *f* glucose
glo|bal /glo'baw/ (*pl* **~bais**) *a* (*mundial*) global; <*preço etc*> overall; **~bo** /o/ *m* globe; **~bo ocular** eyeball
glóbulo /'glɔbulu/ *m* globule; (*do sangue*) corpuscle
glória /'glɔria/ *f* glory
glori|ficar /glorifi'kar/ *vt* glorify; **~oso** /o/ *a* glorious
glossário /glo'sariu/ *m* glossary
glu|tão /glu'tãw/ *m* (*f* **~tona**) glutton □ *a* (*f* **~tona**) greedy
gnomo /gi'nomu/ *m* gnome
godê /go'de/ *a* flared
goela /go'ɛla/ *f* gullet
gogó /go'gɔ/ *m* (*fam*) Adam's apple
goia|ba /goj'aba/ *f* guava; **~bada** *f* guava jelly; **~beira** *f* guava tree
gol /'gow/ (*pl* **~s**) *m* goal
gola /'gɔla/ *f* collar
gole /'gɔli/ *m* mouthful
go|lear /goli'ar/ *vt* thrash; **~leiro** *m* goalkeeper
golfe /'gowfi/ *m* golf
golfinho /gow'fiɲu/ *m* dolphin
golfista /gow'fista/ *m/f* golfer
golo /'golu/ *m* (*Port*) goal
golpe /'gɔwpi/ *m* blow; (*manobra*) trick; **~ (de estado)** coup (d'état); **~ de mestre** masterstroke; **~ de vento** gust of wind; **~ de vista** glance; **~ar** *vt* hit
goma /'goma/ *f* gum; (*para roupa*) starch
gomo /'gomu/ *m* segment
gôndola /'gõdola/ *f* rack
gongo /'gõgu/ *m* gong
gonorréia /gono'xɛja/ *f* gonorrhea
gonzo /'gõzu/ *m* hinge
gorar /go'rar/ *vi* go wrong, fail
gor|do /'gordu/ *a* fat; **~ducho** *a* plump
gordu|ra /gor'dura/ *f* fat; **~rento** *a* greasy; **~roso** /u/ *a* fatty; <*pele*> greasy, oily
gorgolejar /gorgole'ʒar/ *vi* gurgle
gorila /go'rila/ *m* gorilla
gor|jear /gorʒi'ar/ *vi* twitter; **~jeio** *m* twittering
gorjeta /gor'ʒeta/ *f* tip
gorro /'goxu/ *m* hat
gos|ma /'gɔzma/ *f* slime; **~mento** *a* slimy
gos|tar /gos'tar/ *vi* **~tar de** like; **~to** /o/ *m* taste; (*prazer*) pleasure; **para o meu ~to** for my taste; **ter ~to de** taste of; **~toso** *a* nice; <*comida*> nice, tasty; (*fam*) <*pessoa*> gorgeous

go|ta /'gota/ *f* drop; (*que cai*) drip; (*doença*) gout; **foi a ~ta d'água** (*fig*) it was the last straw; **~teira** *f* (*buraco*) leak; (*cano*) gutter; **~tejar** *vi* drip; <*telhado*> leak □ *vt* drip
gótico /'gɔtʃiku/ *a* Gothic
gotícula /go'tʃicula/ *f* droplet
gover|nador /governa'dor/ *m* governor; **~namental** (*pl* **~namentais**) *a* government; **~nanta** *f* housekeeper; **~nante** *a* ruling □ *m/f* ruler; **~nar** *vt* govern; **~nista** *a* government □ *m/f* government supporter; **~no** /e/ *m* government
go|zação /goza'sãw/ *f* joking; (*uma*) send-up; **~zado** *a* funny; **~zar** *vt* **~zar (de)** enjoy; (*fam: zombar de*) make fun of □ *vi* (*ter orgasmo*) come; **~zo** *m* (*prazer*) enjoyment; (*posse*) possession; (*orgasmo*) orgasm; **ser um ~zo** be funny
Grã-Bretanha /grãbre'taɲa/ *f* Great Britain
graça /'grasa/ *f* grace; (*piada*) joke; (*humor*) humour, funny side; (*jur*) pardon; **de ~** for nothing; **sem ~** (*enfadonho*) dull; (*não engraçado*) unfunny; (*envergonhado*) embarrassed; **ser uma ~** be lovely; **ter ~** be funny; **não tem ~ sair sozinho** it's no fun to go out alone; **~s a** thanks to
grace|jar /grase'ʒar/ *vi* joke; **~jo** /e/ *m* joke
graci|nha /gra'siɲa/ *f* **ser uma ~nha** be sweet; **~oso** /o/ *a* gracious
grada|ção /grada'sãw/ *f* gradation; **~tivo** *a* gradual
grade /'gradʒi/ *f* grille, grating; (*cerca*) railings; **atrás das ~s** behind bars; **~ado** *a* <*janela*> barred
grado /'gradu/ *m* **de bom/mau ~** willingly/unwillingly
gradu|ação /gradua'sãw/ *f* graduation; (*mil*) rank; (*variação*) gradation; **~ado** *a* <*escala*> graduated; <*estudante*> graduate; <*militar*> high-ranking; (*eminente*) respected; **~al** (*pl* **~ais**) *a* gradual; **~ar** *vt* graduate <*escala*>; (*ordenar*) grade; (*regular*) regulate; **~ar-se** *vpr* <*estudante*> graduate
grafia /gra'fia/ *f* spelling
gráfi|ca /'grafika/ *f* (*arte*) graphics; (*oficina*) print shop; **~co** *a* graphic □ *m* (*pessoa*) printer; (*diagrama*) graph; *pl* (*de computador*) graphics
grã-fino /grã'finu/ (*fam*) *a* posh, upper-class □ *m* posh person

grafite /gra'fitʃi/ *f* (*mineral*) graphite; (*de lápis*) lead; (*pichação*) piece of graffiti

gra|fologia /grafolo'ʒia/ *f* graphology; **~fólogo** *m* graphologist

grama[1] /'grama/ *m* gramme

grama[2] /'grama/ *f* grass; **~do** *m* lawn; (*campo de futebol*) field

gramática /gra'matʃika/ *f* grammar

gramati|cal /gramatʃi'kaw/ (*pl* **~cais**) *a* grammatical

gram|peador /grãpia'dor/ *m* stapler; **~pear** *vt* staple <*papéis etc*>; tap <*telefone*>; **~po** *m* (*de cabelo*) hairclip; (*para papéis etc*) staple; (*ferramenta*) clamp

grana /'grana/ *f* (*fam*) cash

granada /gra'nada/ *f* (*projétil*) grenade; (*pedra*) garnet

gran|dalhão /grãda'ʎãw/ *a* (*f* **~dalhona**) enormous; **~dão** *a* (*f* **~dona**) huge; **~de** *a* big; (*fig*) <*escritor, amor etc*> great; **~deza** /e/ *f* greatness; (*tamanho*) magnitude; **~dioso** /o/ *a* grand

granel /gra'nɛw/ *m* **a ~** in bulk

granito /gra'nitu/ *m* granite

granizo /gra'nizu/ *m* hail

gran|ja /'grãʒa/ *f* farm; **~jear** *vt* win, gain

granulado /granu'ladu/ *a* granulated

grânulo /'granulu/ *m* granule

grão /grãw/ (*pl* **~s**) *m* grain; (*de café*) bean; **~-de-bico** (*pl* **~s-de-bico**) *m* chickpea

grasnar /graz'nar/ *vi* <*pato*> quack; <*rã*> croak; <*corvo*> caw

grati|dão /gratʃi'dãw/ *f* gratitude; **~ficação** *f* (*dinheiro a mais*) gratuity; (*recompensa*) gratification; **~ficante** *a* gratifying; **~ficar** *vt* (*dar dinheiro a*) give a gratuity to; (*recompensar*) gratify

gratinado /gratʃi'nadu/ *a & m* gratin

grátis /'gratʃis/ *adv* free

grato /'gratu/ *a* grateful

gratuito /gra'tuito/ *a* (*de graça*) free; (*sem motivo*) gratuitous

grau /graw/ *m* degree; **escola de 1°/2° ~** primary/secondary school

graúdo /gra'udu/ *a* big; (*importante*) important

gra|vação /grava'sãw/ *f* (*de som*) recording; (*de desenhos etc*) engraving; **~vador** *m* (*pessoa*) engraver; (*máquina*) tape recorder; **~vadora** *f* record company; **~var** *vt* record <*música, disco*>; (*fixar na memória*) memorize; (*estampar*) engrave

gravata /gra'vata/ *f* tie; (*golpe*) stranglehold; **~ borboleta** bowtie

grave /'gravi/ *a* serious; <*voz, som*> deep; <*acento*> grave

grávida /'gravida/ *f* pregnant

gravidade /gravi'dadʒi/ *f* gravity

gravidez /gravi'des/ *f* pregnancy

gravura /gra'vura/ *f* engraving; (*em livro*) illustration

graxa /'graʃa/ *f* (*de sapatos*) polish; (*de lubrificar*) grease

Grécia /'grɛsia/ *f* Greece

grego /'gregu/ *a & m* Greek

grei /grej/ *f* flock

gre|lha /'grɛʎa/ *f* grill; **~lhado** *a* grilled □ *m* grill; **~lhar** *vt* grill

grêmio /'gremiu/ *m* guild, association

grená /gre'na/ *a & m* dark red

gre|ta /'greta/ *f* crack; **~tar** *vt/i* crack

gre|ve /'grɛvi/ *f* strike; **entrar em ~ve** go on strike; **~ve de fome** hunger strike; **~vista** *m/f* striker

gri|fado /gri'fadu/ *a* in italics; **~far** *vt* italicize

griffe /'grifi/ *f* label, line

gri|lado /gri'ladu/ *a* (*fam*) hung-up; **~lar** (*fam*) *vt* bug; **~lar-se** *vpr* get hung-up (**com** about)

grilhão /gri'ʎãw/ *m* fetter

grilo /'grilu/ *m* (*bicho*) cricket; (*fam*) (*preocupação*) hang-up; (*problema*) hassle; (*barulho*) squeak

grinalda /gri'nawda/ *f* garland

gringo /'grĩgu/ (*fam*) *a* foreign □ *m* foreigner

gri|pado /gri'padu/ *a* **estar/ficar ~pado** have/get the flu; **~par-se** *vpr* get the flu; **~pe** *f* flu, influenza; **~pe das aves** bird flu

grisalho /gri'zaʎu/ *a* grey

gri|tante /gri'tãtʃi/ *a* <*erro*> glaring, gross; <*cor*> loud, garish; **~tar** *vt/i* shout; (*de medo*) scream; **~taria** *f* shouting; **~to** *m* shout; (*de medo*) scream; **aos ~tos** in a loud voice; **no ~to** (*fam*) by force

grogue /'grɔgi/ *a* groggy

grosa /'grɔza/ *f* gross

groselha /gro'zɛʎa/ *f* (*vermelha*) redcurrant; (*espinhosa*) gooseberry; **~ negra** blackcurrant

gros|seiro /gro'seru/ *a* rude; (*tosco, malfeito*) rough; **~seria** *f* rudeness; (*uma*) rude thing; **~so** /o/ *a* thick; <*voz*> deep; (*fam*) <*pessoa, atitude*> rude; **~sura** *f* thickness; (*fam: grosseria*) rudeness

grotesco /gro'tesku/ *a* grotesque

grua /'grua/ *f* crane

gru|dado /gru'dadu/ *a* stuck; (*fig*) very attached (**em** to); **~dar** *vt/i* stick; **~de** *m* glue; **~dento** *a* sticky

gru|nhido /gru'ɲidu/ *m* grunt; **~nhir** *vi* grunt
grupo /'grupu/ *m* group
gruta /'gruta/ *f* cave
guaraná /gwara'na/ *m* guarana
guarani /gwara'ni/ *a & m/f* Guarani
guarda /'gwarda/ *f* guard □ *m/f* guard; (*policial*) policeman (*f*-woman); **~ costeira** coastguard; **~-chuva** *m* umbrella; **~-costas** *m invar* bodyguard; **~dor** *m* parking attendant; **~-florestal** (*pl* **~s-florestais**) *m/f* forest ranger; **~-louça** *m* china cupboard; **~napo** *m* napkin, serviette; **~-noturno** (*pl* **~s-noturnos**) *m* night watchman
guardar /gwar'dar/ *vt* (*pôr no lugar*) put away; (*conservar*) keep; (*vigiar*) guard; (*não esquecer*) remember; **~-se de** guard against
guarda|-redes /'gwarda-'xedʃ/ *m invar* (*Port*) goalkeeper; **~-roupa** *m* wardrobe; **~-sol** (*pl* **~-sóis**) *m* sunshade
guardi|ão /gwardʒi'ãw/ (*pl* **~ães** *ou* **~ões**) *m* (*f* **~ã**) guardian
guarita /gwa'rita/ *f* sentry box
guar|necer /gwarne'ser/ *vt* (*fortificar*) garrison; (*munir*) equip; (*enfeitar*) garnish; **~nição** *f* (*mil*) garrison; (*enfeite*) garnish
Guatemala /gwate'mala/ *f* Guatemala
guatemalteco /gwatemal'tɛku/ *a & m* Guatemalan
gude /'gudʒi/ *m* **bola de ~** marble
guelra /'gɛwxa/ *f* gill
guer|ra /'gɛxa/ *f* war; **~reiro** *m* warrior □ *a* warlike; **~rilha** *f* guerrilla war; **~rilheiro** *a & m* guerrilla
gueto /'getu/ *m* ghetto
guia /'gia/ *m/f* guide □ *m* guide(book) □ *f* delivery note
Guiana /gi'ana/ *f* Guyana
guianense /gia'nẽsi/ *a & m/f* Guyanan
guiar /gi'ar/ *vt* guide; drive <*veículo*> □ *vi* drive; **~-se** *vpr* be guided
guichê /gi'ʃe/ *m* window
guidom /gi'dõ/, (*Port*) **guidão** /gi'dãw/ *m* handlebars
guilhotina /giʎo'tʃina/ *f* guillotine
guimba /'gĩba/ *f* butt
guinada /gi'nada/ *f* change of direction; **dar uma ~** change direction
guinchar[1] /gĩ'ʃar/ *vi* squeal; <*freios*> screech
guinchar[2] /gĩ'ʃar/ *vt* tow <*carro*>; (*içar*) winch
guincho[1] /'gĩʃu/ *m* squeal; (*de freios*) screech
guincho[2] /'gĩʃu/ *m* (*máquina*) winch; (*veículo*) tow truck
guin|dar /gĩ'dar/ *vt* hoist; **~daste** *m* crane
Guiné /gi'nɛ/ *f* Guinea
gui|sado /gi'zadu/ *m* stew; **~sar** *vt* stew
guitar|ra /gi'taxa/ *f* (electric) guitar; **~rista** *m/f* guitarist
guizo /'gizu/ *m* bell
gu|la /'gula/ *f* greed; **~lodice** *f* greed; **~loseima** *f* delicacy; **~loso** /o/ *a* greedy
gume /'gumi/ *m* cutting edge
guri /gu'ri/ *m* boy; **~a** *f* girl
guru /gu'ru/ *m* guru
gutu|ral /gutu'raw/ (*pl* **~rais**) *a* guttural

há|bil /'abiw/ (*pl* **~beis**) *a* clever, skilful
habili|dade /abili'dadʒi/ *f* skill; **ter ~dade com** be good with; **~doso** /o/ *a* skilful; **~tação** *f* qualification; **~tar** *vt* qualify
habi|tação /abita'sãw/ *f* housing; (*casa*) dwelling; **~tacional** (*pl* **~tacionais**) *a* housing; **~tante** *m/f* inhabitant; **~tar** *vt* inhabit □ *vi* live; **~tável** (*pl* **~táveis**) *a* habitable
hábito /'abitu/ *m* habit
habitu|al /abitu'aw/ (*pl* **~ais**) *a* habitual; **~ar** *vt* accustom (**a** to); **~ar-se** *vpr* get accustomed (**a** to)
hadoque /a'dɔki/ *m* haddock
Haia /'aja/ *f* the Hague
Haiti /aj'tʃi/ *m* Haiti
haitiano /ajtʃi'anu/ *a & m* Haitian
hálito /'alitu/ *m* breath
halitose /ali'tɔzi/ *f* halitosis
hall /xɔw/ (*pl* **~s**) *m* hall; (*de hotel*) foyer
halte|re /aw'tɛri/ *m* dumbbell; **~rofilismo** *m* weight lifting; **~rofilista** *m/f* weight lifter
hambúrguer /ã'burger/ *m* hamburger
hangar /ã'gar/ *m* hangar
haras /'aras/ *m invar* stud farm
hardware /'xarduɛr/ *m* hardware
harmo|nia /armo'nia/ *f* harmony; **~nioso** /o/ *a* harmonious; **~nizar** *vt* harmonize; (*conciliar*) reconcile; **~nizar-se** *vpr* (*combinar*) tone in; (*concordar*) coincide
har|pa /'arpa/ *f* harp; **~pista** *m/f* harpist

haste /'astʃi/ *m* pole; (*de planta*) stem, stalk; **~ar** *vt* hoist, raise
Havaí /ava'i/ *m* Hawaii
havaiano /avaj'anu/ *a* & *m* Hawaiian
haver /a'ver/ *m* credit; *pl* possessions ▫ *vt* (*auxiliar*) **havia sido** it had been; (*impessoal*) **há** there is/are; **ele trabalha aqui há anos** he's been working here for years; **ela morreu há vinte anos (atrás)** she died twenty years ago
haxixe /a'ʃiʃi/ *m* hashish
he|braico /e'brajku/ *a* & *m* Hebrew; **~breu** *a* & *m* (*f* **~bréia**) Hebrew
hectare /ek'tari/ *m* hectare
hediondo /edʒi'õdu/ *a* hideous
hein /ẽj/ *int* eh
hélice /'ɛlisi/ *f* propeller
helicóptero /eli'kɔpteru/ *m* helicopter
hélio /'ɛliu/ *m* helium
heliporto /eli'portu/ *m* heliport
hem /ẽj/ *int* eh
hematoma /ema'toma/ *m* bruise
hemisfério /emis'fɛriu/ *m* hemisphere; **Hemisfério Norte/Sul** Northern/ Southern Hemisphere
hemo|filia /emofi'lia/ *f* haemophilia; **~fílico** *a* & *m* haemophiliac; **~globina** *f* haemoglobin; **~grama** *m* blood count
hemor|ragia /emoxa'ʒia/ *f* haemorrhage; **~róidas** *f pl* haemorrhoids
henê /e'ne/ *m* henna
hepatite /epa'tʃitʃi/ *f* hepatitis
hera /'ɛra/ *f* ivy
heráldi|ca /e'rawdʒika/ *f* heraldry; **~co** *a* heraldic
herança /e'rãsa/ *f* inheritance; (*de um povo etc*) heritage
her|bicida /erbi'sida/ *m* weedkiller; **~bívoro** *a* herbivorous ▫ *m* herbivore
her|dar /er'dar/ *vt* inherit; **~-deiro** *m* heir
hereditário /eredʒi'tariu/ *a* hereditary
here|ge /e'rɛʒi/ *m*/*f* heretic; **~sia** *f* heresy
herético /e'rɛtʃiku/ *a* heretical
hermético /er'mɛtʃiku/ *a* airtight; (*fig*) obscure
hérnia /'ɛrnia/ *f* hernia
herói /e'rɔj/ *m* hero; **~co** *a* heroic
hero|ína /ero'ina/ *f* (*mulher*) heroine; (*droga*) heroin; **~ismo** *m* heroism
herpes /'ɛrpis/ *m invar* herpes; **~-zoster** *m* shingles
hesi|tação /ezita'sãw/ *f* hesitation; **~tante** *a* hesitant; **~tar** *vi* hesitate
hetero|doxo /etero'dɔksu/ *a* unorthodox; **~gêneo** *a* heterogeneous
heterossexu|al /eteroseksu'aw/ (*pl* **~ais**) *a* & *m* heterosexual
hexago|nal /eksago'naw/ (*pl* **~nais**) *a* hexagonal
hexágono /ek'sagonu/ *m* hexagon
hiato /i'atu/ *m* hiatus
hiber|nação /iberna'sãw/ *f* hibernation; **~nar** *vi* hibernate
híbrido /'ibridu/ *a* & *m* hybrid
hidrante /i'drãtʃi/ *m* fire hydrant
hidra|tante /idra'tãtʃi/ *a* moisturising ▫ *m* moisturizer; **~tar** *vt* moisturize <*pele*>; **~to** *m* **~to de carbono** carbohydrate
hidráuli|ca /i'drawlika/ *f* hydraulics; **~co** *a* hydraulic
hidrelétri|ca /idre'lɛtrika/ *f* hydroelectric power station; **~co** *a* hydroelectric
hidro|avião /idroavi'ãw/ *m* seaplane; **~carboneto** /e/ *m* hydrocarbon
hidrófilo /i'drɔfilu/ *a* absorbent; **algodão ~** cotton wool, (*Amer*) absorbent cotton
hidrofobia /idrofo'bia/ *f* rabies
hidro|gênio /idro'ʒeniu/ *m* hydrogen; **~massagem** *f* **banheira de ~massagem** jacuzzi; **~via** *f* waterway
hiena /i'ena/ *f* hyena
hierarquia /ierar'kia/ *f* hierarchy
hieróglifo /ie'rɔglifu/ *m* hieroglyphic
hífen /'ifẽ/ *m* hyphen
higi|ene /iʒi'eni/ *f* hygiene; **~ênico** *a* hygienic
hilari|ante /ilari'ãtʃi/ *a* hilarious; **~dade** *f* hilarity
Himalaia /ima'laja/ *m* Himalayas
hin|di /ĩ'dʒi/ *m* Hindi; **~du** *a* & *m*/*f* Hindu; **~duísmo** *m* Hinduism; **~duísta** *a* & *m*/*f* Hindu
hino /'inu/ *m* hymn; **~ nacional** national anthem
hipermercado /ipermer'kadu/ *m* hypermarket
hipersensí|vel /iperse͂'sivew/ (*pl* **~veis**) *a* hypersensitive
hipertensão /iperte͂'sãw/ *f* hypertension
hípico /'ipiku/ *a* horseriding
hipismo /i'pizmu/ *m* horseriding; (*corridas*) horseracing
hip|nose /ipi'nɔzi/ *f* hypnosis; **~nótico** *a* hypnotic; **~notismo** *m* hypnotism; **~notizador** *m* hypnotist; **~notizar** *vt* hypnotize
hipocondríaco /ipokõ'driaku/ *a* & *m* hypochondriac
hipocrisia /ipokri'zia/ *f* hypocrisy
hipócrita /i'pɔkrita/ *m*/*f* hypocrite ▫ *a* hypocritical

hipódromo /i'pɔdromu/ *m* race course, (*Amer*) race track

hipopótamo /ipo'pɔtamu/ *m* hippopotamus

hipote|ca /ipo'tɛka/ *f* mortgage; **~car** *vt* mortgage; **~cário** *a* mortgage

hipotermia /ipoter'mia/ *f* hypothermia

hipótese /i'pɔtezi/ *f* hypothesis; **na ~ de** in the event of; **na pior das ~s** at worst

hipotético /ipo'tɛtʃiku/ *a* hypothetical

hirto /'irtu/ *adj* rigid, stiff

hispânico /is'paniku/ *a* Hispanic

histamina /ista'mina/ *f* histamine

his|terectomia /isterekto'mia/ *f* hysterectomy; **~teria** *f* hysteria; **~térico** *a* hysterical; **~terismo** *m* hysteria

his|tória /is'tɔria/ *f* (*do passado*) history; (*conto*) story; *pl* (*amolação*) trouble; **~toriador** *m* historian; **~tórico** *a* historical; (*marcante*) historic □ *m* history

hoje /'oʒi/ *adv* today; **~ em dia** nowadays; **~ de manhã** this morning; **~ à noite** tonight

Holanda /o'lãda/ *f* Holland

holan|dês /olã'des/ *a* (*f* **~desa**) Dutch □ *m* (*f* **~desa**) Dutchman (*f*-woman); (*língua*) Dutch; **os ~deses** the Dutch

holding /'xɔwdʒĩ/ (*pl* **~s**) *f* holding company

holerite /ole'ritʃi/ *m* pay slip

holo|causto /olo'kawstu/ *m* holocaust; **~fote** /ɔ/ *m* spotlight; **~grama** *m* hologram

homem /'omẽ/ *m* man; **~ de negócios** businessman; **~-rã** (*pl* **homens-rã**) *m* frogman

homena|gear /omenaʒi'ar/ *vt* pay tribute to; **~gem** *f* tribute; **em ~gem a** in honour of

homeo|pata /omio'pata/ *m*/*f* homoeopath; **~patia** *f* homoeopathy; **~pático** *a* homoeopathic

homérico /o'mɛriku/ *a* (*estrondoso*) booming; (*extraordinário*) phenomenal

homi|cida /omi'sida/ *a* homicidal □ *m*/*f* murderer; **~cídio** *m* homicide; **~cídio involuntário** manslaughter

homo|geneizado /omoʒenej'zadu/ *a* <*leite*> homogenized; **~gêneo** *a* homogeneous

homologar /omolo'gar/ *vt* ratify

homólogo /o'mɔlogu/ *m* opposite number □ *a* equivalent

homônimo /o'monimu/ *m* (*xará*) namesake; (*vocábulo*) homonym

homossexu|al /omoseksu'aw/ (*pl* **~ais**) *a* & *m* homosexual; **~alismo** *m* homosexuality

Honduras /õ'duras/ *f* Honduras

hondurenho /õdu'reɲu/ *a* & *m* Honduran

hones|tidade /onestʃi'dadʒi/ *f* honesty; **~to** /ɛ/ *a* honest

hono|rário /ono'rariu/ *a* honorary; **~rários** *m pl* fees; **~rífico** *a* honorific

hon|ra /'õxa/ *f* honour; **~radez** *f* honesty, integrity; **~rado** *a* honourable; **~rar** *vt* honour; **~roso** /o/ *a* honourable

hóquei /'ɔkej/ *m* (field) hockey; **~ sobre gelo** ice hockey; **~ sobre patins** roller hockey

hora /'ɔra/ *f* (*unidade de tempo*) hour; (*ocasião*) time; **que ~s são?** what's the time?; **a que ~s?** at what time?; **às três ~s** at three o'clock; **dizer as ~s** tell the time; **tem ~s?** do you have the time?; **de ~ em ~** every hour; **em cima da ~** at the last minute; **na ~** (*naquele momento*) at the time; (*no ato*) on the spot; (*a tempo*) on time; **está na ~ de ir** it's time to go; **na ~ H** (*no momento certo*) at just the right moment; (*no momento crítico*) at the crucial moment; **meia ~** half an hour; **toda ~** all the time; **fazer ~** kill time; **marcar ~** make an appointment; **perder a ~** lose track of time; **não tenho ~** my time is my own; **não vejo a ~ de ir** I can't wait to go; **~s extras** overtime; **~s vagas** spare time

horário /o'rariu/ *a* hourly; **km ~s** km per hour □ *m* (*hora*) time; (*tabela*) timetable; (*de trabalho etc*) hours; **~ nobre** prime time

horda /'ɔrda/ *f* horde

horista /o'rista/ *a* paid by the hour □ *m*/*f* worker paid by the hour

horizon|tal /orizõ'taw/ (*pl* **~tais**) *a* & *f* horizontal; **~te** *m* horizon

hor|monal /ormo'naw/ (*pl* **~monais**) *a* hormonal; **~mônio** *m* hormone

horóscopo /o'rɔskopu/ *m* horoscope

horrendo /o'xẽdu/ *a* horrid

horripi|lante /oxipi'lãtʃi/ *a* horrifying; **~lar** *vt* horrify

horrí|vel /o'xivew/ (*pl* **~veis**) *a* horrible, awful

horror /o'xor/ *m* horror (**a** of); (*coisa horrorosa*) horrible thing; **ser um ~** be awful; **que ~!** how awful!

horro|rizar /oxori'zar/ *vt*/*i* horrify; **~rizar-se** *vpr* be horrified; **~roso** /o/ *a* horrible

horta /'ɔrta/ *f* vegetable plot; **~ comercial** market garden, (*Amer*) truck farm; **~liça** *f* vegetable

hortelã /orte'lã/ *f* mint; **~-pimenta** peppermint

horti|cultor /ortʃikuw'tor/ *m* horticulturalist; **~cultura** *f* horticulture; **~frutigranjeiros** *m pl* fruit and vegetables; **~granjeiros** *m pl* vegetables

horto /'ortu/ *m* market garden; (*viveiro*) nursery

hospe|dagem /ospe'daʒẽ/ *f* accommodation; **~dar** *vt* put up; **~dar-se** *vpr* stay

hóspede /'ɔspidʒi/ *m/f* guest

hospedei|ra /ospe'dera/ *f* landlady; **~ra de bordo** (*Port*) stewardess; **~ro** *m* landlord

hospício /os'pisiu/ *m* (*de loucos*) asylum

hospi|tal /ospi'taw/ (*pl* **~tais**) *m* hospital; **~talar** *a* hospital; **~taleiro** *a* hospitable; **~talidade** *f* hospitality; **~talizar** *vt* hospitalize

hóstia /'ɔstʃia/ *f* Host, Communion wafer

hos|til /os'tʃiw/ (*pl* **~tis**) *a* hostile; **~tilidade** *f* hostility; **~tilizar** *vt* antagonize

ho|tel /o'tɛw/ (*pl* **~téis**) *m* hotel; **~teleiro** *a* hotel □ *m* hotelier

huma|nidade /umani'dadʒi/ *f* humanity; **~nismo** *m* humanism; **~nista** *a & m/f* humanist; **~nitário** *a & m* humanitarian; **~nizar** *vt* humanize; **~no** *a* human; (*compassivo*) humane; **~nos** *m pl* humans

húmido /'umidu/ *adj* (*Port*) humid

humil|dade /umiw'dadʒi/ *f* humility; **~de** *a* humble

humi|lhação /umiʎa'sãw/ *f* humiliation; **~lhante** *a* humiliating; **~lhar** *vt* humiliate

humor /u'mor/ *m* humour; (*disposição do espírito*) mood; **de bom/mau ~** in a good/bad mood

humo|rismo /umo'rizmu/ *m* humour; **~rista** *m/f* (*no palco*) comedian; (*escritor*) humorist; **~rístico** *a* humorous

húngaro /'ũgaru/ *a & m* Hungarian

Hungria /ũ'gria/ *f* Hungary

hurra /'uxa/ *int* hurrah □ *m* cheer

Ii

ia|te /i'atʃi/ *m* yacht; **~tismo** *m* yachting; **~tista** *m/f* yachtsman (*f*-woman)

ibérico /i'bɛriku/ *a & m* Iberian

ibope /i'bɔpi/ *m* **dar ~** (*fam*) be popular

içar /i'sar/ *vt* hoist

iceberg /ajs'bɛrgi/ (*pl* **~s**) *m* iceberg

ícone /'ikoni/ *m* icon

iconoclasta /ikono'klasta/ *m/f* iconoclast □ *a* iconoclastic

icterícia /ikte'risia/ *f* jaundice

ida /'ida/ *f* going; **na ~** on the way there; **~ e volta** return, (*Amer*) round trip

idade /i'dadʒi/ *f* age; **meia ~** middle age; **homem de meia ~** middle-aged man; **senhor de ~** elderly man; **Idade Média** Middle Ages

ide|al /ide'aw/ (*pl* **~ais**) *a & m* ideal; **~alismo** *m* idealism; **~alista** *m/f* idealist □ *a* idealistic; **~alizar** *vt* (*criar*) devise; (*sublimar*) idealize; **~ar** *vt* devise; **~ário** *m* ideas

idéia /i'dɛja/ *f* idea; **mudar de ~** change one's mind

idem /'idẽ/ *adv* ditto

idêntico /i'dẽtʃiku/ *a* identical

identi|dade /idẽtʃi'dadʒi/ *f* identity; **~ficar** *vt* identify; **~ficar-se** *vpr* identify (**com** with)

ideo|logia /ideolo'ʒia/ *f* ideology; **~lógico** *a* ideological

idílico /i'dʒiliku/ *a* idyllic

idílio /i'dʒiliu/ *m* idyll

idio|ma /idʒi'oma/ *m* language; **~mático** *a* idiomatic

idio|ta /idʒi'ɔta/ *m/f* idiot □ *a* idiotic; **~tice** *f* stupidity; (*uma*) stupid thing

idola|trar /idola'trar/ *vt* idolize; **~tria** *f* idolatry

ídolo /'idulu/ *m* idol

idôneo /i'doniu/ *a* suitable

idoso /i'dozu/ *a* elderly

Iêmen /i'emẽ/ *m* Yemen

iemenita /ieme'nita/ *a & m/f* Yemeni

iene /i'ɛni/ *m* yen

iglu /i'glu/ *m* igloo

ignição /igni'sãw/ *f* ignition

ignomínia /igno'minia/ *f* ignominy

igno|rância /igno'rãsia/ *f* ignorance; **~rante** *a* ignorant; **~rar** (*desconsiderar*) ignore; (*desconhecer*) not know

igreja /i'greʒa/ *f* church

igu|al /i'gwaw/ (*pl* **~ais**) *a* equal; (*em aparência*) identical; (*liso*) even □ *m/f* equal; **por ~al** equally; **~alar** *vt* equal; level <*terreno*>; **~alar(-se) a** be equal to; **~aldade** *f* equality; **~alitário** *a* egalitarian; **~almente** *adv* equally; (*como resposta*) the same to you; **~alzinho** *a* exactly the same (**a** as)

iguaria /igwa'ria/ *f* delicacy

iídiche /i'idiʃi/ *m* Yiddish

ile|gal /ile'gaw/ (*pl* **~gais**) *a* illegal; **~galidade** *f* illegality

ilegítimo /ile'ʒitʃimu/ *a* illegitimate

ilegí|vel /ile'ʒivew/ (*pl* **~veis**) *a* illegible

ileso /i'lɛzu/ *a* unhurt

iletrado /ile'tradu/ *adj* & *m* illiterate

ilha /'iʎa/ *f* island

ilharga /i'ʎarga/ *f* side

ilhéu /i'ʎɛw/ *m* (*f* **ilhoa**) islander

ilhós /i'ʎɔs/ *m invar* eyelet

ilhota /i'ʎɔta/ *f* small island

ilícito /i'lisitu/ *a* illicit

ilimitado /ilimi'tadu/ *a* unlimited

ilógico /i'lɔʒiku/ *a* illogical

iludir /ilu'dʒir/ *vt* delude; **~-se** *vpr* delude o.s.

ilumi|nação /ilumina'sãw/ *f* lighting; (*inspiração*) enlightenment; **~nar** *vt* light up, illuminate; (*inspirar*) enlighten

ilu|são /ilu'zãw/ *f* illusion; (*sonho*) delusion; **~sionista** *m*/*f* illusionist; **~sório** *a* illusory

ilus|tração /ilustra'sãw/ *f* illustration; (*erudição*) learning; **~-trador** *m* illustrator; **~trar** *vt* illustrate; **~trativo** *a* illustrative; **~tre** *a* illustrious; **~tríssimo senhor** Dear Sir

ímã /'imã/ *m* magnet

imaculado /imaku'ladu/ *a* immaculate

imagem /i'maʒẽ/ *f* image; (*da TV*) picture

imagi|nação /imaʒina'sãw/ *f* imagination; **~nar** *vt* imagine; **~nário** *a* imaginary; **~nativo** *a* imaginative; **~nável** (*pl* **~náveis**) *a* imaginable; **~noso** /o/ *a* imaginative

imatu|ridade /imaturi'dadʒi/ *f* immaturity; **~ro** *a* immature

imbatí|vel /ĩba'tʃivew/ (*pl* **~veis**) *a* unbeatable

imbe|cil /ĩbe'siw/ (*pl* **~cis**) *a* stupid □ *m*/*f* imbecile

imberbe /ĩ'berbi/ *adj* (*sem barba*) beardless

imbricar /ĩbri'kar/ *vt* overlap; **~-se** *vpr* overlap

imedia|ções /imedʒia'sõjs/ *f pl* vicinity; **~tamente** *adv* immediately; **~to** *a* immediate

imemori|al /imemori'aw/ (*pl* **~ais**) *a* immemorial

imen|sidão /imẽsi'dãw/ *f* vastness; **~so** *a* immense

imergir /imer'ʒir/ *vt* immerse

imi|gração /imigra'sãw/ *f* immigration; **~grante** *a* & *m*/*f* immigrant; **~grar** *vi* immigrate

imi|nência /imi'nẽsia/ *f* imminence; **~nente** *a* imminent

imiscuir-se /imisku'irsi/ *vpr* interfere

imi|tação /imita'sãw/ *f* imitation; **~tador** *m* imitator; **~tar** *vt* imitate

imobili|ária /imobili'aria/ *f* estate agent's, (*Amer*) realtor; **~ário** *a* property; **~dade** *f* immobility; **~zar** *vt* immobilize

imo|ral /imo'raw/ (*pl* **~rais**) *a* immoral; **~ralidade** *f* immorality

imor|tal /imor'taw/ (*pl* **~tais**) *a* immortal □ *m*/*f* member of the Brazilian Academy of Letters; **~talidade** *f* immortality; **~talizar** *vt* immortalize

imó|vel /i'mɔvew/ (*pl* **~veis**) *a* motionless, immobile □ *m* building, property; *pl* property, real estate

impaci|ência /ĩpasi'ẽsia/ *f* impatience; **~entar-se** *vpr* get impatient; **~ente** *a* impatient

impacto /ĩ'paktu/, (*Port*) **impacte** /ĩ'paktʃi/ *m* impact

impagá|vel /ĩpa'gavew/ (*pl* **~veis**) *a* priceless

ímpar /'ĩpar/ *a* unique; <*número*> odd

imparci|al /ĩparsi'aw/ (*pl* **~ais**) *a* impartial; **~alidade** *f* impartiality

impasse /ĩ'pasi/ *m* impasse

impassí|vel /ĩpa'sivew/ (*pl* **~veis**) *a* impassive

impecá|vel /ĩpe'kavew/ (*pl* **~veis**) *a* impeccable

impe|dido /ĩpe'dʒidu/ *a* <*rua*> blocked; (*Port: ocupado*) engaged, (*Amer*) busy; (*no futebol*) offside; **~dimento** *m* prevention; (*estorvo*) obstruction; (*no futebol*) offside position; **~dir** *vt* stop; (*estorvar*) hinder; block <*rua*>; **~dir alg de ir** *ou* **que alg vá** stop s.o. going

impelir /ĩpe'lir/ *vt* drive

impenetrá|vel /ĩpene'travew/ (*pl* **~veis**) *a* impenetrable

impensá|vel /ĩpẽ'savew/ (*pl* **~veis**) *a* unthinkable

impe|rador /ĩpera'dor/ *m* emperor; **~rar** *vi* reign, rule; **~rativo** *a* & *m* imperative; **~ratriz** *f* empress

imperceptí|vel /ĩpersep'tʃivew/ (*pl* **~veis**) *a* imperceptible

imperdí|vel /ĩper'dʒivew/ (*pl* **~veis**) *a* unmissable

imperdoá|vel /ĩperdo'avew/ (*pl* **~veis**) *a* unforgivable

imperfei|ção /ĩperfej'sãw/ *f* imperfection; **~to** *a* & *m* imperfect

imperi|al /ĩperi'aw/ (*pl* **~ais**) *a* imperial; **~alismo** *m* imperialism; **~alista** *a* & *m*/*f* imperialist

império /ĩ'pɛriu/ *m* empire

imperioso /ĩperi'ozu/ *a* imperious; <*necessidade*> pressing

imperme|abilizar /ĩpermiabili-'zar/ *vt* waterproof; **~ável** (*pl* **~áveis**) *a* waterproof; (*fig*) impervious (**a** to) ▫ *m* raincoat

imperti|nência /ĩpertʃi'nẽsia/ *f* impertinence; **~nente** *a* impertinent

impesso|al /ĩpeso'aw/ (*pl* **~ais**) *a* impersonal

ímpeto /'ĩpetu/ *m* (*vontade*) urge, impulse; (*de emoção*) surge; (*movimento*) start; (*na física*) impetus

impetuo|sidade /ĩpetuozi'dadʒi/ *f* impetuosity; **~so** /o/ *a* impetuous

impiedoso /ĩpie'dozu/ *a* merciless

impingir /ĩpĩ'ʒir/ *vt* foist (**a** on)

implacá|vel /ĩpla'kavew/ (*pl* **~veis**) *a* implacable

implan|tar /ĩplã'tar/ *vt* introduce; (*no corpo*) implant; **~te** *m* implant

implemen|tar /ĩplemẽ'tar/ *vt* implement; **~to** *m* implement

impli|cação /ĩplika'sãw/ *f* implication; **~cância** *f* (*ato*) harassment; (*antipatia*) grudge; **estar de ~cância com** have it in for; **~cante** *a* troublesome ▫ *m/f* troublemaker; **~car** *vt* (*comprometer*) implicate; **~car (em)** (*dar a entender*) imply; (*acarretar, exigir*) involve; **~car com** (*provocar*) pick on; (*antipatizar*) not get on with

implícito /ĩ'plisitu/ *a* implicit

implorar /ĩplo'rar/ *vt* plead for (**a** from)

imponente /ĩpo'nẽtʃi/ *a* imposing

impopular /ĩpopu'lar/ *a* unpopular

impor /ĩ'por/ *vt* impose (**a** on); command <*respeito*>; **~-se** *vpr* assert o.s.

impor|tação /ĩporta'sãw/ *f* import; **~tador** *m* importer; **~tadora** *f* import company; **~tados** *m pl* imported goods; **~tância** *f* importance; (*quantia*) amount; **ter ~tância** be important; **~tante** *a* important; **~tar** *vt* import <*mercadorias*> ▫ *vi* matter; **~tar em** (*montar a*) amount to; (*resultar em*) lead to; **~tar-se (com)** mind

importu|nar /ĩportu'nar/ *vt* bother; **~no** *a* annoying

imposição /ĩpozi'sãw/ *f* imposition

impossibili|dade /ĩposibili'dadʒi/ *f* impossibility; **~tar** *vt* make impossible; **~tar alg de ir, ~tar a alg ir** prevent s.o. from going, make it impossible for s.o. to go

impossí|vel /ĩpo'sivew/ (*pl* **~veis**) *a* impossible

impos|to /ĩ'postu/ *m* tax; **~to de renda** income tax; **~to sobre o valor acrescentado** (*Port*) VAT; **~tor** *m* impostor; **~tura** *f* deception

impo|tência /ĩpo'tẽsia/ *f* impotence; **~tente** *a* impotent

impreci|são /ĩpresi'zãw/ *f* imprecision; **~so** *a* imprecise

impregnar /ĩpreg'nar/ *vt* impregnate

imprensa /ĩ'prẽsa/ *f* press; **~ marrom** gutter press

imprescindí|vel /ĩpresĩ'dʒivew/ (*pl* **~veis**) *a* essential

impres|são /ĩpre'sãw/ *f* impression; (*no prelo*) printing; **~são digital** fingerprint; **~sionante** *a* (*imponente*) impressive; (*comovente*) striking; **~sionar** *vt* (*causar admiração*) impress; (*co-mover*) make an impression on; **~sionar-se** *vpr* be impressed (**com** by); **~sionável** (*pl* **~sionáveis**) *a* impressionable; **~sionismo** *m* impressionism; **~sionista** *a & m/f* impressionist; **~so** *a* printed ▫ *m* printed sheet; *pl* printed matter; **~sor** *m* printer; **~sora** *f* printer

imprestá|vel /ĩpres'tavew/ (*pl* **~veis**) *a* useless

impre|visível /ĩprevi'zivew/ (*pl* **~visíveis**) *a* unpredictable; **~visto** *a* unforeseen ▫ *m* unforeseen circumstance

imprimir /ĩpri'mir/ *vt* print

impropério /ĩpro'pɛriu/ *m* term of abuse; *pl* abuse

impróprio /ĩ'prɔpriu/ *a* improper; (*inadequado*) unsuitable (**para** for)

imprová|vel /ĩpro'vavew/ (*pl* **~veis**) *a* unlikely

improvi|sação /ĩproviza'sãw/ *f* improvisation; **~sar** *vt/i* improvise; **~so** *m* **de ~so** on the spur of the moment

impru|dência /ĩpru'dẽsia/ *f* recklessness; **~dente** *a* reckless

impul|sionar /ĩpuwsio'nar/ *vt* drive; **~sivo** *a* impulsive; **~so** *m* impulse

impu|ne /ĩ'puni/ *a* unpunished; **~nidade** *f* impunity

impu|reza /ĩpu'reza/ *f* impurity; **~ro** *a* impure

imun|dície /imũ'dʒisi/ *f* filth; **~do** *a* filthy

imu|ne /i'muni/ *a* immune (**a** to); **~nidade** *f* immunity; **~nizar** *vt* immunize

inabalá|vel /inaba'lavew/ (*pl* **~veis**) *a* unshakeable

iná|bil /i'nabiw/ (*pl* **~bis**) *a* (*desafeitado*) clumsy

inabitado /inabi'tadu/ *a* uninhabited

inacabado /inaka'badu/ *a* unfinished

inaceitá|vel /inasej'tavew/ (*pl* **~veis**) *a* unacceptable

inacessí|vel /inase'sivew/ (*pl* **~veis**) *a* inaccessible

inacreditá|vel /inakredʒi'tavew/ (*pl* **~veis**) *a* unbelievable

inadequado /inade'kwadu/ *a* unsuitable

inadmissí|vel /inadʒimi'sivew/ (*pl* **~veis**) *a* inadmissible

inadvertência /inadʒiver'tēsia/ *f* oversight

inalar /ina'lar/ *vt* inhale

inalcançá|vel /inawkã'savew/ (*pl* **~veis**) *a* unattainable

inalterá|vel /inawte'ravew/ (*pl* **~veis**) *a* unchangeable

inanição /inani'sãw/ *f* starvation

inanimado /inani'madu/ *a* inanimate

inapto /i'naptu/ *a* (*incapaz*) unfit

inati|vidade /inatʃivi'dadʒi/ *f* inactivity; **~vo** *a* inactive

inato /i'natu/ *a* innate

inaudito /inaw'dʒitu/ *a* unheard of

inaugu|ração /inawgura'sãw/ *f* inauguration; **~ral** (*pl* **~rais**) *a* inaugural; **~rar** *vt* inaugurate

incabí|vel /ĩka'bivew/ (*pl* **~veis**) *a* inappropriate

incalculá|vel /ĩkawku'lavew/ (*pl* **~veis**) *a* incalculable

incandescente /ĩkãde'sẽtʃi/ *a* red-hot

incansá|vel /ĩkã'savew/ (*pl* **~veis**) *a* tireless

incapaci|tado /ĩkapasi'tadu/ *a* <*pessoa*> disabled; **~tar** *vt* incapacitate

incauto /ĩ'kawtu/ *a* reckless

incendi|ar /ĩsẽdʒi'ar/ *vt* set alight; **~ar-se** *vpr* catch fire; **~ário** *a* incendiary; (*fig*) <*discurso*> inflammatory □ *m* arsonist; (*fig*) agitator

incêndio /ĩ'sẽdʒiu/ *m* fire

incenso /ĩ'sẽsu/ *m* incense

incenti|var /ĩsẽtʃi'var/ *vt* encourage; **~vo** *m* incentive

incer|teza /ĩser'teza/ *f* uncertainty; **~to** /ɛ/ *a* uncertain

inces|to /ĩ'sɛstu/ *m* incest; **~tuoso** /o/ *a* incestuous

in|chação /ĩʃa'sãw/ *f* swelling; **~char** *vt/i* swell

inci|dência /ĩsi'dẽsia/ *f* incidence; **~dente** *m* incident; **~dir** *vi* **~dir em** <*luz*> shine on; <*imposto*> be payable on

incinerar /ĩsine'rar/ *vt* incinerate

inci|são /ĩsi'zãw/ *f* incision; **~sivo** *a* incisive

incitar /ĩsi'tar/ *vt* incite

incli|nação /ĩklina'sãw/ *f* (*do chão*) incline; (*da cabeça*) nod; (*propensão*) inclination; **~nado** *a* <*chão*> sloping; <*edifício*> leaning; (*propenso*) inclined (**a** to); **~nar** *vt* tilt; nod <*cabeça*> □ *vi* <*chão*> slope; <*edifício*> lean; (*tender*) incline (**para** towards); **~nar-se** *vpr* lean

inclu|ir /ĩklu'ir/ *vt* include; **~são** *f* inclusion; **~sive** *prep* including □ *adv* inclusive; (*até*) even; **~so** *a* included

incoe|rência /ĩkoe'rẽsia/ *f* (*falta de nexo*) incoherence; (*inconseqüência*) inconsistency; **~rente** *a* (*sem nexo*) incoherent; (*inconseqüente*) inconsistent

incógni|ta /ĩ'kɔgnita/ *f* unknown; **~to** *adv* incognito

incolor /ĩko'lor/ *a* colourless

incólume /ĩ'kɔlumi/ *a* unscathed

incomodar /ĩkomo'dar/ *vt* bother □ *vi* be a nuisance; **~-se** *vpr* (*dar-se ao trabalho*) bother (**em** to); **~-se (com)** be bothered (by), mind

incômodo /ĩ'komodu/ *a* (*desagradável*) tiresome; (*sem conforto*) uncomfortable □ *m* nuisance

incompa|rável /ĩkõpa'ravew/ (*pl* **~ráveis**) *a* incomparable; **~tível** (*pl* **~tíveis**) *a* incompatible

incompe|tência /ĩkõpe'tẽsia/ *f* incompetence; **~tente** *a* incompetent

incompleto /ĩkõ'plɛtu/ *a* incomplete

incompreensí|vel /ĩkõpriẽ'sivew/ (*pl* **~veis**) *a* incomprehensible

inconcebí|vel /ĩkõse'bivew/ (*pl* **~veis**) *a* inconceivable

incondicio|nal /ĩkõdʒisio'naw/ (*pl* **~nais**) *a* unconditional; <*fã, partidário*> firm

inconformado /ĩkõfor'madu/ *a* unreconciled (**com** to)

inconfundí|vel /ĩkõfũ'dʒivew/ (*pl* **~veis**) *a* unmistakeable

inconsciente /ĩkõsi'ẽtʃi/ *a* & *m* unconscious

inconseqüente /ĩkõse'kwẽtʃi/ *a* inconsistent

incons|tância /ĩkõs'tãsia/ *f* changeability; **~tante** *a* changeable

inconstitucio|nal /ĩkõstʃitusio'naw/ (*pl* **~nais**) *a* unconstitutional

incontestá|vel /ĩkõtes'tavew/ (*pl* **~veis**) *a* indisputable

inconveniente /ĩkõveni'ẽtʃi/ *a* (*difícil*) inconvenient; (*desagradável*) annoying, tiresome; (*indecente*) unseemly □ *m* drawback

incorporar /ĩkorpo'rar/ *vt* incorporate

incorrer /ĩko'xer/ *vi* **~ em** <*multa etc*> incur

incorrigí|vel /ĩkoxi'ʒivew/ (*pl* **~veis**) *a* incorrigible

incrédulo /ĩ'krɛdulu/ *a* incredulous

incremen|tado /ĩkremẽ'tadu/ *a* (*fam*) stylish; **~tar** *vt* build up; (*fam*) jazz up; **~to** *m* development, growth

incriminar /ĩkrimi'nar/ *vt* incriminate

incrí|vel /ĩ'krivew/ (*pl* **~veis**) *a* incredible

incu|bação /ĩkuba'sãw/ *f* incubation; **~badora** *f* incubator; **~bar** *vt/i* incubate

inculto /ĩ'kuwtu/ *a* <*pessoa*> uneducated; <*terreno*> uncultivated

incum|bência /ĩkũ'bẽsia/ *f* task; **~bir** *vt* **~bir alg de aco/de ir** assign s.o. sth/to go ▫ *vi* **~bir a** be up to; **~bir-se de** take on

incurá|vel /ĩku'ravew/ (*pl* **~veis**) *a* incurable

incursão /ĩkur'sãw/ *f* incursion

incutir /ĩku'tʃir/ *vt* instil (**em** in)

indagar /ĩda'gar/ *vt* inquire (into)

inde|cência /ĩde'sẽsia/ *f* indecency; **~cente** *a* indecent

indecifrá|vel /ĩdesi'fravew/ (*pl* **~veis**) *a* indecipherable

indeciso /ĩde'sizu/ *a* undecided

indecoroso /ĩdeko'rozu/ *a* indecorous

indefi|nido /ĩdefi'nidu/ *a* indefinite; **~nível** (*pl* **~níveis**) *a* indefinable

indelé|vel /ĩde'lɛvew/ (*pl* **~veis**) *a* indelible

indelica|deza /ĩdelika'deza/ *f* impoliteness; (*uma*) impolite thing; **~do** *a* impolite

indeni|zação /ĩdeniza'sãw/ *f* compensation; **~zar** *vt* compensate

indepen|dência /ĩdepẽ'dẽsia/ *f* independence; **~dente** *a* independent

indescrití|vel /ĩdʒiskri'tʃivew/ (*pl* **~veis**) *a* indescribable

indesculpá|vel /ĩdʒiskuw'pavew/ (*pl* **~veis**) *a* inexcusable

indesejá|vel /ĩdeze'ʒavew/ (*pl* **~veis**) *a* undesirable

indestrutí|vel /ĩdʒistru'tʃivew/ (*pl* **~veis**) *a* indestructible

indeterminado /ĩdetermi'nadu/ *a* indeterminate

indevido /ĩde'vidu/ *a* undue

indexar /ĩdek'sar/ *vt* index; index-link <*salário, preços*>

ndia /'ĩdʒia/ *f* India

indiano /ĩdʒi'anu/ *a* & *m* Indian

indi|cação /ĩdʒika'sãw/ *f* indication; (*do caminho*) directions; (*nomeação*) nomination; (*recomendação*) recommendation; **~-cador** *m* indicator; (*dedo*) index finger ▫ *a* indicative (**de** of); **~car** *vt* indicate; (*para cargo, prêmio*) nominate (**para** for); (*recomendar*) recommend; **~cativo** *a* & *m* indicative

índice /'ĩdʒisi/ *m* (*taxa*) rate; (*em livro etc*) index; **~ de audiência** ratings

indiciar /ĩdʒisi'ar/ *vt* charge

indício /ĩ'dʒisiu/ *m* sign, indication; (*de crime*) clue

indife|rença /ĩdʒife'rẽsa/ *f* indifference; **~rente** *a* indifferent

indígena /ĩ'dʒiʒena/ *a* indigenous, native ▫ *m/f* native

indiges|tão /ĩdʒiʒes'tãw/ *f* indigestion; **~to** *a* indigestible; (*fig*) heavy-going

indig|nação /ĩdʒigna'sãw/ *f* indignation; **~nado** *a* indignant; **~nar** *vt* make indignant; **~-nar-se** *vpr* get indignant (**com** about)

indig|nidade /ĩdʒigni'dadʒi/ *f* indignity; **~no** *a* <*pessoa*> unworthy; <*ato*> despicable

índio /'ĩdʒiu/ *a* & *m* Indian

indire|ta /ĩdʒi'rɛta/ *f* hint; **~to** /ɛ/ *a* indirect

indis|creto /ĩdʒis'krɛtu/ *a* indiscreet; **~crição** *f* indiscretion

indiscriminado /ĩdʒiskrimi'nadu/ *a* indiscriminate

indiscutí|vel /ĩdʒisku'tʃivew/ (*pl* **~veis**) *a* unquestionable

indispensá|vel /ĩdʒispẽ'savew/ (*pl* **~veis**) *a* indispensable

indisponí|vel /ĩdʒispo'nivew/ (*pl* **~veis**) *a* unavailable

indis|por /ĩdʒis'por/ *vt* upset; **~por alg contra** turn s.o. against; **~por-se** *vpr* fall out (**com** with); **~posição** *f* indisposition; **~posto** *a* (*doente*) indisposed

indistinto /ĩdʒis'tʃĩtu/ *a* indistinct

individu|al /ĩdʒividu'aw/ (*pl* **~-ais**) *a* individual; **~alidade** *f* individuality; **~alismo** *m* individualism; **~alista** *a* & *m/f* individualist

indivíduo /ĩdʒi'viduu/ *m* individual

indizí|vel /ĩdʒi'zivew/ (*pl* **~veis**) *a* unspeakable

índole /'ĩdoli/ *f* nature

indo|lência /ĩdo'lẽsia/ *f* indolence; **~lente** *a* indolent

indolor /ĩdo'lor/ *a* painless

Indonésia /ĩdo'nɛzia/ *f* Indonesia

indonésio /ĩdo'nɛziu/ *a* & *m* Indonesian

indubitá|vel /ĩdubi'tavew/ (*pl* **~veis**) *a* undoubted

indul|gência /ĩduw'ʒẽsia/ *f* indulgence; **~gente** *a* indulgent

indulto /ĩ'duwtu/ *m* pardon

indumentária /ĩdumẽ'taria/ *f* outfit

indústria /ĩ'dustria/ *f* industry

industri|al /ĩdustri'aw/ (*pl* **~ais**) *a* industrial ▫ *m/f* industrialist; **~alizado** *a* <*país*> industrialized; <*mercadoria*> manufactured; <*comida*> processed; **~-alizar** *vt* industrialize <*país, agricultura etc*>;

process <*comida, lixo etc*>; **~oso** /o/ *a* industrious

induzir /ĩdu'zir/ *vt* (*persuadir*) induce; (*inferir*) infer (**de** from); **~ em erro** lead astray, mislead s.o.

inebriante /inebri'ãtʃi/ *a* intoxicating

inédito /i'nɛdʒitu/ *a* unheard-of, unprecedented; (*não publicado*) unpublished

ineficaz /inefi'kas/ *a* ineffective

inefici|ência /inefisi'ẽsia/ *f* inefficiency; **~ente** *a* inefficient

inegá|vel /ine'gavew/ (*pl* **~veis**) *a* undeniable

inépcia /i'nɛpsia/ *f* ineptitude

inepto /i'nɛptu/ *a* inept

inequívoco /ine'kivoku/ *a* unmistakeable

inércia /i'nɛrsia/ *f* inertia

inerente /ine'rẽtʃi/ *a* inherent (**a** in)

inerte /i'nɛrtʃi/ *a* inert

inesgotá|vel /inezgo'tavew/ (*pl* **~veis**) *a* inexhaustible

inesperado /inespe'radu/ *a* unexpected

inesquecí|vel /ineske'sivew/ (*pl* **~veis**) *a* unforgettable

inevitá|vel /inevi'tavew/ (*pl* **~-veis**) *a* inevitable

inexato /ine'zatu/ *a* inaccurate

inexis|tência /inezis'tẽsia/ *f* lack; **~tente** *a* non-existent

inexperi|ência /inisperi'ẽsia/ *f* inexperience; **~ente** *a* inexperienced

inexpressivo /inespre'sivu/ *a* expressionless

infalí|vel /ĩfa'livew/ (*pl* **~veis**) *a* infallible

infame /ĩ'fami/ *a* despicable; (*péssimo*) dreadful

infâmia /ĩ'famia/ *f* disgrace

infância /ĩ'fãsia/ *f* childhood

infantaria /ĩfãta'ria/ *f* infantry

infan|til /ĩfã'tʃiw/ *a* <*roupa, livro*> children's; (*bobo*) childish; **~tilidade** *f* childishness; (*uma*) childish thing

infarto /ĩ'fartu/ *m* heart attack

infec|ção /ĩfek'sãw/ *f* infection; **~cionar** *vt* infect; **~cioso** *a* infectious

infeliz /ĩfe'lis/ *a* (*não contente*) unhappy; (*inconveniente*) unfortunate; (*desgraçado*) wretched □ *m* (*desgraçado*) wretch; **~mente** *adv* unfortunately

inferi|or /ĩferi'or/ *a* lower; (*em qualidade*) inferior (**a** to); **~oridade** *f* inferiority

inferir /ĩfe'rir/ *vt* infer

infer|nal /ĩfer'naw/ (*pl* **~nais**) *a* infernal; **~nizar** *vt* **~nizar a vida dele** make his life hell; **~no** /ɛ/ *m* hell

infér|til /ĩ'fɛrtʃiw/ (*pl* **~teis**) *a* infertile

infertilidade /ĩfertʃili'dadʒi/ *f* infertility

infestar /ĩfes'tar/ *vt* infest

infetar /ĩfe'tar/ *vt* infect

infidelidade /ĩfideli'dadʒi/ *f* infidelity

infi|el /ĩfi'ɛw/ (*pl* **~éis**) *a* unfaithful

infiltrar /ĩfiw'trar/ *vt* infiltrate; **~-se em** infiltrate

ínfimo /'ĩfimu/ *a* lowest; (*muito pequeno*) tiny

infindá|vel /ĩfĩ'davew/ (*pl* **~veis**) *a* unending

infinidade /ĩfini'dadʒi/ *f* infinity; **uma ~ de** an infinite number of

infini|tesimal /ĩfinitezi'maw/ (*pl* **~tesimais**) *a* infinitesimal; **~tivo** *a & m* infinitive; **~to** *a* infinite □ *m* infinity

infla|ção /ĩfla'sãw/ *f* inflation; **~cionar** *vt* inflate; **~cionário** *a* inflationary; **~cionista** *a & m/f* inflationist

infla|mação /ĩflama'sãw/ *f* inflammation; **~mar** *vt* inflame; **~mar-se** *vpr* become inflamed; **~matório** *a* inflammatory; **~mável** (*pl* **~máveis**) *a* inflammable

in|flar *vt* inflate; **~flar-se** *vpr* inflate; **~flável** (*pl* **~fláveis**) *a* inflatable

infle|xibilidade /ĩfleksibili'dadʒi/ *f* inflexibility; **~xível** (*pl* **~xíveis**) *a* inflexible

infligir /ĩfli'ʒir/ *vt* inflict (**a** on)

influência /ĩflu'ẽsia/ *f* influence

influen|ciar /ĩfluẽsi'ar/ *vt* **~ciar (em)** influence; **~ciar-se** *vpr* be influenced; **~ciável** (*pl* **~ciáveis**) *a* open to influence; **~te** *a* influential

influir /ĩflu'ir/ *vi* **~ em** *ou* **sobre** influence

informação /ĩforma'sãw/ *f* information; (*uma*) a piece of information; (*mil*) intelligence; *pl* information

infor|mal /ĩfor'maw/ (*pl* **~mais**) *a* informal; **~malidade** *f* informality

infor|mar /ĩfor'mar/ *vt* inform; **~mar-se** *vpr* find out (**de** about); **~mática** *f* information technology; **~mativo** *a* informative; **~matizar** *vt* computerize; **~me** *m* (*mil*) piece of intelligence

infortúnio /ĩfor'tuniu/ *m* misfortune

infração /ĩfra'sãw/ *f* infringement

infra-estrutura /ĩfraistru'tura/ *f* infrastructure

infrator /ĩfra'tor/ *m* offender

infravermelho /ĩfraver'meʎu/ *a* infrared

infringir /ĩfrĩ'ʒir/ *vt* infringe

infrutífero /ĩfru'tʃiferu/ *a* fruitless

infundado /ĩfũ'dadu/ *a* unfounded

infundir /ĩfũ'dʒir/ *vt* (*insuflar*) infuse; (*incutir*) instil

infusão /ĩfu'zãw/ *f* infusion

ingenuidade /ĩʒenui'dadʒi/ *f* naivety

ingênuo /ĩ'ʒenuu/ *a* naive

Inglaterra /ĩgla'tɛxa/ *f* England

ingerir /ĩʒe'rir/ *vt* ingest; (*engolir*) swallow

in|glês /ĩ'gles/ *a* (*f* **~glesa**) English □ *m* (*f* **~glesa**) Englishman (*f*-woman); (*língua*) English; **os ~gleses** the English

ingra|tidão /ĩgratʃi'dãw/ *f* ingratitude; **~to** *a* ungrateful

ingrediente /ĩgredʒi'ẽtʃi/ *m* ingredient

íngreme /'ĩgrimi/ *a* steep

ingres|sar /ĩgre'sar/ *vi* **~sar em** join; **~so** *m* entry; (*bilhete*) ticket

inhame /i'ɲami/ *m* yam

ini|bição /inibi'sãw/ *f* inhibition; **~bir** *vt* inhibit

inici|ado /inisi'adu/ *m* initiate; **~al** (*pl* **~ais**) *a* & *f* initial; **~ar** *vt* (*começar*) begin; (*em ciência, seita etc*) initiate (**em** into) □ *vi* begin; **~ativa** *f* initiative

início /i'nisiu/ *m* beginning

inigualá|vel /inigwa'lavew/ (*pl* **~veis**) *a* unparalleled

inimaginá|vel /inimaʒi'navew/ (*pl* **~veis**) *a* unimaginable

inimi|go /ini'migu/ *a* & *m* enemy; **~zade** *f* enmity

ininterrupto /inĩte'xuptu/ *a* continuous

inje|ção /ĩʒe'sãw/ *f* injection; **~tado** *a* <*olhos*> bloodshot; **~tar** *vt* inject; **~tável** (*pl* **~táveis**) *a* <*droga*> intravenous

injúria /ĩ'ʒuria/ *f* insult

injuriar /ĩʒuri'ar/ *vt* insult

injus|tiça /ĩʒus'tʃisa/ *f* injustice; **~tiçado** *a* wronged; **~to** *a* unfair, unjust

ino|cência /ino'sẽsia/ *f* innocence; **~centar** *vt* clear (**de** of); **~-cente** *a* innocent

inocular /inoku'lar/ *vt* inoculate

inócuo /i'nɔkuu/ *a* harmless

inodoro /ino'dɔru/ *a* odourless

inofensivo /inofẽ'sivu/ *a* harmless

inoportuno /inopor'tunu/ *a* inopportune

inorgânico /inor'ganiku/ *a* inorganic

inóspito /i'nɔspitu/ *a* inhospitable

ino|vação /inova'sãw/ *f* innovation; **~var** *vt/i* innovate

inoxidá|vel /inoksi'davew/ (*pl* **~veis**) *a* <*aço*> stainless

inquérito /ĩ'kɛritu/ *m* inquiry

inquie|tação /ĩkieta'sãw/ *f* concern; **~tador, ~tante** *a* worrying; **~tar** *vt* worry; **~tar-se** *vpr* worry; **~to** /ɛ/ *a* uneasy

inquili|nato /ĩkili'natu/ *m* tenancy; **~no** *m* tenant

inquirir /ĩki'rir/ *vt* cross-examine <*testemunha*>

Inquisição /ĩkizi'sãw/ *f* **a ~** the Inquisition

insaciá|vel /ĩsasi'avew/ (*pl* **~-veis**) *a* insatiable

insalubre /ĩsa'lubri/ *a* unhealthy

insatis|fação /ĩsatʃisfa'sãw/ *f* dissatisfaction; **~fatório** *a* unsatisfactory; **~feito** *a* dissatisfied

ins|crever /ĩskre'ver/ *vt* (*registrar*) register; (*gravar*) inscribe; **~crever-se** *vpr* register; (*em escola etc*) enrol; **~crição** *f* (*registro*) registration; (*em clube, escola*) enrolment; (*em monumento etc*) inscription

insegu|rança /ĩsegu'rãsa/ *f* insecurity; **~ro** *a* insecure

insemi|nação /ĩsemina'sãw/ *f* insemination; **~nar** *vt* inseminate

insen|satez /ĩsẽsa'tes/ *f* folly; **~sato** *a* foolish; **~sibilidade** *f* insensitivity; **~sível** (*pl* **~síveis**) *a* insensitive

insepará|vel /ĩsepa'ravew/ (*pl* **~veis**) *a* inseparable

inserção /ĩser'sãw/ *f* insertion

inserir /ĩse'rir/ *vt* insert; enter <*dados*>

inse|ticida /ĩsetʃi'sida/ *m* insecticide; **~to** /ɛ/ *m* insect

insígnia /ĩ'signia/ *f* insignia

insignifi|cância /ĩsignifi'kãsia/ *f* insignificance; **~cante** *a* insignificant

insincero /ĩsĩ'sɛru/ *a* insincere

insinu|ante /ĩsinu'ãtʃi/ *a* suggestive; **~ar** *vt/i* insinuate

insípido /ĩ'sipidu/ *a* insipid

insis|tência /ĩsis'tẽsia/ *f* insistence; **~tente** *a* insistent; **~tir** *vt/i* insist (**em** on)

insolação /ĩsola'sãw/ *f* sunstroke

inso|lência /ĩso'lẽsia/ *f* insolence; **~lente** *a* insolent

insólito /ĩ'sɔlitu/ *a* unusual

insolú|vel /ĩso'luvew/ (*pl* **~veis**) *a* insoluble

insone /ĩ'sɔni/ *a* <*noite*> sleepless; <*pessoa*> insomniac □ *m/f* insomniac

insônia /ĩ'sonia/ *f* insomnia

insosso /ĩ'sosu/ *a* bland; (*sem sabor*) tasteless; (*sem sal*) unsalted

inspe|ção /ĩspe'sãw/ *f* inspection; **~cionar** *vt* inspect; **~tor** *m* inspector

inspi|ração /ĩspira'sãw/ *f* inspiration; **~rar** *vt* inspire; **~rar-se** *vpr* take inspiration (**em** from)

instabilidade /ĩstabili'dadʒi/ *f* instability

insta|lação /ĩstala'sãw/ *f* installation; **~lar** *vt* install; **~lar-se** *vpr* install o.s.

instan|tâneo /ĩstã'taniu/ *a* instant; **~te** *m* instant

instaurar /ĩstaw'rar/ *vt* set up

instá|vel /ĩ'stavew/ (*pl* **~veis**) *a* unstable; <*tempo*> unsettled

insti|gação /ĩstʃiga'sãw/ *f* instigation; **~gante** *a* stimulating; **~gar** *vt* incite

instin|tivo /ĩstʃĩ'tʃivu/ *a* instinctive; **~to** *m* instinct

institu|cional /ĩstʃitusio'naw/ (*pl* **~cionais**) *a* institutional; **~ição** *f* institution; **~ir** *vt* set up; set <*prazo*>; **~to** *m* institute

instru|ção /ĩstru'sãw/ *f* instruction; **~ir** *vt* instruct; train <*recrutas*>; (*informar*) advise (**sobre** of)

instrumen|tal /ĩstrumẽ'taw/ (*pl* **~tais**) *a* instrumental; **~tista** *m/f* instrumentalist; **~to** *m* instrument

instru|tivo /ĩstru'tʃivu/ *a* instructive; **~tor** *m* instructor

insubstituí|vel /ĩsubistʃitu'ivew/ (*pl* **~veis**) *a* irreplaceable

insucesso /ĩsu'sesu/ *m* failure

insufici|ência /ĩsufisi'ẽsia/ *f* insufficiency; (*dos órgãos*) failure; **~ente** *a* insufficient

insulina /ĩsu'lina/ *f* insulin

insul|tar /ĩsuw'tar/ *vt* insult; **~to** *m* insult

insuperá|vel /ĩsupe'ravew/ (*pl* **~veis**) *a* <*problema*> insurmountable; <*qualidade*> unsurpassed

insuportá|vel /ĩsupor'tavew/ (*pl* **~veis**) *a* unbearable

insur|gente /ĩsur'ʒẽtʃi/ *a* & *m/f* insurgent; **~gir-se** *vpr* rise up, revolt; **~reição** *f* insurrection

intato /ĩ'tatu/ *a* intact

íntegra /'ĩtegra/ *f* full text; **na ~** in full

inte|gração /ĩtegra'sãw/ *f* integration; **~gral** (*pl* **~grais**) *a* whole; **arroz /pão ~gral** brown rice/bread; **~grante** *a* integral □ *m/f* member; **~grar** *vt* make up, form; **~grar-se em** become a part of; **~gridade** *f* integrity

íntegro /'ĩtegru/ *a* honest

intei|ramente /ĩtera'mẽtʃi/ *adv* completely; **~rar** *vt* (*informar*) fill in, inform (**de** about); **~rar-se** *vpr* find out (**de** about); **~riço** *a* in one piece; **~ro** *a* whole

intelec|to /ĩte'lɛktu/ *m* intellect; **~tual** (*pl* **~tuais**) *a* & *m/f* intellectual

inteli|gência /ĩteli'ʒẽsia/ *f* intelligence; **~gente** *a* clever, intelligent; **~gível** (*pl* **~gíveis**) *a* intelligible

intem|périe /ĩtẽ'pɛri/ *f* bad weather; **~pestivo** *a* ill-timed

inten|ção /ĩtẽ'sãw/ *f* intention; **segundas ~ções** ulterior motives

intencio|nado /ĩtẽsio'nadu/ *a* **bem ~nado** well-meaning; **~nal** (*pl* **~nais**) *a* intentional; **~nar** *vt* intend

inten|sidade /ĩtẽsi'dadʒi/ *f* intensity; **~sificar** *vt* intensify; **~sificar-se** *vpr* intensify; **~sivo** *a* intensive; **~so** *a* intense

intento /ĩ'tẽtu/ *m* intention

intera|ção /ĩtera'sãw/ *f* interaction; **~gir** *vi* interact; **~tivo** *a* interactive

inter|calar /ĩterka'lar/ *vt* insert; **~câmbio** *m* exchange; **~ceptar** *vt* intercept

intercontinen|tal /ĩterkõtʃinẽ'taw/ (*pl* **~tais**) *a* intercontinental

interdepen|dência /ĩterdepẽ'dẽsia/ *f* interdependence; **~dente** *a* interdependent

interdi|ção /ĩterdʒi'sãw/ *f* closure; (*jurid*) injunction; **~tar** *vt* close <*rua etc*>; (*proibir*) ban

interes|sante /ĩtere'sãtʃi/ *a* interesting; **~sar** *vt* interest □ *vi* be relevant; **~sar-se** *vpr* be interested (**em** *ou* **por** in); **~se** /e/ *m* interest; (*próprio*) self-interest; **~seiro** *a* self-seeking

interestadu|al /ĩteristadu'aw/ (*pl* **~ais**) *a* interstate

interface /ĩter'fasi/ *f* interface

interfe|rência /ĩterfe'rẽsia/ *f* interference; **~rir** *vi* interfere

interfone /ĩter'fɔni/ *m* intercom

ínterim /'ĩterĩ/ *m* interim; **nesse ~** in the interim

interino /ĩte'rinu/ *a* temporary

interior /ĩteri'or/ *a* inner; (*dentro do país*) internal, domestic □ *m* inside; (*do país*) country, interior

inter|jeição /ĩterʒej'sãw/ *f* interjection; **~ligar** *vt* interconnect; **~locutor** *m* interlocutor; **~-mediário** *a* & *m* intermediary

intermédio /ĩter'mɛdʒiu/ *m* **por ~ de** through

interminá|vel /ĩtermi'navew/ (*pl* **~veis**) *a* interminable

internacio|nal /ĩternasio'naw/ (*pl* **~nais**) *a* international

inter|nar /ĩter'nar/ *vt* intern <*preso*>; admit to hospital <*doente*>; **~-nato** *m* boarding school

internauta /ĩter'nawta/ *m/f* (*comput*) netsurfer

Internet /ĩter'nɛt/ *f* Internet

interno /ĩ'tɛrnu/ *a* internal
interpelar /ĩterpe'lar/ *vt* question
interpor /ĩter'por/ *vt* interpose; **~-se** *vpr* intervene
interpre|tação /ĩterpreta'sãw/ *f* interpretation; **~tar** *vt* interpret; perform <*papel, música*>; **intérprete** *m/f* (*de línguas*) interpreter; (*de teatro etc*) performer
interro|gação /ĩtexoga'sãw/ *f* interrogation; **~gar** *vt* interrogate, question; **~gativo** *a* interrogative; **~gatório** *m* interrogation
inter|romper /ĩtexõ'per/ *vt* interrupt; **~rupção** *f* interruption; **~ruptor** *m* switch
interurbano /ĩterur'banu/ *a* long-distance ▫ *m* trunk call
intervalo /ĩter'valu/ *m* interval
inter|venção /ĩtervẽ'sãw/ *f* intervention; **~vir** *vi* intervene
intesti|nal /ĩtestʃi'naw/ (*pl* **~nais**) *a* intestinal; **~no** *m* intestine
inti|mação /ĩtʃima'sãw/ *f* (*da justiça*) summons; **~mar** *vt* order; (*à justiça*) summon
intimidade /ĩtʃimi'dadʒi/ *f* intimacy; (*entre amigos*) closeness; (*vida íntima*) private life; **ter ~ com** be close to
intimidar /ĩtʃimi'dar/ *vt* intimidate; **~-se** *vpr* be intimidated
íntimo /'ĩtʃimu/ *a* intimate; <*amigo*> close; <*vida*> private ▫ *m* close friend
intitular /ĩtʃitu'lar/ *vt* entitle
intocá|vel /ĩto'kavew/ (*pl* **~veis**) *a* untouchable
intole|rância /ĩtole'rãsia/ *f* intolerance; **~ rável** (*pl* **~ráveis**) *a* intolerable
intoxi|cação /ĩtoksika'sãw/ *f* poisoning; **~cação alimentar** food poisoning; **~car** *vt* poison
intragá|vel /ĩtra'gavew/ (*pl* **~veis**) *a* <*comida*> inedible; <*pessoa*> unbearable
intransigente /ĩtrãzi'ʒẽtʃi/ *a* uncompromising
intransi|tável /ĩtrãzi'tavew/ (*pl* **~táveis**) *a* impassable; **~tivo** *a* intransitive
intratá|vel /ĩtra'tavew/ (*pl* **~veis**) *a* <*pessoa*> difficult
intra-uterino /ĩtraute'rinu/ *a* **dispositivo ~** intra-uterine device, IUD
intrépido /ĩ'trɛpidu/ *a* intrepid
intri|ga /ĩ'triga/ *f* intrigue; (*enredo*) plot; **~gante** *a* intriguing; **~gar** *vt* intrigue
intrincado /ĩtrĩ'kadu/ *a* intricate
intrínseco /ĩ'trĩsiku/ *a* intrinsic
introdu|ção /ĩtrodu'sãw/ *f* introduction; **~tório** *a* introductory; **~zir** *vt* introduce
introme|ter-se /ĩtrome'tersi/ *vpr* interfere; **~tido** *a* interfering ▫ *m* busybody
introspec|ção /ĩtrospek'sãw/ *f* introspection; **~tivo** *a* introspective
introvertido /ĩtrover'tʃidu/ *a* introverted ▫ *m* introvert
intruso /ĩ'truzu/ *a* intrusive ▫ *m* intruder
intu|ição /ĩtui'sãw/ *f* intuition; **~ir** *vt* intuit; **~itivo** *a* intuitive; **~to** *m* purpose
inumano /inu'manu/ *a* inhuman
inumerá|vel /inume'ravew/ (*pl* **~veis**) *a* innumerable
inúmero /i'numeru/ *a* countless
inun|dação /inũda'sãw/ *f* flood; **~dar** *vt/i* flood
inusitado /inuzi'tadu/ *a* unusual
inú|til /i'nutʃiw/ (*pl* **~teis**) *a* useless
inutilmente /inutʃiw'mẽtʃi/ *adv* in vain
inutilizar /inutʃili'zar/ *vt* render useless; damage <*aparelho*>; thwart <*esforços*>
invadir /ĩva'dʒir/ *vt* invade
invali|dar /ĩvali'dar/ *vt* invalidate; disable <*pessoa*>; **~dez** /e/ *f* disability
inválido /ĩ'validu/ *a* & *m* invalid
invariá|vel /ĩvari'avew/ (*pl* **~veis**) *a* invariable
inva|são /ĩva'zãw/ *f* invasion; **~sor** *m* invader ▫ *a* invading
inve|ja /ĩ'vɛʒa/ *f* envy; **~jar** *vt* envy; **~jável** (*pl* **~jáveis**) *a* enviable; **~joso** /o/ *a* envious
inven|ção /ĩvẽ'sãw/ *f* invention; **~tar** *vt* invent; **~tário** *m* inventory; **~tivo** *a* inventive; **~tor** *m* inventor
inver|nar /ĩver'nar/ *vi* winter, spend the winter; **~no** /ɛ/ *m* winter
inverossí|mil /ĩvero'simiw/ (*pl* **~meis**) *a* improbable
inver|são /ĩver'sãw/ *f* inversion; **~so** *a* inverse; <*ordem*> reverse ▫ *m* reverse; **~ter** *vt* reverse; (*colocar de cabeça para baixo*) invert
invertebrado /ĩverte'bradu/ *a* & *m* invertebrate
invés /ĩ'vɛs/ *m* **ao ~ de** instead of
investida /ĩves'tʃida/ *f* attack
investidura /ĩvestʃi'dura/ *f* investiture

investi|gação /ĩvestʃiga'sãw/ *f* investigation; **~gar** *vt* investigate
inves|timento /ĩvestʃi'mẽtu/ *m* investment; **~tir** *vt/i* invest; **~tir contra** attack
inveterado /ĩvete'radu/ *a* inveterate
inviá|vel /ĩvi'avew/ (*pl* **~veis**) *a* impracticable
invicto /ĩ'viktu/ *a* unbeaten
invisí|vel /ĩvi'zivew/ (*pl* **~veis**) *a* invisible
invocar /ĩvo'kar/ *vt* invoke; (*fam*) pester
invólucro /ĩ'vɔlukru/ *m* covering
involuntário /ĩvolũ'tariu/ *a* involuntary
invulnerá|vel /ĩvuwne'ravew/ (*pl* **~veis**) *a* invulnerable
iodo /i'odu/ *m* iodine
ioga /i'ɔga/ *f* yoga
iogurte /io'gurtʃi/ *m* yoghurt
ir /ir/ *vi* go; **~-se** *vpr* go away; **vou voltar** I will come back; **vou melhorando** I am (gradually) getting better
ira /'ira/ *f* wrath
Irã /i'rã/ *m* Iran
iraniano /irani'anu/ *a & m* Iranian
Irão /i'rãw/ *m* (*Port*) Iran
Iraque /i'raki/ *m* Iraq
iraquiano /iraki'anu/ *a & m* Iraqui
Irlanda /ir'lãda/ *f* Ireland
irlan|dês /irlã'des/ *a* (*f* **~desa**) Irish □ *m* (*f* **~desa**) Irishman (*f*-woman); (*língua*) Irish; **os ~deses** the Irish
irmã /ir'mã/ *f* sister
irmandade /irmã'dadʒi/ *f* (*associação*) brotherhood
irmão /ir'mãw/ (*pl* **~s**) *m* brother
ironia /iro'nia/ *f* irony
irônico /i'roniku/ *a* ironic
irracio|nal /ixasio'naw/ (*pl* **~nais**) *a* irrational
irradiar /ixadʒi'ar/ *vt* radiate; (*pelo rádio*) broadcast □ *vi* shine; **~-se** *vpr* spread, radiate
irre|al /ixe'aw/ (*pl* **~ais**) *a* unreal
irreconhecí|vel /ixekoɲe'sivew/ (*pl* **~veis**) *a* unrecognizable
irrecuperá|vel /ixekupe'ravew/ (*pl* **~veis**) *a* irretrievable
irrefletido /ixefle'tʃidu/ *a* rash
irregu|lar /ixegu'lar/ *a* irregular; (*inconstante*) erratic; **~laridade** *f* irregularity
irrelevante /ixele'vãtʃi/ *a* irrelevant
irreparā|vel /ixepa'ravew/ (*pl* **~veis**) *a* irreparable
irrepreensí|vel /ixepriẽ'sivew/ (*pl* **~veis**) *a* irreproachable
irrequieto /ixeki'ɛtu/ *a* restless
irresistí|vel /ixezis'tʃivew/ (*pl* **~veis**) *a* irresistible
irresoluto /ixezo'lutu/ *a* <*questão*> unresolved; <*pessoa*> indecisive
irresponsá|vel /ixespõ'savew/ (*pl* **~veis**) *a* irresponsible
irreverente /ixeve'rẽtʃi/ *a* irreverent
irri|gação /ixiga'sãw/ *f* irrigation; **~gar** *vt* irrigate
irrisório /ixi'zɔriu/ *a* derisory
irri|tação /ixita'sãw/ *f* irritation; **~tadiço** *a* irritable; **~tante** *a* irritating; **~tar** *vt* irritate; **~-tar-se** *vpr* get irritated
irromper /ixõ'per/ *vi* **~ em** burst into
isca /'iska/ *f* bait
isen|ção /izẽ'sãw/ *f* exemption; **~tar** *vt* exempt; **~to** *a* exempt
Islã /iz'lã/ *m* Islam
islâmico /iz'lamiku/ *a* Islamic
isla|mismo /izla'mizmu/ *m* Islam; **~mita** *a & m/f* Muslim
islan|dês /izlã'des/ *a* (*f* **~desa**) Icelandic □ *m* (*f* **~desa**) Icelander; (*língua*) Icelandic
Islândia /iz'lãdʒia/ *f* Iceland
iso|lamento /izola'mẽtu/ *m* isolation; (*eletr*) insulation; **~lante** *a* insulating; **~lar** *vt* isolate; (*eletr*) insulate □ *vi* (*contra azar*) touch wood, (*Amer*) knock on wood
isopor /izo'por/ *m* polystyrene
isqueiro /is'keru/ *m* lighter
Israel /izxa'ɛw/ *m* Israel
israe|lense /izraj'lẽsi/ *a & m/f* Israeli; **~lita** *a & m/f* Israelite
isso /'isu/ *pron* that; **por ~** therefore
isto /'istu/ *pron* this; **~ é** that is
Itália /i'talia/ *f* Italy
italiano /itali'anu/ *a & m* Italian
itálico /i'taliku/ *a & m* italic
item /'itẽ/ *m* item
itine|rante /itʃine'rãtʃi/ *a* itinerant; **~rário** *m* itinerary
Iugoslávia /iugoz'lavia/ *f* Yugoslavia
iugoslavo /iugoz'lavu/ *a & m* Yugoslavian

Jj

já /ʒa/ *adv* already; (*agoraâ*) right away □ *conj* on the other hand; **desde ~** from now on; **~ não** no longer; **~ que** since; **~, ~** in no time

jabuticaba /ʒabutʃi'kaba/ *f* jaboticaba

jaca /'ʒaka/ *f* jack fruit

jacaré /ʒaka'rɛ/ *m* alligator

jacinto /ʒa'sĩtu/ *m* hyacinth

jactância /ʒak'tãsia/ *f* boasting

jade /'ʒadʒi/ *m* jade

jaguar /ʒagu'ar/ *m* jaguar

jagunço /ʒa'gũsu/ *m* hired gunman

jamais /ʒa'majs/ *adv* never

Jamaica /ʒa'majka/ *f* Jamaica

jamaicano /ʒamaj'kanu/ *a & m* Jamaican

jamanta /ʒa'mãta/ *f* juggernaut

janeiro /ʒa'neru/ *m* January

janela /ʒa'nɛla/ *f* window

jangada /ʒã'gada/ *f* (fishing) raft

janta /'ʒãta/ *f* (*fam*) dinner

jantar /ʒã'tar/ *m* dinner □ *vi* have dinner □ *vt* have for dinner

Japão /ʒa'pãw/ *m* Japan

japo|na /ʒa'pɔna/ *f* pea jacket □ *m/f* (*fam*) Japanese; **~nês** *a & m* (*f* **~nesa**) Japanese

jaqueira /ʒa'kera/ *f* jack-fruit tree

jaqueta /ʒa'keta/ *f* jacket

jarda /'ʒarda/ *f* yard

jar|dim /ʒar'dʒĩ/ *m* garden; **~dim-de-infância** (*pl* **~dins-de-infância**) *f* kindergarten

jardi|nagem /ʒardʒi'naʒẽ/ *f* gardening; **~nar** *vi* garden; **~-neira** *f* (*calça*) dungarees; (*vestido*) pinafore dress, (*Amer*) jumper; (*ônibus*) open-sided bus; (*para flores*) flower stand; **~neiro** *m* gardener

jargão /ʒar'gãw/ *m* jargon

jar|ra /'ʒaxa/ *f* pot; **~ro** *m* jug

jasmim /ʒaz'mĩ/ *m* jasmine

jato /'ʒatu/ *m* jet

jaula /'ʒawla/ *f* cage

ja|zer /ʒa'zer/ *vi* lie; **~zida** *f* deposit; **~zigo** *m* grave

jazz /dʒaz/ *m* jazz; **~ista** *m/f* jazz artist; **~ístico** *a* jazzy

jeca /'ʒɛka/ *m/f* country bumpkin □ *a* countrified; (*cafona*) tacky; **~-tatu** *m/f* country bumpkin

jei|tão /ʒej'tãw/ *m* (*fam*) individual style; **~tinho** *m* knack; **~to** *m* way; (*de pessoa*) manner; (*habilidade*) skill; **de qualquer ~to** anyway; **de ~to nenhum** no way; **pelo ~to** by the looks of things; **sem ~to** awkward; **dar um ~to** find a way; **dar um ~to em** (*arrumar*) tidy up; (*consertar*) fix; (*torcer*) twist <*pé etc*>; **ter ~to de** look like; **ter** *ou* **levar ~to para** be good at; **tomar ~to** pull one's socks up; **~toso** /o/ *a* skilful; (*de aparência*) elegant

je|juar /ʒeʒu'ar/ *vi* fast; **~jum** *m* fast

Jeová /ʒio'va/ *m* **testemunha de ~** Jehovah's witness

jérsei /'ʒersej/ *m* jersey

jesuíta /ʒezu'ita/ *a & m/f* Jesuit

Jesus /ʒe'zus/ *m* Jesus

jibóia /ʒi'bɔja/ *f* boa constrictor

jiboiar /ʒiboj'ar/ *vi* have a rest to let one's dinner go down

jiló /ʒi'lɔ/ *m* okra

jipe /'ʒipi/ *m* jeep

jiu-jitsu /ʒiu'ʒitsu/ *m* jiu-jitsu

joa|lheiro /ʒoa'ʎeru/ *m* jeweller; **~lheria** *f* jeweller's (shop)

joaninha /ʒoa'niɲa/ *f* ladybird, (*Amer*) ladybug; (*alfinete*) safety pin

joão-ninguém /ʒoãwnĩ'gẽj/ (*pl* **joões-ninguém**) *m* nobody

jocoso /ʒo'kozu/ *a* jocular

joe|lhada /ʒoe'ʎada/ *f* blow with the knee; **~lheira** *f* kneepad; **~lho** /e/ *m* knee; **de ~lhos** kneeling

jo|gada /ʒo'gada/ *f* move; **~gado** *a* <*pessoa*> flat out; <*papéis, roupa etc*> lying around; **~gador** *m* player; (*no cassino etc*) gambler; **~gar** *vt* play; (*atirar*) throw; (*arriscar no jogo*) gamble □ *vi* play; (*no cassino etc*) gamble; (*balançar*) toss; **~gar fora** throw away; **~gatina** *f* gambling

jogging /'ʒɔgĩ/ *m* (*cooper*) jogging; (*roupa*) track suit

jogo /'ʒogu/ *m* (*partida*) game; (*ação de jogar*) play; (*jogatina*) gambling; (*conjunto*) set; **em ~** at stake; **~ de cintura** (*fig*) flexibility, room to manoeuvre; **~ de luz** lighting effects; **~ do bicho** illegal numbers game; **Jogos Olímpicos** Olympic Games; **~-da-velha** *m* noughts and crosses

joguete /ʒo'getʃi/ *m* plaything

jóia /'ʒɔja/ *f* jewel; (*propina*) entry fee □ *a* (*fam*) great

joio /'ʒoju/ *m* chaff; **separar o ~ do trigo** separate the wheat from the chaff

jóquei /'ʒɔkej/ *m* (*pessoa*) jockey; (*lugar*) race course

Jordânia /ʒor'dania/ *f* Jordan

jordaniano /ʒordani'anu/ *a & m* Jordanian

jor|nada /ʒor'nada/ *f* (*viagem*) journey; **~nada de trabalho** working day; **~nal** (*pl* **~nais**) *m* newspaper; (*na TV*) news

jorna|leco /ʒorna'lɛku/ *m* rag, scandal sheet; **~leiro** *m* (*vendedor*) newsagent, (*Amer*) newsdealer; (*entregador*) paperboy; **~lismo** *m* journalism; **~lista** *m/f* journalist; **~lístico** *a* journalistic

jor|rar /ʒo'xar/ *vi* gush, spurt; **~ro** /'ʒoxu/ *m* spurt

jota /'ʒɔta/ *m* letter J

jovem /'ʒɔvẽ/ *a* young; (*criado por jovens*) youth □ *m/f* young man (*f* -woman); *pl* young people

jovi|al /ʒovi'aw/ (*pl* **~ais**) *a* jovial

juba /'ʒuba/ *f* mane

jubileu /ʒubi'lew/ *m* jubilee

júbilo /'ʒubilu/ *m* joy

ju|daico /ʒu'dajku/ *a* Jewish; **~daísmo** *m* Judaism; **~deu** *a* (*f* **~dia**) Jewish □ *m* (*f* **~dia**) Jew; **~diação** *f* ill-treatment; (*uma*) terrible thing; **~diar** *vi* **~diar de** ill-treat

judici|al /ʒudʒisi'aw/ (*pl* **~ais**) *a* judicial; **~ário** *a* judicial □ *m* judiciary; **~oso** /o/ *a* judicious

judô /ʒu'do/ *m* judo

judoca /ʒu'dɔka/ *m/f* judo player

jugo /'ʒugu/ *m* yoke

juiz /ʒu'is/ *m* (*f* **juíza**) judge; (*em jogos*) referee

juizado /ʒui'zadu/ *m* court

juízo /ʒu'izu/ *m* judgement; (*tino*) sense; (*tribunal*) court; **perder o ~** lose one's head; **ter ~** be sensible; **tomar** *ou* **criar ~** come to one's senses

jujuba /ʒu'ʒuba/ *f* (*bala*) fruit jelly

jul|gamento /ʒuwga'mẽtu/ *m* judgement; **~gar** *vt* judge; pass judgement on <*réu*>; (*imaginar*) think; **~gar-se** *vpr* consider o.s.

julho /'ʒuʎu/ *m* July

jumento /ʒu'mẽtu/ *m* donkey

junção /ʒũ'sãw/ *f* join; (*ação*) joining

junco /'ʒũku/ *m* reed

junho /'ʒuɲu/ *m* June

juni|no /ʒu'ninu/ *a* **festa ~na** St John's Day festival

júnior /'ʒunior/ *a & m* junior

jun|ta /'ʒũta/ *f* board; (*pol*) junta; **~tar** *vt* (*acrescentar*) add; (*uma coisa a outra*) join; (*uma coisa com outra*) combine; save up <*dinheiro*>; gather up <*papéis, lixo etc*> □ *vi* gather; **~tar-se** *vpr* join together; <*multidão*> gather; <*casal*> live together; **~tar-se a** join; **~to** *a* together □ *adv* together; **~to a** next to; **~to com** together with

ju|ra /'ʒura/ *f* vow; **~rado** *m* juror; **~ramentado** *a* accredited; **~ramento** *m* oath; **~rar** *vt/i* swear; **~ra?** (*fam*) really?

júri /'ʒuri/ *m* jury

jurídico /ʒu'ridʒiku/ *a* legal

juris|consulto /ʒuriskõ'suwtu/ *m* legal advisor; **~dição** *f* jurisdiction; **~prudência** *f* jurisprudence; **~ta** *m/f* jurist

juros /'ʒurus/ *m pl* interest

jus /ʒus/ *m* **fazer ~ a** live up to

jusante /ʒu'zãtʃi/ *f* **a ~** downstream

justamente /ʒusta'mẽtʃi/ *adv* exactly; (*com justiça*) fairly

justapor /ʒusta'por/ *vt* juxtapose

justi|ça /ʒus'tʃisa/ *f* (*perante a lei*) justice; (*para com outros*) fairness; (*tribunal*) court; **~-ceiro** *a* fair-minded □ *m* vigilante

justifi|cação /ʒustʃifika'sãw/ *f* justification; **~car** *vt* justify; **~cativa** *f* justification; **~cável** (*pl* **~cáveis**) *a* justifiable

justo /'ʒustu/ *a* fair; (*apertado*) tight □ *adv* just

juve|nil /ʒuve'niw/ (*pl* **~nis**) *a* youthful; (*para jovens*) for young people; <*time, torneio*> junior □ *m* junior championship

juventude /ʒuvẽ'tudʒi/ *f* youth

karaokê /karao'ke/ *m* karaoke

kart /'kartʃi/ (*pl* **~s**) *m* go-kart

ketchup /ke'tʃupi/ *m* ketchup

kit /'kitʃi/ (*pl* **~s**) *m* kit

kitchenette /kitʃe'nɛtʃi/ *f* bedsitter

Kuwait /ku'wajtʃi/ *m* Kuwait

kuwaitiano /kuwajtʃi'anu/ *a & m* Kuwaiti

L

lá /la/ *adv* there; **até ~** <*ir*> there; <*esperar etc*> until then; **por ~** (*naquela direão*) that way; (*naquele lugar*) around there; **~ fora** outside; **sei ~** how should I know?

lã /lã/ *f* wool

labareda /laba'reda/ *f* flame

lábia /'labia/ *f* flannel; **ter ~** have the gift of the gab

lábio /'labio/ *m* lip

labirinto /labi'rĩtu/ *m* labyrinth

laboratório /labora'tɔriu/ *m* laboratory

laborioso /labori'ozu/ *a* hard-working

labu|ta /la'buta/ *f* drudgery; **~tar** *vi* slog

laca /'laka/ *f* lacquer

laçada /la'sada/ *f* slipknot

lacaio /la'kaju/ *m* lackey

la|çar /la'sar/ *vt* lasso <*boi*>; **~ço** *m* bow; (*de vaqueiro*) lasso; (*vínculo*) tie

lacônico /la'koniku/ *a* laconic

lacraia /la'kraja/ *f* centipede

la|crar /la'krar/ *vt* seal; **~cre** *m* (*substância*) sealing wax; (*fechamento*) seal

lacri|mejar /lakrime'ʒar/ *vi* water; **~mogêneo** *a* <*gás*> tear; <*filme*> tearjerking; **~moso** /o/ *a* tearful

lácteo /'laktʃiu/ *a* milk; **Via Láctea** Milky Way

lacticínio /laktʃi'siniu/ *m veja* **laticínio**

lacuna /la'kuna/ *f* gap

ladainha /lada'iɲa/ *f* litany

la|dear /ladʒi'ar/ *vt* flank; sidestep <*dificuldade*>; **~deira** *f* slope

lado /'ladu/ *m* side; **o ~ de cá/lá** this/that side; **ao ~ de** beside; **~ a ~** side by side; **para este ~** this way; **por outro ~** on the other hand

la|drão /la'drãw/ *m* (*f* **~dra**) thief; (*tubo*) overflow pipe □ *a* thieving

ladrar /la'drar/ *vi* bark

ladri|lhar /ladri'ʎar/ *vt* tile; **~lho** *m* tile

ladroagem /ladro'aʒẽ/ *f* stealing

lagar|ta /la'garta/ *f* caterpillar; (*numa roda*) caterpillar track; **~tear** *vi* bask in the sun; **~tixa** *f* gecko; **~to** *m* lizard

lago /'lagu/ *m* lake

lagoa /la'goa/ *f* lagoon

lagos|ta /la'gosta/ *f* lobster; **~tim** *m* crayfish, (*Amer*) crawfish

lágrima /'lagrima/ *f* tear

laia /'laja/ *f* kind

laico /'lajku/ *adj* <*pessoa*> lay; <*ensino*> secular

laivos /'lajvus/ *m pl* traces

laje /'laʒi/ *m* flagstone; **~ar** *vt* pave

lajota /la'ʒɔta/ *f* small paving stone

lama /'lama/ *f* mud; **~çal** (*pl* **~çais**) *m* bog; **~cento** *a* muddy

lamba|da /lã'bada/ *f* lambada; **~teria** *f* lambada club

lam|ber /lã'ber/ *vt* lick; **~bida** *f* lick

lambreta /lã'breta/ *f* moped

lambris /lã'bris/ *m pl* panelling

lambuzar /lãbu'zar/ *vt* smear; **~-se** *vpr* get sticky

lamen|tar /lamẽ'tar/ *vt* (*lastimar*) lament; (*sentir*) be sorry; **~tar-se de** lament; **~tável** (*pl* **~táveis**) *a* lamentable; **~to** *m* lament

lâmina /'lamina/ *f* blade; (*de persiana*) slat

laminar /lami'nar/ *vt* laminate

lâmpada /'lãpada/ *f* light bulb; (*abajur*) lamp

lampe|jar /lãpe'ʒar/ *vi* flash; **~jo** /e/ *m* flash

lampião /lãpi'ãw/ *m* lantern

lamúria /la'muria/ *f* moaning

lamuriar-se /lamuri'arsi/ *vpr* moan (**de** about)

lan|ça /'lãsa/ *f* spear; **~çamento** *m* (*de navio, foguete, produto*) launch; (*de filme, disco*) release; (*novo produto*) new line; (*novo filme, disco*) release; (*novo livro*) new title; (*em livro comercial*) entry; **~çar** *vt* (*atirar*) throw; launch <*navio, foguete, novo produto, livro*>; release <*filme, disco*>; (*em livro comercial*) enter; (*em leilão*) bid; **~çar mão de** make use of; **~ce** *m* (*num filme, jogo*) bit, moment; (*episódio*) episode; (*questão*) matter; (*jogada*) move; (*em leilão*) bid; (*de escada*) flight; (*de casas*) row

lancha /'lãʃa/ *f* launch

lan|char /lã'ʃar/ *vi* have a snack □ *vt* have a snack of; **~che** *m* snack; **~chonete** /ɛ/ *f* snack bar

lancinante /lãsi'nãtʃi/ *a* <*dor*> shooting; <*grito*> piercing

lânguido /'lãgidu/ *a* languid

lantejoula /lãte'ʒola/ *f* sequin

lanter|na /lã'tɛrna/ *f* lantern; (*de bolso*) torch, (*Amer*) flashlight; **~nagem** *f* panel-beating; (*oficina*) body-shop; **~ninha** *m*/*f* usher (*f* usherette)

lanugem /la'nuʒẽ/ *f* down

lapela /la'pɛla/ *f* lapel

lapidar /lapi'dar/ *vt* cut <*pedra preciosa*>; (*fig*) polish

lápide /'lapidʒi/ *f* tombstone

lápis /'lapis/ *m invar* pencil

lapiseira /lapi'zera/ *f* propelling pencil; (*caixa*) pencil box

Lapônia /la'ponia/ *f* Lappland

lapso /'lapsu/ *m* lapse

la|quê /la'ke/ *m* lacquer; **~quear** *vt* lacquer

lar /lar/ *m* home

laran|ja /la'rãʒa/ *f* orange □ *a invar* orange; **~jada** *f* orangeade; **~jeira** *f* orange tree

lareira /la'rera/ *f* hearth, fireplace

lar|gada /lar'gada/ *f* start; **dar a ~gada** start off; **~gar** *vt* (*soltar*) let go of; give up <*estudos, emprego etc*>; **~gar de fumar** give up smoking; **~go** *a* wide; <*roupa*> loose □ *m* (*praça*) square; **ao ~go** (*no alto-mar*) out at sea; **~gura** *f* width

larin|ge /la'rĩʒi/ *f* larynx; **~gite** *f* laryngitis

larva /'larva/ *f* larva

lasanha /la'zaɲa/ *f* lasagna

las|ca /'laska/ *f* chip; **~car** *vt/i* chip; **de ~car** (*fam*) awful

lástima /'lastʃima/ *f* shame

lastro /'lastru/ *m* ballast

la|ta /'lata/ *f* (*material*) tin; (*recipiente*) tin, (*Amer*) can; **~ta de lixo** dustbin, (*Amer*) trash can; **~tão** *m* brass

late|jante /late'ʒãtʃi/ *a* throbbing; **~jar** *vi* throb

latente /la'tẽtʃi/ *a* latent

late|ral /late'raw/ (*pl* **~rais**) *a* side, lateral

laticínio /latʃi'siniu/ *m* dairy product

latido /la'tʃidu/ *m* bark

lati|fundiário /latʃifũdʒi'ariu/ *a* landowning □ *m* landowner; **~-fúndio** *m* estate

latim /la'tʃĩ/ *m* Latin

latino /la'tʃinu/ *a & m* Latin; **~-americano** *a & m* Latin American

latir /la'tʃir/ *vi* bark

latitude /latʃi'tudʒi/ *f* latitude

lauda /'lawda/ *f* side

laudo /'lawdu/ *m* report, findings

lava /'lava/ *f* lava

lava|bo /la'vabu/ *m* toilet; **~dora** *f* washing machine; **~gem** *f* washing; **~gem a seco** dry cleaning; **~gem cerebral** brainwashing

lavanda /la'vãda/ *f* lavender

lavanderia /lavãde'ria/ *f* laundry

lavar /la'var/ *vt* wash; **~ a seco** dry-clean; **~-se** *vpr* wash

lavatório /lava'tɔriu/ *m* (*Port*) washbasin

lavoura /la'vora/ *f* (*agricultura*) farming; (*terreno*) field

lav|rador /lavra'dor/ *m* farmhand; **~rar** *vt* work; draw up <*documento*>

laxante /la'ʃãtʃi/ *a & m* laxative

lazer /la'zer/ *m* leisure

le|al /le'aw/ (*pl* **~ais**) *a* loyal; **~aldade** *f* loyalty

leão /le'ãw/ *m* lion; **Leão** (*signo*) Leo; **~-de-chácara** (*pl* **leões-de-chácara**) *m* bouncer

lebre /'lɛbri/ *f* hare

lecionar /lesio'nar/ *vt/i* teach

le|gação /lega'sãw/ *f* legation; **~gado** *m* (*pessoa*) legate; (*herança*) legacy

le|gal /le'gaw/ (*pl* **~gais**) *a* legal; (*fam*) good; <*pessoa*> nice; **tá ~gal** OK; **~galidade** *f* legality; **~galizar** *vt* legalize

legar /le'gar/ *vt* bequeath

legenda /le'ʒẽda/ *f* (*de quadro*) caption; (*de filme*) subtitle; (*inscrição*) inscription

legi|ão /leʒi'ãw/ *f* legion; **~-onário** *m* (*romano*) legionary; (*da legião estrangeira*) legionnaire

legis|lação /leʒizla'sãw/ *f* legislation; **~lador** *m* legislator; **~-lar** *vi* legislate; **~lativo** *a* legislative □ *m* legislature; **~latura** *f* legislature; **~ta** *m/f* legal expert

legiti|mar /leʒitʃi'mar/ *vt* legitimize; **~midade** *f* legitimacy

legítimo /le'ʒitʃimu/ *a* legitimate

legí|vel /le'ʒivew/ (*pl* **~veis**) *a* legible

légua /'lɛgwa/ *f* league

legume /le'gumi/ *m* vegetable

lei /lej/ *f* law

leigo /'lejgu/ *a* lay □ *m* layman

lei|lão /lej'lãw/ *m* auction; **~loar** *vt* auction; **~loeiro** *m* auctioneer

leitão /lej'tãw/ *m* sucking pig

lei|te /'lejtʃi/ *m* milk; **~te condensado /desnatado** condensed/skimmed milk; **~teira** *f* (*jarro*) milk jug; (*panela*) milk saucepan; **~teiro** *m* milkman □ *a* <*vaca*> dairy

leito /'lejtu/ *m* bed

leitor /lej'tor/ *m* reader

leitoso /lej'tozu/ *a* milky

leitura /lej'tura/ *f* (*ação*) reading; (*material*) reading matter

lema /'lema/ *m* motto

lem|brança /lẽ'brãsa/ *f* memory; (*presente*) souvenir; **~brar** *vt/i* remember; **~brar-se de** remember; **~brar aco a alg** remind s.o. of sth; **~brete** /e/ *m* reminder

leme /'lemi/ *m* rudder

len|ço /'lẽsu/ *m* (*para o nariz*) handkerchief; (*para vestir*) scarf; **~çol** /ɔ/ (*pl* **~çóis**) *m* sheet

len|da /'lẽda/ *f* legend; **~dário** *a* legendary

lenha /'leɲa/ *f* firewood; (*uma*) log; **~dor** *m* woodcutter

lente /'lẽtʃi/ *f* lens; **~ de contato** contact lens

lentidão /lẽtʃi'dãw/ *f* slowness

lentilha /lẽ'tʃiʎa/ *f* lentil

lento /'lẽtu/ *a* slow

leoa /le'oa/ *f* lioness

leopardo /lio'pardu/ *m* leopard

le|pra /'lɛpra/ *f* leprosy; **~proso** /o/ *a* leprous □ *m* leper

leque /'lɛki/ *m* fan; (*fig*) array

ler /ler/ *vt/i* read

ler|deza /ler'deza/ *f* sluggishness; **~do** /ɛ/ *a* sluggish

le|são /le'zãw/ *f* lesion, injury; **~sar** *vt* damage

lésbi|ca /'lɛzbika/ *f* lesbian; **~co** *a* lesbian

lesionar /lezio'nar/ *vt* injure

lesma /'lezma/ *f* slug

leste /'lɛstʃi/ *m* east

le|tal /le'taw/ (*pl* **~tais**) *a* lethal

le|tão /le'tãw/ *a & m* (*f* **~tã**) Latvian

letargia /letar'ʒia/ *f* lethargy

letivo /le'tʃivu/ *a* **ano ~** academic year

Letônia /le'tonia/ *f* Latvia

letra /'letra/ *f* letter; (*de música*) lyrics, words; (*caligrafia*) writing; **Letras** Modern Languages; **ao pé da ~** literally; **com todas as ~s** in no uncertain terms; **tirar de ~** take in one's stride; **~ de fôrma** block letter

letreiro /le'treru/ *m* sign

leucemia /lewse'mia/ *f* leukaemia

leva /ɛ/ *f* batch

levado /le'vadu/ *a* naughty

levan|tamento /levãta'mẽtu/ *m* (*enquete*) survey; (*rebelião*) uprising; **~tamento de pesos** weightlifting; **~tar** *vt* raise; lift <*peso*> □ *vi* get up; **~tar-se** *vpr* get up; (*revoltar-se*) rise up

levante /le'vãtʃi/ *m* east

levar /le'var/ *vt* take; lead <*vida*>; get <*tapa, susto etc*> □ *vi* lead (**a** to)

leve /'lɛvi/ *a* light; (*não grave*) slight; **de ~** lightly

levedura /leve'dura/ *f* yeast

leveza /le'veza/ *f* lightness

levi|andade /leviã'dadʒi/ *f* frivolity; **~ano** *a* frivolous

levitar /levi'tar/ *vi* levitate

lexi|cal /leksi'kaw/ (*pl* **~cais**) *a* lexical

léxico /'leksiku/ *m* lexicon

lexicografia /leksikogra'fia/ *f* lexicography

lhe /ʎi/ *pron* (*a ele*) to him; (*a ela*) to her; (*a você*) to you; **~s** *pron* to them; (*a vocês*) to you

liba|nês /liba'nes/ *a & m* (*f* **~nesa**) Lebanese

Líbano /'libanu/ *m* Lebanon

libélula /li'bɛlula/ *f* dragonfly

libe|ração /libera'sãw/ *f* release; **~ral** (*pl* **~rais**) *a & m* liberal; **~ralismo** *m* liberalism; **~ralizar** *vt* liberalize; **~rar** *vt* release

liberdade /liber'dadʒi/ *f* freedom; **pôr em ~** set free; **~ condicional** probation

líbero /'liberu/ *m* sweeper

liber|tação /liberta'sãw/ *f* liberation; **~tar** *vt* free

Líbia /'libia/ *f* Libya

líbio /'libiu/ *a & m* Libyan

libi|dinoso /libidʒi'nozu/ *a* lecherous; **~do** *f* libido

li|bra /'libra/ *f* pound; **Libra** (*signo*) Libra; **~briano** *a & m* Libran

lição /li'sãw/ *f* lesson

licen|ça /li'sẽsa/ *f* leave; (*documento*) licence; **com ~ça** excuse me; **de ~ça** on leave; **sob ~ça** under licence; **~ciar** *vt* (*autorizar*) license; (*dar férias a*) give leave to; **~ciar-se** *vpr* (*tirar férias*) take leave; (*formar-se*) graduate; **~ciatura** *f* degree; **~cioso** /o/ *a* licentious

liceu /li'sew/ *m* (*Port*) secondary school, (*Amer*) high school

licor /li'kor/ *m* liqueur

lida /'lida/ *f* slog, grind; (*leitura*) read

lidar /li'dar/ *vt/i* **~ com** deal with

lide /'lidʒi/ *f* (*trabalho*) work

líder /'lider/ *m/f* leader

lide|rança /lide'rãsa/ *f* (*de partido etc*) leadership; (*em corrida, jogo etc*) lead; **~rar** *vt* lead

lido /'lidu/ *a* well-read

liga /'liga/ *f* (*aliança*) league; (*tira*) garter; (*presilha*) suspender; (*de metais*) alloy

li|gação /liga'sãw/ *f* connection; (*telefônica*) call; (*amorosa*) liaison; **~gada** *f* call, ring; **~gado** *a* <*luz, TV*> on; **~gado em** attached to <*pessoa*>; hooked on <*droga*>; **~gamento** *m* ligament; **~gar** *vt* join, connect; switch on <*luz, TV etc*>; start up <*carro*>; bind <*amigos*> □ *vi* ring up, call; **~gar para** (*telefonar*) ring, call; (*dar importância*) care about; (*dar atenção*) pay attention to; **~gar-se** *vpr* join

ligeiro /li'ʒeru/ *a* light; <*ferida, melhora*> slight; (*ágil*) nimble

lilás /li'las/ *m* lilac □ *a invar* mauve

lima[1] /'lima/ *f* (*ferramenta*) file

lima[2] /'lima/ *f* (*fruta*) sweet orange

limão /li'mãw/ *m* lime; (*amarelo*) lemon

limar /li'mar/ *vt* file

limeira /li'mera/ *f* sweet orange tree

limiar /limi'ar/ *m* threshold

limi|tação /limita'sãw/ *f* limitation; **~tar** *vt* limit; **~tar-se** *vpr* limit o.s.; **~tar(-se) com** border on; **~te** *m* limit; (*de terreno*) boundary; **passar dos ~tes** go too far; **~te de velocidade** speed limit

limo|eiro /limo'eru/ *m* lime tree; **~nada** *f* lemonade

lim|pador /lĩpa'dor/ *m* **~pador de pára-brisas** windscreen wiper; **~par** *vt* clean; wipe <*lágrimas, suor*>; (*fig*) clean up <*cidade, organização*>; **~peza** /e/ *f* (*ato*) cleaning; (*qualidade*) cleanness; (*fig*) clean-up; **~peza pública** sanitation; **~po** *a* clean; <*céu, consciência*> clear; <*lucro*> net, clear; (*fig*) pure; **passar a ~po** write up <*trabalho*>; (*fig*) sort out <*vida*>; **tirar a ~po** get to the bottom of <*caso*>

limusine /limu'zini/ *f* limousine

lince /'lĩsi/ *m* lynx

lindo /'lĩdu/ *a* beautiful

linear /lini'ar/ *a* linear

lingote /lĩ'gɔtʃi/ *m* ingot

língua /'lĩgwa/ *f* (*na boca*) tongue; (*idioma*) language; **~ materna** mother tongue

linguado /lĩ'gwadu/ *m* sole

lingua|gem /lĩ'gwaʒẽ/ *f* language; **~jar** *m* speech, dialect

lingüeta /lĩ'gweta/ *f* bolt

lingüiça /lĩ'gwisa/ *f* pork sausage

lin|güista /lĩ'gwiʃta/ *m/f* linguist; **~güística** *f* linguistics; **~güístico** *a* linguistic

linha /'liɲa/ *f* line; (*fio*) thread; **perder a ~** lose one's cool; **~ aérea** airline; **~ de fogo** firing line; **~ de montagem** assembly line; **~gem** *f* lineage

linho /'liɲu/ *m* linen; (*planta*) flax

linóleo /li'nɔliu/ *m* lino(leum)

lipoaspiração /lipoaspira'sãw/ *f* liposuction

liqui|dação /likida'sãw/ *f* liquidation; (*de loja*) clearance sale; (*de conta*) settlement; **~dar** *vt* liquidate; settle <*conta*>; pay off <*dívida*>; sell off, clear <*mercadorias*>

liqüidificador /likwidʒifika'dor/ *m* liquidizer

líquido /'likidu/ *a* liquid; <*lucro, salário*> net □ *m* liquid

líri|ca /'lirika/ *f* (*mus*) lyrics; (*poesia*) lyric poetry; **~co** *a* lyrical; <*poesia*> lyric

lírio /'liriu/ *m* lily

Lisboa /liz'boa/ *f* Lisbon

lisboeta /lizbo'eta/ *a & m/f* (person) from Lisbon

liso /'lizu/ *a* smooth; (*sem desenho*) plain; <*cabelo*> straight; (*fam: duro*) broke

lison|ja /li'zõʒa/ *f* flattery; **~jear** *vt* flatter

lista /'lista/ *f* list; (*listra*) stripe; **~ telefônica** telephone directory

listra /'listra/ *f* stripe; **~do** *a* striped, stripey

lite|ral /lite'raw/ (*pl* **~rais**) *a* literal; **~rário** *a* literary; **~ratura** *f* literature

litígio /li'tʃiʒiu/ *m* dispute; (*jurid*) lawsuit

lito|ral /lito'raw/ (*pl* **~rais**) *m* coastline; **~râneo** *a* coastal

litro /'litru/ *m* litre

Lituânia /litu'ania/ *f* Lithuania

lituano /litu'anu/ *a & m* Lithuanian

living /'livĩ/ (*pl* **~s**) *m* living room

livrar /li'vrar/ *vt* free; (*salvar*) save; **~-se** *vpr* escape; **~-se de** get rid of

livraria /livra'ria/ *f* bookshop

livre /'livri/ *a* free; **~ de impostos** tax-free; **~-arbítrio** *m* free will

liv|reiro /li'vreru/ *m* bookseller; **~ro** *m* book; **~ro de consulta** reference book; **~ro de cozinha** cookery book; **~ro de texto** text book; **~ro eletrônico** e-book

li|xa /'liʃa/ *f* (*de unhas*) emery board; (*para madeira etc*) sandpaper; **~xar** *vt* sand <*madeira*>; file <*unhas*>; **estou me ~xando** (*fam*) I couldn't care less

li|xeira /li'ʃera/ *f* dustbin, (*Amer*) garbage can; **~xeiro** *m* dustman, (*Amer*) garbage collector; **~xo** rubbish, (*Amer*) garbage; (*atômico*) waste

lobisomem /lobi'zomẽ/ *m* werewolf

lobo /'lobu/ *m* wolf; **~-marinho** (*pl* **~s-marinhos**) *m* sea lion

lóbulo /'lɔbulu/ *m* lobe

lo|cação /loka'sãw/ *f* (*de imóvel*) lease; (*de carro*) rental; **~cador** *m* (*de casa*) landlord; **~cadora** *f* rental company; (*de vídeos*) video shop

lo|cal /lo'kaw/ (*pl* **~cais**) *a* local □ *m* site; (*de um acidente etc*) scene; **~calidade** *f* locality; **~calização** *f* location; **~calizar** *vt* locate; **~calizar-se** *vpr* (*orientar-se*) get one's bearings

loção /lo'sãw/ *f* lotion; **~ após-barba** aftershave lotion

locatário /loka'tariu/ *m* (*de imóvel*) tenant; (*de carro etc*) hirer

locomo|tiva /lokomo'tʃiva/ *f* locomotive; **~ver-se** *vpr* get around

locu|ção /loku'sãw/ *f* phrase; **~tor** *m* announcer

lodo /'lodu/ *m* mud; **~so** /o/ *a* muddy

logaritmo /loga'ritʃimu/ *m* logarithm

lógi|ca /'lɔʒika/ *f* logic; **~co** *a* logical

logo /'lɔgu/ *adv* (*em seguida*) straightaway; (*em breve*) soon; (*justamente*) just; **~ mais** later; **~ antes/depois** just before/straight after; **~ que** as soon as; **até ~** goodbye

logotipo /logo'tʃipu/ *m* logo

logradouro /logra'doru/ *m* public place

loiro /'lojru/ *a veja* **louro**

lo|ja /'lɔja/ *f* shop, (*Amer*) store; **~ja de departamentos** department store; **~ja maçônica** masonic lodge; **~jista** *m/f* shopkeeper

lom|bada /lõ'bada/ *f* (*de livro*) spine; (*na rua*) speed bump; **~binho** *m* tenderloin; **~bo** *m* back; (*carne*) loin

lona /'lona/ *f* canvas

Londres /'lõdris/ *f* London

londrino /lõ'drinu/ *a* London □ *m* Londoner

longa-metragem /lõgame'traʒẽ/ (*pl* **longas-metragens**) *m* feature film

longe /'lõʒi/ *adv* far, a long way; **de ~** from a distance; (*por muito*) by far; **~ disso** far from it

longevidade /lõʒevi'dadʒi/ *f* longevity

longínquo /lõ'ʒĩkwu/ *a* distant

longitude /lõʒi'tudʒi/ *f* longitude

longo /'lõgu/ *a* long □ *m* long dress; **ao ~ de** along; (*durante*) through, over

lontra /'lõtra/ *f* otter

lorde /'lɔrdʒi/ *m* lord

lorota /lo'rɔta/ (*fam*) *f* fib

losango /lo'zãgu/ *m* diamond

lo|tação /lota'sãw/ *f* capacity; (*ônibus*) bus; **~tação esgotada** full house; **~tado** *a* crowded; <*teatro, ônibus*> full; **~tar** *vt* fill □ *vi* fill up

lote /'lɔtʃi/ *m* (*quinhão*) portion; (*de terreno*) plot, (*Amer*) lot; (*em leilão*) lot; (*porção de coisas*) batch

loteria /lote'ria/ *f* lottery

louça /'losa/ *f* china; (*pratos etc*) crockery; **lavar a ~** wash up, (*Amer*) do the dishes

lou|co /'loku/ *a* mad, crazy □ *m* madman; **estou ~co para ir** (*fam*) I'm dying to go; **~cura** *f* madness; (*uma*) crazy thing

louro /'loru/ *a* blond □ *m* laurel; (*condimento*) bayleaf

lou|var /lo'var/ *vt* praise; **~vável** (*pl* **~váveis**) *a* praiseworthy; **~vor** /o/ *m* praise

lua /'lua/ *f* moon; **~-de-mel** *f* honeymoon

lu|ar /lu'ar/ *m* moonlight; **~arento** *a* moonlit

lubrifi|cação /lubrifika'sãw/ *f* lubrication; **~cante** *a* lubricating □ *m* lubricant; **~car** *vt* lubricate

lucidez /lusi'des/ *f* lucidity

lúcido /'lusidu/ *a* lucid

lu|crar /lu'krar/ *vi* profit (**com** by); **~cratividade** *f* profitability; **~crativo** *a* profitable, lucrative; **~cro** *m* profit

ludibriar /ludʒibri'ar/ *vt* cheat

lúdico /'ludʒiku/ *a* playful

lugar /lu'gar/ *m* place; (*espaço*) room; **em ~ de** in place of; **em primeiro ~** in the first place; **em algum ~** somewhere; **em todo ~** everywhere; **dar ~ a** give rise to; **ter ~** take place

lugarejo /luga'reʒu/ *m* village

lúgubre /'lugubri/ *a* gloomy, dismal

lula /'lula/ *f* squid

lume /'lumi/ *m* fire

luminária /lumi'naria/ *f* light, lamp; *pl* illuminations

luminoso /lumi'nozu/ *a* luminous; <*idéia*> brilliant

lunar /lu'nar/ *a* lunar □ *m* mole

lupa /'lupa/ *f* magnifying glass

lusco-fusco /lusku'fusku/ *m* twilight

lusitano /luzi'tanu/, **luso** /'luzu/ *a* & *m* Portuguese

lus|trar /lus'trar/ *vt* shine, polish; **~tre** *m* shine; (*fig*) lustre; (*luminária*) light, lamp; **~troso** /o/ *a* shiny

lu|ta /'luta/ *f* fight, struggle; **~ta livre** wrestling; **~tador** *m* fighter; (*de luta livre*) wrestler; **~tar** *vi* fight □ *vt* do <*judô etc*>

luto /'lutu/ *m* mourning

luva /'luva/ *f* glove

luxação /luʃa'sãw/ *f* dislocation

Luxemburgo /luʃẽ'burgu/ *m* Luxembourg

luxembur|guês /luʃẽbur'ges/ *a* (*f* **~guesa**) Luxemburg □ *m* (*f* **~guesa**) Luxemburger; (*língua*) Luxemburgish

luxo /'luʃu/ *m* luxury; **hotel de ~** luxury hotel; **cheio de ~** (*fam*) fussy

luxuoso /luʃu'ozu/ *a* luxurious

luxúria /lu'ʃuria/ *f* lust

luxuriante /luʃuri'ãtʃi/ *a* lush

luz /lus/ *f* light; **à ~ de** by the light of <*velas etc*>; in the light of <*fatos etc*>; **dar à ~** give birth to

luzidio /luzi'dʒio/ *a* shiny

luzir /lu'zir/ *vi* shine

Mm

maca /'maka/ *f* stretcher

maçã /ma'sã/ *f* apple

macabro /ma'kabru/ *a* macabre

maca|cão /maka'kãw/ *m* (*de trabalho*) overalls, (*Amer*) coveralls; (*tipo de calça*) dungarees; (*roupa inteiriça*) jumpsuit; (*para bebê*) romper suit; **~co** *m* monkey; (*aparelho*) jack

maçada /ma'sada/ *f* bore

maçaneta /masa'neta/ *f* doorknob

maçante /ma'sãtʃi/ *a* boring

macar|rão /maka'xãw/ *m* pasta; (*espaguete*) spaghetti; **~ronada** *f* pasta with tomato sauce and cheese

macarrônico /maka'xoniku/ *a* broken

macete /ma'setʃi/ *m* trick

machado /ma'ʃadu/ *m* axe

ma|chão /ma'ʃãw/ *a* tough □ *m* tough guy; **~chismo** *m* machismo; **~chista** *a* chauvinistic □ *m* male chauvinist; **~cho** *a* male; <*homem*> macho □ *m* male

machu|cado /maʃu'kadu/ *m* injury; (*na pele*) sore patch; **~car** *vt/i* hurt; **~car-se** *vpr* hurt o.s.

maciço /ma'sisu/ *a* solid; <*dose etc*> massive □ *m* massif

macieira /masi'era/ *f* apple tree

maciez /masi'es/ *f* softness

macilento /masi'lẽtu/ *a* haggard

macio /ma'siu/ *a* soft; <*carne*> tender

maço /'masu/ *m* (*de cigarros*) packet; (*de notas*) bundle

ma|çom /ma'sõ/ *m* freemason; **~çonaria** *f* freemasonry

maconha /ma'koɲa/ *f* marijuana

maçônico /ma'soniku/ *a* masonic

má-criação /makria'sãw/ *f* rudeness

macrobiótico /makrobi'ɔtʃiku/ *a* macrobiotic

macum|ba /ma'kũba/ *f* Afro-Brazilian cult; (*uma*) spell; **~beiro** *m* follower of macumba □ *a* macumba

madame /ma'dami/ *f* lady

Madeira /ma'dera/ *f* Madeira

madeira /ma'dera/ *f* wood □ *m* (*vinho*) Madeira; **~ de lei** hardwood

madeirense /made'rẽsi/ *a* & *m* Madeiran

madeixa /ma'deʃa/ *f* lock

madrasta /ma'drasta/ *f* stepmother

madrepérola /madre'pɛrola/ *f* mother of pearl

madressilva /madre'siwva/ *f* honeysuckle

Madri /ma'dri/ *f* Madrid

madrinha /ma'driɲa/ *f* (*de batismo*) godmother; (*de casamento*) bridesmaid

madru|gada /madru'gada/ *f* early morning; **~gador** *m* early riser; **~gar** *vi* get up early

maduro /ma'duru/ *a* <*fruta*> ripe; <*pessoa*> mature

mãe /mãj/ *f* mother; **~-de-santo** (*pl* **~s-de-santo**) *f* macumba priestess

maes|tria /majs'tria/ *f* expertise; **~tro** *m* conductor

máfia /'mafia/ *f* mafia

magazine /maga'zini/ *m* department store

magia /ma'ʒia/ *f* magic

mági|ca /'maʒika/ *f* magic; (*uma*) magic trick; **~co** *a* magic □ *m* magician

magis|tério /maʒis'tɛriu/ *m* teaching; (*professores*) teachers; **~-trado** *m* magistrate

magnânimo /mag'nanimu/ *a* magnanimous

magnata /mag'nata/ *m* magnate

magnésio /mag'nɛziu/ *m* magnesium

mag|nético /mag'nɛtʃiku/ *a* magnetic; **~netismo** *m* magnetism; **~netizar** *vt* magnetize; (*fig*) mesmerize

mag|nificência /magnifi'sẽsia/ *f* magnificence; **~nífico** *a* magnificent

magnitude /magni'tudʒi/ *f* magnitude

mago /'magu/ *m* magician; **os reis ~s** the Three Wise Men

mágoa /'magoa/ *f* sorrow

magoar /mago'ar/ *vt/i* hurt; **~-se** *vpr* be hurt

ma|gricela /magri'sɛla/ *a* skinny; **~gro** *a* thin; <*leite*> skimmed; <*carne*> lean; (*fig*) meagre

maio /'maju/ *m* May

maiô /ma'jo/ *m* swimsuit

maionese /majo'nɛzi/ *f* mayonnaise

maior /ma'jɔr/ *a* bigger; <*escritor, amor etc*> greater; **o ~ carro** the biggest car; **o ~ escritor** the greatest writer; **~ de idade** of age

Maiorca /ma'jɔrka/ *f* Majorca

maio|ria /majo'ria/ *f* majority; **a ~ria dos brasileiros** most Brazilians; **~ridade** *f* majority, adulthood

mais /majs/ *adv* & *pron* more; **~ dois** two more; **dois dias a ~** two more days; **não trabalho ~** I don't work any more; **~ ou menos** more or less

maisena /maj'zɛna/ *f* cornflour, (*Amer*) cornstarch

maître /mɛtr/ *m* head waiter

maiúscula /ma'juskula/ *f* capital letter

majes|tade /maʒes'tadʒi/ *f* majesty; **~toso** *a* majestic

major /ma'jɔr/ *m* major

majoritário /maʒori'tariu/ *a* majority

mal /maw/ *adv* badly; (*quase não*) hardly □ *conj* hardly □ *m* evil; (*doença*) sickness; **não faz ~** never mind; **levar a ~** take offence at; **passar ~** be sick

mala /'mala/ *f* suitcase; (*do carro*) boot, (*Amer*) trunk; **~ aérea** air courier

malabaris|mo /malaba'rizmu/ *m* juggling act; **~ta** *m/f* juggler

malagradecido /malagrade'sidu/ *a* ungrateful

malagueta /mala'geta/ *f* chilli pepper

malaio /ma'laju/ *a & m* Malay

Malaísia /mala'izia/ *f* Malaysia

malaísio /mala'iziu/ *a & m* Malaysian

malan|dragem /malã'draʒẽ/ *f* hustling; (*uma*) clever trick; **~dro** *a* cunning □ *m* hustler

malária /ma'laria/ *f* malaria

mal-assombrado /malasõ'bradu/ *a* haunted

Malavi /mala'vi/ *m* Malawi

malcriado /mawkri'adu/ *a* rude

mal|dade /maw'dadʒi/ *f* wickedness; (*uma*) wicked thing; **por ~dade** out of spite; **~dição** *f* curse; **~dito** *a* cursed, damned; **~doso** /o/ *a* wicked

maleá|vel /mali'avew/ (*pl* **~veis**) *a* malleable

maledicência /maledi'sẽsia/ *f* malicious gossip

maléfico /ma'lɛfiku/ *a* evil; (*prejudicial*) harmful

mal-encarado /malĩka'radu/ *a* shady, dubious □ *m* shady character

mal-entendido /malĩtẽ'dʒidu/ *m* misunderstanding

mal-estar /malis'tar/ *m* (*doença*) ailment; (*constrangimento*) discomfort

maleta /ma'leta/ *f* overnight bag

malévolo /ma'lɛvolu/ *a* malevolent

malfei|to /maw'fejtu/ *a* badly done; <*roupa etc*> badly made; (*fig*) wrongful; **~tor** *m* wrongdoer; **~toria** *f* wrongdoing

ma|lha /'maʎa/ *f* (*ponto*) stitch; (*tricô*) knitting; (*tecido*) jersey; (*casaco*) jumper, (*Amer*) sweater; (*para ginástica*) leotard; (*de rede*) mesh; **fazer ~lha** knit; **~lhado** *a* <*animal*> dappled; <*roque*> heavy; **~lhar** *vt* beat; thresh <*trigo etc*> □ *vi* (*fam*) work out

mal-humorado /malumo'radu/ *a* in a bad mood, grumpy

malícia /ma'lisia/ *f* (*má índole*) malice; (*astúcia*) guile; (*humor*) innuendo

malicioso /malisi'ozu/ *a* (*mau*) malicious; (*astuto*) crafty; (*que põe malícia*) dirty-minded

maligno /ma'liginu/ *a* malignant

malmequer /mawme'ker/ *m* marigold

maloca /ma'lɔka/ *f* Indian village

malo|grar-se /malo'grarsi/ *vpr* go wrong, fail; **~gro** /o/ *m* failure

mal-passado /mawpa'sadu/ *a* <*carne*> rare

Malta /'mawta/ *f* Malta

malte /'mawtʃi/ *m* malt

maltrapilho /mawtra'piʎu/ *a* scruffy

maltratar /mawtra'tar/ *vt* ill-treat, mistreat

malu|co /ma'luku/ *a* mad, crazy □ *m* madman; **~quice** *f* madness; (*uma*) crazy thing

malvado /maw'vadu/ *a* wicked

malver|sação /mawversa'sãw/ *f* mismanagement; (*de fundos*) misappropriation; **~sar** *vt* mismanage; misappropriate <*dinheiro*>

Malvinas /maw'vinas/ *fpl* Falklands

mamadeira /mama'dera/ *f* (baby's) bottle

mamãe /ma'mãj/ *f* mum

mamão /ma'mãw/ *m* papaya

ma|mar /ma'mar/ *vi* suckle; **~mata** *f* (*fam*) fiddle

mamífero /ma'miferu/ *m* mammal

mamilo /ma'milu/ *m* nipple

mamoeiro /mamo'eru/ *m* papaya tree

manada /ma'nada/ *f* herd

mananci|al /manãsi'aw/ (*pl* **~-ais**) *m* spring; (*fig*) rich source

man|cada /mã'kada/ *f* blunder; **~car** *vi* limp; **~car-se** *vpr* (*fam*) take the hint, get the message

Mancha /'mãʃa/ *f* **o canal da ~** the English Channel

man|cha /'mãʃa/ *f* stain; (*na pele*) mark; **~char** *vt* stain

manchete /mã'ʃɛtʃi/ *f* headline

manco /'mãku/ *a* lame □ *m* cripple

mandachuva /mãda'ʃuva/ *m* (*fam*) bigwig; (*chefe*) boss

man|dado /mã'dadu/ *m* order; **~dado de busca** search warrant; **~dado de prisão** arrest warrant; **~damento** *m* commandment; **~dante** *m/f* person in charge; **~dão** *a* (*f* **~dona**) bossy; **~dar** *vt* (*pedir*) order; (*enviar*) send □ *vi* be in charge; **~dar-se** *vpr* (*fam*) take off; **~dar buscar** fetch; **~dar dizer** send word; **~dar alg ir** tell s.o. to go; **~dar ver** (*fam*) go to town; **~dar em alg** order s.o. about; **~dato** *m* mandate

mandíbula /mã'dʒibula/ *f* (lower) jaw

mandioca /mãdʒi'ɔka/ *f* manioc

maneira /ma'nera/ *f* way; *pl* (*boas*) manners; **desta ~** in this way; **de qualquer ~** anyway

mane|jar /mane'ʒar/ *vt* handle; operate <*máquina*>; **~jável** (*pl* **~jáveis**) *a* manageable; **~jo** /e/ *m* handling

manequim /mane'kĩ/ *m* (*boneco*) dummy; (*medida*) size □ *m/f* mannequin, model

maneta /ma'neta/ *a* one-armed □ *m/f* person with one arm

manga[1] /'mãga/ *f* (*de roupa*) sleeve

manga[2] /'mãga/ *f* (*fruta*) mango

manganês /mãga'nes/ *m* manganese

mangue /'mãgi/ *m* mangrove swamp

mangueira[1] /mã'gera/ *f* (*tubo*) hose

mangueira[2] /mã'gera/ *f* (*árvore*) mango tree

manha /'maɲa/ *f* tantrum

manhã /ma'ɲã/ *f* morning; **de ~** in the morning

manhoso /ma'ɲozu/ *a* wilful

mania /ma'nia/ *f* (*moda*) craze; (*doença*) mania

maníaco /ma'niaku/ *a* manic □ *m* maniac; **~-depressivo** *a & m* manic depressive

manicômio /mani'komiu/ *m* lunatic asylum

manicura /mani'kura/ *f* manicure; (*pessoa*) manicurist

manifes|tação /manifesta'sãw/ *f* manifestation; (*passeata*) demonstration; **~tante** *m/f* demonstrator; **~tar** *vt* manifest, demonstrate; **~tar-se** *vpr* (*revelar-se*) manifest o.s.; (*exprimir-se*) express an opinion; **~to** /ɛ/ *a* manifest, clear □ *m* manifesto

manipular /manipu'lar/ *vt* manipulate

manjedoura /mãʒe'dora/ *f* manger

manjericão /mãʒeri'kãw/ *m* basil

mano|bra /ma'nɔbra/ *f* manoeuvre; **~brar** *vt* manoeuvre; **~brista** *m/f* parking valet

mansão /mã'sãw/ *f* mansion

man|sidão /mãsi'dãw/ *f* gentleness; (*do mar*) calm; **~sinho** *adv* **de ~sinho** (*devagar*) slowly; (*de leve*) gently; (*de fininho*) stealthily; **~so** *a* gentle; <*mar*> calm; <*animal*> tame

manta /'mãta/ *f* blanket; (*casaco*) cloak

mantei|ga /mã'tejga/ *f* butter; **~gueira** *f* butter dish

manter /mã'ter/ *vt* keep; **~-se** *vpr* keep; (*sustentar-se*) keep o.s.

mantimentos /mãtʃi'mẽtus/ *m pl* provisions

manto /'mãtu/ *m* mantle

manu|al /manu'aw/ (*pl* **~ais**) *a & m* manual; **~fatura** *f* manufacture; (*fábrica*) factory; **~faturar** *vt* manufacture

manuscrito /manus'kritu/ *a* handwritten □ *m* manuscript

manu|sear /manuzi'ar/ *vt* handle; **~seio** *m* handling

manutenção /manutẽ'sãw/ *f* maintenance; (*de prédio*) upkeep

mão /mãw/ (*pl* **~s**) *f* hand; (*do trânsito*) direction; (*de tinta*) coat; **abrir ~ de** give up; **agüentar a ~** hang on; **dar a ~ a alg** hold s.o.'s hand; (*cumprimentando*) shake s.o.'s hand; **deixar alg na ~** let s.o. down; **enfiar** *ou* **meter a ~ em** hit, slap; **lançar ~ de** make use of; **escrito à ~** written by hand; **ter à ~** have to hand; **de ~s dadas** hand in hand; **em segunda ~** second-hand; **fora de ~** out of the way; **~ única** one way; **~-de-obra** *f* labour

mapa /'mapa/ *m* map

maquete /ma'kɛtʃi/ *f* model

maqui|agem /maki'aʒẽ/ *f* make-up; **~ar** *vt* make up; **~ar-se** *vpr* put on make-up

maquiavélico /makia'vɛliku/ *a* Machiavellian

maqui|lagem, ~lar, (*Port*) **~-lhagem, ~lhar** *veja* **maqui|agem, ~ar**

máquina /'makina/ *f* machine; (*ferroviária*) engine; **escrever à ~** type; **~ de costura** sewing machine; **~ de escrever** typewriter; **~ de lavar (roupa)** washing machine; **~ de lavar pratos** dishwasher; **~ fotográfica** camera

maqui|nação /makina'sãw/ *f* machination; **~nal** (*pl* **~nais**) *a* mechanical; **~nar** *vt/i* plot; **~naria** *f* machinery; **~nista** *m/f* (*ferroviário*) engine driver; (*de navio*) engineer

mar /mar/ *m* sea

maracu|já /maraku'ʒa/ *m* passion fruit; **~jazeiro** *m* passion-fruit plant

marasmo /ma'razmu/ *f* stagnation

marato|na /mara'tona/ *f* marathon; **~nista** *m/f* marathon runner

maravi|lha /mara'viʎa/ *f* marvel; **às mil ~lhas** wonderfully; **~lhar** *vt* amaze; **~lhar-se** *vpr* marvel (**de** at); **~lhoso** /o/ *a* marvellous

mar|ca /'marka/ *f* (*sinal*) mark; (*de carro, máquina*) make; (*de cigarro, sabão etc*) brand; **~ca registrada** registered trademark; **~cação** *f* marking; (*Port: discagem*) dialling; **~cador** *m* marker; (*em livro*) bookmark; (*placar*) scoreboard; (*jogador*) scorer; **~cante** *a* outstanding; **~capasso** *m* pacemaker; **~car** *vt* mark; arrange <*hora,* *encontro, jantar etc*>; score <*gol, ponto*>; (*Port: discar*) dial; <*relógio, termômetro*> show; brand <*gado*>; (*observar*) keep a close eye on; (*impressionar*) leave one's mark on □ *vi* make one's mark; **~car época** make history; **~car hora** make an appointment; **~car o compasso** beat time; **~car os pontos** keep the score

marce|naria /marsena'ria/ *f* cabinet-making; (*oficina*) cabinet maker's workshop; **~neiro** *m* cabinet maker

mar|cha /'marʃa/ *f* march; (*de carro*) gear; **pôr-se em ~cha** get going; **~cha à ré**, (*Port*) **~cha atrás** reverse; **~char** *vi* march

marci|al /marsi'aw/ (*pl* **~ais**) *a* martial; **~ano** *a & m* Martian

marco[1] /'marku/ *m* (*sinal*) landmark

marco[2] /'marku/ *m* (*moeda*) mark

março /'marsu/ *m* March

maré /ma'rɛ/ *f* tide

mare|chal /mare'ʃaw/ (*pl* **~-chais**) *m* marshal

maresia /mare'zia/ *f* smell of the sea

marfim /mar'fĩ/ *m* ivory

margarida /marga'rida/ *f* daisy; (*para impressora*) daisywheel

margarina /marga'rina/ *f* margarine

mar|gem /'marʒẽ/ *f* (*de rio*) bank; (*de lago*) shore; (*parte em branco, fig*) margin; **~ginal** (*pl* **~-ginais**) *a* marginal; (*delinqüente*) delinquent □ *m/f* delinquent □ *f* (*rua*) riverside road; **~ginalidade** *f* delinquency; **~ginalizar** *vt* marginalize

marido /ma'ridu/ *m* husband

marimbondo /marĩ'bõdu/ *m* hornet

marina /ma'rina/ *f* marina

mari|nha /ma'riɲa/ *f* navy; **~nha mercante** merchant navy; **~-nheiro** *m* sailor; **~nho** *a* marine

marionete /mario'nɛtʃi/ *f* puppet

mariposa /mari'poza/ *f* moth

mariscos /ma'riskus/ *m* seafood

mari|tal /mari'taw/ (*pl* **~tais**) *a* marital

marítimo /ma'ritʃimu/ *a* sea; <*cidade*> seaside

marmanjo /mar'mãʒu/ *m* grown-up

marme|lada /marme'lada/ *f* (*fam*) fix; **~lo** /ɛ/ *m* quince

marmita /mar'mita/ *f* (*de soldado*) mess tin; (*de trabalhador*) lunchbox

mármore /'marmori/ *m* marble

marmóreo /mar'mɔriu/ *a* marble

marquise /mar'kizi/ *f* awning

marreco /ma'xɛku/ *m* wild duck

Marrocos /ma'xɔkus/ *m* Morocco

marrom /ma'xõ/ *a & m* brown

marroquino /maxo'kinu/ *a & m* Moroccan

Marte /'martʃi/ *m* Mars

marte|lada /marte'lada/ *f* hammer blow; **~lar** *vt/i* hammer; **~lar em** (*fig*) go on and on about; **~lo** /ɛ/ *m* hammer

mártir /'martʃir/ *m/f* martyr

mar|tírio /mar'tʃiriu/ *m* martyrdom; (*fig*) torture; **~tirizar** *vt* martyr; (*fig*) torture

marujo /ma'ruʒu/ *m* sailor

mar|xismo /mark'sizmu/ *m* Marxism; **~xista** *a & m/f* Marxist

mas /mas/ *conj* but

mascar /mas'kar/ *vt* chew

máscara /'maskara/ *f* mask; (*tratamento facial*) face-pack

mascarar /maska'rar/ *vt* mask

mascate /mas'katʃi/ *m* street vendor

mascavo /mas'kavu/ *a* **açúcar ~** brown sugar

mascote /mas'kɔtʃi/ *f* mascot

masculino /masku'linu/ *a* male; (*para homens*) men's; <*palavra*> masculine □ *m* masculine

másculo /'maskulu/ *a* masculine

masmorra /maz'moxa/ *f* dungeon

masoquis|mo /mazo'kizmu/ *m* masochism; **~ta** *m/f* masochist □ *a* masochistic

massa /'masa/ *f* mass; (*de pão*) dough; (*de torta, empada*) pastry; (*macarrão etc*) pasta; **cultura de ~** mass culture; **em ~** en masse; **as ~s** the masses

massa|crante /masa'krãtʃi/ *a* gruelling; **~crar** *vt* massacre; (*fig: maçar*) wear out; **~cre** *m* massacre

massa|gear /masaʒi'ar/ *vt* massage; **~gem** *f* massage; **~gista** *m/f* masseur (*f* masseuse)

mastigar /mastʃi'gar/ *vt* chew; (*ponderar*) chew over

mastro /'mastru/ *m* mast; (*de bandeira*) flagpole

mastur|bação /masturba'sãw/ *f* masturbation; **~bar-se** *vpr* masturbate

mata /'mata/ *f* forest

mata-borrão /matabo'xãw/ *m* blotting paper

matadouro /mata'doru/ *m* slaughterhouse

mata|gal /mata'gaw/ (*pl* **~gais**) *m* thicket

mata-moscas /mata'moskas/ *m invar* fly spray

ma|tança /ma'tãsa/ *f* slaughter; **~tar** *vt* kill; satisfy <*fome*>; quench <*sede*>; guess <*charada*>; (*fazer nas coxas*) dash off; (*fam*) skive off <*aula, serviço*> □ *vi* kill

mata-ratos /mata'xatus/ *m invar* rat poison
mate[1] /'matʃi/ *m* (*chá*) maté
mate[2] /'matʃi/ *a invar* matt
matemáti|ca /mate'matʃika/ *f* mathematics; **~co** *a* mathematical □ *m* mathematician
matéria /ma'tɛria/ *f* (*assunto, disciplina*) subject; (*no jornal*) article; (*substância*) matter; (*usada para fazer algo*) material; **em ~ de** in the way of
materi|al /materi'aw/ (*pl* **~ais**) *m* materials □ *a* material; **~alismo** *m* materialism; **~alista** *a* materialistic □ *m/f* materialist; **~alizar-se** *vpr* materialize
matéria-prima /matɛria'prima/ (*pl* **matérias-primas**) *f* raw material
mater|nal /mater'naw/ (*pl* **~-nais**) *a* maternal; **~nidade** *f* maternity; (*clínica*) maternity hospital; **~no** /ɛ/ *a* maternal; **língua ~na** mother tongue
mati|nal /matʃi'naw/ (*pl* **~nais**) *a* morning; **~nê** *f* matinée
matiz /ma'tʃis/ *m* shade; (*político*) colouring; (*pontinha: de ironia etc*) tinge
matizar /matʃi'zar/ *vt* tinge (**de** with)
mato /'matu/ *m* scrubland, bush
matraca /ma'traka/ *f* rattle; (*tagarela*) chatterbox
matreiro /ma'treru/ *a* cunning
matriar|ca /matri'arka/ *f* matriarch; **~cal** (*pl* **~cais**) *a* matriarchal
matrícula /ma'trikula/ *f* enrolment; (*taxa*) enrolment fee; (*Port: de carro*) number plate, (*Amer*) license plate
matricular /matriku'lar/ *vt* enrol; **~-se** *vpr* enrol
matri|monial /matrimoni'aw/ (*pl* **~moniais**) *a* marriage; **~mônio** *m* marriage
matriz /ma'tris/ *f* matrix; (*útero*) womb; (*sede*) head office
maturidade /maturi'dadʒi/ *f* maturity
matutino /matu'tʃinu/ *a* morning □ *m* morning paper
matuto /ma'tutu/ *a* countrified □ *m* country bumpkin
mau /maw/ *a* (*f* **má**) bad; **~-caráter** *m invar* bad lot □ *a invar* no-good; **~-olhado** *m* evil eye
mausoléu /mawzo'lɛw/ *m* mausoleum
maus-tratos /maws'tratus/ *m pl* ill-treatment
maxilar /maksi'lar/ *m* jaw
máxima /'masima/ *f* maxim
maximizar /masimi'zar/ *vt* maximize; (*exagerar*) play up
máximo /'masimu/ *a* (*antes do substantivo*) utmost, greatest; (*depois do substantivo*) maximum □ *m* maximum; **o ~** (*fam: o melhor*) really something; **ao ~** to the maximum; **no ~** at most
maxixe /ma'ʃiʃi/ *m* gherkin
me /mi/ *pron* me; (*indireto*) (to) me; (*reflexivo*) myself
meada /mi'ada/ *f* skein; **perder o fio da ~** lose one's thread
meados /mi'adus/ *m pl* **~ de maio** mid-May
meandro /mi'ãdru/ *f* meander; *pl* (*fig*) twists and turns
mecâni|ca /me'kanika/ *f* mechanics; **~co** *a* mechanical □ *m* mechanic
meca|nismo /meka'nizmu/ *m* mechanism; **~nizar** *vt* mechanize
mecenas /me'sɛnas/ *m invar* patron
mecha /'mɛʃa/ *f* (*de vela*) wick; (*de bomba*) fuse; (*porção de cabelos*) lock; (*cabelo tingido*) highlight; **~do** *a* highlighted
meda|lha /me'daʎa/ *f* medal; **~-lhão** *m* medallion; (*jóia*) locket
média /'mɛdʒia/ *f* average; (*café*) white coffee; **em ~** on average
medi|ação /medʒia'sãw/ *f* mediation; **~ador** *m* mediator; **~-ante** *prep* through, by; **~ar** *vi* mediate
medica|ção /medʒika'sãw/ *f* medication; **~mento** *m* medicine
medição /medʒi'sãw/ *f* measurement
medicar /medʒi'kar/ *vt* treat □ *vi* practise medicine; **~-se** *vpr* dose o.s. up
medici|na /medʒi'sina/ *f* medicine; **~na legal** forensic medicine; **~nal** (*pl* **~nais**) *a* medicinal
médico /'mɛdʒiku/ *m* doctor □ *a* medical; **~-legal** (*pl* **~-legais**) *a* forensic; **~-legista** (*pl* **~s-legistas**) *m/f* forensic scientist
medi|da /me'dʒida/ *f* measure; (*dimensão*) measurement; **à ~da que** as; **sob ~da** made to measure; **tirar as ~das de alg** take s.o.'s measurements; **~dor** *m* meter
medie|val /medʒie'vaw/ (*pl* **~-vais**) *a* medieval
médio /'mɛdʒiu/ *a* (*típico*) average; <*tamanho, prazo*> medium; <*classe, dedo*> middle
medíocre /me'dʒiokri/ *a* mediocre
mediocridade /medʒiokri'dadʒi/ *f* mediocrity
medir /me'dʒir/ *vt* measure; weigh <*palavras*> □ *vi* measure; **~-se** *vpr* measure o.s.; **quanto você mede?** how tall are you?
medi|tação /medʒita'sãw/ *f* meditation; **~tar** *vi* meditate

mediterrâneo /medʒite'xaniu/ *a* Mediterranean □ *m* **o Mediterrâneo** the Mediterranean

médium /'mɛdʒiũ/ *m/f* medium

medo /'medu/ *m* fear; **ter ~ de** be afraid of; **com ~** afraid; **~nho** /o/ *a* frightful

medroso /me'drozu/ *a* fearful, timid

medula /me'dula/ *f* marrow

megalomania /megaloma'nia/ *f* megalomania

meia /'meja/ *f* (*comprida*) stocking; (*curta*) sock; (*seis*) six; **~-calça** (*pl* **~s-calças**) *f* tights, (*Amer*) pantihose; **~-idade** *f* middle age; **~-noite** *f* midnight; **~-volta** (*pl* **~s-voltas**) *f* about-turn

mei|go /'mejgu/ *a* sweet; **~guice** *f* sweetness

meio /'meju/ *a* half □ *adv* rather □ *m* (*centro*) middle; (*ambiente*) environment; (*recurso*) means; **~ litro** half a litre; **dois meses e ~** two and a half months; **em ~ a** amid; **por ~ de** through; **o ~ ambiente** the environment; **os ~s de comunicação** the media; **~-dia** *m* midday; **~-fio** *m* kerb; **~-termo** *m* (*acordo*) compromise

mel /mɛw/ *m* honey

mela|ço /me'lasu/ *m* molasses; **~do** *a* sticky □ *m* treacle

melancia /melã'sia/ *f* watermelon

melan|colia /melãko'lia/ *f* melancholy; **~cólico** *a* melancholy

melão /me'lãw/ *m* melon

melar /me'lar/ *vt* make sticky

melhor /me'ʎɔr/ *a & adv* better; **o ~** the best

melho|ra /me'ʎɔra/ *f* improvement; **~ras!** get well soon!; **~-ramento** *m* improvement; **~rar** *vt* improve □ *vi* improve; <*doente*> get better

melin|drar /melĩ'drar/ *vt* hurt; **~drar-se** *vpr* be hurt; **~droso** /o/ *a* delicate; <*pessoa*> sensitive

melodi|a /melo'dʒia/ *f* melody; **~oso** /o/ *a* melodious

melodra|ma /melo'drama/ *m* melodrama; **~mático** *a* melodramatic

meloso /me'lozu/ *a* sickly sweet

melro /'mɛwxu/ *m* blackbird

membrana /mẽ'brana/ *f* membrane

membro /'mẽbru/ *m* member; (*braço, perna*) limb

memo|rando /memo'rãdu/ *m* memo; **~rável** (*pl* **~ráveis**) *a* memorable

memória /me'mɔria/ *f* memory; *pl* (*autobiografia*) memoirs

men|ção /mẽ'sãw/ *f* mention; **fazer ~ção de** mention; **~cionar** *vt* mention

mendi|cância /mẽdʒi'kãsia/ *f* begging; **~gar** *vi* beg; **~go** *m* beggar

menina /me'nina/ *f* girl; **a ~ dos olhos de alg** the apple of s.o.'s eye

meningite /menĩ'ʒitʃi/ *f* meningitis

meni|nice /meni'nisi/ *f* (*idade*) childhood; **~no** *m* boy

menopausa /meno'pawza/ *f* menopause

menor /me'nɔr/ *a* smaller □ *m/f* minor; **o/a ~** the smallest; (*mínimo*) the slightest, the least

menos /'menos/ *adv & pron* less □ *prep* except; **dois dias a ~** two days less; **a ~ que** unless; **ao** *ou* **pelo ~** at least; **o ~ bonito** the least pretty; **~prezar** *vt* look down upon

mensa|geiro /mẽsa'ʒeru/ *m* messenger; **~gem** *f* message; **~gem de texto** (*telec*) text message

men|sal /mẽ'saw/ (*pl* **~sais**) *a* monthly; **~salidade** *f* monthly payment; **~salmente** *adv* monthly

menstru|ação /mẽstrua'sãw/ *f* menstruation; **~ada** *a* **estar ~ada** be having one's period; **~al** (*pl* **~ais**) *a* menstrual; **~ar** *vi* menstruate

menta /'mẽta/ *f* mint

men|tal /mẽ'taw/ (*pl* **~tais**) *a* mental; **~talidade** *f* mentality; **~te** *f* mind

men|tir /mẽ'tʃir/ *vi* lie; **~tira** *f* lie; **~tiroso** /o/ *a* lying □ *m* liar

mentor /mẽ'tor/ *m* mentor

mercado /mer'kadu/ *m* market; **~ria** *f* commodity; *pl* goods

mercan|te /mer'kãtʃi/ *a* merchant; **~til** (*pl* **~tis**) *a* mercantile

mercê /mer'se/ *f* **à ~ de** at the mercy of

merce|aria /mersia'ria/ *f* grocer's; **~eiro** *m* grocer

mercenário /merse'nariu/ *a & m* mercenary

mercúrio /mer'kuriu/ *m* mercury; **Mercúrio** Mercury

merda /'mɛrda/ *f* (*chulo*) shit

mere|cedor /merese'dor/ *a* deserving; **~cer** *vt* deserve □ *vi* be deserving; **~cimento** *m* merit

merenda /me'rẽda/ *f* packed lunch; **~ escolar** school dinner

mere|trício /mere'trisiu/ *m* prostitution; **~triz** *f* prostitute

mergu|lhador /merguʎa'dor/ *m* diver; **~lhar** *vt* dip (**em** into) □ *vi* (*na água*) dive; (*no trabalho*) bury o.s.; **~lho** *m* dive; (*esporte*) diving; (*banho de mar*) dip

meridi|ano /meridʒi'anu/ *m* meridian; **~onal** (*pl* **~onais**) *a* southern

mérito /'mɛritu/ *m* merit

merluza /mer'luza/ *f* hake

mero /'mɛru/ *a* mere

mês /mes/ (*pl* **meses**) *m* month

mesa /'meza/ *f* table; (*de trabalho*) desk; **~ de centro** coffee table; **~ de jantar** dining table; **~ telefônica** switchboard

mesada /me'zada/ *f* monthly allowance

mescla /'mɛskla/ *f* mixture, blend

mesmice /mez'misi/ *f* sameness

mesmo /'mezmu/ *a* same □ *adv* (*até*) even; (*justamente*) right; (*de verdade*) really; **você ~** you yourself; **hoje ~** this very day; **~ assim** even so; **~ que** even if; **dá no ~** it comes to the same thing; **fiquei na mesma** I'm none the wiser

mesqui|nharia /meskiɲa'ria/ *f* meanness; (*uma*) mean thing; **~nho** *a* mean

mesquita /mes'kita/ *f* mosque

Messias /me'sias/ *m* Messiah

mesti|çagem /mestʃi'saʒẽ/ *f* interbreeding; **~ço** *a* <*pessoa*> of mixed race; <*animal*> crossbred □ *m* (*pessoa*) person of mixed race; (*animal*) mongrel

mes|trado /mes'tradu/ *m* master's degree; **~tre** /ɛ/ *m* (*f* **~tra**) master (*f* mistress); (*de escola*) teacher □ *a* main; <*chave*> master; **~tre-de-obras** (*pl* **~tres-de-obras**) *m* foreman; **~tre-sala** (*pl* **~tres-salas**) *m* master of ceremonies (*in carnival procession*); **~tria** *f* expertise

meta /'mɛta/ *f* (*de corrida*) finishing post; (*gol, fig*) goal

meta|bólico /meta'bɔliku/ *a* metabolic; **~bolismo** *m* metabolism

metade /me'tadʒi/ *f* half; **pela ~** halfway

metafísi|ca /meta'fizika/ *f* metaphysics; **~co** *a* metaphysical

metáfora /me'tafora/ *f* metaphor

metafórico /meta'fɔriku/ *a* metaphorical

me|tal /me'taw/ (*pl* **~tais**) *m* metal; *pl* (*numa orquestra*) brass; **~tálico** *a* metallic

meta|lurgia /metalur'ʒia/ *f* metallurgy; **~lúrgica** *f* metal works; **~lúrgico** *a* metallurgical □ *m* metalworker

metamorfose /metamor'fɔzi/ *f* metamorphosis

metano /me'tanu/ *m* methane

meteórico /mete'ɔriku/ *a* meteoric

meteoro /mete'ɔru/ *m* meteor; **~logia** *f* meteorology; **~lógico** *a* meteorological; **~logista** *m/f* (*cientista*) meteorologist; (*na TV*) weather forecaster

meter /me'ter/ *vt* put; **~-se** *vpr* (*envolver-se*) get (**em** into); (*intrometer-se*) meddle (**em** in); **~ medo** be frightening

meticuloso /metʃiku'lozu/ *a* meticulous

metido /me'tʃidu/ *a* snobbish; **ele é ~ a perito** he thinks he's an expert

metódico /me'tɔdʒiku/ *a* methodical

metodista /meto'dʒista/ *a & m/f* Methodist

método /'mɛtodu/ *m* method

metra|lhadora /metraʎa'dora/ *f* machine gun; **~lhar** *vt* machine-gun

métri|co /'mɛtriku/ *a* metric; **fita ~ca** tape measure

metro[1] /'mɛtru/ *m* metre

metro[2] /'mɛtru/ *m* (*Port. metropolitano*) underground, (*Amer*) subway

metrô /me'tro/ *m* underground, (*Amer*) subway

metrópole /me'trɔpoli/ *f* metropolis

metropolitano /metropoli'tanu/ *a* metropolitan □ *m* (*Port*) underground, (*Amer*) subway

meu /mew/ *a* (*f* **minha**) my □ *pron* (*f* **minha**) mine; **um amigo ~** a friend of mine; **fico na minha** (*fam*) I keep myself to myself

mexer /me'ʃer/ *vt* move; (*com colher etc*) stir □ *vi* move; **~-se** *vpr* move; (*apressar-se*) get a move on; **~ com** (*comover*) affect, get to; (*brincar com*) tease; (*trabalhar com*) work with; **~ em** touch

mexeri|ca /meʃe'rika/ *f* tangerine; **~car** *vi* gossip; **~co** *m* piece of gossip; *pl* gossip; **~queiro** *a* gossiping □ *m* gossip

mexicano /meʃi'kanu/ *a & m* Mexican

México /'mɛʃiku/ *m* Mexico

mexido /me'ʃidu/ *a* **ovos ~s** scrambled eggs

mexilhão /meʃi'ʎãw/ *m* mussel

mi|ado /mi'adu/ *m* miaow; **~ar** *vi* miaow

micreiro /mi'krejru/ *m* pc hacker

micróbio /mi'krɔbiu/ *m* microbe

micro|cosmo /mikro'kɔzmu/ *m* microcosm; **~empresa** /e/ *f* small business; **~empresário** *m* small businessman; **~filme** *m* microfilm; **~fone** *m* microphone; **~onda** *f* microwave; **(forno de) ~s** *m* microwave (oven); **~ônibus** *m invar* minibus; **~processador** *m* microprocessor

microrganismo /mikrorga-'nizmu/ *m* microorganism

microscó|pico /mikros'kɔpiku/ *a* microscopic; **~pio** *m* microscope

mídia /'midʒia/ *f* media

migalha /mi'gaʎa/ *f* crumb

mi|gração /migra'sãw/ *f* migration; **~grar** *vi* migrate

mi|jar /mi'ʒar/ *vi* (*fam*) pee; **~jar-se** *vpr* wet o.s.; **~jo** *m* (*fam*) pee

mil /miw/ *a & m invar* thousan **estar a ~** be on top form
mila|gre /mi'lagri/ *m* miracle; **~groso** /o/ *a* miraculous
milênio /mi'leniu/ *m* millennium
milésimo /mi'lɛzimu/ *a* thousandth
milha /'miʎa/ *f* mile
milhão /mi'ʎãw/ *m* million; **um ~ de dólares** a million dollars
milhar /mi'ʎar/ *m* thousand; **~es de vezes** thousands of times; **aos ~es** in their thousands
milho /'miʎo/ *m* maize, (*Amer*) corn
milico /mi'liku/ *m* (*fam*) military man; **os ~s** the military
mili|grama /mili'grama/ *m* milligram; **~litro** *m* millilitre; **~- metro** /e/ *m* millimetre
milionário /milio'nariu/ *a & m* millionaire
mili|tante /mili'tãtʃi/ *a & m* militant; **~tar** *a* military □ *m* soldier
mim /mĩ/ *pron* me
mimar /mi'mar/ *vt* spoil
mímica /'mimika/ *f* mime; (*brincadeira*) charades
mi|na /'mina/ *f* mine; **~nar** *vt* mine; (*fig: prejudicar*) undermine
mindinho /mĩ'dʒiɲu/ *m* little finger, (*Amer*) pinkie
mineiro /mi'neru/ *a* mining; (*de MG*) from Minas Gerais □ *m* miner; (*de MG*) person from Minas Gerais
mine|ração /minera'sãw/ *f* mining; **~ral** (*pl* **~rais**) *a & m* mineral; **~rar** *vt/i* mine
minério /mi'nɛriu/ *m* ore
mingau /mĩ'gaw/ *m* porridge
mingua /'mĩgwa/ *f* lack
minguante /mĩ'gwãtʃi/ *a* **quarto ~** last quarter
minguar /mĩ'gwar/ *vi* dwindle
minha /'miɲa/ *a & pron veja* **meu**
minhoca /mi'ɲɔka/ *f* worm
miniatura /minia'tura/ *f* miniature
mini|malista /minima'lista/ *a & m/f* minimalist; **~mizar** *vt* minimize; (*subestimar*) play down
mínimo /'minimu/ *a* (*muito pequeno*) tiny; (*mais baixo*) minimum □ *m* minimum; **a mínima idéia** the slightest idea; **no ~** at least
minissaia /mini'saja/ *f* miniskirt
minis|terial /ministeri'aw/ (*pl* **~teriais**) *a* ministerial; **~tério** *m* ministry; **Ministério do Interior** Home Office, (*Amer*) Department of the Interior
minis|trar /minis'trar/ *vt* administer; **~tro** *m* minister; **primeiro ~tro** prime minister
Minorca /mi'nɔrka/ *f* Menorca
mino|ritário /minori'tariu/ *a* minority; **~ria** *f* minority
minúcia /mi'nusia/ *f* detail
minucioso /minusi'ozu/ *a* thorough
minúscu|la /mi'nuskula/ *f* small letter; **~lo** *a* <*letra*> small; (*muito pequeno*) minuscule
minuta /mi'nuta/ *f* (*rascunho*) rough draft
minuto /mi'nutu/ *m* minute
miolo /mi'olu/ *f* (*de fruta*) flesh; (*de pão*) crumb; *pl* brains
míope /'miopi/ *a* short-sighted
miopia /mio'pia/ *f* myopia
mira /'mira/ *f* sight; **ter em ~** have one's sights on
mirabolante /mirabo'lãtʃi/ *a* amazing; <*idéias, plano*> grandiose
mi|ragem /mi'raʒẽ/ *f* mirage; **~rante** *m* lookout; **~rar** *vt* look at; **~rar-se** *vpr* look at o.s.
mirim /mi'rĩ/ *a* little
miscelânea /mise'lania/ *f* miscellany
miscigenação /misiʒena'sãw/ *f* interbreeding
mise-en-plis /mizã'pli/ *m* shampoo and set
miserá|vel /mize'ravew/ (*pl* **~veis**) *a* miserable
miséria /mi'zɛria/ *f* misery; (*pobreza*) poverty; **uma ~** (*pouco dinheiro*) a pittance; **chorar ~** claim poverty
miseri|córdia /mizeri'kɔrdʒia/ *f* mercy; **~cordioso** *a* merciful
misógino /mi'zɔʒinu/ *m* misogynist □ *a* misogynistic
miss /'misi/ *f* beauty queen
missa /'misa/ *f* mass
missão /mi'sãw/ *f* mission
mís|sil /'misiw/ (*pl* **~seis**) *m* missile; **~sil de longo alcance** long-range missile
missionário /misio'nariu/ *m* missionary
missiva /mi'siva/ *f* missive
mis|tério /mis'tɛriu/ *m* mystery; **~terioso** /o/ *a* mysterious; **~-ticismo** *m* mysticism
místico /'mistʃiku/ *m* mystic □ *a* mystical
misto /'mistu/ *a* mixed □ *m* mix; **~ quente** toasted ham and cheese sandwich
mistu|ra /mis'tura/ *f* mixture; **~-rar** *vt* mix; (*confundir*) mix up; **~rar-se** *vpr* mix (**com** with)
mítico /'mitʃiku/ *a* mythical
mito /'mitu/ *m* myth; **~logia** *f* mythology; **~lógico** *a* mythological

miudezas /miu'dezas/ *f pl* odds and ends
miúdo /mi'udu/ *a* tiny, minute; <*chuva*> fine; <*despesas*> minor □ *m* (*criança*) child, little one; *pl* (*de galinha*) giblets; **trocar em ~s** go into detail
mixaria /miʃa'ria/ *f* (*fam*) (*soma irrisória*) pittance
mixórdia /mi'ʃɔrdʒia/ *f* muddle
mnemônico /ne'moniku/ *a* mnemonic
mobilar /mobi'lar/ *vt* (*Port*) furnish
mobília /mo'bilia/ *f* furniture
mobili|ar /mobili'ar/ *vt* furnish; **~ário** *m* furniture
mobili|dade /mobili'dadʒi/ *f* mobility; **~zar** *vt* mobilize
moça /'mosa/ *f* girl
moçambicano /mosãbi'kanu/ *a & m* Mozambican
Moçambique /mosã'biki/ *m* Mozambique
moção /mo'sãw/ *f* motion
mochila /mo'ʃila/ *f* rucksack
moço /'mosu/ *a* young □ *m* boy, lad
moda /'mɔda/ *f* fashion; **na ~** fashionable
modalidade /modali'dadʒi/ *f* (*esporte*) event
mode|lagem /mode'laʒẽ/ *f* modelling; **~lar** *vt* model (**a** on); **~lar-se** *vpr* model o.s. (**a** on) □ *a* model; **~lo** /e/ *m* model
mode|ração /modera'sãw/ *f* moderation; **~rado** *a* moderate; **~rar** *vt* moderate; reduce <*velocidade, despesas*>; **~rar-se** *vpr* restrain oneself
moder|nidade /moderni'dadʒi/ *f* modernity; **~nismo** *m* modernism; **~nista** *a & m/f* modernist; **~nizar** *vt* modernize; **~no** /ɛ/ *a* modern
modess /'mɔdʒis/ *m invar* sanitary towel
modéstia /mo'dɛstʃia/ *f* modesty
modesto /mo'dɛstu/ *a* modest
módico /'mɔdʒiku/ *a* modest
modifi|cação /modʒifika'sãw/ *f* modification; **~car** *vt* modify
mo|dismo /mo'dʒizmu/ *m* idiom; **~dista** *f* dressmaker
modo /'mɔdu/ *m* way; (*ling*) mood; *pl* (*maneiras*) manners
modular /modu'lar/ *vt* modulate □ *a* modular
módulo /'mɔdulu/ *m* module
moeda /mo'ɛda/ *f* (*peça de metal*) coin; (*dinheiro*) currency
mo|edor /moe'dor/ *m* **~edor de café** coffee-grinder; **~edor de carne** mincer; **~er** *vt* grind <*café, trigo*>; squeeze <*cana*>; mince <*carne*>; (*bater*) beat
mo|fado /mo'fadu/ *a* mouldy; **~far** *vi* moulder; **~fo** /o/ *m* mould
mogno /'mɔgnu/ *m* mahogany
moinho /mo'iɲu/ *m* mill; **~ de vento** windmill
moisés /moj'zɛs/ *m invar* carry-cot
moita /'mojta/ *f* bush
mola /'mɔla/ *f* spring
mol|dar /mow'dar/ *vt* mould; cast <*metal*>; **~de** /ɔ/ *m* mould; (*para costura etc*) pattern
moldu|ra /mow'dura/ *f* frame; **~rar** *vt* frame
mole /'mɔli/ *a* soft; <*pessoa*> listless; (*fam*) (*fácil*) easy □ *adv* easily; **é ~?** (*fam*) can you believe it?
molécula /mo'lɛkula/ *f* molecule
moleque /mo'lɛki/ *m* (*menino*) lad; (*de rua*) urchin; (*homem*) scoundrel
molestar /moles'tar/ *vt* bother
moléstia /mo'lɛstʃia/ *f* disease
moletom /mole'tõ/ *m* (*tecido*) knitted cotton; (*blusa*) sweatshirt
moleza /mo'leza/ *f* softness; (*de pessoa*) laziness; **viver na ~** lead a cushy life; **ser ~** be easy
mo|lhado /mo'ʎadu/ *a* wet; **~lhar** *vt* wet; **~lhar-se** *vpr* get wet
molho[1] /'mɔʎu/ *m* (*de chaves*) bunch; (*de palha*) sheaf
molho[2] /'moʎu/ *m* sauce; (*para salada*) dressing; **deixar de ~** leave in soak <*roupa*>; **~ inglês** Worcester sauce
molusco /mo'lusku/ *m* mollusc
momen|tâneo /momẽ'taniu/ *a* momentary; **~to** *m* moment; (*força*) momentum
Mônaco /'monaku/ *m* Monaco
monar|ca /mo'narka/ *m/f* monarch; **~quia** *f* monarchy; **~-quista** *a & m/f* monarchist
monástico /mo'nastʃiku/ *a* monastic
monção /mõ'sãw/ *f* monsoon
mone|tário /mone'tariu/ *a* monetary; **~tarismo** *m* monetarism; **~tarista** *a & m/f* monetarist
monge /'mõʒi/ *m* monk
monitor /moni'tor/ *m* monitor; **~ de vídeo** VDU
monitorar /monito'rar/ *vt* monitor
mono|cromo /mono'krɔmu/ *a* monochrome; **~gamia** *f* monogamy
monógamo /mo'nɔgamu/ *a* monogamous
monograma /mono'grama/ *m* monogram
monólogo /mo'nɔlogu/ *m* monologue
mononucleose /mononukli'ɔzi/ *f* glandular fever
mono|pólio /mono'pɔliu/ *m* monopoly; **~polizar** *vt* monopolize

monossílabo /mono'silabu/ *a* monosyllabic □ *m* monosyllable

monotonia /monoto'nia/ *f* monotony

monótono /mo'nɔtonu/ *a* monotonous

monóxido /mo'nɔksidu/ *m* **~ de carbono** carbon monoxide

mons|tro /'mõstru/ *m* monster; **~truosidade** *f* monstrosity; **~truoso** /o/ *a* monstrous

monta|dor /mõta'dor/ *m* (*de cinema*) editor; **~dora** *f* assembly company; **~gem** *f* assembly; (*de filme*) editing; (*de peça teatral*) production

monta|nha /mõ'taɲa/ *f* mountain; **~nha-russa** (*pl* **~nhas-russas**) *f* roller coaster; **~nhismo** *m* mountaineering; **~nhoso** /o/ *a* mountainous

mon|tante /mõ'tãtʃi/ *m* amount □ *a* rising; **a ~tante** upstream; **~tão** *m* heap; **~tar** *vt* ride <*cavalo, bicicleta*>; assemble <*peças, máquina*>; put up <*barraca*>; set up <*empresa, escritório*>; mount <*guarda, diamante*>; put on <*espetáculo, peça*>; edit <*filme*> □ *vi* ride; **~tar a** <*dívidas etc*> amount to; **~tar em** (*subir em*) mount; **~taria** *f* mount; **~te** *m* heap; **um ~te de coisas** (*fam*) loads of things; **o Monte Branco** Mont Blanc

Montevidéu /mõtʃivi'dɛw/ *f* Montevideo

montra /'mõtra/ *f* (*Port*) shop window

monumen|tal /monumẽ'taw/ (*pl* **~tais**) *a* monumental; **~to** *m* monument

mora|da /mo'rada/ *f* dwelling; (*Port*) address; **~dia** *f* dwelling; **~dor** *m* resident

mo|ral /mo'raw/ (*pl* **~rais**) *a* moral □ *f* (*ética*) morals; (*de uma história*) moral □ *m* (*ânimo*) morale; (*de pessoa*) moral sense; **~ralidade** *f* morality; **~ralista** *a* moralistic □ *m*/*f* moralist; **~ralizar** *vi* moralize

morango /mo'rãgu/ *m* strawberry

morar /mo'rar/ *vi* live

moratória /mora'tɔria/ *f* moratorium

mórbido /'mɔrbidu/ *a* morbid

morcego /mor'segu/ *m* bat

mor|daça /mor'dasa/ *f* gag; (*para cão*) muzzle; **~daz** *a* scathing; **~der** *vt*/*i* bite; **~dida** *f* bite

mordo|mia /mordo'mia/ *f* (*no emprego*) perk; (*de casa etc*) comfort; **~mo** /o/ *m* butler

more|na /mo'rena/ *f* brunette; **~no** *a* dark; (*bronzeado*) brown □ *m* dark person

morfina /mor'fina/ *f* morphine

moribundo /mori'bũdu/ *a* dying

moringa /mo'rĩga/ *f* water jug

morma|cento /morma'sẽtu/ *a* sultry; **~ço** *m* sultry weather

morno /'mornu/ *a* lukewarm

moro|sidade /morozi'dadʒi/ *f* slowness; **~so** /o/ *a* slow

morrer /mo'xer/ *vi* die; <*luz, dia, ardor, esperança etc*> fade; <*carro*> stall

morro /'moxu/ *m* hill; (*fig: favela*) slum

mortadela /morta'dɛla/ *f* mortadella, salami

mor|tal /mor'taw/ (*pl* **~tais**) *a & m* mortal; **~talha** *f* shroud; **~talidade** *f* mortality; **~tandade** *f* slaughter; **~te** /ɔ/ *f* death; **~tífero** *a* deadly; **~tificar** *vt* mortify; **~to** /o/ *a* dead

mosaico /mo'zajku/ *m* mosaic

mosca /'moska/ *f* fly

Moscou /mos'ku/, (*Port*) **Moscovo** /moʃ'kovu/ *f* Moscow

mosquito /mos'kitu/ *m* mosquito

mostarda /mos'tarda/ *f* mustard

mosteiro /mos'teru/ *m* monastery

mos|tra /'mɔstra/ *f* display; **dar ~tras de** show signs of; **pôr à ~tra** show up; **~trador** *m* face, dial; **~trar** *vt* show; **~trar-se** *vpr* (*revelar-se*) show o.s. to be; (*exibir-se*) show off; **~truário** *m* display case

mo|tel /mo'tɛw/ (*pl* **~téis**) *m* motel

motim /mo'tʃĩ/ *m* riot; (*na marinha*) mutiny

moti|vação /motʃiva'sãw/ *f* motivation; **~var** *vt* (*incentivar*) motivate; (*provocar*) cause; **~vo** *m* (*razão*) reason; (*estímulo*) motive; (*na arte, música*) motif; **dar ~vo de** give cause for

moto /'mɔtu/ *f* motorbike; **~ca** /mo'tɔka/ *f* (*fam*) motorbike

motoci|cleta /motosi'klɛta/ *f* motorcycle; **~clismo** *m* motorcycling; **~clista** *m*/*f* motorcyclist

motoqueiro /moto'keru/ *m* (*fam*) biker

motor /mo'tor/ *m* (*de carro, avião etc*) engine; (*elétrico*) motor □ *a* (*f* **motriz**) <*força*> driving; (*anat*) motor; **~ de arranque** starter motor; **~ de popa** outboard motor

moto|rista /moto'rista/ *m*/*f* driver; **~rizado** *a* motorized; **~rizar** *vt* motorize

movedi|ço /move'dʒisu/ *a* unstable, moving; **areia ~ça** quicksand

mó|vel /'mɔvew/ (*pl* **~veis**) *a* <*peça, parte*> moving; <*tropas*> mobile; <*festa*> movable □ *m* piece of furniture; *pl* furniture

mo|ver /mo'ver/ *vt* move; (*impulsionar, fig*) drive; **~ver-se** *vpr* move; **~vido** *a* driven; **~vido a álcool** alcohol-powered

movimen|tação /movimẽta'sãw/ *f* bustle; **~tado** *a* <*rua, loja*> busy; <*música*> up-beat, lively; <*pessoa, sessão*> lively; **~tar** *vt* liven up; **~tar-se** *vpr* move; **~to** *m* movement; (*tecn*) motion; (*na rua etc*) activity

muam|ba /mu'ãba/ *f* contraband; **~beiro** *m* smuggler

muco /'muku/ *m* mucus

muçulmano /musuw'manu/ *a & m* Muslim

mu|da /'muda/ *f* (*planta*) seedling; **~da de roupa** change of clothes; **~dança** *f* change; (*de casa*) move; (*de carro*) transmission; **~dar** *vt/i* change; **~dar de assunto** change the subject; **~dar (de casa)** move (house); **~dar de cor** change colour; **~dar de idéia** change one's mind; **~dar de lugar** change places; **~dar de roupa** change (clothes); **~dar-se** *vpr* move

mu|dez /mu'des/ *f* silence; **~do** *a* silent; (*deficiente*) dumb; <*telefone*> dead □ *m* mute

mu|gido /mu'ʒidu/ *m* moo; **~gir** *vi* moo

muito /'mũitu/ *a* a lot of; *pl* many □ *pron* a lot □ *adv* (*com adjetivo, advérbio*) very; (*com verbo*) a lot; **~ maior** much bigger; **~ tempo** a long time

mula /'mula/ *f* mule

mulato /mu'latu/ *a & m* mulatto

muleta /mu'leta/ *f* crutch

mulher /mu'ʎɛr/ *f* woman; (*esposa*) wife

mulherengo /muʎe'rẽgu/ *a* womanizing □ *m* womanizer, ladies' man

mul|ta /'muwta/ *f* fine; **~tar** *vt* fine

multicolor /muwtʃiko'lor/ *a* multicoloured

multidão /muwtʃi'dãw/ *f* crowd

multinacio|nal /muwtʃinasio'naw/ (*pl* **~nais**) *a & f* multinational

multipli|cação /muwtʃiplika-'sãw/ *f* multiplication; **~car** *vt* multiply; **~car-se** *vpr* multiply; **~cidade** *f* multiplicity

múltiplo /'muwtʃiplu/ *a & m* multiple

multirraci|al /muwtʃixasi'aw/ (*pl* **~ais**) *a* multiracial

múmia /'mumia/ *f* mummy

mun|dano /mũ'danu/ *a* <*prazeres etc*> worldly; <*vida, mulher*> society; **~dial** (*pl* **~diais**) *a* world □ *m* world championship; **~do** *m* world; **todo (o) ~do** everybody

munição /muni'sãw/ *f* ammunition

muni|cipal /munisi'paw/ (*pl* **~cipais**) *a* municipal; **~cípio** *m* (*lugar*) borough, community; (*prédio*) town hall; (*autoridade*) local authority

munir /mu'nir/ *vt* provide (**de** with); **~-se** *vpr* equip o.s. (**de** with)

mu|ral /mu'raw/ (*pl* **~rais**) *a & m* mural; **~ralha** *f* wall

mur|char /mur'ʃar/ *vi* <*planta*> wither, wilt; <*salada*> go limp; <*beleza*> fade □ *vt* wither, wilt <*planta*>; **~cho** *a* <*planta*> wilting; <*pessoa*> broken

mur|murar /murmu'rar/ *vi* murmur; (*queixar-se*) mutter □ *vt* murmur; **~múrio** *m* murmur

muro /'muru/ *m* wall

murro /'muxu/ *m* punch

musa /'muza/ *f* muse

muscu|lação /muskula'sãw/ *f* weight-training; **~lar** *a* muscular; **~latura** *f* musculature

músculo /'muskulu/ *m* muscle

musculoso /musku'lozu/ *a* muscular

museu /mu'zew/ *m* museum

musgo /'muzgu/ *m* moss

música /'muzika/ *f* music; (*uma*) song; **~ de câmara** chamber music; **~ de fundo** background music; **~ clássica** *ou* **erudita** classical music

musi|cal /muzi'kaw/ (*pl* **~cais**) *a & m* musical; **~car** *vt* set to music

músico /'muziku/ *m* musician □ *a* musical

musse /'musi/ *f* mousse

mutilar /mutʃi'lar/ *vt* mutilate; maim <*pessoa*>

mutirão /mutʃi'rãw/ *m* joint effort

mútuo /'mutuu/ *a* mutual

muxoxo /mu'ʃoʃu/ *m* **fazer ~** tut

Nn

na = **em** + **a**

nabo /'nabu/ *m* turnip

nação /na'sãw/ *f* nation

nacio|nal /nasio'naw/ (*pl* **~nais**) *a* national; (*brasileiro*) home-produced; **~nalidade** *f* nationality; **~nalismo** *m* nationalism; **~nalista** *a & m/f* nationalist; **~nalizar** *vt* nationalize

naco /'naku/ *m* chunk

nada /'nada/ *pron* nothing □ *adv* not at all; **de ~** (*não há de quê*) don't mention it; **que ~!, ~ disso!** no way!

na|dadeira /nada'dera/ *f* (*de peixe*) fin; (*de mergulhador*) flipper; **~dador** *m* swimmer; **~dar** *vi* swim

nádegas /'nadegas/ *f pl* buttocks

nado /'nadu/ *m* **~ borboleta** butterfly stroke; **~ de costas** backstroke; **~ de**

peito breaststroke; **atravessar a ~** swim across

náilon /'najlõ/ *m* nylon

naipe /'najpi/ *m* (*em jogo de cartas*) suit

namo|rada /namo'rada/ *f* girlfriend; **~rado** *m* boyfriend; **~-rador** *a* amorous □ *m* ladies' man; **~rar** *vt* (*ter relação com*) go out with; (*cobiçar*) eye up □ *vi* <*casal*> (*ter relação*) go out together; (*beijar-se etc*) kiss and cuddle; <*homem*> have a girlfriend; <*mulher*> have a boyfriend; **~ro** /o/ *m* relationship

nanar /na'nar/ *vi* (*col*) sleep

nanico /na'niku/ *a* tiny

não /nãw/ *adv* not; (*resposta*) no □ *m* no; **~-alinhado** *a* non-aligned; **~-conformista** *a & m/f* non-conformist

naquela, naquele, naquilo = **em** + **aquela, aquele, aquilo**

narci|sismo /narsi'zizmu/ *m* narcissism; **~sista** *m/f* narcissist □ *a* narcissistic; **~so** *m* narcissus

narcótico /nar'kɔtʃiku/ *a & m* narcotic

nari|gudo /nari'gudu/ *a* with a big nose; **ser ~gudo** have a big nose; **~na** *f* nostril

nariz /na'ris/ *m* nose

nar|ração /naxa'sãw/ *f* narration; **~rador** *m* narrator; **~rar** *vt* narrate; **~rativa** *f* narrative; **~rativo** *a* narrative

nas = **em** + **as**

na|sal /na'zaw/ (*pl* **~sais**) *a* nasal; **~salizar** *vt* nasalize

nas|cença /na'sẽsa/ *f* birth; **~cente** *a* nascent □ *f* source; **~cer** *vi* be born; <*dente, espinha*> grow; <*planta*> sprout; <*sol, lua*> rise; <*dia*> dawn; (*fig*) <*empresa, projeto etc*> come into being □ *m* **o ~cer do sol** sunrise; **~cimento** *m* birth

nata /'nata/ *f* cream

natação /nata'sãw/ *f* swimming

Natal /na'taw/ *m* Christmas

na|tal /na'taw/ (*pl* **~tais**) *a* <*país, terra*> native

nata|lício /nata'lisiu/ *a & m* birthday; **~lidade** *f* **índice de ~lidade** birth rate; **~lino** *a* Christmas

nati|vidade /natʃivi'dadʒi/ *f* nativity; **~vo** *a & m* native

nato /'natu/ *a* born

natu|ral /natu'raw/ (*pl* **~rais**) *a* natural; (*oriundo*) originating (**de** from) □ *m* native (**de** of)

natura|lidade /naturali'dadʒi/ *f* naturalness; **com ~lidade** matter-of-factly; **de ~lidade carioca** born in Rio de Janeiro; **~lismo** *m* naturalism; **~lista** *a & m/f* naturalist; **~lizar** *vt* naturalize; **~lizar-se** *vpr* become naturalized

natureza /natu'reza/ *f* nature; **~ morta** still life

naturis|mo /natu'rizmu/ *m* naturism; **~ta** *m/f* naturist

nau|fragar /nawfra'gar/ *vi* <*navio*> be wrecked; <*tripulação*> be shipwrecked; (*fig*) <*plano, casamento etc*> founder; **~frágio** *m* shipwreck; (*fig*) failure

náufrago /'nawfragu/ *m* castaway

náusea /'nawzia/ *f* nausea

nauseabundo /nawzia'bũdu/ *a* nauseating

náuti|ca /'nawtʃika/ *f* navigation; **~co** *a* nautical

na|val /na'vaw/ (*pl* **~vais**) *a* naval; **construção ~val** shipbuilding

navalha /na'vaʎa/ *f* razor; **~da** *f* cut with a razor

nave /'navi/ *f* nave; **~ espacial** spaceship

nave|gação /navega'sãw/ *f* navigation; (*tráfego*) shipping; **~gador** *m* navigator; (comput) browser; **~gante** *m/f* seafarer; **~gar** *vt* navigate; sail <*mar*> □ *vi* sail; (*traçar o rumo*) navigate; **~gável** (*pl* **~gáveis**) *a* navigable

navio /na'viu/ *m* ship; **~ cargueiro** cargo ship; **~ de guerra** warship; **~ petroleiro** oil tanker

nazista /na'zista/, (*Port*) **nazi** /na'zi/ *a & m/f* Nazi

neblina /ne'blina/ *f* mist

nebulo|sa /nebu'lɔza/ *f* nebula; **~sidade** *f* cloud; **~so** /o/ *a* cloudy; (*fig*) obscure

neces|saire /nese'sɛr/ *m* toilet bag; **~sário** *a* necessary; **~sidade** *f* necessity; (*que se impõe*) need; (*pobreza*) need; **~sitado** *a* needy □ *m* person in need; **~sitar** *vt* require; (*tornar necessário*) necessitate; **~sitar de** need

necro|lógio /nekro'lɔʒiu/ *m* obituary column; **~tério** *m* mortuary, (*Amer*) morgue

nectarina /nekta'rina/ *f* nectarine

nefasto /ne'fastu/ *a* fatal

ne|gação /nega'sãw/ *f* denial; (*ling*) negation; **ser uma ~gação em** be hopeless at; **~gar** *vt* deny; **~gar-se a** refuse to; **~gativa** *f* refusal; (*ling*) negative; **~gativo** *a & m* negative

negli|gência /negli'ʒẽsia/ *f* negligence; **~genciar** *vt* neglect; **~gente** *a* negligent

negoci|ação /negosia'sãw/ *f* negotiation; **~ador** *m* negotiator;

~**ante** *m/f* dealer (**de** in); ~**ar** *vt/i* negotiate; ~**ar em** deal in; ~**ata** *f* shady deal; ~**ável** (*pl* ~**áveis**) *a* negotiable

negócio /ne'gɔsiu/ *m* deal; (*fam: coisa*) thing; *pl* business; **a** *ou* **de** ~**s** <*viajar*> on business

negocista /nego'sista/ *m* wheeler-dealer □ *a* wheeler-dealing

ne|grito /ne'gritu/ *m* bold; ~**gro** /e/ *a* & *m* black; (*de raça*) Negro

nela, nele = **em** + **ela, ele**

nem /nẽj/ *adv* not even □ *conj* ~ ... ~ ... neither ... nor ...; ~ **sempre** not always; ~ **todos** not all; ~ **que** not even if; **que** ~ like; ~ **eu** nor do I

nenê /ne'ne/, **neném** /ne'nẽj/ *m* baby

nenhum /ne'ɲũ/ *a* (*f* **nenhuma**) no □ *pron* (*f* **nenhuma**) not one; ~ **dos dois** neither of them; ~ **erro** no mistakes; **erro** ~ no mistakes at all, not a single mistake; ~ **lugar** nowhere

nenúfar /ne'nufar/ *m* waterlily

neologismo /neolo'ʒizmu/ *m* neologism

néon /'nɛõ/ *m* neon

neozelan|dês /neozelã'des/ *a* (*f* ~**desa**) New Zealand □ *m* (*f* ~**desa**) New Zealander

Nepal /ne'paw/ *m* Nepal

nervo /'nervu/ *m* nerve; ~**sismo** *m* (*chateação*) annoyance; (*medo*) nervousness; ~**so** /o/ *a* <*sistema, doença*> nervous; (*chateado*) annoyed; (*medroso*) nervous; **deixar alg** ~**so** get on s.o.'s nerves

nessa(s), nesse(s) = **em** + **essa(s), esse(s)**

nesta(s), neste(s) = **em** + **esta(s), este(s)**

ne|ta /'nɛta/ *f* granddaughter; ~**to** /ɛ/ *m* grandson; *pl* grandchildren

neuro|logia /newrolo'ʒia/ *f* neurology; ~**lógico** *a* neurological; ~**logista** *m/f* neurologist

neu|rose /new'rɔzi/ *f* neurosis; ~**rótico** *a* neurotic

neutrali|dade /newtrali'dadʒi/ *f* neutrality; ~**zar** *vt* neutralize

neutrão /new'trãw/ *m* (*Port*) *veja* **nêutron**

neutro /'newtru/ *a* neutral

nêutron /'newtrõ/ *m* neutron

ne|vada /ne'vada/ *f* snowfall; ~**vado** *a* snow-covered; ~**var** *vi* snow; ~**vasca** *f* snowstorm; ~**ve** /ɛ/ *f* snow

névoa /'nɛvoa/ *f* haze

nevoeiro /nevo'eru/ *m* fog

nexo /'nɛksu/ *m* connection; **sem** ~ incoherent

Nicarágua /nika'ragwa/ *f* Nicaragua

nicaragüense /nikara'gwẽsi/ *a* & *m/f* Nicaraguan

nicho /'niʃu/ *m* niche

nicotina /niko'tʃina/ *f* nicotine

Níger /'niʒer/ *m* Niger

Nigéria /ni'ʒɛria/ *f* Nigeria

nigeriano /niʒeri'anu/ *a* & *m* Nigerian

Nilo /'nilu/ *m* Nile

ninar /ni'nar/ *vt* lull to sleep

ninfa /'nĩfa/ *f* nymph

ninguém /nĩ'gẽj/ *pron* no-one, nobody

ninhada /ni'ɲada/ *f* brood

ninharia /niɲa'ria/ *f* trifle

ninho /'niɲu/ *m* nest

níquel /'nikew/ *m* nickel

nisei /ni'sej/ *a* & *m/f* Japanese Brazilian

nisso = **em** + **isso**

nisto = **em** + **isto**

nitidez /nitʃi'des/ *f* (*de imagem etc*) sharpness

nítido /'nitʃidu/ *a* <*imagem, foto*> sharp; <*diferença, melhora*> distinct, clear

nitrogênio /nitro'ʒeniu/ *m* nitrogen

ní|vel /'nivew/ (*pl* ~**veis**) *m* level; **a** ~**vel de** in terms of

nivelamento /nivela'mẽtu/ *m* levelling

nivelar /nive'lar/ *vt* level

no = **em** + **o**

nó /nɔ/ *m* knot; **dar um** ~ tie a knot; ~ **dos dedos** knuckle; **um** ~ **na garganta** a lump in one's throat

nobre /'nɔbri/ *a* noble; <*bairro*> exclusive □ *m/f* noble; ~**za** /e/ *f* nobility

noção /no'sãw/ *f* notion; *pl* (*rudimentos*) elements

nocaute /no'kawtʃi/ *m* knockout; **pôr alg** ~ knock s.o. out; ~**ar** *vt* knock out

nocivo /no'sivu/ *a* harmful

nódoa /'nodoa/ *f* (*Port*) stain

nogueira /no'gera/ *f* (*árvore*) walnut tree

noi|tada /noj'tada/ *f* night; ~**te** *f* night; (*antes de dormir*) evening; **à** *ou* **de** ~**te** at night; (*antes de dormir*) in the evening; **hoje à** ~**te** tonight; **ontem à** ~**te** last night; **boa** ~**te** (*ao chegar*) good evening; (*ao despedir-se*) good night; ~**te em branco** *ou* **claro** sleepless night

noi|vado /noj'vadu/ *m* engagement; ~**va** *f* fiancée; (*no casamento*) bride; ~**vo** *m* fiancé; (*no casamento*) bridegroom; **os** ~**-vos** the engaged couple; (*no casamento*) the bride and groom; **ficar** ~**vo** get engaged

no|jento /no'ʒẽtu/ *a* disgusting; ~**jo** /o/ *m* disgust

nômade /'nomadʒi/ *m/f* nomad □ *a* nomadic

nome /'nomi/ *m* name; **de** ~ by name; **em** ~ **de** in the name of; ~ **comercial**

trade name; ~ **de batismo** Christian name; ~ **de guerra** professional name

nome|ação /nomia'sãw/ *f* appointment; **~ar** *vt* (*para cargo*) appoint; (*chamar pelo nome*) name

nomi|nal /nomi'naw/ (*pl* **~nais**) *a* nominal

nonagésimo /nona'ʒɛzimu/ *a* ninetieth

nono /'nonu/ *a & m* ninth

nora /'nɔra/ *f* daughter-in-law

nordes|te /nor'dɛstʃi/ *m* northeast; **~tino** *a* Northeastern □ *m* person from the Northeast (*of Brazil*)

nórdico /'nɔrdʒiku/ *a* Nordic

nor|ma /'nɔrma/ *f* norm; **~mal** (*pl* **~mais**) *a* normal

normali|dade /normali'dadʒi/ *f* normality; **~zar** *vt* bring back to normal; normalize <*relações diplomáticas*>; **~zar-se** *vpr* return to normal

noroeste /noro'ɛstʃi/ *a & m* northwest

norte /'nɔrtʃi/ *a & m* north; **~-africano** *a & m* North African; **~-americano** *a & m* North American; **~-coreano** *a & m* North Korean

nortista /nor'tʃista/ *a* Northern □ *m/f* Northerner

Noruega /noru'ɛga/ *f* Norway

norue|guês /norue'ges/ *a & m* (*f* **~guesa**) Norwegian

nos[1] = **em + os**

nos[2] /nus/ *pron* us; (*indireto*) (to) us; (*reflexivo*) ourselves

nós /nɔs/ *pron* we; (*depois de preposição*) us

nos|sa /'nɔsa/ *int* gosh; **~so** /ɔ/ *a* our □ *pron* ours

nos|talgia /nostaw'ʒia/ *f* nostalgia; **~tálgico** *a* nostalgic

nota /'nɔta/ *f* note; (*na escola etc*) mark; (*conta*) bill; **custar uma ~ (preta)** (*fam*) cost a bomb; **tomar ~** take note (**de** of); ~ **fiscal** receipt

no|tação /nota'sãw/ *f* notation; **~tar** *vt* notice, note; **fazer ~tar** point out; **~tável** (*pl* **~táveis**) *a & m/f* notable

notícia /no'tʃisia/ *f* piece of news; *pl* news

notici|ar /notʃi'sjar/ *vt* report; **~ário** *m* (*na TV*) news; (*em jornal*) news section; **~arista** *m/f* (*na TV*) newsreader; (*em jornal*) news reporter; **~oso** /o/ *a* **agência ~osa** news agency

notifi|cação /notʃifika'sãw/ *f* notification; **~car** *vt* notify

notívago /no'tʃivagu/ *a* nocturnal □ *m* night person

notório /no'tɔriu/ *a* well-known

noturno /no'turnu/ *a* night; <*animal*> nocturnal

nova /'nɔva/ *f* piece of news; **~mente** *adv* again

novato /no'vatu/ *m* novice

nove /'nɔvi/ *a & m* nine; **~centos** *a & m* nine hundred

novela /no'vɛla/ *f* (*na TV*) soap opera; (*livro*) novella

novembro /no'vẽbru/ *m* November

noventa /no'vẽta/ *a & m* ninety

noviço /no'visu/ *m* novice

novidade /novi'dadʒi/ *f* novelty; (*notícia*) piece of news; *pl* (*notícias*) news

novilho /no'viʎu/ *m* calf

novo /'novu/ *a* new; (*jovem*) young; **de ~** again; ~ **em folha** brand new

noz /nɔs/ *f* walnut; ~ **moscada** nutmeg

nu /nu/ *a* (*f* **~a**) <*corpo, pessoa*> naked; <*braço, parede, quarto*> bare □ *m* nude; ~ **em pêlo** stark naked; **a verdade ~a e crua** the plain truth

nuança /nu'ãsa/ *f* nuance

nu|blado /nu'bladu/ *a* cloudy; **~blar** *vt* cloud; **~blar-se** *vpr* cloud over

nuca /'nuka/ *f* nape of the neck

nuclear /nukli'ar/ *a* nuclear

núcleo /'nukliu/ *m* nucleus

nu|dez /nu'des/ *f* nakedness; (*na TV etc*) nudity; (*da parede etc*) bareness; **~dismo** *m* nudism; **~dista** *m/f* nudist

nulo /'nulu/ *a* void

num, numa(s) = em + um, uma(s)

nume|ral /nume'raw/ (*pl* **~rais**) *a & m* numeral; **~rar** *vt* number

numérico /nu'mɛriku/ *a* numerical

número /'numeru/ *m* number; (*de jornal, revista*) issue; (*de sapatos*) size; (*espetáculo*) act; **fazer ~** make up the numbers

numeroso /nume'rozu/ *a* numerous

nunca /'nũka/ *adv* never; ~ **mais** never again

nuns = em + uns

nupci|al /nupsi'aw/ (*pl* **~ais**) *a* bridal

núpcias /'nupsias/ *f pl* marriage

nu|trição /nutri'sãw/ *f* nutrition; **~trir** *vt* nourish; (*fig*) harbour <*ódio, esperança*>; **~tritivo** *a* nourishing; <*valor*> nutritional

nuvem /'nuvẽ/ *f* cloud

Oo

o /u/ *artigo* the □ *pron* (*homem*) him; (*coisa*) it; (*você*) you; ~ **que** (*a coisa que*) what; (*aquele que*) the one that; ~ **quê?** what?; **meu livro e ~ do João** my book and John's (one)

ó /ɔ/ *int* (*fam*) look

ô /o/ *int* oh

oásis /o'azis/ *m invar* oasis

oba /'oba/ *int* great

obcecar /obise'kar/ *vt* obsess

obe|decer /obede'ser/ *vt* **~decer a** obey; **~diência** *f* obedience; **~diente** *a* obedient

obe|sidade /obezi'dadʒi/ *f* obesity; **~so** /e/ *a* obese

óbito /'ɔbitu/ *m* death

obituário /obitu'ariu/ *m* obituary

obje|ção /obiʒe'sãw/ *f* objection; **~tar** *vt/i* object (**a** to)

objeti|va /obiʒe'tʃiva/ *f* lens; **~vidade** *f* objectivity; **~vo** *a & m* objective

objeto /obi'ʒɛtu/ *m* object

oblíquo /o'blikwu/ *a* oblique; <*olhar*> sidelong

obliterar /oblite'rar/ *vt* obliterate

oblongo /o'blõgu/ *a* oblong

obo|é /obo'ɛ/ *m* oboe; **~ísta** *m/f* oboist

obra /'ɔbra/ *f* work; **em ~s** being renovated; **~ de arte** work of art; **~ de caridade** charity; **~-prima** (*pl* **~s-primas**) *f* masterpiece

obri|gação /obriga'sãw/ *f* obligation; (*título*) bond; **~gado** *int* thank you; (*não querendo*) no thank you; **~gar** *vt* force, oblige (**a** to); **~gar-se** *vpr* undertake (**a** to); **~gatório** *a* obligatory, compulsory

obsce|nidade /obiseni'dadʒi/ *f* obscenity; **~no** /e/ *a* obscene

obscu|ridade /obiskuri'dadʒi/ *f* obscurity; **~ro** *a* obscure

obséquio /obi'sɛkiu/ *m* favour

obsequioso /obiseki'ozu/ *a* obsequious

obser|vação /obiserva'sãw/ *f* observation; **~vador** *a* observant □ *m* observer; **~vância** *f* observance; **~var** *vt* observe; **~vatório** *m* observatory

obses|são /obise'sãw/ *f* obsession; **~sivo** *a* obsessive

obsoleto /obiso'letu/ *a* obsolete

obstáculo /obis'takulu/ *m* obstacle

obstar /obis'tar/ *vt* stand in the way (**a** of)

obs|tetra /obis'tɛtra/ *m/f* obstetrician; **~tetrícia** *f* obstetrics; **~tétrico** *a* obstetric

obsti|nação /obistina'sãw/ *f* obstinacy; **~nado** *a* obstinate; **~nar-se** *vpr* insist (**em** on)

obstru|ção /obistru'sãw/ *f* obstruction; **~ir** *vt* obstruct

ob|tenção /obitẽ'sãw/ *f* obtaining; **~ter** *vt* obtain

obtu|ração /obitura'sãw/ *f* filling; **~rador** *m* shutter; **~rar** *vt* fill <*dente*>

obtuso /obi'tuzu/ *a* obtuse

óbvio /'ɔbviu/ *a* obvious

ocasi|ão /okazi'ãw/ *f* occasion; (*oportunidade*) opportunity; (*compra*) bargain; **~onal** (*pl* **~onais**) *a* chance; **~onar** *vt* cause

Oceania /osia'nia/ *f* Oceania

oce|ânico /osi'aniku/ *a* ocean; **~ano** *m* ocean

ociden|tal /osidẽ'taw/ (*pl* **~tais**) *a* western □ *m/f* Westerner; **~te** *m* West

ócio /'ɔsiu/ *m* (*lazer*) leisure; (*falta de trabalho*) idleness

ocioso /osi'ozu/ *a* idle □ *m* idler

oco /'oku/ *a* hollow; <*cabeça*> empty

ocor|rência /oko'xẽsia/ *f* occurrence; **~rer** *vi* occur (**a** to)

ocu|lar /oku'lar/ *a* **testemunha ~lar** eye witness; **~lista** *m/f* optician

óculos /'ɔkulus/ *m pl* glasses; **~ de sol** sunglasses

ocul|tar /okuw'tar/ *vt* conceal; **~to** *a* hidden; (*sobrenatural*) occult

ocu|pação /okupa'sãw/ *f* occupation; **~pado** *a* <*pessoa*> busy; <*cadeira*> taken; <*telefone*> engaged, (*Amer*) busy; **~par** *vt* occupy; take up <*tempo, espaço*>; hold <*cargo*>; **~par-se** *vpr* keep busy; **~par-se com** *ou* **de** be involved with <*política, literatura etc*>; take care of <*cliente, doente, problema*>; occupy one's time with <*leitura, palavras cruzadas etc*>

odiar /odʒi'ar/ *vt* hate

ódio /'ɔdʒiu/ *m* hatred, hate; (*raiva*) anger

odioso /odʒi'ozu/ *a* hateful

odontologia /odõtolo'ʒia/ *f* dentistry

odor /o'dor/ *m* odour

oeste /o'ɛstʃi/ *a & m* west

ofe|gante /ofe'gãtʃi/ *a* panting; **~gar** *vi* pant

ofen|der /ofẽ'der/ *vt* offend; **~der-se** *vpr* take offence; **~sa** *f* insult; **~siva** *f* offensive; **~sivo** *a* offensive

ofere|cer /ofere'ser/ *vt* offer; **~cer-se** *vpr* <*pessoa*> offer o.s. (**como** as); <*ocasião*> arise; **~cer-se para ajudar** offer to help; **~cimento** *m* offer

oferenda /ofe'rẽda/ *f* offering

oferta /o'fɛrta/ *f* offer; **em ~** on offer; **a ~ e a demanda** supply and demand

ofici|al /ofisi'aw/ (*pl* **~ais**) *a* official □ *m* officer; **~alizar** *vt* make official; **~ar** *vi* officiate

oficina /ofi'sina/ *f* workshop; (*para carros*) garage, (*Amer*) shop

ofício /o'fisiu/ *m* (*profissão*) trade; (*na igreja*) service

oficioso /ofisi'ozu/ *a* unofficial

ofus|cante /ofus'kãtʃi/ *a* dazzling; **~car** *vt* dazzle <*pessoa*>; obscure <*sol etc*>; (*fig: eclipsar*) outshine

OGM /oʒe'ɛm/ *m* (*biol*) GMO

oi /oj/ *int* (*cumprimento*) hi; (*resposta*) yes?

oi|tavo /oi'tavu/ *a* & *m* eighth; **~tenta** *a* & *m* eighty; **~to** *a* & *m* eight; **~tocentos** *a* & *m* eight hundred

olá /o'la/ *int* hello

olaria /ola'ria/ *f* pottery

óleo /'ɔliu/ *m* oil

oleo|duto /oliu'dutu/ *m* oil pipeline; **~so** /o/ *a* oily

olfato /ow'fatu/ *m* sense of smell

olhada /o'ʎada/ *f* look; **dar uma ~** have a look

olhar /o'ʎar/ *vt* look at; (*assistir*) watch ▫ *vi* look ▫ *m* look; **~ para** look at; **~ por** look after; **e olhe lá** (*fam*) and that's pushing it

olheiras /o'ʎeras/ *f pl* dark rings under one's eyes

olho /'oʎu/ *m* eye; **a ~ nu** with the naked eye; **custar os ~s da cara** cost a fortune; **ficar de ~** keep an eye out; **ficar de ~ em** keep an eye on; **pôr alg no ~ da rua** throw s.o. out; **não pregar o ~** not sleep a wink; **~ gordo** *ou* **grande** envy; **~ mágico** peephole; **~ roxo** black eye

Olimpíada /olĩ'piada/ *f* Olympic Games

olímpico /o'lĩpiku/ *a* <*jogos, vila*> Olympic; (*fig*) blithe

oliveira /oli'vera/ *f* olive tree

olmo /'owmu/ *m* elm

om|breira /õ'brera/ *f* (*para roupa*) shoulder pad; **~bro** *m* shoulder; **dar de ~bros** shrug one's shoulders

omelete /ome'lɛtʃi/, (*Port*) **omeleta** /ome'leta/ *f* omelette

omis|são /omi'sãw/ *f* omission; **~so** *a* negligent, remiss

omitir /omi'tʃir/ *vt* omit

omni- (*Port*) *veja* **oni-**

omoplata /omo'plata/ *f* shoulder blade

onça[1] /'õsa/ *f* (*peso*) ounce

onça[2] /'õsa/ *f* (*animal*) jaguar

onda /'õda/ *f* wave; **pegar ~** (*fam*) surf

onde /'õdʒi/ *adv* where; **por ~?** which way?; **~ quer que** wherever

ondu|lação /õdula'sãw/ *f* undulation; (*do cabelo*) wave; **~lado** *a* wavy; **~lante** *a* undulating; **~lar** *vt* wave <*cabelo*> ▫ *vi* undulate

onerar /one'rar/ *vt* burden

ônibus /'onibus/ *m invar* bus; **~ espacial** space shuttle

onipotente /onipo'tẽtʃi/ *a* omnipotent

onírico /o'niriku/ *a* dreamlike

onisciente /onisi'ẽtʃi/ *a* omniscient

onomatopéia /onomato'pɛja/ *f* onomatopoeia

ontem /'õtẽ/ *adv* yesterday

onze /'õzi/ *a* & *m* eleven

opaco /o'paku/ *a* opaque

opala /o'pala/ *f* opal

opção /opi'sãw/ *f* option

ópera /'ɔpera/ *f* opera

ope|ração /opera'sãw/ *f* operation; (*bancária etc*) transaction; **~rador** *m* operator; **~rar** *vt* operate; operate on <*doente*>; work <*milagre*> ▫ *vi* operate; **~rar-se** *vpr* (*acontecer*) come about; (*fazer operação*) have an operation; **~rário** *a* working ▫ *m* worker

opereta /ope'reta/ *f* operetta

opinar /opi'nar/ *vt* think ▫ *vi* express one's opinion

opinião /opini'ãw/ *f* opinion; **na minha ~** in my opinion; **~ pública** public opinion

ópio /'ɔpiu/ *m* opium

opor /o'por/ *vt* put up <*resistência, argumento*>; (*pôr em contraste*) contrast (**a** with); **~-se a** (*não aprovar*) oppose; (*ser diferente*) contrast with

oportu|nidade /oportuni'dadʒi/ *f* opportunity; **~nista** *a* & *m*/*f* opportunist; **~no** *a* opportune

oposi|ção /opozi'sãw/ *f* opposition (**a** to); **~cionista** *a* opposition ▫ *m*/*f* opposition politician

oposto /o'postu/ *a* & *m* opposite

opres|são /opre'sãw/ *f* oppression; (*no peito*) tightness; **~sivo** *a* oppressive; **~sor** *m* oppressor

oprimir /opri'mir/ *vt* oppress; (*com trabalho*) weigh down ▫ *vi* be oppressive

optar /opi'tar/ *vi* opt (**por** for); **~ por ir** opt to go

óptica, óptico *veja* **ótica, ótico**

opu|lência /opu'lẽsia/ *f* opulence; **~lento** *a* opulent

ora /'ɔra/ *adv* & *conj* now ▫ *int* come; **~ essa!** come now!; **~ ..., ~ ...** first ..., then

oração /ora'sãw/ *f* (*prece*) prayer; (*discurso*) oration; (*frase*) clause

oráculo /o'rakulu/ *m* oracle

orador /ora'dor/ *m* orator

oral /o'raw/ (*pl* **orais**) *a* & *f* oral

orar /o'rar/ *vi* pray

órbita /'ɔrbita/ *f* orbit; (*do olho*) socket

orçamen|tário /orsamẽ'tariu/ *a* budgetary; **~to** *m* (*plano financeiro*) budget; (*previsão dos custos*) estimate

orçar /or'sar/ *vt* estimate (**em** at)

ordeiro /or'deru/ *a* orderly

ordem /'ɔrdẽ/ *f* order; **por ~ alfabética** in alphabetical order; **~ de pagamento** banker's draft; **~ do dia** agenda

orde|nação /ordena'sãw/ *f* ordering; (*de padre*) ordination; **~nado** *a* ordered □ *m* wages; **~nar** *vt* order; put in order <*papéis, livros etc*>; ordain <*padre*>

ordenhar /orde'ɲar/ *vt* milk

ordinário /ordʒi'nariu/ *a* (*normal*) ordinary; (*grosseiro*) vulgar; (*de má qualidade*) inferior; (*sem caráter*) rough

ore|lha /o'reʎa/ *f* ear; **~lhão** *m* phone booth; **~lhudo** *a* with big ears; **ser ~lhudo** have big ears

orfanato /orfa'natu/ *m* orphanage

ór|fão /'ɔrfãw/ (*pl* **~fãos**) *a* & *m* (*f* **~fã**) orphan

orgânico /or'ganiku/ *a* organic

orga|nismo /orga'nizmu/ *m* organism; (*do Estado etc*) institution; **~ geneticamente modificado** GMO; **~nista** *m/f* organist

organi|zação /organiza'sãw/ *f* organization; **~zador** *a* organizing □ *m* organizer; **~zar** *vt* organize

órgão /'ɔrgãw/ (*pl* **~s**) *m* organ; (*do Estado etc*) body

orgasmo /or'gazmu/ *m* orgasm

orgia /or'ʒia/ *f* orgy

orgu|lhar /orgu'ʎar/ *vt* make proud; **~lhar-se** *vpr* be proud (**de** of); **~lho** *m* pride; **~lhoso** /o/ *a* proud

orien|tação /oriẽta'sãw/ *f* orientation; (*direção*) direction; (*vocacional etc*) guidance; **~tador** *m* advisor; **~tal** (*pl* **~tais**) *a* eastern; (*da Ásia*) oriental; **~tar** *vt* direct; (*aconselhar*) advise; (*situar*) position; **~tar-se** *vpr* get one's bearings; **~tar-se por** be guided by; **~te** *m* east; **Oriente Médio** Middle East; **Extremo Oriente** Far East

orifício /ori'fisiu/ *m* opening; (*no corpo*) orifice

origem /o'riʒẽ/ *f* origin; **dar ~ a** give rise to; **ter ~** originate

origi|nal /oriʒi'naw/ (*pl* **~nais**) *a* & *m* original; **~nalidade** *f* originality; **~nar** *vt* give rise to; **~nar-se** *vpr* originate; **~nário** *a* <*planta, animal*> native (**de** to); <*pessoa*> originating (**de** from)

oriundo /o'rjũdu/ *a* originating (**de** from)

orla /'ɔrla/ *f* border; **~ marítima** seafront

ornamen|tação /ornamẽta'sãw/ *f* ornamentation; **~tal** (*pl* **~tais**) *a* ornamental; **~tar** *vt* decorate; **~to** *m* ornament

orques|tra /or'kɛstra/ *f* orchestra; **~tra sinfônica** symphony orchestra; **~tral** (*pl* **~trais**) *a* orchestral; **~trar** *vt* orchestrate

orquídea /or'kidʒia/ *f* orchid

ortodoxo /orto'dɔksu/ *a* orthodox

orto|grafia /ortogra'fia/ *f* spelling, orthography; **~gráfico** *a* orthographic

orto|pedia /ortope'dʒia/ *f* orthopaedics; **~pédico** *a* orthopaedic; **~pedista** *m/f* orthopaedic surgeon

orvalho /or'vaʎu/ *m* dew

os /us/ *artigo & pron veja* **o**

oscilar /osi'lar/ *vi* oscillate

ósseo /'ɔsiu/ *a* bone

os|so /'osu/ *m* bone; **~sudo** *a* bony

ostensivo /ostẽ'sivu/ *a* ostensible

osten|tação /ostẽta'sãw/ *f* ostentation; **~tar** *vt* show off; **~toso** *a* showy, ostentatious

osteopata /ostʃio'pata/ *m/f* osteopath

ostra /'ostra/ *f* oyster

ostracismo /ostra'sizmu/ *m* ostracism

otário /o'tariu/ *m* (*fam*) fool

óti|ca /'ɔtʃika/ *f* (*ciência*) optics; (*loja*) optician's; (*ponto de vista*) viewpoint; **~co** *a* optical

otimis|mo /otʃi'mizmu/ *m* optimism; **~ta** *m/f* optimist □ *a* optimistic

ótimo /'ɔtʃimu/ *a* excellent

otorrino /oto'xinu/ *m* ear, nose and throat specialist

ou /o/ *conj* or; **~ ... ~ ...** either ... or ...; **~ seja** in other words

ouriço /o'risu/ *m* hedgehog; **~-do-mar** (*pl* **~s-do-mar**) *m* sea urchin

ouri|ves /o'rivis/ *m/f invar* jeweller; **~vesaria** *f* (*loja*) jeweller's

ouro /'oru/ *m* gold; *pl* (*naipe*) diamonds; **de ~** golden

ou|sadia /oza'dʒia/ *f* daring; (*uma*) daring step; **~sado** *a* daring; **~sar** *vt/i* dare

outdoor /'awtdor/ (*pl* **~s**) *m* billboard

outo|nal /oto'naw/ (*pl* **~nais**) *a* autumnal; **~no** /o/ *m* autumn, (*Amer*) fall

outorgar /otor'gar/ *vt* grant

ou|trem /o'trẽj/ *pron* (*outro*) someone else; (*outros*) others; **~tro** *a* other □ *pron* (*um*) another (one); *pl* others; **~tro copo** another glass; **~tra coisa** something else; **~tro dia** the other day; **no ~tro dia** the next day; **~tra vez** again; **~trora** *adv* once upon a time; **~trossim** *adv* equally

outubro /o'tubru/ *m* October

ou|vido /o'vidu/ *m* ear; **de ~vido** by ear; **dar ~vidos a** listen to; **~vinte** *m/f* listener; **~vir** *vt* hear; (*atentamente*) listen to □ *vi* hear; **~vir dizer que** hear that; **~vir falar de** hear of

ovação /ova'sãw/ *f* ovation

oval /o'vaw/ (*pl* **ovais**) *a* & *f* oval

ovário /o'variu/ *m* ovary

ovelha /o'veʎa/ *f* sheep

óvni /'ɔvni/ *m* UFO

ovo /'ovu/ *m* egg; **~ cozido /frito/mexido/pochê** boiled/fried /scrambled/poached egg

oxi|genar /oksiʒe'nar/ *vt* bleach <*cabelo*>; **~gênio** *m* oxygen

ozônio /o'zoniu/ *m* ozone

Pp

pá /pa/ *f* spade; (*de hélice*) blade; (*de moinho*) sail ▫ *m* (*Port: fam*) mate

pacato /pa'katu/ *a* quiet

paci|ência /pasi'ẽsia/ *f* patience; **~ente** *a & m/f* patient

pacificar /pasifi'kar/ *vt* pacify

pacífico /pa'sifiku/ *a* peaceful; **Oceano Pacífico** Pacific Ocean; **ponto ~** undisputed point

pacifis|mo /pasi'fizmu/ *m* pacifism; **~ta** *a & m/f* pacifist

paço /'pasu/ *m* palace

pacote /pa'kɔtʃi/ *m* (*de biscoitos etc*) packet; (*mandado pelo correio*) parcel; (*econômico, turístico, software*) package

pacto /'paktu/ *m* pact

padaria /pada'ria/ *f* baker's (shop), bakery

padecer /pade'ser/ *vt/i* suffer

padeiro /pa'deru/ *m* baker

padiola /padʒi'ɔla/ *f* stretcher

padrão /pa'drãw/ *m* standard; (*desenho*) pattern

padrasto /pa'drastu/ *m* stepfather

padre /'padri/ *m* priest

padrinho /pa'driɲu/ *m* (*de batismo*) godfather; (*de casamento*) best man

padroeiro /padro'eru/ *m* patron saint

padronizar /padroni'zar/ *vt* standardize

paga /'paga/ *f* pay; **~mento** *m* payment

pa|gão /pa'gãw/ (*pl* **~gãos**) *a & m* (*f* **~gã**) pagan

pagar /pa'gar/ *vt* pay for <*compra, erro etc*>; pay <*dívida, conta, empregado etc*>; pay back <*empréstimo*>; repay <*gentileza etc*> ▫ *vi* pay; **eu pago para ver** I'll believe it when I see it

página /'paʒina/ *f* page; **~ web** web page

pago /'pagu/ *a* paid ▫ *pp de* **pagar**

pagode /pa'gɔdʒi/ *m* (*torre*) pagoda; (*fam*) singalong

pai /paj/ *m* father; *pl* (*pai e mãe*) parents; **~-de-santo** (*pl* **~s-de-santo**) *m* macumba priest

pai|nel /paj'nɛw/ (*pl* **~néis**) *m* panel; (*de carro*) dashboard

paio /'paju/ *m* pork sausage

pairar /paj'rar/ *vi* hover

país /pa'is/ *m* country; **País de Gales** Wales; **Países Baixos** Netherlands

paisa|gem /paj'zaʒẽ/ *f* landscape; **~gista** *m/f* landscape gardener

paisana /paj'zana/ *f* **à ~** <*policial*> in plain clothes; <*soldado*> in civilian clothes

paixão /pa'ʃãw/ *f* passion

pala /'pala/ *f* (*de boné*) peak; (*de automóvel*) sun visor

palácio /pa'lasiu/ *m* palace

paladar /pala'dar/ *m* palate, taste

palanque /pa'lãki/ *m* stand

palavra /pa'lavra/ *f* word; **pedir a ~** ask to speak; **ter ~** be reliable; **tomar a ~** start to speak; **sem ~** <*pessoa*> unreliable; **~ de ordem** watchword; **~s cruzadas** crossword

palavrão /pala'vrãw/ *m* swearword

palco /'pawku/ *m* stage

palestino /pales'tʃinu/ *a & m* Palestinian

palestra /pa'lɛstra/ *f* lecture

paleta /pa'leta/ *f* palette

paletó /pale'tɔ/ *m* jacket

palha /'paʎa/ *f* straw

palha|çada /paʎa'sada/ *f* joke; **~ço** *m* clown

paliativo /palia'tʃivu/ *a & m* palliative

palidez /pali'des/ *f* paleness

pálido /'palidu/ *a* pale

pali|tar /pali'tar/ *vt* pick ▫ *vi* pick one's teeth; **~teiro** *m* toothpick holder; **~to** *m* (*para dentes*) toothpick; (*de fósforo*) matchstick; (*pessoa magra*) beanpole

pal|ma /'pawma/ *f* palm; *pl* (*aplauso*) clapping; **bater ~mas** clap; **~meira** *f* palm tree; **~mito** *m* palm heart; **~mo** *m* span; **~mo a ~mo** inch by inch

palpá|vel /paw'pavew/ (*pl* **~veis**) *a* palpable

pálpebra /'pawpebra/ *f* eyelid

palpi|tação /pawpita'sãw/ *f* palpitation; **~tante** *a* (*fig*) thrilling; **~tar** *vi* <*coração*> flutter; <*pessoa*> tremble; (*dar palpite*) stick one's oar in; **~te** *m* (*pressentimento*) hunch; (*no jogo etc*) tip; **dar ~te** stick one's oar in

panacéia /pana'sɛja/ *f* panacea

Panamá /pana'ma/ *m* Panama

panamenho /pana'meɲu/ *a & m* Panamanian

pan-americano /panameri'kanu/ *a* Pan-American

pança /'pãsa/ *f* paunch

pancada /pã'kada/ *f* blow; **~ d'água** downpour; **~ria** *f* fight, punch-up

pâncreas /'pãkrias/ *m invar* pancreas

pançudo /pã'sudu/ *a* paunchy

panda /'pãda/ *f* panda

pandarecos /pãda'rɛkus/ *m pl* **aos** *ou* **em ~** battered

pandeiro /pã'deru/ *m* tambourine

pandemônio /pãde'moniu/ *m* pandemonium

pane /'pani/ *f* breakdown

panela /pa'nɛla/ *f* saucepan; **~ de pressão** pressure cooker

panfleto /pã'fletu/ *m* pamphlet

pânico /'paniku/ *m* panic; **em ~** in a panic; **entrar em ~** panic

panifica|ção /panifika'sãw/ *f* bakery; **~dora** *f* bakery

pano /'panu/ *m* cloth; **~ de fundo** backdrop; **~ de pó** duster; **~ de pratos** tea towel

pano|rama /pano'rama/ *m* panorama; **~râmico** *a* panoramic

panqueca /pã'kɛka/ *f* pancake

panta|nal /pãta'naw/ (*pl* **~nais**) *m* marshland

pântano /'pãtanu/ *m* marsh

pantanoso /pãta'nozu/ *a* marshy

pantera /pã'tɛra/ *f* panther

pão /pãw/ (*pl* **pães**) *m* bread; **~ de fôrma** sliced loaf; **~ integral** brown bread; **~-de-ló** *m* sponge cake; **~-duro** (*pl* **pães-duros**) (*fam*) *a* stingy, tight-fisted □ *m/f* skinflint; **~zinho** *m* bread roll

Papa /'papa/ *m* Pope

papa /'papa/ *f* (*de nenem*) food; (*arroz etc*) mush

papagaio /papa'gaju/ *m* parrot

papai /pa'paj/ *m* dad, daddy; **Papai No·l** Father Christmas

papar /pa'par/ *vt/i* (*fam*) eat

papari|car /papari'kar/ *vt* pamper; **~cos** *m pl* pampering

pa|pel /pa'pɛw/ (*pl* **~péis**) *m* (*de escrever etc*) paper; (*um*) piece of paper; (*numa peça, filme*) part; (*fig: função*) role; **de ~pel passado** officially; **~pel de alumínio** aluminium foil; **~pel higiênico** toilet paper; **~pelada** *f* paperwork; **~pelão** *m* cardboard; **~pelaria** *f* stationer's (shop); **~pelzinho** *m* scrap of paper

papo /'papu/ *f* (*fam: conversa*) talk; (*do rosto*) double chin; **bater um ~** (*fam*) have a chat; **~ furado** idle talk

papoula /pa'pola/ *f* poppy

páprica /'paprika/ *f* paprika

paque|ra /pa'kɛra/ *f* (*fam*) pick-up; **~rador** *a* flirtatious □ *m* flirt; **~rar** *vt* flirt with <*pessoa*>; eye up <*vestido, carro etc*> □ *vi* flirt

paquista|nês /pakista'nes/ *a & m* (*f* **~nesa**) Pakistani

Paquistão /pakis'tãw/ *m* Pakistan

par /par/ *a* even □ *m* pair; (*parceiro*) partner; **a ~ de** up to date with <*notícias etc*>; **sem ~** unequalled

para /'para/ *prep* for; (*a*) to; **~ que** so that; **~ quê?** what for?; **~ casa** home; **estar ~ sair** be about to leave; **era ~ eu ir** I was supposed to go

para|benizar /parabeni'zar/ *vt* congratulate (**por** on); **~béns** *m pl* congratulations

parábola /pa'rabola/ *f* (*conto*) parable; (*curva*) parabola

parabóli|co /para'bɔliku/ *a* **antena ~ca** satellite dish

pára|-brisa /para'briza/ *m* windscreen, (*Amer*) windshield; **~-choque** *m* bumper

para|da /pa'rada/ *f* stop; (*interrupção*) stoppage; (*militar*) parade; (*fam: coisa difícil*) ordeal, challenge; **~da cardíaca** cardiac arrest; **~deiro** *m* whereabouts

paradisíaco /paradʒi'ziaku/ *a* idyllic

parado /pa'radu/ *a* <*trânsito, carro*> at a standstill, stopped; (*fig*) <*pessoa*> dull; **ficar ~** <*pessoa*> stand still; <*trânsito*> stop; (*deixar de trabalhar*) stop work

parado|xal /paradok'saw/ (*pl* **~xais**) *a* paradoxical; **~xo** /ɔ/ *m* paradox

parafina /para'fina/ *f* paraffin

paráfrase /pa'rafrazi/ *f* paraphrase

parafrasear /parafrazi'ar/ *vt* paraphrase

parafuso /para'fuzu/ *f* screw; **entrar em ~** get into a state

para|gem /pa'raʒẽ/ *f* (*Port: parada*) stop; **nestas ~gens** in these parts

parágrafo /pa'ragrafu/ *m* paragraph

Paraguai /para'gwaj/ *m* Paraguay

paraguaio /para'gwaju/ *a & m* Paraguayan

paraíso /para'izu/ *m* paradise

pára-lama /para'lama/ *m* (*de carro*) wing, (*Amer*) fender; (*de bicicleta*) mudguard

parale|la /para'lɛla/ *f* parallel; *pl* (*aparelho*) parallel bars; **~lepípedo** *m* paving stone; **~lo** /ɛ/ *a & m* parallel

para|lisar /parali'zar/ *vt* paralyse; bring to a halt <*fábrica, produção*>; **~lisar-se** *vpr* become paralysed; <*fábrica, produção*> grind to a halt; **~lisia** *f* paralysis; **~lítico** *a & m* paralytic **~médico** *m* paramedic

paranói|a /para'nɔja/ *f* paranoia; **~co** *a* paranoid

parapeito /para'pejtu/ *m* (*muro*) parapet; (*da janela*) window-sill

pára-que|das /para'kɛdas/ *m invar* parachute; **~dista** *m/f* parachutist; (*militar*) paratrooper

parar /pa'rar/ *vt/i* stop; **~ de fumar** stop smoking; **ir ~** end up

pára-raios /para'xajus/ *m invar* lightning conductor

parasita /para'zita/ *a & m/f* parasite

parceiro /par'seru/ *m* partner

parce|la /par'sɛla/ *f* (*de terreno*) plot; (*prestação*) instalment; **~lar** *vt* spread <*pagamento*>

parceria /parse'ria/ *f* partnership

parci|al /parsi'aw/ (*pl* **~ais**) *a* partial; (*partidário*) biased; **~alidade** *f* bias

parco /'parku/ *a* frugal; <*recursos*> scant

par|dal /par'daw/ (*pl* **~dais**) *m* sparrow; **~do** *a* <*papel*> brown; <*pessoa*> mulatto

pare|cer /pare'ser/ *vi* (*ter aparência de*) seem; (*ter semelhança com*) be like; **~cer-se com** look like, resemble □ *m* opinion; **~cido** *a* similar (**com** to)

parede /pa'redʒi/ *f* wall

paren|te /pa'rẽtʃi/ *m/f* relative, relation; **~tesco** /e/ *m* relationship

parêntese /pa'rẽtʃizi/ *f* parenthesis; *pl* (*sinais*) brackets

paridade /pari'dadʒi/ *f* parity

parir /pa'rir/ *vt* give birth to □ *vi* give birth

parlamen|tar /parlamẽ'tar/ *a* parliamentary □ *m/f* member of parliament; **~tarismo** *m* parliamentary system; **~to** *m* parliament

parmesão /parme'zãw/ *a & m* **(queijo) ~** Parmesan (cheese)

paródia /pa'rɔdʒia/ *f* parody

parodiar /parodʒi'ar/ *vt* parody

paróquia /pa'rɔkia/ *f* parish

parque /'parki/ *m* park; **~** temático theme park

parte /'partʃi/ *f* part; (*quinhão*) share; (*num litígio, contrato*) party; **a maior ~ de** most of; **à ~** (*de lado*) aside; (*separadamente*) separately; **um erro da sua ~** a mistake on your part; **em ~** in part; **em alguma ~** somewhere; **por toda ~** everywhere; **por ~ do pai** on one's father's side; **fazer ~ de** be part of; **tomar ~ em** take part in

parteira /par'tera/ *f* midwife

partici|pação /partʃisipa'sãw/ *f* participation; (*numa empresa, nos lucros*) share; **~pante** *a* participating □ *m/f* participant; **~par** *vi* take part (**de** *ou* **em** in)

particípio /partʃi'sipiu/ *m* participle

partícula /par'tʃikula/ *f* particle

particu|lar /partʃiku'lar/ *a* private; (*especial*) unusual □ *m* (*pessoa*) private individual; *pl* (*detalhes*) particulars; **em ~lar** (*especialmente*) in particular; (*a sós*) in private; **~laridade** *f* peculiarity

partida /par'tʃida/ *f* (*saída*) departure; (*de corrida*) start; (*de futebol, xadrez etc*) match; **dar ~ em** start up

par|tidário /partʃi'dariu/ *a* partisan □ *m* supporter; **~tido** *a* broken □ *m* (*político*) party; (*casamento, par*) match; **tirar ~tido de** benefit from; **tomar o ~tido de** side with; **~tilha** *f* division; **~tir** *vi* (*sair*) depart; <*corredor*> start □ *vt* break; **~tir-se** *vpr* break; **a ~tir de ...** from ... onwards; **~tir para** (*fam*) resort to; **~tir para outra** do something different, change direction; **~titura** *f* score

parto /'partu/ *m* birth

parvo /'parvu/ *a* (*Port*) stupid

Páscoa /'paskoa/ *f* Easter

pas|mar /paz'mar/ *vt* amaze; **~mar-se** *vpr* be amazed (**com** at); **~mo** *a* amazed □ *m* amazement

passa /'pasa/ *f* raisin

pas|sada /pa'sada/ *f* **dar uma ~sada em** call in at; **~-sadeira** *f* (*mulher*) woman who irons; (*Port: faixa*) zebra crossing, (*Amer*) crosswalk; **~sado** *a* <*ano, mês, semana*> last; <*tempo, particípio etc*> past; <*fruta, comida*> off □ *m* past; **são duas horas ~sadas** it's gone two o'clock; **bem/mal ~sado** <*bife*> well done/rare

passa|geiro /pasa'ʒeru/ *m* passenger □ *a* passing; **~gem** *f* passage; (*bilhete*) ticket; **de ~gem** <*dizer etc*> in passing; **estar de ~gem** be passing through; **~gem de ida e volta** return ticket, (*Amer*) round trip ticket

passaporte /pasa'pɔrtʃi/ *m* passport

passar /pa'sar/ *vt* pass; spend <*tempo*>; cross <*ponte, rio*>; (*a ferro*) iron <*roupa etc*>; (*aplicar*) put on <*creme, batom etc*> □ *vi* pass; <*dor, medo, chuva etc*> go; (*ser aceitável*) be passable □ *m* passing; **~-se** *vpr* happen; **passou a beber muito** he started to drink a lot; **passei dos 30 anos** I'm over thirty; **não passa de um boato** it's nothing more than a rumour; **~ por** go through; go along <*rua*>; (*ser considerado*) be taken for; **fazer-se ~ por** pass o.s. off as; **~ por cima de** (*fig*) overlook; **~ sem** do without

passarela /pasa'rɛla/ *f* (*sobre rua*) footbridge; (*para desfile de moda*) catwalk

pássaro /'pasaru/ *m* bird

passatempo /pasa'tẽpu/ *m* pastime

passe /'pasi/ *m* pass

pas|sear /pasi'ar/ *vi* go out and about; (*viajar*) travel around □ *vt* take for a walk; **~seata** *f* protest march; **~seio** *m* outing; (*volta a pé*) walk; (*volta de carro*) drive; **dar um ~seio** (*a pé*) go for a walk; (*de carro*) go for a drive

passio|nal /pasio'naw/ (*pl* **~nais**) *a* **crime ~nal** crime of passion

passista /pa'sista/ *m/f* dancer

passí|vel /pa'sivew/ (*pl* **~veis**) *a* **~vel de** subject to

passi|vidade /pasivi'dadʒi/ *f* passivity; **~vo** *a* passive □ *m* (*com*) liabilities; (*ling*) passive

passo /'pasu/ *m* step; (*velocidade*) pace; (*barulho*) footstep; **~ a ~** step by step; **a dois ~s de** a stone's throw from; **dar um ~** take a step

pasta /'pasta/ *f* (*matéria*) paste; (*bolsa*) briefcase; (*fichário*) folder; **ministro sem ~** minister without portfolio; **~ de dentes** toothpaste

pas|tagem /pas'taʒẽ/ *f* pasture; **~tar** *vi* graze

pas|tel /pas'tɛw/ (*pl* **~téis**) *m* (*para comer*) samosa; (*Port: doce*) pastry; (*para desenhar*) pastel; **~telão** *m* (*comédia*) slapstick; **~telaria** *f* (*loja*) samosa vendor, (*Port*) pastry shop; (*Port: pastéis*) pastries

pasteurizado /pastewri'zadu/ *a* pasteurized

pastilha /pas'tʃiʎa/ *f* pastille

pas|to /'pastu/ *m* (*erva*) fodder, feed; (*lugar*) pasture; **~tor** *m* (*de gado*) shepherd; (*clérigo*) vicar; **~tor alemão** (*cachorro*) Alsatian; **~toral** (*pl* **~torais**) *a* pastoral

pata /'pata/ *f* paw; **~da** *f* kick

patamar /pata'mar/ *m* landing; (*fig*) level

patê /pa'te/ *m* pâté

patente /pa'tẽtʃi/ *a* obvious □ *f* (*mil*) rank; (*de invenção*) patent; **~ar** *vt* patent <*produto, invenção*>

pater|nal /pater'naw/ (*pl* **~nais**) *a* paternal; **~nidade** *f* paternity; **~no** /ɛ/ *a* paternal

pate|ta /pa'tɛta/ *a* daft, silly □ *m/f* fool; **~tice** *f* stupidity; (*uma*) silly thing

patético /pa'tɛtʃiku/ *a* pathetic

patíbulo /pa'tʃibulu/ *m* gallows

pati|faria /patʃifa'ria/ *f* roguishness; (*uma*) dirty trick; **~fe** *m* scoundrel

patim /pa'tʃĩ/ *m* skate; **~ de rodas** roller skate

pati|nação /patʃina'sãw/ *f* skating; (*rinque*) skating rink; **~nador** *m* skater; **~nar** *vi* skate; <*carro*> skid; **~nete** /ɛ/ *m* skateboard

pátio /'patʃiu/ *m* courtyard; (*de escola*) playground

pato /'patu/ *m* duck

pato|logia /patolo'ʒia/ *f* pathology; **~lógico** *a* pathological; **~logista** *m/f* pathologist

patrão /pa'trãw/ *m* boss

pátria /'patria/ *f* homeland

patriar|ca /patri'arka/ *m* patriarch; **~cal** (*pl* **~cais**) *a* patriarchal

patrimônio /patri'moniu/ *m* (*bens*) estate, property; (*fig: herança*) heritage

patri|ota /patri'ɔta/ *m/f* patriot; **~ótico** *a* patriotic; **~otismo** *m* patriotism

patroa /pa'troa/ *f* boss; (*fam: esposa*) missus, wife

patro|cinador /patrosina'dor/ *m* sponsor; **~cinar** *vt* sponsor; **~cínio** *m* sponsorship

patru|lha /pa'truʎa/ *f* patrol; **~lhar** *vt/i* patrol

pau /paw/ *m* stick; (*fam: cruzeiro*) cruzeiro; (*chulo: pênis*) prick; *pl* (*naipe*) clubs; **a meio ~** at half mast; **rachar ~** (*fam: brigar*) row, fight like cat and dog; **~lada** *f* blow with a stick

paulista /paw'lista/ *a & m/f* (person) from (the state of) São Paulo; **~no** *a & m* (person) from (the city of) São Paulo

pausa /'pawza/ *f* pause; **~do** *a* slow

pauta /'pawta/ *f* (*em papel*) lines; (*de música*) stave; (*fig: de discussão etc*) agenda; **~do** *a* <*papel*> lined

pavão /pa'vãw/ *m* peacock

pavilhão /pavi'ʎãw/ *m* pavilion; (*no jardim*) summerhouse

pavimen|tar /pavimẽ'tar/ *vt* pave; **~to** *m* floor; (*de rua etc*) surface

pavio /pa'viu/ *m* wick

pavor /pa'vor/ *m* terror; **ter ~ de** be terrified of; **~oso** /o/ *a* dreadful

paz /pas/ *f* peace; **fazer as ~es** make up

pé /pɛ/ *m* foot; (*planta*) plant; (*de móvel*) leg; **a ~** on foot; **ao ~ da letra** literally; **estar de ~** <*festa etc*> be on; **ficar de ~** stand up; **em ~** standing (up); **em ~ de igualdade** on an equal footing

peão /pi'ãw/ *m* (*Port: pedestre*) pedestrian; (*no xadrez*) pawn

peça /'pɛsa/ *f* piece; (*de máquina, carro etc*) part; (*teatral*) play; **pregar uma ~ em** play a trick on; **~ de reposição** spare part; **~ de vestuário** item of clothing

pe|cado /pe'kadu/ *m* sin; **~cador** *m* sinner; **~caminoso** /o/ *a* sinful; **~car** *vi* (*contra a religião*) sin; (*fig*) fall down

pechin|cha /pe'ʃĩʃa/ *f* bargain; **~char** *vi* bargain, haggle

peçonhento /peso'ɲẽtu/ *a* **animais ~s** vermin

pecu|ária /peku'aria/ *f* livestock-farming; **~ário** *a* livestock; **~arista** *m/f* livestock farmer

peculi|ar /pekuli'ar/ *a* peculiar; **~aridade** *f* peculiarity

pecúlio /pe'kuliu/ *m* savings

pedaço /pe'dasu/ *m* piece; **aos ~s** in pieces; **cair aos ~s** fall to pieces

pedágio /pe'daʒiu/ *m* toll; (*cabine*) tollbooth

peda|gogia /pedago'ʒia/ *f* education; **~gógico** *a* educational; **~gogo** /o/ *m* educationalist

pe|dal /pe'daw/ (*pl* **~dais**) *m* pedal; **~dalar** *vt/i* pedal

pedante /pe'dãtʃi/ *a* pretentious □ *m/f* pseud

pé|-de-atleta /pɛdʒiat'lɛta/ *m* athlete's foot; **~-de-meia** (*pl* **~s-de-meia**) *m* nest egg; **~-de-pato** (*pl* **~s-de-pato**) *m* flipper

pederneira /peder'nera/ *f* flint

pedes|tal /pedes'taw/ (*pl* **~tais**) *m* pedestal

pedestre /pe'dɛstri/ *a & m/f* pedestrian

pé|-de-vento /pɛdʒi'vẽtu/ (*pl* **~s-de-vento**) *m* gust of wind

pedia|tra /pedʒi'atra/ *m/f* paediatrician; **~tria** *f* paediatrics

pedicuro /pedʒi'kuru/ *m* chiropodist, (*Amer*) podiatrist

pe|dido /pe'dʒidu/ *m* request; (*encomenda*) order; **a ~dido de** at the request of; **~dido de demissão** resignation; **~dido de desculpa** apology; **~dir** *vt* ask for; (*num restaurante etc*) order □ *vi* ask; (*num restaurante etc*) order; **~dir aco a alg** ask s.o. for sth; **~dir para alg ir** ask s.o. to go; **~dir desculpa** apologize; **~dir em casamento** propose to

pedinte /pe'dʒĩtʃi/ *m/f* beggar

pedra /'pɛdra/ stone; **~ de gelo** ice cube; **chuva de ~** hail; **~ pomes** pumice stone

pedregoso /pedre'gozu/ *a* stony

pedreiro /pe'dreru/ *m* builder

pegada /pe'gada/ *f* footprint; (*de goleiro*) save

pegajoso /pega'ʒozu/ *a* sticky

pegar /pe'gar/ *vt* get; catch <*bola, doença, ladrão, ônibus*>; (*segurar*) get hold of; pick up <*emissora, hábito, mania*> □ *vi* (*aderir*) stick; <*doença*> be catching; <*moda*> catch on; <*carro, motor*> start; <*mentira, desculpa*> stick; **~-se** *vpr* come to blows; **~ bem /mal** go down well/badly; **~ fogo** catch fire; **pega essa rua** take that street; **~ em** grab; **~ no sono** get to sleep

pego /'pɛgu/ *pp de* **pegar**

pei|dar /pej'dar/ *vi* (*chulo*) fart; **~do** *m* (*chulo*) fart

pei|to /'pejtu/ *m* chest; (*seio*) breast; (*fig: coragem*) guts; **~toril** (*pl* **~toris**) *m* window-sill; **~tudo** *a* <*mulher*> busty; (*fig: corajoso*) gutsy

pei|xaria /peʃa'ria/ *f* fishmonger's; **~xe** *m* fish; **Peixes** (*signo*) Pisces; **~xeiro** *m* fishmonger

pela = por + a

pelado /pe'ladu/ *a* (*nu*) naked, in the nude

pelan|ca /pe'lãka/ *f* roll of fat; *pl* flab; **~cudo** *a* flabby

pelar /pe'lar/ *vt* peel <*fruta, batata*>; skin <*animal*>; (*fam: tomar dinheiro de*) fleece

pelas = por + as

pele /'pɛli/ *f* skin; (*como roupa*) fur; **~teiro** *m* furrier; **~teria** *f* furrier's

pelica /pe'lika/ *f* **luvas de ~** kid gloves

pelicano /peli'kanu/ *m* pelican

película /pe'likula/ *f* skin

pelo = por + o

pêlo /'pelu/ *m* hair; (*de animal*) coat; **nu em ~** stark naked; **montar em ~** ride bareback

pelos = por + os

pelotão /pelo'tãw/ *m* platoon

pelúcia /pe'lusia/ *f* **bicho de ~** soft toy, fluffy animal

peludo /pe'ludu/ *a* hairy

pena[1] /'pena/ *f* (*de ave*) feather; (*de caneta*) nib

pena[2] /'pena/ *f* (*castigo*) penalty; (*de amor etc*) pang; **é uma ~ que** it's a pity that; **que ~!** what a pity!; **dar ~** be upsetting; **estar com** *ou* **ter ~ de** feel sorry for; **(não) vale a ~** it's (not) worth it; **vale a ~ tentar** it's worth trying; **~ de morte** death penalty

penada /pe'nada/ *f* stroke of the pen

pe|nal /pe'naw/ (*pl* **~nais**) *a* penal; **~nalidade** *f* penalty; **~nalizar** *vt* penalize

pênalti /'penawtʃi/ *m* penalty

penar /pe'nar/ *vi* suffer

pen|dente /pẽ'dẽtʃi/ *a* hanging; (*fig: causa*) pending; **~der** *vi* hang; (*inclinar-se*) slope; (*tender*) be inclined (a to); **~dor** *m* inclination

pêndulo /'pẽdulu/ *m* pendulum

pendu|rado /pẽdu'radu/ *a* hanging; (*fam: por fazer, pagar*) outstanding;

~rar *vt* hang (up); (*fam*) put on the slate <*compra*> □ *vi* (*fam*) pay later; **~ricalho** *m* pendant

penedo /pe'nedu/ *m* rock

penei|ra /pe'nera/ *f* sieve; **~rar** *vt* sieve, sift □ *vi* drizzle

pene|tra /pe'nɛtra/ *m/f* (*fam*) gatecrasher; **~tração** *f* penetration; (*fig*) perspicacity; **~trante** *a* <*som, olhar*> piercing; <*dor*> sharp; <*ferida*> deep; <*frio*> biting; <*análise, espírito*> incisive, perceptive; **~trar** *vt* penetrate □ *vi* **~trar em** enter <*casa*>; (*fig*) penetrate

penhasco /pe'ɲasku/ *m* cliff

penhoar /peɲo'ar/ *m* dressing gown

penhor /pe'ɲor/ *m* pledge; **casa de ~es** pawnshop

penicilina /penisi'lina/ *f* penicillin

penico /pe'niku/ *m* potty

península /pe'nĩsula/ *f* peninsula

pênis /'penis/ *m invar* penis

penitência /peni'tẽsia/ *f* (*arrependimento*) penitence; (*expiação*) penance

penitenciá|ria /penitẽsi'aria/ *f* prison; **~rio** *a* prison □ *m* prisoner

penoso /pe'nozu/ *a* <*experiência, tarefa, assunto*> painful; <*trabalho, viagem*> hard, difficult

pensa|dor /pẽsa'dor/ *m* thinker; **~mento** *m* thought

pensão /pẽ'sãw/ *f* (*renda*) pension; (*hotel*) guesthouse; **~ (alimentícia)** (*paga por ex-marido*) alimony; **~ completa** full board

pen|sar /pẽ'sar/ *vt/i* think (**em** of *ou* about); **~sativo** *a* thoughtful, pensive

pên|sil /'pẽsiw/ (*pl* **~seis**) *a* **ponte ~sil** suspension bridge

penso /'pẽsu/ *m* (*curativo*) dressing

pentágono /pẽ'tagonu/ *m* pentagon

pentatlo /pẽ'tatlu/ *m* pentathlon

pente /'pẽtʃi/ *m* comb; **~adeira** *f* dressing table; **~ado** *m* hairstyle, hairdo; **~ar** *vt* comb; **~ar-se** *vpr* do one's hair; (*com pente*) comb one's hair

Pentecostes /pẽte'kɔstʃis/ *m* Whitsun

pente-fino /pẽtʃi'finu/ *m* **passar a ~** go over with a fine-tooth comb

pente|lhar /pẽte'ʎar/ *vt* (*fam*) bother; **~lho** /e/ *m* pubic hair; (*fam: pessoa inconveniente*) pain (in the neck)

penugem /pe'nuʒẽ/ *f* down

penúltimo /pe'nuwtʃimu/ *a* last but one, penultimate

penumbra /pe'nũbra/ *f* half-light

penúria /pe'nuria/ *f* penury, extreme poverty

pepino /pe'pinu/ *m* cucumber

pepita /pe'pita/ *f* nugget

peque|nez /peke'nes/ *f* smallness; (*fig*) pettiness; **~nininho** *a* tiny; **~no** /e/ *a* small; (*mesquinho*) petty

Pequim /pe'kĩ/ *f* Peking, Beijing

pequinês /peki'nes/ *m* Pekinese

pêra /'pera/ *f* pear

perambular /perãbu'lar/ *vi* wander

perante /pe'rãtʃi/ *prep* before

percalço /per'kawsu/ *m* pitfall

perceber /perse'ber/ *vt* realize; (*Port: entender*) understand; (*psiqu*) perceive

percen|tagem /persẽ'taʒẽ/ *f* percentage; **~tual** (*pl* **~tuais**) *a* & *m* percentage

percep|ção /persep'sãw/ *f* perception; **~tível** (*pl* **~tíveis**) *a* perceptible

percevejo /perse'veʒu/ *m* (*bicho*) bedbug; (*tachinha*) drawing pin, (*Amer*) thumbtack

per|correr /perko'xer/ *vt* cross; cover <*distância*>; (*viajar por*) travel through; **~curso** *m* journey

percus|são /perku'sãw/ *f* percussion; **~sionista** *m/f* percussionist

percutir /perku'tʃir/ *vt* strike

perda /'perda/ *f* loss; **~ de tempo** waste of time

perdão /per'dãw/ *f* pardon

perder /per'der/ *vt* lose; (*não chegar a ver, pegar*) miss <*ônibus, programa na TV etc*>; waste <*tempo*> □ *vi* lose; **~-se** *vpr* get lost; **~-se de alg** lose s.o.; **~ aco de vista** lose sight of sth

perdiz /per'dʒis/ *f* partridge

perdoar /perdo'ar/ *vt* forgive (**aco a alg** s.o. for sth)

perdulário /perdu'lariu/ *a* & *m* spendthrift

perdurar /perdu'rar/ *vi* endure; <*coisa ruim*> persist

pere|cer /pere'ser/ *vi* perish; **~cível** (*pl* **~cíveis**) *a* perishable

peregri|nação /peregrina'sãw/ *f* peregrination; (*romaria*) pilgrimage; **~nar** *vi* roam; (*por motivos religiosos*) go on a pilgrimage; **~no** *m* pilgrim

pereira /pe'rera/ *f* pear tree

peremptório /perẽp'tɔriu/ *a* peremptory

perene /pe'reni/ *a* perennial

perereca /pere'rɛka/ *f* tree frog

perfazer /perfa'zer/ *vt* make up

perfeccionis|mo /perfeksio'nizmu/ *m* perfectionism; **~ta** *a* & *m/f* perfectionist

perfei|ção /perfej'sãw/ *f* perfection; **~to** *a* & *m* perfect

per|fil /per'fiw/ (*pl* **~fis**) *m* profile; **~filar** *vt* line up; **~filar-se** *vpr* line up

perfu|mado /perfu'madu/ *a* <*flor, ar*> fragrant; <*sabonete etc*> scented;

<*pessoa*> with perfume on; **~mar** *vt* perfume; **~mar-se** *vpr* put perfume on; **~maria** *f* perfumery; (*fam*) trimmings, frills; **~me** *m* perfume

perfu|rador /perfura'dor/ *m* punch; **~rar** *vt* punch <*papel, bilhete*>; drill through <*chão*>; perforate <*úlcera, pulmão etc*>; **~ratriz** *f* drill

pergaminho /perga'miɲu/ *m* parchment

pergun|ta /per'gũta/ *f* question; **fazer uma ~ta** ask a question; **~tar** *vt/i* ask; **~tar aco a alg** ask s.o. sth; **~tar por** ask after

perícia /pe'risia/ *f* (*mestria*) expertise; (*inspeção*) investigation; (*peritos*) experts

perici|al /perisi'aw/ (*pl* **~ais**) *a* expert

pericli|tante /perikli'tãtʃi/ *a* precarious; **~tar** *vi* be at risk

peri|feria /perife'ria/ *f* periphery; (*da cidade*) outskirts; **~férico** *a* & *m* peripheral

perigo /pe'rigu/ *m* danger; **~so** /o/ *a* dangerous

perímetro /pe'rimetru/ *m* perimeter

periódico /peri'ɔdʒiku/ *a* periodic □ *m* periodical

período /pe'riodu/ *m* period; **trabalhar meio ~** work part-time

peripécias /peri'pɛsias/ *f pl* ups and downs, vicissitudes

periquito /peri'kitu/ *m* parakeet; (*de estimação*) budgerigar

periscópio /peris'kɔpiu/ *m* periscope

perito /pe'ritu/ *a* & *m* expert (**em** at)

per|jurar /perʒu'rar/ *vi* commit perjury; **~júrio** *m* perjury; **~juro** *m* perjurer

perma|necer /permane'ser/ *vi* remain; **~nência** *f* permanence; (*estadia*) stay; **~nente** *a* permanent □ *f* perm

permeá|vel /permi'avew/ (*pl* **~veis**) *a* permeable

permis|são /permi'sãw/ *f* permission; **~sível** (*pl* **~síveis**) *a* permissible; **~sivo** *a* permissive

permitir /permi'tʃir/ *vt* allow, permit; **~ a alg ir** allow s.o. to go

permutar /permu'tar/ *vt* exchange

perna /'pɛrna/ *f* leg

pernicioso /pernisi'ozu/ *a* pernicious

per|nil /per'niw/ (*pl* **~nis**) *m* leg

pernilongo /perni'lõgu/ *m* (large) mosquito

pernoi|tar /pernoj'tar/ *vi* spend the night; **~te** *m* overnight stay

pérola /'pɛrola/ *f* pearl

perpendicular /perpẽdʒiku'lar/ *a* perpendicular

perpetrar /perpe'trar/ *vt* perpetrate

perpetu|ar /perpetu'ar/ *vt* perpetuate; **~idade** *f* perpetuity

perpétu|o /per'pɛtuu/ *a* perpetual; **prisão ~a** life imprisonment

perple|xidade /perpleksi'dadʒi/ *f* puzzlement; **~xo** /ɛ/ *a* puzzled

persa /'pɛrsa/ *a* & *m/f* Persian

perse|guição /persegi'sãw/ *f* pursuit; (*de minorias etc*) persecution; **~guidor** *m* pursuer; (*de minorias etc*) persecutor; **~guir** *vt* pursue; persecute <*minoria, seita etc*>

perseve|rança /perseve'rãsa/ *f* perseverance; **~rante** *a* persevering; **~rar** *vi* persevere

persiana /persi'ana/ *f* blind

pérsico /'pɛrsiku/ *a* **Golfo Pérsico** Persian Gulf

persignar-se /persig'narsi/ *vt* cross o.s.

persis|tência /persis'tẽsia/ *f* persistence; **~tente** *a* persistent; **~tir** *vi* persist

perso|nagem /perso'naʒẽ/ *m/f* (*pessoa famosa*) personality; (*em livro, filme etc*) character; **~-nalidade** *f* personality; **~-nalizar** *vt* personalize; **~nificar** *vt* personify

perspectiva /perspek'tʃiva/ *f* (*na arte, ponto de vista*) perspective; (*possibilidade*) prospect

perspi|cácia /perspi'kasia/ *f* insight, perceptiveness; **~caz** *a* perceptive

persua|dir /persua'dʒir/ *vt* persuade (**alg a** s.o. to); **~são** *f* persuasion; **~sivo** *a* persuasive

perten|cente /pertẽ'sẽtʃi/ *a* belonging (**a** to); (*que tem a ver com*) pertaining (**a** to); **~cer** *vi* belong (**a** to); (*referir-se*) pertain (**a** to); **~ces** *m pl* belongings

perto /'pɛrtu/ *adv* near (**de** to); **aqui ~** near here, nearby; **de ~** closely; <*ver*> close up

pertur|bação /perturba'sãw/ *f* disturbance; (*do espírito*) anxiety; **~bado** *a* <*pessoa*> unsettled, troubled; **~bar** *vt* disturb; **~bar-se** *vpr* get upset, be perturbed

Peru /pe'ru/ *m* Peru

peru /pe'ru/ *m* turkey

perua /pe'rua/ *f* (*carro grande*) estate car, (*Amer*) station wagon; (*caminhonete*) van; (*para escolares etc*) minibus; (*fam: mulher*) brassy woman

peruano /peru'ano/ *a* & *m* Peruvian

peruca /pe'ruka/ *f* wig

perver|são /perver'sãw/ *f* perversion; **~so** *a* perverse; **~ter** *vt* pervert

pesadelo /peza'delu/ *m* nightmare

pesado /pe'zadu/ *a* heavy; <*estilo, livro*> heavy-going □ *adv* heavily

pêsames /'pezamis/ *m pl* condolences

pesar[1] /pe'zar/ *vt* weigh; (*fig: avaliar*) weigh up □ *vi* weigh; (*influir*) carry weight; **~ sobre** <*ameaça etc*> hang over; **~-se** *vpr* weigh o.s.

pesar² /pe'zar/ *m* sorrow; **~oso** /o/ *a* sorry, sorrowful

pes|ca /'pɛska/ *f* fishing; **ir à ~ca** go fishing; **~cador** *m* fisherman; **~car** *vt* catch; (*retirar da água*) fish out ▫ *vi* fish; (*fam*) (*entender*) understand; (*cochilar*) nod off; **~car de** (*fam*) know all about

pescoço /pes'kosu/ *m* neck

peseta /pe'zeta/ *f* peseta

peso /'pezu/ *m* weight; **de ~** (*fig*) <*pessoa*> influential; <*livro, argumento*> authoritative

pesqueiro /pes'keru/ *a* fishing

pesqui|sa /pes'kiza/ *f* research; (*uma*) study; *pl* research; **~sa de mercado** market research; **~sador** *m* researcher; **~sar** *vt/i* research

pêssego /'pesigu/ *m* peach

pessegueiro /pesi'geru/ *m* peach tree

pessimis|mo /pesi'mizmu/ *m* pessimism; **~ta** *a* pessimistic ▫ *m/f* pessimist

péssimo /'pɛsimu/ *a* terrible, awful

pesso|a /pe'soa/ *f* person; *pl* people; **em ~a** in person; **~al** (*pl* **~ais**) *a* personal ▫ *m* staff; (*fam*) folks

pesta|na /pes'tana/ *f* eyelash; **tirar uma ~na** (*fam*) have a nap; **~nejar** *vi* blink; **sem ~nejar** (*fig*) without batting an eyelid

pes|te /'pɛstʃi/ *f* (*doença*) plague; (*criança etc*) pest; **~ticida** *m* pesticide

pétala /'pɛtala/ *f* petal

peteca /pe'tɛka/ *f* kind of shuttlecock; (*jogo*) kind of badminton played with the hand

peteleco /pete'lɛku/ *m* flick

petição /petʃi'sãw/ *f* petition

petisco /pe'tʃisku/ *m* savoury, titbit

petrificar /petrifi'kar/ *vt* petrify; (*de surpresa*) stun; **~-se** *vpr* be petrified; (*de surpresa*) be stunned

petroleiro /petro'leru/ *a* oil ▫ *m* oil tanker

petróleo /pe'trɔliu/ *m* oil, petroleum; **~ bruto** crude oil

petrolífero /petro'liferu/ *a* oil-producing

petroquími|ca /petro'kimika/ *f* petrochemicals; **~co** *a* petrochemical

petu|lância /petu'lãsia/ *f* cheek; **~lante** *a* cheeky

peúga /pi'uga/ *f* (*Port*) sock

pevide /pe'vidʒi/ *f* (*Port*) pip

pia /'pia/ *f* (*do banheiro*) washbasin; (*da cozinha*) sink; **~ batismal** font

piada /pi'ada/ *f* joke

pia|nista /pia'nista/ *m/f* pianist; **~no** *m* piano; **~no de cauda** grand piano

piar /pi'ar/ *vi* <*pinto*> cheep; <*coruja*> hoot

picada /pi'kada/ *f* (*de agulha, alfinete etc*) prick; (*de abelha, vespa*) sting; (*de mosquito, cobra*) bite; (*de heroína*) shot; (*de avião*) nosedive; **o fim da ~** (*fig*) the limit

picadeiro /pika'deru/ *m* ring

picante /pi'kãtʃi/ *a* <*comida*> hot, spicy; <*piada*> risqué; <*filme, livro*> raunchy

pica-pau /pika'paw/ *m* woodpecker

picar /pi'kar/ *vt* (*com agulha, alfinete etc*) prick; <*abelha, vespa, urtiga*> sting; <*mosquito, cobra*> bite; <*pássaro*> peck; chop <*carne, alho etc*>; shred <*papel*> ▫ *vi* <*peixe*> bite; <*lã, cobertor*> prickle

picareta /pika'reta/ *f* pickaxe

pi|chação /piʃa'sãw/ *f* piece of graffiti; *pl* graffiti; **~char** *vt* spray with graffiti <*muro, prédio*>; spray <*grafite, desenho*>; **~che** *m* pitch

picles /'piklis/ *m pl* pickles

pico /'piku/ *m* peak; **20 anos e ~** (*Port*) just over 20

picolé /piko'lɛ/ *m* ice lolly

pico|tar /piko'tar/ *vt* perforate; **~te** /ɔ/ *m* perforations

pie|dade /pie'dadʒi/ *f* (*religiosidade*) piety; (*compaixão*) pity; **~doso** /o/ *a* merciful, compassionate

pie|gas /pi'ɛgas/ *a invar* <*filme, livro*> sentimental, schmaltzy; <*pessoa*> soppy; **~guice** *f* sentimentality

pifar /pi'far/ *vi* (*fam*) break down, go wrong

pigar|rear /pigaxi'ar/ *vi* clear one's throat; **~ro** *m* frog in the throat

pigmento /pig'mẽtu/ *m* pigment

pig|meu /pig'mew/ *a & m* (*f* **~méia**) pygmy

pijama /pi'ʒama/ *m* pyjamas

pilantra /pi'lãtra/ *m/f* (*fam*) crook

pilão /pi'lãw/ *m* (*na cozinha*) pestle; (*na construção*) ram

pilar /pi'lar/ *m* pillar

pilastra /pi'lastra/ *f* pillar

pileque /pi'lɛki/ *m* drinking session; **tomar um ~** get drunk

pilha /'piʎa/ *f* (*monte*) pile; (*elétrica*) battery

pilhar /pi'ʎar/ *vt* pillage

pilhéria /pi'ʎɛria/ *f* joke

pilotar /pilo'tar/ *vt* fly, pilot <*avião*>; drive <*carro*>

pilotis /pilo'tʃis/ *m pl* pillars

piloto /pi'lotu/ *m* pilot; (*de carro*) driver; (*de gás*) pilot light ▫ *a invar* pilot

pílula /'pilula/ *f* pill

pimen|ta /pi'mẽta/ *f* pepper; **~ta de Caiena** cayenne pepper; **~-ta-do-reino** *f* black pepper; **~ta-malagueta** (*pl* **~tas-malagueta**) *f* chilli pepper; **~tão** *m* (bell) pepper; **~teira** *f* pepper pot

pinacoteca /pinako'tɛka/ *f* art gallery

pin|ça /'pĩsa/ (*para tirar pêlos*) tweezers; (*para segurar*) tongs; (*de siri etc*) pincer; **~çar** *vt* pluck <*sobrancelhas*>

pin|cel /pĩ'sɛw/ (*pl* **~céis**) *m* brush; **~celada** *f* brush stroke; **~celar** *vt* paint

pin|ga /'pĩga/ *f* Brazilian rum; **~gado** *a* <*café*> with a dash of milk; **~gar** *vi* drip; (*começar a chover*) spit (with rain) □ *vt* drip; **~gente** *m* pendant; **~go** *m* drop; (*no i*) dot

pingue-pongue /pĩgi'põgi/ *m* table tennis

pingüim /pĩ'gwĩ/ *m* penguin

pi|nha /'piɲa/ *f* pine cone; **~nheiro** *f* pine tree; **~nho** *m* pine

pino /'pinu/ *m* pin; (*para trancar carro*) lock; **a ~** upright; **bater ~** <*carro*> knock

pin|ta /'pĩta/ *f* (*sinal*) mole; (*fam: aparência*) look; **~tar** *vt* paint; dye <*cabelo*>; put make-up on <*rosto, olhos*> □ *vi* paint; (*fam*) <*pessoa*> show up; <*problema, oportunidade*> crop up; **~tar-se** *vpr* put on make-up

pintarroxo /pĩta'xoʃu/ *m* robin

pinto /'pĩtu/ *m* chick

pin|tor /pĩ'tor/ *m* painter; **~tura** *f* painting

pio[1] /'piu/ *m* (*de pinto*) cheep; (*de coruja*) hoot

pio[2] /'piu/ *a* pious

piolho /pi'oʎu/ *m* louse

pioneiro /pio'neru/ *m* pioneer □ *a* pioneering

pior /pi'ɔr/ *a & adv* worse; **o ~** the worst

pio|ra /pi'ɔra/ *f* worsening; **~rar** *vt* make worse, worsen □ *vi* get worse, worsen

pipa /'pipa/ *f* (*que voa*) kite; (*de vinho*) cask

pipilar /pipi'lar/ *vi* chirp

pipo|ca /pi'pɔka/ *f* popcorn; **~car** *vi* spring up; **~queiro** *m* popcorn seller

pique /'piki/ *m* (*disposição*) energy; **a ~** vertically; **ir a ~** <*navio*> sink

piquenique /piki'niki/ *m* picnic

pique|te /pi'ketʃi/ *m* picket; **~teiro** *m* picket

pirado /pi'radu/ *a* (*fam*) crazy

pirâmide /pi'ramidʒi/ *f* pyramid

piranha /pi'raɲa/ *f* piranha; (*fam: mulher*) maneater

pirar /pi'rar/ (*fam*) *vi* flip out, go mad

pirata /pi'rata/ *a & m/f* pirate; **~ria** *f* piracy

pires /'piris/ *m invar* saucer

pirilampo /piri'lãpu/ *m* glow-worm

Pirineus /piri'news/ *m pl* Pyrenees

pirra|ça /pi'xasa/ *f* spiteful act; **fazer ~ça** be spiteful; **~cento** *a* spiteful

pirueta /piru'eta/ *f* pirouette

pirulito /piru'litu/ *m* lollipop

pi|sada /pi'zada/ *f* step; (*rastro*) footprint; **~sar** *vt* tread on; tread <*uvas, palco*>; (*esmagar*) trample on □ *vi* step; **~sar em** step on; (*entrar*) set foot in

pis|cadela /piska'dɛla/ *f* wink; **~ca-pisca** *m* indicator; **~car** *vi* (*com o olho*) wink; (*pestanejar*) blink; <*estrela, luz*> twinkle; <*motorista*> indicate □ *m* **num ~car de olhos** in a flash

piscicultura /pisikuw'tura/ *f* fish farming; (*lugar*) fish farm

piscina /pi'sina/ *f* swimming pool

piso /'pizu/ *m* floor

pisotear /pizotʃi'ar/ *vt* trample

pista /'pista/ *f* track; (*da estrada*) carriageway; (*para aviões*) runway; (*de circo*) ring; (*dica*) clue; **~ de dança** dancefloor

pistache /pis'taʃi/ *m*, **pistacho** /pis'taʃu/ *m* pistachio (nut)

pisto|la /pis'tɔla/ *f* pistol; (*para pintar*) spray gun; **~lão** *m* influential contact; **~leiro** *m* gunman

pitada /pi'tada/ *f* pinch

piteira /pi'tera/ *f* cigarette-holder

pitoresco /pito'resku/ *a* picturesque

pitu /pi'tu/ *m* crayfish

pivete /pi'vɛtʃi/ *m/f* child thief

pivô /pi'vo/ *m* pivot

pixaim /piʃa'ĩ/ *a* frizzy

pizza /'pitsa/ *f* pizza; **~ria** *f* pizzeria

placa /'plaka/ *f* plate; (*de carro*) number plate, (*Amer*) license plate; (*comemorativa*) plaque; (*em computador*) board; **~ de sinalização** roadsign

placar /pla'kar/ *m* scoreboard; (*escore*) scoreline

plácido /'plasidu/ *a* placid

plagi|ário /plaʒi'ariu/ *m* plagiarist; **~ar** *vt* plagiarize

plágio /'plaʒiu/ *m* plagiarism

plaina /'plajna/ *f* plane

planador /plana'dor/ *m* glider

planalto /pla'nawtu/ *m* plateau

planar /pla'nar/ *vi* glide

planeamento, planear (*Port*) *veja* **planejamento, planejar**

plane|jamento /planeʒa'mẽtu/ *m* planning; **~jamento familiar** family planning; **~jar** *vt* plan

planeta /pla'neta/ *m* planet

planície /pla'nisi/ *f* plain

planificar /planifi'kar/ *vt* (*programar*) plan (out)

planilha /pla'niʎa/ *f* spreadsheet

plano /'planu/ *a* flat □ *m* plan; (*superfície, nível*) plane; **primeiro ~** foreground

planta /'plãta/ *f* plant; (*do pé*) sole; (*de edifício*) ground plan; **~ção** *f* (*ato*) planting; (*terreno*) plantation; **~do** *a* **deixar alg ~do** (*fam*) keep s.o. waiting around

plantão /plã'tãw/ *m* duty; (*noturno*) night duty; **estar de ~** be on duty

plantar /plã'tar/ *vt* plant

plas|ma /'plazma/ *m* plasma; **~mar** *vt* mould, shape

plásti|ca /'plastʃika/ *f* face-lift; **~co** *a* & *m* plastic

plataforma /plata'fɔrma/ *f* platform

plátano /'platanu/ *m* plane tree

platéia /pla'tɛja/ *f* audience; (*parte do teatro*) stalls, (*Amer*) orchestra

platina /pla'tʃina/ *f* platinum; **~dos** *m pl* points

platônico /pla'toniku/ *a* platonic

plausí|vel /plaw'zivew/ (*pl* **~vels**) *a* plausible

ple|be /'plɛbi/ *f* common people; **~beu** *a* (*f* **~béia**) plebeian □ *m* (*f* **~béia**) commoner; **~biscito** *m* plebiscite

plei|tear /plejtʃi'ar/ *vt* contest; **~to** *m* (*litígio*) case; (*eleitoral*) contest

ple|namente /plena'mẽtʃi/ *adv* fully; **~nário** *a* plenary □ *m* plenary assembly; **~no** /e/ *a* full; **em ~no verão** in the middle of summer

plissado /pli'sadu/ *a* pleated

pluma /'pluma/ *f* feather; **~gem** *f* plumage

plu|ral /plu'raw/ (*pl* **~rais**) *a* & *m* plural

plutônio /plu'toniu/ *m* plutonium

pluvi|al /pluvi'aw/ (*pl* **~ais**) *a* rain

pneu /pi'new/ *m* tyre; **~mático** *a* pneumatic □ *m* tyre

pneumonia /pineumo'nia/ *f* pneumonia

pó /pɔ/ *f* powder; (*poeira*) dust; **leite em ~** powdered milk

pobre /'pɔbri/ *a* poor □ *m*/*f* poor man (*f* woman); **os ~s** the poor; **~za** /e/ *f* poverty

poça /'posa/ *f* pool; (*deixada pela chuva*) puddle

poção /po'sãw/ *f* potion

pocilga /po'siwga/ *f* pigsty

poço /'posu/ *f* (*de água, petróleo*) well; (*de mina, elevador*) shaft

podar /po'dar/ *vt* prune

pó-de-arroz /pɔdʒia'xoz/ *m* (face) powder

poder /po'der/ *m* power □ *v aux* can, be able; (*eventualidade*) may; **ele pode /podia/poderá vir** he can/could/ might come; **ele pôde vir** he was able to come; **pode ser que** it may be that; **~ com** stand up to; **em ~ de alg** in sb's possession; **estar no ~** be in power

pode|rio /pode'riu/ *m* might; **~roso** /o/ *a* powerful

pódio /'pɔdʒiu/ *m* podium

podre /'podri/ *a* rotten; (*fam*) (*cansado*) exhausted; (*doente*) grotty; **~ de rico** filthy rich; **~s** *m pl* faults

poei|ra /po'era/ *f* dust; **~rento** *a* dusty

poe|ma /po'ema/ *m* poem; **~sia** *f* (*arte*) poetry; (*poema*) poem; **~ta** *m* poet

poético /po'ɛtʃiku/ *a* poetic

poetisa /poe'tʃiza/ *f* poetess

pois /pojs/ *conj* as, since; **~ é** that's right; **~ não** of course; **~ não?** can I help you?; **~ sim** certainly not

polaco /pu'laku/ (*Port*) *a* Polish □ *m* Pole; (*língua*) Polish

polar /po'lar/ *a* polar

polarizar /polari'zar/ *vt* polarize; **~-se** *vpr* polarize

pole|gada /pole'gada/ *f* inch; **~gar** *m* thumb

poleiro /po'leru/ *m* perch

polêmi|ca /po'lemika/ *f* controversy, debate; **~co** *a* controversial

pólen /'pɔlẽ/ *m* pollen

polícia /po'lisia/ *f* police □ *m*/*f* policeman (*f*-woman)

polici|al /polisi'aw/ (*pl* **~ais**) *a* <*carro, inquérito etc*> police; <*romance, filme*> detective □ *m*/*f* policeman (*f*-woman); **~amento** *m* policing; **~ar** *vt* police

poli|dez /poli'des/ *f* politeness; **~do** *a* polite

poli|gamia /poliga'mia/ *f* polygamy; **~glota** *a* & *m*/*f* polyglot

Polinésia /poli'nɛzia/ *f* Polynesia

polinésio /poli'nɛziu/ *a* & *m* Polynesian

pólio /'pɔliu/ *f* polio

polir /po'lir/ *vt* polish

polissilabo /poli'silabu/ *m* polysyllable

políti|ca /po'litʃika/ *f* politics; (*uma*) policy; **~co** *a* political □ *m* politician

pólo[1] /'pɔlu/ *m* pole

pólo[2] /'pɔlu/ *m* (*jogo*) polo; **~ aquático** water polo

polo|nês /polo'nes/ *a* (*f* **~nesa**) Polish □ *m* (*f* **~nesa**) Pole; (*língua*) Polish

Polônia /po'lonia/ *f* Poland

polpa /'powpa/ *f* pulp

poltrona /pow'trona/ *f* armchair

polu|ente /polu'ẽtʃi/ *a & m* pollutant; **~ição** *f* pollution; **~ir** *vt* pollute

polvilhar /powvi'ʎar/ *vt* sprinkle

polvo /'powvu/ *m* octopus

pólvora /'pɔwvora/ *f* gunpowder

polvorosa /powvo'rɔza/ *f* uproar; **em ~** in uproar; <*pessoa*> in a flap

pomada /po'mada/ *f* ointment

pomar /po'mar/ *m* orchard

pom|ba /'põba/ *f* dove; **~bo** *m* pigeon

pomo-de-Adão /pomudʃia'dãw/ *m* Adam's apple

pom|pa /'põpa/ *f* pomp; **~poso** /o/ *a* pompous

ponche /'põʃi/ *m* punch

ponderar /põde'rar/ *vt/i* ponder

pônei /'ponej/ *m* pony

ponta /'põta/ *f* end; (*de faca, prego*) point; (*de nariz, dedo, língua*) tip; (*de sapato*) toe; (*Cin, Teat: papel curto*) walk-on part; (*no campo de futebol*) wing; (*jogador*) winger; **na ~ dos pés** on tip-toe; **uma ~ de** a touch of <*ironia etc*>; **agüentar as ~s** (*fam*) hold on; **~-cabeça** /e/ *f* **de ~-cabeça** upside down

pontada /põ'tada/ *f* (*dor*) twinge

pontapé /põta'pɛ/ *m* kick; **~ inicial** kick-off

pontaria /põta'ria/ *f* aim; **fazer ~** take aim

ponte /'põtʃi/ *f* bridge; **~ aérea** shuttle; (*em tempo de guerra*) airlift; **~ de safena** heart bypass; **~ pênsil** suspension bridge

ponteiro /põ'teru/ *m* pointer; (*de relógio*) hand

pontiagudo /põtʃia'gudu/ *a* sharp

pontilhado /põtʃi'ʎadu/ *a* dotted

ponto /'põtu/ *m* point; (*de costura, tricô*) stitch; (*no final de uma frase*) full stop, (*Amer*) period; (*sinalzinho, no i*) dot; (*de ônibus*) stop; (*no teatro*) prompter; **a ~ de** on the point of; **ao ~** <*carne*> medium; **até certo ~** to a certain extent; **às duas em ~** at exactly two o'clock; **dormir no ~** (*fam*) miss the boat; **entregar os ~s** (*fam*) give up; **fazer ~** (*fam*) hang out; **dois ~s** colon; **~ de exclamação/interrogação** exclamation/question mark; **~ de táxi** taxi rank, (*Amer*) taxi stand; **~ de vista** point of view; **~ morto** neutral; **~-e-vírgula** *m* semicolon

pontu|ação /põtua'sãw/ *f* punctuation; **~al** (*pl* **~ais**) *a* punctual; **~alidade** *f* punctuality; **~ar** *vt* punctuate

pontudo /põ'tudu/ *a* pointed

popa /'popa/ *f* stern

popu|lação /popula'sãw/ *f* population; **~lacional** (*pl* **~lacionais**) *a* population; **~lar** *a* popular; **~laridade** *f* popularity; **~larizar** *vt* popularize; **~larizar-se** *vpr* become popular

pôquer /'poker/ *m* poker

por /por/ *prep* for; (*através de*) through; (*indicando meio, agente*) by; (*motivo*) out of; **~ ano/mês/** *etc* per year/month/ *etc*; **~ cento** per cent; **~ aqui** (*nesta área*) around here; (*nesta direção*) this way; **~ dentro/fora** on the inside/ outside; **~ isso** for this reason; **~ sorte** luckily; **~ que** why; **~ mais caro que seja** however expensive it may be; **está ~ acontecer/fazer** it is yet to happen/ to be done

pôr /por/ *vt* put; put on <*roupa, chapéu, óculos*>; lay <*mesa, ovos*> □ *m* **o ~ do sol** sunset; **~-se** *vpr* <*sol*> set; **~-se a** start to; **~-se a caminho** set off

porão /po'rãw/ *m* (*de prédio*) basement; (*de casa*) cellar; (*de navio*) hold

porca /'pɔrka/ *f* (*de parafuso*) nut; (*animal*) sow

porção /por'sãw/ *f* portion; **uma ~ de** (*muitos*) a lot of

porcaria /porka'ria/ *f* (*sujeira*) filth; (*coisa malfeita*) piece of trash; *pl* trash

porcelana /porse'lana/ *f* china

porcentagem /porsẽ'taʒẽ/ *f* percentage

porco /'porku/ *a* filthy □ *m* (*animal, fig*) pig; (*carne*) pork; **~-espinho** (*pl* **~s-espinhos**) *m* porcupine

porém /po'rẽj/ *conj* however

pormenor /porme'nɔr/ *m* detail

por|nô /por'no/ *a* porn □ *m* porn film; **~nografia** *f* pornography; **~nográfico** *a* pornographic

poro /'pɔru/ *m* pore; **~so** /o/ *a* porous

por|quanto /por'kwãtu/ *conj* since; **~que** /por'ki/ *conj* because; (*Port: por quê?*) why; **~quê** /por'ke/ *adv* (*Port*) why □ *m* reason why

porquinho|-da-índia /porkiɲuda'ĩdʒia/ (*pl* **~s-da-índia**) *m* guinea pig

porrada /po'xada/ *f* (*fam*) beating

porre /'pɔxi/ *m* (*fam*) drinking session, booze-up; **de ~** drunk; **tomar um ~** get drunk

porta /'pɔrta/ *f* door

porta-aviões /pɔrtavi'õjs/ *m invar* aircraft carrier

portador /porta'dor/ *m* bearer

portagem /por'taʒẽ/ *f* (*Port*) toll

porta|chaves /pɔrta'ʃavis/ *m invar* key-holder *ou* key-ring; **~-jóias** *m invar* jewellery box; **~-lápis** *m invar* pencil holder; **~-luvas** *m invar* glove compartment; **~-malas** *m invar* boot, (*Amer*) trunk; **~-níqueis** *m invar* purse

portanto /por'tãtu/ *conj* therefore

portão /por'tãw/ *m* gate

portar /por'tar/ *vt* carry; **~-se** *vpr* behave

porta|-retrato /pɔrtaxe'tratu/ *m* photo frame; **~-revistas** *m invar* magazine rack

portaria /porta'ria/ *f* (*entrada*) entrance; (*decreto*) decree

portá|til (*pl* **~teis**) *a* portable

porta|-toalhas /pɔrtato'aʎas/ *m invar* towel rail; **~-voz** *m/f* spokesman (*f*-woman)

porte /'pɔrtʃi/ *m* (*frete*) carriage; (*de cartas etc*) postage; (*de pessoa*) bearing; (*dimensão*) scale; **de grande/pequeno ~** large-/small-scale

porteiro /por'teru/ *m* doorman; **~ eletrônico** entryphone

porto /'portu/ *m* port; **o Porto** Oporto; **~ de escala** port of call; **Porto Rico** *m* Puerto Rico; **~-riquenho** /e/ *a & m* Puertorican; porto USB *m* USB port

portuense /portu'ẽsi/ *a & m/f* (person) from Oporto

Portugal /portu'gaw/ *m* Portugal

portu|guês /portu'ges/ *a & m* (*f* **~guesa**) Portuguese

portuário /portu'ariu/ *a* port ▫ *m* dock worker, docker

po|sar /po'zar/ *vi* pose; **~se** /o/ *f* pose; (*de filme*) exposure

pós-datar /pɔzda'tar/ *vt* postdate

pós-escrito /pɔzis'kritu/ *m* postscript

pós-gradua|ção /pɔzgradua'sãw/ *f* postgraduation; **~do** *a & m* postgraduate

pós-guerra /pɔz'gɛxa/ *m* post-war period; **a Europa do ~** post-war Europe

posi|ção /pozi'sãw/ *f* position; **~cionar** *vt* position; **~tivo** *a & m* positive

posologia /pozolo'ʒia/ *f* dosage

pos|sante /po'sãtʃi/ *a* powerful; **~se** /ɔ/ *f* (*de casa etc*) possession, ownership; (*do presidente etc*) swearing in; *pl* (*pertences*) possessions; **tomar ~se** take office; **tomar ~se de** take possession of

posses|são /pose'sãw/ *f* possession; **~sivo** *a* possessive; **~so** /ɛ/ *a* possessed; (*com raiva*) furious

possibili|dade /posibili'dadʒi/ *f* possibility; **~tar** *vt* make possible

possí|vel /po'sivew/ (*pl* **~veis**) *a* possible; **fazer todo o ~vel** do one's best

possuir /posu'ir/ *vt* possess; (*ser dono de*) own

posta /'pɔsta/ *f* (*de peixe*) steak

pos|tal /pos'taw/ (*pl* **~tais**) *a* postal ▫ *m* postcard

postar /pos'tar/ *vt* place; **~-se** *vpr* position o.s.

poste /'pɔstʃi/ *m* post

pôster /'poster/ *m* poster

posteri|dade /posteri'dadʒi/ *f* posterity; **~or** *a* (*no tempo*) subsequent, later; (*no espaço*) rear; **~ormente** *adv* subsequently

postiço /pos'tʃisu/ *a* false

posto /'postu/ *m* post; **~ de gasolina** petrol station, (*Amer*) gas station; **~ de saúde** health centre ▫ *pp de* **pôr**; **~ que** although

póstumo /'pɔstumu/ *a* posthumous

postura /pos'tura/ *f* posture

potá|vel /po'tavew/ (*pl* **~veis**) *a* **água ~vel** drinking water

pote /'pɔtʃi/ *m* pot; (*de vidro*) jar

potência /po'tẽsia/ *f* power

poten|cial /potẽsi'aw/ (*pl* **~ciais**) *a & m* potential; **~te** *a* potent

potro /'potru/ *m* foal

pouco /'poku/ *a & pron* little; *pl* few ▫ *adv* not much ▫ *m* **um ~** a little; **~ a ~** little by little; **aos ~s** gradually; **daqui a ~** shortly; **por ~** almost; **~ tempo** a short time

pou|pança /po'pãsa/ *f* saving; (*conta*) savings account; **~par** *vt* save; spare <*vida*>

pouquinho /po'kiɲu/ *m* **um ~ (de)** a little

pou|sada /po'zada/ *f* inn; **~sar** *vi* land; **~so** *m* landing

po|vão /po'vãw/ *m* common people; **~vo** /o/ *m* people

povo|ação /povoa'sãw/ *f* settlement; **~ar** *vt* populate

poxa /'poʃa/ *int* gosh

pra /pra/ *prep* (*fam*) *veja* **para**

praça /'prasa/ *f* (*largo*) square; (*mercado*) market ▫ *m* (*soldado*) private

prado /'pradu/ *m* meadow

pra-frente /pra'frẽtʃi/ *a invar* (*fam*) with it, modern

praga /'praga/ *f* curse; (*inseto, doença, pessoa*) pest

prag|mático /prag'matʃiku/ *a* pragmatic; **~matismo** *m* pragmatism

praguejar /prage'ʒar/ *vt/i* curse

praia /'praja/ *f* beach

pran|cha /'prãʃa/ *f* plank; (*de surfe*) board; **~cheta** /e/ *f* drawing board

pranto /'prãtu/ *m* weeping

pra|ta /'prata/ *f* silver; **~taria** *f* (*coisas de prata*) silverware; **~teado** *a* silver-plated; (*cor*) silver

prateleira /prate'lera/ *f* shelf

prática /'pratʃika/ *f* practice; **na ~** in practice

prati|cante /pratʃi'kãtʃi/ *a* practising □ *m/f* apprentice; (*de esporte etc*) player; **~car** *vt* practise; (*cometer, executar*) carry out □ *vi* practise; **~cável** (*pl* **~cáveis**) *a* practicable

prático /'pratʃiku/ *a* practical

prato /'pratu/ *m* (*objeto*) plate; (*comida*) dish; (*parte de uma refeição*) course; (*do toca-discos*) turntable; *pl* (*instrumento*) cymbals; **~ fundo** dish; **~ principal** main course

praxe /'praʃi/ *f* normal practice; **de ~** usually

prazer /pra'zer/ *m* pleasure; **muito ~ (em conhecê-lo)** pleased to meet you; **~oso** /o/ *a* pleasurable

prazo /'prazu/ *m* term, time; **a ~** <*compra etc*> on credit; **a curto/longo ~** in the short/long term; **último ~** deadline

preâmbulo /pri'ãbulu/ *m* preamble

precário /pre'kariu/ *a* precarious

precaução /prekaw'sãw/ *f* precaution

preca|ver-se /preka'versi/ *vpr* take precautions (**de** against); **~vido** *a* cautious

prece /'prɛsi/ *f* prayer

prece|dência /prese'dẽsia/ *f* precedence; **~dente** *a* preceding □ *m* precedent; **~der** *vt/i* precede

preceito /pre'sejtu/ *m* precept

precioso /presi'ozu/ *a* precious

precipício /presi'pisiu/ *m* precipice

precipi|tação /presipita'sãw/ *f* haste; (*chuva etc*) precipitation; **~tado** *a* <*fuga*> headlong; <*decisão, ato*> hasty, rash; **~tar** *vt* (*lançar*) throw; (*antecipar*) hasten; **~tar-se** *vpr* (*lançar-se*) throw o.s.; (*apressar-se*) rush; (*agir sem pensar*) act rashly

precisão /presi'zãw/ *f* precision, accuracy

precisamente /presiza'mẽtʃi/ *adv* precisely

preci|sar /presi'zar/ *vt* (*necessitar*) need; (*indicar com exatidão*) specify □ *vi* be necessary; **~sar de** need; **~so ir** I have to go; **~sa-se** wanted; **~so** *a* (*exato*) precise; (*necessário*) necessary

preço /'presu/ *m* price; **~ de custo** cost price; **~ fixo** set price

precoce /pre'kɔsi/ *a* <*fruto*> early; <*velhice, calvície etc*> premature; <*criança*> precocious

precon|cebido /prekõse'bidu/ *a* preconceived; **~ceito** *m* prejudice; **~ceituoso** *a* prejudiced

preconizar /prekoni'zar/ *vt* advocate

precursor /prekur'sor/ *m* forerunner

preda|dor /preda'dor/ *m* predator; **~tório** *a* predatory

predecessor /predese'sor/ *m* predecessor

predestinar /predestʃi'nar/ *vt* predestine

predeterminar /predetermi'nar/ *vt* predetermine

predição /predʒi'sãw/ *f* prediction

predile|ção /predʒile'sãw/ *f* preference; **~to** /ɛ/ *a* favourite

prédio /'prɛdʒiu/ *m* building

predis|por /predʒis'por/ *vt* prepare (**para** for); (*tornar parcial*) prejudice (**contra** against); **~por-se** *vpr* prepare o.s.; **~posto** *a* predisposed; (*contra*) prejudiced

predizer /predʒi'zer/ *vt* predict, foretell

predomi|nância /predomi'nãsia/ *f* predominance; **~nante** *a* predominant; **~nar** *vi* predominate

predomínio /predo'miniu/ *m* predominance

preencher /priẽ'ʃer/ *vt* fill; fill in, (*Amer*) fill out <*formulário*>; meet <*requisitos*>

pré|-escola /prɛis'kɔla/ *f* infant school, (*Amer*) preschool; **~-escolar** *a* pre-school; **~-estréia** *f* preview; **~-fabricado** *a* prefabricated

prefácio /pre'fasiu/ *m* preface

prefei|to /pre'fejtu/ *m* mayor; **~tura** *f* prefecture; (*prédio*) town hall

prefe|rência /prefe'rẽsia/ *f* preference; (*direito no trânsito*) right of way; **de ~rência** preferably; **~rencial** (*pl* **~renciais**) *a* preferential; <*rua*> main; **~-rido** *a* favourite; **~rir** *vt* prefer (**a** to); **~rível** (*pl* **~ríveis**) *a* preferable

prefixo /pre'fiksu/ *m* prefix

prega /'prɛga/ *f* pleat

pregador[1] /prega'dor/ *m* (*de roupa*) peg

pre|gador[2] /prega'dor/ *m* (*quem prega*) preacher; **~gão** *m* (*de vendedor*) cry; **o ~gão** (*na bolsa de valores*) trading; (*em leilão*) bidding

pregar[1] /pre'gar/ *vt* fix; (*com prego*) nail; sew on <*botão*>; **não ~ olho** not sleep a wink; **~ uma peça em** play a trick on; **~ um susto em alg** give s.o. a fright

pregar[2] /pre'gar/ *vt/i* preach

prego /'prɛgu/ *m* nail

pregui|ça /pre'gisa/ *f* laziness; (*bicho*) sloth; **estou com ~ça de ir** I can't be bothered to go; **~çoso** *a* lazy

pré-histórico /prɛjs'tɔriku/ *a* prehistoric

preia-mar /preja'mar/ *f* high tide

prejudi|car /preʒudʒi'kar/ *vt* harm; damage <*saúde*>; **~car-se** *vpr* harm o.s.; **~cial** (*pl* **~ciais**) *a* harmful, damaging (**a** to)

prejuízo /preʒu'izu/ *m* damage; (*financeiro*) loss; **em ~ de** to the detriment of

prejulgar /preʒuw'gar/ *vt* prejudge

preliminar /prelimi'nar/ *a* & *m/f* preliminary

prelo /'prɛlu/ *m* printing press; **no ~** being printed

prelúdio /pre'ludʒiu/ *m* prelude

prematuro /prema'turu/ *a* premature

premeditar /premedʒi'tar/ *vt* premeditate

premente /pre'mẽtʃi/ *a* pressing

premi|ado /premi'adu/ *a* <*romance, atleta etc*> prize-winning; <*bilhete, número etc*> winning □ *m* prize-winner; **~ar** *vt* award a prize to <*romance, atleta etc*>; reward <*honestidade, mérito*>

prêmio /'premiu/ *m* prize; (*de seguro*) premium; **Grande Prêmio** (*de F1*) Grand Prix

premissa /pre'misa/ *f* premiss

premonição /premoni'sãw/ *f* premonition

pré-na|tal /prɛna'taw/ (*pl* **~tais**) *a* antenatal, (*Amer*) prenatal

prenda /'prẽda/ *f* (*Port*) present; **~s domésticas** household chores; **~do** *a* domesticated

pren|dedor /prẽde'dor/ *m* clip; **~dedor de roupa** clothes peg; **~der** *vt* (*pregar*) fix; (*capturar*) arrest; (*atar*) tie up <*cachorro*>; tie back <*cabelo*>; (*restringir*) restrict; (*ligar afetivamente*) bind; **~der (a atenção de) alg** grab s.o.('s attention)

prenhe /'preɲi/ *a* pregnant

prenome /pre'nomi/ *m* first name

pren|sa /'prẽsa/ *f* press; **~sar** *vt* press

preocu|pação /preokupa'sãw/ *f* concern; **~pante** *a* worrying; **~par** *vt* worry; **~par-se** *vpr* worry (**com** about)

prepa|ração /prepara'sãw/ *f* preparation; **~rado** *m* preparation; **~rar** *vt* prepare; **~rar-se** *vpr* prepare, get ready; **~rativos** *m pl* preparations; **~ro** *m* preparation; (*competência*) knowledge; **~ro físico** physical fitness

preponderar /prepõde'rar/ *vi* prevail (**sobre** over)

preposição /prepozi'sãw/ *f* preposition

prerrogativa /prexoga'tʃiva/ *f* prerogative

presa /'preza/ *f* (*de caça*) prey; (*de cobra*) fang; (*de elefante*) tusk; **~ de guerra** spoils of war

prescin|dir /presĩ'dʒir/ *vi* **~dir de** dispense with; **~dível** (*pl* **~díveis**) *a* dispensable

pres|crever /preskre'ver/ *vt* prescribe; **~crição** *f* prescription; (*norma*) rule

presen|ça /pre'zẽsa/ *f* presence; **~ça de espírito** presence of mind; **~ciar** *vt* (*estar presente a*) be present at; (*testemunhar*) witness; **~te** *a* & *m* present; **~tear** *vt* **~tear alg (com aco)** give s.o. (sth as) a present

presépio /pre'zɛpiu/ *m* crib

preser|vação /prezerva'sãw/ *f* preservation; **~var** *vt* preserve, protect; **~vativo** *m* (*em comida*) preservative; (*camisinha*) condom

presi|dência /prezi'dẽsia/ *f* presidency; (*de uma reunião*) chair; **~dencial** (*pl* **~denciais**) *a* presidential; **~dencialismo** *m* presidential system; **~dente** *m* (*f* **~denta**) president; (*de uma reunião*) chairperson

presidiário /prezidʒi'ariu/ *m* convict

presídio /pre'zidʒiu/ *m* prison

presidir /prezi'dʒir/ *vi* preside (**a** over)

presilha /pre'ziʎa/ *f* fastener; (*de cabelo*) slide

preso /'prezu/ *pp de* **prender** □ *m* prisoner; **ficar ~** get stuck; <*saia, corda etc*> get caught

pressa /'prɛsa/ *f* hurry; **às ~s** in a hurry, hurriedly; **estar com** *ou* **ter ~** be in a hurry

presságio /pre'saʒiu/ *m* omen

pressão /pre'sãw/ *f* pressure; **fazer ~ sobre** put pressure on; **~ arterial** blood pressure

pressen|timento /presẽtʃi'mẽtu/ *m* premonition, feeling; **~tir** *vt* sense

pressionar /presio'nar/ *vt* press <*botão*>; pressure <*pessoa*>

pressupor /presu'por/ *vt* <*pessoa*> presume; <*coisa*> presuppose

pressurizado /presuri'zadu/ *a* pressurized

pres|tação /presta'sãw/ *f* repayment, instalment; **~tar** *vt* render <*contas, serviço*> □ *vi* be of use; **não ~ta** he/it is no good; **~tar atenção** pay attention; **~tar juramento** take an oath; **~tativo** *a* helpful; **~tável** (*pl* **~táveis**) *a* serviceable

prestes /'prɛstʃis/ *a invar* **~ a** about to

prestidigita|ção /prestʃidʒiʒita-'sãw/ *f* conjuring; **~dor** *m* conjurer

pres|tigiar /prestʃiʒi'ar/ *vt* give prestige to; **~tígio** *m* prestige; **~tigioso** /o/ *a* prestigious

préstimo /'prɛstʃimu/ *m* merit

presumir /prezu'mir/ *vt* presume

presun|ção /prezũ'sãw/ *f* presumption; **~çoso** /o/ *a* presumptuous

presunto /pre'zũtu/ *m* ham

pretendente /pretẽ'dẽtʃi/ *m/f* (*candidato*) candidate, applicant

preten|der /pretẽ'der/ *vt* intend; **~são** *f* pretension; **~sioso** /o/ *a* pretentious

preterir /prete'rir/ *vt* disregard

pretérito /pre'tɛritu/ *m* preterite

pretexto /pre'testu/ *m* pretext

preto /'pretu/ *a & m* black; **~-e-branco** *a invar* black and white

prevalecer /prevale'ser/ *vi* prevail

prevenção /prevẽ'sãw/ *f* (*impedimento*) prevention; (*parcialidade*) bias

prevenir /preve'nir/ *vt* (*evitar*) prevent; (*avisar*) warn; **~-se** *vpr* take precautions

preventivo /prevẽ'tʃivu/ *a* preventive

prever /pre'ver/ *vt* foresee, predict

previdência /previ'dẽsia/ *f* foresight; **~ social** social security

prévio /'prɛviu/ *a* prior

previ|são /previ'zãw/ *f* prediction, forecast; **~são do tempo** weather forecast; **~sível** (*pl* **~ síveis**) *a* predictable

pre|zado /pre'zadu/ *a* esteemed; **Prezado Senhor** Dear Sir; **~zar** *vt* think highly of; **~zar-se** *vpr* have self-respect

prima /'prima/ *f* cousin

primário /pri'mariu/ *a* primary; (*fundamental*) basic

primata /pri'mata/ *m* primate

primave|ra /prima'vɛra/ *f* spring; (*flor*) primrose; **~ril** (*pl* **~ris**) *a* spring

primazia /prima'zia/ *f* primacy

primei|ra /pri'mera/ *f* (*marcha*) first (gear); **de ~ra** first-rate; <*carne*> prime; **~ra-dama** (*pl* **~ras-damas**) *f* first lady; **~ranista** *m/f* first-year (student); **~ro** *a & adv* first; **no dia ~ro de maio** on the first of May; **em ~ro lugar** (*para começar*) in the first place; (*numa corrida, competição*) in first place; **~ro de tudo** first of all; **~ros socorros** first aid; **~ro-ministro** (*pl* **~ros-ministros**) *m* (*f* **~ra-ministra**) prime-minister

primitivo /primi'tʃivu/ *a* primitive

primo /'primu/ *m* cousin □ *a* **número ~** prime number; **~gênito** *a & m* first-born

primor /pri'mor/ *m* perfection

primordi|al /primordʒi'aw/ (*pl* **~ais**) *a* (*primitivo*) primordial; (*fundamental*) fundamental

primoroso /primo'rozu/ *a* exquisite

princesa /prĩ'seza/ *f* princess

princi|pado /prĩsipi'adu/ *m* principality; **~pal** (*pl* **~pais**) *a* main □ *m* principal

príncipe /'prĩsipi/ *m* prince

principiante /prĩsipi'ãtʃi/ *m/f* beginner

princípio /prĩ'sipiu/ *m* (*início*) beginning; (*regra*) principle; **em ~** in principle; **por ~** on principle

priori|dade /priori'dadʒi/ *f* priority; **~tário** *a* priority

prisão /pri'zãw/ *f* (*ato de prender*) arrest; (*cadeia*) prison; (*encarceramento*) imprisonment; **~ perpétua** life imprisonment; **~ de ventre** constipation

prisioneiro /prizio'neru/ *m* prisoner

prisma /'prizma/ *m* prism

privação /priva'sãw/ *f* deprivation

privacidade /privasi'dadʒi/ *f* privacy

pri|vada /pri'vada/ *f* toilet; **~vado** *a* private; **~vado de** deprived of; **~var** *vt* deprive (**de** of); **~var-se** *vpr* deprive o.s. (**de** of)

privati|vo /priva'tʃivu/ *a* private; **~zar** *vt* privatize

privi|legiado /privileʒi'adu/ *a* privileged; <*tratamento*> preferential; **~legiar** *vt* favour; **~-légio** *m* privilege

pro (*fam*) = **para + o**

pró /prɔ/ *adv* for □ *m* **os ~s e os contras** the pros and cons

proa /'proa/ *f* bow, prow

probabilidade /probabili'dadʒi/ *f* probability

proble|ma /pro'blema/ *m* problem; **~mático** *a* problematic

proce|dência /prose'dẽsia/ *f* origin; **~dente** *a* logical; **~dente de** coming from; **~der** *vi* proceed; (*comportar-se*) behave; (*na justiça*) take legal action; **~der de** come from; **~dimento** *m* procedure; (*comportamento*) behaviour; (*na justiça*) proceedings

proces|sador /prosesa'dor/ *m* processor; **~sador de texto** word processor; **~samento** *m* processing; (*na justiça*) prosecution; **~samento de dados** data processing; **~sar** *vt* process; (*por crime*) prosecute; (*por causa civil*) sue; **~so** /ɛ/ *m* process; (*criminal*) trial; (*civil*) lawsuit

procla|mação /proklama'sãw/ *f* proclamation; **~mar** *vt* proclaim

procri|ação /prokria'sãw/ *f* procreation; **~ar** *vt/i* procreate

procu|ra /pro'kura/ *f* search; (*de produto*) demand; **à ~ra de** in search of; **~ração** *f* power of attorney; **~rado** *a* sought after, in demand; **~rado pela polícia** wanted by the police; **~rador** *m* (*mandatário*) proxy; (*advogado*) public prosecutor; **~rar** *vt* look for; (*contatar*) get in touch with; (*ir visitar*) look up; **~rar saber** try to find out

prodígio /pro'dʒiʒiu/ *m* wonder; (*pessoa*) prodigy

prodigioso /prodʒiʒi'ozu/ *a* prodigious

pródigo /'prɔdigu/ *a* lavish, extravagant

produ|ção /produ'sãw/ *f* production; **~tividade** *f* productivity; **~tivo** *a* productive; **~to** *m* product; (*renda*) proceeds; **~to nacional bruto** gross national product; **~tos agrícolas** agricultural produce; **~tor** *m* producer □ *a* **país ~tor de trigo** wheat-producing country; **~zido** *a* (*fam: arrumado*) done up; **~zir** *vt* produce

proeminente /proemi'nẽtʃi/ *a* prominent

proeza /pro'eza/ *f* achievement

profa|nar /profa'nar/ *vt* desecrate; **~no** *a* profane

profecia /profe'sia/ *f* prophecy

proferir /profe'rir/ *vt* utter; give <*discurso, palestra*>; pass <*sentença*>

profes|sar /profe'sar/ *vt* profess; **~so** /ɛ/ *a* professed; <*político etc*> seasoned; **~sor** *m* teacher; **~sor catedrático** professor

pro|feta /pro'fɛta/ *m* prophet; **~fético** *a* prophetic; **~fetizar** *vt* prophesy

profissão /profi'sãw/ *f* profession

profissio|nal /profisio'naw/ (*pl* **~nais**) *a* & *m*/*f* professional; **~nalismo** *m* professionalism; **~nalizante** *a* vocational; **~nalizar-se** *vpr* <*esportista etc*> turn professional

profun|didade /profũdʒi'dadʒi/ *f* depth; **~do** *a* deep; <*sentimento etc*> profound

profusão /profu'zãw/ *f* profusion

prog|nosticar /prognostʃi'kar/ *vt* forecast; **~nóstico** *m* forecast; (*med*) prognosis

progra|ma /pro'grama/ *m* programme; (*de computador*) program; (*diversão*) thing to do; **~mação** *f* programming; **~mador** *m* programmer; **~mar** *vt* plan; program <*computador etc*>; **~mável** (*pl* **~máveis**) *a* programmable

progredir /progre'dʒir/ *vi* progress

progres|são /progre'sãw/ *f* progression; **~sista** *a* & *m*/*f* progressive; **~sivo** *a* progressive; **~so** /ɛ/ *m* progress

proi|bição /proibi'sãw/ *f* ban (**de** on); **~bido** *a* forbidden; **~bir** *vt* forbid (**alg de** s.o. to); ban <*livro, importações etc*>; **~bitivo** *a* prohibitive

proje|ção /proʒe'sãw/ *f* projection; **~tar** *vt* plan <*viagem, estrada etc*>; design <*casa, carro etc*>; project <*filme, luz*>

proje|til /pro'ʒɛtʃiw/ (*pl* **~teis**) *m* projectile

proje|tista /proʒe'tʃista/ *m*/*f* designer; **~to** /ɛ/ *m* project; (*de casa, carro*) design; **~to de lei** bill; **~tor** *m* projector

prol /prɔw/ *m* **em ~ de** on behalf of

prole /'prɔli/ *f* offspring; **~tariado** *m* proletariat; **~tário** *a* & *m* proletarian

prolife|ração /prolifera'sãw/ *f* proliferation; **~rar** *vi* proliferate

prolífico /pro'lifiku/ *a* prolific

prolixo /pro'liksu/ *a* verbose, long-winded

prólogo /'prɔlogu/ *m* prologue

prolon|gado /prolõ'gadu/ *a* prolonged; **~gar** *vt* prolong; **~-gar-se** *vpr* go on

promessa /pro'mɛsa/ *f* promise

prome|tedor /promete'dor/ *a* promising; **~ter** *vt* promise □ *vi* (*dar esperança*) show promise; **~ter voltar** promise to return

promíscuo /pro'miskuu/ *a* promiscuous

promis|sor /promi'sor/ *a* promising; **~sória** *f* promissory note

promoção /promo'sãw/ *f* promotion

promontório /promõ'tɔriu/ *m* promontory

promo|tor /promo'tor/ *m* promoter; (*advogado*) prosecutor; **~ver** *vt* promote

promulgar /promuw'gar/ *vt* promulgate

prono|me /pro'nomi/ *m* pronoun; **~minal** (*pl* **~minais**) *a* pronominal

pron|tidão /prõtʃi'dãw/ *f* readiness; **com ~tidão** promptly; **estar de ~tidão** be at the ready; **~tificar** *vt* get ready; **~tificar-se** *vpr* volunteer (**a** to; **para** for); **~to** *a* ready; (*rápido*) prompt □ *int* that's that; **~to-socorro** (*pl* **~tos-socorros**) *m* casualty department; (*Port: reboque*) towtruck; **~tuário** *m* (*manual*) manual, handbook; (*médico*) notes; (*policial*) record, file

pronúncia /pro'nũsia/ *f* pronunciation

pronunci|ado /pronũsi'adu/ *a* pronounced; **~amento** *m* pronouncement; **~ar** *vt* pronounce

propagar /propa'gar/ *vt* propagate <*espécie*>; spread <*notícia, idéia, fé*>; **~-se** *vpr* spread; <*espécie*> propagate

propen|são /propẽ'sãw/ *f* propensity; **~so** *a* inclined (**a** to)

pro|piciar /propisi'ar/ *vt* provide; **~pício** *a* propitious

propina /pro'pina/ *f* bribe; (*Port: escolar*) fee

propor /pro'por/ *vt* propose; **~-se** *vpr* set o.s. <*objetivo*>; **~-se a estudar** set out to study

proporção /propor'sãw/ *f* proportion

proporcio|nado /proporsio'nadu/ *a* proportionate (**a** to); **bem ~nado** well proportioned; **~nal** (*pl* **~nais**) *a* proportional; **~nar** *vt* provide

proposi|ção /propozi'sãw/ *f* proposition; **~tado** *a*, **~tal** (*pl* **~tais**) *a* intentional

propósito /pro'pɔzitu/ *m* intention; **a ~** by the way; **a ~ de** on the subject of; **chegar a ~** arrive at the right time; **de ~** on purpose

proposta /pro'pɔsta/ *f* proposal

propriamente /propria'mẽtʃi/ *adv* strictly; **a casa ~ dita** the house proper

proprie|dade /proprie'dadʒi/ *f* property; (*direito sobre bens*) ownership; **~tário** *m* owner; (*de casa alugada*) landlord

próprio /'prɔpriu/ *a* (*de si*) own; <*sentido*> literal; <*nome*> proper; **meu ~ carro** my own car; **um carro ~** a car of my own; **o ~ rei** the king himself; **~** a peculiar to; **~ para** suited to

prorro|gação /proxoga'sãw/ *f* extension; (*de dívida*) deferment; (*em futebol etc*) extra time; **~gar** *vt* extend <*prazo*>; defer <*pagamento*>

pro|sa /'prɔza/ *f* prose; **~sador** *m* prose writer; **~saico** *a* prosaic

proscrever /proskre'ver/ *vt* proscribe

prospecto /pros'pɛktu/ *m* (*livro*) brochure; (*folheto*) leaflet

prospe|rar /prospe'rar/ *vi* prosper; **~ridade** *f* prosperity

próspero /'prɔsperu/ *a* prosperous

prosse|guimento /prosegi'mẽtu/ *m* continuation; **~guir** *vt* continue □ *vi* proceed, go on

prostitu|ição /prostʃitui'sãw/ *f* prostitution; **~ta** *f* prostitute

pros|tração /prostra'sãw/ *f* debility; **~trado** *a* prostrate; **~-trar** *vt* prostrate; (*enfraquecer*) debilitate; **~trar-se** *vpr* prostrate o.s.

protago|nista /protago'nista/ *m/f* protagonist; **~nizar** *vt* be at the centre of <*acontecimento*>; feature in <*peça, filme*>

prote|ção /prote'sãw/ *f* protection; **~cionismo** *m* protectionism; **~cionista** *a & m/f* protectionist; **~ger** *vt* protect; **~gido** *m* protégé

proteína /prote'ina/ *f* protein

protelar /prote'lar/ *vt* put off

protes|tante /protes'tãtʃi/ *a & m/f* Protestant; **~tar** *vt/i* protest; **~to** /ɛ/ *m* protest

protetor /prote'tor/ *m* protector □ *a* protective

protocolo /proto'kɔlu/ *m* protocol; (*registro*) register

protótipo /pro'tɔtʃipu/ *m* prototype

protuberância /protube'rãsia/ *f* bulge

pro|va /'prɔva/ *f* (*que comprova*) proof; (*teste*) trial; (*exame*) exam; (*esportiva*) competition; (*de livro etc*) proof; *pl* (*na justiça*) evidence; **à ~va de bala** bulletproof; **pôr à ~va** put to the test; **~vado** *a* proven; **~var** *vt* try <*comida*>; try on <*roupa*>; try out <*carro, novo sistema etc*>; (*comprovar*) prove

prová|vel /pro'vavew/ (*pl* **~veis**) *a* probable

proveito /pro'vejtu/ *m* profit, advantage; **tirar ~ de** (*beneficiar-se*) profit from; (*explorar*) take advantage of; **~so** /o/ *a* useful

proveni|ência /proveni'ẽsia/ *f* origin; **~ente** *a* originating (**de** from)

proventos /pro'vẽtus/ *m pl* proceeds

prover /pro'ver/ *vt* provide (**de** with)

provérbio /pro'vɛrbiu/ *m* proverb

proveta /pro'veta/ *f* test tube; **bebê de ~** test-tube baby

provi|dência /provi'dẽsia/ *f* (*medida*) measure, step; (*divina*) providence; **tomar ~dências** take steps, take action; **~denciar** *vt* (*prover*) get hold of, provide; (*resolver*) see to, take care of □ *vi* take action

província /pro'vĩsia/ *f* province; (*longe da cidade*) provinces

provinci|al /provĩsi'aw/ (*pl* **~ais**) *a* provincial; **~ano** *a & m* provincial

provir /pro'vir/ *vi* come (**de** from); (*resultar*) be due (**de** to)

provi|são /provi'zãw/ *f* provision; **~sório** *a* provisional

provo|cação /provoka'sãw/ *f* provocation; **~cador, ~cante** *a* provocative; **~car** *vt* provoke; (*ocasionar*) cause

proximidade /prosimi'dadʒi/ *f* closeness; *pl* (*imediações*) vicinity

próximo /'prɔsimo/ *a* (*no tempo*) next; (*perto*) near, close (**de** to); <*parente*> close; <*futuro*> near □ *m* neighbour, fellow man

pru|dência /pru'dẽsia/ *f* prudence; **~dente** *a* prudent

prumo /'prumu/ *m* plumb line; **a ~** vertically

prurido /pru'ridu/ *m* itch

pseudônimo /pisew'donimu/ *m* pseudonym

psica|nálise /pisika'nalizi/ *f* psychoanalysis; **~nalista** *m/f* psychoanalyst

psi|cologia /pisikolo'ʒia/ *f* psychology; **~cológico** *a* psychological; **~cólogo** *m* psychologist

psico|pata /pisiko'pata/ *m/f* psychopath; **~se** /ɔ/ *f* psychosis; **~terapeuta** *m/f* psychotherapist; **~terapia** *f* psychotherapy

psicótico /pisi'kɔtʃiku/ *a & m* psychotic

psique /pi'siki/ *f* psyche

psiqui|atra /pisiki'atra/ *m/f* psychiatrist; **~atria** *f* psychiatry; **~átrico** *a* psychiatric

psíquico /pi'sikiku/ *a* psychological

pua /'pua/ *f* bit

puberdade /puber'dadʒi/ *f* puberty

publi|cação /publika'sãw/ *f* publication; **~car** *vt* publish

publici|dade /publisi'dadʒi/ *f* publicity; (*reclame*) advertising; **~tário** *a* publicity; (*de reclame*) advertising □ *m* advertising executive

público /'publiku/ *a* public □ *m* public; (*platéia*) audience; **em ~** in public; **o grande ~** the general public

pudera /pu'dɛra/ *int* no wonder!

pudico /pu'dʒiku/ *a* prudish

pudim /pu'dʒĩ/ *m* pudding

pudor /pu'dor/ *m* modesty, shame

pue|ril /pue'riw/ (*pl* **~ris**) *a* puerile

pugilis|mo /puʒi'lizmu/ *m* boxing; **~ta** *m* boxer

pu|ído /pu'idu/ *a* worn through; **~ir** *vt* wear through

pujan|ça /pu'ʒãsa/ *f* power; **~te** *a* powerful; (*de saúde*) robust

pular /pu'lar/ *vt* jump (over); (*omitir*) skip □ *vi* jump; **~ de contente** jump for joy; **~ carnaval** celebrate Carnival; **~ corda** skip

pulga /'puwga/ *f* flea

pulmão /puw'mãw/ *m* lung

pulo /'pulu/ *m* jump; **dar um ~ em** drop by; **dar ~s** jump up and down

pulôver /pu'lover/ *m* pullover

púlpito /'puwpitu/ *m* pulpit

pul|sar /puw'sar/ *vi* pulsate; **~seira** *f* bracelet; **~so** *m* (*do braço*) wrist; (*batimento arterial*) pulse

pulular /pulu'lar/ *vi* swarm (**de** with)

pulveri|zador /puwveriza'dor/ *m* spray; **~zar** *vt* spray <*líquido*>; (*reduzir a pó, fig*) pulverize

pun|gente /pũ'ʒẽtʃi/ *a* consuming; **~gir** *vt* afflict

pu|nhado /pu'ɲadu/ *m* handful; **~nhal** (*pl* **~nhais**) *m* dagger; **~nhalada** *f* stab wound; **~nho** *m* fist; (*de camisa etc*) cuff; (*de espada*) hilt

pu|nição /puni'sãw/ *f* punishment; **~nir** *vt* punish; **~nitivo** *a* punitive

pupila /pu'pila/ *f* pupil

purê /pu're/ *m* purée; **~ de batata** mashed potato

pureza /pu'reza/ *f* purity

pur|gante /pur'gãtʃi/ *a & m* purgative; **~gar** *vt* purge; **~- gatório** *m* purgatory

purificar /purifi'kar/ *vt* purify

puritano /puri'tanu/ *a & m* puritan

puro /'puru/ *a* pure; <*aguardente*> neat; **~ e simples** pure and simple; **~-sangue** (*pl* **~s-sangues**) *a & m* thoroughbred

púrpura /'purpura/ *a* purple

purpurina /purpu'rina/ *f* glitter

purulento /puru'lẽtu/ *a* festering

pus /pus/ *m* pus

pusilânime /puzi'lanimi/ *a* faint-hearted

pústula /'pustula/ *f* pimple

puta /'puta/ *f* whore □ *a invar* (*fam*) **um ~ carro** one hell of a car; **filho da ~** (*chulo*) bastard; **~ que (o) pariu!** (*chulo*) fucking hell!

puto /'putu/ *a* (*fam*) furious

putrefazer /putrefa'zer/ *vi* putrefy

puxa /'puʃa/ *int* gosh

pu|xado /pu'ʃadu/ *a* (*fam*) <*exame*> tough; <*trabalho*> hard; <*aluguel, preço*> steep; **~xador** *m* handle; **~xão** *m* pull, tug; **~xa-puxa** *m* toffee; **~xar** *vt* pull; strike up <*conversa*>; bring up <*assunto*>; **~xar de uma perna** limp; **~xar para** (*parecer com*) take after; **~xar por** (*exigir muito de*) push (hard); **~xa-saco** *m* (*fam*) creep

Qq

QI /ke i/ *m* IQ

quadra /'kwadra/ *f* (*de tênis etc*) court; (*quarteirão*) block; **~do** *a & m* square

quadragésimo /kwadra'ʒɛzimu/ *a* fortieth

qua|dril /kwa'driw/ (*pl* **~dris**) *m* hip

quadrilha /kwa'driʎa/ *f* (*bando*) gang; (*dança*) square dance

quadrinho /kwa'driɲu/ *m* frame; **história em ~s** comic strip

quadro /'kwadru/ *m* picture; (*pintado*) painting; (*tabela*) table; (*pessoal*) staff;

(*equipe*) team; (*de uma peça*) scene; **~-negro** (*pl* **~s-negros**) *m* blackboard

quadruplicar /kwadrupli'kar/ *vt/i* quadruple

quádruplo /'kwadruplu/ *a* quadruple; **~s** *m pl* (*crianças*) quads

qual /kwaw/ (*pl* **quais**) *pron* which (one); **o/a ~** (*coisa*) that, which; (*pessoa*) that, who; **~ é o seu nome?** what's your name?; **seja ~ for a decisão** whatever the decision may be

qualidade /kwali'dadʒi/ *f* quality; **na ~ de** in one's capacity as, as

qualifi|cação /kwalifika'sãw/ *f* qualification; **~car** *vt* qualify; (*descrever*) describe (**de** as); **~car-se** *vpr* qualify

qualitativo /kwalita'tʃivu/ *a* qualitative

qualquer /kwaw'kɛr/ (*pl* **quaisquer**) *a* any; **um livro ~** any old book; **~ um** any one

quando /'kwãdu/ *adv & conj* when; **~ quer que** whenever; **~ de** at the time of; **~ muito** at most

quantia /kwã'tʃia/ *f* amount

quanti|dade /kwãtʃi'dadʒi/ *f* quantity; **uma ~dade de** a lot of; **em ~dade** in large amounts; **~ficar** *vt* quantify; **~tativo** *a* quantitative

quanto /'kwãtu/ *adv & pron* how much; *pl* how many; **~ tempo?** how long?; **~ mais barato melhor** the cheaper the better; **tão alto ~ eu** as tall as me; **~ ri!** how I laughed!; **~ a** as for; **~ antes** as soon as possible

quaren|ta /kwa'rẽta/ *a & m* forty; **~tão** *a & m* (*f* **~tona**) forty-year-old; **~tena** /e/ *f* quarantine

quaresma /kwa'rɛzma/ *f* Lent

quarta /'kwarta/ *f* (*dia*) Wednesday; (*marcha*) fourth (gear); **~-de-final** (*pl* **~s-de-final**) *f* quarter final; **~-feira** (*pl* **~s-feiras**) *f* Wednesday

quartanista /kwarta'nista/ *m/f* fourth-year (student)

quarteirão /kwarte'rãw/ *m* block

quar|tel /kwar'tɛw/ (*pl* **~téis**) *m* barracks; **~tel-general** (*pl* **~téis-generais**) *m* headquarters

quarteto /kwar'tetu/ *m* quartet; **~ de cordas** string quartet

quarto /'kwartu/ *a* fourth □ *m* (*parte*) quarter; (*aposento*) bedroom; (*guarda*) watch; **são três e/menos um ~** (*Port*) it's quarter past/to three; **~ de banho** (*Port*) bathroom; **~ de hora** quarter of an hour; **~ de hóspedes** guest room

quartzo /'kwartzu/ *m* quartz

quase /'kwazi/ *adv* almost, nearly; **~ nada/nunca** hardly anything/ever

quatro /'kwatru/ *a & m* four; **de ~** (*no chão*) on all fours; **~-centos** *a & m* four hundred

que /ki/ *a* which, what; **~ dia é hoje?** what's the date today?; **~ homem!** what a man!; **~ triste!** how sad! □ *pron* what; **~ é ~ é?** what is it? □ *pron rel* (*coisa*) which, that; (*pessoa*) who, that; (*interrogativo*) what; **o dia em ~ ...** the day when/that ... □ *conj* that; (*porque*) because; **espero ~ sim/não** I hope so/not

quê /ke/ *pron* what □ *m* **um ~** something; **não tem de ~** don't mention it

quebra /'kɛbra/ *f* break; (*de empresa, banco*) crash; (*de força*) cut; **de ~** in addition; **~-cabeça** *m* jigsaw (puzzle); (*fig*) puzzle; **~diço** *a* breakable; **~do** *a* broken; <*carro*> broken down; **~dos** *m pl* small change; **~-galho** (*fam*) *m* stopgap; **~-mar** *m* breakwater; **~-molas** *m invar* speed bump; **~-nozes** *m invar* nutcrackers; **~-pau** (*fam*) *m* row; **~-quebra** *m* riot

quebrar /ke'brar/ *vt* break □ *vi* break; <*carro etc*> break down; <*banco, empresa etc*> crash, go bust; **~-se** *vpr* break

queda /'kɛda/ *f* fall; **ter uma ~ por** have a soft spot for; **~-de-braço** *f* arm wrestling

quei|jeira /ke'ʒera/ *f* cheese dish; **~jo** *m* cheese; **~jo prato** cheddar; **~jo-de-minas** *m* Cheshire cheese

queima /'kejma/ *f* burning; **~da** *f* forest fire; **~do** *a* burnt; (*bronzeado*) tanned, brown; **cheiro de ~do** smell of burning

queimar /kej'mar/ *vt* burn; (*bronzear*) tan □ *vi* burn; <*lâmpada*> go; <*fusível*> blow; **~-se** *vpr* burn o.s.; (*bronzear-se*) go brown

queima-roupa /kejma'xopa/ *f* **à ~** point-blank

quei|xa /'keʃa/ *f* complaint; **~xar-se** *vpr* complain (**de** about)

queixo /'keʃu/ *m* chin; **bater o ~** shiver

queixoso /ke'ʃozu/ *a* plaintive □ *m* plaintiff

quem /kẽj/ *pron* who; (*a pessoa que*) anyone who, he who; **de ~ é este livro?** whose is this book?; **~ quer que** whoever; **seja ~ for** whoever it is; **~ falou isso fui eu** it was me who said that; **~ me dera (que) ...** I wish ..., if only

Quênia /'kenia/ *m* Kenya

queniano /keni'anu/ *a & m* Kenyan

quen|tão /kẽ'tãw/ *m* mulled wine; **~te** *a* hot; (*com calor agradável*) warm; **~tura** *f* heat

quepe /'kɛpi/ *m* cap

quer /kɛr/ *conj* **~ ... ~ ...** whether ... or ...

querer /ke'rer/ *vt/i* want; **quero ir** I want to go; **quero que você vá** I want you to go; **eu queria falar com o Sr X** I'd like to speak to Mr X; **vai ~ vir amanhã?** do you want to come tomorrow?; **vou ~ um cafezinho** I'd like a coffee; **se você quiser** if you want; **queira sentar** do sit down; **~ dizer** mean; **quer dizer** (*isto é*) that is to say, I mean

querido /ke'ridu/ *a* dear □ *m* darling

quermesse /ker'mɛsi/ *f* fête, fair

querosene /kero'zeni/ *m* kerosene

questão /kes'tãw/ *m* question; (*assunto*) matter; **em ~** in question; **fazer ~ de** really want to; **não faço ~ de ir** I don't mind not going

questio|nar /kestʃio'nar/ *vt/i* question; **~nário** *m* questionnaire; **~nável** (*pl* **~náveis**) *a* questionable

quiabo /ki'abu/ *m* okra

quibe /'kibi/ *m* savoury meatball

quicar /ki'kar/ *vt/i* bounce

quiche /'kiʃi/ *f* quiche

quie|to /ki'ɛtu/ *a* (*calado*) quiet; (*imóvel*) still; **~tude** *f* quiet

quilate /ki'latʃi/ *m* carat; (*fig*) calibre

quilha /'kiʎa/ *f* keel

quilo /'kilo/ *m* kilo; **~grama** *m* kilogram; **~metragem** *f* mileage; **~métrico** *a* mile-long

quilômetro /ki'lometru/ *m* kilometre

quimbanda /kĩ'bãda/ *m* Afro-Brazilian cult

qui|mera /ki'mɛra/ *f* fantasy; **~mérico** *a* fanciful

químí|ca /'kimika/ *f* chemistry; **~co** *a* chemical □ *m* chemist

quimioterapia /kimiotera'pia/ *f* chemotherapy

quimono /ki'mɔnu/ *m* kimono

quina /'kina/ *f* **de ~** edgeways

quindim /kĩ'dʒĩ/ *m* sweet made of coconut, sugar and egg yolks

quinhão /ki'ɲãw/ *m* share

quinhentos /ki'ɲẽtus/ *a & m* five hundred

quinina /ki'nina/ *f* quinine

qüinquagésimo /kwĩkwa'ʒɛzimu/ *a* fiftieth

quinquilharias /kĩkiʎa'rias/ *f pl* knick-knacks

quinta[1] /'kĩta/ *f* (*fazenda*) farm

quinta[2] /'kĩta/ *f* (*dia*) Thursday; **~-feira** (*pl* **~s-feiras**) *f* Thursday

quin|tal /kĩ'taw/ (*pl* **~tais**) *m* back yard

quinteiro /kĩ'tajru/ *m* (*Port*) farmer

quinteto /kĩ'tetu/ *m* quintet

quin|to /'kĩtu/ *a & m* fifth; **~tuplo** *a* fivefold; **~tuplos** *m pl* (*crianças*) quins

quinze /'kĩzi/ *a & m* fifteen; **às dez e ~** at quarter past ten; **são ~ para as dez** it's quarter to ten; **~na** /e/ *f* fortnight; **~nal** (*pl* **~nais**) *a* fortnightly; **~nalmente** *adv* fortnightly

quiosque /ki'ɔski/ *m* (*banca*) kiosk; (*no jardim*) gazebo

quiro|mância /kiro'mãsia/ *f* palmistry; **~mante** *m/f* palmist

quisto /'kistu/ *m* cyst

quitan|da /ki'tãda/ *f* grocer's (shop); **~deiro** *m* grocer

qui|tar /ki'tar/ *vt* pay off <*dívida*>; **~te** *a* **estar ~te** be quits

quociente /kwosi'ẽtʃi/ *m* quotient

quórum /'kwɔrũ/ *m* quorum

Rr

rã /xã/ *f* frog

rabanete /xaba'netʃi/ *m* radish

rabear /xabi'ar/ *vi* <*caminhão*> jack-knife

rabino /xa'binu/ *m* rabbi

rabis|car /xabis'kar/ *vt* scribble □ *vi* (*escrever mal*) scribble; (*fazer desenhos*) doodle; **~co** *m* doodle

rabo /'xabu/ *m* (*de animal*) tail; **com o ~ do olho** out of the corner of one's eye; **~-de-cavalo** (*pl* **~s-de-cavalo**) *m* pony tail

rabugento /xabu'ʒẽtu/ *a* grumpy

raça /'xasa/ *f* (*de homens*) race; (*de animais*) breed

ração /xa'sãw/ *f* (*de comida*) ration; (*para animal*) food

racha /'xaʃa/ *f* crack; **~dura** *f* crack

rachar /xa'ʃar/ *vt* (*dividir*) split; (*abrir fendas em*) crack; chop <*lenha*>; split <*despesas*> □ *vi* (*dividir-se*) split; (*apresentar fendas*) crack; (*ao pagar*) split the cost

raci|al /xasi'aw/ (*pl* **~ais**) *a* racial

racio|cinar /xasiosi'nar/ *vi* reason; **~cínio** *m* reasoning; **~nal** (*pl* **~nais**) *a* rational; **~nalizar** *vt* rationalize

racio|namento /xasiona'mẽtu/ *m* rationing; **~nar** *vt* ration

racis|mo /xa'sizmu/ *m* racism; **~ta** *a & m/f* racist

radar /xa'dar/ *m* radar; (*na estrada*) speed camera

radia|ção /xadʒia'sãw/ *f* radiation; **~dor** *m* radiator

radialista /radʒia'lista/ *m/f* radio announcer

radiante /xadʒi'ãtʃi/ *a* (*de alegria*) overjoyed

radi|cal /xadʒi'kaw/ (*pl* **~cais**) *a & m* radical; **~car-se** *vpr* settle

rádio[1] /'xadʒiu/ *m* radio □ *f* radio station

rádio[2] /'xadʒiu/ *m* (*elemento*) radium

radioati|vidade /xadioatʃivi'dadʒi/ *f* radioactivity; **~vo** *a* radioactive

radiodifusão /xadʒiodʒifu'zãw/ *f* broadcasting

radiogra|far /radʒiogra'far/ *vt* X-ray <*pulmões, osso etc*>; radio <*mensagem*>; **~fia** *f* X-ray

radiolo|gia /radʒiolo'ʒia/ *f* radiology; **~gista** *m/f* radiologist

radio|novela /xadʒiono'vɛla/ *f* radio serial; **~patrulha** *f* patrol car; **~táxi** *m* radio taxi; **~terapia** *f* radiotherapy

raia /'xaja/ *f* (*em corrida*) lane; (*peixe*) ray

rainha /xa'iɲa/ *f* queen; **~-mãe** *f* queen mother

raio /'xaju/ *m* (*de luz etc*) ray; (*de círculo*) radius; (*de roda*) spoke; (*relâmpago*) bolt of lightning; **~ de ação** range

rai|va /'xajva/ *f* rage; (*doença*) rabies; **estar com ~va** be furious (**de** with); **ter ~va de alg** have it in for s.o.; **~voso** *a* furious; <*cachorro*> rabid

raiz /xa'iz/ *f* root; **~ quadrada/cúbica** square/cube root

rajada /xa'ʒada/ *f* (*de vento*) gust; (*de tiros*) burst

ra|lador /xala'dor/ *m* grater; **~lar** *vt* grate

ralé /xa'lɛ/ *f* rabble

ralhar /xa'ʎar/ *vi* scold

ralo[1] /'xalu/ *m* (*ralador*) grater; (*de escoamento*) drain

ralo[2] /'xalu/ *a* <*cabelo*> thinning; <*sopa, tecido*> thin; <*vegetação*> sparse; <*café*> weak

ra|mal /xa'maw/ (*pl* **~mais**) *m* (*telefone*) extension; (*de ferrovia*) branch line

ramalhete /xama'ʎetʃi/ *m* posy, bouquet

ramifi|cação /xamifika'sãw/ *f* branch; **~car-se** *vi* branch off

ramo /'xamu/ *m* branch; (*profissional etc*) field; (*buquê*) bunch; **Domingo de Ramos** Palm Sunday

rampa /'xãpa/ *f* ramp

rancor /xã'kor/ *m* resentment; **~oso** /o/ *a* resentful

rançoso /xã'sozu/ *a* rancid

ran|ger /xã'ʒer/ *vt* grind <*dentes*> □ *vi* creak; **~gido** *m* creak

ranhura /xa'ɲura/ *f* groove; (*para moedas*) slot

ranzinza /xã'zĩza/ *a* cantankerous

rapariga /xapa'riga/ *f* (*Port*) girl

rapaz /xa'pas/ *m* boy

rapé /xa'pɛ/ *m* snuff

rapidez /xapi'des/ *f* speed

rápido /'xapidu/ *a* fast □ *adv* <*fazer*> quickly; <*andar*> fast

rapina /xa'pina/ *f* **ave de ~** bird of prey

rapo|sa /xa'poza/ *f* vixen; **~so** *m* fox

rapsódia /xap'sɔdʒia/ *f* rhapsody

rap|tar /xap'tar/ *vt* abduct, kidnap <*criança*>; **~to** *m* abduction, kidnapping (*de criança*)

raquete /xa'kɛtʃi/ *f*, (*Port*) **raqueta** /xa'keta/ *f* racquet

raquítico /xa'kitʃiku/ *a* puny

ra|ramente /xara'mẽtʃi/ *adv* rarely; **~ridade** *f* rarity; **~ro** *a* rare □ *adv* rarely

rascunho /xas'kuɲu/ *m* rough version, draft

ras|gado /xaz'gadu/ *a* torn; (*fig*) <*elogios etc*> effusive; **~gão** *m* tear; **~gar** *vt* tear; (*em pedaços*) tear up □ *vi*, **~gar-se** *vpr* tear; **~go** *m* tear; (*fig*) burst

raso /'xazu/ *a* <*água*> shallow; <*sapato*> flat; <*colher etc*> level

ras|pão /xas'pãw/ *m* graze; **atingir de ~pão** graze; **~par** *vt* shave <*cabeça, pêlos*>; plane <*madeira*>; (*para limpar*) scrape; (*tocar de leve*) graze; **~par em** scrape

ras|teiro /xas'teru/ *a* <*planta*> creeping; <*animal*> crawling; **~tejante** *a* crawling; <*voz*> slurred; **~tejar** *vi* crawl

rasto /'xastu/ *m veja* **rastro**

ras|trear /xastri'ar/ *vt* track <*satélite etc*>; scan <*céu, corpo etc*>; **~tro** *m* trail

ratear[1] /xatʃi'ar/ *vi* <*motor*> miss

ra|tear[2] /xatʃi'ar/ *vt* share; **~teio** *m* sharing

ratifi|cação /xatʃifika'sãw/ *f* ratification; **~car** *vt* ratify

rato /'xatu/ *m* rat; (*camundongo*) mouse; **~eira** *f* mousetrap

ravina /xa'vina/ *f* ravine

razão /xa'zãw/ *f* reason; (*proporção*) ratio □ *m* ledger; **à ~ de** at the rate of; **em ~ de** on account of; **ter ~** be right; **não ter ~** be wrong

razoá|vel /xazo'avew/ (*pl* **~veis**) *a* reasonable

ré[1] /xɛ/ *f* (*na justiça*) defendant

ré[2] /xɛ/ *f* (*marcha*) reverse; **dar ~** reverse

reabastecer /xeabaste'ser/ *vt/i* refuel

reabilitar /xeabili'tar/ *vt* rehabilitate

rea|ção /xea'sãw/ *f* reaction; **~-ção em cadeia** chain reaction; **~cionário** *a & m* reactionary

readmitir /xeadʒimi'tʃir/ *vt* reinstate <*funcionário*>

reagir /xea'ʒir/ *vi* react; <*doente*> respond

reajus|tar /xeaʒus'tar/ *vt* readjust; **~te** *m* adjustment

re|al /xe'aw/ (*pl* **~ais**) *a* (*verdadeiro*) real; (*da realeza*) royal

real|çar /xeaw'sar/ *vt* highlight; **~ce** *m* prominence

realejo /xea'leʒu/ *m* barrel organ

realeza /xea'leza/ *f* royalty

realidade /xeali'dadʒi/ *f* reality

realimentação /xealimẽta'sãw/ *f* feedback

realis|mo /xea'lizmu/ *m* realism; **~ta** *a* realistic □ *m/f* realist

reali|zado /xeali'zadu/ *a* <*pessoa*> fulfilled; **~zar** *vt* (*fazer*) carry out; (*tornar real*) realize <*sonho, capital*>; **~zar-se** *vpr* <*sonho*> come true; <*pessoa*> fulfil o.s.; <*casamento, reunião etc*> take place

realmente /xeaw'mẽtʃi/ *adv* really

reaparecer /xeapare'ser/ *vi* reappear

reativar /xeatʃi'var/ *vt* reactivate

reaver /xea'ver/ *vt* get back

reavivar /xeavi'var/ *vt* revive

rebaixar /xeba'ʃar/ *vt* lower <*preço*>; (*fig*) demean □ *vi* <*preços*> drop; **~-se** *vpr* demean o.s.

rebanho /xe'baɲu/ *m* herd; (*fiéis*) flock

reba|te /xe'batʃi/ *m* alarm; **~ter** *vt* return <*bola*>; refute <*acusação*>; (*à máquina*) retype

rebelar-se /xebe'larsi/ *vpr* rebel

rebel|de /xe'bɛwdʒi/ *a* rebellious □ *m/f* rebel; **~dia** *f* rebelliousness

rebelião /xebeli'ãw/ *f* rebellion

reben|tar /xebẽ'tar/ *vt/i veja* **arrebentar**; **~to** *m* (*de planta*) shoot; (*descendente*) offspring

rebite /xe'bitʃi/ *m* rivet

rebobinar /xebobi'nar/ *vt* rewind

rebo|cador /xeboka'dor/ *m* tug; **~car** *vt* (*tirar*) tow; (*cobrir com reboco*) plaster; **~co** /o/ *m* plaster

reboque /xe'bɔki/ *m* towing; (*veículo a* **~**) trailer; (*com guindaste*) towtruck; **a ~** on tow

rebuçado /xebu'sadu/ *m* (*Port*) sweet, (*Amer*) candy

rebuliço /xebu'lisu/ *m* commotion

rebuscado /xebus'kadu/ *a* recherché

recado /xe'kadu/ *m* message

reca|ída /xeka'ida/ *f* relapse; **~ir** *vi* relapse; <*acento, culpa*> fall

recal|cado /xekaw'kadu/ *a* repressed; **~car** *vt* repress

recanto /xe'kãtu/ *m* nook, recess

recapitular /xekapitu'lar/ *vt* review □ *vi* recap

recarregar /rekare'gar/ *vt* (*bateria*) recharge; (*crédito*) top up

reca|tado /xeka'tadu/ *a* reserved, withdrawn; **~to** *m* reserve

recear /xesi'ar/ *vt/i* fear (*por* for)

rece|ber /xese'ber/ *vt* receive; entertain <*convidados*> □ *vi* (**~***ber salário*) get paid; (**~***ber convidados*) entertain; **~bimento** *m* receipt

receio /xe'seju/ *m* fear

recei|ta /xe'sejta/ *f* (*de cozinha*) recipe; (*médica*) prescription; (*dinheiro*) revenue; **~tar** *vt* prescribe

recém|-casados /xesẽjka'zadus/ *m pl* newly-weds; **~-chegado** *m* newcomer; **~-nascido** *a* newborn □ *m* newborn child, baby

recente /xe'sẽtʃi/ *a* recent; **~mente** *adv* recently

receoso /xese'ozu/ *a* (*apreensivo*) afraid

recep|ção /xesep'sãw/ *f* reception; (*Port: de carta*) receipt; **~cionar** *vt* receive; **~cionista** *m/f* receptionist; **~táculo** *m* receptacle; **~tivo** *a* receptive; **~tor** *m* receiver

reces|são /xese'sãw/ *f* recession; **~so** /ɛ/ *m* recess

re|chear /xeʃi'ar/ *vt* stuff <*frango, assado*>; fill <*empada*>; **~cheio** *m* (*para frango etc*) stuffing; (*de empada etc*) filling

rechonchudo /xeʃõ'ʃudu/ *a* plump

recibo /xe'sibu/ *m* receipt

reciclar /xesik'lar/ *vt* recycle

recife /xe'sifi/ *m* reef

recinto /xe'sĩtu/ *m* enclosure

recipiente /xesipi'ẽtʃi/ *m* container

reciprocar /xesipro'kar/ *vt* reciprocate

recíproco /xe'siproku/ *a* reciprocal; <*sentimento*> mutual

reci|tal /xesi'taw/ (*pl* **~tais**) *m* recital; **~tar** *vt* recite

recla|mação /xeklama'sãw/ *f* complaint; (*no seguro*) claim; **~mar** *vt* claim □ *vi* complain (**de** about); (*no seguro*) claim; **~me** *m*, (*Port*) **~mo** *m* advertising

reclinar-se /xekli'narsi/ *vpr* recline

recluso /xe'kluzu/ *a* reclusive □ *m* recluse

recobrar /xeko'brar/ *vt* recover; **~-se** *vpr* recover

recolher /xeko'ʎer/ *vt* collect; (*retirar*) withdraw; **~-se** *vpr* retire

recomeçar /xekome'sar/ *vt/i* start again

recomen|dação /xekomẽda'sãw/ *f* recommendation; **~dar** *vt* recommend; **~dável** (*pl* **~dáveis**) *a* advisable

recompen|sa /xekõ'pẽsa/ *f* reward; **~sar** *vt* reward

reconcili|ação /xekõsilia'sãw/ *f* reconciliation; **~ar** *vt* reconcile; **~ar-se** *vpr* be reconciled

reconhe|cer /xekoɲe'ser/ *vt* recognize; (*admitir*) acknowledge; (*mil*) reconnoitre; identify <*corpo*>; **~cimento** *m* recognition; (*gratidão*) gratitude; (*mil*) reconnaissance; (*de corpo*) identification; **~cível** (*pl* **~cíveis**) *a* recognizable

reconsiderar /xekõside'rar/ *vt/i* reconsider

reconstituinte /xekõstʃitu'ĩtʃi/ *m* tonic

reconstituir /xekõstʃitu'ir/ *vt* reform; reconstruct <*crime, cena*>

reconstruir /xekõstru'ir/ *vt* rebuild

recor|dação /xekorda'sãw/ *f* recollection; (*objeto*) memento; **~dar** *vt* recollect; **~dar-se (de)** recall

recor|de /xe'kɔrdʒi/ *a invar & m* record; **~dista** *a* record-breaking □ *m/f* record-holder

recorrer /xeko'xer/ *vi* **~ a** turn to <*médico, amigo*>; resort to <*violência, tática*>; **~ de** appeal against

recor|tar /xekor'tar/ *vt* cut out; **~te** /ɔ/ *m* cutting, (*Amer*) clipping

recostar /xekos'tar/ *vt* lean back; **~-se** *vpr* lean back

recreio /xe'kreju/ *m* recreation; (*na escola*) break

recriar /xekri'ar/ *vt* recreate

recriminação /xekrimina'sãw/ *f* recrimination

recrudescer /xekrude'ser/ *vi* intensify

recru|ta /xe'kruta/ *m/f* recruit; **~tamento** *m* recruitment; **~tar** *vt* recruit

recu|ar /xeku'ar/ *vi* move back; <*tropas*> retreat; (*no tempo*) go back; (*ceder*) back down; (*não cumprir*) back out (**de** of) □ *vt* move back; **~o** *m* retreat; (*fig: de intento*) climbdown

recupe|ração /xekupera'sãw/ *f* recovery; **~rar** *vt* recover; make up <*atraso, tempo perdido*>; **~rar-se** *vpr* recover (**de** from)

recurso /xe'kursu/ *m* resort; (*coisa útil*) resource; (*na justiça*) appeal; *pl* resources

recu|sa /xe'kuza/ *f* refusal; **~sar** *vt* refuse; turn down <*convite, oferta*>; **~sar-se** *vpr* refuse (**a** to)

reda|ção /xeda'sãw/ *f* (*de livro, contrato*) draft; (*pessoal*) editorial staff; (*seção*) editorial department; (*na escola*) composition; **~tor** *m* editor

rede /'xedʒi/ *f* net; (*para deitar*) hammock; (*fig: sistema*) network; **~ corporativa** (*comput*) intranet

rédea /'xɛdʒia/ *f* rein

redemoinho /xedemo'iɲu/ *m veja* **rodamoinho**

reden|ção /xedẽ'sãw/ *f* redemption; **~tor** *a* redeeming □ *m* redeemer

redigir /xedʒi'ʒir/ *vt* draw up <*contrato*>; write <*artigo*>; edit <*dicionário*>

redimir /xedʒi'mir/ *vt* redeem

redobrar /xedo'brar/ *vt* redouble

redon|deza /xedõ'deza/ *f* roundness; *pl* vicinity; **~do** *a* round

redor /xe'dɔr/ *m* **ao** *ou* **em ~ de** around

redução /xedu'sãw/ *f* reduction

redun|dante /xedũ'dãtʃi/ *a* redundant; **~dar** *vi* **~dar em** develop into

redu|zido /xedu'zidu/ *a* limited; (*pequeno*) small; **~zir** *vt* reduce; **~zir-se** *vpr* (*ficar reduzido*) be reduced (**a** to); (*resumir-se*) come down (**a** to)

reeleger /xeele'ʒer/ *vt* re-elect

reeleição /xeelej'sãw/ *f* re-election

reembol|sar /xeẽbow'sar/ *vt* reimburse <*pessoa*>; refund <*dinheiro*>; **~so** /o/ *m* refund; **~so postal** cash on delivery

reencarnação /xeẽkarna'sãw/ *f* reincarnation

reentrância /xeẽ'trãsia/ *f* recess

reescalonar /xeeskalo'nar/ *vt* reschedule

reescrever /xeeskre'ver/ *vt* rewrite

refastelar-se /xefaste'larsi/ *vpr* stretch out

refazer /xefa'zer/ *vt* redo; rebuild <*vida*>; **~-se** *vpr* recover (**de** from)

refei|ção /xefej'sãw/ *f* meal; **~tório** *m* dining hall

refém /xe'fẽj/ *m* hostage

referência /xefe'rẽsia/ *f* reference; **com ~ a** with reference to

referendo /xefe'rẽdũ/ *m* referendum

refe|rente /xefe'rẽtʃi/ *a* **~rente a** regarding; **~rir** *vt* report; **~rir-se** *vpr* refer (**a** to)

refestelar-se /xefeste'larsi/ *vpr* (*Port*) *veja* **refastelar-se**

re|fil /xe'fiw/ (*pl* **~fis**) *m* refill

refi|nado /xefi'nadu/ *a* refined; **~namento** *m* refinement; **~nar** *vt* refine; **~naria** *f* refinery

refle|tido /xefle'tʃidu/ *a* <*decisão*> well-thought-out; <*pessoa*> thoughtful; **~tir** *vt/i* reflect; **~tir-se** *vpr* be reflected; **~xão** /ks/ *f* reflection; **~xivo** /ks/ *a* reflexive; **~xo** /ɛks/ *a* <*luz*> reflected; <*ação*> reflex □ *m* (*de luz etc*) reflection; (*físico*) reflex; (*no cabelo*) streak

refluxo /xe'fluksu/ *m* ebb

refo|gado /xefo'gadu/ *m* lightly fried mixture of onions and garlic; **~gar** *vt* fry lightly

refor|çar /xefor'sar/ *vt* reinforce; **~ço** /o/ *m* reinforcement

refor|ma /xe'fɔrma/ *f* (*da lei etc*) reform; (*na casa etc*) renovation; (*de militar*) discharge; (*pensão*) pension; **~ma ministerial** cabinet reshuffle; **~mado** *a* reformed; (*Port: aposentado*) retired □ *m* (*Port*) pensioner; **~mar** *vt* reform <*lei, sistema etc*>; renovate <*casa, prédio*>; (*Port: aposentar*) retire; **~mar-se** *vpr* (*Port: aposentar-se*) retire; <*criminoso*> reform; **~matório** *m* reform school; **~mista** *a* & *m/f* reformist

refratário /xefra'tariu/ *a* <*tigela etc*> ovenproof, heatproof

refrear /xefri'ar/ *vt* rein in <*cavalo*>; (*fig*) curb, keep in check <*paixões etc*>; **~-se** *vpr* restrain o.s.

refrega /xe'frɛga/ *f* clash, fight

refres|cante /xefres'kãtʃi/ *a* refreshing; **~car** *vt* freshen, cool <*ar*>; refresh <*pessoa, memória etc*> □ *vi* get cooler; **~car-se** *vpr* refresh o.s.; **~co** /e/ *m* (*bebida*) soft drink; *pl* refreshments

refrige|rado /xefriʒe'radu/ *a* cooled; <*casa etc*> air-conditioned; (*na geladeira*) refrigerated; **~rador** *m* refrigerator; **~rante** *m* soft drink; **~rar** *vt* keep cool; (*na geladeira*) refrigerate

refugi|ado /xefuʒi'adu/ *m* refugee; **~ar-se** *vpr* take refuge

refúgio /xe'fuʒiu/ *m* refuge

refugo /xe'fugu/ *m* waste, refuse

refutar /xefu'tar/ *vt* refute

regaço /xe'gasu/ *m* lap

regador /xega'dor/ *m* watering can

regalia /xega'lia/ *f* privilege

regar /xe'gar/ *vt* water

regata /xe'gata/ *f* regatta

regatear /xegatʃi'ar/ *vi* bargain, haggle

re|gência /xe'ʒẽsia/ *f* (*de verbo etc*) government; **~gente** *m/f* (*de orquestra*) conductor; **~ger** *vt* govern □ *vi* rule

região /xeʒi'ãw/ *f* region; (*de cidade etc*) area

regi|me /xe'ʒimi/ *m* regime; (*dieta*) diet; **fazer ~me** diet; **~-mento** *m* (*militar*) regiment; (*regulamento*) regulations

régio /'xɛʒiu/ *a* regal

regio|nal /xeʒio'naw/ (*pl* **~nais**) *a* regional

regis|trador /xeʒistra'dor/ *a* **caixa ~tradora** cash register; **~trar** *vt* register; (*anotar*) record; **~tro** *m* (*lista*) register; (*de um fato, em banco de dados*) record; (*ato de ~trar*) registration

rego /'xegu/ *m* (*de arado*) furrow; (*de roda*) rut; (*para escoamento*) ditch

regozi|jar /xegozi'ʒar/ *vt* delight; **~jar-se** *vpr* be delighted; **~jo** *m* delight

regra /'xɛgra/ *f* rule; *pl* (*menstruações*) periods; **em ~** as a rule

regres|sar /xegre'sar/ *vi* return; **~sivo** *a* regressive; **contagem ~siva** countdown; **~so** /ɛ/ *m* return

régua /'xɛgwa/ *f* ruler

regu|lagem /xegu'laʒẽ/ *f* (*de carro*) tuning; **~lamento** *m* regulations; **~lar** *a* regular; <*estatura, qualidade etc*> average □ *vt* regulate; tune <*carro, motor*>; set <*relógio*> □ *vi* work; **~lar-se por** go by, be guided by; **~laridade** *f* regularity; **~larizar** *vt* regularize

regurgitar /xegurʒi'tar/ *vt* bring up

rei /xej/ *m* king; **~nado** *m* reign

reincidir /xeĩsi'dʒir/ *vi* <*criminoso*> reoffend

reino /'xejnu/ *m* kingdom; (*fig: da fantasia etc*) realm; **Reino Unido** United Kingdom

reiterar /xejte'rar/ *vt* reiterate

reitor /xej'tor/ *m* chancellor, (*Amer*) president

reivindi|cação /xejvĩdʒika'sãw/ *f* demand; **~car** *vt* claim, demand

rejei|ção /xeʒej'sãw/ *f* rejection; **~tar** *vt* reject

rejuvenescer /xeʒuvene'ser/ *vt* rejuvenate □ *vi* be rejuvenated

relação /xela'sãw/ *f* relationship; (*relatório*) account; (*lista*) list; *pl* relations; **com** *ou* **em ~ a** in relation to, regarding

relacio|namento /xelasiona'mẽtu/ *m* relationship; **~nar** *vt* relate (**com** to); (*listar*) list; **~nar-se** *vpr* relate (**com** to)

relações-públicas /xelasõjs'publikas/ *m/f invar* public-relations person

relâmpago /xe'lãpagu/ *m* flash of lightning; *pl* lightning □ *a* lightning; **num ~** in a flash

relampejar /xelãpe'ʒar/ *vi* flash; **relampejou** there was a flash of lightning

relance /xe'lãsi/ *m* glance; **olhar de ~** glance (at)

rela|tar /xela'tar/ *vt* relate; **~tivo** *a* relative; **~to** *m* account; **~tório** *m* report

rela|xado /xela'ʃadu/ *a* relaxed; <*disciplina*> lax; <*pessoa*> lazy, complacent; **~xamento** *m* (*físico*) relaxation; (*de pessoa*) complacency; **~xante** *a* relaxing □ *m* tranquillizer; **~xar** *vt* relax □ *vi* (*descansar*) relax; (*tornar-se omisso*) get complacent; **~xar-se** *vpr* relax; **~xe** *m* relaxation

reles /'xɛlis/ *a invar* <*gente*> common; <*ação*> despicable

rele|vância /xele'vãsia/ *f* relevance; **~vante** *a* relevant; **~-var** *vt* emphasize; **~vo** /e/ *m* relief; (*importância*) prominence

religi|ão /xeliʒi'ãw/ *f* religion; **~oso** /o/ *a* religious

relin|char /xelĩ'ʃar/ *vi* neigh; **~cho** *m* neighing

relíquia /xe'likia/ *f* relic

relógio /xe'lɔʒiu/ *m* clock; (*de pulso*) watch

relu|tância /xelu'tãsia/ *f* reluctance; **~tante** *a* reluctant; **~-tar** *vi* be reluctant (**em** to)

reluzente /xelu'zẽtʃi/ *a* shining, gleaming

relva /'xɛwva/ *f* grass; **~do** *m* lawn

remador /xema'dor/ *m* rower

remanescente /xemane'sẽtʃi/ *a* remaining ▫ *m* remainder

remar /xe'mar/ *vt/i* row

rema|tar /xema'tar/ *vt* finish off; **~te** *m* finish; (*adorno*) finishing touch; (*de piada*) punch line

remediar /xemedʒi'ar/ *vt* remedy

remédio /xe'mɛdʒiu/ *m* (*contra doença*) medicine, drug; (*a problema etc*) remedy

remelento /xeme'lẽtu/ *a* bleary

remen|dar /xemẽ'dar/ *vt* mend; (*com pedaço de pano*) patch; **~do** *m* mend; (*pedaço de pano*) patch

remessa /xe'mɛsa/ *f* (*de mercadorias*) shipment; (*de dinheiro*) remittance

reme|tente /xeme'tẽtʃi/ *m/f* sender; **~ter** *vt* send <*mercadorias, dinheiro etc*>; refer <*leitor*> (**a** to)

remexer /xeme'ʃer/ *vt* shuffle <*papéis*>; stir up <*poeira, lama*>; wave <*braços*> ▫ *vi* rummage; **~-se** *vpr* move around

reminiscência /xemini'sẽsia/ *f* reminiscence

remir /xe'mir/ *vt* redeem; **~-se** *vpr* redeem o.s.

remissão /xemi'sãw/ *f* (*de pecados*) redemption; (*de doença, pena*) remission; (*num livro*) cross-reference

remo /'xemu/ *m* oar; (*esporte*) rowing

remoção /xemo'sãw/ *f* removal

remoinho /xemo'iɲu/ *m* (*Port*) *veja* **rodamoinho**

remontar /xemõ'tar/ *vi* **~ a** <*coisa*> date back to; <*pessoa*> think back to

remorso /xe'mɔrsu/ *m* remorse

remo|to /xe'mɔtu/ *a* remote; **~ver** *vt* remove

remune|ração /xemunera'sãw/ *f* payment; **~rador** *a* profitable; **~rar** *vt* pay

rena /'xena/ *f* reindeer

re|nal /xe'naw/ (*pl* **~nais**) *a* renal, kidney

Renascença /xena'sẽsa/ *f* Renaissance

renas|cer /xena'ser/ *vi* be reborn; **~cimento** *m* rebirth

renda[1] /'xẽda/ *f* (*tecido*) lace

ren|da[2] /'xẽda/ *f* income; (*Port: aluguel*) rent; **~der** bring in, yield <*lucro*>; earn <*juros*>; fetch <*preço*>; bring <*resultado*> ▫ *vi* <*investimento, trabalho, ação*> pay off; <*comida*> go a long way; <*produto comprado*> give value for money; **~der-se** *vpr* surrender; **~dição** *f* surrender; **~dimento** *m* (*renda*) income; (*de investimento, terreno*) yield; (*de motor etc*) output; (*de produto comprado*) value for money; **~doso** /o/ *a* profitable

rene|gado /xene'gadu/ *a & m* renegade; **~gar** *vt* renounce

renhido /xe'ɲidu/ *a* hard-fought

Reno /'xenu/ *m* Rhine

reno|mado /xeno'madu/ *a* renowned; **~me** /o/ *m* renown

reno|vação /xenova'sãw/ *f* renewal; **~var** *vt* renew

renque /'xẽki/ *m* row

ren|tabilidade /xẽtabili'dadʒi/ *f* profitability; **~tável** (*pl* **~táveis**) *a* profitable

rente /'xẽtʃi/ *adv* **~ a** close to ▫ *a* <*cabelo*> cropped

renúncia /xe'nũsia/ *f* renunciation (**a** of); (*a cargo*) resignation (**a** from)

renunciar /xenũsi'ar/ *vi* <*presidente etc*> resign; **~ a** give up; waive <*direito*>

reorganizar /xeorgani'zar/ *vt* reorganize

repa|ração /xepara'sãw/ *f* reparation; (*conserto*) repair; **~rar** *vt* (*consertar*) repair; make up for <*ofensa, injustiça, erro*>; make good <*danos, prejuízo*> ▫ *vi* **~rar (em)** notice; **~ro** *m* (*conserto*) repair

repar|tição /xepartʃi'sãw/ *f* division; (*seção do governo*) department; **~tir** *vt* divide up

repassar /xepa'sar/ *vt* revise <*matéria, lição*>

repatriar /xepatri'ar/ *vt* repatriate

repe|lente /xepe'lẽtʃi/ *a & m* repellent; **~lir** *vt* repel; reject <*idéia, proposta etc*>

repensar /xepẽ'sar/ *vt/i* rethink

repen|te /xe'pẽtʃi/ *m* **de ~te** suddenly; (*fam: talvez*) maybe; **~tino** *a* sudden

reper|cussão /xeperku'sãw/ *f* repercussion; **~cutir** *vi* <*som*> reverberate; (*fig: ter efeito*) have repercussions

repertório /xeper'tɔriu/ *m* (*músico etc*) repertoire; (*lista*) list

repe|tição /xepetʃi'sãw/ *f* repetition; **~tido** *a* repeated; **~tidas vezes** repeatedly; **~tir** *vt* repeat ▫ *vi* (*ao comer*) have seconds; **~tir-se** *vpr* <*pessoa*> repeat o.s.; <*fato, acontecimento*> recur; **~titivo** *a* repetitive

repi|car /xepi'kar/ *vt/i* ring; **~que** *m* ring

replay /xe'plej/ (*pl* **~s**) *m* action replay

repleto /xe'plɛtu/ *a* full up

réplica /'xɛplika/ *f* reply; (*cópia*) replica

replicar /xepli'kar/ *vt* answer ▫ *vi* reply

repolho /xe'poʎu/ *m* cabbage

repor /xe'por/ *vt* (*num lugar*) put back; (*substituir*) replace

reportagem /xepor'taʒẽ/ *f* (*uma*) report; (*ato*) reporting

repórter /xe'pɔrter/ *m/f* reporter

reposição /xepozi'sãw/ *f* replacement

repou|sar /xepo'sar/ *vt/i* rest; **~so** *m* rest

repreen|der /xepriẽ'der/ *vt* rebuke, reprimand; **~são** *f* rebuke, reprimand; **~sível** (*pl* **~síveis**) *a* reprehensible

represa /xe'preza/ *f* dam

represália /xepre'zalia/ *f* reprisal

represen|tação /xeprezẽta'sãw/ *f* representation; (*espetáculo*) performance; (*ofício de ator*) acting; **~tante** *m/f* representative; **~tar** *vt* represent; (*no teatro*) perform <*peça*>; play <*papel, personagem*> ▫ *vi* <*ator*> act; **~tativo** *a* representative

repres|são /xepre'sãw/ *f* repression; **~sivo** *a* repressive

repri|mido /xepri'midu/ *a* repressed; **~mir** *vt* repress

reprise /xe'prizi/ *f* (*na TV*) repeat; (*de filme*) rerun

reprodu|ção /xeprodu'sãw/ *f* reproduction; **~zir** *vt* reproduce; **~zir-se** *vpr* (*multiplicar-se*) reproduce; (*repetir-se*) recur

repro|vação /xeprova'sãw/ *f* disapproval; (*em exame*) failure; **~var** *vt* (*rejeitar*) disapprove of; (*em exame*) fail; **ser ~vado** <*aluno*> fail

rép|til /'xɛptʃiw/ (*pl* **~teis**) *m* reptile

república /xe'publika/ *f* republic; (*de estudantes*) hall of residence

republicano /xepubli'kanu/ *a & m* republican

repudiar /xepudʒi'ar/ *vt* disown; repudiate <*esposa*>

repug|nância /xepug'nãsia/ *f* repugnance; **~nante** *a* repugnant

repul|sa /xe'puwsa/ *f* repulsion; (*recusa*) rejection; **~sivo** *a* repulsive

reputação /xeputa'sãw/ *f* reputation

requebrar /xeke'brar/ *vt* swing; **~-se** *vpr* sway

requeijão /xeke'ʒãw/ *m* cheese spread, cottage cheese

reque|rer /xeke'rer/ *vt* (*pedir*) apply for; (*exigir*) require; **~-rimento** *m* application

requin|tado /xekĩ'tadu/ *a* refined; **~tar** *vt* refine; **~te** *m* refinement

requisi|ção /xekizi'sãw/ *f* requisition; **~tar** *vt* requisition; **~to** *m* requirement

rês /xes/ (*pl* **reses**) *m* head of cattle; *pl* cattle

rescindir /xesĩ'dʒir/ *vt* rescind

rés-do-chão /xɛzdu'ʃãw/ *m invar* (*Port*) ground floor, (*Amer*) first floor

rese|nha /xe'zeɲa/ *f* review; **~-nhar** *vt* review

reser|va /xe'zɛrva/ *f* reserve; (*em hotel, avião etc, ressalva*) reservation; **~var** *vt* reserve; **~- vatório** *m* reservoir; **~vista** *m/f* reservist

resfri|ado /xesfri'ado/ *a* **estar ~ado** have a cold ▫ *m* cold; **~ar** *vt* cool ▫ *vi* get cold; (*tornar-se morno*) cool down; **~ar-se** *vpr* catch a cold

resga|tar /xezga'tar/ *vt* (*salvar*) rescue; (*remir*) redeem; **~te** *m* (*salvamento*) rescue; (*pago por refém*) ransom; (*remissão*) redemption

resguardar /xezgwar'dar/ *vt* protect; **~-se** *vpr* protect o.s. (**de** from)

residência /xezi'dẽsia/ *f* residence

residen|cial /xezidẽsi'aw/ (*pl* **~ciais**) *a* <*bairro*> residential; <*telefone etc*> home; **~te** *a & m/f* resident

residir /xezi'dʒir/ *vi* reside

resíduo /xe'ziduu/ *m* residue

resig|nação /xezigna'sãw/ *f* resignation; **~nado** *a* resigned; **~nar-se** *vpr* resign o.s. (**com** to)

resina /xe'zina/ *f* resin

resis|tência /xezis'tẽsia/ *f* resistance; (*de atleta, mental*) endurance; (*de material, objeto*) toughness; **~tente** *a* strong, tough; <*tecido, roupa*> hard-wearing; <*planta*> hardy; **~-tente a** resistant to; **~tir** *vi* (*opor ~tência*) resist; (*agüentar*) <*pessoa*> hold out; <*objeto*> hold; **~tir a** (*combater*) resist; (*agüentar*) withstand; **~tir ao tempo** stand the test of time

resmun|gar /xezmũ'gar/ *vi* grumble; **~go** *m* grumbling

resolu|ção /xezolu'sãw/ *f* resolution; (*firmeza*) resolve; (*de problema*) solution; **~to** *a* resolute; **~to a** resolved to

resolver /xezow'ver/ *vt* (*esclarecer*) sort out; solve <*problema, enigma*>;

(*decidir*) decide; **~-se** *vpr* make up one's mind (**a** to)

respaldo /xes'pawdu/ *m* (*de cadeira*) back; (*fig: apoio*) backing

respectivo /xespek'tʃivu/ *a* respective

respei|tabilidade /xespejtabili'dadʒi/ *f* respectability; **~tador** *a* respectful; **~tar** *vt* respect; **~tável** (*pl* **~táveis**) *a* respectable; **~to** *m* respect (**por** for); **a ~to de** about; **a este ~to** in this respect; **com ~to a** with regard to; **dizer ~to a** concern; **~toso** /o/ *a* respectful

respin|gar /xespĩ'gar/ *vt/i* splash; **~go** *m* splash

respi|ração /xespira'sãw/ *f* breathing; **~rador** *m* respirator; **~rar** *vt/i* breathe; **~ratório** *a* respiratory; **~ro** *m* breath; (*descanso*) break, breather

resplande|cente /xesplãde'sẽtʃi/ *a* resplendent; **~cer** *vi* shine

resplendor /xesplẽ'dor/ *m* brilliance; (*fig*) glory

respon|dão /xespõ'dãw/ *a* (*f* **~dona**) cheeky; **~der** *vt/i* answer; (*com insolência*) answer back; **~der a** answer; **~der por** answer for, take responsibility for

responsabili|dade /xespõsabili'dadʒi/ *f* responsibility; **~zar** *vt* hold responsible (**por** for); **~zar-se** *vpr* take responsibility (**por** for)

responsá|vel /xespõ'savew/ (*pl* **~veis**) *a* responsible (**por** for)

resposta /xes'pɔsta/ *f* answer

resquício /xes'kisiu/ *m* vestige, remnant

ressabiado /xesabi'adu/ *a* wary, suspicious

ressaca /xe'saka/ *f* (*depois de beber*) hangover; (*do mar*) undertow

ressaltar /xesaw'tar/ *vt* emphasize □ *vi* stand out

ressalva /xe'sawva/ *f* reservation, proviso; (*proteção*) safeguard

ressarcir /xesar'sir/ *vt* refund

resse|cado /xese'kadu/ *a* <*terra*> parched; <*pele*> dry; **~car** *vt/i* dry up

ressen|tido /xesẽ'tʃidu/ *a* resentful; **~timento** *m* resentment; **~tir-se de** (*ofender-se*) resent; (*ser influenciado*) show the effects of

ressequido /xese'kidu/ *a veja* **ressecado**

resso|ar /xeso'ar/ *vi* resound; **~-nância** *f* resonance; **~nante** *a* resonant; **~nar** *vi* (*Port*) snore

ressurgimento /xesurʒi'mẽtu/ *m* resurgence

ressurreição /xesuxej'sãw/ *f* resurrection

ressuscitar /xesusi'tar/ *vt* revive

restabele|cer /xestabele'ser/ *vt* restore; restore to health <*doente*>; **~cer-se** *vpr* recover; **~cimento** *m* restoration; (*de doente*) recovery

res|tante /xes'tãtʃi/ *a* remaining □ *m* remainder; **~tar** *vi* remain; **~ta-me dizer que ...** it remains for me to say that ...

restau|ração /xestawra'sãw/ *f* restoration; **~rante** *m* restaurant; **~rar** *vt* restore

restitu|ição /xestʃitui'sãw/ *f* return, restitution; **~ir** *vt* (*devolver*) return; restore <*forma, força etc*>; reinstate <*funcionário*>

resto /'xɛstu/ *m* rest; *pl* (*de comida*) left-overs; (*de cadáver*) remains; **de ~** besides

restrição /xestri'sãw/ *f* restriction

restringir /xestrĩ'ʒir/ *vt* restrict

restrito /xes'tritu/ *a* restricted

resul|tado /xezuw'tadu/ *m* result; **~tante** *a* resulting (**de** from); **~tar** *vi* result (**de** from; **em** in)

resu|mir /xezu'mir/ *vt* (*abreviar*) summarize; (*conter em poucas palavras*) sum up; **~mir-se** *vpr* (*ser expresso em poucas palavras*) be summed up; **~mir-se em** (*ser apenas*) come down to; **~mo** *m* summary; **em ~mo** briefly

resvalar /xezva'lar/ *vi* (*sem querer*) slip; (*deslizar*) slide

reta /'xɛta/ *f* (*linha*) straight line; (*de pista etc*) straight; **~ final** home straight

retaguarda /xeta'gwarda/ *f* rearguard

retalho /xe'taʎu/ *m* scrap; **a ~** (*Port*) retail

retaliação /xetalia'sãw/ *f* retaliation

retangular /xetãgu'lar/ *a* rectangular

retângulo /xe'tãgulu/ *m* rectangle

retar|dado /xetar'dadu/ *a* retarded □ *m* retard; **~dar** *vt* delay; **~datário** *m* latecomer

retenção /xetẽ'sãw/ *f* retention

reter /xe'ter/ *vt* keep <*pessoa*>; hold back <*águas, riso, lágrimas*>; (*na memória*) retain; **~-se** *vpr* restrain o.s.

rete|sado /xete'zadu/ *a* taut; **~sar** *vt* pull taut

reticência /xetʃi'sẽsia/ *f* reticence

reti|dão /xetʃi'dãw/ *f* rectitude; **~ficar** *vt* rectify

reti|rada /xetʃi'rada/ *f* (*de tropas*) retreat; (*de dinheiro*) withdrawal; **~rado** *a* secluded; **~rar** *vt* withdraw; (*afastar*) move away; **~rar-se** *vpr* <*tropas*> retreat; (*afastar-se*) withdraw; (*de uma atividade*) retire; **~ro** *m* retreat

reto /'xɛtu/ *a* <*linha etc*> straight; <*pessoa*> honest

retocar /xeto'kar/ *vt* touch up <*desenho, maquiagem etc*>; alter <*texto*>

reto|mada /xeto'mada/ *f* (*continuação*) resumption; (*reconquista*) retaking; **~mar** *vt* (*continuar com*) resume; (*conquistar de novo*) retake

retoque /xe'tɔki/ *m* finishing touch

retorcer /xetor'ser/ *vt* twist; **~-se** *vpr* writhe

retóri|ca /xe'tɔrika/ *f* rhetoric; **~co** *a* rhetorical

retor|nar /xetor'nar/ *vi* return; **~no** *m* return; (*na estrada*) turning place; **dar ~no** do a U-turn

retrair /xetra'ir/ *vt* retract, withdraw; **~-se** *vpr* (*recuar*) withdraw; (*encolher-se*) retract

retrasa|do /xetra'zadu/ *a* **a semana ~da** the week before last

retratar[1] /xetra'tar/ *vt* (*desdizer*) retract

retra|tar[2] /xetra'tar/ *vt* (*em quadro, livro*) portray, depict; **~to** *m* portrait; (*foto*) photo; (*representação*) portrayal; **~to falado** identikit picture

retribuir /xetribu'ir/ *vt* return <*favor, visita*>; repay <*gentileza*>

retroativo /xetroa'tʃivu/ *a* retroactive; <*pagamento*> backdated

retro|ceder /xetrose'der/ *vi* retreat; (*desistir*) back down; **~cesso** /ɛ/ *m* retreat; (*ao passado*) regression

retrógrado /xe'trɔgradu/ *a* retrograde

retrospec|tiva /xetrospek'tʃiva/ *f* retrospective; **~tivo** *a* retrospective; **~to** /ɛ/ *m* look back; **em ~to** in retrospect

retrovisor /xetrovi'zor/ *a* & *m* **(espelho) ~** rear-view mirror

retrucar /xetru'kar/ *vt/i* retort

retum|bante /xetũ'bãtʃi/ *a* resounding; **~bar** *vi* resound

réu /'xɛw/ *m* (*f* **ré**) defendant

reumatismo /xewma'tʃizmu/ *m* rheumatism

reu|nião /xeuni'ãw/ *f* meeting; (*descontraída*) get-together; (*de família*) reunion; **~nião de cúpula** summit meeting; **~nir** *vt* bring together <*pessoas*>; combine <*qualidades*>; **~nir-se** *vpr* meet; <*amigos, familiares*> get together; **~nir-se a** join

revanche /xe'vãʃi/ *f* revenge; (*jogo*) return match

reveillon /xeve'jõ/ (*pl* **~s**) *m* New Year's Eve

reve|lação /xevela'sãw/ *f* revelation; (*de fotos*) developing; (*novo talento*) promising newcomer; **~lar** *vt* reveal; develop <*filme, fotos*>; **~lar-se** *vpr* (*vir a ser*) turn out to be

revelia /xeve'lia/ *f* **à ~** by default; **à ~ de** without the knowledge of

reven|dedor /xevẽde'dor/ *m* dealer; **~der** *vt* resell

rever /xe'ver/ *vt* (*ver de novo*) see again; (*revisar*) revise; (*examinar*) check

reve|rência /xeve'resia/ *f* reverence; (*movimento do busto*) bow; (*dobrando os joelhos*) curtsey; **~rente** *a* reverent

reverso /xe'vɛrsu/ *m* reverse; **o ~ da medalha** the other side of the coin

revés /xe'vɛs/ (*pl* **reveses**) *m* setback

reves|timento /xevestʃi'mẽtu/ *m* covering; **~tir** *vt* cover

reve|zamento /xeveza'mẽtu/ *m* alternation; **~zar** *vt/i* alternate; **~zar-se** *vpr* alternate

revi|dar /xevi'dar/ *vt* return <*golpe, insulto*>; refute <*crítica*>; (*retrucar*) retort □ *vi* hit back; **~de** *m* response

revigorar /xevigo'rar/ *vt* strengthen □ *vi*, **~-se** *vpr* regain one's strength

revi|rar /xevi'rar/ *vt* turn out <*bolsos, gavetas*>; turn over <*terra*>; turn inside out <*roupa*>; roll <*olhos*>; **~rar-se** *vpr* toss and turn; **~ravolta** /ɔ/ *f* (*na política etc*) about-face, about-turn; (*da situação*) turnabout, dramatic change

revi|são /xevi'zãw/ *f* (*de lições etc*) revision; (*de máquina, motor*) overhaul; (*de carro*) service; **~são de provas** proofreading; **~sar** *vt* revise <*provas, lições*>, service <*carro*>; **~sor** *m* (*de bilhetes*) ticket inspector; **~sor de provas** proofreader

revis|ta /xe'vista/ *f* (*para ler*) magazine; (*teatral*) revue; (*de tropas etc*) review; **passar ~ta a** review; **~tar** *vt* search

reviver /xevi'ver/ *vt* relive □ *vi* revive

revogar /xevo'gar/ *vt* revoke <*lei*>; cancel <*ordem*>

revol|ta /xe'vɔwta/ *f* (*rebelião*) revolt; (*indignação*) disgust; **~tante** *a* disgusting; **~tar** *vt* disgust; **~tar-se** *vpr* (*rebelar-se*) revolt; (*indignar-se*) be disgusted; **~to** /o/ *a* <*casa, gaveta*> upside down; <*cabelo*> dishevelled; <*mar*> rough; <*mundo, região*> troubled; <*anos*> turbulent

revolu|ção /xevolu'sãw/ *f* revolution; **~cionar** *vt* revolutionize; **~cionário** *a* & *m* re-volutionary

revolver /xevow'ver/ *vt* turn over <*terra*>; roll <*olhos*>; go through <*gavetas, arquivos*>

revólver /xe'vɔwver/ *m* revolver

re|za /'xɛza/ *f* prayer; **~zar** *vi* pray □ *vt* say <*missa, oração*>; (*dizer*) state

riacho /xi'aʃu/ *m* stream
ribalta /xi'bawta/ *f* footlights
ribanceira /xibã'sera/ *f* embankment
ribombar /xibõ'bar/ *vi* rumble
rico /'xiku/ *a* rich □ *m* rich man; **os ~s** the rich
ricochete /xiko'ʃetʃi/ *m* ricochet; **~ar** *vi* ricochet
ricota /xi'kɔta/ *f* curd cheese, ricotta
ridicularizar /xidʒikulari'zar/ *vt* ridicule
ridículo /xi'dʒikulu/ *a* ridiculous
ri|fa /'xifa/ *f* raffle; **~far** *vt* raffle
rifão /xi'fãw/ *m* saying
rifle /'xifli/ *m* rifle
rigidez /xiʒi'des/ *f* rigidity
rígido /'xiʒidu/ *a* rigid
rigor /xi'gor/ *m* severity; (*meticulosidade*) rigour; **vestido a ~** evening dress; **de ~** essential
rigoroso /xigo'rozu/ *a* strict; <*inverno, pena*> severe, harsh; <*lógica, estudo*> rigorous
rijo /'xiʒu/ *a* stiff; <*músculos*> firm
rim /xĩ/ *m* kidney; *pl* (*parte das costas*) small of the back
ri|ma /'xima/ *f* rhyme; **~mar** *vt/i* rhyme
rí|mel /'ximew/ (*pl* **~meis**) *m* mascara
ringue /'xĩgi/ *m* ring
rinoceronte /xinose'rõtʃi/ *m* rhinoceros
rinque /'xĩki/ *m* rink
rio /'xio/ *m* river
riqueza /xi'keza/ *f* wealth; (*qualidade*) richness; *pl* riches
rir /xir/ *vi* laugh (**de** at)
risada /xi'zada/ *f* laugh, laughter; **dar ~** laugh
ris|ca /'xiska/ *f* stroke; (*listra*) stripe; (*do cabelo*) parting; **à ~ca** to the letter; **~car** *vt* (*apagar*) cross out <*erro*>; strike <*fósforo*>; scratch <*mesa, carro etc*>; write off <*amigo etc*>; **~co**[1] *m* (*na parede etc*) scratch; (*no papel*) line; (*esboço*) sketch
risco[2] /'xisku/ *m* risk
riso /'xizu/ *m* laugh; **~nho** /o/ *a* smiling
ríspido /'xispidu/ *a* harsh
rítmico /'xitʃmiku/ *a* rhythmic
ritmo /'xitʃimu/ *m* rhythm
rito /'xitu/ *m* rite
ritu|al /xitu'aw/ (*pl* **~ais**) *a & m* ritual
ri|val /xi'vaw/ (*pl* **~vais**) *a & m/f* rival; **~validade** *f* rivalry; **~valizar** *vt* rival □ *vi* vie (**com** with)
rixa /'xiʃa/ *f* fight
robô /xo'bo/ *m* robot
robusto /xo'bustu/ *a* robust
roça /'xɔsa/ *f* (*campo*) country
rocambole /xokã'bɔli/ *m* roll
roçar /xo'sar/ *vt* graze; **~ em** brush against
ro|cha /'xɔʃa/ *f* rock; **~chedo** /e/ *m* cliff
roda /'xɔda/ *f* (*de carro etc*) wheel; (*de amigos etc*) circle; **~ dentada** cog; **~da** *f* round; **~do a saia ~da** full skirt; **~-gigante** (*pl* **~s-gigantes**) *f* big wheel, (*Amer*) ferris wheel; **~moinho** *m* (*de vento*) whirlwind; (*na água*) whirlpool; (*fig*) whirl, swirl; **~pé** *m* skirting board, (*Amer*) baseboard
rodar /xo'dar/ *vt* (*fazer girar*) spin; (*viajar por*) go round; do <*quilometragem*>; shoot <*filme*>; run <*programa*> □ *vi* (*girar*) spin; (*de carro*) drive round
rodear /xodʒi'ar/ *vt* (*circundar*) surround; (*andar ao redor de*) go round
rodeio /xo'deju/ *m* (*ao falar*) circumlocution; (*de gado*) round-up; **falar sem ~s** talk straight
rodela /xo'dɛla/ *f* (*de limão etc*) slice; (*peça de metal*) washer
rodízio /xo'dʒiziu/ *m* rota
rodo /'xodu/ *m* rake
rodopiar /xodopi'ar/ *vi* spin round
rodovi|a /xodo'via/ *f* highway; **~ária** *f* bus station; **~ário** *a* road; **polícia ~ária** traffic police
ro|edor /xoe'dor/ *m* rodent; **~er** *vt* gnaw; bite <*unhas*>; (*fig*) eat away
rogar /xo'gar/ *vi* request
rojão /xo'ʒãw/ *m* rocket
rol /xɔw/ (*pl* **róis**) *m* roll
rolar /xo'lar/ *vt* roll □ *vi* roll; (*fam*) (*acontecer*) happen
roldana /xow'dana/ *f* pulley
roleta /xo'leta/ *f* (*jogo*) roulette; (*borboleta*) turnstile
rolha /'xoʎa/ *f* cork
roliço /xo'lisu/ *a* <*objeto*> cylindrical; <*pessoa*> plump
rolo /'xolu/ *m* (*de filme, tecido etc*) roll; (*máquina, bobe*) roller; **~ compressor** steamroller; **~ de massa** rolling pin
Roma /'xoma/ *f* Rome
romã /xo'mã/ *f* pomegranate
roman|ce /xo'mãsi/ *m* (*livro*) novel; (*caso*) romance; **~cista** *m/f* novelist
romano /xo'manu/ *a & m* Roman
romântico /xo'mãtʃiku/ *a* romantic
romantismo /xomã'tʃizmu/ *m* (*amor*) romance; (*idealismo*) romanticism
romaria /xoma'ria/ *f* pilgrimage
rombo /'xõbu/ *m* hole
Romênia /xo'menia/ *f* Romania
romeno /xo'menu/ *a & m* Romanian
rom|per /xõ'per/ *vt* break; break off <*relações*> □ *vi* <*dia*> break; <*sol*> rise; **~per com** break up with;

~pimento *m* break; (*de relações*) breaking off

ron|car /xõ'kar/ *vi* (*ao dormir*) snore; <*estômago*> rumble; **~co** *m* snoring; (*um*) snore; (*de motor*) roar

ron|da /'xõda/ *f* round, patrol; **~dar** *vt* (*patrulhar*) patrol; (*espreitar*) prowl around □ *vi* <*vigia etc*> patrol; <*animal, ladrão*> prowl around

ronronar /xõxo'nar/ *vi* purr

roque[1] /'xɔki/ *m* (*em xadrez*) rook

ro|que[2] /'xɔki/ *m* (*música*) rock; **~queiro** *m* rock musician

rosa /'xɔza/ *f* rose □ *a invar* pink; **~do** *a* rosy; <*vinho*> rosé

rosário /xo'zariu/ *m* rosary

rosbife /xoz'bifi/ *m* roast beef

rosca /'xoska/ *f* (*de parafuso*) thread; (*biscoito*) rusk; **farinha de ~** breadcrumbs

roseira /xo'zera/ *f* rosebush

roseta /xo'zeta/ *f* rosette

rosnar /xoz'nar/ *vi* <*cachorro*> growl; <*pessoa*> snarl

rosto /'xostu/ *m* face

rota /'xɔta/ *f* route

rota|ção /xota'sãw/ *f* rotation; **~tividade** *f* turnround; **~tivo** *a* rotating

rotei|rista /xote'rista/ *m/f* scriptwriter; **~ro** *m* (*de viagem*) itinerary; (*de filme, peça*) script; (*de discussão etc*) outline

roti|na /xo'tʃina/ *f* routine; **~neiro** *a* routine

rótula /'xɔtula/ *f* kneecap

rotular /xotu'lar/ *vt* label (**de** as)

rótulo /'xɔtulu/ *m* label

rou|bar /xo'bar/ *vt* steal <*dinheiro, carro etc*>; rob <*pessoa, loja etc*> □ *vi* steal; (*em jogo*) cheat; **~bo** *m* theft, robbery

rouco /'xoku/ *a* hoarse; <*voz*> gravelly

rou|pa /'xopa/ *f* clothes; (*uma*) outfit; **~pa de baixo** underwear; **~pa de cama** bedclothes; **~pão** *m* dressing gown

rouquidão /xoki'dãw/ *f* hoarseness

rouxi|nol /xoʃi'nɔw/ (*pl* **~nóis**) *m* nightingale

roxo /'xoʃu/ *a* purple

rua /'xua/ *f* street

rubéola /xu'bɛola/ *f* German measles

rubi /xu'bi/ *m* ruby

rude /'xudʒi/ *a* rude

rudimentos /xudʒi'mẽtus/ *m pl* rudiments, basics

ruela /xu'ɛla/ *f* backstreet

rufar /xu'far/ *vi* <*tambor*> roll □ *m* roll

ruga /'xuga/ *f* (*na pele*) wrinkle; (*na roupa*) crease

ru|gido /xu'ʒidu/ *m* roar; **~gir** *vi* roar

ruibarbo /xui'barbu/ *m* rhubarb

ruído /xu'idu/ *m* noise

ruidoso /xui'dozu/ *a* noisy

ruim /xu'ĩ/ *a* bad

ruína /xu'ina/ *f* ruin

ruivo /'xuivu/ *a* <*cabelo*> red; <*pessoa*> red-haired □ *m* redhead

rulê /xu'le/ *a* **gola ~** roll-neck

rum /xũ/ *m* rum

ru|mar /xu'mar/ *vi* head (**para** for); **~mo** *m* course; **~mo a** heading for; **sem ~mo** <*vida*> aimless; <*andar*> aimlessly

rumor /xu'mor/ *m* (*da rua, de vozes*) hum; (*do trânsito*) rumble; (*boato*) rumour

ru|ral /xu'raw/ (*pl* **~rais**) *a* rural

rusga /'xuzga/ *f* quarrel, disagreement

rush /xaʃ/ *m* rush hour

Rússia /'xusia/ *f* Russia

russo /'xusu/ *a & m* Russian

rústico /'xustʃiku/ *a* rustic

Ss

Saara /saa'ra/ *m* Sahara

sábado /'sabadu/ *m* Saturday

sabão /sa'bãw/ *m* soap; **~ em pó** soap powder

sabatina /saba'tʃina/ *f* test

sabedoria /sabedo'ria/ *f* wisdom

saber /sa'ber/ *vt/i* know (**de** about); (*descobrir*) find out (**de** about) □ *m* knowledge; **eu sei cantar** I know how to sing, I can sing; **sei lá** I've no idea; **que eu saiba** as far as I know

sabiá /sabi'a/ *m* thrush

sabi|chão /sabi'ʃãw/ *a & m* (*f* **~chona**) know-it-all

sábio /'sabiu/ *a* wise □ *m* wise man

sabone|te /sabo'netʃi/ *m* bar of soap; **~teira** *f* soapdish

sabor /sa'bor/ *m* flavour; **ao ~ de** at the mercy of

sabo|rear /sabori'ar/ *vt* savour; **~roso** *a* tasty

sabo|tador /sabota'dor/ *m* saboteur; **~tagem** *f* sabotage; **~tar** *vt* sabotage

saca /'saka/ *f* sack

sacada /sa'kada/ *f* balcony

sa|cal /sa'kaw/ (*pl* **~cais**) *a* (*fam*) boring

saca|na /sa'kana/ (*fam*) *a* (*desonesto*) devious; (*lascivo*) dirty-minded, naughty □ *m/f* rogue; **~nagem** (*fam*) *f*

(*esperteza*) trickery; (*sexo*) sex; (*uma*) dirty trick; **~near** (*fam*) *vt* (*enganar*) do the dirty on; (*amolar*) take the mickey out of
sacar /sa'kar/ *vt/i* withdraw <*dinheiro*>; draw <*arma*>; (*em tênis, vôlei etc*) serve; (*fam*) (*entender*) understand
saçaricar /sasari'kar/ *vi* play around
sacarina /saka'rina/ *f* saccharine
saca-rolhas /saka'xoʎas/ *m invar* corkscrew
sacer|dócio /saser'dɔsiu/ *m* priesthood; **~dote** /ɔ/ *m* priest; **~dotisa** *f* priestess
sachê /sa'ʃe/ *m* sachet
saciar /sasi'ar/ *vt* satisfy
saco /'saku/ *m* bag; **que ~!** (*fam*) what a pain!; **estar de ~ cheio (de)** (*fam*) be fed up (with), be sick (of); **encher o ~ de alg** (*fam*) get on s.o.'s nerves; **puxar o ~ de alg** (*fam*) suck up to s.o.; **~ de dormir** sleeping bag; **~la** /ɔ/ *f* bag; **~lão** *m* wholesale fruit and vegetable market; **~lejar** *vt* shake
sacramento /sakra'mẽtu/ *m* sacrament
sacri|ficar /sakrifi'kar/ *vt* sacrifice; have put down <*cachorro etc*>; **~fício** *m* sacrifice; **~légio** *m* sacrilege
sacrílego /sa'krilegu/ *a* sacrilegious
sacro /'sakru/ *a* <*música*> religious
sacrossanto /sakro'sãtu/ *a* sacrosanct
sacu|dida /saku'dʒida/ *f* shake; **~dir** *vt* shake
sádico /'sadʒiku/ *a* sadistic □ *m* sadist
sadio /sa'dʒiu/ *a* healthy
sadismo /sa'dʒizmu/ *m* sadism
safa|deza /safa'deza/ *f* (*desonestidade*) deviousness; (*libertinagem*) indecency; (*uma*) dirty trick; **~do** *a* (*desonesto*) devious; (*lascivo*) dirty-minded; (*esperto*) quick; <*criança*> naughty
safena /sa'fɛna/ *f* **ponte de ~** heart bypass; **~do** *m* bypass patient
safira /sa'fira/ *f* sapphire
safra /'safra/ *f* crop
sagitariano /saʒitari'anu/ *a & m* Sagittarian
Sagitário /saʒi'tariu/ *m* Sagittarius
sagrado /sa'gradu/ *a* sacred
saguão /sa'gwãw/ *m* (*de teatro, hotel*) foyer, (*Amer*) lobby; (*de estação, aeroporto*) concourse
saia /'saja/ *f* skirt; **~-calça** (*pl* **~s-calças**) *f* culottes
saída /sa'ida/ *f* (*partida*) departure; (*porta, fig*) way out; **de ~** at the outset; **estar de ~** be on one's way out
sair /sa'ir/ *vi* (*de dentro*) go/come out; (*partir*) leave; (*desprender-se*) come off; <*mancha*> come out; (*resultar*) turn out; **~-se** *vpr* fare; **~-se com** (*dizer*) come out with; **~ mais barato** work out cheaper
sal /saw/ (*pl* **sais**) *m* salt; **~ de frutas** Epsom salts
sala /'sala/ *f* (*numa casa*) lounge; (*num lugar público*) hall; (*classe*) class; **fazer ~ a** entertain; **~ (de aula)** classroom; **~ de embarque** departure lounge; **~ de espera** waiting room; **~ de jantar** dining room; **~ de operação** operating theatre
sala|da /sa'lada/ *f* salad; (*fig*) jumble, mishmash; **~da de frutas** fruit salad; **~deira** *f* salad bowl
sala-e-quarto /sali'kwartu/ *m* two-room flat
sala|me /sa'lami/ *m* salami; **~minho** *m* pepperoni
salão /sa'lãw/ *m* hall; (*de cabeleireiro*) salon; (*de carros*) show; **~ de beleza** beauty salon
salari|al /salari'aw/ (*pl* **~ais**) *a* wage
salário /sa'lariu/ *m* salary
sal|dar /saw'dar/ *vt* settle; **~do** *m* balance
saleiro /sa'leru/ *m* salt cellar
sal|gadinhos /sawga'dʒiɲus/ *m pl* snacks; **~gado** *a* salty; <*preço*> exorbitant; **~gar** *vt* salt
salgueiro /saw'geru/ *m* willow; **~ chorão** weeping willow
saliência /sali'ẽsia/ *f* projection
salien|tar /saliẽ'tar/ *vt* (*deixar claro*) point out; (*acentuar*) highlight; **~tar-se** *vpr* distinguish o.s.; **~te** *a* prominent
saliva /sa'liva/ *f* saliva
salmão /saw'mãw/ *m* salmon
salmo /'sawmu/ *m* psalm
salmonela /sawmo'nɛla/ *f* salmonella
salmoura /saw'mora/ *f* brine
salpicar /sawpi'kar/ *vt* sprinkle; (*sem querer*) spatter
salsa /'sawsa/ *f* parsley
salsicha /saw'siʃa/ *f* sausage
saltar /saw'tar/ *vt* (*pular*) jump; (*omitir*) skip □ *vi* jump; **~ à vista** be obvious; **~ do ônibus** get off the bus
saltear /sawtʃi'ar/ *vt* sauté <*batatas etc*>
saltitar /sawtʃi'tar/ *vi* hop
salto /'sawtu/ *m* (*pulo*) jump; (*de sapato*) heel; **~ com vara** pole vault; **~ em altura** high jump; **~ em distância** long jump; **~-mortal** (*pl* **~s-mortais**) *m* somersault
salu|bre /sa'lubri/ *a* healthy; **~tar** *a* salutary
salva[1] /'sawva/ *f* (*de canhões*) salvo; (*bandeja*) salver; **~ de palmas** round of applause
salva[2] /'sawva/ *f* (*erva*) sage

salva|ção /sawva'sãw/ *f* salvation; **~dor** *m* saviour

salvaguar|da /sawva'gwarda/ *f* safeguard; **~dar** *vt* safeguard

sal|vamento /sawva'mẽtu/ *m* rescue; (*de navio*) salvage; **~var** *vt* save; **~var-se** *vpr* escape; **~va-vidas** *m invar* (*bóia*) lifebelt □ *m/f* (*pessoa*) lifeguard □ *a* **barco ~va-vidas** lifeboat; **~vo** *a* safe □ *prep* save; **a ~vo** safe

samambaia /samã'baja/ *f* fern

sam|ba /'sãba/ *m* samba; **~ba-canção** (*pl* **~bas-canção**) *m* slow samba □ *a invar* **cueca ~ba-canção** boxer shorts; **~ba-enredo** (*pl* **~bas-enredo**) *m* samba story; **~bar** *vi* samba; **~bista** *m/f* (*dançarino*) samba dancer; (*compositor*) composer of sambas; **~bódromo** *m* Carnival parade ground

samovar /samo'var/ *m* tea urn

sanar /sa'nar/ *vt* cure

san|ção /sã'sãw/ *f* sanction; **~cionar** *vt* sanction

sandália /sã'dalia/ *f* sandal

sandes /'sãdiʃ/ *f invar* (*Port*) sandwich

sanduíche /sãdu'iʃi/ *m* sandwich

sane|amento /sania'mẽtu/ *m* (*esgotos*) sanitation; (*de finanças*) rehabilitation; **~ar** *vt* set straight <*finanças*>

sanfona /sã'fona/ *f* (*instrumento*) accordion; (*tricô*) ribbing; **~do** *a* <*porta*> folding; <*pulôver*> ribbed

san|grar /sã'grar/ *vt/i* bleed; **~grento** *a* bloody; <*carne*> rare; **~gria** *f* bloodshed; (*de dinheiro*) extortion

sangue /'sãgi/ *m* blood; **~ pisado** bruise; **~-frio** *m* cool, coolness

sanguessuga /sãgi'suga/ *f* leech

sanguinário /sãgi'nariu/ *a* bloodthirsty

sanguíneo /sã'giniu/ *a* blood

sanidade /sani'dadʒi/ *f* sanity

sanitário /sani'tariu/ *a* sanitary; **~s** *mpl* toilets

san|tidade /sãtʃi'dadʒi/ *f* sanctity; **~tificar** *vt* sanctify; **~to** *a* holy □ *m* saint; **todo ~to dia** every single day; **~tuário** *m* sanctuary

São /sãw/ *a* Saint

são /sãw/ (*pl* **~s**) *a* (*f* **sã**) healthy; (*mentalmente*) sane; <*conselho*> sound

sapato /sa'pata/ *m* shoe; **~ria** *f* shoe shop

sapate|ado /sapatʃi'adu/ *m* tap dancing; **~ador** *m* tap dancer; **~ar** *vi* tap one's feet; (*dançar*) tap-dance

sapa|teiro /sapa'teru/ *m* shoemaker; **~tilha** *f* pump; **~tilha de balé** ballet shoe; **~to** *m* shoe

sapeca /sa'pɛka/ *a* saucy

sa|pinho /sa'piɲu/ *m* thrush; **~po** *m* toad

saque[1] /'saki/ *m* (*do banco*) withdrawal; (*em tênis, vôlei etc*) serve

saque[2] /'saki/ *m* (*de loja etc*) looting; **~ar** *vt* loot

saraiva /sa'rajva/ *f* hail; **~da** *f* hailstorm; **uma ~da de** a hail of

sarampo /sa'rãpu/ *m* measles

sarar /sa'rar/ *vt* cure □ *vi* get better; <*ferida*> heal

sar|casmo /sar'kazmu/ *m* sarcasm; **~cástico** *a* sarcastic

sarda /'sarda/ *f* freckle

Sardenha /sar'deɲa/ *f* Sardinia

sardento /sar'dẽtu/ *a* freckled

sardinha /sar'dʒiɲa/ *f* sardine

sardônico /sar'doniku/ *a* sardonic

sargento /sar'ʒẽtu/ *m* sergeant

sarjeta /sar'ʒeta/ *f* gutter

Satanás /sata'nas/ *m* Satan

satânico /sa'taniku/ *a* satanic

satélite /sa'tɛlitʃi/ *a & m* satellite

sátira /'satʃira/ *f* satire

satírico /sa'tʃiriku/ *a* satirical

satirizar /satʃiri'zar/ *vt* satirize

satisfa|ção /satʃisfa'sãw/ *f* satisfaction; **dar ~ções a** answer to; **~tório** *a* satisfactory; **~zer** *vt* **~zer (a)** satisfy □ *vi* be satisfactory; **~zer-se** *vpr* be satis- fied

satisfeito /satʃis'fejtu/ *a* satisfied; (*contente*) content; (*de comida*) full

saturar /satu'rar/ *vt* saturate

Saturno /sa'turnu/ *m* Saturn

saudação /sawda'sãw/ *f* greeting

saudade /saw'dadʒi/ *f* longing; (*lembrança*) nostalgia; **estar com ~s de** miss; **matar ~s** catch up

saudar /saw'dar/ *vt* greet

saudá|vel /saw'davew/ (*pl* **~veis**) *a* healthy

saúde /sa'udʒi/ *f* health □ *int* (*ao beber*) cheers; (*ao espirrar*) bless you

saudo|sismo /sawdo'zizmu/ *m* nostalgia; **~so** /o/ *a* longing; **estar ~so de** miss; **o nosso ~so amigo** our much-missed friend

sauna /'sawna/ *f* sauna

saxofo|ne /sakso'foni/ *m* saxophone; **~nista** *m/f* saxophonist

sazo|nado /sazo'nadu/ *a* seasoned; **~nal** (*pl* **~nais**) *a* seasonal

se[1] /si/ *conj* if; **não sei ~ ...** I don't know if/whether

se[2] /si/ *pron* (*ele mesmo*) himself; (*ela mesma*) herself; (*você mesmo*) yourself; (*eles/elas*) themselves; (*vocês*) yourselves; (*um ao outro*) each other; **dorme-~ tarde no Brasil** people go to bed late in Brazil; **aqui ~ fala inglês** English is spoken here

sebo /'sebu/ *m* (*sujeira*) grease; (*livraria*) secondhand bookshop; **~so** /o/ *a* greasy; <*pessoa*> slimy

seca /'seka/ *f* drought; **~dor** *m* **~dor de cabelo** hairdryer; **~-dora** *f* tumble dryer

seção /se'sãw/ *f* section; (*de loja*) department

secar /se'kar/ *vt/i* dry

sec|ção /sek'sãw/ *f veja* **seção**; **~cionar** *vt* split up

seco /'seku/ *a* dry; <*resposta, tom*> curt; <*pessoa, caráter*> cold; <*barulho, pancada*> dull; **estar ~ por** I'm dying for

secretaria /sekreta'ria/ *f* (*de empresa*) general office; (*ministério*) department

secretá|ria /sekre'taria/ *f* secretary; **~ria eletrônica** ansaphone; **~rio** *m* secretary

secreto /se'krɛtu/ *a* secret

secular /seku'lar/ *a* (*não religioso*) secular; (*antigo*) age-old

século /'sɛkulu/ *m* century; *pl* (*muito tempo*) ages

secundário /sekũ'dariu/ *a* secondary

secura /se'kura/ *f* dryness; **estar com uma ~ de** be longing for/to

seda /'seda/ *f* silk

sedativo /seda'tʃivu/ *a & m* sedative

sede[1] /'sɛdʒi/ *f* headquarters; (*local do governo*) seat

sede[2] /'sedʒi/ *f* thirst (**de** for); **estar com ~** be thirsty

sedentário /sedẽ'tariu/ *a* sedentary

sedento /se'dẽtu/ *a* thirsty (**de** for)

sediar /sedʒi'ar/ *vt* host

sedimen|tar /sedʒimẽ'tar/ *vt* consolidate; **~to** *m* sediment

sedoso /se'dozu/ *a* silky

sedu|ção /sedu'sãw/ *f* seduction; **~tor** *a* seductive; **~zir** *vt* seduce

segmento /seg'mẽtu/ *m* segment

segredo /se'gredu/ *m* secret; (*de cofre etc*) combination

segregar /segre'gar/ *vt* segregate

segui|da /se'gida/ *f* **em ~da** (*imediatamente*) straight away; (*depois*) next; **~do** *a* followed (**de** by); **cinco horas ~das** five hours running; **~dor** *m* follower; **~mento** *m* continuation; **dar ~mento a** go on with

se|guinte /se'gĩtʃi/ *a* following; <*dia, semana etc*> next; **~guir** *vt/i* follow; (*continuar*) continue; **~guir-se** *vpr* follow; **~guir em frente** (*ir embora*) go; (*indicação na rua*) go straight ahead

segun|da /se'gũda/ *f* (*dia*) Monday; (*marcha*) second; **de ~da** second-rate; **~da-feira** (*pl* **~das-feiras**) *f* Monday; **~do** *a & m* second ▫ *adv* secondly ▫ *prep* according to ▫ *conj* according to what; **~das intenções** ulterior motives; **de ~da mão** second-hand

segu|rança /segu'rãsa/ *f* security; (*estado de seguro*) safety; (*certeza*) assurance ▫ *m/f* security guard; **~rar** *vt* hold; **~rar-se** *vpr* (*controlar-se*) control o.s.; **~rar-se em** hold on to; **~ro** *a* secure; (*fora de perigo*) safe; (*com certeza*) sure ▫ *m* insurance; **estar no ~ro** <*bens*> be insured; **fazer ~ro de** insure; **~ro-desemprego** *m* unemployment benefit

seio /'seju/ *m* breast, bosom; **no ~ de** within

seis /sejs/ *a & m* six; **~centos** *a & m* six hundred

seita /'sejta/ *f* sect

seixo /'sejʃu/ *m* pebble

sela /'sɛla/ *f* saddle

selar[1] /se'lar/ *vt* saddle <*cavalo*>

selar[2] /se'lar/ *vt* seal; (*franquear*) stamp

sele|ção /sele'sãw/ *f* selection; (*time*) team; **~cionar** *vt* select; **~to** /ɛ/ *a* select

selim /se'lĩ/ *m* saddle

selo /'selu/ *m* seal; (*postal*) stamp; (*de discos*) label

selva /'sɛwva/ *f* jungle; **~gem** *a* wild; **~geria** *f* savagery

sem /sẽj/ *prep* without; **~ eu saber** without me knowing; **ficar ~ dinheiro** run out of money

semáforo /se'maforu/ *m* (*na rua*) traffic lights; (*de ferrovia*) signal

sema|na /se'mana/ *f* week; **~nal** (*pl* **~nais**) *a* weekly; **~nalmente** *adv* weekly; **~nário** *m* weekly

semear /semi'ar/ *vt* sow

semelhan|ça /seme'ʎãsa/ *f* similarity; **~te** *a* similar; (*tal*) such

sêmen /'semẽ/ *m* semen

semente /se'mẽtʃi/ *f* seed; (*em fruta*) pip

semestre /se'mɛstri/ *m* six months; (*da faculdade etc*) term, (*Amer*) semester

semi|círculo /semi'sirkulu/ *m* semicircle; **~final** (*pl* **~finais**) *f* semifinal

seminário /semi'nariu/ *m* (*aula*) seminar; (*colégio religioso*) seminary

sem-número /sẽ'numeru/ *m* **um ~ de** innumerable

sempre /'sẽpri/ *adv* always; **como ~** as usual; **para ~** for ever; **~ que** whenever

sem|-terra /sẽ'tɛxa/ *m/f invar* landless labourer; **~-teto** *a* homeless ▫ *m/f* homeless person; **~-vergonha** *a invar* brazen ▫ *m/f invar* scoundrel

sena|do /se'nadu/ *m* senate; **~dor** *m* senator

senão /si'nãw/ *conj* otherwise; (*mas antes*) but rather □ *m* snag
senda /'sẽda/ *f* path
senha /'seɲa/ *f* (*palavra*) password; (*número*) code; (*sinal*) signal
senhor /se'ɲor/ *m* gentleman; (*homem idoso*) older man; (*tratamento*) sir □ *a* (*f* **~a**) mighty; **Senhor** (*com nome*) Mr; (*Deus*) Lord; **o ~** (*você*) you
senho|ra /se'ɲɔra/ *f* lady; (*mulher idosa*) older woman; (*tratamento*) madam; **Senhora** (*com nome*) Mrs; **a ~ra** (*você*) you; **nossa ~ra!** (*fam*) gosh; **~ria** *f* **Vossa Senhoria** you; **~rita** *f* young lady; (*tratamento*) miss; **Senhorita** (*com nome*) Miss
se|nil (*pl* **~nis**) *a* senile; **~nilidade** *f* senility
sensação /sẽsa'sãw/ *f* sensation
sensacio|nal /sẽsasio'naw/ (*pl* **~nais**) *a* sensational; **~nalismo** *m* sensationalism; **~nalista** *a* sensationalist
sen|sato /sẽ'satu/ *a* sensible; **~sibilidade** *f* sensitivity; **~sível** (*pl* **~síveis**) *a* sensitive; (*que se pode sentir*) noticeable; **~so** *m* sense; **~sual** (*pl* **~suais**) *a* sensual
sen|tado /sẽ'tadu/ *a* sitting; **~tar** *vt/i* sit; **~tar-se** *vpr* sit down
sentença /sẽ'tẽsa/ *f* sentence
sentido /sẽ'tʃidu/ *m* sense; (*direção*) direction □ *a* hurt; **fazer** *ou* **ter ~** make sense
sentimen|tal /sẽtʃimẽ'taw/ (*pl* **~tais**) *a* sentimental; **vida ~tal** love life; **~to** *m* feeling
sentinela /sẽtʃi'nɛla/ *f* sentry
sentir /sẽ'tʃir/ *vt* feel; (*notar*) sense; smell <*cheiro*>; taste <*gosto*>; tell <*diferença*>; (*ficar magoado por*) be hurt by □ *vi* feel; **~-se** *vpr* feel; **sinto muito** I'm very sorry
sepa|ração /separa'sãw/ *f* separation; **~rado** *a* separate; <*casal*> separated; **~rar** *vt* separate; **~rar-se** *vpr* separate
séptico /'sɛptʃiku/ *a* septic
sepul|tar /sepuw'tar/ *vt* bury; **~tura** *f* grave
seqüência /se'kwẽsia/ *f* sequence
sequer /se'kɛr/ *adv* **nem ~** not even
seqües|trador /sekwestra'dor/ *m* kidnapper; (*de avião*) hijacker; **~trar** *vt* kidnap <*pessoa*>; hijack <*avião*>; sequestrate <*bens*>; **~tro** /ɛ/ *m* (*de pessoa*) kidnapping; (*de avião*) hijack; (*de bens*) sequestration
ser /ser/ *vi* be □ *m* being; **é** (*como resposta*) yes; **você gosta, não é?** you like it, don't you?; **ele foi morto** he was killed; **será que ele volta?** I wonder if he's coming back; **ou seja** in other words; **a não ~** except; **a não ~ que** unless; **não sou de fofocar** I'm not one to gossip
sereia /se'reja/ *f* mermaid
serenata /sere'nata/ *f* serenade
sereno /se'renu/ *a* serene; <*tempo*> fine
série /'sɛri/ *f* series; (*na escola*) grade; **fora de ~** incredible
seriedade /serie'dadʒi/ *f* seriousness
serin|ga /se'rĩga/ *f* syringe; **~gueiro** *m* rubber tapper
sério /'sɛriu/ *a* serious; (*responsável*) responsible; **~?** really?; **falar ~** be serious; **levar a ~** take seriously
sermão /ser'mãw/ *m* sermon
serpen|te /ser'pẽtʃi/ *f* serpent; **~tear** *vi* wind; **~tina** *f* streamer
serra[1] /'sɛxa/ *f* (*montanhas*) mountain range
serra[2] /'sɛxa/ *f* (*de serrar*) saw; **~gem** *f* sawdust; **~lheiro** *m* locksmith
serrano /se'xanu/ *a* mountain
serrar /se'xar/ *vt* saw
ser|tanejo /serta'neʒu/ *a* from the backwoods □ *m* backwoodsman; **~tão** *m* backwoods
servente /ser'vẽtʃi/ *m/f* labourer
Sérvia /'sɛrvia/ *f* Serbia
servi|çal /servi'saw/ (*pl* **~çais**) *a* helpful □ *m/f* servant; **~ço** *m* service; (*trabalho*) work; (*tarefa*) job; **estar de ~ço** be on duty; **~dor** *m* servant; (*comput*) server; **~ público** civil servant
ser|vil /ser'viw/ (*pl* **~vis**) *a* servile
sérvio /'sɛrviu/ *a & m* Serbian
servir /ser'vir/ *vt* serve □ *vi* serve; (*ser adequado*) do; (*ser útil*) be of use; <*roupa, sapato etc*> fit; **~-se** *vpr* (*ao comer etc*) help o.s. (**de** to); **~-se de** make use of; **~ como** *ou* **de** serve as; **para que serve isso?** what is this (used) for?
sessão /se'sãw/ *f* session; (*no cinema*) showing, performance
sessenta /se'sẽta/ *a & m* sixty
seta /'sɛta/ *f* arrow; (*de carro*) indicator
sete /'sɛtʃi/ *a & m* seven; **~centos** *a & m* seven hundred
setembro /se'tẽbru/ *m* September
setenta /se'tẽta/ *a & m* seventy
sétimo /'sɛtʃimu/ *a* seventh
setuagésimo /setua'ʒɛzimu/ *a* seventieth
setor /se'tor/ *m* sector
seu /sew/ *a* (*f* **sua**) (*dele*) his; (*dela*) her; (*de coisa*) its; (*deles*) their; (*de você, de vocês*) your □ *pron* (*dele*) his; (*dela*) hers; (*deles*) theirs; (*de você, de vocês*) yours; **~ idiota!** you idiot!; **seu João** Mr John

seve|ridade /severi'dadʒi/ *f* severity; **~ro** /ɛ/ *a* severe

sexagésimo /seksa'ʒɛzimu/ *a* sixtieth

sexo /'sɛksu/ *m* sex; **fazer ~** have sex

sex|ta /'sesta/ *f* Friday; **~ta-feira** (*pl* **~tas-feiras**) *f* Friday; **Sexta-feira Santa** Good Friday; **~to** /e/ *a & m* sixth

sexu|al /seksu'aw/ (*pl* **~ais**) *a* sexual; **vida ~al** sex life

sexy /'sɛksi/ *a invar* sexy

shopping /'ʃɔpĩ/ (*pl* **~s**) *m* shopping centre, (*Amer*) mall

short /'ʃɔrtʃi/ *m* (*pl* **~s**) shorts; **um ~** a pair of shorts

show /'ʃou/ (*pl* **~s**) *m* show; (*de música*) concert

si /si/ *pron* (*ele*) himself; (*ela*) herself; (*coisa*) itself; (*você*) yourself; (*eles*) themselves; (*vocês*) yourselves; (*qualquer pessoa*) oneself; **em ~** in itself; **fora de ~** beside o.s.; **cheio de ~** full of o.s.; **voltar a ~** come round

sibilar /sibi'lar/ *vi* hiss

SIDA /'sida/ *f* (*Port*) AIDS

side|ral /side'raw/ (*pl* **~rais**) *a* **espaço ~ral** outer space.

siderurgia /siderur'ʒia/ *f* iron and steel industry

siderúrgi|ca /side'rurʒika/ *f* steelworks; **~co** *a* iron and steel ▫ *m* steelworker

sifão /si'fãw/ *m* syphon

sífilis /'sifilis/ *f* syphilis

sigilo /si'ʒilu/ *m* secrecy; **~so** /o/ *a* secret

sigla /'sigla/ *f* acronym

signatário /signa'tariu/ *m* signatory

signifi|cação /signifika'sãw/ *f* significance; **~cado** *m* meaning; **~car** *vt* mean; **~cativo** *a* significant

signo /'signu/ *m* sign

sílaba /'silaba/ *f* syllable

silenciar /silẽsi'ar/ *vt* silence

silêncio /si'lẽsiu/ *m* silence

silencioso /silẽsi'ozu/ *a* silent ▫ *m* silencer, (*Amer*) muffler

silhueta /siʎu'eta/ *f* silhouette

silício /si'lisiu/ *m* silicon

silicone /sili'kɔni/ *m* silicone

silo /'silu/ *m* silo

silvar /siw'var/ *vi* hiss

sil|vestre /siw'vɛstri/ *a* wild; **~vicultura** *f* forestry

sim /sĩ/ *adv* yes; **acho que ~** I think so

simbólico /sĩ'bɔliku/ *a* symbolic

simbo|lismo /sĩbo'lizmu/ *m* symbolism; **~lizar** *vt* symbolize

símbolo /'sĩbolu/ *m* symbol

si|metria /sime'tria/ *f* symmetry; **~métrico** *a* symmetrical

similar /simi'lar/ *a* similar

sim|patia /sĩpa'tʃia/ *f* (*qualidade*) pleasantness; (*afeto*) fondness (**por** for); (*compreensão, apoio*) sympathy; *pl* sympathies; **ter ~patia por** be fond of; **~- pático** *a* nice

simpati|zante /sĩpatʃi'zãtʃi/ *a* sympathetic ▫ *m/f* sympathizer; **~zar** *vi* **~zar com** take a liking to <*pessoa*>; sympathize with <*idéias, partido etc*>

simples /'sĩplis/ *a invar* simple; (*único*) single ▫ *f* (*no tênis etc*) singles; **~mente** *adv* simply

simpli|cidade /sĩplisi'dadʒi/ *f* simplicity; **~ficar** *vt* simplify

simplório /sĩ'plɔriu/ *a* simple

simpósio /sĩ'pɔziu/ *m* symposium

simu|lação /simula'sãw/ *f* simulation; **~lar** *vt* simulate

simultâneo /simuw'taniu/ *a* simultaneous

sina /'sina/ *f* fate

sinagoga /sina'gɔga/ *f* synagogue

si|nal /si'naw/ (*pl* **~nais**) *m* sign; (*aviso, de rádio etc*) signal; (*de trânsito*) traffic light; (*no telefone*) tone; (*dinheiro*) deposit; (*na pele*) mole; **por ~nal** as a matter of fact; **~nal de pontuação** punctuation mark; **~naleira** *f* traffic lights; **~nalização** *f* (*na rua*) road signs; **~nalizar** *vt* signal; signpost <*rua, cidade*>

since|ridade /sĩseri'dadʒi/ *f* sincerity; **~ro** /ɛ/ *a* sincere

sincro|nia /sĩkro'nia/ *f* synchronization; **~nizar** *vt* synchronize

sindi|cal /sĩdʒi'kaw/ (*pl* **~cais**) *a* trade union; **~calismo** *m* trade unionism; **~calista** *m/f* trade unionist; **~calizar** *vt* unionize; **~cato** *m* trade union

síndico /'sĩdʒiku/ *m* house manager

síndrome /'sĩdromi/ *f* syndrome

sineta /si'neta/ *f* bell

sin|fonia /sĩfo'nia/ *f* symphony; **~fônica** *f* symphony orchestra

singe|leza /sĩʒe'leza/ *f* simplicity; **~lo** /ɛ/ *a* simple

singu|lar /sĩgu'lar/ *a* singular; (*estranho*) peculiar; **~larizar** *vt* single out

sinis|trado /sinis'tradu/ *a* damaged; **~tro** *a* sinister ▫ *m* accident

sino /'sinu/ *m* bell

sinônimo /si'nonimu/ *a* synonymous ▫ *m* synonym

sintaxe /sĩ'taksi/ *f* syntax

síntese /'sĩtezi/ *f* synthesis

sin|tético /sĩ'tɛtʃiku/ *a* (*artificial*) synthetic; (*resumido*) concise; **~tetizar** *vt* summarize

sinto|ma /sĩ'toma/ *m* symptom; **~mático** *a* symptomatic

sintoni|zador /sĩtoniza'dor/ *m* tuner; **~zar** *vt* tune <*rádio, TV*>; tune in to <*emissora*> □ *vi* be in tune (**com** with)

sinuca /si'nuka/ *f* snooker

sinuoso /sinu'ozu/ *a* winding

sinusite /sinu'zitʃi/ *f* sinusitis

siri /si'ri/ *m* crab

Síria /'siria/ *f* Syria

sírio /'siriu/ *a & m* Syrian

siso /'sizu/ *m* good sense

siste|ma /sis'tema/ *m* system; **~mático** *a* systematic

sisudo /si'zudu/ *a* serious

site /sajt/ *m* (*comput*) website

sítio /'sitʃiu/ *m* (*chácara*) farm; (*Port: local*) place; **estado de ~** state of siege

situ|ação /situa'sãw/ *f* situation; (*no governo*) party in power; **~ar** *vt* situate; **~ar-se** *vpr* be situated; <*pessoa*> position o.s.

smoking /iz'mokĩ/ (*pl* **~s**) *m* dinner jacket, (*Amer*) tuxedo

só /sɔ/ *a* alone; (*sentindo solidão*) lonely □ *adv* only; **um ~ voto** one single vote; **~ um carro** only one car; **a ~s** alone; **imagina ~** just imagine; **~ que** except (that)

soalho /so'aʎu/ *m* floor

soar /so'ar/ *vt/i* sound

sob /'sobi/ *prep* under

sobera|nia /sobera'nia/ *f* sovereignty; **~no** *a & m* sovereign

soberbo /so'berbu/ *a* <*pessoa*> haughty; (*magnífico*) splendid

sobra /'sɔbra/ *f* surplus; *pl* leftovers; **tempo de ~** (*muito*) plenty of time; **ficar de ~** be left over; **ter aco de ~** (*sobrando*) have sth left over

sobraçar /sobra'sar/ *vt* carry under one's arm

sobrado /so'bradu/ *m* (*casa*) house; (*andar*) upper floor

sobrancelha /sobrã'seʎa/ *f* eyebrow

so|brar /so'brar/ *vi* be left; **~bram-me dois** I have two left

sobre /'sobri/ *prep* (*em cima de*) on; (*por cima de, acima de*) over; (*acerca de*) about

sobreaviso /sobria'vizu/ *m* **estar de ~** be on one's guard

sobrecapa /sobri'kapa/ *f* dust jacket

sobrecarregar /sobrikaxe'gar/ *vt* overload

sobreloja /sobri'lɔʒa/ *f* mezzanine

sobremesa /sobri'meza/ *f* dessert

sobrenatu|ral /sobrinatu'raw/ (*pl* **~rais**) *a* supernatural

sobrenome /sobri'nomi/ *m* surname

sobrepor /sobri'por/ *vt* superimpose

sobrepujar /sobripu'ʒar/ *vt* (*em altura*) tower over; (*em valor, número etc*) surpass; overwhelm <*adversário*>; overcome <*problemas*>

sobrescritar /sobriskri'tar/ *vt* address

sobressair /sobrisa'ir/ *vi* stand out; **~-se** *vpr* stand out

sobressalente /sobrisa'lẽtʃi/ *a* spare

sobressal|tar /sobrisaw'tar/ *vt* startle; **~tar-se** *vpr* be startled; **~to** *m* (*movimento*) start; (*susto*) fright

sobretaxa /sobri'taʃa/ *f* surcharge

sobretudo /sobri'tudu/ *adv* above all □ *m* overcoat

sobrevir /sobri'vir/ *vi* happen suddenly; (*seguir*) ensue; **~ a** follow

sobrevi|vência /sobrivi'vẽsia/ *f* survival; **~vente** *a* surviving □ *m/f* survivor; **~ver** *vt/i* **~ver (a)** survive

sobrevoar /sobrivo'ar/ *vt* fly over

sobri|nha /so'briɲa/ *f* niece; **~nho** *m* nephew

sóbrio /'sɔbriu/ *a* sober

socar /so'kar/ *vt* (*esmurrar*) punch; (*amassar*) crush

soci|al /sosi'aw/ (*pl* **~ais**) *a* social; **camisa ~al** dress shirt; **~alismo** *m* socialism; **~alista** *a & m/f* socialist; **~alite** /-a'lajtʃi/ *m/f* socialite; **~ável** (*pl* **~áveis**) *a* sociable

sociedade /sosie'dadʒi/ *f* society; (*parceria*) partnership; **~ anônima** limited company

sócio /'sɔsiu/ *m* (*de empresa*) partner; (*de clube*) member

socio-econômico /sosioeko'nomiku/ *a* socio-economic

soci|ologia /sosiolo'ʒia/ *f* sociology; **~ológico** *a* sociological; **~ólogo** *m* sociologist

soco /'soku/ *m* punch; **dar um ~ em** punch

socor|rer /soko'xer/ *vt* help; **~ro** *m* aid □ *int* help; **primeiros ~ros** first aid

soda /'sɔda/ *f* (*água*) soda water; **~ cáustica** caustic soda

sódio /'sɔdʒiu/ *m* sodium

sofá /so'fa/ *m* sofa; **~-cama** (*pl* **~s-camas**) *m* sofa-bed

sofisticado /sofistʃi'kadu/ *a* sophisticated

so|fredor /sofre'dor/ *a* martyred; **~frer** *vt* suffer <*dor, derrota, danos etc*>; have <*acidente*>; undergo <*operação, mudança etc*> □ *vi* suffer; **~frer de** suffer from <*doença*>; have trouble with <*coração etc*>; **~frido** *a* long-suffering; **~frimento** *m* suffering; **~frível** (*pl* **~fríveis**) *a* passable

soft /'sɔftʃi/ (*pl* **~s**) *m* software package; **~ware** *m* software; (*um*) software package

so|gra /'sɔgra/ *f* mother-in-law; **~gro** /o/ *m* father-in-law; **~- gros** /ɔ/ *m pl* in-laws

soja /'sɔʒa/ *f* soya, (*Amer*) soy

sol /sɔw/ (*pl* **sóis**) *m* sun; **faz ~** it's sunny

sola /'sɔla/ *f* sole; **~do** *a* <*bolo*> flat

solapar /sola'par/ *vt* undermine

solar[1] /so'lar/ *a* solar

solar[2] /so'lar/ *vt* sole <*sapato*> □ *vi* <*bolo*> go flat

solavanco /sola'vãku/ *m* jolt; **dar ~s** jolt

soldado /sow'dadu/ *m* soldier

sol|dadura /sowda'dura/ *f* weld; **~dar** *vt* weld

soldo /'sowdu/ *m* pay

soleira /so'lera/ *f* doorstep

sole|ne /so'leni/ *a* solemn; **~nidade** *f* (*cerimônia*) ceremony; (*qualidade*) solemnity

soletrar /sole'trar/ *vt* spell

solici|tação /solisita'sãw/ *f* request (**de** for); (*por escrito*) application (**de** for); **~tante** *m/f* applicant; **~tar** *vt* request; (*por escrito*) apply for

solícito /so'lisitu/ *a* helpful

solidão /soli'dãw/ *f* loneliness

soli|dariedade /solidarie'dadʒi/ *f* solidarity; **~dário** *a* supportive (**com** of)

soli|dez /soli'des/ *f* solidity; **~dificar** *vt* solidify; **~dificar-se** *vpr* solidify

sólido /'sɔlidu/ *a & m* solid

solista /so'lista/ *m/f* soloist

solitá|ria /soli'taria/ *f* (*verme*) tapeworm; (*cela*) solitary confinement; **~rio** *a* solitary

solo[1] /'sɔlu/ *m* (*terra*) soil; (*chão*) ground

solo[2] /'sɔlu/ *m* solo

soltar /sow'tar/ *vt* let go <*prisioneiros, animal etc*>; let loose <*cães*>; (*deixar de segurar*) let go of; loosen <*gravata, corda etc*>; let down <*cabelo*>; let out <*grito, suspiro etc*>; let off <*foguetes*>; tell <*piada*>; take off <*freio*>; **~-se** *vpr* <*peça, parafuso*> come loose; <*pessoa*> let o.s. go

soltei|ra /sow'tera/ *f* single woman; **~rão** *m* bachelor; **~ro** *a* single □ *m* single man; **~rona** *f* spinster

solto /'sowtu/ *a* (*livre*) free; <*cães*> loose; <*cabelo*> down; <*arroz*> fluffy; (*frouxo*) loose; (*à vontade*) relaxed; (*abandonado*) abandoned; **correr ~** run wild

solução /solu'sãw/ *f* solution

soluçar /solu'sar/ *vi* (*ao chorar*) sob; (*engasgar*) hiccup

solucionar /solusio'nar/ *vt* solve

soluço /so'lusu/ *m* (*ao chorar*) sob; (*engasgo*) hiccup; **estar com ~s** have the hiccups

solú|vel /so'luvew/ (*pl* **~veis**) *a* soluble

solvente /sow'vẽtʃi/ *a & m* solvent

som /sõ/ *m* sound; (*aparelho*) stereo; **um ~** (*fam*) (*música*) a bit of music

so|ma /'soma/ *f* sum; **~mar** *vt* add up <*números etc*>; (*ter como soma*) add up to

sombra /'sõbra/ *f* shadow; (*área abrigada do sol*) shade; **à ~ de** in the shade of; **sem ~ de dúvida** without a shadow of a doubt

sombre|ado /sõbri'adu/ *a* shady □ *m* shading; **~ar** *vt* shade

sombrinha /sõ'briɲa/ *f* parasol

sombrio /sõ'briu/ *a* gloomy

somente /so'mẽtʃi/ *adv* only

sonâmbulo /so'nãbulu/ *m* sleepwalker

sonante /so'nãtʃi/ *a* **moeda ~** hard cash

sonata /so'nata/ *f* sonata

son|da /'sõda/ *f* probe; **~dagem** *f* (*no mar*) sounding; (*de terreno*) survey; **~dagem de opinião** opinion poll; **~dar** *vt* probe; sound <*profundeza*>; (*fig*) sound out <*pessoas, opiniões etc*>

soneca /so'nɛka/ *f* nap; **tirar uma ~** have a nap

sone|gação /sonega'sãw/ *f* (*de impostos*) tax evasion; **~gador** *m* tax dodger; **~gar** *vt* with-hold

soneto /so'netu/ *m* sonnet

so|nhador /soɲa'dor/ *a* dreamy □ *m* dreamer; **~nhar** *vt/i* dream (**com** about); **~nho** /'soɲu/ *m* dream; (*doce*) doughnut

sono /'sonu/ *m* sleep; **estar com ~** be sleepy; **pegar no ~** get to sleep; **~lento** *a* sleepy

sono|plastia /sonoplas'tʃia/ *f* sound effects; **~ridade** *f* sound quality; **~ro** /ɔ/ *a* sound; <*voz*> sonorous; <*consoante*> voiced

sonso /'sõsu/ *a* devious

sopa /'sopa/ *f* soup

sopapo /so'papu/ *m* slap; **dar um ~ em** slap

sopé /so'pɛ/ *m* foot

sopeira /so'pera/ *f* soup tureen

soprano /so'pranu/ *m/f* soprano

so|prar /so'prar/ *vt* blow <*folhas etc*>; blow up <*balão*>; blow out <*vela*> □ *vi* blow; **~pro** *m* blow; (*de vento*) puff; **instrumento de ~pro** wind instrument

soquete[1] /so'kɛtʃi/ *f* ankle sock

soquete[2] /so'ketʃi/ *m* socket

sordidez /sordʒi'des/ *f* sordidness; (*imundície*) squalor

sórdido /'sɔrdʒidu/ *a* (*reles*) sordid; (*imundo*) squalid

soro /'soru/ *m* (*remédio*) serum; (*de leite*) whey

sorrateiro /soxa'teru/ *a* crafty

sor|ridente /soxi'dẽtʃi/ *a* smiling; **~rir** *vi* smile; **~riso** *m* smile

sorte /'sɔrtʃi/ *f* luck; (*destino*) fate; **pessoa de ~** lucky person; **por ~** luckily; **ter** *ou* **dar ~** be lucky; **tive a ~ de conhecê-lo** I was lucky enough to meet him; **tirar a ~** draw lots; **trazer** *ou* **dar ~** bring good luck

sor|tear /sortʃi'ar/ *vt* draw for <*prêmio*>; select in a draw <*pessoa*>; **~teio** *m* draw

sorti|do /sor'tʃidu/ *a* assorted; **~mento** *m* assortment

sorumbático /sorũ'batʃiku/ *a* sombre, gloomy

sorver /sor'ver/ *vt* sip <*bebida*>

sósia /'sɔzia/ *m/f* double

soslaio /soz'laju/ *m* **de ~** sideways; <*olhar*> askance

sosse|gado /sose'gadu/ *a* <*vida*> quiet; **ficar ~gado** <*pessoa*> rest assured; **~gar** *vt* reassure □ *vi* rest; **~go** /e/ *m* peace

sótão /'sɔtãw/ (*pl* **~s**) *m* attic, loft

sotaque /so'taki/ *m* accent

soterrar /sote'xar/ *vt* bury

soutien /suti'ã/ (*pl* **~s**) *m* (*Port*) bra

sova|co /so'vaku/ *m* armpit; **~queira** *f* BO, body odour

soviético /sovi'ɛtʃiku/ *a & m* Soviet

sovi|na /so'vina/ *a* stingy, mean, (*Amer*) cheap □ *m/f* cheapskate; **~nice** *f* stinginess, meanness, (*Amer*) cheapness

sozinho /so'ziɲu/ *a* (*sem ninguém*) alone, on one's own; (*por si próprio*) by o.s.; **falar ~** talk to o.s.

spray /is'prej/ (*pl* **~s**) *m* spray

squash /is'kwɛʃ/ *m* squash

stand /is'tãdʒi/ (*pl* **~s**) *m* stand

status /is'tatus/ *m* status

stripper /is'triper/ (*pl* **~s**) *m/f* stripper

strip-tease /istripi'tʃizi/ *m* striptease

sua /'sua/ *a & pron veja* **seu**

su|ado /su'adu/ *a* <*pessoa, roupa*> sweaty; (*fig*) hard-earned; **~ar** *vt/i* sweat; **~ar por/para** (*fig*) work hard for/to; **~ar frio** come out in a cold sweat

sua|ve /su'avi/ *a* <*toque, subida*> gentle; <*gosto, cheiro, dor, inverno*> mild; <*música, voz*> soft; <*vinho*> smooth; <*trabalho*> light; <*prestações*> easy; **~vidade** *f* gentleness; mildness; softness; smoothness; *veja* **suave**; **~vizar** *vt* soften; soothe <*dor, pessoa*>

subalterno /subaw'tɛrnu/ *a & m* subordinate

subconsciente /subikõsi'ẽtʃi/ *a & m* subconscious

subdesenvolvido /subidʒizĩvow'vidu/ *a* underdeveloped

súbdito /'subditu/ *m* (*Port*) *veja* **súdito**

subdividir /subidʒivi'dʒir/ *vt* subdivide

subemprego /subĩ'pregu/ *m* menial job

subemprei|tar /subĩprej'tar/ *vt* subcontract; **~teiro** *m* subcontractor

subenten|der /subĩtẽ'der/ *vt* infer; **~dido** *a* implied □ *m* insinuation

subestimar /subestʃi'mar/ *vt* underestimate

su|bida /su'bida/ *f* (*ação*) ascent; (*ladeira*) incline; (*de preços etc, fig*) rise; **~bir** *vi* go up; <*rio, águas*> rise □ *vt* go up, climb; **~bir em** climb <*árvore*>; get up onto <*mesa*>; get on <*ônibus*>

súbito /'subitu/ *a* sudden; **(de) ~** suddenly

subjacente /subiʒa'sẽtʃi/ *a* underlying

subjeti|vidade /subiʒetʃivi'dadʒi/ *f* subjectivity; **~vo** *a* subjective

subjugar /subiʒu'gar/ *vt* subjugate

subjuntivo /subiʒũ'tʃivu/ *a & m* subjunctive

sublevar-se /suble'varsi/ *vpr* rise up

sublime /su'blimi/ *a* sublime

subli|nhado /subli'ɲadu/ *m* underlining; **~nhar** *vt* underline

sublocar /sublo'kar/ *vt/i* sublet

submarino /subima'rinu/ *a* underwater □ *m* submarine

submer|gir /subimer'ʒir/ *vt* submerge; **~gir-se** *vpr* submerge; **~so** *a* submerged

submeter /subime'ter/ *vt* subject (**a** to); put down, subdue <*povo, rebeldes etc*>; submit <*projeto*>; **~-se** *vpr* (*render-se*) submit; **~-se a** (*sofrer*) undergo

submis|são /subimi'sãw/ *f* submission; **~so** *a* submissive

submundo /subi'mũdu/ *m* underworld

subnutrição /subinutri'sãw/ *f* malnutrition

subordi|nado /subordʒi'nadu/ *a & m* subordinate; **~nar** *vt* subordinate (**a** to)

subor|nar /subor'nar/ *vt* bribe; **~no** /o/ *m* bribe

subproduto /subipro'dutu/ *m* by-product

subs|crever /subiskre'ver/ *vt* sign <*carta etc*>; subscribe to <*opinião*>; subscribe <*dinheiro*> (**para** to); **~crever-se** *vpr* sign one's name; **~crição** *f* subscription; **~crito** *pp de* **~crever**

subseqüente /subise'kwẽtʃi/ *a* subsequent

subserviente /subiservi'ẽtʃi/ *a* subservient
subsidiar /subisidʒi'ar/ *vt* subsidize
subsidiá|ria /subisidʒi'aria/ *f* subsidiary; **~rio** *a* subsidiary
subsídio /subi'sidʒiu/ *m* subsidy
subsistência /subisis'tẽsia/ *f* subsistence
subsolo /subi'sɔlu/ *m* (*porão*) basement
substância /subis'tãsia/ *f* substance
substan|cial /subistãsi'aw/ (*pl* **~ciais**) *a* substantial; **~tivo** *m* noun
substitu|ição /subistʃitui'sãw/ *f* replacement; substitution; **~ir** *vt* (*pôr B no lugar de A*) replace (**A por B** A with B); (*usar B em vez de A*) substitute (**A por B** B for A); **~to** *a & m* substitute
subterfúgio /subiter'fuʒiu/ *m* subterfuge
subterrâneo /subite'xaniu/ *a* underground
sub|til /sub'til/ (*pl* **~tis**) *a* (*Port*) *veja* **sutil**
subtra|ção /subitra'sãw/ *f* subtraction; **~ir** *vt* subtract <*números*>; (*roubar*) steal
suburbano /subur'banu/ *a* suburban
subúrbio /su'burbiu/ *m* suburbs
subven|ção /subivẽ'sãw/ *f* grant, subsidy; **~cionar** *vt* subsidize
subver|são /subiver'sãw/ *f* subversion; **~sivo** *a & m* subversive
suca|ta /su'kata/ *f* scrap metal; **~tear** *vt* scrap
sucção /suk'sãw/ *f* suction
suce|der /suse'der/ *vi* (*acontecer*) happen ▫ *vt* **~der a** succeed <*rei etc*>; (*vir depois*) follow; **~der-se** *vpr* follow on from one another; **~dido** *a* **bem ~dido** successful
suces|são /suse'sãw/ *f* succession; **~sivo** *a* successive; **~so** /ɛ/ *m* success; (*música*) hit; **fazer** *ou* **ter ~so** be successful; **~sor** *m* successor
sucinto /su'sĩtu/ *a* succinct
suco /'suku/ *m* juice
suculento /suku'lẽtu/ *a* juicy
sucumbir /sukũ'bir/ *vi* succumb (**a** to)
sucur|sal /sukur'saw/ (*pl* **~sais**) *f* branch
Sudão /su'dãw/ *m* Sudan
sudário /su'dariu/ *m* shroud
sudeste /su'dɛstʃi/ *a & m* southeast; **o Sudeste Asiático** Southeast Asia
súdito /'sudʒitu/ *m* subject
sudoeste /sudo'ɛstʃi/ *a & m* southwest
Suécia /su'ɛsia/ *f* Sweden
sueco /su'ɛku/ *a & m* Swedish
suéter /su'ɛter/ *m/f* sweater
sufici|ência /sufisi'ẽsia/ *f* sufficiency; **~ente** *a* enough, sufficient; **o ~ente** enough
sufixo /su'fiksu/ *m* suffix
suflê /su'fle/ *m* soufflé
sufo|cante /sufo'kãtʃi/ *a* stifling; **~car** *vt* (*asfixiar*) suffocate; (*fig*) stifle ▫ *vi* suffocate; **~co** /o/ *m* hassle; **estar num ~co** be having a tough time
sufrágio /su'fraʒiu/ *m* suffrage
sugar /su'gar/ *vt* suck
sugerir /suʒe'rir/ *vt* suggest
suges|tão /suʒes'tãw/ *f* suggestion; **dar uma ~tão** make a suggestion; **~tivo** *a* suggestive
Suíça /su'isa/ *f* Switzerland
suíças /su'isas/ *f pl* sideburns
sui|cida /sui'sida/ *a* suicidal ▫ *m/f* suicide (victim); **~cidar-se** *vpr* commit suicide; **~cídio** *m* suicide
suíço /su'isu/ *a & m* Swiss
suíno /su'inu/ *a & m* pig
suíte /su'itʃi/ *f* suite
su|jar /su'ʒar/ *vt* dirty; (*fig*) sully <*reputação etc*> ▫ *vi*, **~jar-se** *vpr* get dirty; **~jar-se com alg** queer one's pitch with s.o.; **~jeira** *f* dirt; (*uma*) dirty trick
sujei|tar /suʒej'tar/ *vt* subject (**a** to); **~tar-se** *vpr* subject o.s. (**a** to); **~to** *a* subject (**a** to) ▫ *m* (*de oração*) subject; (*pessoa*) person
su|jidade /suʒi'dadʒi/ *f* (*Port*) dirt; **~jo** *a* dirty
sul /suw/ *a invar & m* south; **~-africano** *a & m* South African; **~-americano** *a & m* South American; **~-coreano** *a & m* South Korean
sul|car /suw'kar/ *vt* furrow <*testa*>; **~co** *m* furrow
sulfúrico /suw'furiku/ *a* sulphuric
sulista /su'lista/ *a* southern ▫ *m/f* southerner
sultão /suw'tãw/ *m* sultan
sumário /su'mariu/ *a* <*justiça*> summary; <*roupa*> skimpy, brief
su|miço /su'misu/ *m* disappearance; **dar ~miço em** spirit away; **tomar chá de ~miço** disappear; **~mido** *a* <*cor, voz*> faint; **ele anda ~mido** he's disappeared; **~mir** *vi* disappear
sumo /'sumu/ *m* (*Port*) juice
sumptuoso /sũtu'ozu/ *a* (*Port*) *veja* **suntuoso**
sunga /'sũga/ *f* swimming trunks
suntuoso /sũtu'ozu/ *a* sumptuous
suor /su'or/ *m* sweat
superar /supe'rar/ *vt* overcome <*dificuldade etc*>; surpass <*expectativa, pessoa*>

superá|vel /supe'ravew/ (*pl* **~veis**) *a* surmountable; **~vit** (*pl* **~vits**) *m* surplus

superestimar /superestʃi'mar/ *vt* overestimate

superestrutura /superistru'tura/ *f* superstructure

superfici|al /superfisi'aw/ (*pl* **~ais**) *a* superficial

superfície /super'fisi/ *f* surface; (*medida*) area

supérfluo /su'pɛrfluu/ *a* superfluous

superintendência /superĩtẽ'dẽsia/ *f* bureau

superi|or /superi'or/ *a* (*de cima*) upper; <*ensino*> higher; <*número, temperatura etc*> greater (**a** than); (*melhor*) superior (**a** to) ▫ *m* superior; **~oridade** *f* superiority

superlativo /superla'tʃivu/ *a & m* superlative

superlota|ção /superlota'sãw/ *f* overcrowding; **~do** *a* overcrowded

supermercado /supermer'kadu/ *m* supermarket

superpotência /superpo'tẽsia/ *f* superpower

superpovoado /superpovo'adu/ *a* overpopulated

supersecreto /superse'krɛtu/ *a* top secret

supersensí|vel /supersẽ'sivew/ (*pl* **~veis**) *a* oversensitive

supersônico /super'soniku/ *a* supersonic

supersti|ção /superstʃi'sãw/ *f* superstition; **~cioso** /o/ *a* superstitious

supervi|são /supervi'zãw/ *f* supervision; **~sionar** *vt* supervise; **~sor** *m* supervisor

supetão /supe'tãw/ *m* **de ~** all of a sudden

suplantar /suplã'tar/ *vt* supplant

suplemen|tar /suplemẽ'tar/ *a* supplementary ▫ *vt* supplement; **~to** *m* supplement

suplente /su'plẽtʃi/ *a & m/f* substitute

supletivo /suple'tʃivu/ *a* supplementary; **ensino ~** adult education

súplica /'suplika/ *f* plea; **tom de ~** pleading tone

suplicar /supli'kar/ *vt* plead for; (*em juízo*) petition for

suplício /su'plisiu/ *m* torture; (*fig: aflição*) torment

supor /su'por/ *vt* suppose

supor|tar /supor'tar/ *vt* (*sustentar*) support; (*tolerar*) stand, bear; **~tável** (*pl* **~táveis**) *a* bearable; **~te** /ɔ/ *m* support

suposição /supozi'sãw/ *f* supposition

supositório /supozi'tɔriu/ *m* suppository

supos|tamente /suposta'mẽtʃi/ *adv* supposedly; **~to** /o/ *a* supposed; **~to que** supposing that

supre|macia /suprema'sia/ *f* supremacy; **~mo** /e/ *a* supreme

supressão /supre'sãw/ *f* (*de lei, cargo, privilégio*) abolition; (*de jornal, informação, nomes*) suppression; (*de palavras, cláusula*) deletion

suprimento /supri'mẽtu/ *m* supply

suprimir /supri'mir/ *vt* abolish <*lei, cargo, privilégio*>; suppress <*jornal, informação, nomes*>; delete <*palavras, cláusula*>

suprir /su'prir/ *vt* provide for <*família, necessidades*>; make up for <*falta*>; make up <*quantia*>; supply <*o que falta*>; (*substituir*) take the place of; **~ alg de** provide s.o. with; **~ A por B** substitute B for A

supurar /supu'rar/ *vi* turn septic

sur|dez /sur'des/ *f* deafness; **~do** *a* deaf; <*consoante*> voiceless ▫ *m* deaf person; **os ~dos** the deaf; **~do-mudo** (*pl* **~dos-mudos**) *a* deaf and dumb ▫ *m* deaf-mute

sur|fe /'surfi/ *m* surfing; **~fista** *m/f* surfer

sur|gimento /surʒi'mẽtu/ *m* appearance; **~gir** *vi* arise; **~gir à mente** spring to mind

Suriname /suri'nami/ *m* Surinam

surpreen|dente /surpriẽ'dẽtʃi/ *a* surprising; **~der** *vt* surprise ▫ *vi* be surprising; **~der-se** *vpr* be surprised (**de** at)

surpre|sa /sur'preza/ *f* surprise; **de ~sa** by surprise; **~so** /e/ *a* surprised

sur|ra /'suxa/ *f* thrashing; **~rado** *a* <*roupa*> worn-out; **~rar** *vt* thrash <*pessoa*>; wear out <*roupa*>

surrealis|mo /suxea'lizmu/ *m* surrealism; **~ta** *a & m/f* surrealist

surtir /sur'tʃir/ *vt* produce; **~ efeito** be effective

surto /'surtu/ *m* outbreak

suscept- (*Port*) *veja* **suscet-**

susce|tibilidade /susetʃibili-'dadʒi/ *f* (*de pessoa*) sensitivity; **~tível** (*pl* **~tíveis**) *a* <*pessoa*> touchy, sensitive; **~tível de** open to

suscitar /susi'tar/ *vt* cause; raise <*dúvida, suspeita*>

suspei|ta /sus'pejta/ *f* suspicion; **~tar** *vt/i* **~tar (de)** suspect; **~to** *a* suspicious; (*duvidoso*) suspect □ *m* suspect; **~toso** /o/ *a* suspicious

suspen|der /suspẽ'der/ *vt* suspend; **~são** *f* suspension; **~se** *m* suspense; **~so** *a* suspended; **~sórios** *m pl* braces, (*Amer*) suspenders

suspi|rar /suspi'rar/ *vi* sigh; **~rar por** long for; **~ro** *m* sigh; (*doce*) meringue

sussur|rar /susu'xar/ *vt/i* whisper; **~ro** *m* whisper

sustar /sus'tar/ *vt/i* stop

susten|táculo /sustẽ'takulu/ *m* mainstay; **~tar** *vt* support; (*afirmar*) maintain; **~to** *m* support; (*ganha-pão*) livelihood

susto /'sustu/ *m* fright

sutiã /sutʃi'ã/ *m* bra

su|til /su'tʃiw/ (*pl* **~tis**) *a* subtle; **~tileza** /e/ *f* subtlety

sutu|ra /su'tura/ *f* suture; **~rar** *vt* suture

Tt

tá /ta/ *int* (*fam*) OK; *veja* **estar**

taba|caria /tabaka'ria/ *f* tobacconist's; **~co** *m* tobacco

tabefe /ta'bɛfi/ *m* slap

tabe|la /ta'bɛla/ *f* table; **~lar** *vt* tabulate

tablado /ta'bladu/ *m* platform

tabu /ta'bu/ *a & m* taboo

tábua /'tabua/ *f* board; **~ de passar roupa** ironing board

tabuleiro /tabu'leru/ *m* (*de xadrez etc*) board

tabuleta /tabu'lɛta/ *f* (*letreiro*) sign

taça /'tasa/ *f* (*prêmio*) cup; (*de champanhe etc*) glass

ta|cada /ta'kada/ *f* shot; **de uma ~cada** in one go; **~car** *vt* hit <*bola*>; (*fam*) throw

tacha /'taʃa/ *f* tack

tachar /ta'ʃar/ *vt* brand (**de** as)

tachinha /ta'ʃiɲa/ *f* drawing pin, (*Amer*) thumbtack

tácito /'tasitu/ *a* tacit

taciturno /tasi'turnu/ *a* taciturn

taco /'taku/ *m* (*de golfe*) club; (*de bilhar*) cue; (*de hóquei*) stick

tact- (*Port*) *veja* **tat-**

tagare|la /taga'rɛla/ *a* chatty, talkative □ *m/f* chatterbox; **~lar** *vi* chatter

tailan|dês /tajlã'des/ *a & m* (*f* **~desa**) Thai

Tailândia /taj'lãdʒia/ *f* Thailand

tailleur /ta'jɛr/ (*pl* **~s**) *m* suit

Taiti /taj'tʃi/ *m* Tahiti

tal /taw/ (*pl* **tais**) *a* such; **que ~?** what do you think?, (*Port*) how are you?; **que ~ uma cerveja?** how about a beer?; **~ como** such as; **~ qual** just like; **um ~ de João** someone called John; **e ~** and so on

tala /'tala/ *f* splint

talão /ta'lãw/ *m* stub; **~ de cheques** chequebook

talco /'tawku/ *m* talc

talen|to /ta'lẽtu/ *m* talent; **~-toso** /o/ *a* talented

talhar /ta'ʎar/ *vt* slice <*dedo, carne*>; carve <*pedra, imagem*>

talharim /taʎa'rĩ/ *m* tagliatelle

talher /ta'ʎɛr/ *m* set of cutlery; *pl* cutlery

talho /'taʎu/ *m* (*Port*) butcher's

talismã /taliz'mã/ *m* charm, talisman

talo /'talu/ *m* stalk

talvez /taw'ves/ *adv* perhaps; **~ ele venha amanhã** he may come tomorrow

tamanco /ta'mãku/ *m* clog

tamanho /ta'maɲu/ *m* size □ *adj* such

tâmara /'tamara/ *f* date

tamarindo /tama'rĩdu/ *m* tamarind

também /tã'bẽj/ *adv* also; **~ não** not ... either, neither

tam|bor /tã'bor/ *m* drum; **~-borilar** *vi* <*dedos*> drum; <*chuva*> patter; **~borim** *m* tambourine

Tâmisa /'tamiza/ *m* Thames

tam|pa /'tãpa/ *f* lid; **~pão** *m* (*vaginal*) tampon; **~par** *vt* put the lid on <*recipiente*>; (*tapar*) cover; **~pinha** *f* top □ *m/f* (*fam*) shorthouse

tampouco /tã'poku/ *adv* nor, neither

tanga /'tãga/ *f* G-string; (*avental*) loincloth

tangente /tã'ʒẽtʃi/ *f* tangent; **pela ~** (*fig*) narrowly

tangerina /tãʒe'rina/ *f* tangerine

tango /'tãgu/ *m* tango

tanque /'tãki/ *m* tank; (*para lavar roupa*) sink

tanto /'tãtu/ *a & pron* so much; *pl* so many □ *adv* so much; **~ ... como ...** both ... and ...; **~ (...) quanto** as much (...) as; **~ melhor** so much the better; **~ tempo** so long; **vinte e ~s anos** twenty odd years; **nem ~** not as much; **um ~ difícil** somewhat difficult; **~ que** to the extent that

Tanzânia /tã'zania/ *f* Tanzania

tão /tãw/ *adv* so; **~ grande quanto** as big as; **~-somente** *adv* solely

tapa /'tapa/ *m ou f* slap; **dar um ~ em** slap

tapar /ta'par/ *vt* (*cobrir*) cover; block <*luz, vista*>; cork <*garrafa*>
tapeçaria /tapesa'ria/ *f* (*pano*) tapestry; (*loja*) carpet shop
tape|tar /tape'tar/ *vt* carpet; **~te** /e/ *m* carpet
tapioca /tapi'ɔka/ *f* tapioca
tapume /ta'pumi/ *m* fence
taquicardia /takikar'dʒia/ *f* palpitations
taquigra|far /takigra'far/ *vt/i* write in shorthand; **~fia** *f* shorthand
tara /'tara/ *f* fetish; **~do** *a* sex-crazed □ *m* sex maniac; **ser ~do por** be crazy about
tar|dar /tar'dar/ *vi* (*atrasar*) be late; (*demorar muito*) be long □ *vt* delay; **~dar a responder** take a long time to answer, be a long time answering; **o mais ~dar** at the latest; **sem mais ~dar** without further delay; **~de** *adv* late □ *f* afternoon; **hoje à ~de** this afternoon; **~de da noite** late at night; **~dinha** *f* late afternoon;**~dio** *a* late
tarefa /ta'rɛfa/ *f* task, job
tarifa /ta'rifa/ *f* tariff; **~ de embarque** airport tax
tarimbado /tarĩ'badu/ *a* experienced
tarja /'tarʒa/ *f* strip
ta|rô /ta'ro/ *m* tarot; **~rólogo** *m* tarot reader
tartamu|dear /tartamudʒi'ar/ *vi* stammer;**~do** *a* stammering □ *m* stammerer
tártaro /'tartaru/ *m* tartar
tartaruga /tarta'ruga/ *f* (*bicho*) turtle; (*material*) tortoiseshell
tatear /tatʃi'ar/ *vt* feel □ *vi* feel one's way
táti|ca /'tatʃika/ *f* tactics; **~co** *a* tactical
tá|til /'tatʃiw/ (*pl* **~teis**) *a* tactile
tato /'tatu/ *m* (*sentido*) touch; (*diplomacia*) tact
tatu /ta'tu/ *m* armadillo
tatu|ador /tatua'dor/ *m* tattooist; **~agem** *f* tattoo; **~ar** *vt* tattoo
tauromaquia /tawroma'kia/ *f* bullfighting
taxa /'taʃa/ *f* (*a pagar*) charge; (*índice*) rate; **~ de câmbio** exchange rate; **~ de juros** interest rate; **~ rodoviária** road tax
taxar /ta'ʃar/ *vt* tax
taxativo /taʃa'tʃivu/ *a* firm, categorical
táxi /'taksi/ *m* taxi
taxiar /taksi'ar/ *vi* taxi
taxímetro /tak'simetru/ *m* taxi meter
taxista /tak'sista/ *m/f* taxi driver
tchã /tʃã/ *m* (*fam*) special something
tchau /tʃaw/ *int* goodbye, bye
tcheco /'tʃɛku/ *a & m* Czech
Tchecoslováquia /tʃekoslo'vakia/ *f* Czechoslovakia
te /tʃi/ *pron* you; (*a ti*) to you
tear /tʃi'ar/ *m* loom
tea|tral /tʃia'traw/ (*pl* **~trais**) *a* theatrical; <*grupo*> theatre; **~tro** *m* theatre; **~trólogo** *m* playwright
tece|lagem /tese'laʒẽ/ *f* (*trabalho*) weaving; (*fábrica*) textile factory; **~lão** *m* (*f* **~lã**) weaver
te|cer /te'ser/ *vt/i* weave; **~cido** *m* cloth; (*no corpo*) tissue
te|cla /'tɛkla/ *f* key; **~cladista** *m/f* (*músico*) keyboard player; (*de computador*) keyboard operator; **~clado** *m* keyboard; **~clar** *vt* key (in)
técni|ca /'tɛknika/ *f* technique; **~co** *a* technical □ *m* specialist; (*de time*) manager; (*que mexe com máquinas*) technician
tecno|crata /tekno'krata/ *m/f* technocrat; **~logia** *f* technology; **~lógico** *a* technological
teco-teco /tɛku'tɛku/ *m* light aircraft
tecto /'tɛtu/ *m* (*Port*) *veja* **teto**
tédio /'tɛdʒiu/ *m* boredom
tedioso /tedʒi'ozu/ *a* boring, tedious
Teerã /tee'rã/ *f* Teheran
teia /'teja/ *f* web
tei|ma /'tejma/ *f* persistence; **~mar** *vi* insist; **~mar em ir** insist on going; **~mosia** *f* stubbornness; **~moso** /o/ *a* stubborn; <*ruído*> insistent
teixo /'tejʃu/ *m* yew
Tejo /'teʒu/ *m* Tagus
tela /'tɛla/ *f* (*de cinema, TV etc*) screen; (*tecido, pintura*) canvas; **~plana** flat screen
telecoman|dado /telekomã'dadu/ *a* remote-controlled; **~do** *m* remote control
telecomunicação /telekomunika'sãw/ *f* telecommunication
teleférico /tele'fɛriku/ *m* cable car
telefo|nar /telefo'nar/ *vi* telephone; **~nar para alg** phone s.o.; **~ne** /o/ *m* telephone; (*número*) phone number; **~ne celular** cell phone; **~ne sem fio** cordless phone; **~nema** /e/ *m* phone call; **~nia** *f* telephone technology
telefôni|co /tele'foniku/ *a* telephone; **cabine ~ca** phone box, (*Amer*) phone booth; **mesa ~ca** switchboard
telefonista /telefo'nista/ *m/f* (*da companhia telefônica*) operator; (*dentro de empresa etc*) telephonist
tele|grafar /telegra'far/ *vt/i* telegraph; **~gráfico** *a* telegraphic
telégrafo /te'lɛgrafu/ *m* telegraph
tele|grama /tele'grama/ *m* telegram; **~guiado** *a* remote- controlled

telejor|nal /teleʒor'naw/ (*pl* **~nais**) *m* television news
telemóvel /tele'mɔvew/ *m* mobile phone, (*Amer.*) cell phone
tele|novela /teleno'vɛla/ *f* TV soap opera; **~objetiva** *f* telephoto lens
tele|patia /telepa'tʃia/ *f* telepathy; **~pático** *a* telepathic
telescó|pico /teles'kɔpiku/ *a* telescopic; **~pio** *m* telescope
telespectador /telespekta'dor/ *m* television viewer □ *a* viewing
teletrabalho /teletra'baʎu/ *m* teleworking
televi|são /televi'zãw/ *f* television; **~são a cabo** cable television; **~sionar** *vt* televise; **~sivo** *a* television; **~sor** *m* television set
telex /te'lɛks/ *m invar* telex
telha /'teʎa/ *f* tile; **~do** *m* roof
te|ma /'tema/ *m* theme; **~mático** *a* thematic
temer /te'mer/ *vt* fear □ *vi* be afraid; **~ por** fear for
teme|rário /teme'rariu/ *a* reckless; **~ridade** *f* recklessness; **~roso** /o/ *a* fearful
te|mido /te'midu/ *a* feared; **~-mível** (*pl* **~míveis**) *a* fearsome; **~mor** *m* fear
tempão /tẽ'pãw/ *m* **um ~** a long time
temperado /tẽpe'radu/ *a* <*clima*> temperate □ *pp de* **temperar**
temperamen|tal /tẽperamẽ'taw/ (*pl* **~tais**) *a* temperamental; **~to** *m* temperament
temperar /tẽpe'rar/ *vt* season <*comida*>; temper <*aço*>
temperatura /tẽpera'tura/ *f* temperature
tempero /tẽ'peru/ *m* seasoning
tempestade /tẽpes'tadʒi/ *f* storm
templo /'tẽplu/ *m* temple
tempo /'tẽpu/ *m* (*período*) time; (*atmosférico*) weather; (*do verbo*) tense; (*de jogo*) half; **ao mesmo ~** at the same time; **nesse meio ~** in the meantime; **o ~ todo** all the time; **de todos os ~s** of all time; **quanto ~** how long; **muito /pouco ~** a long/short time; **~ integral** full time
tempo|rada /tẽpo'rada/ *f* (*sazão*) season; (*tempo*) while; **~ral** (*pl* **~rais**) *a* temporal □ *m* storm; **~rário** *a* temporary
te|nacidade /tenasi'dadʒi/ *f* tenacity; **~naz** *a* tenacious □ *f* tongs
tenção /tẽ'sãw/ *f* intention
tencionar /tẽsio'nar/ *vt* intend
tenda /'tẽda/ *f* tent
tendão /tẽ'dãw/ *m* tendon; **~ de Aquiles** Achilles tendon
tendência /tẽ'dẽsia/ *f* (*moda*) trend; (*propensão*) tendency
tendencioso /tẽdẽsi'ozu/ *a* tendentious
ten|der /tẽ'der/ *vi* tend (**para** towards); **~de a engordar** he tends to get fat; **o tempo ~de a ficar bom** the weather is improving
tenebroso /tene'brozu/ *a* dark; (*fig: terrível*) dreadful
tenente /te'nẽtʃi/ *m/f* lieutenant
tênis /'tenis/ *m invar* (*jogo*) tennis; (*sapato*) trainer; **um ~** (*par*) a pair of trainers; **~ de mesa** table tennis
tenista /te'nista/ *m/f* tennis player
tenor /te'nor/ *m* tenor
tenro /'tẽxu/ *a* tender
ten|são /tẽ'sãw/ *f* tension; **~são (arterial)** blood pressure; **~so** *a* tense
tentação /tẽta'sãw/ *f* temptation
tentáculo /tẽ'taculu/ *m* tentacle
ten|tador /tẽta'dor/ *a* tempting; **~tar** *vt* try; (*seduzir*) tempt □ *vi* try; **~tativa** *f* attempt; **~-tativo** *a* tentative
tênue /'tenui/ *a* faint
teo|logia /teolo'ʒia/ *f* theology; **~lógico** *a* theological
teólogo /te'ɔlogu/ *m* theologian
teor /te'or/ *m* (*de gordura etc*) content; (*de carta, discurso*) drift
teo|rema /teo'rema/ *m* theorem; **~ria** *f* theory
teórico /te'ɔriku/ *a* theoretical
teorizar /teori'zar/ *vt* theorize
tépido /'tɛpidu/ *a* tepid
ter /ter/ *vt* have; **tenho vinte anos** I am twenty (years old); **~ medo/sede** be afraid/thirsty; **tenho que** *ou* **de ir** I have to go; **tem** (*há*) there is/are; **não tem de quê** don't mention it; **~ a ver com** have to do with
tera|peuta /tera'pewta/ *m/f* therapist; **~pêutico** *a* therapeutic; **~pia** *f* therapy
terça /'tersa/ *f* Tuesday; **~-feira** (*pl* **~s-feiras**) *f* Tuesday; **Terça-Feira Gorda** Shrove Tuesday
tercei|ra /ter'sera/ *f* (*marcha*) third; **~ranista** *m/f* third-year; **~ro** *a* third □ *m* third party
terço /'tersu/ *m* third
ter|çol (*pl* **~çóis**) *m* stye
tergal /ter'gaw/ *m* Terylene
térmi|co /'tɛrmiku/ *a* thermal; **garrafa ~ca** Thermos flask
termi|nal /termi'naw/ (*pl* **~nais**) *a* & *m* terminal; **~nal de vídeo** VDU; **~nante** *a* definite; **~nar** *vt* finish □ *vi* <*pessoa, coisa*> finish; <*coisa*> end; **~nar com alg** (*cortar relação*) break up with s.o.

ter|minologia /terminolo'ʒia/ *f* terminology; **~mo**[1] /'termu/ *m* term; **pôr ~mo a** put an end to; **meio ~mo** compromise

termo[2] /'termu / *m* (*Port*) Thermos flask

ter|mômetro /ter'mometru/ *m* thermometer; **~mostato** *m* thermostat

terno[1] /'tɛrnu/ *m* suit

ter|no[2] / 'tɛrnu/ *a* tender; **~nura** *f* tenderness

terra /'tɛxa/ *f* land; (*solo, elétrico*) earth; (*chão*) ground; **a Terra** Earth; **por ~** on the ground; **~ natal** homeland

terraço /te'xasu/ *m* terrace

terra|cota /texa'kɔta/ *f* terracotta; **~moto** /texa'mɔtu/ *m* (*Port*) earthquake; **~plenagem** *f* earth moving

terreiro /te'xeru/ *m* meeting place for Afro-Brazilian cults

terremoto /texe'mɔtu/ *m* earthquake

terreno /te'xenu/ *a* earthly □ *m* ground; (*geog*) terrain; (*um*) piece of land; **~ baldio** piece of waste ground

térreo /'tɛxiu/ *a* ground-floor; **(andar) ~** ground floor, (*Amer*) first floor

terrestre /te'xɛstri/ *a* <*animal, batalha, forças*> land; (*da Terra*) of the Earth, the Earth's; <*alegrias etc*> earthly

terrificante /texifi'kãtʃi/ *a* terrifying

terrina /te'xina/ *f* tureen

territori|al /texitori'aw/ (*pl* **~ais**) *a* territorial

território /texi'tɔriu/ *m* territory

terrí|vel /te'xivew/ (*pl* **~veis**) *a* terrible

terror /te'xor/ *m* terror; **filme de ~** horror film

terroris|mo /texo'rizmu/ *m* terrorism; **~ta** *a* & *m*/*f* terrorist

tese /'tɛzi/ *f* theory; (*escrita*) thesis

teso /'tezu/ *a* (*apertado*) taut; (*rígido*) stiff

tesoura /te'zora/ *f* scissors; **uma ~** a pair of scissors

tesou|reiro /tezo'reru/ *m* treasurer; **~ro** *m* treasure; (*do Estado*) treasury

testa /'tɛsta/ *f* forehead; **~-de-ferro** (*pl* **~s-de-ferro**) *m* frontman

testamento /testa'mẽtu/ *m* will; (*na Bíblia*) testament

tes|tar /tes'tar/ *vt* test; **~te** /ɛ/ *m* test

testemu|nha /teste'muɲa/ *f* witness; **~nha ocular** eye witness; **~nhar** *vt* bear witness to □ *vi* testify; **~nho** *m* evidence, testimony

testículo /tes'tʃikulu/ *m* testicle

teta /'teta/ *f* teat

tétano /'tɛtanu/ *m* tetanus

teto /'tɛtu/ *m* ceiling; **~ solar** sun roof

tétrico /'tɛtriku/ *a* (*triste*) dismal; (*medonho*) horrible

teu /tew/ (*f* **tua**) *a* your □ *pron* yours

têx|til /'testʃiw/ (*pl* **~teis**) *m* textile

tex|to /'testu/ *m* text; **~tura** *f* texture

texugo /te'ʃugu/ *m* badger

tez /tes/ *f* complexion

ti /tʃi/ *pron* you

tia /'tʃia/ *f* aunt; **~-avó** (*pl* **~s-vós**) *f* great aunt

tiara /tʃi'ara/ *f* tiara

tíbia /'tʃibia/ *f* shinbone

ticar /tʃi'kar/ *vt* tick

tico /'tʃiku/ *m* **um ~ de** a little bit of

tiete /tʃi'ɛtʃi/ *m*/*f* fan

tifo /'tʃifu/ *m* typhoid

tigela /tʃi'ʒɛla/ *f* bowl; **de meia ~** smalltime

tigre /'tʃigri/ *m* tiger; **~sa** /e/ *f* tigress

tijolo /tʃi'ʒolu/ *m* brick

til /tʃiw/ (*pl* **tis**) *m* tilde

tilintar /tʃilĩ'tar/ *vi* jingle □ *m* jingling

timão /tʃi'mãw/ *m* tiller

timbre /'tʃĩbri/ *m* (*insígnia*) crest; (*em papel*) heading; (*de som*) tone; (*de vogal*) quality

time /'tʃimi/ *m* team

timidez /tʃimi'des/ *f* shyness

tímido /'tʃimidu/ *a* shy

tímpano /'tʃĩpanu/ *m* (*tambor*) kettledrum; (*no ouvido*) eardrum

tina /'tʃina/ *f* vat

tingir /tʃĩ'ʒir/ *vt* dye <*tecido, cabelo*>; (*fig*) tinge

ti|nido /tʃi'nidu/ *m* tinkling; **~nir** *vi* tinkle; <*ouvidos*> ring; (*tremer*) tremble; **estar ~nindo** (*fig*) be in peak condition

tino /'tʃinu/ *m* sense, judgement; **ter ~ para** have a flair for

tin|ta /'tʃĩta/ *f* (*para pintar*) paint; (*para escrever*) ink; (*para tingir*) dye; **~teiro** *m* inkwell

tintim /tʃĩ'tʃĩ/ *m* **contar ~ por ~** give a blow-by-blow account of

tin|to /'tʃĩtu/ *a* dyed; <*vinho*> red; **~tura** *f* dye; (*fig*) tinge; **~turaria** *f* dry cleaner's

tio /'tʃiu/ *m* uncle; *pl* (**~** *e tia*) uncle and aunt; **~-avô** (*pl* **~s-avôs**) *m* great uncle

típico /'tʃipiku/ *a* typical

tipo /'tʃipu/ *m* type

tipóia /tʃi'pɔja/ *f* sling

tique /'tʃiki/ *m* (*sinal*) tick; (*do rosto etc*) twitch

tíquete /'tʃiketʃi/ *m* ticket

tiquinho /tʃi'kiɲu/ *m* **um ~ de** a tiny bit of

tira /'tʃira/ *f* strip □ *m*/*f* (*fam*) copper, (*Amer*) cop

tiracolo /tʃira'kɔlu/ *m* **a ~** <*bolsa*> over one's shoulder; <*pessoa*> in tow

tiragem /tʃi'raʒẽ/ *f* (*de jornal*) circulation
tira|-gosto /tʃira'gostu/ *m* snack; **~-manchas** *m invar* stain remover
ti|rania /tʃira'nia/ *f* tyranny; **~rânico** *a* tyrannical; **~rano** *m* tyrant
tirar /tʃi'rar/ *vt* (*afastar*) take away; (*de dentro*) take out; take off <*roupa, sapato, tampa*>; take <*foto, cópia, férias*>; clear <*mesa*>; get <*nota, diploma, salário*>; get out <*mancha*>
tiritar /tʃiri'tar/ *vi* shiver
tiro /'tʃiru/ *m* shot; **~ ao alvo** shooting; **é ~ e queda** (*fam*) it can't fail; **~teio** *m* shoot-out
titânio /tʃi'taniu/ *m* titanium
títere /'tʃiteri/ *m* puppet
ti|tia /tʃi'tʃia/ *f* auntie; **~tio** *m* uncle
tititi /tʃitʃi'tʃi/ *m* (*fam*) talk
titubear /tʃitubi'ar/ *vi* stagger, totter; (*fig: hesitar*) waver
titular /tʃitu'lar/ *m/f* title holder; (*de time*) captain ▫ *vt* title
título /'tʃitulu/ *m* title; (*obrigação*) bond; **a ~ de** on the basis of; **a ~ pessoal** on a personal basis
toa /'toa/ *f* **à ~** (*sem rumo*) aimlessly; (*ao acaso*) at random; (*sem motivo*) without reason; (*em vão*) for nothing; (*desocupado*) at a loose end; (*de repente*) out of the blue
toada /to'ada/ *f* melody
toalete /toa'lɛtʃi/ *m* toilet
toalha /to'aʎa/ *f* towel; **~ de mesa** tablecloth
tobogã /tobo'gã/ *m* (*rampa*) slide; (*trenó*) toboggan
toca /'tɔka/ *f* burrow
toca|-discos /toka'dʒiskus/ *m invar* record player; **~-fitas** *m invar* tape player
tocaia /to'kaja/ *f* ambush
tocante/to'kãtʃi/ *a* (*enternecedor*) moving
tocar /to'kar/ *vt* touch; play <*piano, música, disco etc*>; ring <*campainha*> ▫ *vi* touch; <*pianista, música, disco etc*> play; <*campainha, telefone, sino*> ring; **~-se** *vpr* touch; (*mancar-se*) take the hint; **~ a** (*dizer respeito*) concern; **~ em** touch; touch on <*assunto*>
tocha /'tɔʃa/ *f* torch
toco /'toku/ *m* (*de árvore*) stump; (*de cigarro*) butt
toda /'toda/ *f* **a ~** at full speed
todavia /toda'via/ *conj* however
todo /'todu/ *a* all; (*cada*) every; *pl* all; **~ o dinheiro** all the money; **~ dia, ~s os dias** every day; **~s os alunos** all the pupils; **o dia ~** all day; **em ~ lugar** everywhere; **~ mundo, ~s** everyone; **~s nós** all of us; **ao ~** in all; **~-poderoso** *a* almighty
tofe /'tɔfi/ *m* toffee
toga /'tɔga/ *f* gown; (*de romano*) toga
toicinho /toj'siɲu/ *m* bacon
toldo /'towdu/ *m* awning
tole|rância /tole'rãsia/ *f* tolerance; **~rante** *a* tolerant; **~-rar** *vt* tolerate; **~rável** (*pl* **~ráveis**) *a* tolerable
to|lice /to'lisi/ *f* foolishness; (*uma*) foolish thing; **~lo** /o/ *a* foolish ▫ *m* fool
tom /tõ/ *m* tone
to|mada /to'mada/ *f* (*conquista*) capture; (*elétrica*) plughole; (*de filme*) shot; **~mar** *vt* take; (*beber*) drink; **~mar café** have breakfast
tomara /to'mara/ *int* I hope so; **~ que** let's hope that; **~-que-caia** *a invar* <*vestido*> strapless
tomate /to'matʃi/ *m* tomato
tom|bar /tõ'bar/ *vt* (*derrubar*) knock down; list <*edifício*> ▫ *vi* fall over; **~bo** *m* fall; **levar um ~bo** have a fall
tomilho /to'miʎu/ *m* thyme
tomo /'tomu/ *m* volume
tona /'tona/ *f* **trazer à ~** bring up; **vir à ~** emerge
tonalidade /tonali'dadʒi/ *f* (*de música*) key; (*de cor*) shade
to|nel /to'nɛw/ (*pl* **~néis**) *m* cask; **~nelada** *f* tonne
tôni|ca /'tonika/ *f* tonic; (*fig: assunto*) keynote; **~co** *a & m* tonic
tonificar /tonifi'kar/ *vt* tone up
ton|tear /tõtʃi'ar/ *vt* **~tear alg** make s.o.'s head spin; **~teira** *f* dizziness; **~to** *a* (*zonzo*) dizzy; (*bobo*) stupid; (*atrapalhado*) flustered; **~tura** *f* dizziness
to|pada /to'pada/ *f* trip; **dar uma~pada em** stub one's toe on; **~par** *vt* agree to, accept; **~par com** bump into <*pessoa*>; come across <*coisa*>
topázio /to'paziu/ *m* topaz
topete /to'pɛtʃi/ *m* quiff
tópico /'tɔpiku/ *a* topical ▫ *m* topic
topless /topi'lɛs/ *a invar & adv* topless
topo /'topu/ *m* top
topografia /topogra'fia/ *f* topography
topônimo /to'ponimu/ *m* place name
toque /'tɔki/ *m* touch; (*da campainha, do telefone*) ring; (*de instrumento*) playing; **dar um ~ em** (*fam*) have a word with
Tóquio /'tɔkiu/ *f* Tokyo
tora /'tɔra/ *f* log
toranja /to'rãʒa/ *f* grapefruit
tórax /'tɔraks/ *m invar* thorax
tor|ção /tor'sãw/ *f* (*do braço etc*) sprain; **~cedor** *m* supporter; **~cer** *vt* twist; (*machucar*) sprain; (*espremer*) wring

<*roupa*>; (*centrifugar*) spin <*roupa*> □ *vi* (*gritar*) cheer (**por** for); (*desejar sucesso*) keep one's fingers crossed (**por** for; **para que** that); **~cer-se** *vpr* twist about; **~cicolo** /ɔ/ *m* stiff neck; **~cida** *f* (*torção*) twist; (*torcedores*) supporters; (*gritaria*) cheering

tormen|ta /tor'mẽta/ *f* storm; **~to** *m* torment; **~toso** /o/ *a* stormy

tornado /tor'nadu/ *m* tornado

tornar /tor'nar/ *vt* make; **~-se** *vpr* become

torne|ado /torni'adu/ *a* **bem ~ado** shapely; **~ar** *vt* turn

torneio /tor'neju/ *m* tournament

torneira /tor'nera/ *f* tap, (*Amer*) faucet

torniquete /torni'ketʃi/ *m* (*para ferido*) tourniquet; (*Port: de entrada*) turnstile

torno /'tornu/ *m* lathe; (*de ceramista*) wheel; **em ~ de** around

tornozelo /torno'zelu/ *m* ankle

toró /to'rɔ/ *m* downpour

torpe /'torpi/ *a* dirty

torpe|dear /torpedʒi'ar/ *vt* torpedo; **~do** /e/ *m* torpedo

torpor /tor'por/ *m* torpor

torra|da /to'xada/ *f* piece of toast; *pl* toast; **~deira** *f* toaster

torrão /to'xãw/ *m* (*de terra*) turf; (*de açúcar*) lump

torrar /to'xar/ *vt* toast <*pão*>; roast <*café*>; blow <*dinheiro*>; sell off <*mercadorias*>

torre /'toxi/ *f* tower; (*em xadrez*) rook; **~ de controle** control tower; **~ão** *m* turret

torrefação /toxefa'sãw/ *f* (*ação*) roasting; (*fábrica*) coffee-roasting plant

torren|cial /toxẽsi'aw/ (*pl* **~ciais**) *a* torrential; **~te** *f* torrent

torresmo /to'xezmu/ *m* crackling

tórrido /'tɔxidu/ *a* torrid

torrone /to'xoni/ *m* nougat

torso /'torsu/ *m* torso

torta /'tɔrta/ *f* pie, tart

tor|to /'tortu/ *a* crooked; **a ~ e a direito** left, right and centre; **~tuoso** *a* winding

tortu|ra /tor'tura/ *f* torture; **~rador** *m* torturer; **~rar** *vt* torture

to|sa /'tɔza/ *f* (*de cachorro*) clipping; (*de ovelhas*) shearing; **~são** *m* fleece; **~sar** *vt* clip <*cachorro*>; shear <*ovelhas*>; crop <*cabelo*>

tosco /'tosku/ *a* rough, coarse

tosquiar /toski'ar/ *vt* shear <*ovelha*>

tos|se /'tɔsi/ *f* cough; **~se de cachorro** whooping cough; **~sir** *vi* cough

tostão /tos'tãw/ *m* penny

tostar /tos'tar/ *vt* brown <*carne*>; tan <*pele, pessoa*>; **~-se** *vpr* (*ao sol*) go brown

to|tal /to'taw/ (*pl* **~tais**) *a & m* total

totali|dade /totali'dadʒi/ *f* entirety; **~tário** *a* totalitarian; **~zar** *vt* total

touca /'toka/ *f* bonnet; (*de freira*) wimple; **~ de banho** bathing cap; **~dor** *m* dressing table

toupeira /to'pera/ *f* mole

tou|rada /to'rada/ *f* bullfight; **~reiro** *m* bullfighter; **~ro** *m* bull; **Touro** (*signo*) Taurus

tóxico /'tɔksiku/ *a* toxic □ *m* toxic substance

toxicômano /toksi'komanu/ *m* drug addict

toxina /tok'sina/ *f* toxin

traba|lhador /trabaʎa'dor/ *a* <*pessoa*> hard-working; <*classe*> working □ *m* worker; **~lhar** *vt* work □ *vi* work; (*numa peça, filme*) act; **~lheira** *f* big job; **~lhista** *a* labour; **~lho** *m* work; (*um*) job; (*na escola*) assignment; **dar-se o ~lho de** go to the trouble of; **~lho de parto** labour; **~lhos forçados** hard labour; **~lhoso** *a* laborious

traça /'trasa/ *f* moth

tração /tra'sãw/ *f* traction

tra|çar /tra'sar/ *vt* draw; draw up <*plano*>; set out <*ordens*>; **~ço** *m* stroke; (*entre frases*) dash; (*vestígio*) trace; (*característica*) trait; *pl* (*do rosto*) features

tractor /tra'tor/ *m* (*Port*) *veja* **trator**

tradi|ção /tradʒi'sãw/ *f* tradition; **~cional** (*pl* **~cionais**) *a* traditional

tradu|ção /tradu'sãw/ *f* translation; **~tor** *m* translator; **~zir** *vt/i* translate (**de** from; **para** into)

trafe|gar /trafe'gar/ *vi* run; **~gável** (*pl* **~gáveis**) *a* open to traffic

tráfego /'trafegu/ *m* traffic

trafi|cância /trafi'kãsia/ *f* trafficking; **~cante** *m/f* trafficker; **~car** *vt/i* traffic (**com** in)

tráfico /'trafiku/ *m* traffic

tra|gada /tra'gada/ *f* (*de bebida*) swallow; (*de cigarro*) drag; **~gar** *vt* swallow; inhale <*fumaça*>

tragédia /tra'ʒɛdʒia/ *f* tragedy

trágico /'traʒiku/ *a* tragic

trago /'tragu/ *m* (*de bebida*) swallow; (*de cigarro*) drag; **de um ~** in one go

trai|ção /traj'sãw/ *f* (*ato*) betrayal; (*deslealdade*) treachery; (*da pátria*) treason; **~çoeiro** *a* treacherous; **~dor** *a* treacherous □ *m* traitor

trailer /'trejler/ (*pl* **~s**) *m* (*de filme etc*) trailer; (*casa móvel*) caravan, (*Amer*) trailer

traineira /traj'nera/ *f* trawler

training /'trejnĩ/ (*pl* **~s**) *m* track suit

trair /tra'ir/ *vt* betray; be unfaithful to <*marido, mulher*>; **~-se** *vpr* give o.s. away

tra|jar /tra'ʒar/ *vt* wear; **~jar-se** *vpr* dress (**de** in); **~je** *m* outfit; **~je a rigor** evening dress; **~je espacial** space suit

traje|to /tra'ʒɛtu/ *m* (*percurso*) journey; (*caminho*) route; **~-tória** *f* trajectory; (*fig*) course

tralha /'traʎa/ *f* (*trastes*) junk

tra|ma /'trama/ *f* plot; **~mar** *vt/i* plot

trambi|que /trã'biki/ (*fam*) *m* con; **~queiro** (*fam*) *m* con artist

tramitar /trami'tar/ *vi* be processed

trâmites /'tramitʃis/ *m pl* channels

tramóia /tra'mɔja/ *f* scheme

trampolim /trãpo'lĩ/ *m* (*de ginástica*) trampoline; (*de piscina, fig*) springboard

tranca /'trãka/ *f* bolt; (*em carro*) lock

trança /'trãsa/ *f* (*de cabelo*) plait

tran|cafiar /trãkafi'ar/ *vt* lock up; **~car** *vt* lock; cancel <*matrícula*>

trançar /trã'sar/ *vt* plait <*cabelo*>; weave <*palha etc*>

tranco /'trãku/ *m* jolt; **aos ~s e barrancos** in fits and starts

tranqueira /trã'kera/ *f* junk

tranqüi|lidade /trãkwili'dadʒi/ *f* tranquillity; **~lizador** *a* reassuring; **~lizante** *m* tranquillizer ▫ *a* reassuring; **~lizar** *vt* reassure; **~lizar-se** *vpr* be reassured; **~lo** *a* <*bairro, sono*> peaceful; <*pessoa, voz, mar*> calm; <*consciência*> clear; <*sucesso, lucro*> sure-fire ▫ *adv* with no trouble

transa /'trãza/ *f* (*fam*) (*negócio*) deal; (*caso*) affair; **~ção** *f* transaction; **~do** *a* (*fam*) <*roupa, pessoa, casa*> stylish; <*relação*> healthy

Transamazônica /tranzama'zonika/ *f* trans-Amazonian highway

transar /trã'zar/ (*fam*) *vt* set up; do <*drogas*> ▫ *vi* (*negociar*) deal; (*fazer sexo*) have sex

transatlântico /trãzat'lãtʃiku/ *a* transatlantic ▫ *m* liner

transbordar /trãzbor'dar/ *vi* overflow

transcen|dental /trãsẽdẽ'taw/ (*pl* **~dentais**) *a* transcendental; **~der** *vt/i* **~der (a)** transcend

trans|crever /trãskre'ver/ *vt* transcribe; **~crição** *f* transcription; **~crito** *a* transcribed ▫ *m* transcript

transe /'trãzi/ *m* trance

transeunte /trãzi'ũtʃi/ *m/f* passer-by

transfe|rência /trãsfe'rẽsia/ *f* transfer; **~ridor** *m* protractor; **~rir** *vt* transfer; **~rir-se** *vpr* transfer

transfor|mação /trãsforma'sãw/ *f* transformation; **~mador** *m* transformer; **~mar** *vt* transform; **~mar-se** *vpr* be transformed

trânsfuga /'trãsfuga/ *m/f* deserter; (*de um país*) defector

transfusão /trãsfu'zãw/ *f* transfusion

trans|gredir /trãzgre'dʒir/ *vt* infringe; **~gressão** *f* infringement

transi|ção /trãzi'sãw/ *f* transition; **~cional** (*pl* **~cionais**) *a* transitional

transi|gente /trãzi'ʒẽtʃi/ *a* open to compromise; **~gir** *vi* compromise

transis|tor /trãzis'tor/ *m* transistor; **~torizado** *a* transistorized

transi|tar /trãzi'tar/ *vi* pass; **~tável** (*pl* **~táveis**) *a* passable; **~tivo** *a* transitive

trânsito /'trãzitu/ *m* traffic; **em ~** in transit

transitório /trãzi'tɔriu/ *a* transitory

translúcido /trãz'lusidu/ *a* translucent

transmis|são /trãzmi'sãw/ *f* transmission; **~sor** *m* transmitter

transmitir /trãzmi'tʃir/ *vt* transmit <*programa, calor, doença*>; convey <*notícia, ordens*>; transfer <*herança, direito*>; **~-se** *vpr* <*doença*> be transmitted

transpa|recer /trãspare'ser/ *vi* be visible; (*fig*) <*emoção, verdade*> come out; **~rência** *f* transparency; **~rente** *a* transparent

transpi|ração /trãspira'sãw/ *f* perspiration; **~rar** *vt* exude ▫ *vi* (*suar*) perspire; <*notícia*> trickle through; <*verdade*> come out

transplan|tar /trãsplã'tar/ *vt* transplant; **~te** *m* transplant

transpor /trãs'por/ *vt* cross <*rio, fronteira*>; get over <*obstáculo, dificuldade*>; transpose <*letras, música*>

transpor|tadora /trãsporta'dora/ *f* transport company; **~tar** *vt* transport; (*em contas*) carry forward; **~te** *m* transport; **~-te coletivo** public transport

transposto /trãs'postu/ *pp de* **transpor**

transtor|nar /trãstor'nar/ *vt* mess up <*papéis, casa*>; disrupt <*rotina, ambiente*>; disturb, upset <*pessoa*>; **~nar-se** *vpr* <*pessoa*> be rattled; **~no** /o/ *m* (*de casa, rotina*) disruption; (*de pessoa*) disturbance; (*contratempo*) upset

transver|sal /trãzver'saw/ (*pl* **~sais**) *a* **(rua) ~sal** cross street; **~so** /ɛ/ *a* transverse

transvi|ado /trãzvi'adu/ *a* wayward; **~ar** *vt* lead astray

trapa|ça /tra'pasa/ *f* swindle; **~cear** *vi* cheat; **~ceiro** *a* crooked □ *m* cheat

trapa|lhada /trapa'ʎada/ *f* bungle; **~lhão** *a* (*f* **~lhona**) bungling □ *m* (*f* **~lhona**) bungler

trapézio /tra'pɛziu/ *m* trapeze

trapezista /trape'zista/ *m/f* trapeze artist

trapo /'trapu/ *m* rag

traquéia /tra'kɛja/ *f* windpipe, trachea

traquejo /tra'keʒu/ *m* knack

traquinas /tra'kinas/ *a invar* mischievous

trás /tras/ *adv* **de ~** from behind; **a roda de ~** the back wheel; **de ~ para frente** back to front; **para ~** backwards; **deixar para ~** leave behind; **por ~ de** behind

traseiro /tra'zeru/ *a* rear, back □ *m* bottom

trasladar /trazla'dar/ *vt* transport

traspas|sado /traspa'sadu/ *a* <*paletó*> double-breasted; **~sar** *vt* pierce

traste /'trastʃi/ *m* (*pessoa*) pain; (*coisa*) piece of junk

tra|tado /tra'tadu/ *m* (*pacto*) treaty; (*estudo*) treatise; **~tamento** *m* treatment; (*título*) title; **~tar** *vt* treat; negotiate <*preço, venda*> □ *vi* (*manter relações*) have dealings (**com** with); (*combinar*) negotiate (**com** with); **~tar de** deal with; **~tar alg de** *ou* **por** address s.o. as; **~tar de voltar** (*tentar*) seek to return; (*resolver*) decide to return; **~-tar-se de** be a matter of; **~tável** (*pl* **~táveis**) *a* <*doença*> treatable; <*pessoa*> accommodating; **~tos** *m pl* **maus ~tos** ill-treatment

trator /tra'tor/ *m* tractor

trauma /'trawma/ *m* trauma; **~-tizante** *a* traumatic; **~tizar** *vt* traumatize

tra|vão /tra'vãw/ *m* (*Port*) brake; **~var** *vt* lock <*rodas, músculos*>; stop <*carro*>; block <*passagem*>; strike up <*amizade, conversa*>; wage <*luta, combate*> □ *vi* (*Port*) brake

trave /'travi/ *f* beam, joist; (*do gol*) crossbar

traves|sa /tra'vɛsa/ *f* (*trave*) crossbar; (*rua*) side street; (*prato*) dish; (*pente*) slide; **~são** *m* dash; **~seiro** *m* pillow; **~sia** *f* crossing; **~so** /e/ *a* <*criança*> naughty; **~sura** *f* prank; *pl* mischief

travesti /traves'tʃi/ *m* transvestite; (*artista*) drag artist; **~do** *a* in drag

trazer /tra'zer/ *vt* bring; bear <*nome, ferida*>; wear <*barba, chapéu, cabelo curto*>

trecho /'treʃu/ *m* (*de livro etc*) passage; (*de rua etc*) stretch

treco /'trɛku/ (*fam*) *m* (*coisa*) thing; (*ataque*) turn

trégua /'trɛgwa/ *f* truce; (*fig*) respite

trei|nador /trejna'dor/ *m* trainer; **~namento** *m* training; **~nar** *vt* train <*atleta, animal*>; practise <*língua etc*> □ *vi* <*atleta*> train; <*pianista, principiante*> practise; **~no** *m* training; (*um*) training session

trejeito /tre'ʒejtu/ *m* grimace

trela /'trɛla/ *f* lead, (*Amer*) leash

treliça /tre'lisa/ *f* trellis

trem /trẽj/ *m* train; **~ de aterrissagem** undercarriage; **~ de carga** goods train, (*Amer*) freight train

trema /'trema/ *m* dieresis

treme|deira /treme'dera/ *f* shiver; **~licar** *vi* tremble; **~luzir** *vi* glimmer, flicker

tremendo /tre'mẽdu/ *a* tremendous

tre|mer /tre'mer/ *vi* tremble; <*terra*> shake; **~mor** *m* tremor; (*tremedeira*) shiver; **~mular** *vi* <*bandeira*> flutter; <*luz, estrela*> glimmer, flicker

trêmulo /'tremulu/ *a* trembling; <*luz*> flickering

trena /'trena/ *f* tape measure

trenó /tre'nɔ/ *m* sledge, (*Amer*) sled; (*puxado a cavalos etc*) sleigh

tre|padeira /trepa'dera/ *f* climbing plant; **~par** *vt* climb □ *vi* climb; (*chulo*) fuck

três /tres/ *a & m* three

tresloucado /trezlo'kadu/ *a* deranged

trevas /'trɛvas/ *f pl* darkness

trevo /'trevu/ *m* (*planta*) clover; (*rodoviário*) interchange

treze /'trezi/ *a & m* thirteen

trezentos /tre'zẽtus/ *a & m* three hundred

triagem /tri'aʒẽ/ *f* (*escolha*) selection; (*separação*) sorting; **fazer uma ~ de** sort

tri|angular /triãgu'lar/ *a* triangular; **~ângulo** *m* triangle

tri|bal /tri'baw/ (*pl* **~bais**) *a* tribal; **~bo** *f* tribe

tribu|na /tri'buna/ *f* rostrum; **~nal** (*pl* **~nais**) *m* court

tribu|tação /tributa'sãw/ *f* taxation; **~tar** *vt* tax; **~tário** *a* tax □ *m* tributary; **~to** *m* tribute

tri|cô /tri'ko/ *m* knitting; **artigos de ~cô** knitwear; **~cotar** *vt/i* knit

tridimensio|nal /tridʒimẽsio-'naw/ (*pl* **~nais**) *a* three-dimensional

trigêmeo /tri'ʒemiu/ *m* triplet

trigésimo /tri'ʒɛzimu/ *a* thirtieth

tri|go /'trigu/ *m* wheat; **~gueiro** *a* dark

trilha /'triʎa/ *f* path; (*pista, de disco*) track; **~ sonora** soundtrack

trilhão /triˈʎãw/ *m* billion, (*Amer*) trillion

trilho /ˈtriʎu/ *m* track

trilogia /triloˈʒia/ *f* trilogy

trimes|tral /trimesˈtraw/ (*pl* **~trais**) *a* quarterly; **~tre** /ɛ/ *m* quarter; (*do ano letivo*) term

trincar /trĩˈkar/ *vt/i* crack

trincheira /trĩˈʃera/ *f* trench

trinco /ˈtrĩku/ *m* latch

trindade /trĩˈdadʒi/ *f* trinity

trinta /ˈtrĩta/ *a & m* thirty

trio /ˈtriu/ *m* trio; **~ elétrico** music float

tripa /ˈtripa/ *f* gut

tripé /triˈpɛ/ *m* tripod

tripli|car /tripliˈkar/ *vt/i*, **~car-se** *vpr* treble; **~cata** *f* triplicate

triplo /ˈtriplu/ *a & m* triple

tripu|lação /tripulaˈsãw/ *f* crew; **~lante** *m/f* crew member; **~lar** *vt* man

triste /ˈtristʃi/ *a* sad; **~za** /e/ *f* sadness; **é uma ~za** (*fam*) it's pathetic

tritu|rador /trituraˈdor/ *m* (*de papel*) shredder; **~rador de lixo** waste disposal unit; **~rar** *vt* shred <*legumes, papel*>; grind up <*lixo*>

triun|fal /triũˈfaw/ (*pl* **~fais**) *a* triumphal; **~fante** *a* triumphant; **~far** *vi* triumph; **~fo** *m* triumph

trivi|al /triviˈaw/ (*pl* **~ais**) *a* trivial; **~alidade** *f* triviality; *pl* trivia

triz /tris/ *m* **por um ~** narrowly, by a hair's breadth; **não foi atropelado por um ~** he narrowly missed being knocked down

tro|ca /ˈtrɔka/ *f* exchange; **em ~ca de** in exchange for; **~-cadilho** *m* pun; **~cado** *m* change; **~cador** *m* conductor; **~car** *vt* (*dar e receber*) exchange (**por** for); change <*dinheiro, lençóis, lâmpada, lugares etc*>; (*transpor*) change round; (*confundir*) mix up; **~car-se** *vpr* change; **~car de roupa/trem/lugar** change clothes /trains/places; **~ca-troca** *m* swap; **~-co** /o/ *m* change; **a ~co de quê?** what for?; **dar o ~co em alg** pay s.o. back

troço /ˈtrɔsu/ (*fam*) *m* (*coisa*) thing; (*ataque*) turn; **me deu um ~** I had a funny turn

troféu /troˈfɛw/ *m* trophy

trólebus /ˈtrɔlebus/ *m invar* trolley bus

trom|ba /ˈtrõba/ *f* (*de elefante*) trunk; (*cara amarrada*) long face; **~bada** *f* crash; **~ba-d'água** (*pl* **~bas-d'água**) *f* downpour; **~badinha** *m* bag snatcher; **~bar** *vi* **~bar com** crash into <*poste, carro*>; bump into <*pessoa*>

trombo|ne /trõˈbɔni/ *m* trombone; **~nista** *m/f* trombonist

trompa /ˈtrõpa/ *f* French horn; **~ de Falópio** fallopian tube

trompe|te /trõˈpɛtʃi/ *m* trumpet; **~tista** *m/f* trumpeter

tron|co /ˈtrõku/ *m* trunk; **~cudo** *a* stocky

trono /ˈtronu/ *m* throne

tropa /ˈtrɔpa/ *f* troop; (*exército*) army; *pl* troops; **~ de choque** riot police

trope|ção /tropeˈsãw/ *m* trip; (*erro*) slip-up; **~çar** *vi* trip; (*errar*) slip up; **~ço** /e/ *m* stumbling block

trôpego /ˈtropegu/ *a* unsteady

tropi|cal /tropiˈkaw/ (*pl* **~cais**) *a* tropical

trópico /ˈtrɔpiku/ *m* tropic

tro|tar /troˈtar/ *vi* trot; **~te** /ɔ/ *m* (*de cavalo*) trot; (*de estudantes*) practical joke; (*mentira*) hoax

trouxa /ˈtroʃa/ *f* (*de roupa etc*) bundle ▫ *m/f* (*fam*) sucker ▫ *a* (*fam*) gullible

tro|vão /troˈvãw/ *m* clap of thunder; *pl* thunder; **~vejar** *vi* thunder; **~voada** *f* thunderstorm; **~voar** *vi* thunder

trucidar /trusiˈdar/ *vt* slaughter

trucu|lência /trukuˈlẽsia/ *f* barbarity; **~lento** *a* (*cruel*) barbaric; (*brigão*) belligerent

trufa /ˈtrufa/ *f* truffle

trunfo /ˈtrũfu/ *m* trump; (*fig*) trump card

truque /ˈtruki/ *m* trick

truta /ˈtruta/ *f* trout

tu /tu/ *pron* you

tua /ˈtua/ *veja* **teu**

tuba /ˈtuba/ *f* tuba

tubarão /tubaˈrãw/ *m* shark

tubá|rio /tuˈbariu/ *a* **gravidez ~ria** ectopic pregnancy

tuberculose /tubercuˈlɔzi/ *f* tuberculosis

tubo /ˈtubu/ *m* tube; (*no corpo*) duct

tubulação /tubulaˈsãw/ *f* ducting

tucano /tuˈkanu/ *m* toucan

tudo /ˈtudu/ *pron* everything; **~ bem?** (*cumprimento*) how are things?; **~ de bom** all the best; **em ~ quanto é lugar** all over the place

tufão /tuˈfãw/ *m* typhoon

tulipa /tuˈlipa/ *f* tulip

tumba /ˈtũba/ *f* tomb

tumor /tuˈmor/ *m* tumour; **~ cerebral** brain tumour

túmulo /ˈtumulu/ *m* grave

tumul|to /tuˈmuwtu/ *m* commotion; (*motim*) riot; **~tuado** *a* disorderly, rowdy; **~tuar** *vt* disrupt ▫ *vi* cause a commotion; **~tuoso** *a* tumultuous

tú|nel /ˈtunew/ (*pl* **~neis**) *m* tunnel

túnica /'tunika/ *f* tunic
Tunísia /tu'nizia/ *f* Tunisia
tupiniquim /tupini'kĩ/ *a* Brazilian
turbante /tur'bãtʃi/ *m* turban
turbilhão /turbi'ʎãw/ *m* whirlwind
turbina /tur'bina/ *f* turbine
turbu|lência /turbu'lẽsia/ *f* turbulence; **~lento** *a* turbulent
turco /'turku/ *a & m* Turkish
turfa /'turfa/ *f* peat
turfe /'turfe/ *m* horse-racing
turis|mo /tu'rizmu/ *m* tourism; **fazer ~mo** go sightseeing; **~-ta** *m/f* tourist
turístico /tu'ristʃiku/ *a* <*ponto, indústria*> tourist; <*viagem*> sightseeing
turma /'turma/ *f* group; (*na escola*) class
turnê /tur'ne/ *f* tour
turno /'turnu/ *m* (*de trabalho*) shift; (*de competição, eleição*) round
turquesa /tur'keza/ *m/f & a invar* turquoise
Turquia /tur'kia/ *f* Turkey
turra /'tuxa/ *f* **às ~s com** at loggerheads with
tur|var /tur'var/ *vt* cloud; **~vo** *a* cloudy
tutano /tu'tanu/ *m* marrow
tutela /tu'tɛla/ *f* guardianship
tutor /tu'tor/ *m* guardian
tutu /tu'tu/ *m* (*vestido*) tutu; (*prato*) beans with bacon and manioc flour
TV /te've/ *f* TV

ubíquo /u'bikwu/ *a* ubiquitous
Ucrânia /u'krania/ *f* Ukraine
ucraniano /ukrani'anu/ *a & m* Ukrainian
ué /u'ɛ/ *int* hang on
ufa /'ufa/ *int* phew
ufanis|mo /ufa'nizmu/ *m* chauvinism; **~ta** *a & m/f* chauvinist
Uganda /u'gãda/ *m* Uganda
ui /ui/ *int* (*de dor*) ouch; (*de nojo*) ugh; (*de espanto*) oh
uísque /u'iski/ *m* whisky
ui|var /ui'var/ *vi* howl; **~vo** *m* howl
úlcera /'uwsera/ *f* ulcer
ulterior /uwteri'or/ *a* further
ulti|mamente /uwtʃima'mẽtʃi/ *adv* recently; **~mar** *vt* finalize; **~mato** *m* ultimatum
último /'uwtʃimu/ *a* last; <*moda, notícia etc*> latest; **em ~ caso** as a last resort; **nos ~s anos** in recent years; **por ~** last
ultra|jante /uwtra'ʒãtʃi/ *a* offensive; **~jar** *vt* offend; **~je** *m* outrage
ultraleve /uwtra'lɛvi/ *m* microlite
ultra|mar /uwtra'mar/ *m* overseas; **~marino** *a* overseas
ultrapas|sado /uwtrapa'sadu/ *a* outdated; **~sagem** *f* overtaking, (*Amer*) passing; **~sar** *vt* (*de carro*) overtake, (*Amer*) pass; (*ser superior a*) surpass; (*exceder*) exceed; (*extrapolar*) go beyond □ *vi* overtake, (*Amer*) pass
ultra-sonografia /uwtrasonogra'fia/ *f* ultrasound scan
ultravioleta /uwtravio'leta/ *a* ultraviolet
ulu|lante /ulu'lãtʃi/ *a* (*fig*) blatant; **~lar** *vi* wail
um /ũ/ (*f* **uma**; *m pl* **uns**, *f pl* **umas**) *art* a, an; *pl* some □ *a & pron* one; **~ ao outro** one another; **vieram umas 20 pessoas** about 20 people came
umbanda /ũ'bãda/ *m* Afro-Brazilian cult
umbigo /ũ'bigu/ *m* navel
umbili|cal /ũbili'kaw/ (*pl* **~-cais**) *a* umbilical
umedecer /umede'ser/ *vt* moisten; **~-se** *vpr* moisten
umidade /umi'dadʒi/ *f* moisture; (*desagradável*) damp; (*do ar*) humidity
úmido /'umidu/ *a* moist; <*parede, roupa etc*> damp; <*ar, clima*> humid
unânime /u'nanimi/ *a* unanimous
unanimidade /unanimi'dadʒi/ *f* unanimity
undécimo /ũ'dɛsimu/ *a* eleventh
ungüento /ũ'gwẽtu/ *m* ointment
unha /'uɲa/ *f* nail; (*de animal, utensílio*) claw
união /uni'ãw/ *f* union; (*concórdia*) unity; (*ato de unir*) joining; **União Européia** European Union, EU
unicamente /unika'mẽtʃi/ *adv* only
único /'uniku/ *a* only; (*ímpar*) unique
uni|dade /uni'dadʒi/ *f* unit; **~do** *a* united; <*família*> close
unifi|cação /unifika'sãw/ *f* unification; **~car** *vt* unify
unifor|me /uni'fɔrmi/ *a* uniform; <*superfície*> even □ *m* uniform; **~midade** *f* uniformity; **~mizado** *a* <*policial etc*> uniformed; (*padronizado*) standardized; **~zar** *vt* (*padronizar*) standardize
unilate|ral /unilate'raw/ (*pl* **~rais**) *a* unilateral
unir /u'nir/ *vt* unite <*povo, nações, família etc*>; (*ligar, casar*) join; (*combinar*) combine (**a** *ou* **com** with); **~-se** *vpr* (*aliar-se*) unite (**a** with);

(*juntar-se*) join together; (*combinar-se*) combine (**a** *ou* **com** with)

unissex /uni'sɛks/ *a invar* unisex

uníssono /u'nisonu/ *m* **em ~** in unison

univer|sal /univer'saw/ (*pl* **~sais**) *a* universal

universi|dade /universi'dadʒi/ *f* university; **~tário** *a* university □ *m* university student

universo /uni'vɛrsu/ *m* universe

untar /ũ'tar/ *vt* grease <*fôrma*>; spread <*pão*>; smear <*corpo*>

upa /'upa/ *int* (*incentivando*) upsadaisy; (*ao cair algo etc*) whoops

urânio /u'raniu/ *m* uranium

Urano /u'ranu/ *m* Uranus

urbanis|mo /urba'nizmu/ *m* town planning; **~ta** *m/f* town planner

urbani|zado /urbani'zadu/ *a* built-up; **~zar** *vt* urbanize

urbano /ur'banu/ *a* (*da cidade*) urban; (*refinado*) urbane

urdir /ur'dʒir/ *vt* weave; (*maquinar*) hatch

urdu /ur'du/ *m* Urdu

ur|gência /ur'ʒẽsia/ *f* urgency; **~gente** *a* urgent; **~gir** *vi* be urgent; <*tempo*> press; **~ge irmos** we must go urgently

uri|na /u'rina/ *f* urine; **~nar** *vt* pass □ *vi* urinate; **~nol** (*pl* **~nóis**) *m* (*penico*) chamber pot; (*em banheiro*) urinal

urna /'urna/ *f* (*para cinzas*) urn; (*para votos*) ballot box; *pl* (*fig*) polls

ur|rar /u'xar/ *vt/i* roar; **~ro** *m* roar

urso /'ursu/ *m* bear; **~-branco** (*pl* **~s-brancos**) *m* polar bear

urti|cária /urtʃi'karia/ *f* nettle rash; **~ga** *f* nettle

urubu /uru'bu/ *m* black vulture

Uruguai /uru'gwaj/ *m* Uruguay

uruguaio /uru'gwaju/ *a* & *m* Uruguayan

urze /'urzi/ *f* heather

usado /u'zadu/ *a* used; <*roupa*> worn; <*palavra*> common

usar /u'zar/ *vt* wear <*roupa, óculos, barba etc*>; **~ (de)** (*utilizar*) use

usina /u'zina/ *f* plant; **~ termonuclear** nuclear power station

uso /'uzu/ *m* use; (*de palavras, linguagem*) usage; (*praxe*) practice

usu|al /uzu'aw/ (*pl* **~ais**) *a* common; **~ário** *m* user; **~-fruir** *vt* enjoy <*coisas boas*>; have the use of <*prédio, jardim etc*>; **~fruto** *m* use

usurário /uzu'rariu/ *a* money-grabbing □ *m* money-lender

usurpar /uzur'par/ *vt* usurp

uten|sílio /utẽ'siliu/ *m* utensil; **~te** *m/f* (*Port*) user

útero /'uteru/ *m* uterus, womb

UTI /ute'i/ *f* intensive care unit

útil. /'utʃiw/ (*pl* **úteis**) *a* useful; **dia ~** workday

utili|dade /utʃili'dadʒi/ *f* usefulness; (*uma*) utility; **~tário** *a* utilitarian; **~zar** *vt* (*empregar*) use; (*tornar útil*) utilize; **~zável** (*pl* **~záveis**) *a* usable

utopia /uto'pia/ *f* Utopia

utópico /u'tɔpiku/ *a* Utopian

uva /'uva/ *f* grape

úvula /'uvula/ *f* uvula

Vv

vaca /'vaka/ *f* cow

vaci|lante /vasi'lãtʃi/ *a* wavering; <*luz*> flickering; **~lar** *vi* waver; <*luz*> flicker; (*fam: bobear*) slip up

vaci|na /va'sina/ *f* vaccine; **~-nação** *f* vaccination; **~nar** *vt* vaccinate

vácuo /'vakuu/ *m* vacuum

va|diar /vadʒi'ar/ *vi* (*viver ocioso*) laze around; (*fazer cera*) mess about; **~dio** *a* idle □ *m* idler

vaga /'vaga/ *f* (*posto*) vacancy; (*para estacionar*) parking place

vagabun|dear /vagabũdʒi'ar/ *vi* (*perambular*) roam; (*vadiar*) laze around; **~do** *a* <*pessoa, vida*> idle; <*produto, objeto*> shoddy □ *m* tramp; (*pessoa vadia*) bum

vaga-lume /vaga'lumi/ *m* glow-worm

va|gão /va'gãw/ *m* (*de passageiros*) carriage, (*Amer*) car; (*de carga*) wagon; **~gão-leito** (*pl* **~gões-leitos**) *m* sleeping car; **~gão-restaurante** (*pl* **~gões-restaurantes**) *m* dining car

vagar[1] /va'gar/ *vi* <*pessoa*> wander about; <*barco*> drift

vagar[2] /va'gar/ *vi* <*cargo, apartamento*> become vacant

vagaroso /vaga'rozu/ *a* slow

vagem /'vaʒẽ/ *f* green bean

vagi|na /va'ʒina/ *f* vagina; **~nal** (*pl* **~nais**) *a* vaginal

vago[1] /'vagu/ *a* (*indefinido*) vague

vago[2] /'vagu/ *a* (*desocupado*) vacant; <*tempo*> spare

vaguear /vagi'ar/ *vi* roam

vai|a /'vaja/ *f* boo; **~ar** *vi* boo

vai|dade /vaj'dadʒi/ *f* vanity; **~doso** *a* vain

vaivém /vaj'vẽj/ *m* comings and goings, toing and froing

vala /'vala/ *f* ditch; **~ comum** mass grave

vale[1] /'vali/ *m* (*de rio etc*) valley

vale[2] /'vali/ *m* (*ficha*) voucher; **~ postal** postal order

valen|tão /valẽ'tãw/ *a* (*f* **~tona**) tough □ *m* tough guy; **~te** *a* brave; **~tia** *f* bravery; (*uma*) feat

valer /va'ler/ *vt* be worth □ *vi* be valid; **~ aco a alg** earn s.o. sth; **~-se de** avail o.s. of; **~ a pena** be worth it; **vale a pena tentar** it's worth trying; **mais vale desistir** it's better to give up; **vale tudo** anything goes; **fazer ~** enforce <*lei*>; stand up for <*direitos*>; **para ~** (*a sério*) for real; (*muito*) really

vale|-refeição /valirefej'sãw/ (*pl* **~s-refeição**) *m* luncheon voucher

valeta /va'leta/ *f* gutter

valete /va'lɛtʃi/ *m* jack

valia /va'lia/ *f* value

validar /vali'dar/ *vt* validate

válido /'validu/ *a* valid

valioso /vali'ozu/ *a* valuable

valise /va'lizi/ *f* travelling bag

valor /va'lor/ *m* value; (*valentia*) valour; *pl* (*títulos*) securities; **no ~ de** to the value of; **sem ~** worthless; **objetos de ~** valuables; **~ nominal** face value

valori|zaçao /valoriza'sãw/ *f* (*apreciação*) valuing; (*aumento no valor*) increase in value; **~zado** *a* highly valued; **~zar** *vt* (*apreciar*) value; (*aumentar o valor de*) increase the value of; **~zar-se** *vt* <*coisa*> increase in value; <*pessoa*> value o.s.

val|sa /'vawsa/ *f* waltz; **~sar** *vi* waltz

válvula /'vawvula/ *f* valve

vampiro /vã'piru/ *m* vampire

vandalismo /vãda'lizmu/ *m* vandalism

vândalo /'vãdalu/ *m* vandal

vangloriar-se /vãglori'arsi/ *vpr* brag (**de** about)

vanguarda /vã'gwarda/ *f* vanguard; (*de arte*) avant-garde

vanta|gem /vã'taʒẽ/ *f* advantage; **contar ~gem** boast; **levar ~gem** have the advantage (**a** over); **tirar ~gem de** take advantage of; **~joso** /o/ *a* advantageous

vão /vãw/ (*pl* **~s**) *a* (*f* **vã**) vain □ *m* gap; **em ~** in vain

vapor /va'por/ *m* (*fumaça*) steam; (*gás*) vapour; (*barco*) steamer; **máquina a ~** steam engine; **a todo ~** at full blast

vaporizar /vapori'zar/ *vt* vaporize; (*com spray*) spray

vaqueiro /va'keru/ *m* cowboy

vaquinha /va'kiɲa/ *f* collection, whip-round

vara /'vara/ *f* rod; **~ cívil** civil district; **~ mágica** *ou* **de condão** magic wand

va|ral /va'raw/ (*pl* **~rais**) *m* washing line

varanda /va'rãda/ *f* veranda

varão /va'rãw/ *m* male

varar /va'rar/ *vt* (*furar*) pierce; (*passar por*) sweep through

varejão /vare'ʒãw/ *m* wholesale store

varejeira /vare'ʒera/ *f* bluebottle

vare|jista /vare'ʒista/ *a* retail □ *m*/*f* retailer; **~jo** /e/ *m* retail trade; **vender a ~jo** sell retail

vari|ação /varia'sãw/ *f* variation; **~ado** *a* varied; **~ante** *a* & *f* variant; **~ar** *vt*/*i* vary; **para ~ar** for a change; **~ável** (*pl* **~áveis**) *a* variable; <*tempo*> changeable

varicela /vari'sɛla/ *f* chickenpox

variedade /varie'dadʒi/ *f* variety

vários /'varius/ *a pl* several

varíola /va'riola/ *f* smallpox

variz /va'ris/ *f* varicose vein

varo|nil /varo'niw/ (*pl* **~nis**) *a* manly

var|rer /va'xer/ *vt* sweep; (*fig*) sweep away; **~rido** *a* **um doido ~rido** a raving lunatic

Varsóvia /var'sɔvia/ *f* Warsaw

vasculhar /vasku'ʎar/ *vt* search through

vasectomia /vazekto'mia/ *f* vasectomy

vaselina /vaze'lina/ *f* vaseline

vasilha /va'ziʎa/ *f* jug

vaso /'vazu/ *m* pot; (*para flores*) vase; **~ sanguíneo** blood vessel

vassoura /va'sora/ *f* broom

vas|tidão /vastʃi'dãw/ *f* vastness; **~to** *a* vast

vatapá /vata'pa/ *m* spicy North-Eastern dish

Vaticano /vatʃi'kanu/ *m* Vatican

vati|cinar /vatʃisi'nar/ *vt* prophesy; **~cínio** *m* prophecy

va|zamento /vaza'mẽtu/ *m* leak; **~zante** *f* ebb tide; **~zão** *m* outflow; **dar ~zão a** (*fig*) give vent to; **~zar** *vt*/*i* leak

vazio /va'ziu/ *a* empty □ *m* emptiness; (*um*) void

veado /vi'adu/ *m* deer

ve|dação /veda'sãw/ *f* (*de casa, janela*) insulation; (*em motor etc*) gasket; **~dar** *vt* seal <*recipiente, abertura*>; stanch <*sangue*>; seal off <*saída, área*>; **~dar aco (a alg)** prohibit sth (for s.o.)

vedete /ve'dɛte/ *f* star

vee|mência /vee'mẽsia/ *f* vehemence; **~mente** *a* vehement

vege|tação /veʒeta'sãw/ *f* vegetation; **~tal** (*pl* **~tais**) *a* & *m* vegetable; **~tar** *vi* vegetate; **~tariano** *a* & *m* vegetarian

veia /'veja/ *f* vein

veicular /veiku'lar/ *vt* convey; place <*anúncios*>

veículo /ve'ikulu/ *m* vehicle; (*de comunicação etc*) medium

vela[1] /'vɛla/ *f* (*de barco*) sail; (*esporte*) sailing

vela[2] /'vɛla/ *f* candle; (*em motor*) spark plug; **segurar a ~** (*fam*) play gooseberry

velar[1] /ve'lar/ *vt* (*cobrir*) veil

velar[2] /ve'lar/ *vt* watch over □ *vi* keep vigil

veleidade /velej'dadʒi/ *f* whim

ve|leiro /ve'leru/ *m* sailing boat; **~lejar** *vi* sail

velhaco /ve'ʎaku/ *a* crooked □ *m* crook

ve|lharia /veʎa'ria/ *f* old thing; **~lhice** *f* old age; **~lho** /ɛ/ *a* old □ *m* old man; **~lhote** /ɔ/ *m* old man

velocidade /velosi'dadʒi/ *f* speed; (*Port: marcha*) gear; **a toda ~** at full speed; **~ máxima** speed limit

velocímetro /velo'simetru/ *m* speedometer

velocista /velo'sista/ *m/f* sprinter

velório /ve'lɔriu/ *m* wake

veloz /ve'los/ *a* fast

veludo /ve'ludu/ *m* velvet; **~ cotelê** corduroy

ven|cedor /vẽse'dor/ *a* winning □ *m* winner; **~cer** *vt* win over <*adversário etc*>; win <*partida, corrida, batalha*> □ *vi* (*triunfar*) win; <*prestação, aluguel, dívida*> fall due; <*contrato, passaporte, prazo*> expire; <*apólice*> mature; **~cido** *a* **dar-se por ~cido** give in; **~cimento** *m* (*de dívida, aluguel*) due date; (*de contrato, prazo*) expiry date; (*de alimento, remédio etc*) best before date; (*salário*) payment; *pl* earnings

venda[1] /'vẽda/ *f* sale; (*loja*) general store; **à ~** on sale; **pôr à ~** put up for sale

ven|da[2] /'vẽda/ *f* blindfold; **~dar** *vt* blindfold

venda|val /vẽda'vaw/ (*pl* **~vais**) *m* gale, storm

ven|dável /vẽ'davew/ (*pl* **~dáveis**) *a* saleable; **~dedor** *m* (*de loja*) shop assistant; (*em geral*) seller; **~der** *vt/i* sell; **estar ~dendo saúde** be bursting with health

vendeta /vẽ'deta/ *f* vendetta

veneno /ve'nenu/ *m* poison; (*de cobra etc, malignidade*) venom; **~so** /o/ *a* poisonous; (*maldoso*) venomous

vene|ração /venera'sãw/ *f* reverence; (*de Deus etc*) worship; **~rar** *vt* revere; worship <*Deus etc*>

vené|reo /ve'nɛriu/ *a* **doença ~rea** venereal disease

Veneza /ve'neza/ *f* Venice

veneziana /venezi'ana/ *f* shutter

Venezuela /venezu'ɛla/ *f* Venezuela

venezuelano /venezue'lanu/ *a & m* Venezuelan

venta /'vẽta/ *f* nostril

ven|tania /vẽta'nia/ *f* gale; **~tar** *vi* be windy; **~tarola** /ɔ/ *f* fan

venti|lação /vẽtʃila'sãw/ *f* ventilation; **~lador** *m* fan; **~lar** *vt* ventilate; air <*sala, roupa*>

ven|to /'vẽtu/ *m* wind; **de ~to em popa** smoothly; **~toinha** *f* (*cata-vento*) weather vane; (*Port: ventilador*) fan; **~tosa** /ɔ/ *f* sucker; **~toso** /o/ *a* windy

ven|tre /'vẽtri/ *m* belly; **~tríloquo** *m* ventriloquist

Vênus /'venus/ *f* Venus

ver /ver/ *vt* see; watch <*televisão*>; (*resolver*) see to □ *vi* see □ *m* **a meu ~** in my view; **~-se** *vpr* (*no espelho etc*) see o.s.; (*em estado, condição*) find o.s.; (*um ao outro*) see each other; **ter a ~ com** have to do with; **vai ~ que ela não sabe** (*fam*) I bet she doesn't know; **vê se você não volta tarde** see you don't get back late; **viu?** (*fam*) right?

veracidade /verasi'dadʒi/ *f* truthfulness

vera|near /verani'ar/ *vi* spend the summer; **~neio** *m* summer holiday, (*Amer*) summer vacation; **~nista** *m/f* holidaymaker, (*Amer*) vacationer

verão /ve'rãw/ *m* summer

veraz /ve'ras/ *a* truthful

verbas /'vɛrbas/ *f pl* funds

ver|bal /ver'baw/ (*pl* **~bais**) *a* verbal; **~bete** /e/ *m* entry; **~bo** *m* verb; **~borragia** *f* waffle; **~boso** /o/ *a* verbose

verda|de /ver'dadʒi/ *f* truth; **de ~de** <*coisa*> real; <*fazer*> really; **na ~de** actually; **para falar a ~de** to tell the truth; **~deiro** *a* <*declaração, pessoa*> truthful; (*real*) true

verde /'verdʒi/ *a & m* green; **jogar ~ para colher maduro** fish for information; **~-abacate** *a invar* avocado; **~-amarelo** *a* yellow and green; (*brasileiro*) Brazilian; (*nacionalista*) nationalistic; **~-esmeralda** *a invar* emerald green; **~jar** *vi* turn green

verdu|ra /ver'dura/ *f* (*para comer*) greens; (*da natureza*) greenery; **~reiro** *m* greengrocer, (*Amer*) produce dealer

vereador /veria'dor/ *m* councillor

vereda /ve'reda/ *f* path

veredito /vere'dʒitu/ *m* verdict

vergar /ver'gar/ *vt/i* bend

vergo|nha /ver'goɲa/ *f* (*pudor*) shame; (*constrangimento*) embarrassment; (*timidez*) shyness; (*uma*) disgrace; **ter ~nha** be ashamed; be embarrassed; be shy; **cria** *ou* **tome ~nha na cara!** you should be ashamed of yourself!; **~nhoso** *a* shameful

verídico /ve'ridʒiku/ *a* true

verificar /verifi'kar/ *vt* check, verify <*fatos, dados etc*>; **~ que** ascertain that; **~ se** check that; **~-se** *vpr* <*previsão etc*> come true; <*acidente etc*> happen

verme /'vɛrmi/ *m* worm

verme|lhidão /vermeʎi'dãw/ *f* redness; **~lho** /e/ *a* & *m* red; **no ~lho** (*endividado*) in the red

vernáculo /ver'nakulu/ *a* & *m* vernacular

verniz /ver'nis/ *f* varnish; (*couro*) patent leather

veros|símil /vero'simiw/ (*pl* **~símeis**) *a* plausible; **~similhança** *f* plausibility

verruga /ve'xuga/ *f* wart

ver|sado /ver'sadu/ *a* well-versed (**em** in); **~são** *f* version; **~sar** *vi* **~sar sobre** concern; **~sátil** (*pl* **~sáteis**) *a* versatile; **~satilidade** *f* versatility; **~sículo** *m* (*da Bíblia*) verse; **~so**[1] /ɛ/ *m* verse

verso[2] /ɛ/ *m* (*de página*) reverse, other side; **vide ~** see over

vértebra /'vɛrtebra/ *f* vertebra

verte|brado /verte'bradu/ *a* & *m* vertebrate; **~bral** (*pl* **~brais**) *a* spinal

ver|tente /ver'tẽtʃi/ *f* slope; **~ter** *vt* (*derramar*) pour; shed <*lágrimas, sangue*>; (*traduzir*) render (**para** into)

verti|cal /vertʃi'kaw/ (*pl* **~cais**) *a* & *f* vertical; **~gem** *f* dizziness; **~ginoso** /o/ *a* dizzy

vesgo /'vezgu/ *a* cross-eyed

vesícula /ve'zikula/ *f* gall bladder

vespa /'vespa/ *f* wasp

véspera /'vɛspera/ *f* **a ~** the day before; **a ~ de** the eve of; **a ~ de Natal** Christmas Eve; **nas ~s de** on the eve of

vespertino /vesper'tʃinu/ *a* evening

ves|te /'vɛstʃi/ *f* robe; **~tiário** *m* (*para se trocar*) changing room; (*para guardar roupa*) cloakroom

vestibular /vestʃibu'lar/ *m* university entrance exam

vestíbulo /ves'tʃibulu/ *m* hall(way); (*do teatro*) foyer

vestido /ves'tʃidu/ *m* dress ◻ *a* dressed (**de** in)

vestígio /ves'tʃiʒiu/ *m* trace

ves|timenta /vestʃi'mẽta/ *f* (*de sacerdote*) vestments; **~tir** *vt* (*pôr*) put on; (*usar*) wear; (*pôr roupa em*) dress; (*dar roupa a*) clothe; **~tir-se** *vpr* dress; **~tir-se de branco/de padre** dress in white/as a priest; **~tuário** *m* clothing

vetar /ve'tar/ *vt* veto

veterano /vete'ranu/ *a* & *m* veteran

veterinário /veteri'nariu/ *a* veterinary ◻ *m* vet

veto /'vɛtu/ *m* veto

véu /vɛw/ *m* veil

vexa|me /ve'ʃami/ *m* disgrace; **dar um ~me** make a fool of o.s.; **~minoso** /o/ *a* disgraceful

vexar /ve'ʃar/ *vt* shame; **~-se** *vpr* be ashamed (**de** of)

vez /ves/ *f* (*ocasião*) time; (*turno*) turn; **às ~es** sometimes; **cada ~ mais** more and more; **de ~** for good; **desta ~** this time; **de ~ em quando** now and again, from time to time; **de uma ~** (*ao mesmo tempo*) at once; (*de um golpe*) in one go; **de uma ~ por todas** once and for all; **duas ~es** twice; **em ~ de** instead of; **fazer as ~es de** take the place of; **mais uma ~, outra ~** again; **muitas ~es** (*com muita freqüência*) often; (*repetidamente*) many times; **raras ~es** seldom; **repetidas ~es** repeatedly; **uma ~** once; **uma ~ que** since

via /'via/ *f* (*estrada*) road; (*rumo, meio*) way; (*exemplar*) copy; *pl* (*trâmites*) channels ◻ *prep* via; **em ~s de** on the point of; **por ~ aérea/marítima** by air/sea; **por ~ das dúvidas** just in case; **por ~ de regra** as a rule; **Via Láctea** Milky Way

viabili|dade /viabili'dadʒi/ *f* feasibility; **~zar** *vt* make feasible

viação /via'sãw/ *f* (*transporte*) road transport; (*estradas*) road network; (*companhia*) bus company

viaduto /via'dutu/ *m* viaduct; (*rodoviário*) flyover, (*Amer*) overpass

via|gem /vi'aʒẽ/ *f* (*uma*) trip, journey; (*em geral*) travelling; *pl* (*de uma pessoa*) travels; (*em geral*) travel; **boa ~gem!** have a good trip!; **~gem de negócios** business trip; **~jado** *a* well-travelled; **~jante** *a* travelling ◻ *m/f* traveller; **~jar** *vi* travel; **estar ~jando** (*fam*) (*com o pensamento longe*) be miles away

viário /vi'ariu/ *a* road; **anel ~** ring road

viatura /via'tura/ *f* vehicle

viá|vel /vi'avew/ (*pl* **~veis**) *a* feasible

víbora /'vibora/ *f* viper

vi|bração /vibra'sãw/ *f* vibration; (*fig*) thrill; **~brante** *a* vibrant; **~brar** *vt* shake ◻ *vi* vibrate; (*fig*) be thrilled (**com** by)

vice /'visi/ *m/f* deputy

vice-cam|peão /visikãpi'ãw/ *m* (*f* **~peã**) runner-up

vicejar /vise'ʒar/ *vi* flourish

vice-presiden|te /visiprezi'dẽtʃi/ *m* (*f* **~ta**) vice-president

vice-rei /visi'xej/ *m* viceroy

vice-versa /visi'vɛrsa/ *adv* vice-versa

vici|ado /visi'adu/ *a* addicted (**em** to) □ *m* addict; **um ~ado em drogas** a drug addict; **~ar** *vt* (*falsificar*) tamper with; (*estragar*) ruin □ *vi* <*droga*> be addictive; **~ar-se** *vpr* get addicted (**em** to)

vício /'visiu/ *m* vice

vicioso /visi'ozu/ *a* **círculo ~** vicious circle

vicissitudes /visisi'tudʒis/ *f pl* ups and downs

viço /'visu/ *m* (*de plantas*) exuberance; (*de pessoa, pele*) freshness; **~so** /o/ *a* <*planta*> lush; <*pele, pessoa*> fresh

vida /'vida/ *f* life; **sem ~** lifeless; **dar ~ a** liven up

videira /vi'dera/ *f* vine

vidente /vi'dẽtʃi/ *m/f* clairvoyant

vídeo /'vidʒiu/ *m* video; (*tela*) screen

video|cassete /vidʒiuka'sɛtʃi/ *m* (*fita*) video tape; (*aparelho*) video, (*Amer*) VCR; **~clipe** *m* video; **~clube** *m* video club; **~game** *m* videogame; **~teipe** *m* video tape

vidra|ça /vi'drasa/ *f* window pane; **~çaria** *f* (*fábrica*) glassworks; (*vidraças*) glazing; **~ceiro** *m* glazier

vi|drado /vi'dradu/ *a* glazed; **estar ~drado em** *ou* **por** (*fam*) love; **~drar** *vt* glaze □ *vi* (*fam*) fall in love (**em** *ou* **por** with); **~dro** *m* (*material*) glass; (*pote*) jar; (*janela*) window; **~dro fumê** tinted glass

viela /vi'ɛla/ *f* alley

Viena /vi'ɛna/ *f* Vienna

Vietnã /vietʃi'nã/ *m*, (*Port*) **Vietname** /viet'nam/ *m* Vietnam

vietnamita /vietna'mita/ *a & m/f* Vietnamese

viga /'viga/ *f* joist

vigarice /viga'risi/ *f* swindle

vigário /vi'gariu/ *m* vicar

vigarista /viga'rista/ *m/f* swindler, con artist

vi|gência /vi'ʒẽsia/ *f* (*qualidade*) force; (*tempo*) period in force; **~gente** *a* in force

vigésimo /vi'ʒɛzimu/ *a* twentieth

vigi|a /vi'ʒia/ *f* (*guarda*) watch; (*em navio*) porthole □ *m* night watchman; **~ar** *vt* (*observar*) watch; (*cuidar de*) watch over; (*como sentinela*) guard □ *vi* keep watch

vigi|lância /viʒi'lãsia/ *f* vigilance; **~lante** *a* vigilant

vigília /vi'ʒilia/ *f* vigil

vigor /vi'gor/ *m* vigour; **em ~** in force

vigo|rar /vigo'rar/ *vi* be in force; **~roso** *a* vigorous

vil /viw/ (*pl* **vis**) *a* base, despicable

vila /'vila/ *f* (*cidadezinha*) small town; (*casa elegante*) villa; (*conjunto de casas*) housing estate; **~ olímpica** Olympic village

vi|lania /vila'nia/ *f* villainy; **~lão** *m* (*f* **~lã**) villain

vilarejo /vila'reʒu/ *m* village

vilipendiar /vilipẽdʒi'ar/ *vt* disparage

vime /'vimi/ *m* wicker

vina|gre /vi'nagri/ *m* vinegar; **~grete** /ɛ/ *m* vinaigrette

vin|car /vĩ'kar/ *vt* crease; line <*rosto*>; **~co** *m* crease; (*no rosto*) line

vincular /vĩku'lar/ *vt* bond, tie

vínculo /'vĩkulu/ *m* link, bond; **~ empregatício** contract of employment

vinda /'vĩda/ *f* coming; **dar as boas ~s a** welcome

vindicar /vĩdʒi'kar/ *vt* vindicate

vindima /vĩ'dʒima/ *f* vintage

vin|do /'vĩdu/ *pp e pres de* **vir**; **~douro** *a* coming

vin|gança /vĩ'gãsa/ *f* vengeance, revenge; **~gar** *vt* revenge □ *vi* <*flores*> thrive; <*criança*> survive; <*plano, empreendimento*> be successful; **~gar-se** *vpr* take one's revenge (**de** for; **em** on); **~gativo** *a* vindictive

vinha /'viɲa/ *f* vineyard

vinhedo /vi'ɲedu/ *m* vineyard

vinheta /vi'ɲeta/ *f* (*na TV etc*) sequence

vinho /'viɲu/ *m* wine □ *a invar* maroon; **~ do Porto** port

vinícola /vi'nikola/ *a* wine-growing

vinicul|tor /vinikuw'tor/ *m* wine grower; **~tura** *f* wine-growing

vinil /vi'niw/ *m* vinyl

vinte /'vĩtʃi/ *a & m* twenty; **~na** /e/ *f* score

viola /vi'ɔla/ *f* viola

violação /viola'sãw/ *f* violation

violão /vio'lãw/ *m* guitar

violar /vio'lar/ *vt* violate

vio|lência /vio'lẽsia/ *f* violence; (*uma*) act of violence; **~lentar** *vt* rape <*mulher*>; **~lento** *a* violent

violeta /vio'leta/ *f* violet □ *a invar* violet

violi|nista /violi'nista/ *m/f* violinist; **~no** *m* violin

violonce|lista /violõse'lista/ *m/f* cellist; **~lo** /ɛ/ *m* cello

vir /vir/ *vi* come; **o ano que vem** next year; **venho lendo os jornais** I have been reading the papers; **vem cá** come here; (*fam*) listen; **isso não vem ao caso** that's irrelevant; **~ a ser** turn out to be; **~ com** give <*argumento etc*>

virabrequim /virabre'kĩ/ *m* crankshaft

viração /vira'sãw/ *f* breeze

vira-casaca /viraka'zaka/ *m/f* turncoat

vira|da /vi'rada/ *f* turn; **~do** *a* <*roupa*> inside out; (*de cabeça para baixo*) upside down; **~do para** facing

vira-lata /vira'lata/ *m* mongrel

virar /vi'rar/ *vt* turn; turn over <*disco, barco etc*>; turn inside out <*roupa*>; turn out <*bolsos*>; tip <*balde, água etc*> □ *vi* turn; <*barco*> turn over; (*tornar-se*) become; **~-se** *vpr* turn round; (*na vida*) get by, cope; **~-se para** turn to; **vira e mexe** every so often

viravolta /vira'vɔwta/ *f* about-turn

virgem /'virʒẽ/ *a* <*fita*> blank; <*floresta, noiva etc*> virgin □ *f* virgin; **Virgem** (*signo*) Virgo

virgindade /virʒĩ'dadʒi/ *f* virginity

vírgula /'virgula/ *f* comma; (*decimal*) point

vi|ril /vi'riw/ (*pl* **~ris**) *a* virile

virilha /vi'riʎa/ *f* groin

virilidade /virili'dadʒi/ *f* virility

virtu|al /virtu'aw/ (*pl* **~ais**) *a* virtual

virtude /vir'tudʒi/ *f* virtue

virtuo|sismo /virtuo'zizmu/ *m* virtuosity; **~so** /o/ *a* virtuous □ *m* virtuoso

virulento /viru'lẽtu/ *a* virulent

vírus /'virus/ *m invar* virus

visão /vi'zãw/ *f* vision; (*aspecto, ponto de vista*) view

visar /vi'zar/ *vt* aim at <*caça, alvo*>; **~ (a)** aim for <*objetivo*>; <*medida, ação*> be aimed at

vísceras /'viseras/ *f pl* innards

viscon|de /vis'kõdʒi/ *m* viscount; **~dessa** /e/ *f* viscountess

viscoso /vis'kozu/ *a* viscous

viseira /vi'zera/ *f* visor

visibilidade /vizibili'dadʒi/ *f* visibility

visionário /vizio'nariu/ *a & m* visionary

visi|ta /vi'zita/ *f* visit; (*visitante*) visitor; **fazer uma ~ta a alg** pay s.o. a visit; **~tante** *a* visiting □ *m/f* visitor; **~tar** *vt* visit

visí|vel /vi'zivew/ (*pl* **~veis**) *a* visible

vislum|brar /vizlũ'brar/ *vt* (*entrever*) glimpse; (*imaginar*) envisage; **~bre** *m* glimpse

visom /vi'zõ/ *m* mink

visor /vi'zor/ *m* viewfinder

vis|ta /'vista/ *f* sight; (*dos olhos*) eyesight; (*panorama*) view; **à ~ta** (*visível*) in view; (*em dinheiro*) in cash; **à primeira ~ta** at first sight; **pôr à ~ta** put on show; **de ~ta** <*conhecer*> by sight; **em ~ta de** in view of; **ter em ~ta** have in view; **dar na ~ta** attract attention; **fazer ~ta** look nice; **fazer ~ta grossa** turn a blind eye (**a** to); **perder de ~ta** lose sight of; **a perder de ~ta** as far as the eye can see; **uma ~ta de olhos** a quick look; **~to** *a* seen □ *m* visa; **pelo ~to** by the looks of things; **~to que** seeing that

visto|ria /visto'ria/ *f* inspection; **~riar** *vt* inspect

vistoso /vis'tozu/ *a* eye-catching

visu|al /vizu'aw/ (*pl* **~ais**) *a* visual □ *m* look; **~alizar** *vt* visualize

vi|tal /vi'taw/ (*pl* **~tais**) *a* vital; **~talício** *a* for life; **~talidade** *f* vitality

vita|mina /vita'mina/ *f* vitamin; (*bebida*) liquidized fruit drink; **~minado** *a* with added vitamins; **~mínico** *a* vitamin

vitela /vi'tɛla/ *f* (*carne*) veal

viticultura /vitʃikuw'tura/ *f* viticulture

vítima /'vitʃima/ *f* victim

viti|mar /vitʃi'mar/ *vt* (*matar*) claim the life of; **ser ~mado por** fall victim to

vitória /vi'tɔria/ *f* victory

vitorioso /vitori'ozu/ *a* victorious

vi|tral /vi'traw/ (*pl* **~trais**) *m* stained glass window

vitrine /vi'trini/ *f* shop window

vitrola /vi'trɔla/ *f* jukebox

viú|va /vi'uva/ *f* widow; **~vo** *a* widowed □ *m* widower

viva /'viva/ *f* cheer □ *int* hurray; **~ a rainha** long live the queen

vivacidade /vivasi'dadʒi/ *f* vivacity

vivalma /vi'vawma/ *f* **não há ~ lá fora** there's not a soul outside

vivar /vi'var/ *vt/i* cheer

vivaz /vi'vas/ *a* lively, vivacious; <*planta*> hardy

viveiro /vi'veru/ *m* (*de plantas*) nursery; (*de peixes*) fishpond; (*de aves*) aviary; (*fig*) breeding ground

vivência /vi'vẽsia/ *f* experience

vívido /'vividu/ *a* vivid

viver /vi'ver/ *vt/i* live (**de** on) □ *m* life; **ele vive reclamando** he's always complaining

víveres /'viveris/ *m pl* provisions

vivissecção /vivisek'sãw/ *f* vivisection

vivo /'vivu/ *a* (*que vive*) living; (*animado*) lively; <*cor*> bright □ *m* **os ~s** the living; **ao ~** live; **estar ~** be alive; **dinheiro ~** cash

vizi|nhança /vizi'ɲãsa/ *f* neighbourhood; **~nho** *a* neighbouring □ *m* neighbour

vo|ador /voa'dor/ *a* flying; **~ar** *vi* fly; (*explodir*) blow up; **sair ~ando** rush off
vocabulário /vokabu'lariu/ *m* vocabulary
vocábulo /vo'kabulu/ *m* word
voca|ção /voka'sãw/ *f* vocation; **~cional** (*pl* **~cionais**) *a* vocational; **orientação ~cional** careers guidance
vo|cal /vo'kaw/ (*pl* **~cais**) *a* vocal
você /vo'se/ *pron* you; **~s** *pron* you
vociferar /vosife'rar/ *vi* shout abuse
vodca /'vɔdʒka/ *f* vodka
voga /'vɔga/ *f* (*moda*) vogue
vo|gal /vo'gaw/ (*pl* **~gais**) *f* vowel
volante /vo'lãtʃi/ *m* (*de carro*) steering wheel
volá|til /vo'latʃiw/ (*pl* **~teis**) *a* volatile
vôlei /'volej/ *m*, **voleibol** /volej'bɔw/ *m* volleyball
volt /'vɔwtʃi/ (*pl* **~s**) *m* volt
volta /'vɔwta/ *f* (*retorno*) return; (*da pista*) lap; (*resposta*) response; **às ~s com** tied up with; **de ~** back; **em ~ de** around; **na ~** on the way back; **na ~ do correio** by return of post; **por ~ de** around; **dar a ~ ao mundo** go round the world; **dar a ~ por cima** make a comeback; **dar meia ~** turn round; **dar uma ~** (*a pé*) go for a walk; (*de carro*) go for a drive; **dar uma ~ em** turn round; **dar ~s** spin round; **ter ~** get a response; **~ e meia** every so often; **~do** *a* **~do para** geared towards
voltagem /vow'taʒẽ/ *f* voltage
voltar /vow'tar/ *vi* go/come back, return □ *vt* rewind <*fita*>; **~-se** *vpr* turn round; **~-se para/contra** turn to/against; **~ a si** come to; **~ a fazer** do again; **~ atrás** backtrack
volu|me /vo'lumi/ *m* volume; **~moso** *a* sizeable; <*som*> loud
voluntário /volũ'tariu/ *a & m* volunteer
volúpia /vo'lupia/ *f* sensuality, lust
voluptuoso /voluptu'ozu/ *a* sensual; <*mulher*> voluptuous
volú|vel /vo'luvew/ (*pl* **~veis**) *a* fickle
vomitar /vomi'tar/ *vt/i* vomit
vômito /'vomitu/ *m* vomit; *pl* vomiting
vontade /võ'tadʒi/ *f* will; **à ~** (*bem*) at ease; (*quanto quiser*) as much as one likes; **fique à ~** make yourself at home; **tem comida à ~** there's plenty of food; **estar com ~ de** feel like; **isso me dá ~ de chorar** it makes me feel like crying; **fazer a ~ de alg** do what s.o. wants
vôo /'vou/ *m* flight; **levantar ~** take off; **~ livre** hang-gliding
voraz /vo'ras/ *a* voracious
vos /vus/ *pron* you; (*a vocês*) to you
vós /vɔs/ *pron* you
vosso /'vɔsu/ *a* your □ *pron* yours
vo|tação /vota'sãw/ *f* vote; **~tante** *m/f* voter; **~tar** *vt* vote on <*lei etc*>; (*dedicar*) devote; (*prometer*) vow □ *vi* vote (**em** for)
voto /'vɔtu/ *m* (*em votação*) vote; (*promessa*) vow; *pl* (*desejos*) wishes
vo|vó /vo'vɔ/ *f* grandma; **~vô** *m* grandpa
voz /vɔs/ *f* voice; **dar ~ de prisão a alg** place s.o. under arrest
vozerio /voze'riu/ *m* shouting
vul|cânico /vuw'kaniku/ *a* volcanic; **~cão** *m* volcano
vul|gar /vuw'gar/ *a* ordinary; (*baixo*) vulgar; **~garizar** *vt* popularize; (*tornar baixo*) vulgarize; **~go** *adv* commonly known as
vulne|rabilidade /vuwnerabili'dadʒi/ *f* vulnerability; **~rável** (*pl* **~ráveis**) *a* vulnerable
vul|to /'vuwtu/ *m* (*figura*) figure; (*tamanho*) bulk; (*importância*) importance; **de ~to** important; **~toso** /o/ *a* bulky

Ww

walkie-talkie /uɔki'tɔki/ (*pl* **~s**) *m* walkie-talkie
walkman /uɔk'mɛn/ *m invar* walkman
WAP /uap/ *a* (*telec*) WAP
watt /u'ɔtʃi/ (*pl* **~s**) *m* watt
web /uɛb/ *m* web, WWW
windsur|fe /uĩ'surfi/ *m* windsurfing; **~fista** *m/f* windsurfer

xadrez /ʃa'dres/ *m* (*jogo*) chess; (*desenho*) check; (*fam: prisão*) prison □ *a invar* check
xale /'ʃali/ *m* shawl
xampu /ʃã'pu/ *m* shampoo
xará /ʃa'ra/ *m/f* namesake
xarope /ʃa'rɔpi/ *m* syrup
xaxim /ʃa'ʃĩ/ *m* plant fibre
xenofobia /ʃenofo'bia/ *f* xenophobia
xenófobo /ʃe'nɔfobu/ *a* xenophobic □ *m* xenophobe
xepa /'ʃepa/ *f* scraps
xeque[1] /'ʃɛki/ *m* (*árabe*) sheikh
xeque[2] /'ʃɛki/ *m* (*no xadrez*) check; **∼-mate** *m* checkmate
xere|ta /ʃe'reta/ (*fam*) *a* nosy □ *m/f* nosy parker; **∼tar** (*fam*) *vi* nose around
xerez /ʃe'res/ *m* sherry
xerife /ʃe'rifi/ *m* sheriff
xerocar /ʃero'kar/ *vt* photocopy
xerox /ʃe'rɔks/ *m invar* photocopy
xexelento /ʃeʃe'lẽtu/ (*fam*) *a* scruffy □ *m* scruff
xícara /'ʃikara/ *f* cup
xiita /ʃi'ita/ *a & m/f* Shiite
xilofone /ʃilo'foni/ *m* xylophone
xingar /ʃĩ'gar/ *vt* swear at □ *vi* swear
xis /ʃis/ *m invar* letter X; **o ∼ do problema** the crux of the problem
xixi /ʃi'ʃi/ (*fam*) *m* wee; **fazer ∼** do a wee
xô /ʃo/ *int* shoo
xucro /'ʃukru/ *a* ignorant

Zz

zagueiro /za'geru/ *m* fullback
Zaire /'zajri/ *m* Zaire
Zâmbia /'zãbia/ *f* Zambia
zan|gado /zã'gadu/ *a* cross, annoyed; **∼gar** *vt* annoy; **∼gar-se** *vpr* get cross, get annoyed (**com** with)
zanzar /zã'zar/ *vi* wander
zarpar /zar'par/ *vi* set off; (*de navio*) set sail
zebra /'zebra/ *f* zebra; (*pessoa*) fool; (*resultado*) upset
ze|lador /zela'dor/ *m* caretaker, (*Amer*) janitor; **∼lar** *vt* **∼lar (por)** take care of; **∼lo** /e/ *m* zeal; **∼lo por** devotion to; **∼loso** /o/ *a* zealous
zero /'zɛru/ *m* zero; (*em escores*) nil; **∼-quilômetro** *a invar* brand new
ziguezague /zigi'zagi/ *m* zigzag; **∼ar** *vi* zigzag
Zimbábue /zĩ'babui/ *m* Zimbabwe
zinco /'zĩku/ *m* zinc
zíper /'ziper/ *m* zip, zipper
zodíaco /zo'dʒiaku/ *m* zodiac
zoeira /zo'era/ *f* din
zom|bador /zõba'dor/ *a* mocking; **∼bar** *vi* **∼bar (de)** mock; **∼baria** *f* mockery
zona /'zona/ *f* (*área*) zone; (*de cidade*) district; (*desordem*) mess; (*tumulto*) commotion; (*bairro do meretrício*) red-light district
zonzo /'zõzu/ *a* dizzy
zôo /'zou/ *m* zoo
zoo|logia /zoolo'ʒia/ *f* zoology; **∼lógico** *a* zoological
zoólogo /zo'ɔlogu/ *m* zoologist
zulu /zu'lu/ *a & m/f* Zulu
zum /zũ/ *m* zoom lens
zumbi /zũ'bi/ *m* zombie
zum|bido /zũ'bidu/ *m* buzz; (*no ouvido*) ringing; **∼bir** *vi* buzz
zu|nido /zu'nidu/ *m* (*de vento, bala*) whistle; (*de inseto*) buzz; **∼nir** *vi* <*vento, bala*> whistle; <*inseto*> buzz
zunzum /zũ'zũ/ *m* rumour
Zurique /zu'riki/ *f* Zurich
zurrar /zu'xar/ *vi* bray

Aa

a /ə/; *emphatic* /eɪ/ (*before vowel* **an** /ən/; *emphatic* /æn/) *a* um. **two pounds a metre** duas libras o metro. **sixty miles an hour** sessenta milhas por hora, (*P*) à hora. **once a year** uma vez por ano

aback /əˈbæk/ *adv* **taken ~** desconcertado, (*P*) surpreendido

abandon /əˈbændən/ *vt* abandonar □ *n* abandono *m*. **~ed** *a* abandonado; (*behaviour*) livre, dissoluto. **~ment** *n* abandono *m*

abashed /əˈbæʃt/ *a* confuso, (*P*) atrapalhado

abate /əˈbeɪt/ *vt/i* abater, abrandar, diminuir. **~ment** *n* abrandamento *m*, diminuição *f*

abattoir /ˈæbətwɑ:(r)/ *n* matadouro *m*

abbey /ˈæbɪ/ *n* abadia *f*, mosteiro *m*

abbreviat|e /əˈbri:vɪeɪt/ *vt* abreviar. **~ion** /-ˈeɪʃn/ *n* abreviação *f*; (*short form*) abreviatura *f*

abdicat|e /ˈæbdɪkeɪt/ *vt/i* abdicar. **~ion** /-ˈkeɪʃn/ *n* abdicação *f*

abdom|en /ˈæbdəmən/ *n* abdômen *m*, (*P*) abdómen *m*. **~inal** /-ˈdɒmɪnl/ *a* abdominal

abduct /æbˈdʌkt/ *vt* raptar. **~ion** /-ʃn/ *n* rapto *m*. **~or** *n* raptor, -a *mf*

aberration /æbəˈreɪʃn/ *n* aberração *f*

abet /əˈbet/ *vt* (*pt* **abetted**) (*jur*) instigar; (*aid*) auxiliar

abeyance /əˈbeɪəns/ *n* **in ~** (*matter*) em suspenso; (*custom*) em desuso

abhor /əbˈhɔ:(r)/ *vt* (*pt* **abhorred**) abominar, ter horror a. **~rence** /-ˈhɒrəns/ *n* horror *m*. **~rent** /-ˈhɒrənt/ *a* abominável, execrável

abide /əˈbaɪd/ *vt* (*pt* **abided**) suportar, tolerar. **~ by** (*promise*) manter; (*rules*) acatar

abiding /əˈbaɪdɪŋ/ *a* eterno, perpétuo

ability /əˈbɪlətɪ/ *n* capacidade *f* (**to do** para *or* de fazer); (*cleverness*) habilidade *f*, esperteza *f*

abject /ˈæbdʒekt/ *a* abjeto, (*P*) abjecto

ablaze /əˈbleɪz/ *a* em chamas; (*fig*) aceso, (*P*) excitado

abl|e /ˈeɪbl/ *a* (**~er**, **~est**) capaz (**to** de). **be ~e to** (*have power, opportunity*) ser capaz de, poder; (*know how to*) ser capaz de, saber. **~y** *adv* habilmente

ablutions /əˈblu:ʃnz/ *npl* ablução *f*, abluções *fpl*

abnormal /æbˈnɔ:ml/ *a* anormal. **~ity** /-ˈmælətɪ/ *n* anormalidade *f*. **~ly** *adv* (*unusually*) excepcionalmente

aboard /əˈbɔ:d/ *adv* a bordo □ *prep* a bordo de

abode /əˈbəʊd/ *n* (*old use*) habitação *f*. **place of ~** domicílio *m*

aboli|sh /əˈbɒlɪʃ/ *vt* abolir, extinguir. **~tion** /æbəˈlɪʃn/ *n* abolição *f*, extinção *f*

abominable /əˈbɒmɪnəbl/ *a* abominável, detestável

abominat|e /əˈbɒmɪneɪt/ *vt* abominar, detestar. **~ion** /-ˈneɪʃn/ *n* abominação *f*

abort /əˈbɔ:t/ *vt/i* (fazer) abortar. **~ive** *a* (*attempt etc*) abortado, malogrado

abortion /əˈbɔ:ʃn/ *n* aborto *m*. **have an ~** fazer um aborto, ter um aborto. **~ist** *n* abortad/or, -eira *mf*

abound /əˈbaʊnd/ *vi* abundar (**in** em)

about /əˈbaʊt/ *adv* (*approximately*) aproximadamente, cerca de; (*here and there*) aqui e ali; (*all round*) por todos os lados, em roda, em volta; (*in existence*) por aí □ *prep* acerca de, sobre; (*round*) em torno de; (*somewhere in*) em, por. **~-face**, **~-turn** *ns* reviravolta *f*. **~ here** por aqui. **be ~ to** estar prestes a. **he was ~ to eat** ia comer. **how** *or* **what ~ leaving?** e se nós fôssemos embora? **know/talk ~** saber/falar sobre

above /əˈbʌv/ *adv* acima, por cima □ *prep* sobre. **he's not ~ lying** ele não é de mentir. **~ all** sobretudo. **~-board** *a* franco, honesto □ *adv* com lisura. **~-mentioned** *a* acima, supracitado

abrasion /əˈbreɪʒn/ *n* atrito *m*; (*injury*) escoriação *f*, esfoladura *f*

abrasive /əˈbreɪsɪv/ *a* abrasivo; (*fig*) agressivo □ *n* abrasivo *m*

abreast /əˈbrest/ *adv* lado a lado. **keep ~ of** manter-se a par de

abridge /əˈbrɪdʒ/ *vt* abreviar. **~ment** *n* abreviação *f*, abreviatura *f*, redução *f*; (*abridged text*) resumo *m*

abroad /əˈbrɔ:d/ *adv* no estrangeiro; (*far and wide*) por todo o lado. **go ~** ir para o estrangeiro

abrupt /əˈbrʌpt/ *a* (*sudden, curt*) brusco; (*steep*) abrupto. **~ly** *adv* (*suddenly*) bruscamente; (*curtly*) com brusquidão. **~ness** *n* brusquidão *f*; (*steepness*) declive *m*

abscess /ˈæbsɪs/ *n* abscesso *m*, (*P*) abcesso *m*

abscond /əbˈskɒnd/ *vi* evadir-se, andar fugido

absen|t[1] /ˈæbsənt/ *a* ausente; (*look etc*) distraído. **~ce** *n* ausência *f*; (*lack*) falta *f*. **~t-minded** *a* distraído.

~t-mindedness *n* distração *f*, (*P*) distracção *f*
absent[2] /əb'sent/ *v refl* **~ o.s.** ausentar-se
absentee /æbsen'ti:/ *n* ausente *mf*, (*P*) absentista *mf*. **~ism** *n* absenteísmo *m*, (*P*) absentismo *m*
absolute /'æbsəlu:t/ *a* absoluto; (*colloq: coward etc*) autêntico, (*P*) verdadeiro. **~ly** *adv* absolutamente
absolution /æbsə'lu:ʃn/ *n* absolvição *f*
absolve /əb'zɒlv/ *vt* (*from sin*) absolver (**from** de); (*from vow*) desligar (**from** de)
absor|b /əb'sɔ:b/ *vt* absorver. **~ption** *n* absorção *f*
absorbent /əb'sɔ:bənt/ *a* absorvente. **~ cotton** (*Amer*) algodão hidrófilo *m*
abst|ain /əb'stem/ *vi* abster-se (**from** de). **~ention** /-'stenʃn/ *n* abstenção *f*
abstemious /əb'sti:mɪəs/ *a* abstêmio, (*P*) abstémio, sóbrio
abstinen|ce /'æbstməns/ *n* abstinência *f*. **~t** *a* abstinente
abstract[1] /'æbstrækt/ *a* abstrato, (*P*) abstracto
abstract[2] /əb'strækt/ *vt* (*take out*) extrair; (*separate*) abstrair. **~ed** *a* distraído. **~ion** /-ʃn/ *n* (*of mind*) distração *f*, (*P*) distracção *f*; (*idea*) abstração *f*, (*P*) abstracção *f*
absurd /əb'sɜ:d/ *a* absurdo. **~ity** *n* absurdo *m*
abundan|t /ə'bʌndənt/ *a* abundante. **~ce** *n* abundância *f*
abuse[1] /ə'bju:z/ *vt* (*misuse*) abusar de; (*ill-treat*) maltratar; (*insult*) injuriar, insultar
abus|e[2] /ə'bju:s/ *n* (*wrong use*) abuso *m* (**of** de); (*insults*) insultos *m pl*. **~ive** *a* injurioso, ofensivo
abysmal /ə'bɪzməl/ *a* abismal; (*colloq: bad*) abissal
abyss /ə'bɪs/ *n* abismo *m*
academic /ækə'demɪk/ *a* acadêmico, (*P*) académico, universitário; (*scholarly*) intelectual; (*pej*) acadêmico, (*P*) teórico □ *n* universitário
academy /ə'kædəmɪ/ *n* academia *f*
accede /ək'si:d/ *vi* **~ to** (*request*) aceder a; (*post*) assumir; (*throne*) ascender a, subir a
accelerat|e /ək'seləreɪt/ *vt* acelerar □ *vi* acelerar-se; (*auto*) acelerar. **~ion** /-'reɪʃn/ *n* aceleração *f*
accelerator /ək'seləreɪtə(r)/ *n* (*auto*) acelerador *m*
accent[1] /'æksənt/ *n* acento *m*; (*local pronunciation*) sotaque *m*
accent[2] /æk'sent/ *vt* acentuar
accentuate /æk'sentʃʊeɪt/ *vt* acentuar
accept /ək'sept/ *vt* aceitar. **~able** *a* aceitável. **~ance** *n* aceitação *f*; (*approval*) aprovação *f*
access /'ækses/ *n* acesso *m* (**to** a). **~ible** /ək'sesəbl/ *a* acessível
accessory /ək'sesərɪ/ *a* acessório □ *n* acessório *m*; (*Jur: person*) cúmplice *m*
accident /'æksɪdənt/ *n* acidente *m*, desastre *m*; (*chance*) acaso *m*. **~al** /-'dentl/ *a* acidental, fortuito. **~ally** /-'dentəlɪ/ *adv* acidentalmente, por acaso
acclaim /ə'kleɪm/ *vt* aclamar □ *n* aplauso *m*, aclamações *fpl*
acclimatiz|e /ə'klaɪmətaɪz/ *vt/i* aclimatar(-se). **~ation** /-'zeɪʃn/ *n* aclimatação *f*
accommodat|e /ə'kɒmədeɪt/ *vt* acomodar; (*lodge*) alojar; (*adapt*) adaptar; (*supply*) fornecer; (*oblige*) fazer a vontade de. **~ing** *a* obsequioso, amigo de fazer vontades. **~ion** /-'deɪʃn/ *n* acomodação *f*; (*rooms*) alojamento *m*, quarto *m*
accompan|y /ə'kʌmpənɪ/ *vt* acompanhar. **~iment** *n* acompanhamento *m*. **~ist** *n* (*mus*) acompanhad/or, (*B*) -eira *mf*
accomplice /ə'kʌmplɪs/ *n* cúmplice *mf*
accomplish /ə'kʌmplɪʃ/ *vt* (*perform*) executar, realizar; (*achieve*) realizar, conseguir fazer. **~ed** *a* acabado. **~ment** *n* realização *f*; (*ability*) talento *m*, dote *m*
accord /ə'kɔ:d/ *vi* concordar □ *vt* conceder □ *n* acordo *m*. **of one's own ~** por vontade própria, espontaneamente. **~ance** *n* **in ~ance with** em conformidade com, de acordo com
according /ə'kɔ:dɪŋ/ *adv* **~ to** conforme. **~ly** *adv* (*therefore*) por conseguinte, por consequência; (*appropriately*) conformemente
accordion /ə'kɔ:dɪən/ *n* acordeão *m*
accost /ə'kɒst/ *vt* abordar, abeirar-se de
account /ə'kaʊnt/ *n* (*comm*) conta *f*; (*description*) relato *m*; (*importance*) importância *f* □ *vt* considerar. **~ for** dar contas de, explicar. **on ~ of** por causa de. **on no ~** em caso algum. **take into ~** ter *or* levar em conta. **~able** /-əbl/ *a* responsável (**for** por). **~ability** /-ə'bɪlətɪ/ *n* responsabilidade *f*
accountant /ə'kaʊntənt/ *n* contador(a) *m/f*, (*P*) contabilista *mf*
accrue /ə'kru:/ *vi* acumular-se. **~ to** reverter em favor de
accumulat|e /ə'kju:mjʊleɪt/ *vt/i* acumular(-se). **~ion** /-'leɪʃn/ *n* acumulação *f*, acréscimo *m*
accumulator /ə'kju:mjʊleɪtə(r)/ *n* (*electr*) acumulador *m*

accura|te /'ækjərət/ *a* exato, (*P*) exacto, preciso. **~cy** *n* exatidão *f*, (*P*) exactidão *f*, precisão *f*. **~tely** *adv* com exatidão, (*P*) exactidão

accus|e /ə'kju:z/ *vt* acusar. **the ~ed** o acusado. **~ation** /ækju:-'zeɪʃn/ *n* acusação *f*

accustom /ə'kʌstəm/ *vt* acostumar, habituar. **~ed** *a* acostumado, habituado. **get ~ed to** acostumar-se a, habituar-se a

ace /eɪs/ *n* ás *m*

ache /eɪk/ *n* dor *f* □ *vi* doer. **my leg ~s** dói-me a perna, tenho dores na perna

achieve /ə'tʃi:v/ *vt* realizar, efetuar; (*success*) alcançar. **~ment** *n* realização *f*; (*feat*) feito *m*, façanha *f*, sucesso *m*

acid /'æsɪd/ *a* ácido; (*wine*) azedo; (*words*) áspero □ *n* ácido *m*. **~ity** /ə'sɪdətɪ/ *n* acidez *f*

acknowledge /ək'nɒlɪdʒ/ *vt* reconhecer. **~ (receipt of)** acusar a recepção de. **~ment** *n* reconhecimento *m*; (*letter etc*) acusação *f* de recebimento, (*P*) aviso *m* de recepção

acne /'æknɪ/ *n* acne *mf*

acorn /'eɪkɔ:n/ *n* bolota *f*, glande *f*

acoustic /ə'ku:stɪk/ *a* acústico. **~s** *npl* acústica *f*

acquaint /ə'kweɪnt/ *vt* **~ s.o. with sth** pôr alg a par de alg coisa. **be ~ed with** (*person, fact*) conhecer. **~ance** *n* (*knowledge, person*) conhecimento *m*; (*person*) conhecido *m*

acquiesce /ækwɪ'es/ *vi* consentir. **~nce** /ækwɪ'esns/ *n* aquiescência *f*, consentimento *m*

acqui|re /ə'kwaɪə(r)/ *vt* adquirir. **~sition** /ækwɪ'zɪʃn/ *n* aquisição *f*

acquit /ə'kwɪt/ *vt* (*pt* **acquitted**) *absolver*. **~ o.s. well** sair-se bem. **~tal** *n* absolvição *f*

acrid /'ækrɪd/ *a* acre

acrimon|ious /ækrɪ'məʊnɪəs/ *a* acrimonioso. **~y** /'ækrɪmənɪ/ *n* acrimônia *f*, (*P*) acrimónia *f*

acrobat /'ækrəbæt/ *n* acrobata *mf*. **~ic** /-'bætɪk/ *a* acrobático. **~ics** /-'bætɪks/ *npl* acrobacia *f*

acronym /'ækrənɪm/ *n* sigla *f*

across /ə'krɒs/ *adv & prep* (*side to side*) de lado a lado (de), de um lado para o outro (de); (*on the other side*) do outro lado (de); (*crosswise*) através (de), de través. **go** *or* **walk ~** atravessar. **swim ~** atravessar a nado

act /ækt/ *n* (*deed, theatr*) ato *m*, (*P*) acto *m*; (*in variety show*) número *m*; (*decree*) lei *f* □ *vi* agir, atuar, (*P*) actuar; (*theatr*) representar; (*function*) funcionar; (*pretend*) fingir □ *vt* (*part, role*) desempenhar. **~ as** servir de. **~ing** *a* interino □ *n* (*theatr*) desempenho *m*

action /'ækʃn/ *n* ação *f*, (*P*) acção *f*; (*mil*) combate *m*. **out of ~** fora de combate; (*techn*) avariado. **take ~** agir, atuar, (*P*) actuar

activ|e /'æktɪv/ *a* ativo, (*P*) activo; (*interest*) vivo; (*volcano*) em atividade, (*P*) actividade. **~ity** /-'tɪvətɪ/ *n* atividade *f*, (*P*) actividade *f*

ac|tor /'æktə(r)/ *n* ator *m*, (*P*) actor *m*. **~tress** *n* atriz *f*, (*P*) actriz *f*

actual /'æktʃʊəl/ *a* real, verdadeiro; (*example*) concreto. **the ~ pen which** a própria caneta que. **~ity** /-'ælətɪ/ *n* realidade *f*. **~ly** *adv* (*in fact*) na realidade

acumen /ə'kju:men/ *n* agudeza *f*, perspicácia *f*

acupunctur|e /'ækjʊpʌŋktʃə(r)/ *n* acupuntura *f*, (*P*) acupunctura *f*. **~ist** *n* acupunturador *m*, (*P*) acupuncturista *mf*

acute /ə'kju:t/ *a* agudo; (*mind*) perspicaz; (*emotion*) intenso, vivo; (*shortage*) grande. **~ly** *adv* vivamente.

ad /æd/ *n* (*colloq*) anúncio *m*

AD *abbr* dC

adamant /'ædəmənt/ *a* inflexível

adapt /ə'dæpt/ *vt/i* adaptar(-se). **~ation** /ædæp'teɪʃn/ *n* adaptação *f*. **~or** (*electr*) *n* adaptador *m*

adaptab|le /ə'dæptəbl/ *a* adaptável. **~ility** /-'bɪlətɪ/ *n* adaptabilidade *f*

add /æd/ *vt/i* acrescentar. **~ (up)** somar. **~ up to** (*total*) elevar-se a

adder /'ædə(r)/ *n* víbora *f*

addict /'ædɪkt/ *n* viciado *m*. **drug ~** (*B*) viciado em droga, viciado da droga, (*P*) toxicodependente *mf*

addict|ed /ə'dɪktɪd/ *a* **be ~ed to** (*drink, drugs; fig*) ter o vício de. **~ion** /-ʃn/ *n* (*med*) dependência *f*; (*fig*) vício *m*. **~ive** *a* que produz dependência

addition /ə'dɪʃn/ *n* adição *f*. **in ~** além disso. **in ~ to** além de. **~al** /-ʃənl/ *a* adicional, suplementar

address /ə'dres/ *n* endereço *m*; (*speech*) discurso *m* □ *vt* endereçar; (*speak to*) dirigir-se a

adenoids /'ædɪnɔɪdz/ *npl* adenóides *mpl*

adept /'ædept/ *a & n* especialista (*mf*), perito (*m*) (**at** em)

adequa|te /'ædɪkwət/ *a* adequado; (*satisfactory*) satisfatório. **~cy** *n* adequação *f*; (*of person*) competência *f*. **~tely** *adv* adequadamente

adhere /əd'hɪə(r)/ *vi* aderir (**to** a)

adhesive /əd'hi:sɪv/ *a & n* adesivo (*m*). **~ plaster** esparadrapo *m*, (*P*) adesivo *m*
adjacent /ə'dʒeɪsnt/ *a* adjacente, contíguo (**to** a)
adjective /'ædʒektɪv/ *n* adjetivo *m*, (*P*) adjectivo *m*
adjoin /ə'dʒɔɪn/ *vt* confinar com, ficar contíguo a
adjourn /ə'dʒɜ:n/ *vt* adiar □ *vi* suspender a sessão. **~ to** (*go*) passar a, ir para
adjudicate /ə'dʒu:dɪkeɪt/ *vt/i* julgar; (*award*) adjudicar
adjust /ə'dʒʌst/ *vt/i* (*alter*) ajustar, regular; (*arrange*) arranjar. **~ (o.s.) to** adaptar-se a. **~able** *a* regulável. **~ment** *n* (*techn*) regulação *f*, afinação *f*; (*of person*) adaptação *f*
ad lib /æd'lɪb/ *vi* (*pt* **ad libbed**) (*colloq*) improvisar □ *adv* à vontade
administer /əd'mɪnɪstə(r)/ *vt* administrar
administrat|e /əd'mɪnɪstreɪt/ *vt* administrar, gerir. **~ion** /-'streɪʃn/ *n* administração *f*. **~or** *n* administrador *m*
administrative /əd'mɪnɪstrətɪv/ *a* administrativo
admirable /'ædmərəbl/ *a* admirável
admiral /'ædmərəl/ *n* almirante *m*
admir|e /əd'maɪə(r)/ *vt* admirar. **~ation** /-mɪ'reɪʃn/ *n* admiração *f*. **~er** /-'maɪərə(r)/ *n* admirador *m*
admission /əd'mɪʃn/ *n* admissão *f*; (*to museum, theatre, etc*) ingresso *m*, (*P*) entrada *f*; (*confession*) confissão *f*
admit /əd'mɪt/ *vt* (*pt* **admitted**) (*let in*) admitir, permitir a entrada a; (*acknowledge*) reconhecer, admitir. **~ to** confessar. **~tance** *n* admissão *f*
admoni|sh /əd'mɒnɪʃ/ *vt* admoestar. **~tion** /-ə'nɪʃn/ *n* admoestação *f*
adolescen|t /ædə'lesnt/ *a & n* adolescente (*mf*). **~ce** *n* adolescência *f*
adopt /ə'dɒpt/ *vt* adotar, (*P*) adoptar. **~ed child** filho adotivo, (*P*) adoptivo. **~ion** /-ʃn/ *n* adoção *f*, (*P*) adopção *f*
ador|e /ə'dɔ:(r)/ *vt* adorar. **~able** *a* adorável. **~ation** /ædə'reɪʃn/ *n* adoração *f*
adorn /ə'dɔ:n/ *vt* adornar, enfeitar
adrenalin /ə'drenəlɪn/ *n* adrenalina *f*
adrift /ə'drɪft/ *a & adv* à deriva
adult /'ædʌlt/ *a & n* adulto (*m*). **~hood** *n* idade *f* adulta, (*P*) maioridade *f*
adulterat|e /ə'dʌltəreɪt/ *vt* adulterar. **~ion** /-'reɪʃn/ *n* adulteração *f*
adulter|y /ə'dʌltərɪ/ *n* adultério *m*. **~er, ~ess** *ns* adúlter/o, -a *mf*. **~ous** *a* adúltero

advance /əd'va:ns/ *vt/i* avançar □ *n* avanço *m*; (*payment*) adiantamento *m* □ *a* (*payment, booking*) adiantado. **in ~** com antecedência. **~d** *a* avançado. **~ment** *n* promoção *f*, ascensão *f*
advantage /əd'va:ntɪdʒ/ *n* vantagem *f*. **take ~ of** aproveitar-se de, tirar partido de; (*person*) explorar. **~ous** /ædvən'teɪdʒəs/ *a* vantajoso
adventur|e /əd'ventʃə(r)/ *n* aventura *f*. **~er** *n* aventureiro *m*, explorador *m*. **~ous** *a* aventuroso
adverb /'ædvɜ:b/ *n* advérbio *m*
adversary /'ædvəsərɪ/ *n* adversário *m*, antagonista *mf*
advers|e /'ædvɜ:s/ *a* (*contrary*) adverso; (*unfavourable*) desfavorável. **~ity** /əd'vɜ:sətɪ/ *n* adversidade *f*
advert /'ædvɜ:t/ *n* (*colloq*) anúncio *m*
advertise /'ædvətaɪz/ *vt/i* anunciar, fazer publicidade (de); (*sell*) pôr um anúncio (para). **~ for** procurar **~r** /-ə(r)/ *n* anunciante *mf*
advertisement /əd'vɜ:tɪsmənt/ *n* anúncio *m*; (*advertising*) publicidade *f*
advice /əd'vaɪs/ *n* conselho(s) *mpl*; (*comm*) aviso *m*
advis|e /əd'vaɪz/ *vt* aconselhar; (*inform*) avisar, informar. **~e against** desaconselhar. **~able** *a* aconselhável. **~er** *n* conselheiro *m*; (*in business*) consultor *m*. **~ory** *a* consultivo
advocate[1] /'ædvəkət/ *n* (*jur*) advogado *m*; (*supporter*) defensor(a) *m/f*
advocate[2] /'ædvəkeɪt/ *vt* advogar, defender
aerial /'eərɪəl/ *a* aéreo □ *n* antena *f*
aerobatics /eərə'bætɪks/ *npl* acrobacia *f* aérea
aerobics /eə'rəʊbɪks/ *n* ginástica *f* aeróbica
aerodynamic /eərəʊdaɪ'næmɪk/ *a* aerodinâmico
aeroplane /'eərəpleɪn/ *n* avião *m*
aerosol /'eərəsɒl/ *n* aerossol *m*
aesthetic /i:s'θetɪk/ *a* estético.
affair /ə'feə(r)/ *n* (*business*) negócio *m*; (*romance*) ligação *f*, aventura *f*; (*matter*) asunto *m*. **love ~** paixão *f*
affect /ə'fekt/ *vt* afetar, (*P*) afectar. **~ation** /æfek'teɪʃn/ *n* afetação *f*, (*P*) afectação *f*. **~ed** *a* afetado, (*P*) afectado, pretencioso
affection /ə'fekʃn/ *n* afeição *f*, afeto *m*, (*P*) afecto *m*
affectionate /ə'fekʃənət/ *a* afetuoso, (*P*) afectuoso, carinhoso
affiliat|e /ə'fɪlɪeɪt/ *vt* afiliar. **~ed company** filial *f*. **~ion** /-'eɪʃn/ *n* afiliação *f*

affirm /ə'fɜ:m/ *vt* afirmar. **~ation** /æfə'meɪʃn/ *n* afirmação *f*

affirmative /ə'fɜ:mətɪv/ *a* afirmativo □ *n* afirmativa *f*

afflict /ə'flɪkt/ *vt* afligir. **~ion** /-ʃn/ *n* aflição *f*

affluen|t /'æflʊənt/ *a* rico, afluente. **~ce** *n* riqueza *f*, afluência *f*

afford /ə'fɔ:d/ *vt* (*have money for*) permitir-se, ter meios (para). **can you afford the time?** você teria tempo? **I can't afford a car** eu não posso comprar um carro. **we can't afford to lose** não podemos perder

affront /ə'frʌnt/ *n* afronta *f* □ *vt* insultar

afield /ə'fi:ld/ *adv* **far ~** longe

afloat /ə'fləʊt/ *adv* & *a* à tona, a flutuar; (*at sea*) no mar; (*business*) lançado, (*P*) sem dívidas

afraid /ə'freɪd/ *a* **be ~** ter medo (**of, to** de; **that** que); (*be sorry*) lamentar, ter muita pena. **I'm ~ (that)** (*regret to say*) lamento *or* tenho muita pena de dizer que

afresh /ə'freʃ/ *adv* de novo

Africa /'æfrɪkə/ *n* África *f*. **~n** *a* & *n* africano (*m*)

after /a:ftə(r)/ *adv* depois □ *prep* depois de □ *conj* depois que. **~ all** afinal de contas. **~ doing**, depois de fazer. **be ~** (*seek*) querer, pretender. **~-effect** *n* seqüela *f*, (*P*) sequela *f*, efeito *m* retardado; (*of drug*) efeito *m* secundário

aftermath /'a:ftəmæθ/ *n* conseqüências *fpl*

afternoon /a:ftə'nu:n/ *n* tarde *f*

aftershave /'a:ftəʃeɪv/ *n* loção *f* após-barba, (*P*) loção *f* para a barba

afterthought /'a:ftəθɔ:t/ *n* reflexão *f* posterior. **as an ~** pensando melhor

afterwards /'a:ftəwədz/ *adv* depois, mais tarde

again /ə'gen/ *adv* de novo, outra vez; (*on the other hand*) por outro lado. **then ~** além disso

against /ə'genst/ *prep* contra

age /eɪdʒ/ *n* idade *f*; (*period*) época *f*, idade *f* □ *vt*/*i* (*pres p* **ageing**) envelhecer. **~s** (*colloq: very long time*) há séculos *mpl*. **of ~** (*jur*) maior. **ten years of ~** com/de dez anos. **under ~** menor. **~-group** *n* faixa etária *f*. **~less** *a* sempre jovem

aged[1] /eɪdʒd/ *a* **~ six** de seis anos de idade

aged[2] /'eɪdʒɪd/ *a* idoso, velho

agen|cy /'eɪdʒənsɪ/ *n* agência *f*; (*means*) intermédio *m*. **~t** *n* agente *mf*

agenda /ə'dʒendə/ *n* ordem *f* do dia

aggravat|e /'ægrəveɪt/ *vt* agravar; (*colloq: annoy*) irritar. **~ion** /-'veɪʃn/ *n* (*worsening*) agravamento *m*; (*exasperation*) irritação *f*; (*colloq: trouble*) aborrecimentos *mpl*

aggregate /'ægrɪgeɪt/ *vt*/*i* agregar (-se) □ *a* /'ægrɪgət/ total, global □ *n* (*total, mass, materials*) agregado *m*. **in the ~** no todo

aggress|ive /ə'gresɪv/ *a* agressivo; (*weapons*) ofensivo. **~ion** /-ʃn/ *n* agressão *f*. **~iveness** *n* agressividade *f*. **~or** *n* agressor *m*

aggrieved /ə'gri:vd/ *a* (*having a grievance*) lesado

agil|e /'ædʒaɪl/ *a* ágil. **~ity** /ə'dʒɪlətɪ/ *n* agilidade *f*

agitat|e /'ædʒɪteɪt/ *vt* agitar. **~ion** /-'teɪʃn/ *n* agitação *f*. **~or** *n* agitador *m*

agnostic /æg'nɒstɪk/ *a* & *n* agnóstico (*m*)

ago /ə'gəʊ/ *adv* há. **a month ~** há um mês. **long ~** há muito tempo

agon|y /'ægənɪ/ *n* agonia *f*; (*mental*) angústia *f*. **~ize** *vi* atormentar-se, torturar-se. **~izing** *a* angustiante, (*P*) doloroso

agree /ə'gri:/ *vt*/*i* concordar; (*of figures*) acertar. **~ that** reconhecer que. **~ to do** concordar em *or* aceitar fazer. **~ to sth** concordar com alguma coisa. **seafood doesn't ~ with me** não me dou bem com mariscos. **~d** *a* (*time, place*) combinado. **be ~d** estar de acordo

agreeable /ə'gri:əbl/ *a* agradável. **be ~ to** estar de acordo com

agreement /ə'gri:mənt/ *n* acordo *m*; (*gramm*) concordância *f*; (*contract*) contrato *m*. **in ~** de acordo

agricultur|e /'ægrɪkʌltʃə(r)/ *n* agricultura *f*. **~al** /-'kʌltʃərəl/ *a* agrícola

aground /ə'graʊnd/ *adv* **run ~** (*of ship*) encalhar

ahead /ə'hed/ *adv* à frente, adiante; (*in advance*) adiantado. **~ of sb** diante de alguém, à frente de alguém. **~ of time** antes da hora, adiantado. **straight ~** sempre em frente

aid /eɪd/ *vt* ajudar □ *n* ajuda *f*. **~ and abet** ser cúmplice de. **in ~ of** em auxílio de, a favor de

AIDS /eɪdz/ *n* (*med*) AIDS *f*, (*P*) sida *m*

ail /eɪl/ *vt* **what ~s you?** o que é que você tem? **~ing** *a* doente. **~ment** *n* doença *f*, achaque *m*

aim /eɪm/ *vt* (*gun*) apontar; (*efforts*) dirigir; (*send*) atirar (**at** para) □ *vi* visar □ *n* alvo *m*. **~ at** visar. **~ to** aspirar a, tencionar. **take ~** fazer pontaria. **~less** *a*, **~lessly** *adv* sem objetivo, (*P*) objectivo

air /eə(r)/ *n* ar *m* □ *vt* arejar; (*views*) expor □ *a* (*base etc*) aéreo. **in the ~** (*rumour*) espalhado; (*plans*) no ar. **on the ~** (*radio*) no ar. **~-conditioned** *a* com ar condicionado. **~-conditioning** *n* condicionamento *m* do ar, (*P*) ar *m* condicionado. **~ force** Força *f* Aérea. **~ hostess** aeromoça *f*, (*P*) hospedeira *f* de bordo. **~ raid** ataque *m* aéreo

airborne /'eəbɔ:n/ *a* (*aviat: in flight*) no ar; (*diseases*) levado pelo ar; (*freight*) por transporte aéreo

aircraft /'eəkra:ft/ *n* (*pl invar*) avião *m*. **~-carrier** *n* porta-aviões *m*

airfield /'eəfi:ld/ *n* campo *m* de aviação

airgun /'eəgʌn/ *n* espingarda *f* de pressão

airlift /'eəlɪft/ *n* ponte *f* aérea □ *vt* transportar em ponte aérea

airline /'eəlaɪn/ *n* linha *f* aérea

airlock /'eəlɒk/ *n* câmara *f* de vácuo; (*in pipe*) bolha *f* de ar

airmail /'eəmeɪl/ *n* correio *m* aéreo. **by ~** por avião

airport /'eəpɔ:t/ *n* aeroporto *m*

airsick /'eəsɪk/ *a* enjoado. **~ness** /nɪs/ *n* enjôo *m*, (*P*) enjoo *m*

airstrip /'eəstrɪp/ *n* pista *f* de aterrissagem, (*P*) pista *f* de aterragem

airtight /'eətaɪt/ *a* hermético

airy /'eərɪ/ *a* (**-ier, -iest**) arejado; (*manner*) desenvolto

aisle /aɪl/ *n* (*of church*) nave *f* lateral; (*gangway*) coxia *f*

ajar /ə'dʒa:(r)/ *adv* & *a* entreaberto

alabaster /'æləba:stə(r)/ *n* alabastro *m*

à la carte /a:la:'ka:t/ *adv* & *a* à la carte, (*P*) à lista

alarm /ə'la:m/ *n* alarme *m*; (*clock*) campainha *f* □ *vt* alarmar. **~-clock** *n* despertador *m*. **~-bell** *n* campainha *f* de alarme. **~ing** *a* alarmante. **~ist** *n* alarmista *mf*

alas /ə'læs/ *int* ai! ai de mim!

albatross /'ælbətrɒs/ *n* albatroz *m*

album /'ælbəm/ *n* álbum *m*

alcohol /'ælkəhɒl/ *n* álcool *m*. **~ic** /-'hɒlɪk/ *a* (*person, drink*) alcoólico □ *n* alcoólico *m*. **~ism** *n* alcoolismo *m*

alcove /'ælkəʊv/ *n* recesso *m*, alcova *f*

ale /eɪl/ *n* cerveja *f* inglesa

alert /ə'lɜ:t/ *a* (*lively*) vivo; (*watchful*) vigilante □ *n* alerta *m* □ *vt* alertar. **be on the ~** estar alerta

algebra /'ældʒɪbrə/ *n* álgebra *f*. **~ic** /-'breɪɪk/ *a* algébrico

Algeria /æl'dʒɪərɪə/ *n* Argélia *f*. **~n** *a* & *n* argelino (*m*)

alias /'eɪlɪəs/ *n* (*pl* **-ases**) outro nome *m*, nome falso *m*, (*P*) pseudónimo *m* □ *adv* aliás

alibi /'ælɪbaɪ/ *n* (*pl* **-is**) álibi *m*, (*P*) alibi *m*

alien /'eɪlɪən/ *n* & *a* estrangeiro (*m*). **~ to** (*contrary*) contrário a; (*differing*) alheio a, estranho a

alienat|e /'eɪlɪəneɪt/ *vt* alienar. **~ion** /-'neɪʃn/ *n* alienação *f*

alight[1] /ə'laɪt/ *vi* descer; (*bird*) pousar

alight[2] /ə'laɪt/ *a* (*on fire*) em chamas; (*lit up*) aceso

align /ə'laɪn/ *vt* alinhar. **~ment** *n* alinhamento *m*

alike /ə'laɪk/ *a* semelhante, parecido □ *adv* da mesma maneira. **look** *or* **be ~** parecer-se

alimony /'ælɪmənɪ/ *n* pensão *f* alimentar, (*P*) de alimentos

alive /ə'laɪv/ *a* vivo. **~ to** sensível a. **~ with** fervilhando de, (*P*) a fervilhar de

alkali /'ælkəlaɪ/ *n* (*pl* **-is**) álcali *m*, (*P*) alcali *m*

all /ɔ:l/ *a* & *pron* todo (*f* & *pl* *-a, -os, -as*) □ *pron* (*everything*) tudo □ *adv* completamente, de todo □ *n* tudo *m*. **~ the better/less/more/worse** *etc* tanto melhor/menos/mais/pior *etc*. **~ (the) men** todos os homens. **~ of us** todos nós. **~ but** quase, todos menos. **~ in** (*colloq: exhausted*) estafado. **~-in** *a* tudo incluído. **~ out** a fundo, (*P*) completamente. **~-out** *a* (*effort*) máximo. **~ over** (*in one's body*) todo; (*finished*) acabado; (*in all parts of*) por todo. **~ right** bem; (*as a response*) está bem. **~ round** em tudo; (*for all*) para todos. **~-round** *a* geral. **~ the same** apesar de tudo. **it's ~ the same to me** (para mim) tanto faz

allay /ə'leɪ/ *vt* acalmar

allegation /ælɪ'geɪʃn/ *n* alegação *f*

allege /ə'ledʒ/ *vt* alegar. **~dly** /-ɪdlɪ/ *adv* segundo dizem, alegadamente

allegiance /ə'li:dʒəns/ *n* fidelidade *f*, lealdade *f*

allegor|y /'ælɪgərɪ/ *n* alegoria *f*. **~ical** /-'gɒrɪkl/ *a* alegórico

allerg|y /'ælədʒɪ/ *n* alergia *f*. **~ic** /ə'lɜ:dʒɪk/ *a* alérgico

alleviate /ə'li:vɪeɪt/ *vt* aliviar

alley /'ælɪ/ *n* (*pl* **-eys**) (*street*) viela *f*; (*for bowling*) pista *f*

alliance /ə'laɪəns/ *n* aliança *f*

allied /'ælaɪd/ *a* aliado

alligator /'ælɪgeɪtə(r)/ *n* jacaré *m*

allocat|e /'æləkeɪt/ *vt* (*share out*) distribuir; (*assign*) destinar. **~ion** /-'keɪʃn/ *n* atribuição *f*

allot /ə'lɒt/ *vt* (*pt* **allotted**) atribuir. **~ment** *n* atribuição *f*; (*share*) distribuição *f*; (*land*) horta *f* alugada

allow /ə'laʊ/ *vt* permitir; (*grant*) conceder, dar; (*reckon on*) contar com; (*agree*) admitir, reconhecer. **~ sb to** (+ *inf*) permitir a alg (+ *inf or que* + *subj*). **~ for** levar em conta

allowance /ə'laʊəns/ *n* (*for employees*) ajudas *fpl* de custo; (*monthly, for wife, child*) benefício *m*; (*tax*) desconto *m*. **make ~s for** (*person*) levar em consideração, ser indulgente para com; (*take into account*) atender a, levar em consideração

alloy /ə'lɔɪ/ *n* liga *f*

allude /ə'lu:d/ *vi* **~ to** aludir a

allure /ə'lʊə(r)/ *vt* seduzir, atrair

allusion /ə'lu:ʒn/ *n* alusão *f*

ally[1] /'ælaɪ/ *n* (*pl* **-lies**) aliado *m*

ally[2] /ə'laɪ/ *vt* aliar. **~ oneself with/to** aliar-se com/a

almanac /'ɔ:lmənæk/ *n* almanaque *m*

almighty /ɔ:l'maɪtɪ/ *a* todo-poderoso; (*colloq*) grande, formidável

almond /'a:mənd/ *n* amêndoa *f*. **~ paste** maçapão *m*

almost /'ɔ:lməʊst/ *adv* quase

alone /ə'ləʊn/ *a* & *adv* só. **leave ~** (*abstain from interfering with*) deixar em paz. **let ~** (*without considering*) sem *or* para não falar de

along /ə'lɒŋ/ *prep* ao longo de □ *adv* (*onward*) para diante. **all ~** durante todo o tempo. **~ with** com. **move ~, please** ande, por favor

alongside /əlɒŋ'saɪd/ *adv* (*naut*) atracado. **come ~** acostar □ *prep* ao lado de

aloof /ə'lu:f/ *adv* à parte □ *a* distante. **~ness** *n* reserva *f*

aloud /ə'laʊd/ *adv* em voz alta

alphabet /'ælfəbet/ *n* alfabeto *m*. **~ical** /-'betɪkl/ *a* alfabético

alpine /'ælpaɪn/ *a* alpino, alpestre

Alps /ælps/ *npl* **the ~** os Alpes *mpl*

already /ɔ:l'redɪ/ *adv* já

also /'ɔl:səʊ/ *adv* também

altar /'ɔ:ltə(r)/ *n* altar *m*

alter /'ɔ:ltə(r)/ *vt/i* alterar(-se), modificar(-se). **~ation** /-'reɪʃn/ *n* alteração *f*; (*to garment*) modificação *f*

alternate[1] /ɔ:l'tɜ:nət/ *a* alternado. **~ly** *adv* alternadamente

alternat|e[2] /'ɔ:ltəneɪt/ *vt/i* alternar(-se). **~ing current** (*elect*) corrente *f* alterna. **~or** *n* (*elect*) alternador *m*

alternative /ɔ:l'tɜ:nətɪv/ *a* alternativo □ *n* alternativa *f*. **~ly** *adv* em alternativa. **or ~ly** ou então

although /ɔ:l'ðəʊ/ *conj* embora, conquanto

altitude /'æltɪtju:d/ *n* altitude *f*

altogether /ɔ:ltə'geðə(r)/ *adv* (*completely*) completamente; (*in total*) ao todo; (*on the whole*) de modo geral

aluminium /æljʊ'mɪnɪəm/ (*Amer* **aluminum** /ə'lu:mɪnəm/) *n* alumínio *m*

always /'ɔ:lweɪz/ *adv* sempre

am /æm/ *see* **be**

a.m. /eɪ'em/ *adv* da manhã

amalgamate /ə'mælgəmeɪt/ *vt/i* amalgamar(-se); (*comm*) fundir

amass /ə'mæs/ *vt* amontoar, juntar

amateur /'æmətə(r)/ *n* & *a* amador (*m*). **~ish** *a* (*pej*) de amador, (*P*) amadorístico

amaz|e /ə'meɪz/ *vt* assombrar, espantar. **~ed** *a* assombrado. **~ement** *n* assombro *m*. **~ingly** *adv* espantosamente

Amazon /'æməzən/ *n* **the ~** o Amazonas

ambassador /æm'bæsədə(r)/ *n* embaixador *m*

amber /'æmbə(r)/ *n* âmbar *m*; (*traffic light*) luz *f* amarela

ambigu|ous /æm'bɪgjʊəs/ *a* ambíguo. **~ity** /-'gju:ətɪ/ *n* ambigüidade *f*, (*P*) ambiguidade *f*

ambiti|on /æm'bɪʃn/ *n* ambição *f*. **~ous** *a* ambicioso

ambivalen|t /æm'bɪvələnt/ *a* ambivalente. **~ce** *n* ambivalência *f*

amble /'æmbl/ *vi* caminhar sem pressa

ambulance /'æmbjʊləns/ *n* ambulência *f*

ambush /'æmbʊʃ/ *n* emboscada *f* □ *vt* fazer uma emboscada para, (*P*) fazer uma emboscada a

amenable /ə'mi:nəbl/ *a* **~ to** (*responsive*) sensível a

amend /ə'mend/ *vt* emendar, corrigir. **~ment** *n* (*to rule*) emenda *f*. **~s** *n* **make ~s for** reparar, compensar

amenities /ə'mi:nətɪz/ *npl* (*pleasant features*) atrativos *mpl*, (*P*) atractivos *mpl*; (*facilities*) confortos *mpl*, comodidades *fpl*

America /ə'merɪkə/ *n* América *f*. **~n** *a* & *n* americano (*m*). **~nism** /-nɪzəm/ *n* americanismo *m*. **~nize** *vt* americanizar

amiable /'eɪmɪəbl/ *a* amável

amicable /'æmɪkəbl/ *a* amigável, amigo

amid(st) /'əmɪd(st)/ *prep* entre, no meio de

amiss /ə'mɪs/ *a* & *adv* mal. **sth ~** qq coisa que não está bem. **take sth ~** levar qq coisa a mal

ammonia /ə'məʊnɪə/ *n* amoníaco *m*

ammunition /æmjʊ'nɪʃn/ *n* munições *fpl*

amnesia /æm'ni:zɪə/ *n* amnésia *f*
amnesty /'æmnəstɪ/ *n* anistia *f*, (*P*) amnistia *f*
amok /ə'mɒk/ *adv* **run ~** enlouquecer; (*crowd*) correr desordenadamente
among(st) /ə'mʌŋ(st)/ *prep* entre, no meio de. **~ ourselves** (aqui) entre nós
amoral /eɪ'mɒrəl/ *a* amoral
amorous /'æmərəs/ *a* amoroso
amount /ə'maʊnt/ *n* quantidade *f*; (*total*) montante *m*; (*sum of money*) quantia *f* ▫ *vi* **~ to** elevar-se a; (*fig*) equivaler a
amp /æmp/ *n* (*colloq*) ampère *m*
amphibi|an /æm'fɪbɪən/ *n* anfíbio *m*. **~ous** *a* anfíbio
ampl|e /'æmpl/ *a* (**-er, -est**) (*large, roomy*) amplo; (*enough*) suficiente, bastante. **~y** *adv* amplamente
amplif|y /'æmplɪfaɪ/ *vt* ampliar, amplificar. **~ier** *n* amplificador *m*
amputat|e /'æmpjʊteɪt/ *vt* amputar. **~ion** /-'teɪʃn/ *n* amputação *f*
amus|e /ə'mju:z/ *vt* divertir. **~ement** *n* divertimento *m*. **~- ing** *a* divertido
an /ən, æn/ *see* **a**
anachronism /ə'nækrənɪzəm/ *n* anacronismo *m*
anaem|ia /ə'ni:mɪə/ *n* anemia *f*. **~ic** *a* anêmico, (*P*) anémico
anaesthetic /ænɪs'θetɪk/ *n* anestético *m*, (*P*) anestésico *m*. **give an ~ to** anestesiar
anaesthetist /ə'ni:sθətɪst/ *n* anestesista *mf*
anagram /'ænəgræm/ *n* anagrama *m*
analog(ue) /'ænəlɒg/ *a* análogo
analogy /ə'nælədʒɪ/ *n* analogia *f*
analys|e /'ænəlaɪz/ *vt* analisar. **~t** /-ɪst/ *n* analista *mf*
analysis /ə'næləsɪs/ *n* (*pl* **-yses**) /-əsi:z/ análise *f*
analytic(al) /ænə'lɪtɪk(l)/ *a* analítico
anarch|y /'ænəkɪ/ *n* anarquia *f*. **~ist** *n* anarquista *mf*
anatom|y /ə'nætəmɪ/ *n* anatomia *f*. **~ical** /ænə'tɒmɪkl/ *a* anatômico, (*P*) anatómico
ancest|or /'ænsestə(r)/ *n* antepassado *m*. **~ral** /-'sestrəl/ *a* ancestral (*pl* -ais)
ancestry /'ænsestrɪ/ *n* ascendência *f*, estirpe *f*
anchor /'æŋkə(r)/ *n* âncora *f* ▫ *vt/i* ancorar. **~age** /-rɪdʒ/ *n* ancoradouro *m*
anchovy /'æntʃəvɪ/ *n* enchova *f*, (*P*) anchova *f*
ancient /'eɪnʃənt/ *a* antigo
ancillary /æn'sɪlərɪ/ *a* ancilar, (*P*) subordinado
and /ənd/; *emphatic* /ænd/ *conj* e. **go ~ see** vá ver. **better ~ better/less ~ less** *etc* cada vez melhor/menos *etc*
anecdote /'ænɪkdəʊt/ *n* anedota *f*
angel /'eɪndʒl/ *n* anjo *m*. **~ic** /æn'dʒelɪk/ *a* angélico, angelical
anger /'æŋgə(r)/ *n* cólera *f*, zanga *f* ▫ *vt* irritar
angle[1] /'æŋgl/ *n* ângulo *m*
angle[2] /'æŋgl/ *vi* (*fish*) pescar (à linha). **~ for** (*fig: compliments, information*) andar à procura de. **~r** /-ə(r)/ *n* pescador *m*
anglicism /'æŋglɪsɪzəm/ *n* anglicismo *m*
Anglo- /'æŋgləʊ/ *pref* anglo-
Anglo-Saxon /'æŋgləʊ'sæksn/ *a* & *n* anglo-saxão (*m*)
angr|y /'æŋgrɪ/ *a* (**-ier, -iest**) zangado. **get ~y** zangar-se (**with** com). **~ily** *adv* furiosamente
anguish /'æŋgwɪʃ/ *n* angústia *f*
angular /'æŋgjʊlə(r)/ *a* angular; (*features*) anguloso
animal /'ænɪml/ *a* & *n* animal (*m*)
animate[1] /'ænɪmət/ *a* animado
animat|e[2] /'ænɪmeɪt/ *vt* animar. **~ion** /-'meɪʃn/ *n* animação *f*. **~ed cartoon** filme *m* de bonecos animados, (*P*) de desenhos animados
animosity /ænɪ'mɒsətɪ/ *n* animosidade *f*
aniseed /'ænɪsi:d/ *n* semente *f* de anis
ankle /'æŋkl/ *n* tornozelo *m*. **~ sock** meia *f* soquete
annex /ə'neks/ *vt* anexar. **~ation** /ænek'seɪʃn/ *n* anexação *f*
annexe /'æneks/ *n* anexo *m*
annihilate /ə'naɪəleɪt/ *vt* aniquilar
anniversary /ænɪ'vɜ:sərɪ/ *n* aniversário *m*
announce /ə'naʊns/ *vt* anunciar. **~ment** *n* anúncio *m*. **~r** /-ə(r)/ *n* (*radio, TV*) locutor *m*
annoy /ə'nɔɪ/ *vt* irritar, aborrecer. **~ance** *n* aborrecimento *m*. **~ed** *a* aborrecido (**with** com). **get ~ed** aborrecer-se. **~ing** *a* irritante
annual /'ænjʊəl/ *a* anual ▫ *n* (*bot*) planta *f* anual; (*book*) anuário *m*. **~ly** *adv* anualmente
annuity /ə'nju:ətɪ/ *n* anuidade *f*
annul /ə'nʌl/ *vt* (*pt* **annulled**) anular. **~ment** *n* anulação *f*
anomal|y /ə'nɒməlɪ/ *n* anomalia *f*. **~ous** *a* anômalo, (*P*) anómalo
anonym|ous /ə'nɒnɪməs/ *a* anônimo, (*P*) anónimo. **~ity** /ænə-'nɪmətɪ/ *n* anonimato *m*
anorak /'ænəræk/ *n* anoraque *m*, anorak *m*
another /ə'nʌðə(r)/ *a* & *pron* (um) outro. **~ ten minutes** mais dez minutos. **to one ~** um ao outro, uns aos outros

answer /ˈa:nsə(r)/ *n* resposta *f*; (*solution*) solução *f* □ *vt* responder a; (*prayer*) atender a □ *vi* responder. **~ the door** atender à porta. **~ back** retrucar, (*P*) responder torto. **~ for** responder por. **~able** *a* responsável (**for** por; **to** perante). **~ing machine** *n* secretária *f* eletrónica

ant /ænt/ *n* formiga *f*

antagonis|m /ænˈtægənɪzəm/ *n* antagonismo *m*. **~t** *n* antagonista *mf*. **~tic** /-ˈnɪstɪk/ *a* antagônico, (*P*) antagónico, hostil

antagonize /ænˈtægənaɪz/ *vt* antagonizar, hostilizar

Antarctic /ænˈta:ktɪk/ *n* Antártico, (*P*) Antárctico *m* □ *a* antártico, (*P*) antárctico

ante- /ˈæntɪ/ *pref* ante-

antecedent /æntɪˈsi:dnt/ *a* & *n* antecedente (*m*)

antelope /ˈæntɪləʊp/ *n* antílope *m*

antenatal /æntɪˈneɪtl/ *a* pré-natal

antenna /ænˈtenə/ *n* (*pl* **-ae** /-i:/) antena *f*

anthem /ˈænθəm/ *n* cântico *m*. **national ~** hino *m* nacional

anthology /ænˈθɒlədʒɪ/ *n* antologia *f*

anthropolog|y /ænθrəˈpɒlədʒɪ/ *n* antropologia *f*. **~ist** *n* antropólogo *m*

anti- /æntɪ/ *pref* anti-. **~-aircraft** /-eəkra:ft/ *a* antiaéreo

antibiotic /æntɪbaɪˈɒtɪk/ *n* antibiótico *m*

antibody /ˈæntɪbɒdɪ/ *n* anticorpo *m*

anticipat|e /ænˈtɪsɪpeɪt/ *vt* (*foresee, expect*) prever; (*forestall*) antecipar-se a. **~ion** /-ˈpeɪʃn/ *n* antecipação *f*; (*expectation*) expectativa *f*. **in ~ion of** na previsão *or* expectativa de

anticlimax /æntɪˈklaɪmæks/ *n* anticlímax *m*; (*let-down*) decepção *f*. **it was an ~** não correspondeu à expectativa

anticlockwise /æntɪˈklɒkwaɪz/ *adv* & *a* no sentido contrário ao dos ponteiros dum relógio

antics /ˈæntɪks/ *npl* (*of clown*) palhaçadas *fpl*; (*behaviour*) comportamento *m* bizarro

anticyclone /ˌæntɪˈsaɪkləʊn/ *n* anticiclone *m*

antidote /ˈæntɪdəʊt/ *n* antídoto *m*

antifreeze /ˈæntɪfri:z/ *n* anticongelante *m*

antihistamine /æntɪˈhɪstəmi:n/ *a* & *n* anti-histamínico (*m*)

antipathy /ænˈtɪpəθɪ/ *n* antipatia *f*

antiquated /ˈæntɪkweɪtɪd/ *a* antiquado

antique /ænˈti:k/ *a* antigo □ *n* antiguidade *f*. **~ dealer** antiquário *m*. **~ shop** loja *f* de antiguidades, (*P*) antiquário *m*

antiquity /ænˈtɪkwətɪ/ *n* antiguidade *f*

antiseptic /æntɪˈseptɪk/ *a* & *n* antiséptico (*m*)

antisocial /æntɪˈsəʊʃl/ *a* anti- social; (*unsociable*) insociável

antithesis /ænˈtɪθəsɪs/ *n* (*pl* **-eses**) /-si:z/ antítese *f*.

antlers /ˈæntləz/ *npl* chifres *mpl*, esgalhos *mpl*

antonym /ˈæntənɪm/ *n* antônimo *m*, (*P*) antónimo *m*

anus /ˈeɪnəs/ *n* ânus *m*

anvil /ˈænvɪl/ *n* bigorna *f*

anxiety /æŋˈzaɪətɪ/ *n* ansiedade *f*; (*eagerness*) ânsia *f*

anxious /ˈæŋkʃəs/ *a* (*worried, eager*) ansioso (**to** de, por). **~ly** *adv* ansiosamente; (*eagerly*) impacientemente

any /ˈenɪ/ *a & pron* qualquer, quaisquer; (*in neg and interr sentences*) algum, alguns; (*in neg sentences*) nenhum, nenhuns; (*every*) todo. **at ~ moment** a qualquer momento. **at ~ rate** de qualquer modo, em todo o caso. **in ~ case** em todo o caso. **have you ~ money/friends**? você tem (algum) dinheiro/(alguns) amigos? **I don't have ~ time** não tenho nenhum tempo *or* tempo nenhum *or* tempo algum. **has she ~?** ela tem algum? **she doesn't have ~** ela não tem nenhum □ *adv* (*at all*) de modo algum *or* nenhum; (*a little*) um pouco. **~ the less/the worse** *etc* menos/pior *etc*

anybody /ˈenɪbɒdɪ/ *pron* qualquer pessoa; (*somebody*) alguém; (*after negative*) ninguém. **he didn't see ~** ele não viu ninguém

anyhow /ˈenɪhaʊ/ *adv* (*no matter how*) de qualquer modo; (*badly*) de qualquer maneira, ao acaso; (*in any case*) em todo o caso. **you can try, ~** em todo o caso, você pode tentar

anyone /ˈenɪwʌn/ *pron* = **anybody**

anything /ˈenɪθɪŋ/ *pron* (*something*) alguma coisa; (*no matter what*) qualquer coisa; (*after negative*) nada. **he didn't say ~** não disse nada. **it is ~ but cheap** é tudo menos barato. **~ you do** tudo o que você fizer

anyway /ˈenɪweɪ/ *adv* de qualquer modo; (*in any case*) em todo o caso

anywhere /ˈenɪweə(r)/ *adv* (*some-where*) em qualquer parte; (*after negative*) em parte alguma/nenhuma. **~ else** em qualquer outro lado. **~ you go** onde quer que você vá. **he doesn't go ~** ele não vai a lado nenhum

apart /əˈpa:t/ *adv* à parte; (*separated*) separado; (*into pieces*) aos bocados. **~ from** à parte, além de. **ten metres ~** a dez metros de distância entre si.

come ~ desfazer-se. **keep ~** manter separado. **take ~** desmontar

apartment /ə'pa:tmənt/ *n* (*Amer*) apartamento *m*. **~s** aposentos *mpl*

apath|y /'æpəθɪ/ *n* apatia *f*. **~etic** /-'θetɪk/ *a* apático

ape /eɪp/ *n* macaco *m* □ *vt* macaquear

aperitif /ə'perətɪf/ *n* aperitivo *m*

aperture /'æpətʃə(r)/ *n* abertura *f*

apex /'eɪpeks/ *n* ápice *m*, cume *m*

apiece /ə'pi:s/ *adv* cada, por cabeça

apologetic /əpɒlə'dʒetɪk/ *a* (*tone etc*) apologético, de desculpas. **be ~** desculpar-se. **~ally** /-əlɪ/ *adv* desculpando-se

apologize /ə'pɒlədʒaɪz/ *vi* desculpar-se (**for** de, por; **to** junto de, perante), pedir desculpa (**for**, por; **to**, a)

apology /ə'pɒlədʒɪ/ *n* desculpa *f*; (*defence of belief*) apologia *f*

apostle /ə'pɒsl/ *n* apóstolo *m*

apostrophe /ə'pɒstrəfɪ/ *n* apóstrofe *f*

appal /ə'pɔ:l/ *vt* (*pt* **appalled**) estarrecer. **~ling** *a* estarrecedor

apparatus /æpə'reɪtəs/ *n* aparelho *m*

apparent /ə'pærənt/ *a* aparente. **~ly** *adv* aparentemente

apparition /æpə'rɪʃn/ *n* aparição *f*

appeal /ə'pi:l/ *vi* (*jur*) apelar (**to** para); (*attract*) atrair (**to** a); (*for funds*) angariar □ *n* apelo *m*; (*attractiveness*) atrativo *m*, (*P*) atractivo *m*; (*for funds*) angariação *f*. **~ to sb for sth** pedir uma coisa a alg. **~ing** *a* (*attractive*) atraente

appear /ə'pɪə(r)/ *vi* aparecer; (*seem*) parecer; (*in court, theatre*) apresentar-se. **~ance** *n* aparição *f*; (*aspect*) aparência *f*; (*in court*) comparecimento *m*, (*P*) comparência *f*

appease /ə'pi:z/ *vt* apaziguar

appendage /ə'pendɪdʒ/ *n* apêndice *m*

appendicitis /əpendɪ'saɪtɪs/ *n* apendicite *f*

appendix /ə'pendɪks/ *n* (*pl* **-ices** /-si:z/) (*of book*) apêndice *m*; (*pl* **-ixes** /-ksɪz/) (*anat*) apêndice *m*

appetite /'æpɪtaɪt/ *n* apetite *m*

appetizer /'æpɪtaɪzə(r)/ *n* (*snack*) tira-gosto *m*; (*drink*) aperitivo *m*

appetizing /'æpɪtaɪzɪŋ/ *a* apetitoso

applau|d /ə'plɔ:d/ *vt*/*i* aplaudir. **~se** *n* aplauso(s) *m*(*pl*)

apple /'æpl/ *n* maçã *f*. **~ tree** macieira *f*

appliance /ə'plaɪəns/ *n* aparelho *m*, instrumento *m*, utensílio *m*. **household ~s** utensílios *mpl* domésticos

applicable /'æplɪkəbl/ *a* aplicável

applicant /'æplɪkənt/ *n* candidato *m* (**for** a)

application /æplɪ'keɪʃn/ *n* aplicação *f*; (*request*) pedido *m*; (*form*) formulário *m*; (*for job*) candidatura *f*

appl|y /ə'plaɪ/ *vt* aplicar □ *vi* **~y to** (*refer*) aplicar-se a; (*ask*) dirigir-se a. **~y for** (*job, grant*) candidatar-se a. **~y o.s. to** aplicar-se a. **~ied** *a* aplicado

appoint /ə'pɔɪnt/ *vt* (*to post*) nomear; (*time, date*) marcar. **well-~ed** *a* bem equipado, bem provido. **~ment** *n* nomeação *f*; (*meeting*) entrevista *f*; (*with friends*) encontro *m*; (*with doctor etc*) consulta *f*, (*P*) marcação *f*; (*job*) posto *m*

apprais|e /ə'preɪz/ *vt* avaliar. **~al** *n* avaliação *f*

appreciable /ə'pri:ʃəbl/ *a* apreciável

appreciat|e /ə'pri:ʃɪeɪt/ *vt* (*value*) apreciar; (*understand*) compreender; (*be grateful for*) estar/ficar grato por □ *vi* encarecer. **~ion** /-'eɪʃn/ *n* apreciação *f*; (*rise in value*) encarecimento *m*; (*gratitude*) reconhecimento *m*. **~ive** /ə'pri:ʃɪətɪv/ *a* apreciador; (*grateful*) reconhecido

apprehen|d /æprɪ'hend/ *vt* (*seize, understand*) apreender; (*dread*) recear. **~sion** *n* apreensão *f*

apprehensive /æprɪ'hensɪv/ *a* apreensivo

apprentice /ə'prentɪs/ *n* aprendiz, -a *mf* □ *vt* pôr como aprendiz (**to** de). **~ship** *n* aprendizagem *f*

approach /ə'prəʊtʃ/ *vt* aproximar; (*with request or offer*) abordar □ *vi* aproximar-se □ *n* aproximação *f*. **~ to** (*problem*) abordagem *f* de; (*place*) acesso *m* a; (*person*) diligência junto de. **~able** *a* acessível

appropriate[1] /ə'prəʊprɪət/ *a* apropriado, próprio. **~ly** *adv* apropriadamente, a propósito

appropriate[2] /ə'prəʊprɪeɪt/ *vt* apropriar-se de

approval /ə'pru:vl/ *n* aprovação *f*. **on ~** (*comm*) sob condição, à aprovação

approv|e /ə'pru:v/ *vt*/*i* aprovar. **~e of** aprovar. **~ingly** *adv* com ar de aprovação

approximate[1] /ə'prɒksɪmət/ *a* aproximado. **~ly** *adv* aproximadamente

approximat|e[2] /ə'prɒksɪmeɪt/ *vt*/*i* aproximar(-se) de. **~ion** /-'meɪʃn/ *n* aproximação *f*

apricot /'eɪprɪkɒt/ *n* damasco *m*

April /'eɪprəl/ *n* Abril *m*. **~ Fool's Day** o primeiro de Abril, o dia das mentiras. **make an ~ fool of** pregar uma mentira em, (*P*) pregar uma mentira a

apron /ˈeɪprən/ *n* avental *m*
apt /æpt/ *a* apto; (*pupil*) dotado. **be ~ to** ser propenso a. **~ly** *adv* apropriadamente
aptitude /ˈæptɪtjuːd/ *n* aptidão *f*, (*P*) aptitude *f*
aqualung /ˈækwəlʌŋ/ *n* escafandro autônomo, (*P*) autónomo *m*
aquarium /əˈkweərɪəm/ *n* (*pl* **-ums**) aquário *m*
Aquarius /əˈkwɛərɪəs/ *n* (*astr*) Aquário *m*
aquatic /əˈkwætɪk/ *a* aquático; (*sport*) náutico, aquático
aqueduct /ˈækwɪdʌkt/ *n* aqueduto *m*
Arab /ˈærəb/ *a* & *n* árabe (*mf*). **~ic** *a* & *n* (*lang*) árabe (*m*), arábico (*m*). **a~ic numerals** algarismos *mpl* árabes *or* arábicos
Arabian /əˈreɪbɪən/ *a* árabe
arable /ˈærəbl/ *a* arável
arbitrary /ˈaːbɪtrərɪ/ *a* arbitrário
arbitrat|e /ˈaːbɪtreɪt/ *vi* arbitrar. **~ion** /-ˈtreɪʃn/ *n* arbitragem *f*. **~or** *n* árbitro *m*
arc /aːk/ *n* arco *m*. **~ lamp** lâmpada *f* de arco. **~ welding** soldadura *f* a arco
arcade /aːˈkeɪd/ *n* (*shop*) arcada *f*. **amusement ~** fliperama *m*
arch /aːtʃ/ *n* arco *m*; (*vault*) abóbada *f* □ *vt*/*i* arquear(-se)
arch- /aːtʃ/ *pref* arqui-.
archaeolog|y /aːkɪˈɒlədʒɪ/ *n* arqueologia *f*. **~ical** /-əˈlɒdʒɪkl/ *a* arqueológico. **~ist** *n* arqueólogo *m*
archaic /aːˈkeɪɪk/ *a* arcaico
archbishop /aːtʃˈbɪʃəp/ *n* arcebispo *m*
arch-enemy /aːtʃˈenəmɪ/ *n* inimigo *m* número um
archer /ˈaːtʃə(r)/ *n* arqueiro *m*. **~y** *n* tiro *m* ao arco
archetype /ˈaːkɪtaɪp/ *n* arquétipo *m*
architect /ˈaːkɪtekt/ *n* arquiteto *m*, (*P*) arquitecto *m*
architectur|e /ˈaːkɪtektʃə(r)/ *n* arquitetura *f*, (*P*) arquitectura *f*. **~al** /-ˈtektʃərəl/ *a* arquitetônico, (*P*) arquitectónico
archiv|es /ˈaːkaɪvz/ *npl* arquivo *m*. **~ist** /-ɪvɪst/ *n* arquivista *mf*
archway /ˈaːtʃweɪ/ *n* arcada *f*
Arctic /ˈaːktɪk/ *n* Ártico *m*, (*P*) Árctico *m* □ *a* ártico, (*P*) árctico. **~ weather** tempo *m* glacial
ardent /ˈaːdnt/ *a* ardente. **~ly** *adv* ardentemente
ardour /ˈaːdə(r)/ *n* ardor *m*
arduous /ˈaːdjʊəs/ *a* árduo
are /ə(r)/; *emphatic* /aː(r)/ *see* **be**
area /ˈeərɪə/ *n* área *f*
arena /əˈriːnə/ *n* arena *f*
aren't /aːnt/ = **are not**
Argentin|a /aːdʒənˈtiːnə/ *n* Argentina *f*. **~ian** /-ˈtɪnɪən/ *a* & *n* argentino (*m*)
argu|e /ˈaːgjuː/ *vi* discutir; (*reason*) argumentar, arguir □ *vt* (*debate*) discutir. **~e that** alegar que. **~able** *a* alegável. **it's ~-able that** pode-se sustentar que
argument /ˈaːgjʊmənt/ *n* (*dispute*) disputa *f*; (*reasoning*) argumento *m*. **~ative** /-ˈmentətɪv/ *a* que gosta de discutir, argumentativo
arid /ˈærɪd/ *a* árido
Aries /ˈeəriːz/ *n* (*astr*) Áries *m*, Carneiro *m*
arise /əˈraɪz/ *vi* (*pt* **arose**, *pp* **arisen**) surgir. **~ from** resultar de
aristocracy /ærɪˈstɒkrəsɪ/ *n* aristocracia *f*
aristocrat /ˈærɪstəkræt/ *n* aristocrata *mf*. **~ic** /-ˈkrætɪk/ *a* aristocrático
arithmetic /əˈrɪθmətɪk/ *n* aritmética *f*
ark /aːk/ *n* **Noah's ~** arca *f* de Noé
arm[1] /aːm/ *n* braço *m*. **~ in ~** de braço dado
arm[2] /aːm/ *vt* armar □ *n* (*mil*) arma *f*. **~ed robbery** assalto *m* à mão armada
armament /ˈaːməmənt/ *n* armamento *m*
armchair /ˈaːmtʃeə(r)/ *n* cadeira *f* de braços, poltrona *f*
armistice /ˈaːmɪstɪs/ *n* armistício *m*
armour /ˈaːmə(r)/ *n* armadura *f*; (*on tanks etc*) blindagem *f*. **~ed** *a* blindado
armoury /ˈaːmərɪ/ *n* arsenal *m*
armpit /ˈaːmpɪt/ *n* axila *f*, sovaco *m*
arms /aːmz/ *npl* armas *fpl*. **coat of ~** brasão *m*
army /ˈaːmɪ/ *n* exército *m*
aroma /əˈrəʊmə/ *n* aroma *m*. **~tic** /ærəˈmætɪk/ *a* aromático
arose /əˈrəʊz/ *see* **arise**
around /əˈraʊnd/ *adv* em redor, em volta; (*here and there*) por aí □ *prep* em redor de, em torno de, em volta de; (*approximately*) aproximadamente. **~ here** por aqui
arouse /əˈraʊz/ *vt* despertar; (*excite*) excitar
arrange /əˈreɪndʒ/ *vt* arranjar; (*time, date*) combinar. **~ to do sth** combinar fazer alg coisa. **~ment** *n* arranjo *m*; (*agreement*) acordo *m*. **make ~ments (for)** (*plans*) tomar disposições (para); (*preparations*) fazer preparativos (para)
array /əˈreɪ/ *vt* revestir □ *n* **an ~ of** (*display*) um leque de, uma série de
arrears /əˈrɪəz/ *npl* dívidas *fpl* em atraso, atrasos *mpl*. **in ~** em atraso

arrest /ə'rest/ *vt* (*by law*) deter, prender; (*process, movement*) deter □ *n* captura *f*. **under ~** sob prisão
arrival /ə'raɪvl/ *n* chegada *f*. **new ~** recém-chegado *m*
arrive /ə'raɪv/ *vi* chegar
arrogan|t /'ærəgənt/ *a* arrogante. **~ce** *n* arrogância *f*. **~tly** *adv* com arrogância
arrow /'ærəʊ/ *n* flecha *f*, seta *f*
arsenal /'a:sənl/ *n* arsenal *m*
arsenic /'a:snɪk/ *n* arsênico *m*, (*P*) arsénico *m*
arson /'a:sn/ *n* fogo *m* posto. **~ist** *n* incendiário *m*
art[1] /a:t/ *n* arte *f*. **the ~s** (*univ*) letras *fpl*. **fine ~s** belas-artes *fpl*. **~ gallery** museu *m* (de arte); (*private*) galeria *f* de arte
artery /'a:tərɪ/ *n* artéria *f*
artful /'a:tfl/ *a* manhoso. **~ness** *n* manha *f*
arthritis /a:'θraɪtɪs/ *n* artrite *f*
artichoke /'a:tɪtʃəʊk/ *n* alcachofra *f*. **Jerusalem ~** topinambo *m*
article /'a:tɪkl/ *n* artigo *m*. **~d** *a* (*jur*) em estágio, (*P*) a estagiar
articulate[1] /a:'tɪkjʊlət/ *a* que se exprime com clareza; (*speech*) bem articulado
articulat|e[2] /a:'tɪkjʊleɪt/ *vt/i* articular. **~ed lorry** camião *m* articulado. **~ion** /-'leɪʃn/ *n* articulação *f*
artifice /'a:tɪfɪs/ *n* artifício *m*
artificial /a:tɪ'fɪʃl/ *a* artificial
artillery /a:'tɪlərɪ/ *n* artilharia *f*
artisan /a:tɪ'zæn/ *n* artífice *mf*, artesão *m*, artesã *f*
artist /'a:tɪst/ *n* artista *mf*. **~ic** /-'tɪstɪk/ *a* artístico. **~ry** *n* arte *f*
artiste /a:'ti:st/ *n* artista *mf*
artless /'a:tlɪs/ *a* ingênuo, (*P*) ingénuo, simples
as /əz/; *emphatic* /æz/ *adv & conj* como; (*while*) enquanto; (*when*) quando. **~ a gift** de presente. **~ tall as** tão alto quanto, (*P*) tão alto como □ *pron* que. **I ate the same ~ he** comi o mesmo que ele. **~ for, ~ to** quanto a. **~ from** a partir de. **~ if** como se. **~ much** tanto, tantos. **~ many** quanto, quantos. **~ soon as** logo que. **~ well** (*also*) também. **~ well as** (*in addition to*) assim como
asbestos /æz'bestəs/ *n* asbesto *m*, amianto *m*
ascend /ə'send/ *vt/i* subir. **~ the throne** ascender *or* subir ao trono
ascent /ə'sent/ *n* ascensão *f*; (*slope*) subida *f*, rampa *f*
ascertain /æsə'teɪn/ *vt* certificar-se de. **~ that** certificar-se de que
ascribe /ə'skraɪb/ *vt* atribuir
ash[1] /æʃ/ *n* **~(-tree)** freixo *m*
ash[2] /æʃ/ *n* cinza *f*. **A~ Wednesday** Quarta-feira *f* de Cinzas. **~en** *a* pálido
ashamed /ə'ʃeɪmd/ *a*. **be ~** ter vergonha, ficar envergonhado (**of** de, por)
ashore /ə'ʃɔ:(r)/ *adv* em terra. **go ~** desembarcar
ashtray /'æʃtreɪ/ *n* cinzeiro *m*
Asia /'eɪʃə/ *n* Ásia *f*. **~n** *a & n* asiático (*m*)
aside /ə'saɪd/ *adv* de lado, de parte □ *n* (*theat*) aparte *m*. **~ from** (*Amer*) à parte
ask /a:sk/ *vt/i* pedir; (*a question*) perguntar; (*invite*) convidar. **~ sb sth** pedir uma coisa a alguém. **~ about** informar-se de. **~ after sb** pedir notícias de alg, perguntar por alg. **~ for** pedir. **~ sb in** mandar entrar alg. **~ sb to do sth** pedir alguém para fazer alguma coisa
askew /ə'skju:/ *adv & a* de través, de esguelha
asleep /ə'sli:p/ *adv & a* adormecido; (*numb*) dormente. **fall ~** adormecer
asparagus /ə'spærəgəs/ *n* (*plant*) aspargo *m*, (*P*) espargo *m*; (*culin*) aspargos *mpl*, (*P*) espargo *m*
aspect /'æspekt/ *n* aspecto *m*; (*direction*) exposição *f*
aspersions /ə'spɜ:ʃnz/ *npl* **cast ~ on** caluniar
asphalt /'æsfælt/ *n* asfalto *m* □ *vt* asfaltar
asphyxiat|e /əs'fɪksɪeɪt/ *vt/i* asfixiar. **~ion** /-'eɪʃn/ *n* asfixia *f*
aspir|e /əs'paɪə(r)/ *vi* **~e to** aspirar a. **~ation** /æspə'reɪʃn/ *n* aspiração *f*
aspirin /'æsprɪn/ *n* aspirina *f*
ass /æs/ *n* burro *m*. **make an ~ of o.s.** fazer papel de palhaço, (*P*) fazer figura de parvo
assail /ə'seɪl/ *vt* assaltar, agredir. **~ant** *n* assaltante *mf*, agressor *m*
assassin /ə'sæsɪn/ *n* assassino *m*
assassinat|e /ə'sæsɪneɪt/ *vt* assassinar. **~ion** /-'eɪʃn/ *n* assassinato *m*
assault /ə'sɔ:lt/ *n* assalto *m* □ *vt* assaltar, atacar
assemble /ə'sembl/ *vt* (*people*) reunir; (*fit together*) montar □ *vi* reunir-se
assembly /ə'semblɪ/ *n* assembléia *f*, (*P*) assembleia *f*. **~ line** linha *f* de montagem
assent /ə'sent/ *n* assentimento *m* □ *vi* **~ to** consentir em
assert /ə'sɜ:t/ *vt* afirmar; (*one's rights*) reivindicar. **~ o.s.** impor-se. **~ion** /-ʃn/ *n* asserção *f*. **~ive** *a* dogmático, peremptório. **~iveness** *n* assertividade *f*, (*P*) firmeza *f*

assess /ə'ses/ avaliar; (*payment*) estabelecer o montante de. **~ment** *n* avaliação *f*. **~or** *n* (*valuer*) avaliador *m*
asset /'æset/ *n* (*advantage*) vantagem *f*. **~s** (*comm*) ativo *m*, (*P*) activo *m*; (*possessions*) bens *mpl*
assiduous /ə'sɪdjʊəs/ *a* assíduo
assign /ə'saɪn/ *vt* atribuir, destinar; (*jur*) transmitir. **~ sb to** designar alg para
assignation /æsɪg'neɪʃn/ *n* combinação *f* (de hora e local) de encontro
assignment /ə'saɪnmənt/ *n* tarefa *f*, missão *f*; (*jur*) transmissão *f*
assimilat|e /ə'sɪmɪleɪt/ *vt/i* assimilar(-se). **~ion** /-'eɪʃn/ *n* assimilação *f*
assist /ə'sɪst/ *vt/i* ajudar. **~ance** *n* ajuda *f*, assistência *f*
assistant /ə'sɪstənt/ *n* (*helper*) assistente *mf*, auxiliar *mf*; (*in shop*) ajudante *mf*, empregado *m* □ *a* adjunto
associat|e[1] /ə'səʊʃɪeɪt/ *vt* associar □ *vi* **~e with** conviver com. **~ion** /-'eɪʃn/ *n* associação *f*
associate[2] /ə'səʊʃɪət/ *a* & *n* associado (*m*)
assort|ed /ə'sɔ:tɪd/ *a* variados; (*foods*) sortidos. **~ment** *n* sortimento *m*, (*P*) sortido *m*
assume /ə'sju:m/ *vt* assumir; (*presume*) supor, presumir
assumption /ə'sʌmpʃn/ *n* suposição *f*
assurance /ə'ʃʊərəns/ *n* certeza *f*, garantia *f*; (*insurance*) seguro *m*; (*self-confidence*) segurança *f*, confiança *f*
assure /ə'ʃʊə(r)/ *vt* assegurar. **~d** *a* certo, garantido. **rest ~d that** ficar certo que
asterisk /'æstərɪsk/ *n* asterisco *m*
asthma /'æsmə/ *n* asma *f*. **~tic** /-'mætɪk/ *a* & *n* asmático (*m*)
astonish /ə'stɒnɪʃ/ *vt* espantar. **~ingly** *adv* espantosamente. **~ment** *n* espanto *m*
astound /ə'staʊnd/ *vt* assombrar
astray /ə'streɪ/ *adv* & *a* **go ~** perder-se, extraviar-se. **lead ~** desencaminhar
astride /ə'straɪd/ *adv* & *prep* escarranchado (em)
astringent /ə'strɪndʒənt/ *a* & *n* adstringente (*m*)
astrolog|y /ə'strɒlədʒɪ/ *n* astrologia *f*. **~er** *n* astrólogo *m*
astronaut /'æstrənɔ:t/ *n* astronauta *mf*
astronom|y /ə'strɒnəmɪ/ *n* astronomia *f*. **~er** *n* astrônomo *m*, (*P*) astrónomo *m*. **~ical** /æstrə'nɒmɪkl/ *a* astronômico, (*P*) astronómico
astute /ə'stju:t/ *a* astuto, astucioso. **~ness** *n* astúcia *f*
asylum /ə'saɪləm/ *n* asilo *m*
at /ət/; *emphatic* /æt/ *prep* a, em. **~ sign** *m* arroba. **~ home** em casa. **~ night** à noite. **~ once** imediatamente; (*simultaneously*) ao mesmo tempo. **~ school** na escola. **~ sea** no mar. **~ the door** na porta. **~ times** às vezes. **angry/ surprised ~** zangado/ surpreendido com. **not ~ all** de nada. **no wind ~ all** nenhum vento
ate /et/ *see* **eat**
atheis|t /'eɪθɪɪst/ *n* ateu *m*. **~m** /-zəm/ *n* ateísmo *m*
athlet|e /'æθli:t/ *n* atleta *mf*. **~ic** /-'letɪk/ *a* atlético. **~ics** /-'letɪks/ *n*(*pl*) atletismo *m*
Atlantic /ət'læntɪk/ *a* atlântico □ *n* **~ (Ocean)** Atlântico *m*
atlas /'ætləs/ *n* atlas *m*
atmospher|e /'ætməsfɪə(r)/ *n* atmosfera *f*. **~ic** /-'ferɪk/ *a* atmosférico
atom /'ætəm/ *n* átomo *m*. **~ic** /ə'tɒmɪk/ *a* atômico, (*P*) atómico. **~(ic) bomb** bomba *f* atômica
atomize /'ætəmaɪz/ *vt* atomizar, vaporizar, pulverizar. **~r** /-ə(r)/ *n* pulverizador *m*, vaporizador *m*
atone /ə'təʊn/ *vi* **~ for** expiar. **~ment** *n* expiação *f*
atrocious /ə'trəʊʃəs/ *a* atroz
atrocity /ə'trɒsətɪ/ *n* atrocidade *f*
atrophy /'ætrəfɪ/ *n* atrofia *f* □ *vt/i* atrofiar(-se)
attach /ə'tætʃ/ *vt/i* (*affix*) ligar (-se), prender(-se); (*join*) juntar (-se). **~ed** *a* (*document*) junto, anexo. **be ~ed to** (*like*) estar apegado a. **~ment** *n* ligação *f*; (*affection*) apego *m*; (*accessory*) acessório *m*
attaché /ə'tæʃeɪ/ *n* (*pol*) adido *m*. **~ case** pasta *f*
attack /ə'tæk/ *n* ataque *m* □ *vt/i* atacar. **~er** *n* atacante *mf*
attain /ə'teɪn/ *vt* atingir. **~able** *a* atingível. **~ment** *n* consecução *f*. **~ments** *npl* conhecimentos *mpl*, talentos *mpl* adquiridos
attempt /ə'tempt/ *vt* tentar □ *n* tentativa *f*
attend /ə'tend/ *vt/i* atender (**to** a); (*escort*) acompanhar; (*look after*) tratar; (*meeting*) comparecer a; (*school*) freqüentar, (*P*) frequentar. **~ance** *n* comparecimento *m*; (*times present*) freqüência *f*, (*P*) frequência *f*; (*people*) assistência *f*
attendant /ə'tendənt/ *a* concomitante, que acompanha □ *n* empregado *m*; (*servant*) servidor *m*
attention /ə'tenʃn/ *n* atenção *f*. **~!** (*mil*) sentido! **pay ~** prestar atenção (**to** a)
attentive /ə'tentɪv/ *a* atento; (*considerate*) atencioso

attest /ə'test/ *vt/i* ~ **(to)** atestar. ~ **a signature** reconhecer uma assinatura. ~**ation** /ætə'steɪʃn/ *n* atestação *f*, prova *f*

attic /'ætɪk/ *n* sótão *m*, água-furtada *f*

attitude /'ætɪtju:d/ *n* atitude *f*

attorney /ə'tɜ:nɪ/ *n* (*pl* **-eys**) procurador *m*; (*Amer*) advogado *m*

attract /ə'trækt/ *vt* atrair. ~**ion** /-ʃn/ *n* atração *f*, (*P*) atracção *f*; (*charm*) atrativo *m*, (*P*) atractivo *m*

attractive /ə'træktɪv/ *a* atraente. ~**ly** *adv* atraentemente, agradavelmente

attribute[1] /ə'trɪbju:t/ *vt* ~ **to** atribuir a

attribute[2] /'ætrɪbju:t/ *n* atributo *m*

attrition /ə'trɪʃn/ *n* **war of** ~ guerra *f* de desgaste

aubergine /'əʊbəʒi:n/ *n* berinjela *f*

auburn /'ɔ:bən/ *a* cor de acaju, castanho-avermelhado

auction /'ɔ:kʃn/ *n* leilão *m* □ *vt* leiloar. ~**eer** /-ə'nɪə(r)/ *n* leiloeiro *m*, (*P*) pregoeiro *m*

audaci|ous /ɔ:'deɪʃəs/ *a* audacioso, audaz. ~**ty** /-æsətɪ/ *n* audácia *f*

audible /'ɔ:dəbl/ *a* audível

audience /'ɔ:dɪəns/ *n* auditório *m*; (*theat, radio; interview*) audiência *f*

audiovisual /ɔ:dɪəʊ'vɪʒʊəl/ *a* audio-visual

audit /'ɔ:dɪt/ *n* auditoria *f* □ *vt* fazer uma auditoria

audition /ɔ:'dɪʃn/ *n* audição *f* □ *vt* dar/ fazer uma audição

auditor /'ɔ:dɪtə(r)/ *n* perito-contador *m*, (*P*) perito-contabilista *m*

auditorium /ɔ:dɪ'tɔ:rɪəm/ *n* auditório *m*

augment /ɔ:g'ment/ *vt/i* aumentar(-se)

augur /'ɔ:gə(r)/ *vi* ~ **well/ill** ser de bom ou mau agouro

August /'ɔ:gəst/ *n* Agosto *m*

aunt /a:nt/ *n* tia *f*

au pair /əʊ'peə(r)/ *n* au pair *f*

aura /'ɔ:rə/ *n* aura *f*, emanação *f*

auspices /'ɔ:spɪsɪz/ *npl* **under the** ~ **of** sob os auspícios *or* o patrocínio de

auspicious /ɔ:'spɪʃəs/ *a* auspicioso

auster|e /ɔ:'stɪə(r)/ *a* austero. ~**ity** /-erətɪ/ *n* austeridade *f*

Australia /ɒ'streɪlɪə/ *n* Austrália *f*. ~**n** *a & n* australiano (*m*)

Austria /'ɔstrɪə/ *n* Áustria *f*. ~**n** *a & n* austríaco (*m*)

authentic /ɔ:'θentɪk/ *a* autêntico. ~**ity** /-ən'tɪsətɪ/ *n* autenticidade *f*

authenticate /ɔ:'θentɪkeɪt/ *vt* autenticar

author /'ɔ:θə(r)/ *n* autor *m*, autora *f*. ~**ship** *n* (*origin*) autoria *f*

authoritarian /ɔ:θɒrɪ'teərɪən/ *a* autoritário

authorit|y /ɔ:'θɒrətɪ/ *n* autoridade *f*; (*permission*) autorização *f*. ~**ative** /-ɪtətɪv/ *a* (*trusted*) autorizado; (*manner*) autoritário

authoriz|e /'ɔ:θəraɪz/ *vt* autorizar. ~**ation** /-'zeɪʃn/ *n* autorização *f*

autistic /ɔ:'tɪstɪk/ *a* autista, autístico

autobiography /ɔ:tə'baɪɒgrəfɪ/ *n* autobiografia *f*

autocrat /'ɔ:təkræt/ *n* autocrata *mf*. ~**ic** /-'krætɪk/ *a* autocrático

autograph /'ɔ:təgra:f/ *n* autógrafo *m* □ *vt* autografar

automat|e /'ɔ:təmeɪt/ *vt* automatizar. ~**ion** /ɔ:tə'meɪʃn/ *n* automação *f*

automatic /ɔ:tə'mætɪk/ *a* automático □ *n* (*car*) automático *m*. ~**ally** /-klɪ/ *adv* automaticamente

automobile /'ɔ:təməbi:l/ *n* (*Amer*) automóvel *m*

autonom|y /ɔ:'tɒnəmɪ/ *n* autonomia *f*. ~**ous** *a* autônomo, (*P*) autónomo

autopsy /'ɔ:tɒpsɪ/ *n* autópsia *f*

autumn /'ɔ:təm/ *n* outono *m*. ~**al** /-'tʌmnəl/ *a* outonal

auxiliary /ɔ:g'zɪlɪərɪ/ *a & n* auxiliar (*mf*). ~ **verb** verbo *m* auxiliar

avail /ə'veɪl/ *vt* ~ **o.s. of** servir-se de □ *vi* (*be of use*) valer □ *n* **of no** ~ inútil. **to no** ~ sem resultado, em vão

availab|le /ə'veɪləbl/ *a* disponível. ~**ility** /-'bɪlətɪ/ *n* disponibilidade *f*

avalanche /'ævəla:nʃ/ *n* avalanche *f*

avaric|e /'ævərɪs/ *n* avareza *f*. ~**ious** /-'rɪʃəs/ *a* avarento

avenge /ə'vendʒ/ *vt* vingar

avenue /'ævənju:/ *n* avenida *f*; (*fig: line of approach*) via *f*

average /'ævərɪdʒ/ *n* média *f* □ *a* médio □ *vt* tirar a média de; (*produce, do*) fazer em média □ *vi* ~ **out at** dar de média, dar uma média de. **on** ~ em média

avers|e /ə'vɜ:s/ *a* **be** ~**e to** ser avesso a. ~**ion** /-ʃn/ *n* aversão *f*, repugnância *f*

avert /ə'vɜ:t/ *vt* (*turn away*) desviar; (*ward off*) evitar

aviary /'eɪvɪərɪ/ *n* aviário *m*

aviation /eɪvɪ'eɪʃn/ *n* aviação *f*

avid /'ævɪd/ *a* ávido

avocado /ævə'ka:dəʊ/ *n* (*pl* **-s**) abacate *m*

avoid /ə'vɔɪd/ *vt* evitar. ~**able** *a* que se pode evitar, evitável. ~**ance** *n* evitação *f*

await /ə'weɪt/ *vt* aguardar

awake /ə'weɪk/ *vt/i* (*pt* **awoke**, *pp* **awoken**) acordar □ *a* **be** ~ estar acordado

awaken /ə'weɪkən/ *vt/i* despertar. ~**ing** *n* despertar *m*

award /ə'wɔ:d/ *vt* atribuir, conferir; (*jur*) adjudicar □ *n* recompensa *f*, prêmio *m*, (*P*) prémio *m*; (*scholarship*) bolsa *f*

aware /ə'weə(r)/ *a* ciente, cônscio. **be ~ of** estar consciente de *or* ter consciência de. **become ~ of** tomar consciência de. **make sb ~ of** sensibilizar alg para. **~ness** *n* consciência *f*

away /ə'weɪ/ *adv* (*at a distance*) longe; (*to a distance*) para longe; (*absent*) fora; (*persistently*) sem parar; (*entirely*) completamente. **eight miles ~** a oito milhas (de distância). **four days ~** daí a quatro dias □ *a & n* **~ (match)** jogo *m* fora de casa

awe /ɔ:/ *n* assombro *m*, admiração *f* reverente, terror *m* respeitoso. **~some** *a* assombroso. **~struck** *a* assombrado, aterrado

awful /'ɔ:fl/ *a* terrível. **~ly** *adv* muito, terrivelmente

awhile /ə'waɪl/ *adv* por algum tempo

awkward /'ɔ:kwəd/ *a* difícil; (*clumsy, difficult to use*) desajeitado, maljeitoso; (*inconvenient*) inconveniente; (*embarrassing*)embaraçoso; (*embarrassed*) embaraçado. **an ~ customer** (*colloq*) um preguês perigoso *or* intratàvel

awning /'ɔ:nɪŋ/ *n* toldo *m*

awoke, awoken /ə'wəʊk, ə'wəʊkən/ *see* **awake**

awry /ə'raɪ/ *adv* torto. **go ~** dar errado. **be ~** estar torto

axe /æks/ *n* machado *m* □ *vt* (*pres p* **axing**) (*reduce*) cortar; (*dismiss*) despedir

axiom /'æksɪəm/ *n* axioma *m*

axis /'æksɪs/ *n* (*pl* **axes** /-i:z/) eixo *m*

axle /'æksl/ *n* eixo (de roda) *m*

Azores /ə'zɔ:z/ *n* Açores *mpl*

Bb

BA *abbr see* **Bachelor of Arts**

babble /'bæbl/ *vi* balbuciar; (*baby*) palrar; (*stream*) murmurar □ *n* balbucio *m*; (*of baby*) palrice *f*; (*of stream*) murmúrio *m*

baboon /bə'bu:n/ *n* babuíno *m*

baby /'beɪbɪ/ *n* bebê *m*, (*P*) bebé *m*. **~ carriage** (*Amer*) carrinho *m* de bebê, (*P*) bebé. **~-sit** *vi* tomar conta de crianças. **~-sitter** *n* baby-sitter *mf*, babá *f*

babyish /'beɪbɪɪʃ/ *a* infantil

bachelor /'bætʃələ(r)/ *n* solteiro *m*. **B~of Arts/Science** Bacharel *m* em Letras/ Ciencias

back /bæk/ *n* (*of person, hand, chair*) costas *fpl*; (*of animal*) dorso *m*; (*of car, train*) parte *f* traseira; (*of house, room*) fundo *m*; (*of coin*) reverso *m*; (*of page*) verso *m*; (*football*) beque *m*; zagueiro *m*, (*P*) defesa *m* □ *a* traseiro, posterior; (*taxes*) em atraso □ *adv* atrás, para trás; (*returned*) de volta □ *vt* (*support*) apoiar; (*horse*) apostar em; (*car*) (fazer) recuar □ *vi* recuar. **at the ~ of beyond** em casa do diabo, no fim do mundo. **~-bencher** *n* (*pol*) deputado *m* sem pasta. **~ down** desistir (**from** de). **~ number** número *m* atrasado. **~ out** (*of an undertaking etc*) fugir (ao combinado *etc*). **~ up** (*auto*) fazer marcha à ré, (*P*) atrás; (*comput*) tirar um back-up de. **~-up** *n* apoio *m*; (*comput*) back-up *m*; (*Amer: traffic-jam*) engarrafamento *m* □ *a* de reserva; (*comput*) back-up

backache /'bækeɪk/ *n* dor *f* nas costas

backbiting /'bækbaɪtɪŋ/ *n* maledicência *f*

backbone /'bækbəʊn/ *n* espinha *f* dorsal

backdate /bæk'deɪt/ *vt* antedatar

backer /'bækə(r)/ *n* (*of horse*) apostador *m*; (*of cause*) partidário *m*, apoiante *mf*; (*comm*) patrocinador *m*, financiador *m*

backfire /bæk'faɪə(r)/ *vi* (*auto*) dar explosões no tubo de escape; (*fig*) sair o tiro pela culatra

background /'bækgraʊnd/ *n* (*of picture*) fundo *m*, segundo-plano *m*; (*context*) contexto *m*; (*environment*) meio *m*; (*experience*) formação *f*

backhand /'bækhænd/ *n* (*tennis*) esquerda *f*. **~ed** *a* com as costas da mão. **~ed compliment** cumprimento *m* ambéguo. **~er** /-'hændə(r)/ *n* (*sl: bribe*) suborno *m*, (*P*) luvas *fpl* (*colloq*)

backing /'bækɪŋ/ *n* apoio *m*; (*comm*) patrocínio *m*

backlash /'bæklæʃ/ *n* (*fig*) reação *f* violenta, repercussões *fpl*

backlog /'bæklɒg/ *n* acúmulo *m* (de trabalho *etc*)

backside /'bæksaɪd/ *n* (*colloq: buttocks*) traseiro *m*

backstage /bæk'steɪdʒ/ *a & adv* por detrás dos bastidores

backstroke /'bækstrəʊk/ *n* nado *m* de costas

backtrack /'bæktræk/ *vi* (*fig*) voltar atrás

backward /'bækwəd/ *a* retrógrado; (*retarded*) atrasado; (*step, look, etc*) para trás
backwards /'bækwədz/ *adv* para trás; (*walk*) para trás; (*fall*) de costas, para trás; (*in reverse order*) de trás para diante, às avessas. **go ~ and forwards** ir e vir, andar para trás e para a frente. **know sth ~** saber alg coisa de trás para a frente
backwater /'bækwɔ:tə(r)/ *n* (*pej: place*) lugar *m* atrasado
bacon /'beɪkən/ *n* toucinho *m* defumado; (*in rashers*) bacon *m*
bacteria /bæk'tɪərɪə/ *npl* bactérias *fpl*. **~l** *a* bacteriano
bad /bæd/ *a* (**worse, worst**) mau; (*accident*) grave; (*food*) estragado; (*ill*) doente. **feel ~** sentir-se mal. **~ language** palavrões *mpl*. **~-mannered** *a* mal educado. **~-tempered** *a* mal humorado. **~ly** *adv* mal; (*seriously*) gravemente. **want ~ly** (*desire*) desejar imensamente, ter grande vontade de; (*need*) precisar muito de
badge /bædʒ/ *n* emblema *m*; (*policeman's*) crachá *m*, (*P*) distintivo *m*
badger /'bædʒə(r)/ *n* texugo *m* □ *vt* atormentar; (*pester*) importunar
badminton /'bædmɪntən/ *n* badminton *m*
baffle /'bæfl/ *vt* atrapalhar, desconcertar
bag /bæg/ *n* saco *m*; (*handbag*) bolsa *f*, carteira *f*. **~s** (*luggage*) malas *fpl* □ *vt* (*pt* **bagged**) ensacar; (*colloq: take*) embolsar
baggage /'bægɪdʒ/ *n* bagagem *f*
baggy /'bægɪ/ *a* (*clothes*) muito largo, bufante
bagpipes /'bægpaɪps/ *npl* gaita *f* de foles
Bahamas /bə'ha:məz/ *npl* **the ~** as Bahamas *fpl*
bail[1] /beɪl/ *n* fiança *f* □ *vt* pôr em liberdade sob fiança. **be out on ~** estar solto sob fiança
bail[2] /beɪl/ *vt* **~ (out)** (*naut*) esgotar, tirar água de
bailiff /'beɪlɪf/ *n* (*officer*) oficial *m* de diligências; (*of estate*) feitor *m*
bait /beɪt/ *n* isca *f* □ *vt* pôr isca; (*fig*) atormentar (com insultos), atazanar
bak|e /beɪk/ *vt/i* cozer (no forno); (*bread, cakes, etc*) assar; (*in the sun*) torrar. **~er** *n* padeiro *m*; (*of cakes*) doceiro *m*. **~ing** *n* cozedura *f*; (*batch*) fornada *f*. **~ing-powder** *n* fermento *m* em pó. **~ing tin** forma *f*
bakery /'beɪkərɪ/ *n* padaria *f*; (*cakes*) confeitaria *f*
balance /'bæləns/ *n* equilíbrio *m*; (*scales*) balança *f*; (*sum*) saldo *m*; (*comm*) balanço *m*. **~ of power** equilíbrio *m* político. **~ of trade** balança *f* comercial. **~-sheet** *n* balanço *m* □ *vt* equilibrar; (*weigh up*) pesar; (*budget*) equilibrar □ *vi* equilibrar-se. **~d** *a* equilibrado
balcony /'bælkənɪ/ *n* balcão *m*; (*in a house*) varanda *f*
bald /bɔ:ld/ *a* (**-er, -est**) calvo, careca; (*tyre*) careca. **~ing** *a* **be ~ing** ficar calvo. **~ly** *adv* a nu e cru, (*P*) secamente. **~ness** *n* calvície *f*
bale[1] /beɪl/ *n* (*of straw*) fardo *m*; (*of cotton*) balote *m* □ *vt* enfardar
bale[2] /beɪl/ *vi* **~ out** saltar em páraquedas
balk /bɔ:k/ *vt* frustrar, contrariar □ *vi* **~ at** assustar-se com, recuar perante
ball[1] /bɔ:l/ *n* bola *f*. **~-bearing** *n* rolamento *m* de esferas. **~-cock** *n* válvula *f* de depósito de água. **~-point** *n* esferográfica *f*
ball[2] /bɔ:l/ *n* (*dance*) baile *m*
ballad /'bæləd/ *n* balada *f*
ballast /'bæləst/ *n* lastro *m*
ballerina /bælə'ri:nə/ *n* bailarina *f*
ballet /'bæleɪ/ *n* balé *m*, (*P*) ballet *m*, bailado *m*
balloon /bə'lu:n/ *n* balão *m*
ballot /'bælət/ *n* escrutínio *m*. **~(-paper)** *n* cédula *f* eleitoral, (*P*) boletim *m* de voto. **~-box** *n* urna *f* □ *vi* (*pt* **balloted**) (*pol*) votar □ *vt* (*members*) consultar por voto secreto
ballroom /'bɔ:lru:m/ *n* salão *m* de baile
balm /ba:m/ *n* bálsamo *m*. **~y** *a* balsâmico; (*mild*) suave
balustrade /bælə'streɪd/ *n* balaustrada *f*
bamboo /bæm'bu:/ *n* bambu *m*
ban /bæn/ *vt* (*pt* **banned**) banir. **~ from** proibir de □ *n* proibição *f*
banal /bə'na:l/ *a* banal. **~ity** /-ælətɪ/ *n* banalidade *f*
banana /bə'na:nə/ *n* banana *f*
band /bænd/ *n* (*for fastening*) cinta *f*, faixa *f*; (*strip*) tira *f*, banda *f*; (*mus: mil*) banda *f*; (*mus: dance, jazz*) conjunto *m*; (*group*) bando *m* □ *vi* **~ together** juntar-se
bandage /'bændɪdʒ/ *n* atadura *f*, (*P*) ligadura *f* □ *vt* ligar
bandit /'bændɪt/ *n* bandido *m*
bandstand /'bændstænd/ *n* coreto *m*
bandwagon /'bændwægən/ *n* **climb on the ~** (*fig*) apanhar o trem
bandy /'bændɪ/ *vt* trocar. **~ a story about** espalhar uma história
bandy-legged /'bændɪlegd/ *a* cambaio, de pernas tortas
bang /bæŋ/ *n* (*blow*) pancada *f*; (*loud noise*) estouro *m*, estrondo

m; (*of gun*) detonação *f* ◻ *vt*/*i* (*hit, shut*) bater ◻ *vi* explodir ◻ *int* pum. ~ **in the middle** jogar no meio. **shut the door with a** ~ bater (com) a porta

banger /'bæŋə(r)/ *n* (*firework*) bomba *f*; (*sl: sausage*) salsicha *f*. **(old)** ~ (*sl: car*) calhambeque *m* (*colloq*)

bangle /'bæŋgl/ *n* pulseira *f*, bracelete *m*

banish /'bænɪʃ/ *vt* banir, desterrar

banisters /'bænɪstəz/ *npl* corrimão *m*

banjo /'bændʒəʊ/ *pl* (**-os**) banjo *m*

bank[1] /bæŋk/ *n* (*of river*) margem *f*; (*of earth*) talude *m*; (*of sand*) banco *m* ◻ *vt* amontoar ◻ *vi* (*aviat*) inclinar-se numa curva

bank[2] /bæŋk/ *n* (*comm*) banco *m* ◻ *vt* depositar no banco. ~ **account** conta *f* bancária. ~ **holiday** feriado *m* nacional. ~ **on** contar com. ~ **rate** taxa *f* bancária. ~ **with** ter conta em

bank|er /'bæŋkə(r)/ *n* banqueiro *m*. ~**ing** /-ɪŋ/ *n* operações *fpl* bancárias; (*career*) carreira *f* bancária, banca *f*

banknote /'bæŋknəʊt/ *n* nota *f* de banco

bankrupt /'bæŋkrʌpt/ *a* & *n* falido (*m*). **go** ~ falir ◻ *vt* levar à falência. ~**cy** *n* falência *f*, bancarrota *f*

banner /'bænə(r)/ *n* bandeira *f*, estandarte *m*

banns /bænz/ *npl* proclamas *mpl*, (*P*) banhos *mpl*

banquet /'bæŋkwɪt/ *n* banquete *m*

banter /'bæntə(r)/ *n* gracejo *m*, brincadeira *f* ◻ *vi* gracejar, brincar

baptism /'bæptɪzəm/ *n* batismo *m*, (*P*) baptismo *m*

Baptist /'bæptɪst/ *n* batista *mf*, (*P*) baptista *mf*

baptize /bæp'taɪz/ *vt* batizar, (*P*) baptizar

bar /ba:(r)/ *n* (*of chocolate*) tablette *f*, barra *f*; (*of metal, soap, sand etc*) barra *f*; (*of door, window*) tranca *f*; (*in pub*) bar *m*; (*counter*) balcão *m*, bar *m*; (*mus*) barra *f* de compasso; (*fig: obstacle*) barreira *f*; (*in lawcourt*) teia *f*. **the B**~ a advocacia *f* ◻ *vt* (*pt* **barred**) (*obstruct*) barrar; (*prohibit*) proibir (**from** de); (*exclude*) excluir; (*door, window*) trancar ◻ *prep* salvo, exceto, (*P*) excepto. ~ **none** sem exceção, (*P*) excepção. ~ **code** código *m* de barra. **behind** ~**s** na cadeia

Barbados /ba:'beɪdɒs/ *n* Barbados *mpl*

barbarian /ba:'beərɪən/ *n* bárbaro *m*

barbari|c /ba:'bærɪk/ *a* bárbaro. ~**ty** /-ətɪ/ *n* barbaridade *f*

barbarous /'ba:bərəs/ *a* bárbaro

barbecue /'ba:bɪkju:/ *n* (*grill*) churrasqueira *f*; (*occasion, food*) churrasco *m* ◻ *vt* assar

barbed /ba:bd/ *a* ~ **wire** arame *m* farpado

barber /'ba:bə(r)/ *n* barbeiro *m*

barbiturate /ba:'bɪtjʊrət/ *n* barbitúrico *m*

bare /beə(r)/ *a* (**-er, -est**) nu; (*room*) vazio; (*mere*) mero ◻ *vt* pôr à mostra, pôr a nu, descobrir

bareback /'beəbæk/ *adv* em pêlo

barefaced /'beəfeɪst/ *a* descarado

barefoot /'beə(r)fʊt/ *adv* descalço

barely /'beəlɪ/ *adv* apenas, mal

bargain /'ba:gɪn/ *n* (*deal*) negócio *m*; (*good buy*) pechincha *f* ◻ *vi* negociar; (*haggle*) regatear. ~ **for** esperar

barge /ba:dʒ/ *n* barcaça *f* ◻ *vi* ~ **in** interromper (despropositadamente); (*into room*) irromper

bark[1] /ba:k/ *n* (*of tree*) casca *f*

bark[2] /ba:k/ *n* (*of dog*) latido *m* ◻ *vi* latir. **his** ~ **is worse than his bite** cão que ladra não morde

barley /'ba:lɪ/ *n* cevada *f*. ~ **sugar** *n* açúcar *m* de cevada. ~ **water** *n* água *f* de cevada

barmaid /'ba:meɪd/ *n* empregada *f* de bar

barman /'ba:mən/ *n* (*pl* **-men**) barman *m*, empregado *m* de bar

barmy /'ba:mɪ/ *a* (*sl*) maluco

barn /ba:n/ *n* celeiro *m*

barometer /bə'rɒmɪtə(r)/ *n* barômetro *m*, (*P*) barómetro *m*

baron /'bærən/ *n* barão *m*. ~**ess** *n* baronesa *f*

baroque /bə'rɒk/ *a* & *n* barroco (*m*)

barracks /'bærəks/ *n* quartel *m*, caserna *f*

barrage /'bæra:ʒ/ *n* barragem *f*; (*fig*) enxurrada *f*; (*mil*) fogo *m* de barragem

barrel /'bærəl/ *n* (*of oil, wine*) barril *m*; (*of gun*) cano *m*. ~**-organ** *n* realejo *m*

barren /'bærən/ *a* estéril; (*soil*) árido, estéril

barricade /bærɪ'keɪd/ *n* barricada *f* ◻ *vt* barricar

barrier /'bærɪə(r)/ *n* barreira *f*; (*hindrance*) entrave *m*, barreira *f*

barring /'ba:rɪŋ/ *prep* salvo, exceto, (*P*) excepto

barrister /'bærɪstə(r)/ *n* advogado *m*

barrow /'bærəʊ/ *n* carrinho *m* de mão

barter /'ba:tə(r)/ *n* troca *f* ◻ *vt* trocar

base /beɪs/ *n* base *f* ◻ *vt* basear (**on** em) ◻ *a* baixo, ignóbil. ~**less** *a* infundado

baseball /'beɪsbɔ:l/ *n* beisebol *m*

basement /'beɪsmənt/ *n* porão *m*, (*P*) cave *f*

bash /bæʃ/ *vt* bater com violência ◻ *n* pancada *f* forte. **have a** ~ **at** (*sl*) experimentar

bashful /'bæʃfl/ *a* tímido

basic /'beɪsɪk/ *a* básico, elementar, fundamental. ~**ally** *adv* basicamente, no fundo

basil /'bæzl/ *n* mangericão *m*

basin /'beɪsn/ *n* bacia *f*; (*for food*) tigela *f*; (*naut*) ante-doca *f*; (*for washing*) pia *f*

basis /'beɪsɪs/ *n* (*pl* **bases** /-si:z/) base *f*

bask /ba:sk/ *vi* ~ **in the sun** apanhar sol

basket /'ba:skɪt/ *n* cesto *m*

basketball /'ba:skɪtbɔ:l/ *n* basquete(bol) *m*

Basque /ba:sk/ *a* & *n* basco (*m*)

bass[1] /bæs/ *n* (*pl* **bass**) (*fish*) perca *f*

bass[2] /beɪs/ *a* (*mus*) grave □ *n* (*pl* **basses**) (*mus*) baixo *m*

bassoon /bə'su:n/ *n* fagote *m*

bastard /'ba:stəd/ *n* (*illegitimate child*) bastardo *m*; (*sl: pej*) safado (*sl*) *m*; (*colloq: not pej*) cara (*colloq*) *m*

baste /beɪst/ *vt* (*culin*) regar (com molho)

bastion /'bæstɪən/ *n* bastião *m*, baluarte *m*

bat[1] /bæt/ *n* (*cricket*) pá *f*; (*baseball*) bastão *m*; (*table tennis*) rafuete *f* □ *vt*/*i* (*pt* **batted**) bater (em). **without ~ting an eyelid** sem pestanejar

bat[2] /bæt/ *n* (*zool*) morcego *m*

batch /bætʃ/ *n* (*loaves*) fornada *f*; (*people*) monte *m*; (*goods*) remessa *f*; (*papers, letters etc*) batelada *f*, monte *m*

bated /'beɪtɪd/ *a* **with ~ breath** com a respiração em suspenso, com a respiração suspensa

bath /ba:θ/ *n* (*pl* **-s** /ba:ðz/) banho *m*; (*tub*) banheira *f*. **~s** (*washing*) banho *m* público; (*swimming*) piscina *f* □ *vt* dar banho a □ *vi* tomar banho

bathe /beɪð/ *vt* dar banho em; (*wound*) limpar □ *vi* tomar banho (de mar) □ *n* banho *m* (de mar). **~r** /-ə(r)/ *n* banhista *mf*

bathing /'beɪðɪŋ/ *n* banho *m* de mar. **~-costume/-suit** *n* traje *m* de banho, (*P*) fato *m* de banho

bathrobe /'ba:θrəʊb/ *n* (*Amer*) roupão *m*

bathroom /'ba:θru:m/ *n* banheiro *m*, (*P*) casa *f* de banho

baton /'bætən/ *n* (*mus*) batuta *f*; (*policeman's*) cassetete *m*; (*mil*) bastão *m*

battalion /bə'tælɪən/ *n* batalhão *m*

batter /'bætə(r)/ *vt* bater, espancar, maltratar □ *n* (*culin: for cakes*) massa *f* de bolos; (*culin: for frying*) massa *f* de empanar. **~ed** *a* (car, pan) amassado; (*child, wife*) maltratado, espancado. **~ing** *n* **take a ~ing** levar pancada *or* uma surra

battery /'bætərɪ/ *n* (*mil, auto*) bateria *f*; (*electr*) pilha *f*

battle /'bætl/ *n* batalha *f*; (*fig*) luta *f* □ *vi* combater, batalhar, lutar

battlefield /'bætlfi:ld/ *n* campo *m* de batalha

battlements /'bætlmənts/ *npl* ameias *fpl*

battleship /'bætlʃɪp/ *n* couraçado *m*

baulk /bɔ:lk/ *vt*/*i* = **balk**

bawdy /'bɔ:dɪ/ *a* (**-ier, -iest**) obsceno, indecente

bawl /bɔ:l/ *vt*/*i* berrar

bay[1] /beɪ/ *n* (*bot*) loureiro *m*

bay[2] /beɪ/ *n* (*geog*) baía *f*. **~ window** janela *f* saliente

bay[3] /beɪ/ *n* (*bark*) latido *m* □ *vi* latir. **at ~** (*animal; fig*) cercado, (*P*) em apuros. **keep at ~** manter à distância

bayonet /'beɪənɪt/ *n* baioneta *f*

bazaar /bə'za:(r)/ *n* bazar *m*

BC *abbr* (*before Christ*) a C

be /bi:/ *vi* (*pres* **am, are, is**; *pt* **was, were**; *pp* **been**) (*permanent quality/place*) ser; (*temporary place/state*) estar; (*become*) ficar. **~ hot/right** *etc* ter calor/razão *etc*. **he's 30** (*age*) ele tem 30 anos. **it's fine/cold** *etc* (*weather*) faz bom tempo/ frio *etc*. **how are you?** (*health*) como está? **I'm a doctor — are you?** eu sou médico — é mesmo? **it's pretty, isn't it?** é bonito, não é? **he is to come** (*must*) ele deve vir. **how much is it?** (*cost*) quanto é? **~ reading eating** *etc* estar lendo/comendo *etc*. **the money was found** o dinheiro foi encontrado. **have been to** ter ido a, ter estado em

beach /bi:tʃ/ *n* praia *f*

beacon /'bi:kən/ *n* farol *m*; (*marker*) baliza *f*

bead /bi:d/ *n* conta *f*. **~ of sweat** gota *f* de suor

beak /bi:k/ *n* bico *m*

beaker /'bi:kə(r)/ *n* copo *m* de plástico com bico; (*in lab*) proveta *f*

beam /bi:m/ *n* (*of wood*) trave *f*, viga *f*; (*of light*) raio *m*; (*of torch*) feixe *m* de luz □ *vt*/*i* (*radiate*) irradiar; (*fig*) sorrir radiante. **~ing** *a* radiante

bean /bi:n/ *n* feijão *m*. **broad ~** fava *f*. **coffee ~s** café *m* em grão. **runner ~** feijão *m* verde

bear[1] /beə(r)/ *n* urso *m*

bear[2] /beə(r)/ *vt*/*i* (*pt* **bore**, *pp* **borne**) sustentar, suportar; (*endure*) agüentar, (*P*) aguentar, suportar; (*child*) dar à luz. **~ in mind** ter em mente, lembrar. **~ left** virar à esquerda. **~ on** relacionar-se com, ter a ver com. **~ out** confirmar. **~ up!** coragem! **~able** *a* tolerável, suportável. **~er** *n* portador *m*

beard /bɪəd/ *n* barba *f*. **~ed** *a* barbado, com barba

bearing /'beərɪŋ/ *n* (*manner*) porte *m*; (*relevance*) relação *f*; (*naut*) marcação *f*. **get one's ~s** orientar-se

beast /bi:st/ *n* (*animal, person*) besta *f*, animal *m*; (*in fables*) fera *f*. **~ of burden** besta *f* de carga

beat /bi:t/ *vt*/*i* (*pt* **beat**, *pp* **beaten**) bater □ *n* (*med*) batimento *m*; (*mus*)

compasso *m*, ritmo *m*; (*of drum*) toque *m*; (*of policeman*) ronda *f*, (*P*) giro *m*. **~ about the bush** estar com rodeios. **~ a retreat** bater em retirada. **~ it** (*sl: go away*) pôr-se a andar. **it ~s me** (*colloq*) não consigo entender. **~ up** espancar. **~er** *n* (*culin*) batedeira *f*. **~ing** *n* sova *f*
beautician /bju:'tɪʃn/ *n* esteticista *mf*
beautiful /'bju:tɪfl/ *a* belo, lindo. **~ly** *adv* lindamente
beautify /'bju:tɪfaɪ/ *vt* embelezar
beauty /'bju:tɪ/ *n* beleza *f*. **~ parlour** instituto *m* de beleza. **~ spot** sinal *m* no rosto, mosca *f*; (*place*) local *m* pitoresco
beaver /'bi:və(r)/ *n* castor *m*
became /bɪ'keɪm/ *see* **become**
because /bɪ'kɒz/ *conj* porque □ *adv* **~ of** por causa de
beckon /'bekən/ *vt/i* **~ (to)** fazer sinal (para)
become /bɪ'kʌm/ *vt/i* (*pt* **became**, *pp* **become**) tornar-se; (*befit*) ficar bem a. **what has ~ of her?** que é feito dela?
becoming /bɪ'kʌmɪŋ/ *a* que fica bem, apropriado
bed /bed/ *n* cama *f*; (*layer*) camada *f*; (*of sea*) fundo *m*; (*of river*) leito *m*; (*of flowers*) canteiro *m* □ *vt/i* (*pt* **bedded**) **~ down** ir deitar-se. **~ in** plantar. **~ and breakfast** (**b & b**) quarto *m* com café da manhã. **~-sit(ter)** *n* (*colloq*) mixto *m* de quarto e sala. **go to~** ir para cama. **in ~** na cama. **~ding** *n* roupa *f* de cama
bedclothes /'bedkləʊðz/ *n* roupa *f* de cama
bedlam /'bedləm/ *n* confusão *f*, balbúrdia *f*
bedraggled /bɪ'drægld/ *a* (*wet*) molhado; (*untidy*) desarrumado; (*dishevelled*) desgrenhado
bedridden /'bedrɪdn/ *a* preso ao leito, doente de cama
bedroom /'bedru:m/ *n* quarto *m* de dormir
bedside /'bedsaɪd/ *n* cabeceira *f*. **~ manner** (*doctor's*) modos *mpl* que inspiram confiança
bedspread /'bedspred/ *n* colcha *f*
bedtime /'bedtaɪm/ *n* hora *f* de deitar, hora *f* de ir para a cama
bee /bi:/ *n* abelha *f*. **make a ~-line for** ir direto a
beech /bi:tʃ/ *n* faia *f*
beef /bi:f/ *n* carne *f* de vaca
beefburger /'bi:fbɜ:gə(r)/ *n* hambúrguer *m*
beehive /'bi:haɪv/ *n* colméia *f*
been /bi:n/ *see* **be**
beer /bɪə(r)/ *n* cerveja *f*
beet /bi:t/ *n* beterraba *f*
beetle /'bi:tl/ *n* escaravelho *m*
beetroot /'bi:tru:t/ *n* (raiz de) beterraba *f*
before /bɪ'fɔ:(r)/ *prep* (*time*) antes de; (*place*) em frente de □ *adv* antes; (*already*) já □ *conj* antes que. **~ leaving** antes de partir. **~ he leaves** antes que ele parta, antes de ele partir
beforehand /bɪ'fɔ:hænd/ *adv* de antemão, antecipadamente
befriend /bɪ'frend/ *vt* tornar-se amigo de; (*be helpful to*) auxiliar
beg /beg/ *vt/i* (*pt* **begged**) mendigar; (*entreat*) suplicar. **~ sb's pardon** pedir desculpa a alg. **~ the question** fazer uma petição de princípio. **it's going ~ging** está sobrando
began /bɪ'gæn/ *see* **begin**
beggar /'begə(r)/ *n* mendigo *m*, pedinte *mf*; (*colloq: person*) cara (*colloq*) *m*
begin /bɪ'gɪn/ *vt/i* (*pt* **began**, *pp* **begun**, *pres p* **beginning**) começar, principiar. **~ner** *n* principiante *mf*. **~ning** *n* começo *m*, princípio *m*
begrudge /bɪ'grʌdʒ/ *vt* ter inveja de; (*give*) dar de má vontade. **~ doing** fazer de má vontade *or* a contragosto
beguile /bɪ'gaɪl/ *vt* enganar
begun /bɪ'gʌn/ *see* **begin**
behalf /bɪ'ha:f/ *n* **on ~ of** em nome de; (*in the interest of*) em favor de
behave /bɪ'heɪv/ *vi* portar-se. **~ (o.s.)** portar-se bem
behaviour /bɪ'heɪvjə(r)/ *n* conduta *f*, comportamento *m*
behead /bɪ'hed/ *vt* decapitar
behind /bɪ'haɪnd/ *prep* atrás de □ *adv* atrás; (*late*) com atraso □ *n* (*colloq: buttocks*) traseiro (*colloq*) *m*. **~ the times** antiquado, retrógrado. **leave ~** deixar para trás
behold /bɪ'həʊld/ *vt* (*pt* **beheld**) (*old use*) ver
beholden /bɪ'həʊldən/ *a* em dívida (**to** para com)
beige /beɪʒ/ *a* & *n* bege (*m*), (*P*) beige (*m*)
being /'bi:ɪŋ/ *n* ser *m*. **bring into ~** criar. **come into ~** nascer, originar-se
belated /bɪ'leɪtɪd/ *a* tardio, atrasado
belch /beltʃ/ *vi* arrotar □ *vt* **~ out** (*smoke*) vomitar, lançar □ *n* arroto *m*
belfry /'belfrɪ/ *n* campanário *m*
Belgi|um /'beldʒəm/ *n* Bélgica *f*. **~an** *a* & *n* belga (*mf*)
belief /bɪ'li:f/ *n* crença *f*; (*trust*) confiança *f*; (*opinion*) convicção *f*
believ|e /bɪ'li:v/ *vt/i* acreditar. **~e in** acreditar em. **~able** *a* crível. **~er** /-ə(r)/ *n* crente *mf*
belittle /bɪ'lɪtl/ *vt* depreciar

bell /bel/ *n* sino *m*; (*small*) sineta *f*; (*on door, of phone*) campainha *f*; (*on cat, toy*) guizo *m*

belligerent /bɪ'lɪdʒərənt/ *a* & *n* beligerante (*mf*)

bellow /'beləʊ/ *vt/i* berrar, bramir. **~ out** rugir

bellows /'beləʊz/ *npl* fole *m*

belly /'belɪ/ *n* barriga *f*, ventre *m*. **~-ache** *n* dor *f* de barriga

bellyful /'belɪfʊl/ *n* **have a ~** estar com a barriga cheia

belong /bɪ'lɒŋ/ *vi* **~ (to)** pertencer (a); (*club*) ser sócio (de)

belongings /bɪ'lɒŋɪŋz/ *npl* pertences *mpl*. **personal ~** objetos *mpl* de uso pessoal

beloved /bɪ'lʌvɪd/ *a* & *n* amado (*m*)

below /bɪ'ləʊ/ *prep* abaixo de, debaixo de ▫ *adv* abaixo, em baixo; (*on page*) abaixo

belt /belt/ *n* cinto *m*; (*techn*) correia *f*; (*fig*) zona *f* ▫ *vt* (*sl: hit*) zurzir ▫ *vi* (*sl: rush*) safar-se

bemused /bɪ'mju:zd/ *a* estonteado, confuso; (*thoughtful*) pensativo

bench /bentʃ/ *n* banco *m*; (*seat, working-table*) bancada *f*. **the ~** (*jur*) os magistrados (no tribunal)

bend /bend/ *vt/i* (*pt* & *pp* **bent**) curvar (-se); (*arm, leg*) dobrar; (*road, river*) fazer uma curva, virar ▫ *n* curva *f*. **~ over** debruçar-se *or* inclinar-se sobre

beneath /bɪ'ni:θ/ *prep* abaixo de, debaixo de; (*fig*) abaixo de ▫ *adv* debaixo, em baixo

benediction /benɪ'dɪkʃn/ *n* benção *f*

benefactor /'benɪfæktə(r)/ *n* benfeitor *m*

beneficial /benɪ'fɪʃl/ *a* benéfico, proveitoso

benefit /'benɪfɪt/ *n* (*advantage, performance*) benefício *m*; (*profit*) proveito *m*; (*allowance*) subsídio *m* ▫ *vt/i* (*pt* **benefited**, *pres p* **benefiting**) (*be useful to*) beneficiar (**by** de); (*do good to*) beneficiar, fazer bem a; (*receive benefit*) lucrar, ganhar (**by, from** com)

beneficiary /benɪ'fɪʃərɪ/ *n* beneficiário *m*

benevolen|t /bɪ'nevələnt/ *a* benevolente. **~ce** *n* benevolência *f*

benign /bɪ'naɪn/ *a* (*incl med*) benigno

bent /bent/ *see* **bend** ▫ *n* (**for** para) (*skill*) aptidão *f*, jeito *m*; (*liking*) queda *f* ▫ *a* curvado; (*twisted*) torcido; (*sl: dishonest*) desonesto. **~ on** decidido a

bequeath /bɪ'kwi:ð/ *vt* legar

bequest /bɪ'kwest/ *n* legado *m*

bereave|d /bɪ'ri:vd/ *a* **the ~d wife**/*etc* a esposa/*etc* do falecido. **the ~d family** a familia enlutada. **~ment** *n* luto *m*

bereft /bɪ'reft/ *a* **~ of** privado de

beret /'bereɪ/ *n* boina *f*

Bermuda /bə'mju:də/ *n* Bermudas *fpl*

berry /'berɪ/ *n* baga *f*

berserk /bə'sɜ:k/ *a* **go ~** ficar louco de raiva, perder a cabeça

berth /bɜ:θ/ *n* (*in ship*) beliche *m*; (*in train*) couchette *f*; (*anchorage*) ancoradouro *m* ▫ *vi* atracar. **give a wide ~ to** passar ao largo, (*P*) de largo

beside /bɪ'saɪd/ *prep* ao lado de, junto de. **~ o.s.** fora de si. **be ~ the point** não ter nada a ver com o assunto, não vir ao caso

besides /bɪ'saɪdz/ *prep* além de; (*except*) fora, salvo ▫ *adv* além disso

besiege /bɪ'si:dʒ/ *vt* sitiar, cercar. **~ with** assediar

best /best/ *a* & *n* **(the) ~** (o/a) melhor (*mf*) ▫ *adv* melhor. **~ man** padrinho *m* de casamento. **at (the) ~** na melhor das hipóteses. **do one's ~** fazer o (melhor) que se pode. **make the ~ of** tirar o melhor partido de. **the ~ part of** a maior parte de. **to the ~ of my knowledge** que eu saiba

bestow /bɪ'stəʊ/ *vt* conferir. **~ praise** fazer *or* tecer elogios

best-seller /best'selə(r)/ *n* best-seller *m*

bet /bet/ *n* aposta *f* ▫ *vt/i* (*pt* **bet** *or* **betted**) apostar (**on** em)

betray /bɪ'treɪ/ *vt* trair. **~al** *n* traição *f*

better /'betə(r)/ *a* & *adv* melhor ▫ *vt* melhorar ▫ *n* **our ~s** os nossos superiores *mpl*. **all the ~** tanto melhor. **~ off** (*richer*) mais rico. **he's ~ off at home** é melhor para ele ficar em casa. **I'd ~ go** é melhor ir-me embora. **the ~ part of it** a maior parte disso. **get ~** melhorar. **get the ~ of sb** levar a melhor em relação a alg

betting-shop /'betɪŋʃɒp/ *n* agência *f* de apostas

between /bɪ'twi:n/ *prep* entre ▫ *adv* **in ~** no meio, no intervalo. **~ you and me** aqui entre nós

beverage /'bevərɪdʒ/ *n* bebida *f*

beware /bɪ'weə(r)/ *vi* acautelar-se (**of** com), tomar cuidado (**of** com)

bewilder /bɪ'wɪldə(r)/ *vt* desorientar. **~ment** *n* desorientação *f*, confusão *f*

bewitch /bɪ'wɪtʃ/ *vt* encantar, cativar

beyond /bɪ'jɒnd/ *prep* além de; (*doubt, reach*) fora de ▫ *adv* além. **it's ~ me** isso ultrapassa-me. **he lives ~ his means** ele vive acima dos seus meios

bias /'baɪəs/ *n* parcialidade *f*; (*pej: prejudice*) preconceito *m*; (*sewing*) viés *m* ▫ *vt* (*pt* **biased**) influenciar. **~ed** *a* parcial. **~-ed against** de prevenção contra, (*P*) de pé atrás contra

bib /bɪb/ *n* babeiro *m*, babette *m*
Bible /'baɪbl/ *n* Bíblia *f*
biblical /'bɪblɪkl/ *a* bíblico
bibliography /bɪblɪ'ɒgrəfɪ/ *n* bibliografia *f*
bicarbonate /baɪ'ka:bənət/ *n* ~ **of soda** bicarbonato *m* de soda
biceps /'baɪseps/ *n* bíceps *m*
bicker /'bɪkə(r)/ *vi* questionar, discutir
bicycle /'baɪsɪkl/ *n* bicicleta *f* ◻ *vi* andar de bicicleta
bid /bɪd/ *n* oferta *f*, lançe *m*; (*attempt*) tentativa *f* ◻ *vt/i* (*pt* **bid**, *pres p* **bidding**) fazer uma oferta, lançar, oferecer como lançe. ~**der** *n* licitante *mf*. **the highest ~der** quem dá *or* oferece mais
bide /baɪd/ *vt* ~ **one's time** esperar pelo bom momento
bidet /'bi:deɪ/ *n* bidê *m*, (*P*) bidé *m*
biennial /baɪ'enɪəl/ *a* bienal
bifocals /baɪ'fəʊklz/ *npl* óculos *mpl* bifocais
big /bɪg/ *a* (**bigger, biggest**) grande; (*sl: generous*) generoso ◻ *adv* (*colloq*) em grande. ~**-headed** *a* pretensioso, convencido. ~ **shot** (*sl*) manda-chuva *m*. **talk** ~ gabar-se (*colloq*). **think** ~ (*colloq*) ter grandes planos
bigam|y /'bɪgəmɪ/ *n* bigamia *f*. ~**ist** *n* bígamo *m*. ~**ous** *a* bígamo
bigot /'bɪgət/ *n* fanático *m*, intolerante *mf*. ~**ed** *a* fanático, intolerante. ~**ry** *n* fanatismo *m*, intolerância *f*
bigwig /'bɪgwɪg/ *n* (*colloq*) manda-chuva *m*
bike /baɪk/ *n* (*colloq*) bicicleta *f*
bikini /bɪ'ki:nɪ/ *n* (*pl* **-is**) biquíni *m*
bilberry /'bɪlbərɪ/ *n* arando *m*
bile /baɪl/ *n* bílis *f*
bilingual /baɪ'lɪŋgwəl/ *a* bilíngüe
bilious /'bɪlɪəs/ *a* bilioso
bill[1] /bɪl/ *n* (*invoice*) fatura *f*, (*P*) factura *f*; (*in restaurant*) conta *f*; (*pol*) projeto *m*, (*P*) projecto *m* de lei; (*Amer: banknote*) nota *f* de banco; (*poster*) cartaz *m* ◻ *vt* faturar, (*P*) facturar; (*theatre*) anunciar, pôr no programa. ~ **of exchange** letra *f* de câmbio. ~ **sb for** apresentar a alg a conta de
bill[2] /bɪl/ *n* (*of bird*) bico *m*
billiards /'bɪlɪədz/ *n* bilhar *m*
billion /'bɪlɪən/ *n* (10^9) mil milhões; (10^{12}) um milhão de milhões
bin /bɪn/ *n* (*for storage*) caixa *f*, lata *f*; (*for rubbish*) lata *f* do lixo, (*P*) caixote *m*
bind /baɪnd/ *vt* (*pt* **bound**) (*tie*) atar; (*book*) encadernar; (*jur*) obrigar; (*cover the edge of*) debruar ◻ *n* (*sl: bore*) chatice *f* (*sl*). **be ~ing on** ser obrigatório para
binding /'baɪndɪŋ/ *n* encadernação *f*; (*braid*) debrum *m*
binge /bɪndʒ/ *n* (*sl*) **go on a** ~ cair na farra; (*overeat*) empanturrar-se
bingo /'bɪŋgəʊ/ *n* bingo *m* ◻ *int* acertei!
binoculars /bɪ'nɒkjʊləz/ *npl* binóculo *m*
biochemistry /baɪəʊ'kemɪstrɪ/ *n* bioquímica *f*
biodegradable /baɪəʊdɪ'greɪdəbl/ *a* biodegradável
biograph|y /baɪ'ɒgrəfɪ/ *n* biografia *f*. ~**er** *n* biógrafo *m*
biolog|y /baɪ'ɒlədʒɪ/ *n* biologia *f*. ~**ical** /-ə'lɒdʒɪkl/ *a* biológico. ~**ist** *n* biólogo *m*
biopsy /'baɪɒpsɪ/ *n* biópsia *f*
birch /bɜ:tʃ/ *n* (*tree*) bétula *f*
bird /bɜ:d/ *n* ave *f*, pássaro *m*; (*sl: girl*) garota *f* (*colloq*). ~ **flu** gripe *f* das aves. ~ **sanctuary** refúgio *m* ornitológico. ~**-watcher** *n* ornitófilo *m*
Biro /'baɪərəʊ/ *n* (*pl* **-os**) (caneta) esferográfica *f*, Bic *f*
birth /bɜ:θ/ *n* nascimento *m*. ~ **certificate** certidão *f* de nascimento. ~ **control/rate** controle *m*/índice *m* de natalidade. ~**-place** *n* lugar *m* de nascimento. **give ~ to** dar à luz
birthday /'bɜ:θdeɪ/ *n* aniversário *m*, (*P*) dia *m* de anos. **his ~ is on 9 July** ele faz anos no dia 9 de julho
birthmark /'bɜ:θma:k/ *n* sinal *m*
biscuit /'bɪskɪt/ *n* biscoito *m*, bolacha *f*
bisect /baɪ'sekt/ *vt* dividir ao meio
bishop /'bɪʃəp/ *n* bispo *m*
bit[1] /bɪt/ *n* (*small piece, short time*) pedaço *m*, bocado *m*; (*of bridle*) freio *m*; (*of tool*) broca *f*. **a** ~ um pouco
bit[2] /bɪt/ *see* **bite**
bitch /bɪtʃ/ *n* cadela *f*; (*sl: woman*) peste *f* (*fig*), cadela *f* (*sl*) ◻ *vt/i* (*colloq: criticize*) malhar, (*P*) cortar (em) (*colloq*); (*colloq: grumble*) resmungar. ~**y** *a* (*colloq*) maldoso
bite /baɪt/ *vt/i* (*pt* **bit**, *pp* **bitten**) morder; (*insect*) picar ◻ *n* mordida *f*; (*sting*) picada *f*. **have a ~ (to eat)** comer qualquer coisa
biting /'baɪtɪŋ/ *a* cortante
bitter /'bɪtə(r)/ *a* amargo; (*weather*) glacial. ~**ly** *adv* amargamente. **it's ~ly cold** está um frio de rachar. ~**ness** *n* amargura *f*; (*resentment*) ressentimento *m*
bizarre /bɪ'za:(r)/ *a* bizarro
black /blæk/ *a* (**-er, -est**) negro, preto ◻ *n* negro *m*, preto *m*. **a B~** (*person*) um preto, um negro ◻ *vt* enegrecer; (*goods*) boicotar. ~ **and blue** coberto de nódoas negras. ~ **coffee** café *m* (sem leite). ~ **eye** olho *m* negro. ~ **ice** gelo *m*

negro sobre o asfalto. ~ **market** mercado *m* negro. ~ **spot** *n* (*place*) local *m* perigoso, ponto *m* negro

blackberry /'blækbərɪ/ *n* amora *f* silvestre

blackbird /'blækbɜ:d/ *n* melro *m*

blackboard /'blækbɔ:d/ *n* quadro *m* preto

blackcurrant /'blækkʌrənt/ *n* groselha *f* negra

blacken /'blækən/ *vt/i* escurecer. ~ **sb's name** difamar, denegrir

blackleg /'blækleg/ *n* fura-greves *m*

blacklist /'blæklɪst/ *n* lista *f* negra ◻ *vt* pôr na lista negra

blackmail /'blækmeɪl/ *n* chantagem *f* ◻ *vt* fazer chantagem. ~**er** *n* chantagista *mf*

blackout /'blækaʊt/ *n* (*wartime*) blecaute *m*; (*med*) desmaio *m*; (*electr*) falta *f* de corrente; (*theatr*) apagar *m* de luzes

blacksmith /'blæksmɪθ/ *n* ferreiro *m*

bladder /'blædə(r)/ *n* bexiga *f*

blade /bleɪd/ *n* lâmina *f*; (*of oar, propeller*) pá *f*; (*of grass*) ervinha *f*, folhinha *f* de erva

blame /bleɪm/ *vt* culpar ◻ *n* culpa *f*. **be to** ~ ser o culpado. ~**less** *a* irrepreensível; (*innocent*) inocente

bland /blænd/ *a* (**-er, -est**) (*of manner*) suave; (*mild*) brando; (*insipid*) insípido

blank /blæŋk/ *a* (*space, cheque*) em branco; (*look*) vago; (*wall*) nu ◻ *n* espaço *m* em branco; (*cartridge*) cartucho *m* sem bala

blanket /'blæŋkɪt/ *n* cobertor *m*; (*fig*) manto *m* ◻ *vt* (*pt* **blanketed**) cobrir com cobertor; (*cover thickly*) encobrir, recobrir. **wet** ~ desmancha-prazeres *mf*

blare /bleə(r)/ *vt/i* ressoar, atroar ◻ *n* clangor *m*; (*of horn*) buzinar *m*

blasé /'bla:zeɪ/ *a* blasé

blaspheme /blæs'fi:m/ *vt/i* blasfemar

blasphem|y /'blæsfəmɪ/ *n* blasfêmia *f*, (*P*) blasfémia *f*. ~**ous** *a* blasfemo

blast /bla:st/ *n* (*gust*) rajada *f*; (*sound*) som *m*; (*explosion*) explosão *f* ◻ *vt* dinamitar. ~! droga! ~**ed** *a* maldito. ~**-furnace** *n* alto forno *m*. ~**-off** *n* (*of missile*) lançamento *m*, início *m* de combustão

blatant /'bleɪtnt/ *a* flagrante; (*shameless*) descarado

blaze /bleɪz/ *n* chamas *fpl*; (*light*) clarão *m*; (*outburst*) explosão *f* ◻ *vi* arder; (*shine*) resplandecer, brilhar. ~ **a trail** abrir o caminho, ser pioneiro

blazer /'bleɪzə(r)/ *n* blazer *m*

bleach /bli:tʃ/ *n* descolorante, descorante *m*; (*household*) água *f* sanitária ◻ *vt/i* branquear; (*hair*) oxigenar

bleak /bli:k/ *a* (**-er, -est**) (*place*) desolado; (*chilly*) frio; (*fig*) desanimador

bleary-eyed /'blɪərɪaɪd/ *a* com olhos injetados

bleat /bli:t/ *n* balido *m* ◻ *vi* balir

bleed /bli:d/ *vt/i* (*pt* **bled**) sangrar

bleep /bli:p/ *n* bip *m*. ~**er** *n* bip *m*

blemish /'blemɪʃ/ *n* defeito *m*; (*on reputation*) mancha *f* ◻ *vt* manchar

blend /blend/ *vt/i* misturar(-se); (*go well together*) combinar-se ◻ *n* mistura *f*. ~**er** *n* (*culin*) liquidificador *m*

bless /bles/ *vt* abençoar. **be** ~**ed with** ter a felicidade de ter. ~**ing** *n* benção *f*; (*thing one is glad of*) felicidade *f*. **it's a** ~**ing in disguise** há males que vêm para bem

blessed /'blesɪd/ *a* bem-aventurado; (*colloq: cursed*) maldito

blew /blu:/ *see* **blow**

blight /blaɪt/ *n* doença *f* de plantas; (*fig*) influência *f* maligna ◻ *vt* arruinar, frustrar

blind /blaɪnd/ *a* cego ◻ *vt* cegar ◻ *n* (*on window*) persiana *f*; (*deception*) ardil *m*. ~ **alley** (*incl fig*) beco *m* sem saída. ~ **man/woman** cego *m*/cega *f*. **be** ~ **to** não ver. **turn a** ~ **eye to** fingir não ver, fechar os olhos a. ~**ly** *adv* às cegas. ~**ness** *n* cegueira *f*

blindfold /'blaɪndfəʊld/ *a & adv* de olhos vendados ◻ *n* venda *f* ◻ *vt* vendar os olhos a

blink /blɪŋk/ *vi* piscar

blinkers /'blɪŋkəz/ *npl* antolhos *mpl*

bliss /blɪs/ *n* felicidade *f*, beatitude *f*. ~**ful** *a* felicíssimo. ~**-fully** *adv* maravilhosamente

blister /'blɪstə(r)/ *n* bolha *f*, empola *f* ◻ *vi* empolar

blizzard /'blɪzəd/ *n* tempestade *f* de neve, nevasca *f*

bloated /'bləʊtɪd/ *a* inchado

bloater /'bləʊtə(r)/ *n* arenque *m* salgado e defumado

blob /blɒb/ *n* pingo *m* grosso; (*stain*) mancha *f*

bloc /blɒk/ *n* bloco *m*

block /blɒk/ *n* bloco *m*; (*buildings*) quarteirão *m*; (*in pipe*) entupimento *m*. ~ **(of flats)** prédio *m* (de andares) ◻ *vt* bloquear, obstruir; (*pipe*) entupir. ~ **letters** maiúsculas *fpl*. ~**age** *n* obstrução *f*

blockade /blɒ'keɪd/ *n* bloqueio *m* ▫ *vt* bloquear
bloke /bləʊk/ *n* (*colloq*) sujeito *m* (*colloq*), cara *m* (*colloq*)
blond /blɒnd/ *a & n* louro (*m*)
blonde /blɒnd/ *a & n* loura (*f*)
blood /blʌd/ *n* sangue *m* ▫ *a* (*bank, donor, transfusion, etc*) de sangue; (*poisoning*) do sangue; (*group, vessel*) sangüíneo. **~-curdling** *a* horrendo. **~ pressure** tensão *f* arterial. **~ test** exame *m* de sangue. **~less** *a* (*fig*) pacífico
bloodhound /'blʌdhaʊnd/ *n* sabujo *m*
bloodshed /'blʌdʃed/ *n* derramamento *m* de sangue, carnificina *f*
bloodshot /'blʌdʃɒt/ *a* injetado *or* (*P*) injectado de sangue
bloodstream /'blʌdstri:m/ *n* sangue *m*, fluxo *m* sangüíneo
bloodthirsty /'blʌdθɜ:stɪ/ *a* sanguinário
bloody /'blʌdɪ/ *a* (**-ier, -iest**) ensangüentado; (*with much bloodshed*) sangrento; (*sl*) grande, maldito ▫ *adv* (*sl*) pra burro. **~-minded** *a* (*colloq*) do contra (*colloq*), chato (*sl*)
bloom /blu:m/ *n* flor *f*; (*beauty*) frescura *f*, viço *m* ▫ *vi* florir; (*fig*) vicejar. **in ~** em flor
blossom /'blɒsəm/ *n* flor *f*. **in ~** em flor ▫ *vi* (*flower*) florir, desabrochar; (*develop, flourish*) florescer, desabrochar
blot /blɒt/ *n* mancha *f* ▫ *vt* (*pt* **blotted**) manchar; (*dry*) secar. **~ out** apagar; (*hide*) tapar, toldar. **~ter, ~ting-paper** *n* (papel) mata-borrão *m*
blotch /blɒtʃ/ *n* mancha *f*. **~y** *a* manchado
blouse /blaʊz/ *n* blusa *f*; (*in uniform*) blusão *m*
blow[1] /bləʊ/ *vt/i* (*pt* **blew**, *pp* **blown**) soprar; (*fuse*) fundir-se, queimar; (*sl: squander*) esbanjar; (*trumpet etc*) tocar. **~ a whistle** apitar. **~ away** *or* **off** *vt* levar, soprar ▫ *vi* roar, ir pelos ares (fora). **~-dry** *vt* (*hair*) fazer um brushing ▫ *n* brushing *m*. **~ one's nose** assoar o nariz. **~ out** (*candle*) apagar, soprar. **~-out** *n* (*colloq: of tyre*) rebentar *m*; (*colloq: large meal*) comilança *f* (*colloq*). **~ over** passar. **~ up** *vt* (*explode*) explodir; (*tyre*) encher; (*photograph*) ampliar ▫ *vi* (*explode*) explodir
blow[2] /bləʊ/ *n* pancada *f*; (*slap*) bofetada *f*; (*punch*) murro *m*; (*fig*) golpe *m*
blowlamp /'bləʊlæmp/ *n* maçarico *m*
blown /bləʊn/ *see* **blow**[1]
bludgeon /'blʌdʒən/ *n* moca *f* ▫ *vt* malhar em. **~ to death** matar à pancada
blue /blu:/ *a* (**-er, -est**) azul; (*indecent*) indecente ▫ *n* azul *m*. **come out of the ~** ser inesperado. **~s** *n* (*mus*) blues. **have the ~s** estar deprimido (*colloq*)
bluebell /'blu:bel/ *n* jacinto *m* dos bosques
bluebottle /'blu:bɒtl/ *n* mosca *f* varejeira
blueprint /'blu:prɪnt/ *n* cópia *f* fotográfica de planta; (*fig*) projeto *m*, (*P*) projecto *m*
bluff /blʌf/ *vi* blefar, (*P*) fazer bluff ▫ *vt* enganar (fingindo), blefar ▫ *n* blefe *m*, (*P*) bluff *m*
blunder /'blʌndə(r)/ *vi* cometer um erro crasso; (*move*) avançar às cegas *or* tateando ▫ *n* erro *m* crasso, (*P*) bronca *f*
blunt /blʌnt/ *a* (**-er, -est**) embotado; (*person*) direto, (*P*) directo ▫ *vt* embotar. **~ly** *adv* sem rodeios. **~ness** *n* **franqueza** *f* **rude**
blur /blɜ:(r)/ *n* mancha *f* ▫ *vt* (*pt* **blurred**) (*smear*) manchar; (*make indistinct*) toldar
blurb /blɜ:b/ *n* contracapa *f*, sinopse *f* de um livro
blurt /blɜ:t/ *vt* **~ out** deixar escapar
blush /blʌʃ/ *vi* corar ▫ *n* rubor *m*, vermelhidão *f*
bluster /'blʌstə(r)/ *vi* (*wind*) soprar em rajadas; (*swagger*) andar com ar fanfarrão. **~y** *a* borrascoso
boar /bɔ:(r)/ *n* varrão *m*. **wild ~** javali *m*
board /bɔ:d/ *n* tábua *f*; (*for notices*) quadro *m*, (*P*) placard *m*; (*food*) pensão *f*; (*admin*) conselho *m* ▫ *vt/i* cobrir com tábuas; (*aircraft, ship, train*) embarcar (em); (*bus, train*) subir (em). **full ~** pensão *f* completa. **half ~** meia-pensão *f*. **on ~** a bordo. **~ up** entaipar. **~ with** ser pensionista em casa de. **~er** *n* pensionista *mf*; (*at school*) interno *m*. **~ing-card** *n* cartão *m* de embarque. **~ing-house** *n* pensão *f*. **~ing-school** *n* internato *m*
boast /bəʊst/ *vi* gabar-se ▫ *vt* orgulhar-se de ▫ *n* gabarolice *f*. **~er** *n* gabola *mf*. **~ful** *a* vaidoso. **~fully** *adv* com vaidade, gabando-se
boat /bəʊt/ *n* barco *m*. **in the same ~** nas mesmas circunstâncias. **~ing** *n* passear de barco
bob /bɒb/ *vt/i* (*pt* **bobbed**) (*curtsy*) inclinar-se; (*hair*) cortar pelos ombros, (*P*) cortar à Joãozinho. **~ (up and down)** andar para cima e para baixo
bobbin /'bɒbɪn/ *n* bobina *f*; (*sewing-machine*) canela *f*, bobina *f*
bob-sleigh /'bɒbsleɪ/ *n* trenó *m*
bode /bəʊd/ *vi* **~ well/ill** ser de bom/mau agouro
bodice /'bɒdɪs/ *n* corpete *m*

bodily /'bɒdɪlɪ/ *a* corporal, físico. ◻ *adv* (*in person*) fisicamente, em pessoa; (*lift*) em peso

body /'bɒdɪ/ *n* corpo *m*; (*organization*) organismo *m*. **~(work)** *n* (*of car*) carroçaria *f*. **in a ~** em massa. **the main ~ of** o grosso de. **~-building** *n* body building *m*

bodyguard /'bɒdɪga:d/ *n* guarda-costas *m*; (*escort*) escolta *f*

bog /bɒg/ *n* pântano *m* ◻ *vt* **get ~ged down** atolar-se; (*fig*) ficar emperrado

boggle /'bɒgl/ *vi* **the mind ~s** não da para imaginar

bogus /'bəʊgəs/ *a* falso

boil[1] /bɔɪl/ *n* (*med*) furúnculo *m*

boil[2] /bɔɪl/ *vt/i* ferver. **come to the ~** ferver. **~ down to** resumir-se a. **~ over** transbordar. **~ing hot** fervendo. **~ing point** ponto *m* de ebulição

boiler /'bɔɪlə(r)/ *n* caldeira *f*. **~ suit** macacão *m*, (*P*) fato *m* de macaco

boisterous /'bɔɪstərəs/ *a* turbulento; (*noisy and cheerful*) animado

bold /bəʊld/ *a* (**-er**, **-est**) ousado; (*of colours*) vivo. **~ness** *n* ousadia *f*

Bolivia /bə'lɪvɪə/ *n* Bolívia *f*. **~n** *a* & *n* boliviano (*m*)

bollard /'bɒləd/ *n* (*ship*) abita *f*; (*road*) poste *m*

bolster /'bəʊlstə(r)/ *n* travesseiro *m* ◻ *vt* sustentar; ajudar. **~ one's spirits** levantar o moral

bolt /bəʊlt/ *n* (*on door etc*) ferrolho *m*; (*for nut*) parafuso *m*; (*lightning*) relâmpago *m* ◻ *vt* aferrolhar; (*food*) engolir ◻ *vi* fugir, disparar. **~ upright** reto como um fuso

bomb /bɒm/ *n* bomba *f* ◻ *vt* bombardear. **~er** *n* (*aircraft*) bombardeiro *m*; (*person*) bombista *mf*

bombard /bɒm'ba:d/ *vt* bombardear. **~ment** *n* bombardeamento *m*

bombastic /bɒm'bæstɪk/ *a* bombástico

bombshell /'bɒmʃel/ *n* granada *f*; (*fig*) bomba *f*

bond /bɒnd/ *n* (*agreement*) compromisso *m*; (*link*) laço *m*, vínculo *m*; (*comm*) obrigação *f*. **in ~** em depósito na alfândega

bondage /'bɒndɪdʒ/ *n* escravidão *f*, servidão *f*

bone /bəʊn/ *n* osso *m*; (*of fish*) espinha *f* ◻ *vt* desossar. **~-dry** *a* completamente seco, ressecado. **~ idle** preguiçoso

bonfire /'bɒnfaɪə(r)/ *n* fogueira *f*

bonnet /'bɒnɪt/ *n* chapéu *m*; (*auto*) capô *m* do motor, (*P*) capot *m*

bonus /'bəʊnəs/ *n* bônus *m*, (*P*) bónus *m*

bony /'bəʊnɪ/ *a* (**-ier**, **-iest**) ossudo; (*meat, fish*) cheio de ossos/de espinhas

boo /bu:/ *int* fora ◻ *vt/i* vaiar ◻ *n* vaia *f*

boob /bu:b/ *n* (*sl: mistake*) asneira *f*, disparate *m* ◻ *vi* (*sl*) fazer asneira(s)

booby /'bu:bɪ/ *n* **~ prize** prêmio *m* de consolação. **~ trap** bomba *f* armadilhada

book /bʊk/ *n* livro *m*. **~s** (*comm*) contas *fpl*, escrita *f* ◻ *vt* (*enter*) averbar, registrar; (*comm*) escriturar; (*reserve*) marcar, reservar. **~ of matches** carteira *f* de fósforos. **~ of tickets** (*bus, tube*) caderneta *f* de módulos. **be fully ~ed** ter a lotação esgotada. **~ing office** bilheteria *f*, (*P*) bilheteira *f*

bookcase /'bʊkkeɪs/ *n* estante *f*

bookkeep|er /'bʊkki:pə(r)/ *n* guarda-livros *m*. **~ing** *n* contabilidade *f*, escrituração *f*

booklet /'bʊklɪt/ *n* brochura *f*

bookmaker /'bʊkmeɪkə(r)/ *n* book (maker) *m*

bookmark /'bʊkma:k/ *n* marca *f* de livro, marcador *m* de página

bookseller /'bʊkselə(r)/ *n* livreiro *m*

bookshop /'bʊkʃɒp/ *n* livraria *f*

bookstall /'bʊkstɔ:l/ *n* quiosque *m*

boom /bu:m/ *vi* ribombar; (*of trade*) prosperar ◻ *n* (*sound*) ribombo *m*; (*comm*) boom *m*, prosperidade *f*

boon /bu:n/ *n* benção *f*, vantagem *f*

boost /bu:st/ *vt* desenvolver, promover; (*morale*) levantar; (*price*) aumentar ◻ *n* força *f* (*colloq*). **~er** *n* (*med*) dose suplementar *f*; (*vaccine*) revacinação *f*, (*P*) reforço *m*

boot /bu:t/ *n* bota *f*; (*auto*) portamala *f* ◻ *vt* **~ (up)** (*comput*) dar cargaem. **to ~** (*in addition*) ainda por cima

booth /bu:ð/ *n* barraca *f*; (*telephone, voting*) cabine *f*

booty /'bu:tɪ/ *n* saque *m*, pilhagem *f*

booze /bu:z/ *vi* (*colloq*) embebedar-se (*colloq*), encharcar-se (*colloq*) ◻ *n* (*colloq*) pinga *f* (*colloq*)

border /'bɔ:də(r)/ *n* borda *f*, margem *f*; (*frontier*) fronteira *f*; (*garden bed*) canteiro *m* ◻ *vi* **~ on** confinar com; (*be almost the same as*) atingir as raias de

borderline /'bɔ:dəlaɪn/ *n* linha *f* divisória. **~ case** caso *m* limite

bore[1] /bɔ:(r)/ *see* **bear**[2]

bore[2] /bɔ:(r)/ *vt/i* (*techn*) furar, perfurar ◻ *n* (*of gun barrel*) calibre *m*

bore[3] /bɔ:(r)/ *vt* aborrecer, entediar ◻ *n* maçante *m*; (*thing*) chatice *f*. **be ~d** aborrecer-se, maçar-se. **~dom** *n* tédio *m*. **boring** *a* tedioso, maçante

born /bɔ:n/ *a* nascido. **be ~** nascer

borne /bɔ:n/ *see* **bear**[2]

borough /'bʌrə/ *n* município *m*

borrow /'bɒrəʊ/ *vt* pedir emprestado (**from** a)

bosom /'bʊzəm/ *n* peito *m*; (*woman's; fig: midst*) seio *m*. ~ **friend** amigo *m* íntimo

boss /bɒs/ *n* (*colloq*) patrão *m*, patroa *f*, manda-chuva (*colloq*) *m* □ *vt* mandar. ~ **sb about** (*colloq*) mandar em alg

bossy /'bɒsɪ/ *a* mandão, autoritário

botan|y /'bɒtənɪ/ *n* botânica *f*. ~**ical** /bə'tænɪkl/ *a* botânico. ~**ist** /-ɪst/ *n* botânico *m*

botch /bɒtʃ/ *vt* atamancar; (*spoil*) estragar, escangalhar

both /bəʊθ/ *a* & *pron* ambos, os dois □ *adv* ~ . . . **and** não só . . . mas também, tanto . . . como. ~ **of us** nós dois. ~ **the books** ambos os livros

bother /'bɒðə(r)/ *vt/i* incomodar (-se) □ *n* (*inconvenience*) incômodo *m*, (*P*) incómodo *m*, trabalho *m*; (*effort*) custo *m*, trabalho *m*; (*worry*) preocupação *f*. **don't** ~ não se incomode. **I can't be** ~**ed** não posso me dar o trabalho

bottle /'bɒtl/ *n* garrafa *f*; (*small*) frasco *m*; (*for baby*) mamadeira *f*, (*P*) biberão *m* □ *vt* engarrafar. ~**-opener** *n* sacarolhas *m*. ~ **up** reprimir

bottleneck /'bɒtlnek/ *n* (*obstruction*) entrave *m*; (*traffic-jam*) engarrafamento *m*

bottom /'bɒtəm/ *n* fundo *m*; (*of hill*) sopé *m*; (*buttocks*) traseiro *m* □ *a* inferior; (*last*) último. **from top to** ~ de alto a baixo. ~**less** *a* sem fundo

bough /baʊ/ *n* ramo *m*

bought /bɔ:t/ *see* **buy**

boulder /'bəʊldə(r)/ *n* pedregulho *m*

bounce /baʊns/ *vi* saltar; (*of person*) pular, dar pulos; (*sl: of cheque*) ser devolvido □ *vt* fazer saltar □ *n* (*of ball*) salto *m*, (*P*) ressalto *m*

bound[1] /baʊnd/ *vi* pular; (*move by jumping*) ir aos pulos □ *n* pulo *m*

bound[2] /baʊnd/ *see* **bind** □ *a* **be** ~ **for** ir com destino a, ir para. **be** ~ **to** (*obliged*) ser obrigado a; (*certain*) haver de. **she's** ~ **to like it** ela há de gostar disso

boundary /'baʊndrɪ/ *n* limite *m*

bound|s /baʊndz/ *npl* limites *mpl*. **out of** ~**s** interdito. ~**ed by** limitado por. ~**less** *a* sem limites

bouquet /bʊ'keɪ/ *n* ramo *m* de flores; (*wine*) aroma *m*

bout /baʊt/ *n* período *m*; (*med*) ataque *m*; (*boxing*) combate *m*

boutique /bu:'ti:k/ *n* boutique *f*

bow[1] /bəʊ/ *n* (*weapon, mus*) arco *m*; (*knot*) laço *m*. ~**-legged** *a* de pernas tortas. ~**-tie** *n* gravata borboleta *f*, (*P*) laço *m*

bow[2] /baʊ/ *n* vênia *f*, (*P*) vénia *f* □ *vt/i* inclinar(-se), curvar-se

bow[3] /baʊ/ *n* (*naut*) proa *f*

bowels /'baʊəlz/ *npl* intestinos *mpl*; (*fig*) entranhas *fpl*

bowl[1] /bəʊl/ *n* (*basin*) bacia *f*; (*for food*) tigela *f*; (*of pipe*) fornilho *m*

bowl[2] /bəʊl/ *n* (*ball*) boliche *m*, (*P*) bola *f* de madeira. ~**s** *npl* boliche *m*, (*P*) jogo *m* com bolas de madeira □ *vt* (*cricket*) lançar. ~ **over** siderar, varar. ~**ing** *n* boliche *m*, (*P*) bowling *m*. ~**ing-alley** *n* pista *f*

bowler[1] /'bəʊlə(r)/ *n* (*cricket*) lançador *m*

bowler[2] /'bəʊlə(r)/ *n* ~ **(hat)** (chapéu de) coco *m*

box[1] /bɒks/ *n* caixa *f*; (*theatr*) camarote *m* □ *vt* pôr dentro duma caixa. ~ **in** fechar. ~ **office** *n* bilheteria *f*, (*P*) bilheteira *f*. **Boxing Day** feriado *m* no primeiro dia útil depois do Natal

box[2] /bɒks/ *vt/i* (*sport*) lutar boxe. ~ **the ears of** esbofetear. ~**er** *n* pugilista *m*, boxeur *m*. ~**ing** *n* boxe *m*, pugilismo *m*

boy /bɔɪ/ *n* rapaz *m*. ~**-friend** *n* namorado *m*. ~**hood** *n* infância *f*. ~**ish** *a* de menino

boycott /'bɔɪkɒt/ *vt* boicotar □ *n* boicote *m*

bra /bra:/ *n* soutien *m*

brace /breɪs/ *n* braçadeira *f*; (*dental*) aparelho *m*; (*tool*) berbequim *m*; (*of birds*) par *m*. ~**s** *npl* (*for trousers*) suspensórios *mpl* □ *vt* apoiar, firmar. ~ **o.s.** concentrar as energias, fazer força; (*for blow*) preparar-se

bracelet /'breɪslɪt/ *n* bracelete *m*, pulseira *f*

bracing /'breɪsɪŋ/ *a* tonificante, estimulante

bracken /'brækən/ *n* (*bot*) samambaia *f*, (*P*) feto *m*

bracket /'brækɪt/ *n* suporte *m*; (*group*) grupo *m* □ *vt* (*pt* **bracketed**) pôr entre parênteses; (*put together*) pôr em pé de igualdade, agrupar. **age/income** ~ faixa *f* etária/salarial. **round** ~**s** parênteses *mpl*. **square** ~**s** parênteses *mpl*, colchetes *mpl*

brag /bræg/ *vi* (*pt* **bragged**) gabar-se (**about** de)

braid /breɪd/ *n* galão *m*; (*of hair*) trança *f*

Braille /breɪl/ *n* braile *m*

brain /breɪn/ *n* cérebro *m*, miolos *mpl* (*colloq*); (*fig*) inteligência *f*. ~**s** (*culin*) miolos *mpl*. ~**-child** *n* invenção *f*. ~**less** *a* estúpido

brainwash /'breɪnwɒʃ/ *vt* fazer uma lavagem cerebral

brainwave /'breɪnweɪv/ *n* idéia *f*, (*P*) ideia *f* genial

brainy /ˈbreɪnɪ/ *a* (**-ier, -iest**) inteligente, esperto

braise /breɪz/ *vt* (*culin*) estufar

brake /breɪk/ *n* travão *m* □ *vt*/*i* travar. ~ **light** farol *m* do freio

bran /bræn/ *n* (*husks*) farelo *m*

branch /brɑːntʃ/ *n* ramo *m*; (*of road*) ramificação *f*; (*of railway line*) ramal *m*; (*comm*) sucursal *f*; (*of bank*) balcão *m* □ *vi* ~ (**off**) bifurcar-se, ramificar-se

brand /brænd/ *n* marca *f* □ *vt* marcar. ~ **name** marca *f* de fábrica. ~**-new** *a* novo em folha. ~ **sb as** tachar alg de, (*P*) rotular alg de

brandish /ˈbrændɪʃ/ *vt* brandir

brandy /ˈbrændɪ/ *n* aguardente *f*, conhaque *m*

brass /brɑːs/ *n* latão *m*. **the** ~ (*mus*) os metais *mpl* □ *a* de cobre, de latão. **get down to** ~ **tacks** tratar das coisas sérias. **top** ~ (*sl*) os chefões (*colloq*)

brassière /ˈbræsɪə(r)/ *n* soutien *m*

brat /bræt/ *n* (*pej*) fedelho *m*

bravado /brəˈvɑːdəʊ/ *n* bravata *f*

brave /breɪv/ *a* (**-er, -est**) bravo, valente □ *vt* arrostar. ~**ry** /-ərɪ/ *n* bravura *f*

brawl /brɔːl/ *n* briga *f*, rixa *f*, desordem *f* □ *vi* brigar

brawn /brɔːn/ *n* força *f* muscular, músculo *m*. ~**y** *a* musculoso

bray /breɪ/ *n* zurro *m* □ *vi* zurrar

brazen /ˈbreɪzn/ *a* descarado

brazier /ˈbreɪzɪə(r)/ *n* braseiro *m*

Brazil /brəˈzɪl/ *n* Brasil *m*. ~**ian** *a* & *n* brasileiro (*m*). ~ **nut** castanha *f* do Pará

breach /briːtʃ/ *n* quebra *f*; (*gap*) brecha *f* □ *vt* abrir uma brecha em. ~ **of contract** quebra *f* de contrato. ~ **of the peace** perturbação *f* da ordem pública. ~ **of trust** abuso *m* de confiança

bread /bred/ *n* pão *m*. ~**-winner** *n* ganha-pão *m*

breadcrumbs /ˈbredkrʌmz/ *npl* migalhas *fpl*; (*culin*) farinha *f* de rosca

breadline /ˈbredlaɪn/ *n* **on the** ~ na miséria

breadth /bredθ/ *n* largura *f*; (*of mind, view*) abertura *f*

break /breɪk/ *vt* (*pt* **broke**, *pp* **broken**) partir, quebrar; (*vow, silence, etc*) quebrar; (*law*) transgredir; (*journey*) interromper; (*news*) dar; (*a record*) bater □ *vi* partir-se, quebrar-se; (*voice, weather*) mudar □ *n* quebra *f*, ruptura *f*; (*interval*) intervalo *m*; (*colloq: opportunity*) oportunidade *f*, chance *f*. ~ **one's arm/leg** quebrar o braço/a perna ~ **down** *vt* analisar □ *vi* (*of person*) ir-se abaixo; (*of machine*) avariar-se. ~ **in** forçar uma entrada. ~ **off** *vt* quebrar □ *vi* desligar-se. ~ **out** rebentar. ~ **up** *vt*/*i* terminar □ *vi* (*of schools*) entrar em férias. ~**able** *a* quebrável. ~**age** *n* quebra *f*

breakdown /ˈbreɪkdaʊn/ *n* (*techn*) avaria *f*, pane *f*; (*med*) esgotamento *m* nervoso; (*of figures*) análise *f* □ *a* (*auto*) de pronto-socorro. ~ **van** pronto-socorro *m*

breaker /ˈbreɪkə(r)/ *n* vaga *f* de rebentação

breakfast /ˈbrekfəst/ *n* café *m* da manhã

breakthrough /ˈbreɪkθruː/ *n* descoberta *f* decisiva, avanço *m*

breakwater /ˈbreɪkwɔːtə(r)/ *n* quebra-mar *m*

breast /brest/ *n* peito *m*. ~**-feed** *vt* (*pt* **-fed**) amamentar. ~**-stroke** *n* estilo *m* bruços

breath /breθ/ *n* respiração *f*. **bad** ~ mau hálito *m*. **out of** ~ sem fôlego. **under one's** ~ num murmúrio, baixo. ~**less** *a* ofegante

breathalyser /ˈbreθəlaɪzə(r)/ *n* aparelho *m* para medir o nível de álcool no sangue, bafômetro *m* (*colloq*)

breath|e /briːð/ *vt*/*i* respirar. ~**e in** inspirar. ~ **out** expirar. ~**ing** *n* respiração *f*. ~**ing-space** *n* pausa *f*

breather /ˈbriːðə(r)/ *n* pausa *f* de descanso, momento *m* para respirar

breathtaking /ˈbreθteɪkɪŋ/ *a* assombroso, arrebatador

bred /bred/ *see* **breed**

breed /briːd/ *vt* (*pt* **bred**) criar □ *vi* reproduzir-se □ *n* raça *f*. ~**er** *n* criador *m*. ~**ing** *n* criação *f*; (*fig*) educação *f*

breez|e /briːz/ *n* brisa *f*. ~**y** *a* fresco

brevity /ˈbrevətɪ/ *n* brevidade *f*

brew /bruː/ *vt* (*beer*) fabricar; (*tea*) fazer; (*fig*) armar, tramar □ *vi* fermentar; (*tea*) preparar; (*fig*) armar-se, preparar-se □ *n* decocção *f*; (*tea*) infusão *f*. ~**er** *n* cervejeiro *m*. ~**ery** *n* cervejaria *f*

bribe /braɪb/ *n* suborno *m*, (*P*) peita *f* □ *vt* subornar. ~**ry** /-ərɪ/ *n* suborno *m*, corrupção *f*

brick /brɪk/ *n* tijolo *m*

bricklayer /ˈbrɪkleɪə(r)/ *n* pedreiro *m*

bridal /ˈbraɪdl/ *a* nupcial

bride /braɪd/ *n* noiva *f*

bridegroom /ˈbraɪdgrʊm/ *n* noivo *m*

bridesmaid /ˈbraɪdzmeɪd/ *n* dama *f* de honra, (*P*) honor

bridge[1] /brɪdʒ/ *n* ponte *f*; (*of nose*) cana *f* □ *vt* ~ **a gap** preencher uma lacuna

bridge[2] /brɪdʒ/ *n* (*cards*) bridge *m*

bridle /ˈbraɪdl/ *n* cabeçada *f*, freio *m* □ *vt* refrear. ~**-path** *n* atalho *m*, carreiro *m*

brief[1] /bri:f/ *a* (**-er, -est**) breve. **~s** *npl* (*men's*) cueca *f*, (*P*) slip *m*; (*women's*) calcinhas *fpl*, (*P*) cuecas *fpl*. **~ly** *adv* brevemente

brief[2] /bri:f/ *n* (*jur*) sumário *m*; (*case*) causa *f*; (*instructions*) instruções *fpl* ◻ *vt* dar instruções a

briefcase /'bri:fkeɪs/ *n* pasta *f*

brigad|e /brɪ'geɪd/ *n* brigada *f*. **~ier** /-ə'dɪə(r)/ *n* brigadeiro *m*

bright /braɪt/ *a* (**-er, -est**) brilhante; (*of colour*) vivo; (*of light*) forte; (*room*) claro; (*cheerful*) alegre; (*clever*) inteligente. **~ness** *n* (*sheen*) brilho *m*; (*clarity*) claridade *f*; (*intelligence*) inteligência *f*

brighten /'braɪtn/ *vt* alegrar ◻ *vi* (*of weather*) clarear; (*of face*) animar-se, iluminar-se

brillian|t /'brɪljənt/ *a* brilhante. **~ce** *n* brilho *m*

brim /brɪm/ *n* borda *f*; (*of hat*) aba *f* ◻ *vi* (*pt* **brimmed**) **~ over** transbordar, cair por fora

brine /braɪn/ *n* salmoura *f*

bring /brɪŋ/ *vt* (*pt* **brought**) trazer. **~ about** causar. **~ back** trazer (de volta); (*call to mind*) relembrar. **~ down** trazer para baixo; (*bird, plane*) abater; (*prices*) baixar. **~ forward** adiantar, apresentar. **~ it off** ser bem sucedido (em alg coisa). **~ out** (*take out*) tirar; (*show*) revelar; (*book*) publicar. **~ round** *or* **to** reanimar, fazer voltar a si. **~ to bear** (*pressure etc*) exercer. **~ up** educar; (*med*) vomitar; (*question*) levantar

brink /brɪŋk/ *n* beira *f*, borda *f*

brisk /brɪsk/ *a* (**-er, -est**) (*pace, movement*) vivo, rápido; (*business, demand*) grande

bristl|e /'brɪsl/ *n* pêlo *m*.

Britain /'brɪtən/ *n* Grã-Bretanha *f*

British /'brɪtɪʃ/ *a* britânico. **the ~** o povo *m* britânico, os britânicos *mpl*

brittle /'brɪtl/ *a* frágil

broach /brəʊtʃ/ *vt* abordar, entabular, encetar

broad /brɔ:d/ *a* (**-er, -est**) largo; (*daylight*) pleno. **~band** banda *f* larga **~ bean** fava *f*. **~-minded** *a* tolerante, liberal. **~ly** *adv* de modo geral

broadcast /'brɔ:dka:st/ *vt/i* (*pt* **broadcast**) transmitir, fazer uma transmissão; (*person*) cantar, falar *etc* na rádio *or* na TV ◻ *n* emissão *f*. **~ing** *a* & *n* (de) rádiodifusão (*f*)

broaden /'brɔ:dn/ *vt/i* alargar (-se)

broccoli /'brɒkəlɪ/ *n inv* brócolis *mpl*, (*P*) brócolos *mpl*

brochure /'brəʊʃə(r)/ *n* brochura *f*

broke /brəʊk/ *see* **break** ◻ *a* (*sl*) depenado (*sl*), liso (*sl*), (*P*) teso (*sl*)

broken /'brəʊkən/ *see* **break** ◻ *a* **~ English** inglês *m* estropeado. **~-hearted** *a* com o coração despedaçado

broker /'brəʊkə(r)/ *n* corretor *m*, broker *m*

bronchitis /brɒŋ'kaɪtɪs/ *n* bronquite *f*

bronze /brɒnz/ *n* bronze *m*

brooch /brəʊtʃ/ *n* broche *m*

brood /bru:d/ *n* ninhada *f* ◻ *vi* chocar; (*fig*) cismar. **~y** *a* (*hen*) choca; (*fig*) sorumbático

brook /brʊk/ *n* regato *m*, ribeiro *m*

broom /bru:m/ *n* vassoura *f*; (*bot*) giesta *f*

broth /brɒθ/ *n* caldo *m*

brothel /'brɒθl/ *n* bordel *m*

brother /'brʌðə(r)/ *n* irmão *m*. **~-in-law** *n* (*pl* **~s-in-law**) cunhado *m*. **~hood** *n* irmandade *f*, fraternidade *f*. **~ly** *a* fraternal

brought /brɔ:t/ *see* **bring**

brow /braʊ/ *n* (*forehead*) testa *f*; (*of hill*) cume *m*; (*eyebrow*) sobrancelha *f*

browbeat /'braʊbi:t/ *vt* (*pt* **-beat**, *pp* **-beaten**) intimidar

brown /braʊn/ *a* (**-er, -est**) castanho ◻ *n* castanho *m* ◻ *vt/i* acastanhar; (*in the sun*) bronzear, tostar; (*meat*) alourar

browse /braʊz/ *vi* (*through book*) folhear; (*of animal*) pastar; (*in a shop*) olhar sem comprar. **~r** (*comput*) navegador *m*

bruise /bru:z/ *n* hematoma *m*, contusão *f* ◻ *vt* causar um hematoma. **~d** *a* coberto de hematomas, contuso; (*fruit*) machucado

brunette /bru:'net/ *n* morena *f*

brunt /brʌnt/ *n* **the ~ of** o maior peso de, o pior de

brush /brʌʃ/ *n* escova *f*; (*painter's*) pincel *m*; (*skirmish*) escaramuça *f*. **~ against** roçar. **~ aside** não fazer caso de. **~ off** (*colloq: reject*) mandar passear (*colloq*). **~ up (on)** aperfeiçoar

brusque /bru:sk/ *a* brusco

Brussels /'brʌslz/ *n* Bruxelas *f*. **~ sprouts** couve-de-Bruxelas *f*

brutal /'bru:tl/ *a* brutal. **~ity** /-'tælətɪ/ *n* brutalidade *f*

brute /bru:t/ *n* & *a* (*animal, person*) bruto (*m*). **by ~ force** por força bruta

BSc *abbr see* **Bachelor of Science**

BSE /'bi:ɛs'i:/ *n* EEB, encefalopatia espongiforma bovina

bubb|le /'bʌbl/ *n* bolha *f*; (*of soap*) bola *f* de sabão ◻ *vi* borbulhar. **~le gum** *n* chiclete *m*, (*P*) pastilha *f* elástica. **~le over** transbordar. **~ly** *a* efervescente

buck[1] /bʌk/ *n* macho *m* ◻ *vi* dar galões, (*P*) corcovear. **~ up** *vt/i* (*sl*) animar(-se); (*sl: rush*) apressar-se, despachar-se

buck[2] /bʌk/ *n* (*Amer sl*) *dólar m*

buck[3] /bʌk/ *n* **pass the ~** (*sl*) fazer o jogo do empurra

bucket /'bʌkɪt/ *n* balde *m*

buckle /'bʌkl/ *n* fivela *f* □ *vt/i* afivelar(-se); (*bend*) torcer(-se), vergar. **~ down to** empenhar-se

bud /bʌd/ *n* botão *m*, rebento *m* □ *vi* (*pt* **budded**) rebentar. **in ~** em botão

Buddhis|t /'bʊdɪst/ *a* & *n* budista (*mf*). **~m** /-zəm/ *n* budismo *m*

budding /'bʌdɪŋ/ *a* nascente, em botão, incipiente

budge /bʌdʒ/ *vt/i* mexer(-se)

budgerigar /'bʌdʒərɪga:(r)/ *n* periquito *m*

budget /'bʌdʒɪt/ *n* orçamento *m* □ *vi* (*pt* **budgeted**) **~ for** prever no orçamento *m*

buff /bʌf/ *n* (*colour*) côr *f* de camurça; (*colloq*) fanático *m*, entusiasta *mf* □ *vt* polir

buffalo /'bʌfələʊ/ *n* (*pl* **-oes**) búfalo *m*; (*Amer*) bisão *m*

buffer /'bʌfə(r)/ *n* pára-choque *m*

buffet[1] /'bʊfeɪ/ *n* (*meal, counter*) bufê *m*, (*P*) bufete *m*

buffet[2] /'bʌfɪt/ *vt* (*pt* **buffeted**) esbofetear

buffoon /bə'fu:n/ *n* palhaço *m*

bug /bʌg/ *n* (*insect*) bicho *m*; (*bed-bug*) percevejo *m*; (*sl: germ*) vírus *m*; (*sl: device*) microfone *m* de escuta; (*sl: defect*) defeito *m* □ *vt* (*pt* **bugged**) grampear; (*Amer sl: annoy*) chatear (*sl*)

bugbear /'bʌgbeə(r)/ *n* papão *m*

buggy /'bʌgɪ/ *n* (*for baby*) carrinho *m*

bugle /'bju:gl/ *n* clarim *m*

build /bɪld/ *vt/i* (*pt* **built**) construir, edificar □ *n* físico *m*, compleição *f*. **~ up** *vt/i* criar; (*increase*) aumentar; (*accumulate*) acumular(-se). **~-up** *n* acumulação *f*; (*fig*) publicidade *f*. **~er** *n* construtor *m*, empreiteiro *m*; (*workman*) operário *m*

building /'bɪldɪŋ/ *n* edifício *m*, prédio *m*. **~ site** canteiro *m* de obras. **~ society** sociedade *f* de investimentos imobiliários

built /bɪlt/ *see* **build**. **~-in** *a* incorporado. **~-in wardrobe** armário *m* embutido na parede. **~-up** *a* urbanizado

bulb /bʌlb/ *n* bolbo *m*; (*electr*) lâmpada *f*. **~ous** *a* bolboso

Bulgaria /bʌl'geərɪə/ *n* Bulgária *f*. **~n** *a* & *n* búlgaro (*m*)

bulg|e /bʌldʒ/ *n* bojo *m*, saliência *f* □ *vi* inchar; (*jut out*) fazer uma saliência. **~ing** *a* inchado; (*pocket etc*) cheio

bulk /bʌlk/ *n* quantidade *f*, volume *m*. **in ~** por grosso; (*loose*) a granel. **the ~ of** a maior parte de. **~y** *a* volumoso

bull /bʊl/ *n* touro *m*. **~'s-eye** *n* (*of target*) centro *m* do alvo, mosca *f*

bulldog /'bʊldɒg/ *n* buldogue *m*

bulldoze /'bʊldəʊz/ *vt* terraplanar. **~r** /-ə(r)/ *n* bulldozer *m*

bullet /'bʊlɪt/ *n* bala *f*. **~-proof** *a* à prova de balas; (*vehicle*) blindado

bulletin /'bʊlətɪn/ *n* boletim *m*

bullfight /'bʊlfaɪt/ *n* tourada *f*, corrida *f* de touros. **~er** *n* toureiro *m*. **~ing** *n* tauromaquia *f*

bullring /'bʊlrɪŋ/ *n* arena *f*, (*P*) praça *f* de touros

bully /'bʊlɪ/ *n* mandão *m*, pessoa *f* prepotente; (*schol*) terror *m*, o mau □ *vt* intimidar; (*treat badly*) atormentar; (*coerce*) forçar (**into** a)

bum[1] /bʌm/ *n* (*sl: buttocks*) traseiro *m*, bunda *f* (*sl*)

bum[2] /bʌm/ *n* (*Amer sl*) vagabundo *m*

bump /bʌmp/ *n* choque *m*, embate *m*; (*swelling*) inchaço *m*; (*on head*) galo *m* □ *vt/i* bater, chocar. **~ into** bater em, chocar com; (*meet*) esbarrar com, encontrar. **~y** *a* (*surface*) irregular; (*ride*) aos solavancos

bumper /'bʌmpə(r)/ *n* pára- choques *m* *inv* □ *a* excepcional

bun /bʌn/ *n* pãozinho *m* doce com passas; (*hair*) coque *m*

bunch /bʌntʃ/ *n* (*of flowers*) ramo *m*; (*of keys*) molho *m*; (*of people*) grupo *m*; (*of grapes*) cacho *m*

bundle /'bʌndl/ *n* molho *m* □ *vt* atar num molho; (*push*) despachar

bung /bʌŋ/ *n* batoque *m*, rolha *f* □ *vt* rolhar; (*sl: throw*) atirar, deitar. **~ up** entupir

bungalow /'bʌŋgələʊ/ *n* chalé *m*; (*outside Europe*) bungalô *m*, (*P*) bungalow *m*

bungle /'bʌŋgl/ *vt* fazer mal feito, estragar

bunion /'bʌnjən/ *n* (*med*) joanete *m*

bunk /bʌŋk/ *n* (*in train*) couchette *f*; (*in ship*) beliche *m*. **~-beds** *npl* beliches *mpl*

bunker /'bʌŋkə(r)/ *n* (*mil*) abrigo *m*, casamata *f*, bunker *m*; (*golf*) obstáculo *m* em cova de areia

buoy /bɔɪ/ *n* bóia *f* □ *vt* **~ up** animar

buoyan|t /'bɔɪənt/ *a* flutuante; (*fig*) alegre. **~cy** *n* (*fig*) alegria *f*, exuberância *f*

burden /'bɜ:dn/ *n* fardo *m* □ *vt* collegar, sobrecarregar. **~some** *a* pesado

bureau /'bjʊərəʊ/ *n* (*pl* **-eaux**) /-əʊz/ (*desk*) secretária *f*; (*office*) seção *f*, (*P*) secção *f*

bureaucracy /bjʊə'rɒkrəsɪ/ *n* burocracia *f*
bureaucrat /'bjʊərəkræt/ *n* burocrata *mf*. **~ic** /-'krætɪk/ *a* burocrático
burger /'bɜ:gə(r)/ *n*
burglar /'bɜ:glə(r)/ *n* ladrão *m*, assaltante *mf*. **~ alarm** *n* alarme *m* contra ladrões. **~ize** *vt* (*Amer*) assaltar. **~y** *n* assalto *m*
burgle /'bɜ:gl/ *vt* assaltar
burial /'berɪəl/ *n* enterro *m*
burly /'bɜ:lɪ/ *a* (**-ier**, **-iest**) robusto e corpulento, forte
Burm|a /'bɜ:mə/ *n* Birmânia *f*. **~ese** /-'mi:z/ *a* & *n* birmanês (*m*)
burn /bɜ:n/ *vt* (*pt* **burned** *or* **burnt**) queimar □ *vi* queimar (-se), arder □ *n* queimadura *f*. **~ down** reduzir a cinzas. **~er** *n* (*of stove*) bico *m* de gás. **~ing** *a* (*thirst, desire*) ardente; (*topic*) candente
burnt /bɜ:nt/ *see* **burn**
burp /bɜ:p/ *n* (*colloq*) arroto *m* □ *vi* (*colloq*) arrotar
burrow /'bʌrəʊ/ *n* toca *f* □ *vi* cavar, fazer uma toca
burst /bɜ:st/ *vt*/*i* (*pt* **burst**) arrebentar □ *n* estouro *m*, rebentar *m*; (*of anger, laughter*) explosão *f*; (*of firing*) rajada *f*; (*of energy*) acesso *m*. **~ into** (*flames, room, etc*) irromper em. **~ into tears** desatar num choro, desfazer-se em lágrimas. **~ out laughing** desatar a rir
bury /'berɪ/ *vt* sepultar, enterrar; (*hide*) esconder; (*engross, thrust*) mergulhar
bus /bʌs/ *n* (*pl* **buses**) ônibus *m*, (*P*) autocarro *m*. **~lane** faixa *f* de ônibus, de autocarro (*p*). **~-stop** *n* paragem *f*
bush /bʊʃ/ *n* arbusto *m*; (*land*) mato *m*. **~y** *a* espesso
business /'bɪznɪs/ *n* (*trade, shop, affair*) negócio *m*; (*task*) função *f*; (*occupation*) ocupação *f*. **have no ~ to** não ter o direito de. **it's no ~ of yours** não é da sua conta. **mind your own ~** cuide da sua vida. **that's my ~** isso é meu problema. **~like** *a* eficiente, sistemático. **~man** *n* homem *m* de negócios, comerciante *m*
busker /'bʌskə(r)/ *n* músico *m* ambulante
bust[1] /bʌst/ *n* busto *m*
bust[2] /bʌst/ *vt*/*i* (*pt* **busted** *or* **bust**) (*sl*) = **burst**, **break** □ *a* falido. **~-up** *n* (*sl*) discussão *f*, (*P*) bulha *f*. **go ~** (*sl*) falir
bustl|e /'bʌsl/ *vi* andar numa azáfama; (*hurry*) apressar-se □ *n* azáfama *f*. **~ing** *a* animado, movimentado
bus|y /'bɪzɪ/ *a* (**-ier**, **-iest**) ocupado; (*street*) movimentado; (*day*) atarefado □ *vt* **~y o.s. with** ocupar-se com. **~ily** *adv* ativamente, atarefadamente
busybody /'bɪzɪbɒdɪ/ *n* intrometido *m*, pessoa *f* abelhuda
but /bʌt/ *conj* mas □ *prep* exceto, (*P*) excepto, senão □ *adv* apenas, só. **all ~** todos menos; (*nearly*) quaze, por pouco não. **~ for** sem, se não fosse. **last ~ one/two** penúltimo/antepenúltimo. **nobody ~** ninguém a não ser
butcher /'bʊtʃə(r)/ *n* açougueiro *m*, (*P*) homem *m* do talho; (*fig*) carrasco *m* □ *vt* chacinar. **the ~'s** açougue *m*, (*P*) talho *m*. **~y** *n* chacina *f*
butler /'bʌtlə(r)/ *n* mordomo *m*
butt /bʌt/ *n* (*of gun*) coronha *f*; (*of cigarette*) ponta *f*; (*target*) alvo *m* de troça, de ridículo *etc*; (*cask*) barril *m* □ *vt*/*i* dar cabeçada em. **~ in** interromper
butter /'bʌtə(r)/ *n* manteiga *f* □ *vt* pôr manteiga em. **~-bean** *n* feijão *m* branco
buttercup /'bʌtəkʌp/ *n* botão-de-ouro *m*
butterfly /'bʌtəflaɪ/ *n* borboleta *f*
buttock /'bʌtək/ *n* nádega *f*
button /'bʌtn/ *n* botão *m* □ *vt*/*i* abotoar(-se)
buttonhole /'bʌtnhəʊl/ *n* casa *f* de botão; (*in lapel*) botoeira *f* □ *vt* (*fig*) obrigar a ouvir
buttress /'bʌtrɪs/ *n* contraforte *m*; (*fig*) esteio *m* □ *vt* sustentar
buxom /'bʌksəm/ *a* roliço, rechonchudo
buy /baɪ/ *vt* (*pt* **bought**) comprar (**from** a); (*sl*: *believe*) engolir (*colloq*) □ *n* compra *f*. **~er** *n* comprador *m*
buzz /bʌz/ *n* zumbido *m* □ *vi* zumbir. **~ off** (*sl*) pôr-se a andar. **~er** *n* campainha *f*
by /baɪ/ *prep* (*near*) junto de, perto de; (*along, past, means*) por; (*according to*) conforme; (*before*) antes de. **~ land/sea/air** por terra/mar/ar. **~ bike/car** *etc* de bicicleta/carro *etc*. **~ day/night** de dia/noite. **~ the kilo** por quilo. **~ now** a esta hora. **~ accident/mistake** sem querer. **~ oneself** sozinho □ *adv* (*near*) perto. **~ and ~** muito em breve. **~ and large** no conjunto. **~-election** *n* eleição *f* suplementar. **~-law** *n* regulamento *m*. **~-product** *n* derivado *m*
bye(-bye) /'baɪ(baɪ)/ *int* (*colloq*) adeus, adeusinho
bygone /'baɪgɒn/ *a* passado. **let ~s be ~s** o que passou, passou
bypass /'baɪpa:s/ *n* (estrada) secundária *f*, desvio *m*; (*med*) by-pass *m*, ponte *f* de safema □ *vt* fazer um desvio; (*fig*) contornar
bystander /'baɪstændə(r)/ *n* circumstante *mf*, espectador *m*
byte /baɪt/ *n* byte *m*

Mrs. Dalloway's

2904 College Avenue
Berkeley, CA 94705
(510) 704-8222
www.mrsdalloways.com

Cust: **None**

13-Jul-10 6:09p   Clerk: Admin
Trans # 10099706   Reg: 3

10099706

9780425222447 ***The Oxford New Portugu***

1 @ $6.99 -25% $5.24

Items: 1 *Units: 1*

Sub-total	$5.24
Tax @ 9.75%	$0.51
Discount	$1.75
Total:	**$5.75**

* *Non-Tax Items*

Payment Via:
CASH $11.00

Change (Cash) $5.25

Returns accepted for exchange or store credit with receipt up to 30 days after purchase date.

Cc

cab /kæb/ *n* táxi *m*; (*of lorry, train*) cabina *f*, cabine *f*

cabaret /ˈkæbəreɪ/ *n* variedades *fpl*, cabaré *m*

cabbage /ˈkæbɪdʒ/ *n* couve *f*, repolho *m*

cabin /ˈkæbɪn/ *n* cabana *f*; (*in plane*) cabina *f*; (*in ship*) camarote *m*

cabinet /ˈkæbɪnɪt/ *n* armário *m*. **C~** (*pol*) gabinete *m*

cable /ˈkeɪbl/ *n* cabo *m*. **~-car** *n* funicular *m*, teleférico *m*. **~ railway** funicular *m*. **~ television** televisão *f* a cabo

cache /kæʃ/ *n* (esconderijo *m* de) tesouro *m*, armas *fpl*, provisões *fpl*

cackle /ˈkækl/ *n* cacarejo *m* □ *vi* cacarejar

cactus /ˈkæktəs/ *n* (*pl* **~es** *or* **cacti** /-taɪ/) cacto *m*

caddie /ˈkædɪ/ *n* (*golf*) caddie *m*

caddy /ˈkædɪ/ *n* lata *f* para o chá

cadet /kəˈdet/ *n* cadete *m*

cadge /kædʒ/ *vt*/*i* filar, (*P*) cravar

Caesarean /sɪˈzeərɪən/ *a* **~ (section)** cesariana *f*

café /ˈkæfeɪ/ *n* café *m*

cafeteria /kæfɪˈtɪərɪə/ *n* cafeteria *f*, restaurante *m* self-service

caffeine /ˈkæfi:n/ *n* cafeína *f*

cage /keɪdʒ/ *n* gaiola *f*

cagey /ˈkeɪdʒɪ/ *a* (*colloq: secretive*) misterioso, reservado

cajole /kəˈdʒəʊl/ *vt* **~ sb into doing sth** convencer alguém (com lábia ou lisonjas) a fazer alg coisa

cake /keɪk/ *n* bolo *m*. **~d** *a* empastado. **his shoes were ~d with mud** tinha os sapatos cobertos de lama. **a piece of ~** (*sl*) canja *f* (*sl*)

calamity /kəˈlæmətɪ/ *n* calamidade *f*

calcium /ˈkælsɪəm/ *n* cálcio *m*

calculat|e /ˈkælkjʊleɪt/ *vt*/*i* calcular; (*Amer: suppose*) supor. **~ed** *a* (*action*) deliberado, calculado. **~ing** *a* calculista. **~ion** /-ˈleɪʃn/ *n* cálculo *m*. **~or** *n* calculador *m*, (*P*) maquina *f* de calcular

calendar /ˈkælɪndə(r)/ *n* calendário *m*

calf[1] /ka:f/ *n* (*pl* **calves**) (*young cow or bull*) vitelo *m*, bezerro *m*; (*of other animals*) cria *f*

calf[2] /ka:f/ *n* (*pl* **calves**) (*of leg*) barriga *f* da perna

calibrat|e /ˈkælɪbreɪt/ *vt* calibrar. **~ion** /-breɪʃn/ *n* calibragem *f*

calibre /ˈkælɪbə(r)/ *n* calibre *m*

calico /ˈkælɪkəʊ/ *n* pano *m* de algodão; (*printed*) chita *f*, algodão *m*

call /kɔ:l/ *vt*/*i* chamar; (*summon*) convocar; (*phone*) telefonar. **~ (in** *or* **round)** (*visit*) passar por casa de □ *n* chamada *f*; (*bird's cry*) canto *m*; (*shout*) brado *m*, grito *m*. **be ~ed** (*named*) chamar-se. **be on ~** estar de serviço. **~ back** (*phone*) tornar a telefonar; (*visit*) voltar. **~ for** (*demand*) pedir, requerer; (*fetch*) ir buscar. **~ off** cancelar. **~ on** (*visit*) visitar, fazer uma visita a. **~ out (to)** chamar. **~ up** (*mil*) mobilizar, recrutar; (*phone*) telefonar. **~-box** *n* cabina *f* telefônica, (*P*) telefónica. **~centre** central *f* tele fônica **~er** *n* visitante *f*, visita *f*; (*phone*) chamador *m*, (*P*) pessoa *f* que faz a chamada. **~ing** *n* vocação *f*

callous /ˈkæləs/ *a* insensível. **~ly** *adv* sem piedade.

callow /ˈkæləʊ/ *a* (**-er, -est**) inexperiente, verde

calm /ka:m/ *a* (**-er, -est**) calmo □ *n* calma *f* □ *vt*/*i* **~ (down)** acalmar(-se). **~ness** *n* calma *f*

calorie /ˈkælərɪ/ *n* caloria *f*

camber /ˈkæmbə(r)/ *n* (*of road*) abaulamento *m*

camcorder /ˈkæmkɔ:də(r)/ *n* câmera *f* de filmar

came /keɪm/ *see* **come**

camel /ˈkæml/ *n* camelo *m*

camera /ˈkæmərə/ *n* máquina *f* fotográfica; (*cine, TV*) câmera *f*. **~man** *n* (*pl* **-men**) operador *m*

camouflage /ˈkæməfla:ʒ/ *n* camuflagem *f* □ *vt* camuflar

camp[1] /kæmp/ *n* acampamento *m* □ *vi* acampar. **~-bed** *n* cama *f* de campanha. **~er** *n* campista *mf*; (*car*) auto-caravana *f*. **~ing** *n* campismo *m*

camp[2] /kæmp/ *a* afetado, efeminado

campaign /kæmˈpeɪn/ *n* campanha *f* □ *vi* fazer campanha

campsite /ˈkæmpsaɪt/ *n* área *f* de camping, (*P*) parque *m* de campismo

campus /ˈkæmpəs/ *n* (*pl* **-puses** /-pəsɪz/) campus *m*, (*P*) cidade *f* universitária

can[1] /kæn/ *n* vasilha *f* de lata; (*for food*) lata *f* (de conserva) □ *vt* (*pt* **canned**) enlatar. **~ned music** música *f* em fita para locais públicos. **~-opener** *n* abridor *m* de latas, (*P*) abrelatas *m*

can[2] /kæn/ *v aux* (*be able to*) poder, ser capaz de; (*know how to*) saber. **I ~not/~'t go** não posso ir

Canad|a /'kænədə/ *n* Canadá *m*. **~ian** /kə'neɪdɪən/ *a* & *n* canadense (*mf*), (*P*) canadiano (*m*)

canal /kə'næl/ *n* canal *m*

canary /kə'neərɪ/ *n* canário *m*. **C~ Islands** *npl* as (Ilhas) Canárias

cancel /'kænsl/ *vt* (*pt* **cancelled**) cancelar; (*cross out*) riscar; (*stamps*) inutilizar. **~ out** *vi* (*fig*) neutralizar-se mutuamente. **~lation** /-'leɪʃn/ *n* cancelamento *m*

cancer /'kænsə(r)/ *n* câncer *m*, cancro *m*. **C~** (*astrol*) Caranguejo *m*, Câncer *m*. **~ous** *a* canceroso

candid /'kændɪd/ *a* franco. **~ly** *adv* francamente

candida|te /'kændɪdeɪt/ *n* candidato *m*. **~cy** /-əsɪ/ *n* candidatura *f*

candle /'kændl/ *n* vela *f*; (*in church*) vela *f*, círio *m*. **~-light** *n* luz *f* de velas

candlestick /'kændlstɪk/ *n* castiçal *m*

candour /'kændə(r)/ *n* franqueza *f*, candura *f*

candy /'kændɪ/ *n* bala *f*, (*P*) açúcar cândi; (*Amer: sweet, sweets*) doce(s) *m* (*pl*). **~-floss** *n* algodão-doce *m*

cane /keɪn/ *n* cana *f*; (*walking-stick*) bengala *f*; (*for baskets*) verga *f*; (*school: for punishment*) vergasta *f* □ *vt* vergastar

canine /'keɪnaɪn/ *a* & *n* canino (*m*)

canister /'kænɪstə(r)/ *n* lata *f*

cannabis /'kænəbɪs/ *n* cânhamo *m*, maconha *f*

cannibal /'kænɪbl/ *n* canibal *mf*. **~ism** /-zəm/ *n* canibalismo *m*

cannon /'kænən/ *n inv* canhão *m*. **~-ball** *n* bala *f* de canhão

cannot /'kænət/ = **can not**

canny /'kænɪ/ *a* (**-ier, -iest**) astuto, manhoso

canoe /kə'nu:/ *n* canoa *f* □ *vi* andar de canoa. **~ing** *n* (*sport*) canoagem *f*. **~ist** *n* canoeiro *m*, (*P*) canoísta *mf*

canon /'kænən/ *n* cônego *m*, (*P*) cónego *m*; (*rule*) cânone *m*

canonize /'kænənaɪz/ *vt* canonizar

canopy /'kænəpɪ/ *n* dossel *m*; (*over doorway*) toldo *m*, marquise *f*; (*fig*) abóbada *f*

can't /ka:nt/ = **can not**

cantankerous /kæn'tæŋkərəs/ *a* irascível, intratável

canteen /kæn'ti:n/ *n* cantina *f*; (*flask*) cantil *m*; (*for cutlery*) estojo *m*

canter /'kæntə(r)/ *n* meio galope *m*, cânter *m* □ *vi* andar a meio galope

canton /'kæntɒn/ *n* cantão *m*

canvas /'kænvəs/ *n* lona *f*; (*for painting or tapestry*) tela *f*

canvass /'kænvəs/ *vt/i* angariar votos *or* fregueses

canyon /'kænjən/ *n* canhão *m*, (*P*) desfiladeiro *m*

cap /kæp/ *n* (*with peak*) boné *m*; (*without peak*) barrete *m*; (*of nurse*) touca *f*; (*of bottle, pen, tube, etc*) tampa *f*; (*mech*) tampa *f*, tampão *m* □ *vt* (*pt* **capped**) (*bottle, pen, tube, etc*) tapar, tampar; (*rates*) impôr um limite a; (*outdo*) suplantar; (*sport*) selecionar, (*P*) seleccionar. **~ped with** encimado de, coroado de

capab|le /'keɪpəbl/ *a* (*person*) capaz (**of** de); (*things, situations*) suscetível, (*P*) susceptível (**of** de). **~ility** /-'bɪlətɪ/ *n* capacidade *f*. **~ly** *adv* capazmente

capacity /kə'pæsətɪ/ *n* capacidade *f*. **in one's ~ as** na (sua) qualidade de

cape[1] /keɪp/ *n* (*cloak*) capa *f*

cape[2] /keɪp/ *n* (*geog*) cabo *m*

caper[1] /'keɪpə(r)/ *vi* andar aos pinotes

caper[2] /'keɪpə(r)/ *n* (*culin*) alcaparra *f*

capillary /kə'pɪlərɪ/ *n* (*pl* **-ies**) vaso *m* capilar

capital /'kæpɪtl/ *a* capital □ *n* (*town*) capital *f*; (*money*) capital *m*. **~ (letter)** maiúscula *f*. **~ punishment** pena *f* de morte

capitalis|t /'kæpɪtəlɪst/ *a* & *n* capitalista (*mf*). **~m** /-zəm/ *n* capitalismo *m*

capitalize /'kæpɪtəlaɪz/ *vi* capitalizar; (*finance*) financiar; (*writing*) escrever com maiúscula. **~ on** tirar partido de

capitulat|e /kə'pɪtʃʊleɪt/ *vi* capitular. **~ion** /-'leɪʃn/ *n* capitulação *f*

capricious /kə'prɪʃəs/ *a* caprichoso

Capricorn /'kæprɪkɔ:n/ *n* (*astrol*) Capricórnio *m*

capsicum /'kæpsɪkəm/ *n* pimento *m*

capsize /kæp'saɪz/ *vt/i* virar(-se)

capsule /'kæpsju:l/ *n* cápsula *f*

captain /'kæptɪn/ *n* capitão *m*; (*navy*) capitão-de-mar-e-guerra *m* □ *vt* capitanear, comandar

caption /'kæpʃn/ *n* legenda *f*; (*heading*) título *m*

captivate /'kæptɪveɪt/ *vt* cativar

captiv|e /'kæptɪv/ *a* & *n* cativo (*m*), prisioneiro (*m*). **~ity** /-'tɪvətɪ/ *n* cativeiro *m*

captor /'kæptə(r)/ *n* captor *m*

capture /'kæptʃə(r)/ *vt* capturar; (*attention*) prender □ *n* captura *f*

car /ka:(r)/ *n* carro *m*. **~ ferry** barca *f* para carros. **~-park** *n* (parque *m* de) estacionamento (*m*). **~ phone** telefone *m* de carro. **~-wash** *n* estação *f* de lavagem

carafe /kə'ræf/ *n* garrafa *f* para água ou vinho

caramel /'kærəmel/ *n* caramelo *m*.
carat /'kærət/ *n* quilate *m*
caravan /'kærəvæn/ *n* caravana *f*, reboque *m*
caraway /'kærəweɪ/ *n* ~ **seed** cariz *f*
carbohydrate /ka:bəʊ'haɪdreɪt/ *n* hidrato *m* de carbono
carbon /'ka:bən/ *n* carbono *m*. ~ **copy** cópia *f* em papel carbono, (*P*) químico. ~ **monoxide** óxido *m* de carbono. ~ **paper** papel *m* carbono, (*P*) químico
carburettor /ka:bjʊ'retə(r)/ *n* carburador *m*
carcass /'ka:kəs/ *n* carcaça *f*
card /ka:d/ *n* cartão *m*; (*postcard*) postal *m*; (*playing card*) carta *f*. ~**-game(s)** *n*(*pl*) jogo(s) *m*(*pl*) de cartas. ~ **index** *n* fichário *m*, (*P*) ficheiro *m*
cardboard /'ka:dbɔ:d/ *n* cartão *m*, papelão *m*
cardiac /'ka:dɪæk/ *a* cardíaco
cardigan /'ka:dɪgən/ *n* casaco *m* de lã
cardinal /'ka:dɪnl/ *a* cardeal, principal. ~ **number** numeral *m* cardinal □ *n* (*relig*) cardeal *m*
care /keə(r)/ *n* cuidado *m*; (*concern*) interesse *m* □ *vi* ~ **about** (*be interested*) estar interessado por; (*be worried*) estar preocupado com. ~ **for** (*like*) gostar de; (*look after*) tomar conta de. **take** ~ tomar cuidado. **take** ~ **of** cuidar de; (*deal with*) tratar de. **he couldn't** ~ **less** ele está pouco ligando, ele não dá a menor (*colloq*)
career /kə'rɪə(r)/ *n* carreira *f* □ *vi* ir a toda a velocidade, ir numa carreira
carefree /'keəfri:/ *a* despreocupado
careful /'keəfl/ *a* cuidadoso; (*cautious*) cauteloso. ~! cuidado! ~**ly** *adv* cuidadosamente; (*cautiously*) cautelosamente
careless /'keəlɪs/ *a* descuidado (**about** com). ~**ly** *adv* descuidadamente. ~**ness** *n* descuido *m*, negligência *f*
caress /kə'res/ *n* carícia *f* □ *vt* acariciar
caretaker /'keəteɪkə(r)/ *n* zelador *m* duma casa vizia; (*janitor*) zelador *m*, (*P*) porteiro *m*
cargo /'ka:gəʊ/ *n* (*pl* **-oes**) carregamento *m*, carga *f*
Caribbean /kærɪ'bi:ən/ *a* caraíba. **the** ~ as Caraíbas *fpl*
caricature /'kærɪkətjʊə(r)/ *n* caricatura *f* □ *vt* caricaturar
caring /'keərɪŋ/ *a* carinhoso, afetuoso, (*P*) afectuoso
carnage /'ka:nɪdʒ/ *n* carnificina *f*
carnation /ka:'neɪʃn/ *n* cravo *m*
carnival /'ka:nɪvl/ *n* carnaval *m*
carol /'kærəl/ *n* cântico *m* *or* canto *m* de Natal
carp[1] /ka:p/ *n inv* carpa *f*
carp[2] /ka:p/ *vi* ~ **(at)** criticar
carpent|er /'ka:pɪntə(r)/ *n* carpinteiro *m*. ~**ry** *n* carpintaria *f*
carpet /'ka:pɪt/ *n* tapete *m* □ *vt* (*pt* **carpeted**) atapetar. **with fitted** ~**s** (estar) atapetado. **be on the** ~ (*colloq*) ser chamado à ordem. ~**-sweeper** *n* limpador *m* de tapetes
carport /'ka:pɔ:t/ *n* abrigo *m*, (*P*) telheiro *m* para automóveis
carriage /'kærɪdʒ/ *n* carruagem *f*; (*of goods*) frete *m*, transporte *m*; (*cost, bearing*) porte *m*
carriageway /'kærɪdʒweɪ/ *n* faixa *f* de rodagem, pista *f*
carrier /'kærɪə(r)/ *n* transportador *m*; (*company*) transportadora *f*; (*med*) portador *m*. ~ **(bag)** saco *m* de plástico
carrot /'kærət/ *n* cenoura *f*
carry /'kærɪ/ *vt*/*i* levar; (*goods*) transportar; (*involve*) acarretar; (*have for sale*) ter à venda. **be carried away** entusiasmar-se, deixar-se levar. ~**-cot** *n* moisés *m*. ~ **off** levar à força; (*prize*) incluir. ~ **it off** sair-se bem (de). ~ **on** continuar; (*colloq: flirt*) flertar; (*colloq: behave*) portar-se (mal). ~ **out** executar; (*duty*) cumprir. ~ **through** levar a cabo
cart /ka:t/ *n* carroça *f*, carro *m* □ *vt* acarretar; (*colloq*) carregar com
cartilage /'ka:tɪlɪdʒ/ *n* cartilagem *f*
carton /'ka:tn/ *n* embalagem *f* de cartão *or* de plástico; (*of yogurt*) embalagem *f*, pote *m*; (*of milk*) pacote *m*
cartoon /ka:'tu:n/ *n* desenho *m* humorístico, caricatura *f*; (*strip*) estória *f* em quadrinhos, (*P*) banda *f* desenhada; (*film*) desenhos *mpl* animados. ~**ist** *n* caricaturista *mf*; (*of strip, film*) desenhador *m*
cartridge /'ka:trɪdʒ/ *n* cartucho *m*
carv|e /ka:v/ *vt* esculpir, talhar; (*meat*) trinchar. ~**ing** *n* obra *f* de talha; (*on tree-trunk*) incisão *f*. ~**ing knife** faca *f* de trinchar, trinchante *m*
cascade /kæs'keɪd/ *n* cascata *f* □ *vi* cair em cascata
case[1] /keɪs/ *n* caso *m*; (*jur*) causa *f*, processo *m*; (*phil*) argumentos *mpl*. **in any** ~ em todo caso. **in** ~ **(of)** no caso (de). **in that** ~ nesse caso
case[2] /keɪs/ *n* caixa *f*; (*crate*) caixa *f*, caixote *m*; (*for camera, jewels, spectacles, etc*) estojo *m*; (*suitcase*) mala *f*; (*for cigarettes*) cigarreira *f*
cash /kæʃ/ *n* dinheiro *m*, numerário *m*, cash *m* □ *vt* (*obtain money for*) cobrar, receber; (*give money for*) pagar. **be short of** ~ ter pouco dinheiro. ~ **a cheque** (*receive*/*give*) cobrar/descontar

um cheque. **~ in** receber. **~ in (on)** aproveitar-se de. **in ~** em dinheiro. **pay ~** pagar em dinheiro. **~ desk** caixa *f*. **~ dispenser** caixa *f* electrônica. **~-flow** *n* cash-flow *m*. **~ register** caixa *f* registradora, (*P*) registradora *f*

cashew /kæ'ʃu:/ *n* caju *m*

cashier /kæ'ʃɪə(r)/ *n* caixa *mf*

cashmere /kæʃ'mɪə(r)/ *n* caxemira *f*

casino /kə'si:nəʊ/ *n* (*pl* **-os**) casino *m*

cask /ka:sk/ *n* casco *m*, barril *m*

casket /'ka:skɪt/ *n* pequeno cofre *m*; (*Amer: coffin*) caixão *m*

casserole /'kæsərəʊl/ *n* caçarola *f*; (*stew*) estufado *m*

cassette /kə'set/ *n* cassette *f*. **~ player** gravador *m*. **~ recorder** *n* gravador *m*

cast /ka:st/ *vt* (*pt* **cast**) lançar, arremessar; (*shed*) despojar-se de; (*vote*) dar; (*metal*) fundir; (*shadow*) projetar, (*P*) projectar □ *n* (*theatr*) elenco *m*; (*mould*) molde *m*; (*med*) aparelho *m* de gesso. **~ iron** *n* ferro *m* fundido. **~-iron** *a* de ferro fundido; (*fig*) muito forte. **~-offs** *npl* roupa *f* velha

castanets /kæstə'nets/ *npl* castanholas *fpl*

castaway /'ka:stəweɪ/ *n* náufrago *m*

caste /ka:st/ *n* casta *f*

castigate /'kæstɪgeɪt/ *vt* castigar

castle /'ka:sl/ *n* castelo *m*; (*chess*) torre *f*

castor /'ka:stə(r)/ *n* roda *f* de pé de móvel. **~ sugar** açúcar *m* em pó

castrat|e /kæ'streɪt/ *vt* castrar. **~ion** /-ʃn/ *n* castração *f*

casual /'kæʒʊəl/ *a* (*chance: meeting*) casual; (*careless, unmethodical*) descuidado; (*informal*) informal. **~ clothes** roupa *f* prática *or* de lazer. **~ work** trabalho *m* ocasional. **~ly** *adv* casualmente; (*carelessly*) sem cuidado

casualty /'kæʒʊəltɪ/ *n* (*dead*) morto *m*; (*death*) morte *f*; (*injured*) ferido *m*; (*victim*) vítima *f*; (*mil*) baixa *f*

cat /kæt/ *n* gato *m*. **~'s-eyes** *npl* (*P*) reflectores *mpl*

Catalonia /kætə'ləʊnɪə/ *n* Catalunha *f*

catalogue /'kætəlɒg/ *n* catálogo *m* □ *vt* catalogar

catalyst /'kætəlɪst/ *n* catalisador *m*

catapult /'kætəpʌlt/ *n* (*child's*) atiradeira *f*, (*P*) fisga *f* □ *vt* catapultar

cataract /'kætərækt/ *f* (*waterfall & med*) catarata *f*

catarrh /kə'ta:(r)/ *n* catarro *m*

catastroph|e /kə'tæstrəfɪ/ *n* catástrofe *f*. **~ic** /kætəs'trɒfɪk/ *a* catastrófico

catch /kætʃ/ *vt* (*pt* **caught**) apanhar; (*grasp*) agarrar; (*hear*) perceber □ *vi* prender-se (**in** em); (*get stuck*) ficar preso □ *n* apanha *f*; (*of fish*) pesca *f*; (*trick*) ratoeira *f*; (*snag*) problema *m*; (*on door*) trinco *m*; (*fastener*) fecho *m*. **~ fire** pegar fogo, (*P*) incendiar-se. **~ on** (*colloq*) pegar, tornar-se popular. **~ sb's eye** atrair a atenção de alg. **~ sight of** avistar. **~ up (with)** pôr-se a par (com); (*work*) pôr em dia. **~-phrase** *n* clichê *m*

catching /'kætʃɪŋ/ *a* contagioso, infeccioso

catchment /'kætʃmənt/ *n* **~ area** (*geog*) bacia *f* de captação; (*fig: of school, hospital*) área *f*

catchy /'kætʃɪ/ *a* que pega fácil

categorical /kætɪ'gɒrɪkl/ *a* categórico

category /'kætɪgərɪ/ *n* categoria *f*

cater /'keɪtə(r)/ *vi* fornecer comida (para clubes, casamentos, etc). **~ for** (*pander to*) satisfazer; (*consumers*) dirigir-se a. **~er** *n* fornecedor *m*. **~ing** *n* catering *m*

caterpillar /'kætəpɪlə(r)/ *n* lagarta *f*

cathedral /kə'θi:drəl/ *n* catedral *f*

catholic /'kæθəlɪk/ *a* universal; (*eclectic*) eclético, (*P*) ecléctico. **C~** *a* & *n* católico (*m*). **C ~ism** /kə'θɒlɪsɪzəm/ *n* catolicismo *m*

cattle /'kætl/ *npl* gado *m*

catty /'kætɪ/ *a* (dissimuladamente) maldoso, com perfídia

caught /kɔ:t/ *see* **catch**

cauldron /'kɔ:ldrən/ *n* caldeirão *m*

cauliflower /'kɒlɪflaʊə(r)/ *n* couve-flor *f*

cause /kɔ:z/ *n* causa *f* □ *vt* causar. **~ sth to grow/move** *etc* fazer crescer/mexer *etc* alg coisa

causeway /'kɔ:zweɪ/ *n* estrada *f* elevada, caminho *m* elevado

caustic /'kɔ:stɪk/ *a* cáustico

cauti|on /'kɔ:ʃn/ *n* cautela *f*; (*warning*) aviso *m* □ *vt* avisar. **~ous** /'kɔ:ʃəs/ *a* cauteloso. **~ously** *adv* cautelosamente

cavalry /'kævəlrɪ/ *n* cavalaria *f*

cave /keɪv/ *n* caverna *f*, gruta *f* □ *vi* **~ in** desabar, dar de si

caveman /'keɪvmæn/ *n* (*pl* **-men**) troglodita *m*, homen *m* das cavernas; (*fig*) (tipo) primário *m*

cavern /'kævən/ *n* caverna *f*. **~ous** *a* cavernoso

caviare /'kævɪa:(r)/ *n* caviar *m*

caving /'keɪvɪŋ/ *n* espeleologia *f*

cavity /'kævətɪ/ *n* cavidade *f*

cavort /kə'vɔ:t/ *vi* curvetear; (*person*) andar aos pinotes

CD /si:'di/ *see* **compact disc**

cease /si:s/ *vt/i* cessar. **~-fire** *n* cessar-fogo *m*. **~less** *a* incessante

cedar /'si:də(r)/ *n* cedro *m*

cedilla /sɪ'dɪlə/ *n* cedilha *f*
ceiling /'si:lɪŋ/ *n* (*lit & fig*) teto *m*, (*P*) tecto *m*
celebrat|e /'selɪbreɪt/ *vt/i* celebrar, festejar. **~ion** /-'breɪʃn/ *n* celebração *f*, festejo *m*
celebrated /'selɪbreɪtɪd/ *a* célebre
celebrity /sɪ'lebrətɪ/ *n* celebridade *f*
celery /'selərɪ/ *n* aipo *m*
celiba|te /'selɪbət/ *a* celibatário. **~cy** *n* celibato *m*
cell /sel/ *n* (*of prison, convent*) cela *f*; (*biol, pol, electr*) célula *f* **~phone** (*B*) celular *m*, (*p*) telemóvel
cellar /'selə(r)/ *n* porão *m*, cave *f*; (*for wine*) adega *f*, cave *f*
cell|o /'tʃeləʊ/ *n* (*pl* **-os**) violoncelo *m*. **~ist** *n* violoncelista *mf*
Cellophane /'seləfeɪn/ *n* (*P*) celofane *m*
cellular /'seljʊlə(r)/ *a* celular
Celt /kelt/ *n* celta *mf*. **~ic** *a* celta, céltico
cement /sɪ'ment/ *n* cimento *m* □ *vt* cimentar. **~-mixer** *n* betoneira *f*
cemetery /'semətrɪ/ *n* cemitério *m*
censor /'sensə(r)/ *n* censor *m* □ *vt* censurar. **~ship** *n* censura *f*
censure /'senʃə(r)/ *n* censura *f*, crítica *f* □ *vt* censurar, criticar
census /'sensəs/ *n* recenseamento *m*, censo *m*
cent /sent/ *n* cêntimo *m*
centenary /sen'ti:nərɪ/ *n* centenário *m*
centigrade /'sentɪgreɪd/ *a* centígrado
centilitre /'sentɪli:tə(r)/ *n* centilitro *m*
centimetre /'sentɪmi:tə(r)/ *n* centímetro *m*
centipede /'sentɪpi:d/ *n* centopéia *f*, (*P*) centopeia *f*
central /'sentrəl/ *a* central. **~ heating** aquecimento *m* central. **~ize** *vt* centralizar. **~ly** *adv* no centro
centre /'sentə(r)/ *n* centro *m* □ *vt* (*pt* **centred**) centrar □ *vi* **~ on** concentrar-se em, fixar-se em
centrifugal /sen'trɪfjʊgl/ *a* centrífugo
century /'sentʃərɪ/ *n* século *m*
ceramic /sɪ'ræmɪk/ *a* (*object*) em cerâmica. **~s** *n* cerâmica *f*
cereal /'sɪərɪəl/ *n* cereal *m*
cerebral /'serɪbrəl/ *a* cerebral
ceremonial /serɪ'məʊnɪəl/ *a* de cerimônia □ *n* cerimonial *m*
ceremon|y /'serɪmənɪ/ *n* cerimônia *f*, (*P*) cerimónia *f*. **~ious** /-'məʊnɪəs/ *a* cerimonioso
certain /'sə:tn/ *a* certo. **be ~** ter a certeza. **for ~** com certeza, ao certo. **make ~** confirmar, verificar. **~ly** *adv* com certeza, certamente. **~ty** *n* certeza *f*
certificate /sə'tɪfɪkət/ *n* certificado *m*; (*birth, marriage*) certidão *f*; (*health*) atestado *m*
certif|y /'sɜ:tɪfaɪ/ *vt/i* certificar. **~ied** *a* (*as insane*) declarado
cervical /sɜ:'vaɪkl/ *a* cervical; (*of cervix*) do útero
cesspit, cesspool /'sespɪt, 'sespu:l/ *ns* fossa *f* sanitária
chafe /tʃeɪf/ *vt/i* esfregar; (*make/become sore*) esfolar/ficar esfolado; (*fig*) irritar(-se)
chaff /tʃa:f/ *vt* brincar com □ *n* brincadeira *f*; (*husk*) casca *f*
chaffinch /'tʃæfɪntʃ/ *n* tentilhão *m*
chagrin /'ʃægrɪn/ *n* decepção *f*, desgosto *m*, aborrecimento *m*
chain /tʃeɪn/ *n* corrente *f*, cadeia *f*; (*series*) cadeia *f* □ *vt* acorrentar. **~ reaction** reação *f*, (*P*) reacção *f* em cadeia. **~-smoke** *vi* fumar cigarros um atrás do outro. **~ store** loja *f* pertencente a uma cadeia
chair /tʃeə(r)/ *n* cadeira *f*; (*position of chairman*) presidência *f*; (*univ*) cátedra *f* □ *vt* presidir
chairman /'tʃeəmən/ *n* (*pl* **-men**) presidente *mf*
chalet /'ʃæleɪ/ *n* chalé *m*
chalk /tʃɔ:k/ *n* greda *f*, cal *f*; (*for writing*) giz *m* □ *vt* traçar com giz
challeng|e /'tʃælɪndʒ/ *n* desafio *m*; (*by sentry*) interpelação *f* □ *vt* desafiar; (*question truth of*) contestar. **~er** *n* (*sport*) pretendente *mf* (ao título). **~ing** *a* estimulante, que constitui um desafio
chamber /'tʃeɪmbə(r)/ *n* (*old use*) aposento *m*. **~-maid** *n* arrumadeira *f*. **~ music** música *f* de câmara. **C~ of Commerce** Câmara *f* de Comércio
chamois /'ʃæmɪ/ *n*. **~(-leather)** camurça *f*
champagne /ʃæm'peɪn/ *n* champanhe *m*
champion /'tʃæmpɪən/ *n* campeão *m*, campeã *f* □ *vt* defender. **~ship** *n* campeonato *m*
chance /tʃa:ns/ *n* acaso *m*; (*luck*) sorte *f*; (*opportunity*) oportunidade *f*, chance *f*; (*likelihood*) hipótese *f*, probabilidade *f*; (*risk*) risco *m* □ *a* casual, fortuito □ *vi* calhar □ *vt* arriscar. **by ~** por acaso
chancellor /'tʃa:nsələ(r)/ *n* chanceler *m*. **C~ of the Exchequer** Ministro *m* das Finanças
chancy /'tʃa:nsɪ/ *a* arriscado
chandelier /ʃændə'lɪə(r)/ *n* lustre *m*
change /tʃeɪndʒ/ *vt* mudar; (*exchange*) trocar (**for** por); (*clothes, house, trains, etc*) mudar de □ *vi* mudar; (*clothes*) mudar-se, mudar de roupa □ *n* mudança *f*; (*money*) troco *m*. **a ~ of**

clothes uma muda de roupa. **~ hands** (*ownership*) mudar de dono. **~ into** (*a butterfly etc*) transformar-se em; (*evening dress etc*) pôr. **~ one's mind** mudar de idéia. **~ over** passar, mudar (**to** para). **~-over** *n* mudança *f*. **~able** *a* variável

channel /'tʃænl/ *n* canal *m* □ *vt* (*pt* **channelled**) canalizar. **the C~ Islands** as Ilhas do Canal da Mancha. **the (English) C~** o Canal da Mancha

chant /tʃa:nt/ *n* cântico *m*; (*of crowd etc*) *vt/i* cantar, entoar

chao|s /'keɪɒs/ *n* caos *m*. **~tic** /-'ɒtɪk/ *a* caótico

chap /tʃæp/ *n* (*colloq*) sujeito *m*, (*B*) cara *m*, (*P*) tipo *m*

chapel /'tʃæpl/ *n* capela *f*

chaperon /'ʃæpərəʊn/ *n* pau-de-cabeleira *m*, chaperon *m* □ *vt* servir de pau-de-cabeleira *or* de chaperon

chaplain /'tʃæplɪn/ *n* capelão *m*. **~cy** *n* capelania *f*

chapter /'tʃæptə(r)/ *n* capítulo *m*

char /tʃa:(r)/ *vt* (*pt* **charred**) carbonizar

character /'kærəktə(r)/ *n* caráter *m*, (*P*) carácter *m*; (*in novel, play*) personagem *m*; (*reputation*) fama *f*; (*eccentric person*) excêntrico *m*; (*letter*) caractere *m*, (*P*) carácter *m*. **~ize** *vt* caracterizar

characteristic /kærəktə'rɪstɪk/ *a* característico □ *n* característica *f*. **~ally** *adv* tipicamente

charade /ʃə'ra:d/ *n* charada *f*

charcoal /'tʃa:kəʊl/ *n* carvão *m* de lenha

charge /tʃa:dʒ/ *n* preço *m*; (*electr, mil*) carga *f*; (*jur*) acusação *f*; (*task, custody*) cargo *m* □ *vt/i* (*price*) cobrar; (*enemy*) atacar; (*jur*) incriminar. **be in ~ of** ter a cargo. **take ~ of** encarregar-se de

chariot /'tʃærɪət/ *n* carro *m* de guerra *or* triunfal

charisma /kə'rɪzmə/ *n* carisma *m*. **~tic** /kærɪz'mætɪk/ *a* carismático

charit|y /'tʃærətɪ/ *n* caridade *f*; (*society*) instituição *f* de caridade. **~able** *a* caridoso

charlatan /'ʃa:lətən/ *n* charlatão *m*

charm /tʃa:m/ *n* encanto *m*, charme *m*; (*spell*) feitiço *m*; (*talisman*) amuleto *m* □ *vt* encantar. **~ing** *a* encantador

chart /tʃa:t/ *n* (*naut*) carta *f*; (*table*) mapa *m*, gráfico *m*, tabela *f* □ *vt* fazer o mapa de

charter /'tʃa:tə(r)/ *n* carta *f*. **~ (flight)** (voo) charter *m* □ *vt* fretar. **~ed accountant** *n* perito *m* contador, (*P*) perito *m* de contabilidade

charwoman /'tʃa:wʊmən/ *n* (*pl* **-women**) faxineira *f*, (*P*) mulher *f* a dias

chase /tʃeɪs/ *vt* perseguir □ *vi* (*colloq*) correr (**after** atrás de) □ *n* caça *f*, perseguição *f*. **~ away** *or* **off** afugentar, expulsar

chasm /'kæzm/ *n* abismo *m*

chassis /'ʃæsɪ/ *n* chassi *m*

chaste /tʃeɪst/ *a* casto

chastise /tʃæs'taɪz/ *vt* castigar

chastity /'tʃæstətɪ/ *n* castidade *f*

chat /tʃæt/ *n* conversa *f* □ *vi* (*pt* **chatted**) conversar, cavaquear. **have a ~** bater um papo, (*P*) dar dois dedos de conversa. **~ty** *a* conversador

chatter /'tʃætə(r)/ *vi* tagarelar. **his teeth are ~ing** seus dentes estão tiritando □ *n* tagarelice *f*

chauffeur /'ʃəʊfə(r)/ *n* motorista *m*, chofer (particular) *m*, chauffeur *m*

chauvinis|t /'ʃəʊvɪnɪst/ *n* chauvinista *mf*. **male ~t** (*pej*) machista *m*. **~m** /-zəm/ *n* chauvinismo *m*

cheap /tʃi:p/ *a* (**-er**, **-est**) barato; (*fare, rate*) reduzido. **~(ly)** *adv* barato. **~ness** *n* barateza *f*

cheapen /'tʃi:pən/ *vt* depreciar

cheat /tʃi:t/ *vt* enganar, trapacear □ *vi* (*at games*) roubar, (*P*) fazer batota; (*in exams*) copiar □ *n* intrujão *m*; (*at games*) trapaceiro *m*, (*P*) batoteiro *m*

check[1] /tʃek/ *vt/i* (*examine*) verificar; (*tickets*) revisar; (*restrain*) controlar, refrear □ *n* verificação *f*; (*tickets*) controle *m*; (*curb*) freio *m*; (*chess*) xeque *m*; (*Amer: bill*) conta *f*; (*Amer: cheque*) cheque *m*. **~ in** assinar o registro; (*at airport*) fazer o check-in. **~-in** *n* check-in *m*. **~ out** pagar a conta. **~-out** *n* caixa *f*. **~-up** *n* exame *m* médico, check-up *m*

check[2] /tʃek/ *n* (*pattern*) xadrez *m*. **~ed** *a* de xadrez

checkmate /'tʃekmeɪt/ *n* xeque-mate *m*

cheek /tʃi:k/ *n* face *f*; (*fig*) descaramento *m*. **~y** *a* descarado

cheer /tʃɪə(r)/ *n* alegria *f*; (*shout*) viva *m* □ *vt/i* aclamar, aplaudir. **~s!** à sua, (*P*) vossa (saúde)!; (*thank you*) obrigadinho. **~ (up)** animar(-se). **~ful** *a* bem disposto; alegre

cheerio /tʃɪərɪ'əʊ/ *int* (*colloq*) até logo, (*P*) adeusinho

cheese /tʃi:z/ *n* queijo *m*

cheetah /'tʃi:tə/ *n* chita *f*, lobo- tigre *m*

chef /ʃef/ *n* cozinheiro-chefe *m*

chemical /'kemɪkl/ *a* químico □ *n* produto *m* químico

chemist /'kemɪst/ *n* farmacêutico *m*; (*scientist*) químico *m*. **~'s (shop)** *n* farmácia *f*. **~ry** *n* química *f*

cheque /tʃek/ *n* cheque *m*. **~-book** *n* talão *m* de cheques. **~-card** *n* cartão *m* de banco

cherish /ˈtʃerɪʃ/ *vt* estimar, querer; (*hope*) acalentar

cherry /ˈtʃerɪ/ *n* cereja *f*. **~-tree** *n* cerejeira *f*

chess /tʃes/ *n* jogo *m* de xadrez. **~-board** *n* tabuleiro *m* de xadrez

chest /tʃest/ *n* peito *m*; (*for money, jewels*) cofre *m*. **~ of drawers** cômoda *f*, (*P*) cómoda *f*

chestnut /ˈtʃesnʌt/ *n* castanha *f*. **~-tree** *n* castanheiro *m*

chew /tʃu:/ *vt* mastigar. **~ing-gum** *n* chiclete *m*, (*P*) pastilha *f* elástica

chic /ʃi:k/ *a* chique

chick /tʃɪk/ *n* pinto *m*

chicken /ˈtʃɪkɪn/ *n* galinha *f* □ *vi* **~ out** (*sl*) acovardar-se. **~-pox** *n* catapora *f*, (*P*) varicela *f*

chicory /ˈtʃɪkərɪ/ *n* (*for coffee*) chicória *f*; (*for salad*) endívia *f*

chief /tʃi:f/ *n* chefe *m* □ *a* principal. **~ly** *adv* principalmente

chilblain /ˈtʃɪlblem/ *n* frieira *f*

child /tʃaɪld/ *n* (*pl* **children** /ˈtʃɪldrən/) criança *f*; (*son*) filho *m*; (*daughter*) filha *f*. **~hood** *n* infância *f*, meninice *f*. **~ish** *a* infantil; (*immature*) acriançado, pueril. **~less** *a* sem filhos. **~- like** *a* infantil. **~-minder** *n* babá *f* que cuida de crianças em sua propria casa

childbirth /ˈtʃaɪldbɜ:θ/ *n* parto *m*

Chile /ˈtʃɪlɪ/ *n* Chile *m*. **~an** *a* & *n* chileno (*m*)

chill /tʃɪl/ *n* frio *m*; (*med*) resfriado *m*, (*P*) constipação *f* □ *vt*/*i* arrefecer; (*culin*) refrigerar. **~y** *a* frio. **be** *or* **feel ~y** ter frio

chilli /ˈtʃɪlɪ/ *n* (*pl* **-ies**) malagueta *f*

chime /tʃaɪm/ *n* carrilhão *m*; (*sound*) música *m* de carrilhão □ *vt*/*i* tocar

chimney /ˈtʃɪmnɪ/ *n* (*pl* **-eys**) chaminé *f*. **~-sweep** *n* limpador *m* de chaminés, (*P*) limpa-chaminés *m*

chimpanzee /tʃɪmpænˈzi:/ *n* chimpanzé *m*

chin /tʃɪn/ *n* queixo *m*

china /ˈtʃaɪnə/ *n* porcelana *f*; (*crockery*) louça *f*

Chin|a /ˈtʃaɪnə/ *n* China *f*. **~ese** /-ˈni:z/ *a* & *n* chinês (*m*)

chink[1] /tʃɪŋk/ *n* (*crack*) fenda *f*, fresta *f*

chink[2] /tʃɪŋk/ *n* tinir *m* □ *vt*/*i* (fazer) tinir

chip /tʃɪp/ *n* (*broken piece*) bocado *m*; (*culin*) batata *f* frita em palitos; (*gambling*) ficha *f*; (*electronic*) chip *m*, circuito *m* integrado □ *vt*/*i* (*pt* **chipped**) lascar(-se)

chipboard /ˈtʃɪpbɔ:d/ *n* compensado *m* (de madeira)

chiropodist /kɪˈrɒpədɪst/ *n* calista *mf*

chirp /tʃɜ:p/ *n* pipilar *m*; (*of cricket*) cricri *m* □ *vi* pipilar; (*cricket*) cantar, fazer cricri

chisel /ˈtʃɪzl/ *n* cinzel *m*, escopro *m* □ *vt* (*pt* **chiselled**) talhar

chivalr|y /ˈʃɪvlrɪ/ *n* cavalheirismo *m*. **~ous** *a* cavalheiresco

chive /tʃaɪv/ *n* cebolinho *m*

chlorine /ˈklɔ:ri:n/ *n* cloro *m*

chocolate /ˈtʃɒklɪt/ *n* chocolate *m*

choice /tʃɔɪs/ *n* escolha *f* □ *a* escolhido, seleto, (*P*) seleccionado

choir /ˈkwaɪə(r)/ *n* coro *m*

choirboy /ˈkwaɪəbɔɪ/ *n* menino *m* de coro, corista *m*, (*P*) coralista *m*

choke /tʃəʊk/ *vt*/*i* sufocar; (*on food*) engasgar(-se) □ *n* (*auto*) afogador *m*, (*P*) botão *m* do ar (*colloq*)

cholesterol /kəˈlestərɒl/ *n* colesterol *m*

choose /tʃu:z/ *vt*/*i* (*pt* **chose**, *pp* **chosen**) escolher; (*prefer*) preferir. **~ to do** decidir fazer

choosy /ˈtʃu:zɪ/ *a* (*colloq*) exigente, difícil de contentar

chop /tʃɒp/ *vt*/*i* (*pt* **chopped**) cortar □ *n* (*wood*) machadada *f*; (*culin*) costeleta *f*. **~ down** abater. **~per** *n* cutelo *m*; (*sl: helicopter*) helicóptero *m*

choppy /ˈtʃɒpɪ/ *a* (*sea*) picado

chopstick /ˈtʃɒpstɪk/ *n* fachi *m*, pauzinho *m*

choral /ˈkɔ:rəl/ *a* coral

chord /kɔ:d/ *n* (*mus*) acorde *m*

chore /tʃɔ:(r)/ *n* trabalho *m*; (*unpleasant task*) tarefa *f* maçante. **household ~s** afazeres *mpl* domésticos

choreograph|er /kɒrɪˈɒgrəfə(r)/ *n* coreógrafo *m*. **~y** *n* coreografia *f*

chortle /ˈtʃɔ:tl/ *n* risada *f* □ *vi* rir alto

chorus /ˈkɔ:rəs/ *n* coro *m*; (*of song*) refrão *m*, estribilho *m*

chose, chosen /tʃəʊz, ˈtʃəʊzn/ *see* **choose**

Christ /kraɪst/ *n* Cristo *m*

christen /ˈkrɪsn/ *vt* batizar, (*P*) baptizar. **~ing** *n* batismo *m*, (*P*) baptismo *m*

Christian /ˈkrɪstʃən/ *a* & *n* cristão (*m*). **~ name** nome *m* de batismo, (*P*) baptismo. **~ity** /-stɪˈænətɪ/ *n* cristandade *f*

Christmas /ˈkrɪsməs/ *n* Natal *m* □ *a* do Natal. **~ card** cartão *m* de Boas Festas. **~ Day/Eve** dia *m*/véspera *f* de Natal. **~ tree** árvore *f* de Natal

chrome /krəʊm/ *n* cromo *m*

chromosome /ˈkrəʊməsəʊm/ *n* cromossoma *m*

chronic /ˈkrɒnɪk/ *a* crônico, (*P*) crónico

chronicle /'krɒnɪkl/ *n* crônica *f*
chronological /krɒnə'lɒdʒɪkl/ *a* cronológico
chrysanthemum /krɪ'sænθəməm/ *n* crisântemo *m*
chubby /'tʃʌbɪ/ *a* (**-ier, -iest**) gorducho, rechonchudo
chuck /tʃʌk/ *vt* (*colloq*) deitar, atirar. ~ **out** (*person*) expulsar; (*thing*) jogar fora, (*P*) deitar fora
chuckle /'tʃʌkl/ *n* riso *m* abafado ▫ *vi* rir sozinho
chum /tʃʌm/ *n* (*colloq*) amigo *m* íntimo, camarada *mf*. ~**my** *a* amigável
chunk /tʃʌŋk/ *n* (grande) bocado *m*, naco *m*
church /tʃɜ:tʃ/ *n* igreja *f*
churchyard /'tʃɜ:tʃja:d/ *n* cemitério *m*
churlish /'tʃɜ:lɪʃ/ *a* grosseiro, indelicado
churn /tʃɜ:n/ *n* batedeira *f*; (*milk can*) vasilha *f* de leite ▫ *vt* bater. ~ **out** produzir em série
chute /ʃu:t/ *n* calha *f*; (*for rubbish*) conduta *f* de lixo
chutney /'tʃʌtnɪ/ *n* (*pl* **-eys**) chutney *m*
cider /'saɪdə(r)/ *n* sidra *f*, (*P*) cidra *f*
cigar /sɪ'ga:(r)/ *n* charuto *m*
cigarette /sɪgə'ret/ *n* cigarro *m*. ~**-case** *n* cigarreira *f*
cinder /'sɪndə(r)/ *n* brasa *f*. **burnt to a** ~ estorricado
cinema /'sɪnəmə/ *n* cinema *m*
cinnamon /'sɪnəmən/ *n* canela *f*
cipher /'saɪfə(r)/ *n* cifra *f*
circle /'sɛ:kl/ *n* círculo *m*; (*theat*) balcão *m* ▫ *vt* dar a volta a ▫ *vi* descrever círculos, voltear
circuit /'sɜ:kɪt/ *n* circuito *m*
circuitous /sɜ:'kju:ɪtəs/ *a* indireto, tortuoso
circular /'sɜ:kjʊlə(r)/ *a* circular
circulat|e /'sɜ:kjʊleɪt/ *vt/i* (fazer) circular. ~**ion** /-'leɪʃn/ *n* circulação *f*; (*sales of newspaper*) tiragem *f*
circumcis|e /'sɜ:kəmsaɪz/ *vt* circuncidar. ~**ion** /-'sɪʒn/ *n* circuncisão *f*
circumference /sə'kʌmfərəns/ *n* circunferência *f*
circumflex /'sɜ:kəmfleks/ *n* circunflexo *m*
circumstance /'sɜ:kəmstəns/ *n* circunstância *f*. ~**s** (*means*) situação *f* econômica, (*P*) económica
circus /'sɜ:kəs/ *n* circo *m*
cistern /'sɪstən/ *n* reservatório *m*; (*of WC*) autoclismo *m*
cit|e /saɪt/ *vt* citar. ~**ation** /-'teɪʃn/ *n* citação *f*
citizen /'sɪtɪzn/ *n* cidadão *m*, cidadã *f*; (*of town*) habitante *mf*. ~**ship** *n* cidadania *f*
citrus /'sɪtrəs/ *n* ~ **fruit** citrino *m*
city /'sɪtɪ/ *n* cidade *f*
civic /'sɪvɪk/ *a* cívico
civil /'sɪvl/ *a* civil; (*rights*) cívico; (*polite*) delicado. ~ **servant** funcionário *m* público. **C**~ **Service** Administração *f* Pública. ~ **war** guerra *f* civil. ~**ity** /-'vɪlətɪ/ *n* civilidade *f*, cortesia *f*
civilian /sɪ'vɪlɪən/ *a* & *n* civil (*mf*), paisano *m*
civiliz|e /'sɪvəlaɪz/ *vt* civilizar. ~**ation** /-'zeɪʃn/ *n* civilização *f*
claim /kleɪm/ *vt* reclamar; (*assert*) pretender ▫ *vi* (*from insurance*) reclamar ▫ *n* reivindicação *f*; (*assertion*) afirmação *f*; (*right*) direito *m*; (*from insurance*) reclamação *f*
clairvoyant /kleə'vɔɪənt/ *n* vidente *mf* ▫ *a* clarividente
clam /klæm/ *n* molusco *m*
clamber /'klæmbə(r)/ *vi* trepar
clammy /'klæmɪ/ *a* (**-ier, -iest**) úmido, (*P*) húmido e pegajoso
clamour /'klæmə(r)/ *n* clamor *m*, vociferação *f* ▫ *vi* ~ **for** exigir aos gritos
clamp /klæmp/ *n* grampo *m*; (*for car*) bloqueador *m* ▫ *vt* prender com grampo; (*a car*) bloquear. ~ **down on** apertar, suprimir; (*colloq*) cair em cima de (*colloq*)
clan /klæn/ *n* clã *m*
clandestine /klæn'destɪn/ *a* clandestino
clang /klæŋ/ *n* tinir *m*
clap /klæp/ *vt/i* (*pt* **clapped**) aplaudir; (*put*) meter ▫ *n* aplauso *m*; (*of thunder*) ribombo *m*. ~ **one's hands** bater palmas
claptrap /'klæptræp/ *n* parlapatice *f*
claret /'klærət/ *n* clarete *m*
clarif|y /'klærɪfaɪ/ *vt* esclarecer. ~**ication** /-ɪ'keɪʃn/ *n* esclarecimento *m*
clarinet /klærɪ'net/ *n* clarinete *m*
clarity /'klærətɪ/ *n* claridade *f*
clash /klæʃ/ *n* choque *m*; (*sound*) estridor *m*; (*fig*) conflito *m* ▫ *vt/i* entrechocar(-se); (*of colours*) destoar
clasp /kla:sp/ *n* (*fastener*) fecho *m*; (*hold, grip*) aperto *m* de mão ▫ *vt* apertar, serrar
class /kla:s/ *n* classe *f* ▫ *vt* classificar
classic /'klæsɪk/ *a* & *n* clássico (*m*). ~**s** *npl* letras *fpl* clássicas, (*P*) estudos *mpl* clássicos. ~**al** *a* clássico
classif|y /'klæsɪfaɪ/ *vt* classificar. ~**ication** /-ɪ'keɪʃn/ *n* classificação *f*. ~**ied advertisement** (anúncio *m*) classificado (*m*)

classroom /'kla:sru:m/ *n* sala *f* de aulas
clatter /'klætə(r)/ *n* estardalhaço *m* □ *vi* fazer barulho
clause /klɔ:z/ *n* cláusula *f*; (*gram*) oração *f*
claustrophob|ia /klɔ:strə'fəʊbɪə/ *n* claustrofobia *f*. **~ic** *a* claustrofóbico
claw /klɔ:/ *n* garra *f*; (*of lobster*) tenaz *f*, pinça *f* □ *vt* (*seize*) agarrar; (*scratch*) arranhar; (*tear*) rasgar
clay /kleɪ/ *n* argila *f*, barro *m*
clean /kli:n/ *a* (**-er, -est**) limpo □ *adv* completamente □ *vt* limpar □ *vi* **~ up** fazer a limpeza. **~-shaven** *a* de cara rapada. **~er** *n* faxineira *f*, (*P*) mulher *f* da limpeza; (*of clothes*) empregado *m* da tinturaria. **~ly** *adv* com limpeza, como deve ser
cleans|e /klenz/ *vt* limpar; (*fig*) purificar. **~ing cream** creme *m* de limpeza
clear /klɪə(r)/ *a* (**-er, -est**) claro; (*glass*) transparente; (*without obstacles*) livre; (*profit*) líquido; (*sky*) limpo □ *adv* claramente □ *vt* (*snow, one's name, etc*) limpar; (*the table*) tirar; (*jump*) transpor; (*debt*) saldar; (*jur*) absolver; (*through customs*) despachar □ *vi* (*fog*) dissipar-se; (*sky*) limpar. **~ of** (*away from*) afastado de. **~ off** *or* **out** (*sl*) sair andando, zarpar. **~ out** (*clean*) fazer a limpeza. **~ up** (*tidy*) arrumar; (*mystery*) desvendar; (*of weather*) clarear, limpar. **~ly** *adv* claramente
clearance /'klɪərəns/ *n* autorização *f*; (*for ship*) despacho *m*; (*space*) espaço *m* livre. **~ sale** liquidação *f*, saldos *mpl*
clearing /'klɪərɪŋ/ *n* clareira *f*
clearway /'klɪəweɪ/ *n* rodovia *f* de estacionamento proibido
cleavage /'kli:vɪdʒ/ *n* divisão *f*; (*between breasts*) rego *m*; (*of dress*) decote *m*
cleaver /'kli:və(r)/ *n* cutelo *m*
clef /klef/ *n* (*mus*) clave *f*
cleft /kleft/ *n* fenda *f*
clench /klentʃ/ *vt* (*teeth, fists*) cerrar; (*grasp*) agarrar
clergy /'klɜ:dʒɪ/ *n* clero *m*. **~man** *n* (*pl* **-men**) clérigo *m*, sacerdote *m*
cleric /'klerɪk/ *n* clérigo *m*. **~al** *a* (*relig*) clerical; (*of clerks*) de escritório
clerk /kla:k/ *n* auxiliar *m* de escritório
clever /'klevə(r)/ *a* (**-er, -est**) esperto, inteligente; (*skilful*) hábil, habilidoso. **~ly** *adv* inteligentemente; (*skilfully*) habilmente, habilidosamente. **~ness** *n* esperteza *f*, inteligência *f*
cliché /'kli:ʃeɪ/ *n* chavão *m*, lugar-comum *m*, clichê *m*
click /klɪk/ *n* estalido *m*, clique *m* □ *vi* dar um estalido; (*comput*) clicar
client /'klaɪənt/ *n* cliente *mf*
clientele /kli:ən'tel/ *n* clientela *f*
cliff /klɪf/ *n* penhasco *m*. **~s** *npl* falésia *f*
climat|e /'klaɪmɪt/ *n* clima *m*. **~ic** /-'mætɪk/ *a* climático
climax /'klaɪmæks/ *n* clímax *m*, ponto *m* culminante
climb /klaɪm/ *vt* (*stairs*) subir; (*tree, wall*) subir em, trepar em; (*mountain*) escalar □ *vi* subir, trepar □ *n* subida *f*; (*mountain*) escalada *f*. **~ down** descer; (*fig*) dar a mão à palmatória (*fig*). **~er** *n* (*sport*) alpinista *mf*; (*plant*) trepadeira *f*
clinch /klɪntʃ/ *vt* (*deal*) fechar; (*argument*) resolver
cling /klɪŋ/ *vi* (*pt* **clung**) **~ (to)** agarrar-se (a); (*stick*) colar-se (a)
clinic /'klɪnɪk/ *n* clínica *f*
clinical /'klɪnɪkl/ *a* clínico
clink /klɪŋk/ *n* tinido *m* □ *vt*/*i* (fazer) tilintar
clip[1] /klɪp/ *m* (*for paper*) clipe *m*; (*for hair*) grampo *m*, (*P*) gancho *m*; (*for tube*) braçadeira *f* □ *vt* (*pt* **clipped**) prender
clip[2] /klɪp/ *vt* (*pt* **clipped**) cortar; (*trim*) aparar □ *n* tosquia *f*; (*colloq: blow*) murro *m*. **~ping** *n* recorte *m*
clique /kli:k/ *n* panelinha *f*, facção *f*, conventículo *m*
cloak /kləʊk/ *n* capa *f*, manto *m*
cloakroom /'kləʊkru:m/ *n* vestiário *m*; (*toilet*) toalete *m*, (*P*) lavabo *m*
clock /klɒk/ *n* relógio *m* □ *vi* **~ in/out** marcar o ponto (à entrada/à saída). **~ up** (*colloq: miles etc*) fazer
clockwise /'klɒkwaɪz/ *a* & *adv* no sentido dos ponteiros do relógio
clockwork /'klɒkwɜ:k/ *n* mecanismo *m*. **go like ~** ir às mil maravilhas
clog /klɒg/ *n* tamanco *m*, soco *m* □ *vt*/*i* (*pt* **clogged**) entupir(-se)
cloister /'klɔɪstə(r)/ *n* claustro *m*
close[1] /kləʊs/ *a* (**-er, -est**) próximo (**to** de); (*link, collaboration*) estreito; (*friend*) íntimo; (*weather*) abafado □ *adv* perto. **~ at hand, ~ by** muito perto. **~ together** (*crowded*) espremido. **have a ~ shave** (*fig*) escapar por um triz. **~-up** *n* grande plano *m*. **~ly** *adv* de perto. **~ness** *n* proximidade *f*
close[2] /kləʊz/ *vt*/*i* fechar(-se); (*end*) terminar; (*of shop etc*) fechar □ *n* fim *m*. **~d shop** organização *f* que só admite trabalhadores sindicalizados
closet /'klɒzɪt/ *n* armário *m*
closure /'kləʊʒə(r)/ *n* encerramento *m*
clot /klɒt/ *n* coágulo *m* □ *vi* (*pt* **clotted**) coagular

cloth /klɒθ/ *n* pano *m*; (*tablecloth*) toalha *f* de mesa

cloth|e /kləʊð/ *vt* vestir. **~ing** *n* vestuário *m*, roupa *f*

clothes /kləʊðz/ *npl* roupa *f*, vestuário *m*. **~-line** *n* varal *m* para roupa

cloud /klaʊd/ *n* núvem *f* ▫ *vt/i* toldar(-se). **~y** *a* nublado, toldado; (*liquid*) turvo

clout /klaʊt/ *n* cascudo *m*, (*P*) carolo *m*; (*colloq: power*) poder *m* efectivo ▫ *vt* (*colloq*) bater

clove /kləʊv/ *n* cravo *m*. **~ of garlic** dente *m* de alho

clover /'kləʊvə(r)/ *n* trevo *m*

clown /klaʊn/ *n* palhaço *m* ▫ *vi* fazer palhaçadas

club /klʌb/ *n* clube *m*; (*weapon*) cacete *m*. **~s** (*cards*) paus *mpl* ▫ *vt/i* (*pt* **clubbed**) dar bordoadas *or* cacetadas (em). **~ together** (*share costs*) cotizar-se

cluck /klʌk/ *vi* cacarejar

clue /klu:/ *n* indício *m*, pista *f*; (*in crossword*) definição *f*. **not have a ~** (*colloq*) não fazer a menor idéia

clump /klʌmp/ *n* maciço *m*, tufo *m*

clumsy /'klʌmzɪ/ *a* (**-ier, -iest**) desajeitado

clung /klʌŋ/ *see* **cling**

cluster /'klʌstə(r)/ *n* (pequeno) grupo *m*; (*bot*) cacho *m* ▫ *vt/i* agrupar(-se)

clutch /klʌtʃ/ *vt* agarrar (em), apertar ▫ *vi* agarrar-se (**at** a) ▫ *n* (*auto*) embreagem *f*, (*P*) embraiagem *f*. **~es** *npl* garras *fpl*

clutter /'klʌtə(r)/ *n* barafunda *f*, desordem *f* ▫ *vt* atravancar

coach /kəʊtʃ/ *n* ônibus *m*, (*P*) camioneta *f*; (*of train*) carruagem *f*; (*sport*) treinador *m* ▫ *vt* (*tutor*) dar aulas a; (*sport*) treinar

coagulate /kəʊ'ægjʊleɪt/ *vt/i* coagular(-se)

coal /kəʊl/ *n* carvão *m*

coalfield /'kəʊlfi:ld/ *n* região *f* carbonífera

coalition /kəʊə'lɪʃn/ *n* coligação *f*

coarse /kɔ:s/ *a* (**-er, -est**) grosseiro

coast /kəʊst/ *n* costa *f* ▫ *vi* costear; (*cycle*) descer em roda-livre; (*car*) ir em ponto morto. **~al** *a* costeiro

coastguard /'kəʊstga:d/ *n* polícia *f* marítima

coastline /'kəʊstlaɪn/ *n* litoral *m*

coat /kəʊt/ *n* casaco *m*; (*of animal*) pêlo *m*; (*of paint*) camada *f*, demão *f* ▫ *vt* cobrir. **~ of arms** brasão *m*. **~ing** *n* camada *f*

coax /kəʊks/ *vt* levar com afagos ou lisonjas, convencer

cobble /'kɒbl/ *n* **~(-stone)** *n* pedra *f* de calçada

cobweb /'kɒbweb/ *n* teia *f* de aranha

cocaine /kəʊ'keɪn/ *n* cocaína *f*

cock /kɒk/ *n* (*male bird*) macho *m*; (*rooster*) galo *m* ▫ *vt* (*gun*) engatilhar; (*ears*) fitar. **~-eyed** *a* (*sl: askew*) de esguelha

cockerel /'kɒkərəl/ *n* frango *m*, galo *m* novo

cockle /'kɒkl/ *n* berbigão *m*

cockney /'kɒknɪ/ *n* (*pl* **-eys**) (*person*) londrino *m*; (*dialect*) dialeto *m* do leste de Londres

cockpit /'kɒkpɪt/ *n* cabine *f*

cockroach /'kɒkrəʊtʃ/ *n* barata *f*

cocktail /'kɒkteɪl/ *n* cocktail *m*, coquetel *m*. **fruit ~** salada *f* de fruta

cocky /'kɒkɪ/ *a* (**-ier, -iest**) convencido (*colloq*)

cocoa /'kəʊkəʊ/ *n* cacau *m*

coconut /'kəʊkənʌt/ *n* coco *m*

cocoon /kə'ku:n/ *n* casulo *m*

cod /kɒd/ *n* (*pl invar*) bacalhau *m*. **~-liver oil** óleo *m* de fígado de bacalhau

code /kəʊd/ *n* código *m* ▫ *vt* codificar

coeducational /kəʊedʒʊ'keɪʃənl/ *a* misto

coerc|e /kəʊ'ɜ:s/ *vt* coagir. **~ion** /-ʃn/ *n* coação *f*, (*P*) coacção *f*

coexist /kəʊɪg'zɪst/ *vi* coexistir. **~ence** *n* coexistência *f*

coffee /'kɒfɪ/ *n* café *m*. **~ bar** café *m*. **~-pot** *n* cafeteira *f*. **~-table** *n* mesa *f* baixa

coffin /'kɒfɪn/ *n* caixão *m*

cog /kɒg/ *n* dente *m* de roda. **a ~ in the machine** (*fig*) uma rodinha numa engrenagem

cogent /'kəʊdʒənt/ *a* convincente; (*relevant*) pertinente

cognac /'kɒnjæk/ *n* conhaque *m*

cohabit /kəʊ'hæbɪt/ *vi* coabitar

coherent /kə'hɪərənt/ *a* coerente

coil /kɔɪl/ *vt/i* enrolar(-se) ▫ *n* rolo *m*; (*electr*) bobina *f*; (*one ring*) espiral *f*; (*contraceptive*) dispositivo *m* intra-uterino, DIU

coin /kɔɪn/ *n* moeda *f* ▫ *vt* cunhar

coincide /kəʊɪn'saɪd/ *vi* coincidir

coinciden|ce /kəʊ'ɪnsɪdəns/ *n* coincidência *f*. **~tal** /-'dentl/ *a* que acontece por coincidência

colander /'kʌləndə(r)/ *n* peneira *f*, (*P*) coador *m*

cold /kəʊld/ *a* (**-er, -est**) frio ▫ *n* frio *m*; (*med*) resfriado *m*, constipação *f*. **be** *or* **feel ~** estar com frio. **it's ~** está frio. **~-blooded** *a* (*person*) insensível; (*deed*) a sangue frio. **~ cream** creme *m* para a pele. **~ness** *n* frio *m*; (*of feeling*) frieza *f*

coleslaw /'kəʊlslɔ:/ *n* salada *f* de repolho cru

colic /'kɒlɪk/ *n* cólica(s) *f* (*pl*)
collaborat|e /kə'læbəreɪt/ *vi* colaborar. **~ion** /-'reɪʃn/ *n* colaboração *f*. **~or** *n* colaborador *m*
collapse /kə'læps/ *vi* desabar; (*med*) ter um colapso ▫ *n* colapso *m*
collapsible /kə'læpsəbl/ *a* desmontável, dobrável
collar /'kɒlə(r)/ *n* gola *f*; (*of shirt*) colarinho *m*; (*of dog*) coleira *f* ▫ *vt* (*colloq*) pôr a mão a. **~-bone** *n* clavícula *f*
colleague /'kɒli:g/ *n* colega *mf*
collect /kə'lekt/ *vt* (*gather*) juntar; (*fetch*) ir/vir buscar; (*money, rent*) cobrar; (*as hobby*) colecionar, (*P*) coleccionar ▫ *vi* juntar-se. **call ~** (*Amer*) chamar a cobrar. **~ion** /-ʃn/ *n* coleção *f*, (*P*) colecção *f*; (*in church*) coleta *f*, (*P*) colecta *f*; (*of mail*) tiragem *f*, coleta *f*, (*P*) abertura *f*. **~or** *n* (*as hobby*) colecionador *m*, (*P*) coleccionador *m*
collective /kə'lektɪv/ *a* coletivo, (*P*) colectivo
college /'kɒlɪdʒ/ *n* colégio *m*
collide /kə'laɪd/ *vi* colidir
colliery /'kɒlɪərɪ/ *n* mina *f* de carvão
collision /kə'lɪʒn/ *n* colisão *f*, choque *m*; (*fig*) conflito *m*
colloquial /kə'ləʊkwɪəl/ *a* coloquial. **~ism** *n* expressão *f* coloquial
collusion /kə'lu:ʒn/ *n* conluio *m*
colon /'kəʊlən/ *n* (*gram*) dois pontos *mpl*; (*anat*) cólon *m*
colonel /'kɜ:nl/ *n* coronel *m*
colonize /'kɒlənaɪz/ *vt* colonizar
colon|y /'kɒlənɪ/ *n* colônia *f*, (*P*) colónia *f*. **~ial** /kə'ləʊnɪəl/ *a* & *n* colonial (*mf*)
colossal /kə'lɒsl/ *a* colossal
colour /'kʌlə(r)/ *n* cor *f* ▫ *a* (*photo, TV, etc*) a cores; (*film*) colorido ▫ *vt* colorir, dar cor a ▫ *vi* (*blush*) corar. **~-blind** *a* daltônico, (*P*) daltónico. **~ful** *a* colorido. **~ing** *n* (*of skin*) cor *f*; (*in food*) corante *m*. **~less** *a* descolorido
coloured /'kʌləd/ *a* (*pencil, person*) de cor ▫ *n* pessoa *f* de cor
column /'kɒləm/ *n* coluna *f*
columnist /'kɒləmnɪst/ *n* colunista *mf*
coma /'kəʊmə/ *n* coma *m*
comb /kəʊm/ *n* pente *m* ▫ *vt* pentear; (*search*) vasculhar. **~ one's hair** pentear-se
combat /'kɒmbæt/ *n* combate *m* ▫ *vt* (*pt* **combated**) combater
combination /kɒmbɪ'neɪʃn/ *n* combinação *f*
combine /kəm'baɪn/ *vt*/*i* combinar(-se), juntar(-se), reunir(-se)
combustion /kəm'bʌstʃən/ *n* combustão *f*
come /kʌm/ *vi* (*pt* **came**, *pp* **come**) vir; (*arrive*) chegar; (*occur*) suceder. **~ about** acontecer. **~ across** encontrar, dar com. **~ away** *or* **off** soltar-se. **~ back** voltar. **~-back** *n* regresso *m*; (*retort*) réplica *f*. **~ by** obter. **~ down** descer; (*price*) baixar. **~-down** *n* humilhação *f*. **~ from** vir de. **~ in** entrar. **~ into** (*money*) herdar. **~ off** (*succeed*) ter êxito; (*fare*) sair-se. **~ on!** vamos! **~ out** sair. **~ round** (*after fainting*) voltar a si; (*be converted*) deixar-se convencer. **~ to** (*amount to*) montar a. **~ up** subir; (*seeds*) despontar; (*fig*) surgir. **~ up with** (*idea*) vir com, propor. **~-uppance** *n* castigo *m* merecido
comedian /kə'mi:dɪən/ *n* comediante *mf*
comedy /'kɒmədɪ/ *n* comédia *f*
comet /'kɒmɪt/ *n* cometa *m*
comfort /'kʌmfət/ *n* conforto *m* ▫ *vt* confortar, consolar. **~able** *a* confortável
comic /'kɒmɪk/ *a* cômico, (*P*) cómico ▫ *n* cômico *m*, (*P*) cómico *m*; (*periodical*) estórias *fpl* em quadrinhos, (*P*) revista *f* de banda desenhada. **~ strip** estória *f* em quadrinhos, (*P*) banda *f* desenhada. **~al** *a* cômico, (*P*) cómico
coming /'kʌmɪŋ/ *n* vinda *f* ▫ *a* próximo. **~s and goings** idas e vindas *fpl*
comma /'kɒmə/ *n* vírgula *f*
command /kə'ma:nd/ *n* (*mil*) comando *m*; (*order*) ordem *f*; (*mastery*) domínio *m* ▫ *vt* comandar; (*respect*) inspirar, impor. **~er** *n* comandante *m*. **~ing** *a* imponente
commandeer /kɒmən'dɪə(r)/ *vt* requisitar
commandment /kə'ma:ndmənt/ *n* mandamento *m*
commemorat|e /kə'meməreɪt/ *vt* comemorar. **~ion** /-'reɪʃn/ *n* comemoração *f*. **~ive** *a* comemorativo
commence /kə'mens/ *vt*/*i* começar. **~ment** *n* começo *m*
commend /kə'mend/ *vt* louvar; (*entrust*) confiar. **~able** *a* louvável. **~ation** /kɒmen'deɪʃn/ *n* louvor *m*
comment /'kɒment/ *n* comentário *m* ▫ *vi* comentar. **~ on** comentar, fazer comentários
commentary /'kɒməntrɪ/ *n* comentário *m*; (*radio, TV*) relato *m*
commentat|e /'kɒmənteɪt/ *vi* fazer um relato. **~or** *n* (*radio, TV*) comentarista *mf*, (*P*) comentador *m*
commerce /'kɒmɜ:s/ *n* comércio *m*

commercial /kə'mɜ:ʃl/ *a* comercial □ *n* publicidade (comercial) *f*. **~ize** *vt* comercializar

commiserat|e /kə'mɪzəreɪt/ *vi* **~ with** compadecer-se de. **~ion** /-'reɪʃn/ *n* comiseração *f*, pesar *m*

commission /kə'mɪʃn/ *n* comissão *f*; (*order for work*) encomenda *f* □ *vt* encomendar; (*mil*) nomear. **~ to do** encarregar de fazer. **out of ~** fora de serviço ativo, (*P*) activo. **~er** *n* comissário *m*; (*police*) chefe *m*

commit /kə'mɪt/ *vt* (*pt* **committed**) cometer; (*entrust*) confiar. **~ o.s.** comprometer-se, empenhar-se. **~ suicide** suicidar-se. **~ to memory** decorar. **~ment** *n* compromisso *m*

committee /kə'mɪtɪ/ *n* comissão *f*, comitê *m*, (*P*) comité *m*

commodity /kə'mɒdətɪ/ *n* artigo *m*, mercadoria *f*

common /'kɒmən/ *a* (**-er**, **-est**) comum; (*usual*) usual, corrente; (*pej: ill-bred*) ordinario □ *n* prado *m* público, (*P*) baldio *m*. **~ law** direito *m* consuetudinário. **C~ Market** Mercado *m* Comum. **~-room** *n* sala *f* dos professores. **~ sense** bom senso *m*, senso *m* comum. **House of C~s** Câmara *f* dos Comuns. **in ~** em comum. **~ly** *adv* mais comum

commoner /'kɒmənə(r)/ *n* plebeu *m*

commonplace /'kɒmənpleɪs/ *a* banal □ *n* lugar-comum *m*

commotion /kə'məʊʃn/ *n* agitação *f*, confusão *f*, barulheira *f*

communal /'kɒmjʊnl/ *a* (*of a commune*) comunal; (*shared*) comum

commune /'kɒmju:n/ *n* comuna *f*

communicat|e /kə'mju:nɪkeɪt/ *vt/i* comunicar. **~ion** /-'keɪʃn/ *n* comunicação *f*. **~ion cord** sinal *m* de alarme. **~ive** /-ətɪv/ *a* comunicativo

communion /kə'mju:nɪən/ *n* comunhão *f*

communis|t /'kɒmjʊnɪst/ *n* comunista *mf* □ *a* comunista. **~m** /-zəm/ *n* comunismo *m*

community /kə'mju:nətɪ/ *n* comunidade *f*. **~ centre** centro *m* comunitário

commute /kə'mju:t/ *vi* viajar diariamente para o trabalho. **~r** /-ə(r)/ *n* pessoa *f* que viaja diariamente para o trabalho

compact[1] /kəm'pækt/ *a* compacto. **~ disc** /'kɒmpækt/ cd *m*

compact[2] /'kɒmpækt/ *n* estojo *m* de pó-de-arroz, (*P*) caixa *f*

companion /kəm'pænɪən/ *n* companheiro *m*. **~ship** *n* companhia *f*, convívio *m*

company /'kʌmpənɪ/ *n* companhia *f*; (*guests*) visitas *fpl*. **keep sb ~** fazer companhia a alg

comparable /'kɒmpərəbl/ *a* comparável

compar|e /kəm'peə(r)/ *vt/i* comparar(-se) (**to, with** com). **~ative** /-'pærətɪv/ *a* comparativo; (*comfort etc*) relativo

comparison /kəm'pærɪsn/ *n* comparação *f*

compartment /kəm'pa:tmənt/ *n* compartimento *m*

compass /'kʌmpəs/ *n* bússola *f*. **~es** compasso *m*

compassion /kəm'pæʃn/ *n* compaixão *f*. **~ate** *a* compassivo

compatib|le /kəm'pætəbl/ *a* compatível. **~ility** /-'bɪlətɪ/ *n* compatibilidade *f*

compel /kəm'pel/ *vt* (*pt* **compelled**) compelir, forçar. **~ling** *a* irresistível, convincente

compensat|e /'kɒmpənseɪt/ *vt/i* compensar. **~ion** /-'seɪʃn/ *n* compensação *f*; (*financial*) indenização *f*, (*P*) indemnização *f*

compete /kəm'pi:t/ *vi* competir. **~ with** rivalizar com

competen|t /'kɒmpɪtənt/ *a* competente. **~ce** *n* competência *f*

competition /kɒmpə'tɪʃn/ *n* competição *f*; (*comm*) concorrência *f*

competitive /kəm'petɪtɪv/ *a* (*sport, prices*) competitivo. **~ examination** concurso *m*

competitor /kəm'petɪtə(r)/ *n* competidor *m*, concorrente *mf*

compile /kəm'paɪl/ *vt* compilar, coligir. **~r** /-ə(r)/ *n* compilador *m*

complacen|t /kəm'pleɪsnt/ *a* satisfeito consigo mesmo, (*P*) complacente. **~cy** *n* (auto-)satisfação *f*, (*P*) complacência *f*

complain /kəm'pleɪn/ *vi* queixar-se (**about**, **of** de)

complaint /kəm'pleɪnt/ *n* queixa *f*; (*in shop*) reclamação *f*; (*med*) doença *f*, achaque *m*

complement /'kɒmplɪmənt/ *n* complemento *m* □ *vt* completar, complementar. **~ary** /-'mentrɪ/ *a* complementar

complet|e /kəm'pli:t/ *a* completo; (*finished*) acabado; (*downright*) perfeito □ *vt* completar; (*a form*) preencher. **~ely** *adv* completamente. **~ion** /-ʃn/ *n* conclusão *f*, feitura *f*, realização *f*

complex /'kɒmpleks/ *a* complexo □ *n* complexo *m*. **~ity** /kəm'pleksətɪ/ *n* complexidade *f*

complexion /kəm'plekʃn/ *n* cor *f* da tez; (*fig*) caráter *m*, (*P*) carácter *m*, aspecto *m*

compliance /kəm'plaɪəns/ *n* docilidade *f*; (*agreement*) conformidade *f*. **in ~ with** em conformidade com

complicat|e /'kɒmplɪkeɪt/ *vt* complicar. **~ed** *a* complicado. **~ion** /-'keɪʃn/ *n* complicação *f*

compliment /'kɒmplɪmənt/ *n* cumprimento *m* □ *vt* /'kɒmplɪment/ cumprimentar

complimentary /kɒmplɪ'mentrɪ/ *a* amável, elogioso. **~ copy** oferta *f*. **~ ticket** bilhete *m* grátis

comply /kəm'plaɪ/ *vi* **~ with** agir em conformidade com

component /kəm'pəʊnənt/ *n* componente *m*; (*of machine*) peça *f* □ *a* componente, constituinte

compose /kəm'pəʊz/ *vt* compor. **~ o.s.** acalmar-se, dominar-se. **~d** *a* calmo, senhor de si. **~r** /-ə(r)/ *n* compositor *m*

composition /kɒmpə'zɪʃn/ *n* composição *f*

compost /'kɒmpɒst/ *n* húmus *m*, adubo *m*

composure /kəm'pəʊʒə(r)/ *n* calma *f*, domínio *m* de si mesmo

compound /'kɒmpaʊnd/ *n* composto *m*; (*enclosure*) cercado *m*, recinto *m* □ *a* composto. **~ fracture** fratura *f*, (*P*) fractura *f* exposta

comprehen|d /kɒmprɪ'hend/ *vt* compreender. **~sion** *n* compreensão *f*

comprehensive /kɒmprɪ'hensɪv/ *a* compreensivo, vasto; (*insurance*) contra todos os riscos. **~ school** escola *f* de ensino secundário técnico e acadêmico, (*P*) académico

compress /kəm'pres/ *vt* comprimir. **~ion** /-ʃn/ *n* compressão *f*

comprise /kəm'praɪz/ *vt* compreender, abranger

compromise /'kɒmprəmaɪz/ *n* compromisso *m* □ *vt* comprometer □ *vi* chegar a um meio-termo

compulsion /kəm'pʌlʃn/ *n* (*constraint*) coação *f*; (*psych*) desejo *m* irresistível

compulsive /kəm'pʌlsɪv/ *a* (*psych*) compulsivo; (*liar, smoker etc*) inveterado

compulsory /kəm'pʌlsərɪ/ *a* obrigatório, compulsório

computer /kəm'pju:tə(r)/ *n* computador *m*. **~ science** informática *f*. **~ize** *vt* computerizar

comrade /'kɒmreɪd/ *n* camarada *mf*. **~ship** *n* camaradagem *f*

con[1] /kɒn/ *vt* (*pt* **conned**) (*sl*) enganar □ *n* (*sl*) intrujice *f*, vigarice *f*, burla *f*. **~ man** (*sl*) intrujão *m*, vigarista *m*, burlão *m*

con[2] /kɒn/ *see* **pro**

concave /'kɒŋkeɪv/ *a* côncavo

conceal /kən'si:l/ *vt* ocultar, esconder. **~ment** *n* encobrimento *m*

concede /kən'si:d/ *vt* conceder, admitir; (*in a game etc*) ceder

conceit /kən'si:t/ *n* presunção *f*. **~ed** *a* presunçoso, presumido, cheio de si

conceivabl|e /kən'si:vəbl/ *a* concebível. **~y** *adv* possivelmente

conceive /kən'si:v/ *vt/i* conceber

concentrat|e /'kɒnsntreɪt/ *vt/i* concentrar(-se). **~ion** /-'treɪʃn/ *n* concentração *f*

concept /'kɒnsept/ *n* conceito *m*

conception /kən'sepʃn/ *n* concepção *f*

concern /kən'sɜ:n/ *n* (*worry*) preocupação *f*; (*business*) negócio *m* □ *vt* dizer respeito a, respeitar. **~ o.s. with, be ~ed with** interessar-se por, ocupar-se de; (*regard*) dizer respeito a. **it's no ~ of mine** não me diz respeito. **~ing** *prep* sobre, respeitante a

concerned /kən'sɜ:nd/ *a* inquieto, preocupado (**about** com)

concert /'kɒnsət/ *n* concerto *m*

concerted /kən'sɜ:tɪd/ *a* concertado

concession /kən'seʃn/ *n* concessão *f*

concise /kən'saɪs/ *a* conciso. **~ly** *adv* concisamente

conclu|de /kən'klu:d/ *vt* concluir □ *vi* terminar. **~ding** *a* final. **~sion** *n* conclusão *f*

conclusive /kən'klu:sɪv/ *a* conclusivo. **~ly** *adv* de forma conclusiva

concoct /kən'kɒkt/ *vt* preparar por mistura; (*fig: invent*) fabricar. **~ion** /-ʃn/ *n* mistura *f*; (*fig*) invenção *f*, mentira *f*

concrete /'kɒŋkri:t/ *n* concreto *m*, (*P*) cimento *m* □ *a* concreto □ *vt* concretar, (*P*) cimentar

concur /kən'kɜ:(r)/ *vi* (*pt* **concurred**) concordar; (*of circumstances*) concorrer

concussion /kən'kʌʃn/ *n* comoção *f* cerebral

condemn /kən'dem/ *vt* condenar. **~ation** /kɒndem'neɪʃn/ *n* condenação *f*

condens|e /kən'dens/ *vt/i* condensar(-se). **~ation** /kɒnden'seɪʃn/ *n* condensação *f*

condescend /kɒndɪ'send/ *vi* condescender; (*lower o.s.*) rebaixar-se

condition /kən'dɪʃn/ *n* condição *f* □ *vt* condicionar. **on ~ that** com a condição de que. **~al** *a* condicional. **~er** *n* (*for hair*) condicionador *m*, creme *m* rinse

condolences /kən'dəʊlənsɪz/ *npl* condolências *fpl*, pêsames *mpl*, sentimentos *mpl*

condom /'kɒndəm/ *n* preservativo *m*

condone /kən'dəʊn/ *vt* desculpar, fechar os olhos a

conducive /kən'dju:sɪv/ *a* **be ~ to** contribuir para, ser propício a

conduct[1] /kən'dʌkt/ *vt* conduzir, dirigir; (*orchestra*) reger

conduct[2] /'kɒndʌkt/ *n* conduta *f*

conductor /kən'dʌktə(r)/ *n* maestro *m*; (*electr; of bus*) condutor *m*

cone /kəʊn/ *n* cone *m*; (*bot*) pinha *f*; (*for ice-cream*) casquinha *f*, (*P*) cone *m*

confectioner /kən'fekʃnə(r)/ *n* confeiteiro *m*, (*P*) pasteleiro *m*. **~y** *n* confeitaria *f*, (*P*) pastelaria *f*

confederation /kənfedə'reɪʃn/ *n* confederação *f*

confer /kən'fɜ:(r)/ (*pt* **conferred**) *vt* conferir, outorgar □ *vi* conferenciar

conference /'kɒnfərəns/ *n* conferência *f*. **in ~** em reunião *f*

confess /kən'fes/ *vt/i* confessar; (*relig*) confessar(-se). **~ion** /-ʃn/ *n* confissão *f*. **~ional** *n* confessionário *m*. **~or** *n* confessor *m*

confetti /kən'fetɪ/ *n* confetes *mpl*, (*P*) confetti *mpl*

confide /kən'faɪd/ *vt* confiar □ *vi* **~ in** confiar em

confiden|t /'kɒnfɪdənt/ *a* confiante, confiado. **~ce** *n* confiança *f*; (*boldness*) confiança *f* em si; (*secret*) confidência *f*. **~ce trick** vigarice *f*. **in ~ce** em confidência

confidential /kɒnfɪ'denʃl/ *a* confidencial

confine /kən'faɪn/ *vt* fechar; (*limit*) limitar (**to** a). **~ment** *n* detenção *f*; (*med*) parto *m*

confirm /kən'fɜ:m/ *vt* confirmar. **~ation** /kɒnfə'meɪʃn/ *n* confirmação *f*. **~ed** *a* (*bachelor*) inveterado

confiscat|e /'kɒnfɪskeɪt/ *vt* confiscar. **~ion** /-'keɪʃn/ *n* confiscação *f*

conflict[1] /'kɒnflɪkt/ *n* conflito *m*

conflict[2] /kən'flɪkt/ *vi* estar em contradição. **~ing** *a* contraditório

conform /kən'fɔ:m/ *vt/i* conformar(-se)

confound /kən'faʊnd/ *vt* confundir. **~ed** *a* (*colloq*) maldito

confront /kən'frʌnt/ *vt* confrontar, defrontar, enfrentar. **~ with** confrontar-se com. **~ation** /kɒnfrʌn'teɪʃn/ *n* confrontação *f*

confus|e /kən'fju:z/ *vt* confundir. **~ed** *a* confuso. **~ing** *a* que faz confusão. **~ion** /-ʒn/ *n* confusão *f*

congeal /kən'dʒi:l/ *vt/i* congelar, solidificar

congenial /kən'dʒi:nɪəl/ *a* (*agreeable*) simpático

congenital /kən'dʒenɪtl/ *a* congênito, (*P*) congénito

congest|ed /kən'dʒestɪd/ *a* congestionado. **~ion** /-tʃn/ *n* (*traffic*) congestionamento *m*; (*med*) congestão *f*

congratulat|e /kən'grætjʊleɪt/ *vt* felicitar, dar os parabéns (**on** por). **~ions** /-'leɪʃnz/ *npl* felicitações *fpl*, parabéns *mpl*

congregat|e /'kɒŋgrɪgeɪt/ *vi* reunir-se. **~ion** /-'geɪʃn/ *n* (*in church*) congregação *f*, fiéis *mpl*

congress /'kɒŋgres/ *n* congresso *m*. **C~** (*Amer*) Congresso *m*

conjecture /kən'dʒektʃə(r)/ *n* conjetura *f*, (*P*) conjectura *f* □ *vt/i* conjeturar, (*P*) conjecturar

conjugal /'kɒndʒʊgl/ *a* conjugal

conjugat|e /'kɒndʒʊgeɪt/ *vt* conjugar. **~ion** /-'geɪʃn/ *n* conjugação *f*

conjunction /kən'dʒʌŋkʃn/ *n* conjunção *f*

conjur|e /'kʌndʒə(r)/ *vi* fazer truques mágicos □ *vt* **~e up** fazer aparecer. **~or** *n* mágico *m*, prestidigitador *m*

connect /kə'nekt/ *vt/i* ligar(-se); (*of train*) fazer ligação. **~ed** *a* ligado. **be ~ed with** estar relacionado com

connection /kə'nekʃn/ *n* relação *f*; (*rail; phone call*) ligação *f*; (*electr*) contacto *m*

connoisseur /kɒnə'sɜ:(r)/ *n* conhecedor *m*, apreciador *m*

connotation /kɒnə'teɪʃn/ *n* conotação *f*

conquer /'kɒŋkə(r)/ *vt* vencer; (*country*) conquistar. **~or** *n* conquistador *m*

conquest /'kɒŋkwest/ *n* conquista *f*

conscience /'kɒnʃəns/ *n* consciência *f*

conscientious /kɒnʃɪ'enʃəs/ *a* consciencioso

conscious /'kɒnʃəs/ *a* consciente. **~ly** *adv* conscientemente. **~-ness** *n* consciência *f*

conscript[1] /kən'skrɪpt/ *vt* recrutar. **~ion** /-ʃn/ *n* serviço *m* militar obrigatório

conscript[2] /'kɒnskrɪpt/ *n* recruta *m*

consecrate /'kɒnsɪkreɪt/ *vt* consagrar

consecutive /kən'sekjʊtɪv/ *a* consecutivo, seguido

consensus /kən'sensəs/ *n* consenso *m*

consent /kən'sent/ *vi* consentir (**to** em) □ *n* consentimento *m*

consequence /'kɒnsɪkwəns/ *n* conseqüência *f*, (*P*) consequência *f*

consequent /'kɒnsɪkwənt/ *a* resultante (**on, upon** de). **~ly** *adv* por conseqüência, (*P*) consequência, por consequinte

conservation /kɒnsə'veɪʃn/ *n* conservação *f*

conservative /kən'sɜ:vətɪv/ *a* conservador; (*estimate*) moderado. **C~** *a* & *n* conservador (*m*)

conservatory /kən'sɜːvətrɪ/ *n* (*greenhouse*) estufa *f*; (*house extension*) jardim *m* de inverno

conserve /kən'sɜːv/ *vt* conservar

consider /kən'sɪdə(r)/ *vt* considerar; (*allow for*) levar em consideração. **~ation** / 'reɪʃn/ *n* consideração *f*. **~ing** *prep* em vista de, tendo em conta

considerabl|e /kən'sɪdərəbl/ *a* considerável; (*much*) muito. **~y** *adv* consideravelmente

considerate /kən'sɪdərət/ *a* atencioso, delicado

consign /kən'saɪn/ *vt* consignar. **~ment** *n* consignação *f*

consist /kən'sɪst/ *vi* consistir (**of, in**, em)

consisten|t /kən'sɪstənt/ *a* (*unchanging*) constante; (*not contradictory*) coerente. **~t with** conforme com. **~cy** *n* consistência *f*; (*fig*) coerência *f*. **~tly** *adv* regularmente

consol|e /kən'səʊl/ *vt* consolar. **~ation** /kɒnsə'leɪʃn/ *n* consolação *f*. **~ation prize** prêmio *m* de consolação

consolidat|e /kən'sɒlɪdeɪt/ *vt/i* consolidar(-se). **~ion** /-'deɪʃn/ *n* consolidação *f*

consonant /'kɒnsənənt/ *n* consoante *f*

consortium /kən'sɔːtɪəm/ *n* (*pl* **-tia**) consórcio *m*

conspicuous /kən'spɪkjʊəs/ *a* conspícuo, visível; (*striking*) notável. **make o.s. ~** fazer-se notar, chamar a atenção

conspira|cy /kən'spɪrəsɪ/ *n* conspiração *f*. **~tor** *n* conspirador *m*

conspire /kən'spaɪə(r)/ *vi* conspirar

constable /'kʌnstəbl/ *n* polícia *m*

constant /'kɒnstənt/ *a* constante. **~ly** *adv* constantemente

constellation /kɒnstə'leɪʃn/ *n* constelação *f*

consternation /kɒnstə'neɪʃn/ *n* consternação *f*

constipation /kɒnstɪ'peɪʃn/ *n* prisão *f* de ventre

constituency /kən'stɪtjʊənsɪ/ *n* (*pl* **-cies**) círculo *m* eleitoral

constituent /kən'stɪtjʊənt/ *a* & *n* constituinte (*m*)

constitut|e /'kɒnstɪtjuːt/ *vt* constituir. **~ion** /-'tjuːʃn/ *n* constituição *f*. **~ional** /-'tjuːʃənl/ *a* constitucional

constrain /kən'streɪn/ *vt* constranger

constraint /kən'streɪnt/ *n* constrangimento *m*

constrict /kən'strɪkt/ *vt* constringir, apertar. **~ion** /-ʃn/ *n* constrição *f*

construct /kən'strʌkt/ *vt* construir. **~ion** /-ʃn/ *n* construção *f*. **under ~ion** em construção

constructive /kən'strʌktɪv/ *a* construtivo

consul /'kɒnsl/ *n* cônsul *m*

consulate /'kɒnsjʊlət/ *n* consulado *m*

consult /kən'sʌlt/ *vt* consultar. **~ation** /kɒnsl'teɪʃn/ *n* consulta *f*

consultant /kən'sʌltənt/ *n* consultor *m*; (*med*) especialista *mf*

consume /kən'sjuːm/ *vt* consumir. **~r** /-ə(r)/ *n* consumidor *m*

consumption /kən'sʌmpʃn/ *n* consumo *m*

contact /'kɒntækt/ *n* contacto *m*; (*person*) relação *f*. **~ lenses** lentes *fpl* de contacto □ *vt* contactar

contagious /kən'teɪdʒəs/ *a* contagioso

contain /kən'teɪn/ *vt* conter. **~ o.s.** conter-se. **~er** *n* recipiente *m*; (*for transport*) contentor *m*

contaminat|e /kən'tæmɪneɪt/ *vt* contaminar. **~ion** /-'neɪʃn/ *n* contaminação *f*

contemplat|e /'kɒntempleɪt/ *vt* contemplar; (*intend*) ter em vista; (*consider*) esperar, pensar em. **~ion** /-'pleɪʃn/ *n* contemplação *f*

contemporary /kən'temprərɪ/ *a* & *n* contemporâneo (*m*)

contempt /kən'tempt/ *n* desprezo *m*. **~ible** *a* desprezível. **~uous** /-tʃʊəs/ *a* desdenhoso

contend /kən'tend/ *vt* afirmar, sustentar □ *vi* **~ with** lutar contra. **~er** *n* adversário *m*, contendor *m*

content[1] /kən'tent/ *a* satisfeito, contente □ *vt* contentar. **~ed** *a* satisfeito, contente. **~ment** *n* contentamento *m*, satisfação *f*

content[2] /'kɒntent/ *n* conteúdo *m*. **(table of) ~s** índice *m*

contention /kən'tenʃn/ *n* disputa *f*, contenda *f*; (*assertion*) argumento *m*

contest[1] /'kɒntest/ *n* competição *f*; (*struggle*) luta *f*

contest[2] /kən'test/ *vt* contestar; (*compete for*) disputar. **~ant** *n* concorrente *mf*

context /'kɒntekst/ *n* contexto *m*

continent /'kɒntɪnənt/ *n* continente *m*. **the C~** a Europa (continental) *f*. **~al** /-'nentl/ *a* continental; (*of mainland Europe*) europeu **~al breakfast** café *m* da manhã europeu (*P*) pequeno almoço *m* europeu. **~al quilt** edredom *m*, (*P*) edredão *m*

contingen|t /kən'tɪndʒənt/ *a* & *n* contingente (*m*). **~cy** *n* contingência *f*. **~cy plan** plano *m* de emergência

continual /kən'tɪnjʊəl/ *a* contínuo. **~ly** *adv* continuamente

continu|e /kən'tɪnjuː/ *vt/i* continuar. **~ation** /-tɪnjʊ'eɪʃn/ *n* continuação *f*.

continuity /kɒntɪ'nju:ətɪ/ *n* continuidade *f*

continuous /kən'tɪnjʊəs/ *a* contínuo. **~ly** *adv* continuamente

contort /kən'tɔ:t/ *vt* contorcer; (*fig*) distorcer. **~ion** /-ʃn/ *n* contorção *f*

contour /'kɒntʊə(r)/ *n* contorno *m*

contraband /'kɒntrəbænd/ *n* contrabando *m*

contraception /kɒntrə'sepʃn/ *n* contracepção *f*

contraceptive /kɒntrə'septɪv/ *a & n* contraceptivo (*m*)

contract[1] /'kɒntrækt/ *n* contrato *m*

contract[2] /kən'trækt/ *vt/i* contrair(-se); (*make a contract*) contratar. **~ion** /-ʃn/ *n* contração *f*, (*P*) contracção *f*

contractor /kən'træktə(r)/ *n* empreiteiro *m*; (*firm*) firma *f* empreiteira de serviços, (*P*) recrutadora *f* de mão de obra temporária

contradict /kɒntrə'dɪkt/ *vt* contradizer. **~ion** /-ʃn/ *n* contradição *f*. **~ory** *a* contraditório

contraflow /'kɒntrəfləʊ/ *n* fluxo *m* em sentido contrátio

contrary[1] /'kɒntrərɪ/ *a & n* (*opposite*) contrário (*m*) □ *adv* **~ to** contrariamente a. **on the ~** ao *ou* pelo contrário

contrary[2] /kən'treərɪ/ *a* (*perverse*) do contra, embirrento

contrast[1] /'kɒntra:st/ *n* contraste *m*

contrast[2] /kən'tra:st/ *vt/i* contrastar. **~ing** *a* contrastante

contraven|e /kɒntrə'vi:n/ *vt* infringir. **~tion** /'-venʃn/ *n* contravenção *f*

contribut|e /kən'trɪbju:t/ *vt/i* contribuir (**to** para); (*to newspaper etc*) colaborar (**to** em). **~ion** /kɒntrɪ'bju:ʃn/ *n* contribuição *f*. **~or** /-'trɪbju:tə(r)/ *n* contribuinte *mf*; (*to newspaper*) colaborador *m*

contrivance /kən'traɪvəns/ *n* (*invention*) engenho *m*; (*device*) engenhoca *f*; (*trick*) maquinação *f*

contrive /kən'traɪv/ *vt* imaginar, inventar. **~ to do** conseguir fazer

control /kən'trəʊl/ *vt* (*pt* **controlled**) (*check, restrain*) controlar; (*firm etc*) dirigir □ *n* controle *m*; (*management*) direção *f*, (*P*) direcção *f*. **~s** (*of car, plane*) comandos *mpl*; (*knobs*) botões *mpl*. **be in ~ of** dirigir. **under ~** sob controle

controversial /kɒntrə'vɜ:ʃl/ *a* controverso, discutível

controversy /'kɒntrəvɜ:sɪ/ *n* controvérsia *f*

convalesce /kɒnvə'les/ *vi* convalescer. **~nce** *n* convalescença *f*. **~nt** /-nt/ *a & n* convalescente (*mf*). **~nt home** casa *f* de repouso

convene /kən'vi:n/ *vt* convocar □ *vi* reunir-se

convenience /kən'vi:nɪəns/ *n* conveniência *f*. **~s** (*appliances*) comodidades *fpl*; (*lavatory*) privada *f*, (*P*) casa *f* de banho. **at your ~** quando (e como) lhe convier. **~ foods** alimentos *mpl* semiprontos

convenient /kən'vi:nɪənt/ *a* conveniente. **be ~ for** convir a. **~ly** *adv* sem inconveniente; (*situated*) bem; (*arrive*) a propósito

convent /'kɒnvənt/ *n* convento *m*. **~ school** colégio *m* de freiras

convention /kən'venʃn/ *n* convenção *f*; (*custom*) uso *m*, costume *m*. **~al** *a* convencional

converge /kən'vɜ:dʒ/ *vi* convergir

conversant /kən'vɜ:snt/ *a* **be ~ with** conhecer; (*fact*) saber; (*machinery*) estar familiarizado com

conversation /kɒnvə'seɪʃn/ *n* conversa *f*. **~al** *a* de conversa, coloquial

converse[1] /kən'vɜ:s/ *vi* conversar

converse[2] /'kɒnvɜ:s/ *a & n* inverso (*m*). **~ly** /kən'vɜ:slɪ/ *adv* ao invés, inversamente

conver|t[1] /kən'vɜ:t/ *vt* converter; (*house*) transformar. **~sion** /-ʃn/ *n* conversão *f*; (*house*) transformação *f*. **~tible** *a* convertível, conversível □ *n* (*auto*) conversível *m*

convert[2] /'kɒnvɜ:t/ *n* convertido *m*, converso *m*

convex /'kɒnveks/ *a* convexo

convey /kən'veɪ/ *vt* transmitir; (*goods*) transportar; (*idea, feeling*) comunicar. **~ance** *n* transporte *m*. **~or belt** tapete *m* rolante, correia *f* transportadora

convict[1] /kən'vɪkt/ *vt* declarar culpado. **~ion** /-ʃn/ *n* condenação *f*; (*opinion*) convicção *f*

convict[2] /'kɒnvɪkt/ *n* condenado *m*

convinc|e /kən'vɪns/ *vt* convencer. **~ing** *a* convincente

convoluted /kɒnvə'lu:tɪd/ *a* retorcido; (*fig*) complicado; (*bot*) convoluto

convoy /'kɒnvɔɪ/ *n* escolta *f*

convuls|e /kən'vʌls/ *vt* convulsionar; (*fig*) abalar. **be ~ed with laughter** torcer-se de riso. **~ion** /-ʃn/ *n* convulsão *f*

coo /ku:/ *vi* (*pt* **cooed**) arrulhar □ *n* arrulho *m*

cook /kʊk/ *vt/i* cozinhar □ *n* cozinheira *f*, cozinheiro *m*. **~ up** (*colloq*) cozinhar (*fig*), fabricar

cooker /'kʊkə(r)/ *n* fogão *m*
cookery /'kʊkərɪ/ *n* cozinha *f*. **~ book** livro *m* de culinária
cookie /'kʊkɪ/ *n* (*Amer*) biscoito *m*
cool /ku:l/ *a* (**-er, -est**) fresco; (*calm*) calmo; (*unfriendly*) frio □ *n* frescura *f*; (*sl: composure*) sangue-frio *m* □ *vt*/*i* arrefecer. **~-box** *n* geladeira *f* portátil. **in the ~** no fresco. **~ly** /'ku:llɪ/ *adv* calmamente; (*fig*) friamente. **~ness** *n* frescura *f*; (*fig*) frieza *f*
coop /ku:p/ *n* galinheiro *m* □ *vt* **~ up** engaislar, fechar
co-operat|e /kəʊ'ɒpəreɪt/ *vi* cooperar. **~ion** /-'reɪʃn/ *n* cooperação *f*
cooperative /kəʊ'ɒpərətɪv/ *a* cooperativo □ *n* cooperativa *f*
coordinat|e /kəʊ'ɔ:dɪneɪt/ *vt* co-ordenar. **~ion** /-'neɪʃn/ *n* coordenação *f*
cop /kɒp/ *n* (*sl*) porco *m* (*sl*), (*P*) xui *m* (*sl*)
cope /kəʊp/ *vi* aguentar-se, arranjar-se. **~ with** poder com, dar conta de
copious /'kəʊpɪəs/ *a* copioso
copper[1] /'kɒpə(r)/ *n* cobre *m* □ *a* de cobre
copper[2] /'kɒpə(r)/ *n* (*sl*) porco *m* (*sl*), (*P*) xui *m* (*sl*)
coppice /'kɒpɪs/, **copse** /kɒps/ *ns* mata *f* de corte
copulat|e /'kɒpjʊleɪt/ *vi* copular. **~ion** /-'leɪʃn/ *n* cópula *f*
copy /'kɒpɪ/ *n* cópia *f*; (*of book*) exemplar *m*; (*of newspaper*) número *m* □ *vt*/*i* copiar
copyright /'kɒpɪraɪt/ *n* direitos *mpl* autorais
coral /'kɒrəl/ *n* coral *m*
cord /kɔ:d/ *n* cordão *m*; (*electr*) fio *m*
cordial /'kɔ:dɪəl/ *a* & *n* cordial (*m*)
cordon /'kɔ:dn/ *n* cordão *m* □ *vt* **~ off** fechar (com um cordão de isolamento)
corduroy /'kɔ:dərɔɪ/ *n* veludo *m* cotelé
core /kɔ:(r)/ *n* âmago *m*; (*of apple, pear*) coração *m*
cork /kɔ:k/ *n* cortiça *f*; (*for bottle*) rolha *f* □ *vt* rolhar
corkscrew /'kɔ:kskru:/ *n* saca-rolhas *m*
corn[1] /kɔ:n/ *n* trigo *m*; (*Amer: maize*) milho *m*; (*seed*) grão *m*. **~ on the cob** espiga *f* de milho
corn[2] /kɔ:n/ *n* (*hard skin*) calo *m*
corned /kɔ:nd/ *a* **~ beef** carne *f* de vaca enlatada
corner /'kɔ:nə(r)/ *n* canto *m*; (*of street*) esquina *f*; (*bend in road*) curva *f* □ *vt* encurralar; (*market*) monopolizar □ *vi* dar uma curva, virar
cornet /'kɔ:nɪt/ *n* (*mus*) cornetim *m*; (*for ice-cream*) casquinha *f*, (*P*) cone *m*
cornflakes /'kɔ:nfleɪks/ *npl* cornflakes *mpl*, cereais *mpl*
cornflour /'kɔ:nflaʊə(r)/ *n* fécula *f* de milho, maisena *f*
Corn|wall /'kɔ:nwəl/ *n* Cornualha *f*. **~ish** *a* da Cornualha
corny /'kɔ:nɪ/ *a* (*colloq*) batido, (*P*) estafado
coronary /'kɒrənrɪ/ *n* **~ (thrombosis)** infarto *m*, enfarte *m*
coronation /kɒrə'neɪʃn/ *n* coroação *f*
coroner /'kɒrənə(r)/ *n* magistrado *m* que investiga os casos de morte suspeita
corporal[1] /'kɔ:pərəl/ *n* (*mil*) cabo *m*
corporal[2] /'kɔ:pərəl/ *a* **~ punishment** castigo *m* corporal
corporate /'kɔ:pərət/ *a* coletivo, (*P*) colectivo; (*body*) corporativo
corporation /kɔ:pə'reɪʃn/ *n* corporação *f*; (*of town*) municipalidade *f*
corps /kɔ:(r)/ *n* (*pl* **corps** /kɔ:z/) corpo *m*
corpse /kɔ:ps/ *n* cadáver *m*
corpuscle /'kɔ:pʌsl/ *n* corpúsculo *m*
correct /kə'rekt/ *a* correto, (*P*) correcto. **the ~ time** a hora certa. **you are ~** você tem razão □ *vt* corrigir. **~ion** /-ʃn/ *n* correção *f*, (*P*) correcção *f*, emenda *f*
correlat|e /'kɒrəleɪt/ *vt*/*i* correlacionar(-se). **~ion** /-'leɪʃn/ *n* correlação *f*
correspond /kɒrɪ'spɒnd/ *vi* corresponder (**to, with**, a); (*write letters*) corresponder-se (**with**, com). **~ence** *n* correspondência *f*. **~ent** *n* correspondente *mf*. **~ing** *a* correspondente
corridor /'kɒrɪdɔ:(r)/ *n* corredor *m*
corroborate /kə'rɒbəreɪt/ *vt* corroborar
corro|de /kə'rəʊd/ *vt*/*i* corroer (-se). **~sion** *n* corrosão *f*
corrugated /'kɒrəgeɪtɪd/ *a* corrugado. **~ cardboard** cartão *m* canelado. **~ iron** chapa *f* ondulada
corrupt /kə'rʌpt/ *a* corrupto □ *vt* corromper. **~ion** /-ʃn/ *n* corrupção *f*
corset /'kɔ:sɪt/ *n* espartilho *m*; (*elasticated*) cinta *f* elástica
Corsica /'kɔ:sɪkə/ *n* Córsega *f*
cosmetic /kɒz'metɪk/ *n* cosmético *m* □ *a* cosmético; (*fig*) superficial
cosmonaut /'kɒzmənɔ:t/ *n* cosmonauta *mf*
cosmopolitan /kɒzmə'pɒlɪtən/ *a* & *n* cosmopolita (*mf*)
cosset /'kɒsɪt/ *vt* (*pt* **cosseted**) proteger
cost /kɒst/ *vt* (*pt* **cost**) custar; (*pt* **costed**) fixar o preço de □ *n* custo *m*. **~s** (*jur*) custos *mpl*. **at all ~s** custe o que custar. **to one's ~** à sua custa. **~ of living** custo *m* de vida
costly /'kɒstlɪ/ *a* (**-ier, -iest**) *a* caro; (*valuable*) precioso
costume /'kɒstju:m/ *n* traje *m*

cos|y /'kəʊzɪ/ *a* (**-ier, -iest**) confortável, íntimo ◻ *n* abafador *m* (do bule do chá). **~iness** *n* conforto *m*
cot /kɒt/ *n* cama *f* de bêbê, berço *m*
cottage /'kɒtɪdʒ/ *n* pequena casa *f* de campo. **~ cheese** requeijão *m*, ricota *f*. **~ industry** artesanato *m*. **~ pie** empada *f* de carne picada
cotton /'kɒtn/ *n* algodão *m*; (*thread*) fio *m*, linha *f*. **~ wool** algodão *m* hidrófilo
couch /kaʊtʃ/ *n* divã *m*
couchette /ku:'ʃet/ *n* couchette *f*
cough /kɒf/ *vi* tossir ◻ *n* tosse *f*
could /kʊd, kəd/ *pt of* **can**[2]
couldn't /'kʊdnt/ = **could not**
council /'kaʊnsl/ *n* conselho *m*. **~ house** casa *f* de bairro popular
councillor /'kaʊnsələ(r)/ *n* vereador *m*
counsel /'kaʊnsl/ *n* conselho *m*; (*pl invar*) (*jur*) advogado *m*. **~lor** *n* conselheiro *m*
count[1] /kaʊnt/ *vt/i* contar ◻ *n* conta *f*. **~-down** *n* (*rocket*) contagem *f* regressiva. **~ on** contar com
count[2] /kaʊnt/ *n* (*nobleman*) conde *m*
counter[1] /'kaʊntə(r)/ *n* (*in shop*) balcão *m*; (*in game*) ficha *f*, (*P*) tento *m*
counter[2] /'kaʊntə(r)/ *adv* **~ to** contrário a; (*in the opposite direction*) em sentido contrário a ◻ *a* oposto ◻ *vt* opor; (*blow*) aparar ◻ *vi* ripostar
counter- /'kaʊntə(r)/ *pref* contra-
counteract /kaʊntər'ækt/ *vt* neutralizar, frustrar
counter-attack /'kaʊntərətæk/ *n* contra-ataque *m* ◻ *vt/i* contra-atacar
counterbalance /'kaʊntəbæləns/ *n* contrapeso *m* ◻ *vt* contrabalançar
counterfeit /'kaʊntəfɪt/ *a* falsificado, falso ◻ *n* falsificação *f* ◻ *vt* falsificar
counterfoil /'kaʊntəfɔɪl/ *n* talão *m*, canhoto *m*
counterpart /'kaʊntəpa:t/ *n* equivalente *m*; (*person*) homólogo *m*
counter-productive /'kaʊntəprədʌktɪv/ *a* contraproducente
countersign /'kaʊntəsaɪn/ *vt* subscrever documento já assinado; (*cheque*) contrassinar
countess /'kaʊntɪs/ *n* condessa *f*
countless /'kaʊntlɪs/ *a* sem conta, incontável, inúmero
country /'kʌntrɪ/ *n* país *m*; (*homeland*) pátria *f*; (*countryside*) campo *m*
countryside /'kʌntrɪsaɪd/ *n* campo *m*
county /'kaʊntɪ/ *n* condado *m*
coup /ku:/ *n* **~ (d'état)** golpe *m* (de estado)
couple /'kʌpl/ *n* par *m*, casal *m* ◻ *vt/i* unir(-se), ligar(-se); (*techn*) acoplar. **a ~ of** um par de
coupon /'ku:pɒn/ *n* cupão *m*
courage /'kʌrɪdʒ/ *n* coragem *f*. **~ous** /kə'reɪdʒəs/ *a* corajoso
courgette /kʊə'ʒet/ *n* abobrinha *f*
courier /'kʊrɪə(r)/ *n* correio *m*; (*for tourists*) guia *mf*; (*for parcels, mail*) estafeta *m*
course /kɔ:s/ *n* curso *m*; (*series*) série *f*; (*culin*) prato *m*; (*for golf*) campo *m*; (*fig*) caminho *m*. **in due ~** na altura devida, oportunamente. **in the ~ of** durante. **of ~** está claro, com certeza
court /kɔ:t/ *n* (*of monarch*) corte *f*; (*courtyard*) pátio *m*; (*tennis*) court *m*, quadra *f*, (*P*) campo *m*; (*jur*) tribunal *m* ◻ *vt* cortejar; (*danger*) provocar. **~ martial** (*pl* **courts martial**) conselho *m* de guerra
courteous /'kɜ:tɪəs/ *a* cortês, delicado
courtesy /'kɜ:təsɪ/ *n* cortesia *f*
courtship /'kɔ:tʃɪp/ *n* namoro *m*, corte *f*
courtyard /'kɔ:tja:d/ *n* pátio *m*
cousin /'kʌzn/ *n* primo *m*. **first/second ~** primo *m* em primeiro/segundo grau
cove /kəʊv/ *n* angra *f*, enseada *f*
covenant /'kʌvənənt/ *n* convenção *f*, convénio *m*; (*jur*) contrato *m*; (*relig*) aliança *f*
cover /'kʌvə(r)/ *vt* cobrir ◻ *n* cobertura *f*; (*for bed*) colcha *f*; (*for book, furniture*) capa *f*; (*lid*) tampa *f*; (*shelter*) abrigo *m*. **~ charge** serviço *m*. **~ up** tapar; (*fig*) encobrir. **~-up** *n* (*fig*) encobrimento *m*. **take ~** abrigar-se. **under separate ~** em separado. **~ing** *n* cobertura *f*. **~ing letter** carta *f* (que acompanha um documento)
coverage /'kʌvərɪdʒ/ *n* (*of events*) reportagem *f*, cobertura *f*
covet /'kʌvɪt/ *vt* cobiçar
cow /kaʊ/ *n* vaca *f*
coward /'kaʊəd/ *n* covarde *mf*. **~ly** *a* covarde
cowardice /'kaʊədɪs/ *n* covardia *f*
cowboy /'kaʊbɔɪ/ *n* cowboy *m*, vaqueiro *m*
cower /'kaʊə(r)/ *vi* encolher-se (de medo)
cowshed /'kaʊʃed/ *n* estábulo *m*
coy /kɔɪ/ *a* (**-er, -est**) (falsamente) tímido
crab /kræb/ *n* caranguejo *m*
crack /kræk/ *n* fenda *f*; (*in glass*) rachadura *f*; (*noise*) estalo *m*; (*sl: joke*) piada *f*; (*drug*) crack *m* ◻ *a* (*colloq*) de élite ◻ *vt/i* estalar; (*nut*) quebrar; (*joke*) contar; (*problem*) resolver; (*voice*) mudar. **~ down on** (*colloq*) cair em cima de, arrochar. **get ~ing** (*colloq*) pôr mãos à obra
cracker /'krækə(r)/ *n* busca-pé *m*, bomba *f* de estalo; (*culin*) bolacha *f* de água e sal

crackers /'krækəz/ *a* (*sl*) desmiolado, maluco
crackle /'krækl/ *vi* crepitar □ *n* crepitação *f*
crackpot /'krækpɒt/ *n* (*sl*) desmiolado, maluco
cradle /'kreɪdl/ *n* berço *m* □ *vt* embalar
craft[1] /krɑ:ft/ *n* ofício *m*; (*technique*) arte *f*; (*cunning*) manha *f*, astúcia *f*
craft[2] /krɑ:ft/ *n* (*invar*) (*boat*) embarcação *f*
craftsman /'krɑ:ftsmən/ *n* (*pl* **-men**) artífice *mf*. **~ship** *n* arte *f*
crafty /'krɑ:ftɪ/ *a* (**-ier, -iest**) manhoso, astucioso
crag /kræg/ *n* penhasco *m*. **~gy** *a* escarpado, ingreme
cram /kræm/ *vt* (*pt* **crammed**) **~ (for an exam)** decorar, (*P*) empinar. **~ into/with** entulhar com
cramp /kræmp/ *n* cãimbra *f* □ *vt* restringir, tolher. **~ed** *a* apertado
crane /kreɪn/ *n* grua *f*; (*bird*) grou *m* □ *vt* (*neck*) esticar
crank[1] /kræŋk/ *n* (*techn*) manivela *f*. **~shaft** *n* (*techn*) cambota *f*
crank[2] /kræŋk/ *n* excêntrico *m*. **~y** *a* excêntrico
crash /kræʃ/ *n* acidente *m*; (*noise*) estrondo *m*; (*comm*) falência *f*; (*financial*) colapso *m*, crash *m* □ *vt/i* (*fall/strike*) cair/bater com estrondo; (*two cars*) chocar, bater; (*comm*) abrir falência; (*plane*) cair □ *a* (*course, programme*) intensivo. **~-helmet** *n* capacete *m*. **~-land** *vi* fazer uma aterrissagem forçada
crate /kreɪt/ *n* engradado *m*
crater /'kreɪtə(r)/ *n* cratera *f*
crav|e /kreɪv/ *vt/i* **~e (for)** ansiar por. **~ing** *n* desejo *m* irresistível, ânsia *f*
crawl /krɔ:l/ *vi* rastejar; (*of baby*) engatinhar, (*P*) andar de gatas; (*of car*) mover-se lentamente □ *n* rastejo *m*; (*swimming*) crawl *m*. **be ~ing with** fervilhar de, estar cheio de
crayfish /'kreɪfɪʃ/ *n* (*pl invar*) lagostim *m*
crayon /'kreɪən/ *n* crayon *m*, lápis *m* de pastel
craze /kreɪz/ *n* moda *f*, febre *f*
craz|y /'kreɪzɪ/ *a* (**-ier, -iest**) doido, louco (**about** por). **~iness** *n* loucura *f*
creak /kri:k/ *n* rangido *m* □ *vi* ranger
cream /kri:m/ *n* (*milk fat; fig*) nata *f*; (*cosmetic; culin*) creme *m* □ *a* creme *invar* □ *vt* desnatar. **~ cheese** queijo-creme *m*. **~y** *a* cremoso
crease /kri:s/ *n* vinco *m* □ *vt/i* amarrotar(-se)
creat|e /kri:'eɪt/ *vt* criar. **~ion** /-ʃn/ *n* criação *f*. **~ive** *a* criador. **~or** *n* criador *m*
creature /'kri:tʃə(r)/ *n* criatura *f*
crèche /kreɪʃ/ *n* creche *f*
credentials /krɪ'denʃlz/ *npl* credenciais *fpl*; (*of competence etc*) referências *fpl*
credib|le /'kredəbl/ *a* crível, verosímil, (*P*) verossímil. **~ility** /-'bɪlətɪ/ *n* credibilidade *f*
credit /'kredɪt/ *n* crédito *m*; (*honour*) honra *f*. **~s** (*cinema*) créditos *mpl* □ *vt* (*pt* **credited**) acreditar em; (*comm*) creditar. **~ card** cartão *m* de crédito. **~ sb with** atribuir a alg. **~or** *n* credor *m*
creditable /'kredɪtəbl/ *a* louvável, honroso
credulous /'kredjʊləs/ *a* crédulo
creed /kri:d/ *n* credo *m*
creek /kri:k/ *n* enseada *f* estreita. **be up the ~** (*sl*) estar frito (*sl*)
creep /kri:p/ *vi* (*pt* **crept**) rastejar; (*move stealthily*) mover-se furtivamente □ *n* (*sl*) cara *m* nojento. **give sb the ~s** dar arrepios a alg. **~er** *n* (planta *f*) trepadeira (*f*). **~y** *a* arrepiante
cremat|e /krɪ'meɪt/ *vt* cremar. **~ion** /-ʃn/ *n* cremação *f*
crematorium /kremə'tɔ:rɪəm/ *n* (*pl* **-ia**) crematório *m*
crêpe /kreɪp/ *n* crepe *m*. **~ paper** papel *m* crepom, (*P*) plissado
crept /krept/ *see* **creep**
crescent /'kresnt/ *n* crescente *m*; (*street*) rua *f* em semicírculo
cress /kres/ *n* agrião *m*
crest /krest/ *n* (*of bird, hill*) crista *f*; (*on coat of arms*) timbre *m*
Crete /kri:t/ *n* Creta *f*
crevasse /krɪ'væs/ *n* fenda *f* (em geleira)
crevice /'krevɪs/ *n* racha *f*, fenda *f*
crew[1] /kru:/ *see* **crow**
crew[2] /kru:/ *n* tripulação *f*; (*gang*) bando *m*. **~-cut** *n* corte *m* à escovinha. **~-neck** *n* gola *f* redonda e un pouco subida
crib[1] /krɪb/ *n* berço *m*; (*Christmas*) presépio *m*
crib[2] /krɪb/ *vt/i* (*pt* **cribbed**) (*colloq*) colar (*sl*), (*P*) cabular (*sl*) □ *n* cópia *f*, plágio *m*; (*translation*) burro *m* (*sl*)
cricket[1] /'krɪkɪt/ *n* críquete *m*. **~er** *n* jogador *m* de críquete
cricket[2] /'krɪkɪt/ *n* (*insect*) grilo *m*
crime /kraɪm/ *n* crime *m*; (*minor*) delito *m*; (*collectively*) criminalidade *f*
criminal /'krɪmɪnl/ *a* & *n* criminoso (*m*)
crimp /krɪmp/ *vt* preguear; (*hair*) frisar
crimson /'krɪmzn/ *a* & *n* carmesim (*m*)
cring|e /krɪndʒ/ *vi* encolher-se. **~ing** *a* servil

crinkle /'krɪŋkl/ *vt/i* enrugar(-se) ◻ *n* vinco *m*, ruga *f*
cripple /'krɪpl/ *n* aleijado *m*, coxo *m* ◻ *vt* estropiar; (*fig*) paralisar
crisis /'kraɪsɪs/ *n* (*pl* **crises** /-si:z/) crise *f*
crisp /krɪsp/ *a* (**-er, est**) (*culin*) crocante; (*air*) fresco; (*manners, reply*) decidido. **~s** *npl* batatas *fpl* fritas redondas
criterion /kraɪ'tɪərɪən/ *n* (*pl* **-ia**) critério *m*
critic /'krɪtɪk/ *n* crítico *m*. **~al** *a* crítico. **~ally** *adv* de forma crítica; (*ill*) gravemente
criticism /'krɪtɪsɪzəm/ *n* crítica *f*
criticize /'krɪtɪsaɪz/ *vt/i* criticar
croak /krəʊk/ *n* (*frog*) coaxar *m*; (*raven*) crocitar *m*, crocito *m* ◻ *vi* (*frog*) coaxar; (*raven*) crocitar
crochet /'krəʊʃeɪ/ *n* crochê *m* ◻ *vt* fazer em crochê
crockery /'krɒkərɪ/ *n* louça *f*
crocodile /'krɒkədaɪl/ *n* crocodilo *m*
crocus /'krəʊkəs/ *n* (*pl* **-uses** /-siz/) croco *m*
crony /'krəʊnɪ/ *n* camarada *mf*, amigão *m*, parceiro *m*
crook /krʊk/ *n* (*colloq: criminal*) vigarista *mf*; (*stick*) cajado *m*
crooked /'krʊkɪd/ *a* torcido; (*winding*) tortuoso; (*askew*) torto; (*colloq: dishonest*) desonesto. **~ly** *adv* de través
crop /krɒp/ *n* colheita *f*; (*fig*) quantidade *f*; (*haircut*) corte *m* rente ◻ *vt* (*pt* **cropped**) cortar ◻ *vi* **~ up** aparecer, surgir
croquet /'krəʊkeɪ/ *n* croquet *m*, croqué *m*
cross /krɒs/ *n* cruz *f* ◻ *vt/i* cruzar; (*cheque*) cruzar, (*P*) barrar; (*oppose*) contrariar; (*of paths*) cruzar-se ◻ *a* zangado. **~ off** *or* **out** riscar. **~ o.s.** benzer-se. **~ sb's mind** passar pela cabeça *or* pelo espírito de alg, ocorrer a alg. **talk at ~ purposes** falar sem se entender. **~-country** *a & adv* a corta-mato. **~-examine** *vt* fazer o contra-interrogatório (de testemunhas). **~-eyed** *a* vesgo, estrábico. **~-fire** *n* fogo *m* cruzado. **~-reference** *n* nota *f* remissiva. **~-section** *n* corte *m* transversal; (*fig*) grupo *m* or sector *m* representativo. **~ly** *adv* irritadamente
crossbar /'krɒsba:(r)/ *n* barra *f* transversal *f*; (*of bicycle*) travessão *m*
crossing /'krɒsɪŋ/ *n* cruzamento *m*; (*by boat*) travessia *f*; (*on road*) passagem *f*
crossroads /'krɒsrəʊdz/ *n* encruzilhada *f*, cruzamento *m*
crossword /'krɒswɜ:d/ *n* palavras *fpl* cruzadas
crotch /krɒtʃ/ *n* entrepernas *fpl*
crotchet /'krɒtʃɪt/ *n* (*mus*) semínima *f*
crouch /kraʊtʃ/ *vi* agachar-se
crow /krəʊ/ *n* corvo *m* ◻ *vi* (*cock*) (*pt* **crew**) cantar; (*fig*) rejubilar-se (**over** com). **as the ~ flies** em linha reta, (*P*) recta
crowbar /'krəʊba:(r)/ *n* alavanca *f*, pé-de-cabra *m*
crowd /kraʊd/ *n* multidão *f* ◻ *vi* afluir ◻ *vt* encher. **~ into** apinhar-se em. **~ed** *a* cheio, apinhado
crown /kraʊn/ *n* coroa *f*; (*of hill*) topo *m*, cume *m* ◻ *vt* coroar; (*tooth*) pôr uma coroa em
crucial /'kru:ʃl/ *a* crucial
crucifix /'kru:sɪfɪks/ *n* crucifixo *m*
crucif|y /'kru:sɪfaɪ/ *vt* crucificar. **~ixion** /-'fɪkʃn/ *n* crucificação *f*
crude /kru:d/ *a* (**-er, -est**) (*raw*) bruto; (*rough, vulgar*) grosseiro. **~ oil** petróleo *m* bruto
cruel /krʊəl/ *a* (**crueller, cruellest**) cruel. **~ty** *n* crueldade *f*
cruis|e /kru:z/ *n* cruzeiro *m* ◻ *vi* cruzar; (*of tourists*) fazer um cruzeiro; (*of car*) ir a velocidade de cruzeiro. **~er** *n* cruzador *m*. **~ing speed** velocidade *f* de cruzeiro
crumb /krʌm/ *n* migalha *f*, farelo *m*
crumble /'krʌmbl/ *vt/i* desfazer (-se); (*bread*) esmigalhar(-se); (*collapse*) desmoronar-se
crumple /'krʌmpl/ *vt/i* amarrotar (-se)
crunch /krʌntʃ/ *vt* trincar; (*under one's feet*) fazer ranger
crusade /kru:'seɪd/ *n* cruzada *f*. **~r** /-ə(r)/ *n* cruzado *m*; (*fig*) militante *mf*
crush /krʌʃ/ *vt* esmagar; (*clothes, papers*) amassar, amarrotar ◻ *n* aperto *m*. **a ~ on** (*sl*) uma paixonite, (*P*) paixoneta por.
crust /krʌst/ *n* côdea *f*, crosta *f*. **~y** *a* crocante
crutch /krʌtʃ/ *n* muleta *f*; (*crotch*) entrepernas *fpl*
crux /krʌks/ *n* (*pl* **cruxes**) o ponto crucial
cry /kraɪ/ *n* grito *m* ◻ *vi* (*weep*) chorar; (*call out*) gritar. **a far ~ from** muito diferente de.
crying /'kraɪɪŋ/ *a* **a ~ shame** uma grande vergonha
crypt /krɪpt/ *n* cripta *f*
cryptic /'krɪptɪk/ *a* críptico, enigmático
crystal /'krɪstl/ *n* cristal *m*. **~lize** *vt/i* cristalizar(-se)
cub /kʌb/ *n* cria *f*, filhote *m*. **C~ (Scout)** lobito *m*
Cuba /'kju:bə/ *n* Cuba *f*. **~n** *a & n* cubano (*m*)

cubby-hole /ˈkʌbɪhəʊl/ *n* cochicho *m*; (*snug place*) cantinho *m*

cub|e /kju:b/ *n* cubo *m*. **~ic** *a* cúbico

cubicle /ˈkju:bɪkl/ *n* cubículo *m*, compartimento *m*; (*at swimming pool*) cabine *f*

cuckoo /ˈkʊku:/ *n* cuco *m*

cucumber /ˈkju:kʌmbə(r)/ *n* pepino *m*

cuddl|e /ˈkʌdl/ *vt/i* abraçar com carinho; (*nestle*) aninhar(-se) □ *n* abracinho *m*, festinha *f*. **~y** *a* fofo, aconchegante

cudgel /ˈkʌdʒl/ *n* cacete *m*, moca *f* □ *vt* (*pt* **cudgelled**) dar cacetadas em

cue[1] /kju:/ *n* (*theat*) deixa *f*; (*hint*) sugestão *f*, sinal *m*

cue[2] /kju:/ *n* (*billiards*) taco *m*

cuff /kʌf/ *n* punho *m*; (*blow*) sopapo *m* □ *vt* dar um sopapo. **~-link** *n* botão *m* de punho. **off the ~** de improviso

cul-de-sac /ˈkʌldəsæk/ *n* (*pl* **culs-de-sac**) beco *m* sem saída

culinary /ˈkʌlɪnərɪ/ *a* culinário

cull /kʌl/ *vt* (*select*) escolher; (*kill*) abater seletivamente, (*P*) selectivamente □ *n* abate *m*

culminat|e /ˈkʌlmɪneɪt/ *vi* **~e in** acabar em. **~ion** /-ˈneɪʃn/ *n* auge *m*, ponto *m* culminante

culprit /ˈkʌlprɪt/ *n* culpado *m*

cult /kʌlt/ *n* culto *m*

cultivat|e /ˈkʌltɪveɪt/ *vt* cultivar. **~ion** /-ˈveɪʃn/ *n* cultivo *m*, cultivação *f*

cultural /ˈkʌltʃərəl/ *a* cultural

culture /ˈkʌltʃə(r)/ *n* cultura *f*. **~d** *a* culto

cumbersome /ˈkʌmbəsəm/ *a* (*unwieldy*) pesado, incômodo, (*P*) incómodo

cumulative /ˈkju:mjʊlətɪv/ *a* cumulativo

cunning /ˈkʌnɪŋ/ *a* astuto, manhoso □ *n* astúcia *f*, manha *f*

cup /kʌp/ *n* xícara *f*, (*P*) chávena *f*; (*prize*) taça *f*. **C~ Final** Final de Campeonato *f*

cupboard /ˈkʌbəd/ *n* armário *m*

cupful /ˈkʌpfʊl/ *n* xícara *f* cheia, (*P*) chávena *f* (cheia)

curable /ˈkjʊərəbl/ *a* curável

curator /kjʊəˈreɪtə(r)/ *n* (*museum*) conservador *m*; (*jur*) curador *m*

curb /k3:b/ *n* freio *m* □ *vt* refrear; (*price increase etc*) sustar

curdle /ˈk3:dl/ *vt/i* coalhar

cure /kjʊə(r)/ *vt* curar □ *n* cura *f*

curfew /ˈk3:fju:/ *n* toque *m* de recolher

curio /ˈkjʊərɪəʊ/ *n* (*pl* **-os**) curiosidade *f*

curi|ous /ˈkjʊərɪəs/ *a* curioso. **~osity** /-ˈɒsətɪ/ *n* curiosidade *f*

curl /k3:l/ *vt/i* encaracolar(-se) □ *n* caracol *m*. **~ up** enroscar(-se)

curler /ˈk3:lə(r)/ *n* rolo *m*

curly /ˈk3:lɪ/ *a* (**-ier**, **-iest**) encaracolado, crespo

currant /ˈkʌrənt/ *n* passa *f* de Corinto

currency /ˈkʌrənsɪ/ *n* moeda *f* corrente; (*general use*) circulação *f*. **foreign ~** moeda *f* estrangeita

current /ˈkʌrənt/ *a* (*common*) corrente; (*event, price, etc*) atual, (*P*) actual □ *n* corrente *f*. **~ account** conta *f* corrente. **~ affairs** atualidades *fpl*, (*P*) actualidades *fpl*. **~ly** *adv* atualmente, (*P*) actualmente

curriculum /kəˈrɪkjʊləm/ *n* (*pl* **-la**) currículo *m*, programa *m* de estudos. **~ vitae** *n* curriculum vitae *m*

curry[1] /ˈkʌrɪ/ *n* caril *m*

curry[2] /ˈkʌrɪ/ *vt* **~ favour with** procurar agradar a

curse /k3:s/ *n* maldição *f*, praga *f*; (*bad language*) palavrão *m* □ *vt* amaldiçoar, praguejar contra □ *vi* praguejar; (*swear*) dizer palavrões

cursor /ˈk3:sə(r)/ *n* cursor *m*

cursory /ˈk3:sərɪ/ *a* apressado, superficial. **a ~ look** uma olhada superficial

curt /k3:t/ *a* brusco

curtail /k3:ˈteɪl/ *vt* abreviar; (*expenses etc*) reduzir

curtain /ˈk3:tn/ *n* cortina *f*; (*theat*) pano *m*

curtsy /ˈk3:tsɪ/ *n* reverência *f* □ *vi* fazer uma reverência

curve /k3:v/ *n* curva *f* □ *vt/i* curvar(-se); (*of road*) fazer uma curva

cushion /ˈkʊʃn/ *n* almofada *f* □ *vt* (*a blow*) amortecer; (*fig*) proteger

cushy /ˈkʊʃɪ/ *a* (**-ier**, **-iest**) (*colloq*) fácil, agradável. **~ job** sinecura *f*, boca *f* (*fig*)

custard /ˈkʌstəd/ *n* creme *m*

custodian /kʌˈstəʊdɪən/ *n* guarda *m*

custody /ˈkʌstədɪ/ *n* (*safe keeping*) custódia *f*; (*jur*) detenção *f*; (*of child*) tutela *f*

custom /ˈkʌstəm/ *n* costume *m*; (*comm*) freguesia *f*, clientela *f*. **~ary** *a* habitual

customer /ˈkʌstəmə(r)/ *n* freguês *m*, cliente *mf*

customs /ˈkʌstəmz/ *npl* alfândega *f* □ *a* alfandegário. **~ clearance** desembaraço *m* alfandegário. **~ officer** funcionário *m* da alfândega

cut /kʌt/ *vt/i* (*pt* **cut**, *pres p* **cutting**) cortar; (*prices etc*) reduzir □ *n* corte *m*, golpe *m*; (*of clothes, hair*) corte *m*; (*piece*) pedaço *m*; (*prices etc*) redução *f*, corte *m*; (*sl: share*) comissão *f*, (*P*) talhada *f* (*sl*). **~ back** *or* **down (on)** reduzir. **~-back** *n* corte *m*. **~ in** intrometer-se; (*auto*) cortar. **~ off** cortar; (*fig*) isolar. **~ out** recortar;

(*leave out*) suprimir. **~-out** *n* figura *f* para recortar. **~-price** *a* a preço(s) reduzido(s). **~ short** encurtar, (*P*) atalhar

cute /kju:t/ *a* (**-er, -est**) (*colloq: clever*) esperto; (*attractive*) bonito, (*P*) giro (*colloq*)

cuticle /'kju:tɪkl/ *n* cutícula *f*

cutlery /'kʌtlərɪ/ *n* talheres *mpl*

cutlet /'kʌtlɪt/ *n* costeleta *f*

cutting /'kʌtɪŋ/ *a* cortante ▫ *n* (*from newspaper*) recorte *m*; (*plant*) estaca *f*. **~ edge** gume *m*

CV *abbr see* **curriculum vitae**

cyanide /'saɪənaɪd/ *n* cianeto *m*

cycl|e /'saɪkl/ *n* ciclo *m*; (*bicycle*) bicicleta *f* ▫ *vi* andar de bicicleta. **~lane** cicloria *f*. **~ing** *n* ciclismo *m*. **~ist** *n* ciclista *mf*

cyclone /'saɪkləʊn/ *n* ciclone *m*

cylind|er /'sɪlɪndə(r)/ *n* cilindro *m*. **~rical** *a* cilíndrico

cymbals /'sɪmblz/ *npl* (*mus*) pratos *mpl*

cynic /'sɪnɪk/ *n* cínico *m*. **~al** *a* cínico. **~ism** /-sɪzəm/ *n* cinismo *m*

Cypr|us /'saɪprəs/ *n* Chipre *m*. **~iot** /'sɪprɪət/ *a* & *n* cipriota (*mf*)

cyst /sɪst/ *n* quisto *m*

Czech /tʃek/ *a* & *n* tcheco (*m*), (*P*) checo (*m*)

Dd

dab /dæb/ *vt* (*pt* **dabbed**) aplicar levemente ▫ *n* **a ~ of** uma aplicaçãozinha de. **~ sth on** aplicar qq coisa em gestos leves

dabble /'dæbl/ *vi* **~ in** interessar-se por, fazer um pouco de (como amador). **~r** /-ə(r)/ *n* amador *m*

dad /dæd/ *n* (*colloq*) paizinho *m*. **~dy** *n* (*children's use*) papai *m*, (*P*) papá *m*. **~dy-long-legs** *n* pernilongo *m*

daffodil /'dæfədɪl/ *n* narciso *m*

daft /da:ft/ *a* (**-er, -est**) doido, maluco

dagger /'dægə(r)/ *n* punhal *m*. **at ~s drawn** prestes a lutar (**with** com)

daily /'deɪlɪ/ *a* diário, quotidiano ▫ *adv* diariamente, todos os dias ▫ *n* (*newspaper*) diário *m*; (*colloq: charwoman*) faxineira *f*, (*P*) mulher *f* a dias

dainty /'deɪntɪ/ *a* (**-ier, -iest**) delicado; (*pretty, neat*) gracioso

dairy /'deərɪ/ *n* leiteria *f*. **~ products** laticínios *mpl*

daisy /'deɪzɪ/ *n* margarida *f*

dam /dæm/ *n* barragem *f*, represa *f* ▫ *vt* (*pt* **dammed**) represar

damag|e /'dæmɪdʒ/ *n* estrago(s) *mpl*. **~es** (*jur*) perdas *fpl* e danos *mpl* ▫ *vt* estragar, danificar; (*fig*) prejudicar. **~ing** *a* prejudicial

dame /deɪm/ *n* (*old use*) dama *f*; (*Amer sl*) mulher *f*

damn /dæm/ *vt* (*relig*) condenar aõ inferno; (*swear at*) amaldiçoar, maldizer; (*fig: condemn*) condenar ▫ *int* raios!, bolas! ▫ *n* **not care a ~** (*colloq*) estar pouco ligando (*colloq*), (*P*) estar-se marimbando (*colloq*) ▫ *a* (*colloq*) do diabo, danado ▫ *adv* (*colloq*) muitíssimo. **I'll be ~ed if** que um raio me atinja se. **~ation** /-'neɪʃn/ *n* danação *f*, condenação *f*. **~ing** *a* comprometedor, condenatório

damp /dæmp/ *n* umidade *f*, (*P*) humidade *f* ▫ *a* (**-er, -est**) úmido, (*P*) húmido ▫ *vt* umedecer, (*P*) humedecer. **~en** *vt* = **damp**. **~ness** *n* umidade *f*, (*P*) humidade *f*

dance /da:ns/ *vt*/*i* dançar ▫ *n* dança *f*. **~ hall** sala *f* de baile. **~r** /-ə(r)/ *n* dançarino *m*; (*professional*) bailarino *m*

dandelion /'dændɪlaɪən/ *n* dente-de-leão *m*

dandruff /'dændrʌf/ *n* caspa *f*

Dane /deɪn/ *n* dinamarquês *m*

danger /'deɪndʒə(r)/ *n* perigo *m*. **be in ~ of** correr o risco de. **~ous** *a* perigoso

dangle /'dæŋgl/ *vi* oscilar, pender ▫ *vt* ter *or* trazer dependurado; (*hold*) balançar; (*fig: hopes, etc*) acenar com

Danish /'deɪnɪʃ/ *a* dinamarquês ▫ *n* (*lang*) dinamarquês *m*

dank /dæŋk/ *a* (**-er, -est**) frio e úmido, (*P*) húmido

dare /deə(r)/ *vt* **~ to do** ousar fazer. **~ sb to do** desafiar alg a fazer ▫ *n* desafio *m*. **I ~ say** creio

daredevil /'deədevl/ *n* louco *m*, temerário *m*

daring /'deərɪŋ/ *a* audacioso ▫ *n* audácia *f*

dark /da:k/ *a* (**-er, -est**) escuro, sombrio; (*gloomy*) sombrio; (*of colour*) escuro; (*of skin*) moreno ▫ *n* escuridão *f*, escuro *m*; (*nightfall*) anoitecer *m*, cair *m* da noite. **~ horse** concorrente *mf* que é uma incógnita. **~-room** *n* câmara *f* escura. **be in the ~ about** (*fig*) ignorar. **~ness** *n* escuridão *f*

darken /'da:kən/ *vt*/*i* escurecer

darling /'da:lɪŋ/ *a* & *n* querido (*m*)

darn /da:n/ *vt* serzir, remendar

dart /da:t/ *n* dardo *m*, flecha *f*. **~s** (*game*) jogo *m* de dardos ▫ *vi* lançar-se

dartboard /'da:tbɔ:d/ *n* alvo *m*
dash /dæʃ/ *vi* precipitar-se □ *vt* arremessar; (*hopes*) destruir □ *n* corrida *f*; (*stroke*) travessão *m*; (*Morse*) traço *m*. **a ~ of** um pouco de. **~ off** partir a toda a velocidade; (*letter*) escrever às pressas
dashboard /'dæʃbɔ:d/ *n* painel *m* de instrumentos, quadro *m* de bordo
data /'deɪtə/ *npl* dados *mpl*. **~ capture** aquisição *f* de informações, recolha *f* de dados. **~base** *n* base *f* de dados. **~ processing** processamento *m or* tratamento *m* de dados
date[1] /deɪt/ *n* data *f*; (*colloq*) encontro *m* marcado □ *vt/i* datar; (*colloq*) andar com. **out of ~** desatualizado, (*P*) desactualizado. **to ~** até a data. **up to ~** (*style*) moderno; (*information etc*) em dia. **~d** *a* antiquado
date[2] /deɪt/ *n* (*fruit*) tâmara *f*
daub /dɔ:b/ *vt* borrar, pintar toscamente
daughter /'dɔ:tə(r)/ *n* filha *f*. **~-in-law** *n* (*pl* **~s-in-law**) nora *f*
daunt /dɔ:nt/ *vt* assustar, intimidar, desencorajar
dawdle /'dɔ:dl/ *vi* perder tempo
dawn /dɔ:n/ *n* madrugada *f* □ *vi* madrugar, amanhecer. **~ on** (*fig*) fazer-se luz no espírito de, começar a perceber
day /deɪ/ *n* dia *m*; (*period*) época *f*, tempo *m*. **~-dream** *n* devaneio *m* □ *vi* devanear. **the ~ before** a véspera
daybreak /'deɪbreɪk/ *n* romper *m* do dia, aurora *f*, amanhecer *m*
daylight /'deɪlaɪt/ *n* luz *f* do dia. **~ robbery** roubar descaradamente
daytime /'deɪtaɪm/ *n* dia *m*, dia *m* claro
daze /deɪz/ *vt* aturdir □ *n* **in a ~** aturdido
dazzle /'dæzl/ *vt* deslumbrar; (*with headlights*) ofuscar
dead /ded/ *a* morto; (*numb*) dormente □ *adv* completamente, de todo □ *n* **in the ~ of the night** a horas mortas, na calada da noite. **the ~** os mortos. **in the ~ centre** bem no meio. **stop ~** estacar. **~ beat** *a* (*colloq*) morto de cansaço. **~ end** beco *m* sem saída. **~-pan** *a* inexpressivo
deaden /'dedn/ *vt* (*sound, blow*) amortecer; (*pain*) aliviar
deadline /'dedlaɪn/ *n* prazo *m* final
deadlock /'dedlɒk/ *n* impasse *m*
deadly /'dedlɪ/ *a* (**-ier, -iest**) mortal; (*weapon*) mortífero
deaf /def/ *a* (**-er, -est**) surdo. **turn a ~ ear** fingir que não ouve. **~ mute** surdo-mudo *m*. **~ness** *n* surdez *f*
deafen /'defn/ *vt* ensurdecer. **~ing** *a* ensurdecedor
deal /di:l/ *vt* (*pt* **dealt**) distribuir; (*a blow, cards*) dar □ *vi* negociar □ *n* negócio *m*; (*cards*) vez de dar *f*. **a great ~** muito (**of** de). **~ in** negociar em. **~ with** (*person*) tratar (com); (*affair*) tratar de. **~er** *n* comerciante *m*; (*agent*) concessionário *m*; representante *m*
dealings /'di:lɪŋz/ *npl* relações *fpl*; (*comm*) negócios *mpl*
dealt /delt/ *see* **deal**
dean /di:n/ *n* decano *m*
dear /dɪə(r)/ *a* (**-er, -est**) (*cherished*) caro, querido; (*expensive*) caro □ *n* amor *m* □ *adv* caro □ *int* **oh ~!** meu Deus! **~ly** *adv* (*very much*) muito; (*pay*) caro
dearth /dɜ:θ/ *n* escassez *f*
death /deθ/ *n* morte *f*. **~ certificate** certidão *f* de óbito. **~ penalty** pena *f* de morte. **~ rate** taxa *f* de mortalidade. **~-trap** *n* lugar *m* perigoso, ratoeira *f*. **~ly** *a* de morte, mortal
debase /dɪ'beɪs/ *vt* degradar
debat|e /dɪ'beɪt/ *n* debate *m* □ *vt* debater. **~able** *a* discutível
debauchery /dɪ'bɔ:tʃərɪ/ *n* deboche *m*, devassidão *f*
debility /dɪ'bɪlətɪ/ *n* debilidade *f*
debit /'debɪt/ *n* débito *m* □ *vt* (*pt* **debited**) debitar
debris /'deɪbri:/ *n* destroços *mpl*
debt /det/ *n* dívida *f*. **in ~** endividado. **~or** *n* devedor *m*
debunk /di:'bʌŋk/ *vt* (*colloq*) desmitificar
début /'deɪbju:/ *n* (*of actor, play etc*) estréia *f*
decade /'dekeɪd/ *n* década *f*
decaden|t /'dekədənt/ *a* decadente. **~ce** *n* decadência *f*
decaffeinated /di:'kæfi:neɪtɪd/ *a* sem cafeína
decanter /dɪ'kæntə(r)/ *n* garrafa *f* para vinho, de vidro ou cristal
decapitate /dɪ'kæpɪteɪt/ *vt* decapitar
decay /dɪ'keɪ/ *vi* apodrecer, estragar-se; (*food; fig*) deteriorar-se; (*building*) degradar-se □ *n* apodrecimento *m*; (*of tooth*) cárie *f*; (*fig*) declínio *m*, decadência *f*
deceased /dɪ'si:st/ *a* & *n* falecido (*m*), defunto (*m*)
deceit /dɪ'si:t/ *n* engano *m*. **~ful** *a* enganador
deceive /dɪ'si:v/ *vt* enganar, iludir
December /dɪ'sembə(r)/ *n* dezembro *m*
decen|t /'di:snt/ *a* decente; (*colloq: good*) (bastante) bom; (*colloq: likeable*) simpático. **~cy** *n* decência *f*
decentralize /di:'sentrəlaɪz/ *vt* descentralizar
decept|ive /dɪ'septɪv/ *a* enganador, ilusório. **~ion** /-ʃn/ *n* engano *m*

decibel /'desɪbel/ *n* decibel *m*
decide /dɪ'saɪd/ *vt/i* decidir. ~ **on** decidir-se por. ~ **to do** decidir fazer. ~**d** /-ɪd/ *a* decidido; (*clear*) definido, nítido. ~**dly** /-ɪdlɪ/ *adv* decididamente
decimal /'desɪml/ *a* decimal □ *n* (fração *f*, (*P*) fracção *f*) decimal *m*. ~ **point** vírgula *f* decimal
decipher /dɪ'saɪfə(r)/ *vt* decifrar
decision /dɪ'sɪʒn/ *n* decisão *f*
decisive /dɪ'saɪsɪv/ *a* decisivo; (*manner*) decidido. ~**ly** *adv* decisivamente
deck /dek/ *n* convés *m*; (*of cards*) baralho *m*. ~**-chair** *n* espreguiçadeira *f*
declar|e /dɪ'kleə(r)/ *vt* declarar. ~**ation** /deklə'reɪʃn/ *n* declaração *f*
decline /dɪ'klaɪn/ *vt* (*refuse*) declinar, recusar delicadamente; (*gram*) declinar □ *vi* (*deteriorate*) declinar; (*fall*) baixar □ *n* declínio *m*; (*fall*) abaixamento *m*
decode /di:'kəʊd/ *vt* descodificar
decompos|e /di:kəm'pəʊz/ *vt/i* decompor(-se). ~**ition** /-ɒmpə'zɪʃn/ *n* decomposição *f*
décor /'deɪkɔ:(r)/ *n* decoração *f*
decorat|e /'dekəreɪt/ *vt* decorar, enfeitar; (*paint*) pintar; (*paper*) pôr papel em. ~**ion** /-'reɪʃn/ *n* decoração *f*; (*medal etc*) condecoração *f*. ~**ive** /-ətɪv/ *a* decorativo
decorum /dɪ'kɔ:rəm/ *n* decoro *m*
decoy[1] /'di:kɔɪ/ *n* chamariz *m*, engodo *m*; (*trap*) armadilha *f*
decoy[2] /dɪ'kɔɪ/ *vt* atrair, apanhar
decrease[1] /di:'kri:s/ *vt/i* diminuir
decrease[2] /'di:kri:s/ *n* diminuição *f*
decree /dɪ'kri:/ *n* decreto *m*; (*jur*) decisão *f* judicial □ *vt* decretar
decrepit /dɪ'krepɪt/ *a* decrépito
dedicat|e /'dedɪkeɪt/ *vt* dedicar. ~**ed** *a* dedicado. ~**ion** /-'keɪʃn/ *n* dedicação *f*; (*in book*) dedicatória *f*
deduce /dɪ'dju:s/ *vt* deduzir
deduct /dɪ'dʌkt/ *vt* deduzir; (*from pay*) descontar
deduction /dɪ'dʌkʃn/ *n* dedução *f*; (*from pay*) desconto *m*
deed /di:d/ *n* ato *m*; (*jur*) contrato *m*
deem /di:m/ *vt* julgar, considerar
deep /di:p/ *a* (**-er, -est**) profundo □ *adv* profundamente. ~**-freeze** *n* congelador *m* □ *vt* congelar. **take a** ~ **breath** respirar fundo. ~**ly** *adv* profundamente
deepen /'di:pən/ *vt/i* aprofundar (-se); (*mystery, night*) adensar-se
deer /dɪə(r)/ *n* (*pl invar*) veado *m*
deface /dɪ'feɪs/ *vt* danificar, degradar
defamation /defə'meɪʃn/ *n* difamação *f*
default /dɪ'fɔ:lt/ *vi* faltar □ *n* **by** ~ à revelia. **win by** ~ (*sport*) ganhar por não comparecimento, (*P*) comparência □ *n* (*comput*) default *m*
defeat /dɪ'fi:t/ *vt* derrotar; (*thwart*) malograr □ *n* derrota *f*; (*of plan, etc*) malogro *m*
defect[1] /'di:fekt/ *n* defeito *m*. ~**ive** /dɪ'fektɪv/ *a* defeituoso
defect[2] /dɪ'fekt/ *vi* desertar. ~**ion** *n* defecção *m*. ~**or** *n* trânsfuga *mf*, dissidente *mf*; (*political*) asilado *m* político
defence /dɪ'fens/ *n* defesa *f*. ~**less** *a* indefeso
defend /dɪ'fend/ *vt* defender. ~**ant** *n* (*jur*) réu *m*, acusado *m*. ~**er** *n* advogado *m* de defesa, defensor *m*
defensive /dɪ'fensɪv/ *a* defensivo □ *n* **on the** ~ na defensiva *f*; (*person, sport*) na retranca *f* (*colloq*)
defer /dɪ'fɜ:(r)/ *vt* (*pt* **deferred**) adiar, diferir □ *vi* ~ **to** ceder, deferir
deferen|ce /'defərəns/ *n* deferência *f*. ~**tial** /-'renʃl/ *a* deferente
defian|ce /dɪ'faɪəns/ *n* desafio *m*. **in** ~ **of** sem respeito por. ~**t** *a* de desafio. ~**tly** *adv* com ar de desafio
deficien|t /dɪ'fɪʃnt/ *a* deficiente. **be** ~**t in** ter falta de. ~**cy** *n* deficiência *f*
deficit /'defɪsɪt/ *n* déficit *m*
define /dɪ'faɪn/ *vt* definir
definite /'defɪnɪt/ *a* definido; (*clear*) categórico, claro; (*certain*) certo. ~**ly** *adv* decididamente; (*clearly*) claramente
definition /defɪ'nɪʃn/ *n* definição *f*
definitive /dɪ'fɪnətɪv/ *a* definitivo
deflat|e /dɪ'fleɪt/ *vt* esvaziar; (*person*) desemproar, desinchar. ~**ion** /-ʃn/ *n* esvaziamento *m*; (*econ*) deflação *f*
deflect /dɪ'flekt/ *vt/i* desviar(-se)
deform /dɪ'fɔ:m/ *vt* deformar. ~**ed** *a* deformado, disforme. ~**ity** *n* deformidade *f*
defraud /dɪ'frɔ:d/ *vt* defraudar
defrost /di:'frɒst/ *vt* descongelar
deft /deft/ *a* (**-er, -est**) hábil
defunct /dɪ'fʌŋkt/ *a* (*law etc*) caduco, extinto
defuse /di:'fju:z/ *vt* (*a bomb*) desativar, (*P*) desactivar; (*a situation*) acalmar
defy /dɪ'faɪ/ *vt* desafiar; (*attempts*) resistir a; (*the law*) desobedecer a; (*public opinion*) opor-se a
degenerate /dɪ'dʒenəreɪt/ *vi* degenerar (**into** em)
degrad|e /dɪ'greɪd/ *vt* degradar. ~**ation** /degrə'deɪʃn/ *n* degradação *f*
degree /dɪ'gri:/ *n* grau *m*; (*univ*) diploma *m*. **to a** ~ ao mais alto grau, muito

dehydrate /di:'haɪdreɪt/ *vt/i* desidratar(-se)
de-ice /di:'aɪs/ *vt* descongelar, degelar; (*windscreen*) tirar o gelo de
deign /deɪn/ *vt* ~ **to do** dignar-se (a) fazer
deity /'di:ɪtɪ/ *n* divindade *f*
dejected /dɪ'dʒektɪd/ *a* abatido
delay /dɪ'leɪ/ *vt* atrasar; (*postpone*) retardar □ *vi* atrasar-se □ *n* atraso *m*, demora *f*
delegate[1] /'delɪgət/ *n* delegado *m*
delegat|e[2] /'delɪgeɪt/ *vt* delegar. **~ion** /-'geɪʃn/ *n* delegação *f*
delet|e /dɪ'li:t/ *vt* riscar. **~ion** /-ʃn/ *n* rasura *f*
deliberate[1] /dɪ'lɪbərət/ *a* deliberado; (*steps etc*) compassado. **~ly** *adv* deliberadamente, de propósito
deliberat|e[2] /dɪ'lɪbəreɪt/ *vt/i* deliberar. **~ion** /-'reɪʃn/ *n* deliberação *f*
delica|te /'delɪkət/ *a* delicado. **~cy** *n* delicadeza *f*; (*food*) guloseima *f*, iguaria *f*, (*P*) acepipe *m*
delicatessen /delɪkə'tesn/ *n* (*shop*) mercearias *fpl* finas
delicious /dɪ'lɪʃəs/ *a* delicioso
delight /dɪ'laɪt/ *n* grande prazer *m*, delícia *f*; (*thing*) delícia *f*, encanto *m* □ *vt* deliciar □ *vi* ~ **in** deliciar-se com. **~ed** *a* deliciado, encantado. **~ful** *a* delicioso, encantador
delinquen|t /dɪ'lɪŋkwənt/ *a* & *n* delinqüente *mf*, (*P*) delinquente *mf*. **~cy** *n* delinqüência *f*, (*P*) delinquência *f*
deliri|ous /dɪ'lɪrɪəs/ *a* delirante. **be ~ous** delirar. **~um** /-əm/ *n* delírio *m*
deliver /dɪ'lɪvə(r)/ *vt* entregar; (*letters*) distribuir; (*free*) libertar; (*med*) fazer o parto. **~ance** *n* libertação *f*. **~y** *n* entrega *f*; (*letters*) distribuição *f*; (*med*) parto *m*
delu|de /dɪ'lu:d/ *vt* enganar. **~de o.s.** ter ilusões. **~sion** /-ʒn/ *n* ilusão *f*
deluge /'delju:dʒ/ *n* dilúvio *m* □ *vt* inundar
de luxe /dɪ'lʌks/ *a* de luxo
delve /delv/ *vi* ~ **into** pesquisar, rebuscar
demand /dɪ'ma:nd/ *vt* exigir; (*ask to be told*) perguntar □ *n* exigência *f*; (*comm*) procura *f*; (*claim*) reivindicação *f*. **in ~** procurado. **~ing** *a* exigente; (*work*) puxado, custoso
demean /dɪ'mi:n/ *vt* ~ **o.s.** rebaixar-se
demeanour /dɪ'mi:nə(r)/ *n* comportamento *m*, conduta *f*
demented /dɪ'mentɪd/ *a* louco, demente. **become ~** enlouquecer
demo /'deməʊ/ *n* (*pl* **-os**) (*colloq*) manifestação *f*, (*P*) manif *f*
democracy /dɪ'mɒkrəsɪ/ *n* democracia *f*
democrat /'deməkræt/ *n* democrata *mf*. **~ic** /-'krætɪk/ *a* democrático
demoli|sh /dɪ'mɒlɪʃ/ *vt* demolir. **~tion** /demə'lɪʃn/ *n* demolição *f*
demon /'di:mən/ *n* demônio *m*
demonstrat|e /'demənstreɪt/ *vt* demonstrar □ *vi* (*pol*) fazer uma manifestação, manifestar-se. **~ion** /-'streɪʃn/ *n* demonstração *f*; (*pol*) manifestação *f*. **~or** *n* (*pol*) manifestante *mf*
demonstrative /dɪ'mɒnstrətɪv/ *a* demonstrativo
demoralize /dɪ'mɒrəlaɪz/ *vt* desmoralizar
demote /dɪ'məʊt/ *vt* fazer baixar de posto, rebaixar
demure /dɪ'mjʊə(r)/ *a* recatado, modesto
den /den/ *n* antro *m*, covil *m*; (*room*) cantinho *m*, recanto *m*
denial /dɪ'naɪəl/ *n* negação *f*; (*refusal*) recusa *f*; (*statement*) desmentido *m*
denigrate /'denɪgreɪt/ *vt* denegrir
denim /'denɪm/ *n* brim *m*. **~s** (*jeans*) jeans *mpl*
Denmark /'denma:k/ *n* Dinamarca *f*
denomination /dɪnɒmɪ'neɪʃn/ *n* denominação *f*; (*relig*) confissão *f*, seita *f*; (*money*) valor *m*
denote /dɪ'nəʊt/ *vt* denotar
denounce /dɪ'naʊns/ *vt* denunciar
dens|e /dens/ *a* (**-er**, **-est**) denso; (*colloq: person*) obtuso. **~ely** *adv* (*packed etc*) muito. **~ity** *n* densidade *f*
dent /dent/ *n* mossa *f*, depressão *f* □ *vt* dentear
dental /'dentl/ *a* dentário, dental
dentist /'dentɪst/ *n* dentista *mf*. **~ry** *n* odontologia *f*
denture /'dentʃə(r)/ *n* dentadura *f* (postiça)
denunciation /dɪnʌnsɪ'eɪʃn/ *n* denúncia *f*
deny /dɪ'naɪ/ *vt* negar; (*rumour*) desmentir; (*disown*) renegar; (*refuse*) recusar
deodorant /di:'əʊdərənt/ *n* & *a* desodorante (*m*), (*P*) desodorizante (*m*)
depart /dɪ'pa:t/ *vi* partir. **~ from** (*deviate*) afastar-se de, desviar-se de
department /dɪ'pa:tmənt/ *n* departamento *m*; (*in shop, office*) seção *f*, (*P*) secção *f*; (*government*) repartição *f*. **~ store** loja *f* de departamentos, (*P*) grande armazém *m*
departure /dɪ'pa:tʃə(r)/ *n* partida *f*. **a ~ from** (*custom, diet etc*) uma mudança de. **a new ~** uma nova orientação
depend /dɪ'pend/ *vi* ~ **on** depender de; (*trust*) contar com. **~able** *a* de

confiança. **~ence** *n* dependência *f*. **~ent (on)** *a* dependente (de)
dependant /dɪ'pendənt/ *n* dependente *mf*
depict /dɪ'pɪkt/ *vt* descrever; (*in pictures*) representar
deplete /dɪ'pli:t/ *vt* reduzir; (*use up*) esgotar
deplor|e /dɪ'plɔ:(r)/ *vt* deplorar. **~able** *a* deplorável
deport /dɪ'pɔ:t/ *vt* deportar. **~ation** /di:pɔ:'teɪʃn/ *n* deportação *f*
depose /dɪ'pəʊz/ *vt* depor
deposit /dɪ'pɒzɪt/ *vt* (*pt* **deposited**) depositar □ *n* depósito *m*. **~ account** conta *f* de depósito a prazo. **~or** *n* depositante *mf*
depot /'depəʊ/ *n* (*mil*) depósito *m*; (*buses*) garagem *f*; (*Amer: station*) rodoviária *f*, estação *f* de trem, (*P*) de comboio
deprav|e /dɪ'preɪv/ *vt* depravar. **~ity** /-'prævətɪ/ *n* depravação *f*
depreciat|e /dɪ'pri:ʃɪeɪt/ *vt/i* depreciar(-se). **~ion** /-'eɪʃn/ *n* depreciação *f*
depress /dɪ'pres/ *vt* deprimir; (*press down*) carregar em. **~ion** /-ʃn/ *n* depressão *f*
deprivation /deprɪ'veɪʃn/ *n* privação *f*
deprive /dɪ'praɪv/ *vt* **~ of** privar de. **~d** *a* privado; (*underprivileged*) deserdado (da sorte), destituído; (*child*) carente
depth /depθ/ *n* profundidade *f*. **be out of one's ~** perder pé, (*P*) não ter pé; (*fig*) ficar desnorteado, estar perdido. **in the ~(s) of** no mais fundo de, nas profundezas de
deputation /depjʊ'teɪʃn/ *n* delegação *f*
deputy /'depjʊtɪ/ *n* (*pl* **-ies**) delegado *m* □ *a* adjunto. **~ chairman** vice-presidente *m*
derail /dɪ'reɪl/ *vt* descarrilhar. **be ~ed** descarrilhar. **~ment** *n* descarrilhamento *m*
deranged /dɪ'reɪndʒd/ *a* (*mind*) transtornado, louco
derelict /'derəlɪkt/ *a* abandonado
deri|de /dɪ'raɪd/ *vt* escarnecer de. **~sion** /-'rɪʒn/ *n* escárnio *m*. **~sive** *a* escarninho. **~sory** *a* escarninho; (*offer etc*) irrisório
derivative /dɪ'rɪvətɪv/ *a* derivado; (*work*) pouco original □ *n* derivado *m*
deriv|e /dɪ'raɪv/ *vt* **~e from** tirar de □ *vi* **~e from** derivar de. **~ation** /derɪ'veɪʃn/ *n* derivação *f*
derogatory /dɪ'rɒgətrɪ/ *a* pejorativo; (*remark*) depreciativo
derv /dɜ:v/ *n* gasóleo *m*
descend /dɪ'send/ *vt/i* descer, descender. **be ~ed from** descender de. **~ant** *n* descendente *mf*
descent /dɪ'sent/ *n* descida *f*; (*lineage*) descendência *f*, origem *f*
descri|be /dɪs'kraɪb/ *vt* descrever. **~ption** /-'krɪpʃn/ *n* descrição *f*; **~ptive** /-'krɪptɪv/ *a* descritivo
desecrat|e /'desɪkreɪt/ *vt* profanar. **~ion** /-'kreɪʃn/ *n* profanação *f*
desert[1] /'dezət/ *a* & *n* deserto (*m*). **~ island** ilha *f* deserta
desert[2] /dɪ'zɜ:t/ *vt/i* desertar. **~ed** *a* abandonado. **~er** *n* desertor *m*. **~ion** /-ʃn/ *n* deserção *f*
deserv|e /dɪ'zɜ:v/ *vt* merecer. **~edly** /dɪ'zɜ:vɪdlɪ/ *adv* merecidamente, a justo título. **~ing** *a* (*person*) merecedor; (*action*) meritório
design /dɪ'zaɪn/ *n* desenho *m*; (*artistic*) design *m*; (*style of dress*) modelo *m*; (*pattern*) padrão *m*, motivo *m* □ *vt* desenhar; (*devise*) conceber. **~er** *n* desenhador *m*; (*of dresses*) costureiro *m*; (*of machine*) inventor *m*
designat|e /'dezɪgneɪt/ *vt* designar. **~ion** /'-neɪʃn/ *n* designação *f*
desir|e /dɪ'zaɪə(r)/ *n* desejo *m* □ *vt* desejar. **~able** *a* desejável, atraente
desk /desk/ *n* secretária *f*; (*of pupil*) carteira *f*; (*in hotel*) recepção *f*; (*in bank*) caixa *f*
desolat|e /'desələt/ *a* desolado. **~ion** /-'leɪʃn/ *n* desolação *f*
despair /dɪ'speə(r)/ *n* desespero *m* □ *vi* desesperar (**of** de)
desperate /'despərət/ *a* desesperado; (*criminal*) capaz de tudo. **be ~ for** ter uma vontade doida de. **~ly** *adv* desesperadamente
desperation /despə'reɪʃn/ *n* desespero *m*
despicable /dɪ'spɪkəbl/ *a* desprezível
despise /dɪ'spaɪz/ *vt* desprezar
despite /dɪ'spaɪt/ *prep* apesar de, a despeito de, mau grado
desponden|t /dɪ'spɒndənt/ *a* desanimado. **~cy** *n* desânimo *m*
despot /'despɒt/ *n* déspota *mf*
dessert /dɪ'zɜ:t/ *n* sobremesa *f*. **~-spoon** *n* colher *f* de sobremesa
destination /destɪ'neɪʃn/ *n* destino *m*, destinação *f*
destine /'destɪn/ *vt* destinar
destiny /'destɪnɪ/ *n* destino *m*
destitute /'destɪtju:t/ *a* destituído, indigente
destr|oy /dɪ'strɔɪ/ *vt* destruir. **~uction** /-'strʌkʃn/ *n* destruição *f*. **~uctive** *a* destrutivo, destruidor
detach /dɪ'tætʃ/ *vt* separar, arrancar. **~able** *a* separável; (*lining etc*) solto. **~ed** *a* separado; (*impartial*) imparcial; (*unemotional*) desprendido.

~ed house casa *f* sem parede-meia com outra
detachment /dɪ'tætʃmənt/ *n* separação *f*; (*indifference*) desprendimento *m*; (*mil*) destacamento *m*; (*impartiality*) imparcialidade *f*
detail /'di:teɪl/ *n* pormenor *m*, detalhe *m* □ *vt* detalhar; (*troops*) destacar. **~ed** *a* detalhado
detain /dɪ'teɪn/ *vt* reter; (*in prison*) deter. **~ee** /di:teɪ'ni:/ *n* detido *m*
detect /dɪ'tekt/ *vt* detectar. **~ion** /-ʃn/ *n* detecção *f*. **~or** *n* detector *m*
detective /dɪ'tektɪv/ *n* detective *m*. **~ story** romance *m* policial
detention /dɪ'tenʃn/ *n* detenção *f*. **be given a ~** (*school*) ficar de castigo na escola
deter /dɪ'tɜ:(r)/ *vt* (*pt* **deterred**) dissuadir; (*hinder*) impedir
detergent /dɪ'tɜ:dʒənt/ *a* & *n* detergente (*m*)
deteriorat|e /dɪ'tɪərɪəreɪt/ *vi* deteriorar(-se). **~ion** /-'reɪʃn/ *n* deterioração *f*
determin|e /dɪ'tɜ:mɪn/ *vt* determinar. **~e to do** decidir fazer. **~ation** /-'neɪʃn/ *n* determinação *f*. **~ed** *a* determinado. **~ed to do** decidido a fazer
deterrent /dɪ'terənt/ *n* dissuasivo *m*
detest /dɪ'test/ *vt* detestar. **~able** *a* detestável
detonat|e /'detəneɪt/ *vt/i* detonar. **~ion** /-'neɪʃn/ *n* detonação *f*. **~or** *n* espoleta *f*, detonador *m*
detour /'di:tʊə(r)/ *n* desvio *m*
detract /dɪ'trækt/ *vi* **~ from** depreciar, menosprezar
detriment /'detrɪmənt/ *n* detrimento *m*. **~al** /-'mentl/ *a* prejudicial
devalu|e /di:'vælju:/ *vt* desvalorizar. **~ation** /-'eɪʃn/ *n* desvalorização *f*
devastat|e /'devəsteɪt/ *vi* devastar; (*fig: overwhelm*) arrasar. **~ing** *a* devastador; (*criticism*) de arrasar
develop /dɪ'veləp/ *vt/i* (*pt* **developed**) desenvolver(-se); (*get*) contrair; (*build on*) urbanizar; (*film*) revelar. **~ into** tornar-se. **~ing country** país *m* subdesenvolvido. **~ment** *n* desenvolvimento *m*; (*film*) revelação *f*; (*of land*) urbanização *f*
deviat|e /'di:vɪeɪt/ *vi* desviar-se. **~ion** /-'eɪʃn/ *n* desvio *m*
device /dɪ'vaɪs/ *n* dispositivo *m*; (*scheme*) processo *m*. **left to one's own ~s** entregue a si mesmo
devil /'devl/ *n* diabo *m*
devious /'di:vɪəs/ *a* tortuoso; (*fig: means*) escuso; (*fig: person*) pouco franco
devise /dɪ'vaɪz/ *vt* imaginar, inventar
devoid /dɪ'vɔɪd/ *a* **~ of** desprovido de, destituído de
devot|e /dɪ'vəʊt/ *vt* dedicar, devotar. **~ed** *a* dedicado, devotado. **~ion** /-ʃn/ *n* devoção *f*
devotee /devə'ti:/ *n* **~ of** adepto *m* de, entusiasta *mf* de
devour /dɪ'vaʊə(r)/ *vt* devorar
devout /dɪ'vaʊt/ *a* devota; (*prayer*) fervoroso
dew /dju:/ *n* orvalho *m*
dext|erity /dek'sterətɪ/ *n* destreza *f*, jeito *m*. **~rous** /'dekstrəs/ *a* destro, hábil
diabet|es /daɪə'bi:tiz/ *n* diabetes *f*. **~ic** /-'betɪk/ *a* diabético
diabolical /daɪə'bɒlɪkl/ *a* diabólico
diagnose /'daɪəgnəʊz/ *vt* diagnosticar
diagnosis /daɪəg'nəʊsɪs/ *n* (*pl* **-oses** /-si:z/) diagnóstico *m*
diagonal /daɪ'ægənl/ *a* & *n* diagonal (*f*)
diagram /'daɪəgræm/ *n* diagrama *m*, esquema *m*
dial /'daɪəl/ *n* mostrador *m* □ *vt* (*pt* **dialled**) (*number*) marcar, discar. **~ling code** código *m* de discagem. **~ling tone** sinal *m* de discar
dialect /'daɪəlekt/ *n* dialeto *m*, (*P*) dialecto *m*
dialogue /'daɪəlɒg/ *n* diálogo *m*
diameter /daɪ'æmɪtə(r)/ *n* diâmetro *m*
diamond /'daɪəmənd/ *n* diamante *m*, brilhante *m*; (*shape*) losango *m*. **~s** (*cards*) ouros *mpl*
diaper /'daɪəpə(r)/ *n* (*Amer*) fralda *f*
diaphragm /'daɪəfræm/ *n* diafragma *m*
diarrhoea /daɪə'rɪə/ *n* diarréia *f*, (*P*) diarreia *f*
diary /'daɪərɪ/ *n* agenda *f*; (*record*) diário *m*
dice /daɪs/ *n* (*pl invar*) dado *m*
dictat|e /dɪk'teɪt/ *vt/i* ditar. **~ion** /-ʃn/ *n* ditado *m*
dictator /dɪk'teɪtə(r)/ *n* ditador *m*. **~ship** *n* ditadura *f*
diction /'dɪkʃn/ *n* dicção *f*
dictionary /'dɪkʃənrɪ/ *n* dicionário *m*
did /dɪd/ *see* **do**
diddle /'dɪdl/ *vt* (*colloq*) trapacear, enganar
didn't /'dɪdnt/ = **did not**
die /daɪ/ *vi* (*pres p* **dying**) morrer. **be dying to** estar doido para. **~ down** diminuir, baixar. **~ out** desaparecer, extinguir-se
diesel /'di:zl/ *n* diesel *m*. **~ engine** motor *m* diesel
diet /'daɪət/ *n* dieta *f* □ *vi* fazer dieta, estar de dieta
differ /'dɪfə(r)/ *vi* diferir; (*disagree*) discordar

differen|t /'dɪfrənt/ *a* diferente. **~ce** *n* diferença *f*; (*disagreement*) desacordo *m*. **~ly** *adv* diferentemente
differentiate /dɪfə'renʃɪeɪt/ *vt*/*i* diferençar(-se), diferenciar(-se)
difficult /'dɪfɪkəlt/ *a* difícil. **~y** *n* dificuldade *f*
diffiden|t /'dɪfɪdənt/ *a* acanhado, inseguro. **~ce** *n* acanhamento *m*, insegurança *f*
diffuse[1] /dɪ'fju:s/ *a* difuso
diffus|e[2] /dɪ'fju:z/ *vt* difundir. **~ion** /-ʒn/ *n* difusão *f*
dig /dɪg/ *vt*/*i* (*pt* **dug**, *pres p* **digging**) cavar; (*thrust*) espetar ▫ *n* (*with elbow*) cotovelada *f*; (*with finger*) cutucada *f*, (*P*) espetadela *f*; (*remark*) ferroada *f*; (*archaeol*) excavação *f*. **~s** (*colloq*) quarto *m* alugado. **~ up** desenterrar
digest /dɪ'dʒest/ *vt*/*i* digerir. **~ible** *a* digerível, digestível. **~ion** /-ʃn/ *n* digestão *f*
digestive /dɪ'dʒestɪv/ *a* digestivo
digit /'dɪdʒɪt/ *n* dígito *m*
digital /'dɪdʒɪtl/ *a* digital. **~ camera** câmara *f* digital.**~ clock** relógio *m* digital
dignif|y /'dɪgnɪfaɪ/ *vt* dignificar. **~ied** *a* digno
dignitary /'dɪgnɪtərɪ/ *n* dignitário *m*
dignity /'dɪgnətɪ/ *n* dignidade *f*
digress /daɪ'gres/ *vi* digressar, divagar. **~ from** desviar-se de. **~ion** /-ʃn/ *n* digressão *f*
dike /daɪk/ *n* dique *m*
dilapidated /dɪ'læpɪdeɪtɪd/ *a* (*house*) arruinado, degradado; (*car*) estragado
dilat|e /daɪ'leɪt/ *vt*/*i* dilatar(-se). **~ion** /-ʃn/ *n* dilatação *f*
dilemma /dɪ'lemə/ *n* dilema *m*
diligen|t /'dɪlɪdʒənt/ *a* diligente, aplicado. **~ce** *n* diligência *f*, aplicação *f*
dilute /daɪ'lju:t/ *vt* diluir ▫ *a* diluído
dim /dɪm/ *a* (**dimmer, dimmest**) (*weak*) fraco; (*dark*) sombrio; (*indistinct*) vago; (*colloq: stupid*) burro (*colloq*) ▫ *vt*/*i* (*pt* **dimmed**) (*light*) baixar. **~ly** *adv* (*shine*) fracamente; (*remember*) vagamente
dime /daɪm/ *n* (*Amer*) moeda *f* de dez centavos
dimension /daɪ'menʃn/ *n* dimensão *f*
diminish /dɪ'mɪnɪʃ/ *vt*/*i* diminuir
diminutive /dɪ'mɪnjʊtɪv/ *a* diminuto ▫ *n* diminutivo *m*
dimple /'dɪmpl/ *n* covinha *f*
din /dɪn/ *n* barulheira *f*, (*P*) chinfrim *m*
dine /daɪn/ *vi* jantar. **~r** /-ə(r)/ *n* (*person*) comensal *m*; (*rail*) vagão restaurante *m*; (*Amer: restaurant*) lanchonete *f*
dinghy /'dɪŋgɪ/ *n* (*pl* **-ghies**) bote *m*; (*inflatable*) bote *m* de borracha, (*P*) barco *m* de borracha
dingy /'dɪndʒɪ/ *a* (**-ier, -iest**) com ar sujo, esquálido
dining-room /'daɪnɪŋru:m/ *n* sala *f* de jantar
dinner /'dɪnə(r)/ *n* jantar *m*; (*lunch*) almoço *m*. **~-jacket** *n* smoking *m*
dinosaur /'daɪnəsɔ:(r)/ *n* dinossauro *m*
dip /dɪp/ *vt*/*i* (*pt* **dipped**) mergulhar; (*lower*) baixar ▫ *n* mergulho *m*; (*bathe*) banho *m* rápido, mergulho *m*; (*slope*) descida *f*; (*culin*) molho *m*. **~ into** (*book*) folhear. **~ one's headlights** baixar para médios
diphtheria /dɪf'θɪərɪə/ *n* difteria *f*
diphthong /'dɪfθɒŋ/ *n* ditongo *m*
diploma /dɪ'pləʊmə/ *n* diploma *m*
diplomacy /dɪ'pləʊməsɪ/ *n* diplomacia *f*
diplomat /'dɪpləmæt/ *n* diplomata *mf*. **~ic** /-'mætɪk/ *a* diplomático
dire /daɪə(r)/ *a* (**-er, -est**) terrível; (*need, poverty*) extremo
direct /dɪ'rekt/ *a* direto, (*P*) directo ▫ *adv* diretamente, (*P*) directamente ▫ *vt* dirigir. **~ sb to** indicar a alg o caminho para
direction /dɪ'rekʃn/ *n* direção *f*, (*P*) direcção *f*, sentido *m*. **~s** instruções *fpl*. **~s for use** modo *m* de emprego
directly /dɪ'rektlɪ/ *adv* diretamente, (*P*) directamente; (*at once*) imediatamente, logo
director /dɪ'rektə(r)/ *n* diretor *m*, (*P*) director *m*
directory /dɪ'rektərɪ/ *n* **(telephone) ~** lista *f* telefônica, (*P*) telefónica
dirt /dɜ:t/ *n* sujeira *f*. **~ cheap** (*colloq*) baratíssimo
dirty /'dɜ:tɪ/ *a* (**-ier, -iest**) sujo; (*word*) obsceno ▫ *vt*/*i* sujar(-se). **~ trick** golpe *m* baixo, (*P*) boa partida *f*
disability /dɪsə'bɪlətɪ/ *n* deficiência *f*
disable /dɪs'eɪbl/ *vt* incapacitar. **~d** *a* inválido, deficiente
disadvantage /dɪsəd'va:ntɪdʒ/ *n* desvantagem *f*
disagree /dɪsə'gri:/ *vi* discordar (**with** de). **~ with** (*food, climate*) não fazer bem. **~ment** *n* desacordo *m*; (*quarrel*) desintendimento *m*
disagreeable /dɪsə'gri:əbl/ *a* desagradável
disappear /dɪsə'pɪə(r)/ *vi* desaparecer. **~ance** *n* desaparecimento *m*
disappoint /dɪsə'pɔɪnt/ *vt* desapontar, decepcionar. **~ment** *n* desapontamento *m*, decepção *f*
disapprov|e /dɪsə'pru:v/ *vi* **~e (of)** desaprovar. **~al** *n* desaprovação *f*

disarm /dɪ'sa:m/ *vt/i* desarmar. **~ament** *n* desarmamento *m*

disast|er /dɪ'za:stə(r)/ *n* desastre *m*. **~rous** *a* desastroso

disband /dɪs'bænd/ *vt/i* debandar; (*troops*) dispersar

disbelief /dɪsbɪ'li:f/ *n* incredulidade *f*

disc /dɪsk/ *n* disco *m*. **~ jockey** disc(o) jockey *m*

discard /dɪs'ka:d/ *vt* pôr de lado, descartar(-se) de; (*old clothes etc*) desfazer-se de

discern /dɪ'sɜ:n/ *vt* discernir. **~ible** *a* perceptível. **~ing** *a* perspicaz. **~ment** *n* discernimento *m*, perspicácia *f*

discharge[1] /dɪs'tʃɑ:dʒ/ *vt* descarregar; (*dismiss*) despedir, mandar embora; (*duty*) cumprir; (*liquid*) vazar, (*P*) deitar; (*patient*) dar alta a; (*prisoner*) absolver, pôr em liberdade; (*pus*) purgar, (*P*) deitar

discharge[2] /'dɪstʃa:dʒ/ *n* descarga *f*; (*dismissal*) despedimento *m*; (*of patient*) alta *f*; (*of prisoner*) absolvição *f*; (*med*) secreção *f*

disciple /dɪ'saɪpl/ *n* discípulo *m*

disciplin|e /'dɪsɪplɪn/ *n* disciplina *f* □ *vt* disciplinar; (*punish*) castigar. **~ary** *a* disciplinar

disclaim /dɪs'kleɪm/ *vt* (*jur*) repudiar; (*deny*) negar. **~er** *n* desmentido *m*

disclos|e /dɪs'kləʊz/ *vt* revelar. **~ure** /-ʒə(r)/ *n* revelação *f*

disco /'dɪskəʊ/ *n* (*pl* **-os**) (*colloq*) discoteca *f*

discolour /dɪs'kʌlə(r)/ *vt/i* descolorir(-se); (*in sunlight*) desbotar (-se)

discomfort /dɪs'kʌmfət/ *n* mal- estar *m*; (*lack of comfort*) desconforto *m*

disconcert /dɪskən'sɜ:t/ *vt* desconcertar. **~ing** *a* desconcertante

disconnect /dɪskə'nekt/ *vt* desligar

discontent /dɪskən'tent/ *n* descontentamento *m*. **~ed** *a* descontente

discontinue /dɪskən'tɪnju:/ *vt* descontinuar, suspender

discord /'dɪskɔ:d/ *n* discórdia *f*. **~ant** /-'skɔ:dənt/ *a* discordante

discoth'que /'dɪskətek/ *n* discoteca *f*

discount[1] /'dɪskaʊnt/ *n* desconto *m*

discount[2] /dɪs'kaʊnt/ *vt* descontar; (*disregard*) dar o desconto a

discourage /dɪs'kʌrɪdʒ/ *vt* desencorajar

discourte|ous /dɪs'kə:tɪəs/ *a* indelicado. **~sy** /-sɪ/ *n* indelicadeza *f*

discover /dɪs'kʌvə(r)/ *vt* descobrir. **~y** *n* descoberta *f*; (*of island etc*) descobrimento *m*

discredit /dɪs'kredɪt/ *vt* (*pt* **discredited**) desacreditar □ *n* descrédito *m*

discreet /dɪ'skri:t/ *a* discreto

discrepancy /dɪ'skrepənsɪ/ *n* discrepância *f*

discretion /dɪ'skreʃn/ *n* discrição *f*; (*prudence*) prudência *f*

discriminat|e /dɪs'krɪmɪneɪt/ *vt/i* discriminar. **~e against** tomar partido contra, fazer discriminação contra. **~ing** *a* discriminador; (*having good taste*) com discernimento. **~ion** /-'neɪʃn/ *n* discernimento *m*; (*bias*) discriminação *f*

discus /'dɪskəs/ *n* disco *m*

discuss /dɪ'skʌs/ *vt* discutir. **~ion** /-ʃn/ *n* discussão *f*

disdain /dɪs'deɪn/ *n* desdém *m* □ *vt* desdenhar. **~ful** *a* desdenhoso

disease /dɪ'zi:z/ *n* doença *f*. **~d** *a* (*plant*) atacado por doença; (*person, animal*) doente

disembark /dɪsɪm'ba:k/ *vt/i* desembarcar

disembodied /dɪsɪm'bɒdɪd/ *a* desencarnado

disenchant /dɪsɪn'tʃa:nt/ *vt* desencantar. **~ment** *n* desencantamento *m*

disengage /dɪsɪn'geɪdʒ/ *vt* desprender, soltar; (*mech*) desengatar

disentangle /dɪsɪn'tæŋgl/ *vt* desembaraçar, desenredar

disfavour /dɪs'feɪvə(r)/ *n* desfavor *m*, desgraça *f*

disfigure /dɪs'fɪgə(r)/ *vt* desfigurar

disgrace /dɪs'greɪs/ *n* vergonha *f*; (*disfavour*) desgraça *f* □ *vt* desonrar. **~ful** *a* vergonhoso

disgruntled /dɪs'grʌntld/ *a* descontente

disguise /dɪs'gaɪz/ *vt* disfarçar □ *n* disfarce *m*. **in ~** disfarçado

disgust /dɪs'gʌst/ *n* repugnância *f* □ *vt* repugnar. **~ing** *a* repugnante

dish /dɪʃ/ *n* prato *m* □ *vt* **~ out** (*colloq*) distribuir. **~ up** servir. **the ~es** (*crockery*) a louça *f*

dishcloth /'dɪʃklɒθ/ *n* pano *m* de prato

dishearten /dɪs'ha:tn/ *vt* desencorajar, desalentar

dishevelled /dɪ'ʃevld/ *a* desgrenhado

dishonest /dɪs'ɒnɪst/ *a* desonesto. **~y** *n* desonestidade *f*

dishonour /dɪs'ɒnə(r)/ *n* desonra *f* □ *vt* desonrar. **~able** *a* desonroso

dishwasher /'dɪʃwɒʃə(r)/ *n* lavadora *f* de pratos, (*P*) máquina *f* de lavar a louça

disillusion /dɪsɪ'lu:ʒn/ *vt* desiludir. **~ment** *n* desilusão *f*

disinfect /dɪsɪn'fekt/ *vt* desinfetar, (*P*) desinfectar. **~ant** *n* desinfetante *m*, (*P*) desinfectante *m*

disinherit /dɪsɪn'herɪt/ *vt* deserdar

disintegrate /dɪsˈɪntɪgreɪt/ *vt/i* desintegrar(-se)
disinterested /dɪsˈɪntrəstɪd/ *a* desinteressado
disjointed /dɪsˈdʒɔɪntɪd/ *a* (*talk*) descosido, desconexo
disk /dɪsk/ *n* (*comput*) disco *m*; (*Amer*) = **disc**. ~ **drive** unidade *f* de disco
dislike /dɪsˈlaɪk/ *n* aversão *f*, antipatia *f* □ *vt* não gostar de, antipatizar com
dislocat|e /ˈdɪsləkeɪt/ *vt* (*limb*) deslocar. **~ion** /-ˈkeɪʃn/ *n* deslocação *f*
dislodge /dɪsˈlɒdʒ/ *vt* desalojar
disloyal /dɪsˈlɔɪəl/ *a* desleal. **~ty** *n* deslealdade *f*
dismal /ˈdɪzməl/ *a* tristonho
dismantle /dɪsˈmæntl/ *vt* desmantelar
dismay /dɪsˈmeɪ/ *n* consternação *f* □ *vt* consternar
dismiss /dɪsˈmɪs/ *vt* despedir; (*from mind*) afastar, pôr de lado. **~al** *n* despedimento *m*
dismount /dɪsˈmaʊnt/ *vi* desmontar
disobedien|t /dɪsəˈbiːdɪənt/ *a* desobediente. **~ce** *n* desobediência *f*
disobey /dɪsəˈbeɪ/ *vt/i* desobedecer (a)
disorder /dɪsˈɔːdə(r)/ *n* desordem *f*; (*med*) perturbações *fpl*, disfunção *f*. **~ly** *a* desordenado; (*riotous*) desordeiro
disorganize /dɪsˈɔːgənaɪz/ *vt* desorganizar
disorientate /dɪsˈɔːrɪənteɪt/ *vt* desorientar
disown /dɪsˈəʊn/ *vt* repudiar
disparaging /dɪˈspærɪdʒɪŋ/ *a* depreciativo
disparity /dɪˈspærətɪ/ *n* disparidade *f*
dispatch /dɪˈspætʃ/ *vt* despachar □ *n* despacho *m*
dispel /dɪsˈpel/ *vt* (*pt* **dispelled**) dissipar
dispensary /dɪˈspensərɪ/ *n* dispensário *m*, farmácia *f*
dispense /dɪˈspens/ *vt* dispensar □ *vi* ~ **with** dispensar, passar sem. **~r** /-ə(r)/ *n* (*container*) distribuidor *m*
dispers|e /dɪˈspɜːs/ *vt/i* dispersar (-se). **~al** *n* dispersão *f*
dispirited /dɪˈspɪrɪtɪd/ *a* desanimado
displace /dɪˈspleɪs/ *vt* deslocar; (*take the place of*) substituir. **~d person** deslocado *m* de guerra
display /dɪˈspleɪ/ *vt* exibir, mostrar; (*feeling*) manifestar, dar mostras de □ *n* exposição *f*; (*of computer*) apresentação *f* visual; (*comm*) objetos *mpl* expostos
displeas|e /dɪsˈpliːz/ *vt* desagradar a. **~ed with** descontente com. **~ure** /-ˈpleʒə(r)/ *n* desagrado *m*
disposable /dɪˈspəʊzəbl/ *a* descartável
dispos|e /dɪˈspəʊz/ *vt* dispor □ *vi* **~e of** desfazer-se de. **well ~ed towards** bem disposto para com. **~al** *n* (*of waste*) eliminação *f*. **at sb's ~al** à disposição de alg
disposition /dɪspəˈzɪʃn/ *n* disposição *f*; (*character*) índole *f*
disproportionate /dɪsprəˈpɔːʃənət/ *a* desproporcionado
disprove /dɪsˈpruːv/ *vt* refutar
dispute /dɪˈspjuːt/ *vt* contestar; (*fight for, quarrel*) disputar □ *n* disputa *f*; (*industrial, pol*) conflito *m*. **in ~** em questão
disqualif|y /dɪsˈkwɒlɪfaɪ/ *vt* tornar inapto; (*sport*) desqualificar. **~y from driving** apreender a carteira de motorista. **~ication** /-ɪˈkeɪʃn/ *n* desqualificação *f*
disregard /dɪsrɪˈgaːd/ *vt* não fazer caso de □ *n* indiferença *f* (**for** por)
disrepair /dɪsrɪˈpeə(r)/ *n* mau estado *m*, abandono *m*, degradação *f*
disreputable /dɪsˈrepjʊtəbl/ *a* pouco recomendável; (*in appearance*) com mau aspecto; (*in reputation*) vergonhoso, de má fama
disrepute /dɪsrɪˈpjuːt/ *n* descrédito *m*
disrespect /dɪsrɪˈspekt/ *n* falta *f* de respeito. **~ful** *a* desrespeitoso, irreverente
disrupt /dɪsˈrʌpt/ *vt* perturbar; (*plans*) transtornar; (*break up*) dividir. **~ion** /-ʃn/ *n* perturbação *f*. **~ive** *a* perturbador
dissatisf|ied /dɪˈsætɪsfaɪd/ *a* descontente. **~action** /dɪsætɪsˈfækʃn/ *n* descontentamento *m*
dissect /dɪˈsekt/ *vt* dissecar. **~ion** /-ʃn/ *n* dissecação *f*
dissent /dɪˈsent/ *vi* dissentir, discordar □ *n* dissensão *f*, desacordo *m*
dissertation /dɪsəˈteɪʃn/ *n* dissertação *f*
disservice /dɪsˈsɜːvɪs/ *n* **do sb a ~** prejudicar alg
dissident /ˈdɪsɪdənt/ *a* & *n* dissidente (*mf*)
dissimilar /dɪˈsɪmɪlə(r)/ *a* diferente
dissipate /ˈdɪsɪpeɪt/ *vt* dissipar; (*efforts, time*) desperdiçar. **~d** *a* dissoluto
dissociate /dɪˈsəʊʃɪeɪt/ *vt* dissociar, desassociar
dissolution /dɪsəˈluːʃn/ *n* dissolução *f*
dissolve /dɪˈzɒlv/ *vt/i* dissolver (-se)
dissuade /dɪˈsweɪd/ *vt* dissuadir
distance /ˈdɪstəns/ *n* distância *f*. **from a ~** de longe. **in the ~** ao longe, à distância
distant /ˈdɪstənt/ *a* distante; (*relative*) afastado

distaste /dɪs'teɪst/ *n* aversão *f*. **~ful** *a* desagradável

distemper /dɪ'stempə(r)/ *n* pintura *f* a têmpera; (*animal disease*) cinomose *f* □ *vt* pintar a têmpera

distend /dɪ'stend/ *vt/i* distender (-se)

distil /dɪ'stɪl/ *vt* (*pt* **distilled**) destilar. **~lation** /-'leɪʃn/ *n* destilação *f*

distillery /dɪ'stɪlərɪ/ *n* destilaria *f*

distinct /dɪ'stɪŋkt/ *a* distinto; (*marked*) claro, nítido. **~ion** /-ʃn/ *n* distinção *f*. **~ive** *a* distintivo, característico. **~ly** *adv* distintamente; (*markedly*) claramente

distinguish /dɪ'stɪŋgwɪʃ/ *vt/i* distinguir. **~ed** *a* distinto

distort /dɪ'stɔ:t/ *vt* distorcer; (*misrepresent*) deturpar. **~ion** /-ʃn/ *n* distorção *f*; (*misrepresentation*) deturpação *f*

distract /dɪ'strækt/ *vt* distrair. **~ed** *a* (*distraught*) desesperado, fora de si. **~ing** *a* enlouquecedor. **~ion** /-ʃn/ *n* distração *f*, (*P*) distracção *f*

distraught /dɪ'strɔ:t/ *a* desesperado, fora de si

distress /dɪ'stres/ *n* (*physical*) dor *f*; (*anguish*) aflição *f*; (*poverty*) miséria *f*; (*danger*) perigo *m* □ *vt* afligir. **~ing** *a* aflitivo, doloroso

distribut|e /dɪ'strɪbju:t/ *vt* distribuir. **~ion** /-'bju:ʃn/ *n* distribuição *f*. **~or** *n* distribuidor *m*

district /'dɪstrɪkt/ *n* região *f*; (*of town*) zona *f*

distrust /dɪs'trʌst/ *n* desconfiança *f* □ *vt* desconfiar de

disturb /dɪ'stɜ:b/ *vt* perturbar; (*move*) desarrumar; (*bother*) incomodar. **~ance** *n* (*noise, disorder*) distúrbio *m*. **~ed** *a* perturbado. **~ing** *a* perturbador

disused /dɪs'ju:zd/ *a* fora de uso, desusado, em desuso

ditch /dɪtʃ/ *n* fosso *m* □ *vt* (*sl: abandon*) abandonar, largar

dither /'dɪðə(r)/ *vi* hesitar

ditto /'dɪtəʊ/ *adv* idem

div|e /daɪv/ *vi* mergulhar; (*rush*) precipitar-se □ *n* mergulho *m*; (*of plane*) picada *f*; (*sl: place*) espelunca *f*. **~er** *n* mergulhador *m*. **~ing-board** *n* prancha *f* de saltos. **~ing-suit** *n* escafandro *m*

diverge /daɪ'vɜ:dʒ/ *vi* divergir

divergent /daɪ'vɜ:dʒənt/ *a* divergente

diverse /daɪ'vɜ:s/ *a* diverso

diversify /daɪ'vɜ:sɪfaɪ/ *vt* diversificar

diversity /daɪ'vɜ:sətɪ/ *n* diversidade *f*

diver|t /daɪ'vɜ:t/ *vt* desviar; (*entertain*) divertir. **~sion** /-ʃn/ *n* diversão *f*; (*traffic*) desvio *m*

divide /dɪ'vaɪd/ *vt/i* dividir(-se). **~ in two** (*branch, river, road*) bifurcar-se

dividend /'dɪvɪdend/ *n* dividendo *m*

divine /dɪ'vaɪn/ *a* divino

divinity /dɪ'vɪnətɪ/ *n* divindade *f*; (*theology*) teologia *f*

division /dɪ'vɪʒn/ *n* divisão *f*

divorce /dɪ'vɔ:s/ *n* divórcio *m* □ *vt/i* divorciar(-se) de. **~d** *a* divorciado

divorcee /dɪvɔ:'si:/ *n* divorciado *m*

divulge /daɪ'vʌldʒ/ *vt* divulgar

DIY *abbr see* **do-it-yourself**

dizz|y /'dɪzɪ/ *a* (**-ier, -iest**) tonto. **be** *or* **feel ~y** ter tonturas, sentir-se tonto. **~iness** *n* tontura *f*, vertigem *f*

do /du:/ *vt/i* (*3 sing pres* **does**, *pt* **did**, *pp* **done**) fazer; (*be suitable*) servir; (*be enough*) bastar (a); (*sl: swindle*) enganar, levar (*colloq*). **how ~ you ~?** como vai? **well done** muito bem!, (*P*) bravo!; (*culin*) bem passado. **done for** (*colloq*) liquidado (*colloq*), (*P*) anu-mado (*colloq*) □ *v aux* **~ you see?** vê?; **I ~ not smoke** não fumo. **don't you?, doesn't he?** *etc* não é? □ *n* (*pl* **dos** *or* **do's**) festa *f*. **~-it-yourself** *a* faça-você-mesmo. **~ away with** eliminar, suprimir. **~ in** (*sl*) matar, liquidar (*colloq*). **~ out** limpar. **~ up** (*fasten*) fechar; (*house*) renovar. **I could ~ with a cup of tea** apetecia-me uma xícara de chá. **it could ~ with a wash** precisa de uma lavagem

docile /'dəʊsaɪl/ *a* dócil

dock¹ /dɒk/ *n* doca *f* □ *vt* levar à doca □ *vi* entrar na doca. **~er** *n* estivador *m*

dock² /dɒk/ *n* (*jur*) banco *m* dos réus

dockyard /'dɒkja:d/ *n* estaleiro *m*

doctor /'dɒktə(r)/ *n* médico *m*, doutor *m*; (*univ*) doutor *m* □ *vt* (*cat*) capar; (*fig*) adulterar, falsificar

doctorate /'dɒktərət/ *n* doutorado *m*, (*P*) doutoramento *m*

doctrine /'dɒktrɪn/ *n* doutrina *f*

document /'dɒkjʊmənt/ *n* documento *m* □ *vt* documentar. **~ary** /-'mentrɪ/ *a* documental □ *n* documentário *m*

dodge /dɒdʒ/ *vt/i* esquivar(-se), furtar(-se) a □ *n* (*colloq*) truque *m*

dodgy /'dɒdʒɪ/ *a* (**-ier, -iest**) (*colloq*) delicado, difícil, embaraçoso

does /dʌz/ *see* **do**

doesn't /'dʌznt/ = **does not**

dog /dɒg/ *n* cão *m* □ *vt* (*pt* **dogged**) ir no encalço de, perseguir. **~-eared** *a* com os cantos dobrados

dogged /'dɒgɪd/ *a* obstinado, persistente

dogma /'dɒgmə/ *n* dogma *m*. **~tic** /-'mætɪk/ *a* dogmático

dogsbody /'dɒgzbɒdɪ/ *n* (*colloq*) pau-para-toda-obra *m* (*colloq*), factótum *m*

doldrums /'dɒldrəmz/ *npl* **be in the ~** estar com a neura; (*business*) estar parado

dole /dəʊl/ *vt* **~ out** distribuir □ *n* (*colloq*) auxílio *m* desemprego. **on the ~** (*colloq*) desempregado (titular de auxílio)

doleful /'dəʊlfl/ *a* tristonho, melancólico

doll /dɒl/ *n* boneca *f* □ *vt/i* **~ up** (*colloq*) embonecar(-se)

dollar /'dɒlə(r)/ *n* dólar *m*

dolphin /'dɒlfɪn/ *n* golfinho *m*

domain /dəʊ'meɪn/ *n* domínio *m*

dome /dəʊm/ *n* cúpula *f*; (*vault*) abóbada *f*

domestic /də'mestɪk/ *a* (*of home, animal, flights*) doméstico; (*trade*) interno; (*news*) nacional. **~ated** /-keɪtɪd/ *a* (*animal*) domesticado; (*person*) que gosta de trabalhos caseiros

dominant /'dɒmɪnənt/ *a* dominante

dominat|e /'dɒmɪneɪt/ *vt/i* dominar. **~ion** /-'neɪʃn/ *n* dominação *f*, domínio *m*

domineer /dɒmɪ'nɪə(r)/ *vi* **~ over** mandar (em), ser autocrático (para com). **~ing** *a* mandão, autocrático

dominion /də'mɪnjən/ *n* domínio *m*

domino /'dɒmɪnəʊ/ *n* (*pl* **-oes**) dominó *m*

donat|e /dəʊ'neɪt/ *vt* fazer doação de, doar, dar. **~ion** /-ʃn/ *n* donativo *m*

done /dʌn/ *see* **do**

donkey /'dɒŋkɪ/ *n* burro *m*

donor /'dəʊnə(r)/ *n* (*of blood*) doador *m*, (*P*) dador *m*

don't /dəʊnt/ = **do not**

doodle /'du:dl/ *vi* rabiscar

doom /du:m/ *n* ruína *f*; (*fate*) destino *m*. **be ~ed to** ser/estar condenado a. **~ed (to failure)** condenado ao fracasso

door /dɔ:(r)/ *n* porta *f*

doorman /'dɔ:mən/ *n* (*pl* **-men**) porteiro *m*

doormat /'dɔ:mæt/ *n* capacho *m*

doorstep /'dɔ:step/ *n* degrau *m* da porta

doorway /'dɔ:weɪ/ *n* vão *m* da porta, (*P*) entrada *f*

dope /dəʊp/ *n* (*colloq*) droga *f*; (*sl: idiot*) imbecil *mf* □ *vt* dopar, drogar

dormant /'dɔ:mənt/ *a* dormente; (*inactive*) inativo, (*P*) inactivo; (*latent*) latente

dormitory /'dɔ:mɪtrɪ/ *n* dormitório *m*; (*Amer univ*) residência *f*

dos|e /dəʊs/ *n* dose *f* □ *vt* medicar. **~age** *n* dosagem *f*; (*on label*) posologia *f*

doss /dɒs/ *vi* **~ (down)** dormir sem conforto. **~-house** *n* pensão *f* miserável, asilo *m* noturno, (*P*) nocturno. **~er** *n* vagabundo *m*

dot /dɒt/ *n* ponto *m*. **on the ~** no momento preciso □ *vt* **be ~ted with** estar semeado de. **~ted line** linha *f* pontilhada

dot-com /dɒt'kɒm/ *n* empresa *f* dot.com

dote /dəʊt/ *vi* **~ on** ser louco por

double /'dʌbl/ *a* duplo; (*room, bed*) de casal □ *adv* duas vezes mais □ *n* dobro *m*. **~s** (*tennis*) dupla *f*, (*P*) pares *mpl* □ *vt/i* dobrar, duplicar; (*fold*) dobrar em dois. **at the ~** a passo acelerado. **~-bass** *n* contrabaixo *m*. **~ chin** papada *f*. **~-cross** *vt* enganar. **~-dealing** *n* jogo *m* duplo. **~-decker** *n* ônibus *m*, (*P*) autocarro *m* de dois andares. **~ Dutch** algaraviada *f*, fala *f* incompreensível. **~ glazing** (janela *f* de) vidro (*m*) duplo. **doubly** *adv* duplamente

doubt /daʊt/ *n* dúvida *f* □ *vt* duvidar de. **~ if** *or* **that** duvidar que. **~ful** *a* duvidoso; (*hesitant*) que tem dúvidas. **~less** *adv* sem dúvida, indubitavelmente

dough /dəʊ/ *n* massa *f*

doughnut /'dəʊnʌt/ *n* sonho *n*, (*P*) bola *f* de Berlim

dove /dʌv/ *n* pomba *f*

dowdy /'daʊdɪ/ *a* (**-ier, -iest**) sem graça, sem gosto

down[1] /daʊn/ *n* (*feathers, hair*) penugem *f*

down[2] /daʊn/ *adv* (*to lower place*) abaixo, para baixo; (*in lower place*) em baixo. **be ~** (*level, price*) descer; (*sun*) estar posto □ *prep* por (+*n*) (*n*+) abaixo. **~ the hill/street** *etc* pelo monte/pela rua *etc* abaixo □ *vt* (*colloq: knock down*) jogar abaixo; (*colloq: drink*) esvaziar. **come** *or* **go ~** descer. **~-and-out** *n* marginal *m*. **~-hearted** *a* desencorajado, desanimado. **~-to-earth** *a* terra-a-terra *invar*. **~ under** na Austrália. **~ with** abaixo

downcast /'daʊnka:st/ *a* abatido, deprimido, desmoralizado

downfall /daʊn'fɔ:l/ *n* queda *f*, ruína *f*

downhill /daʊn'hɪl/ *adv* **go ~** descer; (*fig*) ir abaixo □ *a* /'daʊnhɪl/ a descer, descendente

download /daʊn'ləʊd/ *vt* (*comput*) baixar

downpour /'daʊnpɔ:(r)/ *n* aguaceiro *m* forte, (*P*) chuvada *f*

downright /'daʊnraɪt/ *a* franco; (*utter*) autêntico, verdadeiro □ *adv* positivamente

downstairs /daʊn'steəz/ *adv* (*at/to*) em/para baixo, no/para o andar de baixo □ *a* /'daʊnsteəz/ (*flat etc*) de baixo, do andar de baixo

downstream /'daʊnstri:m/ *adv* rio abaixo

downtown /'daʊntaʊn/ *a & adv* (de, em, para) o centro da cidade. ~ **Boston** o centro de Boston

downtrodden /'daʊntrɒdn/ *a* espezinhado, oprimido

downward /'daʊnwəd/ *a* descendente. ~**(s)** *adv* para baixo

dowry /'daʊərɪ/ *n* dote *m*

doze /dəʊz/ *vi* dormitar. ~ **off** cochilar □ *n* soneca *f*, cochilo *m*

dozen /'dʌzn/ *n* dúzia *f*. ~**s of** (*colloq*) dezenas de, dúzias de

Dr *abbr* (*Doctor*) Dr

drab /dræb/ *a* insípido; (*of colour*) morto, apagado

draft[1] /dra:ft/ *n* rascunho *m*; (*comm*) ordem *f* de pagamento □ *vt* fazer o rascunho de; (*draw up*) redigir. **the** ~ (*Amer: mil*) recrutamento *m*

draft[2] /dra:ft/ *n* (*Amer*) = **draught**

drag /dræg/ *vt/i* (*pt* **dragged**) arrastar(-se); (*river*) dragar; (*pull away*) arrancar □ *n* (*colloq: task*) chatice *f* (*sl*); (*colloq: person*) estorvo *m*; (*sl: clothes*) travesti *m*

dragon /'drægən/ *n* dragão *m*

dragonfly /'drægənflaɪ/ *n* libélula *f*

drain /dreɪn/ *vt* drenar; (*vegetables*) escorrer; (*glass, tank*) esvaziar; (*use up*) esgotar □ *vi* ~ (**off**) escoar-se □ *n* cano *m*. ~**s** *npl* (*sewers*) esgotos *mpl*. ~**age** *n* drenagem *f*. ~**(-pipe)** cano *m* de esgoto. ~**ing-board** *n* escorredouro *m*

drama /'dra:mə/ *n* arte *f* dramática; (*play, event*) drama *m*. ~**tic** /drə'mætɪk/ *a* dramático. ~**tist** /'dræmətɪst/ *n* dramaturgo *m*. ~**tize** /'dræmətaɪz/ *vt* dramatizar

drank /dræŋk/ *see* **drink**

drape /dreɪp/ *vt* ~ **round/over** dispor (tecido) em pregas à volta de *or* sobre. ~**s** *npl* (*Amer*) cortinas *fpl*

drastic /'dræstɪk/ *a* drástico, violento

draught /dra:ft/ *n* corrente *f* de ar; (*naut*) calado *m*. ~**s** (*game*) (jogo *m* das) damas *fpl*. ~ **beer** chope *m*, (*P*) cerveja *f* à caneca, imperial *f* (*colloq*). ~**y** *a* com correntes de ar, ventoso

draughtsman /'dra:ftsmən/ *n* (*pl* **-men**) desenhista *m*, (*P*) desenhador *m*

draw /drɔ:/ *vt* (*pt* **drew**, *pp* **drawn**) puxar; (*attract*) atrair; (*picture*) desenhar; (*in lottery*) tirar à sorte; (*line*) traçar; (*open curtains*) abrir; (*close curtains*) fechar □ *vi* desenhar; (*sport*) empatar; (*come*) vir □ *n* (*sport*) empate *m*; (*lottery*) sorteio *m*. ~ **back** recuar. ~ **in** (*of days*) diminuir. ~ **near** aproximar-se. ~ **out** (*money*) levantar. ~ **up** deter-se, parar; (*document*) redigir; (*chair*) aproximar, chegar

drawback /'drɔ:bæk/ *n* inconveniente *m*, desvantagem *f*

drawer /drɔ:(r)/ *n* gaveta *f*

drawing /'drɔ:ɪŋ/ *n* desenho *m*. ~**-board** *n* prancheta *f*. ~**-pin** *n* percevejo *m*

drawl /drɔ:l/ *n* fala *f* arrastada

drawn /drɔ:n/ *see* **draw**

dread /dred/ *n* terror *m* □ *vt* temer

dreadful /'dredfl/ *a* medonho, terrível. ~**ly** *adv* terrivelmente

dream /dri:m/ *n* sonho *m* □ *vt/i* (*pt* **dreamed** *or* **dreamt**) sonhar (**of** com) □ *a* (*ideal*) dos seus sonhos. ~ **up** imaginar. ~**er** *n* sonhador *m*. ~**y** *a* sonhador; (*music*) romântico

dreary /'drɪərɪ/ *a* (**-ier, -iest**) tristonho; (*boring*) aborrecido

dredge /dredʒ/ *n* draga *f* □ *vt/i* dragar. ~**r** /-ə(r)/ *n* draga *f*; (*for sugar*) polvilhador *m*

dregs /dregz/ *npl* depósito *m*, sedimento *m*; (*fig*) escória *f*

drench /drentʃ/ *vt* encharcar

dress /dres/ *n* vestido *m*; (*clothing*) roupa *f* □ *vt/i* vestir(-se); (*food*) temperar; (*wound*) fazer curativo, (*P*) pensar, (*P*) tratar. ~ **rehearsal** ensaio *m* geral. ~ **up as** fantasiar-se de. **get** ~**ed** vestir-se

dresser /'dresə(r)/ *n* (*furniture*) guarda-louça *m*

dressing /'dresɪŋ/ *n* (*sauce*) tempero *m*; (*bandage*) curativo *m*, (*P*) penso *m*. ~**-gown** *n* roupão *m*. ~**-room** *n* (*sport*) vestiário *m*; (*theat*) camarim *m*. ~**-table** *n* toucador *m*

dressmak|er /'dresmeɪkə(r)/ *n* costureira *f*, modista *f*. ~**ing** *n* costura *f*

dressy /'dresɪ/ *a* (**-ier, -iest**) elegante, chique *invar*

drew /dru:/ *see* **draw**

dribble /'drɪbl/ *vi* pingar; (*person*) babar-se; (*football*) driblar

dried /draɪd/ *a* (*fruit etc*) seco

drier /'draɪə(r)/ *n* secador *m*

drift /drɪft/ *vi* ir à deriva; (*pile up*) amontoar-se □ *n* força *f* da corrente; (*pile*) monte *m*; (*of events*) rumo *m*; (*meaning*) sentido *m*. ~**er** *n* pessoa *f* sem rumo

drill /drɪl/ *n* (*tool*) broca *f*; (*training*) exercício *m*, treino *m*; (*routine procedure*) exercícios *mpl* □ *vt* furar, perfurar; (*train*) treinar; (*tooth*) abrir □ *vi* treinar-se

drink /drɪŋk/ *vt/i* (*pt* **drank**, *pp* **drunk**) beber □ *n* bebida *f*. **a** ~ **of water** um copo de água. ~**able** *a* potável; (*palatable*) bebível. ~**er** *n* bebedor *m*. ~**ing water** água *f* potável

drip /drɪp/ *vi* (*pt* **dripped**) pingar □ *n* pingar *m*; (*sl: person*) banana *mf* (*colloq*). ~**-dry** *vt* deixar escorrer □ *a* que não precisa passar

dripping /'drɪpɪŋ/ *n* gordura *f* do assado

drive /draɪv/ *vt* (*pt* **drove**, *pp* **driven** /'drɪvn/) empurrar, impelir, levar; (*car, animal*) dirigir, conduzir, (*P*) guiar; (*machine*) acionar, (*P*) accionar □ *vi* dirigir, conduzir, (*P*) guiar □ *n* passeio *m* de carro; (*private road*) entrada *f* para veículos; (*fig*) energia *f*; (*psych*) drive *m*, compulsão *f*, impulso *m*; (*campaign*) campanha *f*. ~ **at** chegar a. ~ **away** (*car*) partir. ~ **in** (*force in*) enterrar. ~**-in** *n* (*bank, cinema etc*) banco *m*, cinema *m etc* em que se é atendido no carro, drive-in *m*. ~ **mad** (fazer) enlouquecer, pôr fora de si

drivel /'drɪvl/ *n* baboseira *f*, bobagem *f*

driver /'draɪvə(r)/ *n* condutor *m*; (*of taxi, bus*) chofer *m*, motorista *mf*

driving /'draɪvɪŋ/ *n* condução *f*. ~**-licence** *n* carteira *f* de motorista, (*P*) carta *f* de condução. ~ **school** auto-escola *f*; (*P*) **escola** *f* **de condução.** ~ **test** exame *m* de motorista, (*P*) de condução

drizzle /'drɪzl/ *n* chuvisco *m* □ *vi* chuviscar

drone /drəʊn/ *n* zumbido *m*; (*male bee*) zangão *m* □ *vi* zumbir; (*fig*) falar monotonamente

drool /dru:l/ *vi* babar(-se)

droop /dru:p/ *vi* pender, curvar-se

drop /drɒp/ *n* gota *f*; (*fall*) queda *f*; (*distance*) altura *f* de queda □ *vt/i* (*pt* **dropped**) (deixar) cair; (*fall, lower*) baixar. ~ **(off)** (*person from car*) deixar, largar. ~ **a line** escrever duas linhas (**to** a). ~ **in** passar por (**on** em casa de). ~ **off** (*doze*) adormecer. ~ **out** (*withdraw*) retirar-se; (*of student*) abandonar. ~**-out** *n* marginal *mf*, marginalizado *m*

droppings /'drɒpɪŋz/ *npl* excrementos *mpl* de animal; (*of birds*) cocô *m* (*colloq*), porcaria *f* (*colloq*)

dross /drɒs/ *n* escória *f*; (*refuse*) lixo *m*

drought /draʊt/ *n* seca *f*

drove /drəʊv/ *see* **drive**

drown /draʊn/ *vt/i* afogar(-se)

drowsy /'draʊzɪ/ *a* sonolento. **be** *or* **feel** ~ ter vontade de dormir

drudge /drʌdʒ/ *n* mouro *m* de trabalho. ~**ry** /-ərɪ/ *n* trabalho *m* penoso e monótono, estafa *f*

drug /drʌg/ *n* droga *f*; (*med*) medicamento *m*, remédio *m* □ *vt* (*pt* **drugged**) drogar. ~ **addict** drogado *m*, tóxico-dependente *m*

drugstore /'drʌgstɔ:(r)/ *n* (*Amer*) farmácia *f* que vende também sorvetes etc

drum /drʌm/ *n* (*mus*) tambor *m*; (*for oil*) barril *m*, tambor *m*. ~**s** (*mus*) bateria *f* □ *vi* (*pt* **drummed**) tocar tambor; (*with one's fingers*) tamborilar □ *vt* ~ **into sb** fazer entrar na cabeça de alg. ~ **up** (*support*) conseguir obter; (*business*) criar. ~**mer** *n* tambor *m*; (*in pop group etc*) baterista *m*, (*P*) bateria *m*

drunk /drʌŋk/ *see* **drink** □ *a* embriagado, bêbedo. **get** ~ embebedar-se, embriagar-se □ *n* bêbedo *m*. ~**ard** *n* alcoólico *m*, bêbedo *m*. ~**en** *a* embriagado, bêbedo; (*habitually*) bêbedo

dry /draɪ/ *a* (**drier, driest**) seco; (*day*) sem chuva □ *vt/i* secar. **be** *or* **feel** ~ ter sede. ~**-clean** *vt* limpar a seco. ~**-cleaner's** *n* (loja de) lavagem *f* a seco, lavanderia *f*. ~ **up** (*dishes*) secar a louça *f*; (*of supplies*) esgotar-se. ~**ness** *n* secura *f*

dual /'dju:əl/ *a* duplo. ~ **carriageway** estrada *f* dividida por faixa central. ~**-purpose** *a* com fim duplo

dub /dʌb/ *vt* (*pt* **dubbed**) (*film*) dobrar; (*nickname*) apelidar de

dubious /'dju:bɪəs/ *a* duvidoso; (*character, compliment*) dúbio. **feel** ~ **about** ter dúvidas quanto a

duchess /'dʌtʃɪs/ *n* duquesa *f*

duck /dʌk/ *n* pato *m* □ *vi* abaixar-se rapidamente □ *vt* (*head*) baixar; (*person*) batizar, pregar uma amona em. ~**ling** *n* patinho *m*

duct /dʌkt/ *n* canal *m*, tubo *m*

dud /dʌd/ *a* (*sl: thing*) que não presta ou não funciona; (*sl: coin*) falso; (*sl: cheque*) sem fundos, (*P*) careca (*sl*)

due /dju:/ *a* devido; (*expected*) esperado □ *adv* ~ **east**/*etc* exatamente, (*P*) exactamente a leste/*etc* □ *n* devido *m*. ~**s** direitos *mpl*; (*of club*) cota *f*. ~ **to** devido a, por causa de. **in** ~ **course** no tempo devido

duel /'dju:əl/ *n* duelo *m*

duet /dju:'et/ *n* dueto *m*

duffel /'dʌfl/ *a* ~ **bag** saco *m* de lona. ~**-coat** *n* casaco *m* de tecido de lã

dug /dʌg/ *see* **dig**

duke /dju:k/ *n* duque *m*

dull /dʌl/ *a* (**-er, -est**) (*boring*) enfadonho; (*colour*) morto; (*mirror*) embaçado; (*weather*) encoberto; (*sound*) surdo; (*stupid*) burro

duly /'dju:lɪ/ *adv* devidamente; (*in due time*) no tempo devido

dumb /dʌm/ *a* (**-er, -est**) mudo; (*colloq: stupid*) bronco, burro

dumbfound /dʌm'faʊnd/ *vt* pasmar

dummy /'dʌmɪ/ *n* imitação *f*, coisa *f* simulada; (*of tailor*) manequim *m*; (*of baby*) chupeta *f*
dump /dʌmp/ *vt* (*rubbish*) jogar fora; (*put down*) deixar cair; (*colloq: abandon*) largar □ *n* monte *m* de lixo; (*tip*) lixeira *f*; (*mil*) depósito *m*; (*colloq*) buraco *m*
dunce /dʌns/ *n* burro *m*. **~'s cap** orelhas *fpl* de burro
dune /dju:n/ *n* duna *f*
dung /dʌŋ/ *n* esterco *m*; (*manure*) estrume *m*
dungarees /dʌŋgə'ri:z/ *npl* macacão *m*, (*P*) fato *m* de macaco
dungeon /'dʌndʒən/ *n* calabouço *m*, masmorra *f*
dupe /dju:p/ *vt* enganar □ *n* trouxa *m*
duplicate[1] /'dju:plɪkət/ *n* duplicado *m* □ *a* idêntico
duplicate[2] /'dju:plɪkeɪt/ *vt* duplicar, fazer em duplicado; (*on machine*) fotocopiar
duplicity /dju:'plɪsətɪ/ *n* duplicidade *f*
durable /'djʊərəbl/ *a* resistente; (*enduring*) duradouro, durável
duration /djʊ'reɪʃn/ *n* duração *f*
duress /djʊ'res/ *n* **under ~** sob coação *f*, (*P*) coacção *f*
during /'djʊərɪŋ/ *prep* durante
dusk /dʌsk/ *n* crepúsculo *m*, anoitecer *m*
dusky /'dʌskɪ/ *a* (**-ier, -iest**) escuro, sombrio
dust /dʌst/ *n* pó *m*, poeira *f* □ *vt* limpar o pó de; (*sprinkle*) polvilhar. **~-jacket** *n* sobrecapa *f* de livro
dustbin /'dʌstbɪn/ *n* lata *f* do lixo, (*P*) caixote *m*
duster /'dʌstə(r)/ *n* pano *m* do pó
dustman /'dʌstmən/ *n* (*pl* **-men**) lixeiro *m*, (*P*) homem *m* do lixo
dusty /'dʌstɪ/ *a* (**-ier, -iest**) poeirento, empoeirado
Dutch /dʌtʃ/ *a* holandês □ *n* (*lang*) holandês *m*. **~man** *n* holandês *m*. **~woman** *n* holandesa *f*. **go ~** pagar cada um a sua despesa
dutiful /'dju:tɪfl/ *a* cumpridor; (*showing respect*) respeitador
dut|y /'dju:tɪ/ *n* dever *m*; (*tax*) impostos *mpl*. **~ies** (*of official etc*) funções *fpl*. **off ~y** de folga. **on ~y** de serviço. **~y-free** *a* isento de impostos. **~y-free shop** free shop *m*
duvet /'dju:veɪ/ *n* edredom *m*, (*P*) edredão *m* de penas
dwarf /dwɔ:f/ *n* (*pl* **-fs**) anão *m*
dwell /dwel/ *vi* (*pt* **dwelt**) morar. **~ on** alongar-se sobre. **~er** *n* habitante. **~ing** *n* habitação *f*
dwindle /'dwɪndl/ *vi* diminuir, reduzirse
dye /daɪ/ *vt* (*pres p* **dyeing**) tingir □ *n* tinta *f*
dying /'daɪɪŋ/ *see* **die**
dynamic /daɪ'næmɪk/ *a* dinâmico
dynamite /'daɪnəmaɪt/ *n* dinamite *f* □ *vt* dinamitar
dynamo /'daɪnəməʊ/ *n* (*pl* **-os**) dínamo *m*
dynasty /'dɪnəstɪ/ *n* dinastia *f*
dysentery /'dɪsəntrɪ/ *n* disenteria *f*
dyslex|ia /dɪs'leksɪə/ *n* dislexia *f*. **~ic** *a* disléxico

Ee

each /i:tʃ/ *a & pron* cada. **~ one** cada um. **~ other** um ao outro, uns aos outros. **they like ~ other** gostam um do outro/uns dos outros. **know/love**/*etc* **~ other** conhecer-se/amar-se/*etc*
eager /'i:gə(r)/ *a* ansioso (**to** por), desejoso (**for** de); (*supporter*) entusiástico. **be ~ to** ter vontade de. **~ly** *adv* com impaciência, ansiosamente; (*keenly*) com entusiasmo. **~ness** *n* ansiedade *f*, desejo *m*; (*keenness*) entusiasmo *m*
eagle /'i:gl/ *n* águia *f*
ear /ɪə(r)/ *n* ouvido *m*; (*external part*) orelha *f*. **~-drum** *n* tímpano *m*. **~-ring** *n* brinco *m*
earache /'ɪoreɪk/ *n* dor *f* de ouvidos
earl /3:l/ *n* conde *m*
early /'3:lɪ/ (**-ier, -iest**) *adv* cedo □ *a* primeiro; (*hour*) matinal; (*fruit*) temporão; (*retirement*) antecipado. **have an ~ dinner** jantar cedo. **in ~ summer** no princípio do verão
earmark /'ɪəma:k/ *vt* destinar, reservar (**for** para)
earn /3:n/ *vt* ganhar; (*deserve*) merecer
earnest /'3:nɪst/ *a* sério. **in ~** a sério
earnings /'3:nɪŋz/ *npl* salário *m*; (*profits*) ganhos *mpl*, lucros *mpl*
earshot /'ɪəʃɒt/ *n* **within ~** ao alcance da voz
earth /3:θ/ *n* terra *f* □ *vt* (*electr*) ligar à terra. **why on ~?** por que diabo?, por que cargas d'água? **~ly** *a* terrestre, terreno
earthenware /'3:θənweə(r)/ *n* louça *f* de barro, faiança *f*
earthquake /'3:θkweɪk/ *n* tremor *m* de terra, terremoto *m*
earthy /'3:θɪ/ *a* terroso, térreo; (*coarse*) grosseiro

earwig /'ɪəwɪg/ *n* lacrainha *f*, (*P*) bicha-cadela *f*

ease /i:z/ *n* facilidade *f*; (*comfort*) bem-estar *m* □ *vt/i* (*from pain, anxiety*) acalmar(-se); (*slow down*) afrouxar; (*slide*) deslizar. **at ~** à vontade; (*mil*) descansar. **ill at ~** pouco à vontade. **with ~** facilmente. **~ in/out** fazer entrar/sair com cuidado

easel /'i:zl/ *n* cavalete *m*

east /i:st/ *n* este *m*, leste *m*, oriente *m*. **the E~** o Oriente □ *a* este, (de) leste, oriental □ *adv* a/para leste. **~ of** para o leste de **~erly** *a* oriental, leste, a/de leste. **~ward** *a*, **~ward(s)** *adv* para leste

Easter /'i:stə(r)/ *n* Páscoa *f*. **~ egg** ovo *m* de Páscoa

eastern /'i:stən/ *a* oriental, leste

easy /'i:zɪ/ *a* (**-ier, -iest**) fácil; (*relaxed*) natural, descontraído. **take it ~** levar as coisas com calma. **~ chair** poltrona *f*. **~-going** *a* bonacheirão. **easily** *adv* facilmente

eat /i:t/ *vt/i* (*pt* **ate**, *pp* **eaten**) comer. **~ into** corroer. **~able** *a* comestível

eaves /i:vz/ *npl* beiral *m*

eavesdrop /'i:vzdrɒp/ *vi* (*pt* **-dropped**) escutar por detrás da porta

e-book /'i:bʊk/ *n* livro *m* eletrônico

ebb /eb/ *n* vazante *f*, baixa-mar *m* □ *vi* vazar; (*fig*) declinar

EC /i:'si:/ *n* (*abbr of European Commission*) CE *f*

eccentric /ɪk'sentrɪk/ *a* & *n* excêntrico (*m*). **~ity** /eksen'trɪsətɪ/ *n* excentricidade *f*

ecclesiastical /ɪkli:zɪ'æstɪkl/ *a* eclesiástico

echo /'ekəʊ/ *n* (*pl* **-oes**) eco *m* □ *vt/i* (*pt* **echoed**, *pres p* **echoing**) ecoar; (*fig*) repetir

eclipse /ɪ'klɪps/ *n* eclipse *m* □ *vt* eclipsar

ecolog|y /i:'kɒlədʒɪ/ *n* ecologia *f*. **~ical** /i:kə'lɒdʒɪkl/ *a* ecológico

e-commerce /'i:kɒmɜ:s/ *n* comércio *m* eletrônico

economic /i:kə'nɒmɪk/ *a* econômico; (*profitable*) rentável. **~al** *a* econômico. **~s** *n* economia *f* política

economist /ɪ'kɒnəmɪst/ *n* economista *mf*

econom|y /ɪ'kɒnəmɪ/ *n* economia *f*. **~ize** *vt/i* economizar

ecstasy /'ekstəsɪ/ *n* êxtase *m*

ecstatic /ɪk'stætɪk/ *a* extático

ecu /'eɪkju:/ *n* unidade *f* monetária européia

eczema /'ɛksɪmə/ *n* eczema *m*

edge /edʒ/ *n* borda *f*, beira *f*; (*of town*) periferia *f*, limite *m*; (*of knife*) fio *m* □ *vt* debruar □ *vi* (*move*) avançar pouco a pouco

edging /'edʒɪŋ/ *n* borda *f*, (*P*) bordadura *f*

edgy /'edʒɪ/ *a* irritadiço, nervoso

edible /'edɪbl/ *a* comestível

edict /'i:dɪkt/ *n* édito *m*

edifice /'edɪfɪs/ *n* edifício *m*

edit /'edɪt/ *vt* (*pt* **edited**) (*newspaper*) dirigir; (*text*) editar

edition /ɪ'dɪʃn/ *n* edição *f*

editor /'edɪtə(r)/ *n* (*of newspaper*) diretor *m*, (*P*) director *m*, editor *m* responsável; (*of text*) organizador *m* de texto. **the ~ (in chief)** redator-chefe *m*, (*P*) redactor-chefe *m*. **~ial** /edɪ'tɔ:rɪəl/ *a* & *n* editorial (*m*)

educat|e /'edʒʊkeɪt/ *vt* instruir; (*mind, public*) educar. **~ed** *a* instruído; educado. **~ion** /-'keɪʃn/ *n* educação *f*; (*schooling*) ensino *m*. **~ional** /-'keɪʃənl/ *a* educativo, pedagógico

EEC /i:i:'si:/ *n* (*abbr of European Economic Community*) CEE *f*

eel /i:l/ *n* enguia *f*

eerie /'ɪərɪ/ *a* (**-ier, -iest**) arrepiante, misterioso

effect /ɪ'fekt/ *n* efeito *m* □ *vt* efetuar, (*P*) efectuar. **come into ~** entrar em vigor. **in ~** na realidade. **take ~** ter efeito

effective /ɪ'fektɪv/ *a* eficaz, eficiente; (*striking*) sensacional; (*actual*) efetivo, (*P*) efectivo. **~-ly** *adv* (*efficiently*) eficazmente; (*strikingly*) de forma sensacional; (*actually*) efetivamente, (*P*) efectivamente. **~ness** *n* eficácia *f*

effeminate /ɪ'femɪnət/ *a* efeminado, afeminado

effervescent /efə'vesnt/ *a* efervescente

efficien|t /ɪ'fɪʃnt/ *a* eficiente, eficaz. **~cy** *n* eficiência *f*. **~tly** *adv* eficientemente

effigy /'efɪdʒɪ/ *n* efígie *f*

effort /'efət/ *n* esforço *m*. **~less** *a* fácil, sem esforço

effrontery /ɪ'frʌntərɪ/ *n* desfaçatez *f*

effusive /ɪ'fju:sɪv/ *a* efusivo, expansivo

e.g. /i:'dʒi:/ *abbr* por ex

egg[1] /eg/ *n* ovo *m*. **~-cup** *n* copinho *m* para ovo quente, oveiro *m*. **~-plant** *n* beringela *f*

egg[2] /eg/ *vt* **~ on** (*colloq*) incitar

eggshell /'egʃel/ *n* casca *f* de ovo

ego /'egəʊ/ *n* (*pl* **-os**) ego *m*, eu *m*. **~ism** *n* egoísmo *m*. **~ist** *n* egoísta *mf*. **~tism** *n* egotismo *m*. **~tist** *n* egotista *mf*

Egypt /'i:dʒɪpt/ *n* Egito *m*. **~ian** /ɪ'dʒɪpʃn/ *a* & *n* egípcio (*m*)

eh /eɪ/ *int* (*colloq*) hã?

eiderdown /'aɪdədaʊn/ *n* edredão *m*, edredom *m*

eight /eɪt/ *a & n* oito (*m*). **eighth** /eɪtθ/ *a & n* oitavo (*m*)

eighteen /eɪ'ti:n/ *a & n* dezoito (*m*). **~th** *a & n* décimo oitavo (*m*)

eight|y /'eɪtɪ/ *a & n* oitenta (*m*). **~ ieth** *a & n* octogésimo (*m*)

either /'aɪðə(r)/ *a & pron* um e outro; (*with negative*) nem um nem outro; (*each*) cada ▫ *adv* também não ▫ *conj* **~ ... or** ou ... ou; (*with negative*) nem ... nem

ejaculate /ɪ'dʒækjʊleɪt/ *vt/i* ejacular; (*exclaim*) exclamar

eject /ɪ'dʒekt/ *vt* expelir; (*expel*) expulsar, despejar

elaborate[1] /ɪ'læbərət/ *a* elaborado, rebuscado, minucioso

elaborate[2] /ɪ'læbəreɪt/ *vt* elaborar ▫ *vi* entrar em pormenores. **~on** estender-se sobre

elapse /ɪ'læps/ *vi* decorrer

elastic /ɪ'læstɪk/ *a & n* elástico (*m*). **~ band** elástico *m*

elat|ed /ɪ'leɪtɪd/ *a* radiante, exultante. **~ ion** *n* exultação *f*

elbow /'elbəʊ/ *n* cotovelo *m*

elder[1] /'eldə(r)/ *a* mais velho. **~s** *npl* pessoas *fpl* mais velhas

elder[2] /'eldə(r)/ *n* (*tree*) sabugueiro *m*

elderly /'eldəlɪ/ *a* idoso. **the ~** as pessoas de idade

eldest /'eldɪst/ *a & n* o mais velho (*m*)

elect /ɪ'lekt/ *vt* eleger ▫ *a* eleito. **~ion** /-kʃn/ *n* eleição *f*

electric /ɪ'lektrɪk/ *a* elétrico, (*P*) eléctrico.

electrician /ɪlek'trɪʃn/ *n* eletricista *m*, (*P*) electricista *m*

electricity /ɪlek'trɪsətɪ/ *n* eletricidade *f*, (*P*) electricidade *f*

electrify /ɪ'lektrɪfaɪ/ *vt* eletrificar, (*P*) electrificar; (*fig: excite*) eletrizar, (*P*) electrizar

electrocute /ɪ'lektrəkju:t/ *vt* eletrocutar, (*P*) electrocutar

electronic /ɪlek'trɒnɪk/ *a* eletrônico, (*P*) electrónico. **~s** *n* eletrônica *f*, (*P*) electrónica *f*

elegan|t /'elɪgənt/ *a* elegante. **~ce** *n* elegância *f*. **~tly** *adv* elegantemente, com elegância

element /'elɪmənt/ *n* elemento *m*; (*of heater etc*) resistência *f*. **~ary** /-'mentrɪ/ *a* elementar; (*school*) primário

elephant /'elɪfənt/ *n* elefante *m*

elevat|e /'elɪveɪt/ *vt* elevar. **~ion** /-'veɪʃn/ *n* elevação *f*

elevator /'elɪveɪtə(r)/ *n* (*Amer: lift*) elevador *m*, ascensor *m*

eleven /ɪ'levn/ *a & n* onze (*m*). **~th** *a & n* décimo primeiro (*m*). **at the ~th hour** à última hora

elicit /ɪ'lɪsɪt/ *vt* extrair, obter

eligible /'elɪdʒəbl/ *a* (*for office*) idôneo, (*P*) idóneo (**for** para); (*desirable*) aceitável. **be ~ for** (*entitled to*) ter direito a

eliminat|e /ɪ'lɪmɪneɪt/ *vt* eliminar. **~ion** /-'neɪʃn/ *n* eliminação *f*

élite /eɪ'li:t/ *n* elite *f*

ellip|se /ɪ'lɪps/ *n* elipse *f*. **~tical** *a* elíptico

elm /elm/ *n* olmo *m*, ulmeiro *m*

elocution /elə'kju:ʃn/ *n* elocução *f*

elongate /'i:lɒŋgeɪt/ *vt* alongar

elope /ɪ'ləʊp/ *vi* fugir. **~ment** *n* fuga *f* (de amantes), (*P*) (de amorosos)

eloquen|t /'eləkwənt/ *a* eloqüente, (*P*) eloquente. **~ce** *n* eloqüência *f*, (*P*) eloquência *f*

else /els/ *adv* mais. **everybody ~** todos os outros. **nobody ~** mais ninguém. **nothing ~** nada mais. **or ~** ou então, senão. **somewhere ~** noutro lado qualquer. **~where** *adv* noutro lado

elude /ɪ'lu:d/ *vt* escapar a; (*a question*) evadir

elusive /ɪ'lu:sɪv/ *a* (*person*) esquivo, difícil de apanhar; (*answer*) evasivo

emaciated /ɪ'meɪʃɪeɪtɪd/ *a* emaciado, macilento

email /'i:meɪl/ *n* correio *m* eletrônico, e-mail *m*; **~ address** endereço *m* de e-mail

emancipat|e /ɪ'mænsɪpeɪt/ *vt* emancipar. **~ion** /-'peɪʃn/ *n* emancipação *f*

embalm /ɪm'ba:m/ *vt* embalsamar

embankment /ɪm'bæŋkmənt/ *n* (*of river*) dique *m*; (*of railway*) terrapleno *m*, talude *m*, (*P*) aterro *m*

embargo /ɪm'ba:gəʊ/ *n* (*pl* **-oes**) embargo *m*

embark /ɪm'ba:k/ *vt/i* embarcar. **~ on** (*business etc*) embarcar em, meter-se em (*colloq*); (*journey*) começar

embarrass /ɪm'bærəs/ *vt* embaraçar, confundir. **~ment** *n* embaraço *m*, atrapalhação *f*

embassy /'embəsɪ/ *n* embaixada *f*

embellish /ɪm'belɪʃ/ *vt* embelezar, enfeitar. **~ment** *n* embelezamento *m*, enfeite *m*

embezzle /ɪm'bezl/ *vt* desviar (fundos). **~ment** *n* desfalque *m*

embitter /ɪm'bɪtə(r)/ *vt* (*person*) amargurar; (*situation*) azedar

emblem /'embləm/ *n* emblema *m*

embod|y /ɪm'bɒdɪ/ *vt* encarnar; (*include*) incorporar, incluir. **~iment** *n* personificação *f*

emboss /ɪmˈbɒs/ *vt* (*metal*) gravar em relevo; (*paper*) gofrar
embrace /ɪmˈbreɪs/ *vt/i* abraçar (-se); (*offer, opportunity*) acolher □ **~** *n* abraço *m*
embroider /ɪmˈbrɔɪdə(r)/ *vt* bordar. **~y** *n* bordado *m*
embryo /ˈembrɪəʊ/ *n* (*pl* **-os**) embrião *m*. **~nic** /-ˈɒnɪk/ *a* embrionário
emerald /ˈemərəld/ *n* esmeralda *f*
emerge /ɪˈmɜ:dʒ/ *vi* emergir, surgir
emergency /ɪˈmɜ:dʒənsɪ/ *n* emergência *f*; (*urgent case*) urgência *f*. **~ exit** saída *f* de emergência. **in an ~** em caso de urgência
emigrant /ˈemɪgrənt/ *n* emigrante *mf*
emigrat|e /ˈemɪgreɪt/ *vi* emigrar. **~ion** /-ˈgreɪʃn/ *n* emigração *f*
eminen|t /ˈemɪnənt/ *a* eminente. **~tly** *adv* eminentemente
emi|t /ɪˈmɪt/ *vt* (*pt* **emitted**) emitir. **~ssion** /-ʃn/ *n* emissão *f*
emotion /ɪˈməʊʃn/ *n* emoção *f*. **~al** *a* (*person, shock*) emotivo; (*speech, scene*) emocionante
emperor /ˈempərə(r)/ *n* imperador *m*
emphasis /ˈemfəsɪs/ *n* ênfase *f*. **lay ~ on** pôr em relevo
emphasize /ˈemfəsaɪz/ *vt* enfatizar, sublinhar; (*syllable, word*) acentuar
emphatic /ɪmˈfætɪk/ *a* enfático; (*manner*) enérgico. **~ally** *adv* enfaticamente
empire /ˈempaɪə(r)/ *n* império *m*
employ /ɪmˈplɔɪ/ *vt* empregar. **~ee** /emplɔɪˈi:/ *n* empregado *m*. **~er** *n* patrão *m*. **~ment** *n* emprego *m*. **~ment agency** agência *f* de empregos
empower /ɪmˈpaʊə(r)/ *vt* autorizar (**to do** a fazer)
empress /ˈemprɪs/ *n* imperatriz *f*
empt|y /ˈemptɪ/ *a* vazio; (*promise*) falso □ *vt/i* esvaziar(-se). **on an ~y stomach** com o estômago vazio, em jejum. **~ies** *npl* garrafas *fpl* vazias. **~iness** *n* vazio *m*
emulate /ˈemjʊleɪt/ *vt* imitar, rivalizar com, emular com
emulsion /ɪˈmʌlʃn/ *n* emulsão *f*
enable /ɪˈneɪbl/ *vt* **~ sb to do** permitir a alg fazer
enact /ɪˈnækt/ *vt* (*jur*) decretar; (*theat*) representar
enamel /ɪˈnæml/ *n* esmalte *m* □ *vt* (*pt* **enamelled**) esmaltar
enamoured /ɪˈnæməd/ *a* **~ of** enamorado de, apaixonado por
encase /ɪnˈkeɪs/ *vt* encerrar (**in** em); (*cover*) revestir (**in** de)
enchant /ɪnˈtʃa:nt/ *vt* encantar. **~ing** *a* encantador. **~ment** *n* encantamento *m*
encircle /ɪnˈsɜ:kl/ *vt* cercar, rodear
enclose /ɪnˈkləʊz/ *vt* (*land*) cercar; (*with letter*) enviar incluso/junto. **~d** *a* (*space*) fechado; (*with letter*) anexo, incluso, junto
enclosure /ɪnˈkləʊʒə(r)/ *n* cercado *m*, recinto *m*; (*with letter*) documento *m* anexo
encompass /ɪnˈkʌmpəs/ *vt* abranger
encore /ɒŋˈkɔ:(r)/ *int* & *n* bis (*m*)
encounter /ɪnˈkaʊntə(r)/ *vt* encontrar, deparar com □ *n* encontro *m*
encourage /ɪnˈkʌrɪdʒ/ *vt* encorajar. **~ment** *n* encorajamento *m*
encroach /ɪnˈkrəʊtʃ/ *vi* **~ on** (*land*) invadir; (*time*) abusar de
encumb|er /ɪnˈkʌmbə(r)/ *vt* estorvar; (*burden*) sobrecarregar. **~rance** *n* estorvo *m*, empecilho *m*; (*burden*) ônus *m*, (*P*) ónus *m*, encargo *m*
encycloped|ia /ɪnsaɪkləˈpi:dɪə/ *n* enciclopédia *f*. **~ic** *a* enciclopédico
end /end/ *n* fim *m*; (*farthest part*) extremo *m*, ponta *f* □ *vt/i* acabar, terminar. **~ up** (*arrive finally*) ir parar (**in** a/em). **~ up doing** acabar por fazer. **in the ~** por fim. **no ~ of** (*colloq*) muito, enorme, imenso. **on ~** (*upright*) em pé; (*consecutive*) a fio, de seguida
endanger /ɪnˈdeɪndʒə(r)/ *vt* pôr em perigo
endear|ing /ɪnˈdɪərɪŋ/ *a* cativante. **~ment** *n* palavra *f* meiga; (*act*) carinho *m*
endeavour /ɪnˈdevə(r)/ *n* esforço *m* □ *vi* esforçar-se (**to** por)
ending /ˈendɪŋ/ *n* fim *m*; (*of word*) terminação *f*
endless /ˈendlɪs/ *a* interminável; (*times*) sem conta; (*patience*) infinito
endorse /ɪnˈdɔ:s/ *vt* (*document*) endossar; (*action*) aprovar. **~ment** *n* (*auto*) averbamento *m*
endow /ɪnˈdaʊ/ *vt* doar. **~ment** *n* doação *f*
endur|e /ɪnˈdjʊə(r)/ *vt* suportar □ *vi* durar. **~able** *a* suportável. **~ance** *n* resistência *f*
enemy /ˈenəmɪ/ *n* & *a* inimigo (*m*)
energetic /enəˈdʒetɪk/ *a* enérgico
energy /ˈenədʒɪ/ *n* energia *f*
enforce /ɪnˈfɔ:s/ *vt* aplicar
engage /ɪnˈgeɪdʒ/ *vt* (*staff*) contratar; (*mech*) engrenar □ *vi* **~ in** envolver-se em, lançar-se em. **~d** *a* noivo; (*busy*) ocupado. **~ment** *n* noivado *m*; (*undertaking, appointment*) compromisso *m*; (*mil*) combate *m*
engender /ɪnˈdʒendə(r)/ *vt* engendrar, produzir, causar
engine /ˈendʒɪn/ *n* motor *m*; (*of train*) locomotiva *f*

engineer /endʒɪ'nɪə(r)/ *n* engenheiro *m* □ *vt* engenhar. **~ing** *n* engenharia *f*

England /'ɪŋglənd/ *n* Inglaterra *f*

English /'ɪŋglɪʃ/ *a* inglês □ *n* (*lang*) inglês *m*. **the ~** os ingleses *mpl*. **~man** *n* inglês *m*. **~-speaking** *a* de lingua inglesa *f*. **~woman** *n* inglesa *f*

engrav|e /ɪn'greɪv/ *vt* gravar. **~-ing** *n* gravura *f*

engrossed /ɪn'grəʊst/ *a* absorto (**in** em)

engulf /ɪn'gʌlf/ *vt* engolfar, tragar

enhance /ɪn'ha:ns/ *vt* aumentar; (*heighten*) realçar

enigma /ɪ'nɪgmə/ *n* enigma *m*. **~tic** /enɪg'mætɪk/ *a* enigmático

enjoy /ɪn'dʒɔɪ/ *vt* gostar de; (*benefit from*) gozar de. **~ o.s.** divertir-se. **~able** *a* agradável. **~ment** *n* prazer *m*

enlarge /ɪn'la:dʒ/ *vt*/*i* aumentar. **~ upon** alargar-se sobre. **~-ment** *n* ampliação *f*

enlighten /ɪn'laɪtn/ *vt* esclarecer. **~ment** *n* esclarecimento *m*, elucidação *f*

enlist /ɪn'lɪst/ *vt* recrutar; (*fig*) aliciar, granjear □ *vi* alistar-se

enliven /ɪn'laɪvn/ *vt* animar

enmity /'enmətɪ/ *n* inimizade *f*

enormous /ɪ'nɔ:məs/ *a* enorme

enough /ɪ'nʌf/ *a, adv* & *n* bastante (*m*), suficiente (*m*) □ *int* basta!, chega! **have ~ of** estar farto de

enquir|e /ɪn'kwaɪə(r)/ *vt*/*i* perguntar, indagar. **~e about** informar-se de, pedir informações sobre. **~y** *n* pedido *m* de informações

enrage /ɪn'reɪdʒ/ *vt* enfurecer, enraivecer

enrich /ɪn'rɪtʃ/ *vt* enriquecer

enrol /ɪn'rəʊl/ *vt*/*i* (*pt* **enrolled**) inscrever(-se); (*schol*) matricular(-se). **~ment** *n* inscrição *f*; (*schol*) matrícula *f*

ensemble /ɒn'sɒmbl/ *n* conjunto *m*

ensign /'ensən/ *n* pavilhão *m*; (*officer*) guarda-marinha *m*

ensu|e /ɪn'sju:/ *vi* seguir-se. **~-ing** *a* decorrente

ensure /ɪn'ʃʊə(r)/ *vt* assegurar. **~ that** assegurar-se de que

entail /ɪn'teɪl/ *vt* acarretar

entangle /ɪn'tæŋgl/ *vt* emaranhar, enredar

enter /'entə(r)/ *vt* (*room, club etc*) entrar em; (*register*) registar; (*data*) entrar com □ *vi* entrar (**into** em). **~ for** inscrever-se em

enterprise /'entəpraɪz/ *n* empresa *f*, empreendimento *m*; (*fig*) iniciativa *f*

enterprising /'entəpraɪzɪŋ/ *a* empreendedor

entertain /entə'teɪn/ *vt* entreter; (*guests*) receber; (*ideas*) alimentar, nutrir. **~er** *n* artista *mf*. **~ment** *n* entretenimento *m*; (*performance*) espetáculo *m*, (*P*) espectáculo *m*

enthral /ɪn'θrɔ:l/ *vt* (*pt* **enthralled**) fascinar

enthuse /ɪn'θju:z/ *vi* **~ over** entusiasmar-se por

enthusias|m /ɪn'θju:zɪæzm/ *n* entusiasmo *m*. **~t** *n* entusiasta *mf*. **~tic** /-'æstɪk/ *a* entusiástico. **~tically** /-'æstɪkəlɪ/ *adv* entusiasticamente

entice /ɪn'taɪs/ *vt* atrair. **~ to do** induzir a fazer. **~ment** *n* tentação *f*, engodo *m*

entire /ɪn'taɪə(r)/ *a* inteiro. **~ly** *adv* inteiramente

entirety /ɪn'taɪərətɪ/ *n* **in its ~** por inteiro, na (sua) totalidade

entitle /ɪn'taɪtl/ *vt* dar direito. **~d** *a* (*book*) intitulado. **be ~d to sth** ter direito a alg coisa. **~ment** *n* direito *m*

entity /'entətɪ/ *n* entidade *f*

entrance /'entrəns/ *n* entrada *f* (**to** para); (*right to enter*) admissão *f*

entrant /'entrənt/ *n* (*sport*) concorrente *mf*; (*in exam*) candidato *m*

entreat /ɪn'tri:t/ *vt* rogar, suplicar. **~y** *n* rogo *m*, súplica *f*

entrench /ɪn'trentʃ/ *vt* (*mil*) entrincheirar; (*fig*) fincar

entrust /ɪn'trʌst/ *vt* confiar

entry /'entrɪ/ *n* entrada *f*; (*on list*) item *m*; (*in dictionary*) verbete *m*. **~ form** ficha *f* de inscrição, (*P*) boletim *m* de inscrição. **no ~** entrada proibida

enumerate /ɪ'nju:məreɪt/ *vt* enumerar

envelop /ɪn'veləp/ *vt* (*pt* **enveloped**) envolver

envelope /'envələʊp/ *n* envelope *m*, sobrescrito *m*

enviable /'envɪəbl/ *a* invejável

envious /'envɪəs/ *a* invejoso. **be ~ of** ter inveja de. **~ly** *adv* invejosamente, com inveja

environment /ɪn'vaɪərənmənt/ *n* meio *m*; (*ecological*) meio- ambiente *m*. **~al** /-'mentl/ *a* do meio; (*ecological*) do ambiente

envisage /ɪn'vɪzɪdʒ/ *vt* encarar; (*foresee*) prever

envoy /'envɔɪ/ *n* enviado *m*

envy /'envɪ/ *n* inveja *f* □ *vt* invejar, ter inveja de

enzyme /'enzaɪm/ *n* enzima *f*

epic /'epɪk/ *n* epopéia *f* □ *a* épico

epidemic /epɪ'demɪk/ *n* epidemia *f*

epilep|sy /'epɪlepsɪ/ *n* epilepsia *f*. **~tic** /-'leptɪk/ *a* & *n* epiléptico (*m*)
episode /'epɪsəʊd/ *n* episódio *m*
epitaph /'epɪta:f/ *n* epitáfio *m*
epithet /'epɪθet/ *n* epíteto *m*
epitom|e /ɪ'pɪtəmɪ/ *n* (*summary*) epítome *m*; (*embodiment*) modelo *m*. **~ize** *vt* (*fig*) representar, encarnar; (*summarize*) resumir
epoch /'i:pɒk/ *n* época *f*. **~-making** *a* que marca uma época
equal /'i:kwəl/ *a* & *n* igual (*m*) □ *vt* (*pt* **equalled**) igualar, ser igual a. **~ to** (*task*) à altura de. **~ity** /i:'kwɒlətɪ/ *n* igualdade *f*. **~ly** *adv* igualmente; (*similarly*) de igual modo
equalize /'i:kwəlaɪz/ *vt/i* igualar; (*sport*) empatar
equanimity /ekwə'nɪmətɪ/ *n* equanimidade *f*, serenidade *f*
equate /ɪ'kweɪt/ *vt* equacionar (**with** com); (*treat as equal*) equiparar (**with** a)
equation /ɪ'kweɪʒn/ *n* equação *f*
equator /ɪ'kweɪtə(r)/ *n* equador *m*. **~ial** /ekwə'tɔ:rɪəl/ *a* equatorial
equilibrium /i:kwɪ'lɪbrɪəm/ *n* equilíbrio *m*
equip /ɪ'kwɪp/ *vt* (*pt* **equipped**) equipar (**with** com), munir (**with** de). **~ment** *n* equipamento *m*
equitable /'ekwɪtəbl/ *a* eqüitativo, (*P*) equitativo
equity /'ekwətɪ/ *n* eqüidade *f*, (*P*) equidade *f*
equivalent /ɪ'kwɪvələnt/ *a* & *n* eqüivalente (*m*), (*P*) equivalente (*m*)
equivocal /ɪ'kwɪvəkl/ *a* equívoco
era /'ɪərə/ *n* era *f*, época *f*
eradicate /ɪ'rædɪkeɪt/ *vt* erradicar, suprimir
erase /ɪ'reɪz/ *vt* apagar. **~r** /-ə(r)/ *n* borracha *f* (de apagar)
erect /ɪ'rekt/ *a* ereto, (*P*) erecto □ *vt* erigir. **~ion** /-ʃn/ *n* ereção *f*, (*P*) erecção *f*; (*building*) construção *f*, edifício *m*
ero|de /ɪ'rəʊd/ *vt* corroer. **~sion** /ɪ'rəʊʒn/ *n* erosão *f*
erotic /ɪ'rɒtɪk/ *a* erótico
err /ɜ:(r)/ *vi* (*pt* **erred**) errar
errand /'erənd/ *n* recado *m*
erratic /ɪ'rætɪk/ *a* errático, irregular; (*person*) variável, imprevisível
erroneous /ɪ'rəʊnɪəs/ *a* errôneo, (*P*) erróneo, errado
error /'erə(r)/ *n* erro *m*
erudit|e /'eru:daɪt/ *a* erudito. **~ion** /-'dɪʃn/ *n* erudição *f*
erupt /ɪ'rʌpt/ *vi* (*war, fire*) irromper; (*volcano*) entrar em erupção. **~ion** /-ʃn/ *n* erupção *f*
escalat|e /'eskəleɪt/ *vt/i* intensificar(-se); (*of prices*) subir em espiral. **~ion** /-'leɪʃn/ *n* escalada *f*
escalator /'eskəleɪtə(r)/ *n* escada *f* rolante
escapade /eskə'peɪd/ *n* peripécia *f*
escape /ɪ'skeɪp/ *vi* escapar-se □ *vt* escapar a □ *n* fuga *f*; (*of prisoner*) evasão *f*, fuga *f*. **~ from sb** escapar de alguém. **~ to** fugir para. **have a lucky** *or* **narrow ~** escapar por um tris
escapism /ɪ'skeɪpɪzəm/ *n* escapismo *m*
escort[1] /'eskɔ:t/ *n* escolta *f*; (*of woman*) cavalheiro *m*, acompanhante *m*
escort[2] /ɪ'skɔ:t/ *vt* escoltar; (*accompany*) acompanhar
escudo /es'kjudəʊ/ *n* (*pl* **-os**) escudo *m*
Eskimo /'eskɪməʊ/ *n* (*pl* **-os**) esquimó *mf*
especial /ɪ'speʃl/ *a* especial. **~ly** *adv* especialmente
espionage /'espɪəna:ʒ/ *n* espionagem *f*
espouse /ɪ'spaʊz/ *vt* (*a cause etc*) abraçar
espresso /e'spressəʊ/ *n* (*pl* **-os**) (*coffee*) expresso *m*
essay /'eseɪ/ *n* ensaio *m*; (*schol*) redação *f*, (*P*) redacção *f*
essence /'esns/ *n* essência *f*
essential /ɪ'senʃl/ *a* essencial □ *n* **the ~s** o essencial *m*. **~ly** *adv* essencialmente
establish /ɪ'stæblɪʃ/ *vt* estabelecer; (*business, state*) fundar; (*prove*) provar, apurar. **~ment** *n* estabelecimento *m*; (*institution*) instituição *f*. **the E~ment** o Establishment *m*, a classe *f* dirigente
estate /ɪ'steɪt/ *n* propriedade *f*; (*possessions*) bens *mpl*; (*inheritance*) herança *f*. **~ agent** agente *m* imobiliário. **(housing) ~** conjunto *m* habitacional. **~ car** perua *f*
esteem /ɪ'sti:m/ *vt* estimar □ *n* estima *f*
estimate[1] /'estɪmət/ *n* cálculo *m*, avaliação *f*; (*comm*) orçamento *m*, estimativa *f*
estimat|e[2] /'estɪmeɪt/ *vt* calcular, estimar. **~ion** /-'meɪʃn/ *n* opinião *f*
estuary /'estʃʊərɪ/ *n* estuário *m*
etc *abbr* = **et cetera** /ɪt'setərə/ etc
etching /'etʃɪŋ/ *n* água-forte *f*
eternal /ɪ'tɜ:nl/ *a* eterno
eternity /ɪ'tɜ:nətɪ/ *n* eternidade *f*
ethic /'eθɪk/ *n* ética *f*. **~s** ética *f*. **~al** *a* ético
ethnic /'eθnɪk/ *a* étnico
etiquette /'etɪket/ *n* etiqueta *f*
etymology /etɪ'mɒlədʒɪ/ *n* etimologia *f*
eulogy /'ju:lədʒɪ/ *n* elogio *m*

euphemism /'ju:fəmɪzəm/ *n* eufemismo *m*

euphoria /ju'fɔ:rɪə/ *n* euforia *f*

euro /'jʊərəʊ/ *n* euro *m*

Europe /'jʊərəp/ *n* Europa *f*. **~an** /-'pɪən/ *a & n* europeu (*m*). **~an Union** União *f* Européia

euthanasia /ju:θə'neɪzɪə/ *n* eutanásia *f*

evacuat|e /ɪ'vækjʊeɪt / *vt* evacuar. **~ion** /-'eɪʃn/ *n* evacuação *f*

evade /ɪ'veɪd/ *vt* evadir

evaluate /ɪ'væljʊeɪt/ *vt* avaliar

evangelical /i:væn'dʒelɪkl/ *a* evangélico

evaporat|e /ɪ'væpəreɪt/ *vt/i* evaporar(-se). **~ed milk** leite *m* evaporado. **~ion** /-'reɪʃn/ *n* evaporação *f*

evasion /ɪ'veɪʒn/ *n* evasão *f*

evasive /ɪ'veɪsɪv/ *a* evasivo

eve /i:v/ *n* véspera *f*

even /'i:vn/ *a* regular; (*surface*) liso, plano; (*amounts*) igual; (*number*) par □ *vt/i* **~ up** igualar(-se), acertar □ *adv* mesmo. **~ better** ainda melhor. **get ~ with** ajustar contas com. **~ly** *adv* uniformemente

evening /'i:vnɪŋ/ *n* entardecer *m*, anoitecer *m*; (*whole evening*) serão *m*. **~ class** aula *f* à noite (*para adultos*). **~ dress** traje *m* de cerimônia, (*P*) trajo *m* de cerimónia *or* de rigor; (*woman's*) vestido *m* de noite

event /ɪ'vent/ *n* acontecimento *m*. **in the ~ of** no caso de. **~ful** *a* movimentado, memorável

eventual /ɪ'ventʃʊəl/ *a* final. **~ity** /-'æləti/ *n* eventualidade *f*. **~ly** *adv* por fim; (*in future*) eventualmente

ever /'evə(r)/ *adv* jamais; (*at all times*) sempre. **do you ~ go?** você já foi alguma vez?, vais alguma vez? **the best I ~ saw** o melhor que já vi. **~ since** *adv* desde então □ *prep* desde □ *conj* desde que. **~ so** (*colloq*) muitíssimo, tão. **hardly ~** quase nunca

evergreen /'evəgri:n/ *n* sempre-verde *f*, planta *f* de folhas persistentes □ *a* persistente

everlasting /'evəla:stɪŋ/ *a* eterno

every /'evrɪ/ *a* cada. **~ now and then** de vez em quando, volta e meia. **~ one** cada um. **~ other day** dia sim dia não, de dois em dois dias. **~ three days** de três em três dias

everybody /'evrɪbɒdɪ/ *pron* todo mundo, todos

everyday /'evrɪdeɪ/ *a* cotidiano, (*P*) quotidiano, diário; (*common*) do dia a dia, vulgar

everyone /'evrɪwʌn/ *pron* todo mundo, todos

everything /'evrɪθɪŋ/ *pron* tudo

everywhere /'evrɪweə(r)/ *adv* (*position*) em todo lugar, em toda parte; (*direction*) a todo lugar, a toda parte

evict /ɪ'vɪkt/ *vt* expulsar, despejar. **~ion** /-ʃn/ *n* despejo *m*

evidence /'evɪdəns/ *n* evidência *f*; (*proof*) prova *f*; (*testimony*) testemunho *m*, depoimento *m*. **~ of** sinal de. **give ~** testemunhar. **in ~** em evidência

evident /'evɪdənt/ *a* evidente. **~ly** *adv* evidentemente

evil /'i:vl/ *a* mau □ *n* mal *m*

evo|ke /ɪ'vəʊk/ *vt* evocar. **~cative** /ɪ'vɒkətɪv/ *a* evocativo

evolution /i:və'lu:ʃn/ *n* evolução *f*

evolve /ɪ'vɒlv/ *vi* evolucionar, evoluir □ *vt* desenvolver, produzir

ex- /eks/ *pref* ex-

exacerbate /ɪg'zæsəbeɪt/ *vt* exacerbar

exact /ɪg'zækt/ *a* exato, (*P*) exacto □ *vt* exigir (**from** de). **~ing** *a* exigente; (*task*) difícil. **~ly** *adv* exatamente, (*P*) exactamente

exaggerat|e /ɪg'zædʒəreɪt/ *vt/i* exagerar. **~ion** /-'reɪʃn/ *n* exagero *m*

exam /ɪg'zæm/ *n* (*colloq*) exame *m*

examination /ɪgzæmɪ'neɪʃn/ *n* exame *m*; (*jur*) interrogatório *m*

examine /ɪg'zæmɪn/ *vt* examinar; (*witness etc*) interrogar. **~r** /-ə(r)/ *n* examinador *m*

example /ɪg'za:mpl/ *n* exemplo *m*. **for ~** por exemplo. **make an ~ of** castigar para servir de exemplo

exasperat|e /ɪg'zæspəreɪt/ *vt* exasperar. **~ion** /-'reɪʃn/ *n* exaspero *m*

excavat|e /'ekskəveɪt/ *vt* escavar; (*uncover*) desenterrar. **~ion** /-'veɪʃn/ *n* escavação *f*

exceed /ɪk'si:d/ *vt* exceder; (*speed limit*) ultrapassar, exceder

excel /ɪk'sel/ *vi* (*pt* **excelled**) distinguir-se □ *vt* superar, ultrapassar

excellen|t /'eksələnt/ *a* excelente. **~ce** *n* excelência *f*. **~tly** *adv* excelentemente

except /ɪk'sept/ *prep* exceto, (*P*) excepto, fora □ *vt* excetuar, (*P*) exceptuar. **~ for** a não ser, menos, salvo. **~ing** *prep* à exceção de, (*P*) à excepção de. **~ion** /-ʃn/ *n* exceção *f*, (*P*) excepção *f*. **take ~ion to** (*object to*) achar inaceitável; (*be offended by*) achar ofensivo

exceptional /ɪk'sepʃənl/ *a* excepcional. **~ly** *adv* excepcionalmente

excerpt /'eksɜ:pt/ *n* trecho *m*, excerto *m*

excess[1] /ɪk'ses/ *n* excesso *m*

excess[2] /'ekses/ *a* excedente, em excesso. **~ fare** excesso *m*, suplemento *m*. **~ luggage** excesso *m* de peso

excessive /ɪk'sesɪv/ *a* excessivo. **~ly** *adv* excessivamente

exchange /ɪks'tʃeɪndʒ/ *vt* trocar □ *n* troca *f*; (*of currency*) câmbio *m*. **(telephone) ~** central *f* telefônica, (*P*) telefónica. **~ rate** taxa *f* de câmbio

excise /'eksaɪz/ *n* imposto *m* (indireto, (*P*) indirecto)

excit|e /ɪk'saɪt/ *vt* excitar; (*rouse*) despertar; (*enthuse*) entusiasmar. **~able** *a* excitável. **~ed** *a* excitado. **get ~ed** excitar-se, entusiasmar-se. **~ement** *n* excitação *f*. **~ing** *a* excitante, emocionante

exclaim /ɪk'skleɪm/ *vi* exclamar

exclamation /eksklə'meɪʃn/ *n* exclamação *f*. **~ mark** ponto *m* de exclamação

exclu|de /ɪk'sklu:d/ *vt* excluir. **~ding** *prep* excluído. **~sion** /ɪk'sklu:ʒn/ *n* exclusão *f*

exclusive /ɪk'sklu:sɪv/ *a* (*rights etc*) exclusivo; (*club etc*) seleto, (*P*) selecto; (*news item*) (em) exclusivo. **~ of** sem incluir. **~ly** *adv* exclusivamente

excruciating /ɪk'skru:ʃɪeɪtɪŋ/ *a* excruciante, atroz

excursion /ɪk'skɜ:ʃn/ *n* excursão *f*

excus|e[1] /ɪk'skju:z/ *vt* desculpar. **~e me!** desculpe!, com licença! **~e from** (*exempt*) dispensar de. **~able** *a* desculpável

excuse[2] /ɪk'skju:s/ *n* desculpa *f*

ex-directory /eksdɪ'rektərɪ/ *a* que não vem no anuário, (*P*) na lista

execute /'eksɪkju:t/ *vt* executar

execution /eksɪ'kju:ʃn/ *n* execução *f*

executive /ɪg'zekjʊtɪv/ *a* & *n* executivo (*m*)

exemplary /ɪg'zemplərɪ/ *a* exemplar

exemplify /ɪg'zemplɪfaɪ/ *vt* exemplificar, ilustrar

exempt /ɪg'zempt/ *a* isento (**from** de) □ *vt* dispensar, eximir. **~ion** /-ʃn/ *n* isenção *f*

exercise /'eksəsaɪz/ *n* exercício *m* □ *vt* (*powers, restraint etc*) exercer; (*dog*) levar para passear □ *vi* fazer exercício. **~ book** caderno *m*

exert /ɪg'zɜ:t/ *vt* empregar, exercer. **~ o.s.** esforçar-se, fazer um esforço. **~ion** /-ʃn/ *n* esforço *m*

exhaust /ɪg'zɔ:st/ *vt* esgotar □ *n* (*auto*) (tubo de) escape *m*. **~ed** *a* esgotado, exausto. **~ion** /-stʃən/ *n* esgotamento *m*, exaustão *f*

exhaustive /ɪg'zɔ:stɪv/ *a* exaustivo, completo

exhibit /ɪg'zɪbɪt/ *vt* exibir, mostrar; (*thing, collection*) expor □ *n* objeto *m*, (*P*) objecto *m* exposto

exhibition /eksɪ'bɪʃn/ *n* exposição *f*; (*act of showing*) demonstração *f*

exhilarat|e /ɪg'zɪləreɪt/ *vt* regozijar; (*invigorate*) animar, estimular. **~ion** /-'reɪʃn/ *n* animação *f*, alegria *f*

exhort /ɪg'zɔ:t/ *vt* exortar

exile /'eksaɪl/ *n* exílio *m*; (*person*) exilado *m* □ *vt* exilar, desterrar

exist /ɪg'zɪst/ *vi* existir. **~ence** *n* existência *f*. **be in ~ence** existir

exit /'eksɪt/ *n* saída *f*

exonerate /ɪg'zɒnəreɪt/ *vt* exonerar

exorbitant /ɪg'zɔ:bɪtənt/ *a* exorbitante

exorcize /'eksɔ:saɪz/ *vt* esconjurar, exorcisar

exotic /ɪg'zɒtɪk/ *a* exótico

expan|d /ɪk'spænd/ *vt/i* expandir (-se); (*extend*) estender(-se), alargar(-se); (*gas, liquid, metal*) dilatar(-se). **~sion** /ɪk'spænʃn/ *n* expansão *f*; (*extension*) alargamento *m*; (*of gas etc*) dilatação *f*

expanse /ɪk'spæns/ *n* extensão *f*

expatriate /eks'pætrɪət/ *a* & *n* expatriado (*m*)

expect /ɪk'spekt/ *vt* esperar; (*suppose*) crer, supor; (*require*) contar com, esperar; (*baby*) esperar. **~ to do** contar fazer. **~ation** /ekspek'teɪʃn/ *n* expectativa *f*

expectan|t /ɪk'spektənt/ *a* **~t mother** gestante *f*. **~cy** *n* expectativa *f*

expedient /ɪk'spi:dɪənt/ *a* oportuno □ *n* expediente *m*

expedition /ekspɪ'dɪʃn/ *n* expedição *f*

expel /ɪk'spel/ *vt* (*pt* **expelled**) expulsar; (*gas, poison etc*) expelir

expend /ɪk'spend/ *vt* despender. **~able** *a* descartável

expenditure /ɪk'spendɪtʃə(r)/ *n* despesa *f*, gasto *m*

expense /ɪk'spens/ *n* despesa *f*; (*cost*) custo *m*. **at sb's ~** à custa de alg. **at the ~ of** (*fig*) à custa de

expensive /ɪk'spensɪv/ *a* caro, dispendioso; (*tastes, habits*) de luxo

experience /ɪk'spɪərɪəns/ *n* experiência *f* □ *vt* experimentar; (*feel*) sentir. **~d** *a* experiente

experiment /ɪk'sperɪmənt/ *n* experiência *f* □ *vi* /ɪk'sperɪment/ fazer uma experiência. **~al** /-'mentl/ *a* experimental

expert /'ekspɜ:t/ *a* & *n* perito (*m*). **~ly** *adv* com perícia, habilmente

expertise /ekspɜ:'ti:z/ *n* perícia *f*, competência *f*

expir|e /ɪk'spaɪə(r)/ *vi* expirar. **~y** *n* fim *m* de prazo, expiração *f*

expl|ain /ɪk'spleɪn/ *vt* explicar. **~anation** /eksplə'neɪʃn/ *n* explicação *f*. **~anatory** /ɪk'splæ-nətrɪ/ *a* explicativo

expletive /ɪk'spli:tɪv/ *n* imprecação *f*, praga *f*
explicit /ɪk'splɪsɪt/ *a* explícito
explo|de /ɪk'spləʊd/ *vt/i* (fazer) explodir. **~sion** /ɪk'spləʊʒn/ *n* explosão *f*. **~sive** *a & n* explosivo (*m*)
exploit[1] /'eksplɔɪt/ *n* façanha *f*
exploit[2] /ɪk'splɔɪt/ *vt* explorar. **~ation** /eksplɔɪ'teɪʃn/ *n* exploração *f*
exploratory /ɪk'splɒrətrɪ/ *a* exploratório; (*talks*) preliminar
explor|e /ɪk'splɔ:(r)/ *vt* explorar; (*fig*) examinar. **~ation** /eksplə'reɪʃn/ *n* exploração *f*. **~er** *n* explorador *m*
exponent /ɪk'spəʊnənt/ *n* (*person*) expoente *mf*; (*math*) expoente *m*
export[1] /ɪk'spɔ:t/ *vt* exportar. **~er** *n* exportador *m*
export[2] /'ekspɔ:t/ *n* exportação *f*. **~s** *npl* exportações *fpl*
expos|e /ɪk'spəʊz/ *vt* expor; (*disclose*) revelar; (*unmask*) desmascarar. **~ure** /-ʒə(r)/ *n* exposição *f*; (*cold*) frio *m*
expound /ɪk'spaʊnd/ *vt* explanar, expor
express[1] /ɪk'spres/ *a* expresso, categórico □ *adv* (por) expresso □ *n* (*train*) rápido *m*, expresso *m*. **~ly** *adv* expressamente
express[2] /ɪk'spres/ *vt* exprimir. **~ion** /-ʃn/ *n* expressão *f*. **~ive** *a* expressivo
expulsion /ɪk'spʌlʃn/ *n* expulsão *f*
exquisite /'ekskwɪzɪt/ *a* requintado
extempore /ek'stempərɪ/ *a* improvisado □ *adv* de improviso, sem preparação prévia
exten|d /ɪk'stend/ *vt* (*stretch*) estender; (*enlarge*) aumentar, ampliar; (*prolong*) prolongar; (*grant*) oferecer □ *vi* (*stretch*) estender-se; (*in time*) prolongar-se. **~sion** /ɪk'stenʃn/ *n* (*incl phone*) extensão *f*; (*of deadline*) prorrogação *f*; (*building*) anexo *m*
extensive /ɪk'stensɪv/ *a* extenso; (*damage, study*) vasto. **~ly** *adv* muito
extent /ɪk'stent/ *n* extensão *f*; (*degree*) medida *f*. **to some ~** até certo ponto, em certa medida. **to such an ~ that** a tal ponto que
exterior /ɪk'stɪərɪə(r)/ *a & n* exterior (*m*)
exterminat|e /ɪk'stɜ:mɪneɪt/ *vt* exterminar. **~ion** /-'neɪʃn/ *n* exterminação *f*, extermínio *m*
external /ɪk'stɜ:nl/ *a* externo. **~ly** *adv* exteriormente
extinct /ɪk'stɪŋkt/ *a* extinto. **~ion** /-ʃn/ *n* extinção *f*
extinguish /ɪk'stɪŋgwɪʃ/ *vt* extinguir, apagar. **~er** *n* extintor *m*
extol /ɪk'stəʊl/ *vt* (*pt* **extolled**) exaltar, elogiar, louvar
extort /ɪk'stɔ:t/ *vt* extorquir (**from** a). **~ion** /-ʃn/ *n* extorsão *f*
extortionate /ɪk'stɔ:ʃənət/ *a* exorbitante
extra /'ekstrə/ *a* extra, adicional □ *adv* extra, excepcionalmente. **~ strong** extra-forte □ *n* extra *m*; (*cine, theat*) extra *mf*, figurante *mf*. **~ time** (*football*) prorrogação *f*
extra- /'ekstrə/ *pref* extra-
extract[1] /ɪk'strækt/ *vt* extrair; (*promise, tooth*) arrancar; (*fig*) obter. **~ion** /-ʃn/ *n* extração *f*, (*P*) extracção *f*; (*descent*) origem *f*
extract[2] /'ekstrækt/ *n* extrato *m*, (*P*) extracto *m*
extradit|e /'ekstrədaɪt/ *vt* extraditar. **~ion** /-'dɪʃn/ *n* extradição *f*
extramarital /ekstrə'mærɪtl/ *a* extraconjugal, extramatrimonial
extraordinary /ɪk'strɔ:dnrɪ/ *a* extraordinário
extravagan|t /ɪk'strævəgənt/ *a* extravagante; (*wasteful*) esbanjador. **~ce** *n* extravagância *f*; (*wastefulness*) esbanjamento *m*
extrem|e /ɪk'stri:m/ *a & n* extremo (*m*). **~ely** *adv* extremamente. **~ist** *n* extremista *mf*
extremity /ɪk'stremətɪ/ *n* extremidade *f*
extricate /'ekstrɪkeɪt/ *vt* desembaraçar, livrar
extrovert /'ekstrəvɜ:t/ *n* extrovertido *m*
exuberan|t /ɪg'zju:bərənt/ *a* exuberante. **~ce** *n* exuberância *f*
exude /ɪg'zju:d/ *vt* (*charm etc*) destilar, ressumar, (*P*) transpirar
exult /ɪg'zʌlt/ *vi* exultar
eye /aɪ/ *n* olho *m* □ *vt* (*pt* **eyed**, *pres p* **eyeing**) olhar. **keep an ~ on** vigiar. **see ~ to ~** concordar inteiramente. **~-opener** *n* revelação *f*. **~-shadow** *n* sombra *f*
eyeball /'aɪbɔ:l/ *n* globo *m* ocular
eyebrow /'aɪbraʊ/ *n* sobrancelha *f*
eyelash /'aɪlæʃ/ *n* pestana *f*
eyelid /'aɪlɪd/ *n* pálpebra *f*
eyesight /'aɪsaɪt/ *n* vista *f*
eyesore /'aɪsɔ:(r)/ *n* monstruosidade *f*, horror *m*
eyewitness /'aɪwɪtnɪs/ *n* testemunha *f* ocular

Ff

fable /'feɪbl/ *n* fábula *f*
fabric /'fæbrɪk/ *n* tecido *m*; (*structure*) edifício *m*
fabricat|e /'fæbrɪkeɪt/ *vt* fabricar; (*invent*) urdir, inventar. **~ion** /-'keɪʃn/ *n* fabrico *m*; (*invention*) invenção *f*
fabulous /'fæbjʊləs/ *a* fabuloso
façade /fə'sa:d/ *n* fachada *f*
face /feɪs/ *n* face *f*, cara *f*, rosto *m*; (*expression*) face *f*; (*grimace*) careta *f*; (*of clock*) mostrador *m* □ *vt* (*look towards*) encarar; (*confront*) enfrentar □ *vi* (*be opposite*) estar de frente para. **~ up to** enfrentar. **~ to face** cara a cara, frente a frente. **in the ~ of** em vista de. **on the ~ of it** a julgar pelas aparências. **pull ~s** fazer caretas. **~-cloth** *n* toalha *f* de rosto, (*P*) toalhete *m* de rosto. **~-lift** *n* cirurgia *f* plástica do rosto. **~-pack** *n* máscara de beleza *f*
faceless /'feɪslɪs/ *a* (*fig*) anônimo, (*P*) anónimo
facet /'fæsɪt/ *n* faceta *f*
facetious /fə'si:ʃəs/ *a* faceto; (*pej*) engraçadinho (*colloq pej*)
facial /'feɪʃl/ *a* facial
facile /'fæsaɪl/ *a* fácil; (*superficial*) superficial
facilitate /fə'sɪlɪteɪt/ *vt* facilitar
facilit|y /fə'sɪlətɪ/ *n* facilidade *f*. **~ies** (*means*) facilidades *fpl*; (*installations*) instalações *fpl*
facing /'feɪsɪŋ/ *n* revestimento *m*
facsimile /fæk'sɪməlɪ/ *n* facsímile *m*
fact /fækt/ *n* fato *m*, (*P*) facto *m*. **in ~, as a matter of ~** na realidade
faction /'fækʃn/ *n* facção *f*
factor /'fæktə(r)/ *n* fator *m*, (*P*) factor *m*
factory /'fæktərɪ/ *n* fábrica *f*
factual /'fæktʃʊəl/ *a* concreto, real
faculty /'fækltɪ/ *n* faculdade *f*
fad /fæd/ *n* capricho *m*, mania *f*; (*craze*) moda *f*
fade /feɪd/ *vt/i* (*colour*) desbotar; (*sound*) diminuir; (*disappear*) apagar(-se)
fag /fæg/ *n* (*colloq: chore*) estafa *f*; (*sl: cigarette*) cigarro *m*. **~ged** *a* estafado
fail /feɪl/ *vt/i* falhar; (*in an examination*) reprovar; (*omit, neglect*) deixar de; (*comm*) falir □ *n* **without ~** sem falta
failing /'feɪlɪŋ/ *n* deficiência *f* □ *prep* na falta de, à falta de
failure /'feɪljə(r)/ *n* fracasso *m*, (*P*) falhanço *m*; (*of engine*) falha *f*; (*of electricity*) falta *f*; (*person*) fracassado *m*.
faint /feɪnt/ *a* (-**er**, -**est**) (*indistinct*) apagado; (*weak*) fraco; (*giddy*) tonto □ *vi* desmaiar □ *n* desmaio *m*. **~-hearted** *a* tímido. **~ly** *adv* vagamente. **~ness** *n* debilidade *f*; (*indistinctness*) apagado *m*
fair[1] /feə(r)/ *n* feira *f*. **~-ground** *n* parque *m* de diversões, (*P*) largo *m* de feira
fair[2] /feə(r)/ *a* (-**er**, -**est**) (*hair*) louro; (*weather*) bom; (*of moderate quality*) razoável; (*just*) justo. **~ play** jogo *m* limpo, fair play *m*. **~ly** *adv* razoavelmente. **~ness** *n* justiça *f*
fairy /'feərɪ/ *n* fada *f*. **~ story**, **~ tale** conto *m* de fadas
faith /feɪθ/ *n* fé *f*; (*religion*) religião *f*; (*loyalty*) lealdade *f*. **in good ~** de boa fé, (*P*) à boa fé. **~-healer** *n* curandeiro *m*
faithful /'feɪθfl/ *a* fiel. **~ly** *adv* fielmente. **yours ~ly** atenciosamente. **~ness** *n* fidelidade *f*
fake /feɪk/ *n* (*thing*) imitação *f*; (*person*) impostor *m* □ *a* falsificado □ *vt* falsificar; (*pretend*) simular, fingir
falcon /'fɔlkən/ *n* falcão *m*
fall /fɔ:l/ *vi* (*pt* **fell**, *pp* **fallen**) cair □ *n* quedas *f*; (*Amer: autumn*) outono *m*. **~s** *npl* (*waterfall*) queda-d'água *f*. **~ back** bater em retirada. **~ back on** recorrer a. **~ behind** atrasar-se (**with** em). **~ down** *or* **off** cair. **~ flat** falhar, não resultar. **~ flat on one's face** estatelar-se. **~ for** (*a trick*) cair em, deixar-se levar por; (*colloq: a person*) apaixonar-se por, ficar caído por (*colloq*). **~ in** (*roof*) ruir; (*mil*) alinhar-se, pôr-se em forma. **~ out** brigar, (*P*) zangar-se (**with** com). **~-out** *n* poeira *f* radioativa, (*P*) radioactiva. **~ through** (*of plans*) falhar
fallac|y /'fæləsɪ/ *n* falácia *f*, engano *m*. **~ious** /fə'leɪʃəs/ *a* errôneo
fallen /'fɔ:lən/ *see* **fall**
fallible /'fæləbl/ *a* falível
fallow /'fæləʊ/ *a* (*of ground*) de pousio; (*uncultivated*) inculto
false /fɔ:ls/ *a* falso. **~ teeth** dentadwa *f*. **~ly** *adv* falsamente. **~ness** *n* falsidade *f*
falsehood /'fɔ:lshʊd/ *n* falsidade *f*, mentira *f*
falsify /'fɔ:lsɪfaɪ/ *vt* (*pt* -**fied**) falsificar; (*a story*) deturpar
falter /'fɔ:ltə(r)/ *vi* vacilar; (*of the voice*) hesitar
fame /feɪm/ *n* fama *f*. **~d** *a* afamado

familiar /fə'mɪlɪə(r)/ *a* familiar; (*intimate*) íntimo. **be ~ with** estar familiarizado com

familiarity /fəmɪlɪ'ærɪtɪ/ *n* familiaridade *f*

familiarize /fə'mɪlɪəraɪz/ *vt* familiarizar (**with/to** com); (*make well known*) tornar conhecido

family /'fæməlɪ/ *n* família *f*. **~ doctor** médico *m* da familia. **~ tree** árvore *f* genealógica

famine /'fæmɪn/ *n* fome *f*

famished /'fæmɪʃt/ *a* esfomeado, faminto. **be ~** (*colloq*) estar morrendo de fome, (*P*) estar a morrer de fome

famous /'feɪməs/ *a* famoso

fan[1] /fæn/ *n* (*in the hand*) leque *m*; (*mechanical*) ventilador *m*, (*P*) ventoínha *f* ◻ *vt* (*pt* **fanned**) abanar; (*a fire; fig*) atiçar ◻ *vi* **~ out** abrir-se em leque. **~ belt** correia *f* da ventoínhas

fan[2] /fæn/ *n* (*colloq*) fã *mf*. **~ mail** correio *m* de fãs

fanatic /fə'nætɪk/ *n* fanático *m*. **~al** *a* fanático. **~ism** /-sɪzəm/ *n* fanatismo *m*

fanciful /'fænsɪfl/ *a* fantasioso, fantasista

fancy /'fænsɪ/ *n* fantasia *f*; (*liking*) gosto *m* ◻ *a* extravagante, fantástico; (*of buttons etc*) de fantasia; (*of prices*) exorbitante ◻ *vt* imaginar; (*colloq: like*) gostar de; (*colloq: want*) apetecer. **it took my ~** gostei disso, (*P*) deu-me no gosto. **a passing ~** um entusiasmo passageiro. **~ dress** traje *m* fantasia, (*P*) trajo *m* de fantasia

fanfare /'fænfeə(r)/ *n* fanfarra *f*

fang /fæŋ/ *n* presa *f*, dente *m* canino

fantastic /fæn'tæstɪk/ *a* fantástico

fantas|y /'fæntəsɪ/ *n* fantasia *f*. **~ize** *vt* fantasiar, imaginar

far /fa:(r)/ *adv* longe; (*much, very*) muito ◻ *a* distante, longínquo; (*end, side*) outro. **~ away**, **~ off** ao longe. **as ~ as** (*up to*) até. **as ~ as I know** tanto quanto saiba. **the F~ East** o Extremo-Oriente *m*. **~-away** *a* distante, longínquo. **~-fetched** *a* forçado; (*unconvincing*) pouco plausível. **~-reaching** *a* de grande alcance

farc|e /fa:s/ *n* farsa *f*. **~ical** *a* de farsa; ridículo

fare /feə(r)/ *n* preço *m* da passagem; (*in taxi*) tarifa *f*, preço *m* da corrida; (*passenger*) passageiro *m*; (*food*) comida *f* ◻ *vi* (*get on*) dar-se

farewell /feə'wel/ *int* & *n* adeus (*m*)

farm /fa:m/ *n* quinta *f*, fazenda *f* ◻ *vt* cultivar ◻ *vi* ser fazendeiro, (*P*) lavrador. **~ out** (*of work*) delegar a tarefeiros. **~-hand** *n* trabalhador *m* rural. **~er** *n* fazendeiro *m*, (*P*) lavrador *m*. **~ing** *n* **agricultura** *f*, **lavoura** *f*

farmhouse /'fa:mhaʊs/ *n* casa *f* da fazenda, (*P*) quinta

farmyard /'fa:mja:d/ *n* quintal de fazenda *m*, (*P*) pátio *m* de quinta

farth|er /'fa:ðə(r)/ *adv* mais longe ◻ *a* mais distante. **~est** *adv* mais longe ◻ *a* o mais distante

fascinat|e /'fæsɪneɪt/ *vt* fascinar. **~ion** /-'neɪʃn/ *n* fascínio *m*, fascinação *f*

fascis|t /'fæʃɪst/ *n* fascista *mf*. **~m** /-zəm/ *n* fascismo *m*

fashion /'fæʃn/ *n* moda *f*; (*manner*) maneira *f* ◻ *vt* amoldar, (*P*) moldar. **~able** *a* na moda, (*P*) à moda. **~ably** *adv* na moda, (*P*) à moda

fast[1] /fa:st/ *a* (**-er, -est**) rápido; (*colour*) fixo, que não desbota ◻ *adv* depressa; (*firmly*) firmemente. **be ~** (*of clock*) adiantar-se, estar adiantado. **~ asleep** profundamente adormecido, ferrado no sono. **~ food** *n* fast-food *f*

fast[2] /fa:st/ *vi* jejuar ◻ *n* jejum *m*

fasten /'fa:sn/ *vt/i* prender; (*door, window*) fechar(-se); (*seat-belt*) apertar. **~er**, **~ing** *ns* fecho *m*

fastidious /fə'stɪdɪəs/ *a* exigente

fat /fæt/ *n* gordura *f* ◻ *a* (**fatter, fattest**) gordo. **~ness** *n* gordura *f*

fatal /'feɪtl/ *a* fatal. **~ injuries** ferimentos *mpl* mortais. **~ity** /fə'tælətɪ/ *n* fatalidade *f*. **~ly** *adv* fatalmente, mortalmente

fate /feɪt/ *n* (*destiny*) destino *m*; (*one's lot*) destino *m*, sorte *f*. **~ful** *a* fatídico

fated /'feɪtɪd/ *a* predestinado; (*doomed*) condenado (**to**, a)

father /'fa:ðə(r)/ *n* pai *m* ◻ *vt* gerar. **~-in-law** *n* (*pl* **~s-in-law**) sogro *m*. **~ly** *a* paternal

fathom /'fæðəm/ *n* braça *f* ◻ *vt* **~ (out)** (*comprehend*) compreender

fatigue /fə'ti:g/ *n* fadiga *f* ◻ *vt* fatigar

fatten /'fætn/ *vt/i* engordar. **~ing** *a* que engorda

fatty /'fætɪ/ *a* (**-ier, -iest**) gorduroso; (*tissue*) adiposo

fault /fɔ:lt/ *n* defeito *m*, falha *f*; (*blame*) falta *f*, culpa *f*; (*geol*) falha *f*. **at ~** culpado. **it's your ~** é culpa sua. **~less** *a* impecável. **~y** *a* defeituoso

favour /'feɪvə(r)/ *n* favor *m* ◻ *vt* favorecer; (*prefer*) preferir. **do sb a ~** fazer um favor a alg. **~able** *a* favorável. **~ably** *adv* favoravelmente

favourit|e /'feɪvərɪt/ *a* & *n* favorito (*m*). **~ism** /-ɪzəm/ *n* favoritismo *m*

fawn[1] /fɔ:n/ *n* cervo *m* novo ◻ *a* (*colour*) castanho claro

fawn[2] /fɔ:n/ *vi* **~ on** adular, bajular

fax /fæks/ *n* fax *m*, fac-símile *m* □ *vt* mandar um fax. ~ **machine** fax *m*

fear /fɪə(r)/ *n* medo *m*, receio *m*, temor *m*; (*likelihood*) perigo *m* □ *vt* recear, ter medo de. **for ~ of/that** com medo de/que. **~ful** *a* (*terrible*) medonho; (*timid*) medroso, receoso. **~less** *a* destemido, intrépido

feasib|le /'fi:zəbl/ *a* factível, praticável; (*likely*) plausível. **~ility** /-'bɪlətɪ/ *n* possibilidade *f*; (*plausibility*) plausibilidade *f*

feast /fi:st/ *n* festim *m*; (*relig; fig*) festa *f* □ *vt/i* festejar; (*eat and drink*) banquetear-se. ~ **on** regalar-se com

feat /fi:t/ *n* feito *m*, façanha *f*

feather /'feðə(r)/ *n* pena *f*, pluma *f*

feature /'fi:tʃə(r)/ *n* feição *f*, traço *m*; (*quality*) característica *f*; (*film*) longa metragem *f*; (*article*) artigo *m* em destaque □ *vt* representar; (*film*) ter como protagonista □ *vi* figurar

February /'febrʊərɪ/ *n* Fevereiro *m*

fed /fed/ *see* **feed** □ *a* **be ~ up** estar farto (*colloq*) (**with** de)

federa|l /'fedərəl/ *a* federal. **~tion** /-'reɪʃn/ *n* federação *f*

fee /fi:/ *n* preço *m*. **~(s)** (*of doctor, lawyer etc*) honorários *mpl*; (*member's subscription*) quota *f*; (*univ*) (*P*) propinas *fpl*; (*enrolment/registration*) matricula *f*; **school ~s** mensalidades *fpl* escolares, (*P*) mensalidades *fpl*

feeble /'fi:bl/ *a* (**-er, -est**) débil, fraco. **~-minded** *a* débil mental, (*P*) deficiente

feed /fi:d/ *vt* (*pt* **fed**) alimentar, dar de comer a; (*suckle*) alimentar; (*supply*) alimentar, abostecer □ *vi* alimentar-se □ *n* comida *f*; (*breast-feeding*) mamada *f*; (*mech*) alimentação *f*

feedback /'fi:dbæk/ *n* reação *f*, (*P*) reacção *f*; (*electr*) regeneração *f*

feel /fi:l/ *vt* (*pt* **felt**) sentir; (*touch*) apalpar, tatear □ *vi* (*tired, lonely etc*) sentir-se. ~ **hot/thirsty** ter calor/sede. ~ **as if** ter a impressão (de) que. ~ **like** ter vontade de

feeler /'fi:lə(r)/ *n* antena *f*

feeling /'fi:lɪŋ/ *n* sentimento *m*; (*physical*) sensação *f*

feet /fi:t/ *see* **foot**

feign /feɪn/ *vt* fingir

feline /'fi:laɪn/ *a* felino

fell[1] /fel/ *vt* abater, derrubar

fell[2] /fel/ *see* **fall**

fellow /'feləʊ/ *n* companheiro *m*, camarada *m*; (*of society, college*) membro *m*; (*colloq*) cara *m*, (*P*) tipo *m* (*colloq*). **~-traveller** *n* companheiro *m* de viagem. **~- ship** *n* companheirismo *m*, camaradagem *f*; (*group*) associação *f*

felt[1] /felt/ *n* feltro *m*

felt[2] /felt/ *see* **feel**

female /'fi:meɪl/ *a* (*animal etc*) fêmea *f*; (*voice, sex etc*) feminino □ *n* mulher *f*; (*animal*) fêmea *f*

feminin|e /'femənɪn/ *a* & *n* feminino (*m*). **~ity** /-'nɪnətɪ/ *n* feminilidade *f*

feminist /'femɪnɪst/ *n* feminista *mf*

fenc|e /fens/ *n* tapume *m*, cerca *f* □ *vt* cercar □ *vi* esgrimir. **~er** *n* esgrimista *mf*. **~ing** *n* esgrima *f*; (*fences*) tapume *m*

fend /fend/ *vi* ~ **for o.s.** defender-se, virar-se (*colloq*), governar-se □ *vt* ~ **off** defender-se de

fender /'fendə(r)/ *n* guarda-fogo *m*; (*Amer: mudguard*) pára-lama *m*, guarda-lama *m*, (*P*) pára- choques *m*

fennel /'fenl/ *n* (*herb*) funcho *m*, erva-doce *f*

ferment[1] /fə'ment/ *vt/i* fermentar; (*excite*) excitar. **~ation** /fɜ:men'teɪʃn/ *n* fermentação *f*

ferment[2] /'fɜ:ment/ *n* fermento *m*; (*fig*) efervescência *f*

fern /fɜ:n/ *n* feto *m*

feroc|ious /fə'rəʊʃəs/ *a* feroz. **~ity** /-'rɒsətɪ/ *n* ferocidade *f*

ferret /'ferɪt/ *n* furão *m* □ *vi* (*pt* **ferreted**) caçar com furões □ *vt* ~ **out** desenterrar

ferry /'ferɪ/ *n* barco *m* de travessia, ferry(-boat) *m* □ *vt* transportar

fertil|e /'fɜ:taɪl/ *a* fértil, fecundo. **~ity** /fə'tɪlətɪ/ *n* fertilidade *f*, fecundidade *f*. **~ize** /-əlaɪz/ *vt* fertilizar, fecundar

fertilizer /'fɜ:təlaɪzə(r)/ *n* adubo *m*, fertilizante *m*

fervent /'fɜ:vənt/ *a* fervoroso

fervour /'fɜ:və(r)/ *n* fervor *m*, ardor *m*

fester /'festə(r)/ *vt/i* infectar; (*fig*) envenenar

festival /'festɪvl/ *n* festival *m*; (*relig*) festa *f*

festiv|e /'festɪv/ *a* festivo. **~e season** periodo *m* das festas. **~ity** /fes'tɪvətɪ/ *n* festividade *f*, regozijo *m*. **~ities** festas *fpl*, festividades *fpl*

festoon /fe'stu:n/ *vt* engrinaldar

fetch /fetʃ/ *vt* (*go for*) ir buscar; (*bring*) trazer; (*be sold for*) vender-se por, render

fetching /'fetʃɪŋ/ *a* atraente

fête /feɪt/ *n* festa *f* or feira *f* de caridade ao ar livre □ *vt* festejar

fetish /'fetɪʃ/ *n* fetiche *m*, ídolo *m*; (*obsession*) mania *f*

fetter /'fetə(r)/ *vt* agrilhoar. **~s** *npl* ferros *mpl*, grilhões *mpl*, grilhetas *fpl*

feud /fju:d/ *n* discórdia *f*, inimizade *f*. **~al** *a* feudal

fever /'fi:və(r)/ *n* febre *f*. **~ish** *a* febril

few /fju:/ *a & n* poucos (*mpl*). ~ **books** poucos livros. **they are** ~ são poucos. **a** ~ *a & n* alguns (*mpl*). **a good** ~, **quite a** ~ bastantes. ~**er** *a & n* menos (de). **they were** ~**er** eram menos numerosos. ~**est** *a & n* o menor número (de)

fiancé /fɪ'ansei/ *n* noivo *m*. ~**e** *n* noiva *f*

fiasco /fɪ'æskəʊ/ *n* (*pl* **-os**) fiasco *m*

fib /fɪb/ *n* lorota *f*, cascata *f*, peta *f*, (*P*) mentira *f* □ *vi* (*pt* **fibbed**) mentir

fibre /'faɪbə(r)/ *n* fibra *f*

fibreglass /'faɪbəgla:s/ *n* fibra *f* de vidro

fickle /'fɪkl/ *a* leviano, inconstante

fiction /'fɪkʃn/ *n* ficção *f*. **(works of)** ~ romances *mpl*, obras *fpl* de ficção. ~**al** *a* de ficção, fictício

fictitious /fɪk'tɪʃəs/ *a* fictício

fiddle /'fɪdl/ *n* (*colloq*) violino *m*; (*sl: swindle*) trapaça *f* □ *vi* (*sl*) trapacear (*sl*) □ *vt* (*sl: falsify*) falsificar, cozinhar (*sl*). ~ **with** (*colloq*) brincar com, remexer em, (*P*) estar a brincar com, estar a (re)mexer em. ~**r** /-ə(r)/ *n* (*colloq*) violinista *m/f*

fidelity /fɪ'delətɪ/ *n* fidelidade *f*

fidget /'fɪdʒɪt/ *vi* (*pt* **fidgeted**) estar irrequieto, remexer-se. ~ **with** remexer em. ~**y** *a* irrequieto; (*impatient*) impaciente

field /fi:ld/ *n* campo *m* □ *vt/i* (*cricket*) (estar pronto para) apanhar ou interceptar a bola. ~**-day** *n* grande dia *m*. ~**-glasses** *npl* binóculo *m*. **F**~ **Marshal** marechal-de-campo *m*

fieldwork /'fi:ldwɜ:k/ *n* trabalho *m* de campo; (*mil*) fortificação *f* de campanha

fiend /fi:nd/ *n* diabo *m*, demônio *m*, (*P*) demónio *m*. ~**ish** *a* diabólico

fierce /fɪəs/ *a* (**-er, -est**) feroz; (*storm, attack*) violento; (*heat*) intenso, abrasador. ~**ness** *n* ferocidade *f*; (*of storm, attack*) violência *f*; (*of heat*) intensidade *f*

fiery /'faɪərɪ/ *a* (**-ier, -iest**) ardente; (*temper, speech*) inflamado

fifteen /fɪf'ti:n/ *a & n* quinze (*m*). ~**th** *a & n* décimo quinto (*m*)

fifth /fɪfθ/ *a & n* quinto (*m*)

fift|y /'fɪftɪ/ *a & n* cinqüenta (*m*), (*P*) cinquenta (*m*). ~**y-**~**y** *a* meias. ~**ieth** *a & n* qüinquagésimo (*m*), (*P*) quinquagésimo (*m*)

fig /fɪg/ *n* figo *m*. ~**-tree** *n* figueira *f*

fight /faɪt/ *vi* (*pt* **fought**) lutar, combater □ *vt* lutar contra, combater □ *n* luta *f*; (*quarrel, brawl*) briga *f*. ~ **over sth** lutar por alg coisa. ~ **shy of** esquivar-se de, fugir de. ~**er** *n* lutador *m*; (*mil*) combatente *mf*; (*plane*) caça *m*. ~**ing** *n* combate *m*

figment /'fɪgmənt/ *n* ~ **of the imagination** fruto *m or* produto *m* da imaginação

figurative /'fɪgjərətɪv/ *a* figurado. ~**ly** *adv* em sentido figurado

figure /'fɪgə(r)/ *n* (*number*) algarismo *m*; (*diagram, body*) figura *f*. ~**s** *npl* (*arithmetic*) contas *fpl*, aritmética *f* □ *vt* imaginar, supor □ *vi* (*appear*) figurar (**in** em). ~ **of speech** figura *f* de retórica. ~ **out** compreender. ~**-head** *n* figura *f* de proa; (*pej: person*) testa-de-ferro *m*, chefe *m* nominal

filament /'fɪləmənt/ *n* filamento *m*

fil|e[1] /faɪl/ *n* (*tool*) lixa *f*, lima *f* □ *vt* lixar, limar. ~**ings** *npl* limalha *f*

fil|e[2] /faɪl/ *n* fichário *m*, (*P*) dossier *m*; (*box, drawer*) fichário *m*, (*P*) ficheiro *m*; (*comput*) arquivo *m*; (*line*) fila *f* □ *vt* arquivar □ *vi* ~**e (past)** desfilar, marchar em fila. ~**e in/out** entrar/sair em fila. **(in) single** ~**e** (em) fila indiana. ~**ing cabinet** fichário *m*, (*P*) ficheiro *m*

fill /fɪl/ *vt/i* encher(-se); (*vacancy*) preencher □ *n* **eat one's** ~ comer o que quiser. **have one's** ~ estar farto. ~ **in** (*form*) preencher. ~ **out** (*get fat*) engordar. ~ **up** encher até cima; (*auto*) encher o tanque

fillet /'fɪlɪt/ *n* (*meat, fish*) filé *m*, (*P*) filete *m* □ *vt* (*pt* **filleted**) (*meat, fish*) cortar em filés, (*P*) filetes

filling /'fɪlɪŋ/ *n* recheio *m*; (*of tooth*) obturação *f*, (*P*) chumbo *m*. ~ **station** posto *m* de gasolina

film /fɪlm/ *n* filme *m* □ *vt/i* filmar. ~ **star** estrela *f or* vedete *f or* (*P*) vedeta *f* de cinema, astro *m*

filter /'fɪltə(r)/ *n* filtro *m* □ *vt/i* filtrar(-se). ~ **coffee** café *m* filtro. ~**-tip** *n* cigarro *m* com filtro

filth /fɪlθ/ *n* imundície *f*; (*fig*) obscenidade *f*. ~**y** *a* imundo; (*fig*) obsceno

fin /fɪn/ *n* barbatana *f*

final /'faɪnl/ *a* final; (*conclusive*) decisivo □ *n* (*sport*) final *f*. ~**s** *npl* (*exams*) finais *fpl*. ~**ist** *n* finalista *mf*. ~**ly** *adv* finalmente, por fim; (*once and for all*) definitivamente

finale /fɪ'na:lɪ/ *n* final *m*

finalize /'faɪnəlaɪz/ *vt* finalizar

financ|e /'faɪnæns/ *n* finança(s) *f* (*pl*) □ *a* financeiro □ *vt* financiar. ~**ier** /-'nænsɪə(r)/ *n* financeiro *m*

financial /faɪ'nænʃl/ *a* financeiro. ~**ly** *adv* financeiramente

find /faɪnd/ *vt* (*pt* **found**) (*sth lost*) achar, encontrar; (*think*) achar; (*discover*) descobrir; (*jur*) declarar □ *n* achado *m*.

~ **out** *vt* apurar, descobrir □ *vi* informar-se (**about** sobre)

fine[1] /faɪn/ *n* multa *f* □ *vt* multar

fine[2] /faɪn/ *a* (**-er, -est**) fino; (*splendid*) belo, lindo □ *adv* (muito) bem; (*small*) fino, fininho. ~ **arts** belas artes *fpl*. ~ **weather** bom tempo. ~**ly** *adv* lindamente; (*cut*) fininho, aos bocadinhos

finesse /fɪ'nes/ *n* finura *f*, sutileza *f*

finger /'fɪŋgə(r)/ *n* dedo *m* □ *vt* apalpar. ~**-mark** *n* dedada *f*. ~**-nail** *n* unha *f*

fingerprint /'fɪŋgəprɪnt/ *n* impressão *f* digital

fingertip /'fɪŋgətɪp/ *n* ponta *f* do dedo

finicky /'fɪnɪkɪ/ *a* meticuloso, miudinho

finish /'fɪnɪʃ/ *vt/i* acabar, terminar □ *n* fim *m*; (*of race*) chegada *f*; (*on wood, clothes*) acabamento *m*. ~ **doing** acabar de fazer. ~ **up doing** acabar por fazer. ~ **up in** ir parar a, acabar em

finite /'faɪnaɪt/ *a* finito

Fin|land /'fɪnlənd/ *n* Finlândia *f*. ~**n** *n* finlandês *m*. ~**nish** *a* & *n* (*lang*) finlandês (*m*)

fir /fɜ:(r)/ *n* abeto *m*

fire /'faɪə(r)/ *n* fogo *m*; (*conflagration*) incêndio *m*; (*heater*) aquecedor *m* □ *vt* (*bullet, gun, etc*) disparar; (*dismiss*) despedir; (*fig: stimulate*) inflamar □ *vi* atirar, fazer fogo (**at** sobre). **on** ~ em chamas. **set** ~ **to** pôr fogo em. ~**-alarm** *n* alarme *m* de incêndio. ~ **brigade** bombeiros *mpl*. ~**-engine** *n* carro *m* de bombeiro, (*P*) da bomba. ~**-escape** *n* saída *f* de incêndio. ~ **extinguisher** *n* extintor *m* de incêndio. ~ **station** quartel *m* dos bombeiros

firearm /'faɪəra:m/ *n* arma *f* de fogo

fireman /'faɪəmən/ *n* (*pl* **-men**) bombeiro *m*

fireplace /'faɪəpleɪs/ *n* chaminé *f*, lareira *f*

firewood /'faɪəwʊd/ *n* lenha *f*

firework /'faɪəwɜ:k/ *n* fogo *m* de artifício

firing-squad /'faɪərɪŋskwɒd/ *n* pelotão *m* de execução

firm[1] /fɜ:m/ *n* firma *f* comercial

firm[2] /fɜ:m/ *a* (**-er, -est**) firme; (*belief*) firme, inabalável. ~**ly** *adv* firmemente. ~**ness** *n* firmeza *f*

first /fɜ:st/ *a* & *n* primeiro (*m*); (*auto*) primeira (*f*) □ *adv* primeiro, em primeiro lugar. **at** ~ a princípio, no início. ~ **of all** antes de mais nada. **for the** ~ **time** pela primeira vez. ~ **aid** primeiros socorros *mpl*. ~**- class** *a* de primeira classe. ~ **name** nome de batismo *m*, (*P*) baptismo *m*. ~**-rate** *a* excelente. ~**ly** *adv* primeiramente, em primeiro lugar

fiscal /'fɪskl/ *a* fiscal

fish /fɪʃ/ *n* (*pl usually invar*) peixe *m* □ *vt/i* pescar. ~ **out** (*colloq*) tirar. ~**ing** *n* pesca *f*. **go** ~**ing** ir pescar, (*P*) ir à pesca. ~**ing-rod** *n* vara *f* de pescar. ~**y** *a* de peixe; (*fig: dubious*) suspeito

fisherman /'fɪʃəmən/ *n* (*pl* **-men**) *pescador m*

fishmonger /'fɪʃmʌŋgə(r)/ *n* dono *m*/empregado *m* de peixaria. ~**'s (shop)** peixaria *f*

fission /'fɪʃn/ *n* fissão *f*, cisão *f*

fist /fɪst/ *n* punho *m*, mão *f* fechada, (*P*) punho *m*

fit[1] /fɪt/ *n* acesso *m*, ataque *m*; (*of generosity*) rasgo *m*

fit[2] /fɪt/ *a* (**fitter, fittest**) de boa saúde, em forma; (*proper*) próprio; (*good enough*) em condições; (*able*) capaz □ *vt/i* (*pt* **fitted**) (*clothes*) assentar, ficar bem (a); (*into space*) caber; (*match*) ajustar(-se) (a); (*install*) instalar □ *n* **be a good** ~ assentar bem. **be a tight** ~ estar justo. ~ **out** equipar. ~**ted carpet** carpete *m*, (*P*) alcatifa *f*. ~**ness** *n* saúde *f*, (*P*) condição *f* física

fitful /'fɪtfl/ *a* intermitente

fitment /'fɪtmənt/ *n* móvel *m* de parede

fitting /'fɪtɪŋ/ *a* apropriado □ *n* (*clothes*) prova *f*. ~**s** (*fixtures*) instalações *fpl*; (*fitments*) mobiliário *m*. ~ **room** cabine *f*

five /faɪv/ *a* & *n* cinco (*m*)

fix /fɪks/ *vt* fixar; (*mend, prepare*) arranjar □ *n* **in a** ~ em apuros, (*P*) numa alhada. ~ **sb up with sth** conseguir alg coisa para alguém. ~**ed** *a* fixo

fixation /fɪk'seɪʃn/ *n* fixação *f*; (*obsession*) obsessão *f*

fixture /'fɪkstʃə(r)/ *n* equipamento *m*, instalação *f*; (*sport*) (data *f* marcada para) competição *f*

fizz /fɪz/ *vi* efervescer, borbulhar □ *n* efervescência *f*. ~**y** *a* gasoso

fizzle /'fɪzl/ *vi* ~ **out** (*plan etc*) acabar em nada *or* (*P*) em águas de bacalhau (*colloq*)

flab /flæb/ *n* (*colloq*) gordura *f*, banha *f* (*colloq*). ~**by** *a* flácido

flabbergasted /'flæbəga:stɪd/ *a* (*colloq*) espantado, pasmado (*colloq*)

flag[1] /flæg/ *n* bandeira *f* □ *vt* (*pt* **flagged**) fazer sinal. ~ **down** fazer sinal para parar. ~**-pole** *n* mastro *m* (de bandeira)

flag[2] /flæg/ *vi* (*pt* **flagged**) (*droop*) cair, pender, tombar; (*of person*) esmorecer

flagrant /'fleɪgrənt/ *a* flagrante

flagstone /'flægstəʊn/ *n* laje *f*

flair /fleə(r)/ *n* jeito *m*, habilidade *f*

flak|e /fleɪk/ *n* floco *m*; (*paint*) lasca *f* □ *vi* descamar-se, lascar-se. **~y** *a* (*paint*) descamado, lascado

flamboyant /flæm'bɔɪənt/ *a* flamejante; (*showy*) flamante, vistoso; (*of manner*) extravagante

flame /fleɪm/ *n* chama *f*, labareda *f* □ *vi* flamejar. **burst into ~s** incendiar-se

flamingo /flə'mɪŋgəʊ/ *n* (*pl* **-os**) flamingo *m*

flammable /'flæməbl/ *a* inflamável

flan /flæn/ *n* torta *f*, (*P*) tarte *f*

flank /flæŋk/ *n* flanco *m* □ *vt* flanquear

flannel /'flænl/ *n* flanela *f*; (*for face*) toalha *f*, (*P*) toalhete *m* de rosto

flap /flæp/ *vi* (*pt* **flapped**) bater □ *vt* **~ its wings** bater as asas □ *n* (*of table, pocket*) aba *f*; (*sl: panic*) pânico *m*

flare /fleə(r)/ *vi* **~ up** irromper em chamas; (*of war*) rebentar; (*fig: of person*) enfurecer-se □ *n* chamejar *m*; (*dazzling light*) clarão *m*; (*signal*) foguete *m* de sinalização. **~d** *a* (*skirt*) évasé

flash /flæʃ/ *vi* brilhar subitamente; (*on and off*) piscar; (*auto*) fazer sinal com o pisca-pisca □ *vt* fazer brilhar; (*send*) lançar, dardejar; (*flaunt*) fazer alarde de, ostentar □ *n* clarão *m*, lampejo *m*; (*photo*) flash *m*. **~ past** passar como uma bala, (*P*) passar como um bólide

flashback /'flæʃbæk/ *n* cena *f* retrospectiva, flashback *m*

flashlight /'flæʃlaɪt/ *n* lanterna *f* elétrica, (*P*) eléctrica

flashy /'flæʃɪ/ *a* espalhafatoso, que dá na vista

flask /flɑ:sk/ *n* frasco *m*; (*vacuum flask*) garrafa *f* térmica, (*P*) garrafa *f* termos

flat /flæt/ *a* (**flatter, flattest**) plano, chato; (*tyre*) arriado, vazio; (*battery*) fraco; (*refusal*) categórico; (*fare, rate*) fixo; (*monotonous*) monótono; (*mus*) bemol; (*out of tune*) desafinado □ *n* apartamento *m*; (*colloq: tyre*) furo *m* no pneu; (*mus*) bemol *m*. **~ out** (*drive*) em alta velocidade; (*work*) a dar tudo por tudo. **~ly** *adv* categoricamente

flatter /'flætə(r)/ *vt* lisonjear, adular. **~er** *n* lisonjeiro *m*, adulador *m*. **~ing** *a* lisonjeiro, adulador. **~y** *n* lisonja *f*

flatulence /'flætjʊləns/ *n* flatulência *f*

flaunt /flɔ:nt/ *vt/i* pavonear(-se), ostentar

flavour /'fleɪvə(r)/ *n* sabor *m* (**of** a) □ *vt* dar sabor a, temperar. **~ing** *n* aroma *m* sintético; (*seasoning*) tempero *m*

flaw /flɔ:/ *n* falha *f*, imperfeição *f*. **~ed** *a* imperfeito. **~less** *a* perfeito

flea /fli:/ *n* pulga *f*

fled /fled/ *see* **flee**

fledged /fledʒd/ *a* **fully-~** (*fig*) treinado, experiente

flee /fli:/ *vi* (*pt* **fled**) fugir □ *vt* fugir de

fleece /fli:s/ *n* lã *f* de carneiro, velo *m* □ *vt* (*fig*) esfolar, roubar

fleet /fli:t/ *n* (*of warships*) esquadra *f*; (*of merchant ships, vehicles*) frota *f*

fleeting /'fli:tɪŋ/ *a* curto, fugaz

Flemish /'flemɪʃ/ *a* & *n* (*lang*) flamengo (*m*)

flesh /fleʃ/ *n* carne *f*; (*of fruit*) polpa *f*. **~y** *a* carnudo

flew /flu:/ *see* **fly**[2]

flex[1] /fleks/ *vt* flexionar

flex[2] /fleks/ *n* (*electr*) fio *f* flexível

flexib|le /'fleksəbl/ *a* flexível. **~ility** /-'bɪlətɪ/ *n* flexibilidade *f*

flexitime /'fleksɪtaɪm/ *n* horário *m* flexível

flick /flɪk/ *n* (*light blow*) safanão *m*; (*with fingertip*) piparote *m* □ *vt* dar um safanão em; (*with fingertip*) dar um piparote a. **~-knife** *n* navalha *f* de ponta e mola. **~ through** folhear

flicker /'flɪkə(r)/ *vi* vacilar, oscilar, tremular □ *n* oscilação *f*, tremular *m*; (*light*) luz *f* oscilante

flier /'flaɪə(r)/ *n* = **flyer**

flies /flaɪz/ *npl* (*of trousers*) braguilha *f*

flight[1] /flaɪt/ *n* (*flying*) voo *m*. **~ of stairs** lance *m*, (*P*) lanço *m* de escada. **~-deck** *n* cabine *f*, (*P*) cabina *f*

flight[2] /flaɪt/ *n* (*fleeing*) fuga *f*. **put to ~** pôr em fuga. **take ~** pôr-se em fuga

flimsy /'flɪmzɪ/ *a* (**-ier, -iest**) (*material*) fino; (*object*) frágil; (*excuse etc*) fraco, esfarrapado

flinch /flɪntʃ/ *vi* (*wince*) retrair-se; (*draw back*) recuar; (*hesitate*) hesitar

fling /flɪŋ/ *vt/i* (*pt* **flung**) atirar (-se), arremessar(-se); (*rush*) precipitar-se

flint /flɪnt/ *n* sílex *m*; (*for lighter*) pedra *f*

flip /flɪp/ *vt* (*pt* **flipped**) fazer girar com o dedo e o polegar □ *n* pancadinha *f*. **~ through** folhear

flippant /'flɪpənt/ *a* irreverente, petulante

flipper /'flɪpə(r)/ *n* (*of seal*) nadadeira *f*; (*of swimmer*) pé-de-pato *m*

flirt /flɜ:t/ *vt* namoriscar, flertar, (*P*) flartar □ *n* namorador *m*, namoradeira *f*. **~ation** /-'teɪʃn/ *n* namorico *m*, flerte *m*, (*P*) flirt *m*. **~atious** *a* namorador *m*, namoradeira *f*

flit /flɪt/ *vi* (*pt* **flitted**) esvoaçar

float /fləʊt/ *vt/i* (fazer) flutuar; (*company*) lançar □ *n* bóia *f*; (*low cart*) carro *m* de alegórico

flock /flɒk/ *n* (*of sheep; congregation*) rebanho *m*; (*of birds*) bando *m*; (*crowd*) multidão *f* □ *vi* afluir, juntar-se

flog /flɒg/ *vt* (*pt* **flogged**) açoitar; (*sl: sell*) vender

flood /flʌd/ *n* inundação *f*, cheia *f*; (*of tears*) dilúvio *m* □ *vt* inundar, alagar □ *vi* estar inundado; (*river*) transbordar; (*fig: people*) afluir

floodlight /'flʌdlaɪt/ *n* projetor *m*, (*P*) projector *m*, holofote *m* □ *vt* (*pt* **floodlit**) iluminar

floor /flɔ:(r)/ *n* chão *m*, soalho *m*; (*for dancing*) pista *f*; (*storey*) andar *m* □ *vt* assoalhar; (*baffle*) desconcertar, embatucar

flop /flɒp/ *vi* (*pt* **flopped**) (*drop*) (deixar-se) cair; (*move helplessly*) debater-se; (*sl: fail*) ser um fiasco □ *n* (*sl*) fiasco *m*. **~py** *a* mole, tombado. **~py (disk)** disquete *m*

floral /'flɒ:rəl/ *a* floral

florid /'flɒrɪd/ *a* florido

florist /'flɒrɪst/ *n* florista *mf*

flounce /flaʊns/ *n* babado *m*, debrum *m*

flounder /'flaʊndə(r)/ *vi* esbracejar, debater-se; (*fig*) meter os pés pelas mãos

flour /'flaʊə(r)/ *n* farinha *f*. **~y** *a* farinhento

flourish /'flʌrɪʃ/ *vi* florescer, prosperar □ *vt* brandir □ *n* floreado *m*; (*movement*) gesto *m* elegante. **~ing** *a* próspero

flout /flaʊt/ *vt* escarnecer (de)

flow /fləʊ/ *vi* correr, fluir; (*traffic*) mover-se; (*hang loosely*) flutuar; (*gush*) jorrar □ *n* corrente *f*; (*of tide; fig*) enchente *f*. **~ into** (*of river*) desaguar em. **~ chart** organograma *m*, (*P*) organigrama *m*

flower /'flaʊə(r)/ *n* flor *f* □ *vi* florir, florescer. **~-bed** *n* canteiro *m*. **~ed** *a* de flores, (*P*) florido, às flores. **~y** *a* florido

flown /fləʊn/ *see* **fly**[2]

flu /flu:/ *n* (*colloq*) gripe *f*

fluctuat|e /'flʌktʃʊeɪt/ *vi* flutuar, oscilar. **~ion** /-'eɪʃn/ *n* flutuação *f*, oscilação *f*

flue /flu:/ *n* cano *m* de chaminé

fluen|t /'flu:ənt/ *a* fluente. **be ~t (in a language)** falar correntemente (uma língua). **~cy** *n* fluência *f*. **~tly** *adv* fluentemente

fluff /flʌf/ *n* cotão *m*; (*down*) penugem *f* □ *vt* (*colloq: bungle*) estender-se em (*sl*), executar mal. **~y** *a* penugento, fofo

fluid /'flu:ɪd/ *a* & *n* fluido (*m*)

fluke /flu:k/ *n* bambúrrio (*colloq*) *m*, golpe *m* de sorte

flung /flʌŋ/ *see* **fling**

flunk /flʌŋk/ *vt/i* (*Amer colloq*) levar pau (*colloq*), (*P*) chumbar (*colloq*)

fluorescent /flʊə'resnt/ *a* fluorescente

fluoride /'flʊəraɪd/ *n* flúor *m*, fluor *m*

flurry /'flʌrɪ/ *n* rajada *f*, rabanada *f*, lufada *f*; (*fig*) atrapalhação *f*, agitação *f*

flush[1] /flʌʃ/ *vi* corar, ruborizar-se □ *vt* lavar com água, (*P*) lavar a jorros de água □ *n* rubor *m*, vermelhidão *f*; (*fig*) excitação *f*; (*of water*) jorro *m* □ *a* **~ with** ao nível de, rente a. **~ the toilet** dar descarga

flush[2] /flʌʃ/ *vt* **~ out** desalojar

fluster /'flʌstə(r)/ *vt* atarantar, perturbar, enervar

flute /flu:t/ *n* flauta *f*

flutter /'flʌtə(r)/ *vi* esvoaçar; (*wings*) bater; (*heart*) palpitar □ *vt* bater. **~ one's eyelashes** pestanejar □ *n* (*of wings*) batimento *m*; (*fig*) agitação *f*

flux /flʌks/ *n* **in a state of ~** em mudança *f* contínua

fly[1] /flaɪ/ *n* mosca *f*

fly[2] /flaɪ/ *vi* (*pt* **flew**, *pp* **flown**) voar; (*passengers*) ir de/viajar de avião; (*rush*) correr □ *vt* pilotar; (*passengers, goods*) transportar por avião; (*flag*) hastear, (*P*) arvorar □ *n* (*of trousers*) braguilha *f*

flyer /'flaɪə(r)/ *n* aviador *m*; (*Amer: circular*) prospecto *m*

flying /'flaɪɪŋ/ *a* voador. **with ~ colours** com grande êxito, esplendidamente. **~ saucer** disco *m* voador. **~ start** bom arranque *m*. **~ visit** visita *f* de médico

flyleaf /'flaɪli:f/ *n* (*pl* **-leaves**) guarda *f*, folha *f* em branco

flyover /'flaɪəʊvə(r)/ *n* viaduto *m*

foal /fəʊl/ *n* potro *m*

foam /fəʊm/ *n* espuma *f* □ *vi* espumar. **~ (rubber)** *n* espuma *f* de borracha

fob /fɒb/ *vt* (*pt* **fobbed**) **~ off** iludir, entreter com artifícios. **~ off on** impingir a

focus /'fəʊkəs/ *n* (*pl* **-cuses** *or* **-ci** /-saɪ/) foco *m* □ *vt/i* (*pt* **focused**) focar; (*fig*) concentrar(-se). **in ~** focado, em foco. **out of ~** desfocado

fodder /'fɒdə(r)/ *n* forragem *f*

foetus /'fi:təs/ *n* (*pl* **-tuses**) feto *m*

fog /fɒg/ *n* nevoeiro *m* □ *vt/i* (*pt* **fogged**) enevoar(-se). **~-horn** *n* sereia *f* de nevoeiro. **~gy** *a* enevoado, brumoso. **it is ~gy** está nevoento

foible /'fɔɪbl/ *n* fraqueza *f*, ponto *m* fraco

foil[1] /fɔɪl/ *n* papel *m* de alumínio; (*fig*) contraste *m*

foil[2] /fɔɪl/ *vt* frustrar

foist /fɔɪst/ *vt* impingir (**on** a)

fold /fəʊld/ *vt/i* dobrar(-se); (*arms*) cruzar; (*colloq: fail*) falir □ *n* dobra *f*. **~er** *n* pasta *f*; (*leaflet*) prospecto *m* (desdobrável). **~ing** *a* dobrável, dobradiço

foliage /'fəʊlɪɪdʒ/ *n* folhagem *f*

folk /fəʊk/ *n* povo *m*. **~s** (*family, people*) gente *f* (*colloq*) □ *a* folclórico, popular. **~-lore** *n* folclore *m*

follow /'fɒləʊ/ *vt/i* seguir. **it ~s that** quer dizer que. **~ suit** (*cards*) servir o naipe jogado; (*fig*) seguir o exemplo, fazer o mesmo. **~ up** (*letter etc*) dar seguimento a. **~er** *n* partidário *m*, seguidor *m*. **~ing** *n* partidários *mpl* □ *a* seguinte □ *prep* em seguimento a

folly /'fɒlɪ/ *n* loucura *f*

fond /fɒnd/ *a* (**-er -est**) carinhoso; (*hope*) caro. **be ~ of** gostar de, ser amigo de. **~ness** *n* (*for people*) afeição *f*; (*for thing*) gosto *m*

fondle /'fɒndl/ *vt* acariciar

font /fɒnt/ *n* pia *f* batismal, (*P*) baptismal

food /fu:d/ *n* alimentação *f*, comida *f*; (*nutrient*) alimento *m* □ *a* alimentar. **~ poisoning** envenenamento *m* alimentar

fool /fu:l/ *n* idiota *mf*, parvo *m* □ *vt* enganar □ *vi* **~ around** andar sem fazer nada

foolhardy /'fu:lha:dɪ/ *a* imprudente, atrevido

foolish /'fu:lɪʃ/ *a* idiota, parvo. **~ly** *adv* parvamente. **~ness** *n* idiotice *f*, parvoice *f*

foolproof /'fu:lpru:f/ *a* infalível

foot /fʊt/ *n* (*pl* **feet**) (*of person, bed, stairs*) pé *m*; (*of animal*) pata *f*; (*measure*) pé *m* (= 30,48 cm) □ *vt* **~ the bill** pagar a conta. **on ~** a pé. **on** *or* **to one's feet** de pé. **put one's ~ in it** fazer uma gafe. **to be under sb's feet** atrapalhar alg. **~-bridge** *n* passarela *f*

football /'fʊtbɔ:l/ *n* bola *f* de futebol; (*game*) futebol *m*. **~ pools** loteria *f* esportiva, (*P*) totobola *m*. **~er** *n* futebolista *mf*, jogador *m* de futebol

foothills /'fʊthɪlz/ *npl* contrafortes *mpl*

foothold /'fʊthəʊld/ *n* ponto *m* de apoio

footing /'fʊtɪŋ/ *n*: **firm ~** apois seguro **on an equal ~** em pé de igualdade

footlights /'fʊtlaɪts/ *npl* ribalta *f*

footnote /'fʊtnəʊt/ *n* nota *f* de rodapé

footpath /'fʊtpa:θ/ *n* (*pavement*) calçada *f*, (*P*) passeio *m*; (*in open country*) atalho *m*, caminho *m*

footprint /'fʊtprɪnt/ *n* pegada *f*

footstep /'fʊtstep/ *n* passo *m*

footwear /'fʊtweə(r)/ *n* calçado *m*

for /fə(r)/; *emphatic* /fɔ:(r)/ *prep* para; (*in favour of; in place of*) por; (*during*) durante □ *conj* porque, visto que. **a liking ~** gosto por. **he has been away ~ two years** há dois anos que ele está fora. **~ ever** para sempre

forage /'fɒrɪdʒ/ *vi* forragear; (*rummage*) remexer à procura (de) □ *n* forragem *f*

forbade /fə'bæd/ *see* **forbid**

forbear /fɔ:'beə(r)/ *vt/i* (*pt* **forbore**, *pp* **forborne**) abster-se (**from** de). **~ance** *n* paciência *f*, tolerância *f*

forbid /fə'bɪd/ *vt* (*pt* **forbade**, *pp* **forbidden**) proibir. **you are ~den to smoke** você está proibido de fumar, (*P*) estás proibido de fumar. **~ding** *a* severo, intimidante

force /fɔ:s/ *n* força *f* □ *vt* forçar. **~ into** fazer entrar à força. **~ on** impor a. **come into ~** entrar em vigor. **the ~s** as Forças Armadas. **~d** *a* forçado. **~ful** *a* enérgico

force-feed /'fɔ:sfi:d/ *vt* (*pt* **-fed**) alimentar à força

forceps /'fɔ:seps/ *n* (*pl invar*) fórceps *m*

forcibl|e /'fɔ:səbl/ *a* convincente; (*done by force*) à força. **~y** *adv* à força

ford /fɔ:d/ *n* vau *m* □ *vt* passar a vau, vadear

fore /fɔ:(r)/ *a* dianteiro □ *n* **to the ~** em evidência

forearm /'fɔ:ra:m/ *n* antebraço *m*

foreboding /fɔ:'bəʊdɪŋ/ *n* pressentimento *m*

forecast /'fɔ:ka:st/ *vt* (*pt* **forecast**) prever □ *n* previsão *f*. **weather ~** boletim *m* meteorológico, previsão *f* do tempo

forecourt /'fɔ:kɔ:t/ *n* pátio *m* de entrada; (*of garage*) área *f* das bombas de gasolina

forefinger /'fɔ:fɪŋgə(r)/ *n* (dedo) indicador *m*

forefront /'fɔ:frʌnt/ *n* vanguarda *f*

foregone /'fɔ:gɒn/ *a* **~ conclusion** resultado *m* previsto

foreground /'fɔ:graʊnd/ *n* primeiro plano *m*

forehead /'fɒrɪd/ *n* testa *f*

foreign /'fɒrən/ *a* estrangeiro; (*trade*) externo; (*travel*) ao/no estrangeiro. **F~ Office** Ministério *m* dos Negócios Estrangeiros. **~er** *n* estrangeiro *m*.

foreman /'fɔ:mən/ *n* (*pl* **foremen**) contramestre *m*; (*of jury*) primeiro jurado *m*

foremost /'fɔ:məʊst/ *a* principal, primeiro □ *adv* **first and ~** antes de mais nada, em primeiro lugar

forename /'fɔ:neɪm/ *n prenome m*

forensic /fə'rensɪk/ *a* forense. **~ medicine** medicina *f* legal

forerunner /'fɔ:rʌnə(r)/ *n* precursor *m*

foresee /fɔ:'si:/ *vt* (*pt* **-saw**, *pp* **-seen**) prever. **~able** *a* previsível

foreshadow /fɔ:'ʃædəʊ/ *vt* prefigurar, pressagiar

foresight /'fɔ:saɪt/ *n* previsão *f*, previdência *f*

forest /'fɒrɪst/ *n* floresta *f*

forestall /fɔ:'stɔ:l/ *vt* (*do first*) antecipar-se a; (*prevent*) prevenir; (*anticipate*) antecipar
forestry /'fɒrɪstrɪ/ *n* silvicultura *f*
foretell /fɔ:'tel/ *vt* (*pt* **foretold**) predizer, profetizar
forever /fə'revə(r)/ *adv* (*endlessly*) constantemente
foreword /'fɔ:wɜ:d/ *n* prefácio *m*
forfeit /'fɔ:fɪt/ *n* penalidade *f*, preço *m*; (*in game*) prenda *f* □ *vt* perder
forgave /fə'geɪv/ *see* **forgive**
forge[1] /fɔ:dʒ/ *vi* ~ **ahead** tomar a dianteira, avançar
forge[2] /fɔ:dʒ/ *n* forja *f* □ *vt* (*metal, friendship*) forjar; (*counterfeit*) falsificar, forjar. **~r** /-ə(r)/ *n* falsificador *m*, forjador *m*. **~ry** /-ərɪ/ *n* falsificação *f*
forget /fə'get/ *vt*/*i* (*pt* **forgot**, *pp* **forgotten**) esquecer. **~ o.s.** portar-se com menos dignidade, esquecer-se de quem é. **~-me-not** *n* miosótis *m*. **~ful** *a* esquecido. **~fulness** *n* esquecimento *m*
forgive /fə'gɪv/ *vt* (*pt* **forgave**, *pp* **forgiven**) perdoar (**sb for sth** alg coisa a alg). **~ness** *n* perdão *m*
forgo /fɔ:'gəʊ/ *vt* (*pt* **forwent**, *pp* **forgone**) renunciar a
fork /fɔ:k/ *n* garfo *m*; (*for digging etc*) forquilha *f*; (*in road*) bifurcação *f* □ *vi* bifurcar. **~ out** (*sl*) desembolsar. **~-lift truck** empilhadeira *f*. **~ed** *a* bifurcado; (*lightning*) em zigzag
forlorn /fə'lɔ:n/ *a* abandonado, desolado
form /fɔ:m/ *n* forma *f*; (*document*) impresso *m*, formulário *m*; (*schol*) classe *f* □ *vt*/*i* formar(-se)
formal /'fɔ:ml/ *a* formal; (*dress*) de cerimônia, (*P*) cerimónia. **~ity** /-'mælətɪ/ *n* formalidade *f*. **~ly** *adv* formalmente
format /'fɔ:mæt/ *n* formato *m* □ *vt* (*pl* **formatted**) (*disk*) formatar
formation /fɔ:'meɪʃn/ *n* formação *f*
former /'fɔ:mə(r)/ *a* antigo; (*first of two*) primeiro. **the ~** aquele. **~ly** *adv* antigamente
formidable /'fɔ:mɪdəbl/ *a* formidável, tremendo
formula /'fɔ:mjʊlə/ *n* (*pl* **-ae** /-i:/ *or* **-as**) fórmula *f*
formulate /'fɔ:mjʊleɪt/ *vt* formular
forsake /fə'seɪk/ *vt* (*pt* **forsook**, *pp* **forsaken**) abandonar
fort /fɔ:t/ *n* (*mil*) forte *m*
forth /fɔ:θ/ *adv* adiante, para a frente. **and so ~** e assim por diante, etcetera. **go back and ~** andar de trás para diante.
forthcoming /fɔ:θ'kʌmɪŋ/ *a* que está para vir, próximo; (*communicative*) comunicativo, receptivo; (*book*) no prelo
forthright /'fɔ:θraɪt/ *a* franco, direto, (*P*) directo
fortif|y /'fɔ:tɪfaɪ/ *vt* fortificar. **~ication** /-ɪ'keɪʃn/ *n* fortificação *f*
fortitude /'fɔ:tɪtju:d/ *n* fortitude *f*, fortaleza *f*
fortnight /'fɔ:tnaɪt/ *n* quinze dias *mpl*, (*P*) quinzena *f*. **~ly** *a* quinzenal □ *adv* de quinze em quinze dias
fortress /'fɔ:trɪs/ *n* fortaleza *f*
fortuitous /fɔ:'tju:ɪtəs/ *a* fortuito, acidental
fortunate /'fɔ:tʃənət/ *a* feliz, afortunado. **be ~** ter sorte. **~ly** *adv* felizmente
fortune /'fɔ:tʃən/ *n* sorte *f*; (*wealth*) fortuna *f*. **have the good ~ to** ter a sorte de. **~-teller** *n* cartomante *mf*
fort|y /'fɔ:tɪ/ *a* & *n* quarenta (*m*). **~ieth** *a* &*n* quadragésimo (*m*)
forum /'fɔ:rəm/ *n* fórum *m*, foro *m*
forward /'fɔ:wəd/ *a* (*in front*) dianteiro; (*towards the front*) para a frente; (*advanced*) adiantado; (*pert*) atrevido □ *n* (*sport*) atacante *m*, (*P*) avançado *m* □ *adv* **~(s)** para a frente, para diante □ *vt* (*letter*) remeter; (*goods*) expedir; (*fig: help*) favorecer. **come ~** apresentar-se. **go ~** avançar. **~ness** *n* adiantamento *m*; (*pertness*) atrevimento *m*
fossil /'fɒsl/ *a* & *n* fóssil (*m*)
foster /'fɒstə(r)/ *vt* fomentar; (*child*) criar. **~-child** *n* filho *m* adotivo, (*P*) adoptivo. **~-mother** *n* mãe *f* adotiva, (*P*) adoptiva
fought /fɔ:t/ *see* **fight**
foul /faʊl/ *a* (**-er, -est**) infecto; (*language*) obsceno; (*weather*) mau □ *n* (*football*) falta *f* □ *vt* sujar, emporcalhar. **~-mouthed** *a* de linguagem obscena. **~ play** jogo *m* desleal; (*crime*) crime *m*
found[1] /faʊnd/ *see* **find**
found[2] /faʊnd/ *vt* fundar. **~ation** /-'deɪʃn/ *n* fundação *f*; (*basis*) fundamento *m*. **~ations** *npl* (*of building*) alicerces *mpl*
founder[1] /'faʊndə(r)/ *n* fundador *m*
founder[2] /'faʊndə(r)/ *vi* afundar-se
foundry /'faʊndrɪ/ *n* fundição *f*
fountain /'faʊntɪn/ *n* fonte *f*. **~-pen** *n* caneta-tinteiro *f*, (*P*) caneta *f* de tinta permanente
four /fɔ:(r)/ *a* & *n* quatro (*m*). **~fold** *a* quádruplo □ *adv* quadruplamente. **~th** *a* & *n* quarto (*m*)
foursome /'fɔ:səm/ *n* grupo *m* de quatro pessoas

fourteen /fɔ:'ti:n/ *a & n* catorze (*m*). **~th** *a & n* décimo quarto (*m*)

fowl /faʊl/ *n* ave *f* de capoeira

fox /fɒks/ *n* raposa *f* □ *vt* (*colloq*) mistificar, enganar. **be ~ed** ficar perplexo

foyer /'fɔɪeɪ/ *n* foyer *m*

fraction /'frækʃn/ *n* fração *f*, (*P*) fracção *f*; (*small bit*) bocadinho *m*, partícula *f*

fracture /'fræktʃə(r)/ *n* fratura *f*, (*P*) fractura *f* □ *vt/i* fraturar(-se), (*P*) fracturar(-se)

fragile /'frædʒaɪl/ *a* frágil

fragment /'frægmənt/ *n* fragmento *m*. **~ary** /'frægməntrɪ/ *a* fragmentário

fragran|t /'freɪgrənt/ *a* fragrante, perfumado. **~ce** *n* fragrância *f*, perfume *m*

frail /freɪl/ *a* (**-er, -est**) frágil

frame /freɪm/ *n* (*techn; of spectacles*) armação *f*; (*of picture*) moldura *f*; (*of window*) caixilho *m*; (*body*) corpo *m*, (*P*) estrutura *f* □ *vt* colocar a armação em; (*picture*) emoldurar; (*fig*) formular; (*sl*) incriminar falsamente, tramar. **~ of mind** estado *m* de espírito

framework /'freɪmwɜ:k/ *n* estrutura *f*; (*context*) quadro *m*, esquema *m*

France /frɑ:ns/ *n* França *f*

franchise /'fræntʃaɪz/ *n* (*pol*) direito *m* de voto; (*comm*) concessão *f*, franchise *f*

frank[1] /fræŋk/ *a* franco. **~ly** *adv* francamente. **~ness** *n* franqueza *f*

frank[2] /fræŋk/ *vt* franquear

frantic /'fræntɪk/ *a* frenético

fraternal /frə'tɜ:nl/ *a* fraternal

fraternize /'frætənaɪz/ *vi* confraternizar

fraud /frɔ:d/ *n* fraude *f*; (*person*) impostor *m*. **~ulent** /'frɔ:djʊlənt/ *a* fraudulento

fraught /frɔ:t/ *a* **~ with** cheio de

fray[1] /freɪ/ *n* rixa *f*

fray[2] /freɪ/ *vt/i* desfiar(-se), puir, esgarçar(-se)

freak /fri:k/ *n* aberração *f*, anomalia *f* □ *a* anormal. **~ of nature** aborto *m* da natureza. **~ish** *a* anormal

freckle /'frekl/ *n* sarda *f*. **~d** *a* sardento

free /fri:/ *a* (**freer, freest**) livre; (*gratis*) grátis; (*lavish*) liberal □ *vt* (*pt* **freed**) libertar (**from** de); (*rid*) livrar (**of** de). **~ of charge** grátis, de graça. **a ~ hand** carta *f* branca. **~-lance** *a* independente, free-lance. **~-range** *a* (*egg*) de galinha criada em galinheiro. **~ly** *adv* livremente

freedom /'fri:dəm/ *n* liberdade *f*

freez|e /fri:z/ *vt/i* (*pt* **froze**, *pp* **frozen**) gelar; (*culin; finance*) congelar(-se) □ *n* gelo *m*; (*culin; finance*) congelamento *m*. **~er** *n* congelador *m*. **~ing** *a* gélido, glacial. **below ~ing** abaixo de zero

freight /freɪt/ *n* frete *m*

French /frentʃ/ *a* francês □ *n* (*lang*) francês *m*. **the ~** os franceses. **~man** *n* francês *m*. **~-speaking** *a* francófono. **~ window** porta *f* envidraçada. **~woman** *n* francesa *f*

frenz|y /'frenzɪ/ *n* frenesi *m*. **~ied** *a* frenético

frequen|t[1] /'fri:kwənt/ *a* freqüente, (*P*) frequente. **~cy** *n* freqüência *f*, (*P*) frequência *f*. **~tly** *adv* freqüentemente, (*P*) frequentemente

frequent[2] /frɪ'kwent/ *vt* freqüentar, (*P*) frequentar

fresh /freʃ/ *a* (**-er, -est**) fresco; (*different, additional*) novo; (*colloq: cheeky*) descarado, atrevido. **~ly** *adv* recentemente. **~ness** *n* frescura *f*

freshen /'freʃn/ *vt/i* refrescar. **~ up** refrescar-se

fret /fret/ *vt/i* (*pt* **fretted**) ralar (-se). **~ful** *a* rabugento

friar /'fraɪə(r)/ *n* frade *m*; (*before name*) frei *m*

friction /'frɪkʃn/ *n* fricção *f*

Friday /'fraɪdɪ/ *n* sexta-feira *f*. **Good ~** sexta-feira *f* santa

fridge /frɪdʒ/ *n* (*colloq*) geladeira *f*, (*P*) frigorífico *m*

fried /fraɪd/ *see* **fry** □ *a* frito

friend /frend/ *n* amigo *m*. **~ship** *n* amizade *f*

friendl|y /'frendlɪ/ *a* (**-ier, -iest**) amigável, amigo, simpático. **~iness** *n* simpatia *f*, gentileza *f*

frieze /fri:z/ *n* friso *m*

frigate /'frɪgət/ *n* fragata *f*

fright /fraɪt/ *n* medo *m*, susto *m*. **give sb a ~** pregar um susto em alguém. **~ful** *a* medonho, assustador

frighten /'fraɪtn/ *vt* assustar. **~ off** afugentar. **~ed** *a* assustado. **be ~ed (of)** ter medo (de)

frigid /'frɪdʒɪd/ *a* frígido. **~ity** /-'dʒɪdətɪ/ *n* frigidez *f*, frieza *f*; (*psych*) frigidez *f*

frill /frɪl/ *n* babado *m*, (*P*) folho *m*

fringe /frɪndʒ/ *n* franja *f*; (*of area*) borda *f*; (*of society*) margem *f*. **~ benefits** (*work*) regalias *fpl* extras. **~ theatre** teatro *m* alternativo, teatro *m* de vanguarda

frisk /frɪsk/ *vi* pular, brincar □ *vt* revistar

fritter[1] /'frɪtə(r)/ *n* bolinho *m* frito, (*P*) frito *m*

fritter[2] /'frɪtə(r)/ *vt* **~ away** desperdiçar

frivol|ous /'frɪvələs/ *a* frívolo. **~ity** /-'vɒlətɪ/ *n* frivolidade *f*

fro /frəʊ/ *see* **to and fro**

frock /frɒk/ *n* vestido *m*

frog /frɒg/ *n* rã *f*

frogman /'frɒgmən/ *n* (*pl* **-men**) homem-rã *m*

frolic /'frɒlɪk/ *vi* (*pt* **frolicked**) brincar, fazer travessuras □ *n* brincadeira *f*, travessura *f*

from /frəm/; *emphatic* /frɒm/ *prep* de; (*with time, prices etc*) de, a partir de; (*according to*) por, a julgar por

front /frʌnt/ *n* (*meteo, mil, pol; of car, train*) frente *f*; (*of shirt*) peitilho *m*; (*of building; fig*) fachada *f*; (*promenade*) calçada *f* à beira-mar □ *a* da frente; (*first*) primeiro. **in ~ (of)** em frente (de). **~ door** porta *f* da rua. **~-wheel drive** tração *f*, (*P*) tracção *f* dianteira. **~age** *n* frontaria *f*. **~al** *a* **frontal**

frontier /'frʌntɪə(r)/ *n* fronteira *f*

frost /frɒst/ *n* gelo *m*, temperatura *f* abaixo de zero; (*on ground, plants etc*) geada *f* □ *vt/i* cobrir (-se) de geada. **~-bite** *n* queimadura *f* de frio. **~-bitten** *a* queimado pelo frio. **~ed** *a* (*glass*) fosco. **~y** *a* glacial

froth /frɒθ/ *n* espuma *f* □ *vi* espumar, fazer espuma. **~y** *a* espumoso

frown /fraʊn/ *vi* franzir as sobrancelhas □ *n* franzir *m* de sobrancelhas. **~ on** desaprovar

froze, frozen /frəʊz, 'frəʊzn/ *see* **freeze**

frugal /'fru:gl/ *a* poupado; (*meal*) frugal. **~ly** *adv* frugalmente

fruit /fru:t/ *n* fruto *m*; (*collectively*) fruta *f*. **~ machine** caça-níqueis *ms/pl*. **~ salad** salada *f* de frutas. **~y** *a* que tem gosto *or* cheiro de fruta

fruit|ful /'fru:tfl/ *a* frutífero, produtivo. **~less** *a* infrutífero

fruition /fru:'ɪʃn/ *n* **come to ~** realizar-se

frustrat|e /frʌ'streɪt/ *vt* frustrar. **~ion** /-ʃn/ *n* frustração *f*

fry /fraɪ/ *vt/i* (*pt* **fried**) fritar. **~ing-pan** *n* frigideira *f*

fudge /fʌdʒ/ *n* (*culin*) doce *m* de leite, (*P*) doce *m* acaramelado □ *vt/i* **~ (the issue)** lançar a confusão

fuel /'fju:əl/ *n* combustível *m*; (*for car*) carburante *m* □ *vt* (*pt* **fuelled**) abastecer de combustível; (*fig*) atear.

fugitive /'fju:dʒətɪv/ *a & n* fugitivo (*m*)

fulfil /fʊl'fɪl/ *vt* (*pt* **fulfilled**) cumprir, realizar; (*condition*) satisfazer. **~ o.s.** realizar-se. **~ling** *a* satisfatório. **~ment** *n* realização *f*; (*of condition*) satisfação *f*

full /fʊl/ *a* (**-er, -est**) cheio; (*meal*) completo; (*price*) total, por inteiro; (*skirt*) rodado □ *adv* **in ~** integralmente. **at ~ speed** a toda velocidade. **to the ~** ao máximo. **be ~ up** (*colloq: after eating*) estar cheio (*colloq*). **~ moon** lua *f* cheia. **~-scale** *a* em grande. **~-size** *a* em tamanho natural. **~ stop** ponto *m* final. **~-time** *a & adv* a tempo integral, full-time. **~y** *adv* completamente

fulsome /'fʊlsəm/ *a* excessivo

fumble /'fʌmbl/ *vi* tatear, (*P*) tactear; (*in the dark*) andar tateando. **~ with** estar atrapalhado com, andar às voltas com

fume /fju:m/ *vi* defumar, (*P*) deitar fumo, fumegar; (*with anger*) ferver. **~s** *npl* gases *mpl*

fumigate /'fju:mɪgeɪt/ *vt* fumigar

fun /fʌn/ *n* divertimento *m*. **for ~** de brincadeira. **make ~ of** zombar de, fazer troça de. **~-fair** *n* parque *m* de diversões, (*P*) feira *f* de diversões, (*P*) feira *f* popular

function /'fʌŋkʃn/ *n* função *f* □ *vi* funcionar. **~al** *a* funcional

fund /fʌnd/ *n* fundos *mpl* □ *vt* financiar

fundamental /fʌndə'mentl/ *a* fundamental

funeral /'fju:nərəl/ *n* enterro *m*, funeral *m* □ *a* fúnebre

fungus /'fʌŋgəs/ *n* (*pl* **-gi** /-gaɪ/) fungo *m*

funnel /'fʌnl/ *n* funil *m*; (*of ship*) chaminé *f*

funn|y /'fʌnɪ/ *a* (**-ier, -iest**) engraçado, divertido; (*odd*) esquisito. **~ily** *adv* comicamente; (*oddly*) estranhamente. **~ily enough** por incrível que pareça

fur /fɜ:(r)/ *n* pêlo *m*; (*for clothing*) pele *f*; (*in kettle*) depósito *m*, crosta *f*. **~ coat** casaco *m* de pele

furious /'fjʊərɪəs/ *a* furioso. **~ly** *adv* furiosamente

furnace /'fɜ:nɪs/ *n* fornalha *f*

furnish /'fɜ:nɪʃ/ *vt* mobiliar, (*P*) mobilar; (*supply*) prover (**with** de). **~ings** *npl* mobiliário *m* e equipamento *m*

furniture /'fɜ:nɪtʃə(r)/ *n* mobília *f*

furrow /'fʌrəʊ/ *n* sulco *m*; (*wrinkle*) ruga *f* □ *vt* sulcar; (*wrinkle*) enrugar

furry /'fɜ:rɪ/ *a* (**-ier, -iest**) peludo; (*toy*) de pelúcia

furth|er /'fɜ:ðə(r)/ *a* mais distante; (*additional*) adicional, suplementar □ *adv* mais longe; (*more*) mais □ *vt* promover. **~er education** ensino *m* supletivo, cursos *mpl* livres, (*P*) educação *f* superior. **~est** *a* o mais distante □ *adv* mais longe

furthermore /fɜ:ðə'mɔ:(r)/ *adv* além disso

furtive /'fɜ:tɪv/ *a* furtivo

fury /'fjʊərɪ/ *n* fúria *f*, furor *m*

fuse[1] /fju:z/ *vt/i* fundir(-se); (*fig*) amalgamar □ *n* fusível *m*. **the lights ~d** os fusíveis queimaram

fuse[2] /fju:z/ *n* (*of bomb*) espoleta *f*

fuselage /'fju:zəla:ʒ/ *n* fuselagem *f*
fusion /'fju:ʒn/ *n* fusão *f*
fuss /fʌs/ *n* história(s) *f* (*pl*), escarcéu *m* □ *vi* preocupar-se com ninharias. **make a ~ of** ligar demasiado para, criar caso com, fazer um espalhafato com. **~y** *a* exigente, complicado
futile /'fju:taɪl/ *a* fútil
future /'fju:tʃə(r)/ *a* & *n* futuro (*m*). **in ~** no futuro, de agora em diante
futuristic /fju:tʃə'rɪstɪk/ *a* futurista, futurístico
fuzz /fʌz/ *n* penugem *f*; (*hair*) cabelo *m* frisado
fuzzy /'fʌzɪ/ *a* (*hair*) frisado; (*photo*) pouco nítido, desfocado

Gg

gab /gæb/ *n* (*colloq*) **have the gift of the ~** ter o dom da palavra
gabble /'gæbl/ *vt/i* tagarelar, falar, ler muito depressa □ *n* tagarelice *f*, algaravia *f*
gable /'geɪbl/ *n* empena *f*, oitão *m*
gad /gæd/ *vi* (*pt* **gadded**) **~ about** (*colloq*) badalar
gadget /'gædʒɪt/ *n* pequeno utensílio *m*; (*fitting*) dispositivo *m*; (*device*) engenhoca *f* (*colloq*)
Gaelic /'geɪlɪk/ *n* galês *m*
gaffe /gæf/ *n* gafe *f*
gag /gæg/ *n* mordaça *f*; (*joke*) gag *m*, piada *f* □ *vt* (*pt* **gagged**) amordaçar
gaiety /'geɪətɪ/ *n* alegria *f*
gaily /'geɪlɪ/ *adv* alegremente
gain /geɪn/ *vt* ganhar □ *vi* (*of clock*) adiantar-se. **~ weight** aumentar de peso. **~ on** (*get closer to*) aproximar-se de □ *n* ganho *m*; (*increase*) aumento *m*. **~ful** *a* lucrativo, proveitoso
gait /geɪt/ *n* (modo de) andar *m*
gala /'ga:lə/ *n* gala *m*; (*sport*) festival *m*
galaxy /'gæləksɪ/ *n* galáxia *f*
gale /geɪl/ *n* vento *m* forte
gall /gɔ:l/ *n* bílis *f*; (*fig*) fel *m*; (*sl*: *impudence*) descaramento *m*, desplante *m*, (*P*) lata *f* (*sl*). **~-bladder** *n* vesícula *f* biliar. **~-stone** *n* cálculo *m* biliar
gallant /'gælənt/ *a* galhardo, valente; (*chivalrous*) galante, cortês. **~ry** *n* galhardia *f*, valentia *f*; (*chivalry*) galanteria *f*, cortesia *f*
gallery /'gælərɪ/ *n* galeria *f*
galley /'gælɪ/ *n* (*pl* **-eys**) galera *f*; (*ship's kitchen*) cozinha *f*
gallivant /gælɪ'vænt/ *vi* (*colloq*) vadiar, (*P*) andar na paródia
gallon /'gælən/ *n* galão *m* (= *4,546 litros; Amer = 3.785 litros*)
gallop /'gæləp/ *n* galope *m* □ *vi* (*pt* **galloped**) galopar
gallows /'gæləʊz/ *npl* forca *f*
galore /gə'lɔ:(r)/ *adv* a beça, em abundância
galvanize /'gælvənaɪz/ *vt* galvanizar
gambit /'gæmbɪt/ *n* gambito *m*
gambl|e /'gæmbl/ *vt/i* jogar □ *n* jogo (de azar) *m*; (*fig*) risco *m*. **~e on** apostar em. **~er** *n* jogador *m*. **~ing** *n* jogo *m* (de azar)
game /geɪm/ *n* jogo *m*; (*football*) desafio *m*; (*animals*) caça *f* □ *a* bravo. **~ for** pronto para
gamekeeper /'geɪmki:pə(r)/ *n* guarda-florestal *m*
gammon /'gæmən/ *n* presunto *m* defumado
gamut /'gæmət/ *n* gama *f*
gang /gæŋ/ *n* bando *m*, gang *m*; (*of workmen*) turma *f*, (*P*) grupo *m* □ *vi* **~ up** ligar-se (**on** contra)
gangling /'gæŋglɪŋ/ *a* desengonçado
gangrene /'gæŋgri:n/ *n* gangrena *f*
gangster /'gæŋstə(r)/ *n* gângster *m*, bandido *m*
gangway /'gæŋweɪ/ *n* passagem *f*; (*aisle*) coxia *f*; (*on ship*) portaló *m*; (*from ship to shore*) passadiço *m*
gaol /dʒeɪl/ *n* & *vt* = **jail**
gap /gæp/ *n* abertura *f*, brecha *f*; (*in time*) intervalo *m*; (*deficiency*) lacuna *f*
gap|e /geɪp/ *vi* ficar boquiaberto *or* embasbacado. **~ing** *a* escancarado
garage /'gæra:ʒ/ *n* garagem *f*; (*service station*) posto *m* de gasolina, (*P*) estação *f* de serviço □ *vt* pôr na garagem
garbage /'ga:bɪdʒ/ *n* lixo *m*. **~ can** (*Amer*) lata *f* do lixo, (*P*) caixote *m* do lixo
garble /'ga:bl/ *vt* deturpar
garden /'ga:dn/ *n* jardim *m* □ *vi* jardinar. **~er** *n* jardineiro *m*. **~ing** *n* jardinagem *f*
gargle /'ga:gl/ *vi* gargarejar □ *n* gargarejo *m*
gargoyle /'ga:gɔɪl/ *n* gárgula *f*
garish /'geərɪʃ/ *a* berrante, espalhafatoso
garland /'ga:lənd/ *n* grinalda *f*
garlic /'ga:lɪk/ *n* alho *m*
garment /'ga:mənt/ *n* peça *f* de vestuário, roupa *f*
garnish /'ga:nɪʃ/ *vt* enfeitar, guarnecer □ *n* guarnição *f*

garrison /'gærɪsn/ *n* guarnição *f* □ *vt* guarnecer
garrulous /'gærələs/ *a* tagarela
garter /'ga:tə(r)/ *n* liga *f*. ~**-belt** *n* (*Amer*) cinta *f* de ligas
gas /gæs/ *n* (*pl* **gases**) gás *m*; (*med*) anestésico *m*; (*Amer colloq: petrol*) gasolina *f* □ *vt* (*pt* **gassed**) asfixiar; (*mil*) gasear □ *vi* (*colloq*) fazer conversa fiada. ~ **fire** aquecedor *m* a gás. ~ **mask** máscara *f* anti-gás. ~ **meter** medidor *m* do gás
gash /gæʃ/ *n* corte *m*, lanho *m* □ *vt* cortar
gasket /'gæskɪt/ *n* junta *f*
gasoline /'gæsəli:n/ *n* (*Amer*) gasolina *f*
gasp /ga:sp/ *vi* arfar, arquejar; (*fig: with rage, surprise*) ficar sem ar □ *n* arquejo *m*
gassy /'gæsɪ/ *a* gasoso; (*full of gas*) cheio de gás
gastric /'gæstrɪk/ *a* gástrico
gastronomy /gæ'strɒnəmɪ/ *n* gastronomia *f*
gate /geɪt/ *n* portão *m*; (*of wood*) cancela *f*; (*barrier*) barreira *f*; (*airport*) porta *f*
gateau /'gætəʊ/ *n* (*pl* ~**x** /-təʊz/) bolo *m* grande com creme
gatecrash /'geɪtkræʃ/ *vt/i* entrar (numa festa) sem convite
gateway /'geɪtweɪ/ *n* (porta de) entrada *f*
gather /'gæðə(r)/ *vt* reunir, juntar; (*pick up, collect*) apanhar; (*amass, pile up*) acumular, juntar; (*conclude*) deduzir; (*cloth*) franzir □ *vi* reunir-se; (*pile up*) acumular-se. ~ **speed** ganhar velocidade. ~**ing** *n* reunião *f*
gaudy /'gɔ:dɪ/ *a* (**-ier, -iest**) (*bright*) berrante; (*showy*) espalhafatoso
gauge /geɪdʒ/ *n* medida *f* padrão; (*device*) indicador *m*; (*railway*) bitola *f* □ *vt* medir, avaliar
gaunt /gɔ:nt/ *a* emagrecido, macilento; (*grim*) lúgubre, desolado
gauntlet /'gɔ:ntlɪt/ *n* **run the** ~ **of** (*fig*) expor-se a. **throw down the** ~ lançar um desafio, (*P*) atirar a luva
gauze /gɔ:z/ *n* gaze *f*
gave /geɪv/ *see* **give**
gawky /'gɔ:kɪ/ *a* (**-ier, -iest**) desajeitado
gay /geɪ/ *a* (**-er, -est**) alegre; (*colloq: homosexual*) homosexual, gay
gaze /geɪz/ *vi* ~ **(at)** olhar fixamente (para) □ *n* contemplação *f*
gazelle /gə'zel/ *n* gazela *f*
GB *abbr of* **Great Britain**
gear /gɪə(r)/ *n* equipamento *m*; (*techn*) engrenagem *f*; (*auto*) velocidade *f* □ *vt* equipar; (*adapt*) adaptar. **in** ~ engrenado. **out of** ~ em ponto morto. ~**-lever** *n* alavanca *f* de mudanças
gearbox /'gɪəbɒks/ *n* caixa *f* de mudança, caixa *f* de transmissão, (*P*) caixa *f* de velocidades
geese /gi:s/ *see* **goose**
gel /dʒel/ *n* geléia *f*, (*P*) geleia *f*
gelatine /'dʒeləti:n/ *n* gelatina *f*
gelignite /'dʒelɪgnaɪt/ *n* gelignite *f*
gem /dʒem/ *n* gema *f*, pedra *f* preciosa
Gemini /'dʒemmaɪ/ *n* (*astr*) Gêmeos *mpl*, (*P*) Gémeos *mpl*
gender /'dʒendə(r)/ *n* gênero *m*, (*P*) género *m*
gene /dʒi:n/ *n* gene *m*
genealogy /dʒi:nɪ'ælədʒɪ/ *n* genealogia *f*
general /'dʒenrəl/ *a* geral □ *n* general *m*. ~ **election** eleições *fpl* legislativas. ~ **practitioner** *n* clínico-geral *m*, (*P*) médico *m* de família. **in** ~ em geral. ~**ly** *adv* geralmente
generaliz|e /'dʒenrəlaɪz/ *vt/i* generalizar. ~**ation** /-'zeɪʃn/ *n* generalização *f*
generate /'dʒenəreɪt/ *vt* gerar, produzir
generation /dʒenə'reɪʃn/ *n* geração *f*
generator /'dʒenəreɪtə(r)/ *n* gerador *m*
gener|ous /'dʒenərəs/ *a* generoso; (*plentiful*) abundante. ~**osity** /-'rɒsətɪ/ *n* generosidade *f*
genetic /dʒɪ'netɪk/ *a* genético. ~**s** *n* genética *f*
genial /'dʒi:nɪəl/ *a* agradável
genital /'dʒenɪtl/ *a* genital. ~**s** *npl* órgãos *mpl* genitais
genius /'dʒi:nɪəs/ *n* (*pl* **-uses**) gênio *m*, (*P*) génio *m*
genocide /'dʒenəsaɪd/ *n* genocídio *m*
gent /dʒent/ *n* **the G**~**s** (*colloq*) banheiros *mpl* de homens, (*P*) lavabos *mpl* para homens
genteel /dʒen'ti:l/ *a* elegante, fino, refinado
gentl|e /'dʒentl/ *a* (~**er**, ~**est**) brando, suave. ~**eness** *n* brandura *f*, suavidade *f*. ~**y** *adv* brandamente, suavemente
gentleman /'dʒentlmən/ *n* (*pl* **-men**) senhor *m*; (*well-bred*) cavalheiro *m*
genuine /'dʒenjʊɪn/ *a* genuíno, verdadeiro; (*belief*) sincero
geograph|y /dʒɪ'ɒgrəfɪ/ *n* geografia *f*. ~**er** *n* geógrafo *m*. ~**ical** /dʒɪə'græfɪkl/ *a* geográfico
geolog|y /dʒɪ'ɒlədʒɪ/ *n* geologia *f*. ~**ical** /dʒɪə'lɒdʒɪkl/ *a* geológico. ~**ist** *n* geólogo *m*
geometr|y /dʒɪ'ɒmətrɪ/ *n* geometria *f*. ~**ic(al)** /dʒɪə'metrɪk(l)/ *a* geométrico
geranium /dʒə'reɪnɪəm/ *n* gerânio *m*
geriatric /dʒerɪ'ætrɪk/ *a* geriátrico
germ /dʒɜ:m/ *n* germe *m*, micróbio *m*

German /'dʒɜ:mən/ *a* & *n* alemão (*m*), alemã (*f*); (*lang*) alemão (*m*). **~ measles** rubéola *f*. **~ic** /dʒə'mænɪk/ *a* germânico. **~y** *n* Alemanha *f*

germinate /'dʒɜ:mmeɪt/ *vi* germinar

gestation /dʒe'steɪʃn/ *n* gestação *f*

gesticulate /dʒe'stɪkjʊleɪt/ *vi* gesticular

gesture /'dʒestʃə(r)/ *n* gesto *m*

get /get/ *vt* (*pt* **got**, *pres p* **getting**) (*have*) ter; (*receive*) receber; (*catch*) apanhar; (*earn, win*) ganhar; (*fetch*) ir buscar; (*find*) achar; (*colloq: understand*) entender. **~ sb to do sth** fazer com que alguém faça alg coisa □ *vi* ir, chegar; (*become*) ficar. **~ married/ready** casar-se/aprontar-se. **~ about** andar dum lado para o outro. **~ across** atravessar. **~ along** *or* **by** (*manage*) ir indo. **~ along** *or* **on with** entender-se com. **~ at** (*reach*) chegar a; (*attack*) atacar; (*imply*) insinuar. **~ away** ir-se embora; (*escape*) fugir. **~ back** *vi* voltar □ *vt* recuperar. **~ by** (*pass*) passar, escapar; (*manage*) aguentar-se. **~ down** descer. **~ in** entrar. **~ off** *vi* descer; (*leave*) partir; (*jur*) ser absolvido □ *vt* (*remove*) tirar. **~ on** (*succeed*) fazer progressos, ir; (*be on good terms*) dar-se bem. **~ out** sair. **~ out of** (*fig*) fugir de. **~ over** (*illness*) restabelecer-se de. **~ round** (*person*) convencer; (*rule*) contornar. **~ up** *vi* levantar-se □ *vt* (*mount*) montar. **~-up** *n* (*colloq*) apresentação *f*

getaway /'getəweɪ/ *n* fuga *f*

geyser /'gi:zə(r)/ *n* aquecedor *m*; (*geol*) gêiser *m*, (*P*) géiser *m*

Ghana /'ga:nə/ *n* Gana *m*

ghastly /'ga:stlɪ/ *a* (**-ier, -iest**) horrível; (*pale*) lívido

gherkin /'gɜ:kɪn/ *n* pepino *m* pequeno para conservas, cornichão *m*

ghetto /'getəʊ/ *n* (*pl* **-os**) gueto *m*, ghetto *m*

ghost /gəʊst/ *n* fantasma *m*, espectro *m*. **~ly** *a* fantasmagórico, espectral

giant /'dʒaɪənt/ *a* & *n* gigante (*m*)

gibberish /'dʒɪbərɪʃ/ *n* algaravia *f*, linguagem *f* incompreensível

gibe /dʒaɪb/ *n* zombaria *f* □ *vi* **~ (at)** zombar (de)

giblets /'dʒɪblɪts/ *npl* miúdos *mpl*, miudezas *fpl*

giddy /'gɪdɪ/ *a* (**-ier, -iest**) estonteante, vertiginoso. **be** *or* **feel ~** ter tonturas *or* vertigens

gift /gɪft/ *n* presente *m*, dádiva *f*; (*ability*) dom *m*, dote *m*. **~-wrap** *vt* (*pt* **-wrapped**) fazer um embrulho de presente

gifted /'gɪftɪd/ *a* dotado

gig /gɪg/ *n* (*colloq*) show *m*, sessão *f* de jazz etc

gigantic /dʒaɪ'gæntɪk/ *a* gigantesco

giggle /'gɪgl/ *vi* dar risadinhas nervosas □ *n* risinho *m* nervoso

gild /gɪld/ *vt* dourar

gills /gɪlz/ *npl* guelras *fpl*

gilt /gɪlt/ *a* & *n* dourado (*m*). **~-edged** *a* de toda a confiança

gimmick /'gɪmɪk/ *n* truque *m*, artifício *m*

gin /dʒɪn/ *n* gin *m*, genebra *f*

ginger /'dʒɪndʒə(r)/ *n* gengibre *m* □ *a* louro-avermelhado, ruivo. **~ ale, ~ beer** cerveja *f* de gengibre, (*P*) ginger ale *m*

gingerbread /'dʒɪndʒəbred/ *n* pão *m* de gengibre

gingerly /'dʒɪndʒəlɪ/ *adv* cautelosamente

gipsy /'dʒɪpsɪ/ *n* = **gypsy**

giraffe /dʒɪ'ra:f/ *n* girafa *f*

girder /'gɜ:də(r)/ *n* trave *f*, viga *f*

girdle /'gɜ:dl/ *n* cinto *m*; (*corset*) cinta *f* □ *vt* rodear

girl /gɜ:l/ *n* (*child*) menina *f*; (*young woman*) moça *f*, (*P*) rapariga *f*. **~-friend** *n* amiga *f*; (*of boy*) namorada *f*. **~hood** *n* (*of child*) meninice *f*; (*youth*) juventude *f*

giro /'dʒaɪrəʊ/ *n* sistema *m* de transferência de crédito entre bancos; (*cheque*) cheque *m* pago pelo governo a desempregados ou doentes

girth /gɜ:θ/ *n* circumferência *f*, perímetro *m*

gist /dʒɪst/ *n* essencial *m*

give /gɪv/ *vt/i* (*pt* **gave**, *pp* **given**) dar; (*bend, yield*) ceder. **~ away** dar; (*secret*) revelar, trair. **~ back** devolver. **~ in** dar-se por vencido, render-se. **~ off** emitir. **~ out** *vt* anunciar □ *vi* esgotar-se. **~ up** *vt/i* desistir (de), renunciar (a). **~ o.s. up** entregar-se. **~ way** ceder; (*traffic*) dar prioridade; (*collapse*) dar de si

given /'gɪvn/ *see* **give** □ *a* dado. **~ name** nome *m* de batismo, (*P*) baptismo

glacier /'glæsɪə(r)/ *n* glaciar *m*, geleira *f*

glad /glæd/ *a* contente. **~ly** *adv* com (todo o) prazer

gladden /'glædn/ *vt* alegrar

glam|our /'glæmə(r)/ *n* fascinação *f*, encanto *m*. **~orize** *vt* tornar fascinante. **~orous** *a* fascinante, sedutor

glance /gla:ns/ *n* relance *m*, olhar *m* □ *vi* **~ at** dar uma olhada a. **at first ~** à primeira vista

gland /glænd/ *n* glândula *f*

glar|e /gleə(r)/ *vi* brilhar intensamente, faiscar □ *n* luz *f* crua; (*fig*) olhar *m* feroz. **~e at** olhar ferozmente para. **~ing** *a* brilhante; (*obvious*) flagrante

glass /gla:s/ *n* vidro *m*; (*vessel, its contents*) copo *m*; (*mirror*) espelho *m*. **~es** óculos *mpl*. **~y** *a* vítreo

glaze /gleɪz/ *vt* (*door etc*) envidraçar; (*pottery*) vidrar □ *n* vidrado *m*

gleam /gli:m/ *n* raio *m* de luz frouxa; (*fig*) vislumbre *m* □ *vi* luzir, brilhar

glean /gli:n/ *vt* catar

glee /gli:/ *n* alegria *f*. **~ful** *a* cheio de alegria

glib /glɪb/ *a* que tem a palavra fácil, verboso. **~ly** *adv* fluentemente, sem hesitação. **~ness** *n* verbosidade *f*

glide /glaɪd/ *vi* deslizar; (*bird, plane*) planar. **~r** /-ə(r)/ *n* planador *m*

glimmer /'glɪmə(r)/ *n* luz *f* trêmula □ *vi* tremular

glimpse /glɪmps/ *n* vislumbre *m*. **catch a ~ of** entrever, ver de relance

glint /glɪnt/ *n* brilho *m*, reflexo *m* □ *vi* brilhar, cintilar

glisten /'glɪsn/ *vi* reluzir

glitter /'glɪtə(r)/ *vi* luzir, resplandecer □ *n* esplendor *m*, cintilação *f*

gloat /gləʊt/ *vi* **~ over** ter um prazer maligno em, exultar com

global /'gləʊbl/ *a* global

globe /gləʊb/ *n* globo *m*

gloom /glu:m/ *n* obscuridade *f*; (*fig*) tristeza *f*. **~y** *a* sombrio; (*sad*) triste; (*pessimistic*) pessimista

glorif|y /'glɔ:rɪfaɪ/ *vt* glorificar. **a ~ied waitress**/*etc* pouco mais que uma garçonete/*etc*

glorious /'glɔ:rɪəs/ *a* glorioso

glory /'glɔ:rɪ/ *n* glória *f*; (*beauty*) esplendor *m* □ *vi* **~ in** orgulhar-se de

gloss /glɒs/ *n* brilho *m* □ *a* brilhante □ *vt* **~ over** minimizar, encobrir. **~y** *a* brilhante

glossary /'glɒsərɪ/ *n* (*pl* **-ries**) glossário *m*

glove /glʌv/ *n* luva *f*. **~ compartment** porta-luvas *m*. **~d** *a* enluvado

glow /gləʊ/ *vi* arder; (*person*) resplandecer □ *n* brasa *f*. **~ing** *a* (*fig*) entusiástico

glucose /'glu:kəʊs/ *n* glucose *f*

glue /glu:/ *n* cola *f* □ *vt* (*pres p* **gluing**) colar

glum /glʌm/ *a* (**glummer, glummest**) sorumbático; (*dejected*) abatido

glut /glʌt/ *n* superabundância *f*

glutton /'glʌtn/ *n* glutão *m*. **~ous** *a* glutão. **~y** *n* gula *f*

GMO /dʒi:ɛm'əʊ/ *n* OGM, organismo *m* geneticamente modificado

gnarled /na:ld/ *a* nodoso

gnash /næʃ/ *vt* **~ one's teeth** ranger os dentes

gnat /næt/ *n* mosquito *m*

gnaw /nɔ:/ *vt*/*i* roer

gnome /nəʊm/ *n* gnomo *m*

go /gəʊ/ *vi* (*pt* **went**, *pp* **gone**) ir; (*leave*) ir, ir-se; (*mech*) andar, funcionar; (*become*) ficar; (*be sold*) vender-se; (*vanish*) ir-se, desaparecer □ *n* (*pl* **goes**) (*energy*) dinamismo *m*; (*try*) tentativa *f*; (*success*) sucesso *m*; (*turn*) vez *f*. **~ riding** ir andar *or* montar a cavalo. **~ shopping** ir às compras. **be ~ing to do** ir fazer. **~ ahead** ir para diante. **~ away** ir-se embora. **~ back** voltar atrás (**on** com). **~ bad** estragar-se. **~ by** (*pass*) passar. **~ down** descer; (*sun*) pôr-se; (*ship*) afundar-se. **~ for** ir buscar; (*like*) gostar de; (*sl: attack*) atirar-se a, irse a (*colloq*). **~ in** entrar. **~ in for** (*exam*) apresentar-se a. **~ off** ir-se; (*explode*) rebentar; (*sound*) soar; (*decay*) estragar-se. **~ on** continuar; (*happen*) acontecer. **~ out** sair; (*light*) apagar-se. **~ over** *or* **through** verificar, examinar. **~ round** (*be enough*) chegar. **~ under** ir abaixo. **~ up** subir. **~ without** passar sem. **on the ~** em grande atividade. **~-ahead** *n* luz *f* verde □ *a* dinâmico, empreendedor. **~-between** *n* intermediário *m*. **~-kart** *n* kart *m*. **~-slow** *n* operação *f* tartaruga, (*P*) greve *f* de zelo

goad /gəʊd/ *vt* aguilhoar, espicaçar

goal /gəʊl/ *n* meta *f*; (*area*) baliza *f*; (*score*) gol *m*, (*P*) golo *m*. **~-post** *n* trave *f*

goalkeeper /'gəʊlki:pə(r)/ *n* goleiro *m*, (*P*) guarda-redes *m*

goat /gəʊt/ *n* cabra *f*

gobble /'gɒbl/ *vt* comer com sofreguidão, devorar

goblet /'gɒblɪt/ *n* taça *f*, cálice *m*

goblin /'gɒblɪn/ *n* duende *m*

God /gɒd/ *n* Deus *m*. **~-forsaken** *a* miserável, abandonado

god /gɒd/ *n* deus *m*. **~-daughter** *n* afilhada *f*. **~dess** *n* deusa *f*. **~father** *n* padrinho *m*. **~ly** *a* devoto. **~mother** *n* madrinha *f*. **~son** *n* afilhado *m*

godsend /'gɒdsend/ *n* achado *m*, dádiva *f* do céu

goggles /'gɒglz/ *npl* óculos *mpl* de proteção, (*P*) protecção

going /'gəʊɪŋ/ *n* **it is slow/hard ~** é demorado/difícil □ *a* (*price, rate*) corrente, atual, (*P*) actual. **~s-on** *npl* acontecimentos *mpl* estranhos

gold /gəʊld/ *n* ouro *m* □ *a* de/em ouro. **~-mine** *n* mina *f* de ouro

golden /'gəʊldən/ *a* de ouro; (*like gold*) dourado; (*opportunity*) único. **~ wedding** bodas *fpl* de ouro

goldfish /'gəʊldfɪʃ/ *n* peixe *m* dourado/vermelho

goldsmith /'gəʊldsmɪθ/ *n* ourives *m inv*

golf /gɒlf/ *n* golfe *m*. ~ **club** clube *m* de golfe, associação *f* de golfe; (*stick*) taco *m*. ~**-course** *n* campo *m* de golfe. ~**er** *n* jogador *m* de golfe

gone /gɒn/ *see* **go** □ *a* ido, passado. ~ **six o'clock** depois das seis

gong /gɒŋ/ *n* gongo *m*

good /gʊd/ *a* (**better, best**) bom □ *n* bem *m*. **as** ~ **as** praticamente. **for** ~ para sempre. **it is no** ~ não adianta. **it is no** ~ **shouting**/*etc* não adianta gritar/*etc*. ~ **afternoon** *int* boa(s) tarde(s). ~ **evening/night** *int* boa(s) noite(s). **G**~ **Friday** Sexta-feira *f* Santa. ~**-looking** *a* bonito. ~ **morning** *int* **bom dia.** ~ **name** bom nome *m*

goodbye /gʊd'baɪ/ *int & n* adeus (*m*)

goodness /'gʊdnɪs/ *n* bondade *f*. **my** ~**ness!** meu Deus!

goods /gʊdz/ *npl* (*comm*) mercadorias *fpl*. ~ **train** trem *m* de carga, (*P*) comboio *m* de mercadorias

goodwill /gʊd'wɪl/ *n* boa vontade *f*

goose /gu:s/ *n* (*pl* **geese**) ganso *m*. ~**-flesh,** ~**-pimples** *ns* pele *f* de galinha

gooseberry /'gʊzbərɪ/ *n* (*fruit*) groselha *f*; (*bush*) groselheira *f*

gore[1] /gɔ:(r)/ *n* sangue *m* coagulado

gore[2] /gɔ:(r)/ *vt* perfurar

gorge /gɔ:dʒ/ *n* desfiladeiro *m*, garganta *f* □ *vt* ~ **o.s.** empanturrar-se

gorgeous /'gɔ:dʒəs/ *a* magnífico, maravilhoso

gorilla /gə'rɪlə/ *n* gorila *m*

gormless /'gɔ:mlɪs/ *a* (*sl*) estúpido

gorse /gɔ:s/ *n* giesta *f*, tojo *m*, urze *f*

gory /'gɔ:rɪ/ *a* (**-ier, -iest**) sangrento

gosh /gɒʃ/ *int* puxa!, (*P*) caramba!

gospel /'gɒspl/ *n* evangelho *m*

gossip /'gɒsɪp/ *n* bisbilhotice *f*, fofoca *f*; (*person*) bisbilhoteiro *m*, fofoqueiro *m* □ *vi* (*pt* **gossiped**) bisbilhotar. ~**y** *a* bisbilhoteiro, fofoqueiro

got /gɒt/ *see* **get. have** ~ ter. **have** ~ **to do** ter de *or* que fazer

Gothic /'gɒθɪk/ *a* gótico

gouge /gaʊdʒ/ *vt* ~ **out** arrancar

gourmet /'gʊəmeɪ/ *n* gastrônomo *m*, (*P*) gastrónomo *m*, gourmet *m*

gout /gaʊt/ *n* gota *f*

govern /'gʌvn/ *vt/i* governar. ~**ess** *n* preceptora *f*. ~**or** *n* governador *m*; (*of school, hospital etc*) diretor *m*, (*P*) director *m*

government /'gʌvənmənt/ *n* governo *m*. ~**al** /-'mentl/ *a* governamental

gown /gaʊn/ *n* vestido *m*; (*of judge, teacher*) toga *f*

GP *abbr see* **general practitioner**

grab /græb/ *vt* (*pt* **grabbed**) agarrar, apanhar

grace /greɪs/ *n* graça *f* □ *vt* honrar; (*adorn*) ornar. **say** ~ dar graças. ~**ful** *a* gracioso

gracious /'greɪʃəs/ *a* gracioso; (*kind*) amável, afável

grade /greɪd/ *n* categoria *f*; (*of goods*) classe *f*, qualidade *f*; (*on scale*) grau *m*; (*school mark*) nota *f* □ *vt* classificar

gradient /'greɪdɪənt/ *n* gradiente *m*, declive *m*

gradual /'grædʒʊəl/ *a* gradual, progressivo. ~**ly** *adv* gradualmente

graduate[1] /'grædʒʊət/ *n* diplomado *m*, graduado *m*, licenciado *m*

graduat|e[2] /'grædʒʊeɪt/ *vt/i* formar(-se). ~**ion** /-'eɪʃn/ *n* colação *f* de grau, (*P*) formatura *f*

graffiti /grə'fi:ti:/ *npl* graffiti *mpl*

graft /gra:ft/ *n* (*med, bot*) enxerto *m*; (*work*) batalha *f* □ *vt* enxertar; (*work*) batalhar

grain /greɪn/ *n* grão *m*; (*collectively*) cereais *mpl*; (*in wood*) veio *m*. **against the** ~ (*fig*) contra a maneira de ser

gram /græm/ *n* grama *m*

gramm|ar /'græmə(r)/ *n* gramática *f*. ~**atical** /grə'mætɪkl/ *a* gramatical

grand /grænd/ *a* (**-er, -est**) grandioso, magnífico; (*duke, master*) grão. ~ **piano** piano *m* de cauda.

grand|child /'grændtʃaɪld/ *n* (*pl* **-children**) neto *m*. ~**daughter** *n* neta *f*. ~**father** *n* avô *m*. ~**- mother** *n* avó *f*. ~**parents** *npl* avós *mpl*. ~**son** *n* neto *m*

grandeur /'grændʒə(r)/ *n* grandeza *f*

grandiose /'grændɪəʊs/ *a* grandioso

grandstand /'grændstænd/ *n* tribuna *f* principal

granite /'grænɪt/ *n* granito *m*

grant /gra:nt/ *vt* conceder; (*a request*) ceder a; (*admit*) admitir (**that** que) □ *n* subsídio *m*; (*univ*) bolsa *f*. **take for** ~**ed** ter como coisa garantida, contar com

grape /greɪp/ *n* uva *f*

grapefruit /'greɪpfru:t/ *n inv* grapefruit *m*, toronja *f*

graph /gra:f/ *n* gráfico *m*

graphic /'græfɪk/ *a* gráfico; (*fig*) vívido. ~**s** *npl* (*comput*) gráficos *mpl*

grapple /'græpl/ *vi* ~ **with** estar engalfinhado com; (*fig*) estar às voltas com

grasp /gra:sp/ *vt* agarrar; (*understand*) compreender □ *n* domínio *m*; (*reach*) alcance *m*; (*fig: understanding*) compreensão *f*

grasping /'gra:spɪŋ/ *a* ganancioso

grass /gra:s/ *n* erva *f*; (*lawn*) grama *f*, (*P*) relva *f*; (*pasture*) pastagem *f*; (*sl*:

informer) delator *m* ◻ *vt* cobrir com grama; (*sl*: *betray*) delatar. ~ **roots** (*pol*) bases *fpl*. ~**y** *a* coberto de erva

grasshopper /'gra:shɒpə(r)/ *n* gafanhoto *m*

grate[1] /greɪt/ *n* (*fireplace*) lareira *f*; (*frame*) grelha *f*

grate[2] /greɪt/ *vt* ralar ◻ *vi* ranger. ~ **one's teeth** ranger os dentes. ~**r** /-ə(r)/ *n* ralador *m*

grateful /'greɪtfl/ *a* grato, agradecido. ~**ly** *adv* com reconhecimento, com gratidão

gratify /'grætɪfaɪ/ *vt* (*pt* **-fied**) contentar, satisfazer. ~**ing** *a* gratificante

grating /'greɪtɪŋ/ *n* grade *f*

gratis /'greɪtɪs/ *a* & *adv* grátis (*invar*), de graça

gratitude /'grætɪtju:d/ *n* gratidão *f*, reconhecimento *m*

gratuitous /grə'tju:ɪtəs/ *a* gratuito; (*uncalled-for*) sem motivo

gratuity /grə'tju:ətɪ/ *n* gratificação *f*, gorjeta *f*

grave[1] /greɪv/ *n* cova *f*, sepultura *f*, túmulo *m*

grave[2] /greɪv/ *a* (**-er, -est**) grave, sério. ~**ly** *adv* gravemente

grave[3] /gra:v/ *a* ~ **accent** acento *m* grave

gravel /'grævl/ *n* cascalho *m* miúdo, saibro *m*

gravestone /'greɪvstəʊn/ *n* lápide *f*, campa *f*

graveyard /'greɪvja:d/ *n* cemitério *m*

gravity /'grævətɪ/ *n* gravidade *f*

gravy /'greɪvɪ/ *n* molho *m* (de carne)

graze[1] /greɪz/ *vt*/*i* pastar

graze[2] /greɪz/ *vt* roçar; (*scrape*) esfolar ◻ *n* esfoladura *f*, (*P*) esfoladela *f*

greas|e /gri:s/ *n* gordura *f* ◻ *vt* engordurar; (*culin*) untar; (*mech*) lubrificar. ~**e-proof paper** papel *m* vegetal. ~**y** *a* gorduroso

great /greɪt/ *a* (**-er, -est**) grande; (*colloq: splendid*) esplêndido. **G**~ **Britain** Grã-Bretanha *f*. ~**-grandfather** *n* bisavô *m*. ~**-grandmother** *f* bisavó *f*. ~**ly** *adv* grandemente, muito. ~**- ness** *n* grandeza *f*

Great Britain /greɪt'brɪtən/ *n* Grã-Bretanha *f*

Greece /gri:s/ *n* Grécia *f*

greed /gri:d/ *n* cobiça *f*, ganância *f*; (*for food*) gula *f*. ~**y** *a* cobiçoso, ganancioso; (*for food*) guloso

Greek /gri:k/ *a* & *n* grego (*m*)

green /gri:n/ *a* (**-er, -est**) verde ◻ *n* verde *m*; (*grass*) gramado *m*, (*P*) relvado *m*. ~**s** hortaliças *fpl*. ~ **belt** zona *f* verde, paisagem *f* protegida. ~ **light** luz *f* verde. ~**ery** *n* verdura *f*

greengrocer /'gri:ngrəʊsə(r)/ *n* quitandeiro *m*, (*P*) vendedor *m* de hortaliças

greenhouse /'gri:nhaʊs/ *n* estufa *f*. ~ **effect** efeito estufa

Greenland /'gri:nlənd/ *n* Groenlândia *f*

greet /gri:t/ *vt* acolher. ~**ing** *n* saudação *f*; (*welcome*) acolhimento *m*. ~**ings** *npl* cumprimentos *mpl*; (*Christmas etc*) votos *mpl*, desejos *mpl*

gregarious /grɪ'geərɪəs/ *a* gregário; (*person*) sociável

grenade /grɪ'neɪd/ *n* granada *f*

grew /gru:/ *see* **grow**

grey /greɪ/ *a* (**-er, -est**) cinzento; (*of hair*) grisalho ◻ *n* cinzento *m*

greyhound /'greɪhaʊnd/ *n* galgo *m*

grid /grɪd/ *n* (*grating*) gradeamento *m*, grade *f*; (*electr*) rede *f*

grief /gri:f/ *n* dor *f*. **come to** ~ acabar mal

grievance /'gri:vns/ *n* razão *f* de queixa

grieve /gri:v/ *vt* sofrer, afligir ◻ *vi* sofrer. ~ **for** chorar por

grill /grɪl/ *n* grelha *f*; (*food*) grelhado *m*; (*place*) grill *m* ◻ *vt* grelhar; (*question*) submeter a interrogatório cerrado, apertar com perguntas ◻ *vi* grelhar

grille /grɪl/ *n* grade *f*; (*of car*) grelha *f*

grim /grɪm/ *a* (**grimmer, grimmest**) sinistro; (*without mercy*) implacável

grimace /grɪ'meɪs/ *n* careta *f* ◻ *vi* fazer careta(s)

grim|e /graɪm/ *n* sujeira *f*. ~**y** *a* encardido, sujo

grin /grɪn/ *vi* (*pt* **grinned**) sorrir abertamente, dar um sorriso largo ◻ *n* sorriso *m* aberto

grind /graɪnd/ *vt* (*pt* **ground**) triturar; (*coffee*) moer; (*sharpen*) amolar, afiar. ~ **one's teeth** ranger os dentes. ~ **to a halt** parar freando lentamente

grip /grɪp/ *vt* (*pt* **gripped**) agarrar; (*interest*) prender ◻ *n* (*of hands*) aperto *m*; (*control*) controle *m*, domínio *m*. **come to** ~**s with** arcar com. ~**ping** *a* apaixonante

grisly /'grɪzlɪ/ *a* (**-ier, -iest**) macabro, horrível

gristle /'grɪsl/ *n* cartilagem *f*

grit /grɪt/ *n* areia *f*, grão *m* de areia; (*fig: pluck*) coragem *f*, fortaleza *f* ◻ *vt* (*pt* **gritted**) (*road*) jogar areia em; (*teeth*) cerrar

groan /grəʊn/ *vi* gemer ◻ *n* gemido *m*

grocer /'grəʊsə(r)/ *n* dono/a *m*/*f* de mercearia. ~**ies** *npl* artigos *mpl* de mercearia. ~**y** *n* (*shop*) mercearia *f*

groggy /'grɒgɪ/ *a* (**-ier, -iest**) grogue, fraco das pernas

groin /grɔɪn/ *n* virilha *f*

groom /gru:m/ *n* noivo *m*; (*for horses*) moço *m* de estrebaria ▫ *vt* (*horse*) tratar de; (*fig*) preparar
groove /gru:v/ *n* ranhura *f*; (*for door, window*) calha *f*; (*in record*) estria *f*; (*fig*) rotina *f*
grope /grəʊp/ *vi* tatear. ~ **for** procurar às cegas
gross /grəʊs/ *a* (**-er, -est**) (*vulgar*) grosseiro; (*flagrant*) flagrante; (*of error*) crasso; (*of weight, figure etc*) bruto ▫ *n* (*pl invar*) grosa *f*. ~**ly** *adv* grosseiramente; (*very*) extremamente
grotesque /grəʊ'tesk/ *a* grotesco
grotty /'grɒtɪ/ *a* (*sl*) sórdido
grouch /graʊtʃ/ *vi* (*colloq*) ralhar. ~**y** *a* (*colloq*) rabugento
ground[1] /graʊnd/ *n* chão *m*, solo *m*; (*area*) terreno *m*; (*reason*) razão *f*, motivo *m*. ~**s** jardins *mpl*; (*of coffee*) borra(s) *f*(*pl*) ▫ *vt/i* (*naut*) encalhar; (*plane*) reter em terra. ~ **floor** térreo *m*, (*P*) rés-do-chão *m*. ~**less** *a* infundado, sem fundamento
ground[2] /graʊnd/ *see* **grind**
grounding /'graʊndɪŋ/ *n* bases *fpl*, conhecimentos *mpl* básicos
groundsheet /'graʊndʃi:t/ *n* impermeável *m* para o chão
groundwork /'graʊndwɜ:k/ *n* trabalhos *mpl* de base *or* preliminares
group /gru:p/ *n* grupo *m* ▫ *vt/i* agrupar(-se)
grouse[1] /graʊs/ *n* (*pl invar*) galo *m* silvestre
grouse[2] /graʊs/ *vi* (*colloq: grumble*) resmungar; (*colloq: complain*) queixar-se
grovel /'grɒvl/ *vi* (*pt* **grovelled**) humilhar-se; (*fig*) rebaixar-se
grow /grəʊ/ *vi* (*pt* **grew**, *pp* **grown**) crescer; (*become*) tornar-se ▫ *vt* cultivar. ~ **old** envelhecer. ~ **up** crescer, tornar-se adulto. ~**er** *n* cultivador *m*, produtor *m*. ~**ing** *a* crescente
growl /graʊl/ *vi* rosnar ▫ *n* rosnadela *f*
grown /grəʊn/ *see* **grow** ▫ *a* ~ **man** homem feito. ~**-up** *a* adulto ▫ *n* pessoa *f* adulta
growth /grəʊθ/ *n* crescimento *m*; (*increase*) aumento *m*; (*med*) tumor *m*
grub /grʌb/ *n* larva *f*; (*sl: food*) bóia *f*, rango *m*, (*P*) comida *f*
grubby /'grʌbɪ/ *a* (**-ier, -iest**) sujo, porco
grudge /grʌdʒ/ *vt* dar/reconhecer de má vontade ▫ *n* má vontade *f*. ~ **doing** fazer de má vontade. ~ **sb sth** dar alg a alguém má vontade. **have a ~ against** ter ressentimento contra. **grudgingly** *adv* relutantemente
gruelling /'gru:əlɪŋ/ *a* estafante, extenuante
gruesome /'gru:səm/ *a* macabro
gruff /grʌf/ *a* (**-er, -est**) carrancudo, rude
grumble /'grʌmbl/ *vi* resmungar (**at** contra, por)
grumpy /'grʌmpɪ/ *a* (**-ier, -iest**) mal-humorado, rabugento
grunt /grʌnt/ *vi* grunhir ▫ *n* grunhido *m*
guarantee /gærən'ti:/ *n* garantia *f* ▫ *vt* garantir
guard /ga:d/ *vt* guardar, proteger ▫ *vi* ~ **against** precaver-se contra ▫ *n* guarda *f*; (*person*) guarda *m*; (*on train*) condutor *m*. ~**ian** *n* guardião *m*, defensor *m*; (*of orphan*) tutor *m*
guarded /'ga:dɪd/ *a* cauteloso, circunspeto, (*P*) circunspecto
guerrilla /gə'rɪlə/ *n* guerrilheiro *m*, (*P*) guerrilha *m*. ~ **warfare** guerrilha *f*, guerra *f* de guerrilhas
guess /ges/ *vt/i* adivinhar; (*suppose*) supor ▫ *n* suposição *f*, conjetura *f*, (*P*) conjectura *f*
guesswork /'geswɜ:k/ *n* suposição *f*, conjetura(s) *f*(*pl*), (*P*) conjectura(s) *f*(*pl*)
guest /gest/ *n* convidado *m*; (*in hotel*) hóspede *mf*. ~**-house** *n* pensão *f*
guffaw /gə'fɔ:/ *n* gargalhada *f* ▫ *vi* rir à(s) gargalhada(s)
guidance /'gaɪdns/ *n* orientação *f*, direção *f*, (*P*) direcção *f*
guide /gaɪd/ *n* guia *mf* ▫ *vt* guiar. ~**d missile** míssil *m* guiado; (*remote-control*) míssil *m* teleguiado. ~**-dog** *n* cão *m* de cego, cão-guia *m*. ~**-lines** *npl* diretrizes *fpl*, (*P*) directrizes *fpl*
Guide /gaɪd/ *n* Guia *f*
guidebook /'gaɪdbʊk/ *n* guia *m* (turístico)
guild /gɪld/ *n* corporação *f*
guile /gaɪl/ *n* astúcia *f*, manha *f*
guilt /gɪlt/ *n* culpa *f*. ~**y** *a* culpado
guinea-pig /'gɪnɪpɪg/ *n* cobaia *f*, porquinho-da-India *m*
guitar /gɪ'ta:(r)/ *n* guitarra *f*, violão *m*, (*P*) viola *f*. ~**ist** *n* guitarrista *mf*, tocador *m* de violão, (*P*) de viola
gulf /gʌlf/ *n* golfo *m*; (*hollow*) abismo *m*
gull /gʌl/ *n* gaivota *f*
gullible /'gʌləbl/ *a* crédulo
gully /'gʌlɪ/ *n* barranco *m*; (*drain*) sarjeta *f*
gulp /gʌlp/ *vt* engolir, devorar ▫ *vi* engolir em seco ▫ *n* trago *m*
gum[1] /gʌm/ *n* (*anat*) gengiva *f*
gum[2] /gʌm/ *n* goma *f*; (*chewing-gum*) chiclete *m*, goma *f* elástica, (*P*) pastilha *f* ▫ *vt* (*pt* **gummed**) colar
gumboot /'gʌmbu:t/ *n* bota *f* de borracha

gumption /ˈgʌmpʃn/ *n* (*colloq*) iniciativa *f* e bom senso *m*, cabeça *f*, juizo *m*
gun /gʌn/ *n* (*pistol*) pistola *f*; (*rifle*) espingarda *f*; (*cannon*) canhão *m* □ *vt* (*pt* **gunned**) **~ down** abater a tiro
gunfire /ˈgʌnfaɪə(r)/ *n* tiroteio *m*
gunman /ˈgʌnmən/ *n* (*pl* **-men**) bandido *m* armado
gunpowder /ˈgʌnpaʊdə(r)/ *n* pólvora *f*
gunshot /ˈgʌnʃɒt/ *n* tiro *m*
gurgle /ˈgɜ:gl/ *n* gorgolejo *m* □ *vi* gorgolejar
gush /gʌʃ/ *vi* jorrar □ *n* jorro *m*. **~ing** *a* efusivo, derretido
gust /gʌst/ *n* (*of wind*) rajada *f*; (*of smoke*) nuvem *f*. **~y** *a* ventoso
gusto /ˈgʌstəʊ/ *n* gosto *m*, entusiasmo *m*
gut /gʌt/ *n* tripa *f*. **~s** (*belly*) barriga *f*; (*colloq: courage*) coragem *f* □ *vt* (*pt* **gutted**) estripar; (*fish*) limpar; (*fire*) destruir o interior de
gutter /ˈgʌtə(r)/ *n* calha *f*, canaleta *f*; (*in street*) sarjeta *f*, valeta *f*
guy /gaɪ/ *n* (*sl: man*) cara *m*, (*P*) tipo *m* (*colloq*)
guzzle /ˈgʌzl/ *vt/i* comer/beber com sofreguidão, encher-se (de)
gym /dʒɪm/ *n* (*colloq: gymnasium*) ginásio *m*; (*colloq: gymnastics*) ginástica *f*. **~-slip** *n* uniforme *m* escolar
gym|nasium /dʒɪmˈneɪzɪəm/ *n* ginásio *m*. **~nast** /ˈdʒɪmnæst/ *n* ginasta *mf*. **~nastics** /-ˈnæstɪks/ *npl* ginástica *f*
gynaecolog|y /gaɪnɪˈkɒlədʒɪ/ *n* ginecologia *f*. **~ist** *n* ginecologista *mf*
gypsy /ˈdʒɪpsɪ/ *n* cigano *m*
gyrate /dʒaɪˈreɪt/ *vi* girar

Hh

haberdashery /ˈhæbədæʃərɪ/ *n* armarinho *m*, (*P*) retrosaria *f*
habit /ˈhæbɪt/ *n* hábito *m*, costume *m*; (*costume*) hábito *m*. **be in/get into the ~ of** ter/apanhar o hábito de
habit|able /ˈhæbɪtəbl/ *a* habitável. **~ation** /-ˈteɪʃn/ *n* habitação *f*
habitat /ˈhæbɪtæt/ *n* habitat *m*
habitual /həˈbɪtʃʊəl/ *a* habitual, costumeiro; (*smoker, liar*) inveterado. **~ly** *adv* habitualmente
hack[1] /hæk/ *n* (*horse*) cavalo *m* de aluguel; (*writer*) escrevinhador (*pej*) *m*. **~er** (*comput*) micreiro *m*
hack[2] /hæk/ *vt* cortar, despedaçar. **~ to pieces** cortar em pedaços
hackneyed /ˈhæknɪd/ *a* banal, batido
had /hæd/ *see* **have**
haddock /ˈhædək/ *n invar* hadoque *m*, eglefim *m*. **smoked ~** hadoque *m* fumado
haemorrhage /ˈhemərɪdʒ/ *n* hemorragia *f*
haemorrhoids /ˈhemərɔɪdz/ *npl* hemorróidas *fpl*
haggard /ˈhægəd/ *a* desfigurado, com o rosto desfeito, magro e macilento
haggle /ˈhægl/ *vi* **~ (over)** regatear
hail[1] /heɪl/ *vt* saudar; (*taxi*) fazer sinal para, chamar □ *vi* **~ from** vir de
hail[2] /heɪl/ *n* granizo *m*, (*P*) saraiva *f*, (*P*) chuva de pedra *f* □ *vi* chover granizo, (*P*) saraivar
hailstone /ˈheɪlstəʊn/ *n* pedra *f* de granizo
hair /heə(r)/ *n* (*on head*) cabelo(s) *m*(*pl*); (*on body*) pêlos *mpl*; (*single strand*) cabelo *m*; (*of animal*) pêlo *m*. **~-do** *n* (*colloq*) penteado *m*. **~-dryer** *n* secador *m* de cabelo. **~-raising** *a* horripilante, de pôr os cabelos em pé. **~-style** *n* estilo *m* de penteado
hairbrush /ˈheəbrʌʃ/ *n* escova *f* para o cabelo
haircut /ˈheəkʌt/ *n* corte *m* de cabelo
hairdresser /ˈheədresə(r)/ *n* cabeleireiro *m*, cabeleireira *f*
hairpin /ˈheəpɪn/ *n* grampo *m*, (*P*) gancho *m* para o cabelo. **~ bend** curva *f* fechada, quase em W
hairy /ˈheərɪ/ *a* (**-ier**, **-iest**) peludo, cabeludo; (*sl: terrifying*) de pôr os cabelos em pé, horripilante
hake /heɪk/ *n* (*pl invar*) abrótea *f*
half /ha:f/ *n* (*pl* **halves** /ha:vz/) metade *f*, meio *m* □ *a* meio □ *adv* ao meio. **~ a dozen** meia dúzia. **~ an hour** meia hora. **~-caste** *n* mestiço *m*. **~-hearted** *a* sem grande entusiasmo. **~-term** *n* férias *fpl* no meio do trimestre. **~-time** *n* meio-tempo *m*. **~-way** *a* & *adv* a meio caminho. **~-wit** *n* idiota *mf*. **go halves** dividir as despesas
halibut /ˈhælɪbət/ *n* (*pl invar*) halibute *m*
hall /hɔ:l/ *n* sala *f*; (*entrance*) vestíbulo *m*, entrada *f*; (*mansion*) solar *m*. **~ of residence** resi-dência *f* de estudantes
hallmark /ˈhɔ:lma:k/ *n* (*on gold etc*) marca *f* do contraste; (*fig*) cunho *m*, selo *m*
hallo /həˈləʊ/ *int* & *n* (*greeting, surprise*) olá; (*on phone*) está
hallow /ˈhæləʊ/ *vt* consagrar, santificar
Halloween /hæləʊˈi:n/ *n* véspera *f* do Dia de Todos os Santos

hallucination /həlu:sɪ'neɪʃn/ *n* alucinação *f*

halo /'heɪləʊ/ *n* (*pl* **-oes**) halo *m*, auréola *f*

halt /hɔ:lt/ *n* parada *f*, (*P*) paragem *f* ▫ *vt* deter, fazer parar ▫ *vi* fazer alto, parar

halve /ha:v/ *vt* dividir ao meio; (*time etc*) reduzir à metade

ham /hæm/ *n* presunto *m*

hamburger /'hæmbɜ:gə(r)/ *n* hambúrguer *m*, (*P*) hamburgo *m*

hamlet /'hæmlɪt/ *n* aldeola *f*, lugarejo *m*

hammer /'hæmə(r)/ *n* martelo *m* ▫ *vt/i* martelar; (*fig*) bater com força

hammock /'hæmək/ *n* rede *f* (de dormir)

hamper[1] /'hæmpə(r)/ *n* cesto *m*, (*P*) cabaz *m*

hamper[2] /'hæmpə(r)/ *vt* dificultar, atrapalhar

hamster /'hæmstə(r)/ *n* hamster *m*

hand /hænd/ *n* mão *f*; (*of clock*) ponteiro *m*; (*writing*) letra *f*; (*worker*) trabalhador *m*; (*cards*) mão *f*; (*measure*) palmo *m*. **(helping)** ~ ajuda *f*, mão *f* ▫ *vt* dar, entregar. **at** ~ à mão. **~-baggage** *n* bagagem *f* de mão. **~ in** *or* **over** entregar. **~ out** distribuir. **~-out** *n* impresso *m*, folheto *m*; (*money*) esmola *f*, donativo *m*. **on the one ~ . . . on the other ~** por um lado . . . por outro. **out of ~** incontrolável. **to ~** à mão

handbag /'hændbæg/ *n* carteira *f*, bolsa de mão *f*, mala de mão *f*

handbook /'hændbʊk/ *n* manual *m*

handbrake /'hændbreɪk/ *n* freio *m* de mão, (*P*) travão *m* de mão

handcuffs /'hændkʌfs/ *npl* algemas *fpl*

handful /'hændfʊl/ *n* mão-cheia *f*, punhado *m*; (*a few*) punhado *m*; (*difficult task*) mão-de-obra *f*. **she's a ~** (*colloq*) ela é danada

handicap /'hændɪkæp/ *n* (*in competition*) handicap *m*; (*disadvantage*) desvantagem *f* ▫ *vt* (*pt* **handicapped**) prejudicar. **~ped** *a* deficiente. **mentally ~ped** deficiente mental

handicraft /'hændɪkra:ft/ *n* artesanato *m*, trabalho *m* manual

handiwork /'hændɪwɜ:k/ *n* obra *f*, trabalho *m*

handkerchief /'hæŋkətʃɪf/ *n* lenço *m*

handle /'hændl/ *n* (*of door etc*) maçaneta *f*, puxador *m*; (*of cup etc*) asa *f*; (*of implement*) cabo *m*; (*of pan etc*) alça *f*, (*P*) pega *f* ▫ *vt* (*touch*) manusear, tocar; (*operate with hands*) manejar; (*deal in*) negociar em; (*deal with*) tratar de; (*person*) lidar com. **fly off the ~** (*colloq*) perder as estribeiras

handlebar /'hændlba:(r)/ *n* guidão *m*, (*P*) guidador *m*

handmade /'hændmeɪd/ *a* feito à mão

handshake /'hændʃeɪk/ *n* aperto *m* de mão

handsome /'hænsəm/ *a* bonito; (*fig*) generoso

handwriting /'hændraɪtɪŋ/ *n* letra *f*, caligrafia *f*

handy /'hændɪ/ *a* (**-ier, -iest**) *a* (*convenient, useful*) útil, prático; (*person*) jeitoso; (*near*) à mão

handyman /'hændɪmæn/ *n* (*pl* **-men**) faz-tudo *m*

hang /hæŋ/ *vt* (*pt* **hung**) pendurar, suspender; (*head*) baixar; (*pt* **hanged**) (*criminal*) *enforcar* ▫ *vi estar dependurado, pender; (criminal) ser enforcado.* **get the ~ of** (*colloq*) pegar o jeito de, (*P*) apanhar. **~ about** andar por aí. **~ back** hesitar. **~-gliding** *n* asa *f* delta. **~ on** (*wait*) aguardar. **~ on to** (*hold tightly*) agarrar-se a. **~ out** (*sl*: *live*) morar. **~ up** (*phone*) desligar. **~-up** *n* (*sl*) complexo *m*

hangar /'hæŋə(r)/ *n* hangar *m*

hanger /'hæŋə(r)/ *n* (*for clothes*) cabide *m*. **~-on** *n* parasita *mf*

hangover /'hæŋəʊvə(r)/ *n* (*from drinking*) ressaca *f*

hanker /'hæŋkə(r)/ *vi* **~ after** ansiar por, suspirar por

haphazardly /hæp'hæzədlɪ/ *adv ao acaso, à sorte, a fortuito, casual*

happen /'hæpən/ *vi* acontecer, suceder. **he ~s to be out** por acaso ele não está. **~ing** *n* acontecimento *m*

happ|y /'hæpɪ/ *a* (**-ier, -iest**) feliz. **be ~y with** estar contente com. **~y-go-lucky** *a* despreocupado. **~ily** *adv* com satisfação; (*fortunately*) felizmente. **she smiled ~ily** ela sorriu feliz. **~iness** *n* felicidade *f*

harass /'hærəs/ *vt* amofinar, atormentar, perseguir. **~ment** *n* amofinação *f*, perseguição *f*. **sexual ~ment** assédio *m* sexual

harbour /'ha:bə(r)/ *n* porto *m*; (*shelter*) abrigo *m* ▫ *vt* abrigar, dar asilo a; (*fig: in the mind*) ocultar, obrigar

hard /ha:d/ *a* (**-er, -est**) duro; (*difficult*) difícil ▫ *adv* muito, intensamente; (*look*) fixamente; (*pull*) com força; (*think*) a fundo, a sério. **~back** *n* livro *m* encadernado. **~-boiled egg** ovo *m* cozido. **~ by** muito perto. **~ disk** disco *m* rígido, (*P*) duro. **~-headed** *a* realista, prático. **~ of hearing** meio surdo. **~ shoulder** acostamento *m*, (*P*) berma *f* alcatroada. **~ up** (*colloq*) sem dinheiro, teso (*sl*), liso (*sl*). **~ water** água *f* dura

hardboard /'ha:dbɔ:d/ *n* madeira *f* compensada, madeira *f* prensada, (*P*) tabopan *m*

harden /'ha:dn/ *vt/i* endurecer. **~ed** *a* (*callous*) calejado; (*robust*) enrijado

hardly /'ha:dlɪ/ *adv* mal, dificilmente, a custo. **~ ever** quase nunca

hardship /'ha:dʃɪp/ *n* provação *f*, adversidade *f*; (*suffering*) sofrimento *m*; (*financial*) privação *f*

hardware /'ha:dweə(r)/ *n* ferragens *fpl*; (*comput*) hardware *m*

hardy /'ha:dɪ/ *a* (**-ier**, **-iest**) resistente

hare /heə(r)/ *n* lebre *f*

hark /ha:k/ *vi* **~ back to** voltar a, recordar

harm /ha:m/ *n* mal *m* □ *vt* prejudicar, fazer mal a. **~ful** *a* prejudicial, nocivo. **~less** *a* inofen-sivo. **out of ~'s way** a salvo. **there's no ~ in** não há mal em

harmonica /ha:'mɒnɪkə/ *n* gaita *f* de boca, (*P*) beiços

harmon|y /'ha:mənɪ/ *n* harmonia *f*. **~ious** /-'məʊnɪəs/ *a* harmonioso. **~ize** *vt/i* harmonizar(-se)

harness /'ha:nɪs/ *n* arreios *mpl* □ *vt* arrear; (*fig: use*) aproveitar, utilizar

harp /ha:p/ *n* harpa *f* □ *vi* **~ on (about)** repisar. **~ ist** *n* harpista *mf*

harpoon /ha:'pu:n/ *n* arpão *m*

harpsichord /'ha:psɪkɔ:d/ *n* cravo *m*

harrowing /'hærəʊɪŋ/ *a* dilacerante, lancinante

harsh /ha:ʃ/ *a* (**-er**, **-est**) duro, severo; (*texture, voice*) áspero; (*light*) cru; (*colour*) gritante; (*climate*) rigoroso. **~ly** *adv* duramente. **~ness** *n* dureza *f*

harvest /'ha:vɪst/ *n* colheita *f*, ceifa *f* □ *vt* colher, ceifar

has /hæz/ *see* **have**

hash /hæʃ/ *n* picadinho *m*, carne *f* cozida; (*fig: jumble*) bagunça *f*. **make a ~ of** fazer uma bagunça

hashish /'hæʃɪʃ/ *n* haxixe *m*

hassle /'hæsl/ *n* (*colloq: quarrel*) discussão *f*; (*colloq: struggle*) dificuldade *f* □ *vt* (*colloq*) aborrecer

haste /heɪst/ *n* pressa *f*. **make ~** apressar-se

hasten /'heɪsn/ *vt/i* apressar(-se)

hast|y /'heɪstɪ/ *a* (**-ier**, **-iest**) apressado; (*too quick*) precipitado. **~ily** *adv* às pressas, precipitadamente

hat /hæt/ *n* chapéu *m*

hatch[1] /hætʃ/ *n* (*for food*) postigo *m*; (*naut*) escotilha *f*

hatch[2] /hætʃ/ *vt/i* chocar; (*a plot etc*) tramar, urdir

hatchback /'hætʃbæk/ *n* carro *m* de três ou cinco portas

hatchet /'hætʃɪt/ *n* machadinha *f*

hate /heɪt/ *n* ódio *m* □ *vt* odiar, detestar. **~ful** *a* odioso, detestável

hatred /'heɪtrɪd/ *n* ódio *m*

haughty /'hɔ:tɪ/ *a* (**-ier**, **-iest**) altivo, soberbo, arrogante

haul /hɔ:l/ *vt* arrastar, puxar; (*goods*) transportar em camião □ *n* (*booty*) presa *f*; (*fish caught*) apanha *f*; (*distance*) percurso *m*. **~age** *n* transporte *m* de cargas. **~ier** *n* (*firm*) transportadora *f* rodoviária; (*person*) fretador *m*

haunt /hɔ:nt/ *vt* rondar, freqüentar, (*P*) frequentar; (*ghost*) assombrar; (*thought*) obcecar □ *n* lugar *m* favorito. **~ed house** casa *f* mal-assombrada

have /hæv/ *vt* (*3 sing pres* **has**, *pt* **had**) ter; (*bath etc*) tomar; (*meal*) fazer; (*walk*) dar □ *v aux* ter. **~ done** ter feito. **~ it out (with)** pôr a coisa em pratos limpos, pedir uma explicação (para). **~ sth done** mandar fazer alg coisa

haven /'heɪvn/ *n* porto *m*; (*refuge*) refúgio *m*

haversack /'hævəsæk/ *n* mochila *f*

havoc /'hævək/ *n* estragos *mpl*. **play ~ with** causar estragos em

hawk[1] /hɔ:k/ *n* falcão *m*

hawk[2] /hɔ:k/ *vt* vender de porta em porta. **~er** *n* vendedor *m* ambulante

hawthorn /'hɔ:θɔ:n/ *n* pirilteiro *m*, estrepeiro *m*

hay /heɪ/ *n* feno *m*. **~ fever** febre *f* do feno

haystack /'heɪstæk/ *n* palheiro *m*, (*P*) meda *f* de feno

haywire /'heɪwaɪə(r)/ *a* **go ~** (*colloq*) ficar transtornado

hazard /'hæzəd/ *n* risco *m* □ *vt* arriscar. **~ warning lights** pisca-alerta *m*. **~ous** *a* arriscado

haze /heɪz/ *n* bruma *f*, neblina *f*, cerração *f*

hazel /'heɪzl/ *n* aveleira *f*. **~-nut** *n* avelã *f*

hazy /'heɪzɪ/ *a* (**-ier**, **-iest**) brumoso, encoberto; (*fig: vague*) vago

he /hi:/ *pron* ele □ *n* macho *m*

head /hed/ *n* cabeça *f*; (*chief*) chefe *m*; (*of beer*) espuma *f* □ *a* principal □ *vt* encabeçar, estar à frente de □ *vi* **~ for** dirigir-se para. **~-dress** *n* toucador *m*. **~ first** de cabeça. **~-on** *a* frontal □ *adv* de frente. **~s or tails?** cara ou coroa? **~ waiter** chefe de garçons *m*, (*P*) dos criados. **~er** *n* (*football*) cabeçada *f*

headache /'hedeɪk/ *n* dor *f* de cabeça

heading /'hedɪŋ/ *n* cabeçalho *m*, título *m*; (*subject category*) rubrica *f*

headlamp /'hedlæmp/ *n* farol *m*

headland /'hedlənd/ *n* promontório *m*

headlight /'hedlaɪt/ *n* farol *m*

headline /'hedlaɪn/ *n* título *m*, cabeçalho *m*

headlong /'hedlɒŋ/ *a* de cabeça; (*rash*) precipitado □ *adv* de cabeça; (*rashly*) precipitadamente

head|master /hed'ma:stə(r)/ *n* diretor *m*, (*P*) director *m*. **~-mistress** *n* diretora *f*, (*P*) directora *f*

headphone /'hedfəʊn/ *n* fone *m* de cabeça, (*P*) auscultador *m*

headquarters /hed'kwɔ:təz/ *npl* sede *f*; (*mil*) quartel *m* general

headrest /'hedrest/ *n* apoio *m* para a cabeça

headroom /'hedru:m/ *n* (*auto*) espaço *m* para a cabeça; (*bridge*) limite *m* de altura, altura *f* máxima

headstrong /'hedstrɒŋ/ *a* teimoso

headway /'hedweɪ/ *n* progresso *m*. **make ~** fazer progressos

heady /'hedɪ/ *a* (**-ier, -iest**) empolgante

heal /hi:l/ *vt/i* curar(-se), sarar; (*wound*) cicatrizar

health /helθ/ *n* saúde *f*. **~ centre** posto *m* de saúde. **~ foods** alimentos *mpl* naturais. **~y** *a* saudável, sadio

heap /hi:p/ *n* monte *m*, pilha *f* □ *vt* amontoar, empilhar. **~s of money** (*colloq*) dinheiro aos montes (*colloq*)

hear /hɪə(r)/ *vt/i* (*pt* **heard** /hɜ:d/) ouvir. **~, hear!** apoiado! **~ from** ter notícias de. **~ of** *or* **about** ouvir falar de. **I won't ~ of it** nem quero ouvir falar nisso. **~ing** *n* ouvido *m*, audição *f*; (*jur*) audiência *f*. **~ing-aid** *n* aparelho *m* de audição

hearsay /'hɪəseɪ/ *n* boato *m*. **it's only ~** é só por ouvir dizer

hearse /hɜ:s/ *n* carro *m* funerário

heart /ha:t/ *n* coração *m*. **~s** (*cards*) copas *fpl*. **at ~** no fundo. **by ~** de cor. **~ attack** ataque *m* de coração. **~-beat** *n* pulsação *f*, batida *f*. **~-breaking** *a* de cortar o coração. **~-broken** *a* com o coração partido, desfeito. **~-to-heart** *a* com o coração nas mãos. **lose ~** perder a coragem, desanimar

heartburn /'ha:tbɜ:n/ *n* azia *f*

hearten /'ha:tn/ *vt* animar, encorajar

heartfelt /'ha:tfelt/ *a* sincero, sentido

hearth /ha:θ/ *n* lareira *f*

heartless /'ha:tlɪs/ *a* insensível, desalmado, cruel

heart|y /'ha:tɪ/ *a* (**-ier, -iest**) caloroso; (*meal*) abundante. **~ily** *adv* calorosamente; (*eat, laugh*) com vontade

heat /hi:t/ *n* calor *m*; (*fig*) ardor *m*; (*contest*) eliminatória *f* □ *vt/i* aquecer. **~stroke** *n* insolação *f*. **~wave** *n* onda *f* de calor. **~er** *n* aquecedor *m*. **~ing** *n* aquecimento *m*

heated /'hi:tɪd/ *a* (*fig*) acalorado, aceso

heathen /'hi:ðn/ *n* pagão *m*, pagã *f*

heather /'heðə(r)/ *n* urze *f*

heave /hi:v/ *vt/i* (*lift*) içar; (*a sigh*) soltar; (*retch*) ter náuseas; (*colloq: throw*) atirar

heaven /'hevn/ *n* céu *m*. **~ly** *a* celestial; (*colloq*) divino

heav|y /'hevɪ/ *a* (**-ier, -iest**) pesado; (*blow, rain*) forte; (*cold, drinker*) grande; (*traffic*) intenso. **~ily** *adv* pesadamente; (*drink, smoke etc*) inveterado

heavyweight /'hevɪweɪt/ *n* (*boxing*) peso-pesado *m*

Hebrew /'hi:bru:/ *a* hebreu, hebraico □ *n* (*lang*) hebreu *m*

heckle /'hekl/ *vt* interromper, interpelar

hectic /'hektɪk/ *a* muito agitado, febril

hedge /hedʒ/ *n* sebe *f* □ *vt* cercar □ *vi* (*in answering*) usar de evasivas. **~ one's bets** (*fig*) resguardar-se

hedgehog /'hedʒhɒg/ *n* ouriçocacheiro *m*

heed /hi:d/ *vt* prestar atenção a, escutar □ *n* **pay ~ to** prestar atenção a, dar ouvidos a. **~less** *a* **~less of** indiferente a, sem prestar atenção a

heel /hi:l/ *n* calcanhar *m*; (*of shoe*) salto *m*; (*sl*) canalha *m*

hefty /'heftɪ/ *a* (**-ier, -iest**) robusto e corpulento

height /haɪt/ *n* altura *f*; (*of mountain, plane*) altitude *f*; (*fig*) auge *m*, cúmulo *m*

heighten /'haɪtn/ *vt/i* aumentar, elevar(-se)

heir /eə(r)/ *n* herdeiro *m*. **~ess** *n* herdeira *f*

heirloom /'eəlu:m/ *n* peça *f* de família, (*P*) relíquia *f* de família

held /held/ *see* **hold**[1]

helicopter /'helɪkɒptə(r)/ *n* helicóptero *m*

hell /hel/ *n* inferno *m*. **for the ~ of it** só por gozo. **~-bent** *a* decidido a todo o custo (**on** a). **~ish** *a* infernal

hello /hə'ləʊ/ *int & n* = **hallo**

helm /helm/ *n* leme *m*

helmet /'helmɪt/ *n* capacete *m*

help /help/ *vt/i* ajudar □ *n* ajuda *f*. **home ~** empregada *f*, faxineira *f*, (*P*) mulher *f* a dias. **~ o.s. to** servir-se de. **he cannot ~ laughing** ele não pode conter o riso. **it can't be ~ed** não há remédio. **~er** *n* ajudante *mf*. **~ful** *a* útil; (*serviceable*) de grande ajuda. **~less** *a* impotente

helping /'helpɪŋ/ *n* porção *f*, dose *f*

hem /hem/ *n* bainha *f* □ *vt* (*pt* **hemmed**) fazer a bainha. **~ in** cercar, encurralar

hemisphere /ˈhemɪsfɪə(r)/ *n* hemisfério *m*

hemp /hemp/ *n* cânhamo *m*

hen /hen/ *n* galinha *f*

hence /hens/ *adv* (*from now*) a partir desta altura; (*for this reason*) daí, por isso. **a week ~** daqui a uma semana. **~forth** *adv* de agora em diante, doravante

henpecked /ˈhenpekt/ *a* mandado, (*P*) dominado pela mulher

her /hɜ:(r)/ *pron* a (a ela); (*after prep*) ela. **(to) ~** lhe. **I know ~** conheço-a □ *a* seu(s), sua(s); dela

herald /ˈherəld/ *vt* anunciar

heraldry /ˈherəldrɪ/ *n* heráldica *f*

herb /hɜ:b/ *n* erva *f* culinária *or* medicinal

herd /hɜ:d/ *n* manada *f*; (*of pigs*) vara *f* □ □ *vi* **~ together** juntar-se em rebanho

here /hɪə(r)/ *adv* aqui □ *int* tome; aqui está. **to/from ~** para aqui/daqui

hereafter /hɪərˈa:ftə(r)/ *adv* de/para o futuro, daqui em diante □ *n* **the ~** a vida de além-túmulo, (*P*) a vida futura

hereby /hɪəˈbaɪ/ *adv* (*jur*) pelo presente ato ou decreto, etc, (*P*) pelo presente acto ou decreto, etc

hereditary /hɪˈredɪtrɪ/ *a* hereditário

heredity /hɪˈredətɪ/ *n* hereditariedade *f*

here|sy /ˈherəsɪ/ *n* heresia *f*. **~tic** *n* herege *mf*. **~tical** /hɪˈretɪkl/ *a* herético

heritage /ˈherɪtɪdʒ/ *n* herança *f*, patrimônio *m*, (*P*) património *m*

hermit /ˈhɜ:mɪt/ *n* eremita *m*

hernia /ˈhɜ:nɪə/ *n* hérnia *f*

hero /ˈhɪərəʊ/ *n* (*pl* **-oes**) herói *m*

heroic /hɪˈrəʊɪk/ *a* heróico

heroin /ˈherəʊɪn/ *n* heroína *f*

heroine /ˈherəʊɪn/ *n* heroína *f*

heroism /ˈherəʊɪzəm/ *n* heroísmo *m*

heron /ˈherən/ *n* garça *f*

herring /ˈherɪŋ/ *n* arenque *m*

hers /hɜ:z/ *poss pron* o(s) seu(s), a(s) sua(s), o(s) dela, a(s) dela. **it is ~** é (o) dela *or* o seu

herself /hɜ:ˈself/ *pron* ela mesma; (*reflexive*) se. **by ~** sozinha. **for ~** para si mesma. **to ~** a/para si mesma. **Mary ~ said so** foi a própria Maria que o disse

hesitant /ˈhezɪtənt/ *a* hesitante

hesitat|e /ˈhezɪteɪt/ *vt* hesitar. **~ion** /-ˈteɪʃn/ *n* hesitação *f*

heterosexual /hetərəʊˈseksjʊəl/ *a* & *n* heterossexual (*mf*)

hexagon /ˈheksəgən/ *n* hexágono *m*. **~al** /-ˈægənl/ *a* hexagonal

hey /heɪ/ *int* eh, olá

heyday /ˈheɪdeɪ/ *n* auge *m*, apogeu *m*

hi /haɪ/ *int* olá, viva

hibernat|e /ˈhaɪbəneɪt/ *vi* hibernar. **~ion** /-ˈneɪʃn/ *n* hibernação *f*

hiccup /ˈhɪkʌp/ *n* soluço *m* □ *vi* soluçar, estar com soluços

hide[1] /haɪd/ *vt*/*i* (*pt* **hid**, *pp* **hidden**) esconder(-se) (**from** de). **~-and-seek** *n* (*game*) esconde-esconde *m*. **~-out** *n* (*colloq*) esconderijo *m*

hide[2] /haɪd/ *n* pele *f*, couro *m*

hideous /ˈhɪdɪəs/ *a* horrendo, medonho

hiding /ˈhaɪdɪŋ/ *n* (*colloq*: *thrashing*) sova *f*, surra *f*. **go into ~** esconder-se. **~-place** *n* esconderijo *m*

hierarchy /ˈhaɪəra:kɪ/ *n* hierarquia *f*

hi-fi /haɪˈfaɪ/ *a* & *n* (de) alta fidelidade (*f*)

high /haɪ/ *a* (**-er**, **-est**) alto; (*price, number*) elevado; (*voice, pitch*) agudo □ *n* alta *f* □ *adv* alto. **two metres ~** com dois metros de altura. **~ chair** cadeira *f* alta para crianças. **~-handed** *a* autoritário, prepotente. **~ jump** salto *m* em altura. **~-rise building** edifício *m* alto, (*P*) torre *f*. **~ school** escola *f* secundária. **in the ~ season** em plena estação. **~-speed** *a* ultra-rápido. **~-spirited** *a* animado, vivo. **~ spot** (*sl*) ponto *m* culminante. **~ street** rua *f* principal. **~ tide** maré *f* alta. **~er education** ensino *m* superior

highbrow /ˈhaɪbraʊ/ *a* & *n* (*colloq*) intelectual (*m*)

highlight /ˈhaɪlaɪt/ *n* (*fig*) ponto *m* alto □ *vt* salientar, pôr em relevo, realçar

highly /ˈhaɪlɪ/ *adv* altamente, extremamente. **~-strung** *a* muito sensível, nervoso, tenso. **speak ~ of** falar bem de

Highness /ˈhaɪnɪs/ *n* Alteza *f*

highway /ˈhaɪweɪ/ *n* estrada *f*, rodovia *f*. **H~ Code** Código *m* Nacional de Trânsito

hijack /ˈhaɪdʒæk/ *vt* seqüestrar, (*P*) sequestrar □ *n* seqüestro *m*, (*P*) sequestro *m*. **~er** *n* (*of plane*) pirata *m* (do ar)

hike /haɪk/ *n* caminhada no campo *f* □ *vi* fazer uma caminhada. **~r** /-ə(r)/ *n* excursionista *mf*, caminhante *mf*

hilarious /hɪˈleərɪəs/ *a* divertido, desopilante

hill /hɪl/ *n* colina *f*, monte *m*; (*slope*) ladeira *f*, subida *f*. **~y** *a* acidentado

hillside /ˈhɪlsaɪd/ *n* encosta *f*, vertente *f*

hilt /hɪlt/ *n* punho *m*. **to the ~** completamente, inteiramente

him /hɪm/ *pron* o (a ele); (*after prep*) ele. **(to)** ~ lhe. **I know** ~ conheço-o

himself /hɪm'self/ *pron* ele mesmo; (*reflexive*) se. **by** ~ sozinho. **for** ~ para si mesmo. **to** ~ a/para si mesmo. **Peter** ~ **saw it** foi o próprio Pedro que o viu

hind /haɪnd/ *a* traseiro, posterior

hind|er /'hɪndə(r)/ *vt* empatar, estorvar; (*prevent*) impedir. **~rance** *n* estorvo *m*

hindsight /'haɪndsaɪt/ *n* **with** ~ em retrospecto

Hindu /hɪn'du:/ *n* & *a* hindu (*mf*). **~ism** /-ɪzəm/ *n* hinduísmo *m*

hinge /hɪndʒ/ *n* dobradiça *f* ▫ *vi* ~ **on** depender de

hint /hɪnt/ *n* insinuação *f*, indireta *f*, (*P*) indirecta *f*; (*advice*) sugestão *f*, dica *f* (*colloq*) ▫ *vt* dar a entender, insinuar ▫ *vi* ~ **at** fazer alusão a

hip /hɪp/ *n* quadril *m*

hippie /'hɪpɪ/ *n* hippie *mf*

hippopotamus /hɪpə'pɒtəməs/ *n* (*pl* **-muses**) hipopótamo *m*

hire /'haɪə(r)/ *vt* alugar; (*person*) contratar ▫ *n* aluguel *m*, (*P*) aluguer *m*. **~-purchase** *n* compra *f* a prestações, (*P*) crediário *m*

hirsute /'hɜ:sju:t/ *a* hirsuto

his /hɪz/ *a* seu(s), sua(s), dele ▫ *poss pron* o(s) seu(s), a(s) sua(s), o(s) dele, a(s) dele. **it is** ~ é (o) dele *or* o seu

Hispanic /hɪs'pænɪk/ *a* hispânico

hiss /hɪs/ *n* silvo *m*; (*for disapproval*) assobio *m*, vaia *f* ▫ *vt/i* sibilar; (*for disapproval*) assobiar, vaiar

historian /hɪ'stɔ:rɪən/ *n* historiador *m*

histor|y /'hɪstərɪ/ *n* história *f*. **~ic(al)** /hɪ'stɒrɪk(l)/ *a* histórico

hit /hɪt/ *vt* (*pt* **hit**, *pres p* **hitting**) atingir, bater em; (*knock against, collide with*) chocar com, ir de encontro a; (*strike a target*) acertar em; (*find*) descobrir; (*affect*) atingir ▫ *vi* ~ **on** dar com ▫ *n* pancada *f*; (*fig: success*) sucesso *m*. ~ **it off** dar-se bem (**with** com). **~-and-run** *a* (*driver*) que foge depois do desastre. **~-or-miss** *a* ao acaso

hitch /hɪtʃ/ *vt* atar, prender; (*to a hook*) enganchar ▫ *n* sacão *m*; (*snag*) problema *m*. ~ **a lift**, **~-hike** viajar de carona, (*P*) boleia. **~-hiker** *n* o que viaja de carona, boleia. ~ **up** puxar para cima

hive /haɪv/ *n* colméia *f* ▫ *vt* ~ **off** separar e tornar independente

hoard /hɔ:d/ *vt* juntar, açambarcar ▫ *n* provisão *f*; (*of valuables*) tesouro *m*

hoarding /'hɔ:dɪŋ/ *n* tapume *m*, outdoor *m*

hoarse /hɔ:s/ *a* (**-er**, **-est**) rouco. **~ness** *n* rouquidão *f*

hoax /həʊks/ *n* (*malicious*) logro *m*, embuste *m*; (*humorous*) trote *m* ▫ *vt* (*malicious*) engancer, lograr; passar um trote, pregar uma peça em

hob /hɒb/ *n* placa *f* de aquecimento (do fogão)

hobble /'hɒbl/ *vi* coxear ▫ *vt* pear

hobby /'hɒbɪ/ *n* passatempo *m* favorito. **~-horse** *n* (*fig*) tópico *m* favorito

hock /hɒk/ *n* vinho *m* branco do Reno

hockey /'hɒkɪ/ *n* hóquei *m*

hoe /həʊ/ *n* enxada *f* ▫ *vt* trabalhar com enxada

hog /hɒg/ *n* porco *m*; (*greedy person*) glutão *m* ▫ *vt* (*pt* **hogged**) (*colloq*) açambarcar

hoist /hɔɪst/ *vt* içar ▫ *n* guindaste *m*, (*P*) monta-cargas *m*

hold[1] /həʊld/ *vt* (*pt* **held**) segurar; (*contain*) levar; (*possess*) ter, possuir; (*occupy*) ocupar; (*keep, maintain*) conservar, manter; (*affirm*) manter ▫ *vi* (*of rope etc*) agüentar(-se), (*P*) *aguentar(-se)* ▫ *n* (*influence*) domínio *m*. **get** ~ **of** pôr as mãos em; (*fig*) apanhar. ~ **back** reter. ~ **on** (*colloq*) esperar. ~ **on to** guardar; (*cling to*) agarrar-se a. ~ **one's breath** suster a respiração. ~ **one's tongue** calar-se. ~ **the line** não desligar. ~ **out** resistir. ~ **up** (*support*) sustentar; (*delay*) demorar; (*rob*) assaltar. **~-up** *n* atraso *m*; (*auto*) engarrafamento *m*; (*robbery*) assalto *m*. ~ **with** agüentar, (*P*) aguentar. **~er** *n* detentor *m*; (*of post, title etc*) titular *mf*; (*for object*) suporte *m*

hold[2] /həʊld/ *n* (*of ship, plane*) porão *m*

holdall /'həʊldɔ:l/ *n* saco *m* de viagem

holding /'həʊldɪŋ/ *n* (*land*) propriedade *f*; (*comm*) ações *fpl*, (*P*) acções *fpl*, valores *mpl*, holding *m*

hole /həʊl/ *n* buraco *m* ▫ *vt* abrir buraco(s) em, esburacar

holiday /'hɒlədeɪ/ *n* férias *fpl*; (*day off; public*) feriado *m* ▫ *vi* passar férias. **~-maker** *n* pessoa *f* em férias; (*in summer*) veranista *mf*, (*P*) veraneante *mf*

holiness /'həʊlɪnɪs/ *n* santidade *f*

Holland /'hɒlənd/ *n* Holanda *f*

hollow /'hɒləʊ/ *a* oco, vazio; (*fig*) falso; (*cheeks*) fundo; (*sound*) surdo ▫ *n* (*in the ground*) cavidade *f*, (*in the hand*) cova *f*

holly /'hɒlɪ/ *n* azevinho *m*

holster /'həʊlstə(r)/ *n* coldre *m*

holy /'həʊlɪ/ *a* (**-ier**, **-iest**) santo, sagrado; (*water*) benta. **H~ Ghost**, **H~ Spirit** Espírito *m* Santo

homage /'hɒmɪdʒ/ *n* homenagem *f*. **pay** ~ **to** prestar homenagem a

home /həʊm/ *n* casa *f*, lar *m*; (*institution*) lar *m*, asilo *m*; (*country*) país *m* natal □ *a* caseiro, doméstico; (*of family*) de família; (*pol*) nacional, interno; (*football match*) em casa □ *adv* **(at)** ~ en casa. **come/go** ~ vir/ir para casa. **make oneself at** ~ não fazer cerimônia, (*P*) cerimónia. **~-made** *a* caseiro. **H~ Office** Ministério *m* do Interior. **~ town** cidade *f* or terra *f* natal. **~ truth** dura verdade *f*, verdade(s) *f* (*pl*) amarga(s). **~less** *a* sem casa, desabrigado

homeland /ˈhəʊmlænd/ *n* pátria *f*

homely /ˈhəʊmlɪ/ *a* (**-ier, -iest**) (*simple*) simples; (*Amer: ugly*) sem graça

homesick /ˈhəʊmsɪk/ *a* **be** ~ ter saudades

homeward /ˈhəʊmwəd/ *a* (*journey*) de regresso

homework /ˈhəʊmwɜːk/ *n* trabalho *m* de casa, dever *m* de casa

homicide /ˈhɒmɪsaɪd/ *n* homicídio *m*; (*person*) homicida *mf*

homoeopath|y /həʊmɪˈɒpəθɪ/ *n* homeopatia *f*. **~ic** *a* homeopático

homosexual /hɒməˈsekʃʊəl/ *a* & *n* homossexual (*mf*)

honest /ˈɒnɪst/ *a* honesto; (*frank*) franco. **~ly** *adv* honestamente; (*frankly*) francamente. **~y** *n* honestidade *f*

honey /ˈhʌnɪ/ *n* mel *m*; (*colloq: darling*) querido *m*, querida *f*, meu bem *m*

honeycomb /ˈhʌnɪkəʊm/ *n* favo *m* de mel

honeymoon /ˈhʌnɪmuːn/ *n* lua de mel *f*

honorary /ˈɒnərərɪ/ *a* honorário

honour /ˈɒnə(r)/ *n* honra *f* □ *vt* honrar. **~able** *a* honrado, honroso

hood /hʊd/ *n* capuz *m*; (*car roof*) capota *f*, (*P*) tejadilho *m*; (*Amer: bonnet*) capô *m*, (*P*) capot *m*

hoodwink /ˈhʊdwɪŋk/ *vt* enganar

hoof /huːf/ *n* (*pl* **-fs**) casco *m*

hook /hʊk/ *n* gancho *m*; (*on garment*) colchete *m*; (*for fishing*) anzol *m* □ *vt* enganchar; (*fish*) apanhar, pescar. **off the** ~ livre de dificuldades; (*phone*) desligado

hooked /hʊkt/ *a* **be ~ on** (*sl*) ter o vício de, estar viciado em

hookey /ˈhʊkɪ/ *n* **play** ~ (*Amer sl*) fazer gazeta

hooligan /ˈhuːlɪgən/ *n* desordeiro *m*

hoop /huːp/ *n* arco *m*; (*of cask*) cinta *f*

hooray /huːˈreɪ/ *int* & *n* = **hurrah**

hoot /huːt/ *n* (*of owl*) pio *m* de mocho; (*of horn*) buzinada *f*; (*jeer*) apupo *m* □ *vi* (*of owl*) piar; (*of horn*) buzinar; (*jeer*) apupar. **~er** *n* buzina *f*; (*of factory*) sereia *f*

Hoover /ˈhuːvə(r)/ *n* aspirador de pó *m*, (*P*) aspirador *m* □ *vt* passar o aspirador

hop[1] /hɒp/ *vi* (*pt* **hopped**) saltar num pé só, (*P*) ao pé coxinho □ *n* salto *m*. **~ in** (*colloq*) subir, saltar (*colloq*). **~ it** (*sl*) pôr-se a andar (*colloq*). **~ out** (*colloq*) descer, saltar (*colloq*)

hop[2] /hɒp/ *n* (*plant*) lúpulo *m*. **~s** espigas *fpl* de lúpulo

hope /həʊp/ *n* esperança *f* □ *vt*/*i* esperar. **~ for** esperar (ter). **~ful** *a* esperançoso; (*promising*) promissor. **be ~ful (that)** ter esperança (que), confiar (em que). **~fully** *adv* esperançosamente; (*it is hoped that*) é de esperar que. **~less** *a* desesperado, sem esperança; (*incompetent*) incapaz

horde /hɔːd/ *n* horda *f*

horizon /həˈraɪzn/ *n* horizonte *m*

horizontal /hɒrɪˈzɒntl/ *a* horizontal

hormone /ˈhɔːməʊn/ *n* hormônio *m*, (*P*) hormona *f*

horn /hɔːn/ *n* chifre *m*, corno *m*; (*of car*) buzina *f*; (*mus*) trompa *f*. **~y** *a* caloso, calejado

hornet /ˈhɔːnɪt/ *n* vespão *m*

horoscope /ˈhɒrəskəʊp/ *n* horóscopo *m*, (*P*) horoscópio *m*

horrible /ˈhɒrəbl/ *a* horrível, horroroso

horrid /ˈhɒrɪd/ *a* horrível, horripilante

horrific /həˈrɪfɪk/ *a* horrífico

horr|or /ˈhɒrə(r)/ *n* horror *m* □ *a* (*film etc*) de terror. **~ify** *vt* horrorizar, horripilar

horse /hɔːs/ *n* cavalo *m*. **~-chest-nut** *n* castanha *f* da India. **~- racing** *n* corrida *f* de cavalos, hipismo *m*. **~-radish** *n* rábano *m*

horseback /ˈhɔːsbæk/ *n* **on** ~ a cavalo

horseplay /ˈhɔːspleɪ/ *n* brincadeira *f* grosseira, abrutalhada *f*

horsepower /ˈhɔːspaʊə(r)/ *n* cavalo-vapor *m*

horseshoe /ˈhɔːsʃuː/ *n* ferradura *f*

horticultur|e /ˈhɔːtɪkʌltʃə(r)/ *n* horticultura *f*. **~al** /-ˈkʌltʃərəl/ *a* hortícola

hose /həʊz/ *n* **~(-pipe)** mangueira *f* □ *vt* regar com a mangueira

hospice /ˈhɒspɪs/ *n* hospício *m*; (*for travellers*) hospedaria *f*

hospit|able /həˈspɪtəbl/ *a* hospitaleiro. **~ality** /-ˈtælətɪ/ *n* hospitalidade *f*

hospital /ˈhɒspɪtl/ *n* hospital *m*

host[1] /həʊst/ *n* anfitrião *m*, dono *m* da casa. **~ess** *n* anfitriã *f*, dona *f* da casa

host[2] /həʊst/ *n* **a ~ of** uma multidão de, um grande número de

host[3] /həʊst/ *n* (*relig*) hóstia *f*

hostage /ˈhɒstɪdʒ/ *n* refém *m*

hostel /'hɒstl/ *n* residência *f* de estudantes *etc*
hostil|e /'hɒstaɪl/ *a* hostil. **~ity** /hɒ'stɪlətɪ/ *n* hostilidade *f*
hot /hɒt/ *a* (**hotter, hottest**) quente; (*culin*) picante. **be** *or* **feel ~** estar com *or* ter calor. **it is ~** está *or* faz calor □ *vt/i* (*pt* **hotted**) **~ up** (*colloq*) aquecer. **~ dog** cachorro-quente *m*. **~ line** linha direta *f*, (*P*) directa esp entre chefes de estado. **~-water bottle** saco *m* de água quente
hotbed /'hɒtbed/ *n* (*fig*) foco *m*
hotchpotch /'hɒtʃpɒtʃ/ *n* misturada *f*, (*P*) salgalhada *f*
hotel /həʊ'tel/ *n* hotel *m*. **~ier** /-ɪə(r)/ *n* hoteleiro *m*
hound /haʊnd/ *n* cão *m* de caça e de corrida, sabujo *m* □ *vt* acossar, perseguir
hour /'aʊə(r)/ *n* hora *f*. **~ly** *adv* de hora em hora □ *a* de hora em hora. **~ly pay** retribuição *f* horária. **paid ~ly** pago por hora
house[1] /haʊs/ *n* (*pl* **~s** /'haʊzɪz/) *n* casa *f*; (*pol*) câmara *f*. **on the ~** por conta da casa. **~-warming** *n* inauguração *f* da casa
house[2] /haʊz/ *vt* alojar; (*store*) arrecadar, guardar
houseboat /'haʊsbəʊt/ *n* casa *f* flutuante
household /'haʊshəʊld/ *n* família *f*, agregado *m* familiar. **~er** *n* ocupante *mf*; (*owner*) proprietário *m*
housekeep|er /'haʊski:pə(r)/ *n* governanta *f*. **~ing** *n* (*work*) tarefas *fpl* domésticas
housewife /'haʊswaɪf/ *n* (*pl* **-wives**) dona *f* de casa
housework /'haʊswɜ:k/ *n* tarefas *fpl* domésticas
housing /'haʊzɪŋ/ *n* alojamento *m*. **~ estate** zona *f* residencial
hovel /'hɒvl/ *n* casebre *m*, tugúrio *m*
hover /'hɒvə(r)/ *vi* pairar; (*linger*) deixar-se ficar, demorar-se
hovercraft /'hɒvəkra:ft/ *n invar* aerobarco *m*, hovercraft *m*
how /haʊ/ *adv* como. **~ long/old is...?** que comprimento/idade tem...? **~ far?** a que distância? **~ many?** quantos? **~ much?** quanto? **~ often?** com que freqüência, (*P*) frequência? **~ pretty it is** como é lindo. **~ about a walk?** e se fôssemos dar uma volta? **~ are you?** como vai? **~ do you do?** muito prazer! **and ~!** oh se é!
however /haʊ'evə(r)/ *adv* de qualquer maneira; (*though*) contudo, no entanto, todavia. **~ small it may be** por menor que seja
howl /haʊl/ *n* uivo *m* □ *vi* uivar
HP *abbr see* **hire-purchase**
hp *abbr see* **horsepower**
hub /hʌb/ *n* cubo *m* da roda; (*fig*) centro *m*. **~-cap** *n* calota *f*, (*P*) tampão *m* da roda
hubbub /'hʌbʌb/ *n* chinfrim *m*
huddle /'hʌdl/ *vt/i* apinhar(-se). **~ together** aconchegar-se
hue[1] /hju:/ *n* matiz *f*, tom *m*
hue[2] /hju:/ *n* **~ and cry** clamor *m*, alarido *m*
huff /hʌf/ *n* **in a ~** com raiva, zangado
hug /hʌg/ *vt* (*pt* **hugged**) abraçar, apertar nos braços; (*keep close to*) chegar-se a □ *n* abraço *m*
huge /hju:dʒ/ *a* enorme
hulk /hʌlk/ *n* casco (esp de navio desmantelado) *m*. **~ing** *a* (*colloq*) desajeitadão (*colloq*)
hull /hʌl/ *n* (*of ship*) casco *m*
hullo /hə'ləʊ/ *int* & *n* = **hallo**
hum /hʌm/ *vt/i* (*pt* **hummed**) cantar com a boca fechada; (*of insect, engine*) zumbir □ *n* zumbido *m*
human /'hju:mən/ *a* humano □ *n* **~ (being)** ser *m* humano
humane /hju:'meɪn/ *a* humano, compassivo
humanitarian /hju:mænɪ'teərɪən/ *a* humanitário
humanity /hju:'mænətɪ/ *n* humanidade *f*
humbl|e /'hʌmbl/ *a* (**-er, -est**) humilde □ *vt* humilhar. **~y** *adv* humildemente
humdrum /'hʌmdrʌm/ *a* monótono, rotineiro
humid /'hju:mɪd/ *a* úmido, (*P*) húmido. **~ity** /-'mɪdətɪ/ *n* umidade *f*, (*P*) humidade *f*
humiliat|e /hju:'mɪlɪeɪt/ *vt* humilhar. **~ion** /-'eɪʃn/ *n* humilhação *f*
humility /hju:'mɪlətɪ/ *n* humildade *f*
humorist /'hju:mərɪst/ *n* humorista *mf*
hum|our /'hju:mə(r)/ *n* humor *m* □ *vt* fazer a vontade de. **~orous** *a* humorístico; (*person*) divertido, espirituoso
hump /hʌmp/ *n* corcova *f*; (*of the back*) corcunda *f* □ *vt* corcovar, arquear. **the ~** (*sl*) a neura (*colloq*)
hunch[1] /hʌntʃ/ *vt* curvar. **~ed up** curvado
hunch[2] /hʌntʃ/ *n* (*colloq*) palpite *m*
hunchback /'hʌntʃbæk/ *n* corcunda *mf*
hundred /'hʌndrəd/ *a* cem □ *n* centena *f*, cento *m*. **~s of** centenas de. **~fold** *a* cêntuplo □ *adv* cem vezes mais. **~th** *a* & *n* centésimo (*m*)
hundredweight /'hʌndrədweɪt/ *n* quintal *m* (*= 50,8 kg; Amer 45,36 kg*)
hung /hʌŋ/ *see* **hang**

Hungar|y /'hʌŋgərɪ/ *n* Hungria *f*. **~ian** /-'geərɪən/ *a* & *n* húngaro (*m*)
hunger /'hʌŋgə(r)/ *n* fome *f* □ *vi* **~ for** ter fome de; (*fig*) desejar vivamente, ansiar por
hungr|y /'hʌŋgrɪ/ *a* (**ier, -iest**) esfomeado, faminto. **be ~y** ter fome, estar com fome. **~ily** *adv* avidamente
hunk /hʌŋk/ *n* grande naco *m*
hunt /hʌnt/ *vt/i* caçar □ *n* caça *f*. **~ for** andar à caça de, andar à procura de. **~er** *n* caçador *m*. **~ing** *n* caça *f*, caçada *f*
hurdle /'hɜ:dl/ *n* obstáculo *m*
hurl /hɜ:l/ *vt* arremessar, lançar com força
hurrah, hurray /hʊ'ra:, hʊ'reɪ/ *int* & *n* hurra (*m*), viva (*m*)
hurricane /'hʌrɪkən/ *n* furacão *m*
hurried /'hʌrɪd/ *a* apressado. **~ly** *adv* apressadamente, às pressas
hurry /'hʌrɪ/ *vt/i* apressar(-se), despachar(-se) □ *n* pressa *f*. **be in a ~** estar com *or* ter pressa. **do sth in a ~** fazer alg coisa às pressas. **~up!** ande logo
hurt /hɜ:t/ *vt* (*pt* **hurt**) fazer mal a; (*injure, offend*) magoar, ferir □ *vi* doer □ *a* magoado, ferido □ *n* mal *m*; (*feelings*) mágoa *f*. **~ful** *a* prejudicial; (*remark etc*) que magoa
hurtle /'hɜ:tl/ *vi* despenhar-se; (*move rapidly*) precipitar-se □ *vt* arremessar
husband /'hʌzbənd/ *n* marido *m*, esposo *m*
hush /hʌʃ/ *vt* (fazer) calar. **~!** silencio! □ *vi* calar-se □ *n* silêncio *m*. **~-hush** *a* (*colloq*) muito em segredo. **~ up** abafar, encobrir
husk /hʌsk/ *n* casca *f*
husky /'hʌskɪ/ *a* (**-ier, -iest**) (*hoarse*) rouco, enrouquecido; (*burly*) corpulento □ *n* cão *m* esquimó
hustle /'hʌsl/ *vt* empurrar, dar encontrões a □ *n* empurrão *m*. **~ and bustle** grande movimento *m*
hut /hʌt/ *n* cabana *f*, barraca *f* de madeira
hutch /hʌtʃ/ *n* coelheira *f*
hyacinth /'haɪəsɪnθ/ *n* jacinto *m*
hybrid /'haɪbrɪd/ *a* & *n* híbrido (*m*)
hydrant /'haɪdrənt/ *n* hidrante *m*
hydraulic /haɪ'drɔ:lɪk/ *a* hidráulico
hydroelectric /haɪdrəʊɪ'lektrɪk/ *a* hidrelétrico, (*P*) hidroelectrico
hydrofoil /'haɪdrəʊfɔɪl/ *n* hydrofoil *m*
hydrogen /'haɪdrədʒən/ *n* hidrogênio *m*, (*P*) hidrogénio *m*
hyena /haɪ'i:nə/ *n* hiena *f*
hygiene /'haɪdʒi:n/ *n* higiene *f*
hygienic /haɪ'dʒi:nɪk/ *a* higiênico, (*P*) higiénico
hymn /hɪm/ *n* hino *m*, cântico *m*
hyper- /'haɪpə(r)/ *pref* hiper-
hypermarket /'haɪpəma:kɪt/ *n* hipermercado *m*
hyphen /'haɪfn/ *n* hífen *m*, traço-de-união *m*. **~ate** *vt* unir com hífen
hypno|sis /hɪp'nəʊsɪs/ *n* hipnose *f*. **~tic** /-'nɒtɪk/ *a* hipnótico
hypnot|ize /'hɪpnətaɪz/ *vt* hipnotizar. **~ism** /-ɪzəm/ *n* hipnotismo *m*
hypochondriac /haɪpə'kɒndrɪæk/ *n* hipocondríaco *m*
hypocrisy /hɪ'pɒkrəsɪ/ *n* hipocrisia *f*
hypocrit|e /'hɪpəkrɪt/ *n* hipócrita *mf*. **~ical** /-'krɪtɪkl/ *a* hipócrita
hypodermic /haɪpə'dɜ:mɪk/ *a* hipodérmico □ *n* seringa *f*
hypothe|sis /haɪ'pɒθəsɪs/ *n* (*pl* **-theses** /-si:z/) hipótese *f*. **~tical** /-ə'θetɪkl/ *a* hipotético
hyster|ia /hɪ'stɪərɪə/ *n* histeria *f*. **~ical** /hɪ'sterɪkl/ *a* histérico

I /aɪ/ *pron* eu
Iberian /aɪ'bi:rɪən/ *a* ibérico □ *n* íbero *m*
ice /aɪs/ *n* gelo *m* □ *vt/i* gelar; (*cake*) cobrir com glacê □ *vi* **~ up** gelar. **~-box** *n* (*Amer*) geladeira *f*, (*P*) frigorífico *m*. **~(-cream)** *n* sorvete *m*, (*P*) gelado *m*. **~-cube** *n* cubo *m* *or* pedra *f* de gelo. **~ hockey** hóquei *m* sobre o gelo. **~ lolly** picolé *m*. **~-pack** *n* saco *m* de gelo. **~-rink** *n* rinque *m* de patinação, (*P*) patinagem *f* no gelo. **~ skating** *n* patinação *f*, (*P*) patinagem *f* no gelo
iceberg /'aɪsbɜ:g/ *n* iceberg *m*; (*fig*) pedaço *m* de gelo
Iceland /'aɪslənd/ *n* Islândia *f*. **~er** *n* islandês *m*. **~ic** /-'lændɪk/ *a* & *n* islandês (*m*)
icicle /'aɪsɪkl/ *n* pingente *m* de gelo
icing /'aɪsɪŋ/ *n* (*culin*) cobertura *f* de açúcar, glacê *m*
icy /'aɪsɪ/ *a* (**-ier, -iest**) gelado, gélido, glacial; (*road*) com gelo
idea /aɪ'dɪə/ *n* idéia *f*, (*P*) ideia *f*
ideal /aɪ'dɪəl/ *a* & *n* ideal (*m*). **~ize** *vt* idealizar. **~ly** *adv* idealmente
idealis|t /aɪ'dɪəlɪst/ *n* idealista *mf*. **~m** /-zəm/ *n* idealismo *m*. **~tic** /-'lɪstɪk/ *a* idealista
identical /aɪ'dentɪkl/ *a* idêntico

identif|y /aɪ'dentɪfaɪ/ *vt* identificar □ *vi* **~y with** identificar-se com. **~ication** /-ɪ'keɪʃn/ *n* identificação *f*; (*papers*) documentos *mpl* de identificação

identity /aɪ'dentətɪ/ *n* identidade *f*. **~ card** carteira *f* de identidade, (*P*) bilhete *m*. de identidade

ideolog|y /aɪdɪ'ɒlədʒɪ/ *n* ideologia *f*. **~ical** *a* /-ɪə'lɒdʒɪkl/ *a* ideológico

idiom /'ɪdɪəm/ *n* idioma *m*; (*phrase*) expressão *f* idiomática. **~atic** /-'mætɪk/ *a* idiomático

idiosyncrasy /ɪdɪə'sɪŋkrəsɪ/ *n* idiossincrasia *f*, peculiaridade *f*

idiot /'ɪdɪət/ *n* idiota *mf*. **~ic** /-'ɒtɪk/ *a* idiota

idl|e /'aɪdl/ *a* (**-er, -est**) (*not active; lazy*) ocioso; (*unemployed*) sem trabalho; (*of machines*) parado; (*fig: useless*) inútil □ *vt/i* (*of engine*) estar em ponto morto, *P* estar no ralenti. **~eness** *n* ociosidade *f*. **~y** *adv* ociosamente

idol /'aɪdl/ *n* ídolo *m*. **~ize** *vt* idolatrar

idyllic /ɪ'dɪlɪk/ *a* idílico

i.e. *abbr* isto é, quer dizer

if /ɪf/ *conj* se

igloo /'ɪglu:/ *n* iglu *m*

ignite /ɪg'naɪt/ *vt/i* inflamar(-se), acender; (*catch fire*) pegar fogo; (*set fire to*) atear fogo a, (*P*) deitar fogo a

ignition /ɪg'nɪʃn/ *n* (*auto*) ignição *f*. **~ (key)** chave *f* de ignição

ignoran|t /'ɪgnərənt/ *a* ignorante. **~ce** *n* ignorância *f*. **be ~t of** ignorar

ignore /ɪg'nɔ:(r)/ *vt* não fazer caso de, passar por cima de; (*person in the street etc*) fingir não ver

ill /ɪl/ *a* (*sick*) doente; (*bad*) mau □ *adv* mal □ *n* mal *m*. **~-advised** *a* pouco aconselhável. **~ at ease** pouco à vontade. **~-bred** *a* mal educado. **~-fated** *a* malfadado. **~-treat** *vt* maltratar. **~ will** má vontade *f*, animosidade *f*

illegal /ɪ'li:gl/ *a* ilegal

illegible /ɪ'ledʒəbl/ *a* ilegível

illegitima|te /ɪlɪ'dʒɪtɪmət/ *a* ilegítimo. **~cy** *n* ilegitimidade *f*

illitera|te /ɪ'lɪtərət/ *a* analfabeto; (*uneducated*) iletrado. **~cy** *n* analfabetismo *m*

illness /'ɪlnɪs/ *n* doença *f*

illogical /ɪ'lɒdʒɪkl/ *a* ilógico

illuminat|e /ɪ'lu:mɪneɪt/ *vt* iluminar; (*explain*) esclarecer. **~ion** /-'neɪʃn/ *n* iluminação *f*. **~ions** *npl* luminárias *fpl*

illusion /ɪ'lu:ʒn/ *n* ilusão *f*

illusory /ɪ'lu:sərɪ/ *a* ilusório

illustrat|e /'ɪləstreɪt/ *vt* ilustrar. **~ion** /-'streɪʃn/ *n* ilustração *f*. **~ive** /-ətɪv/ *a* ilustrativo

illustrious /ɪ'lʌstrɪəs/ *a* ilustre

image /'ɪmɪdʒ/ *n* imagem *f*. **(public) ~** imagem *f* pública

imaginary /ɪ'mædʒɪnərɪ/ *a* imaginário

imaginat|ion /ɪmædʒɪ'neɪʃn/ *n* imaginação *f*. **~ive** /ɪ'mædʒɪnətɪv/ *a* imaginativo

imagin|e /ɪ'mædʒɪn/ *vt* imaginar. **~able** *a* imaginável

imbalance /ɪm'bæləns/ *n* desequilíbrio *m*

imbecile /'ɪmbəsi:l/ *a* & *n* imbecil (*mf*)

imbue /ɪm'bju:/ *vt* imbuir, impregnar

imitat|e /'ɪmɪteɪt/ *vt* imitar. **~ion** /-'teɪʃn/ *n* imitação *f*

immaculate /ɪ'mækjʊlət/ *a* imaculado; (*impeccable*) impecável

immaterial /ɪmə'tɪərɪəl/ *a* (*of no importance*) irrelevante. **that's ~ to me** para mim tanto faz

immature /ɪmə'tjʊə(r)/ *a* imaturo

immediate /ɪ'mi:dɪət/ *a* imediato. **~ly** *adv* imediatamente □ *conj* logo que, assim que

immens|e /ɪ'mens/ *a* imenso. **~ely** /-slɪ/ *adv* imensamente. **~ity** *n* imensidade *f*

immers|e /ɪ'mɜ:s/ *vt* mergulhar, imergir. **be ~ed in** (*fig*) estar imerso em. **~ion** /-ʃn/ *n* imersão *f*. **~ion heater** aquecedor *m* de água elétrico, (*P*) eléc-trico

immigr|ate /'ɪmɪgreɪt/ *vi* imigrar. **~ant** *n* & *a* imigrante (*mf*), imigrado (*m*). **~ation** /-'greɪʃn/ *n* imigração *f*

imminen|t /'ɪmɪnənt/ *a* iminente. **~ce** *n* iminência *f*

immobil|e /ɪ'məʊbaɪl/ *a* imóvel. **~ize** /-əlaɪz/ *vt* imobilizar

immoderate /ɪ'mɒdərət/ *a* imoderado, descomedido

immoral /ɪ'mɒrəl/ *a* imoral. **~ity** /ɪmə'rælətɪ/ *n* imoralidade *f*

immortal /ɪ'mɔ:tl/ *a* imortal. **~ity** /-'tælətɪ/ *n* imortalidade *f*. **~ize** *vt* imortalizar

immun|e /ɪ'mju:n/ *a* imune, imunizado (**from, to** contra). **~ity** *n* imunidade *f*

imp /ɪmp/ *n* diabrete *m*

impact /'ɪmpækt/ *n* impacto *m*

impair /ɪm'peə(r)/ *vt* deteriorar; (*damage*) prejudicar

impale /ɪm'peɪl/ *vt* empalar

impart /ɪm'pa:t/ *vt* comunicar, transmitir (**to** a)

impartial /ɪm'pa:ʃl/ *a* imparcial. **~ity** /-ʃɪ'ælətɪ/ *n* imparcialidade *f*

impassable /ɪm'pa:səbl/ *a* (*road, river*) impraticável, intransitável; (*barrier etc*) intransponível

impasse /'æmpa:s/ *n* impasse *m*

impatien|t /ɪm'peɪʃənt/ *a* impaciente. **~ce** *n* impaciência *f*. **~tly** *adv* impacientemente
impeach /ɪm'pi:tʃ/ *vt* incriminar, acusar
impeccable /ɪm'pekəbl/ *a* impecável
impede /ɪm'pi:d/ *vt* impedir, estorvar
impediment /ɪm'pedɪmənt/ *n* impedimento *m*, obstáculo *m*. **(speech)** ~ defeito *m* (na fala)
impel /ɪm'pel/ *vt* (*pt* **impelled**) impelir, forçar (**to do** a fazer)
impending /ɪm'pendɪŋ/ *a* iminente
impenetrable /ɪm'penɪtrəbl/ *a* impenetrável
imperative /ɪm'perətɪv/ *a* imperativo; (*need etc*) imperioso □ *n* imperativo *m*
imperceptible /ɪmpə'septəbl/ *a* imperceptível
imperfect /ɪm'pɜ:fɪkt/ *a* imperfeito. **~ion** /-ə'fekʃn/ *n* imperfeição *f*
imperial /ɪm'pɪərɪəl/ *a* imperial; (*of measures*) legal (*na GB*). **~ism** /-lɪzəm/ *n* imperialismo *m*
imperious /ɪm'pɪərɪəs/ *a* imperioso
impersonal /ɪm'pɜ:sənl/ *a* impessoal
impersonat|e /ɪm'pɜ:səneɪt/ *vt* fazer-se passar por; (*theat*) fazer *or* representar (o papel) de. **~ion** /-'neɪʃn/ *n* imitação *f*
impertinen|t /ɪm'pɜ:tɪnənt/ *a* impertinente. **~ce** *n* impertinência *f*. **~tly** *adv* com impertinência
impervious /ɪm'pɜ:vɪəs/ *a* ~ **to** (*water*) impermeável a; (*fig*) insensível a
impetuous /ɪm'petʃʊəs/ *a* impetuoso
impetus /'ɪmpɪtəs/ *n* ímpeto *m*
impinge /ɪm'pɪndʒ/ *vi* ~ **on** afetar, *P* afectar; (*encroach*) infringir
impish /'ɪmpɪʃ/ *a* travesso, malicioso
implacable /ɪm'plækəbl/ *a* implacável
implant /ɪm'pla:nt/ *vt* implantar
implement[1] /'ɪmplɪmənt/ *n* instrumento *m*, utensílio *m*
implement[2] /'ɪmplɪment/ *vt* implementar, executar
implicat|e /'ɪmplɪkeɪt/ *vt* implicar. **~ion** /-'keɪʃn/ *n* implicação *f*
implicit /ɪm'plɪsɪt/ *a* implícito; (*unquestioning*) absoluto, incondicional
implore /ɪm'plɔ:(r)/ *vt* implorar, suplicar, rogar
imply /ɪm'plaɪ/ *vt* implicar; (*hint*) sugerir, dar a entender, insinuar
impolite /ɪmpə'laɪt/ *a* indelicado, incorreto, (*P*) incorrecto
import[1] /ɪm'pɔ:t/ *vt* importar. **~ation** /-'teɪʃn/ *n* importação *f*. **~er** *n* importador *m*
import[2] /'ɪmpɔ:t/ *n* importação *f*; (*meaning*) significado *m*; (*importance*) importância *f*
importan|t /ɪm'pɔ:tnt/ *a* importante. **~ce** *n* importância *f*
impos|e /ɪm'pəʊz/ *vt* impôr; (*inflict*) infligir □ *vi* **~e on** abusar de. **~ition** /-ə'zɪʃn/ *n* imposição *f*; (*unfair burden*) abuso *m*
imposing /ɪm'pəʊzɪŋ/ *a* imponente
impossib|le /ɪm'pɒsəbl/ *a* impossível. **~ility** /-'bɪlətɪ/ *n* impossibilidade *f*
impostor /ɪm'pɒstə(r)/ *n* impostor *m*
impoten|t /'ɪmpətənt/ *a* impotente. **~ce** *n* impotência *f*
impound /ɪm'paʊnd/ *vt* apreender, confiscar
impoverish /ɪm'pɒvərɪʃ/ *vt* empobrecer
impracticable /ɪm'præktɪkəbl/ *a* impraticável
impractical /ɪm'præktɪkl/ *a* pouco prático
imprecise /ɪmprɪ'saɪs/ *a* impreciso
impregnable /ɪm'pregnəbl/ *a* inexpugnável; (*fig*) inabalável, irrefutável
impregnate /'ɪmpregneɪt/ *vt* impregnar (**with** de)
impresario /ɪmprɪ'sa:rɪəʊ/ *n* (*pl* **-os**) empresário *m*
impress /ɪm'pres/ *vt* impressionar, causar impressão a; (*imprint*) imprimir. ~ **sth on s.o.** inculcar algo em alguém
impression /ɪm'preʃn/ *n* impressão *f*. **~able** *a* impressionável. **~ist** *n* impressionista *mf*
impressive /ɪm'presɪv/ *a* impressionante, imponente
imprint[1] /'ɪmprɪnt/ *n* impressão *f*, marca *f*
imprint[2] /ɪm'prɪnt/ *vt* imprimir
imprison /ɪm'prɪzn/ *vt* prender, aprisionar. **~ment** *n* aprisionamento *m*, prisão *f*
improbab|le /ɪm'prɒbəbl/ *a* improvável. **~ility** /-'bɪlətɪ/ *n* improbabilidade *f*
impromptu /ɪm'prɒmptju:/ *a & adv* de improviso □ *n* impromptu *m*
improper /ɪm'prɒpə(r)/ *a* impróprio; (*indecent*) indecente, pouco decente; (*wrong*) incorreto, (*P*) incorrecto
improve /ɪm'pru:v/ *vt/i* melhorar. ~ **on** aperfeiçoar. **~ment** *n* melhoria *f*; (*in house etc*) melhoramento *m*; (*in health*) melhoras *fpl*
improvis|e /'ɪmprəvaɪz/ *vt/i* improvisar. **~ation** /-'zeɪʃn/ *n* improvisação *f*
imprudent /ɪm'pru:dnt/ *a* imprudente
impuden|t /'ɪmpjʊdənt/ *a* descarado, insolente. **~ce** *n* descaramento *m*, insolência *f*
impulse /'ɪmpʌls/ *n* impulso *m*
impulsive /ɪm'pʌlsɪv/ *a* impulsivo

impur|e /ɪm'pjʊə(r)/ *a* impuro. **~ity** *n* impureza *f*

in /ɪn/ *prep* em, dentro de □ *adv* dentro; (*at home*) em casa; (*in fashion*) na moda. **~ Lisbon/English** em Lisboa/inglês. **~ winter** no inverno. **~ an hour** (*at end of, within*) numa hora. **~ the rain** na chuva. **~ doing** ao fazer. **~ the evening** à tardinha. **the best ~** o melhor em. **we are ~ for** vamos ter. **~-laws** *npl* (*colloq*) sogros *mpl*. **~-patient** *n* doente *m* internado. **the ~s and outs** meandros *mpl*

inability /ɪnə'bɪlətɪ/ *n* incapacidade *f* (**to do** para fazer)

inaccessible /ɪnæk'sesəbl/ *a* inacessível

inaccura|te /ɪn'ækjərət/ *a* inexato, (*P*) inexacto. **~cy** *n* inexatidão *f*, (*P*) inexactidão *f*, falta *f* de rigor

inaction /ɪn'ækʃn/ *n* inação *f*, (*P*) inacção *f*

inactiv|e /ɪn'æktɪv/ *a* inativo, (*P*) inactivo. **~ity** /-'tɪvətɪ/ *n* inação *f*, (*P*) inacção *f*

inadequa|te /ɪn'ædɪkwət/ *a* inadequado, impróprio; (*insufficient*) insuficiente. **~cy** *n* inadequação *f*; (*insufficiency*) insuficiência *f*

inadmissible /ɪnəd'mɪsəbl/ *a* inadmissível

inadvertently /ɪnəd'vɜ:təntlɪ/ *adv* inadvertidamente; (*unintentionally*) sem querer, sem ser por mal

inadvisable /ɪnəd'vaɪzəbl/ *a* desaconselhável, não aconselhável

inane /ɪ'neɪn/ *a* tolo, oco

inanimate /ɪn'ænɪmət/ *a* inanimado

inappropriate /ɪnə'prəʊprɪət/ *a* impróprio, inadequado

inarticulate /ɪnɑ:'tɪkjʊlət/ *a* inarticulado; (*of person*) incapaz de se exprimir claramente

inattentive /ɪnə'tentɪv/ *a* desatento

inaugural /ɪ'nɔ:gjʊrəl/ *a* inaugural

inaugurat|e /ɪ'nɔ:gjʊreɪt/ *vt* inaugurar. **~ion** /-'reɪʃn/ *n* inauguração *f*

inauspicious /ɪnɔ:'spɪʃəs/ *a* pouco auspicioso

inborn /ɪn'bɔ:n/ *a* inato

inbred /ɪn'bred/ *a* inato, congênito, (*P*) congénito

incalculable /ɪn'kælkjʊləbl/ *a* incalculável

incapable /ɪn'keɪpəbl/ *a* incapaz

incapacit|y /ɪnkə'pæsətɪ/ *n* incapacidade *f*. **~ate** *vt* incapacitar

incarnat|e /ɪn'kɑ:neɪt/ *a* encarnado. **the devil ~e** o diabo em pessoa. **~ion** /-'neɪʃn/ *n* encarnação *f*

incendiary /ɪn'sendɪərɪ/ *a* incendiário □ *n* bomba *f* incendiária

incense[1] /'ɪnsens/ *n* incenso *m*

incense[2] /ɪn'sens/ *vt* exasperar, enfurecer

incentive /ɪn'sentɪv/ *n* incentivo, estímulo

incessant /ɪn'sesənt/ *a* incessante. **~ly** *adv* incessantemente, sem cessar

incest /'ɪnsest/ *n* incesto *m*. **~uous** /ɪn'sestjʊəs/ *a* incestuoso

inch /ɪntʃ/ *n* polegada *f* (= *2.54 cm*) □ *vt/i* avançar palmo a palmo *or* pouco a pouco. **within an ~ of** a um passo de

incidence /'ɪnsɪdəns/ *n* incidência *f*; (*rate*) percentagem *f*

incident /'ɪnsɪdənt/ *n* incidente *m*

incidental /ɪnsɪ'dentl/ *a* incidental, acessório; (*casual*) acidental; (*expenses*) eventuais; (*music*) de cena, incidental. **~ly** *adv* incidentalmente; (*by the way*) a propósito

incinerat|e /ɪn'sɪnəreɪt/ *vt* incinerar. **~or** *n* incinerador *m*

incision /ɪn'sɪʒn/ *n* incisão *f*

incisive /ɪn'saɪsɪv/ *a* incisivo

incite /ɪn'saɪt/ *vt* incitar, instigar. **~ment** *n* incitamento *m*

inclination /ɪnklɪ'neɪʃn/ *n* inclinação *f*, tendência *f*

incline[1] /ɪn'klaɪn/ *vt/i* inclinar (-se). **be ~d to** inclinar-se para; (*have tendency*) ter tendência para

incline[2] /'ɪnklaɪn/ *n* inclinação *f*, declive *m*

inclu|de /ɪn'klu:d/ *vt* incluir; (*in letter*) enviar junto *or* em anexo. **~ding** *prep* inclusive. **~sion** *n* inclusão *f*

inclusive /ɪn'klu:sɪv/ *a* & *adv* inclusive. **be ~ of** incluir

incognito /ɪnkɒg'ni:təʊ/ *a & adv* incógnito

incoherent /ɪnkə'hɪərənt/ *a* incoerente

income /'ɪŋkʌm/ *n* rendimento *m*. **~ tax** imposto sobre a renda, (*P*) sobre o rendimento

incoming /'ɪnkʌmɪŋ/ *a* (*tide*) enchente; (*tenant etc*) novo

incomparable /ɪn'kɒmpərəbl/ *a* incomparável

incompatible /ɪnkəm'pætəbl/ *a* incompatível

incompeten|t /ɪn'kɒmpɪtənt/ *a* incompetente. **~ce** *n* incompetência *f*

incomplete /ɪnkəm'pli:t/ *a* incompleto

incomprehensible /ɪnkɒmprɪ-'hensəbl/ *a* incompreensível

inconceivable /ɪnkən'si:vəbl/ *a* inconcebível

inconclusive /ɪnkən'klu:sɪv/ *a* inconcludente

incongruous /ɪn'kɒŋgrʊəs/ *a* incongruente; (*absurd*) absurdo

inconsequential /ɪnkɒnsɪ'kwenʃl/ *a* sem importância

inconsiderate /ɪnkən'sɪdərət/ *a* impensado, inconsiderado; (*lacking in regard*) pouco atencioso, sem consideração (pelos sentimentos *etc* de outrem)

inconsisten|t /ɪnkən'sɪstənt/ *a* incoerente; (*at variance*) contraditório. **~t with** incompatível com. **~cy** *n* incoerência *f*. **~cies** *npl* contradições *fpl*

inconspicuous /ɪnkən'spɪkjʊəs/ *a* que não dá nas vistas, que não chama a atenção

incontinen|t /ɪn'kɒntɪnənt/ *a* incontinente. **~ce** *n* incontinência *f*

inconvenien|t /ɪnkən'vi:nɪənt/ *a* inconveniente, incômodo. **~ce** *n* inconveniência *f*; (*drawback*) inconveniente *m* □ *vt* incomodar

incorporate /ɪn'kɔ:pəreɪt/ *vt* incorporar; (*include*) incluir

incorrect /ɪnkə'rekt/ *a* incorreto, (*P*) incorrecto

incorrigible /ɪn'kɒrɪdʒəbl/ *a* incorrigível

increas|e[1] /ɪn'kri:s/ *vt/i* aumentar. **~ing** *a* crescente. **~ingly** *adv* cada vez mais

increase[2] /'ɪnkri:s/ *n* aumento *m*. **on the ~** aumentando, crescendo

incredible /ɪn'kredəbl/ *a* incrível

incredulous /ɪn'kredjʊləs/ *a* incrédulo

increment /'ɪŋkrəmənt/ *n* incremento *m*, aumento *m*

incriminat|e /ɪn'krɪmɪneɪt/ *vt* incriminar. **~ing** *a* comprometedor

incubat|e /'ɪnkjʊbeɪt/ *vt* incubar. **~ion** /-'beɪʃn/ *n* incubação *f*. **~or** *n* incubadora *f*

inculcate /'ɪnkʌlkeɪt/ *vt* inculcar

incumbent /ɪn'kʌmbənt/ *n* (*pol, relig*) titular *mf* □ *a* **be ~ on** incumbir a, caber a

incur /ɪn'kɜ:r/ *vt* (*pt* **incurred**) (*displeasure, expense etc*) incorrer em; (*debts*) contrair

incurable /ɪn'kjʊərəbl/ *a* incurável, que não tem cura

indebted /ɪn'detɪd/ *a* **~ to s.o.** em dívida (para) com alg (**for** por)

indecen|t /ɪn'di:snt/ *a* indecente. **~t assault** atentado *m* contra o pudor. **~cy** *n* indecência *f*

indecision /ɪndɪ'sɪʒn/ *n* indecisão *f*

indecisive /ɪndɪ'saɪsɪv/ *a* inconcludente, não decisivo; (*hesitating*) indeciso

indeed /ɪn'di:d/ *adv* realmente, deveras, mesmo; (*in fact*) de fato, (*P*) facto. **very much ~** muitíssimo

indefinite /ɪn'defɪnət/ *a* indefinido; (*time*) indeterminado. **~ly** *adv* indefinidamente

indelible /ɪn'deləbl/ *a* indelével

indemnify /ɪn'demnɪfaɪ/ *vt* indenizar, (*P*) indemnizar (**for** de); (*safeguard*) garantir (**against** contra)

indemnity /ɪn'demnətɪ/ *n* (*legal exemption*) isenção *f*; (*compensation*) indenização *f*, (*P*) indemnização *f*; (*safeguard*) garantia *f*

indent /ɪn'dent/ *vt* (*notch*) recortar; (*typ*) entrar. **~ation** /-'teɪʃn/ *n* recorte *m*; (*typ*) entrada *f*

independen|t /ɪndɪ'pendənt/ *a* independente. **~ce** *n* independência *f*. **~tly** *adv* independentemente

indescribable /ɪndɪ'skraɪbəbl/ *a* indescritível

indestructible /ɪndɪ'strʌktəbl/ *a* indestrutível

indeterminate /ɪndɪ'tɜ:mɪnət/ *a* indeterminado

index /'ɪndeks/ *n* (*pl* **indexes**) *n* (*in book*) índice *m*; (*in library*) catálogo *m* □ *vt* indexar. **~ card** ficha *f* (de fichário). **~ finger** index *m*, (dedo) indicador *m*. **~-linked** *a* ligado ao índice de inflação

India /'ɪndɪə/ *n* Índia *f*. **~n** *a* & *n* (*of India*) indiano (*m*); (*American*) índio (*m*)

indicat|e /'ɪndɪkeɪt/ *vt* indicar. **~ion** /-'keɪʃn/ *n* indicação *f*. **~or** *n* indicador *m*; (*auto*) pisca-pisca *m*; (*board*) quadro *m*

indicative /ɪn'dɪkətɪv/ *a* & *n* indicativo (*m*)

indict /ɪn'daɪt/ *vt* acusar. **~ment** *n* acusação *f*

indifferen|t /ɪn'dɪfrənt/ *a* indiferente; (*not good*) medíocre. **~ce** *n* indiferença *f*

indigenous /ɪn'dɪdʒɪnəs/ *a* indígena, natural, nativo (**to** de)

indigest|ion /ɪndɪ'dʒestʃən/ *n* indigestão *f*. **~ible** /-təbl/ *a* indigesto

indign|ant /ɪn'dɪgnənt/ *a* indignado. **~ation** /-'neɪʃn/ *n* indignação *f*

indirect /ɪndɪ'rekt/ *a* indireto, (*P*) indirecto. **~ly** *adv* indiretamente, (*P*) indirectamente

indiscr|eet /ɪndɪ'skri:t/ *a* indiscreto; (*not wary*) imprudente. **~etion** /-'eʃn/ *n* indiscrição *f*; (*action, remark etc*) deslize *m*

indiscriminate /ɪndɪ'skrɪmɪnət/ *a* que tem falta de discernimento; (*random*) indiscriminado. **~ly** *adv* sem discernimento; (*at random*) indiscriminadamente, ao acaso

indispensable /ɪndɪ'spensəbl/ *a* indispensável

indispos|ed /ɪndɪ'spəʊzd/ *a* indisposto. **~ition** /-ə'zɪʃn/ *n* indisposição *f*

indisputable /ɪndɪ'spju:təbl/ *a* indisputável, incontestável

indistinct /ɪndɪ'stɪŋkt/ *a* indistinto

indistinguishable /ɪndɪ'stɪŋgwɪʃ-əbl/ *a* indistinguível, imperceptível; (*identical*) indiferenciável

individual /ɪndɪ'vɪdʒʊəl/ *a* individual □ *n* indivíduo *m*. **~ity** /-'æləti/ *n* individualidade *f*. **~ly** *adv* individualmente

indivisible /ɪndɪ'vɪzəbl/ *a* indivisível

indoctrinat|e /ɪn'dɒktrɪneɪt/ *vt* (en)doutrinar. **~ion** /-'neɪʃn/ *n* (en)doutrinação *f*

indolen|t /'ɪndələnt/ *a* indolente. **~ce** *n* indolência *f*

indoor /'ɪndɔ:(r)/ *a* (de) interior, interno; (*under cover*) coberto; (*games*) de salão. **~s** /ɪn'dɔ:z/ *adv* dentro de casa, no interior

induce /ɪn'dju:s/ *vt* induzir, levar; (*cause*) causar, provocar. **~ment** *n* incentivo *m*, encorajamento *m*

indulge /ɪn'dʌldʒ/ *vt* satisfazer; (*spoil*) fazer a(s) vontade(s) de □ *vi* **~ in** entregar-se a

indulgen|t /ɪn'dʌldʒənt/ *a* indulgente. **~ce** *n* (*leniency*) indulgência *f*; (*desire*) satisfação *f*

industrial /ɪn'dʌstrɪəl/ *a* industrial; (*unrest etc*) trabalhista; (*action*) reivindicativo. **~ estate** zona *f* industrial. **~ist** *n* industrial *m*. **~ized** *a* industrializado

industrious /ɪn'dʌstrɪəs/ *a* trabalhador, aplicado

industry /'ɪndəstrɪ/ *n* indústria *f*; (*zeal*) aplicação *f*, diligência *f*, zelo *m*

inebriated /ɪ'ni:brɪeɪtɪd/ *a* embriagado, ébrio

inedible /ɪ'nedɪbl/ *a* não comestível

ineffective /ɪnɪ'fektɪv/ *a* ineficaz; (*person*) ineficiente, incapaz

ineffectual /ɪnɪ'fektʃʊəl/ *a* ineficaz, improfícuo

inefficien|t /ɪnɪ'fɪʃnt/ *a* ineficiente. **~cy** *n* ineficiência *f*

ineligible /ɪn'elɪdʒəbl/ *a* inelegível; (*undesirable*) indesejável. **be ~ for** não ter direito a

inept /ɪ'nept/ *a* inepto

inequality /ɪnɪ'kwɒlətɪ/ *n* desigualdade *f*

inert /ɪ'nɜ:t/ *a* inerte. **~ia** /-ʃə/ *n* inércia *f*

inevitable /ɪn'evɪtəbl/ *a* inevitável, fatal

inexcusable /ɪnɪk'skju:zəbl/ *a* indesculpável, imperdoável

inexhaustible /ɪnɪg'zɔ:stəbl/ *a* inesgotável, inexaurível

inexorable /ɪn'eksərəbl/ *a* inexorável

inexpensive /ɪnɪk'spensɪv/ *a* barato, em conta

inexperience /ɪnɪk'spɪərɪəns/ *n* inexperiência *f*, falta de experiência *f*. **~d** *a* inexperiente

inexplicable /ɪn'eksplɪkəbl/ *a* inexplicável

inextricable /ɪn'ekstrɪkəbl/ *a* inextricável

infallib|le /ɪn'fæləbl/ *a* infalível. **~ility** /-'bɪlətɪ/ *n* infalibilidade *f*

infam|ous /'ɪnfəməs/ *a* infame. **~y** *n* infâmia *f*

infan|t /'ɪnfənt/ *n* bebê *m*, (*P*) bebé *m*; (*child*) criança *f*. **~cy** *n* infância *f*; (*babyhood*) primeira infância *f*

infantile /'ɪnfəntaɪl/ *a* infantil

infantry /'ɪnfəntrɪ/ *n* infantaria *f*

infatuat|ed /ɪn'fætʃʊeɪtɪd/ *a* **~ed with** cego *or* perdido por. **~ion** /-'eɪʃn/ *n* cegueira *f*, paixão *f*

infect /ɪn'fekt/ *vt* infectar. **~ s.o. with** contagiar *or* contaminar alg com. **~ion** /-ʃn/ *n* infecção *f*, contágio *m*. **~ious** /-ʃəs/ *a* infeccioso, contagioso

infer /ɪn'fɜ:(r)/ *vt* (*pt* **inferred**) inferir, deduzir. **~ence** /'ɪnfərəns/ *n* inferência *f*

inferior /ɪn'fɪərɪə(r)/ *a* inferior; (*work etc*) de qualidade inferior □ *n* inferior *mf*; (*in rank*) subalterno *m*. **~ity** /-'ɒrətɪ/ *n* inferioridade *f*

infernal /ɪn'fɜ:nl/ *a* infernal

infertil|e /ɪn'fɜ:taɪl/ *a* infertil, estéril. **~ity** /-ə'tɪlətɪ/ *n* infertilidade *f*, esterilidade *f*

infest /ɪn'fest/ *vt* infestar (**with** de). **~ation** *n* infestação *f*

infidelity /ɪnfɪ'delətɪ/ *n* infidelidade *f*

infiltrat|e /'ɪnfɪltreɪt/ *vt/i* infiltrar (-se). **~ion** /-'treɪʃn/ *n* infiltração *f*

infinite /'ɪnfɪnət/ *a* & *n* infinito (*m*). **~ly** *adv* infinitamente

infinitesimal /ɪnfɪnɪ'tesɪml/ *a* infinitesimal, infinitésimo

infinitive /ɪn'fɪnətɪv/ *n* infinitivo *m*

infinity /ɪn'fɪnətɪ/ *n* infinidade *f*, infinito *m*

infirm /ɪn'fɜ:m/ *a* débil, fraco. **~ity** *n* (*illness*) enfermidade *f*; (*weakness*) fraqueza *f*

inflam|e /ɪn'fleɪm/ *vt* inflamar. **~mable** /-æməbl/ *a* inflamável. **~mation** /-ə'meɪʃn/ *n* inflamação *f*

inflate /ɪn'fleɪt/ *vt* (*balloon etc*) encher de ar; (*prices*) causar inflação de

inflation /ɪn'fleɪʃn/ *n* inflação *f*. **~ary** *a* inflacionário

inflection /ɪn'flekʃn/ *n* inflexão *f*; (*gram*) flexão *f*, desinência *f*

inflexible /ɪn'fleksəbl/ *a* inflexível

inflict /ɪn'flɪkt/ *vt* infligir, impor (**on** a)

influence /'ɪnflʊəns/ *n* influência *f* □ *vt* influenciar, influir sobre

influential /ɪnflʊ'enʃl/ *a* influente

influenza /ɪnflʊ'enzə/ *n* gripe *f*

influx /'ɪnflʌks/ *n* afluência *f*, influxo *m*

inform /ɪn'fɔ:m/ *vt* informar. **~ against** *or* **on** denunciar. **keep ~ed** manter ao corrente *or* a par. **~ant** *n* informante *mf*. **~- er** *n* delator *m*, denunciante *mf*

informal /ɪn'fɔ:ml/ *a* informal; (*simple*) simples, sem cerimônia, (*P*) cerimónia; (*unofficial*) oficioso; (*colloquial*) familiar; (*dress*) de passeio, à vontade; (*dinner, gathering*) íntimo. **~ity** /-'mælətɪ/ *n* informalidade *f*; (*simplicity*) simplicidade *f*; (*intimacy*) intimidade *f*. **~ly** *adv* informalmente, sem cerimônia, (*P*) cerimónia, à vontade

information /ɪnfə'meɪʃn/ *n* informação *f*; (*facts, data*) informações *fpl*. **~ technology** tec-nologia *f* da informação

informative /ɪn'fɔ:mətɪv/ *a* informativo

infra-red /ɪnfrə'red/ *a* infravermelho

infrequent /ɪn'fri:kwənt/ *a* pouco freqüente, (*P*) frequente. **~ly** *adv* raramente

infringe /ɪn'frɪndʒ/ *vt* infringir. **~ on** transgredir; (*rights*) violar. **~ment** *n* infração *f*, (*P*) infracção *f*; (*rights*) violação *f*

infuriat|e /ɪn'fjʊərɪeɪt/ *vt* enfurecer, enraivecer. **~ing** *a* enfurecedor, de enfurecer, de dar raiva

infus|e /ɪn'fju:z/ *vt* infundir, incutir; (*herbs, tea*) pôr de infusão. **~ion** /-ʒn/ *n* infusão *f*

ingen|ious /ɪn'dʒi:nɪəs/ *a* engenhoso, bem pensado. **~uity** /-ɪ'nju:ətɪ/ *n* engenho *m*, habilidade *f*, imaginação *f*

ingenuous /ɪn'dʒenjʊəs/ *a* cândido, ingênuo, (*P*) ingénuo

ingot /'ɪŋgət/ *n* barra *f*, lingote *m*

ingrained /ɪn'greɪnd/ *a* arraigado, enraizado; (*dirt*) entranhado

ingratiate /ɪn'greɪʃɪeɪt/ *vt* **~ o.s. with** insinuar-se junto de, cair nas *or* ganhar as boas graças de

ingratitude /ɪn'grætɪtju:d/ *n* ingratidão *f*

ingredient /ɪn'gri:dɪənt/ *n* ingrediente *m*

inhabit /ɪn'hæbɪt/ *vt* habitar. **~-able** *a* habitável. **~ant** *n* habitante *mf*

inhale /ɪn'heɪl/ *vt* inalar, aspirar. **~r** /-ə(r)/ *n* inalador *m*

inherent /ɪn'hɪərənt/ *a* inerente. **~ly** *adv* inerentemente, em si

inherit /ɪn'herɪt/ *vt* herdar (**from** de). **~ance** *n* herança *f*

inhibit /ɪn'hɪbɪt/ *vt* inibir; (*prevent*) impedir. **be ~ed** ser (um) inibido. **~ion** /-'bɪʃn/ *n* inibição *f*

inhospitable /ɪn'hɒspɪtəbl/ *a* inóspito; (*of person*) inospitaleiro, pouco/nada hospitaleiro

inhuman /ɪn'hju:mən/ *a* desumano. **~ity** /-'mænətɪ/ *n* desumanidade *f*

inhumane /ɪnhju:'meɪn/ *a* inumano, cruel

inimitable /ɪ'nɪmɪtəbl/ *a* inimitável

iniquitous /ɪ'nɪkwɪtəs/ *a* iníquo

initial /ɪ'nɪʃl/ *a* & *n* inicial (*f*) □ *vt* (*pt* **initialled**) assinar com as iniciais, rubricar. **~ly** *adv* inicialmente

initiat|e /ɪ'nɪʃɪeɪt/ *vt* iniciar (**into** em); (*scheme*) lançar. **~ion** /-'eɪʃn/ *n* iniciação *f*; (*start*) início *m*

initiative /ɪ'nɪʃətɪv/ *n* iniciativa *f*

inject /ɪn'dʒekt/ *vt* injetar, (*P*) injectar; (*fig*) insuflar. **~ion** /-ʃn/ *n* injeção *f*, (*P*) injecção *f*

injure /'ɪndʒə(r)/ *vt* (*harm*) fazer mal a, prejudicar, lesar; (*hurt*) ferir

injury /'ɪndʒərɪ/ *n* ferimento *m*, lesão *f*; (*wrong*) mal *m*

injustice /ɪn'dʒʌstɪs/ *n* injustiça *f*

ink /ɪŋk/ *n* tinta *f*. **~-well** *n* tinteiro *m*. **~y** *a* sujo de tinta

inkling /'ɪŋklɪŋ/ *n* idéia *f*, (*P*) ideia *f*, suspeita *f*

inlaid /ɪn'leɪd/ *see* **inlay**[1]

inland /'ɪnlənd/ *a* interior □ *adv* /ɪn'lænd/ no interior, para o interior. **the I~ Revenue** o Fisco, a Receita Federal

inlay[1] /ɪn'leɪ/ *vt* (*pt* **inlaid**) embutir, incrustar

inlay[2] /'ɪnleɪ/ *n* incrustação *f*, obturação *f*

inlet /'ɪnlet/ *n* braço *m* de mar, enseada *f*; (*techn*) admissão *f*

inmate /'ɪnmeɪt/ *n* residente *mf*; (*in hospital*) internado *m*; (*in prison*) presidiário *m*

inn /ɪn/ *n* estalagem *f*

innards /'ɪnədz/ *npl* (*colloq*) tripas (*colloq*) *fpl*

innate /ɪ'neɪt/ *a* inato

inner /'ɪnə(r)/ *a* interior, interno; (*fig*) íntimo. **~ city** centro *m* da cidade. **~most** *a* mais profundo, mais íntimo. **~ tube** *n* câmara *f* de ar

innings /'ɪnɪŋz/ *n* (*cricket*) vez *f* de bater; (*pol*) período *m* no poder

innocen|t /'ɪnəsnt/ *a* & *n* inocente (*mf*). **~ce** *n* inocência *f*

innocuous /ɪ'nɒkjʊəs/ *a* inócuo, inofensivo

innovat|e /'ɪnəveɪt/ *vi* inovar. **~ion** /-'veɪʃn/ *n* inovação *f*. **~or** *n* inovador *m*

innuendo /ɪnju:'endəʊ/ *n* (*pl* **-oes**) insinuação *f*, indireta *f*, (*P*) indirecta *f*

innumerable /ɪ'nju:mərəbl/ *a* inumerável

inoculat|e /ɪ'nɒkjʊleɪt/ *vt* inocular. **~ion** /-'leɪʃn/ *n* inoculação *f*, vacina *f*

inoffensive /ɪnə'fensɪv/ *a* inofensivo

inoperative /ɪn'ɒpərətɪv/ *a* inoperante, ineficaz

inopportune /ɪn'ɒpətju:n/ *a* inoportuno

inordinate /ɪ'nɔ:dɪnət/ *a* excessivo, desmedido. **~ly** *adv* excessivamente, desmedidamente

input /'ɪnpʊt/ *n* (*data*) dados *mpl*; (*electr: power*) energia *f*; (*computer process*) entrada *f*, dados *mpl*

inquest /'ɪnkwest/ *n* inquérito *m*

inquir|e /ɪn'kwaɪə(r)/ *vi* informar-se □ *vt* perguntar, indagar, inquirir. **~e about** procurar informações sobre, indagar. **~e into** inquirir, indagar. **~ing** *a* (*look*) interrogativo; (*mind*) inquisitivo. **~y** *n* (*question*) pergunta *f*; (*jur*) inquérito *m*; (*investigation*) investigação *f*

inquisition /ɪnkwɪ'zɪʃn/ *n* inquisição *f*

inquisitive /ɪn'kwɪzətɪv/ *a* curioso, inquisitivo; (*prying*) intrometido, bisbilhoteiro

insan|e /ɪn'seɪn/ *a* louco, doido. **~ity** /ɪn'sænətɪ/ *n* loucura *f*, demência *f*

insanitary /ɪn'sænɪtrɪ/ *a* insalubre, anti-higiênico, (*P*) anti-higiénico

insatiable /ɪn'seɪʃəbl/ *a* insaciável

inscri|be /ɪn'skraɪb/ *vt* inscrever; (*book*) dedicar. **~ption** /-ɪpʃn/ *n* inscrição *f*; (*in book*) dedicatória *f*

inscrutable /ɪn'skru:təbl/ *a* impenetrável, misterioso

insect /'ɪnsekt/ *n* inseto *m*, (*P*) insecto *m*

insecur|e /ɪnsɪ'kjʊə(r)/ *a* (*not firm*) inseguro, mal seguro; (*unsafe; psych*) inseguro. **~ity** *n* insegurança *f*, falta *f* de segurança

insensible /ɪn'sensəbl/ *a* insensível; (*unconscious*) inconsciente

insensitive /ɪn'sensətɪv/ *a* insensível

inseparable /ɪn'seprəbl/ *a* inseparável

insert[1] /ɪn'sɜ:t/ *vt* inserir; (*key*) meter, colocar; (*add*) pôr, inserir. **~ion** /-ʃn/ *n* inserção *f*

insert[2] /'ɪnsɜ:t/ *n* coisa *f* inserida

inside /ɪn'saɪd/ *n* interior *m*. **~s** (*colloq*) tripas *fpl* (*colloq*) □ *a* interior, interno □ *adv* no interior, dentro, por dentro □ *prep* dentro de; (*of time*) em menos de. **~ out** de dentro para fora, do avesso; (*thoroughly*) por dentro e por fora, a fundo

insidious /ɪn'sɪdɪəs/ *a* insidioso

insight /'ɪnsaɪt/ *n* penetração *f*, perspicácia *f*; (*glimpse*) vislumbre *m*

insignificant /ɪnsɪg'nɪfɪkənt/ *a* insignificante

insincer|e /ɪnsɪn'sɪə(r)/ *a* insincero. **~ity** /-'serətɪ/ *n* insinceridade *f*, falta *f* de sinceridade

insinuat|e /ɪn'sɪnjʊeɪt/ *vt* insinuar. **~ion** /-'eɪʃn/ *n* (*act*) insinuação *f*; (*hint*) indireta *f*, (*P*) indirecta *f*, insinuação *f*

insipid /ɪn'sɪpɪd/ *a* insípido, sem sabor

insist /ɪn'sɪst/ *vt/i* **~ (on/that)** insistir (em/em que)

insisten|t /ɪn'sɪstənt/ *a* insistente. **~ce** *n* insistência *f*. **~tly** *adv* insistentemente

insolen|t /'ɪnsələnt/ *a* insolente. **~ce** *n* insolência *f*

insoluble /ɪn'sɒljʊbl/ *a* insolúvel

insolvent /ɪn'sɒlvənt/ *a* insolvente

insomnia /ɪn'sɒmnɪə/ *n* insônia *f*, (*P*) insónia *f*

inspect /ɪn'spekt/ *vt* inspecionar, (*P*) inspeccionar, examinar; (*tickets*) fiscalizar; (*passport*) controlar; (*troops*) passar revista a. **~ion** /-ʃn/ *n* inspeção *f*, (*P*) inspecção *f*, exame *m*; (*ticket*) fiscalização *f*; (*troops*) revista *f*. **~or** *n* inspetor *m*, (*P*) inspector *m*; (*on train*) fiscal *m*

inspir|e /ɪn'spaɪə(r)/ *vt* inspirar. **~ation** /-ə'reɪʃn/ *n* inspiração *f*

instability /ɪnstə'bɪlətɪ/ *n* instabilidade *f*

install /ɪn'stɔ:l/ *vt* instalar; (*heater etc*) montar, instalar. **~ation** /-ə'leɪʃn/ *n* instalação *f*

instalment /ɪn'stɔ:lmənt/ *n* prestação *f*; (*of serial*) episódio *m*

instance /'ɪnstəns/ *n* exemplo *m*, caso *m*. **for ~** por exemplo. **in the first ~** em primeiro lugar

instant /'ɪnstənt/ *a* imediato; (*food*) instantâneo □ *n* instante *m*. **~ly** *adv* imediatamente, logo

instantaneous /ɪnstən'teɪnɪəs/ *a* instantâneo

instead /ɪn'sted/ *adv* em vez disso, em lugar disso. **~ of** em vez de, em lugar de

instigat|e /'ɪnstɪgeɪt/ *vt* instigar, incitar. **~ion** /-'geɪʃn/ *n* instigação *f*. **~or** *n* instigador *m*

instil /ɪn'stɪl/ *vt* (*pt* **instilled**) instilar, insuflar

instinct /'ɪnstɪŋkt/ *n* instinto *m*. **~ive** /ɪn'stɪŋktɪv/ *a* instintivo

institut|e /'ɪnstɪtju:t/ *n* instituto *m* □ *vt* instituir; (*legal proceedings*) intentar; (*inquiry*) ordenar. **~ion** /-'tju:ʃn/ *n* instituição *f*; (*school*) estabelecimento *m* de ensino; (*hospital*) estabelecimento *m* hospitalar

instruct /ɪn'strʌkt/ *vt* instruir; (*order*) mandar, ordenar; (*a solicitor etc*) dar instruções a. ~ **s.o. in sth** ensinar alg coisa a alguém. **~ion** /-ʃn/ *n* instrução *f*. **~ions** /-ʃnz/ *npl* instruções *fpl*, modo *m* de emprego; (*orders*) ordens *fpl*. **~ive** *a* instrutivo. **~or** *n* instrutor *m*

instrument /'ɪnstrʊmənt/ *n* instrumento *m*. ~ **panel** painel *m* de instrumentos

instrumental /ɪnstrʊ'mentl/ *a* instrumental. **be ~ in** ter um papel decisivo em. **~ist** *n* instrumentalista *mf*

insubordinat|e /ɪnsə'bɔ:dɪnət/ *a* insubordinado. **~ion** /-'neɪʃn/ *n* insubordinação *f*

insufferable /ɪn'sʌfrəbl/ *a* intolerável, insuportável

insufficient /ɪnsə'fɪʃnt/ *a* insuficiente

insular /'ɪnsjʊlə(r)/ *a* insular; (*fig: narrow-minded*) bitolado, limitado, (*P*) tacanho

insulat|e /'ɪnsjʊleɪt/ *vt* isolar. **~ing tape** fita *f* isolante. **~ion** /-'leɪʃn/ *n* isolamento *m*

insulin /'ɪnsjʊlɪn/ *n* insulina *f*

insult[1] /ɪn'sʌlt/ *vt* insultar, injuriar. **~ing** *a* insultante, injurioso

insult[2] /'ɪnsʌlt/ *n* insulto *m*, injúria *f*

insur|e /ɪn'ʃʊə(r)/ *vt* segurar, pôr no seguro; (*Amer*) = **ensure**. **~-ance** *n* seguro *m*. **~ance policy** apólice *f* de seguro

insurmountable /ɪnsə'maʊntəbl/ *a* insuperável

intact /ɪn'tækt/ *a* intato, (*P*) intacto

intake /'ɪnteɪk/ *n* admissão *f*; (*techn*) admissão *f*, entrada *f*; (*of food*) ingestão *f*

intangible /ɪn'tændʒəbl/ *a* intangível

integral /'ɪntɪgrəl/ *a* integral. **be an ~ part of** ser parte integrante de

integrat|e /'ɪntɪgreɪt/ *vt/i* integrar (-se). **~ed circuit** circuito *m* integrado. **~ion** /-'greɪʃn/ *n* integração *f*

integrity /ɪn'tegrətɪ/ *n* integridade *f*

intellect /'ɪntəlekt/ *n* intelecto *m*, inteligência *f*. **~ual** /-'lektʃʊəl/ *a* & *n* intelectual (*mf*)

intelligen|t /ɪn'telɪdʒənt/ *a* inteligente. **~ce** *n* inteligência *f*; (*mil*) informações *fpl*. **~tly** *adv* inteligentemente

intelligible /ɪn'telɪdʒəbl/ *a* inteligível

intend /ɪn'tend/ *vt* tencionar; (*destine*) reservar, destinar. **~ed** *a* intencional, propositado

intens|e /ɪn'tens/ *a* intenso; (*person*) emotivo. **~ely** *adv* intensamente; (*very*) extremamente. **~ity** *n* intensidade *f*

intensif|y /ɪn'tensɪfaɪ/ *vt* intensificar. **~ication** /-ɪ'keɪʃn/ *n* intensificação *f*

intensive /ɪn'tensɪv/ *a* intensivo. **~ care** tratamento *m* intensivo

intent /ɪn'tent/ *n* intento *m*, desígnio *m*, propósito *m* □ *a* atento, concentrado. **~ on** absorto em; (*intending to*) decidido a. **~ly** *adv* atentamente

intention /ɪn'tenʃn/ *n* intenção *f*. **~al** *a* intencional. **~ally** *adv* de propósito

inter /ɪn'tɜ:(r)/ *vt* (*pt* **interred**) enterrar

inter- /'ɪntə(r)/ *pref* inter-

interact /ɪntə'rækt/ *vi* agir uns sobre os outros. **~ion** /-ʃn/ *n* interação *f*, (*P*) interacção *f*

intercede /ɪntə'si:d/ *vi* interceder

intercept /ɪntə'sept/ *vt* interceptar

interchange[1] /ɪntə'tʃeɪndʒ/ *vt* permutar, trocar. **~able** *a* permutável

interchange[2] /'ɪntətʃeɪndʒ/ *n* permuta *f*, intercâmbio *m*; (*road junction*) trevo *m* de trânsito, (*P*) nó *m*

intercom /'ɪntəkɒm/ *n* interfone *m*, (*P*) intercomunicador *m*

interconnected /ɪntəkə'nektɪd/ *a* (*facts, events etc*) ligado

intercourse /'ɪntəkɔ:s/ *n* (*sexual*) relações *fpl* sexuais

interest /'ɪntrəst/ *n* interesse *m*; (*legal share*) título *m*; (*in finance*) juro(s) *m*(*pl*). **rate of ~** taxa *f* de juros □ *vt* interessar. **~ed** *a* interessado. **be ~ed in** interessar-se por. **~ing** *a* interessante

interface /'ɪntəfeɪs/ *n* interface *f*

interfer|e /ɪntə'fɪə(r)/ *vi* interferir, intrometer-se (**in** em); (*meddle, hinder*) interferir (**with** com); (*tamper*) mexer indevidamente (**with** em). **~ence** *n* interferência *f*

interim /'ɪntərɪm/ *n* **in the ~** nesse/ neste ínterim *m*, (*P*) interim *m* □ *a* interino, provisório

interior /ɪn'tɪərɪə(r)/ *a* & *n* interior (*m*)

interjection /ɪntə'dʒekʃn/ *n* interjeição *f*

interlock /ɪntə'lɒk/ *vt/i* entrelaçar; (*pieces of puzzle etc*) encaixar(-se); (*mech: wheels*) engrenar, engatar

interloper /'ɪntələʊpə(r)/ *n* intruso *m*

intermarr|iage /ɪntə'mærɪdʒ/ *n* casamento *m* entre membros de diferentes famílias, raças etc; (*between near relations*) casamento *m* consangüíneo, (*P*) consanguíneo. **~y** *vi* ligar-se por casamento

intermediary /ɪntə'mi:dɪərɪ/ *a* & *n* intermediário (*m*)

intermediate /ɪntə'mi:dɪət/ *a* intermédio, intermediário

interminable /ɪn'tɜ:mɪnəbl/ *a* interminável, infindável

intermission /ɪntə'mɪʃn/ *n* intervalo *m*

intermittent /ɪntə'mɪtnt/ *a* intermitente. **~ly** *adv* intermitentemente

intern /ɪn'tɜ:n/ *vt* internar. **~ee** /-'ni:/ *n* internado *m*. **~ment** *n* internamento *m*

internal /ɪn'tɜ:nl/ *a* interno, interior. (*Amer.*) the **I ~** Revenue o Fisco, a Receita Federal (*B*) **~ly** *adv* internamente, interiormente

international /ɪntə'næʃnəl/ *a* & *n* internacional (*mf*)

Internet /'ɪntənet/ *n* Internet *f*

interpret /ɪn'tɜ:prɪt/ *vt*/*i* interpretar. **~ation** /-'teɪʃn/ *n* interpretação *f*. **~er** *n* intérprete *mf*

interrelated /ɪntərɪ'leɪtɪd/ *a* inter-relacionado, correlacionado

interrogat|e /ɪn'terəgeɪt/ *vt* interrogar. **~ion** /-'geɪʃn/ *n* interrogação *f*; (*of police etc*) interrogatório *m*

interrogative /ɪntə'rɒgətɪv/ *a* interrogativo □ *n* (*pronoun*) pronome *m* interrogativo

interrupt /ɪntə'rʌpt/ *vt* interromper. **~ion** /-ʃn/ *n* interrupção *f*

intersect /ɪntə'sekt/ *vt*/*i* intersectar(-se); (*roads*) cruzar-se. **~ion** /-ʃn/ *n* intersecção *f*; (*crossroads*) cruzamento *m*

intersperse /ɪntə'spɜ:s/ *vt* entremear, intercalar; (*scatter*) espalhar

interval /'ɪntəvl/ *n* intervalo *m*. **at ~s** a intervalos

interven|e /ɪntə'vi:n/ *vi* (*interfere*) intervir; (*of time*) decorrer; (*occur*) sobrevir, intervir. **~tion** /-'venʃn/ *n* intervenção *f*

interview /'ɪntəvju:/ *n* entrevista *f* □ *vt* entrevistar. **~ee** *n* entrevistado *m*. **~er** *n* entrevistador *m*

intestin|e /ɪn'testɪn/ *n* intestino *m*. **~al** *a* intestinal

intima|te[1] /'ɪntɪmət/ *a* íntimo; (*detailed*) profundo. **~cy** *n* intimidade *f*. **~tely** *adv* intimamente

intimate[2] /'ɪntɪmeɪt/ *vt* (*announce*) dar a conhecer, fazer saber; (*imply*) dar a entender

intimidat|e /ɪn'tɪmɪdeɪt/ *vt* intimidar. **~ion** /-'deɪʃn/ *n* intimidação *f*

into /'ɪntə/; *emphatic* /'ɪntʊ/ *prep* para dentro de. **divide ~ three** dividir em tres. **~ pieces** aos bocados. **translate ~** traduzir para

intolerable /ɪn'tɒlərəbl/ *a* intolerável, insuportável

intoleran|t /ɪn'tɒlərənt/ *a* intolerante. **~ce** *n* intolerância *f*

intonation /ɪntə'neɪʃn/ *n* entonação *f*, entoação *f*, inflexão *f*

intoxicat|ed /ɪn'tɒksɪkeɪtɪd/ *a* embriagado, etilizado. **~ion** /-'keɪʃn/ *n* embriaguez *f*

intra- /ɪntrə/ *pref* intra-

intractable /ɪn'træktəbl/ *a* intratável, difícil

intranet /'ɪntrənet/ *n* rede *f* corporativa

intransigent /ɪn'trænsɪdʒənt/ *a* intransigente

intransitive /ɪn'trænsətɪv/ *a* (*verb*) intransitivo

intravenous /ɪntrə'vi:nəs/ *a* intravenoso

intrepid /ɪn'trepɪd/ *a* intrépido, arrojado

intrica|te /'ɪntrɪkət/ *a* intrincado, complexo. **~cy** *n* complexidade *f*

intrigu|e /ɪn'tri:g/ *vt*/*i* intrigar □ *n* intriga *f*. **~ing** *a* intrigante, curioso

intrinsic /ɪn'trɪnsɪk/ *a* intrínseco. **~ally** /-klɪ/ *adv* intrinsecamente

introduce /ɪntrə'dju:s/ *vt* (*programme, question*) apresentar; (*bring in, insert*) introduzir; (*initiate*) iniciar. **~ sb to sb** (*person*) apresentar alg a alguém

introduct|ion /ɪntrə'dʌkʃn/ *n* introdução *f*; (*of/to person*) apresentação *f*. **~ory** /-tərɪ/ *a* introdutório, de introdução; (*letter, words*) de apresentação

introspective /ɪntrə'spektɪv/ *a* introspectivo

introvert /'ɪntrəvɜ:t/ *n* & *a* introvertido (*m*)

intru|de /ɪn'tru:d/ *vi* intrometer-se, ocr a maio. **~der** *n* intruso *m*. **~sion** *n* intrusão *f*. **~sive** *a* intruso

intuit|ion /ɪntju:'ɪʃn/ *n* intuição *f*. **~ive** /ɪn'tju:ɪtɪv/ *a* intuitivo

inundate /'ɪnʌndeɪt/ *vt* inundar (**with** de)

invade /ɪn'veɪd/ *vt* invadir. **~r** /-ə(r)/ *n* invasor *m*

invalid[1] /'ɪnvəlɪd/ *n* inválido *m*

invalid[2] /ɪn'vælɪd/ *a* inválido. **~ate** *vt* invalidar

invaluable /ɪn'væljʊəbl/ *a* inestimável

invariabl|e /ɪn'veərɪəbl/ *a* invariável. **~y** *adv* invariavelmente

invasion /ɪn'veɪʒn/ *n* invasão *f*

invective /ɪn'vektɪv/ *n* invectiva *f*

invent /ɪn'vent/ *vt* inventar. **~ion** *n* invenção *f*. **~ive** *a* inventivo. **~or** *n* inventor *m*

inventory /'ɪnvəntrɪ/ *n* inventário *m*

inverse /ɪn'vɜ:s/ *a* & *n* inverso (*m*). **~ly** *adv* inversamente

inver|t /ɪn'vɜ:t/ *vt* inverter. **~ted commas** aspas *fpl*. **~sion** *n* inversão *f*

invest /ɪn'vest/ *vt* investir; (*time, effort*) dedicar □ *vi* fazer um investimento. **~ in** (*colloq: buy*) gastar dinheiro em.

~**ment** *n* investimento *m*. ~**or** *n* investidor *m*, financiador *m*
investigat|e /ɪn'vestɪgeɪt/ *vt* investigar. ~**ion** /-'geɪʃn/ *n* investigação *f*. **under** ~**ion** em estudo. ~**or** *n* investigador *m*
inveterate /ɪn'vetərət/ *a* inveterado
invidious /ɪn'vɪdɪəs/ *a* antipático, odioso
invigorate /ɪn'vɪgəreɪt/ *vt* revigorar; (*encourage*) estimular
invincible /ɪn'vɪnsəbl/ *a* invencível
invisible /ɪn'vɪzəbl/ *a* invisível
invit|e /ɪn'vaɪt/ *vt* convidar; (*bring on*) pedir, provocar. ~**ation** /ɪnvɪ'teɪʃn/ *n* convite *m*. ~**ing** *a* (*tempting*) tentador; (*pleasant*) acolhedor, convidativo
invoice /'ɪnvɔɪs/ *n* fatura *f*, (*P*) factura *f* □ *vt* faturar, (*P*) facturar
invoke /ɪn'vəʊk/ *vt* invocar
involuntary /ɪn'vɒləntrɪ/ *a* involuntário
involve /ɪn'vɒlv/ *vt* implicar, envolver. ~**d** *a* (*complex*) complicado; (*at stake*) em jogo; (*emotionally*) envolvido. ~**d in** implicado em. ~**ment** *n* envolvimento *m*, participação *f*
invulnerable /ɪn'vʌlnərəbl/ *a* invulnerável
inward /'ɪnwəd/ *a* interior; (*thought etc*) íntimo. ~**(s)** *adv* para dentro, para o interior. ~**ly** *adv* interiormente, intimamente
iodine /'aɪədi:n/ *n* iodo *m*; (*antiseptic*) tintura *f* de iodo
IOU /aɪəʊ'ju:/ *n abbr* vale *m*
IQ /aɪ'kju:/ *abbr* (*intelligence quotient*) QI *m*
Iran /ɪ'ra:n/ *n* Irã *m*. ~**ian** /ɪ'reɪnɪən/ *a* & *n* iraniano (*m*)
Iraq /ɪ'ra:k/ *n* Iraque *m*. ~**i** *a* & *n* iraquiano (*m*)
irascible /ɪ'ræsəbl/ *a* irascível
irate /aɪ'reɪt/ *a* irado, enraivecido
Ireland /'aɪələnd/ *n* Irlanda *f*
iris /'aɪərɪs/ *n* (*anat, bot*) íris *f*
Irish /'aɪərɪʃ/ *a* & *n* (*language*) irlandês (*m*). ~**man** *n* irlandês *m*. ~**woman** *n* irlandesa *f*
irk /ɜ:k/ *vt* aborrecer, incomodar. ~**some** *a* aborrecido
iron /'aɪən/ *n* ferro *m*; (*appliance*) ferro *m* de engomar □ *a* de ferro □ *vt* passar a ferro. ~ **out** fazer desaparecer; (*fig*) aplanar, resolver. ~**ing** *n* **do the** ~**ing** passar a roupa. ~**ing-board** *n* tábua *f* de passar roupa, (*P*) tábua *f* de engomar
ironic(al) /aɪ'rɒnɪk(l)/ *a* irônico, (*P*) irónico
ironmonger /'aɪənmʌŋgə(r)/ *n* ferreiro *m*, (*P*) ferrageiro *m*. ~**'s** *n* (*shop*) loja *f* de ferragens
irony /'aɪərənɪ/ *n* ironia *f*
irrational /ɪ'ræʃənl/ *a* irracional; (*person*) ilógico, que não raciocina
irreconcilable /ɪrekən'saɪləbl/ *a* irreconciliável
irrefutable /ɪrɪ'fju:təbl/ *a* irrefutável
irregular /ɪ'regjʊlə(r)/ *a* irregular. ~**ity** /-'lærətɪ/ *n* irregularidade *f*
irrelevant /ɪ'reləvənt/ *a* irrelevante, que não é pertinente
irreparable /ɪ'repərəbl/ *a* irreparável, irremediável
irreplaceable /ɪrɪ'pleɪsəbl/ *a* insubstituível
irresistible /ɪrɪ'zɪstəbl/ *a* irresistível
irresolute /ɪ'rezəlu:t/ *a* irresoluto
irrespective /ɪrɪ'spektɪv/ *a* ~ **of** sem levar em conta, independente de
irresponsible /ɪrɪ'spɒnsəbl/ *a* irresponsável
irretrievable /ɪrɪ'tri:vəbl/ *a* irreparável
irreverent /ɪ'revərənt/ *a* irreverente
irreversible /ɪrɪ'vɜ:səbl/ *a* irreversível; (*decision*) irrevogável
irrigat|e /'ɪrɪgeɪt/ *vt* irrigar. ~**ion** /-'geɪʃn/ *n* irrigação *f*
irritable /'ɪrɪtəbl/ *a* irritável, irascível
irritat|e /'ɪrɪteɪt/ *vt* irritar. ~**ion** /-'teɪʃn/ *n* irritação *f*
is /ɪz/ *see* **be**
Islam /'ɪzla:m/ *n* Islã *m*. ~**ic** /ɪz'læmɪk/ *a* islâmico
island /'aɪlənd/ *n* ilha *f*. **traffic** ~ abrigo *m* de pedestres, (*P*) placa *f* de refugio
isolat|e /'aɪsəleɪt/ *vt* isolar. ~**ion** /-'leɪʃn/ *n* isolamento *m*
Israel /'ɪzreɪl/ *n* Israel *m*. ~**i** /ɪz'reɪlɪ/ *a* & *n* israelense (*mf*), (*P*) israelita (*mf*)
issue /'ɪʃu:/ *n* questão *f*; (*outcome*) resultado *m*; (*of magazine etc*) número *m*; (*of stamps, money etc*) emissão *f* □ *vt* distribuir, dar; (*stamps, money etc*) emitir; (*orders*) dar □ *vi* ~ **from** sair de. **at** ~ em questão. **take** ~ **with** entrar em discussão com, discutir com
it /ɪt/ *pron* (*subject*) ele, ela; (*object*) o, a; (*non-specific*) isto, isso, aquilo. ~ **is cold** está *or* faz frio. ~ **is the 6th of May** hoje é seis de maio. **that's** ~ é isso. **take** ~ leva isso. **who is** ~? quem é?
italic /ɪ'tælɪk/ *a* itálico. ~**s** *npl* itálico *m*
Ital|y /'ɪtəlɪ/ *n* Itália *f*. ~**ian** /ɪ'tælɪən/ *a* & *n* (*person, lang*) italiano (*m*)
itch /ɪtʃ/ coceira *f*, (*P*) comichão *f*; (*fig: desire*) desejo *m* ardente □ *vi* coçar, sentir comichão, comichar. **my arm** ~**es** estou com coceira no braço. **I am** ~**ing to** estou morto por (*colloq*). ~**y** *a* que dá coceira
item /'aɪtəm/ *n* item *m*, artigo *m*; (*on programme*) número *m*; (*on agenda*)

ponto *m*. **news ~** notícia *f*. **~ize** /-aɪz/ *vt* discriminar, especificar

itinerant /aɪ'tɪnərənt/ *a* itinerante; (*musician, actor*) ambulante

itinerary /aɪ'tɪnərərɪ/ *n* itinerário *m*

its /ɪts/ *a* seu, sua, seus, suas

it's /ɪts/ = **it is, it has**

itself /ɪt'self/ *pron* ele mesmo, ele próprio, ela mesma, ela própria; (*reflexive*) se; (*after prep*) si mesmo, si próprio, si mesma, si própria. **by ~** sozinho, por si

ivory /'aɪvərɪ/ *n* marfim *m*

ivy /'aɪvɪ/ *n* hera *f*

Jj

jab /dʒæb/ *vt* (*pt* **jabbed**) espetar □ *n* espetadela *f*; (*colloq: injection*) picada *f*

jabber /'dʒæbə(r)/ *vi* tagarelar; (*indistinctly*) falar confusamente □ *n* tagarelice *f*; (*indistinct speech*) algaravia *f*; (*indistinct voices*) algaraviada *f*

jack /dʒæk/ *n* (*techn*) macaco *m*; (*cards*) valete *m* □ *vt* **~ up** levantar com macaco. **the Union J~** a bandeira *f* inglesa

jackal /'dʒækl/ *n* chacal *m*

jackdaw /'dʒækdɔ:/ *n* gralha *f*

jacket /'dʒækɪt/ *n* casaco (curto) *m*; (*of book*) sobrecapa *f*; (*of potato*) casca *f*

jack-knife /'dʒæknaɪf/ *vi* (*lorry*) perder o controle

jackpot /'dʒækpɒt/ *n* sorte *f* grande. **hit the ~** ganhar a sorte grande

Jacuzzi /dʒə'ku:zi:/ *n* (*P*) jacuzzi *m*, banheira *f* de hidromassagem

jade /dʒeɪd/ *n* (*stone*) jade *m*

jaded /'dʒeɪdɪd/ *a* (*tired*) estafado; (*bored*) enfastiado

jagged /'dʒægɪd/ *a* recortado, denteado; (*sharp*) pontiagudo

jail /dʒeɪl/ *n* prisão *f* □ *vt* prender, colocar na cadeia. **~er** *n* carcereiro *m*

jam[1] /dʒæm/ *n* geléia *f*, compota *f*

jam[2] /dʒæm/ *vt/i* (*pt* **jammed**) (*wedge*) entalar; (*become wedged*) entalar-se; (*crowd*) apinhar(-se); (*mech*) bloquear; (*radio*) provocar interferências em □ *n* (*crush*) aperto *m*; (*traffic*) engarrafamento *m*; (*colloq: difficulty*) apuro *m*, aperto *m*. **~ one's brakes on** (*colloq*) pôr o pé no freio, (*P*) no travão subitamente, apertar o freio subitamente. **~-packed** *a* (*colloq*) abarrotado (**with** de)

Jamaica /dʒə'meɪkə/ *n* Jamaica *f*

jangle /'dʒæŋgl/ *n* som *m* estridente □ *vi* retinir

janitor /'dʒænɪtə(r)/ *n* porteiro *m*; (*caretaker*) zelador *m*

January /'dʒænjʊərɪ/ *n* Janeiro *m*

Japan /dʒə'pæn/ *n* Japão *m*. **~ese** /dʒæpə'ni:z/ *a & n* japonês (*m*)

jar[1] /dʒa:(r)/ *n* pote *m*. **jam-~** *n* frasco *m* de geléia

jar[2] /dʒa:(r)/ *vt/i* (*pt* **jarred**) ressoar, bater ruidosamente (**against** contra); (*of colours*) destoar; (*disagree*) discordar (**with** de) □ *n* (*shock*) choque *m*. **~ring** *a* dissonante

jargon /'dʒa:gən/ *n* jargão *m*, gíria *f* profissional

jaundice /'dʒɔ:ndɪs/ *n* icterícia *f*. **~d** *a* (*fig*) invejoso, despeitado

jaunt /dʒɔ:nt/ *n* (*trip*) passeata *f*

jaunty /'dʒɔ:ntɪ/ *a* (**-ier, -iest**) (*cheerful*) alegre, jovial; (*sprightly*) desenvolto

javelin /'dʒævlɪn/ *n* dardo *m*

jaw /dʒɔ:/ *n* maxilar *m*, mandíbula *f*

jay /dʒeɪ/ *n* gaio *m*. **~-walker** *n* pedestre *m* imprudente, (*P*) peão *m* indisciplinado

jazz /dʒæz/ *n* jazz *m* □ *vt* **~ up** animar. **~y** *a* (*colloq*) espalhafatoso

jealous /'dʒeləs/ *a* ciumento; (*envious*) invejoso. **~y** *n* ciúme *m*; (*envy*) inveja *f*

jeans /dʒi:nz/ *npl* (blue-)jeans *mpl*, calça *f* de zuarte, (*P*) calças *fpl* de ganga

jeep /dʒi:p/ *n* jipe *m*

jeer /dʒɪə(r)/ *vt/i* **~ at** (*laugh*) fazer troça de; (*scorn*) escarnecer de; (*boo*) vaiar □ *n* (*mockery*) troça *f*; (*booing*) vaia *f*

jell /dʒel/ *vi* tomar consistência, gelatinizar-se

jelly /'dʒelɪ/ *n* gelatina *f*.

jellyfish /'dʒelɪfɪʃ/ *n* água-viva *f*

jeopard|y /'dʒepədɪ/ *n* perigo *m*. **~ize** *vt* comprometer, pôr em perigo

jerk /dʒɜ:k/ *n* solavanco *m*, (*P*) sacão *m*; (*sl: fool*) idiota *mf* □ *vt/i* sacudir; (*move jerkily*) mover-se aos solavancos, (*P*) mover(-se) aos sacões. **~y** *a* sacudido

jersey /'dʒɜ:zɪ/ *n* (*pl* **-eys**) camisola *f*, pulôver *m*, suéter *m*; (*fabric*) jérsei *m*

jest /dʒest/ *n* gracejo *m*, graça *f* □ *vi* gracejar, brincar

Jesus /'dʒi:zəs/ *n* Jesus *m*

jet[1] /dʒet/ *n* azeviche *m*. **~-black** *a* negro de azeviche

jet[2] /dʒet/ *n* jato *m*, (*P*) jacto *m*; (*plane*) (avião a) jato *m*, (*P*) jacto *m*. **~ lag** cansaço *m* provocado pela diferença de fuso horário. **~-propelled** *a* de propulsão a jato, (*P*) jacto

jettison /'dʒetɪsn/ *vt* alijar; (*discard*) desfazer-se de; (*fig*) abandonar

jetty /'dʒetɪ/ *n* (*breakwater*) quebra-mar *m*; (*landing-stage*) desembarcadouro *m*, cais *m*

Jew /dʒu:/ *n* judeu *m*

jewel /'dʒu:əl/ *n* jóia *f*. **~ler** *n* joalheiro *m*. **~ler's (shop)** joalheria *f*. **~lery** *n* jóias *fpl*

Jewish /'dʒu:ɪʃ/ *a* judeu

jib /dʒɪb/ *vi* (*pt* **jibbed**) recusar-se a avançar; (*of a horse*) empacar. **~ at** (*fig*) opor-se a, ter relutância em □ *n* (*sail*) bujarrona *f*

jig /dʒɪg/ *n* jiga *f*

jiggle /'dʒɪgl/ *vt* (*rock*) balançar; (*jerk*) sacolejar

jigsaw /'dʒɪgsɔ:/ *n* **~(-puzzle)** puzzle *m*, quebra-cabeça *m*, (*P*) quebra-cabeças *m*

jilt /dʒɪlt/ *vt* deixar, abandonar, dar um fora em (*colloq*), (*P*) mandar passear (*colloq*)

jingle /'dʒɪŋgl/ *vt/i* tilintar, tinir □ *n* tilintar *m*, tinido *m*; (*advertising etc*) música *f* de anúncio

jinx /dʒɪŋks/ *n* (*colloq*) pessoa *f* or coisa *f* azarenta; (*fig: spell*) azar *m*

jitter|s /'dʒɪtəz/ *npl* **the ~s** (*colloq*) nervos *mpl*. **~y** /-ərɪ/ *a* **be ~y** (*colloq*) estar nervoso, ter os nervos a flor da pele (*colloq*)

job /dʒɒb/ *n* trabalho *m*; (*post*) emprego *m*. **have a ~ doing** ter dificuldade em fazer. **it is a good ~ that** felizmente que. **~less** *a* desempregado

jobcentre /'dʒɔbsentə(r)/ *n* posto *m* de desemprego

jockey /'dʒɒkɪ/ *n* (*pl* **-eys**) jóquei *m*

jocular /'dʒɒkjʊlə(r)/ *a* jocoso, galhofeiro, brincalhão

jog /dʒɒg/ *vt* (*pt* **jogged**) dar um leve empurrão em, tocar em; (*memory*) refrescar □ *vi* (*sport*) fazer jogging. **~ging** *n* jogging *m*

join /dʒɔɪn/ *vt* juntar, unir; (*become member*) fazer-se sócio de, entrar para. **~ sb** juntar-se a alg □ *vi* (*of roads*) juntar-se, entroncar-se; (*of rivers*) confluir □ *n* junção *f*, junta *f*. **~ in** *vt/i* participar (em). **~ up** alistar-se

joiner /'dʒɔɪnə(r)/ *n* marceneiro *m*

joint /dʒɔɪnt/ *a* comum, conjunto; (*effort*) conjunto □ *n* junta *f*, junção *f*; (*anat*) articulação *f*; (*culin*) quarto *m*; (*roast meat*) carne *f* assada; (*sl: place*) espelunca *f*. **~ author** co-autor *m*. **~ly** *adv* conjuntamente

joist /dʒɔɪst/ *n* trave *f*, barrote *m*

jok|e /dʒəʊk/ *n* piada *f*, gracejo *m* □ *vi* gracejar. **~er** *n* brincalhão *m*; (*cards*) curinga *f* de baralho, (*P*) diabo *m*. **~ingly** *adv* brincadeira

joll|y /'dʒɒlɪ/ *a* (**-ier, -iest**) alegre, bem disposto □ *adv* (*colloq*) muito. **~ity** *n* festança *f*, pândega *f*

jolt /dʒəʊlt/ *vt* sacudir, sacolejar □ *vi* ir aos solavancos □ *n* solavanco *m*; (*shock*) choque *m*, sobressalto *m*

jostle /'dʒɒsl/ *vt* dar um encontrão *or* encontrões em, empurrar □ *vi* empurrar, acotovelar-se

jot /dʒɒt/ *n* **(not a) ~** nada □ *vt* (*pt* **jotted**) **~ (down)** apontar, tomar nota de. **~ter** *n* (*pad*) bloco *m* de notas

journal /'dʒɜ:nl/ *n* diário *m*; (*newspaper*) jornal *m*; (*periodical*) periódico *m*, revista *f*. **~ism** *n* jornalismo *m*. **~ist** *n* jornalista *mf*

journey /'dʒɜ:nɪ/ *n* (*pl* **-eys**) viagem *f*; (*distance*) trajeto *m*, (*P*) trajecto *m* □ *vi* viajar

jovial /'dʒəʊvɪəl/ *a* jovial

joy /dʒɔɪ/ *n* alegria *f*. **~-ride** *n* passeio *m* em carro roubado. **~ful**, **~ous** *adjs* alegre

jubil|ant /'dʒu:bɪlənt/ *a* cheio de alegria, jubiloso. **~ation** /-'leɪʃn/ *n* júbilo *m*, regozijo *m*

jubilee /'dʒu:bɪli:/ *n* jubileu *m*

Judaism /'dʒu:deɪɪzəm/ *n* judaísmo *m*

judder /'dʒʌdə(r)/ *vi* trepidar, vibrar □ *n* trepidação *f*, vibração *f*

judge /dʒʌdʒ/ *n* juiz *m* □ *vt* julgar. **~ment** *n* (*judging*) julgamento *m*, juízo *m*; (*opinion*) juízo *m*; (*decision*) julgamento *m*

judic|iary /dʒu:'dɪʃərɪ/ *n* magistratura *f*; (*system*) judiciário *m*. **~ial** *a* judiciário

judicious /dʒu:'dɪʃəs/ *a* judicioso

judo /'dʒu:dəʊ/ *n* judô *m*, (*P*) judo *m*

jug /dʒʌg/ *n* (*tall*) jarro *m*; (*round*) botija *f*; **milk-~** *n* leiteira *f*

juggernaut /'dʒʌgənɔ:t/ *n* (*lorry*) jainanta *f*, (*P*) camião *m* TIR

juggle /'dʒʌgl/ *vt/i* fazer malabarismos (**with** com). **~r** /-ə(r)/ *n* malabarista *mf*

juic|e /dʒu:s/ *n* suco *m*, (*P*) sumo *m*. **~y** *a* suculento; (*colloq: story etc*) picante

juke-box /'dʒu:kbɒks/ *n* juke-box *m*, (*P*) máquina *f* de música

July /dʒu:'laɪ/ *n* julho *m*

jumble /'dʒʌmbl/ *vt* misturar □ *n* mistura *f*. **~ sale** venda *f* de caridade de objetos usados

jumbo /'dʒʌmbəʊ/ *a* **~ jet** (avião) jumbo *m*

jump /dʒʌmp/ *vt/i* saltar; (*start*) sobressaltar(-se); (*of prices etc*) subir repentinamente □ *n* salto *m*; (*start*) sobressalto *m*; (*of prices*) alta *f*. **~ at** aceitar imediatamente. **~ the gun** agir prematuramente. **~ the queue** furar a fila. **~ to conclusions** tirar conclusões apressadas

jumper /'dʒʌmpə(r)/ *n* pulôver *m*, suéter *m*, (*P*) camisada *f* de lã

jumpy /'dʒʌmpɪ/ *a* nervoso

junction /'dʒʌŋkʃn/ *n* junção *f*; (*of roads etc*) entroncamento *m*

June /dʒu:n/ *n* junho *m*

jungle /'dʒʌŋgl/ *n* selva *f*, floresta *f*

junior /'dʒu:nɪə(r)/ *a* júnior; (*in age*) mais novo (**to** que); (*in rank*) subalterno; (*school*) primária □ *n* o mais novo *m*; (*sport*) júnior *mf*. **~ to** (*in rank*) abaixo de

junk /dʒʌŋk/ *n* ferro-velho *m*, velharias *fpl*; (*rubbish*) lixo *m*. **~ food** comida *f* sem valor nutritivo. **~ mail** material *m* impresso, enviado por correio, sem ter sido solicitado. **~ shop** loja *f* de ferro-velho, bricabraque *m*

junkie /'dʒʌŋkɪ/ *n* (*sl*) drogado *m*

jurisdiction /dʒʊərɪs'dɪkʃn/ *n* jurisdição *f*

juror /'dʒʊərə(r)/ *n* jurado *m*

jury /'dʒʊərɪ/ *n* júri *m*

just /dʒʌst/ *a* justo □ *adv* justamente, exatamente, (*P*) exactamente; (*only*) só. **he has ~ left** ele acabou de sair. **~ listen!** escuta só! **~ as** assim como; (*with time*) assim que. **~ as tall as** exatamente, (*P*) exactamente tão alto quanto. **~ as well that** ainda bem que. **~ before** um momento antes (de). **~ly** *adv* com justiça, justamente

justice /'dʒʌstɪs/ *n* justiça *f*. **J~ of the Peace** juiz *m* de paz

justifiabl|e /'dʒʌstɪfaɪəbl/ *a* justificável. **~y** *adv* com razão, justificadamente

justif|y /'dʒʌstɪfaɪ/ *vt* justificar. **~ication** /-ɪ'keɪʃn/ *n* justificação *f*

jut /dʒʌt/ *vi* (*pt* **jutted**) **~ out** fazer saliência, sobressair

juvenile /'dʒu:vənaɪl/ *a* (*youthful*) juvenil; (*childish*) pueril; (*delinquent*) jovem; (*court*) de menores □ *n* jovem *mf*

juxtapose /dʒʌkstə'pəʊz/ *vt* justapor

Kk

kaleidoscope /kə'laɪdəskəʊp/ *n* caleidoscópio *m*

kangaroo /kæŋgə'ru:/ *n* canguru *m*

karate /kə'ra:tɪ/ *n* karatê *m*

kebab /kə'bæb/ *n* churrasquinho *m*, espetinho *m*

keel /ki:l/ *n* quilha *f* □ *vi* **~ over** virar-se

keen /ki:n/ *a* (**-er, -est**) (*sharp*) agudo; (*eager*) entusiástico; (*of appetite*) devorador; (*of intelligence*) vivo; (*of wind*) cortante. **~ly** *adv* vivamente; (*eagerly*) com entusiasmo. **~ness** *n* vivacidade *f*; (*enthusiasm*) entusiasmo *m*

keep /ki:p/ (*pt* **kept**) *vt* guardar; (*family*) sustentar; (*animals*) ter, criar; (*celebrate*) festejar; (*conceal*) esconder; (*delay*) demorar; (*prevent*) impedir (**from** de); (*promise*) cumprir; (*shop*) ter □ *vi* manter-se, conservar-se; (*remain*) ficar. **~ (on)** continuar (**doing** fazendo) □ *n* sustento *m*; (*of castle*) torre *f* de menagem. **~ back** *vt* (*withhold*) reter □ *vi* manter-se afastado. **~ in/out** impedir de entrar/ de sair. **~ up** conservar. **~ up (with)** acompanhar. **~er** *n* guarda *mf*

keeping /'ki:pɪŋ/ *n* guarda *f*, cuidado *m*. **in ~ with** em harmonia com, (*P*) de harmonia com

keepsake /'ki:pseɪk/ *n* (*thing*) lembrança *f*, recordação *f*

keg /keg/ *n* barril *m* pequeno

kennel /'kenl/ *n* casota *f* (de cão). **~s** *npl* canil *m*

kept /kept/ *see* **keep**

kerb /kɜ:b/ *n* meio fio *m*, (*P*) borda *f* do passeio

kernel /'kɜ:nl/ *n* (*of nut*) miolo *m*

kerosene /'kerəsi:n/ *n* (*paraffin*) querosene *m*, (*P*) petróleo *m*; (*aviation fuel*) gasolina *f*

ketchup /'ketʃəp/ *n* molho *m* de tomate, ketchup *m*

kettle /'ketl/ *n* chaleira *f*

key /ki:/ *n* chave *f*; (*of piano etc*) tecla *f*; (*mus*) clave *f* □ *a* chave. **~-ring** *n* chaveiro *m*, porta-chaves *m invar* □ *vt* **~ in** digitar, bater. **~ed up** tenso

keyboard /'ki:bɔ:d/ *n* teclado *m*

keyhole /'ki:həʊl/ *n* buraco *m* da fechadura

khaki /'ka:kɪ/ *a* & *n* cáqui (*invar m*), (*P*) caqui (*invar m*)

kick /kɪk/ *vt/i* dar um pontapé *or* pontapés (a, em); (*ball*) chutar (em); (*of horse*) dar um coice *or* coices, escoicear □ *n* pontapé *m*; (*of gun, horse*) coice *m*; (*colloq: thrill*) excitação *f*, prazer *m*. **~-off** *n* chute *m* inicial, kick-off *m*. **~ out** (*colloq*) pôr na rua. **~ up** (*colloq: fuss, racket*) fazer

kid /kɪd/ *n* (*goat*) cabrito *m*; (*sl: child*) garoto *m*; (*leather*) pelica *f* □ *vt/i* (*pt* **kidded**) (*colloq*) brincar (com)

kidnap /'kɪdnæp/ *vt* (*pt* **kidnapped**) raptar. **~ping** *n* rapto *m*

kidney /'kɪdnɪ/ *n* rim *m*

kill /kɪl/ *vt* matar; (*fig: put an end to*) acabar com ◻ *n* matança *f*. **~er** *n* assassino *m*. **~ing** *n* matança *f*, massacre *m*; (*of game*) caçada *f* ◻ *a* (*colloq: funny*) de morrer de rir; (*colloq: exhausting*) de morte

killjoy /ˈkɪldʒɔɪ/ *n* desmancha-prazeres *mf*

kiln /kɪln/ *n* forno *m*

kilo /ˈki:ləʊ/ *n* (*pl* **-os**) quilo *m*

kilogram /ˈkɪləgræm/ *n* quilograma *m*

kilometre /ˈkɪləmi:tə(r)/ *n* quilômetro *m*, (*P*) quilómetro *m*

kilowatt /ˈkɪləwɒt/ *n* quilowatt *m*, (*P*) quilovate *m*

kilt /kɪlt/ *n* kilt *m*, saiote *m* escocês

kin /kɪn/ *n* família *f*, parentes *mpl*. **next of ~** os parentes mais próximos

kind[1] /kaɪnd/ *n* espécie *f*, gênero *m*, (*P*) género *m*, natureza *f*. **in ~** em gêneros, (*P*) géneros; (*fig: in the same form*) na mesma moeda. **~ of** (*colloq: somewhat*) de certo modo, um pouco

kind[2] /kaɪnd/ *a* (**-er, -est**) (*good*) bom; (*friendly*) gentil, amável. **~-hearted** *a* bom, bondoso. **~ness** *n* bondade *f*

kindergarten /ˈkɪndəga:tn/ *n* jardim de infância *m*, (*P*) infantil

kindle /ˈkɪndl/ *vt/i* acender(-se), atear(-se)

kindly /ˈkaɪndlɪ/ *a* (**-ier, -iest**) benévolo, bondoso ◻ *adv* bondosamente, gentilmente, com sim-patia. **~ wait** tenha a bondade de esperar

kindred /ˈkɪndrɪd/ *a* aparentado; (*fig: connected*) afim. **~ spirit** espírito *m* congênere, alma *f* gêmea

kinetic /kɪˈnetɪk/ *a* cinético

king /kɪŋ/ *n* rei *m*. **~-size(d)** *a* de tamanho grande

kingdom /ˈkɪŋdəm/ *n* reino *m*

kingfisher /ˈkɪŋfɪʃə(r)/ *n* pica-peixe *m*, martim-pescador *m*

kink /kɪŋk/ *n* (*in rope*) volta *f*, nó *m*; (*fig*) perversão *f*. **~y** *a* (*colloq*) excêntrico, pervertido; (*of hair*) encarapinhado

kiosk /ˈki:ɒsk/ *n* quiosque *m*. **telephone ~** cabine telefônica, (*P*) telefónica

kip /kɪp/ *n* (*sl*) sono *m* ◻ *vi* (*pt* **kipped**) (*sl*) dormir

kipper /ˈkɪpə(r)/ *n* arenque *m* defumado

kiss /kɪs/ *n* beijo *m* ◻ *vt/i* beijar (-se)

kit /kɪt/ *n* equipamento *m*; (*set of tools*) ferramenta *f*; (*for assembly*) kit *m* ◻ *vt* (*pt* **kitted**) **~ out** equipar

kitbag /ˈkɪtbæg/ *n* mochila *f* (de soldado etc); saco *m* de viagem

kitchen /ˈkɪtʃɪn/ *n* cozinha *f*. **~ garden** horta *f*. **~ sink** pia *f*, (*P*) lava-louças *m*

kite /kaɪt/ *n* (*toy*) pipa *f*, (*P*) papagaio *m* de papel

kith /kɪθ/ *n* **~ and kin** parentes e amigos *mpl*

kitten /ˈkɪtn/ *n* gatinho *m*

kitty /ˈkɪtɪ/ *n* (*fund*) fundo *m* comum, vaquinha *f*; (*cards*) bolo *m*

knack /næk/ *n* jeito *m*

knapsack /ˈnæpsæk/ *n* mochila *f*

knead /ni:d/ *vt* amassar

knee /ni:/ *n* joelho *m*

kneecap /ˈni:kæp/ *n* rótula *f*

kneel /ni:l/ *vi* (*pt* **knelt**) **~ (down)** ajoelhar(-se)

knelt /nelt/ *see* **kneel**

knew /nju:/ *see* **know**

knickers /ˈnɪkəz/ *npl* calcinhas (de senhora) *fpl*

knife /naɪf/ *n* (*pl* **knives**) faca *f* ◻ *vt* esfaquear, apunhalar

knight /naɪt/ *n* cavaleiro *m*; (*chess*) cavalo *m*. **~hood** *n* grau *m* de cavaleiro

knit /nɪt/ *vt* (*pt* **knitted** *or* **knit**) tricotar ◻ *vi* tricotar, fazer tricô; (*fig: unite*) unir-se; (*of bones*) soldar-se. **~ one's brow** franzir as sobrancelhas. **~ting** *n* malha *f*, tricô *m*

knitwear /ˈnɪtweə(r)/ *n* roupa *f* de malha, malhas *fpl*

knob /nɒb/ *n* (*of door*) maçaneta *f*; (*of drawer*) puxador *m*; (*of radio, TV etc*) botão *m*; (*of butter*) noz *f*. **~bly** *a* nodoso

knock /nɒk/ *vt/i* bater (em); (*sl*: *criticize*) desancar (em). **~ about** *vt* tratar mal ◻ *vi* (*wander*) andar a esmo. **~ down** (*chair, pedestrian*) deitar no chão, derrubar; (*demolish*) jogar abaixo; (*colloq: reduce*) baixar, reduzir; (*at auction*) adjudicar (**to** a). **~-down** *a* (*price*) muito baixo. **~-kneed** *a* de pernas de tesoura. **~ off** *vt* (*colloq: complete quickly*) despachar; (*sl*: *steal*) roubar ◻ *vi* (*colloq*) parar de trabalhar, fechar a loja (*colloq*). **~ out** pôr fora de combate, eliminar; (*stun*) assombrar. **~-out** *n* (*boxing*) nocaute *m*, KO *m*. **~ over** entornar. **~ up** (*meal etc*) arranjar às pressas. **~er** *n* aldrava *f*

knot /nɒt/ *n* nó *m* ◻ *vt* (*pt* **knotted**) atar com nó, dar nó *or* nós em

knotty /ˈnɒtɪ/ *a* (**-ier, -iest**) nodoso, cheio de nós; (*difficult*) complicado, espinhoso

know /nəʊ/ *vt/i* (*pt* **knew**, *pp* **known**) saber (**that** que); (*person, place*) conhecer ◻ *n* **in the ~** (*colloq*) por dentro. **~ about** (*cars etc*) saber sobre, saber de. **~-all** *n* sabe-tudo *m* (*colloq*). **~-how** *n* know-how *m*, conhecimentos *mpl* técnicos, culturais etc. **~ of** ter conhecimento de, ter ouvido falar de. **~ingly** *adv* com ar conhecedor; (*consciously*) conscientemente

knowledge /'nɒlɪdʒ/ *n* conhecimento *m*; (*learning*) saber *m*. **~able** *a* conhecedor, entendido, versado

known /nəʊn/ *see* **know** ▫ *a* conhecido

knuckle /'nʌkl/ *n* nó *m* dos dedos ▫ *vi* **~ under** ceder, submeter-se

Koran /kə'ra:n/ *n* Alcorão *m*, Corão *m*

Korea /kə'rɪə/ *n* Coréia *f*

kosher /'kəʊʃə(r)/ *a* aprovado pela lei judaica; (*colloq*) como deve ser

kowtow /kaʊ'taʊ/ *vi* prosternar-se (**to** diante de); (*act obsequiously*) bajular

lab /læb/ *n* (*colloq*) laboratório *m*

label /'leɪbl/ *n* (*on bottle etc*) rótulo *m*; (*on clothes, luggage*) etiqueta *f* ▫ *vt* (*pt* **labelled**) rotular; etiquetar, pôr etiqueta em

laboratory /lə'bɒrətrɪ/ *n* laboratório *m*

laborious /lə'bɔ:rɪəs/ *a* laborioso, trabalhoso

labour /'leɪbə(r)/ *n* trabalho *m*, labuta *f*; (*workers*) mão-de-obra *f* ▫ *vi* trabalhar; (*try hard*) esforçar-se ▫ *vt* alongar-se sobre, insistir em. **in ~** em trabalho de parto. **~ed** *a* (*writing*) laborioso, sem espontaneidade; (*breathing, movement*) difícil. **~-saving** *a* que poupa trabalho

Labour /'leɪbə(r)/ *n* (*party*) Partido *m* Trabalhista, os trabalhistas ▫ *a* trabalhista

labourer /'leɪbərə(r)/ *n* trabalhador *m*; (*on farm*) trabalhador *m* rural

labyrinth /'læbərɪnθ/ *n* labirinto *m*

lace /leɪs/ *n* renda *f*; (*of shoe*) cordão *m* de sapato, (*P*) atacador *m* ▫ *vt* atar; (*drink*) juntar um pouco (de aguardente, rum etc)

lacerate /'læsəreɪt/ *vt* lacerar, rasgar

lack /læk/ *n* falta *f* ▫ *vt* faltar (a), não ter. **be ~ing** faltar. **be ~ing in** carecer de

lackadaisical /lækə'deɪzɪkl/ *a* lânguido, apático, desinteressado

laconic /lə'kɒnɪk/ *a* lacônico, (*P*) lacónico

lacquer /'lækə(r)/ *n* laca *f*

lad /læd/ *n* rapaz *m*, moço *m*

ladder /'lædə(r)/ *n* escada de mão *f*, (*P*) escadote *m*; (*in stocking*) fio *m* corrido, (*P*) malha *f* caída ▫ *vi* deixar correr um fio, (*P*) cair uma malha ▫ *vt* fazer malhas em

laden /'leɪdn/ *a* carregado (**with** de)

ladle /'leɪdl/ *n* concha (de sopa) *f*

lady /'leɪdɪ/ *n* senhora *f*; (*title*) Lady *f*. **~-in-waiting** *n* dama *f* de companhia, (*P*) dama *f* de honor. **young ~** jovem *f*. **~like** *a* senhoril, elegante. **Ladies** *n* (*toilets*) toalete *m* das Senhoras

ladybird /'leɪdɪbɜ:d/ *n* joaninha *f*

lag[1] /læg/ *vi* (*pt* **lagged**) atrasar-se, ficar para trás ▫ *n* atraso *m*

lag[2] /læg/ *vt* (*pt* **lagged**) (*pipes etc*) revestir com isolante térmico

lager /'la:gə(r)/ *n* cerveja *f* leve e clara, loura *f* (*sl*)

lagoon /lə'gu:n/ *n* lagoa *f*

laid /leɪd/ *see* **lay**[2]

lain /leɪn/ *see* **lie**[2]

lair /leə(r)/ *n* toca *f*, covil *m*

laity /'leɪətɪ/ *n* leigos *mpl*

lake /leɪk/ *n* lago *m*

lamb /læm/ *n* cordeiro *m*, carneiro *m*; (*meat*) carneiro *m*

lambswool /'læmzwʊl/ *n* lã *f*

lame /leɪm/ *a* (**-er, -est**) coxo; (*fig: unconvincing*) fraco. **~ness** *n* claudicação *f*, coxeadura *f*

lament /lə'ment/ *n* lamento *m*, lamentação *f* ▫ *vt/i* lamentar(-se) (de). **~able** *a* lamentável

laminated /'læmɪneɪtɪd/ *a* laminado

lamp /læmp/ *n* lâmpada *f*

lamppost /'læmppəʊst/ *n* poste *m* (do candeeiro) (de iluminação pública)

lampshade /'læmpʃeɪd/ *n* abajur *m*, quebra-luz *m*

lance /la:ns/ *n* lança *f* ▫ *vt* lancetar

lancet /'lan:sɪt/ *n* bisturi *m*, (*P*) lanceta *f*

land /lænd/ *n* terra *f*; (*country*) país *m*; (*plot*) terreno *m*; (*property*) terras *fpl* ▫ *a* de terra, terrestre; (*policy etc*) agrário ▫ *vt/i* desembarcar; (*aviat*) aterrissar, (*P*) aterrar; (*fall*) ir parar (**on** em); (*colloq: obtain*) arranjar; (*a blow*) aplicar, mandar. **~-locked** *a* rodeado de terra

landing /'lændɪŋ/ *n* desembarque *m*; (*aviat*) aterrissagem *f*, (*P*) aterragem *f*; (*top of stairs*) patamar *m*. **~-stage** *n* cais *m* flutuante

land|lady /'lændleɪdɪ/ *n* (*of rented house*) senhoria *f*, proprietária *f*; (*who lets rooms*) dona *f* da casa; (*of boarding-house*) dona *f* da pensão; (*of inn etc*) proprietária *f*, estalajadeira *f*. **~lord** *n* (*of rented house*) senhorio *m*, proprietário *m*; (*of inn etc*) proprietário *m*, estalajadeiro *m*

landmark /'lændma:k/ *n* (*conspicuous feature*) ponto *m* de referência; (*fig*) marco *m*

landscape /'lændskeɪp/ *n* paisagem *f* □ *vt* projetar, (*P*) projectar paisagisticamente
landslide /'lændslaɪd/ *n* desabamento *m or* desmoronamento *m* de terras; (*fig: pol*) vitoria *f* esmagadora
lane /leɪn/ *n* senda *f*, caminho *m*; (*in country*) estrada *f* pequena; (*in town*) viela *f*, ruela *f*; (*of road*) faixa *f*, pista *f*; (*of traffic*) fila *f*; (*aviat*) corredor *m*; (*naut*) rota *f*
language /'læŋgwɪdʒ/ *n* língua *f*; (*speech, style*) linguagem *f*. **bad ~** linguagem *f* grosseira. **~ lab** laboratório *m* de línguas
languid /'læŋgwɪd/ *a* lânguido
languish /'læŋgwɪʃ/ *vi* elanguescer
lank /læŋk/ *a* (*of hair*) escorrido, liso
lanky /'læŋkɪ/ *a* (**-ier, -iest**) desengonçado, escanifrado
lantern /'læntən/ *n* lanterna *f*
lap[1] /læp/ *n* colo *m*; (*sport*) volta *f* completa. **~-dog** *n* cãozinho *m* de estimação
lap[2] /læp/ *vt* **~ up** beber lambendo □ *vi* marulhar
lapel /lə'pel/ *n* lapela *f*
lapse /læps/ *vi* decair, degenerar-se; (*expire*) caducar □ *n* lapso *m*; (*jur*) prescrição *f*. **~ into** (*thought*) mergulhar em; (*bad habit*) adquirir
larceny /'la:sənɪ/ *n* furto *m*
lard /la:d/ *n* banha de porco *f*
larder /'la:də(r)/ *n* despensa *f*
large /la:dʒ/ *a* (**-er, -est**) grande. **at ~** à solta, em liberdade. **by and ~** em geral. **~ly** *adv* largamente, em grande parte. **~ness** *n* grandeza *f*
lark[1] /la:k/ *n* (*bird*) cotovia *f*
lark[2] /la:k/ *n* (*colloq*) pândega *f*, brincadeira *f* □ *vi* **~ about** (*colloq*) fazer travessuras, brincar
larva /'la:və/ *n* (*pl* **-vae** /-vi:/) larva *f*
laryngitis /lærɪn'dʒaɪtɪs/ *n* laringite *f*
larynx /'lærɪŋks/ *n* laringe *f*
lascivious /lə'sɪvɪəs/ *a* lascivo, sensual
laser /'leɪzə(r)/ *n* laser *m*. **~ printer** impressora *f* a laser
lash /læʃ/ *vt* chicotear, açoitar; (*rain*) fustigar □ *n* chicote *m*; (*stroke*) chicotada *f*; (*eyelash*) pestana *f*, cílio *m*. **~ out** atacar, atirar-se a; (*colloq: spend*) esbanjar dinheiro em algo
lashings /'læʃɪŋz/ *npl* **~ of** (*sl*) montes de (*colloq*)
lasso /læ'su:/ *n* (*pl* **-os**) laço *m* □ *vt* laçar
last[1] /la:st/ *a* último □ *adv* no fim, em último lugar; (*most recently*) a última vez □ *n* último *m*. **at (long) ~** por fim, finalmente. **~-minute** *a* de última hora. **~ night** ontem à noite, a noite passada. **the ~ straw** a gota d'água. **to the ~** até o fim. **~ly** *adv* finalmente, em último lugar
last[2] /la:st/ *vt/i* durar, continuar. **~ing** *a* duradouro, durável
latch /lætʃ/ *n* trinco *m*
late /leɪt/ *a* (**-er, -est**) atrasado; (*recent*) recente; (*former*) antigo, ex-, anterior; (*hour, fruit etc*) tardio; (*deceased*) falecido □ *adv* tarde. **in ~ july** no fim de julho. **of ~** ultimamente. **at the ~st** o mais tardar. **~ness** *n* atraso *m*
lately /'leɪtlɪ/ *adv* nos últimos tempos, ultimamente
latent /'leɪtnt/ *a* latente
lateral /'lætərəl/ *a* lateral
lathe /leɪð/ *n* torno *m*
lather /'la:ðə(r)/ *n* espuma *f* de sabão □ *vt* ensaboar □ *vi* fazer espuma
Latin /'lætɪn/ *n* (*lang*) latim *m* □ *a* latino. **~ America** *n* América *f* Latina. **~ American** *a* & *n* latino-americano (*m*)
latitude /'lætɪtju:d/ *n* latitude *f*
latter /'lætə(r)/ *a* último, mais recente □ *n* **the ~** este, esta. **~ly** *adv* recentemente
lattice /'lætɪs/ *n* treliça *f*, (*P*) gradeamento *m* de ripas
laudable /'lɔ:dəbl/ *a* louvável
laugh /la:f/ *vi* rir (**at** de). **~ off** disfarçar com uma piada □ *n* riso *m*. **~able** *a* irrisório, ridículo. **~ing-stock** *n* objeto *m*, (*P*) objecto *m* de troça
laughter /'la:ftə(r)/ *n* riso *m*, risada *f*
launch[1] /lɔ:ntʃ/ *vt* lançar □ *n* lançamento *m*. **~ into** lançar-se *or* meter-se em. **~ing pad** plataforma *f* de lançamento
launch[2] /lɔ:ntʃ/ *n* (*boat*) lancha *f*
launder /'lɔ:ndə(r)/ *vt* lavar e passar
launderette /lɔ:n'dret/ *n* lavanderia *f* automática
laundry /'lɔ:ndrɪ/ *n* lavanderia *f*; (*clothes*) roupa *f*. **do the ~** lavar a roupa
laurel /'lɒrəl/ *n* loureiro *m*, louro *m*
lava /'la:və/ *n* lava *f*
lavatory /'lævətrɪ/ *n* privada *f*, (*P*) retrete *f*; (*room*) toalete *m*, (*P*) lavabo *m*
lavender /'lævəndə(r)/ *n* alfazema *f*, lavanda *f*
lavish /'lævɪʃ/ *a* pródigo; (*plentiful*) copioso, generoso; (*lush*) suntuoso □ *vt* ser pródigoem, encher de. **~ly** *adv* prodigamente; copiosamente; suntuosamente
law /lɔ:/ *n* lei *f*; (*profession, study*) direito *m*. **~-abiding** *a* cumpridor da lei, respeitador da lei. **~ and order** ordem *f* pública. **~-breaker** *n* transgressor *m* da lei. **~ful** *a* legal, legítimo. **~fully** *adv* legalmente. **~less** *a* sem lei; (*act*) ilegal; (*person*) rebelde

lawcourt /'lɔ:kɔ:t/ *n* tribunal *m*

lawn /lɔ:n/ *n* gramado *m*, (*P*) relvado *m*. **~-mower** *n* cortador *m* de grama, (*P*) máquina *f* de cortar a relva

lawsuit /'lɔ:su:t/ *n* processo *m*, ação *f*, (*P*) acção *f* judicial

lawyer /'lɔ:jə(r)/ *n* advogado *m*

lax /læks/ *a* negligente; (*discipline*) frouxo; (*morals*) relaxado. **~ity** *n* negligência *f*; (*of discipline*) frouxidão *f*; (*of morals*) relaxamento *m*

laxative /'læksətɪv/ *n* laxante *m*, laxativo *m*

lay[1] /leɪ/ *a* leigo. **~ opinion** opinião *f* de um leigo

lay[2] /leɪ/ *vt* (*pt* **laid**) pôr, colocar; (*trap*) preparar, pôr; (*eggs, table, siege*) pôr; (*plan*) fazer □ *vi* pôr (ovos). **~ aside** pôr de lado. **~ down** pousar; (*condition, law, rule*) impôr; (*arms*) depor; (*one's life*) oferecer; (*policy*) ditar. **~ hold of** agarrar(-se a). **~ off** *vt* (*worker*) suspender do trabalho □ *vi* (*colloq*) parar, desistir. **~-off** *n* suspensão *f* temporária. **~ on** (*gas, water etc*) instalar, ligar; (*entertainment etc*) organizar, providenciar; (*food*) servir. **~ out** (*design*) traçar, planejar; (*spread out*) estender, espalhar; (*money*) gastar. **~ up** *vt* (*store*) juntar; (*ship, car*) pôr fora de serviço

lay[3] /leɪ/ *see* **lie**

layabout /'leɪəbaʊt/ *n* (*sl*) vadio *m*

lay-by /'leɪbaɪ/ *n* acostamento *m*, (*P*) berma *f*

layer /'leɪə(r)/ *n* camada *f*

layman /'leɪmən/ *n* (*pl* **-men**) leigo *m*

layout /'leɪaʊt/ *n* disposição *f*; (*typ*) composição *f*

laze /leɪz/ *vi* descansar, vadiar

laz|y /'leɪzɪ/ *a* (**-ier**, **-iest**) preguiçoso. **~iness** *n* preguiça *f*. **~y-bones** *n* (*colloq*) vadio *m*, vagabundo *m*

lead[1] /li:d/ *vt/i* (*pt* **led**) conduzir, guiar, levar; (*team etc*) chefiar, liderar; (*life*) levar; (*choir, band etc*) dirigir □ *n* (*distance*) avanço *m*; (*first place*) dianteira *f*; (*clue*) indício *m*, pista *f*; (*leash*) coleira *f*; (*electr*) cabo *m*; (*theatr*) papel *m* principal; (*example*) exemplo *m*. **in the ~** na frente. **~ away** levar. **~ on** (*fig*) encorajar. **~ the way** ir na frente. **~ up to** conduzir a

lead[2] /led/ *n* chumbo *m*; (*of pencil*) grafite *f*. **~en** *a* de chumbo; (*of colour*) plúmbeo

leader /'li:də(r)/ *n* chefe *m*, líder *m*; (*of country, club, union etc*) dirigente *mf*; (*pol*) líder; (*of orchestra*) regente *mf*, maestro *m*; (*in newspaper*) editorial *m*. **~ship** *n* direção *f*, (*P*) direcção *f*, liderança *f*

leading /'li:dɪŋ/ *a* principal. **~ article** artigo *m* de fundo, editorial *m*

leaf /li:f/ *n* (*pl* **leaves**) folha *f*; (*flap of table*) aba *f* □ *vi* **~ through** folhear. **~y** *a* frondoso

leaflet /'li:flɪt/ *n* prospecto *m*, folheto *m* informativo

league /li:g/ *n* liga *f*; (*sport*) campeonato *m* da Liga. **in ~ with** de coligação com, em conluio com

leak /li:k/ *n* (*escape*) fuga *f*; (*hole*) buraco *m* □ *vt/i* (*roof, container*) pingar; (*electr, gas*) ter um escapamento, (*P*) ter uma fuga; (*naut*) fazer água. **~ (out)** (*fig: divulge*) divulgar; (*fig: become known*) transpirar, divulgar-se. **~age** *n* vazamento *m*. **~y** *a* que tem um vazamento

lean[1] /li:n/ *a* (**-er**, **-est**) magro. **~ness** *n* magreza *f*

lean[2] /li:n/ *vt/i* (*pt* **leaned** *or* **leant** /lent/) encostar(-se), apoiar-se (**on** em); (*be slanting*) inclinar(-se). **~ back/forward** *or* **over** inclinar-se para trás/para a frente. **~ on** (*colloq*) pressionar. **~-to** *n* alpendre *m*

leaning /'li:nɪŋ/ *a* inclinado □ *n* inclinação *f*

leap /li:p/ *vt* (*pt* **leaped** *or* **leapt** /lept/) galgar, saltar por cima de □ *vi* saltar □ *n* salto *m*, pulo *m*. **~-frog** *n* eixo-badeixo *m*, (*P*) jogo *m* do eixo. **~ year** ano *m* bissexto

learn /lɜ:n/ *vt/i* (*pt* **learned** *or* **learnt**) aprender; (*be told*) vir a saber, ouvir dizer. **~er** *n* principiante *mf*, aprendiz *m*

learn|ed /'lɜ:nɪd/ *a* erudito. **~ing** *n* saber *m*, erudição *f*

lease /li:s/ *n* arrendamento *m*, aluguel *m*, (*P*) aluguer *m* □ *vt* arrendar, (*P*) alugar

leash /li:ʃ/ *n* coleira *f*

least /li:st/ *a* o menor □ *n* o mínino *m*, o menos *m* □ *adv* o menos. **at ~** pelo menos. **not in the ~** de maneira alguma

leather /'leðə(r)/ *n* couro *m*, cabedal *m*

leave /li:v/ *vt/i* (*pt* **left**) deixar; (*depart from*) sair/partir (de), ir-se (de) □ *n* licença *f*, permissão *f*. **be left (over)** restar, sobrar. **~ alone** deixar em paz, não tocar. **~ out** omitir. **~ of absence** licença *f*. **on ~** (*mil*) de licença. **take one's ~** despedir-se (**of** de)

leavings /'li:vɪŋz/ *npl* restos *mpl*

Leban|on /'lebənən/ *n* Líbano *m*. **~ese** /-'ni:z/ *a* & *n* libanês (*m*)

lecherous /'letʃərəs/ *a* lascivo

lectern /'lektən/ *n* estante *f* (de coro de igreja)

lecture /'lektʃə(r)/ *n* conferência *f*; (*univ*) aula *f* teórica; (*fig*) sermão *m*

□ *vi* dar uma conferência; (*univ*) dar aula(s) □ *vt* pregar um sermão a alg (*colloq*). **~r** /-ə(r)/ *n* conferente *mf*, conferencista *mf*; (*univ*) professor *m*

led /led/ *see* **lead**[1]

ledge /ledʒ/ *n* rebordo *m*, saliência *f*; (*of window*) peitoril *m*

ledger /'ledʒə(r)/ *n* livro-mestre *m*, razão *m*

leech /li:tʃ/ *n* sanguessuga *f*

leek /li:k/ *n* alho-poró *m*, (*P*) alho-porro *m*

leer /lɪə(r)/ *vi* **~ (at)** olhar de modo malicioso *or* manhoso (para) □ *n* olhar *m* malicioso *or* manhoso

leeway /'li:weɪ/ *n* (*naut*) deriva *f*; (*fig*) liberdade *f* de ação, (*P*) acção, margem *f* (*colloq*)

left[1] /left/ *see* **leave**. **~ luggage (office)** depósito *m* de bagagens. **~-overs** *npl* restos *mpl*, sobras *fpl*

left[2] /left/ *a* esquerdo; (*pol*) de esquerda □ *n* esquerda *f* □ *adv* à/para a esquerda. **~-hand** *a* da esquerda; (*position*) à esquerda. **~-handed** *a* canhoto. **~-wing** *a* (*pol*) de esquerda

leg /leg/ *n* perna *f*; (*of table*) pé *m*, perna *f*; (*of journey*) etapa *f*. **pull sb's ~** brincar *or* mexer com alg. **stretch one's ~s** esticar as pernas. **~-room** *n* espaço *m* para as pernas

legacy /'legəsɪ/ *n* legado *m*

legal /'li:gl/ *a* legal; (*affairs etc*) jurídico. **~ adviser** advogado *m*. **~ity** /li:'gæləti/ *n* legalidade *f*. **~ly** *adv* legalmente

legalize /'li:gəlaɪz/ *vt* legalizar

legend /'ledʒənd/ *n* lenda *f*. **~ary** /'ledʒəndrɪ/ *a* lendário

leggings /'legɪŋz/ *npl* perneiras *fpl*; (*women's*) legging *m*

legib|le /'ledʒəbl/ *a* legível. **~ility** /-'bɪlətɪ/ *n* legibilidade *f*

legion /'li:dʒən/ *n* legião *f*

legislat|e /'ledʒɪsleɪt/ *vi* legislar. **~ion** /-'leɪʃn/ *n* legislação *f*

legislat|ive /'ledʒɪslətɪv/ *a* legislativo. **~ure** /-eɪtʃə(r)/ *n* corpo *m* legislativo

legitima|te /lɪ'dʒɪtɪmət/ *a* legítimo. **~cy** *n* legitimidade *f*

leisure /'leʒə(r)/ *n* lazer *m*, tempo livre *m*. **at one's ~** ao bel prazer, (*P*) a seu belo prazer. **~ centre** centro *m* de lazer. **~ly** *a* pausado, compassado □ *adv* sem pressa, devagar

lemon /'lemən/ *n* limão *m*

lemonade /lemə'neɪd/ *n* limonada *f*

lend /lend/ *vt* (*pt* **lent**) emprestar; (*contribute*) dar. **~ a hand to** (*help*) ajudar. **~ itself to** prestar-se a. **~er** *n* pessoa *f* que empresta. **~ing** *n* empréstimo *m*

length /leŋθ/ *n* comprimento *m*; (*in time*) período *m*; (*of cloth*) corte *m*. **at ~** extensamente; (*at last*) por fim, finalmente. **~y** *a* longo, demorado

lengthen /'leŋθən/ *vt/i* alongar (-se)

lengthways /'leŋθweɪz/ *adv* ao comprido, em comprimento, longitudinalmente

lenien|t /'li:nɪənt/ *a* indulgente, clemente. **~cy** *n* indulgência *f*, clemência *f*

lens /lenz/ *n* (*of spectacles*) lente *f*; (*photo*) objetiva *f*, (*P*) objectiva *f*

lent /lent/ *see* **lend**

Lent /lent/ *n* Quaresma *f*

lentil /'lentl/ *n* lentilha *f*

Leo /'li:əʊ/ *n* (*astr*) Leão *m*

leopard /'lepəd/ *n* leopardo *m*

leotard /'li:əʊta:d/ *n* collant(s) *m* (*pl*), (*P*) maillot *m* de ginástica ou dança

leper /'lepə(r)/ *n* leproso *m*

leprosy /'leprəsɪ/ *n* lepra *f*

lesbian /'lezbɪən/ *a* lésbico □ *n* lésbica *f*

less /les/ *a* (*in number*) menor (**than** que); (*in quantity*) menos (**than** que) □ *n, adv* & *prep* menos. **~ and ~** cada vez menos

lessen /'lesn/ *vt/i* diminuir

lesser /'lesə(r)/ *a* menor. **to a ~ degree** em menor grau

lesson /'lesn/ *n* lição *f*

let /let/ *vt* (*pt* **let**, *pres p* **letting**) deixar, permitir; (*lease*) alugar, arrendar □ *v aux* **~'s go** vamos. **~ him do it** que o faça ele. **~ me know** diga-me, avise-me □ *n* aluguel *m*, (*P*) aluguer *m*. **~ alone** deixar em paz; (*not to mention*) sem falar em, para não falar em. **~ down** baixar; (*deflate*) esvaziar; (*disappoint*) desapontar; (*fail to help*) deixar na mão. **~-down** *n* desapontamento *m*. **~ go** *vt/i* soltar. **~ in** deixar entrar. **~ o.s. in for** (*task, trouble*) meter-se em. **~ off** (*gun*) disparar; (*firework*) soltar, (*P*) deitar; (*excuse*) desculpar. **~ on** (*colloq*) *vt* revelar (**that** que) □ *vi* descoser-se (*colloq*), (*P*) descair-se (*colloq*). **~ out** deixar sair. **~ through** deixar passar. **~ up** (*colloq*) abrandar, diminuir. **~-up** *n* (*colloq*) pausa *f*, trégua *f*

lethal /'li:θl/ *a* fatal, mortal

letharg|y /'leθədʒɪ/ *n* letargia *f*, apatia *f*. **~ic** /lɪ'θa:dʒɪk/ *a* letárgico, apático

letter /'letə(r)/ *n* (*symbol*) letra *f*; (*message*) carta *f*. **~-bomb** *n* carta-bomba *f*. **~-box** *n* caixa *f* do correio. **~ing** *n* letras *fpl*

lettuce /'letɪs/ *n* alface *f*

leukaemia /lu:'ki:mɪə/ *n* leucemia *f*

level /'levl/ *a* plano; (*on surface*) horizontal; (*in height*) no mesmo nível (**with** que); (*spoonful etc*) raso □ *n* nível *m* □ *vt* (*pt* **levelled**) nivelar; (*gun, missile*) apontar; (*accusation*) dirigir. **on the ~** (*colloq*) franco, sincero. **~ crossing** passagem *f* de nível. **~-headed** *a* equilibrado, sensato

lever /'li:və(r)/ *n* alavanca *f* □ *vt* **~ up** levantar com alavanca

leverage /'li:vərɪdʒ/ *n* influência *f*

levity /'levətɪ/ *n* frivolidade *f*, leviandade *f*

levy /'levɪ/ *vt* (*tax*) cobrar □ *n* imposto *m*

lewd /lu:d/ *a* (**-er, -est**) libidinoso, obsceno

liabilit|y /laɪə'bɪlətɪ/ *n* responsabilidade *f*; (*colloq: handicap*) desvantagem *f*. **~ies** dívidas *fpl*

liable /'laɪəbl/ *a* **~ to do** suscetível, (*P*) susceptível de fazer; **~ to** (*illness etc*) suscetível, (*P*) susceptível a; (*fine*) sujeito a. **~ for** responsável por

liaise /lɪ'eɪz/ *vi* (*colloq*) servir de intermediário (**between** entre), fazer a ligação (**with** com)

liaison /lɪ'eɪzn/ *n* ligação *f*

liar /'laɪə(r)/ *n* mentiroso *m*

libel /'laɪbl/ *n* difamação *f* □ *vt* (*pt* **libelled**) difamar

liberal /'lɪbərəl/ *a* liberal. **~ly** *adv* liberalmente

Liberal /'lɪbərəl/ *a* & *n* liberal (*mf*)

liberat|e /'lɪbəreɪt/ *vt* libertar. **~ion** /-'reɪʃn/ *n* libertação *f*; (*of women*) emancipação *f*

libert|y /'lɪbətɪ/ *n* liberdade *f*. **at ~y to** livre de. **take ~ies** tomar liberdades

libido /lɪ'bi:dəʊ/ *n* (*pl* **-os**) libido *m*

Libra /'li:brə/ *n* (*astr*) Balança *f*, Libra *f*

librar|y /'laɪbrərɪ/ *n* biblioteca *f*. **~ian** /-'breərɪən/ *n* bibliotecário *m*

Libya /'lɪbɪə/ *n* Líbia *f*. **~n** *a* & *n* líbio (*m*)

lice /laɪs/ *n* *see* **louse**

licence /'laɪsns/ *n* licença *f*; (*for TV*) taxa *f*; (*for driving*) carteira *f*, (*P*) carta *f*; (*behaviour*) libertinagem *f*

license /'laɪsns/ *vt* dar licença para, autorizar □ *n* (*Amer*) = **licence**. **~ plate** placa *f* do carro, (*P*) placa *f* de matrícula

licentious /laɪ'senʃəs/ *a* licencioso

lichen /'laɪkən/ *n* líquen *m*

lick /lɪk/ *vt* lamber; (*sl: defeat*) bater (*colloq*), dar uma surra em (*colloq*) □ *n* lambidela *f*. **a ~ of paint** uma mão de pintura

lid /lɪd/ *n* tampa *f*

lido /'li:dəʊ/ *n* (*pl* **~os**) piscina *f* pública ao ar livre

lie[1] /laɪ/ *n* mentira *f* □ *vi* (*pt* **lied**, *pres p* **lying**) mentir. **give the ~ to** desmentir

lie[2] /laɪ/ *vi* (*pt* **lay**, *pp* **lain**, *pres p* **lying**) estar deitado; (*remain*) ficar; (*be situated*) estar, encontrar-se; (*in grave, on ground*) jazer. **~ down** descansar. **~ in, have a ~-in** dormir até tarde. **~ low** (*colloq: hide*) andar escondido

lieu /lu:/ *n* **in ~ of** em vez de

lieutenant /lef'tenənt/ *n* (*army*) tenente *m*; (*navy*) 1° tenente *m*

life /laɪf/ *n* (*pl* **lives**) vida *f*. **~ cycle** ciclo *m* vital. **~ expectancy** probabilidade *f* de vida. **~-guard** *n* salva-vidas *m*. **~ insurance** seguro *m* de vida. **~-jacket** *n* colete *m* salva-vidas. **~-size(d)** *a* (de) tamanho natural *invar*

lifebelt /'laɪfbelt/ *n* cinto *m* salva- vidas, (*P*) cinto *m* de salvação

lifeboat /'laɪfbəʊt/ *n* barco *m* salva-vidas

lifebuoy /'laɪfbɔɪ/ *n* bóia *f* salva-vidas, (*P*) bóia *f* de salvação

lifeless /'laɪflɪs/ *a* sem vida

lifelike /'laɪflaɪk/ *a* natural, real; (*of portrait*) muito parecido

lifelong /'laɪflɒŋ/ *a* de toda a vida, perpétuo

lifestyle /'laɪfstaɪl/ *n* estilo *m* de vida

lifetime /'laɪftaɪm/ *n* vida *f*. **the chance of a ~** uma oportunidade única

lift /lɪft/ *vt/i* levantar(-se), erguer (-se); (*colloq: steal*) roubar, surripiar (*colloq*); (*of fog*) levantar, dispersar-se □ *n* ascensor *m*, elevador *m*. **give a ~ to** dar carona, (*P*) boleia a (*colloq*). **~-off** *n* decolagem *f*, (*P*) descolagem *f*

ligament /'lɪgəmənt/ *n* ligamento *m*

light[1] /laɪt/ *n* luz *f*; (*lamp*) lâmpada *f*; (*on vehicle*) farol *m*; (*spark*) lume *m* □ *a* claro □ *vt* (*pt* **lit** *or* **lighted**) (*ignite*) acender; (*illuminate*) iluminar. **bring to ~** trazer à luz, revelar. **come to ~** vir à luz. **~ up** iluminar(-se), acender(-se). **~-year** *n* ano-luz *m*

light[2] /laɪt/ *a* & *adv* (**-er, -est**) leve. **~-headed** *a* (*dizzy*) estonteado, tonto; (*frivolous*) leviano. **~-hearted** *a* alegre, despreocupado. **~ly** *adv* de leve, levemente, ligeiramente. **~ness** *n* leveza *f*

lighten[1] /'laɪtn/ *vt/i* iluminar(-se); (*make brighter*) clarear

lighten[2] /'laɪtn/ *vt/i* (*load etc*) aligeirar(-se), tornar mais leve

lighter /'laɪtə(r)/ *n* isqueiro *m*

lighthouse /'laɪthaʊs/ *n* farol *m*

lighting /'laɪtɪŋ/ *n* iluminação *f*

lightning /'laɪtnɪŋ/ *n* relâmpago *m*; (*thunderbolt*) raio *m* □ *a* muito rápido. **like ~** como um relâmpago

lightweight /'laɪtweɪt/ *a* leve

like[1] /laɪk/ *a* semelhante (a), parecido (com) ▫ *prep* como ▫ *conj* (*colloq*) como ▫ *n* igual *m*, coisa *f* parecida. **~-minded** *a* da mesma opinião. **the ~s of you** gente como você(s).

like[2] /laɪk/ *vt* gostar (de). **~s** *npl* gostos *mpl*. **I would ~** gostaria (de), queria. **if you ~** se quiser. **would you ~?** gostaria?, queria? **~able** *a* simpático

like|ly /'laɪklɪ/ *a* (**-ier, -iest**) provável ▫ *adv* provavelmente. **he is ~ly to come** é provável que ele venha. **not ~ly!** (*colloq*) nem morto, nem por sonhos. **~lihood** *n* probabilidade *f*

liken /'laɪkn/ *vt* comparar (**to** com)

likeness /'laɪknɪs/ *n* semelhança *f*

likewise /'laɪkwaɪz/ *adv* também; (*in the same way*) da mesma maneira

liking /'laɪkɪŋ/ *n* gosto *m*, inclinação *f*; (*for person*) afeição *f*. **take a ~ to** (*thing*) tomar gosto por; (*person*) simpatizar com

lilac /'laɪlək/ *n* lilás *m* ▫ *a* lilás *invar*

lily /'lɪlɪ/ *n* lírio *m*, lis *m*. **~ of the valley** lírio *m* do vale

limb /lɪm/ *n* membro *m*

limber /'lɪmbə(r)/ *vi* **~ up** fazer exercícios para desenferrujar (*colloq*)

lime[1] /laɪm/ *n* cal *f*

lime[2] /laɪm/ *n* (*fruit*) limão *m*

lime[3] /laɪm/ *n* **~(-tree)** tília *f*

limelight /'laɪmlaɪt/ *n* **be in the ~** estar em evidência

limerick /'lɪmərɪk/ *n* poema *m* humorístico (*de cinco versos*)

limit /'lɪmɪt/ *n* limite *m* ▫ *vt* limitar. **~ation** /-'teɪʃn/ *n* limitação *f*. **~ed company** sociedade *f* anônima, (*P*) anónima de responsabilidade limitada

limousine /'lɪməzi:n/ *n* limusine *f*

limp[1] /lɪmp/ *vi* mancar, coxear ▫ *n* **have a ~** coxear

limp[2] /lɪmp/ *a* (**-er, -est**) mole, frouxo

line[1] /laɪn/ *n* linha *f*; (*string*) fio *m*; (*rope*) corda *f*; (*row*) fila *f*; (*of poem*) verso *m*; (*wrinkle*) ruga *f*; (*of business*) ramo *m*; (*of goods*) linha *f*; (*Amer: queue*) fila *f*, (*P*) bicha *f* ▫ *vt* marcar com linhas; (*streets etc*) ladear, enfileirar-se ao longo de. **~d paper** papel *m* pautado. **in ~ with** de acordo com. **~ up** alinhar(-se), enfileirar(-se); (*in queue*) pôr(-se) em fila, (*P*) bicha. **~-up** *n* (*players*) formação *f*

line[2] /laɪn/ *vt* (*garment*) forrar (**with** de)

lineage /'lɪnɪɪdʒ/ *n* linhagem *f*

linear /'lɪnɪə(r)/ *a* linear

linen /'lɪnɪn/ *n* (*sheets etc*) roupa *f* (branca) de cama; (*material*) linho *m*

liner /'laɪnə(r)/ *n* navio *m* de linha regular, (*P*) paquete *m*

linesman /'laɪnzmən/ *n* (*football, tennis*) juiz *m* de linha

linger /'lɪŋgə(r)/ *vi* demorar-se, deixar-se ficar; (*of smells etc*) persistir

lingerie /'lænʒərɪ/ *n* roupa *f* de baixo (de senhora), lingerie *f*

linguist /'lɪŋgwɪst/ *n* lingüista *mf*, (*P*) linguista *mf*

linguistic /lɪŋ'gwɪstɪk/ *a* lingüístico, (*P*) linguístico. **~s** *n* lingüística *f*, (*P*) linguística *f*

lining /'laɪnɪŋ/ *n* forro *m*

link /lɪŋk/ *n* laço *m*; (*of chain; fig*) elo *m* ▫ *vt* unir, ligar; (*relate*) ligar; (*arm*) enfiar. **~ up** (*of roads*) juntar-se (**with** a). **~age** *n* ligação *f*

lino, linoleum /'laɪnəʊ, lɪ'nəʊlɪəm/ *n* linóleo *m*

lint /lɪnt/ *n* (*med*) curativo *m* de fibra de algodão; (*fluff*) cotão *m*

lion /'laɪən/ *n* leão *m*. **~ess** *n* leoa *f*

lip /lɪp/ *n* lábio *m*, beiço *m*; (*edge*) borda *f*; (*of jug etc*) bico *m*. **~-read** *vt/i* entender pelos movimentos dos lábios. **pay ~-service to** fingir pena, admiração etc

lipstick /'lɪpstɪk/ *n* batom *m*, (*P*) bâton *m*

liquefy /'lɪkwɪfaɪ/ *vt/i* liquefazer(-se)

liqueur /lɪ'kjʊə(r)/ *n* licor *m*

liquid /'lɪkwɪd/ *n* & *a* líquido (*m*). **~ize** *vt* liqüidificar, (*P*) liquidificar. **~izer** *n* liqüidificador *m*, (*P*) liquidificador *m*

liquidat|e /'lɪkwɪdeɪt/ *vt* liquidar. **~ion** /-'deɪʃn/ *n* liquidação *f*

liquor /'lɪkə(r)/ *n* bebida *f* alcoólica

liquorice /'lɪkərɪs/ *n* alcaçuz *m*

Lisbon /'lɪzbən/ *n* Lisboa *f*

lisp /lɪsp/ *n* ceceio *m* ▫ *vi* cecear

list[1] /lɪst/ *n* lista *f* ▫ *vt* fazer uma lista de; (*enter*) pôr na lista

list[2] /lɪst/ *vi* (*of ship*) adernar ▫ *n* adernamento *m*

listen /'lɪsn/ *vi* escutar, prestar atenção. **~ to, ~ in (to)** escutar, pôr-se à escuta. **~er** *n* ouvinte *mf*

listless /'lɪstlɪs/ *a* sem energia, apático

lit /lɪt/ *see* **light**[1]

literal /'lɪtərəl/ *a* literal. **~ly** *adv* literalmente

litera|te /'lɪtərət/ *a* alfabetizado. **~cy** *n* alfabetização *f*, instrução *f*

literature /'lɪtrətʃə(r)/ *n* literatura *f*; (*colloq: leaflets etc*) folhetos *mpl*

lithe /laɪð/ *a* ágil, flexível

litigation /lɪtɪ'geɪʃn/ *n* litígio *m*

litre /'li:tə(r)/ *n* litro *m*

litter /'lɪtə(r)/ *n* lixo *m*; (*animals*) ninhada *f* ▫ *vt* cobrir de lixo. **~ed with**

coberto de. **~-bin** *n* lata *f*, (*P*) caixote *m* do lixo

little /'lɪtl/ *a* pequeno; (*not much*) pouco ▫ *n* pouco *m* ▫ *adv* pouco, mal, nem. **a ~** um pouco (de). **he ~ knows** ele mal/nem sabe. **~ by ~** pouco a pouco

liturgy /'lɪtədʒɪ/ *n* liturgia *f*

live[1] /laɪv/ *a* vivo; (*wire*) eletrizado; (*broadcast*) em direto, (*P*) directo, ao vivo

live[2] /lɪv/ *vt*/*i* viver; (*reside*) habitar, morar, viver. **~ down** fazer esquecer. **~ it up** cair na farra. **~ on** viver de; (*continue*) continuar a viver. **~ up to** mostrar-se à altura de; (*fulfil*) cumprir

livelihood /'laɪvlɪhʊd/ *n* modo *m* de vida

livel|y /'laɪvlɪ/ *a* (**-ier, -iest**) vivo, animado. **~iness** *n* vivacidade *f*, animação *f*

liven /'laɪvn/ *vt*/*i* **~ up** animar (-se)

liver /'lɪvə(r)/ *n* fígado *m*

livery /'lɪvərɪ/ *n* libré *f*

livestock /'laɪvstɒk/ *n* gado *m*

livid /'lɪvɪd/ *a* lívido; (*colloq: furious*) furioso

living /'lɪvɪŋ/ *a* vivo ▫ *n* vida *f*; (*livelihood*) modo de vida *m*, sustento *m*. **earn** *or* **make a ~** ganhar a vida. **standard of ~** nível *m* de vida. **~-room** *n* sala *f* de estar

lizard /'lɪzəd/ *n* lagarto *m*

llama /'la:mə/ *n* lama *m*

load /ləʊd/ *n* carga *f*; (*of lorry, ship*) carga *f*, carregamento *m*; (*weight, strain*) peso *m*. **~s of** (*colloq*) montes de (*colloq*) ▫ *vt* carregar. **~ed** *a* (*dice*) viciado; (*sl: rich*) cheio da nota

loaf[1] /ləʊf/ *n* (*pl* **loaves**) pão *m*

loaf[2] /ləʊf/ *vi* vadiar. **~er** *n* preguiçoso *m*, vagabundo *m*

loan /ləʊn/ *n* empréstimo *m* ▫ *vt* emprestar. **on ~** emprestado

loath /ləʊθ/ *a* sem vontade de, pouco disposto a, relutante em

loath|e /ləʊð/ *vt* detestar. **~ing** *n* repugnância *f*, aversão *f*.

lobby /'lɒbɪ/ *n* entrada *f*, vestíbulo *m*; (*pol*) lobby *m*, grupo *m* de pressão ▫ *vt* fazer pressão sobre

lobe /ləʊb/ *n* lóbulo *m*

lobster /'lɒbstə(r)/ *n* lagosta *f*

local /'ləʊkl/ *a* local; (*shops etc*) do bairro ▫ *n* pessoa *f* do lugar; (*colloq: pub*) taberna *f*/pub *m* do bairro. **~ government** administração *f* municipal. **~ly** *adv* localmente

locale /ləʊ'ka:l/ *n* local *m*

locality /ləʊ'kælətɪ/ *n* localidade *f*; (*position*) lugar *m*

localization /ləʊə'laɪzeɪʃn/ *n* localização *f*

localized /'ləʊkəlaɪzd/ *a* localizado

locat|e /ləʊ'keɪt/ *vt* localizar; (*situate*) situar. **~ion** /-ʃn/ *n* localização *f*. **on ~ion** (*cinema*) em external, (*P*) no exterior

lock[1] /lɒk/ *n* (*hair*) mecha *f* de cabelo

lock[2] /lɒk/ *n* (*on door etc*) fecho *m*, fechadura *f*; (*on canal*) comporta *f* ▫ *vt*/*i* fechar à chave; (*auto: wheels*) imobilizar(-se). **~ in** fechar à chave, encerrar. **~ out** fechar a porta para, deixar na rua. **~-out** *n* lockout *m*. **~ up** fechar a casa. **under ~ and key** a sete chaves

locker /'lɒkə(r)/ *n* compartimento *m* com chave

locket /'lɒkɪt/ *n* medalhão *m*

locksmith /'lɒksmɪθ/ *n* serralheiro *m*, chaveiro *m*

locomotion /ləʊkə'məʊʃn/ *n* locomoção *f*

locomotive /'ləʊkəməʊtɪv/ *n* locomotiva *f*

locum /'ləʊkəm/ *n* (*med*) substituto *m*

locust /'ləʊkəst/ *n* gafanhoto *m*

lodge /lɒdʒ/ *n* casa *f* do guarda numa propriedade; (*of porter*) portaria *f* ▫ *vt* alojar; (*money*) depositar. **~ a complaint** apresentar uma queixa ▫ *vi* estar alojado (**with** em casa de); (*become fixed*) alojar-se. **~r** /-ə(r)/ *n* hóspede *m*/*f*

lodgings /'lɒdʒɪŋz/ *n* quarto *m* mobiliado; (*flat*) apartamento *m*

loft /lɒft/ *n* sótão *m*

lofty /'lɒftɪ/ *a* (**-ier, -iest**) elevado; (*haughty*) altivo

log /lɒg/ *n* tronco *m*, toro *m*. **~ (-book)** *n* (*naut*) diário *m* de bordo; (*aviat*) diario *m* de vôo. **sleep like a ~** dormir como uma pedra ▫ *vt* (*pt* **logged**) (*naut*/*aviat*) lançar no diário de bordo. **~ off** acabar de usar. **~ on** começar a usar

loggerheads /'lɒgəhedz/ *npl* **at ~** às turras (**with** com)

logic /'lɒdʒɪk/ *a* lógico. **~al** *a* lógico. **~ally** *adv* logicamente

logistics /lə'dʒɪstɪks/ *n* logística *f*

logo /'ləʊgəʊ/ *n* (*pl* **-os**) (*colloq*) emblema *m*, logotipo *m*, (*P*) logótipo *m*

loin /lɔɪn/ *n* (*culin*) lombo *m*, alcatra *f*

loiter /'lɔɪtə(r)/ *vi* andar vagarosamente; (*stand about*) rondar

loll /lɒl/ *vi* refestelar-se

loll|ipop /'lɒlɪpɒp/ *n* pirulito *m*, (*P*) chupa-chupa *m*. **~y** *n* (*colloq*) pirulito *m*, (*P*) chupa-chupa *m*; (*sl: money*) grana *f*

London /'lʌndən/ *n* Londres

lone /ləʊn/ *a* solitário. **~r** /-ə(r)/ *n* solitário *m*. **~some** *a* solitário

lonely /'ləʊnlɪ/ *a* (**-ier, -iest**) solitário; (*person*) só, solitário

long[1] /lɒŋ/ *a* (**-er, -est**) longo, comprido □ *adv* muito tempo, longamente. **how ~ is. . .?** (*in size*) qual é o comprimento de. . .? **how ~?** (*in time*) quanto tempo? **he will not be ~** ele não vai demorar. **a ~ time** muito tempo. **a ~ way** longe. **as** *or* **so ~ as** contanto que, desde que. **~ ago** há muito tempo. **before ~** (*future*) daqui a pouco, dentro em pouco; (*past*) pouco (tempo) depois. **in the ~ run** no fim de contas. **~ before** muito (tempo) antes. **~-distance** *a* (*flight*) de longa distância; (*phone call*) interurbano. **~ face** cara *f* triste. **~ jump** salto *m* em distância. **~-playing record** LP *m*. **~-range** *a* de longo alcance; (*forecast*) a longo prazo. **~-sighted** *a* que enxerga mal a distância. **~-standing** *a* de longa data. **~-suffering** *a* com paciência exemplar/de santo. **~-term** *a* a longo prazo. **~ wave** ondas *fpl* longas. **~-winded** *a* prolixo. **so ~!** (*colloq*) até logo!

long[2] /lɒŋ/ *vi* **~ for** ansiar por, ter grande desejo de. **~ to** desejar. **~ing** *n* desejo *m* ardente

longevity /lɒn'dʒevətɪ/ *n* longevidade *f*, vida *f* longa

longhand /'lɒŋhænd/ *n* escrita *f* à mão

longitude /'lɒndʒɪtju:d/ *n* longitude *f*

loo /lu:/ *n* (*colloq*) banheiro *m*, (*P*) casa *f* de banho

look /lʊk/ *vt/i* olhar; (*seem*) parecer □ *n* olhar *m*; (*appearance*) ar *m*, aspecto *m*. **(good) ~s** beleza *f*. **~ after** tomar conta de, olhar por. **~ at** olhar para. **~ down on** desprezar. **~ for** procurar. **~ forward to** aguardar com impaciência. **~ in on** visitar. **~ into** examinar, investigar. **~ like** parecer-se com, ter ar de. **~ on** (*as spectator*) ver, assistir; (*regard as*) considerar. **~ out** ter cautela. **~ out for** procurar; (*watch*) estar à espreita de. **~-out** *n* (*mil*) posto *m* de observação; (*watcher*) vigia *m*. **~ round** olhar em redor. **~ up** (*word*) procurar; (*visit*) ir ver. **~ up to** respeitar

loom[1] /lu:m/ *n* tear *m*

loom[2] /lu:m/ *vi* surgir indistintamente; (*fig*) ameaçar

loony /'lu:nɪ/ *n* & *a* (*sl*) maluco (*m*), doido (*m*)

loop /lu:p/ *n* laçada *f*; (*curve*) volta *f*, arco *m*; (*aviat*) loop *m* □ *vt* dar uma laçada

loophole /'lu:phəʊl/ *n* (*in rule*) saída *f*, furo *m*

loose /lu:s/ *a* (**-er, -est**) (*knot etc*) frouxo; (*page etc*) solto; (*clothes*) folgado; (*not packed*) a granel; (*inexact*) vago; (*morals*) dissoluto, imoral. **at a ~ end** sem saber o que fazer, sem ocupação definida. **break ~** soltar-se. **~ly** *adv* sem apertar; (*roughly*) vagamente

loosen /'lu:sn/ *vt* (*slacken*) soltar, desapertar; (*untie*) desfazer, desatar

loot /lu:t/ *n* saque *m* □ *vt* pilhar, saquear. **~er** *n* assaltante *mf*. **~ing** *n* pilhagem *f*, saque *m*

lop /lɒp/ *vt* (*pt* **lopped**) **~ off** cortar, podar

lop-sided /lɒp'saɪdɪd/ *a* torto, inclinado para um lado

lord /lɔ:d/ *n* senhor *m*; (*title*) lord *m*. **the L~** o Senhor. **the L~'s Prayer** o Pai-Nosso. **(good) L~!** meu Deus! **~ly** *a* magnífico, nobre; (*haughty*) altivo, arrogante

lorry /'lɒrɪ/ *n* camião *m*, caminhão *m*

lose /lu:z/ *vt/i* (*pt* **lost**) perder. **get lost** perder-se. **get lost** (*sl*) vai passear! (*colloq*). **~r** /-ə(r)/ *n* perdedor *m*

loss /lɒs/ *n* perda *f*. **be at a ~** estar perplexo. **at a ~ for words** sem saber o que dizer

lost /lɒst/ *see* **lose** □ *a* perdido. **~ property** objetos *mpl*, (*P*) objectos *mpl* perdidos (e achados)

lot[1] /lɒt/ *n* sorte *f*; (*at auction, land*) lote *m*. **draw ~s** tirar à sorte

lot[2] /lɒt/ *n* **the ~** tudo; (*people*) todos *mpl*. **a ~ (of), ~s (of)** (*colloq*) uma porção (de) (*colloq*). **quite a ~ (of)** (*colloq*) uma boa porção (de) (*colloq*)

lotion /'ləʊʃn/ *n* loção *f*

lottery /'lɒtərɪ/ *n* loteria *f*, (*P*) lotaria *f*

loud /laʊd/ *a* (**-er, -est**) alto, barulhento, ruidoso; (*of colours*) berrante □ *adv* alto. **~ hailer** *n* megafone *m*. **out ~** em voz alta. **~ly** *adv* alto

loudspeaker /laʊd'spi:kə(r)/ *n* alto-falante *m*

lounge /laʊndʒ/ *vi* recostar-se preguiçosamente □ *n* sala *f*, salão *m*

louse /laʊs/ *n* (*pl* **lice**) piolho *m*

lousy /'laʊzɪ/ *a* (**-ier, -iest**) piolhento; (*sl: very bad*) péssimo

lout /laʊt/ *n* pessoa *f* grosseira, arruaceiro *m*

lovable /'lʌvəbl/ *a* amoroso, adorável

love /lʌv/ *n* amor *m*; (*tennis*) zero *m*, nada *m* □ *vt* amar, estar apaixonado por; (*like greatly*) gostar muito de. **in ~** apaixonado (**with** por). **~ affair** aventura *f* amorosa. **she sends you her ~** ela lhe manda lembranças

lovely /'lʌvlɪ/ *a* (**-ier, -iest**) lindo; (*colloq: delightful*) encantador, delicioso

lover /'lʌvə(r)/ *n* namorado *m*, apaixonado *m*; (*illicit*) amante *m*; (*devotee*) admirador *m*, apreciador *m*

lovesick /'lʌvsɪk/ *a* perdido de amor
loving /'lʌvɪŋ/ *a* amoroso, terno, extremoso
low /ləʊ/ *a* (**-er**, **-est**) baixo □ *adv* baixo □ *n* baixa *f*; (*low pressure*) área de baixa pressão *f*. **~-cut** *a* decotado. **~-down** *a* baixo, reles □ *n* (*colloq*) a verdade autêntica, (*P*) a verdade nua e crua. **~-fat** *a* de baixo teor de gordura. **~-key** *a* (*fig*) moderado, discreto
lower /'ləʊə(r)/ *a* & *adv see* **low** □ *vt* baixar. **~ o.s.** (re)baixar-se (**to** a)
lowlands /'ləʊləndz/ *npl* planície(s) *f* (*pl*)
lowly /'ləʊlɪ/ *a* (**-ier**, **-iest**) humilde, modesto
loyal /'lɔɪəl/ *a* leal. **~ly** *adv* lealmente. **~ty** *n* lealdade *f*
lozenge /'lɒzɪndʒ/ *n* (*shape*) losango *m*; (*tablet*) pastilha *f*
LP *abbr see* **long-playing record**
lubric|ate /'lu:brɪkeɪt/ *vt* lubrificar. **~ant** *n* lubrificante *m*. **~ation** /-'keɪʃn/ *n* lubrificação *f*
lucid /'lu:sɪd/ *a* lúcido. **~ity** /lu:-'sɪdətɪ/ *n* lucidez *f*
luck /lʌk/ *n* sorte *f*. **bad ~** pouca sorte *f*. **for ~** para dar sorte. **good ~!** boa sorte
luck|y /'lʌkɪ/ *a* (**-ier**, **-iest**) sortudo, com sorte; (*event etc*) feliz; (*number etc*) que dá sorte. **~ily** *adv* felizmente
lucrative /'lu:krətɪv/ *a* lucrativo, rentável
ludicrous /'lu:dɪkrəs/ *a* ridículo, absurdo
lug /lʌg/ *vt* (*pt* **lugged**) arrstar
luggage /'lʌgɪdʒ/ *n* bagagem *f*. **~-rack** *n* porta-bagagem *m*. **~-van** *n* furgão *m*
lukewarm /'lu:kwɔ:m/ *a* morno, (*fig*) sem entusiasmo, indiferente
lull /lʌl/ *vt* (*send to sleep*) embalar; (*suspicions*) acalmar □ *n* calmarica *f*, (*P*) acalmia *f*
lullaby /'lʌləbaɪ/ *n* canção *f* de embalar
lumbago /lʌm'beɪgəʊ/ *n* lumbago *m*
lumber /'lʌmbə(r)/ *n* trastes *mpl* velhos; (*wood*) madeira *f* cortada □ *vt* **~ sb with** sobre carregar alguém com
luminous /'lu:mɪnəs/ *a* luminoso
lump /lʌmp/ *n* bocado *m*; (*swelling*) caroço *m*; (*in the throat*) nó *m*; (*in liquid*) grumo *m*; (*of sugar*) torrão *m* □ *vt* **~ together** amontoar, juntar indiscriminadamente. **~ sum** quantia *f* total; (*payment*) pagamento *m* de uma vez. **~y** *a* grumoso, encaroçado
lunacy /'lu:nəsɪ/ *n* loucura *f*
lunar /'lu:nə(r)/ *a* lunar
lunatic /'lu:nətɪk/ *n* lunático *m*. **~ asylum** manicômio *m*, (*P*) manicómio *m*
lunch /lʌntʃ/ *n* almoço *m* □ *vi* almoçar. **~-time** *n* hora *f* do almoço
luncheon /'lʌntʃən/ *n* (*formal*) almoço *m*. **~ meat** carne *f* enlatada, (*P*) 'merenda' *f*. **~ voucher** senha *f* de almoço
lung /lʌŋ/ *n* pulmão *m*
lunge /lʌndʒ/ *n* mergulho *m*, movimento *m* súbito para a frente; (*thrust*) arremetida *f* □ *vi* mergulhar, arremessar-se (**at** para cima de, contra)
lurch[1] /lɜ:tʃ/ *n* **leave sb in the ~** deixar alg em apuros
lurch[2] /lɜ:tʃ/ *vi* ir aos ziguezagues, dar guinadas; (*stagger*) cambalear
lure /lʊə(r)/ *vt* atrair, tentar □ *n* chamariz *m*, engodo *m*. **the ~ of the sea** a atração, (*P*) atracção do mar
lurid /'lʊərɪd/ *a* berrante; (*fig: sensational*) sensacional; (*fig: shocking*) horrífico
lurk /lɔ:k/ *vi* esconder-se à espreita; (*prowl*) rondar; (*be latent*) estar latente
luscious /'lʌʃəs/ *a* apetitoso; (*voluptuous*) desejável
lush /lʌʃ/ *a* viçoso, luxuriante
Lusitanian /lusɪ'teɪnɪən/ *a* & *n* lusitano (*m*)
lust /lʌst/ *n* luxúria *f*, sensualidade *f*; (*fig*) cobiça *f*, desejo *m* ardente □ *vi* **~ after** cobiçar, desejar ardentemente. **~ful** *a* sensual
lustre /'lʌstə(r)/ *n* lustre *m*; (*fig*) prestígio *m*
lusty /'lʌstɪ/ *a* (**-ier**, **-iest**) robusto
lute /lu:t/ *n* alaúde *m*
Luxemburg /'lʌksəmbɜ:g/ *n* Luxemburgo *m*
luxuriant /lʌg'ʒʊərɪənt/ *a* luxuriante
luxurious /lʌg'ʒʊərɪəs/ *a* luxuoso
luxury /'lʌkʃərɪ/ *n* luxo *m* □ *a* de luxo
lying /'laɪɪŋ/ *see* **lie**[1], **lie**[2]
lynch /lɪntʃ/ *vt* linchar
lynx /lɪŋks/ *n* lince *m*
lyre /'laɪə(r)/ *n* lira *f*
lyric /'lɪrɪk/ *a* lírico. **~s** *npl* (*mus*) letra *f*. **~al** *a* lírico

Mm

MA *abbr see* **Master of Arts**
mac /mæk/ *n* (*colloq*) impermeável *m*, gabardine *f*
macabre /mə'ka:brə/ *a* macabro
macaroni /mækə'rəʊnɪ/ *n* macarrão *m*
macaroon /mækə'ru:n/ *n* bolinho *m* seco de amêndoa ralada
mace[1] /meɪs/ *n* (*staff*) maça *f*
mace[2] /meɪs/ *n* (*spice*) macis *m*
machination /mækɪ'neɪʃn/ *n* maquinação *f*
machine /mə'ʃi:n/ *n* máquina *f* □ ~ *vt* fazer à máquina; (*sewing*) coser à máquina. **~-gun** *n* metralhadora *f*. **~-readable** *a* em linguagem de máquina. **~ tool** máquina-ferramenta *f*
machinery /mə'ʃi:nərɪ/ *n* maquinaria *f*; (*working parts; fig*) mecanismo *m*
machinist /mə'ʃi:nɪst/ *n* maquinista *m*
macho /'mætʃəʊ/ *a* machista
mackerel /'mækrəl/ *n* (*pl invar*) cavala *f*
mackintosh /'mækɪntɒʃ/ *n* impermeável *m*, gabardine *f*
mad /mæd/ *a* (**madder, maddest**) doido, louco; (*dog*) raivoso; (*colloq: angry*) furioso (*colloq*). **~ cow disease** doença *f* da vaca louca. **be ~ about** ser doido por. **like ~** como (um) doido. **~ly** *adv* loucamente; (*frantically*) enlouquecidamente. **~ness** *n* loucura *f*
Madagascar /mædə'gæskə(r)/ *n* Madagáscar *m*
madam /'mædəm/ *n* senhora *f*. **no, ~** não senhora
madden /'mædn/ *vt* endoidecer, enlouquecer. **it's ~ing** é de enlouquecer
made /meɪd/ *see* **make**. **~ to measure** feito sob medida
Madeira /mə'dɪərə/ *n* Madeira *f*; (*wine*) Madeira *m*
madman /'mædmən/ *n* (*pl* **-men**) doido *m*
madrigal /'mædrɪgl/ *n* madrigal *m*
Mafia /'mæfɪə/ *n* Máfia *f*
magazine /mægə'zi:n/ *n* revista *f*, magazine *m*; (*of gun*) carregador *m*
magenta /mə'dʒentə/ *a* & *n* magenta (*m*), carmin (*m*)
maggot /'mægət/ *n* larva *f*. **~y** *a* bichento
Magi /'meɪdʒaɪ/ *npl* **the ~** os Reis *mpl* Magos
magic /'mædʒɪk/ *n* magia *f* □ ~ *a* mágico. **~al** *a* mágico
magician /mə'dʒɪʃn/ *n* (*conjuror*) prestidigitador *m*; (*wizard*) feiticeiro *m*
magistrate /'mædʒɪstreɪt/ *n* magistrado *m*
magnanim|ous /mæg'nænɪməs/ *a* magnânimo. **~ity** /-ə'nɪmətɪ/ *n* magnanimidade *f*
magnate /'mægneɪt/ *n* magnata *m*
magnet /'mægnɪt/ *n* ímã *m*, (*P*) íman *m*. **~ic** /-'netɪk/ *a* magnético. **~ism** /-ɪzəm/ *n* magnetismo *m*. **~ize** *vt* magnetizar
magnificen|t /mæg'nɪfɪsnt/ *a* magnífico. **~ce** *n* magnificência *f*
magnif|y /'mægnɪfaɪ/ *vt* aumentar; (*sound*) ampliar, amplificar. **~ication** /-ɪ'keɪʃn/ *n* aumento *m*, ampliação *f*. **~ying glass** lupa *f*
magnitude /'mægnɪtju:d/ *n* magnitude *f*
magpie /'mægpaɪ/ *n* pega *f*
mahogany /mə'hɒgənɪ/ *n* mogno *m*
maid /meɪd/ *n* criada *f*, empregada *f*. **old ~** solteirona *f*
maiden /'meɪdn/ *n* (*old use*) donzela *f* □ *a* (*aunt*) solteira; (*speech, voyage*) inaugural. **~ name** nome *m* de solteira
mail[1] /meɪl/ *n* correio *m*; (*letters*) correio *m*, correspondência *f* □ *a* postal □ *vt* postar, pôr no correio; (*send by mail*) mandar pelo correio. **~-bag** *n* mala *f* postal. **~-box** *n* (*Amer*) caixa *f* do correio. **~ing-list** *n* lista *f* de endereços. **~ order** *n* encomenda *f* por correspondência, (*P*) por correio
mail[2] /meɪl/ *n* (*armour*) cota *f* de malha
mailman /'meɪlmæn/ *n* (*pl* **-men**) (*Amer*) carteiro *m*
maim /meɪm/ *vt* mutilar, aleijar
main[1] /meɪn/ *a* principal □ *n* **in the ~** em geral, essencialmente. **~ road** estrada *f* principal. **~ly** *adv* principalmente, sobretudo
main[2] /meɪn/ *n* **(water/gas) ~** cano *m* de água/gás. **the ~s** (*electr*) a rede *f* elétrica
mainland /'meɪnlənd/ *n* continente *m*
mainstay /'meɪnsteɪ/ *n* (*fig*) esteio *m*
mainstream /'meɪnstri:m/ *n* tendência *f* dominante, linha *f* principal
maintain /meɪn'teɪn/ *vt* manter, sustentar; (*rights*) defender, manter
maintenance /'meɪntənəns/ *n* (*care, continuation*) manutenção *f*; (*allowance*) pensão *f*
maisonette /meɪzə'net/ *n* dúplex *m*
maize /meɪz/ *n* milho *m*
majestic /mə'dʒestɪk/ *a* majestoso. **~ally** *adv* majestosamente
majesty /'mædʒəstɪ/ *n* majestade *f*

major /'meɪdʒə(r)/ *a* maior; (*very important*) de vulto ◻ *n* major *m* ◻ *vi* **~in** (*Amer: univ*) especializar-se em. **~ road** estrada *f* principal

Majorca /mə'dʒɔ:kə/ *n* Maiorca *f*

majority /mə'dʒɒrətɪ/ *n* maioria *f*; (*age*) maioridade *f* ◻ *a* majoritário, (*P*) maioritário. **the ~ of people** a maioria *or* a maior parte das pessoas

make /meɪk/ *vt*/*i* (*pt* **made**) fazer; (*decision*) tomar; (*destination*) chegar a; (*cause to*) fazer (+ *inf*) *or* (com) que (+ *subj*). **you ~ me angry** você me aborrece ◻ *n* (*brand*) marca *f*. **on the ~** (*sl*) oportunista. **be made of** ser feito de. **~ o.s. at home** estar à vontade/como em sua casa. **~ it** chegar; (*succeed*) triunfar. **I ~ it two o'clock** são duas pelo meu relógio. **~ as if to** fazer *ou* fingir que. **~ believe** fingir. **~-believe** *a* fingido ◻ *n* fantasia *f*. **~ do with** arranjar-se com, contentar-se com. **~ for** dirigir-se para; (*contribute to*) ajudar a. **~ good** *vi* triunfar ◻ *vt* compensar; (*repair*) reparar. **~ off** fugir (**with** com). **~ out** avistar, distinguir; (*understand*) entender; (*claim*) pretender; (*a cheque*) passar, emitir. **~ over** ceder, transferir. **~ up** *vt* fazer, compor; (*story*) inventar; (*deficit*) suprir ◻ *vi* fazer as pazes. **~ up (one's face)** maquilar-se, (*P*) maquilhar-se. **~-up** *n* maquilagem *f*, (*P*) maquilhagem *f*; (*of object*) composição *f*; (*psych*) maneira *f* de ser, natureza *f*. **~ up for** compensar. **~ up one's mind** decidir-se

maker /'meɪkə(r)/ *n* fabricante *mf*

makeshift /'meɪkʃɪft/ *n* solução *f* temporária ◻ *a* provisório

making /'meɪkɪŋ/ *n* **be the ~ of** fazer, ser a causa do sucesso de. **in the ~** em formação. **he has the ~s of** ele tem as qualidades essenciais de

maladjusted /mælə'dʒʌstɪd/ *a* desajustado, inadaptado

maladministration /mælədmɪnɪ-'streɪʃn/ *n* mau governo *m*, má gestão *f*

malaise /mæ'leɪz/ *n* mal-estar *m*

malaria /mə'leərɪə/ *n* malária *f*

Malay /mə'leɪ/ *a* & *n* malaio (*m*). **~sia** /-ʒə/ *n* Malásia *f*

male /meɪl/ *a* (*voice, sex*) masculino; (*biol, techn*) macho ◻ *n* (*human*) homem *m*, indivíduo *m* do sexo masculino; (*arrival*) macho *m*

malevolen|t /mə'levələnt/ *a* malévolo. **~ce** *n* malevolência *f*, má vontade *f*

malform|ation /mælfɔ:'meɪʃn/ *n* malformação *f*, deformidade *f*. **~ed** *a* deformado

malfunction /mæl'fʌŋkʃn/ *n* mau funcionamento *m* ◻ *vi* funcionar mal

malice /'mælɪs/ *n* maldade *f*, malícia *f*. **bear sb ~** guardar rancor a alg

malicious /mə'lɪʃəs/ *a* maldoso, malicioso. **~ly** *adv* maldosamente, maliciosamente

malign /mə'laɪn/ *vt* caluniar, difamar

malignan|t /mə'lɪgnənt/ *a* (*tumour*) maligno; (*malevolent*) malévolo. **~cy** *n* malignidade *f*; malevolência *f*

malinger /mə'lɪŋgə(r)/ *vi* fingir-se doente. **~er** *n* pessoa *f* que se finge doente

mallet /'mælɪt/ *n* maço *m*

malnutrition /mælnju:'trɪʃn/ *n* desnutrição *f*, subalimentação *f*

malpractice /mæl'præktɪs/ *n* abuso *m*; (*incompetence*) incompetência *f* profissional, negligência *f*

malt /mɔ:lt/ *n* malte *m*

Malt|a /'mɔ:ltə/ *n* Malta *f*. **~ese** /-'ti:z/ *a* & *n* maltês (*m*)

maltreat /mæl'tri:t/ *vt* maltratar. **~ment** *n* mau(s) trato(s) *m*(*pl*)

mammal /'mæml/ *n* mamífero *m*

mammoth /'mæməθ/ *n* mamute *m* ◻ *a* gigantesco, colossal

man /mæn/ *n* (*pl* **men**) homem *m*; (*in sports team*) jogador *m*; (*chess*) peça *f* ◻ *vt* (*pt* **manned**) prover de pessoal; (*mil*) guarnecer; (*naut*) guarnecer, equipar, tripular; (*be on duty at*) estar de serviço em. **~ in the street** o homem da rua. **~-hour** *n* hora *f* de trabalho per capita, homem-hora *f*. **~-hunt** *n* caça *f* ao homem. **~-made** *a* artificial. **~ to man** de homem para homem

manage /'mænɪdʒ/ *vt* (*household*) governar; (*tool*) manejar; (*boat, affair, crowd*) manobrar; (*shop*) dirigir, gerir. **I could ~ another drink** (*colloq*) até que tomaria mais um drinque (*colloq*) ◻ *vi* arranjar-se. **~ to do** conseguir fazer. **~able** *a* manejável; (*easily controlled*) controlável. **~ment** *n* gerência *f*, direção *f*, (*P*) direcção *f*. **managing director** diretor *m*, (*P*) director *m* geral

manager /'mænɪdʒə(r)/ *n* diretor *m*, (*P*) director *m*; (*of bank, shop*) gerente *m*; (*of actor*) empresário *m*; (*sport*) treinador *m*. **~ess** /-'res/ *n* diretora *f*, (*P*) directora *f*; gerente *f*. **~ial** /-'dʒɪərɪəl/ *a* diretivo, (*P*) directivo, administrativo. **~ial staff** gestores *mpl*

mandarin /'mændərɪn/ *n* mandarim *m*. **~ (orange)** mandarina *f*, tangerina *f*

mandate /'mændeɪt/ *n* mandato *m*

mandatory /'mændətrɪ/ *a* obrigatório

mane /meɪn/ *n* crina *f*; (*of lion*) juba *f*
mangle[1] /ˈmæŋgl/ *n* calandra *f* ▫ *vt* espremer (com a calandra)
mangle[2] /ˈmæŋgl/ *vt* (*mutilate*) mutilar, estropiar
mango /ˈmæŋgəʊ/ *n* (*pl* **-oes**) manga *f*
manhandle /ˈmænhændl/ *vt* mover à força de braço; (*treat roughly*) tratar com brutalidade
manhole /ˈmænhəʊl/ *n* poço *m* de inspeção, (*P*) inspecção
manhood /ˈmænhʊd/ *n* idade adulta *f*; (*quality*) virilidade *f*
mania /ˈmeɪnɪə/ *n* mania *f*. **~c** /-ɪæk/ *n* maníaco *m*
manicur|e /ˈmænɪkjʊə(r)/ *n* manicure *f* ▫ *vt* fazer. **~ist** *n* manicure *m*
manifest /ˈmænɪfest/ *a* manifesto ▫ *vt* manifestar. **~ation** /-ˈsteɪʃn/ *n* manifestação *f*
manifesto /mænɪˈfestəʊ/ *n* (*pl* **-os**) manifesto *m*
manipulat|e /məˈnɪpjʊleɪt/ *vt* manipular. **~ion** /-ˈleɪʃn/ *n* manipulação *f*
mankind /mænˈkaɪnd/ *n* humanidade *f*, gênero *m*, (*P*) género *m* humano
manly /ˈmænlɪ/ *a* viril, másculo
manner /ˈmænə(r)/ *n* maneira *f*, modo *m*; (*attitude*) modo(s) *m* (*pl*); (*kind*) espécie *f*. **~s** maneiras *fpl*. **bad ~s** má-criação *f*, falta *f* de educação. **good ~s** (boa) educação *f*. **~ ed** *a* afetado.
mannerism /ˈmænərɪzəm/ *n* maneirismo *m*
manoeuvre /məˈnuːvə(r)/ *n* manobra *f* ▫ *vt/i* manobrar
manor /ˈmænə(r)/ *n* solar *m*
manpower /ˈmænpaʊə(r)/ *n* mão-de-obra *f*
mansion /ˈmænʃn/ *n* mansão *f*
manslaughter /ˈmænslɔːtə(r)/ *n* homicídio *m* involuntário
mantelpiece /ˈmæntlpiːs/ *n* (*shelf*) consolo *m* da lareira, (*P*) prateleira *f* da chaminé
manual /ˈmænjʊəl/ *a* manual ▫ *n* manual *m*
manufacture /mænjʊˈfæktʃə(r)/ *vt* fabricar ▫ *n* fabrico *m*, fabricação *f*. **~r** /-ə(r)/ *n* fabricante *mf*
manure /məˈnjʊə(r)/ *n* estrume *m*
manuscript /ˈmænjʊskrɪpt/ *n* manuscrito *m*
many /ˈmenɪ/ *a* (**more, most**) muitos ▫ *n* muitos; (*many people*) muita gente *f*. **a great ~** muitíssimos. **~ a man/tear/*etc*** muitos homens/muitas lágrimas/*etc*. **you may take as ~ as you want** você pode levar quantos quiser. **of us/them/you** muitos de nós/deles/de vocês. **how ~?** quantos? **one too ~** um a mais
map /mæp/ *n* mapa *m* ▫ *vt* (*pt* **mapped**) fazer mapa de. **~ out** planear em pormenor; (*route*) traçar
maple /ˈmeɪpl/ *n* bordo *m*
mar /mɑː(r)/ *vt* (*pt* **marred**) estragar; (*beauty*) desfigurar
marathon /ˈmærəθən/ *n* maratona *f*
marble /ˈmɑːbl/ *n* mármore *m*; (*for game*) bola *f* de gude, (*P*) berlinde *m*
March /mɑːtʃ/ *n* março *m*
march /mɑːtʃ/ *vi* marchar ▫ *vt* **~ off** fazer marchar, conduzir à força. **he was ~ed off to prison** fizeram-no marchar para a prisão ▫ *n* marcha *f*. **~-past** *n* desfile *m* em revista militar
mare /meə(r)/ *n* égua *f*
margarine /mɑːdʒəˈriːn/ *n* margarina *f*
margin /ˈmɑːdʒɪn/ *n* margem *f*. **~al** *a* marginal. **~al seat** (*pol*) lugar *m* ganho com pequena maioria. **~ally** *adv* por uma pequena margem, muito pouco
marigold /ˈmærɪgəʊld/ *n* cravo-de-defunto *m*, (*P*) malmequer *m*
marijuana /mærɪˈwɑːnə/ *n* maconha *f*
marina /məˈriːnə/ *n* marina *f*
marinade /mærɪˈneɪd/ *n* vinha d'alho, escalabeche *m* ▫ *vt* pôr na vinha d'alho
marine /məˈriːn/ *a* marinho; (*of ship, trade etc*) marítimo ▫ *n* (*shipping*) marinha *f*; (*sailor*) fuzileiro *m* naval
marionette /mærɪəˈnet/ *n* fantoche *m*, marionete *f*
marital /ˈmærɪtl/ *a* marital, conjugal, matrimonial. **~ status** estado *m* civil
maritime /ˈmærɪtaɪm/ *a* marítimo
mark[1] /mɑːk/ *n* (*currency*) marco *m*
mark[2] /mɑːk/ *n* marca *f*; (*trace*) marca *f*, sinal *m*; (*stain*) mancha *f*; (*schol*) nota *f*; (*target*) alvo *m* ▫ *vt* marcar; (*exam etc*) marcar, classificar. **~ out** marcar. **~ out for** escolher para, designar para. **~ time** marcar passo. **make one's ~** ganhar nome. **~ er** *n* marcador *m*. **~ing** *n* marcas *fpl*, marcação *f*
marked /mɑːkt/ *a* marcado. **~ly** /-ɪdlɪ/ *adv* manifestamente, visivelmente
market /ˈmɑːkɪt/ *n* mercado *m* ▫ *vt* vender; (*launch*) comercializar, lançar. **~ garden** horta *f* de legumes para venda. **~-place** *n* mercado *m*. **~ research** pesquisa *f* de mercado. **on the ~** à venda. **~ ing** *n* marketing *m*
marksman /ˈmɑːksmən/ *n* (*pl* **-men**) atirador *m* especial
marmalade /ˈmɑːməleɪd/ *n* compota *f* de laranja
maroon /məˈruːn/ *a* & *n* bordô (*m*), (*P*) bordeaux (*m*)

marooned /mə'ru:nd/ *a* abandonado em ilha, costa deserta etc; (*fig: stranded*) encalhado (*fig*)
marquee /ma:'ki:/ *n* barraca *f* ou tenda *f* grande; (*Amer: awning*) toldo *m*
marriage /'mærɪdʒ/ *n* casamento *m*, matrimônio *m*, (*P*) matrimónio *m*. **~ certificate** certidão *f* de casamento. **~able** *a* casadouro
marrow /'mærəʊ/ *n* (*of bone*) tutano *m*, medula *f*; (*vegetable*) abóbora *f*. **chilled to the ~** gelado até os ossos
marr|y /'mærɪ/ *vt* casar(-se) com; (*give or unite in marriage*) casar □ *vi* casar-se. **~ied** *a* casado; (*life*) de casado, conjugal. **get ~ied** casar-se
Mars /ma:z/ *n* Marte *m*
marsh /ma:ʃ/ *n* pântano *m*. **~y** *a* pantanoso
marshal /'ma:ʃl/ *n* (*mil*) marechal *m*; (*steward*) mestre *m* de cerimônias, (*P*) cerimónias □ *vt* (*pt* **marshalled**) dispor em ordem, ordenar; (*usher*) conduzir, escoltar
marshmallow /ma:ʃ'mæləʊ/ *n* marshmallow *m*
martial /'ma:ʃl/ *a* marcial. **~ law** lei *f* marcial
martyr /'ma:tə(r)/ *n* mártir *mf* □ *vt* *martirizar*. **~dom** *n* martírio *m*
marvel /'ma:vl/ *n* maravilha *f*, prodígio *m* □ *vi* (*pt* **marvelled**) (*feel wonder*) maravilhar-se (**at** com); (*be astonished*) pasmar (**at** com)
marvellous /'ma:vələs/ *a* maravilhoso
Marxis|t /'ma:ksɪst/ *a* & *n* marxista (*mf*). **~m** /-zəm/ *n* marxismo *m*
marzipan /'ma:zɪpæn/ *n* maçapão *m*
mascara /mæ'ska:rə/ *n* rímel *m*
mascot /'mæskət/ *n* mascote *f*
masculin|e /'mæskjʊlɪn/ *a* masculino □ *n* masculino *m*. **~ity** /-'lɪnətɪ/ *n* masculinidade *f*
mash /mæʃ/ *n* (*pulp*) papa *f* □ *vt* esmagar. **~ed potatoes** purê *m* de batata(s)
mask /ma:sk/ *n* máscara *f* □ *vt* mascarar
masochis|t /'mæsəkɪst/ *n* masoquista *mf*. **~m** /-zəm/ *n* masoquismo *m*
mason /'meɪsn/ *n* maçom *m*; (*building*) pedreiro *m*. **~ry** *n* maçonaria *f*; (*building*) alvenaria *f*
Mason /'meɪsn/ *n* Maçônico *m*, (*P*) Maçónico *m*. **~ic** /mə'sɒnɪk/ *a* Maçônico, (*P*) Maçónico
masquerade /mæ:skə'reɪd/ *n* mascarada *f* □ *vi* **~ as** mascarar-se de, disfarçar-se de
mass[1] /mæs/ *n* (*relig*) missa *f*
mass[2] /mæs/ *n* massa *f*; (*heap*) montão *m* □ *vt*/*i* aglomerar(-se), reunir(-se) em massa. **~-produce** *vt* produzir em série. **the ~es** as massas, a grande massa
massacre /'mæsəkə(r)/ *n* massacre *m* □ *vt* massacrar
massage /'mæsa:ʒ/ *n* massagem *f* □ *vt* massagear, fazer massagens em, (*P*) dar massagens a
masseu|r /mæ'sɜ:(r)/ *n* massagista *m*. **~se** /mæ'sɜ:z/ *n* massagista *f*
massive /'mæsɪv/ *a* (*heavy*) maciço; (*huge*) enorme
mast /ma:st/ *n* mastro *m*; (*for radio etc*) antena *f*
master /'ma:stə(r)/ *n* (*in school*) professor *m*, mestre *m*; (*expert*) mestre *m*; (*boss*) patrão *m*; (*owner*) dono *m*. **M~** (*boy*) menino *m* □ *vt* dominar. **~-key** *n* chave mestra *f*. **~-mind** *n* (*of scheme etc*) cérebro *m* □ *vt* planejar, dirigir. **M~ of Arts**/*etc* Licenciado *m* em Letras/*etc*. **~-stroke** *n* golpe *m* de mestre. **~y** *n* domínio *m* (**over** sobre); (*knowledge*) conhecimento *m*; (*skill*) perícia *f*
masterly /'ma:stəlɪ/ *a* magistral
masterpiece /'ma:stəpi:s/ *n* obraprima *f*
masturbat|e /'mæstəbeɪt/ *vi* masturbar-se. **~ion** /-'beɪʃn/ *n* masturbação *f*
mat /mæt/ *n* tapete *m* pequeno; (*at door*) capacho *m*. (**table-**)**~** *n* (*of cloth*) paninho *m* de mesa; (*for hot dishes*) descanso *m* para pratos
match[1] /mætʃ/ *n* fósforo *m*
match[2] /mætʃ/ *n* (*contest*) competição *f*, torneio *m*; (*game*) partida *f*; (*equal*) par *m*, parceiro *m*, igual *mf*; (*fig: marriage*) casamento *m*; (*marriage partner*) partido *m* □ *vt*/*i* (*set against*) contrapôr (**against** a); (*equal*) igualar; (*go with*) condizer; (*be alike*) ir com, emparceirar com. **her shoes ~ed her bag** os sapatos dela combinavam com a bolsa. **~ing** *a* condizente, a condizer
matchbox /'mætʃbɒks/ *n* caixa *f* de fósforos
mat|e[1] /meɪt/ *n* companheiro *m*, camarada *mf*; (*of birds, animals*) macho *m*, fêmea *f*; (*assistant*) ajudante *mf* □ *vt*/*i* acasalar(-se) (**with** com). **~ing season** *n* época *f* de cio
mate[2] /meɪt/ *n* (*chess*) mate *m*, xeque-mate *m*
material /mə'tɪərɪəl/ *n* material *m*; (*fabric*) tecido *m*; (*equipment*) apetrechos *mpl* □ *a* material; (*significant*) importante
materialis|m /mə'tɪərɪəlɪzəm/ *n* materialismo *m*. **~tic** /-'lɪstɪk/ *a* materialista
materialize /mə'tɪərɪəlaɪz/ *vi* realizar-se, concretizar-se; (*appear*) aparecer
maternal /mə'tɜ:nəl/ *a* maternal

maternity /məˈtɜːnətɪ/ *n* maternidade *f* □ *a* (*clothes*) de grávida. **~ hospital** maternidade *f*. **~ leave** licença *f* de maternidade

mathematic|s /mæθəˈmætɪks/ *n* matemática *f*. **~al** *a* matemático. **~ian** /-əˈtɪʃn/ *n* matemático *m*.

maths /mæθs/ *n* (*colloq*) matemática *f*

matinée /ˈmætɪneɪ/ *n* matinê *f*, (*P*) matinée *f*

matrimon|y /ˈmætrɪmənɪ/ *n* matrimônio *m*, (*P*) matrimónio *m*. **~ial** /-ˈməʊnɪəl/ *a* matrimonial, conjugal

matrix /ˈmeɪtrɪks/ *n* (*pl* **matrices** /-siːz/) matriz *f*

matron /ˈmeɪtrən/ *n* matrona *f*; (*in school*) inspetora *f*; (*former use: senior nursing officer*) enfermeira-chefe *f*. **~ly** *a* respeitável, muito digno

matt /mæt/ *a* fosco, sem brilho

matted /ˈmætɪd/ *a* emaranhado

matter /ˈmætə(r)/ *n* (*substance*) matéria *f*; (*affair*) assunto *m*, caso *m*, questão *f*; (*pus*) pus *m* □ *vi* importar. **as a ~ of fact** na verdade. **it does not ~** não importa. **~-of-fact** *a* prosaico, terra-a-terra. **no ~ what happens** não importa o que acontecer. **what is the ~?** o que é que há? **what is the ~ with you?** o que é que você tem?

mattress /ˈmætrɪs/ *n* colchão *m*

matur|e /məˈtjʊə(r)/ *a* maduro, amadurecido □ *vt/i* amadurecer; (*comm*) vencer-se. **~ity** *n* madureza *f*, maturidade *f*; (*comm*) vencimento *m*

maul /mɔːl/ *vt* maltratar, atacar

Mauritius /məˈrɪʃəs/ *n* Ilha *f* Maurícia

mausoleum /mɔːsəˈlɪəm/ *n* mausoléu *m*

mauve /məʊv/ *a & n* lilás (*m*)

maxim /ˈmæksɪm/ *n* máxima *f*

maxim|um /ˈmæksɪməm/ *a & n* (*pl* **-ima**) máximo (*m*). **~ize** *vt* aumentar ao máximo, maximizar

may /meɪ/ *v aux* (*pt* **might**) poder. **he ~/might come** talvez venha/viesse. **you might have** podia ter. **you ~ leave** pode ir. **~ I smoke?** posso fumar?, dá licença que eu fume? **~ he be happy** que ele seja feliz. **I ~** *or* **might as well go** talvez seja *or* fosse melhor eu ir

May /meɪ/ *n* maio *n*. **~ Day** o primeiro de maio

maybe /ˈmeɪbiː/ *adv* talvez

mayhem /ˈmeɪhem/ *n* (*disorder*) distúrbios *mpl* violentos; (*havoc*) estragos *mpl*

mayonnaise /meɪəˈneɪz/ *n* maionese *f*

mayor /meə(r)/ *n* prefeito *m*. **~ess** *n* prefeita *f*; (*mayor's wife*) mulher *f* do prefeito

maze /meɪz/ *n* labirinto *m*

me /miː/ *pron* me; (*after prep*) mim. **with ~** comigo. **he knows ~** ele me conhece. **it's ~** sou eu

meadow /ˈmedəʊ/ *n* prado *m*, campina *f*

meagre /ˈmiːgə(r)/ *a* (*thin*) magro; (*scanty*) escasso

meal[1] /miːl/ *n* refeição *f*

meal[2] /miːl/ *n* (*grain*) farinha *f* grossa

mean[1] /miːn/ *a* (**-er, -est**) mesquinho; (*unkind*) mau. **~ness** *n* mesquinhez *f*

mean[2] /miːn/ *a* médio □ *n* média *f*. **Greenwich ~ time** tempo *m* médio de Greenwich

mean[3] /miːn/ *vt* (*pt* **meant**) (*intend*) tencionar *or* ter (a) intenção (**to** de); (*signify*) querer dizer, significar; (*entail*) dar em resultado, resultar provavelmente em; (*refer to*) referir-se a. **be meant for** destinar-se a. **I didn't ~ it** desculpe, foi sem querer. **he ~s what he says** ele está falando sério

meander /mɪˈændə(r)/ *vi* serpentear; (*wander*) perambular

meaning /ˈmiːnɪŋ/ *n* sentido *m*, significado *m*. **~ ful** *a* significativo. **~less** *a* sem sentido

means /miːnz/ *n* meio(s) *m*(*pl*) □ *npl* meios *mpl* pecuniários, recursos *mpl*. **by all ~** com certeza. **by ~ of** por meio de, através de. **by no ~** de modo nenhum

meant /ment/ see **mean**[3]

mean|time /ˈmiːntaɪm/ *adv* **(in the) ~time** entretanto. **~- while** /-waɪl/ *adv* entretanto

measles /ˈmiːzlz/ *n* sarampo *m*. **German ~** rubéola *f*

measly /ˈmiːzlɪ/ *a* (*sl*) miserável, ínfimo

measurable /ˈmeʒərəbl/ *a* mensurável

measure /ˈmeʒə(r)/ *n* medida *f* □ *vt/i* medir. **made to ~** feito sob medida. **~ up to** mostrar-se à altura de. **~d** *a* medido, calculado. **~ment** *n* medida *f*

meat /miːt/ *n* carne *f*. **~y** *a* carnudo; (*fig: substantial*) substancial

mechanic /mɪˈkænɪk/ *n* mecânico *m*

mechanic|al /mɪˈkænɪkl/ *a* mecânico. **~s** *n* mecânica *f*; *npl* mecanismo *m*

mechan|ism /ˈmekənɪzəm/ *n* mecanismo *m*. **~ize** *vt* mecanizar

medal /ˈmedl/ *n* medalha *f*. **~list** *n* condecorado *m*. **be a gold ~list** ser medalha de ouro

medallion /mɪˈdælɪən/ *n* medalhão *m*

meddle /ˈmedl/ *vi* (*interfere*) imiscuir-se, intrometer-se (**in** em); (*tinker*) mexer (**with** em). **~some** *a* intrometido, abelhudo

media /ˈmiːdɪə/ *see* **medium** □ *npl* **the ~** a média, os meios de comunicação social *or* de massa

mediat|e /'mi:dɪeɪt/ *vi* servir de intermediário, mediar. **~ion** /-'eɪʃn/ *n* mediação *f*. **~or** *n* mediador *m*, intermediário *m*

medical /'medɪkl/ *a* médico ▫ *n* (*colloq: examination*) exame *m* médico

medicat|ed /'medɪkeɪtɪd/ *a* medicinal. **~ion** /-'keɪʃn/ *n* medicamentação *f*

medicinal /mɪ'dɪsɪnl/ *a* medicinal

medicine /'medsn/ *n* medicina *f*; (*substance*) remédio *m*, medicamento *m*

medieval /medɪ'i:vl/ *a* medieval

mediocr|e /mi:dɪ'əʊkə(r)/ *a* medíocre. **~ity** /-'ɒkrətɪ/ *n* mediocridade *f*

meditat|e /'medɪteɪt/ *vt/i* meditar. **~ion** /-'teɪʃn/ *n* meditação *f*

Mediterranean /medɪtə'reɪnɪən/ *a* mediterrâneo ▫ *n* **the ~** o Mediterrâneo

medium /'mi:dɪəm/ *n* (*pl* **media**) meio *m*; (*pl* **mediums**) (*person*) médium *mf* ▫ *a* médio. **~ wave** (*radio*) onda *f* média. **the happy ~** o meio-termo

medley /'medlɪ/ *n* (*pl* **-eys**) miscelânea *f*

meek /mi:k/ *a* (**-er, -est**) manso, submisso, sofrido

meet /mi:t/ *vt* (*pt* **met**) encontrar; (*intentionally*) encontrar-se com, ir ter com; (*at station etc*) ir esperar, ir buscar; (*make the acquaintance of*) conhecer; (*conform with*) ir ao encontro de, satisfazer; (*opponent, obligation etc*) fazer face a; (*bill, expenses*) pagar ▫ *vi* encontrar-se; (*get acquainted*) familiarizar-se; (*in session*) reunir-se. **~ with** encontrar; (*accident, misfortune*) sofrer, ter

meeting /'mi:tɪŋ/ *n* reunião *f*, encontro *m*; (*between two people*) encontro *m*. **~-place** *n* ponto *m* de encontro

megalomania /megələʊ'meɪnɪə/ *n* megalomania *f*, mania *f* de grandezas

megaphone /'megəfəʊn/ *n* megafone *m*, porta-voz *m*

melancholy /'melənkɒlɪ/ *n* melancolia *f* ▫ *a* melancólico

mellow /'meləʊ/ *a* (**-er, -est**) (*fruit, person*) amadurecido, maduro; (*sound, colour*) quente, suave ▫ *vt/i* amadurecer; (*soften*) suavizar

melodious /mɪ'ləʊdɪəs/ *a* melodioso

melodrama /'melədra:mə/ *n* melodrama *m*. **~tic** /-ə'mætɪk/ *a* melodramático

melod|y /'melədɪ/ *n* melodia *f*. **~ic** /mɪ'lɒdɪk/ *a* melódico

melon /'melən/ *n* melão *m*

melt /melt/ *vt/i* (*metals*) fundir (-se); (*butter, snow etc*) derreter (-se); (*fade away*) desvanecer (-se). **~ing-pot** *n* cadinho *m*

member /'membə(r)/ *n* membro *m*; (*of club etc*) sócio *m*. **M~ of Parliament** deputado *m*. **~ship** *n* qualidade *f* de sócio; (*members*) número *m* de sócios; (*fee*) cota *f*. **~ship card** carteira *f*, (*P*) cartão *m* de sócio

membrane /'membreɪn/ *n* membrana *f*

memento /mɪ'mentəʊ/ *n* (*pl* **-oes**) lembrança *f*, recordação *f*

memo /'meməʊ/ *n* (*pl* **-os**) (*colloq*) nota *f*, apontamento *m*, lembrete *m*

memoir /'memwa:(r)/ *n* (*record, essay*) memória *f*, memorial *m*; **~s** *npl* memórias *fpl*

memorable /'memərəbl/ *a* memorável

memorandum /memə'rændəm/ *n* (*pl* **-da** *or* **-dums**) nota *f*, lembrete *m*; (*diplomatic*) memorando *m*

memorial /mɪ'mɔ:rɪəl/ *n* monumento *m* comemorativo ▫ *a* comemorativo

memorize /'meməraɪz/ *vt* decorar, memorizar, aprender de cor

memory /'memərɪ/ *n* memória *f*. **from ~** de memória, de cor. **in ~ of** em memória de **~ stick** pente *m*. de memória

men /men/ *see* **man**

menac|e /'menəs/ *n* ameaça *f*, (*nuisance*) praga *f*, chaga *f* ▫ *vt* ameaçar. **~ingly** *adv* ameaçadoramente, de modo ameaçador

menagerie /mɪ'nædʒərɪ/ *n* coleção *f*, (*P*) colecção *f* de animais ferozes em jaulas

mend /mend/ *vt* consertar, reparar; (*darn*) remendar ▫ *n* conserto *m*; (*darn*) remendo *m*. **~ one's ways** corrigir-se, emendar-se. **on the ~** melhorando

menial /'mi:nɪəl/ *a* humilde

meningitis /menɪn'dʒaɪtɪs/ *n* meningite *f*

menopause /'menəpɔ:z/ *n* menopausa *f*

menstruation /menstrʊ'eɪʃn/ *n* menstruação *f*

mental /'mentl/ *a* mental; (*hospital*) de doentes mentais, psiquiátrico

mentality /men'tælətɪ/ *n* mentalidade *f*

mention /'menʃn/ *vt* mencionar ▫ *n* menção *f*. **don't ~ it!** não tem de quê, de nada

menu /'menju:/ *n* (*pl* **-us**) menu *m*, (*P*) ementa *f*

mercenary /'mɜ:snərɪ/ *a* & *n* mercenário (*m*)

merchandise /'mɜ:tʃəndaɪz/ *n* mercadorias *fpl* ▫ *vt/i* negociar

merchant /'mɜ:tʃənt/ *n* mercador *m* ▫ *a* (*ship, navy*) mercante. **~ bank** banco *m* comercial

merciful /'mɜ:sɪfl/ *a* misericordioso

merciless /'mɜ:sɪlɪs/ *a* impiedoso, sem dó

mercury /'mɜ:kjʊrɪ/ *n* mercúrio *m*

mercy /'mɜ:sɪ/ *n* piedade *f*, misericórdia *f*. **at the ~ of** à mercê de
mere /mɪə(r)/ *a* mero, simples. **~ly** *adv* meramente, simplesmente, apenas
merge /mɜ:dʒ/ *vt/i* fundir(-se), amalgamar(-se); (*comm: companies*) fundir(-se). **~r** /-ə(r)/ *n* fusão *f*
meringue /mə'ræŋ/ *n* merengue *m*, suspiro *m*
merit /'merɪt/ *n* mérito *m* ▫ *vt* (*pt* **merited**) merecer
mermaid /'mɜ:meɪd/ *n* sereia *f*
merriment /'merɪmənt/ *n* divertimento *m*, alegria *f*, folguedo *m*
merry /'merɪ/ *a* (**-ier, -iest**) alegre, divertido. **~ Christmas** Feliz Natal. **~-go-round** *n* carrossel *m*. **~-making** *n* festa *f*, divertimento *m*. **merrily** *adv* alegremente
mesh /meʃ/ *n* malha *f*. **~es** *npl* (*network; fig*) malhas *fpl*.
mesmerize /'mezməraɪz/ *vt* hipnotizar
mess /mes/ *n* (*disorder*) desordem *f*, trapalhada *f*; (*trouble*) embrulhada *f*, trapalhada *f*; (*dirt*) porcaria *f*; (*mil: place*) cantina *f*; (*mil: food*) rancho *m* ▫ *vt* **~ up** (*make untidy*) desarrumar; (*make dirty*) sujar; (*confuse*) atrapalhar, estragar ▫ *vi* **~ about** perder tempo; (*behave foolishly*) fazer asneiras. **~ about with** (*tinker with*) entreter-se com, andar às voltas com. **make a ~ of** estragar
message /'mesɪdʒ/ *n* mensagem *f*; (*informal*) recado *m*
messenger /'mesɪndʒə(r)/ *n* mensageiro *m*
Messiah /mɪ'saɪə/ *n* Messias *m*
messy /'mesɪ/ *a* (**-ier, -iest**) desarrumado, bagunçado; (*dirty*) sujo, porco
met /met/ *see* **meet**
metabolism /mɪ'tæbəlɪzm/ *n* metabolismo *m*
metal /'metl/ *n* metal *m* ▫ *a* de metal. **~lic** /mɪ'tælɪk/ *a* metálico; (*paint, colour*) metalizado
metamorphosis /metə'mɔ:fəsɪs/ *n* (*pl* **-phoses** /-si:z/) metamorfose *f*
metaphor /'metəfə(r)/ *n* metáfora *f*. **~ical** /-'fɒrɪkl/ *a* metafórico
meteor /'mi:tɪə(r)/ *n* meteoro *m*
meteorolog|y /mi:tɪə'rɒlədʒɪ/ *n* meteorologia *f*. **~ical** /-ə'lɒdʒɪkl/ *a* meteorológico
meter[1] /'mi:tə(r)/ *n* contador *m*
meter[2] /'mi:tə(r)/ *n* (*Amer*) = **metre**
method /'meθəd/ *n* método *m*
methodical /mɪ'θɒdɪkl/ *a* metódico
Methodist /'meθədɪst/ *n* metodista *mf*
methylated /'meθɪleɪtɪd/ *a* **~ spirit** álcool *m* metílico
meticulous /mɪ'tɪkjʊləs/ *a* meticuloso
metre /'mi:tə(r)/ *n* metro *m*
metric /'metrɪk/ *a* métrico. **~ation** /-'keɪʃn/ *n* conversão *f* para o sistema métrico
metropol|is /mə'trɒpəlɪs/ *n* metrópole *f*. **~itan** /metrə'pɒlɪtən/ *a* metropolitano
mettle /'metl/ *n* têmpera *f*, caráter *m*, (*P*) carácter *m*; (*spirit*) brio *m*
mew /mju:/ *n* miado *m* ▫ *vi* miar
Mexic|o /'meksɪkəʊ/ *n* México *m*. **~an** *a & n* mexicano (*m*)
miaow /mi:'aʊ/ *n & vi* = **mew**
mice /maɪs/ *see* **mouse**
mickey /'mɪkɪ/ *n* **take the ~ out of** (*sl*) fazer troça de, gozar (*colloq*)
micro- /'maɪkrəʊ/ *pref* micro-
microbe /'maɪkrəʊb/ *n* micróbio *m*
microchip /'maɪkrəʊtʃɪp/ *n* microchip *m*
microcomputer /'maɪkrəʊkəmpju:tə(r)/ *n* microcomputador *m*
microfilm /'maɪkrəʊfɪlm/ *n* microfilme *m*
microlight /'maɪkrəʊlaɪt/ *n* (*aviat*) ultraleve *m*
microphone /'maɪkrəfəʊn/ *n* microfone *m*
microprocessor /maɪkrəʊ'prəʊsesə(r)/ *n* microprocessador *m*
microscop|e /'maɪkrəskəʊp/ *n* microscópio *m*. **~ic** /-'skɒpɪk/ *a* microscópico
microwave /'maɪkrəʊweɪv/ *n* microonda *f*. **~ oven** forno *m* de microondas
mid /mɪd/ *a* meio. **in ~-air** no ar, em pleno vôo. **in ~-March** em meados de março
midday /mɪd'deɪ/ *n* meio-dia *m*
middle /'mɪdl/ *a* médio, meio; (*quality*) médio, mediano ▫ *n* meio *m*. **in the ~ of** no meio de. **~-aged** *a* de meia idade. **M~ Ages** Idade *f* Média. **~ class** classe *f* média. **~-class** *a* burguês. **M~ East** Médio Oriente *m*. **~ name** segundo nome *m*
middleman /'mɪdlmæn/ *n* (*pl* **-men**) intermediário *m*
midge /mɪdʒ/ *n* mosquito *m*
midget /'mɪdʒɪt/ *n* anão *m* ▫ *a* minúsculo
Midlands /'mɪdləndz/ *npl* região *f* do centro da Inglaterra
midnight /'mɪdnaɪt/ *n* meia-noite *f*
midriff /'mɪdrɪf/ *n* diafragma *m*; (*abdomen*) ventre *m*
midst /mɪdst/ *n* **in the ~ of** no meio de
midsummer /mɪd'sʌmə(r)/ *n* pleno verão *m*; (*solstice*) solstício *m* do verão

midway /mɪd'weɪ/ *adv* a meio caminho
midwife /'mɪdwaɪf/ *n* (*pl* **-wives**) parteira *f*
might[1] /maɪt/ *n* potência *f*; (*strength*) força *f*. **~y** *a* poderoso; (*fig: great*) imenso □ *adv* (*colloq*) muito
might[2] /maɪt/ *see* **may**
migraine /'mi:greɪn/ *n* enxaqueca *f*
migrant /'maɪgrənt/ *a* migratório □ *n* (*person*) migrante *mf*, emigrante *mf*
migrat|e /maɪ'greɪt/ *vi* migrar. **~ion** /-ʃn/ *n* migração *f*
mike /maɪk/ *n* (*colloq*) microfone *m*
mild /maɪld/ *a* (**-er, -est**) brando, manso; (*illness, taste*) leve; (*climate*) temperado; (*weather*) ameno. **~ly** *adv* brandamente, mansamente. **to put it ~ly** para não dizer coisa pior. **~ness** *n* brandura *f*
mildew /'mɪldju:/ *n* bolor *m*, mofo *m*; (*in plants*) míldio *m*
mile /maɪl/ *n* milha *f* (= *1.6 km*). **~s too big**/*etc* (*colloq*) grande demais. **~age** *n* (*loosely*) quilometragem *f*
milestone /'maɪlstəʊn/ *n* marco *m* miliário; (*fig*) data *f* or acontecimento *m* importante
militant /'mɪlɪtənt/ *a* & *n* militante (*mf*)
military /'mɪlɪtrɪ/ *a* militar
militate /'mɪlɪteɪt/ *vi* militar. **~ against** militar contra
milk /mɪlk/ *n* leite *m* □ *a* (*product*) lácteo □ *vt* ordenhar; (*fig: exploit*) explorar. **~-shake** *n* milk-shake *m*, leite *m* batido. **~y** *a* (*like milk*) leitoso; (*tea etc*) com muito leite. **M~ Way** Via *f* Láctea
milkman /'mɪlkmən/ *n* (*pl* **-men**) leiteiro *m*
mill /mɪl/ *n* moinho *m*; (*factory*) fábrica *f* □ *vt* moer □ *vi* **~ around** aglomerar-se; (*crowd*) apinhar-se, (*P*) agitar-se. **~er** *n* moleiro *m*. **pepper-~** *n* moedor *m* de pimenta
millennium /mɪ'lenɪəm/ *n* (*pl* **-iums** *or* **-ia**) milênio *m*, (*P*) milénio *m*
millet /'mɪlɪt/ *n* painço *m*, milhete *m*
milli- /'mɪlɪ/ *pref* mili-
milligram /'mɪlɪgræm/ *n* miligrama *m*
millilitre /'mɪlɪli:tə(r)/ *n* mililitro *m*
millimetre /'mɪlɪmi:tə(r)/ *n* milímetro *m*
million /'mɪlɪən/ *n* milhão *m*. **a ~ pounds** um milhão de libras. **~aire** /-'neə(r)/ *n* milionário *m*
millstone /'mɪlstəʊn/ *n* mó *f*. **a ~ round one's neck** um peso nos ombros
mime /maɪm/ *n* mímica *f*; (*actor*) mímico *m* □ *vt*/*i* exprimir por mímica, mimar
mimic /'mɪmɪk/ *vt* (*pt* **mimicked**) imitar □ *n* imitador *m*, parodiante *mf*. **~ry** *n* imitação *f*.
mince /mɪns/ *vt* picar □ *n* carne *f* moída, (*P*) carne *f* picada. **~-pie** *n* pastel *m* recheado com massa de passas, amêndoas, especiarias etc. **~r** *n* máquina *f* de moer
mincemeat /'mɪnsmi:t/ *n* massa *f* de passas, amêndoas, especiarias etc usada para recheio. **make ~ of** (*colloq*) arrasar, aniquilar
mind *n* espírito *m*, mente *f*; (*intellect*) intelecto *m*; (*sanity*) razão *f* □ *vt* (*look after*) tomar conta de, tratar de; (*heed*) prestar atenção a; (*object to*) importar-se com, incomodar-se com. **do you ~ if I smoke?** você se incomoda que eu fume? **do you ~ helping me?** quer fazer o favor de me ajudar? **never ~** não se importe, não tem importância. **to be out of one's ~** estar fora de si. **have a good ~ to** estar disposto a. **make up one's ~** decidir-se. **presence of ~** presença *f* de espírito. **to my ~** a meu ver. **~ful of** atento a, consciente de. **~less** *a* insensato
minder /'maɪndə(r)/ *n* pessoa *f* que toma conta *mf*; (*bodyguard*) guarda-costa *mf*, (*P*) guarda-costas *mf*
mine[1] /maɪn/ *poss pron* o(s) meu(s), a(s) minha(s). **it is ~** é (o) meu *or* (a) minha
min|e[2] /maɪn/ *n* mina *f* □ *vt* escavar, explorar; (*extract*) extrair; (*mil*) minar. **~er** *n* mineiro *m*. **~ing** *n* exploração *f* mineira □ *a* mineiro
minefield /'maɪnfi:ld/ *n* campo *m* minado
mineral /'mɪnərəl/ *n* mineral *m*; (*soft drink*) bebida *f* gasosa. **~ water** água *f* mineral
minesweeper /'maɪnswi:pə(r)/ *n* caça-minas *m*
mingle /'mɪŋgl/ *vt*/*i* misturar(-se) (**with** com)
mingy /'mɪndʒɪ/ *a* (**-ier, -iest**) (*colloq*) sovina, unha(s)-de-fome (*colloq*)
mini- /'mɪnɪ/ *pref* mini-
miniature /'mɪnɪtʃə(r)/ *n* miniatura *f* □ *a* miniatural
minibus /'mɪnɪbʌs/ *n* (*public*) microônibus *m*, (*P*) autocarro *m* pequeno
minim /'mɪnɪm/ *n* (*mus*) mínima *f*
minim|um /'mɪnɪməm/ *a* & *n* (*pl* **-ma**) mínimo (*m*). **~al** *a* mínimo. **~ize** *vt* minimizar, dar pouca importância a
miniskirt /'mɪnɪskɜ:t/ *n* minissaia *f*
minist|er /'mɪnɪstə(r)/ *n* ministro *m*; (*relig*) pastor *m*. **~erial** /-'stɪərɪəl/ *a* ministerial. **~ry** *n* ministério *m*
mink /mɪŋk/ *n* (*fur*) marta *f*, visão *m*
minor /'maɪnə(r)/ *a* & *n* menor (*mf*)
minority /maɪ'nɒrətɪ/ *n* minoria *f* □ *a* minoritário

mint[1] /mɪnt/ *n* **the M~** a Casa da Moeda. **a ~** uma fortuna □ *vt* cunhar. **in ~ condition** em perfeito estado, como novo, impecável

mint[2] /mɪnt/ *n* (*plant*) hortelã *f*; (*sweet*) pastilha *f* de hortelã

minus /'maɪnəs/ *prep* menos; (*colloq: without*) sem □ *n* menos *m*

minute[1] /'mɪnɪt/ *n* minuto *m*. **~s** (*of meeting*) ata *f*, (*P*) acta *f*

minute[2] /maɪ'nju:t/ *a* diminuto, minúsculo; (*detailed*) minucioso

mirac|le /'mɪrəkl/ *n* milagre *m*. **~ulous** /mɪ'rækjʊləs/ *a* milagroso, miraculoso

mirage /'mɪra:ʒ/ *n* miragem *f*

mire /maɪə(r)/ *n* lodo *m*, lama *f*

mirror /'mɪrə(r)/ *n* espelho *m*; (*in car*) retrovisor *m* □ *vt* refletir, (*P*) reflectir, espelhar

mirth /mɜ:θ/ *n* alegria *f*, hilaridade *f*

misadventure /mɪsəd'ventʃə(r)/ *n* desgraça *f*. **death by ~** morte *f* acidental

misanthropist /mɪs'ænθrəpɪst/ *n* misantropo *m*

misapprehension /mɪsæprɪ'henʃn/ *n* mal-entendido *m*

misbehav|e /mɪsbɪ'heɪv/ *vi* portar-se mal, proceder mal. **~iour** /-'heɪvɪə(r)/ *n* mau comportamento *m*, má conduta *f*

miscalculat|e /mɪs'kælkjʊleɪt/ *vi* calcular mal, enganar-se. **~ion** /-'leɪʃn/ *n* erro *m* de cálculo

miscarr|y /mɪs'kærɪ/ *vi* abortar, ter um aborto; (*fail*) falhar, malograr-se. **~iage** /-ɪdʒ/ *n* aborto *m*. **~iage of justice** erro *m* judiciário

miscellaneous /mɪsə'leɪnɪəs/ *a* variado, diverso

mischief /'mɪstʃɪf/ *n* (*of children*) diabrura *f*, travessura *f*; (*harm*) mal *m*, dano *m*. **get into ~** fazer disparates. **make ~** criar *or* semear discórdias

mischievous /'mɪstʃɪvəs/ *a* endiabrado, travesso

misconception /mɪskən'sepʃn/ *n* idéia *f* errada, falso conceito *m*

misconduct /mɪs'kɒndʌkt/ *n* conduta *f* imprópria

misconstrue /mɪskən'stru:/ *vt* interpretar mal

misdeed /mɪs'di:d/ *n* má ação *f*, (*P*) acção *f*; (*crime*) crime *m*

misdemeanour /mɪsdɪ'mi:nə(r)/ *n* delito *m*

miser /'maɪzə(r)/ *n* avarento *m*, sovina *mf*. **~ly** *a* avarento, sovina

miserable /'mɪzrəbl/ *a* infeliz; (*wretched, mean*) desgraçado, miserável

misery /'mɪzərɪ/ *n* infelicidade *f*

misfire /mɪs'faɪə(r)/ *vi* (*plan, gun, engine*) falhar

misfit /'mɪsfɪt/ *n* inadaptado *m*

misfortune /mɪs'fɔ:tʃən/ *n* desgraça *f*, infelicidade *f*, pouca sorte *f*

misgiving(s) /mɪs'gɪvɪŋ(z)/ *n*(*pl*) dúvida(s) *f*(*pl*), receio(s) *m*(*pl*)

misguided /mɪs'gaɪdɪd/ *a* (*mistaken*) desencaminhado; (*misled*) mal aconselhado, enganado

mishap /'mɪshæp/ *n* contratempo *m*, desastre *m*

misinform /mɪsɪn'fɔ:m/ *vt* informar mal

misinterpret /mɪsɪn'tɜ:prɪt/ *vt* interpretar mal

misjudge /mɪs'dʒʌdʒ/ *vt* julgar mal

mislay /mɪs'leɪ/ *vt* (*pt* **mislaid**) perder, extraviar

mislead /mɪs'li:d/ *vt* (*pt* **misled**) induzir em erro, enganar. **~ing** *a* enganador

mismanage /mɪs'mænɪdʒ/ *vt* dirigir mal. **~ment** *n* má gestão *f*, desgoverno *m*

misnomer /mɪs'nəʊmə(r)/ *n* termo *m* impróprio

misogynist /mɪ'sɒdʒmɪst/ *n* misógino *m*

misprint /'mɪsprɪnt/ *n* erro *m* tipográfico

mispronounce /mɪsprə'naʊns/ *vt* pronunciar mal

misquote /mɪs'kwəʊt/ *vt* citar incorretamente

misread /mɪs'ri:d/ *vt* (*pt* **misread** /-'red/) ler *or* interpretar mal

misrepresent /mɪsreprɪ'zent/ *vt* deturpar, desvirtuar

miss /mɪs/ *vt*/*i* (*chance, bus etc*) perder; (*target*) errar, falhar; (*notice the loss of*) dar pela falta de; (*regret the absence of*) sentir a falta de, ter saudades de. **he ~es her/Portugal**/*etc* ele sente a falta *or* tem saudades dela/de Portugal/*etc* □ *n* falha *f*. **it was a near ~** foi *or* escapou por um triz. **~ out** omitir. **~ the point** não compreender

Miss /mɪs/ *n* (*pl* **Misses**) Senhorita *f*, (*P*) Senhora *f*

misshapen /mɪs'ʃeɪpn/ *a* disforme

missile /'mɪsaɪl/ *n* míssil *m*; (*object thrown*) projétil *m*, (*P*) projéctil *m*

missing /'mɪsɪŋ/ *a* que falta; (*lost*) perdido; (*person*) desaparecido. **a book with a page ~** um livro com uma página a menos

mission /'mɪʃn/ *n* missão *f*

missionary /'mɪʃənrɪ/ *n* missionário *m*

misspell /mɪs'spel/ *vt* (*pt* **misspelt** *or* **misspelled**) escrever mal

mist /mɪst/ *n* neblina *f*, névoa *f*, bruma *f*; (*fig*) névoa *f* □ *vt*/*i* enevoar(-se); (*window*) embaçar(-se)

mistake /mɪ'steɪk/ *n* engano *m*, erro *m* □ *vt* (*pt* **mistook**, *pp* **mistaken**) compreender mal; (*choose wrongly*) enganar-se em. **~ for** confundir com, tomar por. **~n** /-ən/ *a* errado. **be ~n** enganar-se. **~nly** /-ənlɪ/ *adv* por engano

mistletoe /'mɪsltəʊ/ *n* visco *m*

mistreat /mɪs'tri:t/ *vt* maltratar. **~ment** *n* mau trato *m*

mistress /'mɪstrɪs/ *n* senhora *f*, dona *f*; (*teacher*) professora *f*; (*lover*) amante *f*

mistrust /mɪs'trʌst/ *vt* desconfiar de, duvidar de □ *n* desconfiança *f*

misty /'mɪstɪ/ *a* (**-ier, -iest**) enevoado, brumoso; (*window*) embaçado; (*indistinct*) indistinto

misunderstand /mɪsʌndə'stænd/ *vt* (*pt* **-stood**) compreender mal. **~ing** *n* mal-entendido *m*

misuse[1] /mɪs'ju:z/ *vt* empregar mal; (*power etc*) abusar de

misuse[2] /mɪs'ju:s/ *n* mau uso *m*; (*abuse*) abuso *m*; (*of funds*) desvio *m*

mitigat|e /'mɪtɪgeɪt/ *vt* atenuar, mitigar. **~ing circumstances** circunstâncias *fpl* atenuantes

mitten /'mɪtn/ *n* luva *f* com uma única divisão entre o polegar e os dedos

mix /mɪks/ *vt/i* misturar(-se) □ *n* mistura *f*. **~ up** misturar bem; (*fig: confuse*) confundir. **~-up** *n* trapalhada *f*, confusão *f*. **~ with** associar-se com. **~er** *n* (*culin*) batedeira *f*

mixed /mɪkst/ *a* (*school etc*) misto; (*assorted*) sortido. **be ~ up** (*colloq*) estar confuso

mixture /'mɪkstʃə(r)/ *n* mistura *f*. **cough ~** xarope *m* para a tosse

moan /məʊn/ *n* gemido *m* □ *vi* gemer; (*complain*) queixar-se, lastimar-se (**about** de). **~er** *n* pessoa *f* lamurienta

moat /məʊt/ *n* fosso *m*

mob /mɒb/ *n* multidão *f*; (*tumultuous*) turba *f*; (*sl: gang*) bando *m* □ *vt* (*pt* **mobbed**) cercar, assediar

mobil|e /'məʊbaɪl/ *a* móvel. **~e home** caravana *f*, trailer *m*. **~e phone** telemóvel *m*. **~ity** /-'bɪlətɪ/ *n* mobilidade *f*

mobiliz|e /'məʊbɪlaɪz/ *vt/i* mobilizar. **~ation** /-'zeɪʃn/ *n* mobilização *f*

moccasin /'mɒkəsɪn/ *n* mocassim *m*

mock /mɒk/ *vt/i* zombar de, gozar □ *a* falso. **~-up** *n* maqueta *f*

mockery /'mɒkərɪ/ *n* troça *f*, gozação *f*. **a ~ of** uma gozação de

mode /məʊd/ *n* modo *m*; (*fashion*) moda *f*

model /'mɒdl/ *n* modelo *m* □ *a* modelo; (*exemplary*) exemplar; (*toy*) em miniatura □ *vt* (*pt* **modelled**) modelar; (*clothes*) apresentar □ *vi* ser *or* trabalhar como modelo

modem /'məʊdem/ *n* modem *m*

moderate[1] /'mɒdərət/ *a* & *n* moderado (*m*). **~ly** *adv* moderadamente. **~ly good** sofrível

moderat|e[2] /'mɒdəreɪt/ *vt/i* moderar(-se). **~ion** /-'reɪʃn/ *n* moderação *f*. **in ~ion** com moderação

modern /'mɒdn/ *a* moderno. **~ languages** línguas *fpl* vivas. **~ize** *vt* modernizar

modest /'mɒdɪst/ *a* modesto. **~y** *n* modéstia *f*. **~ly** *adv* modestamente

modicum /'mɒdɪkəm/ *n* **a ~ of** um pouco de

modif|y /'mɒdɪfaɪ/ *vt* modificar. **~ication** /-ɪ'keɪʃn/ *n* modificação *f*

modulat|e /'mɒdjʊleɪt/ *vt/i* modular. **~ion** /-'leɪʃn/ *n* modulação *f*

module /'mɒdju:l/ *n* módulo *m*

mohair /'məʊheə(r)/ *n* mohair *m*

moist /mɔɪst/ *a* (**-er, -est**) úmido, (*P*) húmido. **~ure** /'mɔɪstʃə(r)/ *n* umidade *f*, (*P*) humidade *f*. **~urizer** /-tʃəraɪzə(r)/ *n* creme *m* hidratante

moisten /'mɔɪsn/ *vt/i* umedecer, (*P*) humedecer

molasses /mə'læsɪz/ *n* melaço *m*

mole[1] /məʊl/ *n* (*on skin*) sinal na pele *m*

mole[2] /məʊl/ *n* (*animal*) toupeira *f*

molecule /'mɒlɪkju:l/ *n* molécula *f*

molest /mə'lest/ *vt* meter-se com, molestar

mollusc /'mɒləsk/ *n* molusco *m*

mollycoddle /'mɒlɪkɒdl/ *vt* mimar

molten /'məʊltən/ *a* fundido

moment /'məʊmənt/ *n* momento *m*

momentar|y /'məʊməntrɪ/ *a* momentâneo. **~ily** /'məʊməntrəlɪ/ *adv* momentâneamente

momentous /mə'mentəs/ *a* grave, importante

momentum /mə'mentəm/ *n* ímpeto *m*, velocidade *f* adquirida

Monaco /'mɒnəkəʊ/ *n* Mônaco *m*

monarch /'mɒnək/ *n* monarca *mf*. **~y** *n* monarquia *f*

monast|ery /'mɒnəstrɪ/ *n* mosteiro *m*, convento *m*. **~ic** /mə-'næstɪk/ *a* monástico

Monday /'mʌndɪ/ *n* segunda-feira *f*

monetary /'mʌnɪtrɪ/ *a* monetário

money /'mʌnɪ/ *n* dinheiro *m*. **~-box** *n* cofre *m*. **~-lender** *n* agiota *mf*. **~ order** vale *m* postal

mongrel /'mʌŋgrəl/ *n* (cão) vira-lata *m*, (*P*) rafeiro *m*

monitor /'mɒnɪtə(r)/ *n* chefe *m* de turma; (*techn*) monitor *m* □ *vt* controlar; (*a broadcast*) monitorar (a transmissão)

monk /mʌŋk/ *n* monge *m*, frade *m*

monkey /'mʌŋkɪ/ *n* (*pl* **-eys**) macaco *m*. **~-nut** *n* amendoim *m*. **~-wrench** *n* chave *f* inglesa

mono /'mɒnəʊ/ *n* (*pl* **-os**) gravação *f* mono □ *a* mono *invar*

monocle /'mɒnəkl/ *n* monóculo *m*

monogram /'mɒnəgræm/ *n* monograma *m*

monologue /'mɒnəlɒg/ *n* monólogo *m*

monopol|y /mə'nɒpəlɪ/ *n* monopólio *m*. **~ize** *vt* monopolizar

monosyllab|le /'mɒnəsɪləbl/ *n* monossílabo *m*. **~ic** /-'læbɪk/ *a* monossilábico

monotone /'mɒnətəʊn/ *n* tom *m* uniforme

monoton|ous /mə'nɒtənəs/ *a* monótono. **~y** *n* monotonia *f*

monsoon /mɒn'su:n/ *n* monção *f*

monst|er /'mɒnstə(r)/ *n* monstro *m*. **~rous** *a* monstruoso

monstrosity /mɒn'strɒsətɪ/ *n* monstruosidade *f*

month /mʌnθ/ *n* mês *m*

monthly /'mʌnθlɪ/ *a* mensal □ *adv* mensalmente □ *n* (*periodical*) revista *f* mensal

monument /'mɒnjʊmənt/ *n* monumento *m*. **~al** /-'mentl/ *a* monumental

moo /mu:/ *n* mugido *m* □ *vi* mugir

mood /mu:d/ *n* humor *m*, disposição *f*. **in a good/bad ~** de bom/mau humor. **~y** *a* de humor instável; (*sullen*) carrancudo

moon /mu:n/ *n* lua *f*

moon|light /'mu:nlaɪt/ *n* luar *m*. **~lit** *a* iluminado pela lua, enluarado

moonlighting /'mu:nlaɪtɪŋ/ *n* (*colloq*) segundo emprego *m*, esp à noite

moor[1] /mʊə(r)/ *n* charneca *f*

moor[2] /mʊə(r)/ *vt* amarrar, atracar. **~ings** *npl* amarras *fpl*; (*place*) amarradouro *m*, fundeadouro *m*

moose /mu:s/ *n* (*pl invar*) alce *m*

moot /mu:t/ *a* discutível □ *vt* levantar

mop /mɒp/ *n* esfregão *m* □ *vt* (*pt* **mopped**) **~ (up)** limpar. **~ of hair** trunfa *f*

mope /məʊp/ *vi* estar *or* andar abatido e triste

moped /'məʊped/ *n* (bicicleta) motorizada *f*

moral /'mɒrəl/ *a* moral □ *n* moral *f*. **~s** moral *f*, bons costumes *mpl*. **~ize** *vi* moralizar. **~ly** *adv* moralmente

morale /mə'ra:l/ *n* moral *m*

morality /mə'rælətɪ/ *n* moralidade *f*

morass /mə'ræs/ *n* pântano *m*

morbid /'mɔ:bɪd/ *a* mórbido

more /mɔ:(r)/ *a* & *adv* mais (**than** (do) que) □ *n* mais *m*. (**some**) **~ tea/pens/** *etc* mais chá/canetas/*etc*. **there is no ~ bread** não há mais pão. **or less** mais ou menos

moreover /mɔ:'rəʊvə(r)/ *adv* além disso, de mais a mais

morgue /mɔ:g/ *n* morgue *f*, necrotério *m*

moribund /'mɒrɪbʌnd/ *a* moribundo, agonizante

morning /'mɔ:nɪŋ/ *n* manhã *f*. **in the ~** de manhã

Morocc|o /mə'rɒkəʊ/ *n* Marrocos *m*. **~an** *a* & *n* marroquino (*m*)

moron /'mɔ:rɒn/ *n* idiota *mf*

morose /mə'rəʊs/ *a* taciturno e insociável, carrancudo

morphine /'mɔ:fi:n/ *n* morfina *f*

Morse /mɔ:s/ *n* **~ (code)** (alfabeto) Morse *m*

morsel /'mɔ:sl/ *n* bocado *m* (esp de comida)

mortal /'mɔ:tl/ *a* & *n* mortal (*mf*). **~ity** /mɔ:'tælətɪ/ *n* mortalidade *f*

mortar /'mɔ:tə(r)/ *n* argamassa *f*; (*bowl*) almofariz *m*; (*mil*) morteiro *m*

mortgage /'mɔ:gɪdʒ/ *n* hipoteca *f* □ *vt* hipotecar

mortify /'mɔ:tɪfaɪ/ *vt* mortificar

mortuary /'mɔ:tʃərɪ/ *n* casa *f* mortuária

mosaic /məʊ'zeɪɪk/ *n* mosaico *m*

Moscow /'mɔskəʊ/ *n* Moscou *m*, (*P*) Moscovo *m*

mosque /mɒsk/ *n* mesquita *f*

mosquito /mə'ski:təʊ/ *n* (*pl* **-oes**) mosquito *m*

moss /mɒs/ *n* musgo *m*. **~y** *a* musgoso

most /məʊst/ *a* o mais, o maior; (*majority*) a maioria de, a maior parte de □ *n* mais *m*; (*majority*) a maioria, a maior parte, o máximo □ *adv* o mais; (*very*) muito. **at ~** no máximo. **for the ~ part** na maior parte, na grande maioria. **make the ~ of** aproveitar ao máximo, tirar o melhor partido de. **~ly** *adv* sobretudo

motel /məʊ'tel/ *n* motel *m*

moth /mɒθ/ *n* mariposa *f*, (*P*) borboleta *f* nocturna. **(clothes-)~** *n* traça *f*. **~-ball** *n* bola *f* de naftalina. **~-eaten** *a* roído por traças

mother /'mʌðə(r)/ *n* mãe *f* □ *vt* tratar como a um filho. **~hood** *n* maternidade *f*. **~-in-law** *n* (*pl* **~s-in-law**) sogra *f*. **~-of-pearl** *n* madrepérola *f*. **M~'s Day** o Dia das Mães. **~-to-be** *n* futura mãe *f*. **~ly** *a* maternal

motif /məʊ'ti:f/ *n* tema *m*

motion /ˈməʊʃn/ *n* movimento *m*; (*proposal*) moção *f* □ *vt*/*i* ~ **(to) sb to** fazer sinal a alg para. ~**less** *a* imóvel

motivat|e /ˈməʊtɪveɪt / *vt* motivar. ~**ion** /-ˈveɪʃn/ *n* motivação *f*

motive /ˈməʊtɪv/ *n* motivo *m*

motor /ˈməʊtə(r)/ *n* motor *m*; (*car*) automóvel *m* □ *a* (*anat*) motor; (*boat*) a motor □ *vi* ir de automóvel. ~ **bike** (*colloq*) moto *f* (*colloq*). ~ **car** carro *m*. ~ **cycle** motocicleta *f*. ~ **cyclist** motociclista *mf*. ~ **vehicle** veículo *m* automóvel. ~**ing** *n* automobilismo *m*. ~**ized** *a* motorizado

motorist /ˈməʊtərɪst/ *n* motorista *mf*, automobilista *mf*

motorway /ˈməʊtəweɪ/ *n* auto-estrada *f*

mottled /ˈmɒtld/ *a* sarapintado, pintalgado

motto /ˈmɒtəʊ/ *n* (*pl* **-oes**) divisa *f*, lema *m*

mould[1] /məʊld/ *n* (*container*) forma *f*, molde *m*; (*culin*) forma *f* □ *vt* moldar. ~**ing** *n* (*archit*) moldura *f*

mould[2] /məʊld/ *n* (*fungi*) bolor *m*, mofo *m*. ~**y** *a* bolorento

moult /məʊlt/ *vi* estar na muda

mound /maʊnd/ *n* monte *m* de terra *or* de pedras; (*small hill*) montículo *m*

mount /maʊnt/ *vt*/*i* montar □ *n* (*support*) suporte *m*; (*for gem etc*) engaste *m*. ~ **up** aumentar, subir

mountain /ˈmaʊntɪn/ *n* montanha *f*. ~ **bike** mountain bike *f*. ~**-ous** *a* montanhoso

mountaineer /maʊntɪˈnɪə(r)/ *n* alpinista *mf*. ~**ing** *n* alpinismo *m*

mourn /mɔ:n/ *vt*/*i* ~ **(for)** chorar (a morte de). ~ **(over)** sofrer (por). ~**er** *n* pessoa *f* que acompanha o enterro. ~**ing** *n* luto *m*. **in** ~**ing** de luto

mournful /ˈmɔ:nfl/ *a* triste; (*sorrowful*) pesaroso

mouse /maʊs/ *n* (*pl* **mice**) camundongo *m*

mousetrap /ˈmaʊstræp/ *n* ratoeira *f*

mousse /mu:s/ *n* mousse *f*

moustache /məˈsta:ʃ/ *n* bigode *m*

mouth[1] /maʊθ/ *n* boca *f*. ~**-organ** *n* gaita *f* de boca, (*P*) beiços

mouth[2] /maʊð/ *vt*/*i* declamar; (*silently*) articular sem som

mouthful /ˈmaʊθfʊl/ *n* bocado *m*

mouthpiece /ˈmaʊθpi:s/ *n* (*mus*) bocal *m*, boquilha *f*; (*fig: person*) porta-voz *mf*

mouthwash /ˈmaʊθwɒʃ/ *n* líquido *m* para bochecho

movable /ˈmu:vəbl/ *a* móvel

move /mu:v/ *vt*/*i* mover(-se), mexer(-se), deslocar(-se); (*emotionally*) comover; (*incite*) convencer, levar a; (*act*) agir; (*propose*) propor; (*depart*) ir, partir; (*go forward*) avançar. ~ **(out)** mudar-se, sair □ *n* movimento *m*; (*in game*) jogada *f*; (*player's turn*) vez *f*; (*house change*) mudança *f*. ~ **back** recuar. ~ **forward** avançar. ~ **in** mudar-se para. ~ **on!** circulem! ~ **over, please** chegue-se para lá, por favor. **on the** ~ em marcha

movement /ˈmu:vmənt/ *n* movimento *m*

movie /ˈmu:vɪ/ *n* (*Amer*) filme *m*. **the** ~**s** o cinema

moving /ˈmu:vɪŋ/ *a* (*touching*) comovente; (*movable*) móvil; (*in motion*) em movimento

mow /məʊ/ *vt* (*pp* **mowed** *or* **mown**) ceifar; (*lawn*) cortar a grama, (*P*) relva. ~ **down** ceifar. ~**er** *n* (*for lawn*) máquina *f* de cortar a grama, (*P*) relva

MP *abbr see* **Member of Parliament**

Mr /ˈmɪstə(r)/ *n* (*pl* **Messrs**) Senhor *m*. ~ **Smith** o Sr Smith

Mrs /ˈmɪsɪz/ *n* Senhora *f*. ~ **Smith** a Sra Smith. **Mr and** ~ **Smith** o Sr Smith e a mulher

Ms /mɪz/ *n* Senhora D *f*

much /mʌtʃ/ (**more, most**) *a, adv & n* muito (*m*). **very** ~ muito, muitíssimo. **you may have as** ~ **as you need** você pode levar o que precisar. ~ **of it** muito *or* grande parte dele. **so** ~ **the better/worse** tanto melhor/pior. **how** ~? quanto? **not** ~ não muito. **too** ~ demasiado, demais. **he's not** ~ **of a gardener** não é lá grande jardineiro

muck /mʌk/ *n* estrume *m*; (*colloq: dirt*) porcaria *f* □ *vi* ~ **about** (*sl*) entreter-se, perder tempo. ~ **in** (*sl*) ajudar, dar uma mão □ *vt* ~ **up** (*sl*) estragar. ~**y** *a* sujo

mucus /ˈmju:kəs/ *n* muco *m*

mud /mʌd/ *n* lama *f*. ~**dy** *a* lamacento, enlameado

muddle /ˈmʌdl/ *vt* baralhar, atrapalhar, confundir □ *vi* ~ **through** sair-se bem, desenrascar-se (*sl*) □ *n* desordem *f*; (*mix-up*) confusão *f*, trapalhada *f*

mudguard /ˈmʌdga:d/ *n* para-lama *m*

muff /mʌf/ *n* (*for hands*) regalo *m*

muffle /ˈmʌfl/ *vt* abafar. ~ **(up)** agasalhar(-se). ~**d sounds** sons *mpl* abafados. ~**r** /-ə(r)/ *n* cachecol *m*

mug /mʌg/ *n* caneca *f*; (*sl: face*) cara *f*; (*sl: fool*) trouxa *mf* (*colloq*) □ *vt* (*pt* **mugged**) assaltar, agredir. ~**ger** *n* assaltante *mf*. ~**ging** *n* assalto *m*

muggy /ˈmʌgɪ/ *a* abafado

mule /mju:l/ *n* mulo *m*; (*female*) mula *f*

mull /mʌl/ *vt* ~ **over** ruminar; (*fig*) matutar em

multi- /ˈmʌltɪ/ *pref* mult(i)-

multicoloured /ˈmʌltɪkʌləd/ *a* multicolor

multinational /mʌltɪ'næʃnəl/ *a & n* multinacional (*f*)
multiple /'mʌltɪpl/ *a & n* múltiplo (*m*)
multipl|y /'mʌltɪplaɪ/ *vt/i* multiplicar (-se). **~ication** /-ɪ'keɪʃn/ *n* multiplicação *f*
multi-storey /mʌltɪ'stɔ:rɪ/ *a* (*car park*) em vários níveis
multitude /'mʌltɪtju:d/ *n* multidão *f*
mum[1] /mʌm/ *a* **keep ~** (*colloq*) ficar calado
mum[2] /mʌm/ (*B*) mamãe *f* (*colloq*) *n* (*colloq*) (*P*) mamã
mumble /'mʌmbl/ *vt/i* resmungar, resmonear
mummy[1] /'mʌmɪ/ *n* (*body*) múmia *f*
mummy[2] /'mʌmɪ/ *n* (*esp child's lang*) mamã (*B*) mamãe *f* (*colloq*) (*P*) mãezinha *f* (*colloq*), (*P*)
mumps /mʌmps/ *n* parotidite *f*, papeira *f*
munch /mʌntʃ/ *vt* mastigar
mundane /mʌn'deɪn/ *a* banal; (*worldly*) mundano
municipal /mju:'nɪsɪpl/ *a* municipal. **~ity** /-'pælətɪ/ *n* municipalidade *f*
munitions /mju:'nɪʃnz/ *npl* munições *fpl*
mural /'mjʊərəl/ *a & n* mural (*m*)
murder /'mɜ:də(r)/ *n* assassínio *m*, assassinato *m* □ *vt* assassinar. **~er** *n* assassino *m*, assassina *f*. **~ous** *a* assassino, sanguinário; (*of weapon*) mortífero
murky /'mɜ:kɪ/ *a* (**-ier, -iest**) escuro, sombrio
murmur /'mɜ:mə(r)/ *n* murmúrio *m* □ *vt/i* murmurar
muscle /'mʌsl/ *n* músculo *m* □ *vi* **~ in** (*colloq*) impor-se, intrometer-se
muscular /'mʌskjʊlə(r)/ *a* muscular; (*brawny*) musculoso
muse /mju:z/ *vi* meditar, cismar
museum /mju:'zɪəm/ *n* museu *m*
mush /mʌʃ/ *n* papa *f* de farinha de milho. **~y** *a* mole; (*sentimental*) piegas *inv*
mushroom /'mʌʃrʊm/ *n* cogumelo *m* □ *vi* pulular, multiplicar-se com rapidez
music /'mju:zɪk/ *n* música *f*. **~al** *a* musical □ *n* (*show*) comédia *f* musical, musical *m*. **~al box** *n* caixa *f* de música. **~-stand** *n* estante *f* de música
musician /mju:'zɪʃn/ *n* músico *m*
musk /mʌsk/ *n* almíscar *m*
Muslim /'mʊzlɪm/ *a & n* muçulmano (*m*)
muslin /'mʌzlɪn/ *n* musselina *f*
mussel /'mʌsl/ *n* mexilhão *m*
must /mʌst/ *v aux* dever. **you ~ go** é necessário que você parta. **he ~ be old** ele deve ser velho. **I ~ have done it** eu devo tê-lo feito □ *n* **be a ~** (*colloq*) ser imprescindível
mustard /'mʌstəd/ *n* mostarda *f*
muster /'mʌstə(r)/ *vt/i* juntar(-se), reunir(-se). **pass ~** ser aceitável
musty /'mʌstɪ/ *a* (**-ier, -iest**) mofado, bolorento
mutation /mju:'teɪʃn/ *n* mutação *f*
mute /mju:t/ *a & n* mudo (*m*)
muted /'mju:tɪd/ *a* (*sound*) em surdina; (*colour*) suave
mutilat|e /'mju:tɪleɪt/ *vt* mutilar. **~ion** /-'leɪʃn/ *n* mutilação *f*
mutin|y /'mju:tɪnɪ/ *n* motim *f* □ *vi* amotinar-se. **~ous** *a* amotinado
mutter /'mʌtə(r)/ *vt/i* resmungar
mutton /'mʌtn/ *n* (carne de) carneiro *m*
mutual /'mju:tʃʊəl/ *a* mútuo; (*colloq: common*) comum. **~ly** *adv* mutuamente
muzzle /'mʌzl/ *n* focinho *m*; (*device*) focinheira *f*; (*of gun*) boca *f* □ *vt* amordaçar; (*dog*) pôr focinheira em
my /maɪ/ *a* meu(s), minha(s)
myself /maɪ'self/ *pron* eu mesmo, eu próprio; (*reflexive*) me; (*after prep*) mim (próprio, mesmo). **by ~** sozinho
mysterious /mɪ'stɪərɪəs/ *a* misterioso
mystery /'mɪstərɪ/ *n* mistério *m*
mystic /'mɪstɪk/ *a & n* místico (*m*). **~al** *a* místico. **~ism** /-sɪzəm/ *n* misticismo *m*
mystify /'mɪstɪfaɪ/ *vt* deixar perplexo
mystique /mɪ'sti:k/ *n* mística *f*
myth /mɪθ/ *n* mito *m*. **~ical** *a* mítico
mytholog|y /mɪ'θɒlədʒɪ/ *n* mitologia *f*. **~ical** /mɪθə'lɒdʒɪkl/ *a* mitológico

Nn

nab /næb/ *vt* (*pt* **nabbed**) (*sl*) apanhar em flagrante, apanhar com a boca na botija (*colloq*), pilhar
nag /næg/ *vt/i* (*pt* **nagged**) implicar (com), criticar constantemente; (*pester*) apoquentar
nagging /'nægɪŋ/ *a* implicante; (*pain*) constante, contínuo
nail /neɪl/ *n* prego *m*; (*of finger, toe*) unha *f* □ *vt* pregar. **~ -brush** *n* escova *f* de unhas. **~ -file** *n* lixa *f* de unhas. **~ polish** esmalte *m*, (*P*) verniz *m* para as unhas. **hit the ~ on the head** acertar em cheio. **on the ~** sem demora
naïve /naɪ'i:v/ *a* ingênuo, (*P*) ingénuo
naked /'neɪkɪd/ *a* nu. **to the ~ eye** a olho nu, à vista desarmada **~ness** *f* nudez *f*

name /neɪm/ *n* nome *m*; (*fig*) reputação *f*, fama *f* □ *vt* (*mention; appoint*) nomear; (*give a name to*) chamar, dar o nome de; (*a date*) marcar. **be ~d after** ter o nome de. **~less** *a* sem nome, anônimo, (*P*) anónimo

namely /'neɪmlɪ/ *adv* a saber

namesake /'neɪmseɪk/ *n* homônimo *m*, (*P*) homónimo *m*

nanny /'nænɪ/ *n* ama *f*, babá *f*

nap[1] /næp/ *n* soneca *f* □ *vi* (*pt* **napped**) dormitar, tirar um cochilo. **catch ~ping** apanhar desprevenido

nap[2] /næp/ *n* (*of material*) felpa *f*

nape /neɪp/ *n* nuca *f*

napkin /'næpkɪn/ *n* guardanapo *m*; (*for baby*) fralda *f*

nappy /'næpɪ/ *n* fralda *f*. **~-rash** *n* assadura *f*

narcotic /na:'kɒtɪk/ *a* & *n* narcótico (*m*)

narrat|e /nə'reɪt/ *vt* narrar. **~ion** /-ʃn/ *n* narrativa *f*. **~or** *n* narrador *m*

narrative /'nærətɪv/ *n* narrativa *f* □ *a* narrativo

narrow /'nærəʊ/ *a* (**-er, -est**) estreito; (*fig*) restrito □ *vt/i* estreitar(-se); (*limit*) limitar(-se). **~ly** *adv* (*only just*) por pouco; (*closely, carefully*) de perto, com cuidado. **~-minded** a bitolado, de visão limitada. **~ness** *n* estreiteza *f*

nasal /'neɪzl/ *a* nasal

nast|y /'na:stɪ/ *a* (**-ier, -iest**) (*malicious, of weather*) mau; (*unpleasant*) desagradável, intra-gável; (*rude*) grosseiro. **~ily** *adv* maldosamente; (*unpleasantly*) desagradavelmente. **~iness** *f* (*malice*) maldade *f*; (*rudeness*) grosseria *f*

nation /'neɪʃn/ *n* nação *f*. **~-wide** *a* em todo o país, em escala *or* a nível nacional

national /'næʃnəl/ *a* nacional □ *n* natural *mf*. **~ anthem** hino *m* nacional. **~ism** *n* nacionalismo *m*. **~ize** *vt* nacionalizar. **~ly** *adv* em escala nacional

nationality /næʃə'nælətɪ/ *n* nacionalidade *f*

native /'neɪtɪv/ *n* natural *mf*, nativo *m* □ *a* nativo; (*country*) natal; (*inborn*) inato. **be a ~ of** ser natural de. **~ language** língua *f* materna. **~ speaker of Portuguese** pessoa *f* de língua portuguesa, falante *m* nativo de Português

Nativity /nə'tɪvətɪ/ *n* **the ~** a Natividade *f*

natter /'nætə(r)/ *vi* fazer conversa fiada, falar à toa, tagarelar

natural /'nætʃrəl/ *a* natural. **~ history** história *f* natural. **~ist** *n* naturalista *mf*. **~ly** *adv* naturalmente; (*by nature*) por natureza

naturaliz|e /'nætʃrəlaɪz/ *vt/i* naturalizar(-se); (*animal, plant*) aclimatar(-se). **~ation** /-'zeɪʃn/ *n* naturalização *f*

nature /'neɪtʃə(r)/ *n* natureza *f*; (*kind*) gênero *m*, (*P*) género *m*; (*of person*) índole *f*

naughty /'nɔ:tɪ/ *a* (**-ier, -iest**) (*child*) levado; (*indecent*) picante

nause|a /'nɔ:sɪə/ *n* náusea *f*. **~ate** /'nɔ:sɪeɪt/ *vt* nausear. **~ating, ~ous** *a* nauseabundo, repugnante

nautical /'nɔ:tɪkl/ *a* náutico. **~ mile** milha *f* marítima

naval /'neɪvl/ *a* naval; (*officer*) de marinha

nave /neɪv/ *n* nave *f*

navel /'neɪvl/ *n* umbigo *m*

navigable /'nævɪgəbl/ *a* navegável

navigat|e /'nævɪgeɪt/ *vt* (*sea etc*) navegar; (*ship*) pilotar □ *vi* navegar. **~ion** /-'geɪʃn/ *n* navegação *f*. **~or** *n* navegador *m*

navy /'neɪvɪ/ *n* marinha *f* de guerra. **~ (blue)** azul-marinho *m invar*

near /nɪə(r)/ *adv* perto, quaze □ *prep* perto de □ *a* próximo □ *vt* aproximar-se de, chegar-se a. **draw ~** aproximar(-se) (**to** de). **~ by** *adv* perto, próximo. **N~ East** Oriente *m* Próximo. **~ to** perto de. **~ness** *n* proximidade *f*

nearby /'nɪəbaɪ/ *a* & *adv* próximo, perto

nearly /'nɪəlɪ/ *adv* quase, por pouco. **not ~ as pretty**/*etc* **as** longe de ser tão bonita/*etc* como

neat /ni:t/ *a* (**-er, -est**) (bem) cuidado; (*room*) bem arrumado; (*spirits*) puro, sem gelo. **~ly** *adv* (*with care*) com cuidado; (*cleverly*) habilmente. **~ness** *n* aspecto *m* cuidado

nebulous /'nebjʊləs/ *a* nebuloso; (*vague*) vago, confuso

necessar|y /'nesəsərɪ/ *a* necessário. **~ily** *adv* necessariamente

necessitate /nɪ'sesɪteɪt/ *vt* exigir, obrigar a, tornar necessário

necessity /nɪ'sesətɪ/ *n* necessidade *f*; (*thing*) coisa *f* indispensável, artigo *m* de primeira neces-sidade

neck /nek/ *n* pescoço *m*; (*of dress*) gola *f*. **~ and neck** emparelhados

necklace /'neklɪs/ *n* colar *m*

neckline /'neklaɪn/ *n* decote *m*

nectarine /'nektərɪn/ *n* pêssego *m*

née /neɪ/ *a* em solteira. **Ann Jones ~ Drewe** Ann Jones cujo nome de solteira era Drewe

need /ni:d/ *n* necessidade *f* □ *vt* precisar de, necessitar de. **you ~ not come** não tem de *or* não precisa vir. **~less** *a* inútil, desnecessário. **~lessly** *adv* inutilmente, sem necessidade

needle /'ni:dl/ *a* agulha *f* ◻ *vt* (*colloq: provoke*) provocar

needlework /'ni:dlwɜ:k/ *n* costura *f*; (*embroidery*) bordado *m*

needy /'ni:dɪ/ *a* (**-ier, -iest**) necessitado, carenciado

negation /nɪ'geɪʃn/ *n* negação *f*

negative /'negətɪv/ *a* negativo ◻ *n* negativa *f*, negação *f*; (*photo*) negativo *m*. **in the ~** (*answer*) na negativa; (*gram*) na forma negativa. **~ly** *adv* negativamente

neglect /nɪ'glekt/ *vt* descuidar; (*opportunity*) desprezar; (*family*) não cuidar de (*duty*) não cumprir ◻ *n* falta *f* de cuidado(s), descuido *m*. **(state of) ~** abandono *m*. **~ to** (*omit to*) esquecer-se de. **~ful** *a* negligente

negligen|t /'neglɪdʒənt/ *a* negligente. **~ce** *n* negligência *f*, desleixo *m*

negligible /'neglɪdʒəbl/ *a* insignificante, ínfimo

negotiable /nɪ'gəʊʃəbl/ *a* negociável

negotiat|e /nɪ'gəʊʃɪeɪt/ *vt/i* negociar; (*obstacle*) transpor; (*difficulty*) vencer. **~ion** /-sɪ'eɪʃn/ *n* negociação *f*. **~or** *n* negociador *m*

Negro /'ni:grəʊ/ *a* & *n* (*pl* **~oes**) negro (*m*), preto (*m*)

neigh /neɪ/ *n* relincho *m* ◻ *vi* relinchar

neighbour /'neɪbə(r)/ *n* vizinho *m*. **~hood** *n* vizinhança *f*. **~ing** *a* vizinho. **~ly** *a* de boa vizinhança

neither /'naɪðə(r)/ *a* & *pron* nenhum(a) (de dois *ou* duas), nem um nem outro, nem uma nem outra ◻ *adv* tampouco, também não ◻ *conj* nem. **~ big nor small** nem grande nem pequeno. **~ am I** nem eu

neon /'ni:ɒn/ *n* néon *m*

nephew /'nevju:/ *n* sobrinho *m*

nerve /nɜ:v/ *n* nervo *m*; (*fig: courage*) coragem *f*; (*colloq: impudence*) descaramento *m*, (*P*) lata *f* (*colloq*). **get on sb's nerves** irritar, dar nos nervos de alg. **~-racking** *a* de arrasar os nervos, enervante

nervous /'nɜ:vəs/ *a* nervoso. **be** *or* **feel ~** (*afraid*) ter receio/um certo medo. **~ breakdown** esgotamento *m* nervoso. **~ly** *adv* nervosamente. **~ness** *n* nervosismo *m*; (*fear*) receio *m*

nest /nest/ *n* ninho *m* ◻ *vi* aninhar-se, fazer *or* ter ninho. **~-egg** *n* pé-de-meia *m*

nestle /'nesl/ *vi* aninhar-se

net[1] /net/ *n* rede *f* ◻ *vt* (*pt* **netted**) apanhar na rede. **~ting** *n* rede *f*. **wire ~ting** rede *f* de arame

net[2] /net/ *a* (*weight etc*) líquido

Netherlands /'neðələndz/ *npl* **the ~** os Países Baixos

netsurfer /'netsɜ:fə(r)/ *n* internauta *m*/*f*

nettle /'netl/ *n* urtiga *f*

network /'netwɜ:k/ *n* rede *f*, cadeia *f*

neuro|sis /njʊə'rəʊsɪs/ *n* (*pl* **-oses** /-si:z/) neurose *f*. **~tic** /-'rɒtɪk/ *a* & *n* neurótico (*m*)

neuter /'nju:tə(r)/ *a* & *n* neutro (*m*) ◻ *vt* castrar, capar

neutral /'nju:trəl/ *a* neutro. **~ (gear)** ponto *m* morto. **~ity** /-'trælətɪ/ *n* neutralidade *f*

never /'nevə(r)/ *adv* nunca; (*colloq: not*) não. **he ~ refuses** ele nunca recusa. **I ~ saw him** (*colloq*) nunca o vi. **~ mind** não faz mal, deixe para lá. **~-ending** *a* interminável

nevertheless /nevəðə'les/ *adv* & *conj* contudo, no entanto

new /nju:/ *a* (**-er, -est**) novo. **~-born** *a* recém-nascido. **~ moon** lua *f* nova. **~ year** ano *m* novo. **N~ Year's Day** dia *m* de Ano Novo. **N~ Year's Eve** véspera *f* de Ano Novo. **N~ Zealand** Nova Zelândia *f*. **N~ Zealander** neo-zelandês *m*. **~ness** *n* novidade *f*

newcomer /'nju:kʌmə(r)/ *n* recém-chegado *m*, (*P*) recém-vindo *m*

newfangled /nju:'fæŋgld/ *a* (*pej*) moderno

newly /'nju:lɪ/ *adv* há pouco, recentemente. **~-weds** *npl* recém-casados *mpl*

news /nju:z/ *n* notícia(s) *f*(*pl*); (*radio*) noticiário *m*, notícias *fpl*; (*TV*) telejornal *m*. **~-caster, ~-reader** *n* locutor *m*. **~-flash** *n* notícia *f* de última hora

newsagent /'nju:zeɪdʒənt/ *n* jornaleiro *m*

newsletter /'nju:zletə(r)/ *n* boletim *m* informativo

newspaper /'nju:zpeɪpə(r)/ *n* jornal *m*

newsreel /'nju:zri:l/ *n* atualidades *fpl*, (*P*) actualidades *fpl*

newt /nju:t/ *n* tritão *m*

next /nekst/ *a* próximo; (*adjoining*) pegado, ao lado, contíguo; (*following*) seguinte ◻ *adv* a seguir ◻ *n* seguinte *mf*. **~-door** *a* do lado. **~ of kin** parente *m* mais próximo. **~ to** ao lado de. **~ to nothing** quase nada

nib /nɪb/ *n* bico *m*, (*P*) aparo *m*

nibble /'nɪbl/ *vt* mordiscar, dar dentadinhas em

nice /naɪs/ *a* (**-er, -est**) agradável, bom; (*kind*) simpático, gentil; (*pretty*) bonito; (*respectable*) bem educado, correto, (*P*) correcto; (*subtle*) fino, subtil. **~ly** *adv* agradavelmente; (*well*) bem

nicety /ˈnaɪsətɪ/ *n* sutileza *f*, (*P*) subtileza *f*
niche /nɪtʃ/ *n* nicho *m*; (*fig*) bom lugar *m*
nick /nɪk/ *n* corte *m*, chanfradura *f*; (*sl: prison*) cadeia *f* □ *vt* dar um corte em; (*sl: steal*) roubar, limpar (*colloq*); (*sl: arrest*) apanhar, pôr a mão em (*colloq*). **in good ~** (*colloq*) em boa forma, em bom estado. **in the ~ of time** mesmo a tempo
nickel /ˈnɪkl/ *n* níquel *m*; (*Amer*) moeda *f* de cinco cêntimos
nickname /ˈnɪkneɪm/ *n* apelido *m*, (*P*) alcunha *f*; (*short form*) diminutivo *m* □ *vt* apelidar de
nicotine /ˈnɪkəti:n/ *n* nicotina *f*
niece /ni:s/ *n* sobrinha *f*
Nigeria /naɪˈdʒɪərɪə/ *n* Nigéria *f*. **~n** *a* & *n* nigeriano (*m*)
niggardly /ˈnɪgədlɪ/ *a* miserável
night /naɪt/ *n* noite *f* □ *a* de noite, noturno, (*P*) nocturno. **at ~** à/ de noite. **by ~** de noite. **~-cap** *n* (*drink*) bebida *f* na hora de deitar. **~-club** *n* boate *f*, (*P*) boîte *f*. **~-dress**, **~-gown** *ns* camisola *f* de dormir, (*P*) camisa *f* de noite. **~-life** *n* vida *f* noturna, (*P*) nocturna. **~-school** *n* escola *f* noturna, (*P*) nocturna. **~-time** *n* noite *f*. **~-watchman** *n* guarda-noturno *m*, (*P*) guarda-nocturno *m*
nightfall /ˈnaɪtfɔ:l/ *n* anoitecer *m*
nightingale /ˈnaɪtɪŋgeɪl/ *n* rouxinol *m*
nightly /ˈnaɪtlɪ/ *a* noturno, (*P*) nocturno □ *adv* de noite, à noite, todas as noites
nightmare /ˈnaɪtmeə(r)/ *n* pesadelo *m*
nil /nɪl/ *n* nada *m*; (*sport*) zero *m* □ *a* nulo
nimble /ˈnɪmbl/ *a* (**-er**, **-est**) ágil, ligeiro
nin|e /naɪn/ *a* & *n* nove (*m*). **~th** *a* & *n* nono (*m*)
nineteen /naɪnˈti:n/ *a* & *n* dezenove (*m*), (*P*) dezanove (*m*). **~th** *a* & *n* décimo nono (*m*)
ninet|y /ˈnaɪntɪ/ *a* & *n* noventa (*m*). **~ieth** *a* & *n* nonagésimo (*m*)
nip /nɪp/ *vt*/*i* (*pt* **nipped**) apertar, beliscar; (*colloq: rush*) ir correndo, ir num pulo (*colloq*) □ *n* aperto *m*, beliscão *m*; (*drink*) gole *m*, trago *m*. **a ~ in the air** um frio cortante. **~ in the bud** cortar pela raiz
nipple /ˈnɪpl/ *n* mamilo *m*
nippy /ˈnɪpɪ/ *a* (**-ier**, **-iest**) (*colloq: quick*) rápido; (*colloq: chilly*) cortante
nitrogen /ˈnaɪtrədʒən/ *n* azoto *m*, nitrogênio *m*, (*P*) nitrogénio *m*
nitwit /ˈnɪtwɪt/ *n* (*colloq*) imbecil *m*
no /nəʊ/ *a* nenhum □ *adv* não □ *n* (*pl* **noes**) não *m*. **~ entry** entrada *f* proibida. **~ money/time/** *etc* nenhum dinheiro/tempo/*etc*. **~ man's land** terra *f* de ninguém. **~ one** = **nobody**. **~ smoking** é proibido fumar. **~ way!** (*colloq*) de modo nenhum!
nob|le /ˈnəʊbl/ *a* (**-er**, **-est**) nobre. **~ility** /-ˈbɪlətɪ/ *n* nobreza *f*
nobleman /ˈnəʊblmən/ *n* (*pl* **-men**) nobre *m*, fidalgo *m*
nobody /ˈnəʊbɒdɪ/ *pron* ninguém □ *n* nulidade *f*. **he knows ~** ele não conhece ninguém. **~ is there** não tem ninguém lá
nocturnal /nɒkˈtɜ:nl/ *a* noturno, (*P*) nocturno
nod /nɒd/ *vt*/*i* (*pt* **nodded**) **~ (one's head)** acenar (com) a cabeça; **~ (off)** cabecear □ *n* aceno *m* com a cabeça (para dizer que sim *or* para cumprimentar)
noise /nɔɪz/ *n* ruído *m*, barulho *m*. **~less** *a* silencioso
nois|y /ˈnɔɪzɪ/ *a* (**-ier**, **-iest**) ruidoso, barulhento. **~ily** *adv* ruidosamente
nomad /ˈnəʊmæd/ *n* nômade *mf*, (*P*) nómade *mf*. **~ic** /-ˈmædɪk/ *a* nômade, (*P*) nómade
nominal /ˈnɒmɪnl/ *a* nominal; (*fee, sum*) simbólico
nominat|e /ˈnɒmɪneɪt/ *vt* (*appoint*) nomear; (*put forward*) propor. **~ion** /-ˈneɪʃn/ *n* nomeação *f*
non- /nɒn/ *pref* não, sem, in-, a-, anti-, des-. **~-skid** *a* antiderrapante. **~-stick** *a* não-aderente
nonchalant /ˈnɒnʃələnt/ *a* indiferente, desinteressado
non-commissioned /nɒnkəˈmɪʃnd/ *a* **~ officer** sargento *m*, cabo *m*
non-committal /nɒnkəˈmɪtl/ *a* evasivo
nondescript /ˈnɒndɪskrɪpt/ *a* insignificante, medíocre, indefinível
none /nʌn/ *pron* (*person*) nenhum, ninguém; (*thing*) nenhum, nada. **~ of us** nenhum de nós. **I have ~** não tenho nenhum. **~ of that!** nada disso! □ *adv* **~ too** não muito. **he is ~ the happier** nem por isso ele é mais feliz. **~ the less** contudo, no entanto, apesar disso
nonentity /nɒˈnentətɪ/ *n* nulidade *f*, zero *m* à esquerda, João Ninguém *m*
non-existent /nɒnɪgˈzɪstənt/ *a* inexistente
nonplussed /nɒnˈplʌst/ *a* perplexo, pasmado
nonsens|e /ˈnɒnsns/ *n* absurdo *m*, disparate *m*. **~ical** /-ˈsensɪkl/ *a* absurdo, disparatado
non-smoker /nɒnˈsməʊkə(r)/ *n* não-fumante *m*, (*P*) não-fumador *m*
non-stop /nɒnˈstɒp/ *a* ininterrupto, contínuo; (*train*) direto, (*P*) directo; (*flight*) sem escala □ *adv* sem parar

noodles /'nu:dlz/ *npl* talharim *m*, (*P*) macarronete *m*

nook /nʊk/ *n* (re)canto *m*

noon /nu:n/ *n* meio-dia *m*

noose /nu:s/ *n* laço *m* corrediço

nor /nɔ:(r)/ *conj* & *adv* nem, também não. **~ do I** nem eu

norm /nɔ:m/ *n* norma *f*

normal /'nɔ:ml/ *a* & *n* normal (*m*). **above/below ~** acima/abaixo do normal. **~ity** /nɔ:'mælətɪ/ *n* normalidade *f*. **~ly** *adv* normalmente

north /nɔ:θ/ *n* norte *m* ▫ *a* norte, do norte; (*of country, people etc*) setentrional ▫ *adv* a, ao/para o norte. **N~ America** América *f* do Norte. **N~ American** *a* & *n* norte-americano (*m*). **~-east** *n* nordeste *m*. **~erly** /'nɔ:ðəlɪ/ *a* do norte. **~ward** *a* ao norte. **~ward(s)** *adv* para o norte. **~-west** *n* noroeste *m*

northern /'nɔ:ðən/ *a* do norte

Norw|ay /'nɔ:weɪ/ *n* Noruega *f*. **~egian** /nɔ:'wi:dʒən/ *a* & *n* norueguês (*m*)

nose /nəʊz/ *n* nariz *m*; (*of animal*) focinho *m* ▫ *vi* **~ about** farejar. **pay through the ~** pagar um preço exorbitante

nosebleed /'nəʊzbli:d/ *n* hemorragia *f* nasal *or* pelo nariz

nosedive /'nəʊzdaɪv/ *n* vôo *m* picado

nostalg|ia /nɒ'stældʒə/ *n* nostalgia *f*. **~ic** *a* nostálgico

nostril /'nɒstrəl/ *n* narina *f*; (*of horse*) venta *f* (*usually pl*)

nosy /'nəʊzɪ/ *a* (**-ier, -iest**) (*colloq*) bisbilhoteiro

not /nɒt/ *adv* não. **~ at all** nada, de modo nenhum; (*reply to thanks*) de nada. **he is ~ at all bored** ele não está nem um pouco entediado. **~ yet** ainda não. **I suppose ~** creio que não

notable /'nəʊtəbl/ *a* notável ▫ *n* notabilidade *f*

notably /'nəʊtəblɪ/ *adv* notavelmente; (*particularly*) especialmente

notch /nɒtʃ/ *n* corte *m* em V ▫ *vt* marcar com cortes. **~ up** (*score etc*) marcar

note /nəʊt/ *n* nota *f*; (*banknote*) nota (de banco) *f*; (*short letter*) bilhete *m* ▫ *vt* notar

notebook /'nəʊtbʊk/ *n* livrinho *m* de notas, (*P*) bloco-notas *m*

noted /'nəʊtɪd/ *a* conhecido, famoso

notepaper /'nəʊtpeɪpə(r)/ *n* papel *m* de carta

noteworthy /'nəʊtwɜ:ðɪ/ *a* notável

nothing /'nʌθɪŋ/ *n* nada *m*; (*person*) nulidade *f*, zero *m* ▫ *adv* nada, de modo algum *or* nenhum, de maneira alguma *or* nenhuma. **he eats ~** ele não come nada. **~ big**/*etc* nada (de) grande/*etc*. **~ else** nada mais. **~ much** pouca coisa. **for ~** (*free*) de graça; (*in vain*) em vão

notice /'nəʊtɪs/ *n* anúncio *m*, notícia *f*; (*in street, on wall*) letreiro *m*; (*warning*) aviso *m*; (*attention*) atenção *f*. **(advance) ~** pré-aviso *m* ▫ *vt* notar, reparar. **at short ~** num prazo curto. **a week's ~** o prazo de uma semana. **~-board** *n* quadro *m* para afixar anúncios etc. **hand in one's ~** pedir demissão. **take ~** reparar (**of** em). **take no ~** não fazer caso (**of** de)

noticeabl|e /'nəʊtɪsəbl/ *a* visível. **~y** *adv* visivelmente

notif|y /'nəʊtɪfaɪ/ *vt* participar, notificar. **~ication** /-ɪ'keɪʃn/ *n* participação *f*, notificação *f*

notion /'nəʊʃn/ *n* noção *f*

notor|ious /nəʊ'tɔ:rɪəs/ *a* notório. **~iety** /-ə'raɪətɪ/ *n* fama *f*

notwithstanding /nɒtwɪθ'stændɪŋ/ *prep* apesar de, não obstante ▫ *adv* mesmo assim, ainda assim ▫ *conj* embora, conquanto, apesar de que

nougat /'nu:ga:/ *n* nugá *m*, torrone *m*

nought /nɔ:t/ *n* zero *m*

noun /naʊn/ *n* substantivo *m*, nome *m*

nourish /'nʌrɪʃ/ *vt* alimentar, nutrir. **~ing** *a* alimentício, nutritivo. **~ment** *n* alimento *m*, sustento *m*

novel /'nɒvl/ *n* romance *m* ▫ *a* novo, original. **~ist** *n* romancista *mf*. **~ty** *n* novidade *f*

November /nəʊ'vembə(r)/ *n* novembro *m*

novice /'nɒvɪs/ *n* (*beginner*) noviço *m*, novato *m*; (*relig*) noviço *m*

now /naʊ/ *adv* agora ▫ *conj* **~ (that)** agora que. **by ~** a estas horas, por esta altura. **from ~ on** de agora em diante. **~ and again, ~ and then** de vez em quando. **right ~** já

nowadays /'naʊədeɪz/ *adv* hoje em dia, presentemente, atualmente, (*P*) actualmente

nowhere /'nəʊweə(r)/ *adv* (*position*) em lugar nenhum, em lado nenhum; (*direction*) a lado nenhum, a parte alguma *or* nenhuma

nozzle /'nɒzl/ *n* bico *m*, bocal *m*; (*of hose*) agulheta *f*

nuance /'nju:a:ns/ *n* nuance *f*, matiz *m*

nuclear /'nju:klɪə(r)/ *a* nuclear

nucleus /'nju:klɪəs/ *n* (*pl* **-lei** /-lɪaɪ/) núcleo *m*

nud|e /nju:d/ *a* & *n* nu (*m*). **in the ~e** nu. **~ity** *n* nudez *f*

nudge /nʌdʒ/ *vt* tocar com o cotovelo, cutucar ▫ *n* ligeira cotovelada *f*, cutucada *f*

nudis|t /'nju:dɪst/ *n* nudista *mf*. **~m** /-zəm/ *n* nudismo *m*

nuisance /'nju:sns/ *n* aborrecimento *m*, chatice *f* (*sl*); (*person*) chato *m* (*sl*)

null /nʌl/ *a* nulo. **~ and void** (*jur*) írrito e nulo. **~ify** *vt* anular, invalidar

numb /nʌm/ *a* entorpecido, dormente □ *vt* entorpecer, adormecer

number /'nʌmbə(r)/ *n* número *m*; (*numeral*) algarismo *m* □ *vt* numerar; (*amount to*) ser em número de; (*count*) contar, incluir. **~-plate** *n* chapa (do carro) *f*

numeral /'nju:mərəl/ *n* número *m*, algarismo *m*

numerate /'nju:mərət/ *a* que tem conhecimentos básicos de matemática

numerical /nju:'merɪkl/ *a* numérico

numerous /'nju:mərəs/ *a* numeroso

nun /nʌn/ *n* freira *f*, religiosa *f*

nurs|e /nɜ:s/ *n* enfermeira *f*, enfermeiro *m*; (*nanny*) ama(-seca) *f*, babá *f* □ *vt* cuidar de, tratar de; (*hopes etc*) alimentar, acalentar. **~ing** *n* enfermagem *f*. **~ing home** clínica *f* de repouso

nursery /'nɜ:sərɪ/ *n* quarto *m* de crianças; (*for plants*) viveiro *m*. **(day) ~** creche *f*. **~ rhyme** poema *m or* canção *f* infantil. **~ school** jardim *m* de infância

nurture /'nɜ:tʃə(r)/ *vt* educar

nut /nʌt/ *n* (*bot*) noz *f*; (*techn*) porca *f* de parafuso

nutcrackers /'nʌtkrækəz/ *npl* quebra-nozes *m invar*

nutmeg /'nʌtmeg/ *n* noz-moscada *f*

nutrient /'nju:trɪənt/ *n* substância *f* nutritiva, nutriente *m*

nutrit|ion /nju:'trɪʃn/ *n* nutrição *f*. **~ious** *a* nutritivo

nutshell /'nʌtʃel/ *n* casca *f* de noz. **in a ~** em poucas palavras

nuzzle /'nʌzl/ *vt* esfregar com o focinho

nylon /'naɪlɒn/ *n* nylon *m*. **~s** meias *fpl* de nylon

Oo

oaf /əʊf/ *n* (*pl* **oafs**) imbecil *m*, idiota *m*

oak /əʊk/ *n* carvalho *m*

OAP *abbr see* **old-age pensioner**

oar /ɔ:(r)/ *n* remo *m*

oasis /əʊ'eɪsɪs/ *n* (*pl* **oases** /-si:z/) oásis *m*

oath /əʊθ/ *n* juramento *m*; (*swear-word*) praga *f*

oatmeal /'əʊtmi:l/ *n* farinha *f* de aveia; (*porridge*) papa *f* de aveia

oats /əʊts/ *npl* aveia *f*

obedien|t /ə'bi:dɪənt/ *a* obediente. **~ce** *n* obediência *f*. **~tly** *adv* obedientemente

obes|e /əʊ'bi:s/ *a* obeso. **~ity** *n* obesidade *f*

obey /ə'beɪ/ *vt/i* obedecer (a)

obituary /ə'bɪtʃʊərɪ/ *n* necrológio *m*, (*P*) necrologia *f*

object[1] /'ɒbdʒɪkt/ *n* objeto *m*, (*P*) objecto *m*; (*aim*) objetivo *m*, (*P*) objectivo *m*; (*gram*) complemento *m*

object[2] /əb'dʒekt/ *vt/i* objetar, (*P*) objectar (que). **~ to** opor-se a, discordar de. **~ion** /-ʃn/ *n* objeção *f*, (*P*) objecção *f*

objectionable /əb'dʒekʃnəbl/ *a* censurável; (*unpleasant*) desagradável

objectiv|e /əb'dʒektɪv/ *a* objetivo, (*P*) objectivo. **~ity** /-'tɪvətɪ/ *n* objetividade *f*, (*P*) objectividade *f*

obligation /ɒblɪ'geɪʃn/ *n* obrigação *f*. **be under an ~ to sb** dever favores a alg

obligatory /ə'blɪgətrɪ/ *a* obrigatório

oblig|e /ə'blaɪdʒ/ *vt* obrigar; (*do a favour*) fazer um favor a, obsequiar. **~ed** *a* obrigado (to a). **~ed to sb** em dívida (para) com alg. **~ing** *a* prestável, amável. **~ingly** *adv* amavelmente

oblique /ə'bli:k/ *a* oblíquo

obliterat|e /ə'blɪtəreɪt/ *vt* obliterar. **~ion** /-'reɪʃn/ *n* obliteração *f*

oblivion /ə'blɪvɪən/ *n* esquecimento *m*

oblivious /ə'blɪvɪəs/ *a* esquecido, sem consciência (**of/to** de)

oblong /'ɒblɒŋ/ *a* oblongo □ *n* retângulo *m*, (*P*) rectângulo *m*

obnoxious /əb'nɒkʃəs/ *a* ofensivo, detestável

oboe /'əʊbəʊ/ *n* oboé *m*

obscen|e /əb'si:n/ *a* obsceno. **~ity** /-'enətɪ/ *n* obscenidade *f*

obscur|e /əb'skjʊə(r)/ *a* obscuro □ *vt* obscurecer; (*conceal*) encobrir. **~ity** *n* obscuridade *f*

obsequious /əb'si:kwɪəs/ *a* demasiado obsequioso, subserviente

observan|t /əb'zɜ:vənt/ *a* observador. **~ce** *n* observância *f*, cumprimento *m*

observatory /əb'zɜ:vətrɪ/ *n* observatório *m*

observ|e /əb'zɜ:v/ *vt* observar. **~ation** /ɒbzə'veɪʃn/ *n* observação *f*. **keep under ~ation** vigiar. **~er** *n* observador *m*

obsess /əb'ses/ *vt* obcecar. **~ion** /-ʃn/ *n* obsessão *f*. **~ive** *a* obsessivo

obsolete /'ɒbsəli:t/ *a* obsoleto, antiguado

obstacle /'ɒbstəkl/ *n* obstáculo *m*

obstetric|s /əb'stetrɪks/ *n* obstetrícia *f*. **~ian** /ɒbstɪ'trɪʃn/ *n* obstetra *mf*

obstina|te /'ɒbstɪnət/ *a* obstinado. **~cy** *n* obstinação *f*

obstruct /əb'strʌkt/ *vt* obstruir, bloquear; (*hinder*) estorvar, obstruir. **~ion** /-ʃn/ *n* obstrução *f*; (*thing*) obstáculo *m*

obtain /əb'teɪn/ *vt* obter ▫ *vi* prevalecer, estar em vigor. **~able** *a* que se pode obter

obtrusive /əb'tru:sɪv/ *a* importuno; (*thing*) demasiadamente em evidência, que dá muito na vista (*colloq*)

obvious /'ɒbvɪəs/ *a* óbvio, evidente. **~ly** *adv* obviamente

occasion /ə'keɪʒn/ *n* ocasião *f*; (*event*) acontecimento *m* ▫ *vt* ocasionar. **on ~** de vez em quando, ocasionalmente

occasional /ə'keɪʒənl/ *a* ocasional. **~ly** *adv* de vez em quando, ocasionalmente

occult /ɒ'kʌlt/ *a* oculto

occupation /ɒkjʊ'peɪʃn/ *n* ocupação *f*. **~al** *a* profissional; (*therapy*) ocupacional

occup|y /'ɒkjʊpaɪ/ *vt* ocupar. **~ant**, **~ier** *ns* ocupante *mf*

occur /ə'kɜ:(r)/ *vi* (*pt* **occurred**) ocorrer, acontecer, dar-se; (*arise*) apresentar-se, aparecer. **~ to sb** ocorrer a alg

occurrence /ə'kʌrəns/ *n* acontecimento *m*, ocorrência *f*

ocean /'əʊʃn/ *n* oceano *m*

o'clock /ə'klɒk/ *adv* **it is one ~** é uma hora. **it is six ~** são seis horas

octagon /'ɒktəgən/ *n* octógono *m*. **~al** /-'tægənl/ *a* octogonal

octave /'ɒktɪv/ *n* oitava *f*

October /ɒk'təʊbə(r)/ *n* outubro *m*

octopus /'ɒktəpəs/ *n* (*pl* **-puses**) polvo *m*

odd /ɒd/ *a* (**-er, -est**) estranho, singular; (*number*) ímpar; (*left over*) de sobra; (*not of set*) desemparelhado; (*occasional*) ocasional. **~ jobs** (*paid*) biscates *mpl*; (*in garden etc*) trabalhos *mpl* diversos. **twenty ~** vinte e tantos. **~ity** *n* singularidade *f*; (*thing*) curiosidade *f*. **~ly** *adv* de modo estranho

oddment /'ɒdmənt/ *n* resto *m*, artigo *m* avulso

odds /ɒdz/ *npl* probabilidades *fpl*; (*in betting*) ganhos *mpl* líquidos. **at ~** em desacordo; (*quarrelling*) de mal, brigado. **it makes no ~** não faz diferença. **~ and ends** artigos *mpl* avulsos, coisas *fpl* pequenas

odious /'əʊdɪəs/ *a* odioso

odour /'əʊdə(r)/ *n* odor *m*. **~less** *a* inodoro

of /əv/; *emphatic* /ɒv/ *prep* de. **a friend ~ mine** um amigo meu. **the fifth ~ June** (no dia) cinco de junho. **take six ~ them** leve seis deles

off /ɒf/ *adv* embora, fora; (*switched off*) apagado, desligado; (*taken off*) tirado, desligado; (*cancelled*) cancelado; (*food*) estragado ▫ *prep* (fora) de; (*distant from*) a alguma distância de. **be ~** (*depart*) ir-se embora, partir. **be well ~** ser abastado. **be better/worse ~** estar em melhor/pior situação. **a day ~** um dia de folga. **20% ~** redução de 20%. **on the ~ chance that** no caso de. **~ colour** indisposto, adoentado. **~-licence** *n* loja *f* de bebidas alcoólicas. **~-load** *vt* descarregar. **~-putting** *a* desconcertante. **~-stage** *adv* fora de cena. **~-white** *a* branco-sujo

offal /'ɒfl/ *n* miudezas *fpl*, fressura *f*

offence /ə'fens/ *n* (*feeling*) ofensa *f*; (*crime*) delito *m*, transgressão *f*. **give ~ to** ofender. **take ~** ofender-se (**at** com)

offend /ə'fend/ *vt* ofender. **be ~ed** ofender-se (**at** com). **~er** *n* delinqüente *mf*, (*P*) delinquente *mf*

offensive /ə'fensɪv/ *a* ofensivo; (*disgusting*) repugnante ▫ *n* ofensiva *f*

offer /'ɒfə(r)/ *vt* (*pt* **offered**) oferecer ▫ *n* oferta *f*. **on ~** em promoção. **~ing** *n* oferenda *f*

offhand /ɒf'hænd/ *a* espontâneo; (*curt*) seco ▫ *adv* de improviso, sem pensar

office /'ɒfɪs/ *n* escritório *m*; (*post*) cargo *m*; (*branch*) filial *f*. **~ hours** horas *fpl* de expediente. **in ~** no poder. **take ~** assumir o cargo

officer /'ɒfɪsə(r)/ *n* oficial *m*; (*policeman*) agente *m*

official /ə'fɪʃl/ *a* oficial ▫ *n* funcionário *m*. **~ly** *adv* oficialmente

officiate /ə'fɪʃɪeɪt/ *vi* (*relig*) oficiar. **~ as** presidir, exercer as funções de

officious /ə'fɪʃəs/ *a* intrometido

offing /'ɒfɪŋ/ *n* **in the ~** (*fig*) em perspectiva

offset /'ɒfset/ *vt* (*pt* **-set**, *pres p* **-setting**) compensar, contrabalançar

offshoot /'ɔfʃu:t/ *n* rebento *m*; (*fig*) efeito *m* secundário

offshore /'ɒfʃɔ:(r)/ *a* ao largo da costa

offside /ɒf'saɪd/ *a* & *adv* offside, em impedimento, (*P*) fora de jogo

offspring /'ɒfsprɪŋ/ *n* (*pl invar*) descendência *f*, prole *f*

often /'ɒfn/ *adv* muitas vezes, freqüentemente, (*P*) frequentemente. **every so ~** de vez em quando. **how ~?** quantas vezes?

oh /əʊ/ *int* oh, ah

oil /ɔɪl/ *n* óleo *m*; (*petroleum*) petróleo *m* □ *vt* lubrificar. **~-painting** *n* pintura *f* a óleo. **~ rig** plataforma *f* de poço de petróleo. **~ well** poço *m* de petróleo. **~y** *a* oleoso; (*food*) gorduroso

oilfield /'ɔɪlfi:ld/ *n* campo *m* petrolífero

oilskins /'ɔɪlskɪnz/ *npl* roupa *f* de oleado

ointment /'ɔɪntmənt/ *n* pomada *f*

OK /əʊ'keɪ/ *a* & *adv* (*colloq*) (está) bem, (está) certo, (está) legal

old /əʊld/ *a* (**-er, -est**) velho; (*person*) velho, idoso; (*former*) antigo. **how ~ is he?** que idade tem ele? **he is eight years ~** ele tem oito anos (de idade). **of ~** (d)antes, antigamente. **~ age** velhice *f*. **~-age pensioner** reformado *m*, aposentado *m*, pessoa *f* de terceira idade. **~ boy** antigo aluno *m*. **~-fashioned** *a* fora de moda. **~ girl** antiga aluna *f*. **~ maid** solteirona *f*. **~ man** homem *m* idoso, velho *m*. **~-time** *a* antigo. **~ woman** mulher *f* idosa, velha *f*

olive /'ɒlɪv/ *n* azeitona *f* □ *a* de azeitona. **~ oil** azeite *m*

Olympic /ə'lɪmpɪk/ *a* olímpico. **~s** *npl* Olimpíadas *fpl*. **~ Games** Jogos *mpl* Olímpicos

omelette /'ɒmlɪt/ *n* omelete *f*

omen /'əʊmən/ *n* agouro *m*

ominous /'ɒmɪnəs/ *a* agourento

omi|t /ə'mɪt/ *vt* (*pt* **omitted**) omitir. **~ssion** /-ʃn/ *n* omissão *f*

on /ɒn/ *prep* sobre, em cima de, de, em □ *adv* para diante, para a frente; (*switched on*) aceso, ligado; (*tap*) aberto, (*machine*) em funcionamento; (*put on*) posto; (*happening*) em curso. **~ arrival** na chegada, ao chegar. **~ foot** *etc* a pé *etc*. **~ doing** ao fazer. **~ time** na hora, dentro do horário. **~ Tuesday** na terça-feira. **~ Tuesdays** às terças-feiras. **walk**/*etc* **~** continuar a andar/ *etc*. **be ~ at** (*film, TV*) estar levando *or* passando. **~ and off** de vez em quando. **~ and ~** sem parar

once /wʌns/ *adv* uma vez; (*formerly*) noutro(s) tempo(s) □ *conj* uma vez que, desde que. **all at ~** de repente; (*simultaneously*) todos ao mesmo tempo. **just this ~** só esta vez. **~ (and) for all** duma vez para sempre. **~ upon a time** era uma vez. **~-over** *n* (*colloq*) vista *f* de olhos

oncoming /'ɒnkʌmɪŋ/ *a* que se aproxima, próximo. **the ~ traffic** o trânsito que vem do sentido oposto, (*P*) no sentido contrário

one /wʌn/ *a* um(a); (*sole*) único □ *n* um(a) *mf* □ *pron* um(a) *mf*; (*impersonal*) se. **~ by ~** um a um. **a big/red**/*etc* **~** um grande/vermelho/*etc*. **this/that ~** este/esse. **~ another** um ao outro, uns aos outros. **~-sided** *a* parcial. **~-way** *a* (*street*) mão única; (*ticket*) simples

oneself /wʌn'self/ *pron* si, si mesmo/ próprio; (*reflexive*) se. **by ~** sozinho

onion /'ʌnɪən/ *n* cebola *f*

on-line /ɒn'laɪn/ *adj* conectado (à Internet)

onlooker /'ɒnlʊkə(r)/ *n* espectador *m*, circunstante *mf*

only /'əʊnlɪ/ *a* único □ *adv* apenas, só, somente □ *conj* só que. **an ~ child** um filho único. **he ~ has six** ele só tem seis. **not ~ . . . but also** não só . . . mas também. **~ too** muito, mais que

onset /'ɒnset/ *n* começo *m*; (*attack*) ataque *m*

onslaught /'ɒnslɔ:t/ *n* ataque *m* violento, assalto *m*

onward(s) /'ɒnwəd(z)/ *adv* para a frente/ diante

ooze /u:z/ *vt*/*i* escorrer, verter

opal /'əʊpl/ *n* opala *f*

opaque /əʊ'peɪk/ *a* opaco, tosco

open /'əʊpən/ *a* aberto; (*view*) aberto, amplo; (*free to all*) aberto ao público; (*attempt*) franco □ *vt*/*i* abrir(-se); (*of shop, play*) abrir. **in the ~ air** ao ar livre. **keep ~ house** receber muito, abrir a porta para todos. **~ on to** dar para. **~ out** *or* **up** abrir(-se). **~-heart** *a* (*of surgery*) de coração aberto. **~-minded** *a* imparcial. **~-plan** *a* sem divisórias. **~ secret** segredo *m* de polichinelo. **~ sea** mar *m* alto. **~ness** *n* abertura *f*; (*frankness*) franqueza *f*

opener /'əʊpənə(r)/ *n* (*tins*) abridor *m* de latas; (*bottles*) saca-rolhas *m invar*

opening /'əʊpənɪŋ/ *n* abertura *f*; (*beginning*) começo *m*; (*opportunity*) oportunidade *f*; (*job*) vaga *f*

openly /'əʊpənlɪ/ *adv* abertamente

opera /'ɒprə/ *n* ópera *f*. **~-glasses** *npl* binóculo (de teatro) *m*, (*P*) binóculos *mpl*. **~tic** /ɒpə-'rætɪk/ *a* de ópera

operat|e /'ɒpəreɪt/ *vt*/*i* operar; (*techn*) (pôr a) funcionar. **~e on** (*med*) operar. **~ing-theatre** *n* (*med*) anfiteatro *m*, sala *f* de operações. **~ion** /-'reɪʃn/ *n* operação *f*. **in ~ion** em vigor; (*techn*) em funcionamento. **~ional** /-'reɪʃənl/ *a* operacional. **~or** *n* operador *m*; (*telephonist*) telefonista *mf*

operative /'ɒpərətɪv/ *a* (*surgical*) operatório; (*law etc*) em vigor

opinion /ə'pɪnɪən/ *n* opinião *f*, parecer *m*. **in my ~** a meu ver. **~ poll** *n* sondagem (de opinião) *f*. **~ated** /-eɪtɪd/ *a* dogmático

opium /'əʊpɪəm/ *n* ópio *m*

Oporto /ə'pɔ:təʊ/ *n* Porto *m*

opponent /ə'pəʊnənt/ *n* adversário *m*, antagonista *mf*, oponente *mf*
opportune /'ɒpətju:n/ *a* oportuno
opportunity /ɒpə'tju:nətɪ/ *n* oportunidade *f*
oppos|e /ə'pəʊz/ *vt* opor-se a. **~ed to** oposto a. **~ing** *a* oposto
opposite /'ɒpəzɪt/ *a* & *n* oposto (*m*), contrário (*m*) □ *adv* em frente □ *prep* **~ (to)** em frente de
opposition /ɒpə'zɪʃn/ *n* oposição *f*
oppress /ə'pres/ *vt* oprimir. **~ion** /-ʃn/ *n* opressão *f*. **~ive** *a* opressivo. **~or** *n* opressor *m*
opt /ɒpt/ *vi* **~ for** optar por. **~ out** recusar-se a participar (**of** de). **~ to do** escolher fazer
optical /'ɒptɪkl/ *a* óptico. **~ illusion** ilusão *f* óptica
optician /ɒp'tɪʃn/ *n* oculista *mf*
optimis|t /'ɒptɪmɪst/ *n* otimista *mf*, (*P*) optimista *mf*. **~m** /-zəm/ *n* otimismo *m*, (*P*) optimismo *m*. **~tic** /-'mɪstɪk/ *a* otimista, (*P*) optimista. **~tically** /-'mɪstɪklɪ/ *adv* com otimismo, (*P*) optimismo
optimum /'ɒptɪməm/ *a* & *n* (*pl* **-ima**) ótimo (*m*), (*P*) óptimo (*m*)
option /'ɒpʃn/ *n* escolha *f*, opção *f*. **have no ~ (but)** não ter outro remédio (senão)
optional /'ɒpʃənl/ *a* opcional, facultativo
opulen|t /'ɒpjʊlənt/ *a* opulento. **~ce** *n* opulência *f*
or /ɔ:(r)/ *conj* ou; (*with negative*) nem. **~ else** senão
oracle /'ɒrəkl/ *n* oráculo *m*
oral /'ɔ:rəl/ *a* oral
orange /'ɒrɪndʒ/ *n* laranja *f*; (*colour*) laranja *m*, cor *f* de laranja □ *a* de laranja; (*colour*) alaranjado, cor de laranja
orator /'ɒrətə(r)/ *n* orador *m*. **~y** *n* oratória *f*
orbit /'ɔ:bɪt/ *n* órbita *f* □ *vt* (*pt* **orbited**) gravitar em torno de
orchard /'ɔ:tʃəd/ *n* pomar *m*
orchestra /'ɔ:kɪstrə/ *n* orquestra *f*. **~l** /-'kestrəl/ *a* orquestral
orchestrate /'ɔ:kɪstreɪt/ *vt* orquestrar
orchid /'ɔ:kɪd/ *n* orquídea *f*
ordain /ɔ:'deɪn/ *vt* decretar; (*relig*) ordenar
ordeal /ɔ:'di:l/ *n* prova *f*, provação *f*
order /'ɔ:də(r)/ *n* ordem *f*, (*comm*) encomenda *f*, pedido *m* □ *vt* ordenar; (*goods etc*) encomendar. **in ~ that** para que. **in ~ to** para
orderly /'ɔ:dəlɪ/ *a* ordenado, em ordem; (*not unruly*) ordeiro □ *n* (*mil*) ordenança *f*; (*med*) servente *m* de hospital
ordinary /'ɔ:dɪnrɪ/ *a* normal, ordinário, vulgar. **out of the ~** fora do comum
ordination /ɔ:dɪ'neɪʃn/ *n* (*relig*) ordenação *f*
ore /ɔ:(r)/ *n* minério *m*
organ /'ɔ:gən/ *n* órgão *m*. **~ist** *n* organista *mf*
organic /ɔ:'gænɪk/ *a* orgânico
organism /'ɔ:gənɪzəm/ *n* organismo *m*
organiz|e /'ɔ:gənaɪz/ *vt* organizar. **~ation** /-'zeɪʃn/ *n* organização *f*. **~er** *n* organizador *m*
orgasm /'ɔ:gæzəm/ *n* orgasmo *m*
orgy /'ɔ:dʒɪ/ *n* orgia *f*
Orient /'ɔ:rɪənt/ *n* **the ~** o Oriente *m*. **~al** /-'entl/ *a* & *n* oriental (*mf*)
orientat|e /'ɔ:rɪənteɪt/ *vt* orientar. **~ion** /-'teɪʃn/ *n* orientação *f*
orifice /'ɒrɪfɪs/ *n* orifício *m*
origin /'ɒrɪdʒɪn/ *n* origem *f*
original /ə'rɪdʒənl/ *a* original; (*not copied*) original. **~ity** /-'nælətɪ/ *n* originalidade *f*. **~ly** *adv* originalmente; (*in the beginning*) originariamente
originat|e /ə'rɪdʒəneɪt/ *vt/i* originar(-se). **~e from** provir de. **~or** *n* iniciador *m*, criador *m*, autor *m*
ornament /'ɔ:nəmənt/ *n* ornamento *m*; (*object*) peça *f* decorativa. **~al** /-'mentl/ *a* ornamental. **~ation** /-en'teɪʃn/ *n* ornamentação *f*
ornate /ɔ:'neɪt/ *a* florido, floreado
ornitholog|y /ɔ:nɪ'θɒlədʒɪ/ *n* ornitologia *f*. **~ist** *n* ornitólogo *m*
orphan /'ɔ:fn/ *n* órfã(o) *f*(*m*) □ *vt* deixar órfão. **~age** *n* orfanato *m*
orthodox /'ɔ:θədɒks/ *a* ortodoxo
orthopaedic /ɔ:θə'pi:dɪk/ *a* ortopédico
oscillate /'ɒsɪleɪt/ *vi* oscilar, vacilar
ostensibl|e /ɒs'tensəbl/ *a* aparente, pretenso. **~y** *adv* aparentemente, pretensamente
ostentati|on /ɒsten'teɪʃn/ *n* ostentação *f*. **~ous** /-'teɪʃəs/ *a* ostentoso, ostensivo
osteopath /'ɒstɪəpæθ/ *n* osteopata *mf*
ostracize /'ɒstrəsaɪz/ *vt* pôr de lado, marginalizar
ostrich /'ɒstrɪtʃ/ *n* avestruz *mf*
other /'ʌðə(r)/ *a*, *n* & *pron* outro (*m*) □ *adv* **~ than** diferente de, senão. **(some) ~s** outros. **the ~ day** no outro dia. **the ~ one** o outro
otherwise /'ʌðəwaɪz/ *adv* de outro modo □ *conj* senão, caso contrário
otter /'ɒtə(r)/ *n* lontra *f*
ouch /aʊtʃ/ *int* ai!, ui!

ought /ɔ:t/ *v aux* (*pt* **ought**) dever. **you ~ to stay** você devia ficar. **he ~ to succeed** ele deve vencer. **I ~ to have done it** eu devia tê-lo feito

ounce /aʊns/ *n* onça *f* (*= 28,35g*)

our /'aʊə(r)/ *a* nosso(s), nossa(s)

ours /'aʊəz/ *poss pron* o(s) nosso(s), a(s) nossa(s)

ourselves /aʊə'selvz/ *pron* nós mesmos/próprios; (*reflexive*) nos. **by ~** sozinhos

oust /aʊst/ *vt* expulsar, obrigar a sair

out /aʊt/ *adv* fora; (*of light, fire*) apagado; (*in blossom*) aberto, desabrochado; (*of tide*) baixo. **be ~** não estar em casa, estar fora (de casa); (*wrong*) enganar-se. **be ~ to** estar resolvido a. **run**/*etc* **~** sair correndo/*etc*. **~-and-~** *a* completo, rematado. **~ of** fora de; (*without*) sem. **~ of pity**/*etc* por pena/*etc*. **made ~ of** feito de *or* em. **take ~ of** tirar de. **5 ~ of 6** 5 (de) entre 6. **~ of date** fora de moda; (*not valid*) fora do prazo. **~ of doors** ao ar livre. **~ of one's mind** doido. **~ of order** quebrado. **~ of place** deslocado. **~ of the way** afastado. **~-patient** *n* doente *mf* de consulta externa

outboard /'aʊtbɔ:d/ *a* **~ motor** motor *m* de popa

outbreak /'aʊtbreɪk/ *n* (*of flu etc*) surto *m*, epidemia *f*; (*of war*) deflagração *f*

outburst /'aʊtbɜ:st/ *n* explosão *f*

outcast /'aʊtka:st/ *n* pária *m*

outcome /'aʊtkʌm/ *n* resultado *m*

outcry /'aʊtkraɪ/ *n* clamor *m*; (*protest*) protesto *m*

outdated /aʊt'deɪtɪd/ *a* fora da moda, ultrapassado

outdo /aʊt'du:/ *vt* (*pt* **-did**, *pp* **-done**) ultrapassar, superar

outdoor /'aʊtdɔ:(r)/ *a* ao ar livre. **~s** /-'dɔ:z/ *adv* fora de casa, ao ar livre

outer /'aʊtə(r)/ *a* exterior. **~ space** espaço (cósmico) *m*

outfit /'aʊtfɪt/ *n* equipamento *m*; (*clothes*) roupa *f*

outgoing /'aʊtgəʊɪŋ/ *a* que vai sair; (*of minister etc*) demissionário; (*fig*) sociável. **~s** *npl* despesas *fpl*

outgrow /aʊt'grəʊ/ *vt* (*pt* **-grew**, *pp* **-grown**) crescer mais do que; (*clothes*) já não caber em

outhouse /'aʊthaʊs/ *n* anexo *m*, dependência *f*

outing /'aʊtɪŋ/ *n* saída *f*, passeio *m*

outlandish /aʊt'lændɪʃ/ *a* exótico, estranho

outlaw /'aʊtlɔ:/ *n* fora-da-lei *mf*, bandido *m* ▫ *vt* banir, proscrever

outlay /'aʊtleɪ/ *n* despesa(s) *f*(*pl*)

outlet /'aʊtlet/ *n* saída *f*, escoadouro *m*; (*for goods*) mercado *m*, saída *f*; (*for feelings*) escape *m*, vazão *m*; (*electr*) tomada *f*

outline /'aʊtlaɪn/ *n* contorno *m*; (*summary*) plano *m* geral, esquema *m*, esboço *m* ▫ *vt* contornar; (*summarize*) descrever em linhas gerais

outlive /aʊt'lɪv/ *vt* sobreviver a

outlook /'aʊtlʊk/ *n* (*view*) vista *f*; (*mental attitude*) visão *f*; (*future prospects*) perspectiva(s) *f*(*pl*)

outlying /'aʊtlaɪɪŋ/ *a* afastado, remoto

outnumber /aʊt'nʌmbə(r)/ *vt* ultrapassar em número

outpost /'aʊtpəʊst/ *n* posto *m* avançado

output /'aʊtpʊt/ *n* rendimento *m*; (*of computer*) saída *f*, output *m*

outrage /'aʊtreɪdʒ/ *n* atrocidade *f*, crime *m*; (*scandal*) escândalo *m* ▫ *vt* ultrajar

outrageous /aʊt'reɪdʒəs/ *a* (*shocking*) escandaloso; (*very cruel*) atroz

outright /'aʊtraɪt/ *adv* completamente; (*at once*) imediatamente; (*frankly*) abertamente ▫ *a* completo; (*refusal*) claro

outset /'aʊtset/ *n* início *m*, começo *m*, princípio *m*

outside[1] /aʊt'saɪd/ *n* exterior *m* ▫ *adv* (lá) (por) fora ▫ *prep* (para) fora de, além de; (*in front of*) diante de. **at the ~** no máximo

outside[2] /'aʊtsaɪd/ *a* exterior

outsider /aʊt'saɪdə(r)/ *n* estranho *m*; (*in race*) cavalo *m* com poucas probabilidades, azarão *m*

outsize /'aʊtsaɪz/ *a* tamanho extra *invar*

outskirts /'aʊtskɜ:ts/ *npl* arredores *mpl*, subúrbios *mpl*

outspoken /aʊt'spəʊkn/ *a* franco

outstanding /aʊt'stændɪŋ/ *a* saliente, proeminente; (*debt*) por saldar; (*very good*) notável, destacado

outstretched /aʊt'stretʃt/ *a* (*arm*) estendido, esticado

outstrip /aʊt'strɪp/ *vt* (*pt* **-stripped**) ultrapassar, passar à frente de

outward /'aʊtwəd/ *a* para o exterior; (*sign etc*) exterior; (*journey*) de ida. **~ly** *adv* exteriormente. **~s** *adv* para o exterior

outwit /aʊt'wɪt/ *vt* (*pt* **-witted**) ser mais esperto que, enganar

oval /'əʊvl/ *n* & *a* oval (*m*)

ovary /'əʊvərɪ/ *n* ovário *m*

ovation /əʊ'veɪʃn/ *n* ovação *f*

oven /'ʌvn/ *n* forno *m*

over /'əʊvə(r)/ *prep* sobre, acima de, por cima de; (*across*) de para o/do outro lado de; (*during*) durante, em; (*more than*) mais de ▫ *adv* por cima; (*too*) demais, demasiadamente; (*ended*) acabado. **the film is ~** o filme já acabou. **jump**/*etc* **~** saltar/*etc* por cima. **he has some ~** ele tem uns de sobra. **all ~ the country** em/por todo o país. **all ~ the table** por toda a mesa. **~ and above** (*besides, in addition to*) (para) além de. **~ and ~** repetidas vezes. **~ there** ali, lá, acolá

over- /'əʊvə(r)/ *pref* sobre-, super-; (*excessively*) demais, demasiado

overall[1] /'əʊvərɔ:l/ *n* bata *f*. **~s** macacão *m*, (*P*) fato-macaco *m*

overall[2] /'əʊvərɔ:l/ *a* global; (*length etc*) total □ *adv* globalmente

overawe /əʊvər'ɔ:/ *vt* intimidar

overbalance /əʊvə'bæləns/ *vt*/*i* (fazer) perder o equilíbrio

overbearing /əʊvə'beərɪŋ/ *a* autoritário, despótico; (*arrogant*) arrogante

overboard /'əʊvəbɔ:d/ *adv* (pela) borda fora

overcast /əʊvə'ka:st/ *a* encoberto, nublado

overcharge /əʊvə'tʃa:dʒ/ *vt* **~ sb (for)** cobrar demais a alg (por)

overcoat /'əʊvəkəʊt/ *n* casacão *m*; (*for men*) sobretudo *m*

overcome /əʊvə'kʌm/ *vt* (*pt* **-came**, *pp* **-come**) superar, vencer. **~ by** sucumbindo a, dominado *or* vencido por

overcrowded /əʊvə'kraʊdɪd/ *a* apinhado, superlotado; (*country*) superpovoado

overdo /əʊvə'du:/ *vt* (*pt* **-did**, *pp* **-done**) exagerar, levar longe demais. **~ne** (*culin*) cozinhado demais

overdose /'əʊvədəʊs/ *n* dose *f* excessiva

overdraft /'əʊvədra:ft/ *n* saldo *m* negativo

overdraw /əʊvə'drɔ:/ *vt* (*pt* **-drew**, *pp* **-drawn**) sacar a descoberto

overdue /əʊvə'dju:/ *a* em atraso, atrasado; (*belated*) tardio

overestimate /əʊvər'estɪmeɪt/ *vt* sobreestimar, atribuir valor excessivo a

overexpose /əʊvərɪk'spəʊz/ *vt* expor demais

overflow[1] /əʊvə'fləʊ/ *vt*/*i* extravasar, transbordar (**with** de)

overflow[2] /'əʊvəfləʊ/ *n* (*outlet*) descarga *f*; (*excess*) excesso *m*

overgrown /əʊvə'grəʊn/ *a* que cresceu demais; (*garden etc*) invadido pela vegetação

overhang /əʊvə'hæŋ/ *vt* (*pt* **-hung**) estar sobranceiro a, pairar sobre □ *vi* projetar-se, (*P*) projectar-se para fora □ *n* saliência *f*

overhaul[1] /əʊvə'hɔ:l/ *vt* fazer uma revisão em

overhaul[2] /'əʊvəhɔ:l/ *n* revisão *f*

overhead[1] /əʊvə'hed/ *adv* em *or* por cima, ao *or* no alto

overhead[2] /'əʊvəhed/ *a* aéreo. **~s** *npl* despesas *fpl* gerais

overhear /əʊvə'hɪə(r)/ *vt* (*pt* **-heard**) (*eavesdrop*) ouvir sem conhecimento do falante; (*hear by chance*) ouvir por acaso

overjoyed /əʊvə'dʒɔɪd/ *a* radiante, felicíssimo

overlap /əʊvə'læp/ *vt*/*i* (*pt* **-lapped**) sobrepor(-se) parcialmente; (*fig*) coincidir

overleaf /əʊvə'li:f/ *adv* no verso

overload /əʊvə'ləʊd/ *vt* sobrecarregar

overlook /əʊvə'lʊk/ *vt* deixar passar; (*of window*) dar para; (*of building*) dominar

overnight /əʊvə'naɪt/ *adv* durante a noite; (*fig*) dum dia para o outro □ *a* (*train*) da noite; (*stay, journey, etc*) noite, noturno; (*fig*) súbito

overpass /əʊvə'pa:s/ *n* passagem *f* superior

overpay /əʊvə'peɪ/ *vt* (*pt* **-paid**) pagar em excesso

overpower /əʊvə'paʊə(r)/ *vt* dominar, subjugar; (*fig*) esmagar. **~ing** *a* esmagador; (*heat*) sufocante, insuportável

overpriced /əʊvə'praɪst/ *a* muito caro

overrate /əʊvə'reɪt/ *vt* sobreestimar, exagerar o valor de

overrid|e /əʊvə'raɪd/ *vt* (*pt* **-rode**, *pp* **-ridden**) prevalecer sobre, passar por cima de. **~ing** *a* primordial, preponderante; (*importance*) maior

overripe /'əʊvəraɪp/ *a* demasiado maduro

overrule /əʊvə'ru:l/ *vt* anular, rejeitar; (*claim*) indeferir

overrun /əʊvə'rʌn/ *vt* (*pt* **-ran**, *pp* **-run**, *pres p* **-running**) invadir; (*a limit*) exceder, ultrapassar

overseas /əʊvə'si:z/ *a* ultramarino; (*abroad*) estrangeiro □ *adv* no ultramar, no estrangeiro

oversee /əʊvə'si:/ *vt* (*pt* **-saw** *pp* **-seen**) supervisionar. **~r** /'əʊvəsɪə(r)/ *n* capataz *m*

overshadow /əʊvə'ʃædəʊ/ *vt* (*fig*) eclipsar, ofuscar

oversight /'əʊvəsaɪt/ *n* lapso *m*

oversleep /əʊvə'sli:p/ *vi* (*pt* **-slept**) acordar tarde, dormir demais

overt /'əʊvɜ:t/ *a* manifesto, claro, patente

overtake /əʊvə'teɪk/ *vt*/*i* (*pt* **-took**, *pp* **-taken**) ultrapassar

overthrow /əʊvə'θrəʊ/ *vt* (*pt* **-threw**, *pp* **-thrown**) derrubar ▫ *n* /'əʊvəθrəʊ/ (*pol*) derrubada *f*

overtime /'əʊvətaɪm/ *n* horas *fpl* extras

overtones /'əʊvətəʊnz/ *npl* (*fig*) tom *m*, implicação *f*

overture /'əʊvətjʊə(r)/ *n* (*mus*) abertura *f*; (*fig*) proposta *f*, abordagem *f*

overturn /əʊvə'tɜ:n/ *vt*/*i* virar (-se); (*car, plane*) capotar, virar-se

overweight /əʊvə'weɪt/ *a* **be ~** ter excesso de peso

overwhelm /əʊvə'welm/ *vt* oprimir; (*defeat*) esmagar; (*amaze*) assoberbar. **~ing** *a* esmagador; (*urge*) irresistível

overwork /əʊvə'wɜ:k/ *vt*/*i* sobrecarregar(-se) com trabalho ▫ *n* excesso *m* de trabalho

overwrought /əʊvə'rɔ:t/ *a* muito agitado, superexcitado

ow|e /əʊ/ *vt* dever. **~ing** *a* devido. **~ing to** devido a

owl /aʊl/ *n* coruja *f*

own[1] /əʊn/ *a* próprio. **a house**/*etc* **of one's ~** uma casa/*etc* própria. **get one's ~ back** (*colloq*) ir à forra, (*P*) desforrarse. **hold one's ~** agüentar-se, (*P*) aguentar-se. **on one's ~** sozinho

own[2] /əʊn/ *vt* possuir. **~ up (to)** (*colloq*) confessar. **~er** *n* proprietário *m*, dono *m*. **~ership** *n* posse *f*, propriedade *f*

ox /ɒks/ *n* (*pl* **oxen**) boi *m*

oxygen /'ɒksɪdʒən/ *n* oxigênio *m*, (*P*) oxigénio *m*

oyster /'ɔɪstə(r)/ *n* ostra *f*

ozone /'əʊzəʊn/ *n* ozônio *m*, (*P*) ozono *m*. **~ layer** camada *f* de ozônio, (*P*) ozono *m*

pace /peɪs/ *n* passo *m*; (*fig*) ritmo *m* ▫ *vt* percorrer passo a passo ▫ *vi* **~ up and down** andar de um lado para o outro. **keep ~ with** acompanhar, manter-se a par de

pacemaker /'peɪsmeɪkə(r)/ *n* (*med*) marcapasso *m*, (*P*) pacemaker *m*

Pacific /pə'sɪfɪk/ *a* pacífico ▫ *n* **~ (Ocean)** (Oceano) Pacífico *m*

pacifist /'pæsɪfɪst/ *n* pacifista *mf*

pacify /'pæsɪfaɪ/ *vt* pacificar, apaziguar

pack /pæk/ *n* pacote *m*; (*mil*) mochila *f*; (*of hounds*) matilha *f*; (*of lies*) porção *f*; (*of cards*) baralho *m* ▫ *vt* empacotar; (*suitcase*) fazer; (*box, room*) encher; (*press down*) atulhar, encher até não caber mais ▫ *vi* fazer as malas. **~ into** (*cram*) apinhar em, comprimir em. **send ~ing** pôr a andar, mandar passear. **~ed** *a* apinhado. **~ed lunch** merenda *f*

package /'pækɪdʒ/ *n* pacote *m*, embrulho *m* ▫ *vt* embalar. **~ deal** pacote *m* de propostas. **~ holiday** pacote *m* turístico, (*P*) viagem *f* organizada

packet /'pækɪt/ *n* pacote *m*; (*of cigarettes*) maço *m*

pact /pækt/ *n* pacto *m*

pad /pæd/ *n* (*in clothing*) chumaço *m*; (*for writing*) bloco *m* de papel/de notas; (*for ink*) almofada (de carimbo) *f*. **(launching) ~** rampa *f* de lançamento ▫ *vt* (*pt* **padded**) enchumaçar, acolchoar; (*fig: essay etc*) encher linguiça. **~ding** *n* chumaço *m*; (*fig*) linguiça *f*

paddle[1] /'pædl/ *n* remo *m* de canoa. **~-steamer** *n* vapor *m* movido a rodas

paddl|e[2] /'pædl/ *vi* chapinhar, molhar os pés. **~ing pool** piscina *f* de plástico para crianças

paddock /'pædək/ *n* cercado *m*; (*at racecourse*) paddock *m*

padlock /'pædlɒk/ *n* cadeado *m* ▫ *vt* fechar com cadeado

paediatrician /pi:dɪə'trɪʃn/ *n* pediatra *mf*

pagan /'peɪgən/ *a* & *n* pagão (*m*), pagã (*f*)

page[1] /peɪdʒ/ *n* (*of book etc*) página *f*

page[2] /peɪdʒ/ *vt* mandar chamar

pageant /'pædʒənt/ *n* espetáculo *m*, (*P*) espectáculo *m* (histórico); (*procession*) cortejo *m*. **~ry** *n* pompa *f*

pagoda /pə'gəʊdə/ *n* pagode *m*

paid /peɪd/ *see* **pay** ▫ *a* **put ~ to** (*colloq: end*) pôr fim a

pail /peɪl/ *n* balde *m*

pain /peɪn/ *n* dor *f*. **~s** esforços *mpl* ▫ *vt* magoar. **be in ~** sofrer, ter dores. **~-killer** *n* analgésico *m*. **take ~s to** esforçar-se por. **~ful** *a* doloroso; (*grievous, laborious*) penoso. **~less** *a* sem dor, indolor

painstaking /'peɪnzteɪkɪŋ/ *a* cuidadoso, esmerado, meticuloso

paint /peɪnt/ *n* tinta *f*. **~s** (*in box*) tintas *fpl* ▫ *vt*/*i* pintar. **~er** *n* pintor *m*. **~ing** *n* pintura *f*

paintbrush /'peɪntbrʌʃ/ *n* pincel *m*

pair /peə(r)/ *n* par *m*. **a ~ of scissors** uma tesoura. **a ~ of trousers** um par de calças. **in ~s** aos pares ▫ *vi* **~ off** formar pares

Pakistan /pa:kɪ'sta:n/ *n* Paquistão *m*. **~i** *a* & *n* paquistanês (*m*)

pal /pæl/ *n* (*colloq*) colega *mf*, amigo *m*

palace /'pælɪs/ *n* palàcio *m*

palat|e /'pælət/ *n* palato *m*. **~able** *a* saboroso, gostoso; (*fig*) agradável
palatial /pə'leɪʃl/ *a* suntuoso, (*P*) sumptuoso
pale /peɪl/ *a* (**-er, -est**) pálido; (*colour*) claro □ *vi* empalidecer. **~ness** *n* palidez *f*
Palestin|e /'pælɪstaɪn/ *n* Palestina *f*. **~ian** /-'stɪnɪən/ *a* & *n* palestino (*m*)
palette /'pælɪt/ *n* paleta *f*. **~-knife** *n* espátula *f*
pall /pɔ:l/ *vi* tornar-se enfadonho, perder o interesse (**on** para)
pallid /'pælɪd/ *a* pálido
palm /pa:m/ *n* (*of hand*) palma *f*; (*tree*) palmeira *f* □ *vt* **~ off** impingir (**on** a). **P~ Sunday** Domingo *m* de Ramos
palpable /'pælpəbl/ *a* palpável
palpitat|e /'pælpɪteɪt/ *vi* palpitar. **~ion** /-'teɪʃn/ *n* palpitação *f*
paltry /'pɔ:ltrɪ/ *a* (**-ier, -iest**) irrisório
pamper /'pæmpə(r)/ *vt* mimar, paparicar
pamphlet /'pæmflɪt/ *n* panfleto *m*, folheto *m*
pan /pæn/ *n* panela *f*; (*for frying*) frigideira *f* □ *vt* (*pt* **panned**) (*colloq*) criticar severamente
panacea /pænə'sɪə/ *n* panacéia *f*
panache /pæ'næʃ/ *n* brio *m*, estilo *m*, panache *m*
pancake /'pænkeɪk/ *n* crepe *m*, panqueca *f*
pancreas /'pæŋkrɪəs/ *n* pâncreas *m*
panda /'pændə/ *n* panda *m*
pandemonium /pændɪ'məʊnɪəm/ *n* pandemônio *m*, (*P*) pandemónio *m*, caos *m*
pander /'pændə(r)/ *vi* **~ to** prestar-se a servir, ir ao encontro de, fazer concessões a
pane /peɪn/ *n* vidraça *f*
panel /'pænl/ *n* painel *m*; (*jury*) júri *m*; (*speakers*) convidados *mpl*. **(instrument) ~** painel *m* de instrumentos, (*P*) de bordo. **~led** *a* apainelado. **~ling** *n* apainelamento *m*. **~list** *n* convidado *m*
pang /pæŋ/ *n* pontada *f*, dor *f* aguda e súbita. **~s** (*of hunger*) ataques *mpl* de fome. **~s of conscience** remorsos *mpl*
panic /'pænɪk/ *n* pânico *m* □ *vt/i* (*pt* **panicked**) desorientar(-se), (fazer) entrar em pânico. **~-stricken** *a* tomado de pânico
panoram|a /pænə'ra:mə/ *n* panorama *m*. **~ic** /-'ræmɪk/ *a* panorâmico
pansy /'pænzɪ/ *n* amor-perfeito *m*
pant /pænt/ *vi* ofegar, arquejar
panther /'pænθə(r)/ *n* pantera *f*
panties /'pæntɪz/ *npl* (*colloq*) calcinhas *fpl*
pantomime /'pæntəmaɪm/ *n* pantomima *f*
pantry /'pæntrɪ/ *n* despensa *f*
pants /pænts/ *npl* (*colloq: underwear*) cuecas *fpl*; (*colloq: trousers*) calças *fpl*
papal /'peɪpl/ *a* papal
paper /'peɪpə(r)/ *n* papel *m*; (*newspaper*) jornal *m*; (*exam*) prova *f* escrita; (*essay*) comunicação *f*. **~s** *npl* (*for identification*) documentos *mpl* □ *vt* forrar com papel. **on ~** por escrito. **~-clip** *n* clipe *m*
paperback /'peɪpəbæk/ *a* & *n* **~ (book)** livro *m* de capa mole
paperweight /'peɪpəweɪt/ *n* pesa-papéis *m invar*, (*P*) pisa-papéis *m invar*
paperwork /'peɪpəwɜ:k/ *n* trabalho *m* de secretária; (*pej*) papelada *f*
paprika /'pæprɪkə/ *n* páprica *f*
par /pa:(r)/ *n* **be below ~** estar abaixo do padrão desejado. **on a ~ with** em igualdade com
parable /'pærəbl/ *n* parábola *f*
parachut|e /'pærəʃu:t/ *n* pára- quedas *m invar* □ *vi* descer de pára-quedas. **~ist** *n* pára-quedista *mf*
parade /pə'reɪd/ *n* (*mil*) parada *f* militar; (*procession*) procissão *f* □ *vi* desfilar □ *vt* alardear
paradise /'pærədaɪs/ *n* paraíso *m*
paradox /'pærədɒks/ *n* paradoxo *m*. **~ical** /-'dɒksɪkl/ *a* paradoxal
paraffin /'pærəfɪn/ *n* querosene *m*, (*P*) petróleo *m*
paragon /'pærəgən/ *n* modelo *m* de perfeição
paragraph /'pærəgra:f/ *n* parágrafo *m*
parallel /'pærəlel/ *a* & *n* paralelo (*m*) □ *vt* (*pt* **parelleled**) comparar(-se) a
paralyse /'pærəlaɪz/ *vt* paralisar
paraly|sis /pə'ræləsɪs/ *n* paralisia *f*. **~tic** /-'lɪtɪk/ *a* & *n* paralítico (*m*)
paramedic /pærə'medɪk/ *n* paramédico *m*
parameter /pə'ræmɪtə(r)/ *n* parâmetro *m*
paramount /'pærəmaʊnt/ *a* supremo, primordial
parapet /'pærəpɪt/ *n* parapeito *m*
paraphernalia /pærəfə'neɪlɪə/ *n* equipamento *m*, tralha *f* (*colloq*)
paraphrase /'pærəfreɪz/ *n* paráfrase *f* □ *vt* parafrasear
paraplegic /pærə'pli:dʒɪk/ *n* paraplégico *m*
parasite /'pærəsaɪt/ *n* parasita *mf*
parasol /'pærəsɒl/ *n* sombrinha *f*; (*on table*) pára-sol *m*, guarda-sol *m*
parcel /'pa:sl/ *n* embrulho *m*; (*for post*) encomenda *f*
parch /pa:tʃ/ *vt* ressecar. **be ~ed** estar com muita sede

parchment /'pa:tʃmənt/ *n* pergaminho *m*
pardon /'pa:dn/ *n* perdão *m*; (*jur*) perdão *m*, indulto *m* □ *vt* (*pt* **pardoned**) perdoar. **I beg your ~** perdão, desculpe. **(I beg your) ~?** como?
pare /peə(r)/ *vt* aparar, cortar; (*peel*) descascar
parent /'peərənt/ *n* pai *m*, mãe *f*. **~s** *npl* pais *mpl*. **~al** /pə'rentl/ *a* dos pais, paterno, materno
parenthesis /pə'renθəsɪs/ *n* (*pl* **-theses**) /-si:z/ parêntese *m*, parêntesis *m*
Paris /'pærɪs/ *n* Paris *m*
parish /'pærɪʃ/ *n* paróquia *f*; (*municipal*) freguesia *f*. **~ioner** /pə'rɪʃənə(r)/ *n* paroquiano *m*
parity /'pærətɪ/ *n* paridade *f*
park /pa:k/ *n* parque *m* □ *vt* estacionar. **~ing** *n* estacionamento *m*. **no ~ing** estacionamento proibido. **~ing-meter** *n* parquímetro *m*
parliament /'pa:ləmənt/ *n* parlamento *m*, assembléia *f*. **~ary** /-'mentrɪ/ *a* parlamentar
parochial /pə'rəʊkɪəl/ *a* paroquial; (*fig*) provinciano, tacanho
parody /'pærədɪ/ *n* paródia *f* □ *vt* parodiar
parole /pə'rəʊl/ *n* **on ~** em liberdade condicional □ *vt* pôr em liberdade condicional
parquet /'pa:keɪ/ *n* parquê *m*, parquete *m*
parrot /'pærət/ *n* papagaio *m*
parry /'pærɪ/ *vt* (a)parar □ *n* parada *f*
parsimonious /pa:sɪ'məʊnɪəs/ *a* parco; (*mean*) avarento
parsley /'pa:slɪ/ *n* salsa *f*
parsnip /'pa:snɪp/ *n* cherovia *f*, pastinaga *f*
parson /'pa:sn/ *n* pároco *m*, pastor *m*
part /pa:t/ *n* parte *f*; (*of serial*) episódio *m*; (*of machine*) peça *f*; (*theatre*) papel *m*; (*side in dispute*) partido *m* □ *a* parcial □ *adv* em parte □ *vt/i* separar (-se) (**from** de). **in ~** em parte. **on the ~ of** da parte de. **~ -exchange** *n* troca *f* parcial. **~ of speech** categoria *f* gramatical. **~-time** *a & adv* a tempo parcial, part-time. **take ~ in** tomar parte em. **these ~s** estas partes
partial /'pa:ʃl/ *a* (*incomplete, biased*) parcial. **be ~ to** gostar de. **~ity** /-ɪ'ælətɪ/ *n* parcialidade *f*; (*liking*) predileção *f*, (*P*) predilecção *f* (**for** por). **~ly** *adv* parcialmente
particip|ate /pa:'tɪsɪpeɪt/ *vi* participar (**in** em). **~ant** *n* /-ənt/ participante *mf*. **~ation** /-'peɪʃn/ *n* participação *f*
participle /'pa:tɪsɪpl/ *n* particípio *m*
particle /'pa:tɪkl/ *n* partícula *f*; (*of dust*) grão *m*; (*fig*) mínimo *m*
particular /pə'tɪkjʊlə(r)/ *a* especial, particular; (*fussy*) exigente; (*careful*) escrupuloso. **~s** *npl* pormenores *mpl*. **in ~** *adv* em especial, particularmente. **~ly** *adv* particularmente
parting /'pa:tɪŋ/ *n* separação *f*; (*in hair*) risca *f* □ *a* de despedida
partisan /pa:tɪ'zæn/ *n* partidário *m*; (*mil*) guerrilheiro *m*
partition /pa:'tɪʃn/ *n* (*of room*) tabique *m*, divisória *f*; (*pol: division*) partilha *f*, divisão *f* □ *vt* dividir, repartir. **~ off** dividir por meio de tabique
partly /'pa:tlɪ/ *adv* em parte
partner /'pa:tnə(r)/ *n* sócio *m*; (*cards, sport*) parceiro *m*; (*dancing*) par *m*. **~ship** *n* associação *f*; (*comm*) sociedade *f*
partridge /'pa:trɪdʒ/ *n* perdiz *f*
party /'pa:tɪ/ *n* festa *f*, reunião *f*; (*group*) grupo *m*; (*pol*) partido *m*; (*jur*) parte *f*. **~ line** (*telephone*) linha *f* coletiva, (*P*) colectiva
pass /pa:s/ *vt/i* (*pt* **passed**) passar; (*overtake*) ultrapassar; (*exam*) passar; (*approve*) passar; (*law*) aprovar. **~ (by)** passar por □ *n* (*permit, sport*) passe *m*; (*geog*) desfiladeiro *m*, garganta *f*; (*in exam*) aprovação *f*. **make a ~ at** (*colloq*) atirar-se para (*colloq*). **~ away** falecer. **~ out** *or* **round** distribuir. **~ out** (*colloq: faint*) perder os sentidos, desmaiar. **~ over** (*disregard, overlook*) passar por cima de. **~ up** (*colloq: forgo*) deixar perder
passable /'pa:səbl/ *a* passável; (*road*) transitável
passage /'pæsɪdʒ/ *n* passagem *f*, (*voyage*) travessia *f*; (*corridor*) corredor *m*, passagem *f*
passenger /'pæsɪndʒə(r)/ *n* passageiro *m*
passer-by /pa:sə'baɪ/ *n* (*pl* **passers-by**) transeunte *mf*
passion /'pæʃn/ *n* paixão *f*. **~ate** *a* apaixonado, exaltado
passive /'pæsɪv/ *a* passivo. **~ness** *n* passividade *f*
Passover /'pa:səʊvə(r)/ *n* Páscoa *f* dos judeus
passport /'pa:spɔ:t/ *n* passaporte *m*
password /'pa:swɜ:d/ *n* senha *f*
past /pa:st/ *a* passado; (*former*) antigo □ *n* passado □ *prep* para além de; (*in time*) mais de; (*in front of*) diante de □ *adv* em frente. **be ~ it** já não ser capaz. **it's five ~ eleven** são onze e cinco. **these ~ months** estes últimos meses
pasta /'pæstə/ *n* prato *m* de massa(s)
paste /peɪst/ *n* cola *f*; (*culin*) massa(s) *f* (*pl*); (*dough*) massa *f*; (*jewellery*) strass *m* □ *vt* colar

pastel /ˈpæstl/ *n* pastel *m* □ *a* pastel *invar*
pasteurize /ˈpæstʃəraɪz/ *vt* pasteurizar
pastille /ˈpæstɪl/ *n* pastilha *f*
pastime /ˈpɑ:staɪm/ *n* passatempo *m*
pastoral /ˈpɑ:stərəl/ *a* & *n* pastoral (*f*)
pastry /ˈpeɪstrɪ/ *n* massa *f* (de pastelaria); (*tart*) pastel *m*
pasture /ˈpɑ:stʃə(r)/ *n* pastagem *f*
pasty[1] /ˈpæstɪ/ *n* empadinha *f*
pasty[2] /ˈpeɪstɪ/ *a* pastoso
pat /pæt/ *vt* (*pt* **patted**) (*hit gently*) dar pancadinhas em; (*caress*) fazer festinhas a □ *n* pancadinha *f*; (*caress*) festinha *f* □ *adv* a propósito; (*readily*) prontamente □ *a* preparado, pronto
patch /pætʃ/ *n* remendo *m*; (*over eye*) tapa-ôlho *m*; (*spot*) mancha *f*; (*small area*) pedaço *m*; (*of vegetables*) canteiro *m*, (*P*) leira *f* □ *vt* **~ up** remendar. **~ up a quarrel** fazer as pazes. **bad ~** mau bocado *m*. **not be a ~ on** não chegar aos pés de. **~-work** *n* obra *f* de retalhos. **~y** *a* desigual
pâté /ˈpæteɪ/ *n* patê *m*
patent /ˈpeɪtnt/ *a* & *n* patente (*f*) □ *vt* patentear. **~ leather** verniz *m*, polimento *m*. **~ly** *adv* claramente
paternal /pəˈtɜ:nl/ *a* paternal; (*relative*) paterno
paternity /pəˈtɜ:nətɪ/ *n* paternidade *f*
path /pɑ:θ/ *n* (*pl* **-s** /pɑ:ðz/) caminho *m*, trilha *f*; (*in park*) aléia *f*; (*of rocket*) trajetória *f*, (*P*) trajectória *f*
pathetic /pəˈθetɪk/ *a* patético; (*colloq: contemptible*) desgraçado (*colloq*)
patholog|y /pəˈθɒlədʒɪ/ *n* patologia *f*. **~ist** *n* patologista *mf*
pathos /ˈpeɪθɒs/ *n* patos *m*, patético *m*
patience /ˈpeɪʃns/ *n* paciência *f*
patient /ˈpeɪʃnt/ *a* paciente □ *n* doente *mf*, paciente *mf*. **~ly** *adv* pacientemente
patio /ˈpætɪəʊ/ *n* (*pl* **-os**) pátio *m*
patriot /ˈpætrɪət/ *n* patriota *mf*. **~ic** /-ˈɒtɪk/ *a* patriótico. **~ism** /-ɪzəm/ *n* patriotismo *m*
patrol /pəˈtrəʊl/ *n* patrulha *f* □ *vt/i* patrulhar. **~ car** carro *m* de patrulha
patron /ˈpeɪtrən/ *n* (*of the arts etc*) patrocinador *m*, protetor *m*, (*P*) protector *m*; (*of charity*) benfeitor *m*; (*customer*) freguês *m*, cliente *mf*. **~ saint** padroeiro *m*, patrono *m*
patron|age /ˈpætrənɪdʒ/ *n* freguesia *f*, clientela *f*; (*support*) patrocínio *m*. **~ize** *vt* ser cliente de; (*support*) patrocinar; (*condescend*) tratar com ares de superioridade
patter[1] /ˈpætə(r)/ *n* (*of rain*) tamborilar *m*, rufo *m*. **~ of steps** som *m* leve de passos miúdos, corridinha *f* leve
patter[2] /ˈpætə(r)/ *n* (*of class, profession*) gíria *f*, jargão *m*; (*chatter*) conversa *f* fiada
pattern /ˈpætn/ *n* padrão *m*; (*for sewing*) molde *m*; (*example*) modelo *m*
paunch /pɔ:ntʃ/ *n* pança *f*
pause /pɔ:z/ *n* pausa *f* □ *vi* pausar, fazer (uma) pausa
pav|e /peɪv/ *vt* pavimentar. **~e the way** preparar o caminho (for para). **~ing-stone** *n* paralelepípedo *m*, laje *f*
pavement /ˈpeɪvmənt/ *n* passeio *m*
pavilion /pəˈvɪlɪən/ *n* pavilhão *m*
paw /pɔ:/ *n* pata *f* □ *vt* dar patadas em; (*horse*) escarvar; (*colloq: person*) pôr as patas em cima de
pawn[1] /pɔ:n/ *n* (*chess*) peão *m*; (*fig*) joguete *m*
pawn[2] /pɔ:n/ *vt* empenhar. **~-shop** casa *f* de penhores, prego *m* (*colloq*)
pawnbroker /ˈpɔ:nbrəʊkə(r)/ *n* penhorista *mf*, dono *m* de casa de penhores, agiota *mf*
pay /peɪ/ *vt/i* (*pt* **paid**) pagar; (*interest*) render; (*visit, compliment*) fazer □ *n* pagamento *m*; (*wages*) vencimento *m*, ordenado *m*, salário *m*. **in the ~ of** em pagamento de. **~ attention** prestar atenção. **~ back** restituir. **~ for** pagar. **~ homage** prestar homenagem. **~ in** depositar. **~-slip** *n* contracheque *m*, (*P*) folha *f* de pagamento
payable /ˈpeɪəbl/ *a* pagável
payment /ˈpeɪmənt/ *n* pagamento *m*; (*fig: reward*) recompensa *f*
payroll /ˈpeɪrəʊl/ *n* folha *f* de pagamentos. **be on the ~** fazer parte da folha de pagamento de uma firma
pea /pi:/ *n* ervilha *f*
peace /pi:s/ *n* paz *f*. **disturb the ~** perturbar a ordem pública. **~able** *a* pacífico
peaceful /ˈpi:sfl/ *a* pacífico; (*calm*) calmo, sereno
peacemaker /ˈpi:smeɪkə(r)/ *n* mediador *m*, pacificador *m*
peach /pi:tʃ/ *n* pêssego *m*
peacock /ˈpi:kɒk/ *n* pavão *m*
peak /pi:k/ *n* pico *m*, cume *m*, cimo *m*; (*of cap*) pala *f*; (*maximum*) máximo *m*. **~ hours** horas *fpl* de ponta; (*electr*) horas *fpl* de carga máxima. **~ed cap** boné *m* de pala
peaky /ˈpi:ki/ *a* com ar doentio
peal /pi:l/ *n* (*of bells*) repique *m*; (*of laughter*) gargalhada *f*, risada *f*
peanut /ˈpi:nʌt/ *n* amendoim *m*. **~s** (*sl: small sum*) uma bagatela *f*
pear /peə(r)/ *n* pera
pearl /pɜ:l/ *n* pérola *f*. **~y** *a* nacarado
peasant /ˈpeznt/ *n* camponês *m*, aldeão *m*

peat /piːt/ *n* turfa *f*

pebble /ˈpebl/ *n* seixo *m*, calhau *m*

peck /pek/ *vt/i* bicar; (*attack*) dar bicadas (em) □ *n* bicada *f*; (*colloq: kiss*) beijo *m* seco. **~ing order** hierarquia *f*, ordem *f* de importância

peckish /ˈpekɪʃ/ *a* **be ~** (*colloq*) ter vontade de comer

peculiar /pɪˈkjuːlɪə(r)/ *a* bizarro, singular; (*special*) peculiar (**to** a), característico (**to** de). **~ity** /-ˈærətɪ/ *n* singularidade *f*; (*feature*) peculiaridade *f*

pedal /ˈpedl/ *n* pedal *m* □ *vi* (*pt* **pedalled**) pedalar

pedantic /pɪˈdæntɪk/ *a* pedante

peddle /ˈpedl/ *vt* vender de porta em porta; (*drugs*) fazer tráfico de

pedestal /ˈpedɪstl/ *n* pedestal *m*

pedestrian /pɪˈdestrɪən/ *n* pedestre *mf*, (*P*) peão *m* □ *a* pedestre; (*fig*) prosaico. **~ crossing** faixa *f* para pedestres, (*P*) passadeira *f*

pedigree /ˈpedɪgriː/ *n* estirpe *f*, linhagem *f*; (*of animal*) raça *f* □ *a* de raça

pedlar /ˈpedlə(r)/ *n* vendedor *m* ambulante

peek /piːk/ *vi* espreitar □ *n* espreitadela *f*

peel /piːl/ *n* casca *f* □ *vt* descascar □ *vi* (*skin*) pelar; (*paint*) escamar-se, descascar; (*wallpaper*) descolar-se. **~ings** *npl* cascas *fpl*

peep /piːp/ *vi* espreitar □ *n* espreitadela *f*. **~ hole** *n* vigia *f*; (*in door*) olho *m* mágico

peer[1] /pɪə(r)/ *vi* **~ at/into** (*searchingly*) perscrutar; (*with difficulty*) esforçar-se por ver

peer[2] /pɪə(r)/ *n* (*equal, noble*) par *m*. **~age** *n* pariato *m*

peeved /piːvd/ *a* (*sl*) irritado, chateado (*sl*)

peevish /ˈpiːvɪʃ/ *a* irritável

peg /peg/ *n* cavilha *f*; (*for washing*) pregador *m* de roupa, (*P*) mola *f*; (*for coats etc*) cabide *m*; (*for tent*) estaca *f* □ *vt* (*pt* **pegged**) prender com estacas. **off the ~** prêt-à-porter

pejorative /pɪˈdʒɒrətɪv/ *a* pejorativo

pelican /ˈpelɪkən/ *n* pelicano *m*. **~ crossing** passagem *f* com sinais manobrados pelos pedestres

pellet /ˈpelɪt/ *n* bolinha *f*; (*for gun*) grão *m* de chumbo

pelt[1] /pelt/ *n* pele *f*

pelt[2] /pelt/ *vt* bombardear (**with** com) □ *vi* chover a cântaros; (*run fast*) correr em disparada

pelvis /ˈpelvɪs/ *n* (*anat*) pélvis *m*, bacia *f*

pen[1] /pen/ *n* (*enclosure*) cercado *m*. **play-~** *n* cercado *m*, (*P*) pargue *m* □ *vt* (*pt* **penned**) encurralar

pen[2] /pen/ *n* caneta *f* □ *vt* (*pt* **penned**) escrever. **~-friend** *n* correspondente *mf*. **~-name** *n* pseudônimo *m*, (*P*) pseudónimo *m*

penal /ˈpiːnl/ *a* penal. **~ize** *vt* impôr uma penalidade a; (*sport*) penalizar

penalty /ˈpenltɪ/ *n* pena *f*; (*fine*) multa *f*; (*sport*) penalidade *f*. **~ kick** pênalti *m*, (*P*) grande penalidade *f*

penance /ˈpenəns/ *n* penitência *f*

pence /pens/ *see* **penny**

pencil /ˈpensl/ *n* lápis *m* □ *vt* (*pt* **pencilled**) escrever *or* desenhar a lápis. **~-sharpener** *n* apontador *m*, (*P*) apara-lápis *m invar*

pendant /ˈpendənt/ *n* berloque *m*

pending /ˈpendɪŋ/ *a* pendente □ *prep* (*during*) durante; (*until*) até

pendulum /ˈpendjʊləm/ *n* pêndulo *m*

penetrat|e /ˈpenɪtreɪt/ *vt/i* penetrar (em). **~ing** *a* penetrante. **~ion** /-ˈtreɪʃn/ *n* penetração *f*

penguin /ˈpeŋgwɪn/ *n* pingüim *m*, (*P*) pinguin *m*

penicillin /penɪˈsɪlɪn/ *n* penicilina *f*

peninsula /pəˈnɪnsjʊlə/ *n* península *f*

penis /ˈpiːnɪs/ *n* pênis *m*, (*P*) pénis *m*

peniten|t /ˈpenɪtənt/ *a* & *n* penitente (*mf*). **~ce** *n* /-əns/ contrição *f*, penitência *f*

penitentiary /penɪˈtenʃərɪ/ *n* (*Amer*) penitenciária *f*, cadeia *f*

penknife /ˈpennaɪf/ *n* (*pl* **-knives**) canivete *m*

penniless /ˈpenɪlɪs/ *a* sem vintém, sem um tostão

penny /ˈpenɪ/ *n* (*pl* **pennies** *or* **pence**) pêni *m*, (*P*) pêni *m*; (*fig*) centavo *m*, vintém *m*

pension /ˈpenʃn/ *n* pensão *f*; (*in retirement*) aposentadoria *f*, (*P*) reforma *f* □ *vt* **~ off** reformar, aposentar. **~er** *n* **(old-age) ~er** reformado *m*

pensive /ˈpensɪv/ *a* pensativo

Pentecost /ˈpentɪkɒst/ *n* Pentecostes *m*

penthouse /ˈpenthaʊs/ *n* cobertura *f*, (*P*) apartamento de luxo (no último andar)

pent-up /ˈpentʌp/ *a* reprimido

penultimate /penˈʌltɪmət/ *a* penúltimo

people /ˈpiːpl/ *npl* pessoas *fpl* □ *n* gente *f*, povo *m* □ *vt* povoar. **the Portuguese ~** os portugueses *mpl*. **~ say** dizem, diz-se

pep /pep/ *n* vigor *m* □ *vt* **~ up** animar. **~ talk** discurso *m* de encorajamento

pepper /ˈpepə(r)/ *n* pimenta *f*; (*vegetable*) pimentão *m*, (*P*) pimento *m* □ *vt* apimentar. **~y** *a* apimentado, picante

peppermint /ˈpepəmɪnt/ *n* hortelã-pimenta *f*; (*sweet*) bala *f*, (*P*) pastilha *f* de hortelã-pimenta

per /pɜ:(r)/ *prep* por. **~ annum** por ano. **~ cent** por cento. **~ kilo**/*etc* o quilo/*etc*

perceive /pəˈsi:v/ *vt* perceber; (*notice*) aperceber-se de

percentage /pəˈsentɪdʒ/ *n* percentagem *f*

perceptible /pəˈseptəbl/ *a* perceptível

percept|ion /pəˈsepʃn/ *n* percepção *f*. **~ive** /-tɪv/ *a* perceptivo, penetrante, perspicaz

perch[1] /pɜ:tʃ/ *n* poleiro *m* □ *vi* empoleirar-se, pousar

perch[2] /pɜ:tʃ/ *n* (*fish*) perca *f*

percolat|e /ˈpɜ:kəleɪt/ *vt/i* filtrar (-se), passar. **~or** *n* máquina *f* de café com filtro, cafeteira *f*

percussion /pəˈkʌʃn/ *n* percussão *f*

peremptory /pəˈremptərɪ/ *a* peremptório, decisivo

perennial /pəˈrenɪəl/ *a* perene; (*plant*) perene

perfect[1] /ˈpɜ:fɪkt/ *a* perfeito. **~ly** *adv* perfeitamente

perfect[2] /pəˈfekt/ *vt* aperfeiçoar. **~ion** /-ʃn/ *n* perfeição *f*. **~ionist** *n* perfeccionista *mf*

perforat|e /ˈpɜ:fəreɪt/ *vt* perfurar. **~ion** /-ˈreɪʃn/ *n* perfuração *f*; (*line of holes*) pontilhado *m*, picotado *m*

perform /pəˈfɔ:m/ *vt* (*a task; mus*) executar; (*a function; theat*) desempenhar □ *vi* representar; (*function*) funcionar. **~ance** *n* (*of task; mus*) execução *f*; (*of function; theat*) desempenho *m*; (*of car*) performance *f*, comportamento *m*, rendimento *m*; (*colloq: fuss*) drama *m*, cena *f*. **~er** *n* artista *mf*

perfume /ˈpɜ:fju:m/ *n* perfume *m*

perfunctory /pəˈfʌŋktərɪ/ *a* superficial, negligente

perhaps /pəˈhæps/ *adv* talvez

peril /ˈperəl/ *n* perigo *m*. **~ous** *a* perigoso

perimeter /pəˈrɪmɪtə(r)/ *n* perímetro *m*

period /ˈpɪərɪəd/ *n* período *m*, época *f*; (*era*) época *f*; (*lesson*) hora *f* de aula, período *m* letivo, (*P*) lectivo; (*med*) período *m*; (*full stop*) ponto (final) *m* □ *a* (*of novel*) de costumes; (*of furniture*) de estilo. **~ic** /-ˈɒdɪk/ *a* periódico. **~ical** /-ˈɒdɪkl/ *n* periódico *m*. **~ically** /-ˈɒdɪklɪ/ *adv* periodicamente

peripher|y /pəˈrɪfərɪ/ *n* periferia *f*. **~al** *a* periférico; (*fig*) marginal, à margem

perish /ˈperɪʃ/ *vi* morrer, perecer; (*rot*) estragar-se, deteriorar-se. **~able** *a* (*of goods*) deteriorável

perjur|e /ˈpɜ:dʒə(r)/ *vpr* **~e o.s.** jurar falso, perjurar. **~y** *n* perjúrio *m*

perk[1] /pɜ:k/ *vt/i* **~ up** (*colloq*) arrebitar(-se). **~y** *a* (*colloq*) vivo, animado

perk[2] /pɜ:k/ *n* (*colloq*) regalia *f*, extra *m*

perm /pɜ:m/ *n* permanente *f* □ *vt* **have one's hair ~ed** fazer uma permanente

permanen|t /ˈpɜ:mənənt/ *a* permanente. **~ce** *n* permanência *f*. **~tly** *adv* permanentemente, a título permanente

permeable /ˈpɜ:mɪəbl/ *a* permeável

permeate /ˈpɜ:mɪeɪt/ *vt/i* permear, penetrar

permissible /pəˈmɪsəbl/ *a* permissível, admissível

permission /pəˈmɪʃn/ *n* permissão *f*, licença *f*

permissive /pəˈmɪsɪv/ *a* permissivo. **~ society** sociedade *f* permissiva. **~ness** *n* permissividade *f*

permit[1] /pəˈmɪt/ *vt* (*pt* **permitted**) permitir, consentir (**sb to** a alguém que)

permit[2] /ˈpɜ:mɪt/ *n* licença *f*; (*pass*) passe *m*

permutation /pɜ:mju:ˈteɪʃn/ *n* permutação *f*

pernicious /pəˈnɪʃəs/ *a* pernicioso, prejudicial

perpendicular /pɜ:pənˈdɪkjʊlə(r)/ *a* & *n* perpendicular (*f*)

perpetrat|e /ˈpɜ:pɪtreɪt/ *vt* perpetrar. **~or** *n* autor *m*

perpetual /pəˈpetʃʊəl/ *a* perpétuo

perpetuate /pəˈpetʃʊeɪt/ *vt* perpetuar

perplex /pəˈpleks/ *vt* deixar perplexo. **~ed** *a* perplexo. **~ing** *a* confuso. **~ity** *n* perplexidade *f*

persecut|e /ˈpɜ:sɪkju:t/ *vt* perseguir. **~ion** *n* /-ˈkju:ʃn/ *n* perseguição *f*

persever|e /pɜ:sɪˈvɪə(r)/ *vi* perseverar. **~ance** *n* perseverança *f*

Persian /ˈpɜ:ʃn/ *a* & *n* (*lang*) persa (*m*)

persist /pəˈsɪst/ *vi* persistir (**in doing** em fazer). **~ence** *n* persistência *f*. **~ent** *a* persistente; (*obstinate*) teimoso; (*continual*) contínuo, constante. **~ently** *adv* persistentemente

person /ˈpɜ:sn/ *n* pessoa *f*. **in ~** em pessoa

personal /ˈpɜ:sənl/ *a* pessoal; (*secretary*) particular. **~ stereo** estereo *m* pessoal. **~ly** *adv* pessoalmente

personality /pɜ:səˈnælətɪ/ *n* personalidade *f*; (*on TV*) vedete *f*

personify /pəˈsɒnɪfaɪ/ *vt* personificar

personnel /pɜ:sə'nel/ *n* pessoal *m*
perspective /pə'spektɪv/ *n* perspectiva *f*
perspir|e /pə'spaɪə(r)/ *vi* transpirar. **~ation** /-ə'reɪʃn/ *n* transpiração *f*
persua|de /pə'sweɪd/ *vt* persuadir (**to** a). **~sion** /-'sweɪʒn/ *n* persuasão *f*; (*belief*) crença *f*, convicção *f*. **~sive** /-'sweɪsɪv/ *a* persuasivo
pert /pɜ:t/ *a* (*saucy*) atrevido, descarado; (*lively*) vivo
pertain /pə'teɪn/ *vi* **~ to** pertencer a; (*be relevant*) ser pertinente a, (*P*) ser próprio de
pertinent /'pɜ:tɪnənt/ *a* pertinente
perturb /pə'tɜ:b/ *vt* perturbar, transtornar
Peru /pə'ru:/ *n* Peru *m*. **~vian** *a* & *n* peruano (*m*), (*P*) peruviano (*m*)
peruse /pə'ru:z/ *vt* ler com atenção
perva|de /pə'veɪd/ *vt* espalhar-se por, invadir. **~sive** *a* penetrante
pervers|e /pə'vɜ:s/ *a* que insiste no erro; (*wicked*) perverso; (*wayward*) caprichoso. **~ity** *n* obstinação *f*; (*wickedness*) perversidade *f*; (*waywardness*) capricho *m*, birra *f*
perver|t[1] /pə'vɜ:t/ *vt* perverter. **~sion** *n* perversão *f*
pervert[2] /'pɜ:vɜ:t/ *n* pervertido *m*
peseta /pə'seɪtə/ *n* peseta *f*
pessimis|t /'pesɪmɪst/ *n* pessimista *mf*. **~m** /-zəm/ *n* pessimismo *m*. **~tic** /-'mɪstɪk/ *a* pessimista
pest /pest/ *n* inseto *m*, (*P*) insecto *m* nocivo; (*animal*) animal *m* daninho; (*person*) peste *f*
pester /'pestə(r)/ *vt* incomodar (*colloq*)
pesticide /'pestɪsaɪd/ *n* pesticida *m*
pet /pet/ *n* animal *m* de estimação; (*favourite*) preferido *m*, querido *m* □ *a* (*rabbit etc*) de estimação □ *vt* (*pt* **petted**) acariciar. **~ name** nome *m* usado em família
petal /'petl/ *n* pétala *f*
peter /'pi:tə(r)/ *vi* **~ out** extinguir-se, acabar pouco a pouco, morrer (*fig*)
petition /pɪ'tɪʃn/ *n* petição *f* □ *vt* requerer
petrify /'petrɪfaɪ/ *vt* petrificar
petrol /'petrəl/ *n* gasolina *f*. **~ pump** bomba *f* de gasolina. **~ station** posto *m* de gasolina. **~ tank** tanque *m* de gasolina
petroleum /pɪ'trəʊlɪəm/ *n* petróleo *m*
petticoat /'petɪkəʊt/ *n* combinação *f*, anágua *f*
petty /'petɪ/ *a* (**-ier, -iest**) pequeno, insignificante; (*mean*) mesquinho. **~ cash** fundo *m* para pequenas despesas, caixa *f* pequena
petulan|t /'petjʊlənt/ *a* irritável. **~ce** *n* irritabilidade *f*
pew /pju:/ *n* banco (de igreja) *m*
pewter /'pju:tə(r)/ *n* estanho *m*
phallic /'fælɪk/ *a* fálico
phantom /'fæntəm/ *n* fantasma *m*
pharmaceutical /fa:mə'sju:tɪkl/ *a* farmacêutico
pharmac|y /'fa:məsɪ/ *n* farmácia *f*. **~ist** *n* farmacêutico *m*
phase /feɪz/ *n* fase *f* □ *vt* **~ in/out** introduzir/retirar progressivamente
PhD *abbr of* **Doctor of Philosophy** *n* doutorado *m*
pheasant /'feznt/ *n* faisão *m*
phenomen|on /fɪ'nɒmɪnən/ *n* (*pl* **-ena**) fenômeno *m*, (*P*) fenómeno *m*. **~al** *a* fenomenal
philanthrop|ist /fɪ'lænθrəpɪst/ *n* filantropo *m*. **~ic** /-ən'θrɒpɪk/ *a* filantrópico
Philippines /'fɪlɪpi:nz/ *npl* **the ~** as Filipinas *fpl*
philistine /'fɪlɪstaɪn/ *n* filisteu *m*
philosoph|y /fɪ'lɒsəfɪ/ *n* filosofia *f*. **~er** *n* filósofo *m*. **~ical** /-ə'sɒfɪkl/ *a* filosófico
phlegm /flem/ *n* (*med*) catarro *m*, fleuma *f*
phobia /'fəʊbɪə/ *n* fobia *f*
phone /fəʊn/ *n* (*colloq*) telefone *m* □ *vt/i* (*colloq*) telefonar (para). **on the ~** no telefone. **~ back** voltar a telefonar, ligar de volta. **~ book** lista *f* telefônica, (*P*) telefónica. **~ box** cabine *f* telefônica, (*P*) telefónica. **~ call** chamada *f*, telefonema *m*. **~-in** *n* programa *m* de rádio ou tv com participação dos ouvintes
phonecard /'fəʊnka:d/ *n* cartão *m* para uso em telefone público
phonetic /fə'netɪk/ *a* fonetico. **~s** *n* fonética *f*
phoney /'fəʊnɪ/ *a* (**-ier, -iest**) (*sl*) falso, fingido □ *n* (*sl: person*) fingido *m*; (*sl: thing*) falso *m*, (*P*) falsificação *f*
phosphate /'fɒsfeɪt/ *n* fosfato *m*
phosphorus /'fɒsfərəs/ *n* fósforo *m*
photo /'fəʊtəu/ *n* (*pl* **-os**) (*colloq*) retrato *m*, foto *f*
photocop|y /'fəʊtəʊkɒpɪ/ *n* fotocópia *f* □ *vt* fotocopiar. **~ier** *n* fotocopiadora *f*
photogenic /fəʊtəʊ'dʒenɪk/ *a* fotogênico, (*P*) fotogénico
photograph /'fəʊtəgra:f/ *n* fotografia *f* □ *vt* fotografar. **~er** /fə-'tɒgrəfə(r)/ *n* fotógrafo *m*. **~ic** /-'græfɪk/ *a* fotográfico. **~y** /fə-'tɒgrəfɪ/ *n* fotografia *f*
phrase /freɪz/ *n* expressão *f*, frase *f*; (*gram*) locução *f*, frase *f* elíptica □ *vt* exprimir. **~-book** *n* livro *m* de expressões idiomáticas
physical /'fɪzɪkl/ *a* físico

physician /fɪ'zɪʃn/ *n* médico *m*
physicist /'fɪzɪsɪst/ *n* físico *m*
physics /'fɪzɪks/ *n* física *f*
physiology /fɪzɪ'ɒlədʒɪ/ *n* fisiologia *f*
physiotherap|y /fɪzɪəʊ'θerəpɪ/ *n* fisioterapia *f*. **~ist** *n* fisioterapeuta *mf*
physique /fɪ'zi:k/ *n* físico *m*
pian|o /pɪ'ænəʊ/ *n* (*pl* **-os**) piano *m*. **~ist** /'pɪənɪst/ *n* pianista *mf*
pick[1] /pɪk/ *n* (*tool*) picareta *f*
pick[2] /pɪk/ *vt* escolher; (*flowers, fruit etc*) colher; (*lock*) forçar; (*teeth*) palitar □ *n* escolha *f*; (*best*) o/a melhor. **~ a quarrel with** puxar uma briga com. **~ holes in an argument** descobrir os pontos fracos dum argumento. **~ sb's pocket** bater a carteira de alg. **~ off** tirar, arrancar. **~ on** implicar com. **~ out** escolher; (*identify*) identificar, reconhecer. **~ up** *vt* apanhar; (*speed*) ganhar. **take one's ~** escolher livremente
pickaxe /'pɪkæks/ *n* picareta *f*
picket /'pɪkɪt/ *n* piquete *m*; (*single striker*) grevista *mf* de piquete □ *vt* (*pt* **picketed**) colocar um piquete em □ *vi* fazer piquete
pickings /'pɪkɪŋz/ *npl* restos *mpl*
pickle /'pɪkl/ *n* vinagre *m*. **~s** picles *mpl*, (*P*) pickles *mpl* □ *vt* conservar em vinagre. **in a ~** (*colloq*) numa encrenca (*colloq*)
pickpocket /'pɪkpɒkɪt/ *n* batedor *m* de carteiras, (*P*) carteirista *m*
picnic /'pɪknɪk/ *n* piquenique *m* □ *vi* (*pt* **picnicked**) piquenicar, (*P*) fazer um piquenique
pictorial /pɪk'tɔ:rɪəl/ *a* ilustrado
picture /'pɪktʃə(r)/ *n* imagem *f*; (*illustration*) estampa *f*, ilustração *f*; (*painting*) quadro *m*, pintura *f*; (*photo*) fotografia *f*, retrato *m*; (*drawing*) desenho *m*; (*fig*) descrição *f*, quadro *m* □ *vt* imaginar; (*describe*) pintar, descrever. **the ~s** o cinema
picturesque /pɪktʃə'resk/ *a* pitoresco
pidgin /'pɪdʒɪn/ *a* **~ English** inglês *m* estropiado
pie /paɪ/ *n* torta *f*, (*P*) tarte *f*; (*of meat*) empada *f*
piece /pi:s/ *n* pedaço *m*, bocado *m*; (*of machine, in game*) peça *f*; (*of currency*) moeda *f* □ *vt* **~ together** juntar, montar. **a ~ of advice/furniture/***etc* um conselho/um móvel/*etc*. **~-work** *n* trabalho *m* por, (*P*) a peça *or* por, (*P*) a tarefa. **take to ~s** desmontar
piecemeal /'pi:smi:l/ *a* aos poucos, pouco a pouco
pier /pɪə(r)/ *n* molhe *m*
pierc|e /pɪəs/ *vt* furar, penetrar. **~ing** *a* penetrante; (*of scream, pain*) lancinante
piety /'paɪətɪ/ *n* piedade *f*, devoção *f*
pig /pɪg/ *n* porco *m*. **~-headed** *a* cabeçudo, teimoso
pigeon /'pɪdʒɪn/ *n* pombo *m*. **~-hole** *n* escaninho *m*
piggy /'pɪgɪ/ *a* como um porco. **~-back** *adv* nas costas. **~ bank** cofre *m* de criança
pigment /'pɪgmənt/ *n* pigmento *m*. **~ation** /-'teɪʃn/ *n* pigmentação *f*
pigsty /'pɪgstaɪ/ *n* pocilga *f*, chiqueiro *m*
pigtail /'pɪgteɪl/ *n* trança *f*
pike /paɪk/ *n* (*pl invar*) (*fish*) lúcio *m*
pilchard /'pɪltʃəd/ *n* peixe *m* pequeno da família do arenque, sardinha *f* européia
pile /paɪl/ *n* pilha *f*; (*of carpet*) pêlo *m* □ *vt/i* amontoar(-se), empilhar(-se) (**into** em). **a ~ of** (*colloq*) um monte de (*colloq*). **~ up** acumular(-se). **~-up** *n* choque *m* em cadeia
piles /paɪlz/ *npl* hemorróidas *fpl*
pilfer /'pɪlfə(r)/ *vt* furtar. **~age** *n* furto *m* (de coisas pequenas *or* em pequenas quantidades)
pilgrim /'pɪlgrɪm/ *n* peregrino *m*, romeiro *m*. **~age** *n* peregrinação *f*, romaria *f*
pill /pɪl/ *n* pílula *f*, comprimido *m*
pillage /'pɪlɪdʒ/ *n* pilhagem *f*, saque *m* □ *vt* pilhar, saquear
pillar /'pɪlə(r)/ *n* pilar *m*. **~-box** *n* marco *m* do correio
pillion /'pɪlɪən/ *n* assento *m* traseiro de motorizada. **ride ~** ir no assento de trás
pillow /'pɪləʊ/ *n* travesseiro *m*
pillowcase /'pɪləʊkeɪs/ *n* fronha *f*
pilot /'paɪlət/ *n* piloto *m* □ *vt* (*pt* **piloted**) pilotar. **~-light** *n* piloto *m*; (*electr*) lâmpada *f* testemunho; (*gas*) piloto *m*
pimento /pɪ'mentəʊ/ *n* (*pl* **-os**) pimentão *m* vermelho
pimple /'pɪmpl/ *n* borbulha *f*, espinha *f*
pin /pɪn/ *n* alfinete *m*; (*techn*) cavilha *f* □ *vt* (*pt* **pinned**) pregar *or* prender com alfinete(s); (*hold down*) prender, segurar. **have ~s and needles** estar com cãibra. **~ sb down** (*fig*) obrigar alg a definir-se, apertar alg (*fig*). **~-point** *vt* localizar com precisão. **~-stripe** *a* de listras finas. **~ up** pregar. **~-up** *n* (*colloq*) pin-up *f*
pinafore /'pɪnəfɔ:(r)/ *n* avental *m*. **~ dress** veste *f*
pincers /'pɪnsəz/ *npl* (*tool*) torquês *f*, (*P*) alicate *m*; (*med*) pinça *f*; (*zool*) pinça(s) *f*(*pl*), tenaz(es) *f*(*pl*)

pinch /pɪntʃ/ *vt* apertar; (*sl: steal*) surripiar (*colloq*) □ *n* aperto *m*; (*tweak*) beliscão *m*; (*small amount*) pitada *f*. **at a ~** em caso de necessidade

pine[1] /paɪn/ *n* (*tree*) pinheiro *m*; (*wood*) pinho *m*

pine[2] /paɪn/ *vi* **~ away** definhar, consumir-se. **~ for** suspirar por

pineapple /'paɪnæpl/ *n* abacaxi *m*, (*P*) ananás *m*

ping-pong /'pɪŋpɒŋ/ *n* pingue-pongue *m*

pink /pɪŋk/ *a* & *n* rosa (*m*)

pinnacle /'pɪnəkl/ *n* pináculo *m*

pint /paɪnt/ *n* quartilho *m* (= *0,57l*; *Amer* = *0,47l*)

pioneer /paɪə'nɪə(r)/ *n* pioneiro *m* □ *vt* ser o pioneiro em, preparar o caminho para

pious /'paɪəs/ *a* piedoso, devoto

pip /pɪp/ *n* (*seed*) pevide *f*

pipe /paɪp/ *n* cano *m*, tubo *m*; (*of smoker*) cachimbo *m* □ *vt* encanar, canalizar. **~ down** calar a boca

pipeline /'paɪplaɪn/ *n* (*for oil*) oleoduto *m*; (*for gas*) gaseoduto *m*, (*P*) gasoduto *m*. **in the ~** (*fig*) encaminhado

piping /'paɪpɪŋ/ *n* tubagem *f*. **~ hot** muito quente

piquant /'pi:kənt/ *a* picante

pira|te /'paɪərət/ *n* pirata *m*. **~cy** *n* pirataria *f*

Pisces /'paɪsi:z/ *n* (*astr*) Peixe *m*, (*P*) Pisces *m*

pistol /'pɪstl/ *n* pistola *f*

piston /'pɪstən/ *n* êmbolo *m*, pistão *m*

pit /pɪt/ *n* (*hole*) cova *f*, fosso *m*; (*mine*) poço *m*; (*quarry*) pedreira *f* □ *vt* (*pt* **pitted**) picar, esburacar; (*fig*) opor. **~ o.s. against** (*struggle*) medir-se com

pitch[1] /pɪtʃ/ *n* breu *m*. **~-black** *a* escuro como breu

pitch[2] /pɪtʃ/ *vt* (*throw*) lançar; (*tent*) armar □ *vi* cair □ *n* (*slope*) declive *m*; (*of sound*) som *m*; (*of voice*) altura *f*; (*sport*) campo *m*

pitchfork /'pɪtʃfɔ:k/ *n* forcado *m*

pitfall /'pɪtfɔ:l/ *n* (*fig*) cilada *f*, perigo *m* inesperado

pith /pɪθ/ *n* (*of orange*) parte *f* branca da casca, mesocarpo *m*; (*fig: essential part*) cerne *m*, âmago *m*

pithy /'pɪθɪ/ *a* (**-ier, -iest**) preciso, conciso

piti|ful /'pɪtɪfl/ *a* lastimoso; (*contemptible*) miserável. **~less** *a* impiedoso

pittance /'pɪtns/ *n* salário *m* miserável, miséria *f*

pity /'pɪtɪ/ *n* dó *m*, pena *f*, piedade *f* □ *vt* compadecer-se de. **it's a ~** é uma pena. **take ~ on** ter pena de. **what a ~!** que pena!

pivot /'pɪvət/ *n* eixo *m* □ *vt* (*pt* **pivoted**) girar em torno de

placard /'plæka:d/ *n* (*poster*) cartaz *m*

placate /plə'keɪt/ *vt* apaziguar, aplacar

place /pleɪs/ *n* lugar *m*, sítio *m*; (*house*) casa *f*; (*seat, rank etc*) lugar *m* □ *vt* colocar, pôr. **~ an order** fazer uma encomenda. **at/to my ~** em a *or* na minha casa. **~-mat** *n* pano *m* de mesa individual, (*P*) napperon *m* à americana

placid /'plæsɪd/ *a* plácido

plagiar|ize /'pleɪdʒəraɪz/ *vt* plagiar. **~ism** *n* plágio *m*

plague /pleɪg/ *n* peste *f*; (*of insects*) praga *f* □ *vt* atormentar, atazanar

plaice /pleɪs/ *n* (*pl invar*) solha *f*

plain /pleɪn/ *a* (**-er, -est**) claro; (*candid*) franco; (*simple*) simples; (*not pretty*) sem beleza; (*not patterned*) liso □ *adv* com franqueza □ *n* planície *f*. **in ~ clothes** à paisana. **~ly** *adv* claramente; (*candidly*) francamente

plaintiff /'pleɪntɪf/ *n* queixoso *m*

plaintive /'pleɪntɪv/ *a* queixoso

plait /plæt/ *vt* entrançar □ *n* trança *f*

plan /plæn/ *n* plano *m*, projeto *m*, (*P*) projecto *m*; (*of a house, city etc*) plano *m*, planta *f* □ *vt* (*pt* **planned**) planear, planejar □ *vi* fazer planos. **~ to do** ter a intenção de fazer

plane[1] /pleɪn/ *n* (*level*) plano *m*; (*aeroplane*) avião *m* □ *a* plano

plane[2] /pleɪn/ *n* (*tool*) plaina *f* □ *vt* aplainar

planet /'plænɪt/ *n* planeta *m*

plank /plæŋk/ *n* prancha *f*

planning /'plænɪŋ/ *n* planeamento *m*, planejamento *m*. **~ permission** permissão *f* para construir

plant /pla:nt/ *n* planta *f*; (*techn*) aparelhagem *f*; (*factory*) fábrica *f* □ *vt* plantar. **~ a bomb** colocar uma bomba. **~ation** /-'teɪʃn/ *n* plantação *f*

plaque /pla:k/ *n* placa *f*; (*on teeth*) tártaro *m*, pedra *f*

plaster /'pla:stə(r)/ *n* reboco *m*; (*adhesive*) esparadrapo *m*, band-aid *m* □ *vt* rebocar; (*cover*) cobrir (**with** com, de). **in ~** engessado. **~ of Paris** gesso *m*. **~er** *n* rebocador *m*, caiador *m*

plastic /'plæstɪk/ *a* plástico □ *n* plástica *f*. **~ surgery** cirurgia *f* plástica

plate /pleɪt/ *n* prato *m*; (*in book*) gravura *f* □ *vt* revestir de metal

plateau /'plætəʊ/ *n* (*pl* **-eaux** /-əʊz/) planalto *m*, platô *m*

platform /'plætfɔ:m/ *n* estrado *m*; (*for speaking*) tribuna *f*; (*rail*) plataforma *f*, cais *m*; (*fig*) programa *m* de partido político. ~ **ticket** bilhete *m* de gare

platinum /'plætɪnəm/ *n* platina *f*

platitude /'plætɪtju:d/ *n* banalidade *f*, lugar-comum *m*

platonic /plə'tɒnɪk/ *a* platônico, (*P*) platónico

plausible /'plɔ:zəbl/ *a* plausível; (*person*) convincente

play /pleɪ/ *vt*/*i* (*for amusement*) brincar; (*instrument*) tocar; (*cards, game*) jogar; (*opponent*) jogar contra; (*match*) disputar □ *n* jogo *m*; (*theatre*) peça *f*; (*movement*) folga *f*, margem *f*. ~ **down** minimizar. ~ **on** (*take advantage of*) aproveitar-se de. ~ **safe** jogar pelo seguro. ~ **up** (*colloq*) dar problemas (a). ~**-group** *n* jardim *m* de infância, (*P*) jardim *m* infantil. ~**-pen** *n* cercado *m* para crianças

playboy /'pleɪbɔɪ/ *n* play-boy *m*

player /'pleɪə(r)/ *n* jogador *m*; (*theat*) artista *mf*; (*mus*) artista *mf*, executante *mf*, instrumentista *mf*

playful /'pleɪfl/ *a* brincalhão *m*

playground /'pleɪgraʊnd/ *n* pátio *m* de recreio

playing /'pleɪɪŋ/ *n* atuação *f*, (*P*) actuação *f*. ~**-card** *n* carta *f* de jogar. ~**-field** *n* campo *m* de jogos

playwright /'pleɪraɪt/ *n* dramaturgo *m*

plc *abbr* (*of public limited company*) SARL

plea /pli:/ *n* súplica *f*; (*reason*) pretexto *m*, desculpa *f*; (*jur*) alegação *f* da defesa

plead /pli:d/ *vt*/*i* pleitear; (*as excuse*) alegar. ~ **guilty** confessar-se culpado. ~ **with** implorar a

pleasant /'pleznt/ *a* agradável

pleas|e /pli:z/ *vt*/*i* agradar (a), dar prazer (a) □ *adv* por favor, (*P*) se faz favor. **they** ~**e themselves, they do as they** ~**e** eles fazem como bem entendem. ~**ed** *a* contente, satisfeito (**with** com). ~**ing** *a* agradável

pleasur|e /'pleʒə(r)/ *n* prazer *m*. ~**able** *a* agradável

pleat /pli:t/ *n* prega *f* □ *vt* preguear

pledge /pledʒ/ *n* penhor *m*, garantia *f*; (*fig*) promessa *f* □ *vt* prometer; (*pawn*) empenhar

plentiful /'plentɪfl/ *a* abundante

plenty /'plentɪ/ *n* abundância *f*, fartura *f*. ~ **(of)** muito (de); (*enough*) bastante (de)

pliable /'plaɪəbl/ *a* flexível

pliers /'plaɪəz/ *npl* alicate *m*

plight /plaɪt/ *n* triste situação *f*

plimsoll /'plɪmsəl/ *n* alpargata *f*, tênis *m*, (*P*) ténis *m*

plinth /plɪnθ/ *n* plinto *m*

plod /plɒd/ *vi* (*pt* **plodded**) caminhar lentamente; (*work*) trabalhar, marrar (*sl*). ~**der** *n* trabalhador *m* lento mas perseverante. ~**ding** *a* lento

plonk /plɒŋk/ *n* (*sl*) vinho *m* ordinário, (*P*) carrascão *m*

plot /plɒt/ *n* complô *m*, conspiração *f*; (*of novel etc*) trama *f*; (*of land*) lote *m* □ *vt*/*i* (*pt* **plotted**) conspirar; (*mark out*) traçar

plough /plaʊ/ *n* arado *m* □ *vt*/*i* arar. ~ **back** reinvestir. ~ **into** colidir. ~ **through** abrir caminho por

ploy /plɔɪ/ *n* (*colloq*) estratagema *m*

pluck /plʌk/ *vt* apanhar; (*bird*) depenar; (*eyebrows*) depilar; (*mus*) tanger □ *n* coragem *f*. ~ **up courage** ganhar coragem. ~**y** *a* corajoso

plug /plʌg/ *n* tampão *m*; (*electr*) tomada *f*, (*P*) ficha *f* □ *vt* (*pt* **plugged**) tapar com tampão; (*colloq: publicize*) fazer grande propaganda de □ *vi* ~ **away** (*colloq*) trabalhar com afinco. ~ **in** (*electr*) ligar. ~**-hole** *n* buraco *m* do cano

plum /plʌm/ *n* ameixa *f*

plumb /plʌm/ *adv* exatamente, (*P*) exactamente, mesmo □ *vt* sondar. ~**-line** *n* fio *m* de prumo

plumb|er /'plʌmə(r)/ *n* bombeiro *m*, encanador *m*, (*P*) canalizador *m*. ~**ing** *n* encanamento *m*, (*P*) canalização *f*

plummet /'plʌmɪt/ *vi* (*pt* **plummeted**) despencar

plump /plʌmp/ *a* (**-er, -est**) rechonchudo, roliço □ *vi* ~ **for** optar por. ~**ness** *n* gordura *f*

plunder /'plʌndə(r)/ *vt* pilhar, saquear □ *n* pilhagem *f*, saque *m*; (*goods*) despojo *m*

plunge /plʌndʒ/ *vt*/*i* mergulhar, atirar(-se), afundar(-se) □ *n* mergulho *m*. **take the** ~ (*fig*) decidir-se, dar o salto (*fig*)

plunger /'plʌndʒə(r)/ *n* (*of pump*) êmbolo *m*, pistão *m*; (*for sink etc*) desentupidor *m*

pluperfect /plu:'pɜ:fɪkt/ *n* mais-que-perfeito *m*

plural /'plʊərəl/ *a* plural; (*noun*) no plural □ *n* plural *m*

plus /plʌs/ *prep* mais □ *a* positivo □ *n* sinal +; (*fig*) qualidade *f* positiva

plush /plʌʃ/ *n* pelúcia *f* □ *a* de pelúcia; (*colloq*) de luxo

ply /plaɪ/ *vt* (*tool*) manejar; (*trade*) exercer □ *vi* (*ship, bus*) fazer carreira entre dois lugares. ~ **sb with drink** encher alguém de bebidas

plywood /'plaɪwʊd/ *n* madeira *f* compensada

p.m. /pi:'em/ *adv* da tarde, da noite

pneumatic /nju:'mætɪk/ *a* pneumático. ~ **drill** broca *f* pneumática

pneumonia /nju:'məʊnɪə/ *n* pneumonia *f*

PO *abbr see* **Post Office**

poach /pəʊtʃ/ *vt/i* (*steal*) caçar/pescar em propriedade alheia; (*culin*) fazer pochê, (*P*) escalfar. ~**ed eggs** ovos *mpl* pochês, (*P*) ovos *mpl* escalfados

pocket /'pɒkɪt/ *n* bolso *m*, algibeira *f* □ *a* de algibeira □ *vt* meter no bolso. ~**-book** *n* (*notebook*) livro *m* de apontamentos; (*Amer: handbag*) carteira *f*. ~**-money** *n* (*monthly*) mesada *f*; (*weekly*) semanada *f*, dinheiro *m* para pequenas despesas

pod /pɒd/ *n* vagem *f*

poem /'pəʊɪm/ *n* poema *m*

poet /'pəʊɪt/ *n* poeta *m*, poetisa *f*. ~**ic** /-'etɪk/ *a* poético

poetry /'pəʊɪtrɪ/ *n* poesia *f*

poignant /'pɔɪnjənt/ *a* pungente, doloroso

point /pɔɪnt/ *n* ponto *m*; (*tip*) ponta *f*; (*decimal point*) vírgula *f*; (*meaning*) sentido *m*, razão *m*; (*electr*) tomada *f*. ~**s** (*rail*) agulhas *fpl* □ *vt/i* (*aim*) apontar (**at** para); (*show*) apontar, indicar (**at/to** para). **on the** ~ **of** prestes a, quase a. ~**-blank** *a & adv* à *queima-roupa; (fig) categórico.* ~ **of view** ponto *m* de vista. ~ **out** apontar, fazer ver. **that is a good** ~ (*remark*) é uma boa observação. **to the** ~ a propósito. **what is the** ~? de que adianta?

pointed /'pɔɪntɪd/ *a* ponteagudo; (*of remark*) intencional, contundente

pointer /'pɔɪntə(r)/ *n* ponteiro *m*; (*colloq: hint*) sugestão *f*

pointless /'pɔɪntlɪs/ *a* inútil, sem sentido

poise /pɔɪz/ *n* equilíbrio *m*; (*carriage*) porte *m*; (*fig: self-possession*) presença *f*, segurança *f*. ~**d** *a* equilibrado; (*person*) seguro de si

poison /'pɔɪzn/ *n* veneno *m*, peçonha *f* □ *vt* envenenar. **blood-**~**ing** *n* envenenamento *m* do sangue. **food-**~**ing** *n* intoxicação *f* alimentar. ~**ous** *a* venenoso

poke /pəʊk/ *vt/i* espetar; (*with elbow*) acotovelar; (*fire*) atiçar □ *n* espetadela *f*; (*with elbow*) cotovelada *f*. ~ **about** esgaravatar, remexer, procurar. ~ **fun at** fazer troça/pouco de. ~ **out** (*head*) enfiar

poker[1] /'pəʊkə(r)/ *n* atiçador *m*

poker[2] /'pəʊkə(r)/ *n* (*cards*) pôquer *m*, (*P*) póquer *m*

poky /'pəʊkɪ/ *a* (**-ier, -iest**) acanhado, apertado

Poland /'pəʊlənd/ *n* Polônia *f*, (*P*) Polónia *f*

polar /'pəʊlə(r)/ *a* polar. ~ **bear** urso *m* branco

polarize /'pəʊləraɪz/ *vt* polarizar

pole[1] /pəʊl/ *n* vara *f*; (*for flag*) mastro *m*; (*post*) poste *m*

pole[2] /pəʊl/ *n* (*geog*) pólo *m*

Pole /pəʊl/ *n* polaco *m*

polemic /pə'lemɪk/ *n* polêmica *f*, (*P*) polémica *f*

police /pə'li:s/ *n* polícia *f* □ *vt* policiar. ~ **state** estado *m* policial. ~ **station** distrito *m*, delegacia *f*, (*P*) esquadra *f* de polícia

police|man /pə'li:smən/ *n* (*pl* **-men**) policial *m*, (*P*) polícia *m*, guarda *m*, agente *m* de polícia. ~**-woman** (*pl* **-women**) *n* polícia *f* feminina, (*P*) mulher-polícia *f*

policy[1] /'pɒlɪsɪ/ *n* (*plan of action*) política *f*

policy[2] /'pɒlɪsɪ/ *n* (*insurance*) apólice *f* de seguro

polio /'pəʊlɪəʊ/ *n* polio *f*

polish /'pɒlɪʃ/ *vt* polir, dar lustro em; (*shoes*) engraxar; (*floor*) encerar □ *n* (*for shoes*) graxa *f*; (*for floor*) cera *f*; (*for nails*) esmalte *m*, (*P*) verniz *m*; (*shine*) polimento *m*; (*fig*) requinte *m*. ~ **off** acabar (rapidamente). ~ **up** (*language*) aperfeiçoar. ~**ed** *a* requintado, elegante

Polish /'pəʊlɪʃ/ *a & n* polonês (*m*), (*P*) polaco (*m*)

polite /pə'laɪt/ *a* polido, educado, delicado. ~**ly** *adv* delicadamente. ~**ness** *n* delicadeza *f*, cortesia *f*

political /pə'lɪtɪkl/ *a* político

politician /pɒlɪ'tɪʃn/ *n* político *m*

politics /'pɒlətɪks/ *n* política *f*

polka /'pɒlkə/ *n* polca *f*. ~ **dots** bolas *fpl*

poll /pəʊl/ *n* votação *f*; (*survey*) sondagem *f*, pesquisa *f* □ *vt* (*votes*) obter. **go to the** ~**s** votar, ir às urnas. ~**ing-booth** *n* cabine *f* de voto

pollen /'pɒlən/ *n* pólen *m*

pollut|e /pə'lu:t/ *vt* poluir. ~**ion** /-ʃn/ *n* poluição *f*

polo /'pəʊləʊ/ *n* pólo *m*. ~ **neck** gola *f* rolê

polyester /pɒlɪ'estə/ *n* poliéster *m*

polytechnic /pɒlɪ'teknɪk/ *n* politécnica *f*

polythene /'pɒlɪθi:n/ *n* politeno *m*. ~ **bag** *n* saco *m* de plástico

pomegranate /'pɒmɪgrænɪt/ *n* romã *f*

pomp /pɒmp/ *n* pompa *f*

pompon /'pɒmpɒn/ *n* pompom *m*

pomp|ous /'pɒmpəs/ *a* pomposo. ~**osity** /-'pɒsətɪ/ *n* imponência *f*

pond /pɒnd/ *n* lagoa *f*, lago *m*; (*artificial*) tanque *m*, lago *m*

ponder /'pɒndə(r)/ *vt/i* ponderar, meditar (**over** sobre)

pong /pɒŋ/ *n* (*sl*) pivete *m* □ *vi* (*sl*) cheirar mal, tresandar

pony /ˈpəʊnɪ/ *n* pônei *m*, (*P*) pónei *m*. **~-tail** *n* rabo *m* de cavalo. **~-trekking** *n* passeio *m* de pônei, (*P*) pónei

poodle /ˈpu:dl/ *n* cão *m* de água, caniche *m*

pool[1] /pu:l/ *n* (*puddle*) charco *m*, poça *f*; (*for swimming*) piscina *f*

pool[2] /pu:l/ *n* (*fund*) fundo *m* comum; (*econ, comm*) pool *m*; (*game*) forma *f* de bilhar. **~s** loteca *f*, (*P*) totobola *m* □ *vt* pôr num fundo comum

poor /pʊə(r)/ *a* (**-er, -est**) pobre; (*not good*) medíocre. **~ly** *adv* mal □ *a* doente

pop[1] /pɒp/ *n* estalido *m*, ruído *m* seco □ *vt*/*i* (*pt* **popped**) dar um estalido, estalar; (*of cork*) saltar. **~ in/out/off** entrar/sair/ir-se embora. **~ up** aparecer de repente, saltar

pop[2] /pɒp/ *n* música *f* pop □ *a* pop *invar*

popcorn /ˈpɒpkɔ:n/ *n* pipoca *f*

pope /pəʊp/ *n* papa *m*

poplar /ˈpɒplə(r)/ *n* choupo *m*, álamo *m*

poppy /ˈpɒpɪ/ *n* papoula *f*

popular /ˈpɒpjʊlə(r)/ *a* popular; (*in fashion*) em voga, na moda. **be ~ with** ser popular entre. **~ity** /-ˈlærətɪ/ *n* popularidade *f*. **~ize** *vt* popularizar, vulgarizar

populat|e /ˈpɒpjʊleɪt/ *vt* povoar. **~ion** /-ˈleɪʃn/ *n* população *f*

populous /ˈpɒpjʊləs/ *a* populoso

porcelain /ˈpɔ:slɪn/ *n* porcelana *f*

porch /pɔ:tʃ/ *n* alpendre *m*; (*Amer*) varanda *f*

porcupine /ˈpɔ:kjʊpaɪn/ *n* porcoespinho *m*

pore[1] /pɔ:(r)/ *n* poro *m*

pore[2] /pɔ:(r)/ *vi* **~ over** examinar, estudar

pork /pɔ:k/ *n* carne *f* de porco

pornograph|y /pɔ:ˈnɒgrəfɪ/ *n* pornografia *f*. **~ic** /-əˈgræfɪk/ *a* pornográfico

porous /ˈpɔ:rəs/ *a* poroso

porpoise /ˈpɔ:pəs/ *n* toninha *f*, (*P*) golfinho *m*

porridge /ˈpɒrɪdʒ/ *n* (papa *f* de) flocos *mpl* de aveia

port[1] /pɔ:t/ *n* (*harbour*) porto *m*

port[2] /pɔ:t/ *n* (*wine*) (vinho do) Porto *m*

portable /ˈpɔ:təbl/ *a* portátil

porter[1] /ˈpɔ:tə(r)/ *n* (*carrier*) carregador *m*

porter[2] /ˈpɔ:tə(r)/ *n* (*doorkeeper*) porteiro *m*

portfolio /pɔ:tˈfəʊlɪəʊ/ *n* (*pl* **-os**) (*case, post*) pasta *f*; (*securities*) carteira *f* de investimentos

porthole /ˈpɔ:thəʊl/ *n* vigia *f*

portion /ˈpɔ:ʃn/ *n* (*share, helping*) porção *f*; (*part*) parte *f*

portly /ˈpɔ:tlɪ/ *a* (**-ier, -iest**) corpulento e digno

portrait /ˈpɔ:trɪt/ *n* retrato *m*

portray /pɔ:ˈtreɪ/ *vt* retratar, pintar; (*fig*) descrever. **~al** *n* retrato *m*

Portug|al /ˈpɔ:tjʊgl/ *n* Portugal *m*. **~uese** /-ˈgi:z/ *a* & *n invar* português (*m*)

pose /pəʊz/ *vt*/*i* (fazer) posar; (*question*) fazer □ *n* pose *f*, postura *f*. **~ as** fazer-se passar por

poser /ˈpəʊzə(r)/ *n* quebra-cabeças *m*

posh /pɒʃ/ *a* (*sl*) chique *invar*

position /pəˈzɪʃn/ *n* posição *f*; (*job*) lugar *m*, colocação *f*; (*state*) situação *f* □ *vt* colocar

positive /ˈpɒzətɪv/ *a* positivo; (*definite*) categórico, definitivo; (*colloq: downright*) autêntico. **she's ~ that** ela tem certeza que. **~ly** *adv* positivamente; (*absolutely*) completamente

possess /pəˈzes/ *vt* possuir. **~ion** /-ʃn/ *n* posse *f*; (*thing possessed*) possessão *f*. **~or** *n* possuidor *m*

possessive /pəˈzesɪv/ *a* possessivo

possib|le /ˈpɒsəbl/ *a* possível. **~ility** /-ˈbɪlətɪ/ *n* possibilidade *f*

possibly /ˈpɒsəblɪ/ *adv* possivelmente, talvez. **if I ~ can** se me fôr possível. **I cannot ~ leave** estou impossibilitado de partir

post[1] /pəʊst/ *n* (*pole*) poste *m* □ *vt* (*notice*) afixar, pregar

post[2] /pəʊst/ *n* (*station, job*) posto *m* □ *vt* colocar; (*appoint*) colocar

post[3] /pəʊst/ *n* (*mail*) correio *m* □ *a* postal □ *vt* mandar pelo correio. **keep ~ed** manter informado. **~-code** *n* código *m* postal. **P~ Office** agência *f* dos correios, (*P*) estação *f* dos correios; (*corporation*) Departamento *m* dos Correios e Telégrafos, (*P*) Correios, Telégrafos e Telefones *mpl* (CTT)

post- /pəʊst/ *pref* pós-

postage /ˈpəʊstɪdʒ/ *n* porte *m*

postal /ˈpəʊstl/ *a* postal. **~ order** vale *m* postal

postcard /ˈpəʊstka:d/ *n* cartão-postal *m*, (*P*) (bilhete) postal *m*

poster /ˈpəʊstə(r)/ *n* cartaz *m*

posterity /pɒˈsterətɪ/ *n* posteridade *f*

postgraduate /pəʊstˈgrædʒʊet/ *n* pós-graduado *m*

posthumous /ˈpɒstjʊməs/ *a* póstumo. **~ly** *adv* a título póstumo

postman /ˈpəʊstmən/ *n* (*pl* **-men**) carteiro *m*

postmark /'pəʊstma:k/ *n* carimbo *m* do correio
post-mortem /pəʊst'mɔ:təm/ *n* autópsia *f*
postpone /pə'spəʊn/ *vt* adiar. **~ment** *n* adiamento *m*
postscript /'pəʊsskrɪpt/ *n* post scriptum *m*
postulate /'pɒstjʊleɪt/ *vt* postular
posture /'pɒstʃə(r)/ *n* postura *f*, posição *f* □ *vi* posar
post-war /'pəʊstwɔ:(r)/ *a* de após-guerra
posy /'pəʊzɪ/ *n* raminho *m* de flores
pot /pɒt/ *n* pote *m*; (*for cooking*) panela *f*; (*for plants*) vaso *m*; (*sl: marijuana*) maconha *f* □ *vt* (*pt* **potted**) **~ (up)** plantar em vaso. **go to ~** (*sl: business*) arruinar, degringolar (*colloq*); (*sl: person*) estar arruinado *or* liquidado. **~-belly** *n* pança *f*, barriga *f*. **take ~ luck** aceitar o que houver. **take a ~-shot** dar um tiro de perto (**at** em); (*at random*) dar um tiro a esmo (**at** em)
potato /pə'teɪtəʊ/ *n* (*pl* **-oes**) batata *f*
poten|t /'pəʊtnt/ *a* potente, poderoso; (*drink*) forte. **~cy** *n* potência *f*
potential /pə'tenʃl/ *a* & *n* potencial (*m*). **~ly** *adv* potencialmente
pothol|e /'pɒthəʊl/ *n* caverna *f*, caldeirão *m*; (*in road*) buraco *m*. **~ing** *n* espeleologia *f*
potion /'pəʊʃn/ *n* poção *f*
potted /'pɒtɪd/ *a* (*of plant*) de vaso; (*preserved*) de conserva
potter[1] /'pɒtə(r)/ *n* oleiro *m*, ceramista *mf*. **~y** *n* olaria *f*, cerâmica *f*
potter[2] /'pɒtə(r)/ *vi* entreter-se com isto ou aquilo
potty[1] /'pɒtɪ/ *a* (**-ier, -iest**) (*sl*) doido, pirado (*sl*), (*P*) chanfrado (*colloq*)
potty[2] /'pɒtɪ/ *n* (**-ties**) (*colloq*) penico *m* de criança
pouch /paʊtʃ/ *n* bolsa *f*; (*for tobacco*) tabaqueira *f*
poultice /'pəʊltɪs/ *n* cataplasma *f*
poultry /'pəʊltrɪ/ *n* aves *fpl* domésticas
pounce /paʊns/ *vi* atirar-se (**on** sobre, para cima de) □ *n* salto *m*
pound[1] /paʊnd/ *n* (*weight*) libra *f* (*= 453 g*); (*money*) libra *f*
pound[2] /paʊnd/ *n* (*for dogs*) canil municipal *m*; (*for cars*) parque de viaturas rebocadas *m*
pound[3] /paʊnd/ *vt/i* (*crush*) esmagar, pisar; (*of heart*) bater com força; (*bombard*) bombardear; (*on piano etc*) martelar
pour /pɔ:(r)/ *vt* deitar □ *vi* correr; (*rain*) chover torrencialmente. **~ in/out** (*of people*) afluir/sair em massa. **~ off** *or* **out** esvaziar, vazar. **~ing rain** chuva *f* torrencial
pout /paʊt/ *vt/i* **~ (one's lips)** (*sulk*) fazer beicinho; (*in annoyance*) ficar de trombas □ *n* beicinho *m*
poverty /'pɒvətɪ/ *n* pobreza *f*, miséria *f*. **~-stricken** *a* pobre
powder /'paʊdə(r)/ *n* pó *m*; (*for face*) pó-de-arroz *m* □ *vt* polvilhar; (*face*) empoar. **~ed** *a* em pó. **~-room** *n* toalete *m*, toucador *m*. **~y** *a* como pó
power /'paʊə(r)/ *n* poder *m*; (*maths, mech*) potência *f*; (*energy*) energia *f*; (*electr*) corrente *f*. **~ cut** corte *m* de energia, blecaute *m*. **~ station** central *f* elétrica, (*P*) eléctrica. **~ed by** movido a; (*jet etc*) de propulsão. **~ful** *a* poderoso; (*mech*) potente. **~less** *a* impotente
practicable /'præktɪkəbl/ *a* viável
practical /'præktɪkl/ *a* prático. **~ joke** brincadeira *f* de mau gosto
practically /'præktɪklɪ/ *adv* praticamente
practice /'præktɪs/ *n* prática *f*; (*of law etc*) exercício *m*; (*sport*) treino *m*; (*clients*) clientela *f*. **in ~** (*in fact*) na prática; (*well-trained*) em forma. **out of ~** destreinado, sem prática. **put into ~** pôr em prática
practis|e /'præktɪs/ *vt/i* (*skill, sport*) praticar, exercitar-se em; (*profession*) exercer; (*put into practice*) pôr em prática. **~ed** *a* experimentado, experiente. **~ing** *a* (*Catholic etc*) praticante
practitioner /præk'tɪʃənə(r)/ *n* praticante *mf*. **general ~** médico *m* de clínica geral *or* de família
pragmatic /præg'mætɪk/ *a* pragmático
prairie /'preərɪ/ *n* pradaria *f*
praise /preɪz/ *vt* louvar, elogiar □ *n* elogio(s) *m(pl)*, louvor(es) *m(pl)*
praiseworthy /'preɪzwɜ:ðɪ/ *a* louvável, digno de louvor
pram /præm/ *n* carrinho *m* de bebê, (*P*) bebé
prance /pra:ns/ *vi* (*of horse*) curvetear, empinar-se; (*of person*) pavonear-se
prank /præŋk/ *n* brincadeira *f* de mau gosto
prattle /'prætl/ *vi* tagarelar
prawn /prɔ:n/ *n* camarão *m* grande, (*P*) gamba *f*
pray /preɪ/ *vi* rezar, orar
prayer /preə(r)/ *n* oração *f*. **the Lord's P~** o Padre-Nosso. **~-book** *n* missal *m*
pre- /pri:/ *pref* pré-
preach /pri:tʃ/ *vt/i* pregar (**at, to** a). **~er** *n* pregador *m*
preamble /pri:'æmbl/ *n* preâmbulo *m*
prearrange /pri:ə'reɪndʒ/ *vt* combinar *or* arranjar de antemão

precarious /prɪˈkeərɪəs/ *a* precário; (*of position*) instável, inseguro

precaution /prɪˈkɔːʃn/ *n* precaução *f*. **~ary** *a* de precaução

preced|e /prɪˈsiːd/ *vt* preceder. **~ing** *a* precedente

precedent /ˈpresɪdənt/ *n* precedente *m*

precinct /ˈpriːsɪŋkt/ *n* precinto *m*; (*Amer: district*) circunscrição *f*. **(pedestrian) ~** área *f* de pedestres, (*P*) zona *f* para peões

precious /ˈpreʃəs/ *a* precioso

precipice /ˈpresɪpɪs/ *n* precipício *m*

precipitat|e /prɪˈsɪpɪteɪt/ *vt* precipitar □ *a* /-ɪtət/ precipitado. **~ion** /-ˈteɪʃn/ *n* precipitação *f*

precis|e /prɪˈsaɪs/ *a* preciso; (*careful*) meticuloso. **~ely** *adv* precisamente. **~ion** /-ˈsɪʒn/ *n* precisão *f*

preclude /prɪˈkluːd/ *vt* evitar, excluir, impedir

precocious /prɪˈkəʊʃəs/ *a* precoce

preconc|eived /priːkənˈsiːvd/ *a* preconcebido. **~eption** /priːkənˈsepʃn/ *n* idéia *f* preconcebida

precursor /priːˈkɜːsə(r)/ *n* precursor *m*

predator /ˈpredətə(r)/ *n* animal *m* de rapina, predador *m*. **~y** *a* predatório

predecessor /ˈpriːdɪsesə(r)/ *n* predecessor *m*

predicament /prɪˈdɪkəmənt/ *n* situação *f* difícil

predict /prɪˈdɪkt/ *vt* predizer, prognosticar. **~able** *a* previsível. **~ion** /-ʃn/ *n* predição *f*, prognóstico *m*

predominant /prɪˈdɒmɪnənt/ *a* predominante, preponderante. **~ly** *adv* predominantemente, preponderantemente

predominate /prɪˈdɒmɪneɪt/ *vi* predominar

pre-eminent /priːˈemɪnənt/ *a* preeminente, superior

pre-empt /priːˈempt/ *vt* adquirir por preempção. **~ive** *a* antecipado; (*mil*) preventivo

preen /priːn/ *vt* alisar. **~ o.s.** enfeitar-se

prefab /ˈpriːfæb/ *n* (*colloq*) casa *f* pré-fabricada. **~ricated** /-ˈfæbrɪkeɪtɪd/ *a* pré-fabricado

preface /ˈprefɪs/ *n* prefácio *m*

prefect /ˈpriːfekt/ *n* aluno *m* autorizado a disciplinar outros; (*official*) prefeito *m*

prefer /prɪˈfɜː(r)/ *vt* (*pt* **preferred**) preferir. **~able** /ˈprefrəbl/ *a* preferível

preferen|ce /ˈprefrəns/ *n* preferência *f*. **~tial** /-əˈrenʃl/ *a* preferencial, privilegiado

prefix /ˈpriːfɪks/ *n* (*pl* **-ixes**) prefixo *m*

pregnan|t /ˈpregnənt/ *a* (*woman*) grávida; (*animal*) prenhe. **~cy** *n* gravidez *f*

prehistoric /priːhɪˈstɒrɪk/ *a* pré-histórico

prejudice /ˈpredʒʊdɪs/ *n* preconceito *m*, idéia *f* preconcebida, prejuízo *m*; (*harm*) prejuízo *m* □ *vt* influenciar. **~d** *a* com preconceitos

preliminar|y /prɪˈlɪmɪnərɪ/ *a* preliminar. **~ies** *npl* preliminares *mpl*, preâmbulos *mpl*

prelude /ˈpreljuːd/ *n* prelúdio *m*

premarital /priːˈmærɪtl/ *a* antes do casamento, pré-marital

premature /ˈprematjʊə(r)/ *a* prematuro

premeditated /priːˈmedɪteɪtɪd/ *a* premeditado

premier /ˈpremɪə(r)/ *a* primeiro □ *n* (*pol*) primeiro-ministro *m*

premises /ˈpremɪsɪz/ *npl* local *m*, edifício *m*. **on the ~** neste estabelecimento, no local

premium /ˈpriːmɪəm/ *n* prêmio *m*, (*P*) prémio *m*. **at a ~** a peso de ouro

premonition /priːməˈnɪʃn/ *n* pressentimento *m*

preoccup|ation /priːɒkjʊˈpeɪʃn/ *n* preocupação *f*. **~ied** /-ˈɒkjʊpaɪd/ *a* preocupado

preparation /prepəˈreɪʃn/ *n* preparação *f*. **~s** preparativos *mpl*

preparatory /prɪˈpærətrɪ/ *a* preparatório. **~ school** escola *f* primária particular

prepare /prɪˈpeə(r)/ *vt/i* preparar(-se) (**for** para). **~d to** pronto a, preparado para

preposition /prepəˈzɪʃn/ *n* preposição *f*

preposterous /prɪˈpɒstərəs/ *a* absurdo, disparatado, ridículo

prerequisite /priːˈrekwɪzɪt/ *n* condição *f* prévia

prerogative /prɪˈrɒgətɪv/ *n* prerrogativa *f*

Presbyterian /prezbɪˈtɪərɪən/ *a* & *n* presbiteriano (*m*)

prescri|be /prɪˈskraɪb/ *vt* prescrever; (*med*) receitar, prescrever. **~ption** /-ɪpʃn/ *n* prescrição *f*; (*med*) receita *f*

presence /ˈprezns/ *n* presença *f*. **~ of mind** presença *f* de espírito

present[1] /ˈpreznt/ *a* & *n* presente (*mf*). **at ~** no momento, presentemente

present[2] /ˈpreznt/ *n* (*gift*) presente *m*

present[3] /prɪˈzent/ *vt* apresentar; (*film etc*) dar. **~ sb with** oferecer a alg. **~able** *a* apresentável. **~ation** /preznˈteɪʃn/ *n* apresentação *f*. **~er** *n* apresentador *m*

presently /'prezntlɪ/ *adv* dentro em pouco, daqui a pouco; (*Amer: now*) neste momento

preservative /prɪ'zɜ:vətɪv/ *n* preservativo *m*

preserv|e /prɪ'zɜ:v/ *vt* preservar; (*maintain; culin*) conservar □ *n* reserva *f*; (*fig*) área *f*, terreno *m*; (*jam*) compota *f*. **~ation** /prezə'veɪʃn/ *n* conservação *f*

preside /prɪ'zaɪd/ *vi* presidir (**over** a)

presiden|t /'prezɪdənt/ *n* presidente *mf*. **~cy** *n* presidência *f*. **~tial** /-'denʃl/ *a* presidencial

press /pres/ *vt/i* carregar (**on** em); (*squeeze*) espremer; (*urge*) pressionar; (*iron*) passar a ferro □ *n* imprensa *f*; (*mech*) prensa *f*; (*for wine*) lagar *m*. **be ~ed for** estar apertado com falta de. **~ on (with)** continuar (com), prosseguir (com). **~ conference** entrevista *f* coletiva. **~-stud** *n* mola *f*, botão *m* de pressão

pressing /'presɪŋ/ *a* premente, urgente

pressure /'preʃə(r)/ *n* pressão *f* □ *vt* fazer pressão sobre. **~-cooker** *n* panela *f* de pressão. **~ group** grupo *m* de pressão

pressurize /'preʃəraɪz/ *vt* pressionar, fazer pressão sobre

prestige /pre'sti:ʒ/ *n* prestígio *m*

prestigious /pre'stɪdʒəs/ *a* prestigioso

presumably /prɪ'zju:məblɪ/ *adv* provavelmente

presum|e /prɪ'zju:m/ *vt* presumir. **~e to** tomar a liberdade de, atrever-se a. **~ption** /-'zʌmpʃn/ *n* presunção *f*

presumptuous /prɪ'zʌmptʃʊəs/ *a* presunçoso

pretence /prɪ'tens/ *n* fingimento *m*; (*claim*) pretensão *f*; (*pretext*) desculpa *f*, pretexto *m*

pretend /prɪ'tend/ *vt/i* fingir (**to do** fazer). **~ to** (*lay claim to*) ter pretensões a, ser pretendente a; (*profess to have*) pretender ter

pretentious /prɪ'tenʃəs/ *a* pretencioso

pretext /'pri:tekst/ *n* pretexto *m*

pretty /'prɪtɪ/ *a* (**-ier**, **-iest**) bonito, lindo □ *adv* bastante

prevail /prɪ'veɪl/ *vi* prevalecer. **~ on sb to** convencer alguém a. **~ing** *a* dominante

prevalen|t /'prevələnt/ *a* geral, dominante. **~ce** *n* frequência *f*

prevent /prɪ'vent/ *vt* impedir (**from doing** de fazer). **~able** *a* que se pode evitar, evitável. **~ion** /-ʃn/ *n* prevenção *f*. **~ive** *a* preventivo

preview /'pri:vju:/ *n* pré-estréia *f*, (*P*) ante-estréia *f*

previous /'pri:vɪəs/ *a* precedente, anterior. **~ to** antes de. **~ly** *adv* antes, anteriormente

pre-war /pri:'wɔ:(r)/ *a* do pré-guerra, (*P*) de antes da guerra

prey /preɪ/ *n* presa *f* □ *vi* **~ on** dar caça a; (*worry*) preocupar, atormentar. **bird of ~** ave *f* de rapina, predador *m*

price /praɪs/ *n* preço *m* □ *vt* marcar o preço de. **~less** *a* inestimável; (*colloq: amusing*) impagável

prick /prɪk/ *vt* picar, furar □ *n* picada *f*. **~ up one's ears** arrebitar a(s) orelha(s)

prickl|e /'prɪkl/ *n* pico *m*, espinho *m*; (*sensation*) picada *f*. **~y** *a* espinhoso, que pica; (*person*) irritável

pride /praɪd/ *n* orgulho *m* □ *vpr* **~ o.s. on** orgulhar-se de

priest /pri:st/ *n* padre *m*, sacerdote *m*. **~hood** *n* sacerdócio *m*; (*clergy*) clero *m*

prim /prɪm/ *a* (**primmer**, **primmest**) formal, cheio de nove-horas; (*prudish*) pudico

primary /'praɪmərɪ/ *a* primário; (*chief, first*) primeiro. **~ school** escola *f* primária

prime[1] /praɪm/ *a* primeiro, principal; (*first-rate*) de primeira qualidade. **P~ Minister** Primeiro-Ministro *m*. **~ number** número *m* primo

prime[2] /praɪm/ *vt* aprontar, aprestar; (*with facts*) preparar; (*surface*) preparar, aparelhar. **~r** /-ə(r)/ *n* (*paint*) aparelho *m*

primeval /praɪ'mi:vl/ *a* primitivo

primitive /'prɪmɪtɪv/ *a* primitivo

primrose /'prɪmrəʊz/ *n* primavera *f*, prímula *f*

prince /prɪns/ *n* príncipe *m*

princess /prɪn'ses/ *n* princesa *f*

principal /'prɪnsəpl/ *a* principal □ *n* (*schol*) diretor *m*, (*P*) director *m*. **~ly** *adv* principalmente

principle /'prɪnsəpl/ *n* princípio *m*. **in/on ~** em/por princípio

print /prɪnt/ *vt* imprimir; (*write*) escrever em letra de imprensa □ *n* marca *f*, impressão *f*; (*letters*) letra *f* de imprensa; (*photo*) prova (fotográfica) *f*; (*engraving*) gravura *f*. **out of ~** esgotado. **~-out** *n* cópia *f* impressa. **~ed matter** impressos *mpl*

print|er /'prɪntə(r)/ *n* tipógrafo *m*; (*comput*) impressora *f*. **~ing** *n* impressão *f*, tipografia *f*

prior /'praɪə(r)/ *a* anterior, precedente. **~ to** antes de

priority /praɪ'ɒrətɪ/ *n* prioridade *f*

prise /praɪz/ *vt* forçar (com alavanca). **~ open** arrombar

prison /'prɪzn/ *n* prisão *f*. **~er** *n* prisioneiro *m*

pristine /'prɪsti:n/ *a* primitivo; (*condition*) perfeito, como novo

privacy /'prɪvəsɪ/ *n* privacidade *f*, intimidade *f*; (*solitude*) isolamento *m*

private /'praɪvət/ *a* privado; (*confidential*) confidencial; (*lesson, life, house etc*) particular; (*ceremony*) íntimo □ *n* soldado *m* raso. **in ~** em particular; (*of ceremony*) na intimidade. **~ly** *adv* particularmente; (*inwardly*) no fundo, interiormente

privet /'prɪvɪt/ *n* (*bot*) alfena *f*, ligustro *m*

privilege /'prɪvəlɪdʒ/ *n* privilégio *m*. **~d** *a* privilegiado. **be ~d to** ter o privilégio de

prize /praɪz/ *n* prêmio *m*, (*P*) prémio *m* □ *a* premiado; (*fool etc*) perfeito □ *vt* ter em grande apreço, apreciar muito. **~-giving** *n* distribuição *f* de prêmios, (*P*) prémios. **~-winner** *n* premiado *m*, vencedor *m*

pro[1] /prəʊ/ *n* **the ~s and cons** os prós e os contras

pro- /prəʊ/ *pref* (*acting for*) pro-; (*favouring*) pró-

probab|le /'prɒbəbl/ *a* provável. **~ility** /-'bɪlətɪ/ *n* probabilidade *f*. **~ly** *adv* provavelmente

probation /prə'beɪʃn/ *n* (*testing*) estágio *m*, tirocínio *m*; (*jur*) liberdade *f* condicional. **~ary** *a* probatório

probe /prəʊb/ *n* (*med*) sonda *f*; (*fig: investigation*) inquérito *m* □ *vt*/*i* **~ (into)** sondar, investigar

problem /'prɒbləm/ *n* problema *m* □ *a* difícil. **~atic** /-'mætɪk/ *a* problemático

procedure /prə'si:dʒə(r)/ *n* procedimento *m*, processo *m*, norma *f*

proceed /prə'si:d/ *vi* prosseguir, ir para diante, avançar. **~ to do** passar a fazer. **~ with sth** continuar *or* avançar com alguma coisa. **~ing** *n* procedimento *m*

proceedings /prə'si:dɪŋz/ *npl* (*jur*) processo *m*; (*report*) ata *f*, (*P*) acta *f*

proceeds /'prəʊsi:dz/ *npl* produto *m*, luco *m*, proventos *mpl*

process /'prəʊses/ *n* processo *m* □ *vt* tratar; (*photo*) revelar. **in ~** em curso. **in the ~ of doing** sendo feito

procession /prə'seʃn/ *n* procissão *f*, cortejo *m*

procl|aim /prə'kleɪm/ *vt* proclamar. **~amation** /prɒklə'meɪʃn/ *n* proclamação *f*

procure /prə'kjʊə(r)/ *vt* obter

prod /prɒd/ *vt*/*i* (*pt* **prodded**) (*push*) empurrar; (*poke*) espetar; (*fig: urge*) incitar □ *n* espetadela *f*; (*fig*) incitamento *m*

prodigal /'prɒdɪgl/ *a* pródigo

prodigious /prə'dɪdʒəs/ *a* prodigioso

prodigy /'prɒdɪdʒɪ/ *n* prodígio *m*

produc|e[1] /prə'dju:s/ *vt*/*i* produzir; (*bring out*) tirar, extrair; (*show*) apresentar, mostrar; (*cause*) causar, provocar; (*theat*) pôr em cena. **~er** *n* produtor *m*. **~tion** /-'dʌkʃn/ *n* produção *f*; (*theat*) encenação *f*

produce[2] /'prɒdju:s/ *n* produtos (agrícolas) *mpl*

product /'prɒdʌkt/ *n* produto *m*

productiv|e /prə'dʌktɪv/ *a* produtivo. **~ity** /prɒdʌk'tɪvətɪ/ *n* produtividade *f*

profan|e /prə'feɪn/ *a* profano; (*blasphemous*) blasfemo. **~ity** /-'fænətɪ/ *n* profanidade *f*

profess /prə'fes/ *vt* professar. **~ to do** alegar fazer

profession /prə'feʃn/ *n* profissão *f*. **~al** *a* profissional; (*well done*) de profissional; (*person*) que exerce uma profissão liberal □ *n* profissional *mf*

professor /prə'fesə(r)/ *n* professor (universitário) *m*

proficien|t /prə'fɪʃnt/ *a* proficiente, competente. **~cy** *n* proficiência *f*, competência *f*

profile /'prəʊfaɪl/ *n* perfil *m*

profit /'prɒfɪt/ *n* proveito *m*; (*money*) lucro *m* □ *vi* (*pt* **profited**) **~ by** aproveitar-se de; **~ from** tirar proveito de. **~able** *a* proveitoso; (*of business*) lucrativo, rentável

profound /prə'faʊnd/ *a* profundo. **~ly** *adv* profundamente

profus|e /prə'fju:s/ *a* profuso. **~ely** *adv* profusamente, em abundância. **~ion** /-ʒn/ *n* profusão *f*

program /'prəʊgræm/ *n* (**computer**) **~** programa *m* □ *vt* (*pt* **programmed**) programar. **~mer** *n* programador *m*

programme /'prəʊgræm/ *n* programa *m*

progress[1] /'prəʊgres/ *n* progresso *m*. **in ~** em curso, em andamento

progress[2] /prə'gres/ *vi* progredir. **~ion** /-ʃn/ *n* progressão *f*

progressive /prə'gresɪv/ *a* progressivo; (*reforming*) progressista. **~ly** *adv* progressivamente

prohibit /prə'hɪbɪt/ *vt* proibir (**sb from doing** alg de fazer)

project[1] /prə'dʒekt/ *vt* projetar, (*P*) projectar □ *vi* ressaltar, sobressair. **~ion** /-ʃn/ *n* projeção *f*, (*P*) projecção *f*; (*protruding*) saliência *f*, ressalto *m*

project[2] /'prɒdʒekt/ *n* projeto *m*, (*P*) projecto *m*

projectile /prə'dʒektaɪl/ *n* projétil *m*, (*P*) projéctil *m*

projector /prə'dʒektə(r)/ *n* projetor *m*, (*P*) projector *m*

proletari|at /prəʊlɪ'teərɪət/ *n* proletariado *m*. **~an** *a* & *n* proletário (*m*)

proliferat|e /prə'lɪfəreɪt/ *vi* proliferar. **~ion** /-'reɪʃn/ *n* proliferação *f*

prolific /prə'lɪfɪk/ *a* prolífico

prologue /'prəʊlɒg/ *n* prólogo *m*

prolong /prə'lɒŋ/ *vt* prolongar

promenade /prɒmə'nɑ:d/ *n* passeio *m* □ *vt/i* passear

prominen|t /'prɒmɪnənt/ *a* (*projecting; important*) proeminente; (*conspicuous*) bem à vista, conspícuo. **~ce** *n* proeminência *f*. **~tly** *adv* bem à vista

promiscu|ous /prə'mɪskjʊəs/ *a* promíscuo, de costumes livres. **~ity** /prɒmɪs'kju:ətɪ/ *n* promiscuidade *f*, liberdade *f* de costumes

promis|e /'prɒmɪs/ *n* promessa *f* □ *vt/i* prometer. **~ing** *a* prometedor, promissor

promot|e /prə'məʊt/ *vt* promover. **~ion** /-'məʊʃn/ *n* promoção *f*

prompt /prɒmpt/ *a* pronto, rápido, imediato; (*punctual*) pontual □ *adv* em ponto □ *vt* levar; (*theat*) soprar, servir de ponto para. **~er** *n* ponto *m*. **~ly** *adv* prontamente; pontualmente. **~ness** *n* prontidão *f*

prone /prəʊn/ *a* deitado (de bruços). **~ to** propenso a

prong /prɒŋ/ *n* (*of fork*) dente *m*

pronoun /'prəʊnaʊn/ *n* pronome *m*

pron|ounce /prə'naʊns/ *vt* pronunciar; (*declare*) declarar. **~ounced** *a* pronunciado. **~ouncement** *n* declaração *f*. **~unciation** /-ʌnsɪ'eɪʃn/ *n* pronúncia *f*

proof /pru:f/ *n* prova *f*; (*of liquor*) teor *m* alcóolico, graduação *f* □ *a* **~ against** à prova de

prop[1] /prɒp/ *n* suporte *m*; (*lit & fig*) apoio *m*, esteio *m* □ *vt* (*pt* **propped**) sustentar, suportar, apoiar. **~ against** apoiar contra

prop[2] /prɒp/ *n* (*colloq: theat*) acessório *m*, (*P*) adereço *m*

propaganda /prɒpə'gændə/ *n* propaganda *f*

propagat|e /'prɒpəgeɪt/ *vt/i* propagar (-se). **~ion** /-'geɪʃn/ *n* propagação *f*

propel /prə'pel/ *vt* (*pt* **propelled**) propulsionar, impelir

propeller /prə'pelə(r)/ *n* hélice *f*

proper /'prɒpə(r)/ *a* correto, (*P*) correcto; (*seemly*) conveniente; (*real*) propriamente dito; (*colloq: thorough*) belo. **~ noun** substantivo *m* próprio. **~ly** *adv* corretamente, (*P*) correctamente; (*rightly*) com razão, acertadamente; (*accurately*) propriamente

property /'prɒpətɪ/ *n* (*house*) imóvel *m*; (*land, quality*) propriedade *f*; (*possessions*) bens *mpl*

prophecy /'prɒfəsɪ/ *n* profecia *f*

prophesy /'prɒfɪsaɪ/ *vt/i* profetizar. **~ that** predizer que

prophet /'prɒfɪt/ *n* profeta *m*. **~ic** /prə'fetɪk/ *a* profético

proportion /prə'pɔ:ʃn/ *n* proporção *f*. **~al, ~ate** *adjs* proporcional

proposal /prə'pəʊzl/ *n* proposta *f*; (*of marriage*) pedido *m* de casamento

propos|e /prə'pəʊz/ *vt* propor □ *vi* pedir em casamento. **~e to do** propor-se fazer. **~ition** /prɒpə-'zɪʃn/ *n* proposição *f*; (*colloq: matter*) caso *m*, questão *f*

propound /prə'paʊnd/ *vt* propor

proprietor /prə'praɪətə(r)/ *n* proprietário *m*

propriety /prə'praɪətɪ/ *n* propriedade *f*, correção *f*, (*P*) correcção *f*

propulsion /prə'pʌlʃn/ *n* propulsão *f*

prosaic /prə'zeɪɪk/ *a* prosaico

prose /prəʊz/ *n* prosa *f*

prosecut|e /'prɒsɪkju:t/ *vt* (*jur*) processar. **~ion** /-'kju:ʃn/ *n* (*jur*) acusação *f*

prospect[1] /'prɒspekt/ *n* perspectiva *f*

prospect[2] /prə'spekt/ *vt/i* pesquisar, prospectar

prospective /prə'spektɪv/ *a* futuro; (*possible*) provável

prosper /'prɒspə(r)/ *vi* prosperar

prosper|ous /'prɒspərəs/ *a* próspero. **~ity** /-'sperətɪ/ *n* prosperidade *f*

prostitut|e /'prɒstɪtju:t/ *n* prostituta *f*. **~ion** /-'tju:ʃn/ *n* prostituição *f*

prostrate /'prɒstreɪt/ *a* prostrado

protect /prə'tekt/ *vt* proteger. **~ion** /-ʃn/ *n* proteção *f*, (*P*) protecção *f*. **~ive** *a* protetor, (*P*) protector. **~or** *n* protetor *m*, (*P*) protector *m*

protégé /'prɒtɪʒeɪ/ *n* protegido *m*. **~e** *n* protegida *f*

protein /'prəʊti:n/ *n* proteína *f*

protest[1] /'prəʊtest/ *n* protesto *m*

protest[2] /prə'test/ *vt/i* protestar. **~er** *n* (*pol*) manifestante *mf*

Protestant /'prɒtɪstənt/ *a* & *n* protestante (*mf*). **~ism** /-ɪzəm/ *n* protestantismo *m*

protocol /'prəʊtəkɒl/ *n* protocolo *m*

prototype /'prəʊtətaɪp/ *n* protótipo *m*

protract /prə'trækt/ *vt* prolongar, arrastar

protrud|e /prə'tru:d/ *vi* sobressair, sair do alinhamento. **~ing** *a* saliente

proud /praʊd/ *a* (**er**, **-est**) orgulhoso. **~ly** *adv* orgulhosamente

prove /pru:v/ *vt* provar, demonstrar □ *vi* **~ (to be) easy**/*etc* verificar-se ser fácil/ *etc*. **~ o.s.** dar provas de si. **~n** /-n/ *a* provado

proverb /'prɒvɜ:b/ *n* provérbio *m*. **~ial** /prə'vɜ:bɪəl/ *a* proverbial

provid|e /prə'vaɪd/ *vt* prover, munir (**sb with sth** alg de alguma coisa) □ *vi* **~ for** providenciar para; (*person*) prover de, cuidar de; (*allow for*) levar em conta. **~ed, ~ing (that)** *conj* desde que, contanto que

providence /'prɒvɪdəns/ *n* providência *f*

province /'prɒvɪns/ *n* província *f*; (*fig*) competência *f*

provincial /prə'vɪnʃl/ *a* provincial; (*rustic*) provinciano

provision /prə'vɪʒn/ *n* provisão *f*; (*stipulation*) disposição *f*. **~s** (*pl* (*food*) provisões *fpl*

provisional /prə'vɪʒənl/ *a* provisório. **~ly** *adv* provisoriamente

proviso /prə'vaɪzəʊ/ *n* (*pl* **-os**) condição *f*

provo|ke /prə'vəʊk/ *vt* provocar. **~cation** /prɒvə'keɪʃn/ *n* provocação *f*. **~cative** /-'vɒkətɪv/ *a* provocante

prowess /'praʊɪs/ *n* proeza *f*, façanha *f*

prowl /praʊl/ *vi* rondar □ *n* **be on the ~** andar à espreita. **~er** *n* pessoa *f* que anda à espreita

proximity /prɒk'sɪmətɪ/ *n* proximidade *f*

proxy /'prɒksɪ/ *n* **by ~** por procuração

prude /pru:d/ *n* puritano *m*, pudico *m*

pruden|t /'pru:dnt/ *a* prudente. **~ce** *n* prudência *f*

prune[1] /pru:n/ *n* ameixa *f* seca

prune[2] /pru:n/ *vt* podar

pry /praɪ/ *vi* bisbilhotar. **~ into** meter o nariz em, intrometer-se em

psalm /sa:m/ *n* salmo *m*

pseudo- /'sju:dəʊ/ *pref* pseudo-

pseudonym /'sju:dənɪm/ *n* pseudônimo *m*, (*P*) pseudónimo *m*

psychiatr|y /saɪ'kaɪətrɪ/ *n* psiquiatria *f*. **~ic** /-ɪ'ætrɪk/ *a* psiquiátrico. **~ist** *n* psiquiatra *mf*

psychic /'saɪkɪk/ *a* psíquico; (*person*) com capacidade de telepatia

psychoanalys|e /saɪkəʊ'ænəlaɪz/ *vt* psicanalisar. **~t** /-ɪst/ *n* psicanalista *mf*

psychoanalysis /saɪkəʊə'næləsɪs/ *n* psicanálise *f*

psycholog|y /saɪ'kɒlədʒɪ/ *n* psicologia *f*. **~ical** /-ə'lɒdʒɪkl/ *a* psicológico. **~ist** *n* psicólogo *m*

psychopath /'saɪkəʊpæθ/ *n* psicopata *mf*

pub /pʌb/ *n* pub *m*

puberty /'pju:bətɪ/ *n* puberdade *f*

public /'pʌblɪk/ *a* público; (*holiday*) feriado. **in ~** em público. **~ house** pub *m*. **~ relations** relações *fpl* públicas. **~ school** escola *f* particular; (*Amer*) escola *f* oficial. **~-spirited** *a* de espírito cívico, patriótico. **~ly** *adv* publicamente

publication /pʌblɪ'keɪʃn/ *n* publicação *f*

publicity /pʌ'blɪsətɪ/ *n* publicidade *f*

publicize /'pʌblɪsaɪz/ *vt* fazer publicidade de

publish /'pʌblɪʃ/ *vt* publicar. **~er** *n* editor *m*. **~ing** *n* publicação *f*. **~ing house** editora *f*

pucker /'pʌkə(r)/ *vt*/*i* franzir

pudding /'pʊdɪŋ/ *n* pudim *m*; (*dessert*) doce *m*

puddle /'pʌdl/ *n* poça *f* de água, charco *m*

puerile /'pjʊəraɪl/ *a* pueril

puff /pʌf/ *n* baforada *f* □ *vt*/*i* lançar baforadas; (*breathe hard*) arquejar, ofegar. **~ at** (*cigar etc*) dar baforadas em. **~ out** (*swell*) inchar(-se). **~-pastry** *n* massa *f* folhada

puffy /'pʌfɪ/ *a* inchado

pugnacious /pʌg'neɪʃəs/ *a* belicoso, combativo

pull /pʊl/ *vt*/*i* puxar; (*muscle*) distender □ *n* puxão *m*; (*fig: influence*) influência *f*, empenho *m*. **give a ~** dar um puxão. **~ a face** fazer uma careta. **~ one's weight** (*fig*) fazer a sua quota-parte. **~ sb's leg** brincar com alguém, meter-se com alguém. **~ away** *or* **out** (*auto*) arrancar. **~ down** puxar para baixo; (*building*) demolir. **~ in** (*auto*) encostar-se. **~ off** tirar; (*fig*) sair-se bem em, conseguir alcançar. **~ out** partir; (*extract*) arrancar, tirar. **~ through** sair-se bem. **~ o.s. together** recompor-se, refazer-se. **~ up** puxar para cima; (*uproot*) arrancar; (*auto*) parar

pulley /'pʊlɪ/ *n* roldana *f*

pullover /'pʊləʊvə(r)/ *n* pulôver *m*

pulp /pʌlp/ *n* polpa *f*; (*for paper*) pasta *f* de papel

pulpit /'pʊlpɪt/ *n* púlpito *m*

pulsat|e /pʌl'seɪt/ *vi* pulsar, bater, palpitar. **~ion** /-'seɪʃn/ *n* pulsação *f*

pulse /pʌls/ *n* pulso *m*. **feel sb's ~** tirar o pulso de alguém

pulverize /'pʌlvəraɪz/ *vt* (*grind, defeat*) pulverizar

pummel /'pʌml/ *vt* (*pt* **pummelled**) esmurrar

pump[1] /pʌmp/ *n* bomba *f* □ *vt*/*i* bombear; (*person*) arrancar *or* extrair informações de. **~ up** encher com bomba

pump[2] /pʌmp/ *n* (*shoe*) sapato *m*

pumpkin /'pʌmpkɪn/ *n* abóbora *f*

pun /pʌn/ *n* trocadilho *m*, jogo *m* de palavras

punch[1] /pʌntʃ/ *vt* esmurrar, dar um murro *or* soco; (*perforate*) furar, perfurar; (*a hole*) fazer □ *n* murro *m*, soco *m*; (*device*) furador *m*. **~-line** *n* remate *m*. **~-up** *n* (*colloq*) pancadaria *f*

punch[2] /pʌntʃ/ *n* (*drink*) ponche *m*

punctual /'pʌŋktʃʊəl/ *a* pontual. **~ity** /-'ælətɪ/ *n* pontualidade *f*

punctuat|e /'pʌŋktʃʊeɪt/ *vt* pontuar. **~ion** /-'eɪʃn/ *n* pontuação *f*

puncture /'pʌŋktʃə(r)/ *n* (*in tyre*) furo *m* □ *vt/i* furar

pundit /'pʌndɪt/ *n* autoridade *f*, sumidade *f*

pungent /'pʌndʒənt/ *a* acre, pungente

punish /'pʌnɪʃ/ *vt* punir, castigar. **~able** *a* punível. **~ment** *n* punição *f*, castigo *m*

punitive /'pju:nɪtɪv/ *a* (*expedition, measure etc*) punitivo; (*taxation etc*) penalizador

punt /pʌnt/ *n* (*boat*) chalana *f*

punter /'pʌntə(r)/ *n* (*gambler*) jogador *m*; (*colloq: customer*) freguês *m*

puny /'pju:nɪ/ *a* (**-ier, -iest**) fraco, débil

pup(py) /'pʌp(ɪ)/ *n* cachorro *m*, cachorrinho *m*

pupil /'pju:pl/ *n* aluno *m*; (*of eye*) pupila *f*

puppet /'pʌpɪt/ *n* (*lit & fig*) fantoche *m*, marionete *f*

purchase /'pɜ:tʃəs/ *vt* comprar (**from sb** de alg) □ *n* compra *f*. **~r** /-ə(r)/ *n* comprador *m*

pur|e /'pjʊə(r)/ *a* (**-er, -est**) puro. **~ely** *adv* puramente. **~ity** *n* pureza *f*

purgatory /'pɜ:gətrɪ/ *n* purgatório *m*

purge /pɜ:dʒ/ *vt* purgar; (*pol*) sanear □ *n* (*med*) purgante *m*; (*pol*) saneamento *m*

purif|y /'pjʊərɪfaɪ/ *vt* purificar. **~ication** /-ɪ'keɪʃn/ *n* purificação *f*

puritan /'pjʊərɪtən/ *n* puritano *m*. **~ical** /-'tænɪkl/ *a* puritano

purple /'pɜ:pl/ *a* roxo, purpúreo □ *n* roxo *m*, púrpura *f*

purport /pə'pɔ:t/ *vt* dizer-se, (*P*) dar a entender. **~ to be** pretender ser

purpose /'pɜ:pəs/ *n* propósito *m*; (*determination*) firmeza *f*. **on ~** de propósito. **to no ~** em vão. **~-built** *a* construído especialmente.

purposely /'pɜ:pəslɪ/ *adv* de propósito, propositadamente

purr /pɜ:r/ *n* ronrom *m* □ *vi* ronronar

purse /pɜ:s/ *n* carteira *f*; (*Amer*) bolsa *f* □ *vt* franzir

pursue /pə'sju:/ *vt* perseguir; (*go on with*) prosseguir; (*engage in*) entregar-se a, dedicar-se a. **~r** /-ə(r)/ *n* perseguidor *m*

pursuit /pə'sju:t/ *n* perseguição *f*; (*fig*) atividade *f*, (*P*) actividade *f*

pus /pʌs/ *n* pus *m*

push /pʊʃ/ *vt/i* empurrar; (*button*) apertar; (*thrust*) enfiar; (*colloq: recommend*) insistir □ *n* empurrão *m*; (*effort*) esforço *m*; (*drive*) energia *f*. **be ~ed for** (*time etc*) estar com pouco. **be ~ing thirty**/*etc* (*colloq*) estar beirando os trinta/*etc*. **give the ~ to** (*sl*) dar o fora em alguém. **~ s.o. around** fazer alguém de bobo. **~ back** repelir. **~-chair** *n* carrinho *m* (de criança). **~er** *n* fornecedor *m* (de droga). **~ off** (*sl*) dar o fora. **~ on** continuar. **~-over** *n* canja *f*, coisa *f* fácil. **~ up** (*lift*) levantar; (*prices*) forçar o aumento de. **~-up** *n* (*Amer*) flexão *f*. **~y** *a* (*colloq*) agressivo, furão

put /pʊt/ *vt/i* (*pt* **put**, *pres p* **putting**) colocar, pôr; (*question*) fazer. **~ the damage at a million** estimar os danos em um milhão. **I'd ~ it at a thousand** eu diria mil. **~ sth tactfully** dizer alg coisa com tato. **~ across** comunicar. **~ away** guardar. **~ back** repor; (*delay*) retardar, atrasar. **~ by** pôr de lado. **~ down** pôr em lugar baixo; (*write*) anotar; (*pay*) pagar; (*suppress*) sufocar, reprimir. **~ forward** (*plan*) submeter. **~ in** (*insert*) introduzir; (*fix*) instalar; (*submit*) submeter. **~ in for** fazer um pedido, candidatar-se. **~ off** (*postpone*) adiar; (*disconcert*) desanimar; (*displease*) desagradar. **~ s.o. off sth** tirar o gosto de alguém por alg coisa. **~ on** (*clothes*) pôr; (*radio*) ligar; (*light*) acender; (*speed, weight*) ganhar; (*accent*) adotar. **~ out** pôr para fora; (*stretch*) esticar; (*extinguish*) extinguir, apagar; (*disconcert*) desconcertar; (*inconvenience*) incomodar. **~ up** levantar; (*building*) erguer, cons-truir; (*notice*) colocar; (*price*) aumentar; (*guest*) hospedar; (*offer*) oferecer. **~-up job** embuste *m*. **~ up with** suportar

putrefy /'pju:trɪfaɪ/ *vi* putrefazer-se, apodrecer

putty /'pʌtɪ/ *n* massa de vidraceiro *f*, betume *m*

puzzl|e /'pʌzl/ *n* puzzle *m*, quebra-cabeça *m* □ *vt* deixar perplexo, intrigar □ *vi* quebrar a cabeça. **~ing** *a* intrigante

pygmy /'pɪgmɪ/ *n* pigmeu *m*

pyjamas /pə'dʒa:məz/ *npl* pijama *m*

pylon /'paɪlɒn/ *n* poste *m*

pyramid /'pɪrəmɪd/ *n* pirâmide *f*

python /'paɪθn/ *n* píton *m*

Qq

quack[1] /kwæk/ *n* (*of duck*) grasnido *m* □ *vi* grasnar
quack[2] /kwæk/ *n* charlatão *m*
quadrangle /ˈkwɒdræŋgl/ *n* quadrângulo *m*; (*of college*) pátio *m* quadrangular
quadruped /ˈkwɒdrʊped/ *n* quadrúpede *m*
quadruple /ˈkwɒdrʊpl/ *a* & *n* quádruplo (*m*) □ *vt*/*i* /kwɒˈdrʊpl/ quadruplicar. **~ts** /-plɪts/ *npl* quadrigêmeos *mpl*, (*P*) quadrigémeos *mpl*
quagmire /ˈkwægmaɪə(r)/ *n* pântano *m*, lamaçal *m*
quail /kweɪl/ *n* codorniz *f*
quaint /kweɪnt/ *a* (**-er, -est**) pitoresco; (*whimsical*) estranho, bizarro
quake /kweɪk/ *vi* tremer □ *n* (*colloq*) tremor *m* de terra
Quaker /ˈkweɪkə(r)/ *n* quaker *mf*, quacre *m*
qualification /kwɒlɪfɪˈkeɪʃn/ *n* qualificação *f*; (*accomplishment*) habilitação *f*; (*diploma*) diploma *m*, título *m*; (*condition*) requisito *m*, condição *f*; (*fig*) restrição *f*, reserva *f*
qualif|y /ˈkwɒlɪfaɪ/ *vt* qualificar; (*fig: moderate*) atenuar, moderar; (*fig: limit*) pôr ressalvas *or* restrições a □ *vi* (*fig: be entitled to*) ter os requisitos (**for** para); (*sport*) classificar-se. **he ~ied as a vet** ele formou-se em veterinária. **~ied** *a* formado; (*able*) qualificado, habilitado; (*moderated*) atenuado; (*limited*) limitado
quality /ˈkwɒlətɪ/ *n* qualidade *f*
qualm /kwa:m/ *n* escrúpulo *m*
quandary /ˈkwɒndərɪ/ *n* dilema *m*
quantity /ˈkwɒntətɪ/ *n* quantidade *f*
quarantine /ˈkwɒrənti:n/ *n* quarentena *f*
quarrel /ˈkwɒrəl/ *n* zanga *f*, questão *f*, discussão *f* □ *vi* (*pt* **quarrelled**) zangar-se, questionar, discutir. **~some** *a* conflituoso, brigão
quarry[1] /ˈkwɒrɪ/ *n* (*prey*) presa *f*, caça *f*
quarry[2] /ˈkwɒrɪ/ *n* (*excavation*) pedreira *f*
quarter /ˈkwɔ:tə(r)/ *n* quarto *m*; (*of year*) trimestre *m*; (*Amer: coin*) quarto *m* de dólar, 25 cêtimos *mpl*; (*district*) bairro *m*, quarteirão *m*. **~s** (*lodgings*) alojamento *m*, residência *f*; (*mil*) quartel *m* □ *vt* dividir em quarto; (*mil*) aquartelar. **from all ~s** de todos os lados. **~ of an hour** quarto *m* de hora. **(a) ~ past six** seis e quinze. **(a) ~ to seven** quinze para as sete. **~-final** *n* (*sport*) quarta *f* de final. **~ly** *a* trimestral □ *adv* trimestralmente
quartet /kwɔ:ˈtet/ *n* quarteto *m*
quartz /kwɔ:ts/ *n* quartzo *m* □ *a* (*watch etc*) de quartzo
quash /kwɒʃ/ *vt* reprimir; (*jur*) revogar
quaver /ˈkweɪvə(r)/ *vi* tremer, tremular □ *n* (*mus*) colcheia *f*
quay /ki:/ *n* cais *m*
queasy /ˈkwi:zɪ/ *a* delicado. **feel ~** estar enjoado
queen /kwi:n/ *n* rainha *f*; (*cards*) dama *f*
queer /kwɪə(r)/ *a* (**-er, -est**) estranho; (*slightly ill*) indisposto; (*sl: homosexual*) bicha, maricas (*sl*); (*dubious*) suspeito □ *n* (*sl*) bicha *m*, maricas *m* (*sl*)
quell /kwel/ *vt* reprimir, abafar, sufocar
quench /kwentʃ/ *vt* (*fire, flame*) apagar; (*thirst*) matar, saciar
query /ˈkwɪərɪ/ *n* questão *f* □ *vt* pôr em dúvida
quest /kwest/ *n* busca *f*, procura *f*. **in ~ of** em demanda de
question /ˈkwestʃən/ *n* pergunta *f*, interrogação *f*; (*problem, affair*) questão *f* □ *vt* perguntar, interrogar; (*doubt*) pôr em dúvida *or* em causa. **in ~** em questão *or* em causa. **out of the ~** fora de toda a questão. **there's no ~ of** nem pensar em. **without ~** sem dúvida. **~ mark** ponto *m* de interrogação. **~able** *a* discutível
questionnaire /kwestʃəˈneə(r)/ *n* questionário *m*
queue /kju:/ *n* fila *f*, (*P*) bicha *f* □ *vi* (*pres p* **queuing**) fazer fila, (*P*) fazer bicha
quibble /ˈkwɪbl/ *vi* tergiversar, usar de evasivas; (*raise petty objections*) discutir por coisas insignificantes
quick /kwɪk/ *a* (**-er, -est**) rápido □ *adv* depressa. **be ~** despachar-se. **have a ~ temper** exaltar-se facilmente. **~ly** *adv* rapidamente, depressa. **~ness** *n* rapidez *f*
quicken /ˈkwɪkən/ *vt*/*i* apressar (-se)
quicksand /ˈkwɪksænd/ *n* areia *f* movediça
quid /kwɪd/ *n invar* (*sl*) libra *f*
quiet /ˈkwaɪət/ *a* (**-er, -est**) quieto, sossegado, tranquilo □ *n* quietude *f*, sossego *m*, tranqüilidade *f*. **keep ~** calar-se. **on the ~** às escondidas, na calada. **~ly** *adv* sossegadamente, silenciosamente. **~ness** *n* sossego *m*, tranquilidade *f*, calma *f*

quieten /'kwaɪətn/ *vt/i* sossegar, acalmar(-se)
quilt /kwɪlt/ *n* coberta *f* acolchoada. **(continental) ~** edredão *m* de penas □ *vt* acolchoar
quince /kwɪns/ *n* marmelo *m*
quintet /kwɪn'tet/ *n* quinteto *m*
quintuplets /kwɪn'tju:plɪts/ *npl* quíntuplos *mpl*
quip /kwɪp/ *n* piada *f* □ *vt* contar piadas
quirk /kwɜ:k/ *n* mania *f*, singularidade *f*
quit /kwɪt/ *vt* (*pt* **quitted**) deixar □ *vi* ir-se embora; (*resign*) demitir-se. **~ doing** (*Amer*) parar de fazer
quite /kwaɪt/ *adv* completamente, absolutamente; (*rather*) bastante. **~ (so)!** isso mesmo!, exatamente! **~ a few** bastante, alguns/algumas. **~ a lot** bastante
quiver /'kwɪvə(r)/ *vi* tremer, estremecer □ *n* tremor *m*, estremecimento *m*
quiz /kwɪz/ *n* (*pl* **quizzes**) teste *m*; (*game*) concurso *m* □ *vt* (*pt* **quizzed**) interrogar
quizzical /'kwɪzɪkl/ *a* zombeteiro
quorum /'kwɔ:rəm/ *n* quorum *m*
quota /'kwəʊtə/ *n* cota *f*, quota *f*
quotation /kwəʊ'teɪʃn/ *n* citação *f*; (*estimate*) orçamento *m*. **~ marks** aspas *fpl*
quote /kwəʊt/ *vt* citar; (*estimate*) fazer um orçamento □ *n* (*colloq: passage*) citação *f*; (*colloq: estimate*) orçamento *m*

Rr

rabbi /'ræbaɪ/ *n* rabino *m*
rabbit /'ræbɪt/ *n* coelho *m*
rabble /'ræbl/ *n* turba *f*. **the ~** a ralé, a gentalha, o povinho
rabid /'ræbɪd/ *a* (*fig*) fanático, ferrenho; (*dog*) raivoso
rabies /'reɪbi:z/ *n* raiva *f*
race[1] /reɪs/ *n* corrida *f* □ *vt* (*horse*) fazer correr □ *vi* correr, dar uma corrida; (*rush*) ir em grande *or* a toda (a) velocidade. **~-track** *n* pista *f*
race[2] /reɪs/ *n* (*group*) raça *f* □ *a* racial
racecourse /'reɪskɔ:s/ *n* hipódromo *m*
racehorse /'reɪshɔ:s/ *n* cavalo *m* de corrida
racial /'reɪʃl/ *a* racial
racing /'reɪsɪŋ/ *n* corridas *fpl*. **~ car** carro *m* de corridas
racis|t /'reɪsɪst/ *a* & *n* racista (*mf*). **~m** /-zəm/ *n* racismo *m*
rack[1] /ræk/ *n* (*for luggage*) porta-bagagem *m*, bagageiro *m*; (*for plates*) escorredor *m* de prato □ *vt* **~ one's brains** dar tratos à imaginação
rack[2] /ræk/ *n* **go to ~ and ruin** arruinar-se; (*of buildings etc*) cair em ruínas
racket[1] /'rækɪt/ *n* (*sport*) raquete *f*, (*P*) raqueta *f*
racket[2] /'rækɪt/ *n* (*din*) barulheira *f*; (*swindle*) roubalheira *f*; (*sl: business*) negociata *f* (*colloq*)
racy /'reɪsɪ/ *a* (**-ier, -iest**) vivo, vigoroso
radar /'reɪda:(r)/ *n* radar *m* □ *a* de radar
radian|t /'reɪdɪənt/ *a* radiante. **~ce** *n* brilho *m*
radiator /'reɪdɪeɪtə(r)/ *n* radiador *m*
radical /'rædɪkl/ *a* & *n* radical (*m*)
radio /'reɪdɪəʊ/ *n* (*pl* **-os**) rádio *f*; (*set*) (aparelho de) rádio *m* □ *vt* transmitir pelo rádio. **~ station** estação *f* de rádio, emissora *f*
radioactiv|e /reɪdɪəʊ'æktɪv/ *a* radioativo, (*P*) radioactivo. **~ity** /-'tɪvətɪ/ *n* radioatividade *f*, (*P*) radioactividade *f*
radiograph|er /reɪdɪ'ɒgrəfə(r)/ *n* radiologista *mf*. **~y** *n* radiografia *f*
radish /'rædɪʃ/ *n* rabanete *m*
radius /'reɪdɪəs/ *n* (*pl* **-dii** /-dɪaɪ/) raio *m*
raffle /'ræfl/ *n* rifa *f* □ *vt* rifar
raft /ra:ft/ *n* jangada *f*
rafter /'ra:ftə(r)/ *n* trave *f*, viga *f*
rag[1] /ræg/ *n* farrapo *m*; (*for wiping*) trapo *m*; (*pej: newspaper*) jornaleco *m*. **~s** *npl* farrapos *mpl*, andrajos *mpl*. **in ~s** maltrapilho. **~ doll** boneca *f* de trapos
rag[2] /ræg/ *vt* (*pt* **ragged**) zombar de
rage /reɪdʒ/ *n* raiva *f*, fúria *f* □ *vi* estar furioso; (*of storm*) rugir; (*of battle*) estar acesa. **be all the ~** (*colloq*) fazer furor, estar na moda (*colloq*)
ragged /'rægɪd/ *a* (*clothes, person*) esfarrapado, roto; (*edge*) esfiapado, esgarçado
raid /reɪd/ *n* (*mil*) ataque *m*; (*by police*) batida *f*; (*by criminals*) assalto *m* □ *vt* fazer um ataque *or* uma batida *or* um assalto. **~er** *n* atacante *m*, assaltante *m*
rail /reɪl/ *n* (*of stairs*) corrimão *m*; (*of ship*) amurada *f*; (*on balcony*) parapeito *m*; (*for train*) trilho *m*; (*for curtain*) varão *m*. **by ~** por estrada, (*P*) caminho de fer-ro
railings /'reɪlɪŋz/ *npl* grade *f*
railroad /'reɪlrəʊd/ *n* (*Amer*) = **railway**
railway /'reɪlweɪ/ *n* estrada *f*, (*P*) caminho *m* de ferro. **~ line** linha *f* do

trem. ~ **station** estação *f* ferroviária, (*P*) estação *f* de caminho de ferro

rain /reɪn/ *n* chuva *f* □ *vi* chover. ~ **forest** floresta *f* tropical. **~-storm** *n* tempestade *f* com chuva. **~-water** *n* água *f* da chuva

rainbow /ˈreɪnbəʊ/ *n* arco-íris *m*

raincoat /ˈreɪnkəʊt/ *n* impermeável *m*

raindrop /ˈreɪndrɒp/ *n* pingo *m* de chuva

rainfall /ˈreɪnfɔːl/ *n* precipitação *f*, pluviosidade *f*

rainy /ˈreɪnɪ/ *a* (**-ier, -iest**) chuvoso

raise /reɪz/ *vt* levantar, erguer; (*breed*) criar; (*voice*) levantar; (*question*) fazer; (*price etc*) aumentar, subir; (*funds*) angariar; (*loan*) obter □ *n* (*Amer*) aumento *m*

raisin /ˈreɪzn/ *n* passa *f*

rake /reɪk/ *n* ancinho *m* □ *vt* juntar, alisar com ancinho; (*search*) revolver, remexer. ~ **in** (*money*) ganhar a rodos. **~-off** *n* (*colloq*) percentagem *f* (*colloq*). ~ **up** desenterrar, ressuscitar

rally /ˈrælɪ/ *vt/i* reunir(-se); (*reassemble*) reagrupar(-se), reorganizar(-se); (*health*) restabelecer (-se); (*strength*) recuperar as forças □ *n* (*recovery*) recuperação *f*; (*meeting*) comício *m*, assembléia *f*; (*auto*) rally *m*, rali *m*

ram /ræm/ *n* (*sheep*) carneiro *m* □ *vt* (*pt* **rammed**) (*beat down*) calcar; (*push*) meter à força; (*crash into*) bater contra

rambl|e /ˈræmbl/ *n* caminhada *f*, perambulação *f* □ *vi* perambular, vaguear. **~e on** divagar. **~er** *n* caminhante *mf*; (*plant*) trepadeira *f*. **~ing** *a* (*speech*) desconexo

ramp /ræmp/ *n* rampa *f*

rampage /ræmˈpeɪdʒ/ *vi* causar distúrbios violentos

rampant /ˈræmpənt/ *a* **be** ~ vicejar, florescer; (*diseases etc*) grassar

rampart /ˈræmpaːt/ *n* baluarte *m*; (*fig*) defesa *f*

ramshackle /ˈræmʃækl/ *a* (*car*) desconjuntado; (*house*) caindo aos pedaços

ran /ræn/ *see* **run**

ranch /raːntʃ/ *n* rancho *m*, estância *f*. **~er** *n* rancheiro *m*

rancid /ˈrænsɪd/ *a* rançoso

rancour /ˈræŋkə(r)/ *n* rancor *m*

random /ˈrændəm/ *a* feito, tirado *etc* ao acaso □ *n* **at** ~ ao acaso, a esmo, aleatoriamente

randy /ˈrændɪ/ *a* (**-ier, -iest**) lascivo, sensual

rang /ræŋ/ *see* **ring**

range /reɪndʒ/ *n* (*distance*) alcance *m*; (*scope*) âmbito *m*; (*variety*) gama *f*, variedade *f*; (*stove*) fogão *m*; (*of voice*) registro *m*, (*P*) registo *m*; (*of temperature*) variação *f* □ *vt* dispor, ordenar □ *vi* estender-se; (*vary*) variar. ~ **of mountains** cordilheira *f*, serra *f*. **~r** *n* guarda *m* florestal

rank[1] /ræŋk/ *n* fila *f*, fileira *f*; (*mil*) posto *m*; (*social position*) classe *f*, categoria *f* □ *vt/i* ~ **among** contar(-se) entre. **the ~ and file** a massa

rank[2] /ræŋk/ *a* (**-er, -est**) (*plants*) luxuriante; (*smell*) fétido; (*out-and-out*) total

ransack /ˈrænsæk/ *vt* (*search*) espionar, revistar, remexer; (*pillage*) pilhar, saquear

ransom /ˈrænsəm/ *n* resgate *m* □ *vt* resgatar. **hold to** ~ prender como refém

rant /rænt/ *vi* usar linguagem bombástica

rap /ræp/ *n* pancadinha *f* seca □ *vt/i* (*pt* **rapped**) bater, dar uma pancada seca em

rape /reɪp/ *vt* violar, estuprar □ *n* violação *f*, estupro *m*

rapid /ˈræpɪd/ *a* rápido. **~ity** /rəˈpɪdətɪ/ *n* rapidez *f*

rapids /ˈræpɪdz/ *npl* rápidos *mpl*

rapist /ˈreɪpɪst/ *n* violador *m*, estuprador *m*

rapport /ræˈpɔː(r)/ *n* bom relacionamento *m*

rapt /ræpt/ *a* absorto. ~ **in** mergulhado em

raptur|e /ˈræptʃə(r)/ *n* êxtase *m*. **~ous** *a* extático; (*welcome etc*) entusiástico

rar|e[1] /reə(r)/ *a* (**-er, -est**) raro. **~ely** *adv* raramente, raras vezes. **~ity** *n* raridade *f*

rare[2] /reə(r)/ *a* (**-er, -est**) (*culin*) mal passado

rarefied /ˈreərɪfaɪd/ *a* rarefeito; (*refined*) requintado

raring /ˈreərɪŋ/ *a* ~ **to** (*colloq*) impaciente por, louco por (*colloq*)

rascal /ˈraːskl/ *n* (*dishonest*) patife *m*; (*mischievous*) maroto *m*

rash[1] /ræʃ/ *n* erupção *f* cutânea, irritação *f* na pele (*colloq*)

rash[2] /ræʃ/ *a* (**-er, -est**) imprudente, precipitado. **~ly** *adv* imprudentemente, precipitadamente

rasher /ˈræʃə(r)/ *n* fatia *f* (de presunto *or* de bacon)

rasp /raːsp/ *n* lixa *f* grossa, (*P*) lima *f* grossa

raspberry /ˈraːzbrɪ/ *n* framboesa *f*

rasping /ˈraːspɪŋ/ *a* áspero

rat /ræt/ *n* rato *m*, (*P*) ratazana *f*. ~ **race** (*fig*) luta renhida para vencer na vida, arrivismo *m*

rate /reɪt/ *n* (*ratio*) razão *f*; (*speed*) velocidade *f*; (*price*) tarifa *f*; (*of exchange*) (taxa *m* de) câmbio *m*; (*of interest*) taxa *f*. **~s** (*taxes*) impostos *mpl* municipais, taxas *fpl* ▫ *vt* avaliar; (*fig: consider*) considerar. **at any ~** de qualquer modo, pelo menos. **at the ~ of** à razão de. **at this ~** desse jeito, desse modo

ratepayer /ˈreɪtpeɪə(r)/ *n* contribuinte *mf*

rather /ˈrɑːðə(r)/ *adv* (*by preference*) antes; (*fairly*) muito, bastante; (*a little*) um pouco. **I would ~ go** preferia ir

ratif|y /ˈrætɪfaɪ/ *vt* ratificar. **~ication** /-ɪˈkeɪʃn/ *n* ratificação *f*

rating /ˈreɪtɪŋ/ *n* (*comm*) rating *m*, (*P*) valor *m*; (*sailor*) praça *f*, marinheiro *m*; (*radio, TV*) índice *m* de audiência

ratio /ˈreɪʃɪəʊ/ *n* (*pl* **-os**) proporção *f*

ration /ˈræʃn/ *n* ração *f* ▫ *vt* racionar

rational /ˈræʃnəl/ *a* racional; (*person*) sensato, razoável. **~ize** *vt* racionalizar

rattle /ˈrætl/ *vt/i* matraquear; (*of door, window*) bater; (*of bottles*) chocalhar; (*colloq*) agitar, mexer com os nervos de ▫ *n* (*baby's toy*) guizo *m*, chocalho *m*; (*of football fan*) matraca *f*; (*sound*) matraquear *m*, chocalhar *m*. **~ off** despejar (*colloq*)

rattlesnake /ˈrætlsneɪk/ *n* cobra *f* cascavel

raucous /ˈrɔːkəs/ *a* áspero, rouco

ravage /ˈrævɪdʒ/ *vt* devastar, causar estragos a. **~s** *npl* devastação *f*, estragos *mpl*

rave /reɪv/ *vi* delirar; (*in anger*) urrar. **~ about** delirar (de entusiasmo) com

raven /ˈreɪvn/ *n* corvo *m*

ravenous /ˈrævənəs/ *a* esfomeado; (*greedy*) voraz

ravine /rəˈviːn/ *n* ravina *f*, barranco *m*

raving /ˈreɪvɪŋ/ *a* **~ lunatic** doido *m* varrido ▫ *adv* **~ mad** loucamente

ravish /ˈrævɪʃ/ *vt* (*rape*) violar; (*enrapture*) arrebatar, encantar. **~ing** *a* arrebatador, encantador

raw /rɔː/ *a* (**-er, -est**) cru; (*not processed*) bruto; (*wound*) em carne viva; (*weather*) frio e úmido, (*P*) húmido; (*immature*) inexperiente, verde. **~ deal** tratamento *m* injusto. **~ material** matéria-prima *f*

ray /reɪ/ *n* raio *m*

raze /reɪz/ *vt* arrasar

razor /ˈreɪzə(r)/ *n* navalha *f* de barba. **~-blade** *n* lâmina *f* de barbear

re /riː/ *prep* a respeito de, em referência a, relativo a

re- /ri/ *pref* re-

reach /riːtʃ/ *vt* chegar a atingir; (*contact*) contatar; (*pass*) passar ▫ *vi* estender-se, chegar ▫ *n* alcance *m*. **out of ~** fora de alcance. **~ for** estender a mão para agarrar. **within ~ of** ao alcance de; (*close to*) próximo de

react /rɪˈækt/ *vi* reagir

reaction /rɪˈækʃn/ *n* reação *f*, (*P*) reacção *f*. **~ary** *a* & *n* reacionário (*m*), (*P*) reaccionário (*m*)

reactor /rɪˈæktə(r)/ *n* reator *m*, (*P*) reactor *m*

read /riːd/ *vt/i* (*pt* **read** /red/) ler; (*fig: interpret*) interpretar; (*study*) estudar; (*of instrument*) marcar, indicar ▫ *n* (*colloq*) leitura *f*. **~ about** ler um artigo sobre. **~ out** ler em voz alta. **~able** *a* agradável *or* fácil de ler; (*legible*) legível. **~er** *n* leitor *m*; (*book*) livro *m* de leitura. **~ing** *n* leitura *f*; (*of instrument*) registro *m*, (*P*) registo *m*

readily /ˈredɪlɪ/ *adv* de boa vontade, prontamente; (*easily*) facilmente

readiness /ˈredɪnɪs/ *n* prontidão *f*. **in ~** pronto (**for** para)

readjust /riːəˈdʒʌst/ *vt* reajustar ▫ *vi* readaptar-se

ready /ˈredɪ/ *a* (**-ier, -iest**) pronto ▫ *n* **at the ~** pronto para disparar. **~-made** *a* pronto. **~ money** dinheiro *m* vivo, (*P*) dinheiro *m* de contado, pagamento *m* à vista. **~-to-wear** *a* prêt-à-porter

real /rɪəl/ *a* real, verdadeiro; (*genuine*) autêntico ▫ *adv* (*Amer: colloq*) realmente. **~ estate** bens *mpl* imobiliários

realis|t /ˈrɪəlɪst/ *n* realista *mf*. **~m** /-zəm/ *n* realismo *m*. **~tic** /-ˈlɪstɪk/ *a* realista. **~tically** /-ˈlɪstɪkəlɪ/ *adv* realisticamente

reality /rɪˈælətɪ/ *n* realidade *f*

realiz|e /ˈrɪəlaɪz/ *vt* dar-se conta de, aperceber-se de, perceber; (*fulfil; turn into cash*) realizar. **~ation** /-ˈzeɪʃn/ *n* consciência *f*, noção *f*; (*fulfilment*) realização *f*

really /ˈrɪəlɪ/ *adv* realmente, na verdade

realm /relm/ *n* reino *m*; (*fig*) domínio *m*, esfera *f*

reap /riːp/ *vt* (*cut*) ceifar; (*gather; fig*) colher

reappear /riːəˈpɪə(r)/ *vi* reaparecer. **~ance** *n* reaparição *f*

rear[1] /rɪə(r)/ *n* traseira *f*, retaguarda *f* ▫ *a* traseiro, de trás, posterior. **bring up the ~** ir na retaguarda, fechar a marcha. **~-view mirror** espelho *m* retrovisor

rear[2] /rɪə(r)/ *vt* levantar, erguer; (*children, cattle*) criar ▫ *vi* (*of horse etc*) empinar-se. **~ one's head** levantar a cabeça

rearrange /ri:ə'reɪndʒ/ *vt* arranjar doutro modo, reorganizar

reason /'ri:zn/ *n* razão *f* □ *vt/i* raciocinar, argumentar. ~ **with sb** procurar convencer alguém. **within** ~ razoável. ~**ing** *n* raciocínio *m*

reasonable /'ri:znəbl/ *a* razoável

reassur|e /ri:ə'ʃʊə(r)/ *vt* tranqüilizar, sossegar. ~**ance** *n* garantia *f*. ~**ing** *a* animador, reconfortante

rebate /'ri:beɪt/ *n* (*refund*) reimbolso *m*; (*discount*) desconto *m*, abatimento *m*

rebel[1] /'rebl/ *n* rebelde *mf*

rebel[2] /rɪ'bel/ *vi* (*pt* **rebelled**) rebelar-se, revoltar-se, sublevar-se. ~**lion** *n* rebelião *f*, revolta *f*. ~**lious** *a* rebelde

rebound[1] /rɪ'baʊnd/ *vi* repercutir, ressoar; (*fig: backfire*) recair (**on** sobre)

rebound[2] /'ri:baʊnd/ *n* ricochete *m*

rebuff /rɪ'bʌf/ *vt* receber mal, repelir (*colloq*) □ *n* rejeição *f*

rebuild /ri:'bɪld/ *vt* (*pt* **rebuilt**) reconstruir

rebuke /rɪ'bju:k/ *vt* repreender □ *n* reprimenda *f*

recall /rɪ'kɔ:l/ *vt* chamar, mandar regressar; (*remember*) lembrar-se de □ *n* (*summons*) ordem *f* de regresso

recant /rɪ'kænt/ *vi* retratar-se, (*P*) retractar-se

recap /'ri:kæp/ *vt/i* (*pt* **recapped**) (*colloq*) recapitular □ *n* recapitulação *f*

recapitulat|e /ri:kə'pɪtʃʊleɪt/ *vt/i* recapitular. ~**ion** /-'leɪʃn/ *n* recapitulação *f*

reced|e /rɪ'si:d/ *vi* recuar, retroceder. **his hair is** ~**ing** ele está ficando com entradas. ~**ing** *a* (*forehead, chin*) recuado, voltado para dentro

receipt /rɪ'si:t/ *n* recibo *m*; (*receiving*) recepção *f*. ~**s** (*comm*) receitas *fpl*

receive /rɪ'si:v/ *vt* receber. ~**r** /-ə(r)/ *n* (*of stolen goods*) receptador *m*; (*phone*) fone *m*, (*P*) auscultador *m*; (*radio/TV*) receptor *m*. (**official**) ~**r** síndico *m* de massa falida

recent /'ri:snt/ *a* recente. ~**ly** *adv* recentemente

receptacle /rɪ'septəkl/ *n* recipiente *m*, receptáculo *m*

reception /rɪ'sepʃn/ *n* recepção *f*; (*welcome*) acolhimento *m*. ~**ist** *n* recepcionista *mf*

receptive /rɪ'septɪv/ *a* receptivo

recess /rɪ'ses/ *n* recesso *m*; (*of legislature*) recesso *m*; (*Amer: schol*) recreio *m*

recession /rɪ'seʃn/ *n* recessão *f*, depressão *f*

recharge /ri:'tʃa:dʒ/ *vt* tornar a carregar, recarregar

recipe /'resəpɪ/ *n* (*culin*) receita *f*

recipient /rɪ'sɪpɪənt/ *n* recipiente *mf*; (*of letter*) destinatário *m*

reciprocal /rɪ'sɪprəkl/ *a* recíproco

reciprocate /rɪ'sɪprəkeɪt/ *vt/i* reciprocar(-se), retribuir, fazer o mesmo

recital /rɪ'saɪtl/ *n* (*music etc*) recital *m*

recite /rɪ'saɪt/ *vt* recitar; (*list*) enumerar

reckless /'reklɪs/ *a* inconsciente, imprudente, estouvado

reckon /'rekən/ *vt/i* calcular; (*judge*) considerar; (*think*) supor, pensar. ~ **on** contar com, depender de. ~ **with** contar com, levar em conta. ~**ing** *n* conta(s) *f* (*pl*)

reclaim /rɪ'kleɪm/ *vt* (*demand*) reclamar; (*land*) recuperar

reclin|e /rɪ'klaɪn/ *vt/i* reclinar (-se). ~**ing** *a* (*person*) reclinado; (*chair*) reclinável

recluse /rɪ'klu:s/ *n* solitário *m*, recluso *m*

recognition /rekəg'nɪʃn/ *n* reconhecimento *m*. **beyond** ~ irreconhecível. **gain** ~ ganhar nome, ser reconhecido

recogniz|e /'rekəgnaɪz/ *vt* reconhecer. ~**able** /'rekəgnaɪzəbl/ *a* reconhecível

recoil /rɪ'kɔɪl/ *vi* recuar; (*gun*) dar coice □ *n* recuo *m*; (*gun*) coice *m*. ~ **from doing** recusar-se a fazer

recollect /rekə'lekt/ *vt* recordar-se de. ~**ion** /-ʃn/ *n* recordação *f*

recommend /rekə'mend/ *vt* recomendar. ~**ation** /-'deɪʃn/ *n* recomendação *f*

recompense /'rekəmpens/ *vt* recompensar □ *n* recompensa *f*

reconcil|e /'rekənsaɪl/ *vt* (*people*) reconciliar; (*facts*) conciliar. ~**e o.s. to** resignar-se a, conformar-se com. ~**iation** /-sɪlɪ'eɪʃn/ *n* reconciliação *f*

reconnaissance /rɪ'kɒnɪsns/ *n* reconhecimento *m*

reconnoitre /rekə'nɔɪtə(r)/ *vt/i* (*pres p* **-tring**) (*mil*) reconhecer, fazer um reconhecimento (de)

reconsider /ri:kən'sɪdə(r)/ *vt* reconsiderar

reconstruct /ri:kən'strʌkt/ *vt* reconstruir. ~**ion** /-ʃn/ *n* reconstrução *f*

record[1] /rɪ'kɔ:d/ *vt* registar; (*disc, tape etc*) gravar. ~ **that** referir/relatar que. ~**ing** *n* (*disc, tape etc*) gravação *f*

record[2] /'rekɔ:d/ *n* (*register*) registro *m*, (*P*) registo *m*; (*mention*) menção *f*, nota *f*; (*file*) arquivo *m*; (*mus*) disco *m*; (*sport*) record(e) *m* □ *a* record(e) *invar*. **have a (criminal)** ~ ter cadastro. **off the** ~ (*unofficial*) oficioso; (*secret*) confidencial. ~**-player** *n* toca-discos *m invar*, (*P*) gira-discos *m invar*

recorder /rɪ'kɔ:də(r)/ *n* (*mus*) flauta *f* de ponta; (*techn*) instrumento *m* registrador
recount /rɪ'kaʊnt/ *vt* narrar em pormenor, relatar
re-count /'ri:kaʊnt/ *n* (*pol*) nova contagem *f*
recoup /rɪ'ku:p/ *vt* compensar; (*recover*) recuperar
recourse /rɪ'kɔ:s/ *n* recurso *m*. **have ~ to** recorrer a
recover /rɪ'kʌvə(r)/ *vt* recuperar □ *vi* restabelecer-se. **~y** *n* recuperação *f*; (*health*) recuperação *f*, restabelecimento *m*
recreation /rekrɪ'eɪʃn/ *n* recreação *f*, recreio *m*; (*pastime*) passatempo *m*. **~al** *a* recreativo
recrimination /rɪkrɪmɪ'neɪʃn/ *n* recriminação *f*
recruit /rɪ'kru:t/ *n* recruta *m* □ *vt* recrutar. **~ment** *n* recrutamento *m*
rectang|le /'rektæŋgl/ *n* retângulo *m*, (*P*) rectângulo *m*. **~ular** /-'tæŋgjʊlə(r)/ *a* retangular, (*P*) rectangular
rectify /'rektɪfaɪ/ *vt* retificar, (*P*) rectificar
recuperate /rɪ'kju:pəreɪt/ *vt/i* recuperar(-se)
recur /rɪ'kɜ:(r)/ *vi* (*pt* **recurred**) repetir-se; (*come back*) voltar (**to** a)
recurren|t /rɪ'kʌrənt/ *a* freqüente, (*P*) frequente, repetido, periódico. **~ce** *n* repetição *f*
recycle /ri:'saɪkl/ *vt* reciclar
red /red/ *a* (**redder, reddest**) encarnado, vermelho; (*hair*) ruivo □ *n* encarnado *m*, vermelho *m*. **in the ~** em déficit. **~ carpet** (*fig*) recepção *f* solene, tratamento *m* especial. **R~ Cross** Cruz *f* Vermelha. **~-handed** *a* em flagrante (delito), com a boca na botija (*colloq*). **~ herring** (*fig*) pista *f* falsa. **~-hot** *a* escaldante, incandescente. **~ light** luz *f* vermelha. **~ tape** (*fig*) papelada *f*, burocracia *f*. **~ wine** vinho *m* tinto
redden /'redn/ *vt/i* avermelhar (-se); (*blush*) corar, ruborizar-se
redecorate /ri:'dekəreɪt/ *vt* decorar/ pintar de novo
red|eem /rɪ'di:m/ *vt* (*sins etc*) redimir; (*sth pawned*) tirar do prego (*colloq*); (*voucher etc*) resgatar. **~emption** /rɪ'dempʃn/ *n* resgate *m*; (*of honour*) salvação *f*
redirect /ri:daɪ'rekt/ *vt* (*letter*) reendereçar
redness /'rednɪs/ *n* vermelhidão *f*, cor *f* vermelha
redo /ri:'du:/ *vt* (*pt* **-did**, *pp* **-done**) refazer
redress /rɪ'dres/ *vt* reparar; (*set right*) remediar, emendar. **~ the balance** restabelecer o equilíbrio □ *n* reparação *f*
reduc|e /rɪ'dju:s/ *vt* reduzir; (*temperature etc*) baixar. **~tion** /rɪ-'dʌkʃən/ *n* redução *f*
redundan|t /rɪ'dʌndənt/ *a* redundante, supérfluo; (*worker*) desempregado. **be made ~t** ficar desempregado. **~cy** *n* demissão *f* por excesso de pessoal
reed /ri:d/ *n* cana *f*, junco *m*; (*mus*) palheta *f*
reef /ri:f/ *n* recife *m*
reek /ri:k/ *n* mau cheiro *m* □ *vi* cheirar mal, tresandar. **he ~s of wine** ele está com cheiro de vinho
reel /ri:l/ *n* carretel *m*; (*spool*) bobina *f* □ *vi* cambalear, vacilar □ *vt* **~ off** recitar (*colloq*)
refectory /rɪ'fektərɪ/ *n* refeitório *m*
refer /rɪ'fɜ:(r)/ *vt/i* (*pt* **referred**) **~ to** referir-se a; (*concern*) aplicar-se a, dizer respeito a; (*consult*) consultar; (*direct*) remeter a
referee /refə'ri:/ *n* árbitro *m*; (*for job*) pessoa *f* que dá referências □ *vt* (*pt* **refereed**) arbitrar
reference /'refrəns/ *n* referência *f*; (*testimonial*) referências *fpl*. **in ~ or with ~ to** com referência a. **~ book** livro *m* de consulta
referendum /refə'rendəm/ *n* (*pl* **-dums** *or* **-da**) referendo *m*, plebiscito *m*
refill[1] /ri:'fɪl/ *vt* encher de novo; (*pen etc*) pôr carga nova em
refill[2] /'ri:fɪl/ *n* (*pen etc*) carga *f* nova, (*P*) recarga *f*
refine /rɪ'faɪn/ *vt* refinar. **~d** *a* refinado; (*taste, manners etc*) requintado. **~ment** *n* (*taste, manners etc*) refinamento *m*, requinte *m*; (*tech*) refinação *f*. **~ry** /-ərɪ/ *n* refinaria *f*
reflect /rɪ'flekt/ *vt/i* refletir, (*P*) reflectir (**on/upon** em). **~ion** /-ʃn/ *n* reflexão *f*; (*image*) reflexo *m*. **~or** *n* refletor *m*, (*P*) reflector *m*
reflective /rɪ'flektɪv/ *a* refletor, (*P*) reflector; (*thoughtful*) refletido, (*P*) reflectido, ponderado
reflex /'ri:fleks/ *a & n* reflexo (*m*)
reflexive /rɪ'fleksɪv/ *a* (*gram*) reflexivo, (*P*) reflexo
reform /rɪ'fɔ:m/ *vt/i* reformar(-se) □ *n* reforma *f*. **~er** *n* reformador *m*
refract /rɪ'frækt/ *vt* refratar, (*P*) refractar
refrain[1] /rɪ'freɪn/ *n* refrão *m*, estribilho *m*
refrain[2] /rɪ'freɪn/ *vi* abster-se (**from** de)
refresh /rɪ'freʃ/ *vt* refrescar; (*of rest etc*) restaurar. **~ one's memory** avivar *or*

refrescar a memória. **~ing** *a* refrescante; (*of rest etc*) reparador. **~ments** *npl* refeição *f* leve; (*drinks*) refrescos *mpl*

refresher /rɪ'freʃə(r)/ *n* **~ course** curso *m* de reciclagem

refrigerat|e /rɪ'frɪdʒəreɪt/ *vt* refrigerar. **~or** *n* frigorífico *m*, refrigerador *m*, geladeira *f*

refuel /ri:'fju:əl/ *vt/i* (*pt* **refuelled**) reabastecer(-se) (de combustível)

refuge /'refju:dʒ/ *n* refúgio *m*, asilo *m*. **take ~** refugiar-se

refugee /refjʊ'dʒi:/ *n* refugiado *m*

refund[1] /rɪ'fʌnd/ *vt* reembolsar

refund[2] /'ri:fʌnd/ *n* reembolso *m*

refus|e[1] /rɪ'fju:z/ *vt/i* recusar(-se). **~al** *n* recusa *f*. **first ~al** preferência *f*, primeira opção *f*

refuse[2] /'refju:s/ *n* refugo *m*, lixo *m*. **~-collector** *n* lixeiro *m*, (*P*) homem *m* do lixo

refute /rɪ'fju:t/ *vt* refutar

regain /rɪ'geɪn/ *vt* recobrar, recuperar

regal /'ri:gl/ *a* real, régio

regalia /rɪ'geɪlɪə/ *npl* insígnias *fpl*

regard /rɪ'ga:d/ *vt* considerar; (*gaze*) olhar □ *n* consideração *f*, estima *f*; (*gaze*) olhar *m*. **~s** cumprimentos *mpl*; (*less formally*) lembranças *fpl*, saudades *fpl*. **as ~s, ~ing** *prep* no que diz respeito a, quanto a. **~less** *adv* apesar de tudo. **~less of** apesar de

regatta /rɪ'gætə/ *n* regata *f*

regenerate /rɪ'dʒenəreɪt/ *vt* regenerar

regen|t /'ri:dʒənt/ *n* regente *mf*. **~cy** *n* regência *f*

regime /reɪ'ʒi:m/ *n* regime *m*

regiment /'redʒɪmənt/ *n* regimento *m*. **~al** /-'mentl/ *a* de regimento, regimental. **~ation** /-en'teɪʃn/ *n* arregimentação *f*, disciplina *f* excessiva

region /'ri:dʒən/ *n* região *f*. **in the ~ of** por volta de. **~al** *a* regional

regist|er /'redʒɪstə(r)/ *n* registro *m*, (*P*) registo *m* □ *vt* (*record*) anotar; (*notice*) fixar, registar, prestar atenção a; (*birth, letter*) registrar, (*P*) registar; (*vehicle*) matricular; (*emotions etc*) exprimir □ *vi* inscrever-se. **~er office** registro *m*, (*P*) registo *m*. **~ration** /-'streɪʃn/ *n* registro *m*, (*P*) registo *m*; (*for course*) inscrição *f*, matrícula *f*. **~ration (number)** número *m* de placa

registrar /redʒɪ'stra:(r)/ *n* oficial *m* do registro, (*P*) registo civil; (*univ*) secretário *m*

regret /rɪ'gret/ *n* pena *f*, pesar *m*; (*repentance*) remorso *m*. **I have no ~s** não estou arrependido □ *vt* (*pt* **regretted**) lamentar, sentir (**to do** fazer); (*feel repentance*) arrepender-se de, lamentar. **~fully** *adv* com pena, pesarosamente. **~table** *a* lamentável. **~tably** *adv* infelizmente

regular /'regjʊlə(r)/ *a* regular; (*usual*) normal; (*colloq: thorough*) perfeito, verdadeiro, autêntico □ *n* (*colloq: client*) cliente *mf* habitual. **~ity** /-'lærətɪ/ *n* regularidade *f*. **~ly** *adv* regularmente

regulat|e /'regjʊleɪt/ *vt* regular. **~ion** /-'leɪʃn/ *n* regulação *f*; (*rule*) regulamento *m*, regra *f*

rehabilitat|e /ri:ə'bɪlɪteɪt/ *vt* reabilitar. **~ion** /-'teɪʃn/ *n* reabilitação *f*

rehash[1] /ri:'hæʃ/ *vt* apresentar sob nova forma, (*P*) cozinhar (*colloq*)

rehash[2] /'ri:hæʃ/ *n* (*fig*) apanhado *m*, (*P*) cozinhado *m* (*colloq*)

rehears|e /rɪ'hɜ:s/ *vt* ensaiar. **~al** *n* ensaio *m*. **dress ~al** ensaio *m* geral

reign /reɪn/ *n* reinado *m* □ *vi* reinar (**over** em)

reimburse /ri:ɪm'bɜ:s/ *vt* reembolsar. **~ment** *n* reembolso *m*

rein /reɪn/ *n* rédea *f*

reincarnation /ri:ɪnka:'neɪʃn/ *n* reencarnação *f*

reindeer /'reɪndɪə(r)/ *n invar* rena *f*

reinforce /ri:ɪn'fɔ:s/ *vt* reforçar. **~ment** *n* reforço *m*. **~ments** reforços *mpl*. **~d concrete** concreto *m* armado, (*P*) cimento *m or* betão *m* armado

reinstate /ri:ɪn'steɪt/ *vt* reintegrar

reiterate /ri:'ɪtəreɪt/ *vt* reiterar

reject[1] /rɪ'dʒekt/ *vt* rejeitar. **~ion** /-ʃn/ *n* rejeição *f*

reject[2] /'ri:dʒekt/ *n* (artigo de) refugo *m*

rejoic|e /rɪ'dʒɔɪs/ *vi* regozijar-se (**at/over** com). **~ing** *n* regozijo *m*

rejuvenate /ri:'dʒu:vəneɪt/ *vt* rejuvenescer

relapse /rɪ'læps/ *n* recaída *f* □ *vi* recair

relate /rɪ'leɪt/ *vt* relatar; (*associate*) relacionar □ *vi* **~ to** ter relação com, dizer respeito a; (*get on with*) entender-se com. **~d** *a* aparentado; (*ideas etc*) afim, relacionado

relation /rɪ'leɪʃn/ *n* relação *f*; (*person*) parente *mf*. **~ship** *n* parentesco *m*; (*link*) relação *f*; (*affair*) ligação *f*

relative /'relətɪv/ *n* parente *mf* □ *a* relativo. **~ly** *adv* relativamente

relax /rɪ'læks/ *vt/i* relaxar(-se); (*fig*) descontrair(-se). **~ation** /ri:læk'seɪʃn/ *n* relaxamento *m*; (*fig*) descontração *f*, (*P*) descontracção *f*; (*recreation*) distração *f*, (*P*) distracção *f*. **~ing** *a* relaxante

relay[1] /'ri:leɪ/ *n* turma *f*, (*P*) turno *m*. **~ race** corrida *f* de revezamento, (*P*) estafetas

relay[2] /rɪ'leɪ/ *vt* (*message*) retransmitir

release /rɪ'li:s/ *vt* libertar, soltar; (*mech*) desengatar, soltar; (*bomb, film, record*) lançar; (*news*) dar, publicar; (*gas, smoke*) soltar □ *n* libertação *f*; (*mech*) desengate *m*; (*bomb, film, record*) lançamento *m*; (*news*) publicação *f*; (*gas, smoke*) emissão *f*. **new ~** estréia *f*

relegate /'relɪgeɪt/ *vt* relegar

relent /rɪ'lent/ *vi* ceder. **~less** *a* implacável, inexorável, inflexível

relevan|t /'reləvənt/ *a* relevante, pertinente, a propósito. **be ~ to** ter a ver com. **~ce** *n* pertinência *f*, relevância *f*

reliab|le /rɪ'laɪəbl/ *a* de confiança, com que se pode contar; (*source etc*) fidedigno; (*machine etc*) seguro, confiável. **~ility** /-'bɪlətɪ/ *n* confiabilidade *f*

reliance /rɪ'laɪəns/ *n* (*dependence*) segurança *f*; (*trust*) confiança *f*, fé *f* (**on** em)

relic /'relɪk/ *n* relíquia *f*. **~s** vestígios *mpl*, ruínas *fpl*

relief /rɪ'li:f/ *n* alívio *m*; (*assistance*) auxílio *m*, assistência *f*; (*outline, design*) relevo *m*. **~ road** estrada *f* alternativa

relieve /rɪ'li:v/ *vt* aliviar; (*help*) socorrer; (*take over from*) revezar, substituir; (*mil*) render

religion /rɪ'lɪdʒən/ *n* religião *f*

religious /rɪ'lɪdʒəs/ *a* religioso

relinquish /rɪ'lɪŋkwɪʃ/ *vt* abandonar, renunciar a

relish /'relɪʃ/ *n* prazer *m*, gosto *m*; (*culin*) molho *m* condimentado □ *vt* saborear, apreciar, gostar de

relocate /ri:ləʊ'keɪt/ *vt/i* transferir(-se), mudar(-se)

reluctan|t /rɪ'lʌktənt/ *a* relutante (**to** em), pouco inclinado (**to** a). **~ce** *n* relutância *f*. **~tly** *adv* a contragosto, relutantemente

rely /rɪ'laɪ/ *vi* **~ on** contar com; (*depend*) depender de

remain /rɪ'meɪn/ *vi* ficar, permanecer. **~s** *npl* restos *mpl*; (*ruins*) ruínas *fpl*. **~ing** *a* restante

remainder /rɪ'meɪndə(r)/ *n* restante *m*, remanescente *m*

remand /rɪ'ma:nd/ *vt* reconduzir à prisão para detenção provisória □ *n* **on ~** sob prisão preventiva

remark /rɪ'ma:k/ *n* observação *f*, comentário *m* □ *vt* observar, comentar □ *vi* **~ on** fazer observações *or* comentários sobre. **~able** *a* notável

remarr|y /ri:'mærɪ/ *vt/i* tornar a casar(-se) (com). **~iage** *n* novo casamento *m*

remed|y /'remədɪ/ *n* remédio *m* □ *vt* remediar. **~ial** /rɪ'mi:dɪəl/ *a* (*med*) corretivo, (*P*) correctivo

rememb|er /rɪ'membə(r)/ *vt* lembrar-se de, recordar-se de. **~rance** *n* lembrança *f*, recordação *f*

remind /rɪ'maɪnd/ *vt* (fazer) lembrar (**sb of sth** alg coisa a alguém). **~ sb to do** lembrar a alguém que faça. **~er** *n* o que serve para fazer lembrar; (*note*) lembrete *m*

reminisce /remɪ'nɪs/ *vi* (re)lembrar (coisas passadas). **~nces** *npl* reminiscências *fpl*

reminiscent /remɪ'nɪsnt/ *a* **~ of** que faz lembrar, evocativo de

remiss /rɪ'mɪs/ *a* negligente, descuidado

remission /rɪ'mɪʃn/ *n* remissão *f*; (*jur*) comutação *f* (de pena)

remit /rɪ'mɪt/ *vt* (*pt* **remitted**) (*money*) remeter. **~tance** *n* remessa *f* (de dinheiro)

remnant /'remnənt/ *n* resto *m*; (*trace*) vestígio *m*; (*of cloth*) retalho *m*

remorse /rɪ'mɔ:s/ *n* remorso *m*. **~ful** *a* arrependido, com remorsos. **~less** *a* implacável

remote /rɪ'məʊt/ *a* remoto, distante; (*person*) distante; (*slight*) vago, leve. **~ control** comando *m* à distância, telecomando *m*. **~ly** *adv* de longe; vagamente

remov|e /rɪ'mu:v/ *vt* tirar, remover; (*lead away*) levar; (*dismiss*) demitir; (*get rid of*) eliminar. **~al** *n* remoção *f*; (*dismissal*) desmissão *f*; (*from house*) mudança *f*

remunerat|e /rɪ'mju:nəreɪt/ *vt* remunerar. **~ion** /-'reɪʃn/ *n* remuneração *f*

rename /ri:'neɪm/ *vt* rebatizar, (*P*) rebaptizar

render /'rendə(r)/ *vt* retribuir; (*services*) prestar; (*mus*) interpretar; (*translate*) traduzir. **~ing** *n* (*mus*) interpretação *f*; (*plaster*) reboco *m*

renegade /'renɪgeɪd/ *n* renegado *m*

renew /rɪ'nju:/ *vt* renovar; (*resume*) retomar. **~able** *a* renovável. **~al** *n* renovação *f*; (*resumption*) reatamento *m*

renounce /rɪ'naʊns/ *vt* renunciar a; (*disown*) renegar, repudiar

renovat|e /'renəveɪt/ *vt* renovar. **~ion** /-'veɪʃn/ *n* renovação *f*

renown /rɪ'naʊn/ *n* renome *m*. **~ed** *a* conceituado, célebre, de renome

rent /rent/ *n* aluguel *m*, (*P*) aluguer *m*, renda *f* □ *vt* alugar, arrendar. **~al** *n* (*charge*) aluguel *m*, (*P*) aluguer *m*, renda *f*; (*act of renting*) aluguel *m*, (*P*) aluguer *m*

renunciation /rɪnʌnsɪ'eɪʃn/ *n* renúncia *f*

reopen /ri:'əʊpən/ *vt/i* reabrir (-se). **~ing** *n* reabertura *f*

reorganize /ri:'ɔ:gənaɪz/ *vt/i* reorganizar(-se)

rep /rep/ *n* (*colloq*) vendedor *m*, caixeiro-viajante *m*

repair /rɪ'peə(r)/ *vt* reparar, consertar □ *n* reparo *m*, conserto *m*. **in good ~** em bom estado (de conservação)

repartee /repa:'ti:/ *n* resposta *f* pronta e espirituosa

repatriat|e /ri:'pætrɪeɪt/ *vt* repatriar. **~ion** /-'eɪʃn/ *n* repatriamento *m*

repay /ri:'peɪ/ *vt* (*pt* **repaid**) pagar, devolver, reembolsar; (*reward*) recompensar. **~ment** *n* pagamento *m*, reembolso *m*

repeal /rɪ'pi:l/ *vt* revogar □ *n* revogação *f*

repeat /rɪ'pi:t/ *vt/i* repetir(-se) □ *n* repetição *f*; (*broadcast*) retransmissão *f*. **~edly** *adv* repetidas vezes, repetidamente

repel /rɪ'pel/ *vt* (*pt* **repelled**) repelir. **~lent** *a* & *n* repelente (*m*)

repent /rɪ'pent/ *vi* arrepender-se (**of** de). **~ance** *n* arrependimento *m*. **~ant** *a* arrependido

repercussion /ri:pə'kʌʃn/ *n* repercussão *f*

repertoire /'repətwa:(r)/ *n* repertório *m*

repertory /'repətrɪ/ *n* repertório *m*

repetit|ion /repɪ'tɪʃn/ *n* repetição *f*. **~ious** /-'tɪʃəs/, **~ive** /rɪ-'petətɪv/ *a* repetitivo

replace /rɪ'pleɪs/ *vt* colocar no mesmo lugar, repor; (*take the place of*) substituir. **~ment** *n* reposição *f*; (*substitution*) substituição *f*; (*person*) substituto *m*

replenish /rɪ'plenɪʃ/ *vt* voltar a encher, reabastecer; (*renew*) renovar

replica /'replɪkə/ *n* réplica *f*, cópia *f*, reprodução *f*

reply /rɪ'plaɪ/ *vt/i* responder, replicar □ *n* resposta *f*, réplica *f*

report /rɪ'pɔ:t/ *vt* relatar; (*notify*) informar; (*denounce*) denunciar, apresentar queixa de □ *vi* fazer um relatório. **~ (on)** (*news item*) fazer uma reportagem (sobre). **~ to** (*go*) apresentar-se a □ *n* (*in newspapers*) reportagem *f*; (*of company, doctor*) relatório *m*; (*schol*) boletim *m* escolar; (*sound*) detonação *f*; (*rumour*) rumores *mpl*. **~edly** *adv* segundo consta. **~er** *n* repórter *m*

repose /rɪ'pəʊz/ *n* repouso *m*

repossess /ri:pə'zes/ *vt* reapossar-se de, retomar de

represent /reprɪ'zent/ *vt* representar. **~ation** /-'teɪʃn/ *n* representação *f*

representative /reprɪ'zentətɪv/ *a* representativo □ *n* representante *mf*

repress /rɪ'pres/ *vt* reprimir. **~ion** /-ʃn/ *n* repressão *f*. **~ive** *a* repressor, repressivo

reprieve /rɪ'pri:v/ *n* suspensão *f* temporária; (*temporary relief*) tréguas *fpl* □ *vt* suspender temporariamente; (*fig*) dar tréguas a

reprimand /'reprɪma:nd/ *vt* repreender □ *n* repreensão *f*, reprimenda *f*

reprint /'ri:prɪnt/ *n* reimpressão *f*, reedição *f* □ *vt* /ri:'prɪnt/ reimprimir

reprisals /rɪ'praɪzlz/ *npl* represálias *fpl*

reproach /rɪ'prəʊtʃ/ *vt* censurar, repreender (**sb for sth** alguém por alg coisa, alg coisa a alguém) □ *n* censura *f*. **above ~** irrepreensível. **~ful** *a* repreensivo, reprovador. **~fully** *adv* reprovadoramente

reproduc|e /ri:prə'dju:s/ *vt/i* reproduzir(-se). **~tion** /-'dʌkʃn/ *n* reprodução *f*. **~tive** /-'dʌktɪv/ *a* reprodutivo, reprodutor

reptile /'reptaɪl/ *n* réptil *m*

republic /rɪ'pʌblɪk/ *n* república *f*. **~an** *a* & *n* republicano (*m*)

repudiate /rɪ'pju:dɪeɪt/ *vt* repudiar, rejeitar

repugnan|t /rɪ'pʌgnənt/ *a* repugnante. **~ce** *n* repugnância *f*

repuls|e /rɪ'pʌls/ *vt* repelir, repulsar. **~ion** /-ʃn/ *n* repulsa *f*. **~ive** *a* repulsivo, repelente, repugnante

reputable /'repjʊtəbl/ *a* respeitado, honrado; (*firm, make etc*) de renome, conceituado

reputation /repjʊ'teɪʃn/ *n* reputação *f*

repute /rɪ'pju:t/ *n* reputação *f*. **~d** /-ɪd/ *a* suposto, putativo. **~d to be** tido como, tido na conta de. **~dly** /-ɪdlɪ/ *adv* segundo consta, com fama de

request /rɪ'kwest/ *n* pedido *m* □ *vt* pedir, solicitar (**of, from** a)

requiem /'rekwɪəm/ *n* réquiem *m*; (*mass*) missa *f* de réquiem

require /rɪ'kwaɪə(r)/ *vt* requerer. **~d** *a* requerido; (*needed*) necessário, preciso. **~ment** *n* (*fig*) requisito *m*; (*need*) necessidade *f*; (*demand*) exigência *f*

requisite /'rekwɪzɪt/ *a* necessário □ *n* coisa necessária *f*, requisito *m*. **~s** (*for travel etc*) artigos *mpl*

requisition /rekwɪ'zɪʃn/ *n* requisição *f* □ *vt* requisitar

resale /'ri:seɪl/ *n* revenda *f*

rescue /'reskju:/ *vt* salvar, socorrer (**from** de) □ *n* salvamento *m*; (*help*) socorro *m*, ajuda *f*. **~r** /-ə(r)/ *n* salvador *m*

research /rɪ'sɜ:tʃ/ *n* pesquisa *f*, investigação *f* □ *vt/i* pesquisar, fazer investigação (**into** sobre). **~er** *n* investigador *m*

resembl|e /rɪ'zembl/ *vt* assemelhar-se a, parecer-se com. **~ance** *n* semelhança *f*, similaridade *f* (**to** com)

resent /rɪ'zent/ *vt* ressentir(-se de), ficar ressentido com. **~ful** *a* ressentido. **~ment** *n* ressentimento *m*

reservation /rezə'veɪʃn/ *n* (*booking*) reserva *f*; (*Amer*) reserva *f* (de índios)

reserve /rɪ'zɜ:v/ *vt* reservar □ *n* reserva *f*; (*sport*) suplente *mf*. **in ~** de reserva. **~d** *a* reservado

reservoir /'rezəvwa:(r)/ *n* (*lake, supply etc*) reservatório *m*; (*container*) depósito *m*

reshape /ri:'ʃeɪp/ *vt* remodelar

reshuffle /ri:'ʃʌfl/ *vt* (*pol*) remodelar □ *n* (*pol*) reforma *f* (do Ministério)

reside /rɪ'zaɪd/ *vi* residir

residen|t /'rezɪdənt/ *a* residente □ *n* morador *m*, habitante *mf*; (*foreigner*) residente *mf*; (*in hotel*) hóspede *mf*. **~ce** *n* residência *f*; (*of students*) residência *f*, lar *m*. **~ce permit** visto *m* de residência

residential /rezɪ'denʃl/ *a* residencial

residue /'rezɪdju:/ *n* resíduo *m*

resign /rɪ'zaɪn/ *vt* (*post*) demitir-se. **~ o.s. to** resignar-se a □ *vi* demitir-se de. **~ation** /rezɪg'neɪʃn/ *n* resignação *f*; (*from job*) demissão *f*. **~ed** *a* resignado

resilien|t /rɪ'zɪlɪənt/ *a* (*springy*) elástico; (*person*) resistente. **~ce** *n* elasticidade *f*; (*of person*) resistência *f*

resin /'rezɪn/ *n* resina *f*

resist /rɪ'zɪst/ *vt/i* resistir (a). **~ance** *n* resistência *f*. **~ant** *a* resistente

resolut|e /'rezəlu:t/ *a* resoluto. **~ion** /-'lu:ʃn/ *n* resolução *f*

resolve /rɪ'zɒlv/ *vt* resolver. **~ to do** resolver fazer □ *n* resolução *f*. **~d** *a* (*resolute*) resoluto; (*decided*) resolvido (**to** a)

resonan|t /'rezənənt/ *a* ressonante. **~ce** *n* ressonância *f*

resort /rɪ'zɔ:t/ *vi* **~ to** recorrer a, valer-se de □ *n* recurso *m*; (*place*) estância *f*, local *m* turístico. **as a last ~** em último recurso. **seaside ~** praia *f*, balneário *m*, (*P*) estância *f* balnear

resound /rɪ'zaʊnd/ *vi* reboar, ressoar (**with** com). **~ing** *a* ressoante; (*fig*) retumbante

resource /rɪ'sɔ:s/ *n* recurso *m*. **~s** recursos *mpl*, riquezas *fpl*. **~ful** *a* expedito, engenhoso, desembaraçado. **~fulness** *n* expediente *m*, engenho *m*

respect /rɪ'spekt/ *n* respeito *m* □ *vt* respeitar. **with ~ to** a respeito de, com respeito a, relativamente a. **~ful** *a* respeitoso

respectab|le /rɪ'spektəbl/ *a* respeitável; (*passable*) passável, aceitável. **~ility** /-'bɪlətɪ/ *n* respeitabilidade *f*

respective /rɪ'spektɪv/ *a* respectivo. **~ly** *adv* respectivamente

respiration /respə'reɪʃn/ *n* respiração *f*

respite /'respaɪt/ *n* pausa *f*, trégua *f*, folga *f*

respond /rɪ'spɒnd/ *vi* responder (**to** a); (*react*) reagir (**to** a)

response /rɪ'spɒns/ *n* resposta *f*; (*reaction*) reação *f*, (*P*) reacção *f*

responsib|le /rɪ'spɒnsəbl/ *a* responsável; (*job*) de responsabilidade. **~ility** /-'bɪlətɪ/ *n* responsabilidade *f*

responsive /rɪ'spɒnsɪv/ *a* receptivo, que reage bem. **~ to** sensível a

rest[1] /rest/ *vt/i* descansar, repousar; (*lean*) apoiar(-se) □ *n* descanso *m*, repouso *m*; (*support*) suporte *m*. **~-room** *n* (*Amer*) banheiro *m*, (*P*) toaletes *mpl*

rest[2] /rest/ *vi* (*remain*) ficar □ *n* (*remainder*) resto *m* (**of** de). **the ~ (of the)** (*others*) os outros. **it ~s with him** cabe a ele

restaurant /'restrɒnt/ *n* restaurante *m*

restful /'restfl/ *a* sossegado, repousante, tranqüilo, (*P*) tranquilo

restitution /restɪ'tju:ʃn/ *n* restituição *f*; (*for injury*) indenização *f*, (*P*) indemnização *f*

restless /'restlɪs/ *a* agitado, desassossegado

restor|e /rɪ'stɔ:(r)/ *vt* restaurar; (*give back*) restituir, devolver. **~ation** /restə'reɪʃn/ *n* restauração *f*

restrain /rɪ'streɪn/ *vt* conter, reprimir. **~ o.s.** controlar-se. **~ sb from** impedir alguém de. **~ed** *a* comedido, reservado. **~t** *n* controle *m*; (*moderation*) moderação *f*, comedimento *m*

restrict /rɪ'strɪkt/ *vt* restringir, limitar. **~ion** /-ʃn/ *n* restrição *f*. **~ive** *a* restritivo

result /rɪ'zʌlt/ *n* resultado *m* □ *vi* resultar (**from** de). **~ in** resultar em

resum|e /rɪ'zju:m/ *vt/i* reatar, retomar; (*work, travel*) recomeçar. **~ption** /rɪ'zʌmpʃn/ *n* reatamento *m*, retomada *f*; (*of work*) recomeço *m*

résumé /'rezju:meɪ/ *n* resumo *m*

resurgence /rɪ'sɜ:dʒəns/ *n* reaparecimento *m*, ressurgimento *m*
resurrect /rezə'rekt/ *vt* ressuscitar. **~ion** /-ʃn/ *n* ressureição *f*
resuscitat|e /rɪ'sʌsɪteɪt/ *vt* ressuscitar, reanimar. **~ion** /-'teɪʃn/ *n* reanimação *f*
retail /'ri:teɪl/ *n* retalho *m* □ *a* & *adv* a retalho □ *vt*/*i* vender(-se) a retalho. **~er** *n* retalhista *mf*
retain /rɪ'teɪn/ *vt* reter; (*keep*) conservar, guardar
retaliat|e /rɪ'tælɪeɪt/ *vi* retaliar, exercer represálias, desforrar-se. **~ion** /-'eɪʃn/ *n* retaliação *f*, represália *f*, desforra *f*
retarded /rɪ'ta:dɪd/ *a* retardado, atrasado
retch /retʃ/ *vi* fazer esforço para vomitar, estar com ânsias de vômito
retention /rɪ'tenʃn/ *n* retenção *f*
retentive /rɪ'tentɪv/ *a* retentivo. **~ memory** boa memória *f*
reticen|t /'retɪsnt/ *a* reticente. **~ce** *n* reticência *f*
retina /'retɪnə/ *n* retina *f*
retinue /'retɪnju:/ *n* séquito *m*, comitiva *f*
retire /rɪ'taɪə(r)/ *vi* reformar-se, aposentar-se; (*withdraw*) retirar-se; (*go to bed*) ir deitar-se □ *vt* reformar, aposentar. **~d** *a* reformado, aposentado. **~ment** *n* reforma *f*, aposentadoria *f*, (*P*) aposentação *f*
retiring /rɪ'taɪərɪŋ/ *a* reservado, retraído
retort /rɪ'tɔ:t/ *vt*/*i* retrucar, retorquir □ *n* réplica *f*
retrace /ri:'treɪs/ *vt* **~ one's steps** refazer o mesmo caminho; (*fig*) recordar, recapitular
retract /rɪ'trækt/ *vt*/*i* retratar (-se); (*wheels*) recolher; (*claws*) encolher, recolher
retreat /ri'tri:t/ *vi* retirar-se; (*mil*) retirar, bater em retirada □ *n* retirada *f*; (*seclusion*) retiro *m*
retrial /ri:'traɪəl/ *n* novo julgamento *m*
retribution /retrɪ'bju:ʃn/ *n* castigo (merecido) *m*; (*vengeance*) vingança *f*
retriev|e /rɪ'tri:v/ *vt* ir buscar; (*rescue*) salvar; (*recover*) recuperar; (*put right*) reparar. **~al** *n* recuperação *f*. **information ~al** (*comput*) acesso *m* à informação. **~er** *n* (*dog*) perdigueiro *m*, (*P*) cobrador *m*
retrograde /'retrəgreɪd/ *a* retrógrado □ *vt* retroceder, recuar
retrospect /'retrəspekt/ *n* **in ~** em retrospecto, (*P*) retrospectivamente. **~ive** /-'spektɪv/ *a* retrospectivo; (*of law, payment*) retroativo, (*P*) retroactivo
return /rɪ'tɜ:n/ *vi* voltar, regressar, retornar (**to**, a) □ *vt* devolver; (*compliment, visit*) retribuir; (*put back*) pôr de volta □ *n* volta *f*, regresso *m*, retorno *m*; (*profit*) lucro *m*, rendimento *m*; (*restitution*) devolução *f*. **in ~ for** em troca de. **~ journey** viagem *f* de volta. **~ match** (*sport*) desafio *m* de desforra. **~ ticket** bilhete *m* de ida e volta. **many happy ~s (of the day)** muitos parabéns
reunion /ri:'ju:nɪən/ *n* reunião *f*
reunite /ri:ju:'naɪt/ *vt* reunir
rev /rev/ *n* (*colloq: auto*) rotação *f* □ *vt*/*i* (*pt* **revved**) **~ (up)** (*colloq: auto*) acelerar (o motor)
reveal /rɪ'vi:l/ *vt* revelar; (*display*) expor. **~ing** *a* revelador
revel /'revl/ *vi* (*pt* **revelled**) divertir-se. **~ in** deleitar-se com. **~ry** *n* festas *fpl*, festejos *mpl*
revelation /revə'leɪʃn/ *n* revelação *f*
revenge /rɪ'vendʒ/ *n* vingança *f*; (*sport*) desforra *f* □ *vt* vingar
revenue /'revənju:/ *n* receita *f*, rendimento *m*. **Inland R~** Fisco *m*
reverberate /rɪ'vɜ:bəreɪt/ *vi* ecoar, repercutir
revere /rɪ'vɪə(r)/ *vt* reverenciar, venerar
reverend /'revərənd/ *a* reverendo. **R~** Reverendo
reveren|t /'revərənt/ *a* reverente. **~ce** *n* reverência *f*, veneração *f*
revers|e /rɪ'vɜ:s/ *a* contrário, inverso □ *n* contrário *m*; (*back*) reverso *m*; (*gear*) marcha *f* à ré, (*P*) atrás □ *vt* virar ao contrário; (*order*) inverter; (*turn inside out*) virar do avesso; (*decision*) anular □ *vi* (*auto*) fazer marcha à ré, (*P*) atrás. **~al** *n* inversão *f*, mudança *f* em sentido contrário; (*of view etc*) mudança *f*
revert /rɪ'vɜ:t/ *vi* **~ to** reverter a
review /rɪ'vju:/ *n* (*inspection; magazine*) revista *f*; (*of a situation*) revisão *f*; (*critique*) crítica *f* □ *vt* revistar, passar revista em; (*situation*) rever; (*book, film etc*) fazer a crítica de. **~er** *n* crítico *m*
revis|e /rɪ'vaɪz/ *vt* rever; (*amend*) corrigir. **~ion** /-ɪʒn/ *n* revisão *f*; (*amendment*) correção *f*
reviv|e /rɪ'vaɪv/ *vt*/*i* ressuscitar, reavivar; (*play*) reapresentar; (*person*) reanimar(-se). **~al** *n* reflorescimento *m*, renascimento *m*
revoke /rɪ'vəʊk/ *vt* revogar, anular, invalidar
revolt /rɪ'vəʊlt/ *vt*/*i* revoltar(-se) □ *n* revolta *f*
revolting /rɪ'vəʊltɪŋ/ *a* (*disgusting*) repugnante
revolution /revə'lu:ʃn/ *n* revolução *f*. **~ary** *a* & *n* revolucionário (*m*). **~ize** *vt* revolucionar

revolv|e /rɪˈvɒlv/ *vi* girar. **~ing door** porta *f* giratória

revolver /rɪˈvɒlvə(r)/ *n* revólver *m*

revulsion /rɪˈvʌlʃn/ *n* repugnância *f*, repulsa *f*

reward /rɪˈwɔːd/ *n* prêmio *m*, (*P*) prémio *m*; (*for criminal, for lost/stolen property*) recompensa *f* □ *vt* recompensar. **~ing** *a* compensador; (*task etc*) gratificante

rewind /riːˈwaɪnd/ *vt* (*pt* **rewound**) rebobinar

rewrite /riːˈraɪt/ *vt* (*pt* **rewrote**, *pp* **rewritten**) reescrever

rhetoric /ˈretərɪk/ *n* retórica *f*. **~al** /rɪˈtɒrɪkl/ *a* retórico; (*question*) pro forma

rheumati|c /ruːˈmætɪk/ *a* reumático. **~sm** /ˈruːmətɪzm/ *n* reumatismo *m*

rhinoceros /raɪˈnɒsərəs/ *n* (*pl* **-oses**) rinoceronte *m*

rhubarb /ˈruːbaːb/ *n* ruibarbo *m*

rhyme /raɪm/ *n* rima *f*; (*poem*) versos *mpl* □ *vt/i* (fazer) rimar

rhythm /ˈrɪðəm/ *n* ritmo *m*. **~ic(al)** /ˈrɪðmɪk(l)/ *a* rítmico, compassado

rib /rɪb/ *n* costela *f*

ribbon /ˈrɪbən/ *n* fita *f*. **in ~s** em tiras

rice /raɪs/ *n* arroz *m*

rich /rɪtʃ/ *a* (**-er**, **-est**) rico; (*food*) rico em açucar e gordura. **~es** *npl* riquezas *fpl*. **~ly** *adv* ricamente. **~ness** *n* riqueza *f*

rickety /ˈrɪkətɪ/ *a* (*shaky*) desconjuntado

ricochet /ˈrɪkəʃeɪ/ *n* ricochete *m* □ *vi* (*pt* **ricocheted** /-ʃeɪd/) fazer ricochete, ricochetear

rid /rɪd/ *vt* (*pt* **rid**, *pres p* **ridding**) desembaraçar (**of** de). **get ~ of** desembaraçar-se de, livrar-se de

riddance /ˈrɪdns/ *n* **good ~!** que alívio!, vai com Deus!

ridden /ˈrɪdn/ *see* **ride**

riddle[1] /ˈrɪdl/ *n* enigma *m*; (*puzzle*) charada *f*

riddle[2] /ˈrɪdl/ *vt* **~ with** crivar de

ride /raɪd/ *vi* (*pt* **rode**, *pp* **ridden**) andar (de bicicleta, a cavalo, de carro) □ *vt* (*horse*) montar; (*bicycle*) andar de; (*distance*) percorrer □ *n* passeio *m or* volta *f* (de carro, a cavalo etc); (*distance*) percurso *m*. **~r** /-ə(r)/ *n* cavaleiro *m*, amazona *f*; (*cyclist*) ciclista *mf*; (*in document*) aditamento *m*

ridge /rɪdʒ/ *n* aresta *f*; (*of hill*) cume *m*

ridicule /ˈrɪdɪkjuːl/ *n* ridículo *m* □ *vt* ridicularizar

ridiculous /rɪˈdɪkjʊləs/ *a* ridículo

riding /ˈraɪdɪŋ/ *n* equitação *f*

rife /raɪf/ *a* **be ~** estar espalhado; (*of illness*) grassar. **~ with** cheio de

riff-raff /ˈrɪfræf/ *n* gentinha *f*, povinho *m*, ralé *f*

rifle /ˈraɪfl/ *n* espingarda *f* □ *vt* revistar e roubar, saquear

rift /rɪft/ *n* fenda *f*, brecha *f*; (*fig: dissension*) desacordo *m*, desavença *f*, desentendimento *m*

rig[1] /rɪg/ *vt* (*pt* **rigged**) equipar □ *n* (*for oil*) plataforma *f* de poço de petróleo. **~ out** enfarpelar (*colloq*). **~-out** *n* (*colloq*) roupa *f*, farpela *f* (*colloq*). **~ up** arranjar

rig[2] /rɪg/ *vt* (*pt* **rigged**) (*pej*) manipular. **~ged** *a* (*election*) fraudulento

right /raɪt/ *a* (*correct, moral*) certo, correto, (*P*) correcto; (*fair*) justo; (*not left*) direito; (*suitable*) certo, próprio □ *n* (*entitlement*) direito *m*; (*not left*) direita *f*; (*not evil*) o bem □ *vt* (*a wrong*) reparar; (*sth fallen*) endireitar □ *adv* (*not left*) à direita; (*directly*) direito; (*exactly*) mesmo, bem; (*completely*) completamente. **be ~** (*person*) ter razão (**to** em). **be in the ~** ter razão. **on the ~** à direita. **put ~** acertar, corrigir. **~ of way** (*auto*) prioridade *f*. **~ angle** *n* ângulo reto *m*, (*P*) recto. **~ away** logo, imediatamente. **~-hand** *a* à *or* de direita. **~-handed** *a* (*person*) destro. **~-wing** *a* (*pol*) de direita

righteous /ˈraɪtʃəs/ *a* justo, virtuoso

rightful /ˈraɪtfl/ *a* legítimo. **~ly** *adv* legitimamente, legalmente

rightly /ˈraɪtlɪ/ *adv* devidamente, corretamente, (*P*) correctamente; (*with reason*) justificadamente

rigid /ˈrɪdʒɪd/ *a* rígido. **~ity** /rɪˈdʒɪdətɪ/ *n* rigidez *f*

rigmarole /ˈrɪgmərəʊl/ *n* (*speech: procedure*) embrulhada *f*

rig|our /ˈrɪgə(r)/ *n* rigor *m*. **~orous** *a* rigoroso

rile /raɪl/ *vt* (*colloq*) irritar, exasperar

rim /rɪm/ *n* borda *f*; (*of wheel*) aro *m*

rind /raɪnd/ *n* (*on cheese, fruit*) casca *f*; (*on bacon*) pele *f*

ring[1] /rɪŋ/ *n* (*on finger*) anel *m*; (*for napkin, key etc*) argola *f*; (*circle*) roda *f*, círculo *m*; (*boxing*) ringue *m*; (*arena*) arena *f*; (*of people*) quadrilha *f* □ *vt* rodear, cercar. **~ road** *n* estrada *f* periférica *or* perimetral

ring[2] /rɪŋ/ *vt/i* (*pt* **rang**, *pp* **rung**) tocar; (*of words etc*) soar □ *n* toque *m*; (*colloq: phone call*) telefonadela *f* (*colloq*). **~ the bell** tocar a campaínha. **~ back** telefonar de volta. **~ off** desligar. **~ up** telefonar (a)

ringleader /ˈrɪŋliːdə(r)/ *n* cabeça *m*, cérebro *m*

rink /rɪŋk/ *n* rinque *m* de patinação
rinse /rɪns/ *vt* enxaguar ◻ *n* enxaguada *f*, (*P*) enxaguadela *f*; (*hair tint*) rinsagem *f*
riot /ˈraɪət/ *n* distúrbio *m*, motim *m*; (*of colours*) festival *m* ◻ *vi* fazer distúrbios *or* motins. **run ~** desenfrear-se, descontrolar-se; (*of plants*) crescer em matagal. **~er** *n* desordeiro *m*
riotous /ˈraɪətəs/ *a* desenfreado, turbulento, desordeiro
rip /rɪp/ *vt/i* (*pt* **ripped**) rasgar (-se) ◻ *n* rasgão *m*. **~ off** (*sl*: *defraud*) defraudar, enrolar (*sl*). **~-off** *n* (*sl*) roubalheira *f* (*colloq*)
ripe /raɪp/ *a* (**-er, -est**) maduro. **~ness** *n* madureza *f*, (*P*) amadurecimento *m*
ripen /ˈraɪpən/ *vt/i* amadurecer
ripple /ˈrɪpl/ *n* ondulação *f* leve; (*sound*) murmúrio *m* ◻ *vt/i* encrespar(-se), agitar(-se), ondular
rise /raɪz/ *vi* (*pt* **rose**, *pp* **risen**) subir, elevar-se; (*stand up*) erguer-se, levantar-se; (*rebel*) sublevar-se; (*sun*) nascer; (*curtain, prices*) subir ◻ *n* (*increase*) aumento *m*; (*slope*) subida *f*, ladeira *f*; (*origin*) origem *f*. **give ~ to** originar, causar, dar origem a. **~r** /-ə(r)/ *n* **early ~r** madrugador *m*
rising /ˈraɪzɪŋ/ *n* (*revolt*) insurreição *f* ◻ *a* (*sun*) nascente
risk /rɪsk/ *n* risco *m* ◻ *vt* arriscar. **at ~** em risco, em perigo. **at one's own ~** por sua conta e risco. **~ doing** (*venture*) arriscar-se a fazer. **~y** *a* arriscado
risqué /ˈriːskeɪ/ *a* picante
rite /raɪt/ *n* rito *m*. **last ~s** últimos sacramentos *mpl*
ritual /ˈrɪtʃʊəl/ *a* & *n* ritual (*m*)
rival /ˈraɪvl/ *n* & *a* rival (*mf*); (*fig*) concorrente (*mf*), competidor (*m*) ◻ *vt* (*pt* **rivalled**) rivalizar com. **~ry** *n* rivalidade *f*
river /ˈrɪvə(r)/ *n* rio *m* ◻ *a* fluvial
rivet /ˈrɪvɪt/ *n* rebite *m* ◻ *vt* (*pt* **riveted**) rebitar; (*fig*) prender, cravar. **~ing** *a* fascinante
road /rəʊd/ *n* estrada *f*; (*in town*) rua *f*; (*small; fig*) caminho *m*. **~-block** *n* barricada *f*. **~-map** *n* mapa *m* das estradas. **~ sign** *n* sinal *m*, placa *f* de sinalização. **~ tax** imposto *m* de circulação. **~-works** *npl* obras *fpl*
roadside /ˈrəʊdsaɪd/ *n* beira *f* da estrada
roadway /ˈreʊdweɪ/ *n* pista *f* de rolamento, (*P*) rodagem
roadworthy /ˈreʊdwɜːðɪ/ *a* em condições de ser utilizado na rua/estrada
roam /rəʊm/ *vi* errar, andar sem destino ◻ *vt* percorrer
roar /rɔː(r)/ *n* berro *m*, rugido *m*; (*of thunder*) ribombo *m*, troar *m*; (*of sea, wind*) bramido *m* ◻ *vt/i* berrar, rugir; (*of lion*) rugir; (*of thunder*) ribombar, troar; (*of sea, wind*) bramir. **~ with laughter** rir às gargalhadas
roaring /ˈrɔːrɪŋ/ *a* (*trade*) florescente; (*success*) enorme; (*fire*) com grandes chamas
roast /rəʊst/ *vt/i* assar ◻ *a* & *n* assado (*m*)
rob /rɒb/ *vt* (*pt* **robbed**) roubar (**sb of sth** alg coisa de alguém); (*bank*) assaltar; (*deprive*) privar (**of** de). **~ber** *n* ladrão *m*. **~bery** *n* roubo *m*; (*of bank*) assalto *m*
robe /rəʊb/ *n* veste *f* comprida e solta; (*dressing-gown*) robe *m*. **~s** *npl* (*of judge etc*) toga *f*
robin /ˈrɒbɪn/ *n* papo-roxo *m*, (*P*) pintarroxo *m*
robot /ˈrəʊbɒt/ *n* robô *m*, (*P*) robot *m*, autômato *m*, (*P*) autómato *m*
robust /rəʊˈbʌst/ *a* robusto
rock[1] /rɒk/ *n* rocha *f*; (*boulder*) penhasco *m*, rochedo *m*; (*sweet*) pirulito *m*, (*P*) chupa-chupa *m* comprido. **on the ~s** (*colloq: of marriage*) em crise; (*colloq: of drinks*) com gelo. **~-bottom** *n* ponto *m* mais baixo ◻ *a* (*of prices*) baixíssimo (*colloq*)
rock[2] /rɒk/ *vt/i* balouçar(-se); (*shake*) abanar, sacudir; (*child*) embalar ◻ *n* (*mus*) rock *m*. **~ing-chair** *n* cadeira *f* de balanço, (*P*) cadeira *f* de balouço. **~ing-horse** *n* cavalo *m* de balanço, (*P*) cavalo *m* de balouço
rocket /ˈrɒkɪt/ *n* foguete *m*
rocky /ˈrɒkɪ/ *a* (**-ier, -iest**) (*ground*) pedregoso; (*hill*) rochoso; (*colloq: unsteady*) instável; (*colloq: shaky*) tremido (*colloq*)
rod /rɒd/ *n* vara *f*, vareta *f*; (*mech*) haste *f*; (*for curtains*) bastão *m*, (*P*) varão *m*; (*for fishing*) vara (de pescar) *f*
rode /rəʊd/ *see* **ride**
rodent /ˈrəʊdnt/ *n* roedor *m*
rodeo /rəʊˈdeɪəʊ/ *n* (*pl* **-os**) rode(i)o *m*
roe /rəʊ/ *n* ova(s) *f* (*pl*) de peixe
rogue /rəʊg/ *n* (*dishonest*) patife *m*, velhaco *m*; (*mischievous*) brincalhão *m*
role /rəʊl/ *n* papel *m*
roll /rəʊl/ *vt/i* (fazer) rolar; (*into ball or cylinder*) enrolar(-se) ◻ *n* rolo *m*; (*list*) rol *m*, lista *f*; (*bread*) pãozinho *m*; (*of ship*) balanço *m*; (*of drum*) rufar *m*; (*of thunder*) ribombo *m*. **be ~ing in money** (*colloq*) nadar em dinheiro (*colloq*). **~ over** (*turn over*) virar-se ao contrário. **~ up** *vi* (*colloq*) aparecer ◻ *vt* (*sleeves*) arregaçar; (*umbrella*) fechar. **~-call** *n* chamada *f*. **~ing-pin** *n* rolo *m* de pastel
roller /ˈrəʊlə(r)/ *n* cilindro *m*; (*wave*) vagalhão *m*; (*for hair*) rolo *m*. **~-blind**

n estore *m*. **~-coaster** *n* montanha *f* russa. **~-skate** *n* patim *m* de rodas

rolling /'rəʊlɪŋ/ *a* ondulante

Roman /'rəʊmən/ *a* & *n* romano (*m*). **R~ Catholic** *a* & *n* católico (*m*). **~ numerals** algarismos *mpl* romanos

romance /rəʊ'mæns/ *n* (*love affair*) romance *m*; (*fig*) poesia *f*

Romania /rʊ'meɪnɪə/ *n* Romênia *f*, (*P*) Roménia *f*. **~n** *a* & *n* romeno (*m*)

romantic /rəʊ'mæntɪk/ *a* romântico. **~ally** *adv* românticamente. **~ism** *n* romantismo *m*. **~ize** *vi* fazer romance □ *vt* romantizar

romp /rɒmp/ *vi* brincar animadamente □ *n* brincadeira *f* animada. **~ers** *npl* macacão *m* de bebê, (*P*) fato *m* de bebé

roof /ru:f/ *n* (*pl* **roofs**) telhado *m*; (*of car*) teto *m*, (*P*) capota *f*; (*of mouth*) palato *m*, céu *m* da boca □ *vt* cobrir com telhado. **hit the ~** (*colloq*) ficar furioso. **~ing** *n* material *m* para telhados. **~-rack** *n* porta-bagagem *m*. **~-top** *n* cimo *m* do telhado

rook[1] /rʊk/ *n* (*bird*) gralha *f*

rook[2] /rʊk/ *n* (*chess*) torre *f*

room /rʊ:m/ *n* quarto *m*, divisão *f*; (*bedroom*) quarto *m* de dormir; (*large hall*) sala *f*; (*space*) espaço *m*, lugar *m*. **~s** (*lodgings*) apartamento *m*, cômodos *mpl*. **~-mate** *n* companheiro *m* de quarto. **~y** *a* espaçoso; (*clothes*) amplo, largo

roost /ru:st/ *n* poleiro *m* □ *vi* empoleirar-se. **~er** *n* (*Amer*) galo *m*

root[1] /ru:t/ *n* raiz *f*; (*fig*) origem *f* □ *vt*/*i* enraizar(-se), radicar(-se). **~ out** extirpar, erradicar. **take ~** criar raízes. **~less** *a* sem raízes, desenraizado

root[2] /ru:t/ *vi* **~ about** revolver, remexer. **~ for** (*Amer sl*) torcer por

rope /rəʊp/ *n* corda *f* □ *vt* atar. **know the ~s** estar por dentro (do assunto). **~ in** convencer a participar de

rosary /'rəʊzərɪ/ *n* rosário *m*

rose[1] /rəʊz/ *n* rosa *f*; (*nozzle*) ralo *m* (de regador). **~-bush** *n* roseira *f*

rose[2] /rəʊz/ *see* **rise**

rosé /'rəʊzeɪ/ *n* rosé *m*

rosette /rəʊ'zet/ *n* roseta *f*

rosewood /'rəʊzwʊd/ *n* pau-rosa *m*

roster /'rɒstə(r)/ *n* lista (de serviço) *f*, escala *f* (de serviço)

rostrum /'rɒstrəm/ *n* tribuna *f*; (*for conductor*) estrado *m*; (*sport*) podium *m*

rosy /'rəʊzɪ/ *a* (**-ier**, **-iest**) rosado; (*fig*) risonho

rot /rɒt/ *vt*/*i* (*pt* **rotted**) apodrecer □ *n* putrefação *f*, podridão *f*; (*sl*: *nonsense*) disparate *m*, asneiras *fpl*

rota /'rəʊtə/ *n* escala *f* de serviço

rotary /'rəʊtərɪ/ *a* rotativo, giratório

rotat|e /rəʊ'teɪt/ *vt*/*i* (fazer) girar, (fazer) revolver; (*change round*) alternar. **~ing** *a* rotativo. **~ion** /-ʃn/ *n* rotação *f*

rote /rəʊt/ *n* **by ~** de cor, maquinalmente

rotten /'rɒtn/ *a* podre; (*corrupt*) corrupto; (*colloq*: *bad*) mau, ruim. **~ eggs** ovos *mpl* podres. **feel ~** (*ill*) não se sentir nada bem

rotund /rəʊ'tʌnd/ *a* rotundo, redondo

rough /rʌf/ *a* (**-er**, **-est**) rude; (*to touch*) áspero, rugoso; (*of ground*) acidentado, irregular; (*violent*) violento; (*of sea*) agitado, encapelado; (*of weather*) tempestuoso; (*not perfect*) tosco, rudimentar; (*of estimate etc*) aproximado □ *n* (*ruffian*) rufia *m*, desordeiro *m* □ *adv* (*live*) ao relento; (*play*) bruto □ *vt* **~ it** viver de modo primitivo, não ter onde morar (*colloq*). **~ out** fazer um esboço preliminar de. **~-and-ready** *a* grosseiro mas eficiente. **~ paper** rascunho *m*, borrão *m*. **~ly** *adv* asperamente, rudemente; (*approximately*) aproximadamente. **~ness** *n* rudeza *f*, aspereza *f*; (*violence*) brutalidade *f*

roughage /'rʌfɪdʒ/ *n* alimentos *mpl* fibrosos

roulette /ru:'let/ *n* roleta *f*

round /raʊnd/ *a* (**-er**, **-est**) redondo □ *n* (*circle*) círculo *m*; (*slice*) fatia *f*; (*postman's*) entrega *f*; (*patrol*) ronda *f*; (*of drinks*) rodada *f*; (*competition*) partida *f*, rodada *f*; (*boxing*) round *m*; (*of talks*) ciclo *m*, série *f* □ *prep* & *adv* em volta (de), em torno (de) □ *vt* arredondar; (*cape, corner*) dobrar, virar. **come ~** (*into consciousness*) voltar a si. **go** *or* **come ~ to** (*a friend etc*) dar um pulo na casa de. **~ about** (*nearby*) por aí; (*fig*) mais ou menos. **~ of applause** salva *f* de palmas. **~ off** terminar. **~-shouldered** *a* curvado. **~ the clock** noite e dia sem parar. **~ trip** viagem *f* de ida e volta. **~ up** (*gather*) juntar; (*a figure*) arredondar. **~-up** *n* (*of cattle*) rodeio *m*; (*of suspects*) captura *f*

roundabout /'raʊndəbaʊt/ *n* carrossel *m*; (*for traffic*) rotatória *f*, (*P*) rotunda *f* □ *a* indireto, (*P*) indirecto

rous|e /raʊz/ *vt* acordar, despertar. **be ~ed** (*angry*) exaltar-se, inflamar-se, ser provocado. **~ing** *a* (*speech*) inflamado, exaltado; (*music*) vibrante; (*cheers*) frenético

rout /raʊt/ *n* derrota *f*; (*retreat*) debandada *f* □ *vt* derrotar; (*cause to retreat*) pôr em debandada

route /ru:t/ *n* percurso *m*, itinerário *m*; (*naut, aviat*) rota *f*

routine /ru:'ti:n/ *n* rotina *f*; (*theat*) número *m* □ *a* de rotina, rotineiro. **daily ~** rotina *f* diária

rov|e /rəʊv/ *vt/i* errar (por), vaguear (em/por). **~ing** *a* (*life*) errante

row[1] /rəʊ/ *n* fila *f*, fileira *f*; (*in knitting*) carreira *f*. **in a ~** (*consecutive*) em fila

row[2] /rəʊ/ *vt/i* remar. **~ing** *n* remo *m*. **~ing-boat** *n* barco *m* a remo

row[3] /raʊ/ *n* (*colloq: noise*) barulho *m*, bagunça *f*, banzé *m* (*colloq*); (*colloq: quarrel*) discussão *f*, briga *f*. **~ (with)** *vi* (*colloq*) brigar (com), discutir (com)

rowdy /'raʊdɪ/ *a* (**-ier, -iest**) desordeiro

royal /'rɔɪəl/ *a* real

royalty /'rɔɪəltɪ/ *n* família real *f*; (*payment*) direitos *mpl* (de autor, de patente, etc)

rub /rʌb/ *vt/i* (*pt* **rubbed**) esfregar; (*with ointment etc*) esfregar, friccionar □ *n* esfrega *f*; (*with ointment etc*) fricção *f*. **~ it in** repisar/insistir em. **~ off on** comunicar-se a, transmitir-se a. **~ out** (*with rubber*) apagar

rubber /'rʌbə(r)/ *n* borracha *f*. **~ band** elástico *m*. **~ stamp** carimbo *m*. **~-stamp** *vt* aprovar sem questionar. **~y** *a* semelhante à borracha

rubbish /'rʌbɪʃ/ *n* (*refuse*) lixo *m*; (*nonsense*) disparates *mpl*. **~ dump** *n* lixeira *f*. **~y** *a* sem valor

rubble /'rʌbl/ *n* entulho *m*

ruby /'ru:bɪ/ *n* rubi *m*

rucksack /'rʌksæk/ *n* mochila *f*

rudder /'rʌdə(r)/ *n* leme *m*

ruddy /'rʌdɪ/ *a* (**-ier, -iest**) avermelhado; (*of cheeks*) corado, vermelho; (*sl: damned*) maldito (*colloq*)

rude /ru:d/ *a* (**-er, -est**) mal-educado, malcriado, grosseiro. **~ly** *adv* grosseiramente, malcriadamente. **~ness** *n* má-educação *f*, má-criação *f*, grosseria *f*

rudiment /'ru:dɪmənt/ *n* rudimento *m*. **~ary** /-'mentrɪ/ *a* rudimentar

rueful /'ru:fl/ *a* contrito, pesaroso

ruffian /'rʌfɪən/ *n* desordeiro *m*

ruffle /'rʌfl/ *vt* (*feathers*) eriçar; (*hair*) despentear; (*clothes*) amarrotar; (*fig*) perturbar □ *n* (*frill*) franzido *m*, (*P*) folho *m*

rug /rʌg/ *n* tapete *m*; (*covering*) manta *f*

rugged /'rʌgɪd/ *a* rude, irregular; (*coast, landscape*) acidentado; (*character*) forte; (*features*) marcado

ruin /'ru:ɪn/ *n* ruína *f* □ *vt* arruinar; (*fig*) estragar. **~ous** *a* desastroso

rule /ru:l/ *n* regra *f*; (*regulation*) regulamento *m*; (*pol*) governo *m* □ *vt* governar; (*master*) dominar; (*jur*) decretar; (*decide*) decidir □ *vi* governar. **as a ~** regra geral, por via de regra. **~ out** excluir. **~d paper** papel *m* pautado. **~r** /-ə(r)/ *n* (*sovereign*) soberano *m*; (*leader*) governante *m*; (*measure*) régua *f*

ruling /'ru:lɪŋ/ *a* (*class*) dirigente; (*pol*) no poder □ *n* decisão *f*

rum /rʌm/ *n* rum *m*

rumble /'rʌmbl/ *vi* ribombar, ressoar; (*of stomach*) roncar □ *n* ribombo *m*, estrondo *m*

rummage /'rʌmɪdʒ/ *vt* revistar, remexer

rumour /'ru:mə(r)/ *n* boato *m*, rumor *m* □ *vt* **it is ~ed that** corre o boato de que, consta que

rump /rʌmp/ *n* (*of horse etc*) garupa *f*; (*of fowl*) mitra *f*. **~ steak** *n* bife *m* de alcatra

run /rʌn/ *vi* (*pt* **ran**, *pp* **run**, *pres p* **running**) correr; (*flow*) correr; (*pass*) passar; (*function*) andar, funcionar; (*melt*) derreter, pingar; (*bus etc*) circular; (*play*) estar em cartaz; (*colour*) desbotar; (*in election*) candidatar-se (**for** a) □ *vt* (*manage*) dirigir, gerir; (*a risk*) correr; (*a race*) participar em; (*water*) deixar correr; (*a car*) ter, manter □ *n* corrida *f*; (*excursion*) passeio *m*, ida *f*; (*rush*) corrida *f*, correria *f*; (*in cricket*) ponto *m*. **be on the ~** estar foragido. **have the ~ of** ter à sua disposição. **in the long ~** a longo prazo. **~ across** encontrar por acaso, dar com. **~ away** fugir. **~ down** descer correndo; (*of vehicle*) atropelar; (*belittle*) dizer mal de, denegrir. **be ~ down** estar exausto. **~ in** (*engine*) ligar. **~ into** (*meet*) encontrar por acaso; (*hit*) bater em, ir de encontro a. **~ off** *vt* (*copies*) tirar; (*water*) deixar correr □ *vi* fugir. **~-of-the-mill** *a* vulgar. **~ out** esgotar-se; (*lease*) expirar. **I ran out of sugar** o açúcar acabou. **~ over** (*of vehicle*) atropelar. **~ up** deixar acumular. **the ~-up to** o período que precede

runaway /'rʌnəweɪ/ *n* fugitivo *m* □ *a* fugitivo; (*horse*) desembestado; (*vehicle*) desarvorado; (*success*) grande

rung[1] /rʌŋ/ *n* (*of ladder*) degrace *m*

rung[2] /rʌŋ/ *see* **ring**[2]

runner /'rʌnə(r)/ *n* (*person*) corredor *m*; (*carpet*) passadeira *f*. **~ bean** feijão *m* verde. **~-up** *n* segundo classificado *m*

running /'rʌnɪŋ/ *n* corrida *f*; (*functioning*) funcionamento *m* □ *a* consecutivo, seguido; (*water*) corrente. **be in the ~** (*competitor*) ter probabilidades de êxito. **four days ~** quatro dias seguidos *or* a fio. **~ commentary** reportagem *f*, comentário *m*

runny /'rʌnɪ/ *a* derretido

runway /'rʌnweɪ/ *n* pista *f* de decolagem, (*P*) descolagem
rupture /'rʌptʃə(r)/ *n* ruptura *f*; (*med*) hérnia *f* □ *vt/i* romper (-se), rebentar
rural /'rʊərəl/ *a* rural
ruse /ru:z/ *n* ardil *m*, estratagema *m*, manha *f*
rush[1] /rʌʃ/ *n* (*plant*) junco *m*
rush[2] /rʌʃ/ *vi* (*move*) precipitar-se, (*be in a hurry*) apressar-se □ *vt* fazer, mandar *etc* a toda a pressa; (*person*) pressionar; (*mil*) tomar de assalto □ *n* tropel *m*; (*haste*) pressa *f*. **in a ~** as pressas. **~ hour** rush *m*, (*P*) hora *f* de ponta
rusk /rʌsk/ *n* bolacha *f*, biscoito *m*
russet /'rʌsɪt/ *a* castanho avermelhado □ *n* maçã *f* reineta
Russia /'rʌʃə/ *n* Rússia *f*. **~n** *a* & *n* russo (*m*)
rust /rʌst/ *n* (*on iron, plants*) ferrugem *f* □ *vt/i* enferrujar(-se). **~-proof** *a* inoxidável. **~y** *a* ferrugento, enferrujado; (*fig*) enferrujado
rustic /'rʌstɪk/ *a* rústico
rustle /'rʌsl/ *vt/i* restolhar, (fazer) farfalhar; (*Amer: steal*) roubar. **~ up** (*colloq: food etc*) arranjar
rut /rʌt/ *n* sulco *m*; (*fig*) rotina *f*. **in a ~** numa vida rotineira
ruthless /'ru:θlɪs/ *a* implacável
rye /raɪ/ *n* centeio *m*

Ss

sabbath /'sæbəθ/ *n* (*Jewish*) sábado *m*; (*Christian*) domingo *m*
sabbatical /sə'bætɪkl/ *n* (*univ*) período *m* de licença
sabot|age /'sæbəta:ʒ/ *n* sabotagem *f* □ *vt* sabotar. **~eur** /-'tɜ:(r)/ *n* sabotador *m*
sachet /'sæʃeɪ/ *n* saché *m*
sack /sæk/ *n* saco *m*, saca *f* □ *vt* (*colloq*) despedir. **get the~** (*colloq*) ser despedido
sacrament /'sækrəmənt/ *n* sacramento *m*
sacred /'seɪkrɪd/ *a* sagrado
sacrifice /'sækrɪfaɪs/ *n* sacrifício *m*; (*fig*) sacrifício *m* □ *vt* sacrificar
sacrileg|e /'sækrɪlɪdʒ/ *n* sacrilégio *m*. **~ious** /-'lɪdʒəs/ *a* sacrílego
sad /sæd/ *a* (**sadder, saddest**) (*person*) triste; (*story, news*) triste. **~ly** *adv* tristemente; (*unfortunately*) infelizmente. **~ness** *n* tristeza *f*
sadden /'sædn/ *vt* entristecer
saddle /'sædl/ *n* sela *f* □ *vt* (*horse*) selar. **~ sb with** sobrecarregar alguém com
sadis|m /'seɪdɪzəm/ *n* sadismo *m*. **~t** /-ɪst/ *n* sádico *m*. **~tic** /sə'dɪstɪk/ *a* sádico
safe /seɪf/ *a* (**-er, -est**) (*not dangerous*) seguro; (*out of danger*) fora de perigo; (*reliable*) confiável. **~ from** salvo de risco de □ *n* cofre *m*, caixa-forte *f*. **~ and sound** são e salvo. **~ conduct** salvo-conduto *m*. **~ keeping** custódia *f*, (*P*) protecção *f*. **to be on the ~ side** por via das dúvidas. **~ly** *adv* (*arrive etc*) em segurança; (*keep*) seguro
safeguard /'seɪfga:d/ *n* salvaguarda *f* □ *vt* salvaguardar
safety /'seɪftɪ/ *n* segurança *f*. **~-belt** *n* cinto *m* de segurança. **~-pin** *n* alfinete *m* de fralda. **~-valve** *n* válvula *f* de segurança
sag /sæg/ *vi* (*pt* **sagged**) afrouxar
saga /'sa:gə/ *n* saga *f*
sage[1] /seɪdʒ/ *n* (*herb*) salva *f*
sage[2] /seɪdʒ/ *a* sensato, prudente □ **~** *n* sábio *m*
Sagittarius /sædʒɪ'teərɪəs/ *n* (*astrol*) Sagitário *m*
said /sed/ *see* **say**
sail /seɪl/ *n* vela *f*; (*trip*) viagem *f* em barco à vela □ *vi* navegar; (*leave*) partir; (*sport*) velejar □ *vt* navegar. **~ing** *n* navegação *f* à vela. **~ing-boat** *n* barco *m* à vela
sailor /'seɪlə(r)/ *n* marinheiro *m*
saint /seɪnt/ *n* santo *m*. **~ly** *a* santo, santificado
sake /seɪk/ *n* **for the ~ of** em consideração a. **for my/your/ its own ~** por mim/por você/por isso
salad /'sæləd/ *n* salada *f*. **~-dressing** *n* molho *m* para salada
salary /'sælərɪ/ *n* salário *m*
sale /seɪl/ *n* venda *f*; (*at reduced prices*) liquidação *f*. **for ~** vende-se. **on ~** à venda. **~s assistant**, (*Amer*) **~s clerk** vendedor *m*. **~s department** departamento *m* de vendas
sales|man /'seɪlzmən/ *n* (*pl* **- men**) (*in shop*) vendedor *m*; (*traveller*) caixeiro-viajante *m*. **~woman** *n* (*pl* **-women**) (*in shop*) vendedora *f*; (*traveller*) caixeira-viajante *f*
saline /'seɪlaɪn/ *a* salino □ *n* salina *f*
saliva /sə'laɪvə/ *n* saliva *f*
sallow /'sæləʊ/ *a* (**-er, -est**) amarelado
salmon /'sæmən/ *n* (*pl invar*) salmão *m*
saloon /sə'lu:n/ *n* (*on ship*) salão *m*; (*bar*) botequim *m*. **~ (car)** sedã *m*

salt /sɔ:lt/ *n* sal *m* ▫ *a* salgado ▫ *vt* (*season*) salgar; (*cure*) pôr em salmoura. **~-cellar** *n* saleiro *m*. **~ water** água *f* salgada, água *f* do mar. **~y** *a* salgado

salutary /'sæljʊtrɪ/ *a* salutar

salute /sə'lu:t/ *n* saudação *f* ▫ *vt/i* saudar

salvage /'sælvɪdʒ/ *n* (*naut*) salvamento *m*; (*of waste*) reciclagem *f* ▫ *vt* salvar

salvation /sæl'veɪʃn/ *n* salvação *f*

same /seɪm/ *a* mesmo (**as** que) ▫ *pron* **the ~** o mesmo ▫ *adv* **the ~** o mesmo. **all the ~** (*nevertheless*) mesmo assim, apesar de tudo. **at the ~ time** (*at once*) ao mesmo tempo

sample /'sa:mpl/ *n* amostra *f* ▫ *vt* experimentar, provar

sanatorium /sænə'tɔ:rɪəm/ *n* (*pl* **-iums**) sanatório *m*

sanctify /'sæŋktɪfaɪ/ *vt* santificar

sanctimonious /sæŋktɪ'məʊnɪəs/ *a* santarrão, carola

sanction /'sæŋkʃn/ *n* (*approval*) aprovação *f*; (*penalty*) pena *f*, sanção *f* ▫ *vt* sancionar

sanctity /'sæŋktɪtɪ/ *n* santidade *f*

sanctuary /'sæŋktʃʊərɪ/ *n* (*relig*) santuário *m*; (*refuge*) refúgio *m*; (*for animals*) reserva *f*

sand /sænd/ *n* areia *f*; (*beach*) praia *f* ▫ *vt* (*with sandpaper*) lixar

sandal /'sændl/ *n* sandália *f*

sandbag /'sændbæg/ *n* saco *m* de areia

sandbank /'sændbæŋk/ *n* banco *m* de areia

sandcastle /'sændka:sl/ *n* castelo *m* de areia

sandpaper /'sændpeɪpə(r)/ *n* lixa *f* ▫ *vt* lixar

sandpit /'sændpɪt/ *n* caixa *f* de areia

sandwich /'sænwɪdʒ/ *n* sanduíche *m*, (*P*) sandes *f invar* ▫ *vt* **~ed between** encaixado entre. **~ course** curso *m* profissionalizante envolvendo estudo teórico e estágio em local de trabalho

sandy /'sændɪ/ *a* (**-ier, iest**) arenoso; (*beach*) arenoso; (*hair*) ruivo

sane /seɪn/ *a* (**-er, -est**) (*not mad*) são *m*; (*sensible*) sensato, ajuizado

sang /sæŋ/ *see* **sing**

sanitary /'sænɪtrɪ/ *a* sanitário; (*system*) sanitário. **~ towel,** (*Amer*) **~ napkin** toalha *f* absorvente

sanitation /sænɪ'teɪʃn/ *n* condições *fpl* sanitárias, saneamento *m*

sanity /'sænɪtɪ/ *n* sanidade *f*

sank /sæŋk/ *see* **sink**

Santa Claus /'sæntəklɔ:z/ *n* Papai Noel *m*

sap /sæp/ *n* seiva *f* ▫ *vt* (*pt* **sapped**) esgotar, minar

sapphire /'sæfaɪə(r)/ *n* safira *f*

sarcas|m /'sa:rkæzəm/ *n* sarcasmo *m*. **~tic** /sa:r'kæstɪk/ *a* sarcástico

sardine /sa:'di:n/ *n* sardinha *f*

sardonic /sa:'dɒnɪk/ *a* sardônico

sash /sæʃ/ *n* (*around waist*) cinto *m*; (*over shoulder*) faixa *f*. **~-window** *n* janela *f* de guilhotina

sat /sæt/ *see* **sit**

satanic /sə'tænɪk/ *a* satânico

satchel /'sætʃl/ *n* sacola *f*

satellite /'sætəlaɪt/ *n* satélite *m*. **~ dish** antena *f* de satélite. **~ television** televisão *f* via satélite

satin /'sætɪn/ *n* cetim *m*

satir|e /'sætaɪə(r)/ *n* sátira *f*. **~ical** /sə'tɪrɪkl/ *a* satirical. **~ist** /'sætərɪst/ *n* satirista *mf*. **~ize** *vt* satirizar

satisfact|ion /sætɪs'fækʃn/ *n* satisfação *f*. **~ory** /-'fæktərɪ/ *a* satisfatório

satisfy /'sætɪsfaɪ/ *vt* satisfazer; (*convince*) convencer; (*fulfil*) atender. **~ing** *a* satisfatório

saturat|e /'sætʃəreɪt/ *vt* saturar; (*fig*) cansar. **~ed** *a* (*wet*) encharcado; (*fat*) saturado. **~ion** /-'reɪʃn/ *n* saturação *f*

Saturday /'sætədɪ/ *n* sábado *m*

sauce /sɔ:s/ *n* molho *m*; (*colloq: cheek*) atrevimento *m*

saucepan /'sɔ:spən/ *n* panela *f*, (*P*) caçarola *f*

saucer /'sɔ:sə(r)/ *n* pires *m invar*

saucy /'sɔ:sɪ/ *a* (**-ier, -iest**) picante

Saudi Arabia /saʊdɪə'reɪbɪə/ *n* Arábia *f* Saudita

sauna /'sɔ:nə/ *n* sauna *f*

saunter /'sɔ:ntə(r)/ *vi* perambular

sausage /'sɒsɪdʒ/ *n* salsicha *f*, linguiça *f*; (*precooked*) salsicha *f*

savage /'sævɪdʒ/ *a* (*wild*) selvagem; (*fierce*) cruel; (*brutal*) brutal ▫ *n* selvagem *mf* ▫ *vt* atacar ferozmente. **~ry** *n* selvageria *f*, ferocidade *f*

sav|e /seɪv/ *vt* (*rescue*) salvar; (*keep*) guardar; (*collect*) (*P*) colecionar; (*money*) economizar; (*time*) ganhar; (*prevent*) evitar, impedir (**from** de) ▫ *n* (*sport*) salvamento *m* ▫ *prep* salvo, exceto. **~er** *n* poupador *m*. **~ing** *n* economia *f*, poupança *f*. **~ings** *npl* economias *fpl*

saviour /'seɪvɪə(r)/ *n* salvador *m*

savour /'seɪvə(r)/ *n* sabor *m* ▫ *vt* saborear. **~y** *a* (*tasty*) saboroso; (*not sweet*) salgado

saw[1] /sɔ:/ *see* **see**[1]

saw[2] /sɔ:/ *n* serra *f* ▫ *vt* (*pt* **sawed**, *pp* **sawn** *or* **sawed**) serrar

sawdust /'sɔ:dʌst/ *n* serragem *f*

saxophone /'sæksəfəʊn/ *n* saxofone *m*

say /seɪ/ *vt/i* (*pt* **said** /sed/) dizer, falar ▫ *n* **have a ~ (in sth)** opinar sobre alg coisa. **have one's ~** exprimir sua opinião. **I ~!** olhe! *or* escute! **~ing** *n* ditado *m*, provérbio *m*

scab /skæb/ *n* casca *f*, crosta *f*; (*colloq: blackleg*) fura-greve *mf invar*

scaffold /'skæfəʊld/ *n* cadafalso *m*, andaime *m*. **~ing** /-əldɪŋ/ *n* andaime *m*

scald /skɔ:ld/ *vt* escaldar, queimar ◻ *n* escaldadura *f*

scale[1] /skeɪl/ *n* (*of fish etc*) escama *f*

scale[2] /skeɪl/ *n* (*ratio, size*) escala *f*; (*mus*) escala *f*; (*of salaries, charges*) tabela *f*. **on a small/large**/*etc* **~** numa pequena/grande/*etc* escala ◻ *vt* (*climb*) escalar. **~ down** reduzir

scales /skeɪlz/ *npl* (*for weighing*) balança *f*

scallop /'skɒləp/ *n* (*culin*) concha *f* de vieira; (*shape*) concha *f* de vieira

scalp /skælp/ *n* couro *m* cabeludo ◻ *vt* escalpar

scalpel /'skælpl/ *n* bisturi *m*

scamper /'skæmpə(r)/ *vi* sair correndo

scampi /'skæmpɪ/ *npl* camarões *mpl* fritos

scan /skæn/ *vt* (*pt* **scanned**) (*intently*) perscrutar, esquadrinhar; (*quickly*) passar os olhos em; (*med*) examinar; (*radar*) explorar ◻ *n* (*med*) exame *m*

scandal /'skændl/ *n* (*disgrace*) escândalo *m*; (*gossip*) fofoca *f*. **~ous** *a* escandaloso

Scandinavia /skændɪ'neɪvɪə/ *n* Escandinávia *f*. **~n** *a* & *n* escandinavo (*m*)

scanty /'skæntɪ/ *a* (**-ier, -iest**) escasso; (*clothing*) sumário

scapegoat /'skeɪpgəʊt/ *n* bode *m* expiatório

scar /ska:(r)/ *n* cicatriz *f* ◻ *vt* (*pt* **scarred**) marcar; (*fig*) deixar marcas

scarc|e /skeəs/ *a* (**-er, -est**) escasso, raro. **make o.s. ~e** (*colloq*) sumir, dar o fora (*colloq*). **~ity** *n* escassez *f*. **~ely** *adv* mal, apenas

scare /skeə(r)/ *vt* assustar, apavorar. **be ~d** estar com medo (**of** de) ◻ *n* pavor *m*, pânico *m*. **bomb ~** pânico *m* causado por suspeita de bomba num local

scarecrow /'skeəkrəʊ/ *n* espantalho *m*

scarf /ska:f/ *n* (*pl* **scarves**) (*oblong*) cachecol *m*; (*square*) lenço *m* de cabelo

scarlet /'ska:lət/ *a* escarlate *m*

scary /'skeərɪ/ *a* (**-ier, -iest**) (*colloq*) assustador, apavorante

scathing /'skeɪðɪŋ/ *a* mordaz

scatter /'skætə(r)/ *vt* (*strew*) espalhar; (*disperse*) dispersar ◻ *vi* espalhar-se

scavenge /'skævɪndʒ/ *vi* procurar comida *etc* no lixo. **~r** /-ə(r)/ *n* (*person*) que procura comida *etc* no lixo; (*animal*) que se alimenta de carniça

scenario /sɪ'na:rɪəʊ/ *n* (*pl* **-os**) sinopse *f*, resumo *m* detalhado

scene /si:n/ *n* cena *f*; (*of event*) cenário *m*; (*sight*) vista *f*, panorama *m*. **behind the ~s** nos bastidores. **make a ~** fazer um escândalo

scenery /'si:nərɪ/ *n* cenário *m*, paisagem *f*; (*theat*) cenário *m*

scenic /'si:nɪk/ *a* pitoresco, cênico

scent /sent/ *n* (*perfume*) perfume *m*, fragância *f*; (*trail*) rastro *m*, pista *f* ◻ *vt* (*discern*) sentir. **~ed** *a* perfumado

sceptic /'skeptɪk/ *n* cético *m*. **~al** *a* cético. **~ism** /-sɪzəm/ *n* ceticismo *m*

schedule /'ʃedju:l/ *n* programa *m*; (*timetable*) horário *m* ◻ *vt* marcar, programar. **according to ~** conforme planejado. **behind ~** atrasado. **on ~** (*train*) na hora; (*work*) em dia. **~d flight** *n* vôo *m* regular

scheme /ski:m/ *n* esquema *m*; (*plan of work*) plano *m*; (*plot*) conspiração *f*, maquinação *f* ◻ *vi* planejar, (*P*) planear; (*pej*) intrigar, maquinar, tramar

schism /'sɪzəm/ *n* cisma *m*

schizophreni|a /skɪtsəʊ'fri:nɪə/ *n* esquizofrenia *f*. **~c** /-'frenɪk/ *a* esquizofrênico, (*P*) esquizofrénico

scholar /'skɒlə(r)/ *n* erudito *m*, estudioso *m*, escolar *m*. **~ly** *a* erudito. **~ship** *n* erudição *f*, saber *m*; (*grant*) bolsa *f* de estudo

school /sku:l/ *n* escola *f*; (*of university*) escola *f*, faculdade *f* ◻ *a* (*age, year, holidays*) escolar ◻ *vt* ensinar; (*train*) treinar, adestrar. **~ing** *n* instrução *f*; (*attendance*) escolaridade *f*

school|boy /'sku:lbɔɪ/ *n* aluno *m*. **~girl** *n* aluna *f*

school|master /'sku:lma:stə(r)/, **~mistress, ~teacher** *ns* professor *m*, professora *f*

schooner /'sku:nə(r)/ *n* escuna *f*; (*glass*) copo *m* alto

sciatica /saɪ'ætɪkə/ *n* ciática *f*

scien|ce /'saɪəns/ *n* ciência *f*. **~ce fiction** ficção *f* científica. **~tific** /-'tɪfɪk/ *a* científico

scientist /'saɪəntɪst/ *n* cientista *mf*

scintillate /'sɪntɪleɪt/ *vi* cintilar; (*fig: person*) brilhar

scissors /'sɪzəz/ *npl* (**pair of**) **~** tesoura *f*

scoff[1] /skɒf/ *vi* **~ at** zombar de, (*P*) troçar de

scoff[2] /skɒf/ *vt* (*sl: eat*) devorar, tragar

scold /skəʊld/ *vt* ralhar com. **~ing** *n* repreensão *f*, (*P*) descompostura *f*

scone /skɒn/ *n* (*culin*) scone *m*, bolinho *m* para o chá

scoop /sku:p/ *n* (*for grain, sugar etc*) pá *f*; (*ladle*) concha *f*; (*news*) furo *m* ◻ *vt* ~ **out** (*hollow out*) escavar, tirar com concha *or* pá. ~ **up** (*lift*) apanhar

scoot /sku:t/ *vi* (*colloq*) fugir, mandar-se (*colloq*), (*P*) pôr-se a milhas (*colloq*)

scooter /ˈsku:tə(r)/ *n* (*child's*) patinete *f*, (*P*) trotinete *m*; (*motor cycle*) motoreta *f*, lambreta *f*

scope /skəʊp/ *n* âmbito *m*; (*fig: opportunity*) oportunidade *f*

scorch /skɔ:tʃ/ *vt/i* chamuscar (-se), queimar de leve. ~**ing** *a* (*colloq*) escaldante, abrasador

score /skɔ:(r)/ *n* (*sport*) contagem *f*, escore *m*; (*mus*) partitura *f* ◻ *vt* marcar com corte(s), riscar; (*a goal*) marcar; (*mus*) orquestrar ◻ *vi* marcar pontos; (*keep score*) fazer a contagem; (*football*) marcar um gol, (*P*) golo. **a** ~ (**of**) (*twenty*) uma vintena (de), vinte. ~**s** muitos, dezenas. **on that** ~ nesse respeito, quanto a isso. ~**-board** *n* marcador *m*. ~**r** /-ə(r)/ *n* (*score-keeper*) marcador *m*; (*of goals*) autor *m*

scorn /skɔ:n/ *n* desprezo *m* ◻ *vt* desprezar. ~**ful** *a* desdenhoso, escarninho. ~**fully** *adv* com desdém, desdenhosamente

Scorpio /ˈskɔ:pɪəʊ/ *n* (*astr*) Escorpião *m*

scorpion /ˈskɔ:pɪən/ *n* escorpião *m*

Scot /skɒt/ *n*, ~**tish** *a* escocês (*m*)

Scotch /skɒtʃ/ *a* escocês ◻ *n* uísque *m*

scotch /skɒtʃ/ *vt* pôr fim a, frustrar

scot-free /skɒtˈfri:/ *a* impune ◻ *adv* impunemente

Scotland /ˈskɒtlənd/ *n* Escócia *f*

Scots /skɒts/ *a* escocês. ~**man** *n* escocês *m*. ~**woman** *n* escocesa *f*

scoundrel /ˈskaʊndrəl/ *n* patife *m*, canalha *m*

scour[1] /ˈskaʊə(r)/ *vt* (*clean*) esfregar, arear. ~**er** *n* esfregão *m* de palha de aço *or* de nylon

scour[2] /ˈskaʊə(r)/ *vt* (*search*) percorrer, esquadrinhar

scourge /skɜ:dʒ/ *n* açoite *m*; (*fig*) flagelo *m*

scout /skaʊt/ *n* (*mil*) explorador *m* ◻ *vi* ~ **about (for)** andar à procura de

Scout /skaʊt/ *n* escoteiro *m*, (*P*) escuteiro *m*. ~**ing** *n* escotismo *m*, (*P*) escutismo *m*

scowl /skaʊl/ *n* carranca *f*, ar *m* carrancudo ◻ *vi* fazer um ar carrancudo

scraggy /ˈskrægɪ/ *a* (-**ier**, -**iest**) descarnado, ossudo

scramble /ˈskræmbl/ *vi* trepar; (*crawl*) avançar de rastros, rastejar, arrastar-se ◻ *vt* (*eggs*) mexer ◻ *n* luta *f*, confusão *f*

scrap[1] /skræp/ *n* bocadinho *m*. ~**s** *npl* restos *mpl* ◻ *vt* (*pt* **scrapped**) jogar fora, (*P*) deitar fora; (*plan etc*) abandonar, pôr de lado. ~**-book** *n* álbum *m* de recortes. ~ **heap** monte *m* de ferro-velho. ~**-iron** *n* ferro *m* velho, sucata *f*. ~ **merchant** sucateiro *m*. ~**-paper** *n* papel *m* de rascunho. ~**py** *a* fragmentário

scrap[2] /skræp/ *n* (*colloq: fight*) briga *f*, pancadaria *f* (*colloq*), rixa *f*

scrape /skreɪp/ *vt* raspar; (*graze*) esfolar, arranhar ◻ *vi* (*graze, rub*) roçar ◻ *n* (*act of scraping*) raspagem *f*; (*mark*) raspão *m*, esfoladura *f*; (*fig*) encrenca *f*, maus lençóis *mpl*. ~ **through** escapar pela tangente, (*P*) à tangente; (*exam*) passar pela tangente, (*P*) à tangente. ~ **together** conseguir juntar. ~**r** /-ə(r)/ *n* raspadeira *f*

scratch /skrætʃ/ *vt/i* arranhar (-se); (*a line*) riscar; (*to relieve itching*) coçar(-se) ◻ *n* arranhão *m*; (*line*) risco *m*; (*wound with claw, nail*) unhada *f*. **start from** ~ começar do princípio. **up to** ~ à altura, ao nível requerido

scrawl /skrɔ:l/ *n* rabisco *m*, garrancho *m*, garatuja *f* ◻ *vt/i* rabiscar, fazer garranchos, garatujar

scrawny /ˈskrɔ:nɪ/ *a* (-**ier**, -**iest**) descarnado, ossudo, magricela

scream /skri:m/ *vt/i* gritar ◻ *n* grito *m* (agudo)

screech /skri:tʃ/ *vi* guinchar, gritar; (*of brakes*) chiar, guinchar ◻ *n* guincho *m*, grito *m* agudo

screen /skri:n/ *n* écran *m*, tela *f*; (*folding*) biombo *m*; (*fig: protection*) manto *m* (*fig*), capa *f* (*fig*) ◻ *vt* resguardar, tapar; (*film*) passar; (*candidates etc*) fazer a triagem de. ~**ing** *n* (*med*) exame *m* médico

screw /skru:/ *n* parafuso *m* ◻ *vt* aparafusar, atarraxar. ~ **up** (*eyes, face*) franzir; (*sl: ruin*) estragar. ~ **up one's courage** cobrar coragem

screwdriver /ˈskru:draɪvə(r)/ *n* chave *f* de parafusos *or* de fenda

scribble /ˈskrɪbl/ *vt/i* rabiscar, garatujar ◻ *n* rabisco *m*, garatuja *f*

script /skrɪpt/ *n* escrita *f*; (*of film*) roteiro *m*, (*P*) guião *m*. ~**-writer** *n* (*film*) roteirista *m*, (*P*) autor *m* do guião

Scriptures /ˈskrɪptʃəz/ *npl* **the** ~ a Sagrada Escritura

scroll /skrəʊl/ *n* rolo *m* (de papel ou pergaminho); (*archit*) voluta *f* ◻ *vt/i* (*comput*) passar na tela

scrounge /skraʊndʒ/ *vt* (*colloq: cadge*) filar (*sl*), (*P*) cravar (*sl*) □ *vi* (*beg*) parasitar, viver às custas de alguém. **~r** /-ə(r)/ *n* parasita *mf*, filão *m* (*sl*), (*P*) crava *mf* (*sl*)

scrub[1] /skrʌb/ *n* (*land*) mato *m*

scrub[2] /skrʌb/ *vt/i* (*pt* **scrubbed**) esfregar, lavar com escova e sabão; (*colloq: cancel*) cancelar □ *n* esfrega *f*

scruff /skrʌf/ *n* **by the ~ of the neck** pelo cangote, (*P*) pelo cachaço

scruffy /ˈskrʌfɪ/ *a* (**-ier, -iest**) desmazelado, desleixado, mal ajambrado (*colloq*)

scrum /skrʌm/ *n* rixa *f*; (*Rugby*) placagem *f*

scruple /ˈskru:pl/ *n* escrúpulo *m*

scrupulous /ˈskru:pjʊləs/ *a* escrupuloso. **~ly** *adv* escrupulosamente. **~ly clean** impecavelmente limpo

scrutin|y /ˈskru:tɪnɪ/ *n* averiguação *f*, escrutínio *m*. **~ize** *vt* examinar em detalhes

scuff /skʌf/ *vt* (*scrape*) esfolar, safar □ *n* esfoladura *f*

scuffle /ˈskʌfl/ *n* tumulto *m*, briga *f*

sculpt /skʌlpt/ *vt/i* esculpir. **~or** *n* escultor *m*. **~ure** /-tʃə(r)/ *n* escultura *f* □ *vt/i* esculpir

scum /skʌm/ *n* (*on liquid*) espuma *f*; (*pej: people*) gentinha *f*, escumalha *f*, ralé *f*

scurf /skɜ:f/ *n* películas *fpl*; (*dandruff*) caspa *f*

scurrilous /ˈskʌrɪləs/ *a* injurioso, insultuoso

scurry /ˈskʌrɪ/ *vi* dar corridinhas; (*hurry*) apressar- se. **~ off** escapulir-se

scurvy /ˈskɜ:vɪ/ *n* escorbuto *m*

scuttle[1] /ˈskʌtl/ *n* (*bucket, box*) balde *m* para carvão

scuttle[2] /ˈskʌtl/ *vt* (*ship*) afundar abrindo rombos *or* as torneiras de fundo

scuttle[3] /ˈskʌtl/ *vi* **~ away** *or* **off** fugir, escapulir-se

scythe /saɪð/ *n* gadanha *f*, foice *f* grande

sea /si:/ *n* mar *m* □ *a* do mar, marinho, marítimo. **at ~** no alto mar, ao largo. **all at ~** desnorteado. **by ~** por mar. **~ bird** ave *f* marinha. **~-green** *a* verde-mar. **~ horse** cavalo-marinho *m*, hipocampo *m*. **~ level** nível *m* do mar. **~lion** leão-marinho *m*. **~ shell** concha *f*. **~-shore** *n* litoral *m*; (*beach*) praia *f*. **~ water** água *f* do mar

seaboard /ˈsi:bɔ:d/ *n* litoral *m*, costa *f*

seafarer /ˈsi:feərə(r)/ *n* marinheiro *m*, navegante *m*

seafood /ˈsi:fu:d/ *n* marisco(s) *m* (*pl*)

seagull /ˈsi:gʌl/ *n* gaivota *f*

seal[1] /si:l/ *n* (*animal*) foca *f*

seal[2] /si:l/ *n* selo *m*, sinete *m* □ *vt* selar; (*with wax*) lacrar. **~ing-wax** *n* lacre *m*. **~off** (*area*) vedar

seam /si:m/ *n* (*in cloth etc*) costura *f*; (*of mineral*) veio *m*, filão *m*. **~less** *a* sem costura

seaman /ˈsi:mən/ *n* (*pl* **-men**) marinheiro *m*, marítimo *m*

seamy /ˈsi:mɪ/ *a* **~ side** lado *m* (do) avesso; (*fig*) lado *m* sórdido

seance /ˈseɪa:ns/ *n* sessão *f* espírita

seaplane /ˈsi:pleɪn/ *n* hidroavião *m*

seaport /ˈsi:pɔ:t/ *n* porto *m* de mar

search /sɜ:tʃ/ *vt/i* revistar, dar busca (a); (*one's heart, conscience etc*) examinar □ *n* revista *f*, busca *f*; (*quest*) procura *f*, busca *f*; (*official*) inquérito *m*. **in ~ of** à procura de. **~ for** procurar. **~-party** *n* equipe *f* de busca. **~-warrant** *n* mandado *m* de busca. **~ing** *a* (*of look*) penetrante; (*of test etc*) minucioso

searchlight /ˈsɜ:tʃlaɪt/ *n* holofote *m*

seasick /ˈsi:sɪk/ *a* enjoado. **~ness** *n* enjôo *m*, *P* enjoo *m*

seaside /ˈsi:saɪd/ *n* costa *f*, praia *f*, beira-mar *f*. **~ resort** *n* balneário *m*, praia *f*

season /ˈsi:zn/ *n* (*of year*) estação *f*; (*proper time*) época *f*; (*cricket, football etc*) temporada *f* □ *vt* temperar; (*wood*) secar. **in ~** na época. **~able** *a* próprio da estação. **~al** *a* sazonal. **~ed** *a* (*of people*) experimentado. **~ing** *n* tempero *m*. **~-ticket** *n* (*train etc*) passe *m*; (*theatre etc*) assinatura *f*

seat /si:t/ *n* assento *m*; (*place*) lugar *m*; (*of bicycle*) selim *m*; (*of chair*) assento *m*; (*of trousers*) fundilho *m* □ *vt* sentar; (*have seats for*) ter lugares sentados para. **be ~ed, take a ~** sentar-se. **~ of learning** centro *m* de cultura. **~-belt** *n* cinto *m* de segurança

seaweed /ˈsi:wi:d/ *n* alga *f* marinha

seaworthy /ˈsi:wɜ:ðɪ/ *a* navegável, em condições de navegabilidade

secateurs /ˈsekətɜ:z/ *npl* tesoura *f* de poda

seclu|de /sɪˈklu:d/ *vt* isolar. **~ded** *a* isolado, retirado. **~sion** /sɪˈklu:ʒn/ *n* isolamento *m*

second[1] /ˈsekənd/ *a* segundo □ *n* segundo *m*; (*in duel*) testemunha *f*. **~ (gear)** (*auto*) segunda *f* (velocidade). **the ~ of April** dois de Abril. **~s** (*goods*) artigos *mpl* de segunda *or* de refugo □ *adv* (*in race etc*) em segundo lugar □ *vt* secundar. **~-best** *a* escolhido em segundo lugar. **~-class** *a* de segunda classe. **~-hand** *a* de segunda mão □ *n* (*on clock*) ponteiro *m* dos segundos. **~-rate** *a* medíocre, de segunda ordem. **~ thoughts** dúvidas *fpl*. **on**

~ thoughts pensando melhor. **~ly** *adv* segundo, em segundo lugar

second[2] /sɪ'kɒnd/ *vt* (*transfer*) destacar (**to** para)

secondary /'sekəndrɪ/ *a* secundário. **~ school** escola *f* secundária

secrecy /'si:krəsɪ/ *n* segredo *m*

secret /'si:krɪt/ *a* secreto □ *n* segredo *m*. **in ~** em segredo. **~ agent** *n* agente *mf* secreto. **~ly** *adv* em segredo, secretamente

secretar|y /'sekrətrɪ/ *n* secretário *m*, secretária *f*. **S~y of State** ministro *m* de Estado, (*P*) Secretário *m* de Estado; (*Amer*) ministro *m* dos Negócios Estrangeiros. **~ial** /-'teərɪəl/ *a* (*work, course etc*) de secretária

secret|e /sɪ'kri:t/ *vt* segregar; (*hide*) esconder. **~ion** /-ʃn/ *n* secreção *f*

secretive /'si:krətɪv/ *a* misterioso, reservado

sect /sekt/ *n* seita *f*. **~arian** /-'teərɪən/ *a* sectário

section /'sekʃn/ *n* seção *f*, (*P*) secção *f*; (*of country, community etc*) setor *m*, (*P*) sector *m*; (*district of town*) zona *f*

sector /'sektə(r)/ *n* setor *m*, (*P*) sector *m*

secular /'sekjʊlə(r)/ *a* secular, leigo, *P* laico; (*art, music etc*) profano

secure /sɪ'kjʊə(r)/ *a* seguro, em segurança; (*firm*) seguro, sólido; (*in mind*) tranqüilo, *P* tranquilo □ *vt* prender bem *or* com segurança; (*obtain*) conseguir, arranjar; (*ensure*) assegurar; (*windows, doors*) fechar bem. **~ly** *adv* solidamente; (*safely*) em segurança

securit|y /sɪ'kjʊərətɪ/ *n* segurança *f*; (*for loan*) fiança *f*, caução *f*. **~ies** *npl* (*finance*) títulos *mpl*

sedate /sɪ'deɪt/ *a* sereno, comedido □ *vt* (*med*) tratar com sedativos

sedation /sɪ'deɪʃn/ *n* (*med*) sedação *f*. **under ~** sob o efeito de sedativos

sedative /'sedətɪv/ *n* (*med*) sedativo *m*

sedentary /'sedntrɪ/ *a* sedentário

sediment /'sedɪmənt/ *n* sedimento *m*, depósito *m*

seduce /sɪ'dju:s/ *vt* seduzir

seduct|ion /sɪ'dʌkʃn/ *n* sedução *f*. **~ive** /-tɪv/ *a* sedutor, aliciante

see[1] /si:/ *vt/i* (*pt* **saw**, *pp* **seen**) ver; (*escort*) acompanhar. **~ about** *or* **to** tratar de, encarregar-se de. **~ off** *vt* (*wave goodbye*) ir despedir-se de; (*chase*) acompanhar. **~ through** (*task*) levar a cabo; (*not be deceived by*) não se deixar enganar por. **~ (to it) that** assegurar que, tratar de fazer com que. **~ing that** visto que, uma vez que. **~ you later!** (*colloq*) até logo! (*colloq*)

see[2] /si:/ *n* sé *f*, bispado *m*

seed /si:d/ *n* semente *f*; (*fig: origin*) germe(n) *m*; (*tennis*) cabeça *f* de série; (*pip*) caroço *m*. **go to ~** produzir sementes; (*fig*) desmazelar-se (*colloq*). **~ling** *n* planta *f* brotada a partir da semente

seedy /'si:dɪ/ *a* (**-ier, -iest**) (com um ar) gasto, surrado; (*colloq: unwell*) abatido, deprimido, em baixo astral (*colloq*)

seek /si:k/ *vt* (*pt* **sought**) procurar; (*help etc*) pedir

seem /si:m/ *vi* parecer. **~ingly** *adv* aparentemente, ao que parece

seemly /'si:mlɪ/ *adv* decente, conveniente, próprio

seen /si:n/ *see* **see**[1]

seep /si:p/ *vi* (*ooze*) filtrar-se; (*trickle*) pingar, escorrer, passar. **~age** *n* infiltração *f*

see-saw /'si:sɔ:/ *n* gangorra *f*, (*P*) balanço *m*

seethe /si:ð/ *vi* **~ with** (*anger*) ferver de; (*people*) fervilhar de

segment /'segmənt/ *n* segmento *m*; (*of orange*) gomo *m*

segregat|e /'segrɪgeɪt/ *vt* segregar, separar. **~ion** /-'geɪʃn/ *n* segregação *f*

seize /si:z/ *vt* agarrar, (*P*) deitar a mão a, apanhar; (*take possession by force*) apoderar-se de; (*by law*) apreender, confiscar, (*P*) apresar □ *vi* **~ on** (*opportunity*) aproveitar. **~ up** (*engine etc*) grimpar, emperrar. **be ~d with** (*fear, illness*) ter um ataque de

seizure /'si:ʒə(r)/ *n* (*med*) ataque *m*, crise *f*; (*law*) apreensão *f*, captura *f*

seldom /'seldəm/ *adv* raras vezes, raramente, raro

select /sɪ'lekt/ *vt* escolher, selecionar, (*P*) seleccionar □ *a* seleto, (*P*) selecto. **~ion** /-ʃn/ *n* seleção *f*, (*P*) selecção *f*; (*comm*) sortido *m*

selective /sɪ'lektɪv/ *a* seletivo, (*P*) selectivo

self /self/ *n* (*pl* **selves**) **the ~** o eu, o ego

self- /self/ *pref* **~-assurance** *n* segurança *f*. **~-assured** *a* seguro de si. **~-catering** *a* em que os hóspedes tem facilidades de cozinhar. **~-centred** *a* egocêntrico. **~-confidence** *n* autoconfiança *f*, confiança *f* em si mesmo. **~-confident** *a* que tem confiança em si mesmo. **~-conscious** *a* inibido, constrangido. **~-contained** *a* independente. **~-control** *n* auto-domínio *m*. **~-controlled** *a* senhor de si. **~-defence** *n* legítima defesa *f*. **~-denial** *n* abnegação *f*. **~-employed** *a* autónomo. **~-esteem** *n* amor *m* próprio. **~-evident** *a* evidente. **~-indulgent** *a* que não resiste a tentações; (*for ease*) comodista.

~-interest *n* interesse *m* pessoal. **~-portrait** *n* auto-retrato *m*. **~-possessed** *a* senhor de si. **~-reliant** *a* independente, seguro de si. **~-respect** *n* amor *m* próprio. **~-righteous** *a* que se tem em boa conta. **~-sacrifice** *n* abnegação *f*, sacrifício *m*. **~-satisfied** *a* cheio de si, convencido (*colloq*). **~-seeking** *a* egoísta. **~-service** *a* auto-serviço, self-service. **~-styled** *a* pretenso. **~-sufficient** *a* auto-suficiente. **~-willed** *a* voluntarioso

selfish /'selfɪʃ/ *a* egoísta; (*motive*) interesseiro. **~ness** *n* egoísmo *m*

selfless /'selflɪs/ *a* desinteressado

sell /sel/ *vt/i* (*pt* **sold**) vender(-se). **~-by date** válido até. **~ off** liquidar. **be sold out** estar esgotado. **~-out** *n* (*show*) sucesso *m*; (*colloq: betrayal*) traição *f*. **~er** *n* vendedor *m*

Sellotape /'seləʊteɪp/ *n* fita *f* adesiva, (*P*) fitacola *f*

semantic /sɪ'mæntɪk/ *a* semântico. **~s** *n* semântica *f*

semblance /'sembləns/ *n* aparência *f*

semen /'si:mən/ *n* sêmen *m*, (*P*) sémen *m*, esperma *m*

semester /sɪ'mestə(r)/ *n* (*Amer: univ*) semestre *m*

semi- /'semɪ/ *pref* semi-, meio

semibreve /'semɪbri:v/ *n* (*mus*) semibreve *f*

semicirc|le /'semɪsɜ:kl/ *n* semicírculo *m*. **~ular** /-sɜ:kjʊlə(r)/ *a* semicircular

semicolon /semɪ'kəʊlən/ *n* ponto-e-vírgula *m*

semi-detached /semɪdɪ'tætʃt/ *a* **~ house** casa *f* geminada

semifinal /semɪ'faɪnl/ *n* semifinal *f*, (*P*) meiafinal *f*

seminar /'semɪna:(r)/ *n* seminário *m*

semiquaver /'semɪkweɪvə(r)/ *n* (*mus*) semicolcheia *f*

Semit|e /'si:maɪt/ *a* & *n* semita (*mf*). **~ic** /sɪ'mɪtɪk/ *a* & *n* (*lang*) semítico (*m*)

semitone /'semɪtəʊn/ *n* (*mus*) semitom *m*

semolina /semə'li:nə/ *n* sêmola *f*, (*P*) sémola *f*, semolina *f*

senat|e /'senɪt/ *n* senado *m*. **~or** /-ətə(r)/ *n* senador *m*

send /send/ *vt/i* (*pt* **sent**) enviar, mandar. **~ back** devolver. **~ for** (*person*) chamar, mandar vir; (*help*) pedir. **~ (away** *or* **off) for** encomendar, mandar vir (por carta). **~-off** *n* despedida *f*, bota-fora *m*. **~ up** (*colloq*) parodiar. **~er** *n* expedidor *m*, remetente *m*

senil|e /'si:naɪl/ *a* senil. **~ity** /sɪ'nɪlətɪ/ *n* senilidade *f*

senior /'si:nɪə(r)/ *a* mais velho, mais idoso (**to** que); (*in rank*) superior; (*in service*) mais antigo; (*after surname*) sênior, (*P*) sénior □ *n* pessoa *f* mais velha; (*schol*) finalista *mf*. **~ citizen** pessoa *f* de idade *or* da terceira idade. **~ity** /-'ɒrətɪ/ *n* (*in age*) idade *f*; (*in service*) antiguidade *f*

sensation /sen'seɪʃn/ *n* sensação *f*. **~al** *a* sensacional. **~alism** *n* sensacionalismo *m*

sense /sens/ *n* sentido *m*; (*wisdom*) bom senso *m*; (*sensation*) sensação *f*; (*mental impression*) sentimento *m*. **~s** (*sanity*) razão *f* □ *vt* pressentir. **make ~** fazer sentido. **make ~ of** compreender. **~less** *a* disparatado, sem sentido; (*med*) sem sentidos, inconsciente

sensible /'sensəbl/ *a* sensato, razoável; (*clothes*) prático

sensitiv|e /'sensətɪv/ *a* sensível (**to** a); (*touchy*) susceptível. **~ity** /-'tɪvətɪ/ *n* sensibilidade *f*

sensory /'sensərɪ/ *a* sensorial

sensual /'senʃʊəl/ *a* sensual. **~ity** /-'ælətɪ/ *n* sensualidade *f*

sensuous /'senʃʊəs/ *a* sensual

sent /sent/ *see* **send**

sentence /'sentəns/ *n* frase *f*; (*jur: decision*) sentença *f*; (*punishment*) pena *f* □ *vt* **~ to** condenar a

sentiment /'sentɪmənt/ *n* sentimento *m*; (*opinion*) modo *m* de ver

sentimental /sentɪ'mentl/ *a* sentimental. **~ity** /-men'tælətɪ/ *n* sentimentalidade *f*, sentimentalismo *m*. **~ value** valor *m* estimativo

sentry /'sentrɪ/ *n* sentinela *f*

separable /'sepərəbl/ *a* separável

separate[1] /'seprət/ *a* separado, diferente. **~s** *npl* (*clothes*) conjuntos *mpl*. **~ly** *adv* separadamente, em separado

separat|e[2] /'sepəreɪt/ *vt/i* separar (-se). **~ion** /-'reɪʃn/ *n* separação *f*

September /sep'tembə(r)/ *n* setembro *m*

septic /'septɪk/ *a* séptico, infectado

sequel /'si:kwəl/ *n* resultado *m*, seqüela *f*, (*P*) sequela *f*; (*of novel, film*) continuação *f*

sequence /'si:kwəns/ *n* seqüência *f*, (*P*) sequência *f*

sequin /'si:kwɪn/ *n* lantejoula *f*

serenade /serə'neɪd/ *n* serenata *f* □ *vt* fazer uma serenata para

seren|e /sɪ'ri:n/ *a* sereno. **~ity** /-'enətɪ/ *n* serenidade *f*

sergeant /'sa:dʒənt/ *n* sargento *m*

serial /'sɪərɪəl/ *n* folhetim *m* □ *a* (*number*) de série. **~ize** /-laɪz/ *vt* publicar em folhetim

series /'sɪəri:z/ *n invar* série *f*
serious /'sɪərɪəs/ *a* sério; (*very bad, critical*) grave, sério. **~ly** *adv* seriamente, gravemente, a sério. **take ~ly** levar a sério. **~ness** *n* seriedade *f*, gravidade *f*
sermon /'sɜ:mən/ *n* sermão *m*
serpent /'sɜ:pənt/ *n* serpente *f*
serrated /sɪ'reɪtɪd/ *a* (*edge*) serr(e)ado, com serrilha
serum /'sɪərəm/ *n* (*pl* **-a**) soro *m*
servant /'sɜ:vənt/ *n* criado *m*, criada *f*, empregado *m*, empregada *f*
serv|e /sɜ:v/ *vt/i* servir; (*a sentence*) cumprir; (*jur: a writ*) entregar; (*mil*) servir, prestar serviço; (*apprenticeship*) fazer □ *n* (*tennis*) saque *m*, (*P*) serviço *m*. **~e as/to** servir de/para. **~e its purpose** servir para o que é (*colloq*), servir os seus fins. **it ~es you/him** *etc* **right** é bem feito. **~ing** *n* (*portion*) dose *f*, porção *f*
server /'sɜ:və(r)/ *n* (*comput*) servidor *m*
service /'sɜ:vɪs/ *n* serviço *m*; (*relig*) culto *m*; (*tennis*) saque *m*, (*P*) serviço *m*; (*maintenance*) revisão *f*. **~s** (*mil*) forças *fpl* armadas □ *vt* (*car etc*) fazer a revisão de. **of ~ to** útil a, de utilidade a. **~ area** área *f* de serviço. **~ charge** serviço *m*. **~ station** posto *m* de gasolina
serviceable /'sɜ:vɪsəbl/ *a* útil, prático; (*durable*) resistente
serviceman /'sɜ:vɪsmən/ *n* (*pl* **-men**) militar *m*
serviette /sɜ:vɪ'et/ *n* guardanapo *m*
session /'seʃn/ *n* sessão *f*; (*univ*) ano *m* acadêmico, (*P*) académico; (*Amer: univ*) semestre *m*. **in ~** (*sitting*) em sessão, reunidos
set /set/ *vt* (*pt* **set**, *pres p* **setting**) pôr, colocar; (*put down*) pousar; (*limit etc*) fixar; (*watch, clock*) regular; (*example*) dar; (*exam, task*) marcar; (*in plaster*) engessar □ *vi* (*of sun*) pôr-se; (*of jelly*) endurecer, solidificar(-se) □ *n* (*of people*) circulo *m*, roda *f*; (*of books*) coleção *f*, (*P*) colecção *f*; (*of tools, chairs etc*) jogo *m*; (*TV, radio*) aparelho *m*; (*hair*) mise *f*; (*theat*) cenário *m*; (*tennis*) partida *f*, set *m* □ *a* fixo; (*habit*) inveterado; (*jelly*) duro, sólido; (*book*) do programa, (*P*) adoptado; (*meal*) a preço fixo. **be ~ on doing** estar decidido a fazer. **~ about** *or* **to** começar a, pôr-se a. **~ back** (*plans etc*) atrasar; (*sl: cost*) custar. **~-back** *n* revés *m*, contratempo *m*, atraso *m* de vida (*colloq*). **~ fire to** atear fogo a, (*P*) deitar fogo a. **~free** pôr em liberdade. **~ in** (*rain etc*) pegar. **~off** *or* **out** partir, começar a viajar. **~ off** (*mechanism*) pôr para funcionar, (*P*) pôr a funcionar; (*bomb*) explodir; (*by contrast*) realçar. **~ out** (*state*) expor; (*arrange*) dispôr. **~ sail** partir, içar as velas. **~ square** esquadro *m*. **~ the table** pôr a mesa. **~ theory** teoria *f* de conjuntos. **~-to** *n* briga *f*. **~ up** (*establish*) fundar, estabelecer. **~-up** *n* (*system*) sistema *m*, organização *f*; (*situation*) situação *f*
settee /se'ti:/ *n* sofá *m*
setting /'setɪŋ/ *n* (*framework*) quadro *m*; (*of jewel*) engaste *m*; (*typ*) composição *f*; (*mus*) arranjo *m* musical
settle /'setl/ *vt* (*arrange*) resolver; (*date*) marcar; (*nerves*) acalmar; (*doubts*) esclarecer; (*new country*) colonizar, povoar; (*bill*) pagar □ *vi* assentar; (*in country*) estabelecer-se; (*in house, chair etc*) instalar-se; (*weather*) estabilizar-se. **~ down** acalmar-se; (*become orderly*) assentar; (*sit, rest*) instalar-se. **~ for** aceitar. **~ up (with)** fazer contas (com); (*fig*) ajustar contas (com). **~r** /-ə(r)/ *n* colono *m*, colonizador *m*
settlement /'setlmənt/ *n* (*agreement*) acordo *m*; (*payment*) pagamento *m*; (*colony*) colônia *f*, (*P*) colónia *f*; (*colonization*) colonização *f*
seven /'sevn/ *a* & *n* sete (*m*). **~th** *a* & *n* sétimo (*m*)
seventeen /sevn'ti:n/ *a* & *n* dezessete (*m*), (*P*) dezassete (*m*). **~th** *a* & *n* décimo sétimo (*m*)
sevent|y /'sevntɪ/ *a* & *n* setenta (*m*). **~ieth** *a* & *n* septuagésimo (*m*)
sever /'sevə(r)/ *vt* cortar. **~ance** *n* corte *m*
several /'sevrəl/ *a* & *pron* vários, diversos
sever|e /sɪ'vɪə(r)/ *a* (**-er, -est**) severo; (*pain*) forte, violento; (*illness*) grave; (*winter*) rigoroso. **~ely** *adv* severamente; (*seriously*) gravemente. **~ity** /sɪ-'verɪtɪ/ *n* severidade *f*; (*seriousness*) gravidade *f*
sew /səʊ/ *vt/i* (*pt* **sewed**, *pp* **sewn** *or* **sewed**) coser, costurar. **~ing** *n* costura *f*. **~ing-machine** *n* máquina *f* de costura
sewage /'sju:ɪdʒ/ *n* efluentes *mpl* dos esgotos, detritos *mpl*
sewer /'sju:ə(r)/ *n* cano *m* de esgoto
sewn /səʊn/ *see* **sew**
sex /seks/ *n* sexo *m* □ *a* sexual. **have ~** ter relações. **~ maniac** tarado *m* sexual. **~y** *a* sexy *invar*, que tem sex-appeal
sexist /'seksɪst/ *a* & *n* sexista *mf*
sexual /'sekʃʊəl/ *a* sexual. **~ harassment** assédio *m* sexual. **~ intercourse** relações *fpl* sexuais. **~ity** /-'ælətɪ/ *n* sexualidade *f*

shabb|y /ˈʃæbɪ/ *a* (**-ier, -iest**) (*clothes, object*) gasto, surrado; (*person*) maltrapilho, mal vestido; (*mean*) miserável. **~ily** *adv* miseravelmente

shack /ʃæk/ *n* cabana *f*, barraca *f*

shackles /ˈʃæklz/ *npl* grilhões *mpl*, algemas *fpl*

shade /ʃeɪd/ *n* sombra *f*; (*of colour*) tom *m*, matiz *m*; (*of opinion*) matiz *m*; (*for lamp*) abat-jour *m*, quebra-luz *m*; (*Amer: blind*) estore *m* □ *vt* resguardar da luz; (*darken*) sombrear. **a ~ bigger**/*etc* ligeiramente maior/*etc*. **in the ~** à sombra

shadow /ˈʃædəʊ/ *n* sombra *f* □ *vt* cobrir de sombra; (*follow*) seguir, vigiar. **S~ Cabinet** gabinete *m* formado pelo partido da oposição. **~y** *a* ensombrado, sombreado; (*fig*) vago, indistinto

shady /ˈʃeɪdɪ/ *a* (**-ier, -iest**) sombreiro, (*P*) que dá sombra; (*in shade*) à sombra; (*fig: dubious*) suspeito, duvidoso

shaft /ʃɑːft/ *n* (*of arrow, spear*) haste *f*; (*axle*) eixo *m*, veio *m*; (*of mine, lift*) poço *m*; (*of light*) raio *m*

shaggy /ˈʃægɪ/ *a* (**-ier, -iest**) (*beard*) hirsuto; (*hair*) desgrenhado; (*animal*) peludo, felpudo

shake /ʃeɪk/ *vt* (*pt* **shook**, *pp* **shaken**) abanar, sacudir; (*bottle*) agitar; (*belief, house etc*) abalar □ *vi* estremecer, tremer □ *n* (*violent*) abanão *m*, safanão *m*; (*light*) sacudidela *f*. **~ hands with** apertar a mão de. **~ off** (*get rid of*) sacudir, livrar-se de. **~ one's head** (*to say no*) fazer que não com a cabeça. **~ up** agitar. **~-up** *n* (*upheaval*) reviravolta *f*

shaky /ˈʃeɪkɪ/ *a* (**-ier, -iest**) (*hand, voice*) trêmulo, (*P*) trémulo; (*unsteady, unsafe*) pouco firme, inseguro; (*weak*) fraco

shall /ʃæl/; *unstressed* /ʃəl/ *v aux* **I/we ~ do** (*future*) farei/faremos. **I/you/he ~ do** (*command*) eu hei de/você há de/tu hás de/ele há de fazer

shallot /ʃəˈlɒt/ *n* cebolinha *f*, (*P*) chalota *f*

shallow /ˈʃæləʊ/ *a* (**-er, -est**) pouco fundo, raso; (*fig*) superficial

sham /ʃæm/ *n* fingimento *m*; (*jewel etc*) imitação *f*; (*person*) impostor *m*, fingido *m* □ *a* fingido; (*false*) falso □ *vt* (*pt* **shammed**) fingir

shambles /ˈʃæmblz/ *npl* (*colloq: mess*) balbúrdia *f*, trapalhada *f*

shame /ʃeɪm/ *n* vergonha *f* □ *vt* (fazer) envergonhar. **it's a ~** é uma pena. **what a ~!** que pena! **~ful** *a* vergonhoso. **~less** *a* sem vergonha, descarado; (*immodest*) despudorado, desavergonhado

shamefaced /ˈʃeɪmfeɪst/ *a* envergonhado

shampoo /ʃæmˈpuː/ *n* xampu *m*, (*P*) champô *m*, shampoo *m* □ *vt* lavar com xampu, (*P*) champô *or* shampoo

shan't /ʃɑːnt/ = **shall not**

shanty /ˈʃæntɪ/ *n* barraca *f*. **~ town** favela *f*, (*P*) bairro(s) *m*(*pl*) da lata

shape /ʃeɪp/ *n* forma *f* □ *vt* moldar □ *vi* **~ (up)** andar bem, fazer progressos. **take ~** concretizar-se, avançar. **~less** *a* informe, sem forma; (*of body*) deselegante, disforme

shapely /ˈʃeɪplɪ/ *a* (**-ier, -iest**) (*leg, person*) bem feito, elegante

share /ʃeə(r)/ *n* parte *f*, porção *f*; (*comm*) ação *f*, (*P*) acção *f* □ *vt/i* partilhar (**with** com, **in** de)

shareholder /ˈʃeəhəʊldə(r)/ *n* acionista *mf*, (*P*) accionista *mf*

shark /ʃɑːk/ *n* tubarão *m*

sharp /ʃɑːp/ *a* (**-er, -est**) (*knife, pencil etc*) afiado; (*pin, point etc*) pontiagudo, aguçado; (*words, reply*) áspero; (*of bend*) fechado; (*acute*) agudo; (*sudden*) brusco; (*dishonest*) pouco honesto; (*well-defined*) nítido; (*brisk*) rápido, vigoroso; (*clever*) vivo □ *adv* (*stop*) de repente □ *n* (*mus*) sustenido *m*. **six o'clock ~** seis horas em ponto. **~ly** *adv* (*harshly*) rispidamente; (*suddenly*) de repente

sharpen /ˈʃɑːpən/ *vt* aguçar; (*pencil*) fazer a ponta de, (*P*) afiar; (*knife etc*) afiar, amolar. **~er** *n* afiadeira *f*; (*for pencil*) apontador *m*, (*P*) apára-lápis *m*, (*P*) afia-lápis *m*

shatter /ˈʃætə(r)/ *vt/i* despedaçar (-se), esmigalhar(-se); (*hopes*) destruir(-se); (*nerves*) abalar(-se). **~ed** *a* (*upset*) passado; (*exhausted*) estourado (*colloq*)

shav|e /ʃeɪv/ *vt/i* barbear(-se), fazer a barba (de) □ *n* **have a ~e** barbear-se. **have a close ~e** (*fig*) escapar por um triz. **~en** *a* raspado, barbeado. **~er** *n* aparelho *m* de barbear, (*P*) máquina *f* de barbear. **~ing-brush** *n* pincel *m* para a barba. **~ing-cream** *n* creme *m* de barbear

shaving /ˈʃeɪvɪŋ/ *n* apara *f*

shawl /ʃɔːl/ *n* xale *m*, (*P*) xaile *m*

she /ʃiː/ *pron* ela □ *n* fêmea *f*

sheaf /ʃiːf/ *n* (*pl* **sheaves**) feixe *m*; (*of papers*) maço *m*, molho *m*

shear /ʃɪə(r)/ *vt* (*pp* **shorn** *or* **sheared**) (*sheep etc*) tosquiar

shears /ʃɪəz/ *npl* tesoura *f* para jardim

sheath /ʃiːθ/ *n* (*pl* **~s** /ʃiːðz/) bainha *f*; (*condom*) preservativo *m*, camisa-de-Vênus *f*

sheathe /ʃiːð/ *vt* embainhar

shed[1] /ʃed/ *n* (*hut*) casinhola *f*; (*for cows*) estábulo *m*

shed[2] /ʃed/ (*pt* **shed**, *pres p* **shedding**) perder, deixar cair; (*spread*) espalhar; (*blood, tears*) deitar, derramar. ~ **light on** lançar luz sobre

sheen /ʃi:n/ *n* brilho *m*, lustre *m*

sheep /ʃi:p/ *n* (*pl invar*) carneiro *m*, ovelha *f*. ~**-dog** *n* cão *m* de pastor

sheepish /ˈʃi:pɪʃ/ *a* encabulado. ~**ly** *adv* com um ar encabulado

sheepskin /ˈʃi:pskɪn/ *n* pele *f* de carneiro; (*leather*) carneira *f*

sheer /ʃɪə(r)/ *a* mero, simples; (*steep*) íngreme, a pique; (*fabric*) diáfano, transparente □ *adv* a pique, verticalmente

sheet /ʃi:t/ *n* lençol *m*; (*of glass, metal*) chapa *f*, placa *f*; (*of paper*) folha *f*

sheikh /ʃeɪk/ *n* xeque *m*, sheik *m*

shelf /ʃelf/ *n* (*pl* **shelves**) prateleira *f*

shell /ʃel/ *n* (*of egg, nut etc*) casca *f*; (*of mollusc*) concha *f*; (*of ship, tortoise*) casco *m*; (*of building*) estrutura *f*, armação *f*; (*of explosive*) cartucho *m* □ *vt* descascar; (*mil*) bombardear

shellfish /ˈʃelfɪʃ/ *n* (*pl invar*) crustáceo *m*; (*as food*) marisco *m*

shelter /ˈʃeltə(r)/ *n* abrigo *m*, refúgio *m* □ *vt* abrigar; (*protect*) proteger; (*harbour*) dar asilo a □ *vi* abrigar-se, refugiar-se. ~**ed** *a* (*life etc*) protegido; (*spot*) abrigado

shelve /ʃelv/ *vt* pôr em prateleiras; (*fit with shelves*) pôr prateleiras em; (*fig*) engavetar, pôr de lado

shelving /ˈʃelvɪŋ/ *n* (*shelves*) prateleiras *fpl*

shepherd /ˈʃepəd/ *n* pastor *m* □ *vt* guiar. ~**'s pie** empadão *m* de batata e carne moída

sheriff /ˈʃerɪf/ *n* xerife *m*

sherry /ˈʃerɪ/ *n* Xerez *m*

shield /ʃi:ld/ *n* (*armour, heraldry*) escudo *m*; (*screen*) anteparo *m* □ *vt* proteger (**from** contra, de)

shift /ʃɪft/ *vt/i* mudar de posição, deslocar(-se); (*exchange, alter*) mudar de □ *n* mudança *f*; (*workers; work*) turno *m*. **make** ~ arranjar-se

shiftless /ˈʃɪftlɪs/ *a* (*lazy*) molengão, preguiçoso

shifty /ˈʃɪftɪ/ *a* (**-ier, -iest**) velhaco, duvidoso

shimmer /ˈʃɪmə(r)/ *vi* luzir suavemente □ *n* luzir *m*

shin /ʃɪn/ *n* perna *f*. ~**-bone** *n* tíbia *f*, canela *f*. ~**-pad** *n* (*football*) caneleira *f*

shin|e /ʃaɪn/ *vt/i* (*pt* **shone**) (fazer) brilhar, (fazer) reluzir; (*shoes*) engraxar □ *n* lustro *m*. ~**e a torch (on)** iluminar com uma lanterna de mão. **the sun is** ~**ing** faz sol

shingle /ˈʃɪŋgl/ *n* (*pebbles*) seixos *mpl*

shingles /ˈʃɪŋglz/ *npl med* zona *f*, herpes-zóster *f*

shiny /ˈʃaɪnɪ/ *a* (**-ier, -iest**) brilhante; (*of coat, trousers*) lustroso

ship /ʃɪp/ *n* barco *m*, navio *m* □ *vt* (*pt* **shipped**) transportar; (*send*) mandar por via marítima; (*load*) embarcar. ~**ment** *n* (*goods*) carregamento *m*; (*shipping*) embarque *m*. ~**per** *n* expedidor *m*. ~**ping** *n* navegação *f*; (*ships*) navios *mpl*

shipbuilding /ˈʃɪpbɪldɪŋ/ *n* construção *f* naval

shipshape /ˈʃɪpʃeɪp/ *adv* & *a* em (perfeita) ordem, impecável

shipwreck /ˈʃɪprek/ *n* naufrágio *m*. ~**ed** *a* naufragado. **be** ~**ed** naufragar

shipyard /ˈʃɪpja:d/ *n* estaleiro *m*

shirk /ʃɜ:k/ *vt* fugir a, furtar-se a, (*P*) baldar-se a (*sl*). ~**er** *n* parasita *mf*

shirt /ʃɜ:t/ *n* camisa *f*; (*of woman*) blusa *f*. **in** ~**-sleeves** em mangas de camisa

shiver /ˈʃɪvə(r)/ *vi* arrepiar-se, tiritar □ *n* arrepio *m*

shoal /ʃəʊl/ *n* (*of fish*) cardume *m*

shock /ʃɒk/ choque *m*, embate *m*; (*electr*) choque *m* elétrico, (*P*) eléctrico; (*med*) choque *m* □ *a* de choque □ *vt* chocar. ~ **absorber** (*mech*) amortecedor *m*. ~**ing** *a* chocante; (*colloq: very bad*) horrível

shod /ʃɒd/ *see* **shoe**

shodd|y /ˈʃɒdɪ/ *a* (**-ier, -iest**) mal feito, ordinário, de má qualidade. ~**ily** *adv* mal

shoe /ʃu:/ *n* sapato *m*; (*footwear*) calçado *m*; (*horse*) ferradura *f*; (*brake*) sapata *f*, (*P*) calço *m* (de travão) □ *vt* (*pt* **shod**, *pres p* **shoeing**) (*horse*) ferrar. ~**-polish** *n* pomada *f*, (*P*) graxa *f* para sapatos. ~**-shop** *n* sapataria *f*. **on a** ~**-string** (*colloq*) com/por muito pouco dinheiro, na pindaíba (*colloq*)

shoehorn /ˈʃu:hɔ:n/ *n* calçadeira *f*

shoelace /ˈʃu:leɪs/ *n* cordão *m* de sapato, (*P*) atacador *m*

shoemaker /ˈʃu:meɪkə(r)/ *n* sapateiro *m*

shone /ʃɒn/ *see* **shine**

shoo /ʃu:/ *vt* enxotar □ *int* xô

shook /ʃuk/ *see* **shake**

shoot /ʃu:t/ *vt* (*pt* **shot**) (*gun*) disparar; (*glance, missile*) lançar; (*kill*) matar a tiro; (*wound*) ferir a tiro; (*execute*) executar, fuzilar; (*hunt*) caçar; (*film*) filmar, rodar □ *vi* disparar, atirar (**at** contra, sobre); (*bot*) rebentar; (*football*) rematar □ *n* (*bot*) rebento *m*. ~ **down** abater (a tiro). ~ **in/out** (*rush*) entrar/sair correndo *or* disparado. ~ **up** (*spurt*) jorrar; (*grow quickly*) crescer a olhos vistos, dar um pulo;

(*prices*) subir em disparada. **~ing** *n* (*shots*) tiroteio *m*. **~ing-range** *n* carreira *f* de tiro. **~ing star** estrela *f* cadente

shop /ʃɒp/ *n* loja *f*; (*workshop*) oficina *f* □ *vi* (*pt* **shopped**) fazer compras. **~ around** procurar, ver o que há. **~ assistant** empregado *m*, caixeiro *m*; vendedor *m*. **~-floor** *n* (*workers*) trabalhadores *mpl*. **~per** *n* comprador *m*. **~-soiled**, (*Amer*) **~-worn** *adjs* enxovalhado. **~ steward** delegado *m* sindical. **~ window** vitrina *f*, (*P*) montra *f*. **talk ~** falar de coisas profissionais

shopkeeper /ˈʃɒpki:pə(r)/ *n* lojista *mf*, comerciante *mf*

shoplift|er /ˈʃɒplɪftə(r)/ *n* gatuno *m* de lojas. **~ing** *n* furto *m* em lojas

shopping /ˈʃɒpɪŋ/ *n* (*goods*) compras *fpl*. **go ~** ir às compras. **~ bag** sacola *f* de compras. **~ centre** centro *m* comercial

shore /ʃɔ:(r)/ *n* (*of sea*) praia *f*, costa *f*; (*of lake*) margem *f*

shorn /ʃɔ:n/ *see* **shear** □ *a* tosquiado. **~ of** despojado de

short /ʃɔ:t/ *a* (**-er, -est**) curto; (*person*) baixo; (*brief*) breve, curto; (*curt*) seco, brusco. **be ~ of** (*lack*) ter falta de □ *adv* (*abruptly*) bruscamente, de repente. **cut ~** abreviar; (*interrupt*) interromper □ *n* (*electr*) curto-circuito *m*; (*film*) curta-metragem *f*, short *m*. **~s** (*trousers*) calção *m*, (*P*) calções *mpl*, short *m*, (*P*) shorts *mpl*. **a ~ time** pouco tempo. **he is called Tom for ~** o diminutivo dele é Tom. **in ~** em suma. **~-change** *vt* (*cheat*) enganar. **~ circuit** (*electr*) curto-circuito *m* **~-circuit** *vt/i* (*electr*) fazer *or* dar um curto-circuito (em). **~ cut** atalho *m*. **~-handed** *a* com falta de pessoal. **~ list** pré-seleção *f*, (*P*) pré-selecção *f*. **~-lived** *a* de pouca duração. **~-sighted** *a* míope, (*P*) curto de vista. **~-tempered** *a* irritadiço. **~ story** conto *m*. **~ wave** (*radio*) onda(s) *f*(*pl*) curta(s)

shortage /ˈʃɔ:tɪdʒ/ *n* falta *f*, escassez *f*

shortbread /ˈʃɔ:tbred/ *n* shortbread *m*, biscoito *m* de massa amanteigada

shortcoming /ˈʃɔ:tkʌmɪŋ/ *n* falha *f*, imperfeição *f*

shorten /ˈʃɔ:tn/ *vt/i* encurtar(-se), abreviar(-se), diminuir

shorthand /ˈʃɔ:thænd/ *n* estenografia *f*. **~ typist** estenodactilógrafa *f*

shortly /ˈʃɔ:tlɪ/ *adv* (*soon*) em breve, dentro em pouco

shot /ʃɒt/ *see* **shoot** □ *n* (*firing, bullet*) tiro *m*; (*person*) atirador *m*; (*pellets*) chumbo *m*; (*photograph*) fotografia *f*; (*injection*) injeção *f*, (*P*) injecção *f*; (*in golf, billiards*) tacada *f*. **go like a ~** ir disparado. **have a ~ (at sth)** experimentar (fazer alg coisa). **~-gun** *n* espingarda *f*, caçadeira *f*

should /ʃʊd; *unstressed* /ʃəd/ *v aux* **you ~ help me** você devia me ajudar. **I ~ have stayed** devia ter ficado. **I ~ like to** gostaria de *or* gostava de. **if he ~ come** se ele vier

shoulder /ˈʃəʊldə(r)/ *n* ombro *m* □ *vt* (*responsibility*) tomar, assumir; (*burden*) carregar, arcar com. **~-blade** *n* (*anat*) omoplata *f*. **~-pad** *n* enchimento *m* de ombro, ombreira *f*

shout /ʃaʊt/ *n* grito *m*, brado *m*; (*very loud*) berro *m* □ *vt/i* gritar (**at** com); (*very loudly*) berrar (**at** com). **~ down** fazer calar com gritos. **~ing** *n* gritaria *f*, berraria *f*

shove /ʃʌv/ *n* empurrão *m* □ *vt/i* empurrar; (*colloq: put*) meter, enfiar. **~ off** (*colloq: depart*) começar a andar (*colloq*), dar o fora (*colloq*), (*P*) cavar (*colloq*)

shovel /ˈʃʌvl/ *n* pá *f*; (*machine*) escavadora *f* □ *vt* (*pt* **shovelled**) remover com pá

show /ʃəʊ/ *vt* (*pt* **showed**, *pp* **shown**) mostrar; (*of dial, needle*) marcar; (*put on display*) expor; (*film*) dar, passar □ *vi* ver-se, aparecer, estar à vista □ *n* mostra *f*, demonstração *f*, manifestação *f*; (*ostentation*) alarde *m*, espalhafato *m*; (*exhibition*) mostra *f*, exposição *f*; (*theatre, cinema*) espetáculo *m*, (*P*) espectáculo *m*, show *m*. **for ~** para fazer vista. **on ~** exposto, em exposição. **~-down** *n* confrontação *f*. **~-jumping** *n* concurso *m* hípico. **~ in** mandar entrar. **~ off** *vt* exibir, ostentar □ *vi* exibir-se, querer fazer figura. **~-off** *n* exibicionista *mf*. **~ out** acompanhar à porta. **~-piece** *n* peça *f* digna de se expor. **~ up** ser claramente visível, ver-se bem; (*colloq: arrive*) aparecer. **~ing** *n* (*performance*) atuação *f*, performance *f*; (*cinema*) exibição *f*

shower /ˈʃaʊə(r)/ *n* (*of rain*) aguaceiro *m*, chuvarada *f*; (*of blows etc*) saraivada *f*; (*in bathroom*) chuveiro *m*, ducha *f*, (*P*) duche *m* □ *vt* **~ with** cumular de, encher de □ *vi* tomar um banho de chuveiro *or* uma ducha, (*P*) um duche. **~y** *a* chuvoso

showerproof /ˈʃaʊəpru:f/ *a* impermeável

shown /ʃəʊn/ *see* **show**

showroom /ˈʃəʊrʊm/ *n* espaço *m* de exposição, show-room *m*; (*for cars*) stand *m*

showy /ˈʃəʊɪ/ *a* (**-ier, -iest**) vistoso; (*too bright*) berrante; (*pej*) espalhafatoso

shrank /ʃræŋk/ *see* **shrink**

shred /ʃred/ *n* tira *f*, retalho *m*, farrapo *m*; (*fig*) mínimo *m*, sombra *f* □ *vt* (*pt* **shredded**) reduzir a tiras, estrançalhar; (*culin*) desfiar. **~der** *n* trituradora *f*; (*for paper*) fragmentadora *f*

shrewd /ʃru:d/ *a* (**-er, -est**) astucioso, fino, perspicaz. **~ness** *n* astúcia *f*, perspicácia *f*

shriek /ʃri:k/ *n* grito *m* agudo, guincho *m* □ *vt/i* gritar, guinchar

shrift /ʃrɪft/ *n* **give sb short ~** tratar alguém com brusquidão, despachar alguém sem mais cerimônias, (*P*) cerimónias

shrill /ʃrɪl/ *a* estridente, agudo

shrimp /ʃrɪmp/ *n* camarão *m*

shrine /ʃraɪn/ *n* (*place*) santuário *m*; (*tomb*) túmulo *m*; (*casket*) re licário *m*

shrink /ʃrɪŋk/ *vt/i* (*pt* **shrank**, *pp* **shrunk**) encolher; (*recoil*) encolher-se. **~ from** esquivar-se a, fugir a (+ *inf*)/de (+ *noun*), retrair-se de. **~age** *n* encolhimento *m*; (*comm*) contração *f*

shrivel /ˈʃrɪvl/ *vt/i* (*pt* **shrivelled**) encarquilhar(-se)

shroud /ʃraʊd/ *n* mortalha *f* □ *vt* (*veil*) encobrir, envolver

Shrove /ʃrəʊv/ *n* **~ Tuesday** Terça-feira *f* gorda *or* de Carnaval

shrub /ʃrʌb/ *n* arbusto *m*. **~bery** *n* arbustos *mpl*

shrug /ʃrʌg/ *vt* (*pt* **shrugged**) **~ one's shoulders** encolher os ombros □ *n* encolher *m* de ombros. **~ off** não dar importância a

shrunk /ʃrʌŋk/ *see* **shrink**. **~en** *a* encolhido; (*person*) mirrado, chupado

shudder /ˈʃʌdə(r)/ *vi* arrepiar-se, estremecer, tremer □ *n* arrepio *m*, tremor *m*, estremecimento *m*. **I ~ to think** tremo só de pensar

shuffle /ˈʃʌfl/ *vt* (*feet*) arrastar; (*cards*) embaralhar □ *vi* arrastar os pés □ *n* marcha *f* arrastada

shun /ʃʌn/ *vt* (*pt* **shunned**) evitar, fugir de

shunt /ʃʌnt/ *vt/i* (*train*) mudar de linha, manobrar

shut /ʃʌt/ *vt* (*pt* **shut**, *pres p* **shutting**) fechar □ *vi* fechar-se; (*shop, bank etc*) encerrar, fechar. **~ down** *or* **up** fechar. **~-down** *n* encerramento *m*. **~ in** *or* **up** trancar. **~ up** *vi* (*colloq: stop talking*) calar-se □ *vt* (*colloq: silence*) mandar calar. **~ up!** (*colloq*) cale-se!, cale a boca!

shutter /ˈʃʌtə(r)/ *n* taipais *mpl*, (*P*) portada *f* de madeira; (*of laths*) persiana *f*; (*in shop*) taipais *mpl*; (*photo*) obturador *m*

shuttle /ˈʃʌtl/ *n* (*of spaceship*) ônibus *m* espacial. **~ service** (*plane*) ponte *f* aérea; (*bus*) navete *f*

shuttlecock /ˈʃʌtlkɒk/ *n* volante *m*

shy /ʃaɪ/ *a* (**-er, -est**) tímido, acanhado, envergonhado □ *vi* (*horse*) espantar-se (**at** com); (*fig*) assustar-se (**at** *or* **away from** com). **~ness** *n* timidez *f*, acanhamento *m*, vergonha *f*

Siamese /saɪəˈmi:z/ *a* & *n* siamês (*m*). **~ cat** gato *m* siamês

Sicily /ˈsɪsɪlɪ/ *n* Sicília *f*

sick /sɪk/ *a* doente; (*humour*) negro. **be ~** (*vomit*) vomitar. **be ~ of** estar farto de. **feel ~** estar enjoado. **~-bay** *n* enfermaria *f*. **~-leave** *n* licença *f* por doença **~-room** *n* quarto *m* de doente

sicken /ˈsɪkn/ *vt* (*distress*) desesperar; (*disgust*) repugnar □ *vi* **be ~ing for flu** *etc* começar a pegar uma gripe (*colloq*)

sickle /ˈsɪkl/ *n* foice *f*

sickly /ˈsɪklɪ/ *a* (**-ier, -iest**) (*person*) doentio, achacado; (*smell*) enjoativo; (*pale*) pálido

sickness /ˈsɪknɪs/ *n* doença *f*; (*vomiting*) náusea *f*, vômito *m*, (*P*) vómito *m*

side /saɪd/ *n* lado *m*; (*of road, river*) beira *f*; (*of hill*) encosta *f*; (*sport*) equipe *f*, (*P*) equipa *f* □ *a* lateral □ *vi* **~ with** tomar o partido de. **on the ~** (*extra*) nas horas vagas; (*secretly*) pela calada. **~ by ~** lado a lado. **~-car** *n* sidecar *m*. **~-effect** *n* efeito *m* secundário. **~-show** *n* espetáculo *m*, (*P*) espectáculo *m* suplementar. **~-step** *vt* (*pt* **-stepped**) evitar. **~-track** *vt* (fazer) desviar dum propósito

sideboard /ˈsaɪdbɔ:d/ *n* aparador *m*

sideburns /ˈsaɪdbɜ:nz/ *npl* suíças *fpl*, costeletas *fpl*, (*P*) patilhas *fpl*

sidelight /ˈsaɪdlaɪt/ *n* (*auto*) luz *f* lateral, (*P*) farolim *m*

sideline /ˈsaɪdlaɪn/ *n* atividade *f*, (*P*) actividade *f* secundária; (*sport*) linha *f* lateral

sidelong /ˈsaɪdlɒŋ/ *adv* & *a* de lado

sidewalk /ˈsaɪdwɔ:k/ *n* (*Amer*) passeio *m*

sideways /ˈsaɪdweɪz/ *adv* & *a* de lado

siding /ˈsaɪdɪŋ/ *n* desvio *m*, ramal *m*

sidle /ˈsaɪdl/ *vi* **~ up (to)** avançar furtivamente (para), chegar-se furtivamente (a)

siege /si:dʒ/ *n* cerco *m*

siesta /sɪˈestə/ *n* sesta *f*

sieve /sɪv/ *n* peneira *f*; (*for liquids*) coador *m* □ *vt* peneirar; (*liquids*) passar, coar

sift /sɪft/ *vt* peneirar; (*sprinkle*) polvilhar. **~ through** examinar minuciosamente, esquadrinhar

sigh /saɪ/ *n* suspiro *m* □ *vt/i* suspirar

sight /saɪt/ *n* vista *f*; (*scene*) cena *f*; (*on gun*) mira *f* □ *vt* avistar, ver, divisar. **at** *or* **on ~** à vista. **catch ~ of** avistar. **in ~** à vista, visível. **lose ~ of** perder de vista. **out of ~** longe dos olhos

sightsee|ing /'saɪtsi:ɪŋ/ *n* visita *f*, turismo *m*. **go ~ing** visitar lugares turísticos. **~r** /'saɪtsi:ə(r)/ *n* turista *mf*

sign /saɪn/ *n* sinal *m*; (*symbol*) signo *m* □ *vt* (*in writing*) assinar □ *vi* (*make a sign*) fazer sinal. **~ on** *or* **up** (*worker*) assinar contrato. **~-board** *n* tabuleta *f*. **~ language** *n* mímica *f*

signal /'sɪgnəl/ *n* sinal *m* □ *vi* (*pt* **signalled**) fazer signal □ *vt* comunicar (por sinais); (*person*) fazer sinal para. **~-box** *n* cabine *f* de sinalização

signature /'sɪgnətʃə(r)/ *n* assinatura *f*. **~ tune** indicativo *m* musical

signet-ring /'sɪgnɪtrɪŋ/ *n* anel *m* de sinete

significan|t /sɪg'nɪfɪkənt/ *a* importante; (*meaningful*) significativo. **~ce** *n* importância *f*; (*meaning*) significado *m*. **~tly** *adv* (*much*) sensivelmente

signify /'sɪgnɪfaɪ/ *vt* significar

signpost /'saɪnpəʊst/ *n* poste *m* de sinalização □ *vt* sinalizar

silence /'saɪləns/ *n* silêncio *m* □ *vt* silenciar, calar. **~r** /-ə(r)/ *n* (*on gun*) silenciador *m*; (*on car*) silencioso *m*

silent /'saɪlənt/ *a* silencioso; (*not speaking*) calado; (*film*) mudo. **~ly** *adv* silenciosamente

silhouette /sɪlu'et/ *n* silhueta *f* □ *vt* **be ~d against** estar em silhueta contra

silicon /'sɪlɪkən/ *n* silicone *m*. **~ chip** circuito *m* integrado

silk /sɪlk/ *n* seda *f*. **~en, ~y** *adjs* sedoso

sill /sɪl/ *n* (*of window*) parapeito *m*; (*of door*) soleira *f*, limiar *m*

sill|y /'sɪlɪ/ *a* (**-ier, -iest**) tolo, idiota. **~iness** *n* tolice *f*, idiotice *f*

silo /'saɪləʊ/ *n* (*pl* **-os**) silo *m*

silt /sɪlt/ *n* aluvião *m*, sedimento *m*

silver /'sɪlvə(r)/ *n* prata *f*; (*silverware*) prataria *f*, pratas *fpl* □ *a* de prata. **~ papel** papel *m* prateado. **~ wedding** bodas *fpl* de prata. **~y** *a* prateado; (*sound*) argentino

silversmith /'sɪlvəsmɪθ/ *n* ourives *m*

silverware /'sɪlvəweə(r)/ *n* prataria *f*, pratas *fpl*

similar /'sɪmɪlə(r)/ *a* **~ (to)** semelhante (a), parecido (com). **~ity** /-ə'lærətɪ/ *n* semelhança *f*. **~ly** *adv* de igual modo, analogamente

simile /'sɪmɪlɪ/ *n* símile *m*, comparação *f*

simmer /'sɪmə(r)/ *vt/i* cozinhar em fogo brando; (*fig: smoulder*) ferver, fremir; **~ down** acalmar(-se)

simpl|e /'sɪmpl/ *a* (**-er, -est**) simples. **~e-minded** *a* simples; (*feeble-minded*) pobre de espírito, tolo. **~icity** /-'plɪsətɪ/ *n* simplicidade *f*. **~y** *adv* simplesmente; (*absolutely*) absolutamente, simplesmente

simpleton /'sɪmpltən/ *n* simplório *m*

simplif|y /'sɪmplɪfaɪ/ *vt* simplificar. **~ication** /-ɪ'keɪʃn/ *n* simplificação *f*

simulat|e /'sɪmjʊleɪt/ *vt* simular, imitar. **~ion** /-'leɪʃn/ *n* simulação *f*, imitação *f*

simultaneous /sɪml'teɪnɪəs/ *a* simultâneo, concomitante. **~ly** *adv* simultaneamente

sin /sɪn/ *n* pecado *m* □ *vi* (*pt* **sinned**) pecar

since /sɪns/ *prep* desde □ *adv* desde então □ *conj* desde que; (*because*) uma vez que, visto que. **~ then** desde então

sincer|e /sɪn'sɪə(r)/ *a* sincero. **~ely** *adv* sinceramente. **~ity** /-'serətɪ/ *n* sinceridade *f*

sinew /'sɪnju:/ *n* (*anat*) tendão *m*. **~s** músculos *mpl*. **~y** *a* forte, musculoso

sinful /'sɪnfl/ *a* (*wicked*) pecaminoso; (*shocking*) escandaloso

sing /sɪŋ/ *vt/i* (*pt* **sang**, *pp* **sung**) cantar. **~er** *n* cantor *m*

singe /sɪndʒ/ *vt* (*pres p* **singeing**) chamuscar

single /'sɪŋgl/ *a* único, só; (*unmarried*) solteiro; (*bed*) de solteiro; (*room*) individual; (*ticket*) de ida, simples □ *n* (*ticket*) bilhete *m* de ida *or* simples; (*record*) disco *m* de 45 r.p.m. **~s** (*tennis*) singulares *mpl* □ *vt* **~ out** escolher. **in ~ file** em fila indiana. **~-handed** *a* sem ajuda, sozinho. **~-minded** *a* decidido, aferrado à sua idéia, tenaz. **~ parent** pai *m* solteiro, mãe *f* solteira. **singly** *adv* um a um, um por um

singsong /'sɪŋsɒŋ/ *n* **have a ~** cantar em coro □ *a* (*voice*) monótono, monocórdico

singular /'sɪŋgjʊlə(r)/ *n* singular *m* □ *a* (*uncommon; gram*) singular; (*noun*) no singular. **~ly** *adv* singularmente

sinister /'sɪnɪstə(r)/ *a* sinistro

sink /sɪŋk/ *vt* (*pt* **sank**, *pp* **sunk**) (*ship*) afundar, ir a pique; (*well*) abrir; (*invest money*) empatar; (*lose money*) enterrar □ *vi* afundar-se; (*of ground*) ceder; (*of voice*) baixar □ *n* pia *f*, (*P*) lava-louça *m*. **~ in** (*fig*) ficar gravado, entrar (*colloq*). **~ or swim** ou vai ou racha

sinner /'sɪnə(r)/ *n* pecador *m*

sinuous /'sɪnjʊəs/ *a* sinuoso

sinus /'saɪnəs/ *n* (*pl* **-es**) (*anat*) seio (nasal) *m*. **~itis** /saɪnə-'saɪtɪs/ *n* sinusite *f*

sip /sɪp/ *n* gole *m* □ *vt* (*pt* **sipped**) bebericar, beber aos golinhos

siphon /'saɪfn/ *n* sifão *m* ▫ *vt* **~ off** extrair por meio de sifão
sir /sɜ:(r)/ *n* senhor *m*. **S~** (*title*) Sir *m*. **Dear S~** Exmo Senhor. **excuse me, ~** desculpe, senhor. **no, ~** não, senhor
siren /'saɪərən/ *n* sereia *f*, sirene *f*
sirloin /'sɜ:lɔɪn/ *n* lombo *m* de vaca
sissy /'sɪsɪ/ *n* maricas *m*
sister /'sɪstə(r)/ *n* irmã *f*; (*nun*) irmã *f*, freira *f*; (*nurse*) enfermeira-chefe *f*. **~-in-law** (*pl* **~s- in-law**) cunhada *f*. **~ly** *a* fraterno, fraternal
sit /sɪt/ *vt/i* (*pt* **sat**, *pres p* **sitting**) sentar(-se); (*of committee etc*) reunir-se. **~ for an exam** fazer um exame, prestar uma prova. **be ~ting** estar sentado. **~ around** não fazer nada. **~ down** sentar-se. **~-in** *n* ocupação *f*. **~ting** *n* reunião *f*, sessão *f*; (*in restaurant*) serviço *m*. **~ting-room** *n* sala *f* de estar. **~ up** endireitar-se na cadeira; (*not go to bed*) passar a noite acordado
site /saɪt/ *n* local *m*. **(building) ~** terreno *m* para construção, lote *m* ▫ *vt* localizar, situar
situat|e /'sɪtʃʊeɪt/ *vt* situar. **be ~ed** estar situado. **~ion** /-'eɪʃn/ *n* (*position, condition*) situação *f*; (*job*) emprego *m*, colocação *f*
six /sɪks/ *a* & *n* seis (*m*). **~th** *a* & *n* sexto (*m*)
sixteen /sɪk'sti:n/ *a* & *n* dezesseis *m*, (*P*) dezasseis (*m*). **~th** *a* & *n* décimo sexto (*m*)
sixt|y /'sɪkstɪ/ *a* & *n* sessenta (*m*). **~ieth** *a* & *n* sexagésimo (*m*)
size /saɪz/ *n* tamanho *m*; (*of person, garment etc*) tamanho *m*, medida *f*; (*of shoes*) número *m*; (*extent*) grandeza *f* ▫ *vt* **~ up** calcular o tamanho de; (*colloq: judge*) formar um juízo sobre, avaliar. **~able** *a* bastante grande, considerável
sizzle /'sɪzl/ *vi* chiar, rechinar
skate[1] /skeɪt/ *n* (*pl invar*) (*fish*) (ar)raia *f*
skat|e[2] /skeɪt/ *n* patim *m* ▫ *vi* patinar. **~er** *n* patinador *m*. **~ing** *n* patinação *f*. **~ing-rink** *n* rinque *m* de patinação
skateboard /'skeɪtbɔ:d/ *n* skate *m*
skelet|on /'skelɪtən/ *n* esqueleto *m*; (*framework*) armação *f*. **~on crew** *or* **staff** pessoal *m* reduzido. **~on key** chave *f* mestra. **~al** *a* esquelético
sketch /sketʃ/ *n* esboço *m*, croqui(s) *m*; (*theat*) sketch *m*, peça *f* curta e humorística; (*outline*) idéia *f* geral, esboço *m* ▫ *vt* esboçar, delinear ▫ *vi* fazer esboços. **~-book** *n* caderno *m* de desenho
sketchy /'sketʃɪ/ *a* (**-ier, -iest**) incompleto, esboçado
skewer /'skjʊə(r)/ *n* espeto *m*
ski /ski:/ *n* (*pl* **-s**) esqui *m* ▫ *vi* (*pt* **ski'd** *or* **skied**, *pres p* **skiing**) esquiar; (*go skiing*) fazer esqui. **~er** *n* esquiador *m*. **~ing** *n* esqui *m*
skid /skɪd/ *vi* (*pt* **skidded**) derrapar, patinar ▫ *n* derrapagem *f*
skilful /'skɪlfl/ *a* hábil, habilidoso. **~ly** *adv* habilmente, com perícia
skill /skɪl/ *n* habilidade *f*, jeito *m*; (*craft*) arte *f*. **~s** aptidões *fpl*. **~ed** *a* hábil, habilidoso; (*worker*) especializado
skim /skɪm/ *vt* (*pt* **skimmed**) tirar a espuma de; (*milk*) desnatar, tirar a nata de; (*pass or glide over*) deslizar sobre, roçar ▫ *vi* **~ through** ler por alto, passar os olhos por. **~med milk** leite *m* desnatado
skimp /skɪmp/ *vt* (*use too little*) poupar em ▫ *vi* ser poupado
skimpy /'skɪmpɪ/ *a* (**-ier, -iest**) (*clothes*) sumário; (*meal*) escasso, racionado (*fig*)
skin /skɪn/ *n* (*of person, animal*) pele *f*; (*of fruit*) casca *f* ▫ *vt* (*pt* **skinned**) (*animal*) esfolar, tirar a pele de; (*fruit*) descascar. **~-diving** *n* mergulho *m*, caça *f* submarina
skinny /'skɪnɪ/ *a* (**-ier, -iest**) magricela, escanzelado
skint /skɪnt/ *a* (*sl*) sem dinheiro, na última lona (*sl*), (*P*) nas lonas
skip[1] /skɪp/ *vi* (*pt* **skipped**) saltar, pular; (*jump about*) saltitar; (*with rope*) pular corda ▫ *vt* (*page*) saltar; (*class*) faltar a ▫ *n* salto *m*. **~ping rope** *n* corda *f* de pular
skip[2] /skɪp/ *n* (*container*) container *m* grande para entulho
skipper /'skɪpə(r)/ *n* capitão *m*
skirmish /'skɜ:mɪʃ/ *n* escaramuça *f*
skirt /skɜ:t/ *n* saia *f* ▫ *vt* contornar, ladear. **~ing-board** *n* rodapé *m*
skit /skɪt/ *n* (*theat*) paródia *f*, sketch *m* satírico
skittle /'skɪtl/ *n* pino *m*. **~s** *npl* boliche *m*, (*P*) jogo *m* de laranjinha
skive /skaɪv/ *vi* (*sl*) eximir-se de um dever, evitar trabalhar (*sl*)
skulk /skʌlk/ *vi* (*move*) rondar furtivamente; (*hide*) esconder-se
skull /skʌl/ *n* caveira *f*, crânio *m*
skunk /skʌŋk/ *n* (*animal*) gambá *m*
sky /skaɪ/ *n* céu *m*. **~-blue** *a* & *n* azul-celeste (*m*)
skylight /'skaɪlaɪt/ *n* clarabóia *f*
skyscraper /'skaɪskreɪpə(r)/ *n* arranha-céus *m invar*
slab /slæb/ *n* (*of marble*) placa *f*; (*of paving-stone*) laje *f*; (*of metal*) chapa *f*; (*of cake*) fatia *f* grossa

slack /slæk/ *a* (**-er, -est**) (*rope*) bambo, frouxo; (*person*) descuidado, negligente; (*business*) parado, fraco; (*period, season*) morto □ *n* **the ~** (*in rope*) a parte bamba □ *vt/i* (*be lazy*) estar com preguiça, fazer cera (*fig*)

slacken /'slækən/ *vt/i* (*speed, activity etc*) afrouxar, abrandar

slacks /slæks/ *npl* calças *fpl*

slag /slæg/ *n* escória *f*

slain /sleɪn/ *see* **slay**

slam /slæm/ *vt* (*pt* **slammed**) bater violentamente com; (*throw*) atirar; (*sl: criticize*) criticar, malhar □ *vi* (*door etc*) bater violentamente □ *n* (*noise*) bater *m*, pancada *f*

slander /'sla:ndə(r)/ *n* calúnia *f*, difamação *f* □ *vt* caluniar, difamar. **~ous** *a* calunioso, difamatório

slang /slæŋ/ *n* calão *m*, gíria *f*. **~y** *a* de calão

slant /sla:nt/ *vt/i* inclinar(-se); (*news*) apresentar de forma tendenciosa □ *n* inclinação *f*; (*bias*) tendência *f*; (*point of view*) ângulo *m*. **be ~ing** ser/estar inclinado *or* em declive

slap /slæp/ *vt* (*pt* **slapped**) (*strike*) bater, dar uma palmada em; (*on face*) esbofetear, dar uma bofetada em; (*put forcefully*) atirar com □ *n* palmada *f*, bofetada *f* □ *adv* em cheio. **~-up** *a* (*sl: excellent*) excelente

slapdash /'slæpdæʃ/ *a* descuidado; (*impetuous*) precipitado

slapstick /'slæpstɪk/ *n* farsa *f* com palhaçadas

slash /slæʃ/ *vt* (*cut*) retalhar, dar golpes em; (*sever*) cortar; (*a garment*) golpear; (*fig: reduce*) reduzir drasticamente, fazer um corte radical em □ *n* corte *m*, golpe *m*

slat /slæt/ *n* (*in blind*) ripa *f*, (*P*) lâmina *f*

slate /sleɪt/ *n* ardósia *f* □ *vt* (*colloq: criticize*) criticar severamente

slaughter /'slɔ:tə(r)/ *vt* chacinar, massacrar; (*animals*) abater □ *n* chacina *f*, massacre *m*, mortandade *f*; (*animals*) abate *m*

slaughterhouse /'slɔ:təhaʊs/ *n* matadouro *m*

slave /sleɪv/ *n* escravo *m* □ *vi* mourejar, trabalhar como um escravo. **~-driver** *n* (*fig*) o que obriga os outros a trabalharem como escravos, condutor *m* de escravos. **~ry** /-ərɪ/ *n* escravatura *f*

slavish /'sleɪvɪʃ/ *a* servil

slay /sleɪ/ *vt* (*pt* **slew**, *pp* **slain**) matar

sleazy /'sli:zɪ/ *a* (**-ier, -iest**) (*colloq*) esquálido, sórdido

sledge /sledʒ/ *n* trenó *m*. **~-hammer** *n* martelo *m* de forja, marreta *f*

sleek /sli:k/ *a* (**-er, -est**) liso, macio e lustroso

sleep /sli:p/ *n* sono *m* □ *vi* (*pt* **slept**) dormir □ *vt* ter lugar para, alojar. **go to ~** ir dormir, adormecer. **put to ~** (*kill*) mandar matar. **~ around** ser promíscuo. **~er** *n* aquele que dorme; (*rail: beam*) dormente *m*; (*berth*) couchette *f*. **~ing-bag** *n* saco *m* de dormir. **~ing-car** *n* carro-dormitório *m*, carruagem-cama *f*, (*P*) vagon-lit *m*. **~less** *a* insone; (*night*) em claro, insone. **~-walker** *n* sonâmbulo *m*

sleep|y /'sli:pɪ/ *a* (**-ier, -iest**) sonolento. **be ~y** ter *or* estar com sono. **~ily** *adv* meio dormindo

sleet /sli:t/ *n* geada *f* miúda □ *vi* cair geada miúda

sleeve /sli:v/ *n* manga *f*; (*of record*) capa *f*. **up one's ~** de reserva, escondido. **~less** *a* sem mangas

sleigh /sleɪ/ *n* trenó *m*

sleight /slaɪt/ *n* **~ of hand** prestidigitação *f*, passe *m* de mágica

slender /'slendə(r)/ *a* esguio, esbelto; (*fig: scanty*) escasso. **~-ness** *n* aspecto *m* esguio, esbelteza *f*, elegância *f*; (*scantiness*) escassez *f*

slept /slept/ *see* **sleep**

sleuth /slu:θ/ *n* (*colloq*) detective *m*

slew[1] /slu:/ *vi* (*turn*) virar-se

slew[2] /slu:/ *see* **slay**

slice /slaɪs/ *n* fatia *f* □ *vt* cortar em fatias; (*golf, tennis*) cortar

slick /slɪk/ *a* (*slippery*) escorregadio; (*cunning*) astuto, habilidoso; (*unctuous*) melífluo □ *n* **(oil) ~** mancha *f* de óleo

slid|e /slaɪd/ *vt/i* (*pt* **slid**) escorregar, deslizar □ *n* escorregadela *f*, escorregão *m*; (*in playground*) escorrega *m*; (*for hair*) prendedor *m*, (*P*) travessa *f*; (*photo*) diapositivo *m*, slide *m*. **~e-rule** *n* régua *f* de cálculo. **~ing** *a* (*door, panel*) corrediço, de correr. **~-ing scale** escala *f* móvel

slight /slaɪt/ *a* (**-er, -est**) (*slender, frail*) delgado, franzino; (*inconsiderable*) leve, ligeiro □ *vt* desconsiderar, desfeitear □ *n* desconsideração *f*, desfeita *f*. **the ~est** *a* o/a menor. **not in the ~est** em absoluto. **~ly** *adv* ligeiramente, um pouco

slim /slɪm/ *a* (**slimmer, slimmest**) magro, esbelto; (*chance*) pequeno, remoto □ *vi* (*pt* **slimmed**) emagrecer. **~ness** *n* magreza *f*, esbelteza *f*

slim|e /slaɪm/ *n* lodo *m*. **~y** *a* lodoso; (*slippery*) escorregadio; (*fig: servile*) servil, bajulador

sling /slɪŋ/ *n* (*weapon*) funda *f*; (*for arm*) tipóia *f* □ *vt* (*pt* **slung**) atirar, lançar

slip /slɪp/ *vt*/*i* (*pt* **slipped**) escorregar; (*move quietly*) mover-se de mansinho □ *n* escorregadela *f*, escorregão *m*; (*mistake*) engano *m*, lapso *m*; (*petticoat*) combinação *f*; (*of paper*) tira *f* de papel. **give the ~ to** livrar-se de, escapar(-se) de. **~ away** esgueirar-se. **~ by** passar sem se dar conta, passar despercebido. **~-cover** *n* (*Amer*) capa *f* para móveis. **~ into** (*go*) entrar de mansinho, enfiar-se em; (*clothes*) enfiar. **~ of the tongue** lapso *m*. **~ped disc** disco *m* deslocado. **~- road** *n* acesso *m* a autoestrada. **~ sb's mind** passar pela cabeça de alguém. **~ up** (*colloq*) cometer uma gafe. **~-up** *n* (*colloq*) gafe *f*

slipper /'slɪpə(r)/ *n* chinelo *m*

slippery /'slɪpərɪ/ *a* escorregadio; (*fig: person*) que não é de confiança, sem escrúpulos

slipshod /'slɪpʃɒd/ *a* (*person*) desleixado, desmazelado; (*work*) feito sem cuidado, desleixado

slit /slɪt/ *n* fenda *f*; (*cut*) corte *m*; (*tear*) rasgão *m* □ *vt* (*pt* **slit**, *pres p* **slitting**) fender; (*cut*) fazer um corte em, cortar

slither /'slɪðə(r)/ *vi* escorregar, resvalar

sliver /'slɪvə(r)/ *n* (*of cheese etc*) fatia *f*; (*splinter*) lasca *f*

slobber /'slɒbə(r)/ *vi* babar-se

slog /slɒg/ *vt* (*pt* **slogged**) (*hit*) bater com força □ *vi* (*walk*) caminhar com passos pesados e firmes; (*work*) trabalhar duro □ *n* (*work*) trabalheira *f*; (*walk, effort*) estafa *f*

slogan /'sləʊgən/ *n* slogan *m*, lema *m*, palavra *f* de ordem

slop /slɒp/ *vt*/*i* (*pt* **slopped**) transbordar, entornar. **~s** *npl* (*dirty water*) água(s) *f* (*pl*) suja(s); (*liquid refuse*) despejos *mpl*

slop|e /sləʊp/ *vt*/*i* inclinar(-se), formar declive □ *n* (*of mountain*) encosta *f*; (*of street*) rampa *f*, ladeira *f*. **~ing** *a* inclinado, em declive

sloppy /'slɒpɪ/ *a* (**-ier, -iest**) (*ground*) molhado, com poças de água; (*food*) aguado; (*clothes*) desleixado; (*work*) descuidado, feito de qualquer jeito *or* maneira (*colloq*); (*person*) desmazelado; (*maudlin*) piegas

slosh /slɒʃ/ *vt* entornar; (*colloq: splash*) esparrinhar; (*sl: hit*) bater em, dar (uma) sova em □ *vi* chapinhar

slot /slɒt/ *n* ranhura *f*; (*in timetable*) horário *m*; (*TV*) espaço *m*; (*aviat*) slot *m* □ *vt*/*i* (*pt* **slotted**) enfiar(-se), meter(-se), encaixar (-se). **~-machine** *n* (*for stamps, tickets etc*) distribuidor *m* automático; (*for gambling*) caça-níqueis *m*, (*P*) slot machine *f*

sloth /sləʊθ/ *n* preguiça *f*, indolência *f*; (*zool*) preguiça *f*

slouch /slaʊtʃ/ *vi* (*stand, move*) andar com as costas curvadas; (*sit*) sentar em má postura

slovenly /'slʌvnlɪ/ *a* desmazelado, desleixado

slow /sləʊ/ *a* (**-er, -est**) lento, vagaroso □ *adv* devagar, lentamente □ *vt*/*i* **~ (up** *or* **down)** diminuir a velocidade, afrouxar; (*auto*) desacelerar. **be ~** (*clock etc*) atrasar-se, estar atrasado. **in ~ motion** em câmara lenta. **~ly** *adv* devagar, lentamente, vagarosamente

slow|coach /'sləʊkəʊtʃ/, (*Amer*) **~poke** *ns* lesma *m*/*f*, pastelão *m* (*fig*)

sludge /slʌdʒ/ *n* lama *f*, lodo *m*

slug /slʌg/ *n* lesma *f*

sluggish /'slʌgɪʃ/ *a* (*slow*) lento, moroso; (*lazy*) indolente, preguiçoso

sluice /slu:s/ *n* (*gate*) comporta *f*; (*channel*) canal *m* □ *vt* lavar com jorros de água

slum /slʌm/ *n* favela *f*, (*P*) bairro *m* da lata; (*building*) cortiço *m*

slumber /'slʌmbə(r)/ *n* sono *m* □ *vi* dormir

slump /slʌmp/ *n* (*in prices*) baixa *f*, descida *f*; (*in demand*) quebra *f* na procura; (*econ*) depressão *f* □ *vi* (*fall limply*) cair, afundar-se; (*of price*) baixar bruscamente

slung /slʌŋ/ *see* **sling**

slur /slɜ:(r)/ *vt*/*i* (*pt* **slurred**) (*speech*) pronunciar indistintamente, mastigar □ *n* (*in speech*) som *m* indistinto; (*discredit*) nódoa *f*, estigma *m*

slush /slʌʃ/ *n* (*snow*) neve *f* meio derretida. **~fund** (*comm*) fundo *m* para subornos. **~y** *a* (*road*) coberto de neve derretida, lamacento

slut /slʌt/ *n* (*dirty woman*) porca *f*, desmazelada *f*; (*immoral woman*) desavergonhada *f*

sly /slaɪ/ *a* (**slyer, slyest**) (*crafty*) manhoso; (*secretive*) sonso □ *n* **on the ~** na calada. **~ly** *adv* (*craftily*) astutamente; (*secretively*) sonsamente

smack[1] /smæk/ *n* palmada *f*; (*on face*) bofetada *f* □ *vt* dar uma palmada *or* tapa em; (*on the face*) esbofetear, dar uma bofetada em □ *adv* (*colloq*) em cheio, direto

smack[2] /smæk/ *vi* **~ of sth** cheirar a alg coisa

small /smɔ:l/ *a* (**-er, -est**) pequeno □ *n* **~ of the back** zona *f* dos rins □ *adv* (*cut etc*) em pedaços pequenos, aos bocadinhos. **~ change** trocado *m*, dinheiro *m* miúdo. **~ talk** conversa *f* fiada, bate-papo *m*. **~ness** *n* pequenez *f*

smallholding /'smɔ:lhəʊldɪŋ/ *n* pequena propriedade *f*

smallpox /'smɔ:lpɒks/ *n* varíola *f*

smarmy /'sma:mɪ/ *a* (**-ier, -iest**) (*colloq*) bajulador, puxa-saco (*colloq*)

smart /sma:t/ *a* (**-er, -est**) elegante; (*clever*) esperto, vivo; (*brisk*) rápido □ *vi* (*sting*) arder, picar. **~ly** *adv* elegantemente, com elegância; (*cleverly*) com esperteza, vivamente; (*briskly*) rapidamente. **~ness** *n* elegância *f*

smarten /'sma:tn/ *vt/i* **~ (up)** arranjar, dar um ar mais cuidado a. **~ (o.s.) up** embelezar-se, arrumar-se, (*P*) pôr-se elegante/bonito; (*tidy*) arranjar-se

smash /smæʃ/ *vt/i* (*to pieces*) despedaçar(-se), espatifar(-se) (*colloq*); (*a record*) quebrar; (*opponent*) esmagar; (*ruin*) (fazer) falir; (*of vehicle*) espatifar (-se) □ *n* (*noise*) estrondo *m*; (*blow*) pancada *f* forte, golpe *m*; (*collision*) colisão *f*; (*tennis*) smash *m*

smashing /'smæʃɪŋ/ *a* (*colloq*) formidável, estupendo (*colloq*)

smattering /'smætərɪŋ/ *n* leves noções *fpl*

smear /smɪə(r)/ *vt* (*stain; discredit*) manchar; (*coat*) untar, besuntar □ *n* mancha *f*, nódoa *f*; (*med*) esfregaço *m*

smell /smel/ *n* cheiro *m*, odor *m*; (*sense*) cheiro *m*, olfato *m*, (*P*) olfacto *m* □ *vt/i* (*pt* **smelt** *or* **smelled**) **~ (of)** cheirar (a). **~y** *a* malcheiroso

smelt[1] /smelt/ *see* **smell**

smelt[2] /smelt/ *vt* (*ore*) fundir

smil|e /smaɪl/ *n* sorriso *m* □ *vi* sorrir. **~ing** *a* sorridente, risonho

smirk /smɜ:k/ *n* sorriso *m* falso *or* afetado, (*P*) afectado

smithereens /smɪðə'ri:nz/ *npl* **to** *or* **in ~** em pedaços *mpl*

smock /smɒk/ *n* guarda-pó *m*

smog /smɒg/ *n* mistura *f* de nevoeiro e fumaça, smog *m*

smoke /sməʊk/ *n* fumo *m*, fumaça *f* □ *vt* fumar; (*bacon etc*) fumar, defumar □ *vi* fumar, fumegar. **~-screen** *n* (*lit & fig*) cortina *f* de fumaça. **~less** *a* (*fuel*) sem fumo. **~r** /-ə(r)/ *n* (*person*) fumante *mf*, (*P*) fumador *m*. **smoky** *a* (*air*) enfumaçado, fumacento

smooth /smu:ð/ *a* (**-er, -est**) liso; (*soft*) macio; (*movement*) regular, suave; (*manners*) lisonjeiro, conciliador, suave □ **~***vt* alisar. **~ out** (*fig*) aplanar, remover. **~ly** *adv* suavemente, facilmente

smother /'smʌðə(r)/ *vt* (*stifle*) abafar, sufocar; (*cover, overwhelm*) cobrir (**with** de); (*suppress*) abafar, reprimir

smoulder /'sməʊldə(r)/ *vi* (*lit & fig*) arder, abrasar-se

smudge /smʌdʒ/ *n* mancha *f*, borrão *m* □ *vt/i* sujar(-se), manchar(-se), borrar(-se)

smug /smʌg/ *a* (**smugger, smuggest**) presunçoso, convencido (*colloq*). **~ly** *adv* presunçosamente. **~ness** *n* presunção *f*

smuggl|e /'smʌgl/ *vt* contrabandear, fazer contrabando de. **~er** *n* contrabandista *mf*. **~ing** *n* contrabando *m*

smut /smʌt/ *n* fuligem *f*. **~ty** *a* cheio de fuligem; (*colloq: obscene*) indecente, sujo (*colloq*)

snack /snæk/ *n* refeição *f* ligeira. **~-bar** *n* lanchonete *f*, (*P*) snack(-bar) *m*

snag /snæg/ *n* (*obstacle*) obstáculo *m*; (*drawback*) problema *m*, contra *m*; (*in cloth*) rasgão *m*; (*in stocking*) fio *m* puxado

snail /sneɪl/ *n* caracol *m*. **at a ~'s pace** em passo de tartaruga

snake /sneɪk/ *n* serpente *f*, cobra *f*

snap /snæp/ *vt/i* (*pt* **snapped**) (*whip, fingers*) (fazer) estalar; (*break*) estalar(-se), partir(-se) com um estalo, rebentar; (*say*) dizer irritadamente □ *n* estalo *m*; (*photo*) instantâneo *m*; (*Amer: fastener*) mola *f* □ *a* súbito, repentino. **~ at** (*bite*) abocanhar, tentar morder; (*speak angrily*) retrucar asperamente. **~ up** (*buy*) comprar rapidamente

snappish /'snæpɪʃ/ *a* irritadiço

snappy /'snæpɪ/ *a* (**-ier, -iest**) (*colloq*) vivo, animado. **make it ~** (*colloq*) vai rápido!, apresse-se! (*colloq*)

snapshot /'snæpʃɒt/ *n* instantâneo *m*

snare /sneə(r)/ *n* laço *m*, cilada *f*, armadilha *f*

snarl /sna:l/ *vi* rosnar □ *n* rosnadela *f*

snatch /snætʃ/ *vt* (*grab*) agarrar, apanhar; (*steal*) roubar. **~ from sb** arrancar de alguém □ *n* (*theft*) roubo *m*; (*bit*) bocado *m*, pedaço *m*

sneak /sni:k/ *vi* (*slink*) esgueirar-se furtivamente; (*sl: tell tales*) fazer queixa, delatar □ *vt* (*sl: steal*) rapinar (*colloq*) □ *n* (*sl*) dedo-duro *m*, queixinhas *mf* (*sl*). **~ing** *a* secreto. **~y** *a* sonso

sneer /snɪə(r)/ *n* sorriso *m* de desdém □ *vi* sorrir desdenhosamente

sneeze /sni:z/ *n* espirro *m* □ *vi* espirrar

snide /snaɪd/ *a* (*colloq*) sarcástico

sniff /snɪf/ *vi* fungar □ *vt/i* **~ (at)** (*smell*) cheirar; (*dog*) farejar. **~ at** (*fig: in contempt*) desprezar □ *n* fungadela *f*

snigger /'snɪgə(r)/ *n* riso *m* abafado □ *vi* rir dissimuladamente

snip /snɪp/ *vt* (*pt* **snipped**) cortar com tesoura ◻ *n* pedaço *m*, retalho *m*; (*sl: bargain*) pechincha *f*

snipe /snaɪp/ *vi* dar tiros de emboscada. **~r** /-ə(r)/ *n* franco-atirador *m*

snivel /'snɪvl/ *vi* (*pt* **snivelled**) choramingar, lamuriar-se

snob /snɒb/ *n* esnobe *mf*, (*P*) snob *mf*. **~bery** *n* esnobismo *m*, (*P*) snobismo *m*. **~bish** *a* esnobe, (*P*) snob

snooker /'snu:kə(r)/ *n* snooker *m*, sinuca *f*

snoop /snu:p/ *vi* (*colloq*) bisbilhotar, meter o nariz em toda a parte. **~ on** espiar, espionar. **~er** *n* bisbilhoteiro *m*

snooty /'snu:tɪ/ *a* (**-ier, -iest**) (*colloq*) convencido, arrogante (*colloq*)

snooze /snu:z/ *n* (*colloq*) soneca *f* (*colloq*) ◻ *vi* (*colloq*) tirar uma soneca

snore /snɔ:(r)/ *n* ronco *m* ◻ *vi* roncar

snorkel /'snɔ:kl/ *n* tubo *m* de respiração, snorkel *m*

snort /snɔ:t/ *n* resfôlego *m* , bufido *m* ◻ *vi* resfolegar, bufar

snout /snaʊt/ *n* focinho *m*

snow /snəʊ/ *n* neve *f* ◻ *vi* nevar. **be ~ed under** (*fig: be overwhelmed*) estar sobrecarregado (*fig*). **~board** *n* snowboard *m* **~-bound** *a* bloqueado pela neve. **~-drift** *n* banco *m* de neve. **~-plough** *n* limpa-neve *m*. **~y** *a* nevado, coberto de neve

snowball /'snəʊbɔ:l/ *n* bola *f* de neve ◻ *vi* atirar bolas de neve (em); (*fig*) acumular-se, ir num crescendo, aumentar rapidamente

snowdrop /'snəʊdrɒp/ *n* (*bot*) fura-neve *m*

snowfall /'snəʊfɔ:l/ *n* nevada *f*, (*P*) nevão *m*

snowflake /'snəʊfleɪk/ *n* floco *m* de neve

snowman /'snəʊmæn/ *n* (*pl* **-men**) boneco *m* de neve

snub /snʌb/ *vt* (*pt* **snubbed**) desdenhar, tratar com desdém ◻ *n* desdém *m*

snuff[1] /'snʌf/ *n* rapé *m*

snuff[2] /snʌf/ *vt* **~ out** (*candles, hopes etc*) apagar, extinguir

snuffle /'snʌfl/ *vi* fungar

snug /snʌg/ *a* (**snugger, snuggest**) (*cosy*) aconchegado; (*close-fitting*) justo

snuggle /'snʌgl/ *vt*/*i* (*nestle*) aninhar-se, aconchegar-se; (*cuddle*) aconchegar

so /səʊ/ *adv* tão, de tal modo; (*thus*) assim, deste modo ◻ *conj* por isso, portanto, por conseguinte. **~ am I** eu também. **~ does he** ele também. **that is ~** é isso. **I think ~** acho que sim. **five or ~** uns cinco. **~ as to** de modo a. **~ far** até agora, até aqui. **~ long!** (*colloq*) até já! (*colloq*). **~ many** tantos. **~much** tanto. **~ that** para que, de modo que. **~-and-~** fulano *m*. **~-called** *a* pretenso, soi-disant. **~-so** *a & adv* assim assim, mais ou menos

soak /səʊk/ *vt*/*i* molhar(-se), ensopar(-se), enchacar(-se). **leave to ~** pôr de molho. **~ in** *or* **up** *vt* absorver, embeber. **~ through** repassar. **~ing** *a* ensopado, encharcado

soap /səʊp/ *n* sabão *m*. (**toilet**) **~** sabonete *m* ◻ *vt* ensaboar. **~ opera** (*radio*) novela *f* radiofônica, (*P*) radiofónica; (*TV*) telenovela *f*. **~ flakes** flocos *mpl* de sabão. **~ powder** sabão *m* em pó. **~y** *a* ensaboado

soar /sɔ:(r)/ *vi* voar alto; (*go high*) elevar-se; (*hover*) pairar

sob /sɒb/ *n* soluço *m* ◻ *vi* (*pt* **sobbed**) soluçar

sober /'səʊbə(r)/ *a* (*not drunk, calm, of colour*) sóbrio; (*serious*) sério, grave ◻ *vt*/*i* **~ up** (fazer) ficar sóbrio, (fazer) curar a bebedeira (*colloq*)

soccer /'sɒkə(r)/ *n* (*colloq*) futebol *m*

sociable /'səʊʃəbl/ *a* sociável

social /'səʊʃl/ *a* social; (*sociable*) sociável; (*gathering, life*) de sociedade ◻ *n* reunião *f* social. **~ly** *adv* socialmente; (*meet*) em sociedade. **~ security** previdência *f* social; (*for old age*) pensão *f*. **~ worker** assistente *mf* social

socialis|t /'səʊʃəlɪst/ *n* socialista *mf*. **~m** /-zəm/ *n* socialismo *m*

socialize /'səʊʃəlaɪz/ *vi* socializar-se, reunir-se em sociedade. **~ with** freqüentar, (*P*) frequentar, conviver com

society /sə'saɪətɪ/ *n* sociedade *f*

sociolog|y /səʊsɪ'ɒlədʒɪ/ *n* sociologia *f*. **~ical** /-ə'lɒdʒɪkl/ *a* sociológico. **~ist** *n* sociólogo *m*

sock[1] /sɒk/ *n* meia *f* curta; (*men's*) meia *f* (curta), (*P*) peuga *f*; (*women's*) soquete *f*

sock[2] /sɒk/ *vt* (*sl: hit*) esmurrar, dar um murro em (*colloq*)

socket /'sɒkɪt/ *n* cavidade *f*; (*for lamp*) suporte *m*; (*electr*) tomada *f*; (*of tooth*) alvéolo *m*

soda /'səʊdə/ *n* soda *f*. **(baking) ~** (*culin*) bicarbonato *m* de soda. **~(-water)** água *f* gasosa, soda *f* limonada, (*P*) água *f* gaseificada

sodden /'sɒdn/ *a* ensopado, empapado

sodium /'səʊdɪəm/ *n* sódio *m*

sofa /'səʊfə/ *n* sofá *m*

soft /sɒft/ *a* (**-er, -est**) (*not hard, feeble*) mole; (*not rough, not firm*) macio; (*gentle, not loud, not bright*) suave; (*tender-hearted*) sensível; (*fruit*) sem caroço; (*wood*) de coníferas; (*drink*) não alcoólico. **~-boiled** *a* (*egg*) quente.

~ **spot** (*fig*) fraco *m*. ~**ly** *adv* docemente. ~**ness** *n* moleza *f*; (*to touch*) maciez *f*; (*gentleness*) suavidade *f*, brandura *f*

soften /'sɒfn/ *vt/i* amaciar, amolecer; (*tone down, lessen*) abrandar

software /'sɒftweə(r)/ *n* software *m*

soggy /'sɒgɪ/ *a* (**-ier, -iest**) ensopado, empapado

soil[1] /sɔɪl/ *n* solo *m*, terra *f*

soil[2] /sɔɪl/ *vt/i* sujar(-se). ~**ed** *a* sujo

solace /'sɒlɪs/ *n* consolo *m*; (*relief*) alívio *m*

solar /'səʊlə(r)/ *a* solar

sold /səʊld/ *see* **sell** □ *a* ~ **out** esgotado

solder /'səʊldə(r)/ *n* solda *f* □ *vt* soldar

soldier /'səʊldʒə(r)/ *n* soldado *m* □ *vi* ~ **on** (*colloq*) perseverar com afinco, batalhar (*colloq*)

sole[1] /səʊl/ *n* (*of foot*) planta *f*, sola *f* do pé; (*of shoe*) sola *f*

sole[2] /səʊl/ *n* (*fish*) solha *f*

sole[3] /səʊl/ *a* único. ~**ly** *adv* unicamente

solemn /'sɒləm/ *a* solene. ~**ity** /sə'lemnətɪ/ *n* solenidade *f*. ~**ly** *adv* solenemente

solicit /sə'lɪsɪt/ *vt* (*seek*) solicitar □ *vi* (*of prostitute*) aproximar-se de homens na rua

solicitor /sə'lɪsɪtə(r)/ *n* advogado *m*

solicitous /sə'lɪsɪtəs/ *a* solícito

solid /'sɒlɪd/ *a* sólido; (*not hollow*) maciço, cheio, compacto; (*gold etc*) maciço; (*meal*) substancial □ *n* sólido *m* ~**s** (*food*) alimentos *mpl* sólidos. ~**ity** /sə'lɪdətɪ/ *n* solidez *f*. ~**ly** *adv* solidamente

solidarity /sɒlɪ'dærətɪ/ *n* solidariedade *f*

solidify /sə'lɪdɪfaɪ/ *vt/i* solidificar (-se)

soliloquy /sə'lɪləkwɪ/ *n* monólogo *m*, solilóquio *m*

solitary /'sɒlɪtrɪ/ *a* solitário, só; (*only one*) um único. ~ **confinement** prisão *f* celular, solitária *f*

solitude /'sɒlɪtju:d/ *n* solidão *f*

solo /'səʊləʊ/ *n* (*pl* **-os**) solo *m* □ *a* solo. ~ **flight** vôo *m* solo. ~**ist** *n* solista *mf*

soluble /'sɒljʊbl/ *a* solúvel

solution /sə'lu:ʃn/ *n* solução *f*

solv|e /sɒlv/ *vt* resolver, solucionar. ~**able** *a* resolúvel, solúvel

solvent /'sɒlvənt/ *a* (dis)solvente; (*comm*) solvente □ *n* (dis)solvente *m*

sombre /'sɒmbə(r)/ *a* sombrio

some /sʌm/ *a* (*quantity*) algum(a); (*number*) alguns, algumas, uns, umas; (*unspecified, some or other*) um(a)... qualquer, uns... quaisquer, umas... quaisquer; (*a little*) um pouco de, algum; (*a certain*) um certo; (*contrasted with others*) uns, umas, alguns, algumas, certos, certas □ *pron* uns, umas, algum(a), alguns, algumas; (*a little*) um pouco, algum □ *adv* (*approximately*) uns, umas. **will you have ~ coffee**/*etc*? você quer café/*etc*? ~ **day** algum dia. ~ **of my friends** alguns dos meus amigos. ~ **people say...** algumas pessoas dizem... ~ **time ago** algum tempo atrás

somebody /'sʌmbədɪ/ *pron* alguém □ *n* **be a** ~ ser alguém

somehow /'sʌmhaʊ/ *adv* (*in some way*) de algum modo, de alguma maneira; (*for some reason*) por alguma razão

someone /'sʌmwʌn/ *pron & n* = **somebody**

somersault /'sʌməsɔ:lt/ *n* cambalhota *f*; (*in the air*) salto *m* mortal □ *vi* dar uma cambalhota/um salto mortal

something /'sʌmθɪŋ/ *pron & n* uma /alguma/qualquer coisa *f*, algo. ~ **good**/*etc* uma coisa boa/*etc*, qualquer coisa de bom/*etc*. ~ **like** um pouco como

sometime /'sʌmtaɪm/ *adv* a certa altura, um dia □ *a* (*former*) antigo. ~ **last summer** a certa altura no verão passado. **I'll go** ~ hei de ir um dia

sometimes /'sʌmtaɪmz/ *adv* às vezes, de vez em quando

somewhat /'sʌmwɒt/ *adv* um pouco, um tanto (ou quanto)

somewhere /'sʌmweə(r)/ *adv* (*position*) em algum lugar; (*direction*) para algum lugar

son /sʌn/ *n* filho *m*. ~**-in-law** *n* (*pl* ~**s-in-law**) genro *m*

sonar /'səʊna:(r)/ *n* sonar *m*

sonata /sə'na:tə/ *n* (*mus*) sonata *f*

song /sɒŋ/ *n* canção *f*. ~**-bird** *n* ave *f* canora

sonic /'sɒnɪk/ *a* ~ **boom** estrondo *m* sônico, (*P*) sónico

sonnet /'sɒnɪt/ *n* soneto *m*

soon /su:n/ *adv* (**-er, -est**) em breve, dentro em pouco, daqui a pouco; (*early*) cedo. **as ~ as possible** o mais rápido possível. **I would ~er stay** preferia ficar. ~ **after** pouco depois. ~**er or later** mais cedo ou mais tarde

soot /sʊt/ *n* fuligem *f*. ~**y** *a* coberto de fuligem

sooth|e /su:ð/ *vt* acalmar, suavizar; (*pain*) aliviar. ~**ing** *a* (*remedy*) calmante, suavizante; (*words*) confortante

sophisticated /sə'fɪstɪkeɪtɪd/ *a* sofisticado, refinado, requintado; (*machine etc*) sofisticado

soporific /sɒpə'rɪfɪk/ *a* soporífico

sopping /'sɒpɪŋ/ *a* encharcado, ensopado

soppy /'sɒpɪ/ *a* (**-ier, -iest**) (*colloq: sentimental*) piegas; (*colloq: silly*) bobo

soprano /sə'pra:nəʊ/ *n* (*pl* **~s**) & *adj* soprano (*mf*)

sorbet /'sɔ:beɪ/ *n* (*water-ice*) sorvete *m* feito sem leite

sorcerer /'sɔ:sərə(r)/ *n* feiticeiro *m*

sordid /'sɔ:dɪd/ *a* sórdido

sore /sɔ:(r)/ *a* (**-er, -est**) dolorido; (*vexed*) aborrecido (**at, with** com) ◻ *n* ferida *f*. **have a ~ throat** ter a garganta inflamada, ter dores de garganta

sorely /'sɔ:lɪ/ *adv* fortemente, seriamente

sorrow /'sɒrəʊ/ *n* dor *f*, mágoa *f*, pesar *m*. **~ful** *a* pesaroso, triste

sorry /'sɒrɪ/ *a* (**-ier, -iest**) (*state, sight etc*) triste. **be ~ to/that** (*regretful*) sentir muito/que, lamentar que; **be ~ about/for** (*repentant*) ter pena de, estar arrependido de. **feel ~ for** ter pena de. **~!** desculpe!, perdão!

sort /sɔ:t/ *n* gênero *m*, (*P*) género *m*, espécie *f*, qualidade *f*. **of ~s** (*colloq*) uma espécie de (*colloq, pej*). **out of ~s** indisposto ◻ *vt* separar por grupos; (*tidy*) arrumar. **~ out** (*problem*) resolver; (*arrange, separate*) separar, distribuir

soufflé /'su:fleɪ/ *n* (*culin*) suflê *m*, (*P*) soufflé *m*

sought /sɔ:t/ *see* **seek**

soul /səʊl/ *n* alma *f*. **the life and ~ of** (*fig*) a alma *f* de (*fig*)

soulful /'səʊlfl/ *a* emotivo, expressivo, cheio de sentimento

sound[1] /saʊnd/ *n* som *m*, barulho *m*, ruído *m* ◻ *vt/i* soar; (*seem*) dar a impressão de, parecer (**as if** que). **~ a horn** tocar uma buzina, buzinar. **~ barrier** barreira *f* de som. **~ like** parecer ser, soar como. **~-proof** *a* à prova de som ◻ *vt* fazer o isolamento sonoro de, isolar. **~-track** *n* (*of film*) trilha *f* sonora, (*P*) banda *f* sonora

sound[2] /saʊnd/ *a* (**-er, -est**) (*healthy*) saudável, sadio; (*sensible*) sensato, acertado; (*secure*) firme, sólido. **~ asleep** profundamente adormecido. **~ly** *adv* solidamente

sound[3] /saʊnd/ *vt* (*test*) sondar; (*med; views*) auscultar

soup /su:p/ *n* sopa *f*

sour /'saʊə(r)/ *a* (**-er, -est**) azedo ◻ *vt/i* azedar, envinagrar

source /sɔ:s/ *n* fonte *f*; (*of river*) nascente *f*

souse /saʊs/ *vt* (*throw water on*) atirar água em cima de; (*pickle*) pôr em vinagre; (*salt*) pôr em salmoura

south /saʊθ/ *n* sul *m* ◻ *a* sul, do sul; (*of country, people etc*) meridional ◻ *adv* a, ao/para o sul. **S~ Africa/America** África *f*/América *f* do Sul. **S~ African/American** *a* & *n* sul-africano (*m*)/sul-americano (*m*). **~-east** *n* sudeste *m*. **~erly** /'sʌðəlɪ/ *a* do sul, meridional. **~ward** *a* ao sul. **~ward(s)** *adv* para o sul. **~-west** *n* sudoeste *m*

southern /'sʌðən/ *a* do sul, meridional, austral

souvenir /su:və'nɪə(r)/ *n* recordação *f*, lembrança *f*

sovereign /'sɒvrɪn/ *n* & *a* soberano (*m*). **~ty** *n* soberania *f*

Soviet /'səʊvɪət/ *a* soviético. **the S~ Union** a União Soviética

sow[1] /səʊ/ *vt* (*pt* **sowed**, *pp* **sowed** *or* **sown**) semear

sow[2] /saʊ/ *n* (*zool*) porca *f*

soy /'sɔɪ/ *n* **~ sauce** molho *m* de soja

soya /'sɔɪə/ *n* soja *f*. **~-bean** semente *f* de soja

spa /spa:/ *n* termas *fpl*

space /speɪs/ *n* espaço *m*; (*room*) lugar *m*; (*period*) espaço *m*, período *m* ◻ *a* (*research etc*) espacial ◻ *vt* **~ out** espaçar

space|craft /'speɪskra:ft/ *n* (*pl invar*), **~ship** *n* nave espacial *f*

spacious /'speɪʃəs/ *a* espaçoso

spade /speɪd/ *n* (*gardener's*) pá *f* de ferro; (*child's*) pá *f*. **~s** (*cards*) espadas *fpl*

spadework /'speɪdwɜ:k/ *n* (*fig*) trabalho *m* preliminar

spaghetti /spə'getɪ/ *n* espaguete *m*, (*P*) esparguete *m*

Spain /speɪn/ *n* Espanha *f*

span[1] /spæn/ *n* (*of arch*) vão *m*; (*of wings*) envergadura *f*; (*of time*) espaço *m*, duração *f*; (*measure*) palmo *m* ◻ *vt* (*pt* **spanned**) (*extend across*) transpor; (*measure*) medir em palmos; (*in time*) abarcar, abranger, estender-se por

span[2] /spæn/ *see* **spick**

Spaniard /'spænɪəd/ *n* espanhol *m*

Spanish /'spænɪʃ/ *a* espanhol ◻ *n* (*lang*) espanhol *m*

spaniel /'spænɪəl/ *n* spaniel *m*, epagneul *m*

spank /spæŋk/ *vt* dar palmadas *or* chineladas no. **~ing** *n* (*with hand*) palmada *f*; (*with slipper*) chinelada *f*

spanner /'spænə(r)/ *n* (*tool*) chave *f* de porcas; (*adjustable*) chave *f* inglesa

spar /spa:(r)/ *vi* (*pt* **sparred**) jogar boxe, esp para treino; (*fig: argue*) discutir

spare /speə(r)/ *vt* (*not hurt; use with restraint*) poupar; (*afford to give*) dispensar, ceder ◻ *a* (*in reserve*) de reserva, de sobra; (*tyre*) sobressalente; (*bed*) extra; (*room*) de hóspedes ◻ *n* (*part*) sobressalente *m*. **~ time** horas *fpl* vagas. **have an hour to ~** dispôr de

uma hora. **have no time to ~** não ter tempo a perder
sparing /'speərɪŋ/ *a* poupado. **be ~ of** poupar em, ser poupado com. **~ly** *adv* frugalmente
spark /spa:k/ *n* centelha *f*, faísca *f* □ *vt* lançar faíscas. **~ off** (*initiate*) desencadear, provocar. **~(ing)-plug** *n* vela *f* de ignição
sparkle /'spa:kl/ *vi* cintilar, brilhar □ *n* brilho *m*, cintilação *f*
sparkling /'spa:klɪŋ/ *a* (*wine*) espumante
sparrow /'spærəʊ/ *n* pardal *m*
sparse /spa:s/ *a* esparso; (*hair*) ralo. **~ly** *adv* (*furnished etc*) escassamente
spasm /'spæzəm/ *n* (*of muscle*) espasmo *m*; (*of coughing, anger etc*) ataque *m*, acesso *m*
spasmodic /spæz'mɒdɪk/ *a* espasmódico; (*at irregular intervals*) intermitente
spastic /'spæstɪk/ *n* deficiente *mf* motor
spat /spæt/ *see* **spit**[1]
spate /speɪt/ *n* (*in river*) enxurrada *f*, cheia *f*. **a ~ of** (*letters etc*) uma avalanche de
spatter /'spætə(r)/ *vt* salpicar (**with** de, com)
spawn /spɔ:n/ *n* ovas *fpl* □ *vi* desovar □ *vt* gerar em quantidade
speak /spi:k/ *vt/i* (*pt* **spoke**, *pp* **spoken**) falar (**to/with sb about sth** com alguém de/sobre alg coisa); (*say*) dizer. **~ out/up** falar abertamente; (*louder*) falar mais alto. **~ one's mind** dizer o que se pensa. **so to ~** por assim dizer. **English/Portuguese spoken** fala-se português/inglês
speaker /'spi:kə(r)/ *n* (*in public*) orador *m*; (*loudspeaker*) alto-falante *m*; (*of a language*) pessoa *f* de língua nativa
spear /spɪə(r)/ *n* lança *f*
spearhead /'spɪəhed/ *n* ponta *f* de lança □ *vt* (*lead*) estar à frente de, encabeçar
special /'speʃl/ *a* especial. **~ity** /-ɪ'ælətɪ/ *n* especialidade *f*. **~ly** *adv* especialmente. **~ty** *n* especialidade *f*
specialist /'speʃəlɪst/ *n* especialista *mf*
specialize /'speʃəlaɪz/ *vi* especializar-se (**in** em). **~d** *a* especializado
species /'spi:ʃɪz/ *n* (*pl invar*) espécie *f*
specific /spə'sɪfɪk/ *a* específico. **~ally** *adv* especificamente, explicitamente
specif|y /'spesɪfaɪ/ *vt* especificar. **~ication** /-ɪ'keɪʃn/ *n* especificação *f*. **~ications** *npl* (*of work etc*) caderno *m* de encargos
specimen /'spesɪmɪn/ *n* espécime(n) *m*, amostra *f*
speck /spek/ *n* (*stain*) mancha *f* pequena; (*dot*) pontinho *m*, pinta *f*; (*particle*) grão *m*
speckled /'spekld/ *a* salpicado, manchado
specs /speks/ *npl* (*colloq*) óculos *mpl*
spectacle /'spektəkl/ *n* espetáculo *m*, (*P*) espectáculo *m*. **(pair of) ~s** (par *m* de) óculos *mpl*
spectacular /spek'tækjʊlə(r)/ *a* espetacular, (*P*) espectacular
spectator /spek'teɪtə(r)/ *n* espectador *m*
spectre /'spektə(r)/ *n* espectro *m*, fantasma *m*
spectrum /'spektrəm/ *n* (*pl* **-tra**) espectro *m*; (*of ideas etc*) faixa *f*, gama *f*, leque *m*
speculat|e /'spekjʊleɪt/ *vi* especular, fazer especulações *or* conjeturas, (*P*) conjecturas (**about** sobre); (*comm*) especular, fazer especulação (**in** em). **~ion** /-'leɪʃn/ *n* especulação *f*, conjetura *f*, (*P*) conjectura *f*; (*comm*) especulação *f*. **~or** *n* especulador *m*
speech /spi:tʃ/ *n* (*faculty*) fala *f*; (*diction*) elocução *f*; (*dialect*) falar *m*; (*address*) discurso *m*. **~less** *a* mudo, sem fala (**with** com, de)
speed /spi:d/ *n* velocidade *f*, rapidez *f* □ *vt/i* (*pt* **sped** /sped/) (*move*) ir depressa *or* a grande velocidade; (*send*) despedir, mandar; (*pt* **speeded**) (*drive too fast*) ultrapassar o limite de velocidade. **~ camera** radar *m*. **~ limit** limite *m* de velocidade. **~ up** acelerar (-se). **~ing** *n* excesso *m* de velocidade
speedometer /spi:'dɒmɪtə(r)/ *n* velocímetro *m*, (*P*) conta-quilómetros *m inv*
speed|y /'spi:dɪ/ *a* (**-ier**, **-iest**) rápido; (*prompt*) pronto. **~ily** *adv* rapidamente; (*promptly*) prontamente
spell[1] /spel/ *n* (*magic*) sortilégio *m*
spell[2] /spel/ *vt/i* (*pt* **spelled** *or* **spelt**) escrever; (*fig: mean*) significar, ter como resultado. **~ out** soletrar; (*fig: explain*) explicar claramente. **~ing** *n* ortografia *f*
spell[3] /spel/ *n* (*short period*) período *m* curto, breve espaço *m* de tempo; (*turn*) turno *m*
spend /spend/ *vt* (*pt* **spent**) (*money, energy*) gastar (**on** em); (*time, holiday*) passar. **~er** *n* gastador *m*
spendthrift /'spendθrɪft/ *n* perdulário *m*, esbanjador *m*
spent /spent/ *see* **spend** □ *a* gasto
sperm /spɜ:m/ *n* (*pl* **sperms** *or* **sperm**) (*semen*) esperma *m*, sêmen *m*, (*P*) sémen *m*; (*cell*) espermatozóide *m*
spew /spju:/ *vt/i* vomitar, lançar
sphere /sfɪə(r)/ *n* esfera *f*
spherical /'sferɪkl/ *a* esférico

spic|e /spaɪs/ *n* especiaria *f*, condimento *m*; (*fig*) picante *m* □ *vt* condimentar. **~y** *a* condimentado; (*fig*) picante

spick /spɪk/ *a* **~ and span** novo em folha, impecável

spider /'spaɪdə(r)/ *n* aranha *f*

spik|e /spaɪk/ *n* (*of metal etc*) bico *m*, espigão *m*, ponta *f*. **~y** *a* guarnecido de bicos *or* pontas

spill /spɪl/ *vt*/*i* (*pt* **spilled** *or* **spilt**) derramar(-se), entornar (-se), espalhar(-se). **~ over** transbordar, extravasar

spin /spɪn/ *vt*/*i* (*pt* **spun**, *pres p* **spinning**) (*wool, cotton*) fiar; (*web*) tecer; (*turn*) (fazer) girar, (fazer) rodopiar. **~ out** (*money, story*) fazer durar; (*time*) (fazer) parar □ *n* volta *f*; (*aviat*) parafuso *m*. **go for a ~** dar uma volta *or* um giro. **~-drier** *n* centrifugadora *f* para a roupa, secadora *f*. **~ning-wheel** *n* roda *f* de fiar. **~-off** *n* bônus *m*, (*P*) bónus *m* inesperado; (*by-product*) derivado *m*

spinach /'spɪnɪdʒ/ *n* (*plant*) espinafre *m*; (*as food*) espinafres *mpl*

spinal /'spaɪnl/ *a* vertebral. **~ cord** espina *f* dorsal

spindl|e /'spɪndl/ *n* roca *f*, fuso *m*; (*mech*) eixo *m*. **~y** *a* alto e magro; (*of plant*) espigado

spine /spaɪn/ *n* espinha *f*, coluna *f* vertebral; (*prickle*) espinho *m*, pico *m*; (*of book*) lombada *f*

spineless /'spaɪnlɪs/ *a* (*fig: cowardly*) covarde, sem fibra (*fig*)

spinster /'spɪnstə(r)/ *n* solteira *f*; (*pej*) solteirona *f*

spiral /'spaɪərəl/ *a* (em) espiral; (*staircase*) em caracol □ *n* espiral *f* □ *vi* (*pt* **spiralled**) subir em espiral

spire /'spaɪə(r)/ *n* agulha *f*, flecha *f*

spirit /'spɪrɪt/ *n* espírito *m*; (*boldness*) coragem *f*, brio *m*. **~s** (*morale*) moral *m*; (*drink*) bebidas *fpl* alcoólicas, (*P*) bebidas *fpl* espirituosas. **in high ~s** alegre □ *vt* **~ away** dar sumiço em, arrebatar. **~-level** *n* nível *m* de bolha de ar

spirited /'spɪrɪtɪd/ *a* fogoso; (*attack, defence*) vigoroso, enérgico

spiritual /'spɪrɪtʃʊəl/ *a* espiritual

spiritualism /'spɪrɪtʃʊəlɪzəm/ *n* espiritismo *m*

spit[1] /spɪt/ *vt*/*i* (*pt* **spat** *or* **spit**, *pres p* **spitting**) cuspir; (*of rain*) chuviscar; (*of cat*) bufar □ *n* cuspe *m*, (*P*) cuspo *m*. **the ~ting image of** o retrato vivo de, a cara chapada de (*colloq*)

spit[2] /spɪt/ *n* (*for meat*) espeto *m*; (*of land*) restinga *f*, (*P*) lingua *f* de terra

spite /spaɪt/ *n* má vontade *f*, despeito *m*, rancor *m* □ *vt* aborrecer, mortificar. **in ~ of** a despeito de, apesar de. **~ful** *a* rancoroso, maldoso. **~fully** *adv* rancorosamente, maldosamente

spittle /'spɪtl/ *n* cuspe *m*, (*P*) cuspo *m*, saliva *f*

splash /splæʃ/ *vt* salpicar, respingar □ *vi* esparrinhar, esparramar-se. **~ (about)** chapinhar □ *n* (*act, mark*) salpico *m*; (*sound*) chape *m*; (*of colour*) mancha *f*. **make a ~** (*striking display*) fazer um vistão, causar furor

spleen /spli:n/ *n* (*anat*) baço *m*. **vent one's ~ on sb** descarregar a neura em alguém (*colloq*)

splendid /'splendɪd/ *a* esplêndido, magnífico; (*excellent*) estupendo (*colloq*), ótimo, (*P*) óptimo

splendour /'splendə(r)/ *n* esplendor *m*

splint /splɪnt/ *n* (*med*) tala *f*

splinter /'splɪntə(r)/ *n* lasca *f*, estilhaço *m*; (*under the skin*) farpa *f*, lasca *f* □ *vi* estilhaçar-se, lascar-se. **~ group** grupo *m* dissidente

split /splɪt/ *vt*/*i* (*pt* **split**, *pres p* **splitting**) rachar, fender(-se); (*divide, share*) dividir; (*tear*) romper(-se) □ *n* racha *f*, fenda *f*; (*share*) quinhão *m*, parte *f*; (*pol*) cisão *f*. **~ on** (*sl: inform on*) denunciar. **~ one's sides** rebentar de risa. **~ up** (*of couple*) separar-se. **a ~ second** uma fração de segundo. **~ting headache** dor *f* de cabeça forte

splurge /splɜ:dʒ/ *n* (*colloq*) espalhafato *m*, estardalhaço *m* □ *vi* (*colloq: spend*) gastar os tubos, (*P*) gastar à doida (*colloq*)

spool /spu:l/ *n* (*of sewing machine*) bobina *f*; (*for cotton thread*) carretel *m*, carrinho *m*; (*naut; fishing*) carretel *m*

splutter /'splʌtə(r)/ *vi* falar cuspindo; (*engine*) cuspir; (*fat*) crepitar

spoil /spɔɪl/ *vt* (*pt* **spoilt** *or* **spoiled**) estragar; (*pamper*) mimar □ *n* **~(s)** (*plunder*) despojo(s) *m*(*pl*), espólios *mpl*. **~-sport** *n* desmancha-prazeres *mf invar.* **~t** *a* (*pampered*) mimado, estragado com mimos

spoke[1] /spəʊk/ *n* raio *m*

spoke[2], **spoken** /spəʊk, 'spəʊkən/ *see* **speak**

spokes|man /'spəʊksmən/ *n* (*pl* **-men**) **~woman** *n* (*pl* **-women**) porta-voz *mf*

sponge /spʌndʒ/ *n* esponja *f* □ *vt* (*clean*) lavar com esponja; (*wipe*) limpar com esponja □ *vi* **~ on** (*colloq: cadge*) viver à custa de. **~ bag** bolsa *f* de toalete. **~ cake** pão-de-ló *m*. **~r** /-ə(r)/ *n* parasita *mf* (*colloq*) (*sl*). **spongy** *a* esponjoso

sponsor /'spɒnsə(r)/ *n* patrocinador *m*; (*for membership*) (sócio) proponente *m*

□ *vt* patrocinar; (*for membership*) propor. **~ship** *n* patrocínio *m*

spontaneous /spɒn'teɪnɪəs/ *a* espontâneo

spoof /spu:f/ *n* (*colloq*) paródia *f*

spooky /'spu:kɪ/ *a* (**-ier, -iest**) (*colloq*) fantasmagórico, que dá arrepios

spool /spu:l/ *n* (*of sewing machine*) bobina *f*; (*for thread, line*) carretel *m*, (*P*) carrinho *m*

spoon /spu:n/ *n* colher *f*. **~-feed** *vt* (*pt* **-fed**) alimentar de colher; (*fig: help*) dar na bandeja para (*fig*). **~ful** *n* (*pl* **~fuls**) colherada *f*

sporadic /spə'rædɪk/ *a* esporádico, acidental

sport /spɔ:t/ *n* esporte *m*, (*P*) desporto *m*. **(good) ~** (*sl: person*) gente *f* fina, (*P*) bom tipo *m* (*colloq*), (*P*) tipo *m* bestial □ *vt* (*display*) exibir, ostentar. **~s car/coat** carro *m*/casaco *m* esporte, (*P*) de desporto. **~y** *a* (*colloq*) esportivo, (*P*) desportivo

sporting /'spɔ:tɪŋ/ *a* esportivo, (*P*) desportivo. **a ~ chance** uma certa possibilidade de sucesso, uma boa chance

sports|man /'spɔ:tsmən/ *n* (*pl* **-men**), **~woman** (*pl* **-women**) desportista *mf*. **~manship** *n* (*spirit*) espírito *m* esportivo, (*P*) desportivo; (*activity*) esportismo *m*, (*P*) desportismo *m*

spot /spɒt/ *n* (*mark, stain*) mancha *f*; (*in pattern*) pinta *f*, bola *f*; (*drop*) gota *f*; (*place*) lugar *m*, ponto *m*; (*pimple*) borbulha *f*, espinha *f*; (*TV*) spot *m* televisivo □ *vt* (*pt* **spotted**) manchar; (*colloq: detect*) descobrir, detectar (*colloq*). **a ~ of** (*colloq*) um pouco de. **be in a ~** (*colloq*) estar numa encrenca (*colloq*), (*P*) estar metido numa alhada (*colloq*). **on the ~** no local; (*there and then*) ali mesmo, logo ali. **~-on** *a* (*colloq*) certo. **~ check** inspeção *f*, (*P*) inspecção *f* de surpresa; (*of cars*) fiscalização *f* de surpresa. **~ted** *a* manchado; (*with dots*) de pintas, de bolas; (*animal*) malhado. **~ty** *a* (*with pimples*) com borbulhas

spotless /'spɒtlɪs/ *a* impecável, imaculado

spotlight /'spɒtlaɪt/ *n* foco *m*; (*cine, theat*) refletor *m*, holofote *m*

spouse /spaʊz/ *n* cônjuge *mf*, esposo *m*

spout /spaʊt/ *n* (*of vessel*) bico *m*; (*of liquid*) esguicho *m*, jorro *m*; (*pipe*) cano *m* □ *vi* jorrar, esguichar. **up the ~** (*sl: ruined*) liquidado (*sl*)

sprain /spreɪn/ *n* entorse *f*, mau jeito *m* □ *vt* torcer, dar um mau jeito a

sprang /spræŋ/ *see* **spring**

sprawl /sprɔ:l/ *vi* (*sit*) estirar-se, esparramar-se; (*fall*) estatelar-se; (*town*) estender-se, espraiar-se

spray[1] /spreɪ/ *n* (*of flowers*) raminho *m*, ramalhete *m*

spray[2] /spreɪ/ *n* (*water*) borrifo *m*, salpico *m*; (*from sea*) borrifo *m* de espuma; (*device*) bomba *f*, aerossol *m*; (*for perfume*) vaporizador *m*, atomizador *m* □ *vt* aspergir, borrifar, pulverizar; (*with insecticide*) pulverizar. **~-gun** *n* (*for paint*) pistola *f*

spread /spred/ *vt/i* (*pt* **spread**) (*extend, stretch*) estender(-se); (*news, fear, illness etc*) alastrar (-se), espalhar(-se), propagar(-se); (*butter etc*) passar; (*wings*) abrir □ *n* (*expanse*) expansão *f*, extensão *f*; (*spreading*) propagação *f*; (*paste*) pasta *f* para passar pão; (*colloq: meal*) banquete *m*. **~-eagled** *a* de braços e pernas abertos. **~sheet** *n* (*comput*) folha *f* de cálculo

spree /spri:/ *n* **go on a ~** (*colloq*) cair na farra

sprig /sprɪg/ *n* raminho *m*

sprightly /'spraɪtlɪ/ *a* (**-ier, -iest**) vivo, animado

spring /sprɪŋ/ *vi* (*pt* **sprang**, *pp* **sprung**) (*arise*) nascer; (*jump*) saltar, pular □ *vt* (*produce suddenly*) sair-se com; (*a surprise*) fazer (**on sb** a alguém) □ *n* salto *m*, pulo *m*; (*device*) mola *f*; (*season*) primavera *f*; (*of water*) fonte *f*, nascente *f*. **~ from** vir de, originar-se de, provir de. **~-clean** *vt* fazer limpeza geral. **~ onion** cebolinha *f*. **~ up** surgir

springboard /'sprɪŋbɔ:d/ *n* trampolim *m*

springtime /'sprɪŋtaɪm/ *n* primavera *f*

springy /'sprɪŋɪ/ *a* (**-ier, -iest**) elástico

sprinkle /'sprɪŋkl/ *vt* (*with liquid*) borrifar, salpicar; (*with salt, flour*) polvilhar (**with** de). **~ sand**/*etc* espalhar areia/*etc*. **~r** /-ə(r)/ *n* (*in garden*) regador *m*; (*for fires*) sprinkler *m*

sprinkling /'sprɪŋklɪŋ/ *n* (*amount*) pequena quantidade *f*; (*number*) pequeno número *m*

sprint /sprɪnt/ *n* (*sport*) corrida *f* de pequena distância, sprint *m* □ *vi* correr em sprint *or* a toda a velocidade; (*sport*) correr

sprout /spraʊt/ *vt/i* brotar, germinar; (*put forth*) deitar □ *n* (*on plant etc*) broto *m*. **(Brussels) ~s** couves *f* de Bruxelas

spruce /spru:s/ *a* bem arrumado □ *vt* **~ o.s. up** arrumar(-se)

sprung /sprʌŋ/ *see* **spring** □ *a* (*mattress etc*) de molas

spry /spraɪ/ *a* (**spryer, spryest**) vivo, ativo, (*P*) activo; (*nimble*) ágil

spud /spʌd/ *n* (*sl*) batata *f*

spun /spʌn/ *see* **spin**

spur /spɜ:(r)/ *n* (*of rider*) espora *f*; (*fig: stimulus*) aguilhão *m*; (*fig*) espora *f* (*fig*) □ *vt* (*pt* **spurred**) esporear, picar com esporas; (*fig: incite*) aguilhoar, esporear. **on the ~ of the moment** impulsivamente

spurious /'spjʊərɪəs/ *a* falso, espúrio

spurn /spɜ:n/ *vt* desdenhar, desprezar, rejeitar

spurt /spɜ:t/ *vi* jorrar, esguichar; (*fig: accelerate*) acelerar subitamente, dar um arranco súbito □ *n* jorro *m*, esguicho *m*; (*of energy, speed*) arranco *m*, surto *m*

spy /spaɪ/ *n* espião *m* □ *vt* (*make out*) avistar, descortinar □ *vi* **~ (on)** espiar, espionar. **~ out** descobrir. **~ing** *n* espionagem *f*

squabble /'skwɒbl/ *vi* discutir, brigar □ *n* briga *f*, disputa *f*

squad /skwɒd/ *n* (*mil*) pelotão *m*; (*team*) equipe *f*, (*P*) equipa *f*. **firing ~** pelotão *m* de fuzilamento. **flying ~** brigada *f* móvel

squadron /'skwɒdrən/ *n* (*mil*) esquadrão *m*; (*aviat*) esquadrilha *f*; (*naut*) esquadra *f*

squal|id /'skwɒlɪd/ *a* esquálido, sórdido. **~or** *n* sordidez *f*

squall /skwɔ:l/ *n* borrasca *f*

squander /'skwɒndə(r)/ *vt* desperdiçar

square /skweə(r)/ *n* quadrado *m*; (*in town*) largo *m*, praça *f*; (*T-square*) régua-tê *f*; (*set-square*) esquadro *m* □ *a* (*of shape*) quadrado; (*metre, mile etc*) quadrado; (*honest*) direito, honesto; (*of meal*) abundante, substancial. **(all) ~** (*quits*) quite(s) □ *vt* (*math*) elevar ao quadrado; (*settle*) acertar □ *vi* (*agree*) concordar. **go back to ~ one** recomeçar tudo do princípio, voltar à estaca zero. **~ brackets** parênteses *mpl* retos, (*P*) rectos. **~ up to** enfrentar. **~ly** *adv* diretamente, (*P*) directamente; (*fairly*) honestamente

squash /skwɒʃ/ *vt* (*crush*) esmagar; (*squeeze*) espremer; (*crowd*) comprimir, apertar □ *n* (*game*) squash *m*; (*Amer: marrow*) abóbora *f*. **lemon ~** limonada *f*. **orange ~** laranjada *f*. **~y** *a* mole

squat /skwɒt/ *vi* (*pt* **squatted**) acocorar-se, agachar-se; (*be a squatter*) ser ocupante ilegal □ *a* (*dumpy*) atarracado. **~ter** *n* ocupante *mf* ilegal de casa vazia, posseiro *m*

squawk /skwɔ:k/ *n* grasnido *m*, crocito *m* □ *vi* grasnar, crocitar

squeak /skwi:k/ *n* guincho *m*, chio *m*; (*of door, shoes etc*) rangido *m* □ *vi* guinchar, chiar; (*of door, shoes etc*) ranger. **~y** *a* (*shoe etc*) que range; (*voice*) esganiçado

squeal /skwi:l/ *vi* dar gritos agudos, guinchar □ *n* grito *m* agudo, guincho *m*. **~ (on)** (*sl: inform on*) delatar, (*P*) denunciar

squeamish /'skwi:mɪʃ/ *a* (*nauseated*) que enjoa à toa

squeeze /skwi:z/ *vt* (*lemon, sponge etc*) espremer; (*hand, arm*) apertar; (*extract*) arrancar, extorquir (**from** de) □ *vi* (*force one's way*) passar à força, meter-se por □ *n* aperto *m*, apertão *m*; (*hug*) abraço *m*; (*comm*) restrições *fpl* de crédito

squelch /skweltʃ/ *vi* chapinhar *or* fazer chape-chape na lama

squid /skwɪd/ *n* lula *f*

squiggle /'skwɪgl/ *n* rabisco *m*, floreado *m*

squint /skwɪnt/ *vi* ser estrábico *or* vesgo; (*with half-shut eyes*) franzir os olhos □ *n* (*med*) estrabismo *m*

squirm /skwɜ:m/ *vi* (re)torcer-se, contorcer-se

squirrel /'skwɪrəl/ *n* esquilo *m*

squirt /skwɜ:t/ *vt/i* esguichar □ *n* esguicho *m*

stab /stæb/ *vt* (*pt* **stabbed**) apunhalar; (*knife*) esfaquear □ *n* punhalada *f*; (*with knife*) facada *f*; (*of pain*) pontada *f*; (*colloq: attempt*) tentativa *f*

stabilize /'steɪbəlaɪz/ *vt* estabilizar

stab|le[1] /steɪbl/ *a* (**-er**, **-est**) estável. **~ility** /stə'bɪlətɪ/ *n* estabilidade *f*

stable[2] /'steɪbl/ *n* cavalariça *f*, estrebaria *f*. **~-boy** *n* moço *m* de estrebaria

stack /stæk/ *n* pilha *f*, montão *m*; (*of hay etc*) meda *f* □ *vt* **~ (up)** empilhar, amontoar

stadium /'steɪdɪəm/ *n* estádio *m*

staff /sta:f/ *n* pessoal *m*; (*in school*) professores *mpl*; (*mil*) estado-maior *m*; (*stick*) bordão *m*, cajado *m*; (*mus*) (*pl* **staves**) pauta *f* □ *vt* prover de pessoal

stag /stæg/ *n* veado (macho) *m*, cervo *m*. **~-party** *n* (*colloq*) reunião *f* masculina; (*before wedding*) despedida *f* de solteiro

stage /steɪdʒ/ *n* (*theatre*) palco *m*; (*phase*) fase *f*, ponto *m*; (*platform in hall*) estrado *m* □ *vt* encenar, pôr em cena; (*fig: organize*) organizar. **go on the ~** seguir a carreira teatral, ir para o teatro (*colloq*). **~ door** entrada *f* dos artistas. **~-fright** *n* nervosismo *m*

stagger /'stægə(r)/ *vi* vacilar, cambalear □ *vt* (*shock*) atordoar, chocar; (*holidays etc*) escalonar. **~ing** *a* atordoador, chocante

stagnant /'stægnənt/ *a* estagnado, parado

stagnat|e /stæg'neɪt/ *vi* estagnar. **~ion** /-ʃn/ *n* estagnação *f*

staid /steɪd/ *a* sério, sensato, estável

stain /steɪn/ *vt* manchar, pôr nódoa em; (*colour*) tingir, dar cor a □ *n* mancha *f*, nódoa *f*; (*colouring*) corante *m*. **~ed glass window** vitral *m*. **~less steel** aço *m* inoxidável

stair /steə(r)/ *n* degrau *m*. **~s** escada(s) *f*(*pl*)

stair|case /'steəkeɪs/, **~way** /-weɪ/ *ns* escada(s) *f*(*pl*), escadaria *f*

stake /steɪk/ *n* (*post*) estaca *f*, poste *m*; (*wager*) parada *f*, aposta *f* □ *vt* (*area*) demarcar, delimitar; (*wager*) jogar, apostar. **at ~** em jogo. **have a ~ in** ter interesse em. **~ a claim to** reivindicar

stale /steɪl/ *a* (**-er**, **-est**) estragado, velho; (*bread*) duro, mofado; (*smell*) rançoso; (*air*) viciado; (*news*) velho

stalemate /'steɪlmeɪt/ *n* (*chess*) empate *m*; (*fig: deadlock*) impasse *m*, beco-sem-saída *m*

stalk[1] /stɔ:k/ *n* (*of plant*) caule *m*

stalk[2] /stɔ:k/ *vi* andar com ar empertigado □ *vt* (*prey*) perseguir furtivamente, tocaiar

stall /stɔ:l/ *n* (*in stable*) baia *f*; (*in market*) tenda *f*, barraca *f*. **~s** (*theat*) poltronas *fpl* de orquestra; (*cinema*) platéia *f*, (*P*) plateia *f* □ *vt*/*i* (*auto*) enguiçar, (*P*) ir abaixo. **~ (for time)** ganhar tempo

stalwart /'stɔ:lwət/ *a* forte, rijo; (*supporter*) fiel

stamina /'stæmɪnə/ *n* resistência *f*

stammer /'stæmə(r)/ *vt*/*i* gaguejar □ *n* gagueira *f*, (*P*) gaguez *f*

stamp /stæmp/ *vt*/*i* **~ (one's foot)** bater com o pé (no chão), pisar com força □ *vt* estampar; (*letter*) estampilhar, selar; (*with rubber stamp*) carimbar. **~ out** (*fire, rebellion etc*) esmagar; (*disease*) erradicar □ *n* estampa *f*; (*for postage*) selo *m*; (*fig: mark*) cunho *m*. **(rubber) ~** carimbo *m*. **~-collecting** *n* filatelia *f*

stampede /stæm'pi:d/ *n* (*scattering*) debandada *f*; (*of horses, cattle etc*) debandada *f*; (*fig: rush*) corrida *f* □ *vt*/*i* (fazer) debandar; (*horses, cattle etc*) tresmalhar

stance /stæns/ *n* posição *f*, postura *f*

stand /stænd/ *vi* (*pt* **stood**) estar em pé; (*keep upright position*) ficar em pé; (*rise*) levantar-se; (*be situated*) encontrar-se, ficar, situar-se; (*pol*) candidatar-se (**for** por) □ *vt* pôr (de pé), colocar; (*tolerate*) suportar, agüentar, (*P*) aguentar □ *n* posição *f*; (*support*) apoio *m*; (*mil*) resistência *f*; (*at fair*) stand *m*, pavilhão *m*; (*in street*) quiosque *m*; (*for spectators*) arquibancada *f*, (*P*) bancada *f*; (*Amer: witness-box*) banco *m* das testemunhas. **~ a chance** ter uma possibilidade. **~ back** recuar. **~ by** *or* **around** estar parado sem fazer nada. **~ by** (*be ready*) estar a postos; (*promise, person*) manter-se fiel a. **~ down** desistir, retirar-se. **~ for** representar, simbolizar; (*colloq: tolerate*) aturar. **~ in for** substituir. **~ out** (*be conspicuous*) sobressair. **~ still** estar/ficar imóvel. **~ still!** não se mexa!, quieto! **~ to reason** ser lógico. **~ up** levantar-se, pôr-se em *or* de pé. **~ up for** defender, apoiar. **~ up to** enfrentar. **~-by** *a* (*for emergency*) de reserva; (*ticket*) de stand-by □ *n* (*at airport*) stand-by *m*. **on ~-by** (*mil*) de prontidão; (*med*) de plantão. **~-in** *n* substituto *m*, suplente *mf*. **~-offish** *a* (*colloq: aloof*) reservado, distante

standard /'stændəd/ *n* norma *f*, padrão *m*; (*level*) nível *m*; (*flag*) estandarte *m*, bandeira *f*. **~s** (*morals*) princípios *mpl* □ *a* regulamentar; (*average*) standard, normal. **~ lamp** abajur *m* de pé. **~ of living** padrão *m* de vida, (*P*) nível *m* de vida

standardize /'stændədaɪz/ *vt* padronizar

standing /'stændɪŋ/ *a* em pé, de pé *invar*; (*army, committee etc*) permanente □ *n* posição *f*; (*reputation*) prestígio *m*; (*duration*) duração *f*. **~ order** (*at bank*) ordem *f* permanente. **~-room** *n* lugares *mpl* em pé

standpoint /'stændpɔɪnt/ *n* ponto *m* de vista

standstill /'stændstɪl/ *n* paralisação *f*. **at a ~** parado, paralisado. **bring/come to a ~** (fazer) parar, paralisar(-se), imobilizar (-se)

stank /stæŋk/ *see* **stink**

staple[1] /'steɪpl/ *n* (*for paper*) grampo *m*, (*P*) agrafo *m* □ *vt* (*paper*) grampear, (*P*) agrafar. **~r** /-ə(r)/ *n* grampeador *m*, (*P*) agrafador *m*

staple[2] /'steɪpl/ *a* principal, básico □ *n* (*comm*) artigo *m* básico

star /sta:(r)/ *n* estrela *f*; (*cinema*) estrela *f*, vedete *f*; (*celebrity*) celebridade *f* □ *vt* (*pt* **starred**) (*of film*) ter no papel principal, (*P*) ter como actor principal □ *vi* **~ in** ser a vedete *or* ter o papel principal em. **~dom** *n* celebridade *f*, estrelato *m*

starch /sta:tʃ/ *n* amido *m*, fécula *f*; (*for clothes*) goma *f* □ *vt* pôr em goma, engomar. **~y** *a* (*of food*) farináceo, feculento; (*fig: of person*) rígido, formal

stare /steə(r)/ *vi* **~ at** olhar fixamente □ *n* olhar *m* fixo

starfish /'sta:fɪʃ/ *n* (*pl invar*) estrela-do-mar *f*

stark /sta:k/ *a* (**-er, -est**) (*desolate*) árido, desolado; (*severe*) austero, severo; (*utter*) completo, rematado; (*fact etc*) brutal □ *adv* completamente. **~ naked** nu em pêlo, (*P*) em pelota (*colloq*)

starling /'sta:lɪŋ/ *n* estorninho *m*

starlit /'sta:lɪt/ *a* estrelado

starry /'sta:rɪ/ *a* estrelado. **~-eyed** *a* (*colloq*) sonhador, idealista

start /sta:t/ *vt/i* começar; (*machine*) ligar, pôr em andamento; (*fashion etc*) lançar; (*leave*) partir; (*cause*) causar, provocar; (*jump*) sobressaltar-se, estremecer; (*of car*) arrancar, partir □ *n* começo *m*, início *m*; (*of race*) largada *f*, partida *f*; (*lead*) avanço *m*; (*jump*) sobressalto *m*, estremecimento *m*. **by fits and ~s** aos arrancos, intermitentemente. **for a ~** para começar. **give sb a ~** sobressaltar alguém, pregar um susto a alguém. **~ to do** começar a *or* pôr-se a fazer. **~er** *n* (*auto*) arranque *m*; (*competitor*) corredor *m*; (*culin*) entrada *f*. **~ing-point** *n* ponto *m* de partida

startl|e /'sta:tl/ *vt* (*make jump*) sobressaltar, pregar um susto a; (*shock*) alarmar, chocar. **~ing** *a* alarmante; (*surprising*) surpreendente

starv|e /sta:v/ *vi* (*suffer*) passar fome; (*die*) morrer de fome. **be ~ing** (*colloq: very hungry*) ter muita fome, morrer de fome (*colloq*) □ *vt* fazer passar fome a; (*deprive*) privar. **~ation** /-'veɪʃn/ *n* fome *f*

stash /stæʃ/ *vt* (*sl*) guardar, esconder, enfurnar (*colloq*)

state /steɪt/ *n* estado *m*, condição *f*; (*pomp*) pompa *f*, gala *f*; (*pol*) Estado *m* □ *a* de Estado, do Estado; (*school*) público; (*visit etc*) oficial □ *vt* afirmar (**that** que); (*views*) exprimir; (*fix*) marcar, fixar. **in a ~** muito abalado

stateless /'steɪtlɪs/ *a* apátrida

stately /'steɪtlɪ/ *a* (**-ier, -iest**) majestoso. **~ home** solar *m*, palácio *m*

statement /'steɪtmənt/ *n* declaração *f*; (*of account*) extrato *m*, (*P*) extracto *m* de conta

statesman /'steɪtsmən/ *n* (*pl* **-men**) homem *m* de estado, estadista *m*

static /'stætɪk/ *a* estático □ *n* (*radio, TV*) estática *f*, interferência *f*

station /'steɪʃn/ *n* (*position*) posto *m*; (*rail, bus, radio*) estação *f*; (*rank*) condição *f*, posição *f* social □ *vt* colocar. **~-wagon** *n* perua *f*, (*P*) carrinha *f*. **~ed at** *or* **in** (*mil*) estacionado em

stationary /'steɪʃnrɪ/ *a* estacionário, parado, imóvel; (*vehicle*) estacionado, parado

stationer /'steɪʃənə(r)/ *n* dono *m* de papelaria. **~'s shop** papelaria *f*. **~y** *n* artigos *mpl* de papelaria; (*writing-paper*) papel *m* de carta

statistic /stə'tɪstɪk/ *n* dado *m* estatístico. **~s** *n* (*as a science*) estatística *f*. **~al** *a* estatístico

statue /'stætʃu:/ *n* estátua *f*

stature /'stætʃə(r)/ *n* estatura *f*

status /'steɪtəs/ *n* (*pl* **-uses**) situação *f*, posição *f*, categoria *f*; (*prestige*) prestígio *m*, importância *f*, status *m*. **~ quo** status quo *m*. **~ symbol** símbolo *m* de status

statut|e /'stætju:t/ *n* estatuto *m*, lei *f*. **~ory** /-ʊtrɪ/ *a* estatutário, regulamentar; (*holiday*) legal

staunch /stɔ:ntʃ/ *a* (**-er, -est**) (*friend*) fiel, leal

stave /steɪv/ *n* (*mus*) pauta *f* □ *vt* **~ off** (*keep off*) conjurar, evitar; (*delay*) adiar

stay /steɪ/ *vi* estar, ficar, permanecer; (*dwell temporarily*) ficar, alojar-se, hospedar-se; (*spend time*) demorar-se □ *vt* (*hunger*) enganar □ *n* estada *f*, visita *f*, permanência *f*. **~ behind** ficar para trás. **~ in** ficar em casa. **~ put** (*colloq*) não se mexer (*colloq*). **~ up (late)** deitar-se tarde. **~ing-power** *n* resistência *f*

stead /sted/ *n* **in my/your**/*etc* **~** no meu/teu/*etc* lugar. **stand in good ~** ser muito útil

steadfast /'stedfa:st/ *a* firme, constante

stead|y /'stedɪ/ *a* (**-ier, -iest**) (*stable*) estável, firme, seguro; (*regular*) regular, constante; (*hand, voice*) firme □ *vt* firmar, fixar, estabilizar; (*calm*) acalmar. **go ~y with** (*colloq*) namorar. **~ily** *adv* firmemente; (*regularly*) regularmente, de modo constante

steak /steɪk/ *n* bife *m*

steal /sti:l/ *vt/i* (*pt* **stole**, *pp* **stolen**) roubar (**from sb** de alguém). **~ away** /**in**/*etc* sair/entrar/*etc* furtivamente, esgueirar-se. **~ the show** pôr os outros na sombra

stealth /stelθ/ *n* **by ~** furtivamente, na calada, às escondidas. **~y** *a* furtivo

steam /sti:m/ *n* vapor *m* de água; (*on window*) condensação *f* □ *vt* (*cook*) cozinhar a vapor. **~ up** (*window*) embaciar □ *vi* soltar vapor, fumegar; (*move*) avançar. **~-engine** *n* máquina *f* a vapor; (*locomotive*) locomotiva *f* a vapor. **~ iron** ferro *m* a vapor. **~y** *a* (*heat*) úmido, (*P*) húmido

steamer /'sti:mə(r)/ *n* (*ship*) (barco a) vapor *m*; (*culin*) utensílio *m* para cozinhar a vapor

steamroller /'sti:mrəʊlə(r)/ *n* cilindro *m* a vapor, rolo *m* compressor

steel /sti:l/ *n* aço *m* □ *a* de aço □ *vpr* ~ **o.s.** endurecer-se, fortalecer-se. ~ **industry** siderurgia *f*

steep[1] /sti:p/ *vt* (*soak*) mergulhar, pôr de molho; (*permeate*) passar, impregnar. ~**ed in** (*fig: vice, misery etc*) mergulhado em; (*fig: knowledge, wisdom etc*) impregnado de, repassado de

steep[2] /sti:p/ *a* (**-er, -est**) íngreme, escarpado; (*colloq*) exagerado, exorbitante. **rise** ~**ly** (*slope*) subir a pique; (*price*) disparar

steeple /'sti:pl/ *n* campanário *m*, torre *f*

steeplechase /'sti:pltʃeɪs/ *n* (*race*) corrida *f* de obstáculos

steer /stɪə(r)/ *vt/i* guiar, conduzir, dirigir; (*ship*) governar; (*fig*) guiar, orientar. ~ **clear of** evitar passar perto de. ~**ing** *n* (*auto*) direção *f*, (*P*) direcção *f*. ~**ing-wheel** *n* (*auto*) volante *m*

stem[1] /stem/ *n* caule *m*, haste *f*; (*of glass*) pé *m*; (*of pipe*) boquilha *f*; (*of word*) radical *m* □ *vi* (*pt* **stemmed**) ~ **from** provir de, vir de

stem[2] /stem/ *vt* (*pt* **stemmed**) (*check*) conter; (*stop*) estancar

stench /stentʃ/ *n* mau cheiro *m*, fedor *m*

stencil /'stensl/ *n* estênsil *m*, (*P*) stencil *m* □ *vt* (*pt* **stencilled**) (*document*) policopiar

step /step/ *vi* (*pt* **stepped**) ir andar □ *vt* ~ **up** aumentar □ *n* passo *m*, passada *f*; (*of stair, train*) degrau *m*; (*action*) medida *f*, passo *m*. ~**s** (*ladder*) escada *f*. **in** ~ no mesmo passo, a passo certo; (*fig*) em conformidade (**with** com). ~ **down** (*resign*) demitir-se. ~ **in** (*intervene*) intervir. ~**-ladder** *n* escada *f* portátil. ~**ping-stone** *n* (*fig: means to an end*) ponte *f*, trampolim *m*

stepbrother /'stepbrʌðə(r)/ *n* meio-irmão *m*. ~**daughter** *n* nora *f*, (*P*) enteada *f*. ~**father** *n* padrasto *m*. ~**mother** *n* madrasta *f*. ~**sister** *n* meio-irmã *f*. ~**son** *n* genro *m*, (*P*) enteado *m*

stereo /'sterɪəʊ/ *n* (*pl* **-os**) estéreo *m*; (*record-player etc*) equipamento *m* or sistema *m* estéreo □ *a* estéreo *invar*. ~**phonic** /-ə'fɒnɪk/ *a* estereofônico, (*P*) estereofónico

stereotype /'sterɪətaɪp/ *n* estereótipo *m*. ~**d** *a* estereotipado

steril|e /'steraɪl/ *a* estéril. ~**ity** /stə'rɪlətɪ/ *n* esterilidade *f*

steriliz|e /'sterəlaɪz/ *vt* esterilizar. ~**ation** /-'zeɪʃn/ *n* esterilização *f*

sterling /'stɜ:lɪŋ/ *n* libra *f* esterlina □ *a* esterlino; (*silver*) de lei; (*fig*) excelente, de (primeira) qualidade

stern[1] /stɜ:n/ *a* (**-er, -est**) severo

stern[2] /stɜ:n/ *n* (*of ship*) popa *f*, ré *f*

stethoscope /'steθəskəʊp/ *n* estetoscópio *m*

stew /stju:/ *vt/i* estufar, guisar; (*fruit*) cozer □ *n* ensopado *m*. ~**ed fruit** compota *f*

steward /'stjʊəd/ *n* (*of club etc*) ecônomo *m*, (*P*) ecónomo *m*, administrador *m*; (*on ship etc*) camareiro *m* (de bordo), (*P*) criado *m* (de bordo). ~**ess** /-'des/ *n* aeromoça *f*, (*P*) hospedeira *f*

stick[1] /stɪk/ *n* pau *m*; (*for walking*) bengala *f*; (*of celery*) talo *m*

stick[2] /stɪk/ *vt* (*pt* **stuck**) (*glue*) colar; (*thrust*) cravar, espetar; (*colloq: put*) enfiar, meter; (*sl: endure*) agüentar, (*P*) aguentar, aturar, suportar □ *vi* (*adhere*) colar, aderir; (*remain*) ficar enfiado *or* metido; (*be jammed*) emperrar, ficar engatado. ~ **in one's mind** ficar na memória. **be stuck with sb/sth** (*colloq*) não conseguir descartar-se de alguém/alg coisa (*colloq*). ~ **out** *vt* (*head*) esticar; (*tongue etc*) mostrar □ *vi* (*protrude*) sobressair. ~ **to** (*promise*) ser fiel a. ~**-up** *n* (*sl*) assalto *m* à mão armada. ~ **up for** (*colloq*) tomar o partido de, defender. ~**ing-plaster** *n* esparadrapo *m*, (*P*) adesivo *m*

sticker /'stɪkə(r)/ *n* adesivo *m*, etiqueta *f* (adesiva)

stickler /'stɪklə(r)/ *n* **be a** ~ **for** fazer grande questão de, insistir em

sticky /'stɪkɪ/ *a* (**-ier, -iest**) pegajoso; (*label, tape*) adesivo; (*weather*) abafado, mormacento

stiff /stɪf/ *a* (**-er, -est**) teso, hirto, rígido; (*limb, joint; hard*) duro, (*unbending*) inflexível; (*price*) elevado, puxado (*colloq*); (*penalty*) severo; (*drink*) forte; (*manner*) reservado, formal. **be bored/scared** ~ (*colloq*) estar muito aborrecido/com muito medo (*colloq*). ~ **neck** torcicolo *m*. ~**ness** *n* rigidez *f*

stiffen /'stɪfn/ *vt/i* (*harden*) endurecer; (*limb, joint*) emperrar

stifl|e /'staɪfl/ *vt/i* abafar, sufocar. ~**ing** *a* sufocante

stigma /'stɪgmə/ *n* estigma *m*. ~**tize** *vt* estigmatizar

stile /staɪl/ *n* degrau *m* para passar por cima de cerca

stiletto /stɪ'letəʊ/ *n* (*pl* **-os**) estilete *m*. ~ **heel** *n* salto *m* alto fino

still[1] /stɪl/ *a* imóvel, quieto; (*quiet*) sossegado □ *n* silêncio *m*, sossego *m* □ *adv* ainda; (*nevertheless*) apesar disso, apesar de tudo. **keep** ~! fique quieto!, não se mexa! ~ **life** natureza *f* morta. ~**ness** *n* calma *f*

still[2] /stɪl/ *n* (*apparatus*) alambique *m*

stillborn /'stɪlbɔ:n/ *a* natimorto, (*P*) nado-morto
stilted /'stɪltɪd/ *a* afetado, (*P*) afectado
stilts /stɪlts/ *npl* pernas de pau *fpl*, (*P*) andas *fpl*
stimul|ate /'stɪmjʊleɪt/ *vt* estimular. **~ant** *n* estimulante *m*. **~ating** *a* estimulante. **~ation** /-'leɪʃn/ *n* estimulação *f*
stimulus /'stɪmjʊləs/ *n* (*pl* **-li** /-laɪ/) (*spur*) estímulo *m*
sting /stɪŋ/ *n* picada *f*; (*organ*) ferrão *m* □ *vt* (*pt* **stung**) picar □ *vi* picar, arder. **~ing nettle** urtiga *f*
stingy /'stɪndʒɪ/ *a* (**-ier**, **-iest**) pão-duro *m*, sovina (**with** com)
stink /stɪŋk/ *n* fedor *m*, catinga *f*, mau cheiro *m* □ *vi* (*pt* **stank** *or* **stunk**, *pp* **stunk**) **~ (of)** cheirar (a), tresandar (a) □ *vt* **~ out** (*room etc*) empestar. **~ing** *a* malcheiroso. **~ing rich** (*sl*) podre de rico (*colloq*)
stinker /'stɪŋkə(r)/ *n* (*sl: person*) cara *m* horroroso (*colloq*); (*sl: sth difficult*) osso *m* duro de moer
stint /stɪnt/ *vi* **~ on** poupar em, apertar em □ *n* (*work*) tarefa *f*, parte *f*, quinhão *m*
stipulat|e /'stɪpjʊleɪt/ *vt* estipular. **~ion** /-'leɪʃn/ *n* condição *f*, estipulação *f*
stir /stɜ:r/ *vt/i* (*pt* **stirred**) (*move*) mexer(-se), mover(-se); (*excite*) excitar; (*a liquid*) mexer □ *n* agitação *f*, rebuliço *m*. **~ up** (*trouble etc*) provocar, fomentar. **~ring** *a* excitante
stirrup /'stɪrəp/ *n* estribo *m*
stitch /stɪtʃ/ *n* (*in sewing; med*) ponto *m*; (*in knitting*) malha *f*, ponto *m*; (*pain*) pontada *f* □ *vt* coser. **in ~es** (*colloq*) às gargalhadas (*colloq*)
stoat /stəʊt/ *n* arminho *m*
stock /stɒk/ *n* (*comm*) estoque *m*, (*P*) stock *m*, provisão *f*; (*finance*) valores *mpl*, fundos *mpl*; (*family*) família *f*, estirpe *f*; (*culin*) caldo *m*; (*flower*) goivo *m* □ *a* (*goods*) corrente, comum; (*hackneyed*) estereotipado □ *vt* (*shop etc*) abastecer, fornecer; (*sell*) vender □ *vi* **~ up with** abastecer-se de. **in ~** em estoque. **out of ~** esgotado. **take ~** (*fig*) fazer um balanço. **~-car** *n* stock-car *m*. **~-cube** *n* cubo *m* de caldo. **~ market** Bolsa *f* (de Valores). **~-still** *a*, *adv* imóvel. **~-taking** *n* (*comm*) inventário *m*
stockbroker /'stɒkbrəʊkə(r)/ *n* corretor *m* da Bolsa
stocking /'stɒkɪŋ/ *n* meia *f*
stockist /'stɒkɪst/ *n* armazenista *m*
stockpile /'stɒkpaɪl/ *n* reservas *fpl* □ *vt* acumular reservas de, estocar
stocky /'stɒkɪ/ *a* (**-ier**, **-iest**) atarracado
stodg|e /stɒdʒ/ *n* (*colloq*) comida *f* pesada (*colloq*). **~y** *a* (*of food, book*) pesado, maçudo
stoic /'stəʊɪk/ *n* estóico *m*. **~al** *a* estoico. **~ism** /-sɪzəm/ *n* estoicismo *m*
stoke /stəʊk/ *vt* (*boiler, fire*) alimentar, carregar
stole[1] /stəʊl/ *n* (*garment*) estola *m*
stole[2], **stolen** /stəʊl, 'stəʊlən/ *see* **steal**
stomach /'stʌmək/ *n* estômago *m*; (*abdomen*) barriga *f*, ventre *m* □ *vt* (*put up with*) aturar. **~-ache** *n* dor *f* de estômago; (*abdomen*) dores *fpl* de barriga
ston|e /stəʊn/ *n* pedra *f*; (*pebble*) seixo *m*; (*in fruit*) caroço *m*; (*weight*) 6,348 kg; (*med*) cálculo *m*, pedra *f* □ *vt* apedrejar; (*fruit*) tirar o caroço de. **within a ~e's throw (of)** muito perto (de). **~e-cold** gelado. **~e-deaf** totalmente surdo. **~ed** *a* (*colloq: drunk*) bebão *m* (*colloq*); (*colloq: drugged*) drogado. **~y** *a* pedregoso. **~y-broke** *a* (*sl*) duro, liso (*sl*)
stonemason /'stəʊnmeɪsn/ *n* pedreiro *m*
stood /stʊd/ *see* **stand**
stooge /stu:dʒ/ *n* (*colloq: actor*) ajudante *mf*; (*colloq: puppet*) antoche *m*, (*P*) comparsa *mf*, parceiro *m*
stool /stu:l/ *n* banco *m*, tamborete *m*
stoop /stu:p/ *vi* (*bend*) curvar-se, baixar-se; (*condescend*) condescender, dignar-se. **~ to sth** rebaixar-se para (fazer) alg coisa □ *n* **walk with a ~** andar curvado
stop /stɒp/ *vt/i* (*pt* **stopped**) parar; (*prevent*) impedir (**from** de); (*hole, leak etc*) tapar, vedar; (*pain, noise etc*) parar; (*colloq: stay*) ficar □ *n* (*of bus*) parada *f*, (*P*) paragem *f*; (*full stop*) ponto *m* final. **put a ~ to** pôr fim a. **~ it!** acabe logo com isso! **~-over** *n* (*break in journey*) parada *f*, (*P*) paragem *f*; (*port of call*) escala *f*. **~press** *n* notícia *f* de última hora. **~-watch** *n* cronômetro *m*, (*P*) cronómetro *m*
stopgap /'stɒpgæp/ *n* substituto *m* provisório, tapa-buracos *mpl* (*colloq*) □ *a* temporário
stoppage /'stopɪdʒ/ *n* parada *f*, (*P*) paragem *f*; (*of work*) paralisação *f* de trabalho; (*of pay*) suspensão *f*
stopper /'stɒpə(r)/ *n* rolha *f*, tampa *f*
storage /'stɔ:rɪdʒ/ *n* (*of goods, food etc*) armazenagem *f*, armazenamento *m*. **in cold ~** em frigorífico
store /stɔ:(r)/ *n* reserva *f*, provisão *f*; (*warehouse*) armazém *m*, entreposto *m*; (*shop*) grande armazém *m*; (*Amer*) loja *f*; (*in computer*) memória *f* □ *vt* (*for future*) pôr de reserva, juntar, fazer provisão de; (*in warehouse*) armazenar.

be in ~ estar guardado. **have in ~ for** reservar para. **set ~ by** dar valor a. **~-room** *n* depósito *m*, almortarifado *m*, (*P*) armazém *m*

storey /'stɔ:rɪ/ *n* (*pl* **-eys**) andar *m*

stork /stɔ:k/ *n* cegonha *f*

storm /stɔ:m/ *n* tempestade *f* □ *vt* tomar de assalto □ *vi* enfurecer-se. **a ~ in a teacup** uma tempestade num copo de água. **~y** *a* tempestuoso

story /'stɔ:rɪ/ *n* estória *f*, (*P*) história *f*; (*in press*) artigo *m*, matéria *f*; (*Amer: storey*) andar *m*; (*colloq: lie*) cascata *f*, (*P*) peta *f*. **~-teller** *n* contador *m* de estórias, (*P*) histórias

stout /staʊt/ *a* (**-er, -est**) (*fat*) gordo, corpulento; (*strong, thick*) resistente, sólido, grosso; (*brave*) resoluto □ *n* cerveja *f* preta forte

stove /stəʊv/ *n* (*for cooking*) fogão *m* (de cozinha)

stow /stəʊ/ *vt* **~ (away)** (*put away*) guardar, arrumar; (*hide*) esconder □ *vi* **~ away** viajar clandestinamente

stowaway /'stəʊəweɪ/ *n* passageiro *m* clandestino

straddle /'strædl/ *vt* (*sit*) escarranchar-se em, montar; (*stand*) pôr-se de pernas abertas sobre

straggle /'strægl/ *vi* (*lag behind*) desgarrar-se, ficar para trás; (*spread*) estender-se desordenadamente. **~r** /-ə(r)/ *n* retardatário *m*

straight /streɪt/ *a* (**-er, -est**) direito; (*tidy*) em ordem; (*frank*) franco, direto, (*P*) directo; (*of hair*) liso; (*of drink*) puro □ *adv* (*in straight line*) reto; (*directly*) direito, direto, (*P*) directo, diretamente, (*P*) directamente □ *n* linha *f* reta, (*P*) recta. **~ ahead** *or* **on** (sempre) em frente. **~ away** logo, imediatamente. **go ~** viver honestamente. **keep a ~ face** não se desmanchar, manter um ar sério

straighten /'streɪtn/ *vt* endireitar; (*tidy*) arrumar, pôr em ordem

straightforward /streɪt'fɔ:wəd/ *a* franco, sincero; (*easy*) simples

strain[1] /streɪn/ *n* (*breed*) raça *f*; (*streak*) tendência *f*, veia *f*

strain[2] /streɪn/ *vt* (*rope*) esticar, puxar; (*tire*) cansar; (*filter*) filtrar, passar; (*vegetables, tea etc*) coar; (*med*) distender, torcer; (*fig*) forçar, pôr à prova □ *vi* esforçar-se □ *n* tensão *f*; (*fig: effort*) esforço *m*; (*med*) distensão *f*. **~s** (*music*) melodias *fpl*. **~ one's ears** apurar o ouvido. **~ed** *a* forçado; (*relations*) tenso. **~er** *n* coador *m*, (*P*) passador *m*

strait /streɪt/ *n* estreito *m*. **~s** estreito *m*; (*fig*) apuros *mpl*, dificuldades *fpl*.

~-jacket *n* camisa-de-força *f*. **~-laced** *a* severo, puritano

strand /strænd/ *n* (*thread*) fio *m*; (*lock of hair*) mecha *f*, madeixa *f*

stranded /'strændɪd/ *a* (*person*) em dificuldades, deixado para trás, abandonado

strange /streɪndʒ/ *a* (**-er, -est**) estranho. **~ly** *adv* estranhamente. **~ness** *n* estranheza *f*

stranger /'streɪndʒə(r)/ *n* estranho *m*, desconhecido *m*

strangle /'strængl/ *vt* estrangular, sufocar

stranglehold /'strænglhəʊld/ *n* **have a ~ on** ter domínio sobre

strangulation /strængjʊ'leɪʃn/ *n* estrangulamento *m*

strap /stræp/ *n* (*of leather etc*) correia *f*; (*of dress*) alça *f*; (*of watch*) pulseira *f* com correia □ *vt* (*pt* **strapped**) prender com correia

strapping /'stræpɪŋ/ *a* robusto, grande

strata /'streɪtə/ *see* **stratum**

stratagem /'strætədʒəm/ *n* estratagema *m*

strategic /strə'ti:dʒɪk/ *a* estratégico; (*of weapons*) de longo alcance

strategy /'strætədʒɪ/ *n* estratégia *f*

stratum /'stra:təm/ *n* (*pl* **strata**) estrato *m*, camada *f*

straw /strɔ:/ *n* palha *f*; (*for drinking*) canudo *m*, (*P*) palhinha *f*. **the last ~** a última gota *f*

strawberry /'strɔ:brɪ/ *n* (*fruit*) morango *m*; (*plant*) morangueiro *m*

stray /streɪ/ *vi* (*deviate from path etc*) extraviar-se, desencaminhar-se, afastar-se (**from** de); (*lose one's way*) perder-se; (*wander*) vagar, errar □ *a* perdido, extraviado; (*isolated*) isolado, raro, esporádico □ *n* animal *m* perdido *or* vadio

streak /stri:k/ *n* risca *f*, lista *f*; (*strain*) veia *f*; (*period*) período *m*. **~ of lightning** relâmpago *m* □ *vt* listrar, riscar □ *vi* ir como um raio. **~er** *n* (*colloq*) pessoa *f* que corre nua em lugares públicos. **~y** *a* listrado, riscado. **~y bacon** toucinho *m* entremeado com gordura

stream /stri:m/ *n* riacho *m*, córrego *m*, regato *m*; (*current*) corrente *f*; (*fig: flow*) jorro *m*, torrente *f*; (*schol*) nível *m*, grupo *m* □ *vi* correr; (*of banner, hair*) flutuar; (*sweat*) escorrer, pingar

streamer /'stri:mə(r)/ *n* (*of paper*) serpentina *f*; (*flag*) flâmula *f*, bandeirola *f*

streamline /'stri:mlaɪn/ *vt* dar forma aerodinâmica a; (*fig*) racionalizar. **~d** *a* (*shape*) aerodinâmico

street /stri:t/ *n* rua *f.* **the man in the ~** (*fig*) o homem da rua. **~ lamp** poste *m* de iluminação

streetcar /'stri:tka:(r)/ *n* (*Amer*) bonde *m*, (*P*) carro *m* eléctrico

strength /streŋθ/ *n* força *f*; (*of wall*) solidez *f*; (*of fabric etc*) resistência *f.* **on the ~ of** à base de, em virtude de

strengthen /'streŋθn/ *vt* fortificar, fortalecer, reforçar

strenuous /'strenjʊəs/ *a* enérgico; (*arduous*) árduo, estrênuo, (*P*) estrénuo; (*tiring*) fatigante, esgotante. **~ly** *adv* esforçadamente, energicamente

stress /stres/ *n* acento *m*; (*pressure*) pressão *f*, tensão *f*; (*med*) stress *m* □ *vt* acentuar, sublinhar; (*sound*) acentuar. **~ful** *a* estressante

stretch /stretʃ/ *vt* (*pull taut*) esticar; (*arm, leg, neck*) estender, esticar; (*clothes*) alargar; (*truth*) forçar, torcer □ *vi* estender-se; (*after sleep etc*) espreguiçar-se; (*of clothes*) alargar-se □ *n* extensão *f*, trecho *m*; (*period*) período *m*; (*of road*) troço *m* □ *a* (*of fabric*) com elasticidade. **at a ~** sem parar. **~ one's legs** esticar as pernas

stretcher /'stretʃə(r)/ *n* maca *f*, padiola *f.* **~-bearer** *n* padioleiro *m*, (*P*) maqueiro *m*

strew /stru:/ *vt* (*pt* **strewed**, *pp* **strewed** *or* **strewn**) (*scatter*) espalhar; (*cover*) juncar, cobrir

stricken /'strɪkən/ *a* **~ with** atacado *or* acometido de

strict /strɪkt/ *a* (**-er, -est**) estrito, rigoroso. **~ly** *adv* estritamente. **~ly speaking** a rigor. **~ness** *n* severidade *f*, rigor *m*

stride /straɪd/ *vi* (*pt* **strode**, *pp* **stridden**) caminhar a passos largos □ *n* passada *f.* **make great ~s** (*fig*) fazer grandes progressos. **take sth in one's ~** fazer alg coisa sem problemas

strident /'straɪdnt/ *a* estridente

strife /straɪf/ *n* conflito *m* , dissensão *f*, luta *f*

strike /straɪk/ *vt* (*pt* **struck**) bater (em); (*blow*) dar; (*match*) riscar, acender; (*gold etc*) descobrir; (*of clock*) soar, dar, bater (horas); (*of lightning*) atingir □ *vi* fazer greve; (*attack*) atacar □ *n* (*of workers*) greve *f*; (*mil*) ataque *m*; (*find*) descoberta *f.* **on ~** em greve. **~ a bargain** fechar negócio. **~ off** *or* **out** riscar. **~ up** (*mus*) começar a tocar; (*friendship*) travar

striker /'straɪkə(r)/ *n* grevista *mf*

striking /'straɪkɪŋ/ *a* notável, impressionante; (*attractive*) atraente

string /strɪŋ/ *n* corda *f*, fio *m*; (*of violin, racket etc*) corda *f*; (*of pearls*) fio *m*; (*of onions, garlic*) réstia *f*; (*of lies etc*) série *f*; (*row*) fila *f* □ *vt* (*pt* **strung**) (*thread*) enfiar. **pull ~s** usar pistolão, (*P*) puxar os cordelinhos. **~ out** espaçar-se. **~ed** *a* (*instrument*) de cordas. **~y** *a* filamentoso, fibroso; (*meat*) com nervos

stringent /'strɪndʒənt/ *a* rigoroso, estrito

strip[1] /strɪp/ *vt*/*i* (*pt* **stripped**) (*undress*) despir(-se); (*machine*) desmontar; (*deprive*) despojar, privar. **~per** *n* artista *mf* de strip-tease; (*solvent*) removedor *m*

strip[2] /strɪp/ *n* tira *f*; (*of land*) faixa *f.* **comic ~** história *f* em quadrinhos, (*P*) banda *f* desenhada. **~ light** tubo *m* de luz fluorescente

stripe /straɪp/ *n* risca *f*, lista *f*, barra *f.* **~d** *a* listrado, com listras

strive /straɪv/ *vi* (*pt* **strove**, *pp* **striven**) esforçar-se (**to** por)

strode /strəʊd/ *see* **stride**

stroke[1] /strəʊk/ *n* golpe *m*; (*of pen*) penada *f*, (*P*) traço *m*; (*in swimming*) braçada *f*; (*in rowing*) remada *f*; (*med*) ataque *m*, congestão *f.* **~ of genius** rasgo *m* de genialidade. **~ of luck** golpe *m* de sorte

stroke[2] /strəʊk/ *vt* (*with hand*) acariciar, fazer festas em

stroll /strəʊl/ *vi* passear, dar uma volta □ *n* volta *f*, (*P*) giro *m*. **~ in**/*etc* entrar/*etc* tranquilamente

strong /strɒŋ/ *a* (**-er, -est**) forte; (*shoes, fabric etc*) resistente. **be a hundred**/*etc* **~** ser em número de cem/*etc*. **~-box** *n* cofre-forte *m*. **~ language** linguagem *f* grosseira, palavrões *mpl*. **~-minded** *a* resoluto, firme. **~-room** *n* casa-forte *f.* **~ly** *adv* (*greatly*) fortemente, grandemente; (*with energy*) com força; (*deeply*) profundamente

stronghold /'strɒŋhəʊld/ *n* fortaleza *f*; (*fig*) baluarte *m*, bastião *m*

strove /strəʊv/ *see* **strive**

struck /strʌk/ *see* **strike** □ *a* **~ on** (*sl*) apaixonado por

structur|e /'strʌktʃə(r)/ *n* estrutura *f*; (*of building etc*) edifício *m*, construção *f.* **~al** *a* estrutural, de estrutura, de construção

struggle /'strʌgl/ *vi* (*to get free*) debater-se; (*contend*) lutar; (*strive*) esforçar-se (**to, for** por) □ *n* luta *f*; (*effort*) esforço *m*. **have a ~ to** ter dificuldade em. **~ to one's feet** levantar-se a custo

strum /strʌm/ *vt* (*pt* **strummed**) (*banjo etc*) dedilhar

strung /strʌŋ/ *see* **string**

strut /strʌt/ *n* (*support*) suporte *m*, escora *f* □ *vi* (*pt* **strutted**) (*walk*) pavonear-se

stub /stʌb/ *n* (*of pencil, cigarette*) ponta *f*; (*of tree*) cepo *m*, toco *m*; (*counterfoil*) talão *m*, canhoto *m* □ *vt* (*pt* **stubbed**) **~ one's toe** dar uma topada. **~ out** esmagar

stubble /'stʌbl/ *n* (*on chin*) barba *f* por fazer; (*of crop*) restolho *m*

stubborn /'stʌbən/ *a* teimoso, obstinado. **~ly** *adv* obstinadamente, teimosamente. **~ness** *n* teimosia *f*, obstinação *f*

stubby /'stʌbɪ/ *a* (**-ier, -iest**) (*finger*) curto e grosso; (*person*) atarracado

stuck /stʌk/ *see* **stick**[2] □ *a* emperrado. **~-up** *a* (*colloq: snobbish*) convencido, esnobe

stud[1] /stʌd/ *n* tacha *f*; (*for collar*) botão *m* de colarinho □ *vt* (*pt* **studded**) enfeitar com tachas. **~ded with** salpicado de

stud[2] /stʌd/ *n* (*horses*) haras *m*. **~(-farm)** *n* coudelaria *f*. **~ (-horse)** *n* garanhão *m*

student /'stju:dnt/ *n* (*univ*) estudante *mf*, aluno *m*; (*schol*) aluno *m* □ *a* (*life, residence*) universitário

studied /'stʌdɪd/ *a* estudado

studio /'stju:dɪəʊ/ *n* (*pl* **-os**) estúdio *m*. **~ flat** estúdio *m*

studious /'stju:dɪəs/ *a* (*person*) estudioso; (*deliberate*) estudado. **~ly** *adv* (*carefully*) cuidadosamente

study /'stʌdɪ/ *n* estudo *m*; (*office*) escritório *m* □ *vt/i* estudar

stuff /stʌf/ *n* substância *f*, matéria *f*; (*sl: things*) coisa(s) *f* (*pl*) □ *vt* encher; (*animal*) empalhar; (*cram*) apinhar, encher ao máximo; (*culin*) rechear; (*block up*) entupir; (*put*) enfiar, meter. **~ing** *n* enchimento *m*, (*culin*) recheio *m*

stuffy /'stʌfɪ/ *a* (**-ier, -iest**) abafado, mal arejado; (*dull*) enfadonho

stumbl|e /'stʌmbl/ *vi* tropeçar. **~e across** *or* **on** dar com, encontrar por acaso, topar com. **~ing-block** *n* obstáculo *m*

stump /stʌmp/ *n* (*of tree*) cepo *m*, toco *m*; (*of limb*) coto *m*; (*of pencil, cigar*) ponta *f*

stumped /stʌmpt/ *a* (*colloq: baffled*) atrapalhado, perplexo

stun /stʌn/ *vt* (*pt* **stunned**) aturdir, estontear

stung /stʌŋ/ *see* **sting**

stunk /stʌŋk/ *see* **stink**

stunning /'stʌnɪŋ/ *a* atordoador; (*colloq: delightful*) fantástico, sensacional

stunt[1] /stʌnt/ *vt* (*growth*) atrofiar. **~ed** *a* atrofiado

stunt[2] /stʌnt/ *n* (*feat*) façanha *f*, proeza *f*; (*trick*) truque *m*; (*aviat*) acrobacia *f* aérea. **~ man** *n* dublê *m*, (*P*) duplo *m*

stupefy /'stju:pɪfaɪ/ *vt* estupefazer, (*P*) estupeficar

stupendous /stju:'pendəs/ *a* estupendo, assombroso, prodigioso

stupid /'stju:pɪd/ *a* estúpido, obtuso. **~ity** /-'pɪdətɪ/ *n* estupidez *f*. **~ly** *adv* estupidamente

stupor /'stju:pə(r)/ *n* estupor *m*, torpor *m*

sturdy /'stɜ:dɪ/ *a* (**-ier, -iest**) robusto, vigoroso, forte

stutter /'stʌtə(r)/ *vi* gaguejar □ *n* gagueira *f*, (*P*) gaguez *f*

sty /staɪ/ *n* (*pigsty*) pocilga *f*, chiqueiro *m*

stye /staɪ/ *n* (*on eye*) terçol *m*, terçolho *m*

styl|e /staɪl/ *n* estilo *m*; (*fashion*) moda *f*; (*kind*) gênero *m*, (*P*) género *m*, tipo *m*; (*pattern*) feitio *m*, modelo *m* □ *vt* (*design*) desenhar, criar. **in ~e** (*live*) em grande estilo; (*do things*) com classe. **~e sb's hair** fazer um penteado em alguém. **~ist** *n* (*of hair*) cabeleireiro *m*

stylish /'staɪlɪʃ/ *a* elegante, na moda

stylized /'staɪlaɪzd/ *a* estilizado

stylus /'staɪləs/ *n* (*pl* **-uses**) (*of record-player*) agulha *f*, safira *f*

suave /swa:v/ *a* polido, de fala mansa, (*P*) melífluo

sub- /sʌb/ *pref* sub-

subconscious /sʌb'kɒnʃəs/ *a* & *n* subconsciente (*m*)

subcontract /sʌbkən'trækt/ *vt* dar de subempreitada

subdivide /sʌbdɪ'vaɪd/ *vt* subdividir

subdue /səb'dju:/ *vt* (*enemy, feeling*) dominar, subjugar; (*sound, voice*) abrandar. **~d** *a* (*weak*) submisso; (*quiet*) recolhido; (*light*) velado

subject[1] /'sʌbdʒɪkt/ *a* (*state etc*) dominado □ *n* sujeito *m*; (*schol, univ*) disciplina *f*, matéria *f*; (*citizen*) súdito *m*. **~-matter** *n* conteúdo *m*, tema *m*, assunto *m*. **~ to** sujeito a

subject[2] /səb'dʒekt/ *vt* submeter. **~ion** /-kʃn/ *n* submissão *f*

subjective /sʌb'dʒektɪv/ *a* subjetivo, (*P*) subjectivo

subjunctive /səb'dʒʌŋktɪv/ *a* & *n* subjuntivo (*m*), (*P*) conjuntivo (*m*)

sublime /sə'blaɪm/ *a* sublime

submarine /sʌbmə'ri:n/ *n* submarino *m*

submerge /səb'mɜ:dʒ/ *vt* submergir □ *vi* submergir, mergulhar

submissive /səb'mɪsɪv/ *a* submisso

submi|t /səb'mɪt/ *vt/i* (*pt* **submitted**) submeter(-se) (**to a**); (*jur: argue*) alegar. **~ssion** /-'mɪʃn/ *n* submissão *f*

subnormal /sʌb'nɔ:ml/ *a* subnormal; (*temperature*) abaixo do normal

subordinate[1] /sə'bɔ:dɪnət/ *a* subordinado, subalterno; (*gram*) subordinado □ *n* subordinado *m*, subalterno *m*

subordinate[2] /sə'bɔ:dɪneɪt/ *vt* subordinar (**to** a)

subpoena /səb'pi:nə/ *n* (*pl* **-as**) (*jur*) citação *f*, intimação *f*

subscribe /səb'skraɪb/ *vt/i* subscrever, contribuir (**to** para). ~ **to** (*theory, opinion*) subscrever, aceitar; (*newspaper*) assinar. ~**r** /-ə(r)/ *n* subscritor *m*, assinante *m*

subscription /səb'skrɪpʃn/ *n* subscrição *f*; (*to newspaper*) assinatura *f*

subsequent /'sʌbsɪkwənt/ *a* subseqüente, (*P*) subsequente, posterior. ~**ly** *adv* subsequentemente, a seguir, posteriormente

subservient /səb'sɜ:vɪənt/ *a* servil, subserviente

subside /səb'saɪd/ *vi* (*flood, noise etc*) baixar; (*land*) ceder, afundar; (*wind, storm, excitement*) abrandar. ~**nce** /-əns/ *n* (*of land*) afundamento *m*

subsidiary /səb'sɪdɪərɪ/ *a* subsidiário □ *n* (*comm*) filial *f*, sucursal *f*

subsid|y /'sʌbsədɪ/ *n* subsídio *m*, subvenção *f*. ~**ize** /-ɪdaɪz/ *vt* subsidiar, subvencionar

subsist /səb'sɪst/ *vi* subsistir. ~ **on** viver de. ~**ence** *n* subsistência *f*. ~**ence allowance** ajudas *fpl* de custo

substance /'sʌbstəns/ *n* substância *f*

substandard /sʌb'stændəd/ *a* de qualidade inferior

substantial /səb'stænʃl/ *a* substancial. ~**ly** *adv* substancialmente

substantiate /səb'stænʃɪeɪt/ *vt* comprovar, fundamentar

substitut|e /'sʌbstɪtju:t/ *n* (*person*) substituto *m*, suplente *mf* (**for** de); (*thing*) substituto *m* (**for** de) □ *vt* substituir (**for** por). ~**ion** /-'tju:ʃn/ *n* substituição *f*

subterfuge /'sʌbtəfju:dʒ/ *n* subterfúgio *m*

subtitle /'sʌbtaɪtl/ *n* subtitulo *m*

subtle /'sʌtl/ *a* (**-er, -est**) sutil, (*P*) subtil. ~**ty** *n* sutileza *f*, (*P*) subtileza *f*

subtotal /'sʌbtəʊtl/ *n* soma *f* parcial

subtract /səb'trækt/ *vt* subtrair, diminuir. ~**ion** /-kʃn/ *n* subtração *f*, diminuição *f*

suburb /'sʌbɜ:b/ *n* subúrbio *m*, arredores *mpl*. ~**an** /sə'bɜ:bən/ *a* dos subúrbios, suburbano. ~**ia** /sə'bɜ:bɪə/ *n* (*pej*) os arredores

subver|t /səb'vɜ:t/ *vt* subverter. ~**sion** /-ʃn/ *n* subverção *f*. ~**sive** /-sɪv/ *a* subversivo

subway /'sʌbweɪ/ *n* passagem *f* subterrânea; (*Amer: underground*) metropolitano *m*

succeed /sək'si:d/ *vi* ser bem sucedido, ter êxito. ~ **in doing sth** conseguir fazer alg coisa □ *vt* (*follow*) suceder a. ~**ing** *a* seguinte, sucessivo

success /sək'ses/ *n* sucesso *m*, êxito *m*

succession /sək'seʃn/ *n* sucessão *f*; (*series*) série *f*. **in** ~ seguidos, consecutivos

successive /sək'sesɪv/ *a* sucessivo, consecutivo

successor /sək'sesə(r)/ *n* sucessor *m*

succinct /sək'sɪŋkt/ *a* sucinto

succulent /'sʌkjʊlənt/ *a* suculento

succumb /sə'kʌm/ *vi* sucumbir

such /sʌtʃ/ *a & pron* tal, semelhante, assim; (*so much*) tanto □ *adv* tanto. ~ **a book**/*etc* un tal livro/*etc or* um livro/*etc* assim. ~ **books**/*etc* tais livros/*etc or* livros/*etc* assim. ~ **courage**/ *etc* tanta coragem/*etc*. ~ **a big house** uma casa tão grande. **as** ~ como tal. ~ **as** como, tal como. **there's no** ~ **thing** uma coisa dessa não existe. ~**-and-such** *a & pron* tal e tal

suck /sʌk/ *vt* chupar; (*breast*) mamar. ~ **in** *or* **up** (*absorb*) absorver, aspirar; (*engulf*) tragar. ~ **up to** puxar o saco a (*colloq*). ~ **one's thumb** chupar o dedo. ~**er** *n* (*sl: greenhorn*) trouxa *mf* (*colloq*); (*bot*) broto *m*

suckle /'sʌkl/ *vt* amamentar, dar de mamar a

suction /'sʌkʃn/ *n* sucção *f*

sudden /'sʌdn/ *a* súbito, repentino. **all of a** ~ de repente, de súbito. ~**ly** *adv* subitamente, repentinamente. ~**ness** *n* subitaneidade *f*, brusquidão *f*

suds /sʌdz/ *npl* espuma *f* de sabão; (*soapy water*) água *f* de sabão

sue /su:/ *vt* (*pres p* **suing**) processar

suede /sweɪd/ *n* camurça *f*

suet /'su:ɪt/ *n* sebo *m*

suffer /'sʌfə(r)/ *vt/i* sofrer; (*tolerate*) tolerar, suportar. ~**er** *n* sofredor *m*, o que sofre; (*patient*) doente *mf*, vítima *f*. ~**ing** *n* sufrimento *m*

suffice /sə'faɪs/ *vi* bastar, chegar, ser suficiente

sufficien|t /sə'fɪʃnt/ *a* suficiente, bastante. ~**cy** *n* suficiência *f*, quantidade *f* suficiente. ~**tly** *adv* suficientemente

suffix /'sʌfɪx/ *n* sufixo *m*

suffocat|e /'sʌfəkeɪt/ *vt/i* sufocar. ~**ion** /-'keɪʃn/ *n* sufocação *f*, asfixia *f*. ~**ing** *a* sufocante, asfixiante

sugar /'ʃʊgə(r)/ *n* açucar *m* □ *vt* adoçar, pôr açúcar em. ~**-bowl** *n* açucareiro *m*.

~-lump *n* torrão *m* de açúcar, (*P*) quadradinho *m* de açúcar. **brown ~** açúcar *m* preto, (*P*) açúcar *m* amarelo. **~y** *a* açucarado; (*fig: too sweet*) delicodoce

suggest /sə'dʒest/ *vt* sugerir. **~ion** /-tʃn/ *n* sugestão *f*. **~ive** *a* sugestivo; (*improper*) brejeiro, picante. **be ~ive of** sugerir, fazer lembrar

suicid|e /'su:ɪsaɪd/ *n* suicídio *m*. **commit ~e** suicidar-se. **~al** /-'saɪdl/ *a* suicida

suit /su:t/ *n* terno *m*, (*P*) fato *m*; (*woman's*) costume *m*, (*P*) saia-casaco *m*; (*cards*) naipe *m* □ *vt* convir a; (*of garment, style*) ficar bem em; (*adapt*) adaptar. **follow ~** (*fig*) seguir o exemplo. **~-ability** *n* (*of action*) conveniência *f*, oportunidade *f*; (*of candidate*) aptidão *f*. **~able** *a* conveniente, apropriado (**for** para). **~ably** *adv* convenientemente. **~ed** *a* **be ~ed to** ser feito para, servir para. **be well ~ed** (*matched*) combinar-se bem; (*of people*) ser o ideal

suitcase /'su:tkeɪs/ *n* mala *f* (de viagem)

suite /swi:t/ *n* (*of rooms; mus*) suíte *f*, (*P*) suite *f*; (*of furniture*) mobília *f*

suitor /'su:tə(r)/ *n* pretendente *m*

sulk /sʌlk/ *vi* amuar, ficar emburrado. **~y** *a* amuado, emburrado (*colloq*)

sullen /'sʌlən/ *a* carrancudo

sulphur /'sʌlfə(r)/ *n* enxofre *m*. **~ic** /-'fjʊərɪk/ *a* **~ic acid** ácido *m* sulfúrico

sultan /'sʌltən/ *n* sultão *m*

sultana /sʌl'ta:nə/ *n* (*fruit*) passa *f* branca, (*P*) sultana *f*

sultry /'sʌltrɪ/ *a* (**-ier, -iest**) abafado, opressivo; (*fig*) sensual

sum /sʌm/ *n* soma *f*; (*amount of money*) soma *f*, quantia *f*, importância *f*; (*in arithmetic*) conta *f* □ *vt* (*pt* **summed**) somar. **~ up** recapitular, resumir; (*assess*) avaliar, medir

summar|y /'sʌmərɪ/ *n* sumário *m*, resumo *m* □ *a* sumário. **~ize** *vt* resumir

summer /'sʌmə(r)/ *n* verão *m*, estio *m* □ *a* de verão. **~-time** *n* verão *m*, época *f* de verão. **~y** *a* estival, próprio de verão

summit /'sʌmɪt/ *n* cume *m*, cimo *m*. **~ conference** (*pol*) conferência *f* de cúpula, (*P*) reunião *f* de cimeira

summon /'sʌmən/ *vt* mandar chamar; (*to meeting*) convocar. **~ up** (*strength, courage etc*) chamar a si, fazer apelo a

summons /'sʌmənz/ *n* (*jur*) citação *f*, intimação *f* □ *vt* citar, intimar

sump /sʌmp/ *n* (*auto*) cárter *m*

sumptuous /'sʌmptʃʊəs/ *a* suntuoso, (*P*) sumptuoso, luxuoso

sun /sʌn/ *n* sol *m* □ *vt* (*pt* **sunned**) **~ o.s.** aquecer-se ao sol. **~glasses** *npl* óculos *mpl* de sol. **~-roof** *n* teto *m* solar. **~-tan** *n* bronzeado *m*. **~-tanned** *a* bronzeado. **~-tan oil** *n* óleo *m* de bronzear

sunbathe /'sʌnbeɪð/ *vi* tomar um banho de sol

sunburn /'sʌnbɜ:n/ *n* queimadura *f* de sol. **~t** *a* queimado pelo sol

Sunday /'sʌndɪ/ *n* domingo *m*. **~ school** catecismo *m*

sundial /'sʌndaɪəl/ *n* relógio *m* de sol

sundown /'sʌndaʊn/ *n* = **sunset**

sundr|y /'sʌndrɪ/ *a* vários, diversos. **~ies** *npl* artigos *mpl* diversos. **all and ~y** todo o mundo

sunflower /'sʌnflaʊə(r)/ *n* girassol *m*

sung /sʌŋ/ *see* **sing**

sunk /sʌŋk/ *see* **sink**

sunken /'sʌŋkən/ *a* (*ship etc*) afundado; (*eyes*) fundo

sunlight /'sʌnlaɪt/ *n* luz *f* do sol, sol *m*

sunny /'sʌnɪ/ *a* (**-ier, -iest**) (*room, day etc*) ensolarado

sunrise /'sʌnraɪz/ *n* nascer *m* do sol

sunset /'sʌnset/ *n* pôr *m* do sol

sunshade /'sʌnʃeɪd/ *n* (*awning*) toldo *m*; (*parasol*) pára-sol *m*, (*P*) guarda-sol *m*

sunshine /'sʌnʃaɪn/ *n* sol *m*, luz *f* do sol

sunstroke /'sʌnstrəʊk/ *n* (*med*) insolação *f*

super /'su:pə(r)/ *a* (*colloq: excellent*) formidável

superb /su:'pɜ:b/ *a* soberbo, esplêndido

supercilious /su:pə'sɪlɪəs/ *a* (*haughty*) altivo; (*disdainful*) desdenhoso

superficial /su:pə'fɪʃl/ *a* superficial. **~ity** /-ɪ'ælətɪ/ *n* superficialidade *f*. **~ly** *adv* superficialmente

superfluous /su'pɜ:flʊəs/ *a* supérfluo

superhuman /su:pə'hju:mən/ *a* sobre-humano

superimpose /su:pərɪm'pəʊz/ *vt* sobrepor (**on** a)

superintendent /su:pərɪn'tendənt/ *n* superintendente *m*; (*of police*) comissário *m*, chefe *m* de polícia

superior /su:'pɪərɪə(r)/ *a* & *n* superior (*m*). **~ity** /-'ɒrətɪ/ *n* superioridade *f*

superlative /su:'pɜ:lətɪv/ *a* supremo, superlativo □ *n* (*gram*) superlativo *m*

supermarket /'su:pəma:kɪt/ *n* supermercado *m*

supernatural /su:pə'nætʃrəl/ *a* sobrenatural

superpower /'su:pəpaʊə(r)/ *n* superpotência *f*

supersede /su:pə'si:d/ *vt* suplantar, substituir

supersonic /su:pə'sɒnɪk/ *a* supersônico, (*P*) supersónico

superstiti|on /su:pə'stɪʃn/ *n* superstição *f*. **~ous** *a* /-'stɪʃəs/ supersticioso

superstore /'su:pəstɔ:(r)/ *n* hipermercado *m*

supertanker /'su:pətæŋkə(r)/ *n* superpetroleiro *m*

supervis|e /'su:pəvaɪz/ *vt* supervisar, fiscalizar. **~ion** /-'vɪʒn/ *n* supervisão *f*. **~or** *n* supervisor *m*; (*shop*) chefe *mf* de seção; (*firm*) chefe *mf* de serviço. **~ory** /'su:pəvaɪzərɪ/ *a* de supervisão

supper /'sʌpə(r)/ *n* jantar *m*; (*late at night*) ceia *f*

supple /'sʌpl/ *a* flexível, maleável

supplement[1] /'sʌplɪmənt/ *n* suplemento *m*. **~ary** /-'mentrɪ/ *a* suplementar

supplement[2] /'sʌplɪment/ *vt* suplementar

supplier /sə'plaɪə(r)/ *n* fornecedor *m*

suppl|y /sə'plaɪ/ *vt* suprir, prover; (*comm*) fornecer, abastecer □ *n* provisão *f*; (*of goods, gas etc*) fornecimento *m*, abastecimento *m* □ *a* (*teacher*) substituto. **~ies** (*food*) víveres *mpl*; (*mil*) suprimentos *mpl*. **~y and demand** oferta e procura

support /sə'pɔ:t/ *vt* (*hold up, endure*) suportar; (*provide for*) sustentar, suster; (*back*) apoiar, patrocinar; (*sport*) torcer por □ *n* apoio *m*; (*techn*) suporte *m*. **~er** *n* partidário *m*; (*sport*) torcedor *m*

suppos|e /sə'pəʊz/ *vt/i* supor. **~e that** supondo que, na hipótese de que. **~ed** *a* suposto. **he's ~ed to do** ele deve fazer; (*believed to*) consta que ele faz. **~edly** /-ɪdlɪ/ *adv* segundo dizem; (*probably*) supostamente, em princípio. **~ing** *conj* se. **~ition** /sʌpə-'zɪʃn/ *n* suposição *f*

suppress /sə'pres/ *vt* (*put an end to*) suprimir; (*restrain*) conter, reprimir; (*stifle*) abafar, sufocar; (*psych*) recalcar. **~ion** /-ʃn/ *n* supressão *f*; (*restraint*) repressão *f*; (*psych*) recalque *m*, (*P*) recalcamento *m*

suprem|e /su:'pri:m/ *a* supremo. **~acy** /-eməsɪ/ *n* supremacia *f*

surcharge /'sɜ:tʃa:dʒ/ *n* sobretaxa *f*; (*on stamp*) sobrecarga *f*

sure /ʃʊə(r)/ *a* (**-er, -est**) seguro, certo □ *adv* (*colloq: certainly*) deveras, não há dúvida que, de certeza. **be ~ about** *or* **of** ter a certeza de. **be ~ to** (*not fail*) não deixar de. **he is ~ to find out** ele vai descobrir com certeza. **make ~** assegurar. **~ly** *adv* com certeza, certamente

surety /'ʃʊərətɪ/ *n* (*person*) fiador *m*; (*thing*) garantia *f*

surf /sɜ:f/ *n* (*waves*) ressaca *f*, rebentação *f*. **~er** *n* surfista *mf*. **~ing** *n* surfe *m*, (*P*) surf *m*, jacaré-na-praia *m*

surface /'sɜ:fɪs/ *n* superficie *f* □ *a* superficial □ *vt/i* revestir; (*rise, become known*) emergir. **~ mail** via *f* marítima

surfboard /'sɜ:fbɔ:d/ *n* prancha *f* de surfe, (*P*) surf

surfeit /'sɜ:fɪt/ *n* excesso *m* (**of** de)

surge /sɜ:dʒ/ *vi* (*waves*) ondular, encapelar-se; (*move forward*) avançar □ *n* (*wave*) onda *f*, vaga *f*; (*motion*) arremetida *f*

surgeon /'sɜ:dʒən/ *n* cirurgião *m*

surg|ery /'sɜ:dʒərɪ/ *n* cirurgia *f*; (*office*) consultório *m*; (*session*) consulta *f*; (*consulting hours*) horas *fpl* de consulta. **~ical** *a* cirúrgico

surly /'sɜ:lɪ/ *a* (**-ier, -iest**) carrancudo, trombudo

surmise /sə'maɪz/ *vt* imaginar, supor, calcular □ *n* conjetura *f*, (*P*) conjectura *f*; hipótese *f*

surmount /sə'maʊnt/ *vt* sobrepujar, vencer, (*P*) superar

surname /'sɜ:neɪm/ *n* sobrenome *m*, (*P*) apelido *m*

surpass /sə'pa:s/ *vt* superar, ultrapassar, exceder

surplus /'sɜ:pləs/ *n* excedente *m*, excesso *m*; (*finance*) saldo *m* positivo □ *a* excedente, em excesso

surpris|e /sə'praɪz/ *n* surpresa *f* □ *vt* surpreender. **~ed** *a* surpreendido, admirado (**at** com). **~ing** *a* surpreendente. **~ingly** *adv* surpreendentemente

surrender /sə'rendə(r)/ *vi* render-se □ *vt* (*hand over; mil*) entregar □ *n* (*mil*) rendição *f*; (*of rights*) renúncia *f*

surreptitious /sʌrep'tɪʃəs/ *a* sub-reptício, furtivo

surrogate /'sʌrəgeɪt/ *n* delegado *m*. **~ mother** mãe *f* de aluguel, (*P*) aluguer

surround /sə'raʊnd/ *vt* rodear, cercar; (*mil etc*) cercar. **~ing** *a* circundante, vizinho. **~ings** *npl* arredores *mpl*; (*setting*) meio *m*, ambiente *m*

surveillance /sɜ:'veɪləns/ *n* vigilância *f*

survey[1] /sə'veɪ/ *vt* (*landscape etc*) observar; (*review*) passar em revista; (*inquire about*) pesquisar; (*land*) fazer o levantamento de; (*building*) vistoriar, inspecionar, (*P*) inspeccionar. **~or** *n* (*of buildings*) fiscal *m*; (*of land*) agrimensor *m*

survey[2] /'sɜ:veɪ/ *n* (*inspection*) vistoria *f*, inspeção *f*, (*P*) inspecção *f*; (*general view*) panorâmica *f*; (*inquiry*) pesquisa *f*

survival /sə'vaɪvl/ *n* sobrevivência *f*; (*relic*) relíquia *f*, vestígio *m*

surviv|e /sə'vaɪv/ *vt/i* sobreviver (a). **~or** *n* sobrevivente *mf*

susceptib|le /sə'septəbl/ *a* (*prone*) susceptível (**to** a); (*sensitive,* *impressionable*) susceptível, sensível. **~ility** /-'bɪlətɪ/ *n* susceptibilidade *f*

suspect[1] /sə'spekt/ *vt* suspeitar; (*doubt, distrust*) desconfiar de, suspeitar de

suspect[2] /'sʌspekt/ *a & n* suspeito (*m*)

suspen|d /sə'spend/ *vt* (*hang, stop*) suspender; (*from duty etc*) suspender. **~ded sentence** suspensão *f* de pena. **~sion** *n* suspensão *f*. **~sion bridge** ponte *f* suspensa *or* pênsil

suspender /sə'spendə(r)/ *n* (presilha de) liga *f*. **~ belt** *n* cinta-liga *f*, (*P*) cinta *f* de ligas. **~s** (*Amer: braces*) suspensórios *mpl*

suspense /sə'spens/ *n* ansiedade *f*, incerteza *f*; (*in book etc*) suspense *m*, tensão *f*

suspicion /sə'spɪʃn/ *n* suspeita *f*; (*distrust*) desconfiança *f*; (*trace*) vestígio *m*, (*P*) traço *m*

suspicious /səs'pɪʃəs/ *a* desconfiado; (*causing suspicion*) suspeito. **be ~ of** desconfiar de. **~ly** *adv* de modo suspeito

sustain /sə'steɪn/ *vt* (*support*) suster, sustentar; (*suffer*) sofrer; (*keep up*) sustentar; (*jur: uphold*) sancionar; (*interest, effort*) manter. **~ed effort** esforço *m* contínuo

sustenance /'sʌstɪnəns/ *n* (*food*) alimento *m*, sustento *m*

swagger /'swægə(r)/ *vi* pavonear-se, andar com arrogância

swallow[1] /'swɒləʊ/ *vt*/*i* engolir. **~ up** (*absorb, engulf*) devorar, tragar

swallow[2] /'swɒləʊ/ *n* (*bird*) andorinha *f*

swam /swæm/ *see* **swim**

swamp /swɒmp/ *n* pântano *m*, brejo *m* □ *vt* (*flood, overwhelm*) inundar, submergir. **~y** *a* pantanoso

swan /swɒn/ *n* cisne *m*

swank /swœŋk/ *vi* (*colloq: show off*) gabar-se, mostrar-se (*colloq*)

swap /swɒp/ *vt*/*i* (*pt* **swapped**) (*colloq*) trocar (**for** por) □ *n* (*colloq*) troca *f*

swarm /swɔ:m/ *n* (*of insects, people*) enxame *m* □ *vi* formigar. **~ into** *or* **round** invadir

swarthy /'swɔ:ðɪ/ *a* (**-ier, -iest**) moreno, trigueiro

swat /swɒt/ *vt* (*pt* **swatted**) (*fly etc*) esmagar, esborrachar

sway /sweɪ/ *vt*/*i* oscilar, balançar (-se); (*influence*) mover, influenciar □ *n* oscilação *f*, balanceio *m*; (*rule*) domínio *m*, poder *m*

swear /sweə(r)/ *vt*/*i* (*pt* **swore**, *pp* **sworn**) jurar; (*curse*) praguejar, rogar pragas (**at** contra). **~ by** jurar por; (*colloq: recommend*) ter grande fé em. **~-word** *n* palavrão *m*

sweat /swet/ *n* suor *m* □ *vi* suar. **~y** *a* suado

sweater /'swetə(r)/ *n* suéter *m*, (*P*) camisola *f*

sweatshirt /'swetʃɜ:t/ *n* suéter *m* de malha *or* algodão

swede /swi:d/ *n* couve-nabo *f*

Swed|e /swi:d/ *n* sueco *m*. **~en** *n* Suécia *f*. **~ish** *a & n* sueco (*m*)

sweep /swi:p/ *vt*/*i* (*pt* **swept**) varrer; (*go majestically*) avançar majestosamente; (*carry away*) arrastar; (*chimney*) limpar □ *n* (*with broom*) varredela *f*; (*curve*) curva *f*; (*movement*) gesto *m* largo. (**chimney-**)**~** limpa-chaminés *m*. **~ing** *a* (*gesture*) largo; (*action*) de grande alcance. **~ing statement** generalização *f* fácil

sweet /swi:t/ *a* (**-er, -est**) doce; (*colloq: charming*) doce, gracinha; (*colloq: pleasant*) agradável □ *n* doce *m*. **~ corn** milho *m*. **~ pea** ervilha-de-cheiro *f*. **~ shop** confeitaria *f*. **have a ~ tooth** gostar de doce. **~ly** *adv* docemente. **~ness** *n* doçura *f*

sweeten /'swi:tn/ *vt* adoçar; (*fig: mitigate*) suavizar. **~er** *n* (*for tea, coffee*) adoçante *m* (artificial); (*colloq: bribe*) agrado *m*

sweetheart /'swi:tha:t/ *n* namorado *m*, namorada *f*; (*term of endearment*) querido *m*, querida *f*, amor *m*

swell /swel/ *vt*/*i* (*pt* **swelled**, *pp* **swollen** *or* **swelled**) (*expand*) inchar; (*increase*) aumentar □ *n* (*of sea*) ondulação *f* □ *a* (*colloq: excellent*) excelente; (*colloq: smart*) chique. **~ing** *n* (*med*) inchação *f*, inchaço *m*

swelter /'sweltə(r)/ *vi* fazer um calor abrasador; (*person*) abafar (com calor)

swept /swept/ *see* **sweep**

swerve /swɜ:v/ *vi* desviar-se, dar uma guinada

swift /swɪft/ *a* (**-er, -est**) rápido, veloz. **~ly** *adv* rapidamente. **~ness** *n* rapidez *f*

swig /swɪg/ *vt* (*pt* **swigged**) (*colloq: drink*) emborcar, beber em longos tragos □ *n* (*colloq*) trago *m*, gole *m*

swill /swɪl/ *vt* passar por água □ *n* (*pig-food*) lavagem *f*, (*P*) lavadura *f*

swim /swɪm/ *vi* (*pt* **swam**, *pp* **swum**, *pres p* **swimming**) nadar; (*room, head*) rodar □ *vt* atravessar a nado; (*distance*) nadar □ *n* banho *m*. **~mer** *n* nadador *m*. **~ming** *n* natação *f*. **~ming-bath**, **~ming-pool** *ns* piscina *f*. **~ming-cap** *n* touca *f* de banho. **~ming-costume**, **~-suit** *ns* maiô *m*, (*P*) fato *m* de banho. **~ming-trunks** *npl* calção *m* de banho

swindle /'swɪndl/ *vt* trapacear, fraudar, (*P*) vigarizar □ *n* vigarice *f*. **~r** /-ə(r)/ *n* vigarista *mf*
swine /swaɪn/ *npl* (*pigs*) porcos *mpl* □ *n* (*pl invar*) (*colloq: person*) animal *m*, canalha *m* (*colloq*)
swing /swɪŋ/ *vt/i* (*pt* **swung**) balançar(-se); (*turn round*) girar □ *n* (*seat*) balanço *m*; (*of opinion*) reviravolta *f*; (*mus*) swing *m*; (*rhythm*) ritmo *m*. **in full ~** no máximo, em plena atividade, (*P*) actividade. **~ round** (*of person*) virar-se. **~-bridge/door** *ns* ponte *f*/porta *f* giratória
swipe /swaɪp/ *vt* (*colloq: hit*) bater em, dar uma pancada em (*colloq*); (*colloq: steal*) afanar, roubar (*colloq*) □ *n* (*colloq: hit*) pancada *f* (*colloq*). **~ card** cartão *m* magnético
swirl /swɜ:l/ *vi* rodopiar, redemoinhar □ *n* turbilhão *m*, redemoinho *m*
swish /swɪʃ/ *vt/i* sibilar, zunir, (fazer) cortar o ar; (*with brushing sound*) roçar □ *a* (*colloq*) chique
Swiss /swɪs/ *a* & *n* suiço (*m*)
switch /swɪtʃ/ *n* interruptor *m*; (*change*) mudança *f* □ *vt* (*transfer*) transferir; (*exchange*) trocar □ *vi* desviar-se. **~ off** desligar
switchboard /'swɪtʃbɔ:d/ *n* (*telephone*) PBX *m*, mesa *f* telefônica
Switzerland /'swɪtsələnd/ *n* Suiça *f*
swivel /'swɪvl/ *vt/i* (*pt* **swivelled**) (fazer) girar. **~ chair** cadeira *f* giratória
swollen /'swəʊlən/ *see* **swell** □ *a* inchado
swoop /swu:p/ *vi* (*bird*) lançar-se, cair (**down on** sobre); (*police*) dar uma batida policial, (*P*) rusga
sword /sɔ:d/ *n* espada *f*
swore /swɔ:(r)/ *see* **swear**
sworn /swɔ:n/ *see* **swear** □ *a* (*enemy*) jurado, declarado; (*ally*) fiel
swot /swɒt/ *vt/i* (*pt* **swotted**) (*colloq: study*) estudar muito, (*P*) marrar (*sl*) □ *n* (*colloq*) estudante *m* muito aplicado, (*P*) marrão *m* (*sl*)
swum /swʌm/ *see* **swim**
swung /swʌŋ/ *see* **swing**
sycamore /'sɪkəmɔ:(r)/ *n* (*maple*) sicômoro *m*, (*P*) sicómoro *m*; (*Amer: plane*) plátano *m*
syllable /'sɪləbl/ *n* sílaba *f*
syllabus /'sɪləbəs/ *n* (*pl* **-uses**) programa *m*
symbol /'sɪmbl/ *n* símbolo *m*. **~ic(al)** /-'bɒlɪk(l)/ *a* simbólico. **~ism** *n* simbolismo *m*
symbolize /'sɪmbəlaɪz/ *vt* simbolizar
symmetr|y /'sɪmətrɪ/ *n* simetria *f*. **~ical** /sɪ'metrɪkl/ *a* simétrico
sympathize /'sɪmpəθaɪz/ *vi* **~ with** ter pena de, condoer-se de; (*fig*) compartilhar os sentimentos de. **~r** *n* simpatizante *mf*
sympath|y /'sɪmpəθɪ/ *n* (*pity*) pena *f*, compaixão *f*; (*solidarity*) solidariedade *f*; (*condolences*) pêsames *mpl*, condolências *fpl*. **be in ~y with** estar de acordo com. **~etic** /-'θetɪk/ *a* comprensivo, simpático; (*likeable*) simpático; (*showing pity*) compassivo. **~etically** /-'θetɪklɪ/ *adv* compassivamente; (*fig*) compreensivamente
symphon|y /'sɪmfənɪ/ *n* sinfonia *f* □ *a* sinfônico, (*P*) sinfónico. **~ic** /-'fɒnɪk/ *a* sinfônico, (*P*) sinfónico
symptom /'sɪmptəm/ *n* sintoma *m*. **~atic** /-'mætɪk/ *a* sintomático (**of** de)
synagogue /'sɪnəgɒg/ *n* sinagoga *f*
synchronize /'sɪŋkrənaɪz/ *vt* sincronizar
syndicate /'sɪndɪkət/ *n* sindicato *m*
syndrome /'sɪndrəʊm/ *n* (*med*) síndrome *m*, (*P*) sindroma *m*
synonym /'sɪnənɪm/ *n* sinônimo *m*, (*P*) sinónimo *m*. **~ous** /sɪ'nɒnɪməs/ *a* sinônimo, (*P*) sinónimo (**with** de)
synopsis /sɪ'nɒpsɪs/ *n* (*pl* **-opses** /-si:z/) sinopse *f*, resumo *m*
syntax /'sɪntæks/ *n* sintaxe *f*
synthesis /'sɪnθəsɪs/ *n* (*pl* **-theses** /-si:z/) síntese *f*
synthetic /sɪn'θetɪk/ *a* sintético
syphilis /'sɪfɪlɪs/ *n* sífilis *f*
Syria /'sɪrɪə/ *n* Síria *f*. **~n** *a* & *n* sírio (*m*)
syringe /sɪ'rɪndʒ/ *n* seringa *f* □ *vt* seringar
syrup /'sɪrəp/ *n* (*liquid*) xarope *m*; (*treacle*) calda *f* de açúcar. **~y** *a* (*fig*) melado, enjoativo
system /'sɪstəm/ *n* sistema *m*; (*body*) organismo *m*; (*order*) método *m*. **~atic** /sɪstə'mætɪk/ *a* sistemático

Tt

tab /tæb/ *n* (*flap*) lingueta *f*; (*for fastening, hanging*) aba *f*; (*label*) etiqueta *f*; (*loop*) argola *f*; (*Amer colloq: bill*) conta *f*. **keep ~s on** (*colloq*) vigiar

table /ˈteɪbl/ *n* mesa *f*; (*list*) tabela *f*, lista *f* □ *vt* (*submit*) apresentar; (*postpone*) adiar. **at ~** à mesa. **lay** *or* **set the ~** pôr a mesa. **~ of contents** índice *m* (das matérias). **turn the ~s** inverter as posições. **~-cloth** *n* toalha de mesa *f*. **~-mat** *n* descanso *m*. **~ tennis** pingue-pongue *m*

tablespoon /ˈteɪblspu:n/ *n* colher *f* grande de sopa. **~ful** *n* (*pl* **~fuls**) colher *f* de sopa cheia

tablet /ˈtæblɪt/ *n* (*of stone*) lápide *f*, placa *f*; (*drug*) comprimido *m*

tabloid /ˈtæblɔɪd/ *n* tablóide *m*. **~ journalism** (*pej*) jornalismo *m* sensacionalista, imprensa *f* marron

taboo /təˈbu:/ *n* & *a* tabu (*m*)

tacit /ˈtæsɪt/ *a* tácito

taciturn /ˈtæsɪtɜ:n/ *a* taciturno

tack /tæk/ *n* (*nail*) tacha *f*; (*stitch*) ponto *m* de alinhavo; (*naut*) amura *f*; (*fig: course of action*) rumo *m* □ *vt* (*nail*) pregar com tachas; (*stitch*) alinhavar □ *vi* (*naut*) bordejar. **~ on** (*add*) acrescentar, juntar

tackle /ˈtækl/ *n* equipamento *m*, apetrechos *mpl*; (*sport*) placagem *f* □ *vt* (*problem etc*) atacar; (*sport*) placar; (*a thief etc*) agarrar-se a

tacky /ˈtækɪ/ *a* (**-ier, -iest**) peganhento, pegajoso

tact /tækt/ *n* tato *m*, (*P*) tacto *m*. **~ful** *a* cheio de tato, (*P*) tacto, diplomático. **~fully** *adv* com tato, (*P*) tacto. **~less** *a* sem tato, (*P*) tacto. **~lessly** *adv* sem tato, (*P*) tacto

tactic /ˈtæktɪk/ *n* (*expedient*) tática *f*, (*P*) táctica *f*. **~s** *n(pl)* (*procedure*) tática *f*, (*P*) táctica *f*. **~al** *a* tático, (*P*) táctico

tadpole /ˈtædpəʊl/ *n* girino *m*

tag /tæg/ *n* (*label*) etiqueta *f*; (*on shoelace*) agulheta *f*; (*phrase*) chavão *m*, clichê *m* □ *vi* (*pt* **tagged**) etiquetar; (*add*) juntar □ *vi* **~ along** (*colloq*) andar atrás, seguir

Tagus /ˈteɪgʌs/ *n* Tejo *m*

tail /teɪl/ *n* cauda *f*, rabo *m*; (*of shirt*) fralda *f*. **~s!** (*tossing coin*) coroa! □ *vt* (*follow*) seguir, vigiar □ *vi* **~ away** *or* **off** diminuir, baixar. **~-back** *n* (*traffic*) fila *f*, (*P*) bicha *f*. **~-end** *n* parte *f* traseira, cauda *f*. **~-light** *n* (*auto*) farolete *m* traseiro, (*P*) farolim *m* da rectaguarda

tailor /ˈteɪlə(r)/ *n* alfaiate *m* □ *vt* (*garment*) fazer; (*fig: adapt*) adaptar. **~-made** *a* feito sob medida, (*P*) por medida. **~-made for** (*fig*) feito para, talhado para

tainted /ˈteɪntɪd/ *a* (*infected*) contaminado; (*decayed*) estragado; (*fig*) manchado

take /teɪk/ *vt/i* (*pt* **took**, *pp* **taken**) (*get hold of*) agarrar em, pegar em; (*capture*) tomar; (*a seat, a drink; train, bus etc*) tomar; (*carry*) levar (**to** a, para); (*contain, escort*) levar; (*tolerate*) suportar, agüentar, (*P*) aguentar; (*choice, exam*) fazer; (*photo*) tirar; (*require*) exigir. **be ~n by** *or* **with** ficar encantado com. **be ~n ill** adoecer. **it ~s time to** leva tempo para. **~ after** parecer-se a. **~-away** *n* (*meal*) comida *f* para levar, take-away *m*; (*shop*) loja *f* que só vende comida para ser consumida em outro lugar. **~ away** levar. **~ away from sb/sth** tirar de alguém/de alg coisa. **~ back** aceitar de volta; (*return*) devolver; (*accompany*) acompanhar; (*statement*) retirar, retratar. **~ down** (*object*) tirar para baixo; (*notes*) tirar, tomar. **~ in** (*garment*) meter para dentro; (*include*) incluir; (*cheat*) enganar, levar (*colloq*); (*grasp*) compreender; (*receive*) receber. **~ it that** supor que. **~ off** *vt* (*remove*) tirar; (*mimic*) imitar, macaquear □ *vi* (*aviat*) decolar, levantar vôo. **~-off** *n* imitação *f*; (*aviat*) decolagem *f*, (*P*) descolagem *f*. **~ on** (*task*) encarregar-se de; (*staff*) admitir, contratar. **~ out** tirar; (*on an outing*) levar para sair. **~ over** *vt* tomar conta de, assumir a direção, (*P*) direcção de □ *vi* tomar o poder. **~ over from** (*relieve*) render, substituir; (*succeed*) suceder a. **~-over** *n* (*pol*) tomada *f* de poder; (*comm*) take-over *m*. **~ part** participar *or* tomar parte (**in** em). **~ place** ocorrer, suceder. **~ sides** tomar partido. **~ sides with** tomar o partido de. **~ to** gostar de, simpatizar com; (*activity*) tomar gosto por, entregar-se a. **~ up** (*object*) apanhar, pegar em; (*hobby*) dedicar-se a; (*occupy*) ocupar, tomar

takings /ˈteɪkɪŋz/ *npl* receita *f*

talcum /ˈtælkəm/ *n* talco *m*. **~ powder** pó *m* talco

tale /teɪl/ *n* conto *m*, história *f*

talent /'tælənt/ *n* talento *m*. **~ed** *a* talentoso, bem dotado

talk /tɔ:k/ *vt*/*i* falar; (*chat*) conversar □ *n* conversa *f*; (*mode of speech*) fala *f*; (*lecture*) palestra *f*. **small ~** conversa *f* banal. **~ into doing** convencer a fazer. **~ nonsense** dizer disparates. **~ over** discutir. **~ shop** falar de assuntos profissionais. **~to o.s.** falar sozinho, falar com os seus botões. **there's ~ of** fala-se de. **~er** *n* conversador *m*. **~ing-to** *n* (*colloq*) descompostura *f*

talkative /'tɔ:kətɪv/ *a* falador, conversador, tagarela

tall /tɔ:l/ *a* (**-er, -est**) alto. **~ story** (*colloq*) história *f* do arco-da-velha

tallboy /'tɔ:lbɔɪ/ *n* cômoda *f*, (*P*) cómoda *f* alta

tally /'tælɪ/ *vi* corresponder (**with** a), conferir (**with** com)

tambourine /tæmbə'ri:n/ *n* tamborim *m*, pandeiro *m*

tame /teɪm/ *a* (**-er, -est**) manso; (*domesticated*) domesticado; (*dull*) insípido □ *vt* amansar, domesticar

tamper /'tæmpə(r)/ *vi* **~ with** mexer indevidamente em; (*text*) alterar

tampon /'tæmpən/ *n* (*med*) tampão *m*; (*sanitary towel*) toalha *f* higiênica

tan /tæn/ *vt*/*i* (*pt* **tanned**) queimar, bronzear; (*hide*) curtir □ *n* bronzeado *m* □ *a* castanho amarelado

tandem /'tændəm/ *n* (*bicycle*) tandem *m*. **in ~** em tandem, um atrás do outro

tang /tæŋ/ *n* (*taste*) sabor *m* *or* gosto *m* característico; (*smell*) cheiro *m* característico

tangent /'tændʒənt/ *n* tangente *f*

tangerine /tændʒə'ri:n/ *n* tangerina *f*

tangible /'tændʒəbl/ *a* tangível

tangle /'tæŋgl/ *vt* emaranhar, enredar □ *n* emaranhado *m*. **become ~d** emaranhar-se, enredar-se

tank /tæŋk/ *n* tanque *m*, reservatório *m*; (*for petrol*) tanque *m*, (*P*) depósito *m*; (*for fish*) aquário *m*; (*mil*) tanque *m*

tankard /'tæŋkəd/ *n* caneca *f* grande

tanker /'tæŋkə(r)/ *n* carro-tanque *m*, camião-cisterna *m*; (*ship*) petroleiro *m*

tantaliz|e /'tæntəlaɪz/ *vt* atormentar, tantalizar. **~ing** *a* tentador

tantamount /'tæntəmaʊnt/ *a* **be ~ to** equivaler a

tantrum /'tæntrəm/ *n* chilique *m*, ataque *m* de mau gênio, (*P*) génio, birra *f*

tap[1] /tæp/ *n* (*for water etc*) torneira *f* □ *vt* (*pt* **tapped**) (*resources*) explorar; (*telephone*) grampear. **on ~** (*colloq*: *available*) disponível

tap[2] /tæp/ *vt*/*i* (*pt* **tapped**) bater levemente. **~-dance** *n* sapateado *m*

tape /teɪp/ *n* (*for dressmaking*) fita *f*; (*sticky*) fita *f* adesiva. **(magnetic) ~** fita *f* (magnética) □ *vt* (*tie*) atar, prender; (*stick*) colar; (*record*) gravar. **~-measure** *n* fita *f* métrica. **~ recorder** gravador *m*

taper /'teɪpə(r)/ *n* vela *f* comprida e fina □ *vt*/*i* **~ (off)** estreitar (-se), afilar(-se). **~ed**, **~ing** *adjs* (*fingers etc*) afilado; (*trousers*) afunilado

tapestry /'tæpɪstrɪ/ *n* tapeçaria *f*

tapioca /tæpɪ'əʊkə/ *n* tapioca *f*

tar /ta:(r)/ *n* alcatrão *m* □ *vt* (*pt* **tarred**) alcatroar

target /'ta:gɪt/ *n* alvo *m* □ *vt* ter como alvo

tariff /'tærɪf/ *n* tarifa *f*; (*on import*) direitos *mpl* aduaneiros

Tarmac /'ta:mæk/ *n* macadame (alcatroado) *m*; (*runway*) pista *f*

tarnish /'ta:nɪʃ/ *vt*/*i* (fazer) perder o brilho; (*stain*) manchar

tarpaulin /ta:'pɔ:lɪn/ *n* lona *f* impermeável (alcatroada *or* encerada)

tart[1] /ta:t/ *a* (**-er, -est**) ácido; (*fig: cutting*) mordaz, azedo

tart[2] /ta:t/ *n* (*culin*) torta *f* de fruta, (*P*) tarte *f*; (*sl: prostitute*) prostituta *f*, mulher *f* da vida (*sl*) □ *vt* **~ up** (*colloq*) embonecar(-se)

tartan /'ta:tn/ *n* tecido *m* escocês □ *a* escocês

tartar /'ta:tə(r)/ *n* (*on teeth*) tártaro *m*, (*P*) pedra *f*. **~ sauce** molho *m* tártaro

task /ta:sk/ *n* tarefa *f*, trabalho *m*. **take to ~** repreender, censurar. **~ force** (*mil*) força-tarefa *f*

tassel /'tæsl/ *n* borla *f*

taste /teɪst/ *n* gosto *m*; (*fig: sample*) amostra *f* □ *vt* (*eat, enjoy*) saborear; (*try*) provar; (*perceive taste of*) sentir o gosto de □ *vi* **~ of** *or* **like** ter o sabor de. **have a ~ of** (*experience*) provar. **~ful** *a* de bom gosto. **~fully** *adv* com bom gosto. **~less** *a* insípido, insosso; (*fig: not in good taste*) sem gosto; (*fig: in bad taste*) de mau gosto

tasty /'teɪstɪ/ *a* (**-ier, -iest**) saboroso, gostoso

tat /tæt/ *see* **tit**[2]

tatter|s /'tætəz/ *npl* farrapos *mpl*. **~ed** /-əd/ *a* esfarrapado

tattoo /tə'tu:/ *vt* tatuar □ *n* tatuagem *f*

tatty /'tætɪ/ *a* (**-ier, -iest**) (*colloq*) enxovalhado, em mau estado

taught /tɔ:t/ *see* **teach**

taunt /tɔ:nt/ *vt* escarnecer de, zombar de □ *n* escárnio *m*. **~ing** *a* escarninho

Taurus /'tɔ:rəs/ *n* (*astr*) Touro *m*, (*P*) Taurus *m*

taut /tɔ:t/ *a* esticado, retesado; (*fig: of nerves*) tenso

tawdry /'tɔ:drɪ/ *a* (**-ier, -iest**) espalhafatoso e ordinário

tawny /'tɔ:nɪ/ *a* fulvo

tax /tæks/ *n* taxa *f*, imposto *m*; (*on income*) imposto *m* de renda, (*P*) sobre o rendimento □ *vt* taxar, lançar impostos sobre, tributar; (*fig: put to test*) pôr à prova. **~-collector** *n* cobrador *m* de impostos. **~-free** *a* isento de imposto. **~ relief** isenção *f* de imposto. **~ return** declaração *f* do imposto de renda, (*P*) sobre o rendimento. **~ year** ano *m* fiscal. **~able** *a* tributável, passível de imposto. **~ation** /-'seɪʃn/ *n* impostos *mpl*, tributação *f*. **~ing** *a* penoso, difícil

taxi /'tæksɪ/ *n* (*pl* **-is**) táxi *m* □ *vi* (*pt* **taxied**, *pres p* **taxiing**) (*aviat*) rolar na pista, taxiar. **~-cab** *n* táxi *m*. **~-driver** *n* motorista *mf* de táxi. **~ rank**, (*Amer*) **~ stand** ponto *m* de táxis, (*P*) praça *f* de táxis

taxpayer /'tækspeɪə(r)/ *n* contribuinte *mf*

tea /ti:/ *n* chá *m*. **high ~** refeição *f* leve à noite. **~-bag** *n* saquinho *m* de chá. **~-break** *n* intervalo *m* para o chá. **~-cosy** *n* abafador *m*. **~-leaf** *n* folha *f* de chá. **~-set** *n* serviço *m* de chá. **~-shop** *n* salão *m* or casa *f* de chá. **~-time** *n* hora *f* do chá. **~- towel** *n* pano *m* de prato

teach /ti:tʃ/ *vt* (*pt* **taught**) ensinar, lecionar, (*P*) leccionar (**sb sth** alg coisa a alguém) □ *vi* ensinar, ser professor. **~er** *n* professor *m*. **~ing** *n* ensino *m*; (*doctrines*) ensinamento(s) *m* (*pl*) *a* pedagógico, de ensino; (*staff*) docente

teacup /'ti:kʌp/ *n* xícara *f* de chá, (*P*) chávena *f*

teak /ti:k/ *n* teca *f*

team /ti:m/ *n* equipe *f*, (*P*) equipa *f*; (*of oxen*) junta *f*; (*of horses*) parelha *f* □ *vi* **~ up** juntar-se, associar-se (**with** a). **~-work** *n* trabalho *m* de equipe, (*P*) equipa

teapot /'ti:pɒt/ *n* bule *m*

tear[1] /teə(r)/ *vt/i* (*pt* **tore**, *pp* **torn**) rasgar(-se); (*snatch*) arrancar, puxar; (*rush*) lançar-se, ir numa correria; (*fig*) dividir □ *n* rasgão *m*. **~ o.s. away** arrancar-se (**from** de)

tear[2] /tɪə(r)/ *n* lágrima *f*. **~-gas** *n* gases *mpl* lacrimogênios, (*P*) lacrimogénios

tearful /'tɪəfl/ *a* lacrimoso, choroso. **~ly** *adv* choroso, com (as) lágrimas nos olhos

tease /ti:z/ *vt* implicar; (*make fun of*) caçoar de

teaspoon /'ti:spu:n/ *n* colher *f* de chá. **~ful** *n* (*pl* **-fuls**) colher *f* de chá cheia

teat /ti:t/ *n* (*of bottle*) bico *m*; (*of animal*) teta *f*

technical /'teknɪkl/ *a* técnico. **~ity** /-'kælətɪ/ *n* questão *f* de ordem técnica. **~ly** *adv* tecnicamente

technician /tek'nɪʃn/ *n* técnico *m*

technique /tek'ni:k/ *n* técnica *f*

technolog|y /tek'nɒlədʒɪ/ *n* tecnologia *f*. **~ical** /-ə'lɒdʒɪkl/ *a* tecnológico

teddy /'tedɪ/ *a* **~ (bear)** ursinho *m* de pelúcia, (*P*) peluche

tedious /'ti:dɪəs/ *a* maçante

tedium /'ti:dɪəm/ *n* tédio *m*

tee /ti:/ *n* (*golf*) tee *m*

teem[1] /ti:m/ *vi* **~ (with)** (*swarm*) pulular (de), fervilhar (de), abundar (em)

teem[2] /ti:m/ *vi* **~ (with rain)** chover torrencialmente

teenage /'ti:neɪdʒ/ *a* juvenil, de/para adolescente. **~r** /-ə(r)/ *n* jovem *mf*, adolescente *mf*

teens /ti:nz/ *npl* **in one's ~** na adolescência, entre os 13 e os 19 anos

teeter /'ti:tə(r)/ *vi* cambalear

teeth /ti:θ/ *see* **tooth**

teeth|e /ti:ð/ *vi* começar a ter dentes. **~ing troubles** (*fig*) problemas *mpl* iniciais

teetotaller /ti:'təʊtlə(r)/ *n* abstêmio *m*, (*P*) abstémio *m*

telecommunications /telɪkəmju:nɪ'keɪʃnz/ *npl* telecomunicações *fpl*

telegram /'telɪgræm/ *n* telegrama *m*

telegraph /'telɪgra:f/ *n* telégrafo *m* □ *a* telegráfico. **~ic** /-'græfɪk/ *a* telegráfico

telepath|y /tɪ'lepəθɪ/ *n* telepatia *f*. **~ic** /telɪ'pæθɪk/ *a* telepático

telephone /'telɪfəʊn/ *n* telefone *m* □ *vt* (*person*) telefonar a; (*message*) telefonar □ *vi* telefonar. **~ book** lista *f* telefônica, (*P*) telefónica, guia *m* telefônico, (*P*) telefónico. **~ box**, **~ booth** cabine *f* telefônica, (*P*) telefónica. **~ call** chamada *f*. **~ directory** lista *f* telefônica, (*P*) telefónica, guia *m* telefônico, (*P*) telefónico. **~ number** número *m* de telefone

telephonist /tɪ'lefənɪst/ *n* (*in exchange*) telefonista *mf*

telephoto /telɪ'fəʊtəʊ/ *n* **~ lens** teleobjetiva *f*, (*P*) teleobjectiva *f*

telescop|e /'telɪskəʊp/ *n* telescópio *m* □ *vt/i* encaixar(-se). **~ic** /-'skɒpɪk/ *a* telescópico

teletext /'telɪtekst/ *n* teletexto *m*

televise /'telɪvaɪz/ *vt* televisionar

television /ˈtelɪvɪʒn/ *n* televisão *f*. ~ **set** aparelho *m* de televisão, televisor *m*

teleworking /ˈtelɪwɜːkɪŋ/ *n* teletrabalho *m*

telex /ˈteleks/ *n* telex *m* □ *vt* transmitir por telex, telexar

tell /tel/ *vt* (*pt* **told**) dizer (**sb sth** alg coisa a alguém); (*story*) contar; (*distinguish*) distinguir, diferençar □ *vi* (*know*) ver-se, saber. **I told you so** bem lhe disse. ~ **of** falar de. ~ **off** (*colloq: scold*) ralhar, dar uma bronca em. ~ **on** (*have effect on*) afetar, (*P*) afectar; (*colloq: inform on*) fazer queixa de (*colloq*). ~**-tale** *n* mexeriqueiro *m*, fofoqueiro *m* □ *a* (*revealing*) revelador. ~ **tales** mexericar, fofocar

telly /ˈtelɪ/ *n* (*colloq*) TV *f* (*colloq*)

temp /temp/ *n* (*colloq*) empregado *m* temporário

temper /ˈtempə(r)/ *n* humor *m*, disposição *f*; (*anger*) mau humor *m* □ *vt* temperar. **keep/lose one's** ~ manter a calma/perder a calma *or* a cabeça, zangar-se

temperament /ˈtemprəmənt/ *n* temperamento *m*. ~**al** /-ˈmentl/ *a* caprichoso

temperance /ˈtempərəns/ *n* (*in drinking*) sobriedade *f*

temperate /ˈtempərət/ *a* moderado, comedido; (*climate*) temperado

temperature /ˈtemprətʃə(r)/ *n* temperatura *f*. **have a** ~ estar com *or* ter febre

tempest /ˈtempɪst/ *n* tempestade *f*, temporal *m*

tempestuous /temˈpestʃʊəs/ *a* tempestuoso

template /ˈtempl(e)ɪt/ *n* molde *m*

temple[1] /ˈtempl/ *n* templo *m*

temple[2] /ˈtempl/ *n* (*anat*) têmpora *f*, fonte *f*

tempo /ˈtempəʊ/ *n* (*pl* **-os**) (*mus*) tempo *m*; (*pace*) ritmo *m*

temporar|y /ˈtemprərɪ/ *a* temporário, provisório. ~**ily** *adv* temporariamente, provisoriamente

tempt /tempt/ *vt* tentar. ~ **sb to do** dar a alguém vontade de fazer, tentar alguém a fazer. ~**ation** /-ˈteɪʃn/ *n* tentação *f*. ~**ing** *a* tentador

ten /ten/ *a* & *n* dez (*m*)

tenac|ious /tɪˈneɪʃəs/ *a* tenaz. ~**ity** /-æsətɪ/ *n* tenacidade *f*

tenant /ˈtenənt/ *n* inquilino *m*, locatário *m*

tend[1] /tend/ *vt* tomar conta de, cuidar de

tend[2] /tend/ *vi* ~ **to** (*be apt to*) tender a, ter tendência para

tendency /ˈtendənsɪ/ *n* tendência *f*

tender[1] /ˈtendə(r)/ *a* (*soft, delicate*) terno; (*sore, painful*) sensível, dolorido; (*loving*) terno, meigo. ~**-hearted** *a* compassivo. ~**ly** *adv* (*lovingly*) ternamente, meigamente; (*delicately*) delicadamente. ~**ness** *n* (*love*) ternura *f*, meiguice *f*

tender[2] /ˈtendə(r)/ *vt* (*money*) oferecer; (*apologies, resignation*) apresentar □ *vi* ~ **(for)** apresentar orçamento (para) □ *n* (*comm*) orçamento *m*. **legal** ~ (*money*) moeda *f* corrente

tendon /ˈtendən/ *n* tendão *m*

tenement /ˈtenəmənt/ *n* prédio *m* de apartamentos de renda moderada; (*Amer: slum*) prédio *m* pobre

tenet /ˈtenɪt/ *n* princípio *m*, dogma *m*

tennis /ˈtenɪs/ *n* tênis *m*, (*P*) ténis *m*. ~ **court** quadra *f* de tênis, (*P*) court *m* de ténis

tenor /ˈtenə(r)/ *n* (*meaning*) teor *m*; (*mus*) tenor *m*

tense[1] /tens/ *n* (*gram*) tempo *m*

tense[2] /tens/ *a* (**-er**, **-est**) tenso □ *vt* (*muscles*) retesar

tension /ˈtenʃn/ *n* tensão *f*

tent /tent/ *n* tenda *f*, barraca *f*. ~**-peg** *n* estaca *f*

tentacle /ˈtentəkl/ *n* tentáculo *m*

tentative /ˈtentətɪv/ *a* provisório; (*hesitant*) hesitante. ~**ly** *adv* tentativamente, a título experimental; (*hesitantly*) hesitantemente

tenterhooks /ˈtentəhʊks/ *npl* **on** ~ em suspense

tenth /tenθ/ *a* & *n* décimo (*m*)

tenuous /ˈtenjʊəs/ *a* tênue, (*P*) ténue

tepid /ˈtepɪd/ *a* tépido, morno

term /tɜːm/ *n* (*word*) termo *m*; (*limit*) prazo *m*, termo *m*; (*schol etc*) período *m*, trimestre *m*; (*Amer*) semestre *m*; (*of imprisonment*) (duração de) pena *f*. ~**s** (*conditions*) condições *fpl* □ *vt* designar, denominar, chamar. **on good/bad** ~**s** de boas/más relações. **not on speaking** ~**s** de relações cortadas. **come to** ~**s with** chegar a um acordo com; (*become resigned to*) resignar-se a. ~ **of office** (*pol*) mandato *m*

terminal /ˈtɜːmɪnl/ *a* terminal, final; (*illness*) fatal, mortal □ *n* (*oil, computer*) terminal *m*; (*rail*) estação *f* terminal; (*electr*) borne *m*. **(air)** ~ terminal *m* (de avião)

terminat|e /ˈtɜːmɪneɪt/ *vt* terminar, pôr termo a □ *vi* terminar. ~**ion** /-ˈneɪʃn/ *n* término *m*, (*P*) terminação *f*, termo *m*

terminology /tɜːmɪˈnɒlədʒɪ/ *n* terminologia *f*

terminus /ˈtɜːmɪnəs/ *n* (*pl* **-ni** /-naɪ/) (*rail, coach*) estação *f* terminal

terrace /'terəs/ *n* terraço *m*; (*in cultivation*) socalco *m*; (*houses*) casas *fpl* em fileira contínua, lance *m* de casas. **the ~s** (*sport*) arquibancada *f*. **~d house** casa *f* ladeada por outras casas

terrain /te'reɪn/ *n* terreno *m*

terribl|e /'terəbl/ *a* terrível. **~y** *adv* terrivelmente; (*colloq: very*) extremamente, espantosamente

terrific /tə'rɪfɪk/ *a* terrífico, tremendo; (*colloq: excellent; great*) tremendo. **~ally** *adv* (*colloq: very*) tremendamente (*colloq*); (*colloq: very well*) lindamente, maravilhosamente

terrif|y /'terɪfaɪ/ *vt* aterrar, aterrorizar. **be ~ied of** ter pavor de

territorial /terɪ'tɔ:rɪəl/ *a* territorial

territory /'terɪtərɪ/ *n* território *m*

terror /'terə(r)/ *n* terror *m*, pavor *m*

terroris|t /'terərɪst/ *n* terrorista *mf*. **~m** /-zəm/ *n* terrorismo *m*

terrorize /'terəraɪz/ *vt* aterrorizar, aterrar

terse /tɜ:s/ *a* conciso, lapidar; (*curt*) lacônico, (*P*) lacónico

test /test/ *n* teste *m*, exame *m*, prova *f*; (*schol*) prova *f*, teste *m*; (*of goods*) controle *m*; (*of machine etc*) ensaio *m*; (*of strength*) prova *f* □ *vt* examinar; (*check*) controlar; (*try*) ensaiar; (*pupil*) interrogar. **put to the ~** pôr à prova. **~ match** jogo *m* internacional. **~-tube** *n* proveta *f*. **~-tube baby** bebê *m* de proveta

testament /'testəmənt/ *n* testamento *m*. **Old/New T~** Antigo/Novo Testamento *m*

testicle /'testɪkl/ *n* testículo *m*

testify /'testɪfaɪ/ *vt/i* testificar, testemunhar, depôr

testimonial /testɪ'məʊnɪəl/ *n* carta *f* de recomendação

testimony /'testɪmənɪ/ *n* testemunho *m*

tetanus /'tetənəs/ *n* tétano *m*

tether /'teðə(r)/ *vt* prender com corda □ *n* **be at the end of one's ~** estar nas últimas

text /tekst/ *n* texto *m*. **~ message** mensagem *f* escrita □ *vt* enviar um mensagem de texto a

textbook /'tekstbʊk/ *n* compêndio *m*, manual *m*, livro *m* de texto

textile /'tekstaɪl/ *n* & *a* têxtil (*m*)

texture /'tekstʃə(r)/ *n* (*of fabric*) textura *f*; (*of paper*) grão *m*

Thai /taɪ/ *a* & *n* tailandês (*m*). **~-land** *n* Tailândia *f*

Thames /temz/ *n* Tâmisa *m*

than /ðæn/; *unstressed* /ðən/ *conj* que, do que; (*with numbers*) de. **more/less ~ ten** mais/menos de dez

thank /θæŋk/ *vt* agradecer. **~ you!** obrigado! **~s!** (*colloq*) (*P*) obrigadinho! (*colloq*). **~s** *npl* agradecimentos *mpl*. **~s to** graças a. **T~sgiving (Day)** (*Amer*) Dia *m* de Ação, (*P*) Acção de Graças

thankful /'θæŋkfl/ *a* grato, agradecido, reconhecido (**for** por). **~ly** *adv* com gratidão; (*happily*) felizmente

thankless /'θæŋklɪs/ *a* ingrato

that /ðæt/; *unstressed* /ðət/ *a* & *pron* (*pl* **those**) esse/essa, esses/essas; (*more distant*) aquele/aquela, aqueles/aquelas; (*neuter*) isso *invar*; (*more distant*) aquilo *invar* □ *adv* tão, tanto, de tal modo □ *rel pron* que □ *conj* que. **~ boy** esse/aquele rapaz. **what is ~?** o que é isso? **who is ~?** quem é? **is ~ you?** é você? **give me ~ (one)** dá-me esse. **~ is (to say)** isto é, quer dizer. **after ~** depois disso. **the day ~** o dia em que. **~ much** tanto assim, tanto como isto

thatch /θætʃ/ *n* colmo *m*. **~ed** *a* de colmo. **~ed cottage** casa *f* com telhado de colmo

thaw /θɔ:/ *vt/i* derreter(se), degelar; (*food*) descongelar □ *n* degelo *m*, derretimento *m*

the /*before vowel* ðɪ, *before consonant* ðə, *stressed* ði:/ *a* o, a (*pl* os, as). **of ~, from ~** do, da (*pl* dos, das). **at ~, to ~** ao, à (*pl* aos, às), para o/a/os/as. **in ~** no, na (*pl* nos, nas). **by ~ hour** a cada hora □ *adv* **all ~ better** tanto melhor. **~ more... ~ more...** quanto mais... tanto mais...

theatre /'θɪətə(r)/ *n* teatro *m*

theatrical /θɪ'ætrɪkl/ *a* teatral

theft /θeft/ *n* roubo *m*

their /ðeə(r)/ *a* deles, delas, seu

theirs /ðeəz/ *poss pron* o(s) seu(s), a(s) sua(s), o(s) deles, a(s) delas. **it is ~** é (o) deles/delas *or* o seu

them /ðem/; *unstressed* /ðəm/ *pron* os, as; (*after prep*) eles, elas. **(to) ~** lhes

theme /θi:m/ *n* tema *m*. **~ park** parque *m* temático

themselves /ðəm'selvz/ *pron* eles mesmos/próprios, elas mesmas/próprias; (*reflexive*) se; (*after prep*) si (mesmos, próprios). **by ~** sozinhos. **with ~** consigo

then /ðen/ *adv* (*at that time*) então, nessa altura; (*next*) depois, em seguida; (*in that case*) então, nesse caso; (*therefore*) então, portanto, por conseguinte

theolog|y /θɪ'ɒlədʒɪ/ *n* teologia *f*. **~ian** /θɪə'ləʊdʒən/ *n* teólogo *m*

theorem /ˈθɪərəm/ *n* teorema *m*
theor|y /ˈθɪərɪ/ *n* teoria *f*. **~etical** /-ˈretɪkl/ *a* teórico
therapeutic /θerəˈpju:tɪk/ *a* terapêutico
therap|y /ˈθerəpɪ/ *n* terapia *f*. **~ist** *n* terapeuta *mf*
there /ðeə(r)/ *adv* aí, ali, lá; (*over there*) lá, acolá □ *int* (*triumphant*) pronto, aí está; (*consoling*) então, vamos lá. **he goes ~** ele vai aí *or* lá. **~ he goes** aí vai ele. **~ is, ~ are** há. **~ you are** (*giving*) toma. **~ and then** logo ali. **~abouts** *adv* por aí. **~after** *adv* daí em diante, depois disso. **~by** *adv* desse modo
therefore /ˈðeəfɔ:(r)/ *adv* por isso, portanto, por conseguinte
thermal /ˈθɜ:ml/ *a* térmico
thermometer /θəˈmɒmɪtə(r)/ *n* termômetro *m*, (*P*) termómetro *m*
Thermos /ˈθɜ:məs/ *n* garrafa *f* térmica, (*P*) termo *m*
thermostat /ˈθɜ:məstæt/ *n* termostato *m*
thesaurus /θɪˈsɔ:rəs/ *n* (*pl* **-ri** /-raɪ/) dicionário *m* de sinônimos, (*P*) sinónimos
these /ði:z/ *see* **this**
thesis /ˈθi:sɪs/ *n* (*pl* **theses** /-si:z/) tese *f*
they /ðeɪ/ *pron* eles, elas. **~ say (that)...** diz-se *or* dizem que...
thick /θɪk/ *a* (**-er, -est**) espesso, grosso; (*colloq: stupid*) estúpido □ *adv* = **thickly** □ *n* **in the ~ of** no meio de. **~-skinned** *a* insensível. **~ly** *adv* espessamente; (*spread*) em camada espessa. **~ness** *n* espessura *f*, grossura *f*
thicken /ˈθɪkən/ *vt/i* engrossar, espessar (-se). **the plot ~s** o enredo complica-se
thickset /θɪkˈset/ *a* (*person*) atarracado
thief /θi:f/ *n* (*pl* **thieves** /θi:vz/) ladrão *m*, gatuno *m*
thigh /θaɪ/ *n* coxa *f*
thimble /ˈθɪmbl/ *n* dedal *m*
thin /θɪn/ *a* (**thinner, thinnest**) (*slender*) estreito, fino, delgado; (*lean, not plump*) magro; (*sparse*) ralo, escasso; (*flimsy*) leve, fino; (*soup*) aguado; (*hair*) ralo □ *adv* = **thinly** □ *vt/i* (*pt* **thinned**) (*of liquid*) diluir(-se); (*of fog etc*) dissipar(-se); (*of hair*) rarear. **~ out** (*in quantity*) diminuir, reduzir; (*seedlings etc*) desbastar. **~ly** *adv* (*sparsely*) esparsamente. **~ness** *n* (*of board, wire etc*) finura *f*; (*of person*) magreza *f*
thing /θɪŋ/ *n* coisa *f*. **~s** (*belongings*) pertences *mpl*. **the best ~ is to** o melhor é. **for one ~** em primeiro lugar. **just the ~** exatamente o que era preciso. **poor ~** coitado
think /θɪŋk/ *vt/i* (*pt* **thought**) pensar (**about, of** em); (*carefully*) refletir, (*P*) reflectir (**about, of** em). **I ~ so** eu acho que sim. **~ better of it** (*change one's mind*) pensar melhor. **~ nothing of** achar natural. **~ of** (*hold opinion of*) pensar de, achar de. **~ over** pensar bem em. **~-tank** *n* comissão *f* de peritos. **~ up** inventar. **~er** *n* pensador *m*
third /θɜ:d/ *a* terceiro □ *n* terceiro *m*; (*fraction*) terço *m*. **~-party insurance** seguro *m* contra terceiros. **~-rate** *a* inferior, medíocre. **T~ World** Terceiro Mundo *m*. **~ly** *adv* em terceiro lugar
thirst /θɜ:st/ *n* sede *f*. **~y** *a* sequioso, sedento. **be ~y** estar com *or* ter sede. **~ily** *adv* sofregamente
thirteen /θɜ:ˈti:n/ *a & n* treze (*m*). **~th** *a & n* décimo terceiro (*m*)
thirt|y /ˈθɜ:tɪ/ *a & n* trinta (*m*). **~ieth** *a & n* trigésimo (*m*)
this /ðɪs/ *a & pron* (*pl* **these**) este, esta □ *pron* isto *invar*. **~ one** este, esta. **these ones** estes, estas. **~ boy** este rapaz. **~ is** isto é. **after ~** depois disto. **like ~** assim. **~ is the man** este é o homem. **~ far** até aqui. **~ morning** esta manhã. **~ Wednesday** esta quarta-feira
thistle /ˈθɪsl/ *n* cardo *m*
thorn /θɔ:n/ *n* espinho *m*, pico *m*. **~y** *a* espinhoso; (*fig*) bicudo, espinhoso
thorough /ˈθʌrə/ *a* consciencioso; (*deep*) completo, profundo; (*cleaning, washing*) a fundo. **~ly** *adv* (*clean, study etc*) completo, a fundo; (*very*) perfeitamente, muito bem
thoroughbred /ˈθʌrəbred/ *n* (*horse etc*) puro-sangue *m invar*
thoroughfare /ˈθʌrəfeə(r)/ *n* artéria *f*. **no ~** passagem *f* proibida
those /ðəʊz/ *see* **that**
though /ðəʊ/ *conj* se bem que, embora, conquanto □ *adv* (*colloq*) contudo, no entanto
thought /θɔ:t/ *see* **think** □ *n* pensamento *m*; idéia *f*. **on second ~s** pensando bem
thoughtful /ˈθɔ:tfl/ *a* pensativo; (*considerate*) atencioso, solícito. **~ly** *adv* pensativamente; (*considerately*) com consideração, atenciosamente
thoughtless /ˈθɔ:tlɪs/ *a* irrefletido, (*P*) irreflectido; (*inconsiderate*) pouco atencioso. **~ly** *adv* sem pensar; (*inconsiderately*) sem consideração
thousand /ˈθaʊznd/ *a & n* mil (*m*). **~s of** milhares de. **~th** *a & n* milésimo (*m*)
thrash /θræʃ/ *vt* surrar, espancar; (*defeat*) dar uma surra *or* sova em. **~ about** debater-se. **~ out** debater a fundo, discutir bem

thread /θred/ *n* fio *m*; (*for sewing*) linha *f* de coser; (*of screw*) rosca *f* □ *vt* enfiar. ~ **one's way** abrir caminho, furar

threadbare /'θredbeə(r)/ *a* puído, surrado

threat /θret/ *n* ameaça *f*

threaten /'θretn/ *vt/i* ameaçar. ~**ingly** *adv* com ar ameaçador, ameaçadoramente

three /θri:/ *a* & *n* três (*m*)

thresh /θreʃ/ *vt* (*corn etc*) malhar, debulhar

threshold /'θreʃəʊld/ *n* limiar *m*, soleira *f*; (*fig*) limiar *m*

threw /θru:/ *see* **throw**

thrift /θrɪft/ *n* economia *f*, poupança *f*. ~**y** *a* econômico, (*P*) económico, poupado

thrill /θrɪl/ *n* arrepio *m* de emoção, frêmito *m*, (*P*) frémito *m* □ *vt* excitar(-se), emocionar(-se), (fazer) vibrar. **be** ~**ed** estar/ficar encantado. ~**ing** *a* excitante, emocionante

thriller /'θrɪlə(r)/ *n* livro *m or* filme *m* de suspense

thriv|e /θraɪv/ *vi* (*pt* **thrived** *or* **throve**, *pp* **thrived** *or* **thriven**) prosperar, florescer; (*grow strong*) crescer, dar-se bem (**on** com). ~**ing** *a* próspero

throat /θrəʊt/ *n* garganta *f*. **have a sore** ~ ter dores de garganta

throb /θrɒb/ *vi* (*pt* **throbbed**) (*wound, head*) latejar; (*heart*) palpitar, bater; (*engine; fig*) vibrar, trepidar □ *n* (*of pain*) latejo *m*, espasmo *m*; (*of heart*) palpitação *f*, batida *f*; (*of engine*) vibração *f*, trepidação *f*. ~**bing** *a* (*pain*) latejante

throes /θrəʊz/ *npl* **in the** ~ **of** (*fig*) às voltas com, no meio de

thrombosis /θrɒm'bəʊsɪs/ *n* trombose *f*

throne /θrəʊn/ *n* trono *m*

throng /θrɒŋ/ *n* multidão *f* □ *vt/i* apinhar(-se); (*arrive*) afluir

throttle /'θrɒtl/ *n* (*auto*) válvula-borboleta *f*, estrangulador *m*, acelerador *m* de mão □ *vt* estrangular

through /θru:/ *prep* através de, por; (*during*) durante; (*by means or way of, out of*) por; (*by reason of*) por, por causa de □ *adv* através; (*entirely*) completamente, até o fim □ *a* (*train, traffic etc*) direto, (*P*) directo. **be** ~ ter acabado (**with** com); (*telephone*) estar ligado. **come** *or* **go** ~ (*cross, pierce*) atravessar. **get** ~ (*exam*) passar. **be wet** ~ estar ensopado *or* encharcado

throughout /θru:'aʊt/ *prep* durante, por todo. ~ **the country** por todo o país afora. ~ **the day** durante todo a dia, pelo dia afora □ *adv* completamente; (*place*) por toda a parte; (*time*) durante todo o tempo

throw /θrəʊ/ *vt* (*pt* **threw**, *pp* **thrown**) atirar, jogar, lançar; (*colloq: baffle*) desconcertar □ *n* lançamento *m*; (*of dice*) lançe *m*. ~ **a party** (*colloq*) dar uma festa. ~ **away** jogar fora, (*P*) deitar fora. ~ **off** (*get rid of*) livrar-se de. ~ **out** (*person*) expulsar; (*reject*) rejeitar. ~ **over** (*desert*) abandonar, deixar. ~ **up** (*one's arms*) levantar; (*resign from*) abandonar; (*colloq: vomit*) vomitar

thrush /θrʌʃ/ *n* (*bird*) tordo *m*

thrust /θrʌst/ *vt* (*pt* **thrust**) arremeter, empurrar, impelir □ *n* empurrão *m*, arremetida *f*. ~ **into** (*put*) enfiar em, mergulhar em. ~ **upon** (*force on*) impôr a

thud /θʌd/ *n* som *m* surdo, baque *m*

thug /θʌg/ *n* bandido *m*, facínora *m*, malfeitor *m*

thumb /θʌm/ *n* polegar *m* □ *vt* (*book*) manusear. ~ **a lift** pedir carona, (*P*) boleia. **under sb's** ~ completamente dominado por alguém. ~**-index** *n* índice *m* de dedo

thumbtack /'θʌmtæk/ *n* (*Amer*) percevejo *m*

thump /θʌmp/ *vt/i* bater (em), dar pancadas (em); (*with fists*) dar murros (em); (*piano*) martelar (em); (*of heart*) bater com força □ *n* pancada *f*; (*thud*) baque *m*. ~**ing** *a* (*colloq*) enorme

thunder /'θʌndə(r)/ *n* trovão *m*, trovoada *f*; (*loud noise*) estrondo *m* □ *vi* (*weather, person*) trovejar. ~ **past** passar como um raio. ~**y** *a* (*weather*) tempestuoso

thunderbolt /'θʌndəbəʊlt/ *n* raio *m* e ribombo *m* de trovão; (*fig*) raio *m* fulminante (*fig*)

thunderstorm /'θʌndəstɔ:m/ *n* tempestade *f* com trovoadas, temporal *m*

Thursday /'θɜ:zdɪ/ *n* quinta-feira *f*

thus /ðʌs/ *adv* assim, desta maneira. ~ **far** até aqui

thwart /θwɔ:t/ *vt* frustrar, contrariar

thyme /taɪm/ *n* tomilho *m*

tiara /tɪ'a:rə/ *n* tiara *f*, diadema *m*

tic /tɪk/ *n* tique *m*

tick[1] /tɪk/ *n* (*sound*) tique-taque *m*; (*mark*) sinal *m*; (*colloq: moment*) instantinho *m* □ *vi* fazer tique-taque □ *vt* ~ (**off**) marcar com sinal. ~ **off** (*colloq: scold*) dar uma bronca em (*colloq*). ~ **over** (*engine, factory*) funcionar em marcha lenta, (*P*) no "ralenti"

tick[2] /tɪk/ *n* (*insect*) carrapato *m*

ticket /'tɪkɪt/ *n* bilhete *m*; (*label*) etiqueta *f*; (*for traffic offence*) aviso *m* de multa. **~-collector** *n* (*railway*) guarda *m*. **~-office** *n* bilheteira *f*

tickle /'tɪkl/ *vt* fazer cócegas; (*fig: amuse*) divertir □ *n* cócegas *fpl*, comichão *m*

ticklish /'tɪklɪʃ/ *a* coceguento, sensível a cócegas; (*fig*) delicado, melindroso

tidal /'taɪdl/ *a* de marés, que tem marés. **~ wave** onda *f* gigantesca; (*fig*) onda *f* de sentimento popular

tiddly-winks /'tɪdlɪwɪŋks/ *n* (*game*) jogo *m* da pulga

tide /taɪd/ *n* maré *f*; (*of events*) marcha *f*, curso *m*. **high ~** maré *f* cheia, preia-mar *f*. **low ~** maré *f* baixa, baixa-mar *f* □ *vt* **~ over** (*help temporarily*) agüentar, (*P*) aguentar

tid|y /'taɪdɪ/ *a* (**-ier, -iest**) (*room*) arrumado; (*appearance, work*) asseado, cuidado; (*methodical*) bem ordenado; (*colloq: amount*) belo (*colloq*) □ *vt* arrumar, arranjar. **~ily** *adv* com cuidado. **~iness** *n* arrumação *f*, ordem *f*

tie /taɪ/ *vt* (*pres p* **tying**) atar, amarrar, prender; (*link*) ligar, vincular; (*a knot*) dar, fazer □ *vi* (*sport*) empatar □ *n* fio *m*, cordel *m*; (*necktie*) gravata *f*; (*link*) laço *m*, vínculo *m*; (*sport*) empate *m*. **~ in with** estar ligado com, relacionar-se com. **~ up** amarrar, atar; (*animal*) prender; (*money*) imobilizar; (*occupy*) ocupar

tier /tɪə(r)/ *n* cada fila *f*, camada *f*, prateleira *f etc* colocada em cima de outra; (*in stadium*) bancada *f*; (*of cake*) andar *m*; (*of society*) camada *f*

tiff /tɪf/ *n* arrufo *m*

tiger /'taɪgə(r)/ *n* tigre *m*

tight /taɪt/ *a* (**-er, -est**) (*clothes*) apertado, justo; (*rope*) esticado, tenso; (*control*) rigoroso; (*knot, schedule, lid*) apertado; (*colloq: drunk*) embriagado (*colloq*) □ *adv* = **tightly. be in a ~ corner** (*fig*) estar em apuros *or* num aperto, (*P*) estar entalado (*colloq*). **~-fisted** *a* sovina, pão-duro, (*P*) agarrado (*colloq*). **~ly** *adv* bem; (*squeeze*) com força

tighten /'taɪtn/ *vt/i* (*rope*) esticar; (*bolt, control*) apertar. **~ up on** apertar o cinto

tightrope /'taɪtrəʊp/ *n* corda *f* (de acrobacias). **~ walker** funâmbulo *m*

tights /taɪts/ *npl* collants *mpl*, meias-colant *fpl*

tile /taɪl/ *n* (*on wall, floor*) ladrilho *m*, azulejo *m*; (*on roof*) telha *f* □ *vt* ladrilhar, pôr azulejos em; (*roof*) telhar, cobrir com telhas

till[1] /tɪl/ *vt* (*land*) cultivar

till[2] /tɪl/ *prep & conj* = **until**

till[3] /tɪl/ *n* caixa (registadora) *f*

tilt /tɪlt/ *vt/i* inclinar(-se), pender □ *n* (*slope*) inclinação *f*. **(at) full ~** a toda a velocidade

timber /'tɪmbə(r)/ *n* madeira *f* (de construção); (*trees*) árvores *fpl*

time /taɪm/ *n* tempo *m*; (*moment*) momento *m*; (*epoch*) época *f*, tempo *m*; (*by clock*) horas *fpl*; (*occasion*) vez *f*; (*rhythm*) compasso *m*. **~s** (*multiplying*) vezes □ *vt* escolher a hora para; (*measure*) marcar o tempo de; (*sport*) cronometrar; (*regulate*) acertar. **at ~s** às vezes. **for the ~ being** por agora, por enquanto. **from ~ to ~** de vez em quando. **have a good ~** divertir-se. **have no ~ for** não ter paciência para. **in no ~** num instante. **in ~** a tempo; (*eventually*) com o tempo. **in two days' ~** daqui a dois dias. **on ~** na hora, (*P*) a horas. **take your ~** não se apresse. **what's the ~?** que horas são? **~ bomb** bomba-relógio *f*. **~-limit** *n* prazo *m*. **~ off** tempo *m* livre. **~-sharing** *n* time-sharing *m*. **~ zone** fuso *m* horário

timeless /'taɪmlɪs/ *a* intemporal; (*unending*) eterno

timely /'taɪmlɪ/ *a* oportuno

timer /'taɪmə(r)/ *n* (*techn*) relógio *m*; (*with sand*) ampulheta *f*

timetable /'taɪmteɪbl/ *n* horário *m*

timid /'tɪmɪd/ *a* tímido; (*fearful*) assustadiço, medroso. **~ly** *adv* timidamente

timing /'taɪmɪŋ/ *n* (*measuring*) cronometragem *f*; (*of artist*) ritmo *m*; (*moment*) cálculo *m* do tempo, timing *m*. **good/bad ~** (*moment*) momento *m* bem/mal escolhido

tin /tɪn/ *n* estanho *m*; (*container*) lata *f* □ *vt* (*pt* **tinned**) estanhar; (*food*) enlatar. **~ foil** papel *m* de alumínio. **~-opener** *n* abridor *m* de latas, (*P*) abre-latas *m*. **~ plate** lata *f*, folha(-de-Flandes) *f*. **~ned foods** conservas *fpl*. **~ny** *a* (*sound*) metálico

tinge /tɪndʒ/ *vt* **~ (with)** tingir (de); (*fig*) dar um toque (de) □ *n* tom *m*, matiz *m*; (*fig*) toque *m*

tingle /'tɪŋgl/ *vi* (*sting*) arder; (*prickle*) picar □ *n* ardor *m*; (*prickle*) picadela *f*

tinker /'tɪŋkə(r)/ *n* latoeiro *m* ambulante □ *vi* **~ (with)** mexer (em), tentar consertar

tinkle /'tɪŋkl/ *n* tinido *m*, tilintar *m* □ *vt/i* tilintar

tinsel /'tɪnsl/ *n* fio *m* prateado/dourado, enfeites *mpl* metálicos de Natal; (*fig*) falso brilho *m*, ouropel *m*

tint /tɪnt/ *n* tom *m*, matiz *m*; (*for hair*) tintura *f*, tinta *f* □ *vt* tingir, colorir

tiny /'taɪnɪ/ *a* (**-ier, -iest**) minúsculo, pequenino

tip[1] /tɪp/ *n* ponta *f*. **(have sth) on the ~ of one's tongue** ter alg coisa na ponta de língua

tip[2] /tɪp/ *vt/i* (*pt* **tipped**) (*tilt*) inclinar(-se); (*overturn*) virar(-se); (*pour*) colocar, (*P*) deitar; (*empty*) despejar(-se) □ *n* (*money*) gorjeta *f*; (*advice*) sugestão *f*, dica *f* (*colloq*); (*for rubbish*) lixeira *f*. **~ off** avisar, prevenir. **~-off** *n* (*warning*) aviso *m*; (*information*) informação *f*

tipsy /'tɪpsɪ/ *a* ligeiramente embriagado, alegre, tocado

tiptoe /'tɪptəʊ/ *n* **on ~** na ponta dos pés

tir|e[1] /'taɪə(r)/ *vt/i* cansar(-se) (**of** de). **~eless** *a* incansável, infatigável. **~ing** *a* fatigante, cansativo

tire[2] /'taɪə(r)/ *n* (*Amer*) pneu *m*

tired /taɪəd/ *a* cansado, fatigado. **~ of** (*sick of*) farto de. **~ out** morto de cansaço

tiresome /'taɪəsəm/ *a* maçador, aborrecido, chato (*sl*)

tissue /'tɪʃu:/ *n* tecido *m*; (*handkerchief*) lenço *m* de papel. **~-paper** *n* papel *m* de seda

tit[1] /tɪt/ *n* (*bird*) chapim *m*, canário-da-terra *m*

tit[2] /tɪt/ *n* **give ~ for tat** pagar na mesma moeda

titbit /'tɪtbɪt/ *n* petisco *m*

titillate /'tɪtɪleɪt/ *vt* excitar, titilar, (*P*) dar gozo a

title /'taɪtl/ *n* título *m*. **~-deed** *n* título *m* de propriedade. **~-page** *n* página *f* de rosto, (*P*) frontispício *m*. **~-role** *n* papel *m* principal

titter /'tɪtə(r)/ *vi* rir com riso abafado

to /tu:/; *unstressed* /tə/ *prep* a, para; (*as far as*) até; (*towards*) para; (*of attitude*) para (com) □ *adv* **push** *or* **pull ~** (*close*) fechar. **~ Portugal** (*for a short time*) a Portugal; (*to stay*) para Portugal. **~ the baker's** para o padeiro, (*P*) ao padeiro. **~ do/sit/***etc* (*infinitive*) fazer/sentar-se/*etc*; (*expressing purpose*) para fazer/para se sentar/*etc*. **it's ten ~ six** são dez para as seis, faltam dez para as seis. **go ~ and** fro andar de um lado para outro. **husband/***etc***-~-be** *n* futuro marido *m*/*etc*. **~-do** *n* (*fuss*) agitação *f*, alvoroço *m*

toad /təʊd/ *n* sapo *m*

toadstool /'təʊdstu:l/ *n* cogumelo *m* venenoso

toady /'təʊdɪ/ *n* lambe-botas *mf*, puxa-saco *m* □ *vi* puxar saco

toast /təʊst/ *n* fatia *f* de pão torrado, torrada *f*; (*drink*) brinde *m*, saúde *f* □ *vt* (*bread*) torrar; (*drink to*) brindar, beber à saúde de. **~er** *n* torradeira *f*

tobacco /tə'bækəʊ/ *n* tabaco *m*

tobacconist /tə'bækənɪst/ *n* vendedor *m* de tabaco, homem *m* da tabacaria (*colloq*). **~'s shop** tabacaria *f*

toboggan /tə'bɒgən/ *n* tobogã *m*, (*P*) toboggan *m*

today /tə'deɪ/ *n* & *adv* hoje (*m*)

toddler /'tɒdlə(r)/ *n* criança *f* que está aprendendo a andar

toe /təʊ/ *n* dedo *m* do pé; (*of shoe, stocking*) biqueira *f* □ *vt* **~ the line** andar na linha. **on one's ~s** alerta, vigilante. **~-hold** *n* apoio (precário) *m*. **~nail** *n* unha *f* do dedo do pé

toffee /'tɒfɪ/ *n* puxa-puxa *m*, (*P*) caramelo *m*. **~-apple** *n* maçã *f* caramelizada

together /tə'geðə(r)/ *adv* junto, juntamente, juntos; (*at the same time*) ao mesmo tempo. **~ with** juntamente com. **~ness** *n* camaradagem *f*, companheirismo *m*

toil /tɔɪl/ *vi* labutar □ *n* labuta *f*, labor *m*

toilet /'tɔɪlɪt/ *n* banheiro *m*, (*P*) casa *f* de banho; (*grooming*) toalete *f*. **~-paper** *n* papel *m* higiênico, (*P*) higiénico. **~-roll** *n* rolo *m* de papel higiênico, (*P*) higiénico. **~ water** água-de-colônia *f*

toiletries /'tɔɪlɪtrɪz/ *npl* artigos *mpl* de toalete

token /'təʊkən/ *n* sinal *m*, prova *f*; (*voucher*) cheque *m*; (*coin*) ficha *f* □ *a* simbólico

told /təʊld/ *see* **tell** □ *a* **all ~** (*all in all*) ao todo

tolerabl|e /'tɒlərəbl/ *a* tolerável; (*not bad*) sofrível, razoável. **~y** *adv* (*work, play*) razoavelmente

toleran|t /'tɒlərənt/ *a* tolerante (**of** para com). **~ce** *n* tolerância *f*. **~tly** *adv* com tolerância

tolerate /'tɒləreɪt/ *vt* tolerar

toll[1] /təʊl/ *n* pedágio *m*, (*P*) portagem *f*. **death ~** número *m* de mortos. **take its ~** (*of age*) fazer sentir o seu peso

toll[2] /təʊl/ *vt/i* (*of bell*) dobrar

tomato /tə'ma:təʊ/ *n* (*pl* **-oes**) tomate *m*

tomb /tu:m/ *n* túmulo *m*, sepultura *f*

tomboy /'tɒmbɔɪ/ *n* menina *f* levada (e masculinizada), (*P*) maria-rapaz *f*

tombstone /'tu:mstəʊn/ *n* lápide *f*, pedra *f* tumular

tome /təʊm/ *n* tomo *m*, volume *m*

tomfoolery /tɒm'fu:lərɪ/ *n* disparates *mpl*, imbecilidades *fpl*

tomorrow /tə'mɒrəʊ/ *n* & *adv* amanhã (*m*). **~ morning/night** amanhã de manhã/à noite

ton /tʌn/ *n* tonelada *f* (= *1016 kg*). **(metric) ~** tonelada *f* (= *1000 kg*). **~s of**

(*colloq*) montes de (*colloq*), (*P*) carradas de (*colloq*)

tone /təʊn/ *n* tom *m*; (*of radio, telephone etc*) sinal *m*; (*colour*) tom *m*, tonalidade *f*; (*med*) tonicidade *f* □ *vt* ~ **down** atenuar □ *vi* ~ **in** combinar-se, harmonizar-se (**with** com). ~ **up** (*muscles*) tonificar. ~**-deaf** *a* sem ouvido musical

tongs /tɒŋz/ *n* tenaz *f*; (*for sugar*) pinça *f*; (*for hair*) pinça *f*

tongue /tʌŋ/ *n* língua *f*. ~**-in-cheek** *a* & *adv* sem ser a sério, com ironia. ~**-tied** *a* calado. ~**-twister** *n* travalíngua *m*

tonic /'tɒnɪk/ *n* (*med*) tônico *m*, (*P*) tónico *m*; (*mus*) tônica *f*, (*P*) tónica *f* □ *a* tônico, (*P*) tónico

tonight /tə'naɪt/ *adv* & *n* hoje à noite, logo à noite, esta noite (*f*)

tonne /tʌn/ *n* (*metric*) tonelada *f*

tonsil /'tɒnsl/ *n* amígdala *f*

tonsillitis /tɒnsɪ'laɪtɪs/ *n* amigdalite *f*

too /tu:/ *adv* demasiado, demais; (*also*) também, igualmente; (*colloq: very*) muito. ~ **many** *a* demais, demasiados. ~ **much** *a* & *adv* demais, demasiado

took /tʊk/ *see* **take**

tool /tu:l/ *n* (*carpenter's, plumber's etc*) ferramenta *f*; (*gardener's*) utensílio *m*; (*fig: person*) joguete *m*. ~**-bag** *n* saco *m* de ferramenta

toot /tu:t/ *n* toque *m* de buzina □ *vt*/*i* ~ **(the horn)** buzinar

tooth /tu:θ/ *n* (*pl* **teeth**) dente *m*. ~**less** *a* desdentado

toothache /'tu:θeɪk/ *n* dor *f* de dentes

toothbrush /'tu:θbrʌʃ/ *n* escova *f* de dentes

toothpaste /'tu:θpeɪst/ *n* pasta *f* de dentes, dentifrício *m*

toothpick /'tu:θpɪk/ *n* palito *m*

top[1] /tɒp/ *n* (*highest point; upper part*) alto *m*, cimo *m*, topo *m*; (*of hill; fig*) cume *m*; (*upper surface*) cimo *m*, topo *m*; (*surface of table*) tampo *m*; (*lid*) tampa *f*; (*of bottle*) rolha *f*; (*of list*) cabeça *f* □ *a* (*shelf etc*) de cima, superior; (*in rank*) primeiro; (*best*) melhor; (*distinguished*) eminente; (*maximum*) máximo □ *vt* (*pt* **topped**) (*exceed*) ultrapassar, ir acima de. **from ~ to bottom** de alto a baixo. **on ~ of** em cima de; (*fig*) além de. **on ~ of that** ainda por cima. ~ **gear** (*auto*) a velocidade mais alta. ~ **hat** chapéu *m* alto. ~**-heavy** *a* mais pesado na parte de cima. ~ **secret** ultra-secreto. ~ **up** encher; (*mobiles*) recarregar ~**ped with** coberto de

top[2] /tɒp/ *n* (*toy*) pião *m*. **sleep like a ~** dormir como uma pedra

topic /'tɒpɪk/ *n* tópico *m*, assunto *m*

topical /'tɒpɪkl/ *a* da atualidade, (*P*) actualidade, corrente

topless /'tɒplɪs/ *a* com o peito nu, topless

topple /'tɒpl/ *vt*/*i* (fazer) desabar, (fazer) tombar, (fazer) cair

torch /tɔ:tʃ/ *n* (*electric*) lanterna *f* elétrica, (*P*) eléctrica; (*flaming*) archote *m*, facho *m*

tore /tɔ:(r)/ *see* **tear**[1]

torment[1] /'tɔ:mənt/ *n* tormento *m*

torment[2] /tɔ:'ment/ *vt* atormentar, torturar; (*annoy*) aborrecer, chatear

torn /tɔ:n/ *see* **tear**[1]

tornado /tɔ:'neɪdəʊ/ *n* (*pl* **-oes**) tornado *m*

torpedo /tɔ:'pi:dəʊ/ *n* (*pl* **-oes**) torpedo *m* □ *vt* torpedear

torrent /'tɒrənt/ *n* torrente *f*. ~**ial** /tə'renʃl/ *a* torrencial

torrid /'tɒrɪd/ *a* (*climate etc*) tórrido; (*fig*) intenso, ardente

torso /'tɔ:səʊ/ *n* (*pl* **-os**) torso *m*

tortoise /'tɔ:təs/ *n* tartaruga *f*

tortoiseshell /'tɔ:təsʃel/ *n* (*for ornaments etc*) tartaruga *f*

tortuous /'tɔ:tʃʊəs/ *a* (*of path etc*) que dá muitas voltas, sinuoso; (*fig*) tortuoso, retorcido

torture /'tɔ:tʃə(r)/ *n* tortura *f*, suplício *m* □ *vt* torturar. ~**r** /-ə(r)/ *n* carrasco *m*, algoz *m*, torturador *m*

Tory /'tɔ:rɪ/ *a* & *n* (*colloq*) conservador (*m*), (*P*) tóri (*m*)

toss /tɒs/ *vt* atirar, jogar, (*P*) deitar; (*shake*) agitar, sacudir □ *vi* agitar-se, debater-se. ~ **a coin**, ~ **up** tirar cara ou coroa

tot[1] /tɒt/ *n* criancinha *f*; (*colloq: glass*) copinho *m*

tot[2] /tɒt/ *vt*/*i* (*pt* **totted**) ~ **up** (*colloq*) somar

total /'təʊtl/ *a* & *n* total (*m*) □ *vt* (*pt* **totalled**) (*find total of*) totalizar; (*amount to*) elevar-se a, montar a. ~**ity** /-'tælətɪ/ *n* totalidade *f*. ~**ly** *adv* totalmente

totalitarian /təʊtælɪ'teərɪən/ *a* totalitário

totter /'tɒtə(r)/ *vi* cambalear, andar aos tombos; (*of tower etc*) oscilar

touch /tʌtʃ/ *vt*/*i* tocar; (*of ends, gardens etc*) tocar-se; (*tamper with*) mexer em; (*affect*) comover □ *n* (*sense*) tato *m*, (*P*) tacto *m*; (*contact*) toque *m*; (*of colour*) toque *m*, retoque *m*. **a ~ of** (*small amount*) um pouco de. **get in ~ with** entrar em contato, (*P*) contacto com. **lose ~** perder contato, (*P*) contacto. ~ **down** (*aviat*) aterrissar, (*P*) aterrar. ~ **off** disparar; (*cause*) dar início a, desencadear. ~ **on** (*mention*) tocar em.

~ **up** retocar. ~**-and-go** *a* (*risky*) arriscado; (*uncertain*) duvidoso, incerto. ~**-line** *n* linha *f* lateral

touching /'tʌtʃɪŋ/ *a* comovente, comovedor

touchy /'tʌtʃɪ/ *a* melindroso, suscetível, (*P*) susceptível, que se ofende facilmente

tough /tʌf/ *a* (**-er, -est**) (*hard, difficult; relentless*) duro; (*strong*) forte, resistente □ *n* ~ **(guy)** valentão *m*, durão *m* (*colloq*). ~ **luck!** (*colloq*) pouca sorte! ~**ness** *n* dureza *f*; (*strength*) força *f*, resistência *f*

toughen /'tʌfn/ *vt*/*i* (*person*) endurecer; (*strengthen*) reforçar

tour /tʊə(r)/ *n* viagem *f*; (*visit*) visita *f*; (*by team etc*) tournée *f* □ *vt* visitar. **on** ~ em tournée

tourism /'tʊərɪzəm/ *n* turismo *m*

tourist /'tʊərɪst/ *n* turista *mf* □ *a* turístico. ~ **office** agência *f* de turismo

tournament /'tʊərnəmənt/ *n* torneio *m*

tousle /'taʊzl/ *vt* despentear, esguedelhar

tout /taʊt/ *vi* angariar clientes (**for** para) □ *vt* (*try to sell*) tentar revender □ *n* (*hotel etc*) angariador *m*; (*ticket*) cambista *m*, (*P*) revendedor *m*

tow /təʊ/ *vt* rebocar □ *n* reboque *m*. **on** ~ a reboque. ~ **away** (*vehicle*) rebocar. ~**-path** *n* caminho *m* de sirga. ~**-rope** *n* cabo *m* de reboque

toward(s) /tə'wɔ:d(z)/ *prep* para, em direção, (*P*) direcção a, na direção, (*P*) direcção de; (*of attitude*) para com; (*time*) por volta de

towel /'taʊəl/ *n* toalha *f*; (*tea towel*) pano *m* de prato □ *vt* (*pt* **towelled**) esfregar com a toalha. ~**-rail** *n* toalheiro *m*. ~**ling** *n* atoalhado *m*, (*P*) pano *m* turco

tower /'taʊə(r)/ *n* torre *f* □ *vi* ~ **above** dominar. ~ **block** prédio *m* alto. ~**ing** *a* muito alto; (*fig: of rage etc*) violento

town /taʊn/ *n* cidade *f*. **go to** ~ (*colloq*) perder a cabeça (*colloq*). ~ **council** município *m*. ~ **hall** câmara *f* municipal. ~ **planning** urbanização *f*

toxic /'tɒksɪk/ *a* tóxico

toy /tɔɪ/ *n* brinquedo *m* □ *vi* ~ **with** (*object*) brincar com; (*idea*) considerar, cogitar

trace /treɪs/ *n* traço *m*, rastro *m*, sinal *m*; (*small quantity*) traço *m*, vestígio *m* □ *vt* seguir *or* encontrar a pista de; (*draw*) traçar; (*with tracing-paper*) decalcar

tracing /'treɪsɪŋ/ *n* decalque *m*, desenho *m*. ~**-paper** *n* papel *m* vegetal

track /træk/ *n* (*of person etc*) rastro *m*, pista *f*; (*race-track, of tape*) pista *f*; (*record*) faixa *f*; (*path*) trilho *m*, carreiro *m*; (*rail*) via *f* □ *vt* seguir a pista *or* a trajetória, (*P*) trajectória de. **keep** ~ **of** manter-se em contato com; (*keep oneself informed*) seguir. ~ **down** (*find*) encontrar, descobrir; (*hunt*) seguir a pista de. ~ **suit** conjunto *m* de jogging, (*P*) fato *m* de treino

tract /trækt/ *n* (*land*) extensão *f*; (*anat*) aparelho *m*

tractor /'træktə(r)/ *n* trator *m*, (*P*) tractor *m*

trade /treɪd/ *n* comércio *m*; (*job*) ofício *m*, profissão *f*; (*swap*) troca *f* □ *vt*/*i* comerciar (em), negociar (em) □ *vt* (*swap*) trocar. ~ **in** (*used article*) trocar. ~**-in** *n* troca *f*. ~ **mark** marca *f* de fábrica. ~ **on** (*exploit*) tirar partido de, abusar de. ~ **union** sindicato *m*. ~**r** /-ə(r)/ *n* negociante *mf*, comerciante *mf*

tradesman /'treɪdzmən/ *n* (*pl* **-men**) comerciante *m*

trading /'treɪdɪŋ/ *n* comércio *m*. ~ **estate** zona *f* industrial

tradition /trə'dɪʃn/ *n* tradição *f*. ~**al** *a* tradicional

traffic /'træfɪk/ *n* (*trade*) tráfego *m*, tráfico *m*; (*on road*) trânsito *m*, tráfego *m*; (*aviat*) tráfego *m* □ *vi* (*pt* **trafficked**) traficar (**in** em). ~ **circle** (*Amer*) giratória *f*, (*P*) rotunda *f*. ~ **island** ilha *f* de pedestres, (*P*) refúgio *m* para peões. ~ **jam** engarrafamento *m*. ~**-lights** *npl* sinal *m* luminoso, (*P*) semáforo *m*. ~ **warden** guarda *mf* de trânsito. ~**ker** *n* traficante *mf*

tragedy /'trædʒədɪ/ *n* tragédia *f*.

tragic /'trædʒɪk/ *a* trágico

trail /treɪl/ *vt*/*i* arrastar(-se), rastejar; (*of plant, on ground*) rastejar; (*of plant, over wall*) trepar; (*track*) seguir □ *n* (*of powder, smoke etc*) esteira *f*, rastro *m*, (*P*) rasto *m*; (*track*) pista *f*; (*beaten path*) trilho *m*

trailer /'treɪlə(r)/ *n* reboque *m*; (*Amer: caravan*) reboque *m*, caravana *f*, trailer *m*; (*film*) trailer *m*, apresentação *f* de filme

train /treɪn/ *n* (*rail*) trem *m*, (*P*) comboio *m*; (*procession*) fila *f*; (*of dress*) cauda *f*; (*retinue*) comitiva *f* □ *vt* (*instruct, develop*) educar, formar, treinar; (*plant*) guiar; (*sportsman, animal*) treinar; (*aim*) assestar, apontar □ *vi* estudar, treinar-se. ~**ed** *a* (*skilled*) qualificado; (*doctor etc*) diplomado. ~**er** *n* (*sport*) treinador *m*; (*shoe*) tênis *m*. ~**ing** *n* treino *m*

trainee /treɪ'ni:/ *n* estagiário *m*

trait /treɪ(t)/ *n* traço *m*, característica *f*

traitor /'treɪtə(r)/ *n* traidor *m*

tram /træm/ *n* bonde *m*, (*P*) (carro) eléctrico *m*

tramp /træmp/ *vi* marchar (com passo pesado) □ *vt* percorrer, palmilhar □ *n* som *m* de passos pesados; (*vagrant*) vagabundo *m*, andarilho *m*; (*hike*) longa caminhada *f*

trample /'træmpl/ *vt/i* ~ **(on)** pisar com força; (*fig*) menosprezar

trampoline /'træmpəli:n/ *n* (lona *f* usada como) trampolim *m*

trance /tra:ns/ *n* (*hypnotic*) transe *m*; (*ecstasy*) êxtase *m*, arrebatamento *m*; (*med*) estupor *m*

tranquil /'træŋkwɪl/ *a* tranqüilo, (*P*) tranquilo, sossegado. **~lity** /-'kwɪlətɪ/ *n* tranqüilidade *f*, (*P*) tranquilidade *f*, sossego *m*

tranquillizer /'træŋkwɪlaɪzə(r)/ *n* (*drug*) tranqüilizante *m*, (*P*) tranquilizante *m*, calmante *m*

transact /træn'zækt/ *vt* (*business*) fazer, efetuar, (*P*) efectuar. **~ion** /-kʃn/ *n* transação *f*, (*P*) transacção *f*

transcend /træn'send/ *vt* transcender. **~ent** *a* transcendente

transcri|be /træn'skraɪb/ *vt* transcrever. **~pt, ~ption** /-ɪpʃn/ *ns* transcrição *f*

transfer[1] /træns'fɜ:(r)/ *vt* (*pt* **transferred**) transferir; (*power, property*) transmitir □ *vi* mudar, ser transferido; (*change planes etc*) fazer transferência. **~ the charges** (*telephone*) ligar a cobrar

transfer[2] /'trænsfɜ:(r)/ *n* transferência *f*; (*of power, property*) transmissão *f*; (*image*) decalcomania *f*

transfigure /træns'fɪgə(r)/ *vt* transfigurar

transform /træns'fɔ:m/ *vt* transformar. **~ation** /-ə'meɪʃn/ *n* transformação *f*. **~er** *n* (*electr*) transformador *m*

transfusion /træns'fju:ʒn/ *n* (*of blood*) transfusão *f*

transient /'trænzɪənt/ *a* transitório, transiente, efêmero, (*P*) efémero, passageiro

transistor /træn'zɪstə(r)/ *n* (*device, radio*) transistor *m*

transit /'trænsɪt/ *n* trânsito *m*. **in ~** em trânsito

transition /træn'zɪʃn/ *n* transição *f*. **~al** *a* transitório

transitive /'trænsətɪv/ *a* transitivo

transitory /'trænsɪtərɪ/ *a* transitório

translat|e /trænz'leɪt/ *vt* traduzir. **~ion** /-ʃn/ *n* tradução *f*. **~or** *n* tradutor *m*

translucent /trænz'lu:snt/ *a* translúcido

transmi|t /trænz'mɪt/ *vt* (*pt* **transmitted**) transmitir. **~ssion** *n* transmissão *f*. **~tter** *n* transmissor *m*

transparen|t /træns'pærənt/ *a* transparente. **~cy** *n* transparência *f*; (*photo*) diapositivo *m*

transpire /træn'spaɪə(r)/ *vi* (*secret etc*) transpirar; (*happen*) suceder, acontecer

transplant[1] /træns'pla:nt/ *vt* transplantar

transplant[2] /'trænspla:nt/ *n* (*med*) transplantação *f*, transplante *m*

transport[1] /træn'spɔ:t/ *vt* (*carry, delight*) transportar. **~ation** /-'teɪʃn/ *n* transporte *m*

transport[2] /'trænspɔ:t/ *n* (*of goods, delight etc*) transporte *m*

transpose /træn'spəʊz/ *vt* transpor

transverse /'trænzvɜ:s/ *a* transversal

transvestite /trænz'vestaɪt/ *n* travesti *mf*

trap /træp/ *n* armadilha *f*, ratoeira *f*, cilada *f* □ *vt* (*pt* **trapped**) apanhar na armadilha; (*cut off*) prender, bloquear. **~per** *n* caçador *m* de armadilha (esp de peles)

trapdoor /træp'dɔ:(r)/ *n* alçapão *m*

trapeze /trə'pi:z/ *n* trapézio *m*

trash /træʃ/ *n* (*worthless stuff*) porcaria *f*; (*refuse*) lixo *m*; (*nonsense*) disparates *mpl*. **~ can** *n* (*Amer*) lata *f* do lixo, (*P*) caixote *m* do lixo. **~y** *a* que não vale nada, porcaria

trauma /'trɔ:mə/ *n* trauma *m*, traumatismo *m*. **~tic** /-'mætɪk/ *a* traumático

travel /'trævl/ *vi* (*pt* **travelled**) viajar; (*of vehicle, bullet, sound*) ir □ *vt* percorrer □ *n* viagem *f*. **~ agent** agente *mf* de viagem. **~ler** *n* viajante *mf*. **~ler's cheque** cheque *m* de viagem. **~ling** *n* viagem *f*, viagens *fpl*, viajar *m*

travesty /'trævəstɪ/ *n* paródia *f*, caricatura *f*

trawler /'trɔ:lə(r)/ *n* traineira *f*, (*P*) arrastão *m*

tray /treɪ/ *n* tabuleiro *m*, bandeja *f*

treacherous /'tretʃərəs/ *a* traiçoeiro

treachery /'tretʃərɪ/ *n* traição *f*, perfídia *f*, deslealdade *f*

treacle /'tri:kl/ *n* melaço *m*

tread /tred/ *vt/i* (*pt* **trod**, *pp* **trodden**) (*step*) pisar; (*walk*) andar, caminhar; (*walk along*) seguir □ *n* passo *m*, maneira *f* de andar; (*of tyre*) trilho *m*. **~ sth into** (*carpet*) esmigalhar alg coisa sobre/em

treason /'tri:zn/ *n* traição *f*

treasure /'treʒə(r)/ *n* tesouro *m* □ *vt* ter o maior apreço por; (*store*) guardar bem guardado. **~r** *n* tesoureiro *m*

treasury /'treʒərɪ/ *n* (*building*) tesouraria *f*; (*department*) Ministério *m* das Finanças *or* da Fazenda; (*fig*) tesouro *m*

treat /tri:t/ *vt/i* tratar □ *n* (*pleasure*) prazer *m*, regalo *m*; (*present*) mimo *m*, gentileza *f*. ~ **sb to sth** convidar alguém para alg coisa
treatise /'tri:tɪz/ *n* tratado *m*
treatment /'tri:tmənt/ *n* tratamento *m*
treaty /'tri:tɪ/ *n* (*pact*) tratado *m*
trebl|e /'trebl/ *a* triplo □ *vt/i* triplicar □ *n* (*mus: voice*) soprano *m*. ~**y** *adv* triplamente
tree /tri:/ *n* árvore *f*
trek /trek/ *n* viagem *f* penosa; (*walk*) caminhada *f* □ *vi* (*pt* **trekked**) viajar penosamente; (*walk*) caminhar
trellis /'trelɪs/ *n* grade *f* para trepadeiras, treliça *f*
tremble /'trembl/ *vi* tremer
tremendous /trɪ'mendəs/ *a* (*fearful, huge*) tremendo; (*colloq: excellent*) fantástico, formidável
tremor /'tremə(r)/ *n* tremor *m*, estremecimento *m*. **(earth)** ~ abalo (sísmico) *m*, tremor *m* de terra
trench /trentʃ/ *n* fossa *f*, vala *f*; (*mil*) trincheira *f*
trend /trend/ *n* tendência *f*; (*fashion*) moda *f*. ~**y** *a* (*colloq*) na última moda, (*P*) na berra (*colloq*)
trepidation /trepɪ'deɪʃn/ *n* (*fear*) receio *m*, apreensão *f*
trespass /'trespəs/ *vi* entrar ilegalmente (**on** em). **no** ~**ing** entrada *f* proibida. ~**er** *n* intruso *m*
trestle /'tresl/ *n* cavalete *m*, armação *f* de mesa. ~**-table** *n* mesa *f* de cavaletes
trial /'traɪəl/ *n* (*jur*) julgamento *m*, processo *m*; (*test*) ensaio *m*, experiência *f*, prova *f*; (*ordeal*) provação *f*. **on** ~ em julgamento. ~ **and error** tentativas *fpl*
triang|le /'traɪæŋgl/ *n* triângulo *m*. ~**ular** /-'æŋgjʊlə(r)/ *a* triangular
trib|e /traɪb/ *n* tribo *f*. ~**al** *a* tribal
tribulation /trɪbjʊ'leɪʃn/ *n* tribulação *f*
tribunal /traɪ'bju:nl/ *n* tribunal *m*
tributary /'trɪbjʊtərɪ/ *n* afluente *m*, tributário *m*
tribute /'trɪbju:t/ *n* tributo *m*. **pay** ~ **to** prestar homenagem a, render tributo a
trick /trɪk/ *n* truque *m*; (*prank*) partida *f*; (*habit*) jeito *m* □ *vt* enganar. **do the** ~ (*colloq: work*) dar resultado
trickery /'trɪkərɪ/ *n* trapaça *f*
trickle /'trɪkl/ *vi* pingar, gotejar, escorrer □ *n* fio *m* de água *etc*; (*fig: small number*) punhado *m*
tricky /'trɪkɪ/ *a* (*crafty*) manhoso; (*problem*) delicado, complicado
tricycle /'traɪsɪkl/ *n* triciclo *m*
trifle /'traɪfl/ *n* ninharia *f*, bagatela *f*; (*sweet*) sobremesa *f* feita de pão-de-ló e frutas e creme □ *vi* ~ **with** brincar com. **a** ~ um pouquinho, (*P*) um poucochinho
trifling /'traɪflɪŋ/ *a* insignificante
trigger /'trɪgə(r)/ *n* (*of gun*) gatilho *m* □ *vt* ~ **(off)** (*initiate*) desencadear, despoletar
trill /trɪl/ *n* trinado *m*, gorjeio *m*
trilogy /'trɪlədʒɪ/ *n* trilogia *f*
trim /trɪm/ *a* (**trimmer, trimmest**) bem arranjado, bem cuidado; (*figure*) elegante, esbelto □ *vt* (*pt* **trimmed**) (*cut*) aparar; (*sails*) orientar, marear; (*ornament*) enfeitar, guarnecer (**with** com) □ *n* (*cut*) aparadela *f*, corte *m* leve; (*decoration*) enfeite *m*; (*on car*) acabamento(s) *m*(*pl*), estofado *m*. **in** ~ em ordem; (*fit*) em boa forma. ~**ming(s)** *n*(*pl*) (*dress*) enfeite *m*; (*culin*) guarnição *f*, acompanhamento *m*
Trinity /'trɪnətɪ/ *n* **the (Holy)** ~ a Santíssima Trindade
trinket /'trɪŋkɪt/ *n* bugiganga *f*; (*jewel*) bijuteria *f*, berloque *m*
trio /'tri:əʊ/ *n* (*pl* **-os**) trio *m*
trip /trɪp/ *vi* (*pt* **tripped**) (*stumble*) tropeçar, dar um passo em falso; (*go or dance lightly*) andar/dançar com passos leves □ *vt* ~ **(up)** fazer tropeçar, passar uma rasteira a □ *n* (*journey*) viagem *f*; (*outing*) passeio *m*, excursão *f*; (*stumble*) tropeção *m*, passo *m* em falso
tripe /traɪp/ *n* (*food*) dobrada *f*, tripas *fpl*; (*colloq: nonsense*) disparates *mpl*
triple /'trɪpl/ *a* triplo, tríplice □ *vt/i* triplicar. ~**ts** /-plɪts/ *npl* trigêmeos *mpl*, (*P*) trigémeos *mpl*
triplicate /'trɪplɪkət/ *n* **in** ~ em triplicata
tripod /'traɪpɒd/ *n* tripé *m*
trite /traɪt/ *a* banal, corriqueiro
triumph /'traɪəmf/ *n* triunfo *m* □ *vi* triunfar (**over** sobre); (*exult*) exultar, rejubilar-se. ~**al** /-'ʌmfl/ *a* triunfal. ~**ant** /-'ʌmfənt/ *a* triunfante. ~**antly** /-'ʌmfəntlɪ/ *adv* em triunfo, triunfantemente
trivial /'trɪvɪəl/ *a* insignificante
trod, trodden /trɒd, 'trɒdn/ *see* **tread**
trolley /'trɒlɪ/ *n* carrinho *m*. **(tea-)** ~ carrinho *m* de chá
trombone /trɒm'bəʊn/ *n* (*mus*) trombone *m*
troop /tru:p/ *n* bando *m*, grupo *m*. ~**s** (*mil*) tropas *fpl* □ *vi* ~ **in/out** entrar/sair em bando *or* grupo. ~**ing the colour** a saudação da bandeira. ~**er** *n* soldado *m* de cavalaria
trophy /'trəʊfɪ/ *n* troféu *m*
tropic /'trɒpɪk/ *n* trópico *m*. ~**s** trópicos *mpl*. ~**al** *a* tropical

trot /trɒt/ *n* trote *m* □ *vi* (*pt* **trotted**) trotar; (*of person*) correr em passos curtos, ir num *or* a trote (*colloq*). **on the ~** (*colloq*) a seguir, a fio. **~ out** (*colloq: produce*) exibir; (*colloq: state*) desfiar

trouble /'trʌbl/ *n* (*difficulty*) dificuldade(s) *f* (*pl*), problema(s) *m* (*pl*); (*distress*) desgosto(s) *m* (*pl*), aborrecimento(s) *m* (*pl*); (*pains, effort*) cuidado *m*, trabalho *m*, maçada *f*; (*inconvenience*) transtorno *m*, incômodo *m*, (*P*) incómodo *m*; (*med*) doença *f*. **~(s)** (*unrest*) agitação *f*, conflito(s) *m* (*pl*) □ *vt/i* (*bother*) incomodar(-se), (*P*) maçar(-se); (*worry*) preocupar(-se); (*agitate*) perturbar. **be in ~** estar em apuros, estar em dificuldades. **get into ~** meter-se em encrenca/apuros. **it is not worth the ~** não vale a pena. **~-maker** *n* desordeiro *m*, provocador *m*. **~-shooter** *n* mediador *m*, negociador *m*. **~d** *a* agitado, perturbado; (*of sleep*) agitado; (*of water*) turvo

troublesome /'trʌblsəm/ *a* problemático, importuno, (*P*) maçador

trough /trɒf/ *n* (*drinking*) bebedouro *m*; (*feeding*) comedouro *m*. **~ (of low pressure)** depressão *f*, linha *f* de baixa pressão

trounce /traʊns/ *vt* (*defeat*) esmagar; (*thrash*) espancar

troupe /tru:p/ *n* (*theat*) companhia *f*, troupe *f*

trousers /'traʊzəz/ *npl* calça *f*, (*P*) calças *fpl*. **short ~** calções *mpl*

trousseau /'tru:səʊ/ *n* (*pl* **-s** /-əʊz/) (*of bride*) enxoval *m* de noiva

trout /traʊt/ *n* (*pl invar*) truta *f*

trowel /'traʊəl/ *n* (*garden*) colher *f* de jardineiro; (*for mortar*) trolha *f*

truan|t /'tru:ənt/ *n* absenteísta *mf*, (*P*) absentista *mf*; (*schol*) gazeteiro *m*. **play ~t** fazer gazeta. **~cy** *n* absenteísmo *m*, (*P*) absentismo *m*

truce /tru:s/ *n* trégua(s) *f* (*pl*), armistício *m*

truck /trʌk/ *n* (*lorry*) camião *m*; (*barrow*) carro *m* de bagageiro; (*wagon*) vagão *m* aberto. **~-driver** *n* motorista *mf* de camião, (*P*) camionista *mf*

truculent /'trʌkjʊlənt/ *a* agressivo, brigão

trudge /trʌdʒ/ *vi* caminhar com dificuldade, caminhar a custo, arrastar-se

true /tru:/ *a* (**-er, -est**) verdadeiro; (*accurate*) exato, (*P*) exacto; (*faithful*) fiel. **come ~** (*happen*) realizar-se, concretizar-se. **it is ~** é verdade

truffle /'trʌfl/ *n* trufa *f*

truism /'tru:ɪzəm/ *n* truísmo *m*, verdade *f* evidente, (*P*) verdade *f* do Amigo Banana (*colloq*)

truly /'tru:lɪ/ *adv* verdadeiramente; (*faithfully*) fielmente; (*truthfully*) sinceramente

trump /trʌmp/ *n* trunfo *m* □ *vt* jogar trunfo, trunfar. **~ up** forjar, inventar. **~ card** carta *f* de trunfo; (*colloq: valuable resource*) trunfo *m*

trumpet /'trʌmpɪt/ *n* trombeta *f*

truncheon /'trʌntʃən/ *n* cassetete *m*, (*P*) cassetête *m*

trundle /'trʌndl/ *vt/i* (fazer) rolar ruidosamente/pesadamente

trunk /trʌŋk/ *n* (*of tree, body*) tronco *m*; (*of elephant*) tromba *f*; (*box*) mala *f* grande; (*Amer, auto*) mala *f*. **~s** (*for swimming*) calção *m* de banho. **~ call** *n* chamada *f* interurbana. **~ road** *n* estrada *f* nacional

truss /trʌs/ *n* (*med*) funda *f* □ *vt* atar, amarrar

trust /trʌst/ *n* confiança *f*; (*association*) truste *m*, (*P*) trust *m*, consórcio *m*; (*foundation*) fundação *f*; (*responsibility*) responsabilidade *f*; (*jur*) fideicomisso *m* □ *vt* (*rely on*) ter confiança em, confiar em; (*hope*) esperar □ *vi* **~ in** *or* **to** confiar em. **in ~** em fideicomisso. **on ~** (*without proof*) sem verificação prévia; (*on credit*) a crédito. **~ sb with** confiar em alguém. **~ed** *a* (*friend etc*) de confiança, seguro. **~ful**, **~ing** *adjs* confiante. **~y** *a* fiel

trustee /trʌs'ti:/ *n* administrador *m*; (*jur*) fideicomissório *m*

trustworthy /'trʌstwɜ:ðɪ/ *a* (digno) de confiança

truth /tru:θ/ *n* (*pl* **-s** /tru:ðz/) verdade *f*. **~ful** *a* (*account etc*) verídico; (*person*) verdadeiro, que fala verdade. **~fully** *adv* sinceramente

try /traɪ/ *vt/i* (*pt* **tried**) tentar, experimentar; (*be a strain on*) cansar, pôr à prova; (*jur*) julgar □ *n* (*attempt*) tentativa *f*, experiência *f*; (*Rugby*) ensaio *m*. **~ for** (*post, scholarship*) candidatar-se a; (*record*) tentar alcançar. **~ on** (*clothes*) provar. **~ out** experimentar. **~ to do** tentar fazer. **~ing** *a* difícil

tsar /za:(r)/ *n* czar *m*

T-shirt /'ti:ʃɜ:t/ *n* T-shirt *f*, camiseta *f* de algodão de mangas curtas

tub /tʌb/ *n* selha *f*; (*colloq: bath*) tina *f*, banheira *f*

tuba /'tju:bə/ *n* (*mus*) tuba *f*

tubby /'tʌbɪ/ *a* (**-ier, -iest**) baixote e gorducho

tub|e /tju:b/ *n* tubo *m*; (*colloq: railway*) metrô *m*. **inner ~e** câmara *f* de ar. **~ing** *n* tubos *mpl*, tubagem *f*

tuber /'tju:bə(r)/ *n* tubérculo *m*

tuberculosis /tju:bɜ:kjʊ'ləʊsɪs/ *n* tuberculose *f*
tubular /'tju:bjʊlə(r)/ *a* tubular
tuck /tʌk/ *n* (*fold*) prega *f* cosida; (*for shortening or ornament*) refego *m* □ *vt/i* fazer pregas; (*put*) guardar, meter, enfiar; (*hide*) esconder. ~ **in** *or* **into** (*colloq: eat*) atacar. ~ **in** (*shirt*) meter as fraldas para dentro; (*blanket*) prender em; (*person*) cobrir bem, aconchegar. ~**-shop** *n* (*schol*) loja *f* de balas, (*P*) pastelaria *f* (junto à escola)
Tuesday /'tju:zdɪ/ *n* terça-feira *f*
tuft /tʌft/ *n* tufo *m*
tug /tʌg/ *vt/i* (*pt* **tugged**) puxar com força; (*vessel*) rebocar □ *n* (*boat*) rebocador *m*; (*pull*) puxão *m*. ~ **of war** cabo-de-guerra *m*, (*P*) jogo *m* da guerra
tuition /tju:'ɪʃn/ *n* ensino *m*
tulip /'tju:lɪp/ *n* tulipa *f*
tumble /'tʌmbl/ *vi* tombar, baquear, dar um trambolhão □ *n* tombo *m*, trambolhão *m*. ~**-drier** *n* máquina *f* de secar (roupa)
tumbledown /'tʌmbldaʊn/ *a* em ruínas
tumbler /'tʌmblə(r)/ *n* copo *m*
tummy /'tʌmɪ/ *n* (*colloq: stomach*) estômago *m*; (*colloq: abdomen*) barriga *f*. ~**-ache** *n* (*colloq*) dor *f* de barriga/de estômago
tumour /'tju:mə(r)/ *n* tumor *m*
tumult /'tju:mʌlt/ *n* tumulto *m*. ~**uous** /-'mʌltʃʊəs/ *a* tumultuado, barulhento, agitado
tuna /'tju:nə/ *n* (*pl invar*) atum *m*
tune /tju:n/ *n* melodia *f* □ *vt* (*engine*) regular; (*piano etc*) afinar □ *vi* ~ **in (to)** (*radio, TV*) ligar (em), (*P*) sintonizar. ~ **up** afinar. **be in** ~**/out of** ~ (*instrument*) estar afinado/desafinado; (*singer*) cantar afinado/desafinado. ~**ful** *a* melodioso, harmonioso. ~**r** *n* afinador *m*; (*radio*) sintonizador *m*
tunic /'tju:nɪk/ *n* túnica *f*
Tunisia /tju:'nɪzɪə/ *n* Tunísia *f*. ~**n** *a* & *n* tunisiano (*m*), (*P*) tunisino (*m*)
tunnel /'tʌnl/ *n* túnel *m* □ *vi* (*pt* **tunnelled**) abrir um túnel (**into** em)
turban /'tɜ:bən/ *n* turbante *m*
turbine /'tɜ:baɪn/ *n* turbina *f*
turbo- /'tɜ:bəʊ/ *pref* turbo-
turbot /'tɜ:bət/ *n* rodovalho *m*
turbulen|t /'tɜ:bjʊlənt/ *a* turbulento. ~**ce** *n* turbulência *f*
tureen /tə'ri:n/ *n* terrina *f*
turf /tɜ:f/ *n* (*pl* **turfs** *or* **turves**) gramado *m*, (*P*) relva *f*, relvado *m* □ *vt* ~ **out** (*colloq*) jogar fora, (*P*) deitar fora. **the** ~ (*racing*) turfe *m*, hipismo *m*. ~ **accountant** corretor *m* de apostas
turgid /'tɜ:dʒɪd/ *a* (*speech, style*) pomposo, empolado
Turk /tɜ:k/ *n* turco *m*. ~**ey** *n* Turquia *f*. ~**ish** *a* turco *m* □ *n* (*lang*) turco *m*
turkey /'tɜ:kɪ/ *n* peru *m*
turmoil /'tɜ:mɔɪl/ *n* agitação *f*, confusão *f*, desordem *f*. **in** ~ em ebulição
turn /tɜ:n/ *vt/i* virar(-se), voltar (-se), girar; (*change*) transformar (-se) (**into** em); (*become*) ficar, tornar-se; (*corner*) virar, dobrar; (*page*) virar, voltar □ *n* volta *f*; (*in road*) curva *f*; (*of mind, events*) mudança *f*; (*occasion, opportunity*) vez *f*; (*colloq*) ataque *m*, crise *f*; (*colloq: shock*) susto *m*. **do a good** ~ prestar (um) serviço. **in** ~ por sua vez, sucessivamente. **speak out of** ~ dizer o que não se deve, cometer uma indiscrição. **take** ~**s** revezar-se. ~ **of the century** virada *f* do século. ~ **against** virar-se *or* voltar-se contra. ~ **away** *vi* virar-se *or* voltar-se para o outro lado □ *vt* (*avert*) desviar; (*reject*) recusar; (*send back*) mandar embora. ~ **back** *vi* (*return*) devolver; (*vehicle*) dar meia volta, voltar para trás □ *vt* (*fold*) dobrar para trás. ~ **down** recusar; (*fold*) dobrar para baixo; (*reduce*) baixar. ~ **in** (*hand in*) entregar; (*colloq: go to bed*) deitar-se. ~ **off** (*light etc*) apagar; (*tap*) fechar; (*road*) virar (para rua transversal). ~ **on** (*light etc*) acender, ligar; (*tap*) abrir. ~ **out** *vt* (*light*) apagar; (*empty*) esvaziar, despejar; (*pocket*) virar do avesso; (*produce*) produzir □ *vi* (*transpire*) vir a saber-se, descobrir-se; (*colloq: come*) aparecer. ~ **round** virar-se, voltar-se. ~ **up** *vi* aparecer, chegar; (*be found*) aparecer □ *vt* (*find*) desenterrar; (*increase*) aumentar; (*collar*) levantar. ~**-out** *n* assis-tência *f*. ~**-up** *n* (*of trousers*) dobra *f*
turning /'tɜ:nɪŋ/ *n* rua *f* transversal; (*corner*) esquina *f*. ~**-point** *n* momento *m* decisivo
turnip /'tɜ:nɪp/ *n* nabo *m*
turnover /'tɜ:nəʊvə(r)/ *n* (*pie, tart*) pastel *m*, empada *f*; (*money*) faturamento *m*, (*P*) facturação *f*; (*of staff*) rotatividade *f*
turnpike /'tɜ:npaɪk/ *n* (*Amer*) auto-estrada *f* com pedágio, (*P*) portagem
turnstile /'tɜ:nstaɪl/ *n* (*gate*) torniquete *m*, borboleta *f*
turntable /'tɜ:nteɪbl/ *n* (*for record*) prato *m* do toca-disco, (*P*) giradiscos; (*record-player*) toca-disco *m*, (*P*) giradiscos *m*
turpentine /'tɜ:pəntaɪn/ *n* terebentina *f*, aguarrás *m*
turquoise /'tɜ:kwɔɪz/ *a* turquesa *invar*
turret /'tʌrɪt/ *n* torreão *m*, torrinha *f*

turtle /'tɜ:tl/ *n* tartaruga-do-mar *f*. **~-neck** *a* de gola alta
tusk /tʌsk/ *n* (*tooth*) presa *f*; (*elephant's*) defesa *f*, dente *m*
tussle /'tʌsl/ *n* luta *f*, briga *f*
tutor /'tju:tə(r)/ *n* professor *m* particular; (*univ*) professor *m* universitário
tutorial /tju:'tɔ:rɪəl/ *n* (*univ*) seminário *m*
TV /ti:'vi:/ *n* tevê *f*
twaddle /'twɒdl/ *n* disparates *mpl*
twang /twæŋ/ *n* (*mus*) som *m* duma corda esticada; (*in voice*) nasalação *f* □ *vt/i* (*mus*) (fazer) vibrar, dedilhar
tweet /twi:t/ *n* pio *m*, pipilo *m* □ **~** *vi* pipilar
tweezers /'twi:zəz/ *npl* pinça *f*
twel|ve /twelv/ *a & n* doze (*m*). **~ (o'clock)** doze horas. **~fth** *a & n* décimo segundo (*m*). **T~fth Night** véspera *f* de Reis
twent|y /'twentɪ/ *a & n* vinte (*m*). **~ieth** *a & n* vigésimo (*m*)
twice /twaɪs/ *adv* duas vezes
twiddle /'twɪdl/ *vt/i* **~ (with)** (*fiddle with*) torcer, brincar (com). **~ one's thumbs** girar os polegares
twig /twɪg/ *n* galho *m*, graveto *m*
twilight /'twaɪlaɪt/ *n* crepúsculo *m* □ *a* crepuscular
twin /twɪn/ *n & a* gêmeo (*m*), (*P*) gémeo (*m*) □ *vt* (*pt* **twinned**) (*pair*) emparelhar, emparceirar. **~ beds** par *m* de camas de solteiro. **~ning** *n* emparelhamento *m*
twine /twaɪn/ *n* guita *f*, cordel *m* □ *vt/i* (*weave together*) entrançar; (*wind*) enroscar(-se)
twinge /twɪndʒ/ *n* dor *f* aguda e súbita, pontada *f*; (*fig*) pontada *f*, (*P*) ferroada *f*
twinkle /'twɪŋkl/ *vi* cintilar, brilhar □ *n* cintilação *f*, brilho *m*
twirl /twɜ:l/ *vt/i* (fazer) girar; (*moustache*) torcer
twist /twɪst/ *vt* torcer; (*weave together*) entrançar; (*roll*) enrolar; (*distort*) torcer, deturpar □ *vi* (*rope etc*) torcer-se, enrolar-se; (*road*) dar voltas *or* curvas, serpentear □ *n* (*act of twisting*) torcedura *f*, (*P*) torcedela *f*; (*of rope*) nó *m*; (*of events*) reviravolta *f*. **~ sb's arm** (*fig*) forçar alguém
twit /twɪt/ *n* (*colloq*) idiota *mf*
twitch /twɪtʃ/ *vt/i* contrair(-se) □ *n* (*tic*) tique *m*; (*jerk*) puxão *m*
two /tu:/ *a & n* dois (*m*). **in** *or* **of ~ minds** indeciso. **put ~ and ~ together** tirar conclusões. **~-faced** *a* de duas caras, hipócrita. **~-piece** *n* (*garment*) duas-peças *m invar*. **~-seater** *n* (*car*) carro *m* de dois lugares. **~-way** *a* (*of road*) mão dupla
twosome /'tu:səm/ *n* par *m*
tycoon /taɪ'ku:n/ *n* magnata *m*
tying /'taɪɪŋ/ *see* **tie**
type /taɪp/ *n* (*example, print*) tipo *m*; (*kind*) tipo *m*, gênero *m*, (*P*) género *m*; (*colloq: person*) cara *m*, (*P*) tipo *m* (*colloq*) □ *vt/i* (*write*) bater à máquina, datilografar, (*P*) dactilografar
typescript /'taɪpskrɪpt/ *n* texto *m* datilografado, (*P*) dactilografado
typewrit|er /'taɪpraɪtə(r)/ *n* máquina *f* de escrever. **~ten** /-ɪtn/ *a* batido à máquina, datilografado, (*P*) dactilografado
typhoid /'taɪfɔɪd/ *n* **~ (fever)** febre *f* tifóide
typhoon /taɪ'fu:n/ *n* tufão *m*
typical /'tɪpɪkl/ *a* típico. **~ly** *adv* tipicamente
typify /'tɪpɪfaɪ/ *vt* ser o (protó)tipo de, tipificar
typing /'taɪpɪŋ/ *n* datilografia *f*, (*P*) dactilografia *f*
typist /'taɪpɪst/ *n* datilógrafa *f*, (*P*) dactilógrafa *f*
tyrann|y /'tɪrənɪ/ *n* tirania *f*. **~ical** /tɪ'rænɪkl/ *a* tirânico
tyrant /'taɪərənt/ *n* tirano *m*
tyre /'taɪə(r)/ *n* pneu *m*

Uu

ubiquitous /ju:'bɪkwɪtəs/ *a* ubíquo, omnipresente
udder /'ʌdər/ *n* úbere *m*
UFO /'ju:fəʊ/ *n* OVNI *m*
ugl|y /'ʌglɪ/ *a* (**-ier, -iest**) feio. **~iness** *n* feiúra *f*, (*P*) fealdade *f*
UK *abbr see* **United Kingdom**
ulcer /'ʌlsə(r)/ *n* úlcera *f*
ulterior /ʌl'tɪərɪə(r)/ *a* ulterior. **~ motive** razão *f* inconfessada, segundas intenções *fpl*
ultimate /'ʌltɪmət/ *a* último, derradeiro; (*definitive*) definitivo; (*maximum*) supremo; (*basic*) fundamental. **~ly** *adv* finalmente
ultimatum /ʌltɪ'meɪtəm/ *n* (*pl* **-ums**) ultimato *m*
ultra- /'ʌltrə/ *pref* ultra-, super-
ultraviolet /ʌltrə'vaɪələt/ *a* ultravioleta
umbilical /ʌm'bɪlɪkl/ *a* **~ cord** cordão *m* umbilical
umbrage /'ʌmbrɪdʒ/ *n* **take ~ (at sth)** ofender-se *or* melindrar-se (com alg coisa)

umbrella /ʌm'brelə/ *n* guarda-chuva *m*
umpire /'ʌmpaɪə(r)/ *n* (*sport*) àrbitro *m* ▫ *vt* arbitrar
umpteen /'ʌmpti:n/ *a* (*sl*) sem conta, montes de (*colloq*). **for the ~th time** (*sl*) pela centésima *or* enésima vez
UN *abbr* (*United Nations*) ONU *f*
un- /ʌn/ *pref* não, pouco
unable /ʌn'eɪbl/ *a* **be ~ to do** ser incapaz de/não poder fazer
unabridged /ʌnə'brɪdʒd/ *a* (*text*) integral
unacceptable /ʌnək'septəbl/ *a* inaceitável, inadmissível
unaccompanied /ʌnə'kʌmpənɪd/ *a* só, desacompanhado
unaccountable /ʌnə'kaʊntəbl/ *a* (*strange*) inexplicável; (*not responsible*) que não tem que dar contas
unaccustomed /ʌnə'kʌstəmd/ *a* desacostumado. **~ to** não acostumado *or* não habituado a
unadulterated /ʌnə'dʌltəreɪtɪd/ *a* (*pure, sheer*) puro
unaided /ʌn'eɪdɪd/ *a* sem ajuda, sozinho, por si só
unanim|ous /ju:'nænɪməs/ *a* unânime. **~ity** /-ə'nɪmətɪ/ *n* unanimidade *f*. **~ously** *adv* unânimemente, por unanimidade
unarmed /ʌn'a:md/ *a* desarmado, indefeso
unashamed /ʌnə'ʃeɪmd/ *a* desavergonhado, sem vergonha. **~ly** /-ɪdlɪ/ *adv* sem vergonha
unassuming /ʌnə'sju:mɪŋ/ *a* modesto, despretencioso
unattached /ʌnə'tætʃt/ *a* (*person*) livre
unattainable /ʌnə'teɪnəbl/ *a* inacessível
unattended /ʌnə'tendɪd/ *a* (*person*) desacompanhado; (*car, luggage*) abandonado
unattractive /ʌnə'træktɪv/ *a* sem atrativos, (*P*) atractivos; (*offer*) de pouco interesse
unauthorized /ʌn'ɔ:θəraɪzd/ *a* não-autorizado, sem autorização
unavoidabl|e /ʌnə'vɔɪdəbl/ *a* inevitável. **~y** *adv* inevitavelmente
unaware /ʌnə'weə(r)/ *a* **be ~ of** desconhecer, ignorar, não ter consciência de. **~s** /-eəz/ *adv* (*unexpectedly*) inesperadamente. **catch sb ~s** apanhar alguém desprevenido
unbalanced /ʌn'bælənst/ *a* (*mind, person*) desequilibrado
unbearable /ʌn'beərəbl/ *a* insuportável
unbeat|able /ʌn'bi:təbl/ *a* imbatível. **~en** *a* não vencido, invicto; (*unsurpassed*) insuperado
unbeknown(st) /ʌnbɪ'nəʊn(st)/ *a* **~ to** (*colloq*) sem o conhecimento de
unbelievable /ʌnbɪ'lɪ:vəbl/ *a* inacreditável, incrível
unbend /ʌn'bend/ *vi* (*pt* **unbent**) (*relax*) descontrair. **~ing** *a* inflexível
unbiased /ʌn'baɪəst/ *a* imparcial
unblock /ʌn'blɒk/ *vt* desbloquear, desobstruir; (*pipe*) desentupir
unborn /'ʌnbɔ:n/ *a* por nascer; (*future*) vindouro, futuro
unbounded /ʌn'baʊndɪd/ *a* ilimitado
unbreakable /ʌn'breɪkəbl/ *a* inquebrável
unbridled /ʌn'braɪdld/ *a* desequilibrado, (*P*) desenfreado
unbroken /ʌn'brəʊkən/ *a* (*intact*) intato, (*P*) intacto, inteiro; (*continuous*) ininterrupto
unburden /ʌn'bɜ:dn/ *vpr* **~ o.s.** (*open one's heart*) desabafar (**to** com)
unbutton /ʌn'bʌtn/ *vt* desabotoar
uncalled-for /ʌn'kɔ:ldfɔ:(r)/ *a* injustificável, gratuito
uncanny /ʌn'kænɪ/ *a* (**-ier, -iest**) estranho, misterioso
unceasing /ʌn'si:sɪŋ/ *a* incessante
unceremonious /ʌnserɪ'məʊnɪəs/ *a* sem cerimônia, (*P*) cerimónia, brusco
uncertain /ʌn'sɜ:tn/ *a* incerto. **be ~ whether** não saber ao certo se, estar indeciso quanto a. **~ty** *n* incerteza *f*
unchang|ed /ʌn'tʃeɪndʒd/ *a* inalterado, sem modificação. **~ing** *a* inalterável, imutável
uncivilized /ʌn'sɪvɪlaɪzd/ *a* não civilizado, bárbaro
uncle /'ʌŋkl/ *n* tio *m*
uncomfortable /ʌn'kʌmfətəbl/ *a* (*thing*) desconfortável, incômodo, (*P*) incómodo; (*unpleasant*) desagradável. **feel** *or* **be ~** (*uneasy*) sentir-se *or* estar pouco à vontade
uncommon /ʌn'kɒmən/ *a* pouco vulgar, invulgar, fora do comum. **~ly** *adv* invulgarmente, excepcionalmente
uncompromising /ʌn'kɒmprəmaɪzɪŋ/ *a* intransigente
unconcerned /ʌnkən'sɜ:nd/ *a* (*indifferent*) indiferente (**by** a)
unconditional /ʌnkən'dɪʃənl/ *a* incondicional
unconscious /ʌn'kɒnʃəs/ *a* inconsciente (**of** de). **~ly** *adv* inconscientemente. **~ness** *n* inconsciência *f*
unconventional /ʌnkən'venʃənl/ *a* não convencional, fora do comum
uncooperative /ʌnkəʊ'ɒpərətɪv/ *a* (*person*) pouco cooperativo, do contra (*colloq*)

uncork /ʌn'kɔ:k/ *vt* desarolhar, tirar a rolha de

uncouth /ʌn'ku:θ/ *a* rude, grosseiro

uncover /ʌn'kʌvə(r)/ *vt* descobrir, revelar

unctuous /'ʌŋktʃʊəs/ *a* untuoso, gorduroso; (*fig*) melífluo

undecided /ʌndɪ'saɪdɪd/ *a* (*irresolute*) indeciso; (*not settled*) por decidir, pendente

undeniable /ʌndɪ'naɪəbl/ *a* inegável, incontestável

under /'ʌndə(r)/ *prep* debaixo de, sob; (*less than*) com menos de; (*according to*) conforme, segundo □ *adv* por baixo, debaixo. **~ age** menor de idade. **~ way** em preparo

under- /'ʌndə(r)/ *pref* sub-

undercarriage /'ʌndəkærɪdʒ/ *n* (*aviat*) trem *m* de aterrissagem, (*P*) trem *m* de aterragem

underclothes /'ʌndəkləʊðz/ *npl see* **underwear**

undercoat /'ʌndəkəʊt/ *n* (*of paint*) primeira mão *f*, (*P*) primeira demão *f*

undercover /ʌndə'kʌvə(r)/ *a* (*agent, operation*) secreto

undercurrent /'ʌndəkʌrənt/ *n* corrente *f* subterrânea; (*fig*) filão *m* (*fig*), tendência *f* oculta

undercut /ʌndə'kʌt/ *vt* (*pt* **undercut**, *pres p* **undercutting**) (*comm*) vender a preços mais baixos que

underdeveloped /ʌndədɪ'veləpt/ *a* atrofiado; (*country*) subdesenvolvido

underdog /ʌndə'dɒg/ *n* desprotegido *m*, o mais fraco (*colloq*)

underdone /'ʌndədʌn/ *a* (*of meat*) mal passado

underestimate /ʌndə'restɪmeɪt/ *vt* subestimar, não dar o devido valor a

underfed /ʌndə'fed/ *a* subalimentado, subnutrido

underfoot /ʌndə'fʊt/ *adv* debaixo dos pés; (*on the ground*) no chão

undergo /ʌndə'gəʊ/ *vt* (*pt* **-went**, *pp* **-gone**) (*be subjected to*) sofrer; (*treatment*) ser submetido a

undergraduate /ʌndə'grædʒʊət/ *n* estudante *mf* universitário

underground[1] /ʌndə'graʊnd/ *adv* debaixo da terra; (*fig: secretly*) clandestinamente

underground[2] /'ʌndəgraʊnd/ *a* subterrâneo; (*fig: secret*) clandestino □ *n* (*rail*) metro(politano) *m*

undergrowth /'ʌndəgrəʊθ/ *n* mato *m*

underhand /'ʌndəhænd/ *a* (*deceitful*) sonso, dissimulado

under|lie /ʌndə'laɪ/ *vt* (*pt* **-lay**, *pp* **-lain**, *pres p* **-lying**) estar por baixo de. **~lying** *a* subjacente

underline /ʌndə'laɪn/ *vt* sublinhar

undermine /ʌndə'maɪn/ *vt* minar, solapar

underneath /ʌndə'ni:θ/ *prep* sob, debaixo de, por baixo de □ *adv* abaixo, em baixo, por baixo

underpaid /ʌndə'peɪd/ *a* mal pago

underpants /'ʌndəpænts/ *npl* (*man's*) cuecas *fpl*

underpass /'ʌndəpa:s/ *n* (*for cars, people*) passagem *f* inferior

underprivileged /ʌndə'prɪvɪlɪdʒd/ *a* desfavorecido

underrate /ʌndə'reɪt/ *vt* subestimar, depreciar

underside /'ʌndəsaɪd/ *n* lado *m* inferior, base *f*

underskirt /'ʌndəskɜ:t/ *n* anágua *f*

understand /ʌndə'stænd/ *vt/i* (*pt* **-stood**) compreender, entender. **~able** *a* compreensível. **~ing** *a* compreensivo □ *n* compreensão *f*; (*agreement*) acordo *m*, entendimento *m*

understatement /'ʌndəsteɪtmənt/ *n* versão *f* atenuada da verdade, litotes *f*

understudy /'ʌndəstʌdɪ/ *n* substituto *m*

undertak|e /ʌndə'teɪk/ *vt* (*pt* **-took**, *pp* **-taken**) empreender; (*responsibility*) assumir. **~e to** encarregar-se de. **~ing** *n* (*task*) empreendimento *m*; (*promise*) compromisso *m*

undertaker /'ʌndəteɪkə(r)/ *n* agente *m* funerário, papa-defuntos *m* (*colloq*)

undertone /'ʌndətəʊn/ *n* **in an ~** a meia voz

undervalue /ʌndə'vælju:/ *vt* avaliar por baixo, subestimar

underwater /ʌndə'wɔ:tə(r)/ *a* submarino □ *adv* debaixo de água

underwear /'ʌndəweə(r)/ *n* roupa *f* interior *or* de baixo

underweight /'ʌndəweɪt/ *a* **be ~** estar com o peso abaixo do normal, ter peso a menos

underwent /ʌndə'went/ *see* **undergo**

underworld /'ʌndəwɜ:ld/ *n* (*of crime*) submundo *m*, bas-fonds *mpl*

underwriter /'ʌndəraɪtə(r)/ *n* segurador *m*; (*marine*) underwriter *m*

undeserved /ʌndɪ'zɜ:vd/ *a* imerecido, injusto

undesirable /ʌndɪ'zaɪərəbl/ *a* indesejável, inconveniente

undies /'ʌndɪz/ *npl* (*colloq*) roupa *f* de baixo *or* interior

undignified /ʌn'dɪgnɪfaɪd/ *a* pouco digno, sem dignidade

undisputed /ʌndɪ'spju:tɪd/ *a* incontestado
undo /ʌn'du:/ *vt* (*pt* **-did**, *pp* **-done** /dʌn/) desfazer; (*knot*) desfazer, desatar; (*coat, button*) abrir. **leave ~ne** não fazer, deixar por fazer. **~ing** *n* desgraça *f*, ruína *f*
undoubted /ʌn'daʊtɪd/ *a* indubitável. **~ly** *adv* indubitavelmente
undress /ʌn'dres/ *vt/i* despir(-se). **get ~ed** despir-se
undu|e /ʌn'dju:/ *a* excessivo, indevido. **~ly** *adv* excessivamente, indevidamente
undulate /'ʌndjʊleɪt/ *vi* ondular
undying /ʌn'daɪɪŋ/ *a* eterno, perene
unearth /ʌn'ɜ:θ/ *vt* desenterrar; (*fig*) descobrir
unearthly /ʌn'ɜ:θlɪ/ *a* sobrenatural, misterioso. **~ hour** (*colloq*) hora *f* absurda *or* inconveniente
uneasy /ʌn'i:zɪ/ *a* (*ill at ease*) pouco à vontade; (*worried*) preocupado
uneconomic /ʌni:kə'nɒmɪk/ *a* antieconômico. **~al** *a* antieconõmico
uneducated /ʌn'edʒʊkeɪtɪd/ *a* (*person*) inculto, sem instrução
unemploy|ed /ʌnɪm'plɔɪd/ *a* desempregado. **~ment** *n* desemprego *m*. **~ment benefit** auxílio-desemprego *m*
unending /ʌn'endɪŋ/ *a* interminável, sem fim
unequal /ʌn'i:kwəl/ *a* desigual. **~led** *a* sem igual, inigualável
unequivocal /ʌnɪ'kwɪvəkl/ *a* inequívoco, claro
uneven /ʌn'i:vn/ *a* desigual, irregular
unexpected /ʌnɪk'spektɪd/ *a* inesperado. **~ly** *a* inesperadamente
unfair /ʌn'feə(r)/ *a* injusto (**to** com). **~ness** *n* injustiça *f*
unfaithful /ʌn'feɪθfl/ *a* infiel
unfamiliar /ʌnfə'mɪlɪə(r)/ *a* estranho, desconhecido. **be ~ with** desconhecer, não conhecer, não estar familiarizado com
unfashionable /ʌn'fæʃənəbl/ *a* fora de moda
unfasten /ʌn'fa:sn/ *vt* (*knot*) desatar, soltar; (*button*) abrir
unfavourable /ʌn'feɪvərəbl/ *a* desfavorável
unfeeling /ʌn'fi:lɪŋ/ *a* insensível
unfinished /ʌn'fɪnɪʃt/ *a* incompleto, inacabado
unfit /ʌn'fɪt/ *a* sem preparo físico, fora de forma; (*unsuitable*) impróprio (**for** para)
unfold /ʌn'fəʊld/ *vt* desdobrar; (*expose*) expor, revelar □ *vi* desenrolar-se
unforeseen /ʌnfɔ:'si:n/ *a* imprevisto, inesperado
unforgettable /ʌnfə'getəbl/ *a* inesquecível
unforgivable /ʌnfə'gɪvəbl/ *a* imperdoável, indesculpável
unfortunate /ʌn'fɔ:tʃənət/ *a* (*unlucky*) infeliz; (*regrettable*) lamentável. **it was very ~ that** foi uma pena que **~ly** *adv* infelizmente
unfounded /ʌn'faʊndɪd/ *a* (*rumour etc*) infundado, sem fundamento
unfriendly /ʌn'frendlɪ/ *a* pouco amável, antipático, frio
unfurnished /ʌn'fɜ:nɪʃt/ *a* sem mobília
ungainly /ʌn'gemlɪ/ *a* desajeitado, desgracioso
ungodly /ʌn'gɒdlɪ/ *a* ímpio. **~ hour** (*colloq*) hora *f* absurda, às altas horas (*colloq*)
ungrateful /ʌn'greɪtfl/ *a* ingrato
unhapp|y /ʌn'hæpɪ/ *a* (**-ier, -iest**) infeliz, triste; (*not pleased*) descontente, pouco contente (**with** com). **~ily** *adv* infelizmente. **~iness** *n* infelicidade *f*, tristeza *f*
unharmed /ʌn'ha:md/ *a* incólume, são e salvo, ileso
unhealthy /ʌn'helθɪ/ *a* (**-ier, -iest**) (*climate etc*) doentio, insalubre; (*person*) adoentado, com pouca saúde
unheard-of /ʌn'hɜ:dɒv/ *a* inaudito, sem precedentes
unhinge /ʌn'hɪndʒ/ *vt* (*person, mind*) desequilibrar
unholy /ʌn'həʊlɪ/ *a* (**-ier, -iest**) (*person, act etc*) ímpio; (*colloq: great*) incrível, espantoso
unhook /ʌn'hʊk/ *vt* desenganchar; (*dress*) desapertar
unhoped /ʌn'həʊpt/ *a* **~ for** inesperado
unhurt /ʌn'hɜ:t/ *a* ileso, incólume
unicorn /'ju:nɪkɔ:n/ *n* unicórnio *m*
uniform /'ju:nɪfɔ:m/ *n* uniforme *m* □ *a* uniforme, sempre igual. **~ity** /-'fɔ:mətɪ/ *n* uniformidade *f*. **~ly** *adv* uniformemente
unif|y /'ju:nɪfaɪ/ *vt* unificar. **~ication** /-ɪ'keɪʃn/ *n* unificação *f*
unilateral /ju:nɪ'lætrəl/ *a* unilateral
unimaginable /ʌnɪ'mædʒɪnəbl/ *a* inimaginável
unimportant /ʌnɪm'pɔ:tnt/ *a* sem importância, insignificante
uninhabited /ʌnɪn'hæbɪtɪd/ *a* desabitado
unintentional /ʌnɪn'tenʃənl/ *a* involuntário, não propositado
uninterest|ed /ʌn'ɪntrəstɪd/ *a* desinteressado (**in** em), indiferente

(in a). **~ing** *a* desinteressante, sem interesse

union /'ju:nɪən/ *n* união *f*; (*trade union*) sindicato *m*. **~ist** *n* sindicalista *mf*; (*pol*) unionista *mf*. **U~ Jack** bandeira *f* britânica

unique /ju:'ni:k/ *a* único, sem igual

unisex /'ju:nɪseks/ *a* unisexo

unison /'ju:nɪsn/ *n* **in ~** em uníssono

unit /'ju:nɪt/ *n* unidade *f*; (*of furniture*) peça *f*, unidade *f*, (*P*) módulo *m*

unite /ju:'naɪt/ *vt/i* unir(-se). **U~d Kingdom** *n* Reino *m* Unido. **U~d Nations (Organization)** *n* Organização *f* das Nações Unidas. **U~ States (of America)** Estados *mpl* Unidos (da América)

unity /'ju:nətɪ/ *n* unidade *f*; (*fig: harmony*) união *f*

universal /ju:nɪ'vɜ:sl/ *a* universal

universe /'ju:nɪvɜ:s/ *n* universo *m*

university /ju:nɪ'vɜ:sətɪ/ *n* universidade *f* □ *a* universitário; (*student, teacher*) universitário, da universidade

unjust /ʌn'dʒʌst/ *a* injusto

unkempt /ʌn'kempt/ *a* desmazelado, desleixado; (*of hair*) despenteado, desgrenhado

unkind /ʌn'kaɪnd/ *a* desagradável, duro. **~ly** *adv* mal

unknowingly /ʌn'nəʊɪŋlɪ/ *adv* sem saber, inconscientemente

unknown /ʌn'nəʊn/ *a* desconhecido □ *n* **the ~** o desconhecido

unleaded /ʌn'ledɪd/ *a* sem chumbo

unless /ʌn'les/ *conj* a não ser que, a menos que, salvo se, se não

unlike /ʌn'laɪk/ *a* diferente □ *prep* ao contrário de

unlikely /ʌn'laɪklɪ/ *a* improvável

unlimited /ʌn'lɪmɪtɪd/ *a* ilimitado

unload /ʌn'ləʊd/ *vt* descarregar

unlock /ʌn'lɒk/ *vt* abrir (com chave)

unluck|y /ʌn'lʌkɪ/ *a* (**-ier, -iest**) infeliz, sem sorte; (*number*) que dá azar. **be ~y** ter pouca sorte. **~ily** *adv* infelizmente

unmarried /ʌn'mærɪd/ *a* solteiro, celibatário

unmask /ʌn'ma:sk/ *vt* desmascarar

unmistakable /ʌnmɪs'teɪkəbl/ *a* (*voice etc*) inconfundível; (*clear*) claro, inequívoco

unmitigated /ʌn'mɪtɪgeɪtɪd/ *a* (*absolute*) completo, absoluto

unmoved /ʌn'mu:vd/ *a* impassível; (*indifferent*) indiferente (**by** a), insensível (**by** a)

unnatural /ʌn'nætʃrəl/ *a* que não é natural; (*wicked*) desnaturado

unnecessary /ʌn'nesəserɪ/ *a* desnecessário; (*superfluous*) supérfluo, dispensável

unnerve /ʌn'nɜ:v/ *vt* desencorajar, desmoralizar, intimidar

unnoticed /ʌn'nəʊtɪst/ *a* **go ~** passar despercebido

unobtrusive /ʌnəb'tru:sɪv/ *a* discreto

unofficial /ʌnə'fɪʃl/ *a* oficioso, que não é oficial; (*strike*) ilegal, inautorizado

unorthodox /ʌn'ɔ:θədɒks/ *a* pouco ortodoxo, não ortodoxo

unpack /ʌn'pæk/ *vt* (*suitcase etc*) desfazer; (*contents*) desembalar, desempacotar □ *vi* desfazer a mala

unpaid /ʌn'peɪd/ *a* não remunerado; (*bill*) a pagar

unpalatable /ʌn'pælətəbl/ *a* (*food, fact etc*) desagradável, intragável

unparalleled /ʌn'pærəleld/ *a* sem paralelo, incomparável

unpleasant /ʌn'pleznt/ *a* desagradável (**to** com); (*person*) antipático

unplug /ʌn'plʌg/ *vt* (*pt* **-plugged**) (*electr*) desligar a tomada, (*P*) tirar a ficha da tomada

unpopular /ʌn'pɒpjʊlə(r)/ *a* impopular

unprecedented /ʌn'presɪdentɪd/ *a* sem precedentes, inaudito, nunca visto

unpredictable /ʌnprə'dɪktəbl/ *a* imprevisível

unprepared /ʌnprɪ'peəd/ *a* sem preparação, improvisado; (*person*) desprevenido

unpretentious /ʌnprɪ'tenʃəs/ *a* despretencioso, sem pretensões

unprincipled /ʌn'prɪnsəpld/ *a* sem princípios, sem escrúpulos

unprofessional /ʌnprə'feʃənl/ *a* (*work*) de amador; (*conduct*) sem consciência profissional

unprofitable /ʌn'prɒfɪtəbl/ *a* não lucrativo

unqualified /ʌn'kwɒlɪfaɪd/ *a* sem habilitações; (*success etc*) total, absoluto. **be ~ to** não estar habilitado para

unquestionable /ʌn'kwestʃənəbl/ *a* incontestável, indiscutível

unravel /ʌn'rævl/ *vt* (*pt* **unravelled**) desenredar, desemaranhar; (*knitting*) desmanchar

unreal /ʌn'rɪəl/ *a* irreal

unreasonable /ʌn'ri:znəbl/ *a* pouco razoável, disparatado; (*excessive*) excessivo

unrecognizable /ʌn'rekəgnaɪzəbl/ *a* irreconhecível

unrelated /ʌnrɪ'leɪtɪd/ *a* (*facts*) desconexo, sem relação (**to** com); (*people*) não aparentado (**to** com)

unreliable /ʌnrɪ'laɪəbl/ *a* que não é de confiança
unremitting /ʌnrɪ'mɪtɪŋ/ *a* incessante, infatigável
unreservedly /ʌnrɪ'zɜ:vɪdlɪ/ *adv* sem reservas
unrest /ʌn'rest/ *n* agitação *f*, distúrbios *mpl*
unrivalled /ʌn'raɪvld/ *a* sem igual, incomparável
unroll /ʌn'rəʊl/ *vt* desenrolar
unruffled /ʌn'rʌfld/ *a* calmo, tranqüilo, imperturbável
unruly /ʌn'ru:lɪ/ *a* indisciplinado, turbulento
unsafe /ʌn'seɪf/ *a* (*dangerous*) que não é seguro, perigoso; (*person*) em perigo
unsaid /ʌn'sed/ *a* **leave ~** não mencionar, não dizer, deixar algo por dizer
unsatisfactory /ʌnsætɪs'fæktərɪ/ *a* insatisfatório, pouco satisfatório
unsavoury /ʌn'seɪvərɪ/ *a* desagradável, repugnante
unscathed /ʌn'skeɪðd/ *a* ileso, incólume
unscrew /ʌn'skru:/ *vt* desenroscar, desparafusar
unscrupulous /ʌn'skru:pjʊləs/ *a* sem escrúpulos, pouco escrupuloso, sem consciência
unseemly /ʌn'si:mlɪ/ *a* inconveniente, indecoroso, impróprio
unsettle /ʌn'setl/ *vt* perturbar, agitar. **~d** *a* perturbado; (*weather*) instável, variável; (*bill*) não saldado
unshakeable /ʌn'ʃeɪkəbl/ *a* (*person, belief etc*) inabalável
unshaven /ʌn'ʃeɪvn/ *a* com a barba por fazer, por barbear
unsightly /ʌn'saɪtlɪ/ *a* feio
unskilled /ʌn'skɪld/ *a* inexperiente; (*work, worker*) não especializado; (*labour*) mão-de-obra *f* não especializada
unsociable /ʌn'səʊʃəbl/ *a* insociável, misantropo
unsophisticated /ʌnsə'fɪstɪkeɪtɪd/ *a* insofisticado, simples
unsound /ʌn'saʊnd/ *a* pouco sólido. **of ~ mind** (*jur*) não estar em plena posse das suas faculdades mentais (*jur*)
unspeakable /ʌn'spi:kəbl/ *a* indescritível; (*bad*) inqualificável
unspecified /ʌn'spesɪfaɪd/ *a* não especificado, indeterminado
unstable /ʌn'steɪbl/ *a* instável
unsteady /ʌn'stedɪ/ *a* (*step*) vacilante, incerto; (*ladder*) instável; (*hand*) pouco firme
unstuck /ʌn'stʌk/ *a* (*not stuck*) descolado. **come ~** (*colloq: fail*) falhar
unsuccessful /ʌnsək'sesfl/ *a* (*candidate*) mal sucedido; (*attempt*) malogrado, fracassado. **be ~** não ter êxito. **~ly** *adv* em vão
unsuit|able /ʌn's(j)u:təbl/ *a* impróprio, pouco apropriado, inadequado (**for** para). **~ed** *a* inadequado (**to** para)
unsure /ʌn'ʃʊə(r)/ *a* incerto
unsuspecting /ʌnsə'spektɪŋ/ *a* sem desconfiar de nada, insuspeitado
untangle /ʌn'tæŋgl/ *vt* desemaranhar, desenredar
unthinkable /ʌn'θɪŋkəbl/ *a* impensável, inconcebível
untid|y /ʌn'taɪdɪ/ *a* (**-ier, -iest**) (*room, desk etc*) desarrumado; (*appearance*) desleixado, desmazelado; (*hair*) despenteado. **~ily** *adv* sem cuidado. **~iness** *n* desordem *f*; (*of appearance*) desmazelo *m*
untie /ʌn'taɪ/ *vt* (*knot, parcel*) desatar, desfazer; (*person*) desamarrar
until /ən'tɪl/ *prep* até. **not ~** não antes de □ *conj* até que
untimely /ʌn'taɪmlɪ/ *a* inoportuno, intempestivo; (*death*) prematuro
untold /ʌn'təʊld/ *a* incalculável
untoward /ʌntə'wɔ:d/ *a* inconveniente, desagradável
untrue /ʌn'tru:/ *a* falso
unused[1] /ʌn'ju:zd/ *a* (*new*) novo, por usar; (*not in use*) não utilizado
unused[2] /ʌn'ju:st/ *a* **~ to** não habituado a, não acostumado a
unusual /ʌn'ju:ʒʊəl/ *a* insólito, fora do comum. **~ly** *adv* excepcionalmente
unveil /ʌn'veɪl/ *vt* descobrir; (*statue, portrait etc*) desvelar
unwanted /ʌn'wɒntɪd/ *a* (*useless*) que já não serve; (*child*) indesejado
unwarranted /ʌn'wɒrəntɪd/ *a* injustificado
unwelcome /ʌn'welkəm/ *a* desagradável; (*guest*) indesejável
unwell /ʌn'wel/ *a* indisposto
unwieldy /ʌn'wi:ldɪ/ *a* difícil de manejar, pouco jeitoso
unwilling /ʌn'wɪlɪŋ/ *a* relutante (**to** em), pouco disposto (**to** a)
unwind /ʌn'waɪnd/ *vt/i* (*pt* **unwound** /ʌn'waʊnd/) desenrolar (-se); (*colloq: relax*) descontrair (-se)
unwise /ʌn'waɪz/ *a* imprudente, insensato
unwittingly /ʌn'wɪtɪŋlɪ/ *adv* sem querer
unworthy /ʌn'wɜ:ðɪ/ *a* indigno
unwrap /ʌn'ræp/ *vt* (*pt* **unwrapped**) desembrulhar, abrir, desfazer
unwritten /ʌn'rɪtn/ *a* (*agreement*) verbal, tácito

up /ʌp/ *adv* (*to higher place*) cima, para cima, para o alto; (*in higher place*) em cima, no alto; (*out of bed*) acordado, de pé; (*up and dressed*) pronto; (*finished*) acabado; (*sun*) alto ◻ *prep* no cimo de, em cima de, no alto de. **~ the street/river**/*etc* pela rua/pelo rio/*etc* acima ◻ *vt* (*pt* **upped**) (*increase*) aumentar. **be ~ against** defrontar, enfrentar. **be ~ in** (*colloq*) saber. **be ~ to** (*do*) estar fazendo; (*plot*) estar tramando; (*task*) estar à altura de. **feel ~ to doing** (*able*) sentir-se capaz de fazer. **it is ~ to you** depende de você. **come** *or* **go ~** subir. **have ~s and downs** (*fig*) ter (os seus) altos e baixos. **walk ~ and down** andar dum lado para o outro *or* para a frente e para trás. **~-and-coming** *a* prometedor. **~-market** *a* requintado, fino

upbringing /'ʌpbrɪŋɪŋ/ *n* educação *f*

update /ʌp'deɪt/ *vt* atualizar, (*P*) actualizar

upheaval /ʌp'hi:vl/ *n* pandemônio *m*, (*P*) pandemónio *m*, revolução *f* (*fig*); (*social, political*) convulsão *f*

uphill /'ʌphɪl/ *a* ladeira acima, ascendente; (*fig: difficult*) árduo ◻ *adv* /ʌp'hɪl/ **go ~** subir

uphold /ʌp'həʊld/ *vt* (*pt* **upheld**) sustentar, manter, apoiar

upholster /ʌp'həʊlstə(r)/ *vt* estofar. **~y** *n* estofados *mpl*, (*P*) estofo(s) *m*(*pl*)

upkeep /'ʌpki:p/ *n* manutenção *f*

upon /ə'pɒn/ *prep* sobre

upper /'ʌpə(r)/ *a* superior ◻ *n* (*of shoe*) gáspea *f*. **have the ~ hand** estar por cima, estar em posição de superioridade. **~ class** aristocracia *f*. **~most** *a* (*highest*) o mais alto, superior

upright /'ʌpraɪt/ *a* vertical; (*honourable*) honesto, honrado, (*P*) recto

uprising /'ʌpraɪzɪŋ/ *n* insurreição *f*, sublevação *f*, levantamento *m*

uproar /'ʌprɔ:(r)/ *n* tumulto *m*, alvoroço *m*

uproot /ʌp'ru:t/ *vt* desenraizar; (*fig*) erradicar, desarraigar

upset[1] /ʌp'set/ *vt* (*pt* **upset**, *pres p* **upsetting**) (*overturn*) entornar, virar; (*plan*) contrariar, transtornar; (*stomach*) desarranjar; (*person*) contrariar, transtornar, incomodar ◻ *a* aborrecido

upset[2] /'ʌpset/ *n* transtorno *m*; (*of stomach*) indisposição *f*; (*distress*) choque *m*

upshot /'ʌpʃɒt/ *n* resultado *m*

upside-down /ʌpsaɪd'daʊn/ *adv* (*lit & fig*) ao contrário, de pernas para o ar

upstairs /ʌp'steəz/ *adv* (*at/to*) em/para cima, no/para o andar de cima ◻ *a* /'ʌpsteəz/ (*flat etc*) de cima, do andar de cima

upstart /'ʌpsta:t/ *n* arrivista *mf*

upstream /ʌp'stri:m/ *adv* rio acima, contra a corrente

upsurge /'ʌpsɜ:dʒ/ *n* recrudescência *f*, recrudescimento *m*; (*of anger*) acesso *m*, ataque *m*

uptake /'ʌpteɪk/ *n* **be quick on the ~** pegar rapidamente as coisas; (*fig*) ser de compreensão rápida, ser vivo

up-to-date /'ʌptədeɪt/ *a* moderno, atualizado, (*P*) actualizado

upturn /'ʌptɜ:n/ *n* melhoria *f*

upward /'ʌpwəd/ *a* ascendente, voltado para cima. **~s** *adv* para cima

uranium /jʊ'reɪnɪəm/ *n* urânio *m*

urban /'ɜ:bən/ *a* urbano

urbane /ɜ:'beɪn/ *a* delicado, cortês, urbano

urge /ɜ:dʒ/ *vt* aconselhar vivamente (**to** a) ◻ *n* (*strong desire*) grande vontade *f*. **~ on** (*impel*) incitar

urgen|t /'ɜ:dʒənt/ *a* urgente. **be ~t** urgir. **~cy** *n* urgência *f*

urinal /jʊə'raɪnl/ *n* urinol *m*

urin|e /'jʊərɪn/ *n* urina *f*. **~ate** *vi* urinar

urn /ɜ:n/ *n* urna *f*; (*for tea, coffee*) espécie *f* de samovar

us /ʌs/; *unstressed* /əs/ *pron* nos; (*after preps*) nós. **with ~** conosco. **he knows ~** ele nos conhece

US *abbr* **United States**

USA *abbr* **United States of America**

USB port /ju:esbi:pɔ:t/ *n* porto *m* USB

usable /'ju:zəbl/ *a* utilizável

usage /'ju:zɪdʒ/ *n* uso *m*

use[1] /ju:z/ *vt* usar, utilizar, servir-se de; (*exploit*) servir-se de; (*consume*) gastar, usar, consumir. **~ up** esgotar, consumir. **~r** /-ə(r)/ *n* usuário *m*, (*P*) utente *mf*. **~r-friendly** *a* fácil de usar

use[2] /ju:s/ *n* uso *m*, emprego *m*. **in ~** em uso. **it is no ~ shouting**/*etc* não serve de nada *or* não adianta gritar/*etc*. **make ~ of** servir-se de. **of ~** útil

used[1] /ju:zd/ *a* (*second-hand*) usado

used[2] /ju:st/ *pt* **he ~ to** ele costumava, ele tinha por costume *or* hábito ◻ *a* **~ to** acostumado a, habituado a

use|ful /'ju:sfl/ *a* útil. **~less** *a* inútil; (*person*) incompetente

usher /'ʌʃə(r)/ *n* vagalume *m*, (*P*) arrumador *m* ◻ *vt* **~ in** mandar entrar. **~ette** *n* vagalume *m*, (*P*) arrumadora *f*

usual /'ju:ʒʊəl/ *a* usual, habitual, normal. **as ~** como de costume, como habitualmente. **at the ~ time** na hora de costume, (*P*) à(s) hora(s) de costume. **~ly** *adv* habitualmente, normalmente

USSR *abbr* URSS

usurp /ju:'zɜ:p/ *vt* usurpar
utensil /ju:'tensl/ *n* utensílio *m*
uterus /'ju:tərəs/ *n* útero *m*
utilitarian /ju:tɪlɪ'teərɪən/ *a* utilitário
utility /ju:'tɪlətɪ/ *n* utilidade *f*. **(public)** ~ serviço *m* público. ~ **room** área *f* de serviço (para as máquinas de lavar a roupa e a louça)
utilize /'ju:tɪlaɪz/ *vt* utilizar
utmost /'ʌtməʊst/ *a* (*furthest, most intense*) extremo. **the** ~ **care**/*etc* (*greatest*) o maior cuidado/*etc* □ *n* **do one's** ~ fazer todo o possível
utter[1] /'ʌtə(r)/ *a* completo, absoluto. ~**ly** *adv* completamente
utter[2] /'ʌtə(r)/ *vt* proferir; (*sigh, shout*) dar. ~**ance** *n* expressão *f*
U-turn /'ju:tɜ:n/ *n* retorno *m*

vacan|t /'veɪkənt/ *a* (*post, room, look*) vago; (*mind*) vazio; (*seat, space, time*) desocupado, livre. ~**cy** *n* (*post*) vaga *f*; (*room in hotel*) vago *m*
vacate /və'keɪt/ *vt* vagar, deixar vago
vacation /və'keɪʃn/ *n* férias *fpl*
vaccinat|e /'væksɪmeɪt/ *vt* vacinar. ~**ion** /-'neɪʃn/ *n* vacinação *f*
vaccine /'væksi:n/ *n* vacina *f*
vacuum /'vækjʊəm/ *n* (*pl* **-cuums** *or* **-cua**) vácuo *m*, vazio *m*. ~ **flask** garrafa *f* térmica, (*P*) termo(s) *m*. ~ **cleaner** aspirador *m* de pó
vagina /və'dʒaɪnə/ *n* vagina *f*
vagrant /'veɪgrənt/ *n* vadio *m*, vagabundo *m*
vague /veɪg/ *a* (**-er, -est**) vago; (*outline*) impreciso. **be** ~ **about** ser vago acerca de, não precisar. ~**ly** *adv* vagamente
vain /veɪn/ *a* (**-er, -est**) (*conceited*) vaidoso; (*useless*) vão, inútil; (*fruitless*) infrutífero. **in** ~ em vão. ~**ly** *adv* em vão
valentine /'væləntaɪn/ *n* (*card*) cartão *m* do dia de São Valentin
valet /'vælɪt, 'væleɪ/ *n* (*manservant*) criado *m* de quarto; (*of hotel*) camareiro *m* □ *vt* (*car*) lavar e limpar o interior
valiant /'vælɪənt/ *a* corajoso, valente
valid /'vælɪd/ *a* válido. ~**ity** /və'lɪdətɪ/ *n* validade *f*
validate /'vælɪdeɪt/ *vt* validar, confirmar, ratificar
valley /'vælɪ/ *n* vale *m*
valuable /'væljʊəbl/ *a* (*object*) valioso, de valor; (*help, time etc*) precioso. ~**s** *npl* objetos *mpl*, (*P*) objectos *mpl* de valor
valuation /vælju'eɪʃn/ *n* avaliação *f*
value /'vælju:/ *n* valor *m* □ *vt* avaliar; (*cherish*) dar valor a. ~ **added tax** imposto *m* de valor adicional, (*P*) acrescentado. ~**r** /-ə(r)/ *n* avaliador *m*
valve /vælv/ *n* (*anat, techn, of car tyre*) válvula *f*; (*of bicycle tyre*) pipo *m*; (*of radio*) lâmpada *f*, válvula *f*
vampire /'væmpaɪə(r)/ *n* vampiro *m*
van /væn/ *n* (*large*) camião *m*; (*small*) camionete *f*, comercial *m*; (*milkman's, baker's etc*) camionete *f*; (*rail*) bagageiro *m*, (*P*) furgão *m*
vandal /'vændl/ *n* vândalo *m*. ~**ism** /-əlɪzəm/ *n* vandalismo *m*
vandalize /'vændəlaɪz/ *vt* destruir, estragar
vanguard /'væŋga:d/ *n* vanguarda *f*
vanilla /və'nɪlə/ *n* baunilha *f*
vanish /'vænɪʃ/ *vi* desaparecer, sumir-se, desvanecer-se
vanity /'vænətɪ/ *n* vaidade *f*. ~ **case** bolsa *f* de maquilagem
vantage-point /'va:ntɪdʒpɔɪnt/ *n* (bom) ponto *m* de observação
vapour /'veɪpə(r)/ *n* vapor *m*; (*mist*) bruma *f*
vari|able /'veərɪəbl/ *a* variável. ~**ation** /-'eɪʃn/ *n* variação *f*. ~**ed** /-ɪd/ *a* variado
variance /'veərɪəns/ *n* **at** ~ em desacordo (**with** com)
variant /'veərɪənt/ *a* diverso, diferente □ *n* variante *f*
varicose /'værɪkəʊs/ *a* ~ **veins** varizes *fpl*
variety /və'raɪətɪ/ *n* variedade *f*; (*entertainment*) variedades *fpl*
various /'veərɪəs/ *a* vários, diversos, variados
varnish /'va:nɪʃ/ *n* verniz *m* □ *vt* envernizar; (*nails*) pintar
vary /'veərɪ/ *vt*/*i* variar. ~**ing** *a* variado
vase /va:z/ *n* vaso *m*, jarra *f*
vast /va:st/ *a* vasto, imenso. ~**ly** *adv* imensamente, infinitamente. ~**ness** *n* vastidão *f*, imensidão *f*, imensidade *f*
vat /væt/ *n* tonel *m*, dorna *f*, cuba *f*
VAT /vi:eɪ'ti:, væt/ *abbr* ICM *m*, (*P*) IVA *m*
vault[1] /vɔ:lt/ *n* (*roof*) abóbada *f*; (*in bank*) casa-forte *f*; (*tomb*) cripta *f*; (*cellar*) adega *f*
vault[2] /vɔ:lt/ *vt*/*i* saltar □ *n* salto *m*
vaunt /vɔ:nt/ *vt*/*i* gabar(-se), ufanar(-se) (de), vangloriar(-se)
VD *abbr see* **venereal disease**
VDU *abbr see* **visual display unit**
veal /vi:l/ *n* (*meat*) vitela *f*

veer /vɪə(r)/ *vi* virar, mudar de direção, (*P*) direcção
vegan /ˈviːgən/ *a & n* vegetariano (*m*) estrito
vegetable /ˈvedʒɪtəbl/ *n* hortaliça *f*, legume *m* □ *a* vegetal
vegetarian /vedʒɪˈteərɪən/ *a & n* vegetariano (*m*)
vegetate /ˈvedʒɪteɪt/ *vi* vegetar
vegetation /vedʒɪˈteɪʃn/ *n* vegetação *f*
vehement /ˈviːəmənt/ *a* veemente. **~ly** *adv* veementemente
vehicle /ˈviːɪkl/ *n* veículo *m*
veil /veɪl/ *n* véu *m* □ *vt* velar, cobrir com véu; (*fig*) esconder, disfarçar
vein /veɪn/ *n* (*in body; mood*) veia *f*; (*in rock*) veio *m*, filão *m*; (*of leaf*) nervura *f*
velocity /vɪˈlɒsətɪ/ *n* velocidade *f*
velvet /ˈvelvɪt/ *n* veludo *m*. **~y** *a* aveludado
vendetta /venˈdetə/ *n* vendeta *f*
vending-machine /ˈvendɪŋməʃiːn/ *n* vendedora *f* automática, (*P*) máquina *f* de distribuição
vendor /ˈvendə(r)/ *n* vendedor *m*. **street ~** vendedor *m* ambulante
veneer /vəˈnɪə(r)/ *n* folheado *m*; (*fig*) fachada *f*, máscara *f*
venerable /ˈvenərəbl/ *a* venerável
venereal /vəˈnɪərɪəl/ *a* venéreo. **~ disease** doença *f* venérea
venetian /vəˈniːʃn/ *a* **~ blinds** persiana *f*
Venezuela /venɪzˈweɪlə/ *n* Venezuela *f*. **~n** *a & n* venezuelano (*m*)
vengeance /ˈvendʒəns/ *n* vingança. **with a ~** furiosamente, em excesso, com mais força do que se pretende
venison /ˈvenɪzn/ *n* carne *f* de veado
venom /ˈvenəm/ *n* veneno *m*. **~ous** /ˈvenəməs/ *a* venenoso
vent[1] /vent/ *n* (*in coat*) abertura *f*
vent[2] /vent/ *n* (*hole*) orifício *m*, abertura *f*; (*for air*) respiradouro *m* □ *vt* (*anger*) descarregar (**on** para cima de). **give ~ to** (*fig*) desabafar, dar vazão a
ventilat|e /ˈventɪleɪt/ *vt* ventilar. **~ion** /-ˈleɪʃn/ *n* ventilação *f*. **~or** *n* ventilador *m*
ventriloquist /venˈtrɪləkwɪst/ *n* ventríloquo *m*
venture /ˈventʃə(r)/ *n* emprendimento *m* arriscado, aventura *f* □ *vt/i* arriscar(-se)
venue /ˈvenjuː/ *n* porto *m* de encontro
veranda /vəˈrændə/ *n* varanda *f*
verb /vɜːb/ *n* verbo *m*
verbal /ˈvɜːbl/ *a* verbal; (*literal*) literal
verbatim /vɜːˈbeɪtɪm/ *adv* literalmente, palavra por palavra
verbose /vɜːˈbəʊs/ *a* palavroso, prolixo
verdict /ˈvɜːdɪkt/ *n* veredicto *m*; (*opinion*) opinião *f*
verge /vɜːdʒ/ *n* beira *f*, borda *f* □ *vi* **~ on** estar à beira de. **on the ~ of doing** prestes a fazer
verify /ˈverɪfaɪ/ *vt* verificar
veritable /ˈverɪtəbl/ *a* autêntico, verdadeiro
vermicelli /vɜːmɪˈselɪ/ *n* aletria *f*
vermin /ˈvɜːmɪn/ *n* animais *mpl* nocivos; (*lice, fleas etc*) parasitas *mpl*
vermouth /ˈvɜːməθ/ *n* vermute *m*
vernacular /vəˈnækjʊlə(r)/ *n* vernáculo *m*; (*dialect*) dialeto *m*, (*P*) dialecto *m*
versatil|e /ˈvɜːsətaɪl/ *a* versátil; (*tool*) que serve para vários fins. **~ity** /-ˈtɪlətɪ/ *n* versatilidade *f*
verse /vɜːs/ *n* (*poetry*) verso *m*, poesia *f*; (*stanza*) estrofe *f*; (*of Bible*) versículo *m*
versed /vɜːst/ *a* **~ in** versado em, conhecedor de
version /ˈvɜːʃn/ *n* versão *f*
versus /ˈvɜːsəs/ *prep* contra
vertebra /ˈvɜːtɪbrə/ *n* (*pl* **-brae** /-briː/) vértebra *f*
vertical /ˈvɜːtɪkl/ *a* vertical. **~ly** *adv* verticalmente
vertigo /ˈvɜːtɪgəʊ/ *n* vertigem *f*
verve /vɜːv/ *n* verve *f*, vivacidade *f*
very /ˈverɪ/ *adv* muito □ *a* (*actual*) mesmo, próprio; (*exact*) preciso, exato, (*P*) exacto. **the ~ day**/*etc* o próprio *or* o mesmo dia/*etc*. **at the ~ end** mesmo *or* precisamente no fim. **the ~ first/best**/*etc* (*emph*) o primeiro/melhor/*etc* de todos. **~ much** muito. **~ well** muito bem
vessel /ˈvesl/ *n* vaso *m*
vest[1] /vest/ *n* corpete *m*, (*P*) camisola *f* interior; (*Amer: waistcoat*) colete *m*
vest[2] /vest/ *vt* conferir (**in** a). **~ed interests** interesses *mpl*
vestige /ˈvestɪdʒ/ *n* vestígio *m*
vestry /ˈvestrɪ/ *n* sacristia *f*
vet /vet/ *n* (*colloq*) veterinário *m* □ *vt* (*pt* **vetted**) (*candidate etc*) examinar atentamente, estudar
veteran /ˈvetərən/ *n* veterano *m*. **(war) ~** veterano *m* de guerra
veterinary /ˈvetərɪnərɪ/ *a* veterinário. **~ surgeon** veterinário *m*
veto /ˈviːtəʊ/ *n* (*pl* **-oes**) veto *m*; (*right*) direito *m* de veto □ *vt* vetar, opor o veto a
vex /veks/ *vt* aborrecer, irritar, contrariar. **~ed question** questão *f* muito debatida, assunto *m* controverso
via /ˈvaɪə/ *prep* por, via
viab|le /ˈvaɪəbl/ *a* viável. **~ility** /-ˈbɪlətɪ/ *n* viabilidade *f*

viaduct /'vaɪədʌkt/ *n* viaduto *m*
vibrant /'vaɪbrənt/ *a* vibrante
vibrat|e /vaɪ'breɪt/ *vt/i* (fazer) vibrar. **~ion** /-ʃn/ *n* vibração *f*
vicar /'vɪkə(r)/ *n* (*Anglican*) pastor *m*; (*Catholic*) vigário *m*, pároco *m*. **~age** *n* presbitério *m*
vicarious /vɪ'keərɪəs/ *a* vivido indiretamente, (*P*) indirectamente
vice[1] /vaɪs/ *n* (*depravity*) vício *m*
vice[2] /vaɪs/ *n* (*techn*) torno *m*
vice- /vaɪs/ *pref* vice-. **~- chairman** vice-presidente *m*. **~-chancellor** *n* vice-chanceler *m*; (*univ*) reitor *m*. **~-consul** *n* vice-cônsul *m*. **~-president** *n* vice-presidente *mf*
vice versa /'vaɪsɪ'vɜ:sə/ *adv* vice-versa
vicinity /vɪ'sɪnətɪ/ *n* vizinhança *f*, cercania(s) *fpl*, arredores *mpl*. **in the ~ of** nos arredores de
vicious /'vɪʃəs/ *a* (*spiteful*) mau, maldoso; (*violent*) brutal, feroz. **~ circle** círculo *m* vicioso. **~ly** *adv* maldosamente; (*violently*) brutalmente, ferozmente
victim /'vɪktɪm/ *n* vítima *f*
victimiz|e /'vɪktɪmaɪz/ *vt* perseguir. **~ation** /-'zeɪʃn/ *n* perseguição *f*
victor /'vɪktə(r)/ *n* vencedor *m*
victor|y /'vɪktərɪ/ *n* vitória *f*. **~ious** /-'tɔ:rɪəs/ *a* vitorioso
video /'vɪdɪəʊ/ *a* vídeo □ *n* (*pl* **-os**) (*colloq*) vídeo □ *vt* (*record*) gravar em vídeo. **~ cassette** videocassete *m* **~ recorder** videocassete *m*
vie /vaɪ/ *vi* (*pres p* **vying**) rivalizar, competir (**with** com)
view /vju:/ *n* vista *f* □ *vt* ver; (*examine*) examinar; (*consider*) considerar, ver; (*a house*) visitar, ver. **in my ~** a meu ver, na minha opinião. **in ~ of** em vista de. **on ~** em exposição, à mostra; (*open to the public*) aberto ao público. **with a ~ to** com a intenção de, com o fim de. **~er** *n* (*TV*) telespectador *m*; (*for slides*) visor *m*
viewfinder /'vju:faɪndə(r)/ *n* visor *m*
viewpoint /'vju:pɔɪnt/ *n* ponto *m* de vista
vigil /'vɪdʒɪl/ *n* vigília *f*; (*over corpse*) velório *m*; (*relig*) vigília *f*
vigilan|t /'vɪdʒɪlənt/ *a* vigilante. **~ce** *n* vigilância *f*. **~te** /vɪdʒɪ'læntɪ/ *n* vigilante *m*
vig|our /'vɪgə(r)/ *n* vigor *m*. **~orous** /'vɪgərəs/ *a* vigoroso
vile /vaɪl/ *a* (*base*) infame, vil; (*colloq: bad*) horroroso, péssimo
vilify /'vɪlɪfaɪ/ *vt* difamar
villa /'vɪlə/ *n* vivenda *f*, vila *f*; (*country residence*) casa *f* de campo
village /'vɪlɪdʒ/ *n* aldeia *f*, povoado *m*. **~r** *n* aldeão *m*, aldeã *f*
villain /'vɪlən/ *n* patife *m*, mau-caráter *m*. **~y** *n* infâmia *f*, vilania *f*
vindicat|e /'vɪndɪkeɪt/ *vt* vindicar, justificar. **~ion** /-'keɪʃn/ *n* justificação *f*
vindictive /vɪn'dɪktɪv/ *a* vingativo
vine /vaɪn/ *n* (*plant*) vinha *f*
vinegar /'vɪnɪgə(r)/ *n* vinagre *m*
vineyard /'vɪnjəd/ *n* vinha *f*, vinhedo *m*
vintage /'vɪntɪdʒ/ *n* (*year*) ano *m* de colheita de qualidade excepcional □ *a* (*wine*) de colheita excepcional e de um determinado ano; (*car*) de museu (*colloq*), fabricado entre 1917 e 1930
vinyl /'vaɪnɪl/ *n* vinil *m*
viola /vɪ'əʊlə/ *n* (*mus*) viola *f*, violeta *f*
violat|e /'vaɪəleɪt/ *vt* violar. **~ion** /-'leɪʃn/ *n* violação *f*
violen|t /'vaɪələnt/ *a* violento. **~ce** *n* violência *f*. **~tly** *adv* violentamente, com violência
violet /'vaɪələt/ *n* (*bot*) violeta *f*; (*colour*) violeta *m* □ *a* violeta
violin /vaɪə'lɪn/ *n* violino *m*. **~ist** *n* violinista *mf*
VIP /vi:aɪ'pi:/ *abbr* (*very important person*) VIP *m*, personalidade *f* importante
viper /'vaɪpə(r)/ *n* víbora *f*
virgin /'vɜ:dʒɪn/ *a & n* virgem (*f*); **~ity** /və'dʒɪnətɪ/ *n* virgindade *f*
Virgo /'vɜ:gəʊ/ *n* (*astr*) Virgem *f*, (*P*) virgo *m*
viril|e /'vɪraɪl/ *a* viril, varonil. **~ity** /vɪ'rɪlətɪ/ *n* virilidade *f*
virtual /'vɜ:tʃʊəl/ *a* que é na prática embora não em teoria, verdadeiro. **a ~ failure**/*etc* praticamente um fracasso/*etc*. **~ly** *adv* praticamente
virtue /'vɜ:tʃu:/ *n* (*goodness, chastity*) virtude *f*; (*merit*) mérito *m*. **by** *or* **in ~ of** por *or* em virtude de
virtuos|o /vɜ:tʃʊ'əʊsəʊ/ *n* (*pl* **-si** /-si:/) virtuoso *m*, virtuose *mf*. **~ity** /-'ɒsətɪ/ *n* virtuosidade *f*, virtuosismo *m*
virtuous /'vɜ:tʃʊəs/ *a* virtuoso
virulen|t /'vɪrʊlənt/ *a* virulento. **~ce** /-ləns/ *n* virulência *f*
virus /'vaɪərəs/ *n* (*pl* **-es**) vírus *m*; (*colloq: disease*) virose *f*
visa /'vi:zə/ *n* visto *m*
viscount /'vaɪkaʊnt/ *n* visconde *m*. **~ess** /-ɪs/ *n* viscondessa *f*
viscous /'vɪskəs/ *a* viscoso
vise /vaɪs/ *n* (*Amer: vice*) torno *m*
visib|le /'vɪzəbl/ *a* visível. **~ility** /-'bɪlətɪ/ *n* visibilidade *f*. **~ly** *adv* visivelmente
vision /'vɪʒn/ *n* (*dream, insight*) visão *f*; (*seeing, sight*) vista *f*, visão *f*

visionary /'vɪʒənərɪ/ *a* visionário; (*plan, scheme etc*) fantasista, quimérico ▫ *n* visionário *m*

visit /'vɪzɪt/ *vt* (*pt* **visited**) (*person*) visitar, fazer uma visita a; (*place*) visitar ▫ *vi* estar de visita ▫ *n* (*tour, call*) visita *f*; (*stay*) estada *f*, visita *f*. **~or** *n* visitante *mf*; (*guest*) visita *f*

visor /'vaɪzə(r)/ *n* viseira *f*; (*in vehicle*) visor *m*

vista /'vɪstə/ *n* vista *f*, panorama *m*

visual /'vɪʒʊəl/ *a* visual. **~ display unit** terminal *m* de vídeo. **~ly** *adv* visualmente

visualize /'vɪʒʊəlaɪz/ *vt* visualizar; (*foresee*) imaginar, prever

vital /'vaɪtl/ *a* vital. **~ statistics** estatísticas *fpl* demográficas; (*colloq: woman*) medidas *fpl*

vitality /vaɪ'tælətɪ/ *n* vitalidade *f*

vitamin /'vɪtəmɪn/ *n* vitamina *f*

vivac|ious /vɪ'veɪʃəs/ *a* cheio de vida, vivo, animado. **~ity** /-'væsətɪ/ *n* vivacidade *f*, animação *f*

vivid /'vɪvɪd/ *a* vívido; (*imagination*) vivo. **~ly** *adv* vividamente

vivisection /vɪvɪ'sekʃn/ *n* vivissecção *f*

vixen /'vɪksn/ *n* raposa *f* fêmea

vocabulary /və'kæbjʊlərɪ/ *n* vocabulário *m*

vocal /'vəʊkl/ *a* vocal; (*fig: person*) eloqüente, (*P*) eloquente. **~ cords** cordas *fpl* vocais. **~ist** *n* vocalista *mf*

vocation /və'keɪʃn/ *n* vocação *f*; (*trade*) profissão *f*. **~al** *a* vocacional, profissional

vociferous /və'sɪfərəs/ *a* vociferante

vodka /'vɒdkə/ *n* vodka *m*

vogue /vəʊg/ *n* voga *f*, moda *f*, popularidade *f*. **in ~** em voga, na moda

voice /vɔɪs/ *n* voz *f* ▫ *vt* (*express*) exprimir

void /vɔɪd/ *a* vazio; (*jur*) nulo, sem validade ▫ *n* vácuo *m*, vazio *m*. **make ~** anular, invalidar. **~ of** sem, destituído de

volatile /'vɒlətaɪl/ *a* (*substance*) volátil; (*fig: changeable*) instável

volcan|o /vɒl'keɪnəʊ/ *n* (*pl* **-oes**) vulcão *m*. **~ic** /-ænɪk/ *a* vulcânico

volition /və'lɪʃn/ *n* **of one's own ~** de sua própria vontade

volley /'vɒlɪ/ *n* (*of blows etc*) saraivada *f*; (*of gunfire*) salva *f*; (*tennis*) voleio *m*. **~ball** *n* voleibol *m*, vôlei *m*

volt /vəʊlt/ *n* volt *m*. **~age** *n* voltagem *f*

voluble /'vɒljʊbl/ *a* falante, loquaz

volume /'vɒlju:m/ *n* (*book, sound*) volume *m*; (*capacity*) capacidade *f*

voluntar|y /'vɒləntərɪ/ *a* voluntário; (*unpaid*) não-remunerado. **~ily** /-trəlɪ/ *adv* voluntariamente

volunteer /vɒlən'tɪə(r)/ *n* voluntário *m* ▫ *vi* oferecer-se (**to do** para fazer); (*mil*) alistar-se como voluntário ▫ *vt* oferecer espontaneamente

voluptuous /və'lʌptʃʊəs/ *a* voluptuoso, sensual

vomit /'vɒmɪt/ *vt*/*i* (*pt* **vomited**) vomitar ▫ *n* vômito *m*, (*P*) vómito *m*

voodoo /'vu:du:/ *n* vodu *m*

voraci|ous /və'reɪʃəs/ *a* voraz. **~ously** *adv* vorazmente. **~ty** /və'ræsətɪ/ *n* voracidade *f*

vot|e /vəʊt/ *n* voto *m*; (*right*) direito *m* de voto ▫ *vt*/*i* votar. **~er** *n* eleitor *m*. **~ing** *n* votação *f*; (*poll*) escrutínio *m*

vouch /vaʊtʃ/ *vi* **~ for** responder por, garantir

voucher /'vaʊtʃə(r)/ *n* (*for meal, transport*) vale *m*; (*receipt*) comprovante *m*

vow /vaʊ/ *n* voto *m* ▫ *vt* (*loyalty etc*) jurar (**to** a). **~ to do** jurar fazer

vowel /'vaʊəl/ *n* vogal *f*

voyage /'vɔɪɪdʒ/ *n* viagem (por mar) *f*. **~r** /-ə(r)/ *n* viajante *m*

vulgar /'vʌlgə(r)/ *a* ordinário, grosseiro; (*in common use*) vulgar. **~ity** /-'gærətɪ/ *n* (*behaviour*) grosseria *f*, vulgaridade *f*

vulnerab|le /'vʌlnərəbl/ *a* vulnerável. **~ility** /-'bɪlətɪ/ *n* vulnerabilidade *f*

vulture /'vʌltʃə(r)/ *n* abutre *m*, urubu *m*

vying /'vaɪɪŋ/ *see* **vie**

Ww

wad /wɒd/ *n* bucha *f*, tampão *m*; (*bundle*) maço *m*, rolo *m*

wadding /'wɒdɪŋ/ *n* enchimento *m*

waddle /'wɒdl/ *vi* bambolear-se, rebolar-se, gingar

wade /weɪd/ *vi* **~ through** (*fig*) avançar a custo por; (*mud, water*) patinhar em

wafer /'weɪfə(r)/ *n* (*biscuit*) bolacha *f* de baunilha; (*relig*) hóstia *f*

waffle[1] /'wɒfl/ *n* (*colloq: talk*) lengalenga *f*, papo *m*, conversa *f*; (*colloq: writing*) lenga-lenga ▫ *vi* (*colloq*) escrever muito sem dizer nada de importante

waffle[2] /'wɒfl/ *n* (*culin*) waffle *m*

waft /wɒft/ *vi* flutuar ▫ *vt* espalhar, levar suavemente

wag /wæg/ *vt*/*i* (*pt* **wagged**) abanar, agitar, sacudir

wage[1] /weɪdʒ/ *vt* (*campaign, war*) fazer

wage[2] /weɪdʒ/ *n* **~(s)** (*weekly, daily*) salário *m*, ordenado *m*. **~-claim** *n* pedido *m* de aumento de salário. **~-earner** *n* trabalhador *m* assalariado. **~-freeze** *n* congelamento *m* de salários

wager /ˈweɪdʒə(r)/ *n* (*bet*) aposta *f* □ *vt* apostar (**that** que)

waggle /ˈwægl/ *vt/i* abanar, agitar, sacudir

wagon /ˈwægən/ *n* (*horse-drawn*) carroça *f*; (*rail*) vagão *m* de mercadorias

waif /weɪf/ *n* criança *f* abandonada

wail /weɪl/ *vi* lamentar-se, gemer lamentosamente □ *n* lamentação *f*, gemido *m* lamentoso

waist /weɪst/ *n* cintura *f*. **~-line** *n* cintura *f*

waistcoat /ˈweɪskəʊt/ *n* colete *m*

wait /weɪt/ *vt/i* esperar □ *n* espera *f*. **~ for** esperar. **~ on** servir. **lie in ~ (for)** estar escondido à espera (de), armar uma emboscada (para). **keep sb ~ing** fazer alguém esperar. **~ing-list** *n* lista *f* de espera. **~ing-room** *n* sala *f* de espera

wait|er /ˈweɪtə(r)/ *n* garçon *m*, (*P*) criado *m* (de mesa). **~ress** *n* garçonete *f*, (*P*) criada *f* (de mesa)

waive /weɪv/ *vt* renunciar a, desistir de

wake[1] /weɪk/ *vt/i* (*pt* **woke**, *pp* **woken**) **~ (up)** acordar, despertar □ *n* (*before burial*) velório *m*

wake[2] /weɪk/ *n* (*ship*) esteira (de espuma) *f*. **in the ~ of** (*following*) atrás de, em seguida a

waken /ˈweɪkən/ *vt/i* acordar, despertar

Wales /weɪlz/ *n* País *m* de Gales

walk /wɔːk/ *vi* andar, caminhar; (*not ride*) ir a pé; (*stroll*) passear □ *vt* (*streets*) andar por, percorrer; (*distance*) andar, fazer a pé, percorrer; (*dog*) (levar para) passear □ *n* (*stroll*) passeio *m*, volta *f*; (*excursion*) caminhada *f*; (*gait*) passo *m*, maneira *f* de andar; (*pace*) passo *m*; (*path*) caminho *m*. **it's a 5-minute ~** são 5 minutos a pé. **~ of life** meio *m*, condição *f* social. **~ out** (*go away*) sair; (*go on strike*) fazer greve. **~ out on** abandonar. **~-over** *n* vitória *f* fácil

walker /ˈwɔːkə(r)/ *n* caminhante *mf*

walkie-talkie /wɔːkɪˈtɔːkɪ/ *n* walkie-talkie *m*

walking /ˈwɔːkɪŋ/ *n* andar (a pé) *m*, marcha (a pé) *f* □ *a* (*colloq: dictionary*) vivo. **~-stick** *n* bengala *f*

Walkman /ˈwɔːkmæn/ *n* walkman *m*

wall /wɔːl/ *n* parede *f*; (*around land*) muro *m*; (*of castle, town; fig*) muralha *f*; (*of stomach etc*) parede(s) *f* (*pl*) □ *vt* (*city*) fortificar; (*property*) murar. **go to the ~** sucumbir, falir; (*firm*) ir à falência. **up the ~** (*colloq*) fora de si

wallet /ˈwɒlɪt/ *n* carteira *f*

wallflower /ˈwɔːlflaʊə(r)/ *n* (*bot*) goivo *m*. **be a ~** (*fig*) tomar chá de cadeira, (*P*) levar banho de cadeira

wallop /ˈwɒləp/ *vt* (*pt* **walloped**) (*sl*) espancar (*colloq*) □ *n* (*sl*) pancada *f* forte

wallow /ˈwɒləʊ/ *vi* (*in mud*) chafurdar; (*fig*) regozijar-se

wallpaper /ˈwɔːlpeɪpə(r)/ *n* papel *m* de parede □ *vt* forrar com papel de parede

walnut /ˈwɔːlnʌt/ *n* (*nut*) noz *f*; (*tree*) nogueira *f*

walrus /ˈwɔːlrəs/ *n* morsa *f*

waltz /wɔːls/ *n* valsa *f* □ *vi* valsar

wan /wɒn/ *a* pálido

wand /wɒnd/ *n* (*magic*) varinha *f* mágica *or* de condão

wander /ˈwɒndə(r)/ *vi* andar ao acaso, vagar, errar; (*river*) serpentear; (*mind, speech*) divagar; (*stray*) extraviar-se. **~er** *n* vagabundo *m*, andarilho *m*. **~ing** *a* errante

wane /weɪn/ *vi* diminuir, minguar; (*decline*) declinar □ *n* **on the ~** em declínio; (*moon*) no quarto minguante

wangle /ˈwæŋgl/ *vt* (*colloq*) conseguir algo através de pistolão

want /wɒnt/ *vt* querer (**to do** fazer); (*need*) precisar (de); (*ask for*) exigir, requerer □ *vi* **~ for** ter falta de □ *n* (*need*) necessidade *f*, precisão *f*; (*desire*) desejo *m*; (*lack*) falta *f*, carência *f*. **for ~ of** por falta de. **I ~ you to go** eu quero que você vá. **~ed** *a* (*criminal*) procurado pela polícia; (*in ad*) precisa(m)-se

wanting /ˈwɒntɪŋ/ *a* falho, falto (**in** de). **be found ~** não estar à altura

wanton /ˈwɒntən/ *a* (*playful*) travesso, brincalhão; (*cruelty, destruction etc*) gratuito; (*woman*) despudorado

WAP /wæp/ *a* WAP

war /wɔː(r)/ *n* guerra *f*. **at ~** em guerra. **on the ~-path** em pé de guerra

warble /ˈwɔːbl/ *vt/i* gorjear

ward /wɔːd/ *n* (*in hospital*) enfermaria *f*; (*jur: minor*) pupilo *m*; (*pol*) círculo *m* eleitoral □ *vt* **~ off** (*a blow*) aparar; (*anger*) desviar; (*danger*) prevenir, evitar

warden /ˈwɔːdn/ *n* (*of institution*) diretor *m*, (*P*) director *m*; (*of park*) guarda *m*

warder /ˈwɔːdə(r)/ *n* guarda (de prisão) *m*, carcereiro *m*

wardrobe /ˈwɔːdrəʊb/ *n* (*place*) armário *m*, guarda-roupa *m*, (*P*) guarda-fato *m*,

(*P*) roupeiro *m*; (*clothes*) guarda-roupa *m*

warehouse /'weəhaʊs/ *n* (*pl* **-s** /-haʊzɪz/) armazém *m*, depósito *m* de mercadorias

wares /weəz/ *npl* (*goods*) mercadorias *fpl*, artigos *mpl*

warfare /'wɔ:feə(r)/ *n* guerra *f*

warhead /'wɔ:hed/ *n* ogiva (de combate) *f*

warlike /'wɔ:laɪk/ *a* marcial, guerreiro; (*bellicose*) belicoso

warm /wɔ:m/ *a* (**-er, -est**) quente; (*hearty*) caloroso, cordial. **be** *or* **feel ~** estar com *or* ter *or* sentir calor □ *vt*/*i* **~ (up)** aquecer(-se). **~-hearted** *a* afetuoso, (*P*) afectuoso, com calor humano. **~ly** *adv* (*heartily*) calorosamente. **wrap up ~ly** agasalhar-se bem. **~th** *n* calor *m*

warn /wɔ:n/ *vt* avisar, prevenir. **~ sb off sth** (*advise against*) pôr alguém de prevenção *or* de pé atrás com alg coisa; (*forbid*) proibir alg coisa a alguém. **~ing** *n* aviso *m*. **~ing light** lâmpada *f* de advertência. **without ~ing** sem aviso, sem prevenir

warp /wɔ:p/ *vt*/*i* (*wood etc*) empenar; (*fig: pervert*) torcer, deformar, desvirtuar. **~ed** *a* (*fig*) deturpado, pervertido

warrant /'wɒrənt/ *n* autorização *f*; (*for arrest*) mandato (de captura) *m*; (*comm*) título *m* de crédito, warrant *m* □ *vt* justificar; (*guarantee*) garantir

warranty /'wɒrəntɪ/ *n* garantia *f*

warring /'wɔ:rɪŋ/ *a* em guerra; (*rival*) contrário, antagônico, (*P*) antagónico

warrior /'wɒrɪə(r)/ *n* guerreiro *m*

warship /'wɔ:ʃɪp/ *n* navio *m* de guerra

wart /wɔ:t/ *n* verruga *f*

wartime /'wɔ:taɪm/ *n* **in ~** em tempo de guerra

wary /'weərɪ/ *a* (**-ier, -iest**) cauteloso, prudente

was /wɒz/; *unstressed* /wəz/ *see* **be**

wash /wɒʃ/ *vt*/*i* lavar(-se); (*flow over*) molhar, inundar □ *n* lavagem *f*; (*dirty clothes*) roupa *f* para lavar; (*of ship*) esteira *f*; (*of paint*) fina camada *f* de tinta. **have a ~** lavar-se. **~-basin** *n* pia *f*, (*P*) lavatório *m*. **~-cloth** *n* (*Amer: face-cloth*) toalha *f* de rosto. **~ one's hands of** lavar as mãos de. **~ out** (*cup etc*) lavar; (*stain*) tirar lavando. **~-out** *n* (*sl*) fiasco *m*. **~-room** *n* (*Amer*) banheiro *m*, (*P*) casa *f* de banho. **~ up** lavar a louça; (*Amer: wash oneself*) lavar-se. **~able** *a* lavável. **~ing** *n* (*dirty*) roupa *f* suja; (*clean*) roupa *f* lavada. **~ing-machine** *n* máquina *f* de lavar roupa. **~ing-powder** *n* detergente *m* em pó. **~ing-up** *n* lavagem *f* da louça

washed-out /wɒʃt'aʊt/ *a* (*faded*) desbotado; (*exhausted*) exausto

washer /'wɒʃə(r)/ *n* (*machine*) máquina *f* de lavar roupa, louça *f*, (*P*) loiça *f*; (*ring*) anilha *f*

wasp /wɒsp/ *n* vespa *f*

wastage /'weɪstɪdʒ/ *n* desperdício *m*, perda *f*. **natural ~** desgaste *m* natural

waste /weɪst/ *vt* desperdiçar, esbanjar; (*time*) perder □ *vi* **~ away** consumir-se □ *a* (*useless*) inútil; (*material*) de refugo □ *n* desperdício *m*, perda *f*; (*of time*) perda *f*; (*rubbish*) lixo *m*. **lay ~** assolar, desvastar. **~ (land)** (*desolate*) região *f* desolada, ermo *m*; (*unused*) (terreno) baldio *m*. **~-disposal unit** triturador *m* de lixo. **~ paper** papéis *mpl* velhos. **~-paper basket** cesto *m* de papéis

wasteful /'weɪstfl/ *a* dispendioso; (*person*) esbanjador, gastador, perdulário

watch /wɒtʃ/ *vt*/*i* ver bem, olhar com atenção, observar; (*game, TV*) ver; (*guard, spy on*) vigiar; (*be careful about*) tomar cuidado com □ *n* vigia *f*, vigilância *f*; (*naut*) quarto *m*; (*for telling time*) relógio *m*. **~-dog** *n* cão *m* de guarda. **~ out** (*look out*) estar à espreita (**for** de); (*take care*) acautelar-se. **~-strap** *n* correia *f*, pulseira *f* do relógio. **~- tower** *n* torre *f* de observação. **~ful** *a* atento, vigilante

watchmaker /'wɒtʃmeɪkə(r)/ *n* relojoeiro *m*

watchman /'wɒtʃmən/ *n* (*pl* **-men**) (*of building*) guarda *m*. **(night-) ~** guarda-noturno *m*

watchword /'wɒtʃwɜ:d/ *n* lema *m*, divisa *f*

water /'wɔ:tə(r)/ *n* água *f* □ *vt* regar □ *vi* (*of eyes*) lacrimejar, chorar. **~ down** juntar água a, diluir; (*milk, wine*) aguar, batizar, (*P*) baptizar (*colloq*); (*fig: tone down*) suavizar. **~-closet** *n* WC *m*, banheiro *m*, (*P*) lavabos *mpl*. **~-colour** *n* aquarela *f*. **~-ice** *n* sorvete *m*. **~-lily** *n* nenúfar *m*. **~-main** *n* cano *m* principal da rede. **~-melon** *n* melancia *f*. **~-pistol** *n* pistola *f* de água. **~ polo** pólo *m* aquático. **~-skiing** *n* esqui *m* aquático. **~-wheel** *n* roda *f* hidráulica

watercress /'wɔ:təkres/ *n* agrião *m*

waterfall /'wɔ:təfɔ:l/ *n* queda *f* de água, cascata *f*

watering-can /'wɔ:tərɪŋkæn/ *n* regador *m*

waterlogged /'wɔ:təlɒgd/ *a* saturado de água; (*land*) empapado, alagado; (*vessel*) inundado, alagado

watermark /'wɔ:təma:k/ *n* (*in paper*) marca-d'água *f*, filigrana *f*

waterproof /'wɔ:təpru:f/ *a* impermeável; (*watch*) à prova d'água

watershed /'wɔ:təʃed/ *n* (*fig*) momento *m* decisivo; (*in affairs*) ponto *m* crítico

watertight /'wɔ:tətaɪt/ *a* à prova d'água, hermético; (*fig: argument etc*) inequívoco, irrefutável

waterway /'wɔ:təweɪ/ *n* via *f* navegável

waterworks /'wɔ:təwɜ:ks/ *n* (*place*) estação *f* hidráulica

watery /'wɔ:tərɪ/ *a* (*colour*) pálido; (*eyes*) lacrimoso; (*soup*) aguado; (*tea*) fraco

watt /wɒt/ *n* watt *m*

wav|e /weɪv/ *n* onda *f*; (*in hair; radio*) onda *f*; (*sign*) aceno *m* □ *vt* acenar com; (*sword*) brandir; (*hair*) ondular □ *vi* acenar (com a mão); (*hair etc*) ondular; (*flag*) tremular. **~eband** *n* faixa *f* de onda. **~e goodbye** dizer adeus. **~elength** *n* comprimento *m* de onda. **~y** *a* ondulado

waver /'weɪvə(r)/ *vi* vacilar; (*hesitate*) hesitar

wax[1] /wæks/ *n* cera *f* □ *vt* encerar; (*car*) polir. **~en, ~y** *adjs* de cera

wax[2] /wæks/ *vi* (*of moon*) aumentar, crescer

waxwork /'wækswɜ:k/ *n* (*dummy*) figura *f* de cera. **~s** *npl* (*exhibition*) museu *m* de figuras de cera

way /weɪ/ *n* (*road, path*) caminho *m*, estrada *f*, rua *f* (**to** para); (*distance*) percurso *m*; (*direction*) (*P*) direcção *f*; (*manner*) modo *m*, maneira *f*; (*means*) meios *mpl*; (*respect*) respeito *m*. **~s** (*habits*) costumes *mpl* □ *adv* (*colloq*) consideravelmente, de longe. **be in the ~** atrapalhar. **be on one's** *or* **the ~** estar a caminho. **by the ~** a propósito. **by ~ of** por, via, através. **get one's own ~** conseguir o que quer. **give ~** (*yield*) ceder; (*collapse*) desabar; (*auto*) dar a preferência. **in a ~** de certo modo. **make one's ~** ir. **that ~** dessa maneira. **this ~** desta maneira. **~ in** entrada *f*. **~ out** saída *f*. **~-out** *a* (*colloq*) excêntrico

waylay /weɪ'leɪ/ *vt* (*pt* **-laid**) (*assail*) armar uma cilada para; (*stop*) interceptar

wayward /'weɪwəd/ *a* (*wilful*) teimoso; (*perverse*) caprichoso, difícil

WC /dʌb(ə)lju:'si:/ *n* WC *m*, banheiro *m*, (*P*) casa *f* de banho

we /wi:/ *pron* nós

weak /wi:k/ *a* (**-er, -est**) fraco; (*delicate*) frágil. **~en** *vt/i* enfraquecer; (*give way*) fraquejar. **~ly** *adv* fracamente. **~ness** *n* fraqueza *f*; (*fault*) ponto *m* fraco. **a ~ness for** (*liking*) um fraco por

weakling /'wi:klɪŋ/ *n* fraco *m*

wealth /welθ/ *n* riqueza *f*; (*riches, resources*) riquezas *fpl*; (*quantity*) abundância *f*

wealthy /'welθɪ/ *a* (**-ier, -iest**) rico

wean /wi:n/ *vt* (*baby*) desmamar; (*from habit etc*) desabituar

weapon /'wepən/ *n* arma *f*

wear /weə(r)/ *vt* (*pt* **wore**, *pp* **worn**) (*have on*) usar, trazer; (*put on*) pôr; (*expression*) ter; (*damage*) gastar. **~ black/red/***etc* vestir-se de preto/vermelho/*etc* □ *vi* (*last*) durar; (*become old, damaged etc*) gastar-se □ *n* (*use*) uso *m*; (*deterioration*) gasto *m*, uso *m*; (*endurance*) resistência *f*; (*clothing*) roupa *f*. **~ and tear** desgaste *m*. **~ down** gastar; (*person*) extenuar. **~ off** passar. **~ on** (*time*) passar lentamente. **~ out** gastar; (*tire*) esgotar

wear|y /'wɪərɪ/ *a* (**-ier, -iest**) fatigado, cansado; (*tiring*) fatigante, cansativo □ *vi* **~y of** cansar-se de. **~ily** *adv* com lassidão, cansadamente. **~iness** *n* fadiga *f*

weasel /'wi:zl/ *n* doninha *f*

weather /'weðə(r)/ *n* tempo *m* □ *a* meteorológico □ *vt* (*survive*) agüentar, (*P*) aguentar, resistir a. **under the ~** (*colloq: ill*) indisposto, achacado. **~-beaten** *a* curtido pelo tempo. **~ forecast** *n* boletim *m* meteorológico. **~-vane** *n* cata-vento *m*

weathercock /'weðəkɒk/ *n* (*lit & fig*) cata-vento *m*

weav|e[1] /wi:v/ *vt* (*pt* **wove**, *pp* **woven**) (*cloth etc*) tecer; (*plot*) urdir, criar □ *n* (*style*) tipo *m* de tecido. **~er** /-ə(r)/ *n* tecelão *m*, tecelã *f*. **~ing** *n* tecelagem *f*

weave[2] /wi:v/ *vi* (*move*) serpear; (*through traffic, obstacles*) ziguezaguear

web /web/ *n* (*of spider*) teia *f*; (*fabric*) tecido *m*; (*comput*) web *m*; (*on foot*) membrana *f* interdigital. **~bed** *a* (*foot*) palmado. **~bing** *n* (*in chair*) tira *f* de tecido forte. **~-footed** *a* palmípede. **~page** página *f* web. **~site** site *m*

wed /wed/ *vt/i* (*pt* **wedded**) casar (-se)

wedding /'wedɪŋ/ *n* casamento *m*. **~-cake** *n* bolo *m* de noiva. **~-ring** *n* aliança (de casamento) *f*

wedge /wedʒ/ *n* calço *m*, cunha *f*; (*cake*) fatia *f*; (*of lemon*) quarto *m*; (*under wheel etc*) calço *m*, cunha *f* □ *vt* calçar; (*push*) meter *or* enfiar à força; (*pack in*) entalar

Wednesday /'wenzdɪ/ *n* quartafeira *f*

weed /wi:d/ *n* erva *f* daninha □ *vt/i* arrancar as ervas, capinar. **~-killer** *n* herbicida *m*. **~ out** suprimir, arrancar. **~y** *a* (*fig: person*) fraco

week /wi:k/ *n* semana *f*. **a ~ today/tomorrow** de hoje/de amanhã a oito dias. **~ly** *a* semanal □ *a* & *n* (*periodical*) (jornal) semanário (*m*) □ *adv* semanalmente, todas as semanas

weekday /'wi:kdeɪ/ *n* dia *m* de semana

weekend /'wi:kend/ *n* fim-de- semana *m*

weep /wi:p/ *vt*/*i* (*pt* **wept**) chorar (**for sb** por alguém). **~ing willow** (salgueiro-)chorão *m*

weigh /weɪ/ *vt*/*i* pesar. **~ anchor** levantar âncora *or* ferro, zarpar. **~ down** (*weight*) sobrecarregar; (*bend*) envergar; (*fig*) acabrunhar. **~ up** (*colloq: examine*) pesar

weight /weɪt/ *n* peso *m*. **lose ~** emagrecer. **put on ~** engordar. **~less** *a* imponderável. **~-lifter** *n* halterofilista *m*. **~-lifting** *n* halterofilia *f*. **~y** *a* pesado; (*subject etc*) de peso; (*influential*) influente

weighting /'weɪtɪŋ/ *n* suplemento *m* salarial

weir /wɪə(r)/ *n* represa *f*, açude *m*

weird /wɪəd/ *a* (**-er, -est**) misterioso; (*strange*) estranho, bizarro

welcom|e /'welkəm/ *a* agradável; (*timely*) oportuno □ *int* (seja) benvindo! □ *n* acolhimento *m* □ *vt* acolher, receber; (*as greeting*) dar as boas vindas a. **be ~e** ser bem-vindo. **you're ~e!** (*after thank you*) não tem de quê!, de nada! **~e to do** livre para fazer. **~ing** *a* acolhedor

weld /weld/ *vt* soldar □ *n* solda *f*. **~er** *n* soldador *m*. **~ing** *n* soldagem *f*, soldadura *f*

welfare /'welfeə(r)/ *n* bem-estar *m*; (*aid*) assistência *f*, previdência *f* social. **W~ State** Estado-Providência *m*

well[1] /wel/ *n* (*for water, oil*) poço *m*; (*of stairs*) vão *m*; (*of lift*) poço *m*

well[2] /wel/ *adv* (**better, best**) bem □ *a* bem (*invar*) □ *int* bem! **as ~** também. **we may as ~ go** é melhor irnos andando. **as ~ as** tão bem como; (*in addition*) assim como. **be ~** (*healthy*) ir *or* passar bem. **do ~** (*succeed*) sair-se bem, ser bem sucedido. **very ~** muito bem. **~ done!** bravo!, muito bem! **~-behaved** *a* bem comportado, educado. **~-being** *n* bem-estar *m*. **~-bred** *a* (bem) educado. **~-done** *a* (*of meat*) bem passado. **~-dressed** *a* bem vestido. **~-heeled** *a* (*colloq: wealthy*) rico. **~-informed** *a* versado, bem informado. **~-known** *a* (bem-) conhecido. **~-meaning** *a* bem intencionado. **~-off** *a* rico, próspero. **~-read** *a* instruído. **~-spoken** *a* bem-falante. **~-timed** *a* oportuno. **~-to-do** *a* rico. **~-wisher** *n* admirador *m*, simpatizante *mf*

wellington /'welɪŋtən/ *n* (*boot*) bota *f* alta de borracha

Welsh /welʃ/ *a* galês □ *n* (*lang*) galês *m*. **~man** *n* galês *m*. **~ woman** *n* galesa *f*

wend /wend/ *vt* **~ one's way** dirigir-se, seguir o seu caminho

went /went/ *see* **go**

wept /wept/ *see* **weep**

were /wɜ:(r)/; *unstressed* /wə(r)/ *see* **be**

west /west/ *n* oeste *m*. **the W~** (*pol*) o Oeste, o Ocidente □ *a* ocidental, do oeste □ *adv* ao oeste, para o oeste. **W~ Indian** *a* & *n* antilhano (*m*). **the W~ Indies** as Antilhas. **~erly** *a* ocidental, oeste. **~ward** *a* para o oeste. **~ward(s)** *adv* para o oeste

western /'westən/ *a* ocidental, do oeste; (*pol*) ocidental □ *n* (*film*) filme *m* de cowboys, bangue- bangue *m*

westernize /'westənaɪz/ *vt* ocidentalizar

wet /wet/ *a* (**wetter, wettest**) molhado; (*of weather*) chuvoso, de chuva; (*colloq: person*) fraco. **get ~** molhar-se □ *vt* (*pt* **wetted**) molhar. **~ blanket** (*colloq*) desmancha-prazeres *mf invar* (*colloq*). **~ paint** pintado de fresco. **~ suit** roupa *f* de mergulho

whack /wæk/ *vt* (*colloq*) bater em □ *n* (*colloq*) pancada *f*. **~ed** *a* (*colloq*) morto de cansaço, rebentado (*colloq*). **~ing** *a* (*sl*) enorme, de todo o tamanho

whale /weɪl/ *n* baleia *f*

wharf /wɔ:f/ *n* (*pl* **wharfs**) cais *m*

what /wɒt/ *a* (*interr, excl*) que. **~ time is it?** que horas são? **~ an idea!** que idéia! □ *pron* (*interr*) (o) quê, como, o que, qual, quais; (*object*) o que; (*after prep*) que; (*that which*) o que, aquilo que. **~?** (o) quê?, como? **~ is it?** o que é? **~ is your address?** qual é o seu endereço? **~ is your name?** como se chama? **~ can you see?** o que é que você pode ver? **this is ~ I write with** é com isto que escrevo. **that's ~ I need** é disso que eu preciso. **do ~ you want** faça o que *or* aquilo que quiser. **~ about me/him/***etc*? e eu/ele/*etc*? **~ about doing sth?** e se fizéssemos alg coisa? **~ for?** para quê?

whatever /wɒt'evə(r)/ *a* **~ book**/*etc* qualquer livro/*etc* que seja □ *pron* (*no matter what*) qualquer que seja; (*anything that*) o que quer que, tudo o que. **nothing ~** absolutamente nada. **~ happens** aconteça o que acontecer. **do ~ you like** faça o que quiser

whatsoever /wɒtsəʊ'evə(r)/ *a* & *pron* = **whatever**

wheat /wi:t/ *n* trigo *m*

wheedle /ˈwi:dl/ *vt* convencer, persuadir, levar a

wheel /wi:l/ *n* roda *f* □ *vt* empurrar □ *vi* rodar, rolar. **at the ~** (*of vehicle*) ao volante; (*helm*) ao leme

wheelbarrow /ˈwi:lbærəʊ/ *n* carrinho *m* de mão

wheelchair /ˈwi:ltʃeə(r)/ *n* cadeira *f* de rodas

wheeze /wi:z/ *vi* respirar ruidosamente □ *n* respiração *f* difícil

when /wen/ *adv, conj & pron* quando. **the day/moment ~** o dia/momento em que

whenever /wenˈevə(r)/ *conj & adv* (*at whatever time*) quando quer que, quando; (*every time that*) (de) cada vez que, sempre que

where /weə(r)/ *adv, conj & pron* onde, aonde; (*in which place*) em que, onde; (*whereas*) enquanto que, ao passo que. **~ is he going?** aonde é que ele vai? **~-abouts** *adv* onde □ *n* paradeiro *m*. **~by** *adv* pelo que. **~upon** *adv* após o que, depois do que

whereas /weərˈæz/ *conj* enquanto que, ao passo que

wherever /weərˈevə(r)/ *conj & adv* onde quer que. **~ can it be?** onde pode estar?

whet /wet/ *vt* (*pt* **whetted**) (*appetite, desire*) aguçar, despertar

whether /ˈweðə(r)/ *conj* se. **not know ~** não saber se. **~ I go or not** caso eu vá ou não

which /wɪtʃ/ *interr a & pron* qual, que **~ bag is yours?** qual das malas é a sua? **~ is your coat?** qual é o seu casaco? **do you know ~ he's taken?** sabe qual/quais é que ele levou? □ *rel pron* que, o qual; (*referring to whole sentence*) o que; (*after prep*) que, o qual, cujo. **at ~** em qual/que. **from ~** do qual/que. **of ~** do qual/de que. **to ~** para o qual/o que

whichever /wɪtʃˈevə(r)/ *a* **~ book**/*etc* qualquer livro/*etc* que seja, seja que livro/*etc* for. **take ~ book you wish** leve o livro que quiser □ *pron* qualquer, quaisquer

whiff /wɪf/ *n* (*of fresh air*) sopro *m*, lufada *f*; (*smell*) baforada *f*

while /waɪl/ *n* (espaço de) tempo *m*, momento *m*. **once in a ~** de vez em quando □ *conj* (*when*) enquanto; (*although*) embora; (*whereas*) enquanto que □ *vt* **~ away** (*time*) passar

whim /wɪm/ *n* capricho *m*

whimper /ˈwɪmpə(r)/ *vi* gemer; (*baby*) choramingar □ *n* gemido *m*; (*baby*) choro *m*

whimsical /ˈwɪmzɪkl/ *a* (*person*) caprichoso; (*odd*) bizarro

whine /waɪn/ *vi* lamuriar-se, queixar-se; (*dog*) ganir □ *n* lamúria *f*, queixume *m*; (*dog*) ganido *m*

whip /wɪp/ *n* chicote *m* □ *vt* (*pt* **whipped**) chicotear; (*culin*) bater □ *vi* (*move*) ir a toda a pressa. **~-round** *n* (*colloq*) coleta *f*, vaquinha *f*. **~ up** excitar; (*cause*) provocar; (*colloq: meal*) preparar rapidamente. **~ped cream** creme *m* chantilly

whirl /wɜ:l/ *vt/i* (fazer) rodopiar, girar □ *n* rodopio *m*

whirlpool /ˈwɜ:lpu:l/ *n* redemoinho *m*

whirlwind /ˈwɜ:lwɪnd/ *n* redemoinho *m* de vento, turbilhão *m*

whirr /wɜ:(r)/ *vi* zunir, zumbir

whisk /wɪsk/ *vt/i* (*snatch*) levar/tirar bruscamente; (*culin*) bater; (*flies*) sacudir □ *n* (*culin*) batedeira *f*. **~ away** (*brush away*) sacudir

whisker /ˈwɪskə(r)/ *n* fio *m* de barba. **~s** *npl* (*of animal*) bigode *m*; (*beard*) barba *f*; (*sideboards*) suiças *fpl*

whisky /ˈwɪskɪ/ *n* uísque *m*

whisper /ˈwɪspə(r)/ *vt/i* sussurrar, murmurar; (*of stream, leaves*) sussurrar □ *n* sussurro *m*, murmúrio *m*. **in a ~** baixinho, em voz baixa

whist /wɪst/ *n* uíste *m*, (*P*) whist *m*

whistle /ˈwɪsl/ *n* assobio *m*; (*instrument*) apito *m* □ *vt/i* assobiar; (*with instrument*) apitar

Whit /wɪt/ *a* **~ Sunday** domingo *m* de Pentecostes

white /waɪt/ *a* (**-er, -est**) branco, alvo; (*pale*) pálido □ *n* (*colour; of eyes; person*) branco *m*; (*of egg*) clara (de ovo) *f*. **go ~** (*turn pale*) empalidecer; (*of hair*) branquear, embranquecer. **~ coffee** café *m* com leite. **~-collar worker** empregado *m* de escritório. **~ elephant** (*fig*) trambolho *m*, elefante *m* branco. **~ lie** mentirinha *f*. **~ness** *n* brancura *f*, alvura *f*

whiten /ˈwaɪtn/ *vt/i* branquear

whitewash /ˈwaɪtwɒʃ/ *n* cal *f*; (*fig*) encobrimento *m* □ *vt* caiar; (*fig*) encobrir

Whitsun /ˈwɪtsn/ *n* Pentecostes *m*

whittle /ˈwɪtl/ *vt* **~ down** aparar, cortar aparas; (*fig*) reduzir gradualmente

whiz /wɪz/ *vi* (*pt* **whizzed**) (*through air*) zunir, sibilar; (*rush*) passar a toda a velocidade. **~-kid** *n* (*colloq*) prodígio *m*

who /hu:/ *interr pron* quem □ *rel pron* que, o(a) qual, os(as) quais

whoever /hu:ˈevə(r)/ *pron* (*no matter who*) quem quer que, seja quem for; (*the one who*) aquele que

whole /həʊl/ *a* inteiro, todo; (*not broken*) intacto. **the ~ house**/*etc* toda a casa/*etc* □ *n* totalidade *f*; (*unit*) todo *m*. **as a ~** no conjunto, como um todo. **on the ~** de um modo geral. **~-hearted** *a* de todo o coração; (*person*) dedicado. **~-heartedly** *adv* sem reservas, sinceramente

wholefood /'həʊlfu:d/ *n* comida *f* integral

wholemeal /'həʊlmi:l/ *a* **~ bread** pão *m* integral

wholesale /'həʊlseɪl/ *n* venda *f* por grosso *or* por atacado □ *a* (*firm*) por grosso, por atacado; (*fig*) sistemático, em massa □ *adv* (*in large quantities*) por atacado; (*fig*) em massa, em grande escala. **~r** /-ə(r)/ *n* grossista *mf*, atacadista *mf*

wholesome /'həʊlsəm/ *a* sadio, saudável

wholewheat /'həʊlwi:t/ *a* = **wholemeal**

wholly /'həʊlɪ/ *adv* inteiramente, completamente

whom /hu:m/ *interr pron* quem □ *rel pron* (*that*) que; (*after prep*) quem, que, o qual

whooping cough /'hu:pɪŋkɒf/ *n* coqueluche *f*

whore /hɔ:(r)/ *n* prostituta *f*

whose /hu:z/ *rel pron* & *a* cujo, de quem □ *interr pron* de quem. **~ hat is this?**, **~ is this hat?** de quem é este chapéu? **~ son are you?** de quem é que o senhor é filho?

why /waɪ/ *adv* porque, por que motivo, por que razão, porquê. **she doesn't know ~ he's here** ela não sabe porque *or* por que motivo ele está aqui. **she doesn't know ~** ela não sabe porquê. **do you know ~?** você sabe porquê? □ *int* (*protest*) ora, ora essa; (*discovery*) oh. **~ yes**/*etc* ah, sim

wick /wɪk/ *n* torcida *f*, mecha *f*, pavio *m*

wicked /'wɪkɪd/ *a* mau, malvado; (*mischievous, spiteful*) maldoso. **~ly** *adv* maldosamente. **~ness** *n* maldade *f*, malvadeza *f*

wicker /'wɪkə(r)/ *n* verga *f*, vime *m*. **~-work** *n* trabalho *m* de verga *or* de vime

wicket /'wɪkɪt/ *n* (*cricket*) arco *m*

wide /waɪd/ *a* (**-er**, **-est**) largo; (*extensive*) vasto, grande, extenso. **two metres ~** com dois metros de largura □ *adv* longe; (*fully*) completamente. **open ~** (*door, window*) abrir(-se) de par em par, escancarar(-se); (*mouth*) abrir bem. **~ awake** desperto, acordado. **far and ~** por toda a parte. **~ly** *adv* largamente; (*travel, spread*) muito; (*generally*) geralmente; (*extremely*) extremamente

widen /'waɪdn/ *vt*/*i* alargar(-se)

widespread /'waɪdspred/ *a* muito espalhado, difundido

widow /'wɪdəʊ/ *n* viúva *f*. **~ed** *a* (*man*) viúvo; (*woman*) viúva. **be ~ed** enviuvar, ficar viúvo *or* viúva. **~er** *n* viúvo *m*. **~hood** *n* viuvez *f*

width /wɪdθ/ *n* largura *f*

wield /wi:ld/ *vt* (*axe etc*) manejar; (*fig: power*) exercer

wife /waɪf/ *n* (*pl* **wives**) mulher *f*, esposa *f*

wig /wɪg/ *n* cabeleira (postiça) *f*; (*judge's etc*) peruca *f*

wiggle /'wɪgl/ *vt*/*i* remexer(-se), retorcer(-se), mexer(-se) dum lado para outro

wild /waɪld/ *a* (**-er**, **-est**) selvagem; (*of plant*) silvestre; (*mad*) louco; (*enraged*) furioso, violento □ *adv* a esmo; (*without control*) à solta. **~s** *npl* regiões *fpl* selvagens. **~-goose chase** falsa pista *f*, tentativa *f* inútil. **~ly** *adv* violentamente; (*madly*) loucamente

wildcat /'waɪldkæt/ *a* **~ strike** greve *f* ilegal

wilderness /'wɪldənɪs/ *n* deserto *m*

wildlife /'waɪldlaɪf/ *n* animais *mpl* selvagens

wile /waɪl/ *n* artimanha *f*; (*cunning*) astúcia *f*, manha *f*

wilful /'wɪlfl/ *a* (*person*) voluntarioso; (*act*) intencional, propositado

will[1] /wɪl/ *v aux* **you ~ sing**/**he ~ do**/*etc* tu cantarás/ele fará/*etc*. (*1st person: future expressing will or intention*) **I ~ sing**/**we ~ do**/*etc* eu cantarei/nós faremos/*etc*. **~ you have a cup of coffee?** quer tomar um cafézinho? **~ you shut the door?** quer fazer o favor de fechar a porta?

will[2] /wɪl/ *n* vontade *f*; (*document*) testamento *m*. **at ~** à vontade, quando *or* como se quiser □ *vt* (*wish*) querer; (*bequeath*) deixar em testamento. **~-power** *n* força *f* de vontade

willing /'wɪlɪŋ/ *a* pronto, de boa vontade. **~ to** disposto a. **~ly** *adv* (*with pleasure*) de boa vontade, de bom grado; (*not forced*) voluntariamente. **~ness** *n* boa vontade *f*, disposição *f* (**to do** em fazer)

willow /'wɪləʊ/ *n* salgueiro *m*

willy-nilly /wɪlɪ'nɪlɪ/ *adv* de bom ou de mau grado, quer queira ou não

wilt /wɪlt/ *vi* murchar, definhar

wily /'waɪlɪ/ *a* (**-ier**, **-iest**) manhoso, matreiro

win /wɪn/ *vt*/*i* (*pt* **won**, *pres p* **winning**) ganhar □ *n* vitória *f*. **~ over** *vt* convencer, conquistar

winc|e /wɪns/ *vi* estremecer, contrair-se.

winch /wɪntʃ/ *n* guincho *m* □ *vt* içar com guincho

wind[1] /wɪnd/ *n* vento *m*; (*breath*) fôlego *m*; (*flatulence*) gases *mpl*. **get ~ of** (*fig*) ouvir rumor de. **put the ~ up** (*sl*) assustar. **in the ~** no ar. **~ farm** central *f* eólica. **~ instrument** (*mus*) instrumento *m* de sopro. **~-swept** *a* varrido pelo vento

wind[2] /waɪnd/ *vt/i* (*pt* **wound**) enrolar(-se); (*wrap*) envolver, pôr em volta; (*of path, river*) serpentear. **~ (up)** (*clock etc*) dar corda em. **~ up** (*end*) terminar, acabar; (*fig: speech etc*) concluir; (*firm*) liquidar. **he'll ~ up in jail** (*colloq*) ele vai acabar na cadeia. **~ing** *a* (*path*) sinuoso; (*staircase*) em caracol

windfall /ˈwɪndfɔːl/ *n* fruta *f* caída; (*fig: money*) sorte *f* grande

windmill /ˈwɪndmɪl/ *n* moinho *m* de vento

window /ˈwɪndəʊ/ *n* janela *f*; (*of shop*) vitrine *f*, (*P*) montra *f*; (*counter*) guichê *m*, (*P*) guichet *m*. **~-box** *n* jardineira *f*, (*P*) floreira *f*. **~-cleaner** *n* limpador *m* de janelas. **~-dressing** *n* decoração *f* de vitrines; (*fig*) apresentação *f* cuidadosa. **~-ledge** *n* peitoril *m*. **~-pane** *n* vidro *m*, vidraça *f*. **go ~-shopping** ir ver vitrines. **~-sill** *n* peitoril *m*

windpipe /ˈwɪndpaɪp/ *n* traquéia *f*, (*P*) traqueia *f*

windscreen /ˈwɪndskriːn/ *n* pára-brisa *m*, (*P*) pára-brisas *m invar*. **~-wiper** /-waɪpə(r)/ *n* limpador *m* de pára-brisa

windshield /ˈwɪndʃiːld/ *n* (*Amer*) **= windscreen**

windsurf|er /ˈwɪndsɜːfə(r)/ *n* surfista *mf*. **~ing** *n* surfe *m*

windy /ˈwɪndɪ/ *a* (**-ier, -iest**) ventoso. **it is very ~** está ventando muito

wine /waɪn/ *n* vinho *m*. **~ bar** bar *m* para degustação de vinhos. **~-cellar** *n* adega *f*, cave *f*. **~-grower** *n* vinicultor *m*. **~-growing** *n* vinicultura *f*. **~-list** *n* lista *f* de vinhos. **~-tasting** *n* prova *f* *or* degustação *f* de vinhos. **~ waiter** garçon *m*

wineglass /ˈwaɪnglɑːs/ *n* copo *m* de vinho; (*with stem*) cálice *m*

wing /wɪŋ/ *n* asa *f*; (*mil*) flanco *m*; (*archit*) ala *f*; (*auto*) pára-lamas *m invar*, (*P*) guarda-lamas *m invar*. **~s** (*theat*) bastidores *mpl*. **under sb's ~** debaixo das asas de alguém. **~ed** *a* alado

wink /wɪŋk/ *vi* piscar o olho; (*light, star*) cintilar, piscar □ *n* piscadela *f*. **not sleep a ~** não pregar olho

winner /ˈwɪnə(r)/ *n* vencedor *m*

winning /ˈwɪnɪŋ/ *see* **win** □ *a* vencedor, vitorioso; (*number*) premiado; (*smile*) encantador, atraente. **~-post** *n* meta *f*, poste de chegada *f*. **~s** *npl* ganhos *mpl*

wint|er /ˈwɪntə(r)/ *n* inverno *m* □ *vi* hibernar. **~ry** *a* de inverno, invernoso; (*smile*) glacial

wipe /waɪp/ *vt* limpar; (*dry*) enxugar, limpar □ *n* limpadela *f*. **~ off** limpar. **~ out** (*destroy*) aniquilar, limpar (*colloq*); (*cancel*) cancelar. **~ up** enxugar

wir|e /ˈwaɪə(r)/ *n* arame *m*; (*colloq: telegram*) telegrama *m*. **(electric) ~e** fio elétrico *m*, (*P*) eléctrico □ *vt* (*a house*) montar a instalação elétrica em; (*colloq: telegraph*) telegrafar. **~e netting** rede *f* de arame. **~ing** *n* (*electr*) instalação *f* elétrica, (*P*) eléctrica

wireless /ˈwaɪəlɪs/ *n* rádio *f*; (*set*) rádio *m*

wiry /ˈwaɪərɪ/ *a* (**-ier, -iest**) magro e rijo

wisdom /ˈwɪzdəm/ *n* sagacidade *f*, sabedoria *f*; (*common sense*) bom senso *m*, sensatez *f*. **~ tooth** dente *m* (do) sizo

wise /waɪz/ *a* (**-er, -est**) (*person*) sábio, avisado, sensato; (*look*) entendedor. **~ guy** (*colloq*) sabichão *m* (*colloq*), sabe-tudo *m* (*colloq*). **none the ~r** sem entender nada. **~ly** *adv* sensatamente

wisecrack /ˈwaɪzkræk/ *n* (*colloq*) (boa) piada *f*

wish /wɪʃ/ *n* (*desire, aspiration*) desejo *m*, vontade *f*; (*request*) pedido *m*; (*greeting*) desejo *m*, voto *m*. **I have no ~ to go** não tenho nenhum desejo *or* nenhuma vontade de ir □ *vt* (*desire, bid*) desejar; (*want*) apetecer, ter vontade de, desejar (**to do** fazer) □ *vi* **~ for** desejar. **~ sb well** desejar felicidades a alguém. **I don't ~ to go** não me apetece ir, não tenho vontade de ir, não desejo ir. **I ~ he'd leave** eu gostaria que ele partisse. **with best ~es** (*formal: in letter*) com os melhores cumprimentos, com saudações cordiais; (*on greeting card*) com desejos *or* votos (**for** de)

wishful /ˈwɪʃfl/ *a* **~ thinking** sonhar acordado

wishy-washy /ˈwɪʃɪwɒʃɪ/ *a* sem expressão, fraco, inexpressivo

wisp /wɪsp/ *n* (*of hair*) pequena mecha *f*; (*of smoke*) fio *m*

wistful /ˈwɪstfl/ *a* melancólico, saudoso

wit /wɪt/ *n* inteligência *f*; (*humour*) presença *f* de espírito, humor *m*; (*person*) senso *m* de humor. **be at one's ~'s** *or* **~s' end** não saber o que fazer. **keep one's ~s about one** estar alerta. **live by one's ~s** ganhar a vida de maneira suspeita. **scared out of one's ~s** apavorado

witch /wɪtʃ/ *n* feiticeira *f*, bruxa *f*. **~craft** *n* feitiçaria *f*, bruxaria *f*, magia *f*

with /wɪð/ *prep* com; (*having*) de; (*because of*) de; (*at the house of*) em casa de. **the man ~ the beard** o homem de barbas. **fill**/*etc* **~** encher/*etc* de. **laughing/shaking/** *etc* **~** a rir/a tremer/*etc* de. **I'm not ~ you** (*colloq*) não estou compreendendo-o

withdraw /wɪð'drɔ:/ *vt*/*i* (*pt* **withdrew**, *pp* **withdrawn**) retirar (-se); (*money*) tirar. **~al** *n* retirada *f*; (*med*) estado *m* de privação. **~n** *a* (*person*) retraído, fechado

wither /'wɪðə(r)/ *vt*/*i* murchar, secar. **~ed** *a* (*person*) mirrado. **~ing** *a* (*fig: scornful*) desdenhoso

withhold /wɪð'həʊld/ *vt* (*pt* **withheld**) negar, recusar; (*retain*) reter; (*conceal, not tell*) esconder (**from** de)

within /wɪ'ðɪn/ *prep* & *adv* dentro (de), por dentro (de); (*in distances*) a menos de. **~ a month** (*before*) dentro de um mês. **~ sight** à vista

without /wɪ'ðaʊt/ *prep* sem. **~ fail** sem falta. **go ~ saying** não ser preciso dizer

withstand /wɪð'stænd/ *vt* (*pt* **withstood**) resistir a, opor-se a

witness /'wɪtnɪs/ *n* testemunha *f*; (*evidence*) testemunho *m* □ *vt* testemunhar, presenciar; (*document*) assinar como testemunha. **bear ~ to** testemunhar, dar testemunho de. **~-box** *n* banco *m* das testemunhas

witticism /'wɪtɪsɪzəm/ *n* dito *m* espirituoso

witty /'wɪtɪ/ *a* (**-ier, -iest**) espirituoso

wives /waɪvz/ *see* **wife**

wizard /'wɪzəd/ *n* feiticeiro *m*; (*fig: genius*) gênio *m*, (*P*) génio *m*

wizened /'wɪznd/ *a* encarquilhado

wobbl|e /'wɒbl/ *vi* (*of jelly, voice, hand*) tremer; (*stagger*) cambalear, vacilar; (*of table, chair*) balançar. **~y** *a* (*trembling*) trêmulo; (*staggering*) cambaleante, vacilante; (*table, chair*) pouco firme

woe /wəʊ/ *n* dor *f*, infortúnio *m*

woke, woken /wəʊk, 'wəʊkən/ *see* **wake**[1]

wolf /wʊlf/ *n* (*pl* **wolves** /wʊlvz/) lobo *m* □ *vt* (*food*) devorar. **cry ~** dar alarme falso. **~-whistle** *n* assobio *m* de admiração

woman /'wʊmən/ *n* (*pl* **women**) mulher *f*. **~hood** *n* as mulheres, o sexo feminino; (*maturity*) maturidade *f*. **~ly** *a* feminino

womb /wu:m/ *n* seio *m*, ventre *m*; (*med*) útero *m*; (*fig*) seio *m*

women /'wɪmɪn/ *see* **woman**. **~'s movement** movimento *m* feminista

won /wʌn/ *see* **win**

wonder /'wʌndə(r)/ *n* admiração *f*; (*thing*) maravilha *f* □ *vt* perguntar-se a si mesmo (**if** se) □ *vi* admirar-se (**at** de, com), ficar admirado, espantar-se (**at** com); (*reflect*) pensar (**about** em). **it is no ~** não admira (**that** que)

wonderful /'wʌndəfl/ *a* maravilhoso. **~ly** *adv* maravilhosamente. **it works ~ly** funciona às mil maravilhas

won't /wəʊnt/ = **will not**

wood /wʊd/ *n* madeira *f*, pau *m*; (*for burning*) lenha *f*. **~(s)** *n* (*pl*) (*area*) bosque *m*, mata *f*, floresta *f*. **~ed** *a* arborizado. **~en** *a* de *or* em madeira, de pau; (*fig: stiff*) rígido; (*fig: inexpressive*) inexpressivo, de pau

woodcut /'wʊdkʌt/ *n* gravura *f* em madeira

woodland /'wʊdlənd/ *n* região *f* arborizada, bosque *m*, mata *f*

woodlouse /'wʊdlaʊs/ *n* (*pl* **-lice** /laɪs/) baratinha *f*, tatuzinho *m*

woodpecker /'wʊdpekə(r)/ *n* (*bird*) pica-pau *m*

woodwind /'wʊdwɪnd/ *n* (*mus*) instrumentos *mpl* de sopro de madeira

woodwork /'wʊdwɜ:k/ *n* (*of building*) madeiramento *m*; (*carpentry*) carpintaria *f*

woodworm /'wʊdwɜ:m/ *n* caruncho *m*

woody /'wʊdɪ/ *a* (*wooded*) arborizado; (*like wood*) lenhoso

wool /wʊl/ *n* lã *f*. **~len** *a* de lã. **~lens** *npl* roupas *fpl* de lã. **~ly** *a* de lã; (*vague*) confuso □ *n* (*colloq: garment*) roupa *f* de lã

word /wɜ:d/ *n* palavra *f*; (*news*) notícia(s) *f* (*pl*); (*promise*) palavra *f* □ *vt* exprimir, formular. **by ~ of mouth** de viva voz. **have a ~ with** dizer duas palavras a. **in other ~s** em outras palavras. **~-perfect** *a* que sabe de cor seu papel, a lição etc. **~ processor** processador *m* de textos. **~ing** *n* termos *mpl*, redação *f*, (*P*) redacção *f*. **~y** *a* prolixo

wore /wɔ:(r)/ *see* **wear**

work /wɜ:k/ *n* trabalho *m*; (*product, book etc*) obra *f*; (*building etc*) obras *fpl*. **at ~** no trabalho. **out of ~** desempregado. **~s** *npl* (*techn*) mecanismo *m*; (*factory*) fábrica *f* □ *vt*/*i* (*of person*) trabalhar; (*techn*) (fazer) funcionar, (fazer) andar; (*of drug etc*) agir, fazer efeito; (*farm, mine*) explorar; (*land*) lavrar. **~ sb** (*make work*) fazer alguém trabalhar. **~ in**

introduzir, inserir. **~ loose** soltar-se. **~ off** (*get rid of*) descarregar. **~ out** *vt* (*solve*) resolver; (*calculate*) calcular; (*devise*) planejar □ *vi* (*succeed*) resultar; (*sport*) treinar-se. **~-station** *n* estação *f* de trabalho. **~-to-rule** *n* greve *f* de zelo. **~ up** *vt* criar □ *vi* (*to climax*) ir num crescendo. **~ed up** (*person*) enervado, transtornado, agitado

workable /ˈwɜːkəbl/ *a* viável, praticável

workaholic /wɜːkəˈhɒlɪk/ *n* **be a ~** (*colloq*) trabalhar como um possesso (*colloq*)

worker /ˈwɜːkə(r)/ *n* trabalhador *m*, trabalhadora *f*; (*factory*) operário *m*

working /ˈwɜːkɪŋ/ *a* (*day, clothes, hypothesis, lunch etc*) de trabalho. **the ~ class(es)** a classe operária, a(s) class(es) trabalhadora(s), o proletariado. **~-class** *a* operário, trabalhador. **~ mother** mãe *f* que trabalha. **~ party** comissão *f* consultiva, de estudo *etc*. **~s** *npl* mecanismo *m*. **in ~ order** em condições de funcionamento

workman /ˈwɜːkmən/ *n* (*pl* **-men**) trabalhador *m*; (*factory*) operário *m*. **~ship** *n* trabalho *m*, execução *f*, mão-de-obra *f*; (*skill*) arte *f*, habilidade *f*

workshop /ˈwɜːkʃɒp/ *n* oficina *f*

world /wɜːld/ *n* mundo *m* □ *a* mundial. **a ~ of** muito(s), grande quantidade de, um mundo de. **~-wide** *a* mundial, universal

worldly /ˈwɜːldlɪ/ *a* terreno; (*devoted to the affairs of life*) mundano. **~ goods** bens *mpl* materiais. **~-wise** *a* com experiência do mundo

worm /wɜːm/ *n* verme *m*; (*earthworm*) minhoca *f* □ *vt* **~ one's way into** insinuar-se, introduzir-se, enfiar-se. **~-eaten** *a* (*wood*) carunchoso; (*fruit*) bichado, bichoso

worn /wɔːn/ *see* **wear** □ *a* usado. **~-out** *a* (*thing*) completamente gasto; (*person*) esgotado

worr|y /ˈwʌrɪ/ *vt/i* preocupar(-se) □ *n* preocupação *f*. **don't ~y** fique descansado, não se preocupe. **~ied** *a* preocupado. **~ying** *a* preocupante, inquietante

worse /wɜːs/ *a* & *adv* pior □ *n* pior *m*. **get ~** piorar. **from bad to ~** de mal a pior. **~ luck** pouca sorte, pena

worsen /ˈwɜːsn/ *vt/i* piorar

worship /ˈwɜːʃɪp/ *n* (*reverence*) reverência *f*, veneração *f*; (*religious*) culto *m* □ *vt* (*pt* **worshipped**) adorar, venerar □ *vi* fazer as suas devoções, praticar o culto. **~per** *n* (*in church*) fiel *m*. **Your/His W~** Vossa/Sua Excelência *f*

worst /wɜːst/ *a* & *n* **(the) ~** (o/a) pior (*mf*) □ *adv* pior. **if the ~ comes to the ~** se o pior acontecer, na pior das hipóteses. **do one's ~** fazer todo o mal que se quiser. **get the ~ of it** ficar a perder. **the ~ (thing) that** o pior que

worth /wɜːθ/ *a* **be ~** valer; (*deserving*) merecer □ *n* valor *m*, mérito *m*. **ten pounds ~ of** dez libras de. **it's ~ it, it's ~ while** vale a pena. **it's not ~ my while** não vale a pena. **it's ~ waiting**/*etc* vale a pena esperar/*etc*. **for all one's ~** (*colloq*) dando tudo por tudo. **~less** *a* sem valor

worthwhile /ˈwɜːθwaɪl/ *a* que vale a pena; (*cause*) louvável, meritório

worthy /ˈwɜːðɪ/ *a* (**-ier, -iest**) (*deserving*) digno, merecedor (**of** de); (*laudable*) meritório, louvável □ *n* (*person*) pessoa *f* ilustre

would /wʊd/; *unstressed* /wəd/ *v aux* **he ~ do/you ~ sing**/*etc* (*conditional tense*) ele faria/você cantaria/*etc*. **he ~ have done** ele teria feito. **she ~ come every day** (*used to*) ela vinha *or* costumava vir aqui todos os dias. **~ you please come here?** chegue aqui por favor. **~ you like some tea?** você quer um chazinho? **he ~n't go** (*refused to*) ele não queria ir. **~-be author/doctor**/*etc* aspirante a autor/médico/*etc*

wound[1] /wuːnd/ *n* ferida *f* □ *vt* ferir. **the ~ed** os feridos *mpl*

wound[2] /waʊnd/ *see* **wind**[2]

wove, woven /wəʊv, ˈwəʊvn/ *see* **weave**

wrangle /ˈræŋgl/ *vi* disputar, discutir, brigar □ *n* disputa *f*, discussão *f*, briga *f*

wrap /ræp/ *vt* (*pt* **wrapped**) **~ (up)** embrulhar (**in** em); (*in cotton wool, mystery etc*) envolver (**in** em) □ *vi* **~ up** (*dress warmly*) abrigar-se bem, agasalhar-se bem □ *n* xale *m*. **~ped up in** (*engrossed*) absorto em, mergulhado em. **~per** *n* (*of sweet*) papel *m*; (*of book*) capa *f* de papel. **~ing** *n* embalagem *f*

wrath /rɒθ/ *n* ira *f*. **~ful** *a* irado

wreak /riːk/ *vt* **~ havoc** (*of storm etc*) fazer estragos

wreath /riːθ/ *n* (*pl* **-s** /-ðz/) (*of flowers, leaves*) coroa *f*, grinalda *f*

wreck /rek/ *n* (*sinking*) naufrágio *m*; (*ship*) navio *m* naufragado; restos *mpl* de navio; (*remains*) destroços *mpl*; (*vehicle*) veículo *m* destroçado □ *vt* destruir; (*ship*) fazer naufragar, afundar; (*fig: hope*) acabar. **be a**

nervous ~ estar com os nervos arrasados. **~age** *n* (*pieces*) destroços *mpl*

wren /ren/ *n* (*bird*) carriça *f*

wrench /rentʃ/ *vt* (*pull*) puxar; (*twist*) torcer; (*snatch*) arrancar (**from** a) ◻ *n* (*pull*) puxão *m*; (*of ankle, wrist*) torcedura *f*; (*tool*) chave *f* inglesa; (*fig*) dor *f* de separação

wrest /rest/ *vt* arrancar (**from** a)

wrestl|e /'resl/ *vi* lutar, debater-se (**with** com *or* contra). **~er** *n* lutador *m*. **~ing** *n* luta *f*

wretch /retʃ/ *n* desgraçado *m*, miserável *mf*; (*rascal*) miserável *mf*

wretched /'retʃɪd/ *a* (*pitiful, poor*) miserável; (*bad*) horrível, desgraçado

wriggle /'rɪgl/ *vt/i* remexer(-se), contorcer-se

wring /rɪŋ/ *vt* (*pt* **wrung**) (*twist; clothes*) torcer. **~ out of** (*obtain from*) arrancar a. **~ing wet** encharcado; (*of person*) encharcado até os ossos

wrinkle /'rɪŋkl/ *n* (*on skin*) ruga *f*; (*crease*) prega *f* ◻ *vt/i* enrugar (-se)

wrist /rɪst/ *n* pulso *m*. **~-watch** *n* relógio *m* de pulso

writ /rɪt/ *n* (*jur*) mandado *m* judicial

write /raɪt/ *vt/i* (*pt* **wrote**, *pp* **written**) escrever. **~ back** responder. **~ down** escrever, tomar nota de. **~ off** (*debt*) dar por liquidado; (*vehicle*) destinar à sucata. **~-off** *n* perda *f* total. **~ out** (*in full*) escrever por extenso. **~ up** (*from notes*) redigir. **~-up** *n* relato *m*; (*review*) crítica *f*

writer /'raɪtə(r)/ *n* escritor *m*, autor *m*

writhe /raɪð/ *vi* contorcer(-se)

writing /'raɪtɪŋ/ *n* escrita *f*. **~(s)** (*works*) escritos *mpl*, obras *fpl*. **in ~** por escrito. **~-paper** *n* papel *m* de carta

written /'rɪtn/ *see* **write**

wrong /rɒŋ/ *a* (*incorrect, mistaken*) mal, errado; (*unfair*) injusto; (*wicked*) mau; (*amiss*) que não está bem; (*mus: note*) falso; (*clock*) que não está certo ◻ *adv* mal ◻ *n* mal *m*; (*injustice*) injustiça *f* ◻ *vt* (*be unfair to*) ser injusto com; (*do a wrong to*) fazer mal a. **what's ~?** qual é o problema? **what's ~ with it?** (*amiss*) o que é que não vai bem?; (*morally*) que mal há nisso?, que mal tem? **he's in the ~** (*his fault*) ele não tem razão. **go ~** (*err*) desencaminhar-se; (*fail*) ir mal; (*vehicle*) quebrar. **~ly** *adv* mal; (*blame etc*) sem razão, injustamente

wrongful /'rɒŋfl/ *a* injusto, ilegal

wrote /rəʊt/ *see* **write**

wrought /rɔ:t/ *a* **~ iron** ferro *m* forjado. **~-up** *a* excitado

wrung /rʌŋ/ *see* **wring**

wry /raɪ/ *a* (**wryer, wryest**) torto; (*smile*) forçado. **~ face** careta *f*

Xerox /'zɪərɒks/ *n* fotocópia *f*, xerox *m* ◻ *vt* fotocopiar, xerocar, tirar um xerox de

Xmas /'krɪsməs/ *n* **Christmas**

X-ray /'eksreɪ/ *n* raio X *m*; (*photograph*) radiografia *f* ◻ *vt* radiografar. **have an ~** tirar uma radiografia

xylophone /'zaɪləfəʊn/ *n* xilofone *m*

yacht /jɒt/ *n* iate *m*. **~ing** *n* iatismo *m*, andar *m* de iate; (*racing*) regata *f* de iate

yank /jæŋk/ *vt* (*colloq*) puxar bruscamente ◻ *n* (*colloq*) puxão *m*

Yank /jæŋk/ *n* (*colloq*) ianque *mf*

yap /jæp/ *vi* (*pt* **yapped**) latir

yard[1] /ja:d/ *n* (*measure*) jarda *f* (*= 0,9144 m*). **~age** *n* medida *f* em jardas

yard[2] /ja:d/ *n* (*of house*) pátio *m*; (*Amer: garden*) jardim *m*; (*for storage*) depósito *m*

yardstick /'ja:dstɪk/ *n* jarda *f*; (*fig*) bitola *f*, craveira *f*

yarn /ja:n/ *n* (*thread*) fio *m*; (*colloq: tale*) longa história *f*

yawn /jɔ:n/ *vi* bocejar; (*be wide open*) abrir-se, escancarar-se ◻ *n* bocejo *m*. **~ing** *a* escancarado

year /jɪə(r)/ *n* ano *m*. **school/tax ~** ano *m* escolar/fiscal. **be ten/***etc* **~s old** ter dez/*etc* anos de idade. **~-book** *n* anuário *m*. **~ly** *a* anual ◻ *adv* anualmente

yearn /jɜ:n/ *vi* **~ for, to** desejar, ansiar por, suspirar por. **~ing** *n* desejo *m*, anseio *m* (**for** de)

yeast /ji:st/ *n* levedura *f*

yell /jel/ *vt/i* gritar, berrar ◻ *n* grito *m*, berro *m*

yellow /'jeləʊ/ *a* amarelo; (*colloq: cowardly*) covarde, poltrão ▫ *n* amarelo *m*

yelp /jelp/ *n* (*of dog etc*) ganido *m* ▫ *vi* ganir

yen /jen/ *n* (*colloq: yearning*) grande vontade *f* (**for** de)

yes /jes/ *n* & *adv* sim (*m*). **~-man** *n* (*colloq*) lambe-botas *m invar*, puxa-saco *m*

yesterday /'jestədɪ/ *n* & *adv* ontem (*m*). **~ morning/afternoon/evening** ontem de manhã/à tarde/à noite. **the day before ~** anteontem. **~ week** há oito dias, há uma semana

yet /jet/ *adv* ainda; (*already*) já ▫ *conj* contudo, no entanto. **as ~** até agora, por enquanto. **his best book ~** o seu melhor livro até agora

yew /ju:/ *n* teixo *m*

Yiddish /'jɪdɪʃ/ *n* ídiche *m*

yield /ji:ld/ *vt* (*produce*) produzir, dar; (*profit*) render; (*surrender*) entregar ▫ *vi* (*give way*) ceder ▫ *n* produção *f*; (*comm*) rendimento *m*

yoga /'jəʊgə/ *n* ioga *f*

yoghurt /'jɒgət/ *n* iogurte *m*

yoke /jəʊk/ *n* jugo *m*, canga *f*; (*of garment*) pala *f* ▫ *vt* jungir; (*unite*) unir, ligar

yokel /'jəʊkl/ *n* caipira *m*, labrego *m*

yolk /jəʊk/ *n* gema (de ovo) *f*

yonder /'jɒndə(r)/ *adv* acolá, além

you /ju:/ *pron* (*familiar*) tu, você (*pl* vocês); (*polite*) vós, o(s) senhor(es), a(s) senhora(s); (*object: familiar*) te, lhe (*pl* vocês); (*polite*) o(s), a(s), lhes, vós, o(s) senhor(es), a(s) senhora(s); (*after prep*) ti, si, você (*pl* vocês); (*polite*) vós, o senhor, a senhora (*pl* os senhores, as senhoras); (*indefinite*) se; (*after prep*) si, você. **with ~** (*familiar*) contigo, consigo, com você (*pl* com vocês); (*polite*) com o senhor/a senhora (*pl* convosco, com os senhores/as senhoras). **I know ~** (*familiar*) eu te conheço, eu o/a conheço (*pl* eu os/as conheço); (*polite*) eu vos conheço, conheço o senhor/a senhora (*pl* conheço os senhores/as senhoras). **~ can see the sea** você pode ver o mar

young /jʌŋ/ *a* (**-er**, **-est**) jovem, novo, moço ▫ *n* (*people*) jovens *mpl*, a juventude *f*, a mocidade *f*; (*of animals*) crias *fpl*, filhotes *mpl*

youngster /'jʌŋstə(r)/ *n* jovem *mf*, moço *m*, rapaz *m*

your /jɔ:(r)/ *a* (*familiar*) teu, tua, seu, sua (*pl* teus, tuas, seus, suas); (*polite*) vosso, vossa, do senhor, da senhora (*pl* vossos, vossas, dos senhores, das senhoras)

yours /jɔ:z/ *poss pron* (*familiar*) o teu, a tua, o seu, a sua (*pl* os teus, as tuas, os seus, as suas); (*polite*) o vosso, a vossa, o/a do senhor, o/a da senhora (*pl* os vossos, as vossas; os/as do(s) senhor(es), os/as da(s) senhora(s)). **a book of ~** um livro seu. **~ sincerely/faithfully** atenciosamente, com os cumprimentos de

yourself /jɔ:'self/ (*pl* **-selves** /-'selvz/) *pron* (*familiar*) tu mesmo/a, você mesmo/a (*pl* vocês mesmos/as); (*polite*) vós mesmo/a, o senhor mesmo, a senhora mesma (*pl* vós mesmos/as, os senhores mesmos, as senhoras mesmas); (*reflexive: familiar*) te, a ti mesmo/a, se, a si mesmo/a (*pl* a vocês mesmos/as); (*polite*) ao senhor mesmo, à senhora mesma (*pl* aos senhores mesmos, às senhoras mesmas); (*after prep: familiar*) ti mesmo/a, si mesmo/a, você mesmo/a (*pl* vocês mesmos/as); (*after prep: polite*) vós mesmo/a, o senhor mesmo, a senhora mesma (*pl* vós mesmos/as, os senhores mesmos, as senhoras mesmas). **with ~** (*familiar*) contigo mesmo/a, consigo mesmo/a, com você (*pl* com vocês); (*polite*) convosco, com o senhor, com a senhora (*pl* com os senhores, com as senhoras). **by ~** sozinho

youth /ju:θ/ *n* (*pl* **-s** /-ðz/) mocidade *f*, juventude *f*; (*young man*) jovem *m*, moço *m*. **~ club** centro *m* de jovens. **~ hostel** albergue *m* da juventude. **~ful** *a* juvenil, jovem

yo-yo /'jəʊjəʊ/ *n* (*pl* **-os**) ioiô *m*

Yugoslav /'ju:gəsla:v/ *a* & *n* iogoslavo (*m*), (*P*) jugoslavo (*m*). **~ia** /-'sla:vɪə/ *n* Iogoslávia *f*, (*P*) Jugoslávia *f*

Zz

zany /'zeɪnɪ/ *a* (**-ier**, **-iest**) tolo, bobo

zeal /zi:l/ *n* zelo *m*

zealous /'zeləs/ *a* zeloso. **~ly** *adv* zelosamente

zebra /'zebrə, 'zi:brə/ *n* zebra *f*. **~ crossing** faixa *f* para pedestres, (*P*) passagem *f* para peões

zenith /'zenɪθ/ *n* zênite *m*, (*P*) zénite *m*, auge *m*

zero /'zɪərəʊ/ *n* (*pl* **-os**) zero *m*. **~ hour** a hora H. **below ~** abaixo de zero

zest /zest/ *n* (*gusto*) entusiasmo *m*; (*fig: spice*) sabor *m* especial; (*lemon or* *orange peel*) casca *f* de limão/laranja ralada

zigzag /'zɪgzæg/ *n* ziguezague *m* □ *a* & *adv* em ziguezague □ *vi* (*pt* **zigzagged**) ziguezaguear

zinc /zɪŋk/ *n* zinco *m*

zip /zɪp/ *n* (*vigour*) energia *f*, alma *f*. **~(-fastener)** fecho *m* ecler □ *vt* (*pt* **zipped**) fechar o fecho eclerde □ *vi* ir a toda a velocidade. **Z~ code** (*Amer*) CEP de endereçamento postal *m*, (*P*) código *m* postal

zipper /'zɪpə(r)/ *n* = **zip(-fastener)**

zodiac /'zəʊdɪæk/ *n* zodíaco *m*

zombie /'zɒmbɪ/ *n* zumbi *m*; (*colloq*) zumbi *m*, (*P*) autómato *m*

zone /zəʊn/ *n* zona *f*

zoo /zu:/ *n* jardim *m* zoológico

zoolog|y /zəʊ'ɒlədʒɪ/ *n* zoologia *f*. **~ical** /-ə'lɒdʒɪkl/ *a* zoológico. **~ist** *n* zoólogo *m*

zoom /zu:m/ *vi* (*rush*) sair roando **~ lens** zum *m*, zoom *m*. **~ off** *or* **past** passar zunindo

zucchini /zu:'ki:nɪ/ *n* (*pl invar*) (*Amer*) courgette *f*

Portuguese verbs

Portuguese verbs can be divided into three categories: regular verbs, those with spelling peculiarities determined by their sound and irregular verbs.

Regular verbs:

in **-ar** (e.g. **comprar**)

Present: compr|o, **~as, ~a, ~amos, ~ais, ~am**
Future: comprar|ei, **~ás, ~á, ~emos, ~eis, ~ão**
Imperfect: compr|ava, **~avas, ~ava, ~ávamos, ~áveis, ~avam**
Preterite: compr|ei, **~aste, ~ou, ~amos (P: ~ámos), ~astes, ~aram**
Pluperfect: compr|ara, **~aras, ~ara, ~áramos, ~áreis, ~aram**
Present subjunctive: compr|e, **~es, ~e, ~emos, ~eis, ~em**
Imperfect subjunctive: compr|asse, **~asses, ~asse, ~ássemos, ~ásseis, ~assem**
Future subjunctive: compr|ar, **~ares, ~ar, ~armos, ~ardes, ~arem**
Conditional: comprar|ia, **~ias, ~ia, ~íamos, ~íeis, ~iam**
Personal infinitive: comprar, **~es, ~, ~mos, ~des, ~em**
Present participle: comprando
Past participle: comprado
Imperative: compra, comprai

in **~er** (e.g. **bater**)

Present: bat|o, **~es, ~e, ~emos, ~eis, ~em**
Future: bater|ei, **~ás, ~á, ~emos, ~eis, ~ão**
Imperfect: bat|ia, **~ias, ~ia, ~íamos, ~íeis, ~iam**
Preterite: bat|i, **~este, ~eu, ~emos, ~estes, ~eram**
Pluperfect: bat|era, **~eras, ~era, ~êramos, ~êreis, ~eram**
Present subjunctive: bat|a, **~as, ~a, ~amos, ~ais, ~am**
Imperfect subjunctive: bat|esse, **~esses, ~esse, ~êssemos, ~êsseis, ~essem**
Future subjunctive: bat|er, **~eres, ~er, ~ermos, ~erdes, ~erem**
Conditional: bater|ia, **~ias, ~ia, ~íamos, ~íeis, ~iam**
Personal infinitive: bater, **~es, ~, ~mos, ~des, ~em**
Present participle: batendo
Past participle: batido
Imperative: bate, batei

in **~ir** (e.g. **admitir**)

Present: admit|o, **~es, ~e, ~imos, ~is, ~em**
Future: admitir|ei, **~ás, ~á, ~emos, ~eis, ~ão**
Imperfect: admit|ia, **~ias, ~ia, ~íamos, ~íeis, ~iam**
Preterite: admit|i, **~iste, ~iu, ~imos, ~istes, ~iram**
Pluperfect: admit|ira, **~iras, ~ira, ~íramos, ~íreis, ~iram**
Present subjunctive: admit|a, **~as, ~a, ~amos, ~ais, ~am**
Imperfect subjunctive: admit|isse, **~isses, ~isse, ~íssemos, ~ísseis, ~issem**
Future subjunctive: admit|ir, **~ires, ~ir, ~irmos, ~irdes, ~irem**
Conditional: admitir|ia, **~ias, ~ia, ~íamos, ~íeis, ~iam**
Personal infinitive: admitir, **~es, ~, ~mos, ~des, ~em**
Present participle: admitindo
Past participle: admitido
Imperative: admite, admiti

Regular verbs with spelling changes:

-ar verbs:

in **-car** (e.g. **ficar**)

Preterite: fiquei, ficaste, ficou, ficamos (P: ficámos), ficais, ficam
Present subjunctive: fique, fiques, fique, fiquemos, fiqueis, fiquem

in **-çar** (e.g. **abraçar**)

Preterite: abracei, abraçaste, abraçou, abraçamos (P: abraçámos), abraçastes, abraçaram
Present subjunctive: abrace, abraces, abrace, abracemos, abraceis, abracem

in **-ear** (e.g. **passear**)

Present: passeio, passeias, passeia, passeamos, passeais, passeiam
Present subjunctive: passeie, passeies, passeie, passeemos, passeeis, passeiem
Imperative: passeia, passeai

in **-gar** (e.g. **apagar**)

Preterite: apaguei, apagaste, apagou, apagamos (P: apagámos), apagastes, apagaram
Present subjunctive: apague, apagues, apague, apaguemos, apagueis, apaguem

in **-oar** (e.g. **voar**)

Present: vôo (P: voo), voas, voa, voamos, voais, voam

averiguar

Preterite: averigüei (P: averiguei), averiguaste, averiguou, averiguamos (P: averiguámos), averiguastes, averiguaram
Present subjunctive: averigúe, averigúes, averigúe, averigüemos (P: averiguemos), averigüeis (P: averigueis), averigúem

enxaguar

Present: enxáguo, enxáguas, enxágua, enxaguamos, enxaguais, enxáguam
Preterite: enxagüei (P: enxaguei), enxaguaste, enxaguou, enxaguamos (P: enxaguámos), enxaguastes, enxaguaram
Present subjunctive: enxágüe, enxágües, enxágüe, enxagüemos, enxagüeis, enxágüem (P: enxágue, enxágues, enxágue, enxaguemos, enxagueis, enxáguem)
Similarly: aguar, desaguar

saudar

Present: saúdo, saúdas, saúda, saudamos, saudais, saúdam
Present subjunctive: saúde, saúdes, saúde, saudemos, saudeis, saúdem
Imperative: saúda, saudai

-er verbs:

in **-cer** (e.g. **tecer**)

Present: teço, teces, tece, tecemos, teceis, tecem
Present subjunctive: teça, teças, teça, teçamos, teçais, teçam

in **-ger** (e.g. **proteger**)

Present: protejo, proteges, protege, protegemos, protegeis, protegem
Present subjunctive: proteja, protejas, proteja, protejamos, protejais, protejam

in **-guer** (e.g. **erguer**)

Present: ergo, ergues, ergue, erguemos, ergueis, erguem
Present subjunctive: erga, ergas, erga, ergamos, ergais, ergam

in **-oer** (e.g. **roer**)

Present: rôo (P: roo), róis, rói, roemos, roeis, roem
Imperfect: roía, roías, roía, roíamos, roíeis, roíam
Preterite: roí, roeste, roeu, roemos, roestes, roeram
Past participle: roído
Imperative: rói, roei

-ir verbs:

in **-ir** with **-e-** in stem (e.g. **vestir**)

Present: visto, vestes, veste, vestimos, vestis, vestem
Present subjunctive: vista, vistas, vista, vistamos, vistais, vistam
Similarly: mentir, preferir, refletir, repetir, seguir, sentir, servir

in **-ir** with **-o-** in stem (e.g. **dormir**)

Present: durmo, dormes, dorme, dormimos, dormis, dormem
Present subjunctive: durma, durmas, durma, durmamos, durmais, durmam
Similarly: cobrir, descobrir, tossir

in **-ir** with **-u-** in stem (e.g. **subir**)

Present: subo, sobes, sobe, subimos, subis, sobem
Similarly: consumir, cuspir, fugir, sacudir, sumir

in **-air** (e.g. **sair**)

Present: saio, sais, sai, saímos, saís, saem
Imperfect: saía, saías, saía, saíamos, saíeis, saíam
Preterite: saí, saíste, saiu, saímos, saístes, saíram
Pluperfect: saíra, saíras, saíra, saíramos, saíreis, saíram
Present subjunctive: saia, saias, saia, saiamos, saiais, saiam
Imperfect subjunctive: saísse, saísses, saísse, saíssemos, saísseis, saíssem
Future subjunctive: sair, saíres, sair, sairmos, sairdes, saírem
Personal infinitive: sair, saíres, sair, sairmos, sairdes, saírem
Present participle: saindo
Past participle: saído
Imperative: sai, saí

in **-gir** (e.g. **dirigir**)

Present: dirijo, diriges, dirige, dirigimos, dirigis, dirigem
Present subjunctive: dirija, dirijas, dirija, dirijamos, dirijais, dirijam

in **-guir** (e.g. **distinguir**)

Present: distingo, distingues, distingue, distinguimos, distinguis, distinguem
Present subjunctive: distinga, distingas, distinga, distingamos, distingais, distingam

in **-uir** (e.g. **atribuir**)

Present: atribuo, atribuis, atribui, atribuímos, atribuís, atribuem
Imperfect: atribuía, atribuías, atribuía, atribuíamos, atribuíeis, atribuíam
Preterite: atribuí, atribuíste, atribuiu, atribuímos, atribuístes, atribuíram
Pluperfect: atribuíra, atribuíras, atribuíra, atribuíramos, atribuíreis, atribuíram
Present subjunctive: atribua, atribuas, atribua, atribuamos, atribuais, atribuam
Imperfect subjunctive: atribuísse, atribuísses, atribuísse, atribuíssemos, atribuísseis, atribuíssem
Future subjunctive: atribuir, atribuíres, atribuir, atribuirmos, atribuirdes, atribuírem
Personal infinitive: atribuir, atribuíres, atribuir, atribuirmos, atribuirdes, atribuírem
Present participle: atribuindo

Past participle: atribuído
Imperative: atribui, atribuí

proibir

Present: proíbo, proíbes, proíbe, proibimos, proibis, proíbem
Present subjunctive: proíba, proíbas, proíba, proibamos, proibais, proíbam
Imperative: proíbe, proibi
Similarly: coibir

reunir

Present: reúno, reúnes, reúne, reunimos, reunis, reúnem
Present subjunctive: reúna, reúnas, reúna, reunamos, reunais, reúnam
Imperative: reúne, reuni

in **-struir** (e.g. **construir**) – like **atribuir** except:

Present: construo, constróis/construis, constrói/construi, construímos, construís, constroem/construem
Imperative: constrói/construi, construí

in **-duzir** (e.g. **produzir**)

Present: produzo, produzes, produz, produzimos, produzis, produzem
Imperative: produz(e), produzi
Similarly: luzir, reluzir

Irregular verbs

caber

Present: caibo, cabes, cabe, cabemos, cabeis, cabem
Preterite: coube, coubeste, coube, coubemos, coubestes, couberam
Pluperfect: coubera, couberas, coubera, coubéramos, coubéreis, couberam
Present subjunctive: caiba, caibas, caiba, caibamos, caibais, caibam
Imperfect subjunctive: coubesse, coubesses, coubesse, coubéssemos, coubésseis, coubessem
Future subjunctive: couber, couberes, couber, coubermos, couberdes, couberem

dar

Present: dou, dás, dá, damos, dais, dão
Preterite: dei, deste, deu, demos, destes, deram
Pluperfect: dera, deras, dera, déramos, déreis, deram
Present subjunctive: dê, dês, dê, demos, deis, dêem
Imperfect subjunctive: desse, desses, desse, déssemos, désseis, dessem
Future subjunctive: der, deres, der, dermos, derdes, derem
Imperative: dá, dai

dizer

Present: digo, dizes, diz, dizemos, dizeis, dizem
Future: direi, dirás, dirá, diremos, direis, dirão
Preterite: disse, disseste, disse, dissemos, dissestes, disseram
Pluperfect: dissera, disseras, dissera, disséramos, disséreis, disseram
Present subjunctive: diga, digas, diga, digamos, digais, digam
Imperfect subjunctive: dissesse, dissesses, dissesse, disséssemos, dissésseis, dissessem
Future subjunctive: disser, disseres, disser, dissermos, disserdes, disserem
Conditional: diria, dirias, diria, diríamos, diríeis, diriam
Present participle: dizendo
Past participle: dito
Imperative: diz, dizei

estar

Present: estou, estás, está, estamos, estais, estão
Preterite: estive, estiveste, esteve, estivemos, estivestes, estiveram
Pluperfect: estivera, estiveras, estivera, estivéramos, estivéreis, estiveram

Present subjunctive: esteja, estejas, esteja, estejamos, estejais, estejam
Imperfect subjunctive: estivesse, estivesses, estivesse, estivéssemos, estivésseis, estivessem
Future subjunctive: estiver, estiveres, estiver, estivermos, estiverdes, estiverem
Imperative: está, estai

fazer

Present: faço, fazes, faz, fazemos, fazeis, fazem
Future: farei, farás, fará, faremos, fareis, farão
Preterite: fiz, fizeste, fez, fizemos, fizestes, fizeram
Pluperfect: fizera, fizeras, fizera, fizéramos, fizéreis, fizeram
Present subjunctive: faça, faças, faça, façamos, façais, façam
Imperfect subjunctive: fizesse, fizesses, fizesse, fizéssemos, fizésseis, fizessem
Future subjunctive: fizer, fizeres, fizer, fizermos, fizerdes, fizerem
Conditional: faria, farias, faria, faríamos, faríeis, fariam
Present participle: fazendo
Past participle: feito
Imperative: faz(e), fazei

frigir

Present: frijo, freges, frege, frigimos, frigis, fregem
Present subjunctive: frija, frijas, frija, frijamos, frijais, frijam
Imperative: frege, frigi

haver

Present: hei, hás, há, hemos/havemos, haveis/heis, hão
Preterite: houve, houveste, houve, houvemos, houvestes, houveram
Pluperfect: houvera, houveras, houvera, houvéramos, houvéreis, houveram
Present subjunctive: haja, hajas, haja, hajamos, hajais, hajam
Imperfect subjunctive: houvesse, houvesses, houvesse, houvéssemos, houvésseis, houvessem
Future subjunctive: houver, houveres, houver, houvermos, houverdes, houverem
Imperative: há, havei

ir

Present: vou, vais, vai, vamos, ides, vão
Imperfect: ia, ias, ia, íamos, íeis, iam
Preterite: fui, foste, foi, fomos, fostes, foram
Pluperfect: fora, foras, fora, fôramos, fôreis, foram
Present subjunctive: vá, vás, vá, vamos, vades, vão
Imperfect subjunctive: fosse, fosses, fosse, fôssemos, fôsseis, fossem
Future subjunctive: for, fores, for, formos, fordes, forem
Present participle: indo
Past participle: ido
Imperative: vai, ide

ler

Present: leio, lês, lê, lemos, ledes, lêem
Imperfect: lia, lias, lia, líamos, líeis, liam
Preterite: li, leste, leu, lemos, lestes, leram
Pluperfect: lera, leras, lera, lêramos, lêreis, leram
Present subjunctive: leia, leias, leia, leiamos, leiais, leiam
Imperfect subjunctive: lesse, lesses, lesse, lêssemos, lêsseis, lessem
Future subjunctive: ler, leres, ler, lermos, lerdes, lerem
Present participle: lendo
Past participle: lido
Imperative: lê, lede
Similarly: crer

odiar

Present: odeio, odeias, odeia, odiamos, odiais, odeiam

Present subjunctive: odeie, odeies, odeie, odiemos, odieis, odeiem
Imperative: odeia, odiai
Similarly: incendiar

ouvir

Present: ouço (P also: oiça), ouves, ouve, ouvimos, ouvis, ouvem
Present subjunctive: ouça, ouças, ouça, ouçamos, ouçais, ouçam (P also: oiça, oiças, oiça, oiçamos, oiçais, oiçam)

pedir

Present: peço, pedes, pede, pedimos, pedis, pedem
Present subjunctive: peça, peças, peça, peçamos, peçais, peçam
Similarly: despedir, impedir, medir

perder

Present: perco, perdes, perde, perdemos, perdeis, perdem
Present subjunctive: perca, percas, perca, percamos, percais, percam

poder

Present: posso, podes, pode, podemos, podeis, podem
Preterite: pude, pudeste, pôde, pudemos, pudestes, puderam
Pluperfect: pudera, puderas, pudera, pudéramos, pudéreis, puderam
Present subjunctive: possa, possas, possa, possamos, possais, possam
Imperfect subjunctive: pudesse, pudesses, pudesse, pudéssemos, pudésseis, pudessem
Future subjunctive: puder, puderes, puder, pudermos, puderdes, puderem

polir

Present: pulo, pules, pule, polimos, polis, pulem
Present subjunctive: pula, pulas, pula, pulamos, pulais, pulam
Imperative: pule, poli

pôr

Present: ponho, pões, põe, pomos, pondes, põãm
Future: porei, porás, porá, poremos, poreis, poráo
Imperfect: punha, punhas, punha, púnhamos, púnheis, punham
Preterite: pus, puseste, pôs, pusemos, pusestes, puseram
Pluperfect: pusera, puseras, pusera, puséramos, puséreis, puseram
Present subjunctive: ponha, ponhas, ponha, ponhamos, ponhais, ponham
Imperfect subjunctive: pusesse, pusesses, pusesse, puséssemos, pusésseis, pusessem
Future subjunctive: puser, puseres, puser, pusermos, puserdes, puserem
Conditional: poria, porias, poria, poríamos, poríeis, poriam
Present participle: pondo
Past participle: posto
Imperative: põe, ponde
Similarly: compor, depor, dispor, opor, supor etc

prover

Present: provejo, provês, provê, provemos, provedes, provêem
Present subjunctive: proveja, provejas, proveja, provejamos, provejais, provejam
Imperative: provê, provede

querer

Present: quero, queres, quer, queremos, quereis, querem
Preterite: quis, quiseste, quis, quisemos, quisestes, quiseram
Pluperfect: quisera, quiseras, quisera, quiséramos, quiséreis, quiseram
Present subjunctive: queira, queiras, queira, queiramos, queirais, queiram
Imperfect subjunctive: quisesse,

quisesses, quisesse, quiséssemos, quisésseis, quisessem
Future subjunctive: quiser, quiseres, quiser, quisermos, quiserdes, quiserem
Imperative: quer, querei

requerer

Present: requeiro, requeres, requer, requeremos, requereis, requerem
Present subjunctive: requeira, requeiras, requeira, requeiramos, requeirais, requeiram
Imperative: requer, requerei

rir

Present: rio, ris, ri, rimos, rides, riem
Present subjunctive: ria, rias, ria, riamos, riais, riam
Imperative: ri, ride
Similarly: sorrir

saber

Present: sei, sabes, sabe, sabemos, sabeis, sabem
Preterite: soube, soubeste, soube, soubemos, soubestes, souberam
Pluperfect: soubera, souberas, soubera, soubéramos, soubéreis, souberam
Present subjunctive: saiba, saibas, saiba, saibamos, saibais, saibam
Imperfect subjunctive: soubesse, soubesses, soubesse, soubéssemos, soubésseis, soubessem
Future subjunctive: souber, souberes, souber, soubermos, souberdes, souberem
Imperative: sabe, sabei

ser

Present: sou, és, é, somos, sois, são
Imperfect: era, eras, era, éramos, éreis, eram
Preterite: fui, foste, foi, fomos, fostes, foram
Pluperfect: fora, foras, fora, fôramos, fôreis, foram
Present subjunctive: seja, sejas, seja, sejamos, sejais, sejam
Imperfect subjunctive: fosse, fosses, fosse, fôssemos, fôsseis, fossem
Future subjunctive: for, fores, for, formos, fordes, forem
Present participle: sendo
Past participle: sido
Imperative: sê, sede

ter

Present: tenho, tens, tem, temos, tendes, têm
Imperfect: tinha, tinhas, tinha, tínhamos, tínheis, tinham
Preterite: tive, tiveste, teve, tivemos, tivestes, tiveram
Pluperfect: tivera, tiveras, tivera, tivéramos, tivéreis, tiveram
Present subjunctive: tenha, tenhas, tenha, tenhamos, tenhais, tenham
Imperfect subjunctive: tivesse, tivesses, tivesse, tivéssemos, tivésseis, tivessem
Future subjunctive: tiver, tiveres, tiver, tivermos, tiverdes, tiverem
Present participle: tendo
Past participle: tido
Imperative: tem, tende

trazer

Present: trago, trazes, traz, trazemos, trazeis, trazem
Future: trarei, trarás, trará, traremos, trareis, trarão
Preterite: trouxe, trouxeste, trouxe, trouxemos, trouxestes, trouxeram
Pluperfect: trouxera, trouxeras, trouxera, trouxéramos, trouxéreis, trouxeram
Present subjunctive: traga, tragas, traga, tragamos, tragais, tragam
Imperfect subjunctive: trouxesse, trouxesses, trouxesse, trouxéssemos, trouxésseis, trouxessem
Future subjunctive: trouxer, trouxeres, trouxer, trouxermos, trouxerdes, trouxerem

Conditional: traria, trarias, traria, traríamos, traríeis, trariam
Imperative: traze, trazei

valer

Present: valho, vales, vale, valemos, valeis, valem
Present subjunctive: valha, valhas, valha, valhamos, valhais, valham

ver

Present: vejo, vês, vê, vemos, vedes, vêem
Imperfect: via, vias, via, víamos, víeis, viam
Preterite: vi, viste, viu, vimos, vistes, viram
Pluperfect: vira, viras, vira, víramos, víreis, viram
Present subjunctive: veja, vejas, veja, vejamos, vejais, vejam
Imperfect subjunctive: visse, visses, visse, víssemos, vísseis, vissem
Future subjunctive: vir, vires, vir, virmos, virdes, virem
Present participle: vendo
Past participle: visto
Imperative: vê, vede

vir

Present: venho, vens, vem, vimos, vindes, vêm
Imperfect: vinha, vinhas, vinha, vínhamos, vínheis, vinham
Preterite: vim, vieste, veio, viemos, viestes, vieram
Pluperfect: viera, vieras, viera, viéramos, viéreis, vieram
Present subjunctive: venha, venhas, venha, venhamos, venhais, venham
Imperfect subjunctive: viesse, viesses, viesse, viéssemos, viésseis, viessem
Future subjunctive: vier, vieres, vier, viermos, vierdes, vierem
Present participle: vindo
Past participle: vindo
Imperative: vem, vinde